Morality in Criminal Justice

An Introduction to Ethics

Daryl Close
Nicholas Meier

CENGAGE
Learning™

Australia • Brazil • Japan • Korea • Mexico • Singapore • Spain • United Kingdom • United States

CENGAGE
Learning™

**Morality in
Criminal Justice:
An Introduction to Ethics**

Daryl Close
Nicholas Meier

Executive Editors:
Michele Baird

Maureen Staudt

Michael Stranz

Project Development Manager:
Linda deStefano

Senior Marketing Coordinators:
Sara Mecurio

Lindsay Shapiro

Production/Manufacturing Manager:
Donna M. Brown

PreMedia Services Supervisor:
Rebecca A. Walker

Rights & Permissions Specialist:
Kalina Hintz

Cover Image:
Getty Images*

* Unless otherwise noted, all
cover images used by Custom
Solutions, a part of Cengage
Learning, have been supplied
courtesy of Getty Images with
the exception of the Earthview
cover image, which has been
supplied by the National
Aeronautics and Space
Administration (NASA).

For product information and
technology assistance, contact us at **Cengage Learning
Customer & Sales Support, 1-800-354-9706**

For permission to use material from this text or product,
submit all requests online at **cengage.com/permissions**
Further permissions questions can be emailed to
permissionrequest@cengage.com

ISBN-13: 978-0-534-14366-4

ISBN-10: 0-534-14366-0

Cengage Learning

5191 Natorp Boulevard
Mason, Ohio 45040
USA

Cengage Learning is a leading provider of customized learning
solutions with office locations around the globe, including
Singapore, the United Kingdom, Australia, Mexico, Brazil, and Japan.
Locate your local office at: **international.cengage.com/region**

Cengage Learning products are represented in Canada by
Nelson Education, Ltd.

For your lifelong learning solutions, visit **custom.cengage.com**

Visit our corporate website at **cengage.com**

Printed in the United States of America

Because the understanding and support of our families was so important, we thank them and dedicate this book to them—Donna, Julia, Meredith, Hilary, Betsy, and Kathleen.

Contents

Chapter 3: *The Individual: Discretion and Decision-making*

Chapter 4: *Loyalty*

Chapter 5: *Truth*   218

Chapter 6: *Corruption*   271

Chapter 7: *Force* 348

Chapter 8: *Punishment* 422

Preface

As MOST CRIMINAL JUSTICE EDUCATORS are aware, there has been a tremendous growth in interest in criminal justice ethics in the past 10 years. Interest in the moral issues encountered in policing, corrections, probation, parole, prosecution, and criminal defense is reflected in conference programs as well as graduate theses and dissertations in criminal justice ethics. And a growing body of critical literature is evident in such journals as *Criminal Justice Ethics*.

Although relatively recent in the area of criminal justice, a deep interest in the philosophical analysis of ethical issues is also present in many other professions whose practitioners are regularly confronted with ethically charged decisions. For example, medical ethics has matured into an entire subdiscipline of ethics, with journals devoted exclusively to ethical problems in medicine. Growing numbers of hospitals employ staff ethicists to assist health care professionals in analyzing the moral choices confronting them. Similarly, business ethics has generated a tremendous amount of literature. Ethical consultants are retained to counsel senior management in the ethical dilemmas they encounter. Engineering ethics, too, is growing rapidly. Other professional areas that are emerging as distinct research interests in ethics include computer ethics, journalistic ethics, and legal ethics. Some of these areas of decision-making allow ample time for reflection. Other areas, including medical ethics and criminal justice ethics, have such broad ranges of cases that the practitioner does not have that luxury.

As one of the five traditional branches of philosophy, ethics is normally divided into metaethics, the study of the meaning of ethical concepts, and normative ethics, the study of specific ethical theories. During the early 1960s, a branch of normative ethics, now usually referred to broadly as "applied ethics," began to emerge (or, to reemerge after several hundred years of dormancy). Research in applied ethics is characterized by the analysis of specific actions performed by persons in specific situations, usually demarcated by professional boundaries such as those mentioned above. Although applied ethics must be concerned with conceptual issues, the goal is always the practical application of the results of philosophical analysis. Applied ethics may begin in the armchair, but it always ends up in the trenches.

One of us is a criminal justice educator as well as an experienced police officer, and the other is a philosopher with many years of experience in designing and teaching a variety of applied ethics courses. While the absence of an undergraduate-level text in criminal justice ethics was initially a prime consideration in developing this book, we have since become even more convinced of the criminal justice student's need for a systematic and thorough treatment of the moral dimension of criminal justice practice.

By definition, that treatment must be philosophically informed. At the same time, it must not assume a background in philosophy that most criminal justice students are unlikely to have. For this reason, a very basic, but essential, introduction to ethical theory is presented in Chapter 1.

Teachers of applied ethics will notice that we have adopted the popular reader format found in applied ethics texts. We have provided brief introductions to each chapter and, as noted in the case of Chapter 1, an introduction to ethical theory. The readings and cases have been selected to provoke reflection about the thematic topic of each chapter. Readings and cases are followed by discussion questions. We have deliberately chosen readings not only from the philosophical literature but also from criminal justice, criminology, and sociology.

We have attempted to provide a balanced treatment of ethical issues in the various areas of criminal justice practice. For example, readings that focus primarily on law enforcement and on corrections are present in almost equal numbers. Still, the fact remains that there is currently far more ethics research in policing than in other areas such as juvenile justice, probation, and parole. We have tried to provide a more even coverage of those areas by asking practitioners outside of law enforcement to write many of the cases in this book. Readers will find that many of the selections that appear by the title to pertain only to ethical issues in policing in fact apply equally well to the entire area of criminal justice practice.

Finally, it should be noted that in some cases, we have selected readings that include empirical research that is now outdated or mooted by new statutory or case law. We have chosen all of the readings for the ethical issues raised, and we hope that readers will find the selections thought-provoking, stimulating, even controversial. Such an atmosphere allows ethical analysis to flourish.

Applied ethical analysis must be grounded in a theoretical framework, but the student needs a foil to test his or her assumptions, conjectures, and conclusions. To assist in this essential aspect of teaching applied ethics, each chapter includes several extended cases. Although a handful of books concerning criminal justice ethics have recently been published, as of this writing none of those texts uses cases as a major pedagogical feature. We believe that this combination of theory and practical case applications is essential to applied ethics instruction. Based on actual events, our cases have been written specifically for this book by a wide range of practitioners in the justice system, including police and corrections officers, judges, youth counselors, and social workers. Because existing research in criminal justice ethics has tended to concentrate on law enforcement and corrections, we have attempted to balance this by including cases from other areas of criminal justice practice. Names, places, and some details have been changed for reasons of privacy and, in a few instances, to ensure safety, both physical and legal. Some cases are horrific, some are pathetic, while others have a streak of humor. All involve decision-making, rough and unadorned. A case can only approximate "what it's really like out there" and we do not dispute the value of experience. But in the past, much instruction in criminal justice "ethics" has been based on the traditional "war story" in a context of peer-group socialization, rather than one of critical inquiry.

We feel strongly that the criminal justice professional who has not had formal exposure to analysis of the moral issues in his or her work is in many ways as ill-equipped as a patrol officer who goes on duty without a weapon. It is no exaggeration to say that in both cases, personal careers, social welfare, and even lives are unnecessarily jeopardized. No course in ethics can bring about instant changes in professional behavior. However, a thoughtful and realistic criminal justice ethics course can help to initiate a career-long sensitivity to the complex moral issues with which the criminal justice professional must routinely grapple.

We believe that an applied ethics course is best approached with a focus on discussion and critical examination of ideas, arguments, and perspectives rather than relying on the traditional lecture method. We think you will find the extensive use of cases, for example, to be very supportive of a discussion-oriented course. Small group problem-solving (both in class and out of class), group paper writing, formal case presentations, debates, and other cooperative learning pedagogies, as well as individual assignments, can all be easily implemented using the materials in this book.

We have arranged the chapters to allow some flexibility. Chapters 1 through 3 should be completed in sequence. Chapters 4 through 10 may be ordered at the instructor's preference, but Chapter 11 should conclude the course. If time limitations emerge, we recommend briefer treatment of Chapters 6, 7, and 8 rather than complete omission of any chapter.

To aid in case analysis, and ultimately in making decisions on the job, instructors will notice the focus on the basic moral principles of decision-making presented in Chapters 1, 2, and 3. In the introduction to Chapter 3, a brief decision-making "checklist" is presented. Such a checklist of moral principles is not a moral calculus, but rather seeks to provide the criminal justice professional with a procedure for identifying the moral component of a given policy or situation. The checklist explicitly avoids the "Dos and Don'ts" approach of a professional code of ethics while equipping the practitioner for the broad range of decisions that ethics codes simply cannot handle. The cases provide the student with practice in applying such a decision-making checklist so that an ethically sensitive perspective is internalized and is carried beyond the classroom. Our goal is to make the adoption of that perspective seem a natural and obvious part of criminal justice education. A related goal is to aid in dismantling the popular view that there is a morally relevant distinction between "personal" and "professional" ethics. In this sense, we would argue that the study of applied ethics is never simply about profession-specific decision-making. Instead, it is about the struggle to gain a general moral perspective that is guided by reason, and never simply by social role or status. But we leave that issue for you to explore with your students!

We are eager to assist you in designing your course around this text. We encourage you to write to us, either through the publisher or at our respective institutions. If you prefer, you may correspond by electronic mail at the following Internet addresses: 76170.2351@compuserve.com for Daryl Close, and meier01@vax.kvcc.edu for Nicholas Meier.

Acknowledgments

Many people contributed to this book and we are deeply grateful to them. We are indebted to both those whose work is reprinted here and to those who wrote cases specifically for this volume. In addition to the contributors who wish to remain anonymous, we want to thank Professor Michael Barrett, Ashland University; Hon. Frederick R. Daniel, Jr., Tiffin Municipal Court, Tiffin, Ohio; R. Scott Distel, Tiffin University; Rev. Richard Lawrence; John Myers, J.D.; Hon. William G. Schma, Ninth Judicial Circuit, State of Michigan; Marilyn S. Stalsworth; and Carol Wiseman for their contributions and assistance. We appreciate the extended comments on the draft by Kalamazoo Valley Community College criminal justice students Scott Locey, Laura Mackey, Dale Richardson, Rita Robertson, and Coleen Roelofs. A special thanks must go to Annette Staunton for voluminous typing, photocopying, and correspondence, and to reference librarians Frances Fleet, Tiffin University, and Pam Fox and Gene Radtke, Kalamazoo Valley Community College. We also want to thank our friends at Wadsworth, including the anonymous reviewers. Special thanks go to Wadsworth's Criminal Justice editor, Brian Gore, whose guidance and suggestions have helped to make this a better book.

We appreciate the comments, proofreading, and manuscript preparation support of our spouses, Donna Close and Julia Meier.

Finally, a special thanks to Bob Cooper for the gift of confidence; and, to Bill Tafoya for the gift of closure. Both of these gifts will be treasured and shared.

DARYL CLOSE
NICHOLAS MEIER

Chapter 1

Introduction to Ethics in Criminal Justice

YOUR CITY HAS BEGUN A PROGRAM designed to reduce the supply of cheap hand-guns available to potential young offenders. Cash seized in drug arrests is used to buy handguns, shotguns, and semiautomatic rifles from any person who turns a weapon in at a police station. The impact of the program has been dramatic—it has reduced the number of gang shootings and virtually eliminated handguns in the area schools. You are a probation officer. You stop by a precinct station to visit an old friend. As you enter the station, you see one of your probationers, Robinson, through an open door. He is turning in a handgun. You continue down the hall undetected by Robin-son, but you now have a problem. Robinson's possession of a handgun is a clear viola-tion of his probation, but from what you know of Robinson, the $50 he earns will go toward the care of his family. If you report him, he will have to serve at least six months, possibly a year. He will lose a job that could have gotten him completely off support. What should you do?

What concerns are relevant in this case? Does it really matter what Robinson plans to do with the money he earns? What if you are reasonably sure that he will spend the money "irresponsibly" instead of providing for his family? Should you contact his case worker at Children's Services about the income even though you know that doing so will probably reduce his monthly support? What if the gun-buying policy promises anonymity to the seller? If the door had been closed, as it should have been according to policy, you wouldn't have seen Robinson at all. What if Robinson had been reported by an informer as having turned in a handgun two weeks ago?

No book or scholarly paper can provide you with a moral formula to determine what action to take. No policy manual or code of ethics can identify the correct action. This much is certain. But it is equally certain that deep moral issues are present in the case above, and that it makes sense to wrestle with them. In this chapter, we will try to show you the most prominent features of the moral terrain. By learning the landscape in a general way, you will be better prepared to travel it on your own. We will try to show you that moral issues can be approached rationally and that bad answers to ethical questions can be separated from plausible answers. Throughout this book you will have an opportunity to engage with the moral reflections of philosophers, sociologists, and criminal justice practitioners. You will study cases like the one above to challenge your moral reasoning abilities.

Moral Problems in Criminal Justice

Criminal justice includes four somewhat distinct areas of practice: police, courts, corrections, and juvenile justice.[1] Ethical issues that arise in these four areas are nonetheless very similar. Discretion, due process, the use of force, loyalty to fellow officers, and deceptive practices are examples of fundamental moral problems confronted by the criminal justice practitioner. Although different professions are faced with moral decisions that may appear to be unique to that area, the underlying moral issues are usually generic ones. For example, the issue of loyalty to fellow officers involved in misconduct is not significantly different in a morally relevant sense from the issue of loyalty to fellow physicians involved in questionable medical care.

The criminal justice system exists to protect the public and to secure those things on which our society places the greatest value, particularly life, liberty, and property. The criminal law and the threat of punishment are designed to serve as preventatives. Whether we apprehend and punish violators to validate the threat, or for some other purpose, will be discussed in more detail in Chapter 9. At any rate, the fundamental task of a criminal justice practitioner is to administer the criminal law. This is accomplished by apprehending the violator, demonstrating his or her guilt in court, and applying the prescribed sanction.

To the practitioner, this conception of one's job is not very helpful. We could as easily say that the task of the physician is to cure the patient. Sometimes the practice of criminal justice is straightforward and sometimes it is impossible. The real difficulties arise in determining how the officer (police, probation, parole, and correctional) can perform these vital social functions in a way that is both legal and morally correct.

At the same time, how can the officer ensure that official activities not directly connected with the enforcement or administration of the criminal law are performed in a way that is consistent with the legal and moral principles that guide one's professional conduct? For example, administrative actions such as hiring and promoting may well involve the same moral decision-making processes with respect to race and sex that are involved in an arrest decision. The officer responsible for hiring may believe that affirmative action guidelines discriminate unfairly against white males. This belief could easily have an impact on the number of applications from women and minority members that are rejected. Officers who hold such views may be inclined to engage in overly aggressive enforcement in African-American or Hispanic communities, or even in vice enforcement activities.

We cannot expect officers to maintain two separate sets of moral values, one reserved for one's personal life and one to be applied professionally. This would deny persons of their ability to act as autonomous moral agents. An **autonomous moral agent** can be defined as a person who can make moral decisions on the basis of personal values independently of what other persons believe, but in which the values are held to be universally true, not just "true-for-me." Our goal for moral education in criminal justice is to allow officers to function as autonomous moral agents.[2] Therefore, officers must be willing to treat their moral values as part of a single system of universal ethical values. This system of values must by definition be present in both the private and professional behavior of the officer.

Ethics

Dictionaries sometimes define ethics as the science of morals, but that doesn't help much since both "ethics" and "moral" have similar root meanings. The Greek word *ethos* means pertaining to custom or character, and the Latin word *moralis* means the same. The plural, *mores* (pronounced "mor-ayz"), still exists in English with its original meaning. For example, a cultural anthropologist might refer to the mores of the native peoples of the Pacific Northwest during the 1800s as involving elaborate gift-giving customs. The word "morality" is often used in a similar way to refer to the actual customs or practices of human beings.

Ethics as a branch of study is one of the five traditional areas of philosophy.[3] Ethics concerns the study of right and wrong, duty, responsibility, and personal character. You should regard all of the concepts just mentioned as having an implicit modifier—"moral"—attached to them. Ethics is concerned with **moral** duty, what is **morally** right and wrong, etc.

Words like "duty" and "right" can have many applications that are **nonmoral**. What that means is that they have nothing to do with morality at all. For instance, one of the duties of elementary school cooks might be to make coffee for the staff every morning; although making coffee is a duty, it's not a moral duty. Likewise, it might be the responsibility—but not the moral responsibility—of the school engineer to see that adequate hot water is available for the kitchen, the shower rooms, and the lavatories.

You may have already guessed that it's not always easy to distinguish between actions that are nonmoral and those that have moral content. For example, the cooks do not have a moral responsibility to make coffee for the staff, but they do have a moral responsibility to make the coffee in a safe and healthful manner. Similarly, the school engineer has a moral duty to ensure that the hot water is not too hot. If the engineer fails in his or her duty, someone could be badly injured. If the engineer is careless and pays no attention to the water temperature, we might say that he or she did something morally wrong, or behaved unethically or unprofessionally.

Being able to identify actions or situations that have moral content is a very important part of ethics. Everyone can spot the easy ones, but the rest require careful examination. For example, every defense attorney knows that she has a duty to zealously represent her client. It is equally obvious that this duty has moral content; the attorney should not allow—or worse, counsel—her client to commit perjury.[4]

Moral Decision-Making

What constitutes a morally correct decision? A decision that reflects an officer's religious upbringing is one candidate. Others might base their decisions strictly on professional codes of ethics, departmental policy, statutory law, or constitutional law. Still others might refer to the consequences of their actions as the operative criterion for right behavior. Other common criteria include informal reference to peer group mores, community mores, or individual "conscience." Historically, human beings have based moral decision-making on the position of the planets, tea leaves, and even the entrails of birds. And, really, isn't all morality just a matter of personal opinion, anyway? So why spend so much time and effort on issues for which one person's answer is just as good as anyone else's? Don't all of us have a right to our own personal opinions when it comes to issues of right and wrong?

At least some of the above moral criteria are logically irrelevant to the decision-making process. But which are relevant and which are not? Having determined that issue as best we can, how can the relevant criteria be coordinated into a practical model for moral decision-making?

Moral Relativism

The questions of moral criteria, their relevancy and irrelevancy, and the consistent application of moral principles seem to assume that morality is subject to the same procedures of rational investigation as are other areas of human life. But how can this be? Who are *you* to tell *me* what I should or should not do? Aren't we all entitled to our own opinions about what is morally right and what is morally wrong? Isn't morality relative to, and dependent on, the beliefs of individuals and their culture?

Many people in our society believe that morality is just a matter of personal opinion. According to this view, if you *believe* very firmly that abortion is morally wrong, then abortion *is* morally wrong. If you *believe* very strongly that abortion is sometimes (or always) morally permissible, then it *is* morally permissible. Consequently, the moral rightness or wrongness of an act is entirely relative to the individual assessing the act. Often, this position is associated with a destructive general relativism, first characterized by Stephen Satris as "student relativism":

> There is really nothing true or false—or nothing really good or bad—it's all relative. One person has an opinion or feeling, and another person has a different one. What is true for one person might not be true for another. After all, who's to say? Everybody has [his or her] own feelings.[5]

We might call this view of morality the "Peter Pan" principle. You may remember how in the play, *Peter Pan*, Peter invites the Darling children to associate believing that one can fly with actually flying. The idea that we can cause moral statements to become true merely by wishing or believing that they are true is known in ethics as **moral relativism**.[6] The moral relativist claims that moral standards are simply what persons believe about morality. The moral absolutist, on the other hand, draws a distinction between what *is* true and what one *believes* to be true. The moral relativist is captivated by the idea that "each of us has a right to his or her own opinion." This makes morality a matter of choosing what one wishes to believe, much like choosing which flavor of ice cream one wants. Since no one has a right to choose my ice cream for me, then, in a similar way, no one has a right to choose my moral values for me.

This is an extremely popular view of morality in our society. But just because a view is popular doesn't mean that it is correct. The fatal flaw with this view is that one simply can't choose a moral statement to be true or false. The statement "Torturing children for pleasure is morally wrong" is either true or false quite independently of my choice. If the statement is false, I can "choose" it to be true all I want, but the statement will still be false. Likewise, if the statement is true, I can "choose" it to be false, but that will not affect the truth of the statement. A person who *truly* believes that torturing a child is morally permissible simply because "Everyone has a right to his own opinion" and "After all, morality is just a matter of opinion" would be regarded not just as wrong, but as mentally ill. Someone who truly thinks this way, and is willing to act on the conviction of that belief, will be regarded as having lost the capacity for rational thought. Such a person has not simply offered a counter-thesis to be discussed by other thoughtful human beings. That person has abandoned rational discourse altogether.

Are people who say that they are moral relativists really relativists, then? Or do they have a core of basic beliefs the truth of which they hold to be independent of individual or cultural beliefs? We can use moral axioms such as "Torturing a child is wrong" as a litmus test to smoke out the Sunday soldiers in the relativist camp. Ask the alleged relativist whether she *really* believes that the sentence "Torturing children for pleasure is morally wrong" can be changed from true to false by merely willing it to be false.[7]

The Peter Pan view of morality is simply inconsistent with the way that human beings really regard moral issues. We take moral issues seriously and spend great effort, expense, and emotion debating and analyzing them. The fact that we debate and disagree shows that we have some public conception of moral knowledge. Our arguments may not prevail—they may even veer off the course of rational discussion from time to time. But human beings have persisted in moral conversion and debate for thousands of years, and the hope of progress seems to underlie that persistence. On the other hand, if moral relativism were true, the very idea of rationally investigating moral statements would be impossible. That is, relativism is opposed to the rational investigation of the truth or falsity of moral claims because truth or falsity itself becomes relative to, and dependent on, the beliefs of persons, or of a culture. If I can make a moral statement true or false merely by the act of believing it to be true or false, then the possibility of determining what human beings should or should not do in various circumstances becomes academic. What possible reason would you have for talking with me about moral issues?

This does not mean that we have proved relativism to be false. But we want to stimulate ethical conversation, and at the very least, relativism thwarts such conversation. This reason alone is sufficient to reject relativism as an ethical perspective, even if we could find a person who really is a relativist.

Walter T. Stace's selection, "Ethical Relativity," presents a detailed criticism of moral relativism. Stace examines two arguments in support of moral relativism. The first is based on anthropological research into the widely varying beliefs held by different cultures throughout history. This argument has been called the **argument from cultural relativism.** It claims that moral relativism must be true because human beings in fact have held very different views about what is morally right and wrong— that is, moral beliefs are in fact relative to one's culture. The second argument in support of moral relativism is that no one has discovered a completely satisfactory way to determine the truth or falsity of moral statements. Therefore, the relativist argues, moral absolutism (the opposite of moral relativism) must be rejected. As a defense of moral relativism, this argument commits the logical fallacy known as the argument from ignorance. This fallacy argues that if there is no evidence that a statement is true, then it must be false, and therefore its opposite must be true.

Ethical Theories

We will assume that there is a point to rational discussion of moral issues. The next task, then, is to formulate some principles that can guide our discussion. Over the centuries, philosophers have proposed different theories about the nature of morality, what morally justifies an action, what makes an action morally wrong, what contributes to the moral character of a person, and so on. First, we'll look at some basic terminology.

To say that an action is morally wrong is to say that you are not morally permitted to do it; it is morally impermissible. If an action is morally right, we may mean that it is an obligation or duty, or we may simply mean that it is permissible. Most commonly in English, "do the right thing" means "do your duty" or "do what you are obligated to do." The exceptions to this are acts that are *above* the call of duty, such as acts of heroism. Philosophers call this type of act **supererogatory.**[8]

A supererogatory act is an act that is morally praiseworthy but not morally obligatory. For example, if you are driving by a burning house, you are under no moral obligation to risk your own life by entering the house to see whether anyone is inside. If you do so, and suffer severe burns while rescuing an occupant, you have done something morally praiseworthy and you would very likely be recognized for your heroic action. But we would not say, "We're very happy that you saved a person's life, but after all, you were only doing your duty."

On the other hand, if you drove past an evidently unreported fire without even making the effort to dial 911 on your car phone, we would very likely chastise you for not having done what you ought—perform your moral duty. You may be familiar with a dramatic example of such a failure: the 1964 case of the Queens, New York, woman, Kitty Genovese, who was fatally attacked on the steps of her apartment building while her neighbors looked on in safety several stories above. Not a single witness so much as picked up the phone to call the police to her aid.[9]

So you can see that "morally right" sometimes means "good, but not an obligation," but usually it means "good *and* you have a duty to do it." The adequacy of a moral theory is determined in part by whether it can correctly distinguish morally right actions from morally wrong actions. But many philosophers feel that it is equally critical that a moral theory be able to distinguish between right actions that are duties and those that are supererogatory.

It might seem odd to you that the criminal justice system is society's way of identifying people who fail (dramatically) in their moral duties, but that we have very little systematic recognition of those who do their duties. One reason appears to be that doing what one should do is not particularly praiseworthy. In fact, we typically lavish praise only on those who not only do what they are obliged to do, but who go far beyond obligation. Even in those cases, only the most outstanding examples of supererogation are recognized, and more modest sacrifices are ignored. Exceptions to this practice include recognition of persons for years of service (is the consistent meeting of one's duties supererogatory?), and moral training, e.g., with children. In the latter case, we praise the person for simply doing what he or she has a duty to do (telling the truth, not hitting one's sibling, respecting another child's possessions, etc.), because the person has not yet learned what should and should not be done. That fundamental distinction has always been the focus of most ethical theories.

Now we will consider the moral theories themselves. First, we'll split moral theories into two categories: **teleological** theories and **deontological** theories. Teleological theories are also often referred to as **consequentialist.** The term "teleological" derives from the Greek root *telos,* which means *end* or *goal,* thus referring to the ends or consequences of an action. Deontological theories also derive their name from a Greek word (*deon*), meaning that which is binding. Deontological theories are sometimes referred to as nonconsequentialist or formalist theories of ethics.

Teleological theories state that the rightness or wrongness of an action is determined by the consequences of that action. Deontological theories, such as Kant's categorical imperative, rights-based theories, and divine command codes like the Ten Commandments, state that the rightness or wrongness of an action is intrinsic to the act itself. Such theories reject the moral relevance of an action's consequences in the moral assessment of the action. They generally try to ground the moral value of an action in the nature of the action itself rather than in something external to the action.

Teleological Theories

Have you ever heard the expression "the greatest good for the greatest number"? This is a common formulation of **utilitarianism,** the most popular variety of teleological moral theories. Utilitarianism has also been called the "the greatest happiness" principle, but that is just one form of utilitarianism. Utilitarianism states that the morally right action (or rule) is that action or rule that creates the greatest balance of good consequences over bad consequences for *all* those who are affected by the action. When we say "all" we mean it. *Every* person who is in any way affected by the action must be taken into consideration. When we say "greatest" we mean in comparison to all the alternative actions possible in those circumstances. To determine the correct action, we must determine the total amount of good (happiness, for example) that will be produced and the total amount of bad (unhappiness) that will be produced.

Suppose that I have promised to pick you up at the airport. The top two alternatives might be (1) to keep my promise and pick you up (e.g., 200 units of good for you, and 125 units of bad for me for the inconvenience, plus 25 units of good for me because I like to drive); or (2) to break my promise and go golfing (300 units of bad for you and 500 units of good for me, plus 50 units of bad for me because I feel guilty about breaking my promise). The net balance of alternative (1) is 100 units of good, while the net balance of alternative (2) is 150 units of good. Therefore, in this analysis, alternative (2)—breaking your promise—is the morally correct action to take (see Figure 1).

Let's apply a utilitarian analysis to the case of Robinson, the gun-selling probationer. This case is more complex because we have more details to consider: the effect of writing up Robinson's violation on him, on his family, and on you. You must also consider the effects of not writing up the violation. What will be the impact on you professionally if word gets out that you are willing to "overlook" violations? What will be the impact on the deterrence effect of your conduct with respect to your other probationers? Will they be more inclined to violate their probation terms? Examine Figure 2 to see what conclusion might be drawn by a utilitarian. Is the table complete? Does it reflect all of the outcomes of the action? Are the numbers accurate estimates? Do the numbers have any validity at all? These are questions that the utilitarian must be prepared to answer.

One of the first things you should notice about utilitarianism is that the words "good" and "bad" are *used* to define the concept of a morally right action. This means that "good" and "bad" must be *nonmoral* ideas. Otherwise, our definition would be circular (think about it). Over the centuries, philosophers have proposed many different ideas about what makes the consequences of an action good or bad.

A very ancient view about this issue is that "good" refers to what is pleasurable, and "bad" refers to what is painful. Such a view is called **hedonism**. That is why people who pursue pleasure as the main goal of their lives are sometimes called hedonists. Hedonists may not be utilitarians, but utilitarians who define "good" and "bad" in terms of pleasure and pain are called hedonistic utilitarians. Remember, the defining characteristic of a utilitarian is that our actions should produce the maximum amount of good and the minimum amount of bad for *everyone*, not just for oneself.

Sometimes "good" and "bad" are associated with the concepts of happiness and unhappiness instead of pleasure and pain. Or the utilitarian may define good and bad in terms of preferences, such as those that are indicated in economic behavior. On the economic scale in the example above, the disutility to you of breaking my promise

	KEEP PROMISE (Pick you up at the airport)	BREAK PROMISE (Play golf)
UNITS OF GOOD	+200 You need the ride. + 25 I like to drive.	+500 I love golf.
UNITS OF BAD	−125 Inconvenience to me.	−300 Waiting, cabfare, etc. − 50 I feel guilty.
BALANCE	+100	+150

FIGURE 1   A Utilitarian Calculation of Keeping a Promise

	WRITE UP ROBINSON'S VIOLATION	DON'T WRITE UP ROBINSON
UNITS OF GOOD	+800 Your example of Robinson deters your other probationers from violating their probation. +200 AFDC payments are increased to Robinson's family. +400 You feel good about not being "soft" on violators. +800 You protect your professional reputation and job security.	+ 100 AFDC is not reduced. + 500 Robinson continues to support his family. +1000 Family remains intact. Positive husband and father presence increases strength of family unit.
UNITS OF BAD	−1500 Struggling family unit is broken; husband, father, and breadwinner are lost. − 500 Mrs. Robinson's emotional and physical health decline. − 800 You experience severe stress because of your direct causal involvement in harm to innocent family members.	−500 Your professionalism is compromised. Stress over job security is experienced. −200 Robinson is positively reinforced to violate probation again. −200 Conflict of role as officer of the court with officer/client loyalty decreases your overall job effectiveness.
BALANCE	−600	+700

FIGURE 2   A Utilitarian Probation Officer Makes a Decision

would be the money you spend on a phone call for a cab and the cost of the cab ride. If you miss a vital appointment that costs you a $200,000 contract, that would be added to the "bad" side of the ledger, too. You can see that defining and counting units of good and bad presents a major problem for the utilitarian. For instance, what is the dollar cost of turning in our probationer, Robinson, for selling a weapon? How many units of bad result from a third-grader losing her father for six months?

Stop here and ask yourself, "Am I a utilitarian?" If you think the consequences of your actions are of the highest moral importance, you must be able to answer the questions in the paragraph above. *All* of the consequences of an action must be taken into account, however far and wide the "ripples" may spread. Moreover, since utilitarianism is an inherently *quantitative* moral theory, you must be able to count the consequences, even if you can only approximate. How would *you* measure the suffering of Robinson's family?

Some Practical Problems With Utilitarianism

How are happiness and unhappiness to be measured? What are the units of measurement? Jeremy Bentham (1748-1832), the father of utilitarianism, proposed seven different characteristics of good (pleasure) and bad (pain) that must be taken into account. These include (1) the intensity of the pleasure or pain, (2) its duration, (3) the certainty or uncertainty of pleasure or pain actually resulting from the stimulus, (4) the propinquity (nearness) or remoteness, i.e., how long it will be before the pain or the pleasure is experienced, (5) the fecundity (how likely it is to be followed by a similar sensation), (6) the purity of the sensation, and (7) the extent of the sensation (the number of persons who will be affected by the pleasure or pain).[10]

After we've solved the problem of measurement of specific pleasures and pains, how do we compare different pleasures and pains? How should the pleasure of a fine wine be compared with the pleasure of receiving emergency medical care? Is the medical care twice as good as the wine, 10 times as good, or 87 times as good? Further problems loom for the utilitarian. For instance, what is pleasant to one human being may be unpleasant to another. What constitutes happiness to me may make you unhappy. This means that we need precise and extensive knowledge about all the persons affected by an action. Think back to the example in which I promise to pick you up at the airport. If you suffer anxiety from a childhood trauma of being abandoned in an airport terminal, the cost of breaking my promise suddenly escalates. If I don't know this fact about you, my calculation of the consequences of my action will be wrong. As a result, I will choose to perform what is in fact the morally wrong alternative. Or think of Robinson's family—perhaps Mrs. Robinson is handicapped and depends on her husband for assistance in daily living activities. Turning in your probationer begins to appear to be very wrong from the utilitarian perspective (see Figure 2).

Act and Rule Utilitarianism

As you can imagine, applying the utilitarian principle to individual actions in everyday life is very difficult. It could take days, even years, of intensive research to determine whether a specific action is morally right or wrong. This kind of utilitarianism is called **act utilitarianism.** A major defect is practicality. In daily life, we are accustomed to making decisions by referring to *rules*, rather than to long, involved processes of reasoning. For example, the entire justice system is itself a system of rules. Only in unusual cases do the rules fail, calling for specific analysis of the situation. This is part of the function of the state and federal supreme courts. The act utilitarian can, of course, appeal to rules. But he or she cannot appeal to them on utilitarian grounds, since it is only the consequences of *this* particular action that are relevant. Hence, if the act utilitarian appeals to rules at all, it will essentially be out of laziness, since the rules can only express very crude guesses about what the consequences of *this* action will be.

Given the impracticality of act utilitarianism proper, philosophers have proposed a modified version called **rule utilitarianism.** This variety of utilitarianism highlights those *rules* that produce the greatest amount of happiness, rather than specific actions. Rule utilitarianism states that an individual act is morally right if it falls under a rule that is morally right. In turn, the morality of the rule is determined on utilitarian grounds. A morally sound rule is one that in the long run produces the greatest balance of good over bad. The idea of "the long run" is somewhat vague, but we certainly cannot employ a rule once or twice and then throw it out because of bad results. A rule must have a history of applications in a variety of circumstances if we are to evaluate the effects of following it.

Rule utilitarians may employ any rule at all, including laws, religious teachings, or personal rules. The definition simply requires that the rule be one that, when followed, maximizes the balance of good over bad. What this means is that laborious calculation is not needed for each individual action that you might take. If the action falls under a rule that tends to produce more good than bad, the action is morally correct, even if the specific consequences are not good themselves. Likewise, even though the specific consequences of an action might be good, the action could still be morally wrong.

Let's look at the airport example from the perspective of a rule utilitarian. In our original example, my breaking my promise to pick you up had good results in the balance. But it's easy to see that *as a rule,* breaking a promise to pick up a person is a bad rule. Keeping one's promises is just not something one does if it is convenient. Under normal circumstances, we keep our promises even if there is a net result of inconvenience and discomfort.

This does not mean that rules have no exceptions. It simply means that the exceptions are not strictly determined by the consequences in each specific case. For instance, a sensible rule for the case above might be, "Keep your promise to pick up a person at the airport unless doing so poses a significant threat to the health or well-being of another person." If my daughter has just broken her leg and I must take her to the hospital, an exception to the rule has occurred.

Another example of a rule utilitarian line of reasoning concerns search and seizure. Suppose that in the U.S., we had a rule that said that the state need not have any reason for detaining and/or searching a citizen. Now, it might be true that a random strip search of citizens entering city limits would produce good consequences. Persons possessing illegal drugs, illegal weapons, driving with suspended licenses, etc., would no doubt be discovered. Yet most of us would agree that life under such conditions would be intolerable in a free society. The search without cause would be morally wrong to the rule utilitarian because the rule under which the specific act falls is not a good rule. That is, if this hypothetical rule were consistently followed, the bad consequences would, in the long run, outweigh the good consequences.

Or consider interrogation techniques. Beating and torture can be effective methods of extracting statements from a suspect or inmate. The act utilitarian would simply assess the consequences of beating and torture in each case. In some cases, such actions would be morally justified, while in other cases they would not. But there is no principle that would prevent the act utilitarian from selecting and beating citizens, particularly if the action were carried out in a secretive way with few witnesses and little or no permanent injury to the victim.[11]

Rule utilitarianism also solves the "free rider" problem with act utilitarianism. This problem involves "what would happen if everyone did that?" sorts of situations. Consider A. K. Stout's water ban example discussed by J. J. C. Smart.[12] Suppose that I live in an arid area of the country and that because of unusually severe water shortages, a ban has been placed on washing cars, watering lawns and gardens, and so on. Imagine also that I have a small, secret garden that I cannot bear to see destroyed by the drought. If I were to water my secret garden during the water use restrictions, without anyone knowing, the harm would be minuscule, perhaps even nonexistent, and the benefit (my pleasure derived from the garden) would be considerable. On an act utilitarian analysis, it is morally permissible for me to water my garden. However, what if I live in a world consisting mostly of act utilitarians? What will be the consequences of everyone reasoning in the same way? Obviously, the collective effect of small violations of the water ban will be a considerable amount of harm.

Or consider a corrections officer who overlooks an inmate's violation of a minor rule because it will put the inmate "in debt" for a valuable favor regarding inmate drug use. If other corrections officers reason in the same way, the entire system of prison rules may be jeopardized. These difficulties are resolved by a rule utilitarian approach, since the consequences of everyone following a rule over a period of time must be considered.[13]

Some version of rule utilitarianism is probably the most plausible type of teleological moral theory currently available. The advantages of the theory include (1) much easier application in real life than act utilitarianism, and (2) the ability to look at moral issues from a familiar perspective—rule-following. What rule utilitarianism provides is a way to separate the good rules from the bad rules. For the utilitarian, the consequences of following the rule are what count.

A Deep Problem with Utilitarianism

The most serious problem with utilitarianism in any form is that it allows violations of moral principles that we ordinarily take as basic, such as fairness. The classic example is punishment of an innocent person. In the utilitarian view, punishing an innocent person is morally correct as long as it produces more good than bad for all concerned. If great social benefits such as deterrence can be obtained by punishing a person, the moral guilt or innocence of the prisoner will be only a minor consideration, far outweighed by the great social good to be accomplished. The protest that punishment of an innocent person is unjust falls on deaf ears. Scapegoating is perfectly acceptable to the utilitarian as long as the balance of good over bad consequences arising from the act (or rule) is greater than that from the available alternatives.

Resolution of this difficulty lies in acknowledging that utilitarianism is an incomplete moral theory. In fact, this can be seen in the very formulation of the principle of utility. Did you notice that utilitarianism *assumes* that in weighing the consequences, all persons are to be counted equally? Utilitarianism itself seems to rest on a higher-level moral principle of fairness, in which the happiness of one person cannot count for more than the happiness of another. In Bentham's words, "each is to count as one." Or consider the "peeping Tom" problem. Suppose that a voyeur gains, on balance,

200 units of pleasure by peeping in the neighbor's window. Suppose further that this act is undetected by anyone, including the neighbor. Since no one but the voyeur knows of the act, it appears that no one else is harmed by the action on a utilitarian basis. Yet most of us would probably agree that the neighbor has been harmed because her privacy has been invaded. Similar cases can be generated regarding unauthorized access of confidential personal information (reading someone else's mail, examining medical records or bank records, etc.).

John Stuart Mill's "What Utilitarianism Is" is the classic statement of the utilitarian position. The selection begins with Mill's definition of the "greatest happiness principle" (the principle of utility): "... actions are right in proportion as they tend to promote happiness; wrong as they tend to produce the reverse of happiness." Even from this brief definition it is clear that Mill is a rule utilitarian. He appears to be speaking of *types* of actions and their *tendencies* to have good consequences. Mill proceeds to distinguish among grades of happiness and of "higher" and "lower" pleasures. In this section you will find Mill's famous statement, "It is better to be a human being dissatisfied than a pig satisfied ..." Mill then considers several other objections to utilitarianism, distinguishes between good actions and good persons, argues that motive is irrelevant to the morality of an action, and refutes the charge that utilitarianism is a "godless doctrine."

Ethical Egoism

Do you know someone whose basic principle of life is summed up by "Looking out for Number One"? This variety of consequentialism is called ethical egoism. The ethical egoist holds that the morally correct action is the action that produces the greatest balance of good consequences over bad consequences for him or her. Some egoists have attempted to formulate the theory in general terms, i.e., that *one* should seek to maximize *one's own* good. The difficulty with this approach is that it seems unlikely that it would be in the egoist's best interest for other people to pursue their interests. If I am a consistent egoist, I would want you to pursue my interests alone. Consequently, egoism seems to be difficult or impossible to teach to another person. How would you proceed? If teaching the theory to another person would produce good consequences for you, you ought to teach the theory. If the other person's practice of ethical egoism could adversely affect your own interests, you should keep the theory to yourself.

Such problems have convinced many philosophers that egoism is just not an ethical theory at all. They claim that for anything to qualify as a moral theory, that theory must take other people into consideration. Since ethical egoism by definition cannot take others into account, it is not a moral theory at all. At the very least, egoism strikes most of us as being very odd, since one's own interests and needs are only part of the moral picture.

There are obviously serious conceptual problems in formulating ethical egoism as a viable moral theory, and we will not pursue it further. However, we should note that moral decisions may still legitimately refer to one's own personal interests. As you know, utilitarians consider the consequences of an act or rule regardless of who is involved. So how my acts affect me is definitely morally relevant. In a somewhat similar way, deontologists have typically held that we have moral duties to ourselves. The choices are not just between looking out for Number One, and being a selfless saint who pays no attention to personal interests. It's just that personal interests cannot form the exclusive basis for moral decision-making.

Deontological Theories

Deontological theories do not typically consider the consequences of one's actions to be morally significant. At first, this may seem to be very odd. After all, aren't the consequences really what matters, morally speaking? In what else could the morality of an action lie? Notice also that we have hedged our definition a bit here, by saying that deontologists *typically* ignore consequences. This reflects a general unwillingness among contemporary philosophers to argue that teleological and deontological theories are mutually exclusive. But the deontologist generally analyzes moral duty without referring to some nonmoral good that is produced when a person performs his or her duty. Like teleological theories, deontological theories can be divided into act- and rule-based approaches. However, since act deontological theories involve several serious inadequacies, we will devote most of our attention to rule deontological theories.

Kant's Categorical Imperative

The most influential deontologist by far has been the German philosopher, Immanuel Kant (1724-1804). Kant is credited with several revolutionary ideas for solving ancient philosophical problems. One problem attacked by Kant was the possibility of a rational basis for morality. Kant believed that a system of morality that depends on a person's own inclination or desire to do good things is an inadequate motive for acting morally. Kant knew that some people are naturally inclined to help others, for example, but that this inclination varies from person to person. Likewise, Kant knew that the basic human motivation of selfishness can conflict with the desire to help others.

For these reasons, Kant wanted to identify a basis for morally correct action that was free of the erratic and varying psychological motivations that often guide our actions. Kant proposed, instead, that **a morally correct action is one that is performed from duty alone.** My actions derive their moral worth from the fact that I perform them out of duty, not out of inclination. Consequently, when I perform an action out of duty, rather than on the basis of the results I hope to produce, Kant believed that I am exercising my free will in the best way possible.

What is my moral duty, then, in Kant's view? If we are supposed to act from duty alone, and not on kindly impulse, self-interest, or consequences that are produced by our actions, how can our duty be determined?

Kant's proposal here might be phrased, "What is the principle that is the foundation for all morality?" (Kant's quest for precision in ethics was matched by personal habit. It is said that in Kant's hometown of Koenigsberg, Germany, the townspeople could set their clocks by observing when Kant left his house for his afternoon walk.)

Kant proposed as the "supreme principle of morality" what he called the **categorical imperative**. An imperative is something that one must do, i.e., a *duty*. One of Kant's many formulations of the categorical imperative is

> Act as if the maxim of your action were to become through your will a universal law of nature.

We will use two of Kant's examples to illustrate how to apply the categorical imperative. Suppose someone has suffered so much that they no longer want to live. Is suicide morally permissible? The person's maxim of action is described by Kant: "From self-love I make it my principle to shorten my life if its continuance threatens more evil than it promises pleasure."

Now we must simply apply the categorical imperative to this maxim. Can this maxim hold as a universal law of nature? The answer is, "No." Self love is quite plausibly regarded by Kant as a natural law about human beings. This law of nature is part of the basis of the preservation of the human species. A rational universe could therefore not contain both the law that self love preserves life and, at the same time, that self love could be the basis for ending life. As one commentator points out, "...it would be irrational if one and the same principle or instinct could lead to diametrically opposed types of behavior."[14] There is an internal contradiction in the maxim; its validity would undercut the possibility of it existing in the first place.

As you can see, Kant's view of morality has very practical applications, for example, in the area of euthanasia and the "right to die." You may not agree with Kant's conclusion regarding suicide here. For example, you might not agree with Kant that human beings have an instinct toward self preservation. If self love is not a law of nature whose purpose is to preserve life, then suicide may be permissible in such cases as terminal cancer. Even if you don't agree with Kant in this particular example, you can see how Kant places rationality and logical consistency at the center of his ethical theory. What counts is not the consequences of your action, but whether your action is fundamentally rational. That is, could the maxim of your action become a **real** law of nature in our universe? If not, your action is fundamentally irrational, and therefore is morally wrong.

Another of Kant's examples involves a man who needs to borrow money. In order to borrow it, he must promise to pay it back, even though he knows that he will never be able to do so. Is it morally acceptable for the man to make a promise that he has no intention of keeping? Kant describes the man's maxim of action like this: "Whenever I believe myself short of money, I will borrow money and promise to pay it back, though I know this will never be done."

Again, we must simply apply the categorical imperative to this maxim. Could it become a universal law of nature? Kant's answer is worth quoting:

> ... this maxim can never rank as a universal law of nature and be self consistent, but must necessarily contradict itself. For the universality of a law that every one believing himself to be in need can make any promise he pleases with the intention not to keep it would make promising, and the very purpose of promising, itself impossible, since no one would believe he was being promised anything, but would laugh at utterances of this kind as empty shams.[15]

One of the difficulties with Kant's categorical imperative is how to correctly formulate a maxim of action. If the maxim of action is too broadly stated, then certain apparently unobjectionable actions are incorrectly identified as morally wrong. For example, suppose you want to construct a maxim regarding loyalty to fellow officers. The maxim "I will always corroborate my fellow officer's sworn testimony" could make it morally wrong for you to testify that you observed the officer commit a felony. On the other hand, if a maxim of action is made very specific to the circumstances, then many actions that are obviously morally wrong will turn out to be morally right. An example would be the maxim, "I will corroborate my fellow officer's testimony only if the testimony pertains to a Miranda warning." This maxim would make it morally right for you to corroborate another officer's testimony that the suspect was properly "Mirandized," when you know that the suspect was given no warning at all.

Perhaps the most understandable of Kant's formulations of the categorical imperative is the *Formula of the End in Itself.* We will not attempt to work through Kant's argument, which connects the general form of the categorical imperative to the "practical" imperative below. (Nevertheless, you may be able to see the connection for yourself.) Here is what Kant says:

> Act in such a way that you always treat humanity, whether in your own person or in the person of any other, never simply as a means, but always at the same time as an end.

You can see that most types of criminal behavior involve treating other persons as means to achieve selfish ends. This is what is meant by the expression "using people." Criminal justice practitioners, along with the rest of humanity, face Kant's challenge here to never simply "use" other persons to achieve a goal, even if that goal is an admirable one. For example, a police officer may have to depend on an informant in order to obtain information essential to making an arrest. How should the officer treat the informant? What moral obligations does the officer have toward the informant? In Kant's view, the informant can never be simply "used." As a human being, the informant must be treated at the same time as an end in himself or herself, even if doing so compromises the investigation. For Kant, as well as other deontologists, a good end result does not justify an objectionable means to that end.

The Divine Command Theory

Now let's consider a view known in ethics as the **divine command** theory (also known as theological voluntarism). This approach to morality is quite common in our society, and in many other societies. The divine command theory says simply that morally correct actions are those that conform with the commandments of the religious person's chosen deity, e.g., Jehovah, Yahweh, Allah, Shiva, Krishna, or even Satan.[16] For the divine command theorist, the morality of an action originates in the will of God. By definition, this approach denies the moral relevance of the consequences of one's actions. For example, if I am a mainstream Christian, I may subscribe to the Ten Commandments (and the Golden Rule, for that matter) because I believe that they are the word of God, i.e., they are divine commands. Whether following

God's commandments will produce more good consequences than bad consequences is irrelevant. I cannot, in this view of morality, choose to obey or disobey the Ten Commandments on the basis of the consequences of my doing so. The Ten Commandments are correct in and of themselves, by virtue of their divine source.

Note that someone (religious or not) might follow the Ten Commandments on utilitarian grounds. That is, a person might believe that following the Ten Commandments will produce the greatest balance of good over evil for all those affected by the action. This person does not embrace those commandments *per se*; rather, the consequences of following the rules are what counts, not the fact that they may be of divine origin.

More to the point, what if God commanded the Ten Commandments to human beings because He perceived that following them would result in the greatest balance of good over bad consequences? Would the rightness of an action still be grounded in divine will?

The Greek philosopher Plato (428-347 B.C.) wrote about his teacher Socrates' (470-399 B.C.) approach to the problem of divine commands. In a conversation on the steps of the Athens courthouse, Socrates asks the following question of Euthyphro:

> Is what is holy holy because the gods approve it, or do they approve it because it is holy?[17]

Putting Socrates' question in more contemporary terms, can God *make* an action morally right or morally wrong, or does God merely identify those rights and wrongs? For example, could God make it a serious moral wrong to wear a necktie? The common sense answer to Socrates' question would appear to be that divine commands don't create morality. Given this conclusion, the basis for morality must exist outside of the will of God. God can report what is morally right and morally wrong to human beings, but God cannot, by an act of divine will, simply *make* certain actions right and others wrong. Part of Socrates' point in posing the question to Euthyphro was to establish that through rational investigation, human beings can gain knowledge about morality. You should note that this would be impossible if morality were just a matter of divine whim. Attempting to rationally investigate moral issues would be pointless since there would be no independent principles that could be used to predict what God will command next. For the divine command theorist, we couldn't use reason to discover what is right, since *whatever* God commands would *be* morally right, not *vice versa*.

The Golden Rule

Another perspective on morality that is common in our society is "Do unto others as you would have them do unto you..." This principle, known in Christianity as the Golden Rule, is found in the literature of many diverse cultures throughout history. It proposes a simple rule of equity, which is the basis of the concept of equal treatment. That we should not treat others differently from the interests that we would obtain for ourselves is a compelling moral concept. Like any other rule, the Golden Rule may be adopted just as plausibly by the rule utilitarian as by the deontologist.

So, there is no special reason that the Golden Rule should be regarded as a type of deontological moral theory. Nevertheless, this principle is quite often treated from the deontological perspective in that it is held to capture a fundamental principle of morality. Other philosophers have argued that the Golden Rule is a truism, merely stating a logical point about morality that any moral theory must acknowledge.

In the selection, "Morality vs. Slogans," Bernard Gert argues that the Golden Rule is a very poor basic moral rule because it gives us the wrong answers in too many cases. For example, can a police officer expect the Golden Rule to serve reliably in all the professional and personal circumstances he or she might encounter? Few of us wish to be arrested and jailed. This includes police officers themselves, obviously. Now imagine an officer who observes a serious violation, for example, an armed robbery. If the police officer were to employ the Golden Rule, he or she would have to reason, "Would I like to be arrested, if I were the robber?" Since the officer would probably not like to have an arrest "done unto" him or her, the officer would conclude that making the arrest would be morally wrong. Arrest could quickly become a rare event.

Ethical Codes and Canons

We have seen that both utilitarians and deontologists may appeal to rules in order to determine what is morally right. Perhaps because no basic set of moral rules exists in our culture, many professional organizations attempt to regulate the behavior of their members by enumerating which actions are morally permissible and which actions are impermissible. Like Moses, these organizations dictate their "Ten Commandments" to their members, often with little explanation or discussion. These lists of Dos and Don'ts are called **codes of ethics** or ethical **canons**. There is rarely any attempt in a code of ethics to present a rational justification of the rules of the code. Consequently, codes of ethics are not ethical *theories* at all. As mere lists of rules, they may be justified on either teleological or deontological grounds. In some professional codes, for example, the rules may be viewed as justified only insofar as they tend to protect the profession from external review and regulation. Generally, though, codes of ethics embody moral ideals that are basic and uncontroversial from the perspective of the members of the profession.

Because the moral theory justifying the rules of a code of ethics is usually not stated in the code, conflicts among the rules have little chance of being resolved unless there is a "super rule" that tells the professional how to resolve the conflict. This difficulty is obviously not unique to codes of ethics, but it is often the most dramatic weakness of those codes.

A related problem is that codes of ethics do not typically state a hierarchy indicating which rule is to be followed first, second, third, etc. For example, a code of police ethics might require honesty and it might also require "relentless pursuit" of criminals. May the officer lie to a narcotics dealer as part of an undercover operation? Unless the code provides a hierarchy of rules and a means of resolving conflicts, either the code of ethics goes out the window or the undercover operation does. How can a code of ethics play any useful role in assisting the criminal justice practitioner in making morally sound decisions?

First, we must not assume that the code by itself is sufficient in providing guidance to the officer. But, as we will see in Chapter 3, a code of ethics can nonetheless contribute to the decision-making process. Second, professional codes of ethics represent discipline-specific knowledge gleaned from experience. This practical experience will be reflected in a well-written code of ethics. If a code of ethics poses ideal norms that are generally unattainable in practice, the code is likely to be seen as "textbook" material irrelevant to the day-to-day problems of the professional.

Consequently, many (or most) codes of ethics fail miserably in making contact with real situations when taken by themselves. But, together with other moral considerations that are based on rationally examined grounds, the codes of ethics can play an important role in orienting the officer's sense of moral direction. An ethical code might be viewed as a compass. A compass can point you in the right direction, but it is not by itself a means of getting you to the destination.

For example, the "International Chiefs of Police Canons of Police Ethics" demands that an officer's decisions never be influenced by personal opinion. This injunction appears to bar the use of discretion in day-to-day enforcement. It also seems to suggest that ethical considerations other than those explicitly stated in the code cannot be brought into the decision-making process. "Code-bashing" has a long and venerable history, but the weaknesses of specific codes are not really the point. What is important is that codes represent an effort to capture the ideals of professional behavior. They cannot be followed blindly. Instead, the codes can be used as one of several components in making a decision. Codes of ethics for criminal justice practitioners are discussed in more detail in Chapter 3.

Conscience as a Moral Guide

In the film version of Carlo Collodi's children's classic, *The Adventures of Pinocchio*, Jiminy Cricket advises Pinocchio to "Always let your conscience be your guide." Jiminy Cricket's theory is that morally right and wrong actions are to be identified by appealing to one's conscience. Some philosophers might not regard this as a theory of morality at all since it does not state what *constitutes* right and wrong. Instead, it merely provides a criterion for *identifying* right and wrong. For our purposes, this appeal to conscience or moral intuition can be best classified as an act deontological theory, in contrast to the rule deontological theories above.[18]

What the word "conscience" refers to is itself a serious problem. Some people claim that human beings are born with an innate sense of morality. This view is usually based on religious beliefs about the origin and composition of human beings. For example, some people believe that human beings have been created in "the image of God" and therefore retain a "divine spark" of moral sense. Regardless of the question of divine origin, the view that humans possess a uniform set of moral intuitions just seems to be false. Or, if there are such intuitions, many of them are relatively weak and subject to corruption. A quick review of human behavior throughout history and in various cultures shows widely differing views about morally acceptable behavior. A more plausible approach is this: an appeal to one's conscience for guidance will produce desirable results only if one's conscience has been conditioned by a set of morally acceptable practices. If the person's conscience is malformed for whatever reasons, then appealing to it isn't going to be of much use.

How can we tell if our moral sense (or anyone else's moral sense) is in working order? If we say that the consciences of Adolph Hitler and Charles Manson are damaged, it would appear that we are employing some moral criterion other than conscience, in which case an appeal to conscience is superfluous at best. Do not mistakenly conclude that one's moral intuitions are of no value in ethical reasoning. In fact, moral intuitions are essential to begin analysis, but the dictates of individual conscience are clearly inadequate to complete that analysis. So-called **situational ethics** encounters a related problem. In that view, every situation is unique and consequently, previous experience, moral rules, and other guides are either useless or of limited value. One must employ one's moral "sense" in light of the current circumstances and come to a decision. Decisions do not flow from rules. Instead, if rules are of any use at all, they are mere generalizations from individual, unrelated decisions of the past. Conscience or intuition in the given situation forms the basis of the decision-making process. Since every situation is unique, according to this view, it would appear that we have no reason to expect consistency in decision-making. In fact, the concept of consistency seems not to apply at all. If this criticism is successful, it may be fatal to situationalism. Consistency, uniformity, and reliability are plausible requirements for any ethical theory.

In general, the appeal to conscience as a moral guide to action seems to simply push back the problem of moral justification of actions to the problem of moral justification of conscience. This move is certainly permissible, but it clearly raises the question of moral relativism. When the criteria for moral truths are based solely on personal opinion, any alternative based on publicly inspectable reasoning will be inadmissible in the court of ethics. That is, if you want to morally ground your actions on a foundation of personal opinion, then no one can comment about the results. As was argued earlier, the moral relativist's position collapses as a view of morality.

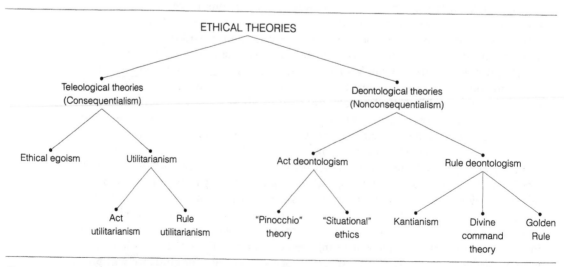

FIGURE 3   Overview of Ethical Theories

Even if conscience cannot operate as a basis of morality, our moral intuitions do play an important role in the development of axioms for a given moral theory. The selection of axioms for a theory is a separate topic that arises in all areas of human investigation. Other areas in which human beings seek understanding—whether it is medicine, economics, mathematics, or physics—will involve theorizing. Those theories are based on axioms. Axioms are statements that are assumed to be true without further proof. Like investigations into any other area of human interest, moral theories must rest on axioms. Quite often, those axioms will emerge from our moral intuitions and, though this is not the same thing as always acting on one's conscience, it does show how our moral intuitions play a role in the rational investigation of moral claims.

More on Consequences and Justice

Think back a moment to the "greatest happiness" idea of utilitarianism. Let's look again at the utilitarian's apparent lack of concern for basic principles of fairness. For example, consider the *distribution* of the happiness and unhappiness that results from performing an action or following a rule. Suppose that you are trying to decide between two alternative actions (or rules), A and B. Alternative A will produce 100 units of happiness and 10 units of unhappiness, so the overall balance is +90. Alternative B will produce 200 units of happiness and 50 units of unhappiness, for an overall balance of +150. According to utilitarianism, alternative B is the morally better choice. However, suppose that in alternative A, the happiness and unhappiness will be fairly evenly distributed. Everyone suffers a bit, but everyone also benefits. Alternative B, on the other hand, will reward the happiness to just a few persons. No one else will benefit at all, but they will have to suffer.

Even though alternative B produces the greatest happiness for all concerned, it appears to be unjust or unfair, relative to alternative A. A Kantian would probably agree, pointing out that alternative B appears to treat most of the people affected purely as a means to the happiness of a few. In other words, utilitarianism does not provide us with a principle of justice or of human rights. To emphasize the point with an extreme case, consider the following example from the American psychologist and philosopher William James (1842–1910).

> ... if the hypothesis were offered us of a world in which ... millions of us [were] kept permanently happy on the one simple condition that a certain lost soul on the far-off edge of things should lead a life of lonely torture, what except a specifical and independent sort of emotion can it be which would make us immediately feel, even though an impulse arose within us to clutch at the happiness so offered, how hideous a thing would be its enjoyment when deliberately accepted as the fruit of such a bargain?[19]

What compromise can be worked out between the utilitarian and the Kantian? It seems plausible to suppose with Kant that human beings have a fundamental right not to be merely used or sacrificed for some greater good benefiting other human beings. For example, we can't kill a person and harvest his or her organs simply to save the lives of three other people. The utilitarian calculations of happiness just don't seem to work correctly in such cases. But, at the same time, most of us are reluctant to dismiss the consequences of our actions as being morally irrelevant.

A balancing of overall good consequences with a respect for the rights of individuals seems necessary. When grotesque violations of basic human rights (however those are defined) are the only means to achieve some social good, a red flag must obviously be raised. Kant's Formula of the End in Itself provides a limiting control on our actions and on the rules that we follow.

The difficult cases arise when the consequences are very good and the abridgement of rights is minimal. It should not be surprising that some of the most controversial social issues in the administration of justice involve precisely this conflict. Consider the constitutional right of American citizens to keep and bear arms. This right is currently in dramatic conflict with the socially desirable consequences of outlawing Teflon bullets, assault rifles, and other armaments that are used almost exclusively by criminals against their victims and against police officers.

Moral Rights and Legal Rights

For criminal justice practitioners, we propose that a fundamental principle of justice guiding one's professional performance is *due process*. The consequences of one's actions, or of following a rule, will always be limited by consideration of the rights of individuals, so the right to due process forms a grounding or *prima facie* duty for the practitioner. A prima facie duty is a duty that one is obligated to perform if other competing moral considerations do not arise.[20]

In many countries, due process is a legal right, but there are good reasons for supposing that human beings have a moral right to due process. When rights are denied by a repressive political regime, the right to due process is often one of the first rights to be denied. Due process requires society to treat individuals in such a way that the autonomy of the individual is always firmly in view. Due process challenges the view that the individual may be sacrificed for the good of the whole. To deprive a person of his or her autonomy, or to limit autonomy, without due process is to violate the Kantian imperative.

Other rights that must be considered by the criminal justice practitioner are legal rights, such as the right to have counsel present during interrogation. Most, if not all, basic legal rights can be traced to what the founding fathers saw as the moral right to freedom. As you already know, Kant had a great deal to say about freedom and autonomy, but since much of his work in ethics coincided with the framing of the U.S. Constitution, there was no actual connection. One of the framers' chief influences in this regard was the British philosopher, John Locke.

At any rate, there is a direct connection between legal rights and moral rights. This connection is not a necessary one though, because legal rights are not required to have any moral foundation at all. Or the moral foundation may be inconsistent. This is certainly true in the earlier "right" to own slaves. The legal right to be free to do with one's property as one wishes was not correctly balanced against the moral right of every human being to never be treated as a means to an end. The legal rule giving a right to property and the Kantian moral imperative were not correctly balanced by the founding fathers (backing down on a constitutional ban on slavery was viewed as a necessary compromise during the constitutional conventions).

As we move from chapter to chapter, we will refer frequently to the balancing of good consequences with the basic rights of persons and to the balancing of competing rights. The next chapter deals specifically with the right to due process, which, as you will see, is at the very foundation of criminal justice.

Notes

1. References to the courts include prosecutors, defense attorneys, judges, law administrators, probation officers, and other court personnel. Judicial and legal ethics form a distinct area of applied ethics and are outside the scope of this book. Even though we limit our treatment primarily to policing, probation, corrections, juvenile justice, and parole, much of what we have to say has relevance to the court system generally.

2. Psychologists such as Lawrence Kohlberg believe that people progress along a scale of moral development. In Kohlberg's theory, many persons never develop to the final stage of autonomous moral agency. See Lawrence Kohlberg, "Moral Development: A Modern Statement of the Platonic View," in James M. Gustafson, et al., *Moral Education: Five Lectures.* (Cambridge: Harvard University Press, 1970). In a continuing debate on Kohlberg's theory, psychologist Carol Gilligan has argued persuasively that the Kohlberg theory of development is seriously biased toward males. See Carol Gilligan, *In a Different Voice: Psychological Theory and Women's Development.* (Cambridge: Harvard University Press, 1982).

3. The other areas are logic, epistemology, metaphysics, and aesthetics.

4. There is an excellent discussion of how to resolve the conflict between legal advocacy and moral duty in Elliot D. Cohen, "Pure Legal Advocacy and Moral Agents: Two Concepts of a Lawyer in an Adversary System," *Criminal Justice Ethics,* Vol. 4:1 (Winter/Spring 1985), pp. 38–59.

5. Stephen A. Satris, "Student Relativism," *Teaching Philosophy,* Vol. 9:3 (September 1986), p. 193.

6. There are several varieties of moral relativism, many of which collapse into what is known as moral subjectivism. We do not attempt to draw distinctions among these alternative characterizations in this text. Our aim is simply to reject a very common, and destructive, form of relativism that is commonly held. For a brief and accessible discussion of moral relativism, see Richard B. Brandt's entry, "Ethical Relativism," in Paul Edwards (ed.), *The Encyclopedia of Philosophy.* (New York: Macmillan, 1967), vol. 3. Also see Jonathan Harrison's entries, "Ethical Objectivism" and "Ethical Subjectivism," *ibid.*

7. The Greek philosopher Socrates argued over 2,300 years ago that not even a god could make what is unholy, holy. To the religious person, at least, it seems implausible to suppose that humans could do what God cannot. Socrates' argument will be examined in more detail later in this chapter.

8. There is a large amount of literature on the concept of supererogation. See J. O. Urmson's paper, "Saints and Heroes," in A. I. Meldon (ed.), *Essays in Moral Philosophy.* (Seattle: University of Washington Press, 1958), and Joel Feinberg, "Supererogation and Rules," *Ethics,* vol. 71 (1961), pp. 276–288.

9. See A. M. Rosenthal, *The Thirty-Eight Witnesses.* (New York: McGraw-Hill, 1964).

10. Jeremy Bentham, *Fragment on Government and Introduction to the Principles of Morals and Legislation,* Wilfred Harrison, ed. (Oxford: Oxford University Press, 1948), Ch. 4.

11. For example, see *Hudson v. McMillian* (1992), reprinted in Chapter 8.

12. See J. J. C. Smart, "Extreme and Restricted Utilitarianism," *The Philosophical Quarterly,* vol. 6 (1956), pp. 344-354.

13. Similar examples can be produced showing, for example, that an act utilitarian approach fails to justify not voting when one could have voted. It might be argued here that there is an act utilitarian justification for not voting, violating the water restrictions, etc., if most or all of the rest of society does not make decisions on act utilitarian grounds. The only difficulty would be the disutility of the example I set for others. If my actions motivate others to convert to act utilitarianism, then I'll no longer be able to justify not voting or breaking the water ban.

14. J. Kemp, "Kant's Examples of the Categorical Imperative," *Philosophical Quarterly* 8 (1958), p. 67.

15. Immanuel Kant, *Groundwork of the Metaphysic of Morals.* Translated and analyzed by H. J. Paton. (New York: Harper Torchbooks, 1964), p. 90.

16. Sometimes this theory is confused with "natural law" theory, the thesis that minimally, what is legal is not identical with what is just, and that the norms of justice are grounded in nature. A divine command theorist will very likely be a natural law theorist, but not vice versa.

17. Plato, *Euthyphro,* 10a, Lane Cooper (trans.) as reprinted in Edith Hamilton and Huntington Cairns (eds.), *The Collected Dialogues of Plato* (Princeton: Princeton University Press, 1961).

18. Cf. William K. Frankena, *Ethics.* Second edition. (Englewood Cliffs: Prentice-Hall, 1973), pp. 16 ff. In this classic book, Frankena distinguishes between rule and act deontology, identifying moral intuitionism, appeals to conscience, and "situational" ethics as varieties of act deontologism. Frankena argues that act deontological theories all fail to provide any moral guidance whatsoever because those theories deny the inherent generality of moral judgments.

19. William James, "The Moral Philosopher and the Moral Life," *International Journal of Ethics,* Vol. I, April 1891. Republished in William James, *The Will to Believe and Other Essays in Popular Philosophy* (New York: Longmans, Green and Company, 1897), pp. 184-215. The original source of this paper was derived from an editorial note in John K. Roth (ed.), *The Moral Philosophy of William James* (New York: Thomas Y. Crowell, 1969), p. 169.

20. See W. D. Ross, *The Right and the Good.* (Oxford: Oxford University Press, 1930). Reprinted by Hackett Publishing Company, 1988. Ross, who created the concept of a prima facie duty, speaks of these duties as 'conditional'.

Ethical Relativity and Ethical Absolutism

WALTER T. STACE

ANY ETHICAL POSITION WHICH denies that there is a single moral standard equally applicable to all men at all times may fairly be called a species of ethical relativity. There is not, the relativist asserts, merely one moral law, one code, one standard. There are many moral laws, codes, standards. What morality ordains in one place or age may be quite different from what morality ordains in another place or age. The moral code of Chinamen is quite different from that of Europeans, that of African savages quite different from both. Any morality, therefore, is relative to the age, the place, and the circumstances in which it is found. It is in no sense absolute.

This does not mean merely—as one might at first sight be inclined to suppose—that the very same kind of action which is *thought* right in one country and period may be *thought* wrong in another. This would be a mere platitude, the truth of which everyone would have to admit. Even the absolutist would admit this—would even wish to emphasize it—since he is well aware that different peoples have different sets of moral ideas, and his whole point is that some of these sets of ideas are false. What the relativist means to assert is, not this platitude, but that the very same kind of action which *is* right in one country and period may *be* wrong in another. And this, far from being a platitude, is a very startling assertion.

It is very important to grasp thoroughly the difference between the two ideas. For there is reason to think that many minds tend to find ethical relativity attractive because they fail to keep them clearly apart. It is so very obvious that moral ideas differ from country to country and from age to age. And it is so very easy, if you are mentally lazy, to suppose that to say this means the same as to say that no universal moral standard exists,—or in other words that it implies ethical relativity. We fail to see that the word "standard" is used in two different senses. It is perfectly true that, in one sense, there are many variable moral standards. We speak of judging a man by the standard of his time. And this implies that different times have different standards. And this, of course, is quite true. But when the word "standard" is used in this sense it means simply the set of moral ideas current during the period in question. It means what people *think* right, whether as a matter of fact it *is* right or not. On the other hand when the absolutist asserts that there exists a single universal moral "standard," he is not using the word in this sense at all. He means by "standard" what *is* right as distinct from what people merely think right. His point is that although what people think right varies in different countries and periods, yet what actually is right is everywhere and always the same. And it follows that when the ethical relativist disputes the position of the absolutist and denies that any universal moral standard exists he too means by "standard" what actually is right. But it is exceedingly easy, if we are not careful, to slip loosely from using the word in the first sense to using it in the second sense; and to suppose that the variability of moral beliefs is the same thing as the variability of what really is moral. And unless we keep the two senses of the word "standard" distinct, we are likely to think the creed of ethical relativity much more plausible than it actually is.

The genuine relativist, then, does not merely mean that Chinamen may think right what Frenchmen think wrong. He means that what *is* wrong for the Frenchman may *be* right for the Chinaman. And if one enquires how, in those circumstances, one is to know what actually is right in China or in France, the answer comes quite glibly. What is right in China is the same as what people think right in China; and what is right in France is the same as what people think right in France. So that, if you want to know what is moral in any particular country or age all you have to do is to ascertain what are the moral ideas current in that age or country. Those ideas are, *for that age or country,* right. Thus what is morally right is identified with what is thought to be morally right, and the distinction which we made above between these two is simply denied. To put the same thing in another way, it is denied that there can be or ought to be any distinction between the two senses of the word "standard." There is only one kind of standard of right and wrong, namely, the moral ideas current in any particular age or country.

Moral right *means* what people think morally right. It has no other meaning. What Frenchmen think right is, therefore, right *for Frenchmen.* And evidently one must conclude—though I am not aware that relativists are anxious to draw one's attention to such unsavoury but yet absolutely necessary conclusions from their creed—that cannibalism is right for people who believe in it, that human sacrifice is right for those races which practice it, and that burning widows alive was right for Hindus until the British stepped in and compelled the Hindus to behave immorally by allowing their widows to remain alive....

The relativist does not, of course, mean that there actually is an objective moral standard in France and a different objective standard in England, and that French and British opinions respectively give us correct information about these different standards. His point is rather that there are no objectively true moral standards at all. There is no single universal objective standard. Nor are there a variety of local objective standards. All standards are subjective. People's subjective feelings about morality are the only standards which exist.

To sum up. The ethical relativist consistently denies, it would seem, whatever the ethical absolutist asserts. For the absolutist there is a single universal moral standard. For the relativist there is no such standard. There are only local, ephemeral, and variable standards. For the absolutist there are two senses of the word "standard."

Standards in the sense of sets of current moral ideas are relative and changeable. But the standard in the sense of what is actually morally right is absolute and unchanging. For the relativist no such distinction can be made. There is only one meaning of the word standard, namely, that which refers to local and variable sets of moral ideas. Or if it is insisted that the word must be allowed two meanings, then the relativist will say that there is at any rate no actual example of a standard in the absolute sense, and that the word as thus used is an empty name to which nothing in reality corresponds; so that the distinction between the two meanings becomes empty and useless. Finally—though this is merely saying the same thing in another way—the absolutist makes a distinction between what actually is right and what is thought right. The relativist rejects this distinction and identifies what is moral with what is thought moral by certain human beings or groups of human beings....

I shall now proceed to consider, first, the main arguments which can be urged in favour of ethical relativity; and secondly the arguments which can be urged against it....

There are, I think, [two] main arguments in favour of ethical relativity. The first is that which relies upon the actual varieties of moral "standards" found in the world. It was easy enough to believe in a single absolute morality in older times when there was no anthropology, when all humanity was divided clearly into two groups, Christian peoples and the "heathen." Christian peoples knew and possessed the one true morality. The rest were savages whose moral ideas could be ignored. But all this is changed. Greater knowledge has brought greater tolerance. We can no longer exalt our own morality as alone true, while dismissing all other moralities as false or inferior. The investigations of anthropologists have shown that there exist side by side in the world a bewildering variety of moral codes. On this topic endless volumes have been written, masses of evidence piled up. Anthropologists have ransacked the Melanesian Islands, the jungles of New Guinea, the steppes of Siberia, the deserts of Australia, the forests of central Africa, and have brought back with them countless examples of weird, extravagant, and fantastic "moral" customs with which to confound us. We learn that all kinds of horrible practices are, in this, that, or the other place, regarded as essential to virtue. We find that there is nothing, or next to nothing, which has always and everywhere been regarded as morally good by all men. Where then is our universal morality? Can we, in face of all this evidence, deny that it is nothing but an empty dream ?

This argument, taken by itself, is a very weak one. It relies upon a single set of facts—the variable moral customs of the world. But this variability of moral ideas is admitted by both parties to the dispute, and is capable of ready explanation upon the hypothesis of either party. The relativist says that the facts are to be explained by the non-existence of any absolute moral standard. The absolutist says that they are to be explained by human ignorance of what the absolute moral standard is. And he can truly point out that men have differed widely in their opinions about all manner of topics including the subject matters of the physical sciences—just as much as they differ about morals. And if the various different opinions which men have held about the shape of the earth do not prove that it has no one real shape, neither do the various opinions which they have held about morality prove that there is no one true morality.

Thus the facts can be explained equally plausibly on either hypothesis. There is nothing in the facts themselves which compels us to prefer the relativistic hypothesis to that of the absolutist.

And therefore the argument fails to prove the relativist conclusion. If that conclusion is to be established, it must be by means of other considerations. . . .

The [second] argument in favour of ethical relativity is also a very strong one. . . . It consists in alleging that no one has ever been able to discover upon what foundation an absolute morality could rest, or from what source a universally binding moral code could derive its authority.

If, for example, it is an absolute and unalterable moral rule that all men ought to be unselfish, from whence does this *command* issue? For a command it certainly is, phrase it how you please. There is no difference in meaning between the sentence "You ought to be unselfish" and the sentence "Be unselfish." Now a command implies a commander. An obligation implies some authority which obliges. Who is this commander, what [is] this authority? Thus the vastly difficult question is raised of *the basis of moral obligation.* Now the argument of the relativist would be that it is impossible to find any basis for a universally binding moral law; but that it is quite easy to discover a basis for morality if moral codes are admitted to be variable, ephemeral, and relative to time, place, and circumstance. . . .

No such easy solution of the basis of moral obligation is open to the absolutist. He believes in moral commands obedience to which is obligatory on all men, whether they know it or not, whatever they feel, and whatever their customs may be. Such uniform obligation cannot be founded upon feelings, because feelings are—or are said to be—variable. And there is no set of customs which is more than local in its operation. The will of God as the source of a universal law is no longer a feasible suggestion. And there is obviously no mundane authority, king, or Pope, or super-state, to which all men admit allegiance, and which could have the recognized right to issue universally binding decrees. Where then is the absolutist to turn for an answer to the question? And if he cannot find one, he will have to admit the claims of the ethical relativist; or at least he will have to give up his own claims. . . .

This argument is undoubtedly very strong. It *is* absolutely essential to solve the problem of the basis of moral obligation if we are to believe in any kind of moral standards other than those provided by mere custom or by irrational emotions. It is idle to talk about a universal morality unless we can point to the source of its authority—or at least to do so is to indulge in a faith which is without rational ground. To cherish a blind faith in morality may be, for the average man whose business is primarily to live aright and not to theorize, sufficient. Perhaps it is his wisest course. But it will not do for the philosopher. His function, or at least one of his functions, is precisely to discover the rational grounds of our everyday beliefs—if they have any. Philosophically and intellectually, then, we cannot accept belief in a universally binding morality unless we can discover upon what foundation its obligatory character rests.

But in spite of the strength of the argument thus posed in favour of ethical relativity, it is not impregnable. For it leaves open one loophole. It is always possible that some theory, not yet examined, may provide a basis for a universal moral obligation. The argument rests upon the negative proposition that *there is no theory which can provide a basis for a universal morality*. But it is notoriously difficult to prove a negative. How can you prove that there are no green swans? All you can show is that none have been found so far. And then it is always possible that one will be found tomorrow. So it is here. The relativist shows that no theory of the basis of moral obligation has yet been discovered which could validate a universal morality. Perhaps. But it is just conceivable that one might be discovered in the course of this book.

It is time that we turned our attention from the case in favour of ethical relativity to the case against it. Now the case against it consists, to a very large extent, in urging that, if taken seriously and pressed to its logical conclusion, ethical relativity can only end in destroying the conception of morality altogether, in undermining its practical efficacy, in rendering meaningless many almost universally accepted truths about human affairs, in robbing human beings of any incentive to strive for a better world, in taking the life-blood out of every ideal and every aspiration which has ever ennobled the life of man....

First of all, then, ethical relativity, in asserting that the moral standards of particular social groups are the only standards which exist, renders meaningless all propositions which attempt to compare these standards with one another in respect of their moral worth. And this is a very serious matter indeed. We are accustomed to think that the moral ideas of one nation or social group may be "higher" or "lower" than those of another. We believe, for example, that Christian ethical ideals are nobler than those of the savage races of central Africa. Probably most of us would think that the Chinese moral standards are higher than those of the inhabitants of New Guinea. In short we habitually compare one civilization with another and judge the sets of ethical ideas to be found in them to be some better, some worse. The fact that such judgments are very difficult to make with any justice, and that they are frequently made on very superficial and prejudiced grounds, has no bearing on the question now at issue. The question is whether such judgments have any *meaning*. We habitually assume that they have.

But on the basis of ethical relativity they can have none whatever. For the relativist must hold that there is no *common* standard which can be applied to the various civilizations judged. Any such comparison of moral standards implies the existence of some superior standard which is applicable to both. And the existence of any such standard is precisely what the relativist denies. According to him the Christian standard is applicable only to Christians, the Chinese standard only to Chinese, the New Guinea standard only to the inhabitants of New Guinea.

What is true of comparisons between the moral standards of different races will also be true of comparisons between those of different ages. It is not unusual to ask such questions as whether the standard of our own day is superior to that which existed among our ancestors five hundred years ago. And when we remember that our ancestors employed slaves, practiced barbaric physical tortures, and burnt people alive, we may be inclined to think that it is. At any rate we assume that the question is one which has meaning and is capable of rational discussion. But if the ethical relativist is right, whatever we assert on this subject must be totally meaningless. For here again there is no common standard which could form the basis of any such judgments. . . .

There is indeed one way in which the ethical relativist can give some sort of meaning to judgments of higher or lower as applied to the moral ideas of different races or ages. What he will have to say is that we assume *our* standards to be the best simply because they are ours. And we judge other standards by our own. If we say that Chinese moral codes are better than those of African cannibals, what we *mean* by this is that they are better *according to our standards*. We mean, that is to say, that Chinese standards are *more like our own* than African standards are. "Better" accordingly *means* "more like us." "Worse" means "less like us." It thus becomes clear that judgments of better and worse in such cases do not express anything that is really true at all. They merely give expression to our perfectly groundless satisfaction with our own ideas. In short, they give expression to nothing but our egotism and self-conceit. Our moral ideals are not really better than those of the savage. We are simply deluded by our egotism into thinking they are. The African savage has just as good a right to think his morality the best as we have to think ours the best. His opinion is just as well grounded as ours, or rather both opinions are equally groundless. . . .

Thus the ethical relativist must treat all judgments comparing different moralities as either entirely meaningless; or, if this course appears too drastic, he has the alternative of declaring that they have for their meaning-content nothing except the vanity and egotism of those who pass them. . . .

I come now to a second point. Up to the present I have allowed it to be taken tacitly for granted that, though judgments comparing different races and ages in respect of the worth of their moral codes are impossible for the ethical relativist, yet judgments of comparison between individuals living within the same social group would be quite possible. For individuals living within the same social group would presumably be subject to the same moral code, that of their group, and this would therefore constitute, as between these individuals, a common standard by which they could both be measured. We have not here, as we had in the other case, the difficulty of the absence of any common standard of comparison. It should therefore be possible for the ethical relativist to say quite meaningfully that President Lincoln was a better man than some criminal or moral imbecile of his own time and country, or that Jesus was a better man than Judas Iscariot.

But is even this minimum of moral judgment really possible on relativist grounds? It seems to me that it is not. For when once the whole of humanity is abandoned as the area covered by a single moral standard, what smaller areas are to be adopted as the *loci* of different standards? Where are we to draw the lines of demarcation? We can split up humanity, perhaps,—though the procedure will be very arbitrary—into races, races into nations, nations into tribes, tribes into families, families into individuals. Where are we going to draw the *moral* boundaries? Does the *locus* of a particular moral standard reside in a race, a nation, a tribe, a family, or an individual? Perhaps the blessed phrase "social group" will be dragged in to save the situation. Each such group, we shall be told, has its own moral code which is, for it, right. But what *is* a "group"? Can anyone define it or give its boundaries? . . .

The difficulty is not, as might be thought, merely an academic difficulty of logical definition. If that were all, I should not press the point. But the ambiguity has practical consequences which are disastrous for morality. No one is likely to say that moral codes are confined within the arbitrary limits of the geographical divisions of countries. Nor are the notions of race, nation, or political state likely to help us.

To bring out the essentially practical character of the difficulty let us put it in the form of concrete questions. Does the American nation constitute a "group" having a single moral standard? Or does the standard of what I ought to do change continuously as I cross the continent in a railway train? Do different States of the Union have different moral codes? Perhaps every town and village has its own peculiar standard. This may at first sight seem reasonable enough. "In Rome do as Rome does" may seem as good a rule in morals as it is in etiquette. But can we stop there? Within the village are numerous cliques each having its own set of ideas. Why should not each of these claim to be bound only by its own special and peculiar moral standards? And if it comes to that, why should not the gangsters of Chicago claim to constitute a group having its own morality, so that its murders and debaucheries must be viewed as "right" by the only standard which can legitimately be applied to it? And if it be answered that the nation will not tolerate this, that may be so. But this is to put the foundation of right simply in the superior force of the majority. In that case whoever is stronger will be right, however monstrous his ideas and actions. And if we cannot deny to any set of people the right to have its own morality, is it not clear that, in the end, we cannot even deny this right to the individual? Every individual man and woman can put up, on this view, an irrefutable claim to be judged by no standard except his or her own.

If these arguments are valid, the ethical relativist cannot really maintain that there is anywhere to be found a moral standard binding upon anybody against his will. And he cannot maintain that, even within the social group, there is a common standard as between individuals. And if that is so, then even judgments to the effect that one man is morally better than another become meaningless. All moral valuation thus vanishes. There is nothing to prevent each man from being a rule unto himself. The result will be moral chaos and the collapse of all effective standards.

Perhaps, in regard to the difficulty of defining the social group, the relativist may make the following suggestion. If we admit, he may say, that it is impossible or very difficult to define a group territorially or nationally or geographically, it is still possible to define it logically. We will simply define an ethical group as any set of persons (whether they live together in one place or are scattered about in many places over the earth) who recognize one and the same moral standard. As a matter of fact such groups will as a rule be found occupying each something like a single locality. The people in one country, or at least in one village, tend to think much alike. But theoretically at least the members of an ethical group so defined might be scattered all over the face of the globe. However that may be, it will now be possible to make meaningful statements to the effect that one individual is morally better or worse than another, so long as we keep within the ethical group so defined. For the individuals of the ethical group will have as their common standard the ethical belief or beliefs the acknowledgment of which constitutes the defining characteristic of the group. By this common standard they can be judged and compared with one another. Therefore it is not true that ethical relativity necessarily makes all such judgments of moral comparison between individuals meaningless.

I admit the logic of this. Theoretically judgments of comparison can be given meaning in this way. Nevertheless there are fatal objections to the suggestion....

But even if we assume that the difficulty about defining moral groups has been surmounted, a further difficulty presents itself. Suppose that we have now definitely decided what are the exact boundaries of the social group within which a moral standard is to be operative. And we will assume—as is invariably done by relativists themselves—that this group is to be some actually existing social community such as a tribe or nation. How are we to know, even then, what actually *is* the moral standard within that group? How is anyone to know? How is even a member of the group to know? For there are certain to be within the group—at least this will be true among advanced peoples—wide differences of opinion as to what is right, what wrong. Whose opinion, then, is to be taken as representing *the* moral standard of the group? Either we must take the opinion of the majority within the group, or the opinion of some minority. If we rely upon the ideas of the majority, the results will be disastrous. Wherever there is found among a people a small band of select spirits, or perhaps one man, working for the establishment of higher and nobler ideals than those commonly accepted by the group, we shall be compelled to hold that, for that people at that time, the majority are right, and that the reformers are wrong and are preaching what is immoral....

The ethical relativists are great empiricists. *What* is the actual moral standard of any group can only be discovered, they tell us, by an examination on the ground of the moral opinions and customs of that group. But will they tell us how they propose to decide, when they get to the ground, which of the many moral opinions they are sure to find there is *the* right one in that group? To some extent they will be able to do this for the Melanesian Islanders—from whom apparently all lessons in the nature of morality are in future to be taken. But it is certain that they cannot do it for advanced peoples whose members have learnt to think for themselves and to entertain among themselves a wide variety of opinions. They cannot do it unless they accept the calamitous view that the ethical opinion of the majority is always right. We are left therefore once more with the conclusion that, even within a particular social group, anybody's moral opinion is as good as anybody else's, and that every man is entitled to be judged by his own standards.

Finally, not only is ethical relativity disastrous in its consequences for moral theory. It cannot be doubted that it must tend to be equally disastrous in its impact upon practical conduct. If men come really to believe that one moral standard is as good as another, they will conclude that their own moral standard has nothing special to recommend it. They might as well then slip down to some lower and easier standard. It is true that, for a time, it may be possible to hold one view in theory and to act practically upon another. But ideas, even philosophical ideas, are not so ineffectual that they can remain for ever idle in the upper chambers of the intellect. In the end they seep down to the level of practice. They get themselves acted on....

These, then, are the main arguments which the antirelativist will urge against ethical relativity. And perhaps finally he will attempt a diagnosis of the social, intellectual, and psychological conditions of our time to which the emergence of ethical relativism is to be attributed.

Study Questions

1. For the ethical absolutist or objectivist, there are two senses of the word "standard." What are they?

2. What form of relativism does Stace view as a "mere platitude" that everyone agrees with? Define the form of relativism that Stace finds "startling." Is it startling to you? Why?

3. What are the two main arguments for ethical relativism identified by Stace? How does Stace counter these arguments? Do you think that Stace's attack is successful? Why?

4. Do you believe that anyone's moral opinion is as valid as anybody else's? Why? How does Stace answer this question?

5. In cases of moral controversy, people often ask the question, "Who is to decide?" Do you believe that a moral statement can be made true (or false) simply by deciding that it is? Why?

What Utilitarianism Is

JOHN STUART MILL

A PASSING REMARK IS all that needs be given to the ignorant blunder of supposing that those who stand up for utility as the test of right and wrong use the term in that restricted and merely colloquial sense in which utility is opposed to pleasure. An apology is due to the philosophical opponents of utilitarianism for even the momentary appearance of confounding them with anyone capable of so absurd a misconception; which is the more extraordinary, inasmuch as the contrary accusation, of referring everything to pleasure, and that, too, in its grossest form, is another of the common charges against utilitarianism: and, as has been pointedly remarked by an able writer, the same sort of persons, and often the very same persons, denounce the theory "as impracticably dry when the word 'utility' precedes the word 'pleasure,' and as too practicably voluptuous when the word 'pleasure' precedes the word 'utility.'" Those who know anything about the matter are aware that every writer, from Epicurus to Bentham, who maintained the theory of utility meant by it, not something to be contradistinguished from pleasure, but pleasure itself, together with exemption from pain; and instead of opposing the useful to the agreeable or the ornamental, have always declared that the useful means these, among other things. Yet the common herd, including the herd of writers, not only in newspapers and periodicals, but in books of weight and pretension, are perpetually falling into this shallow mistake. Having caught up the word "utilitarian," while knowing nothing whatever about it but its sound, they habitually express by it the rejection or the neglect of pleasure in some of its forms: of beauty, of ornament, or of amusement. Nor is the term thus ignorantly misapplied solely in disparagement, but occasionally in compliment, as though it implied superiority to frivolity and the mere pleasures of the moment. And this perverted use is the only one in which the word is popularly known, and the one from which the new generation are acquiring their sole notion of its meaning. Those who introduced the word, but who had for many years discontinued it as a distinctive appellation, may well feel themselves called upon to resume it if by doing so they can hope to contribute anything toward rescuing it from this utter degradation.[1]

The creed which accepts as the foundation of morals "utility" or the "greatest happiness principle" holds that actions are right in proportion as they tend to promote happiness; wrong as they tend to produce the reverse of happiness. By happiness is intended pleasure and the absence of pain; by unhappiness, pain and the privation of pleasure. To give a clear view of the moral standard set up by the theory, much more requires to be said; in particular, what things it includes in the ideas of pain and pleasure, and to what extent this is left an open question. But these supplementary explanations do not affect the theory of life on which this theory of morality is grounded— namely, that pleasure and freedom from pain are the only things desirable as ends; and that all desirable things (which are as numerous in the utilitarian as in any other scheme) are desirable either for pleasure inherent in themselves or as means to the promotion of pleasure and the prevention of pain.

From John Stuart Mill, Utilitarianism, edited, with an introduction, by George Sher. (Indianapolis: Hackett Publishing Company, 1979). Used by permission of Hackett Publishing Company. Utilitarianism was originally published in 1861.

Now such a theory of life excites in many minds, and among them in some of the most estimable in feeling and purpose, inveterate dislike. To suppose that life has (as they express it) no higher end than pleasure—no better and nobler object of desire and pursuit—they designate as utterly mean and groveling, as a doctrine worthy only of swine, to whom the followers of Epicurus were, at a very early period, contemptuously likened; and modern holders of the doctrine are occasionally made the subject of equally polite comparisons by its German, French, and English assailants.

When thus attacked, the Epicureans have always answered that it is not they, but their accusers, who represent human nature in a degrading light, since the accusation supposes human beings to be capable of no pleasures except those of which swine are capable. If this supposition were true, the charge could not be gainsaid, but would then be no longer an imputation; for if the sources of pleasure were precisely the same to human beings and to swine, the rule of life which is good enough for the one would be good enough for the other. The comparison of the Epicurean life to that of beasts is felt as degrading, precisely because a beast's pleasures do not satisfy a human being's conceptions of happiness. Human beings have faculties more elevated than the animal appetites and, when once made conscious of them, do not regard anything as happiness which does not include their gratification. I do not indeed, consider the Epicureans to have been by any means faultless in drawing out their scheme of consequences from the utilitarian principle. To do this in any sufficient manner, many Stoic, as well as Christian, elements require to be included. But there is no known Epicurean theory of life which does not assign to the pleasures of the intellect, of the feelings and imagination, and of the moral sentiments a much higher value as pleasures than to those of mere sensation. It must be admitted, however, that utilitarian writers in general have placed the superiority of mental over bodily pleasures chiefly in the greater permanency, safety, uncostliness, etc., of the former—that is, in their circumstantial advantages rather than in their intrinsic nature. And on all these points utilitarians have fully proved their case; but they might have taken the other and, as it may be called, higher ground with entire consistency. It is quite compatible with the principle of utility to recognize the fact that some kinds of pleasure are more desirable and more valuable than others. It would be absurd that, while in estimating all other things quality is considered as well as quantity, the estimation of pleasure should be supposed to depend on quantity alone.

If I am asked what I mean by difference of quality in pleasures, or what makes one pleasure more valuable than another, merely as a pleasure, except its being greater in amount, there is but one possible answer. Of two pleasures, if there be one to which all or almost all who have experience of both give a decided preference, irrespective of any feeling of moral obligation to prefer it, that is the more desirable pleasure. If one of the two is, by those who are competently acquainted with both, placed so far above the other that they prefer it, even though knowing it to be attended with a greater amount of discontent, and would not resign it for any quantity of the other pleasure which their nature is capable of, we are justified in ascribing to the preferred enjoyment a superiority in quality so far outweighing quantity as to render it, in comparison, of small account.

Now it is an unquestionable fact that those who are equally acquainted with and equally capable of appreciating and enjoying both do give a most marked preference to the manner of existence which employs their higher faculties. Few human creatures would consent to be changed into any of the lower animals for a promise of the fullest allowance of a beast's pleasures; no intelligent human being would consent to be a fool, no instructed person would be an ignoramus, no person of feeling and conscience would be selfish and base, even though they should be persuaded that the fool, the dunce, or the rascal is better satisfied with his lot than they are with theirs. They would not resign what they possess more than he for the most complete satisfaction of all the desires which they have in common with him. If they ever fancy they would, it is only in cases of unhappiness so extreme that to escape from it they would exchange their lot for almost any other, however undesirable in their own eyes. A being of higher faculties requires more to make him happy, is capable probably of more acute suffering, and certainly accessible to it at more points, than one of an inferior type; but in spite of these liabilities, he can never really wish to sink into what he feels to be a lower grade of existence. We may give what explanation we please of this unwillingness; we may attribute it to pride, a name which is given indiscriminately to some of the most and to some of the least estimable feelings of which mankind are capable; we may refer it to the love of liberty and personal independence, an appeal to which was with the Stoics one of the most effective means for the inculcation of it; to the love of power or to the love of excitement, both of which do really enter into and contribute to it; but its most appropriate appellation is a sense of dignity, which all human beings possess in one form or other, and in some, though by no means in exact, proportion to their higher faculties, and which is so essential a part of the happiness of those in whom it is strong that nothing which conflicts with it could be otherwise than momentarily an object of desire to them. Whoever supposes that this preference takes place at a sacrifice of happiness—that the superior being, in anything like equal circumstances, is not happier than the inferior—confounds the two very different ideas of happiness and content. It is indisputable that the being whose capacities of enjoyment are low has the greatest chance of having them fully satisfied; and a highly endowed being will always feel that any happiness which he can look for, as the world is constituted, is imperfect. But he can learn to bear its imperfections, if they are at all bearable; and they will not make him envy the being who is indeed unconscious of the imperfections, but only because he feels not at all the good which those imperfections qualify. It is better to be a human being dissatisfied than a pig satisfied; better to be Socrates dissatisfied than a fool satisfied. And if the fool, or the pig, are of a different opinion, it is because they only know their own side of the question. The other party to the comparison knows both sides.

It may be objected that many who are capable of the higher pleasures occasionally, under the influence of temptation, postpone them to the lower. But this is quite compatible with a full appreciation of the intrinsic superiority of the higher. Men often, from infirmity of character, make their election for the nearer good, though they know it to be the less valuable; and this no less when the choice is between two bodily pleasures than when it is between bodily and mental. They pursue sensual indulgences to the injury of health, though perfectly aware that health is the greater good. It may be further objected that many who begin with youthful enthusiasm for everything noble, as they advance in years, sink into indolence and selfishness. But I do not believe that those who undergo this very common change voluntarily choose the lower description of pleasures in preference to the higher. I believe that, before they devote themselves exclusively to the one, they have already become incapable of the other. Capacity for the nobler feelings is in most natures a very tender plant, easily killed, not only by hostile influences, but by mere want of sustenance; and in the majority of young persons it speedily dies away if the occupations to which their position in life has devoted them, and the society into which it has thrown them, are not favorable to keeping that higher capacity in exercise. Men lose their high aspirations as they lose their intellectual tastes, because they have not time or opportunity for indulging them; and they addict themselves to inferior pleasures, not because they deliberately prefer them, but because they are either the only ones to which they have access or the only ones which they are any longer capable of enjoying. It may be questioned whether anyone who has remained equally susceptible to both classes of pleasure ever knowingly and calmly preferred the lower, though many, in all ages, have broken down in an ineffectual attempt to combine both.

From this verdict of the only competent judges, I apprehend there can be no appeal. On a question which is the best worth having of two pleasures, or which of two modes of existence is the most grateful to the feelings, apart from its moral attributes and from its consequences, the judgment of these who are qualified by knowledge of both, or, if they differ, that of the majority among them, must be admitted as final. And there needs be the less hesitation to accept this judgment respecting the quality of pleasures, since there is no other tribunal to be referred to even on the question of quantity. What means are there of determining which is the acutest of two pains, or the intensest of two pleasurable sensations, except the general suffrage of those who are familiar with both? Neither pains nor pleasures are homogeneous, and pain is always heterogeneous with pleasure. What is there to decide whether a particular pleasure is worth purchasing at the cost of a particular pain, except the feelings and judgment of the experienced? When, therefore, those feelings and judgment declare the pleasures derived from the higher faculties to be preferable in kind, apart from the question of intensity, to those of which the animal nature, disjoined from the higher faculties, is susceptible, they are entitled on this subject to the same regard.

I have dwelt on this point as being part of a perfectly just conception of utility or happiness considered as the directive rule of human conduct. But it is by no means an indispensable condition to the acceptance of the utilitarian standard; for that standard is not the agent's own greatest happiness, but the greatest amount of happiness altogether; and if it may possibly be doubted whether a noble character is always the happier for its nobleness, there can be no doubt that it makes other people happier, and that the world in general is immensely a gainer by it. Utilitarianism, therefore, could only attain its end by the general cultivation of nobleness of character, even if each individual were only

benefited by the nobleness of others, and his own, so far as happiness is concerned, were a sheer deduction from the benefit. But the bare enunciation of such an absurdity as this last renders refutation superfluous.

According to the greatest happiness principle, as above explained, the ultimate end, with reference to and for the sake of which all other things are desirable—whether we are considering our own good or that of other people—is an existence exempt as far as possible from pain, and as rich as possible in enjoyments, both in point of quantity and quality; the test of quality and the rule for measuring it against quantity being the preference felt by those who, in their opportunities of experience, to which must be added their habits of self-consciousness and self-observation, are best furnished with the means of comparison. This, being according to the utilitarian opinion the end of human action, is necessarily also the standard of morality, which may accordingly be defined "the rules and precepts for human conduct," by the observance of which an existence such as has been described might be, to the greatest extent possible, secured to all mankind; and not to them only, but, so far as the nature of things admits, to the whole sentient creation.

Against this doctrine, however, arises another class of objectors who say that happiness, in any form, cannot be the rational purpose of human life and action; because, in the first place, it is unattainable; and they contemptuously ask, What right hast thou to be happy?—a question which Mr. Carlyle clinches by the addition, What right, a short time ago, hadst thou even *to be*? Next they say that men can do *without* happiness; that all noble human beings have felt this, and could not have become noble but by learning the lesson of *Entsagen,* or renunciation; which lesson, thoroughly learned and submitted to, they affirm to be the beginning and necessary condition of all virtue.

The first of these objections would go to the root of the matter were it well founded; for if no happiness is to be had at all by human beings, the attainment of it cannot be the end of morality or of any rational conduct. Though, even in that case, something might still be said for the utilitarian theory, since utility includes not solely the pursuit of happiness, but the prevention or mitigation of unhappiness; and if the former aim be chimerical, there will be all the greater scope and more imperative need for the latter, so long at least as mankind think fit to live and do not take refuse in the simultaneous act of suicide recommended under certain conditions by Novalis. When, however, it is thus positively asserted to be impossible that human life should be happy, the assertion, if not something like a verbal quibble, is at least an exaggeration. If by happiness be meant a continuity of highly pleasurable excitement, it is evident enough that this is impossible. A state of exalted pleasure lasts only moments or in some cases, and with some intermissions, hours or days, and is the occasional brilliant flash of enjoyment, not its permanent and steady flame. Of this the philosophers who have taught that happiness is the end of life were as fully aware as those who taunt them. The happiness which they meant was not a life of rapture, but moments of such, in an existence made up of few and transitory pains, many and various pleasures, with a decided predominance of the active over the passive, and having as the foundation of the whole not to expect more from life than it is capable of bestowing. A life thus composed, to those who have been fortunate enough to obtain it, has always appeared worthy of the name of happiness. And such an existence is even now the lot of many during some considerable portion of their lives. The present wretched education and wretched social arrangements are the only real hindrance to its being attainable by almost all.

The objectors perhaps may doubt whether human beings, if taught to consider happiness as the end of life, would be satisfied with such a moderate share of it. But great numbers of mankind have been satisfied with much less. The main constituents of a satisfied life appear to be two, either of which by itself is often found sufficient for the purpose: tranquillity and excitement. With much tranquillity, many find that they can be content with very little pleasure; with much excitement, many can reconcile themselves to a considerable quantity of pain. There is assuredly no inherent impossibility of enabling even the mass of mankind to unite both, since the two are so far from being incompatible that they are in natural alliance, the prolongation of either being a preparation for, and exciting a wish for, the other. It is only those in whom indolence amounts to a vice that do not desire excitement after an interval of response; it is only those in whom the need of excitement is a disease that feel the tranquillity which follows excitement dull and insipid, instead of pleasurable in direct proportion to the excitement which preceded it. When people who are tolerably fortunate in their outward lot do not find in life sufficient enjoyment to make it valuable to them, the cause generally is caring for nobody but themselves. To those who have neither public nor private affections, the excitements of life are much curtailed, and in any case dwindle in value as the time approaches when all selfish interests must be terminated by death; while those who leave after them objects of personal affection, and especially those who have also cultivated a fellow-feeling with the collective interests of mankind, retain as lively an interest in life on the eve of death as in the vigor of youth and health. Next to selfishness, the principal cause which makes life unsatisfactory is want of mental cultivation. A cultivated mind—I do not mean that of a philosopher, but any mind to which the fountains of knowledge have been opened, and which has been taught, in any tolerable degree, to exercise its faculties—finds sources of inexhaustible interest in all that surrounds it: in the objects of nature, the achievements of art, the imaginations of poetry, the incidents of history, the ways of mankind, past and present, and their prospects in the future. It is possible, indeed, to become indifferent to all this, and that too without having exhausted a thousandth part of it, but only when one has had from the beginning no moral or human interest in these things and has sought in them only the gratification of curiosity.

Now there is absolutely no reason in the nature of things why an amount of mental culture sufficient to give an intelligent interest in these objects of contemplation should not be the inheritance of every one born in a civilized country. As little is there an inherent necessity that any human being should be a selfish egotist, devoid of every feeling or care but those which center in his own miserable individuality. Something far superior to this is sufficiently common even now, to give ample earnest of what the human species may be made. Genuine private affections and a sincere interest in the public good are possible, though in unequal degrees, to every rightly brought up human being. In a world in which there is so much to interest, so much to enjoy, and so much also to correct and improve, everyone who has this moderate amount of moral and intellectual requisites is capable of an existence which may be called enviable; and unless such a person, through bad laws or subjection to the will of others, is denied the liberty to use the sources of happiness within his reach, he will not fail to find this enviable existence, if he escapes the positive evils of life, the great sources of physical and mental suffering—such as indigence, disease, and the unkindness, worthlessness, or premature loss of objects of affection. The main stress of the problem lies, therefore, in the contest with these calamities from which it is a rare good fortune entirely to escape; which, as things now are, cannot be obviated, and often cannot be in any material degree mitigated. Yet no one whose opinion deserves a moment's consideration can doubt that most of the great positive evils of the world are in themselves removable, and will, if human affairs continue to improve, be in the end reduced within narrow limits. Poverty, in any sense implying suffering, may be completely extinguished by the wisdom of society combined with the good sense and providence of individuals. Even that most intractable of enemies, disease, may be indefinitely reduced in dimensions by good physical and moral education and proper control of noxious influences, while the progress of science holds out a promise for the future of still more direct conquests over this detestable foe. And every advance in that direction relieves us from some, not only of the chances which cut short our own lives, but, what concerns us still more, which deprive us of those in whom our happiness is wrapt up. As for vicissitudes of fortune and other disappointments connected with worldly circumstances, these are principally the effect either of gross imprudence, of ill-regulated desires, or of bad or imperfect social institutions. All the grand sources, in short, of human suffering are in a great degree, many of them almost entirely, conquerable by human care and effort; and though their removal is grievously slow—though a long succession of generations will perish in the breach before the conquest is completed, and this world becomes all that, if will and knowledge were not wanting, it might easily be made—yet every mind sufficiently intelligent and generous to bear a part, however small and inconspicuous, in the endeavor will draw a noble enjoyment from the contest itself, which he would not for any bribe in the form of selfish indulgence consent to be without.

And this leads to the true estimation of what is said by the objectors concerning the possibility and the obligation of learning to do without happiness. Unquestionably it is possible to do without happiness; it is done involuntarily by nineteen-twentieths of mankind, even in those parts of our present world which are least deep in barbarism; and it often has to be done voluntarily by the hero or the martyr, for the sake of something which he prizes more than his individual happiness. But this something, what is it, unless the happiness of others or some of the requisites of happiness? It is noble to be capable of resigning entirely one's own portion of happiness, or chances of it; but, after all, this self-sacrifice must be for some end; it is not its own end; and if we are told that its end is not happiness but virtue, which is better than happiness, I ask, would the sacrifice be made if the hero or martyr did not believe that it would earn for others immunity from similar sacrifices? Would it be made if he thought that his renunciation of happiness for himself would produce no fruit for any of his fellow creatures, but to make their lot like his and place them also in the condition of persons who have renounced happiness? All honor to those who can abnegate for themselves the personal enjoyment of life when by such renunciation they contribute worthily to increase the amount of happiness in the world; but he who does it or professes to do it for any other purpose is no more deserving of admiration than the ascetic mounted on his pillar. He may be an inspiriting proof of what men *can* do, but assuredly not an example of what they *should*.

Though it is only in a very imperfect state of the world's arrangements that anyone can best serve the happiness of others by the absolute sacrifice of his own, yet, so long as the world is in that imperfect state, I fully acknowledge that the readiness to make such a sacrifice is the highest virtue which can be found in man. I will add that in this condition of the world, paradoxical as the assertion may be, the conscious ability to do without happiness gives the best prospect of realizing such happiness as is attainable. For nothing except that consciousness can raise a person above the chances of life by making him feel that, let fate and fortune do their worst, they have not power to subdue him; which, once felt, frees him from excess of anxiety concerning the evils of life and enables him, like many a Stoic in the worst times of the Roman Empire, to cultivate in tranquillity the sources of satisfaction accessible to him, without concerning himself about the uncertainty of their duration any more than about their inevitable end.

Meanwhile, let utilitarians never cease to claim the morality of self-devotion as a possession which belongs by as good a right to them as either to the Stoic or to the Transcendentalist. The utilitarian morality does recognize in human beings the power of sacrificing their own greatest good for the good of others. It only refuses to admit that the sacrifice is itself a good. A sacrifice which does not increase or tend to increase the sum total of happiness, it considers as wasted. The only self-renunciation which it applauds is devotion to the happiness, or to some of the means of happiness, of others, either of mankind collectively or of individuals within the limits imposed by the collective interests of mankind.

I must again repeat what the assailants of utilitarianism seldom have the justice to acknowledge, that the happiness which forms the utilitarian standard of what is right in conduct is not the agent's own happiness but that of all concerned. As between his own happiness and that of others, utilitarianism requires him to be as strictly impartial as a disinterested and benevolent spectator. In the golden rule of Jesus of Nazareth, we read the complete spirit of the ethics of utility. "To do as you would be done by," and "to love your neighbor as yourself," constitute the ideal perfection of utilitarian morality. As the means of making the nearest approach to this ideal, utility would enjoin, first, that laws and social arrangements should place the happiness or (as, speaking practically, it may be called) the interest of every individual as nearly as possible in harmony with the interest of the whole; and, secondly, that education and opinion, which have so vast a power over human character, should so use that power as to establish in the mind of every individual an indissoluble association between his own happiness and the good of the whole, especially between his own happiness and the practice of such modes of conduct, negative and positive, as regard for the universal happiness prescribes; so that not only he may be unable to conceive the possibility of happiness to himself, consistently with conduct opposed to the general good, but also that a direct impulse to promote the general good may be in every individual one of the habitual motives of action, and the sentiments connected therewith may fill a large and prominent place in every human being's sentient existence. If the impugners of the utilitarian morality represented it to their own minds in this its true character, I know not what recommendation possessed by any other morality they could possibly affirm to be wanting to it; what more beautiful or more exalted developments of human nature any other ethical system can be supposed to foster, or what springs of action, not accessible to the utilitarian, such systems rely on for giving effect to their mandates.

The objectors to utilitarianism cannot always be charged with representing it in a discreditable light. On the contrary, those among them who entertain anything like a just idea of its disinterested character sometimes find fault with its standard as being too high for humanity. They say it is exacting too much to require that people shall always act from the inducement of promoting the general interest of society. But this is to mistake the very meaning of a standard of morals and confound the rule of action with the motive of it. It is the business of ethics to tell us what are our duties, or by what test we may know them; but no system of ethics requires that the sole motive of all we do shall be a feeling of duty; on the contrary, ninety-nine hundredths of all our actions are done from other motives, and rightly so done if the rule of duty does not condemn them. It is the more unjust to utilitarianism that this particular misapprehension should be made a ground of objection to it, inasmuch as utilitarian moralists have gone beyond almost all others in affirming that the motive has nothing to do with the morality of the action, though much with the worth of the agent. He who saves a fellow creature from drowning does what is morally right, whether his motive be duty or the hope of being paid for his trouble; he who betrays the friend that trusts him is guilty of a crime, even if his object be to serve another friend to whom he is under greater obligations.[2] But to speak only of actions done from the motive of duty, and in direct obedience to principle: it is a misapprehension of the utilitarian mode of thought to conceive it as implying that people should fix their minds upon so wide a generality as the world, or society at large. The great majority of good actions are intended not for the benefit of the world, but for that of individuals, of which the good of the world is made up; and the thoughts of the most virtuous man need not on these occasions travel beyond the particular persons concerned, except so far as is necessary to assure himself that in benefiting them he is not violating the rights, that is, the legitimate and authorized expectations, of anyone else. The multiplication of happiness is, according to the utilitarian ethics, the object of virtue: the occasions on which any person (except one in a thousand) has it in his power to do this on an extended scale—in other words, to be a public benefactor—are but exceptional; and on these occasions alone is he called on to consider public utility; in every other case, private utility, the interest or happiness of some few persons, is all he has to attend to. Those alone the influence of whose actions extends to society in general need concern themselves habitually about so large an object. In the case of abstinences indeed—of things which people forbear to do from moral considerations, though the consequences in the particular case might be beneficial—it would be unworthy of an intelligent agent not to be consciously aware that the action is of a class which, if practiced generally, would be generally injurious, and that this is the ground of the obligation to abstain from it. The amount of regard for the public interest implied in this recognition is no greater than is demanded by every system of morals, for they all enjoin to abstain from whatever is manifestly pernicious to society.

The same considerations dispose of another reproach against the doctrine of utility, founded on a still grosser misconception of the purpose of a standard of morality and of the very meaning of the words "right" and "wrong." It is often affirmed that utilitarianism renders men cold and unsympathizing; that it chills their moral feelings toward individuals; that it makes them regard only the dry and hard consideration of the consequences of actions, not taking into their moral estimate the qualities from which those actions emanate. If the assertion means that they do not allow their judgment respecting the rightness or wrongness of an action to be influenced by their opinion of the qualities of the person who does it, this is a complaint not against utilitarianism, but against any standard or morality at all; for certainly no known ethical standard decides an action to be good or bad because it is done by a good or bad man, still less because done by an amiable, a brave, or a benevolent man, or the contrary. These considerations are relevant, not to the estimation of actions, but of persons; and there is nothing in the utilitarian theory inconsistent with the fact that there are other things which interest us in persons besides the rightness and wrongness of their actions. The Stoics, indeed, with the paradoxical misuse of language which was part of their system, and by which they strove to raise themselves above all concern about anything but virtue, were fond of saying that he who has that has everything; that he, and only he, is rich, is beautiful, is a king. But no claim of this description is made for the virtuous man by the utilitarian doctrine. Utilitarians are quite aware that there are other desirable possessions and qualities besides virtue, and are perfectly willing to allow to all of them their full worth. They are also aware that a right action does not necessarily indicate a virtuous character, and that actions which are blamable often proceed from qualities entitled to praise. When this is apparent in any particular case, it modifies their estimation, not certainly of the act, but of the agent. I grant that they are, notwithstanding, of opinion that in the long run the best proof of a good character is good actions; and resolutely refuse to consider any mental disposition as good of which the predominant tendency is to produce bad conduct. This makes them unpopular with many people, but it is an unpopularity which they must share with everyone who regards the distinction between right and wrong in a serious light; and the reproach is not one which a conscientious utilitarian need be anxious to repel.

If no more be meant by the objection than that many utilitarians look on the morality of actions, as measured by the utilitarian standards, with too exclusive a regard, and do not lay sufficient stress upon the other beauties of character which go toward making a human being lovable or admirable, this may be admitted. Utilitarians who have cultivated their moral feelings, but not their sympathies, nor their artistic perceptions, do fall into this mistake; and so do all other moralists under the same conditions. What can be said in excuse for other moralists is equally available for them, namely, that, if there is to be any error, it is better that it should be on that side. As a matter of fact, we may affirm that among utilitarians, as among adherents of other systems, there is every imaginable degree of rigidity and of laxity in the application of their standard; some are even puritanically rigorous, while others are as indulgent as can possibly be desired by sinner or by sentimentalist. But on the whole, a doctrine which brings prominently forward the interest that mankind have in the repression and prevention of conduct which violates the moral law is likely to be inferior to no other in turning the sanctions of opinion against such violations. It is true, the question "What does violate the moral law?" is one on which those who recognize different standards of morality are likely now and then to differ. But difference of opinion on moral questions was not first introduced into the world by utilitarianism, while that doctrine does supply, if not always an easy, at all events a tangible and intelligible, mode of deciding such differences.

It may not be superfluous to notice a few more of the common misapprehensions of utilitarian ethics, even those which are so obvious and gross that it might appear impossible for any person of candor and intelligence to fall into them; since persons, even of considerable mental endowment, often give themselves so little trouble to understand the bearings of any opinion against which they entertain a prejudice, and men are in general so little conscious of this voluntary ignorance as a defect that the vulgarest misunderstandings of ethical doctrines are continually met with in the deliberate writings of persons of the greatest pretensions both to high principle and to philosophy. We not uncommonly hear the doctrine of utility inveighed against as a *godless* doctrine. If it be necessary to say anything at all against so mere an assumption, we may say that the question depends upon what idea we have formed of the moral character of the Deity. If it be a true belief that God desires, above all things, the happiness of his creatures, and that this was his purpose in their creation, utility is not only not a godless doctrine, but more profoundly religious than any other. If it be meant that utilitarianism does not recognize the revealed will of God as the supreme law of morals, I answer that a utilitarian who believes in the perfect goodness and wisdom of *God* necessarily believes that whatever God has thought fit to reveal on the subject of morals must fulfill the requirements of utility in a supreme degree. But others besides utilitarians have been of opinion that the Christian revelation was intended, and is fitted, to inform the hearts and minds of mankind with a spirit which should enable them to find for themselves what is right, and incline them to do it when found, rather than to tell them, except in a very general way, what it is; and that we need a doctrine of ethics, carefully followed out, to *interpret* to us the will of God. Whether this opinion is correct or not, it is superfluous here to discuss; since whatever aid religion, either natural or revealed, can afford to ethical investigation is as open to the utilitarian moralist as to any other. He can use it as the testimony of God to the usefulness or hurtfulness of any given course of action by as good a right as others can use it for the indication of a transcendental law having no connection with usefulness or with happiness.

Again, utility is often summarily stigmatized as an immoral doctrine by giving it the name of "expediency," and taking advantage of the popular use of that term to contrast it with principle. But the expedient, in the sense in which it is opposed to the right, generally means that which is expedient for the particular interest of the agent himself; as when a minister sacrifices the interests of his country to keep himself in place. When it means anything better than this, it means that which is expedient for some immediate object, some temporary purpose, but which violates a rule whose observance is expedient in a much higher degree. The expedient, in this sense, instead of being the same thing with the

useful, is a branch of the hurtful. Thus it would often be expedient, for the purpose of getting over some momentary embarrassment, or attaining some object immediately useful to ourselves or others, to tell a lie. But inasmuch as the cultivation in ourselves of a sensitive feeling on the subject of veracity is one of the most useful, and the enfeeblement of that feeling one of the most hurtful, things to which our conduct can be instrumental; and inasmuch as any, even unintentional, deviation from truth does that much toward weakening the trustworthiness of human assertion, which is not only the principal support of all present social well-being, but the insufficiency of which does more than any one thing that can be named to keep back civilization, virtue, everything on which human happiness on the largest scale depends—we feel that the violation, for a present advantage, of a rule of such transcendent expediency is not expedient, and that he who, for the sake of convenience to himself or to some other individual, does what depends on him to deprive mankind of the good, and inflict upon them the evil, involved in the greater or less reliance which they can place in each other's words, acts the part of one of their worst enemies. Yet that even this rule, sacred as it is, admits of possible exceptions is acknowledged by all moralists; the chief of which is when the withholding of some fact (as of information from a malefactor, or of bad news from a person dangerously ill) would save an individual (especially an individual other than oneself) from great and unmerited evil, and when the withholding can only be effected by denial. But in order that the exception may not extend itself beyond the need, and may have the least possible effect in weakening reliance on veracity, it ought to be recognized and, if possible, its limits defined; and, if the principle of utility is good for anything, it must be good for weighing these conflicting utilities against one another and marking out the region within which one or the other preponderates.

Again, defenders of utility often find themselves called upon to reply to such objections as this—that there is not time, previous to action, for calculating and weighing the effects of any line of conduct on the general happiness. This is exactly as if anyone were to say that it is impossible to guide our conduct by Christianity because there is not time, on every occasion on which anything has to be done, to read through the Old and New Testaments. The answer to the objection is that there has been ample time, namely, the whole past duration of the human species. During all that time mankind have been learning by experience the tendencies of actions; on which experience all the prudence as well as all the morality of life are dependent. People talk as if the commencement of this course of experience had hitherto been put off, and as if, at the moment when some man feels tempted to meddle with the property or life of another, he had to begin considering for the first time whether murder and theft are injurious to human happiness. Even then I do not think that he would find the question very puzzling; but, at all events, the matter is now done to his hand. It is truly a whimsical supposition that, if mankind were agreed in considering utility to be the test of morality, they would remain without any agreement as to what is useful, and would take no measures for having their notions on the subject taught to the young and enforced by law and opinion. There is no difficulty in proving any ethical standard whatever to work ill if we suppose universal idiocy to be conjoined with it; but on any hypothesis short of that, mankind must by this time have acquired positive beliefs as to the effects of some actions on their happiness; and the beliefs which have thus come down are the rules of morality for the multitude, and for the philosopher until he has succeeded in finding better. That philosophers might easily do this, even now, on many subjects; that the received code of ethics is by no means of divine right; and that mankind have still much to learn as to the effects of actions on the general happiness, I admit or rather earnestly maintain. The corollaries from the principle of utility, like the precepts of every practical art, admit of indefinite improvement, and, in a progressive state of the human mind, their improve-ment is perpetually going on. But to consider the rules of morality as improvable is one thing; to pass over the intermediate generalization entirely and endeavor to test each individual action directly by the first principle is another. It is a strange notion that the acknowledgment of a first principle is inconsistent with the admission of secondary ones. To inform a traveler respecting the place of his ultimate destination is not to forbid the use of landmarks and direction posts on the way. The proposition that happiness is the end and aim of morality does not mean that no road ought to be laid down to that goal, or that persons going thither should not be advised to take one direction rather than another. Men really ought to leave off talking a kind of nonsense on this subject, which they would neither talk nor listen to on other matters of practical concernment. Nobody argues that the art of navigation is not founded on astronomy because sailors cannot wait to calculate the Nautical Almanac. Being rational creatures, they go to sea with it ready calculated; and all rational creatures go out upon the sea of life with their minds made up on the common questions of right and wrong, as well as on many of the far more difficult questions of wise and foolish. And this, as long as foresight is a human quality, it is to be presumed they will continue to do. Whatever we adopt as the fundamental principle of morality, we require subordinate principles to apply it by; the impossibility of doing without them, being common to all systems, can afford no argument against any one in particular; but gravely to argue as if no such secondary principles could be had, and as if mankind had remained till now, and always must remain, without drawing any general conclusions from the experience of human life is as high a pitch, I think, as absurdity has ever reached in philosophical controversy.

The remainder of the stock arguments against utilitarianism mostly consist in laying to its charge the common infirmities of human nature, and the general difficulties which embarrass conscientious persons in shaping their course through life. We are told that a utilitarian will be apt to make his own particular case an exception to moral rules, and, when under temptation, will see a utility in the breach of a rule, greater than he will see in its observance. But is utility the only creed which is able to furnish us with excuses for evil-doing and means of cheating our own conscience? They are afforded in abundance by all doctrines which recognize as a fact in morals the existence of conflicting considerations, which all doctrines do that have been believed by sane persons. It is not the fault of any creed, but of the complicated nature of human affairs, that rules of conduct cannot be so framed as to require no exceptions, and that hardly any kind of action can safely be laid down as either always obligatory or always condemnable. There is no ethical creed which does not temper the rigidity of its laws by giving a certain latitude, under the moral responsibility of the agent, for accommodation to peculiarities of circumstances; and under every creed, at the opening thus made, self-deception and dishonest casuistry get in. There exists no moral system under which there do not arise unequivocal cases of conflicting obligation. These are the real difficulties, the knotty points both in the theory of ethics and in the conscientious guidance of personal conduct. They are overcome practically, with greater or with less success, according to the intellect and virtue of the individual; but it can hardly be pretended that anyone will be the less qualified for dealing with them, from possessing an ultimate standard to which conflicting rights and duties can be referred. If utility is the ultimate source of moral obligations, utility may be invoked to decide between them when their demands are incompatible. Though the application of the standard may be difficult, it is better than none at all; while in other systems, the moral laws all claiming independent authority, there is no common umpire entitled to interfere between them; their claims to precedence one over another rest on little better than sophistry, and, unless determined, as they generally are, by the unacknowledged influence of consideration of utility, afford a free scope for the action of personal desires and partialities. We must remember that only in these cases of conflict between secondary principles is it requisite that first principles should be appealed to. There is no case of moral obligation in which some secondary principle is not involved; and if only one, there can seldom be any real doubt which one it is, in the mind of any person by whom the principle itself is recognized.

NOTES

1. The author of this essay has reason for believing himself to be the first person who brought the word "utilitarian" into use. He did not invent it, but adopted it from a passing expression in Mr. Galt's *Annals of the Parish*. After using it as a designation for several years, he and others abandoned it from a growing dislike to anything resembling a badge or watchword of sectarian distinction. But as a name for one single opinion, not a set of opinions—to denote the recognition of utility as a standard, not any particular way of applying it—the term supplies a want in the language, and offers, in many cases, a convenient mode of avoiding tiresome circumlocutions.

2. An opponent, whose intellectual and moral fairness it is a pleasure to acknowledge (the Rev. J. Llewellyn Davies), has objected to this passage, saying, "Surely the rightness or wrongness of saving a man from drowning does depend very much upon the motive with which it is done. Suppose that a tyrant, when his enemy jumped into the sea to escape from him, saved him from drowning simply in order that he might inflict upon him more exquisite tortures, would it tend to clearness to speak of that rescue as a 'morally right action'? Or suppose again, according to one of the stock illustrations of ethical inquiries, that a man betrayed a trust received from a friend, because the discharge of it would fatally injure that friend himself or someone belonging to him, would utilitarianism compel one to call the betrayal 'a crime' as much as if it had been done from the meanest motive?"

I submit that he who saves another from drowning in order to kill him by torture afterwards does not differ only in motive from him who does the same thing from duty or benevolence; the act itself is different. The rescue of the man is, in the case supposed, only the necessary first step of an act far more atrocious than leaving him to drown would have been. Had Mr. Davies said, "The rightness or wrongness of saving a man from drowning does depend very much"—not upon the motive, but—"upon the *intention*," no utilitarian would have differed from him. Mr. Davies, by an oversight too common not to be quite venial, has in this case confounded the very different ideas of Motive and Intention. There is no point which utilitarian thinkers (and Bentham pre-eminently) have taken more pains to illustrate than this. The morality of the action depends entirely upon the intention—that is, upon what the agent *wills to do*. But the motive, that is, the feeling which makes him will so to do, if it makes no difference in the act, makes none in the morality: though it makes a great difference in our moral estimation of the agent, especially if it indicates a good or a bad habitual *disposition*—a bent of character from which useful, or from which hurtful actions are likely to arise.

Study Questions

1. In the first paragraph of the essay, Mill attacks "the common herd" for continually making a "shallow" mistake. What is that mistake? Mill goes on to describe the relationship between utility and pleasure. What is the relationship?

2. Would you consent to be changed into a lower animal for a promise of the fullest allowance of that animal's pleasures? Why? What does Mill say about such an exchange? What point do you think Mill is making here?

3. How do you think the typical criminal would respond to Mill's statement that it is better to be a human being dissatisfied than a pig satisfied? Why? How does this bear on the question of corruption in criminal justice practice?

4. Reread the paragraph that begins on page 34. Mill claims that the capacity for the nobler feelings in young persons "speedily dies away" in some occupations. Do you think that criminal justice practice is one of those occupations? Why?

5. Is utilitarianism a "godless doctrine" in Mill's view? Do you agree? Why?

6. Does Mill think that utilitarianism justifies telling a lie if some present advantage can be gained? Is Mill's position that of an act utilitarian or a rule utilitarian? Explain.

The Categorical Imperative

IMMANUEL KANT

IN SOLVING THIS PROBLEM, we want first to inquire whether perhaps the mere concept of a categorical imperative may not also supply us with the formula containing the proposition that can alone be a categorical imperative. For even when we know the purpose of such an absolute command, the question as to how it is possible will still require a special and difficult effort, which we postpone to the last section.[8]

If I think of a hypothetical imperative in general, I do not know beforehand what it will contain until its condition is given. But if I think of a categorical imperative, I know immediately what it contains. For since, besides the law, the imperative contains only the necessity that the maxim[9] should accord with this law, while the law contains no condition to restrict it, there remains nothing but the universality of a law as such with which the maxim of the action should conform. This conformity alone is properly what is represented as necessary by the imperative.

Hence there is only one categorical imperative and it is this: Act only according to that maxim whereby you can at the same time will that it should become a universal law.[10]

Now if all imperatives of duty can be derived from this one imperative as their principle, then there can at least be shown what is understood by the concept of duty and what it means, even though there is left undecided whether what is called duty may not be an empty concept.

The universality of law according to which effects are produced constitutes what is properly called nature in the most general sense (as to form), i.e., the existence of things as far as determined by universal laws. Accordingly, the universal imperative of duty may be expressed thus: Act

as if the maxim of your action were to become through your will a universal law of nature.[11]

We shall now enumerate some duties, following the usual division of them into duties to ourselves and to others and into perfect and imperfect duties.[12]

1. A man reduced to despair by a series of misfortunes feels sick of life but is still so far in possession of his reason that he can ask himself whether taking his own life would not be contrary to his duty to himself.[13] Now he asks whether the maxim of his action could become a universal law of nature. But his maxim is this: from self-love I make as my principle to shorten my life when its continued duration threatens more evil than it promises satisfaction. There only remains the question as to whether this principle of self-love can become a universal law of nature. One sees at once a contradiction in a system of nature whose law would destroy life by means of the very same feeling that acts so as to stimulate the furtherance of life, and hence there could be no existence as a system of nature. Therefore, such a maxim cannot possibly hold as a universal law of nature and is, consequently, wholly opposed to the supreme principle of all duty.

2. Another man in need finds himself forced to borrow money. He knows well that he won't be able to repay it, but he sees also that he will not get any loan unless he firmly promises to repay it within a fixed time. He wants to make such a promise, but he still has conscience enough to ask himself whether it is not permissible and is contrary to duty to get out of difficulty in this way. Suppose, however, that he

From Immanuel Kant, Grounding for the Metaphysics of Morals, *trans. by James W. Ellington (Indianapolis: Hackett Publishing Company, 1981). Bracket notes are provided by James W. Ellington.*

decides to do so. The maxim of his action would then be expressed as follows: when I believe myself to be in need of money, I will borrow money and promise to pay it back, although I know that I can never do so. Now this principle of self-love or personal advantage may perhaps be quite compatible with one's entire future welfare, but the question is now whether it is right.[14] I then transform the requirement of self-love into a universal law and put the question thus: how would things stand if my maxim were to become a universal law? He then sees at once that such a maxim could never hold as a universal law of nature and be consistent with itself, but must necessarily be self-contradictory. For the universality of a law which says that anyone believing himself to be in difficulty could promise whatever he pleases with the intention of not keeping it would make promising itself and the end to be attained thereby quite impossible, inasmuch as no one would believe what was promised him but would merely laugh at all such utterances as being vain pretenses.

3. A third finds in himself a talent whose cultivation could make him a man useful in many respects. But he finds himself in comfortable circumstances and prefers to indulge in pleasure rather than to bother himself about broadening and improving his fortunate natural aptitudes. But he asks himself further whether his maxim of neglecting his natural gifts, besides agreeing of itself with his propensity to indulgence, might agree also with what is called duty.[15] He then sees that a system of nature could indeed always subsist according to such a universal law, even though every man (like South Sea Islanders) should let his talents rust and resolve to devote his life entirely to idleness, indulgence, propagation, and, in a word, to enjoyment. But he cannot possibly will that this should become a universal law of nature or be implanted in us as such a law by a natural instinct. For as a rational being he necessarily wills that all his faculties should be developed, inasmuch as they are given him for all sorts of possible purposes.

4. A fourth man finds things going well for himself but sees others (whom he could help) struggling with great hardships; and he thinks: what does it matter to me? Let everybody be as happy as Heaven wills or as he can make himself; I shall take nothing from him nor even envy him; but I have no desire to contribute anything to his well-being or to his assistance when in need. If such a way of thinking were to become a universal law of nature, the human race admittedly could very well subsist and doubtless could subsist even better than when everyone prates about sympathy and benevolence and even on occasion exerts himself to practice them but, on the other hand, also cheats when he can, betrays the rights of man, or otherwise violates them. But even though it is possible that a universal law of nature could subsist in accordance with that maxim, still it is impossible to will that such a principle should hold everywhere as a law of nature.[16] For a will which resolved in this way would contradict itself, inasmuch as cases might often arise in which one would have need of the love and sympathy of others and in which he would deprive himself, by such a law of nature springing from his own will, of all hope of the aid he wants for himself.

These are some of the many actual duties, or at least what are taken to be such, whose derivation from the single principle cited above is clear. We must be able to will that a maxim of our action become a universal law; this is the canon for morally estimating any of our actions. Some actions are so constituted that their maxims cannot without contradiction even be thought as a universal law of nature, much less be willed as what should become one. In the case of others this internal impossibility is indeed not found, but there is still no possibility of willing that their maxim should be raised to the universality of a law of nature, because such a will would contradict itself. There is no difficulty in seeing that the former kind of action conflicts with strict or narrow [perfect] (irremissible) duty, while the second kind conflicts only with broad [imperfect] (meritorious) duty.[17] By means of these examples there has thus been fully set forth how all duties depend as regards the kind of obligation (not the object of their action) upon the one principle.

If we now attend to ourselves in any transgression of a duty, we find that we actually do not will that our maxim should become a universal law—because this is impossible for us—but rather that the opposite of this maxim should remain a law universally.[18] We only take the liberty of making an exception to the law for ourselves (or just for this one time) to the advantage of our inclination. Consequently, if we weighed up everything from one and the same standpoint, namely, that of reason, we would find a contradiction in our own will, viz., that a certain principle be objectively necessary as a universal law and yet subjectively not hold universally but should admit of exceptions. But since we at one moment regard our action from the standpoint of a will wholly in accord with reason and then at another moment regard the very same action from the standpoint of a will affected by inclination, there is really no contradiction here. Rather, there is an opposition (*antagonismus*) of inclination to the precept of reason, whereby the universality (*universalitas*) of the principle is changed into a mere generality (*generalitas*) so that the practical principle of reason may meet the maxim halfway. Although this procedure cannot be justified in our own impartial judgment, yet it does show that we actually acknowledge the validity of the categorical imperative and (with all respect for it) merely allow ourselves a few exceptions which, as they seem to us, are unimportant and forced upon us.

We have thus at least shown that if duty is a
425   concept which is to have significance and real legislative authority for our actions, then such duty can be expressed only in categorical imperatives but not at all in hypothetical ones. We have also—and this is already a great deal—exhibited clearly and definitely for every application what is the content of the categorical imperative, which must contain the principle of all duty (if there is such a thing at all). But we have not yet advanced far enough to prove a priori that there

actually is an imperative of this kind, that there is a practical law which of itself commands absolutely and without any incentives, and that following this law is duty.

In order to attain this proof there is the utmost importance in being warned that we must not take it into our mind to derive the reality of this principle from the special characteristics of human nature. For duty has to be a practical, unconditioned necessity of action; hence it must hold for all rational beings (to whom alone an imperative is at all applicable) and for this reason only can it also be a law for all human wills. On the other hand, whatever is derived from the special natural condition of humanity, from certain feelings and propensities, or even, if such were possible, from some special tendency peculiar to human reason and not holding necessarily for the will of every rational being—all of this can indeed yield a maxim valid for us, but not a law. This is to say that such can yield a subjective principle according to which we might act if we happen to have the propensity and inclination, but cannot yield an objective principle according to which we would be directed to act even though our every propensity, inclination, and natural tendency were opposed to it. In fact, the sublimity and inner worth of the command are so much the more evident in a duty, the fewer subjective causes there are for it and the more they oppose it; such causes do not in the least weaken the necessitation exerted by the law or take away anything from its validity.

Here philosophy is seen in fact to be put in a precarious position, which should be firm even though there is neither in heaven nor on earth anything upon which it depends or is based. Here philosophy must show its purity as author of its laws, and not as the herald of such laws as are whispered to it by an implanted sense or by who knows what tutelary nature. Such laws may be better than nothing at all, but they can never give us principles dictated by reason. These prin-   426
ciples must have an origin that is completely a priori and must at the same time derive from such origin their authority to command. They

expect nothing from the inclination of men but, rather, expect everything from the supremacy of the law and from the respect owed to the law. Without the latter expectation, these principles condemn man to self-contempt and inward abhorrence.

Hence everything empirical is not only quite unsuitable as a contribution to the principle of morality, but is even highly detrimental to the purity of morals. For the proper and inestimable worth of an absolutely good will consists precisely in the fact that the principle of action is free of all influences from contingent grounds, which only experience can furnish. This lax or even mean way of thinking which seeks its principle among empirical motives and laws cannot too much or too often be warned against, for human reason in its weariness is glad to rest upon this pillow. In a dream of sweet illusions (in which not Juno but a cloud is embraced) there is substituted for morality some bastard patched up from limbs of quite varied ancestry and looking like anything one wants to see in it but not looking like virtue to him who has once beheld her in her true form.[19]

Therefore, the question is this: is it a necessary law for all rational beings always to judge their actions according to such maxims as they can themselves will that such should serve as universal laws? If there is such a law, then it must already be connected (completely a priori) with the concept of the will of a rational being in general. But in order to discover this connection we must, however reluctantly, take a step into metaphysics, although into a region of it different from speculative philosophy, i.e., we must enter the metaphysics of morals. In practical philosophy the concern is not with accepting 427 grounds for what happens but with accepting laws of what ought to happen, even though it never does happen—that is, the concern is with objectively practical laws. Here there is no need to inquire into the grounds as to why something pleases or displeases, how the pleasure of mere sensation differs from taste, and whether taste differs from a general satisfaction of reason, upon what does the feeling of pleasure and dis-

pleasure rest, and how from this feeling desires and inclinations arise, and how, finally, from these there arise maxims through the cooperation of reason. All of this belongs to an empirical psychology, which could constitute the second part of the doctrine of nature, if this doctrine is regarded as the philosophy of nature insofar as this philosophy is grounded on empirical laws. But here the concern is with objectively practical laws, and hence with the relation of a will to itself insofar as it is determined solely by reason. In this case everything related to what is empirical falls away of itself, because if reason entirely by itself determines conduct (and the possibility of such determination we now wish to investigate), then reason must necessarily do so a priori.

The will is thought of as a faculty of determining itself to action in accordance with the representation of certain laws, and such a faculty can be found only in rational beings. Now what serves the will as the objective ground of its self-determination is an end; and if this end is given by reason alone, then it must be equally valid for all rational beings. On the other hand, what contains merely the ground of the possibility of the action, whose effect is an end, is called the means. The subjective ground of desire is the incentive; the objective ground of volition is the motive. Hence there arises the distinction between subjective ends, which rest on incentives, and objective ends, which depend on motives valid for every rational being. Practical principles are formal when they abstract from all subjective ends; they are material, however, when they are founded upon subjective ends, and hence upon certain incentives. The ends which a rational being arbitrarily proposes to himself as effects of this action (material ends) are all merely relative, for only their relation to a specially constituted faculty of desire in the subject gives them their worth. Consequently, such worth cannot provide any universal principles, which are valid and necessary for all rational beings and, furthermore, are valid for every voli- 428 tion, i.e., cannot provide any practical laws. Therefore, all such relative ends can be grounds only for hypothetical imperatives.

But let us suppose that there were something whose existence has in itself an absolute worth, something which as an end in itself could be a ground of determinate laws. In it, and in it alone, would there be the ground of a possible categorical imperative, i.e., of a practical law.

Now I say that man, and in general every rational being, exists as an end in himself and not merely as a means to be arbitrarily used by this or that will. He must in all his actions, whether directed to himself or to other rational beings, always be regarded at the same time as an end. All the objects of inclinations have only a conditioned value; for if there were not these inclinations and the needs founded on them, then their object would be without value. But the inclinations themselves, being sources of needs, are so far from having an absolute value such as to render them desirable for their own sake that the universal wish of every rational being must be, rather, to be wholly free from them. Accordingly, the value of any object obtainable by our action is always conditioned. Beings whose existence depends not on our will but on nature have, nevertheless, if they are not rational beings, only a relative value as means and are therefore called things. On the other hand, rational beings are called persons inasmuch as their nature already marks them out as ends in themselves, i.e., as something which is not to be used merely as means and hence there is imposed thereby a limit on all arbitrary use of such beings, which are thus objects of respect. Persons are, therefore, not merely subjective ends, whose existence as an effect of our actions has a value for us; but such beings are objective ends, i.e., exist as ends in themselves. Such an end is one for which there can be substituted no other end to which such beings should serve merely as means, for otherwise nothing at all of absolute value would be found anywhere. But if all value were conditioned and hence contingent, then no supreme practical principle could be found for reason at all.

If then there is to be a supreme practical principle and, as far as the human will is concerned, a

categorical imperative, then it must be such that from the conception of what is necessarily an end for everyone because this end is an end in itself it constitutes an objective principle of the will and can hence serve as a practical law. The ground of such a principle is this: rational nature exists as an end in itself. In this way man necessarily thinks of his own existence; thus far is it a subjective principle of human actions. But in this way also does every other rational being think of his existence on the same rational ground that holds also for me;[20] hence it is at the same time an objective principle, from which, as a supreme practical ground, all laws of the will must be able to be derived. The practical imperative will therefore be the following: Act in such a way that you treat humanity, whether in your own person or in the person of another, always at the same time as an end and never simply as a means.[21] We now want to see whether this can be carried out in practice.

Let us keep to our previous examples.[22]

First, as regards the concept of necessary duty to oneself, the man who contemplates suicide will ask himself whether his action can be consistent with the idea of humanity as an end in itself. If he destroys himself in order to escape from a difficult situation, then he is making use of his person merely as a means so as to maintain a tolerable condition till the end of his life. Man, however, is not a thing and hence is not something to be used merely as a means; he must in all his actions always be regarded as an end in himself. Therefore, I cannot dispose of man in my own person by mutilating, damaging, or killing him. (A more exact determination of this principle so as to avoid all misunderstanding, e.g., regarding the amputation of limbs in order to save oneself, or the exposure of one's life to danger in order to save it, and so on, must here be omitted; such questions belong to morals proper.)

Second, as concerns necessary or strict duty to others, the man who intends to make a false promise will immediately see that he intends to make use of another man merely as a means to an end which the latter does not likewise hold. For the man whom I want to use for my own

429

430 purposes by such a promise cannot possibly concur with my way of acting toward him and hence cannot himself hold the end of this action. This conflict with the principle of duty to others becomes even clearer when instances of attacks on the freedom and property of others are considered. For then it becomes clear that a transgressor of the rights of men intends to make use of the persons of others merely as a means, without taking into consideration that, as rational beings, they should always be esteemed at the same time as ends, i.e., be esteemed only as beings who must themselves be able to hold the very same action as an end.[23]

Third, with regard to contingent (meritorious) duty to oneself, it is not enough that the action does not conflict with humanity in our own person as an end in itself; the action must also harmonize with this end. Now there are in humanity capacities for greater perfection which belong to the end that nature has in view as regards humanity in our own person. To neglect these capacities might perhaps be consistent with the maintenance of humanity as an end in itself, but would not be consistent with the advancement of this end.

Fourth, concerning meritorious duty to others, the natural end that all men have is their own happiness. Now humanity might indeed subsist if nobody contributed anything to the happiness of others, provided he did not intentionally impair their happiness. But this, after all, would harmonize only negatively and not positively with humanity as an end in itself, if everyone does not also strive, as much as he can, to further the ends of others. For the ends of any subject who is an end in himself must as far as possible be my ends also, if that conception of an end in itself is to have its full effect in me.

NOTES

8. [See below Ak. 446-63.]

9. A maxim is the subjective principle of acting and must be distinguished from the objective principle, viz., the practical law. A maxim contains the practical rule which reason determines in accordance with the conditions of the subject (often his ignorance or his inclinations) and is thus the principle according to which the subject does act. But the law is the objective principle valid for every rational being, and it is the principle according to which he ought to act, i.e., an imperative.

10. [This formulation of the categorical imperative is often referred to as the formula of universal law.]

11. [This is often called the formula of the law of nature.]

12. There should be noted here that I reserve the division of duties for a future *Metaphysics of Morals* [in Part II of the *Metaphysics of Morals*, entitled *The Metaphysical Principles of Virtue*, Ak. 417-474]. The division presented here stands as merely an arbitrary one (in order to arrange my examples). For the rest, I understand here by a perfect duty one which permits no exception in the interest of inclination. Accordingly, I have perfect duties which are external [to others], while other ones are internal [to oneself]. This classification runs contrary to the accepted usage of the schools, but I do not intend to justify it here, since there is no difference for my purpose whether this classification is accepted or not.

13. [Not committing suicide is an example of a perfect duty to oneself. See Metaphysical Principles of Virtue, Ak. 422-24.]

14. [Keeping promises is an example of a perfect duty to others. See *ibid.*, Ak. 423-31.]

15. [Cultivating one's talents is an example of an imperfect duty to oneself. See *ibid.*, Ak. 444-46.]

16. [Benefiting others is an example of an imperfect duty to others. See *ibid.*, Ak. 452-54.]

17. [Compare *ibid.*, Ak. 390-94, 410-411, 421-51.]

18. [This is to say, for example, that when you tell a lie, you do so on the condition that others are truthful and believe that what you are saying is true, because otherwise your lie will never work to get you what you want. When you tell a lie, you simply take exception to the general rule that says everyone should always tell the truth.]

19. To behold virtue in her proper form is nothing other than to present morality stripped of all admixture of what is sensuous and of every spurious adornment of reward or self-love. How much she then eclipses all else that appears attractive to the inclinations can be easily seen by everyone with the least effort of his reason, if it be not entirely ruined for all abstraction.

20. This proposition I here put forward as a postulate. The grounds for it will be found in the last section [See below Ak. 446-63.]

21. [This oft-quoted version of the categorical imperative is usually referred to as the formula of the end in itself.]

22. [See above Ak. 422-23.]

23. Let it not be thought that the trivial *quod tibi non vis fieri, etc.* [do not do to others what you do not want done to yourself] can here serve as a standard or principle. For it is merely derived from our principle, although with several limitations. It cannot be a universal law, for it contains the ground neither of duties to oneself nor of duties of love toward others (for many a man would gladly consent that others should not benefit him, if only he might be excused from benefiting them). Nor, finally, does it contain the ground of strict duties toward others, for the criminal would on this ground be able to dispute with the judges who punish him; and so on.

Study Questions

1. Locate three statements of the categorical imperative and the Formula of the End in Itself. Construct an example in criminal justice practice that you think violates the categorical imperative.

2. What is a maxim of action in Kant's sense of the expression? What does Kant mean when he says that I should act as though my maxim of action were to become a "universal law of nature"? In your example from Question 1, formulate as precisely as you can the maxim of action. Explain why, in your view, that maxim could not exist as a universal law of nature.

3. What does Kant mean when he says that "man is not a thing"? Do you agree with Kant here? Why? What impact does Kant's view have for punishment that seeks to deter other people from committing a crime?

4. Explain why Kant's ethical theory is classified as a nonconsequentialist view.

5. In what does an absolutely good will consist (hint: see 426)? What is the bastard that is substituted for morality, according to Kant?

Morality Versus Slogans

BERNARD GERT

I AM NOT GOING to say anything that everyone doesn't already know. I think of myself as simply making explicit some points that people may have overlooked, and clarifying some points that are confusing because people may not have taken enough time to think about them sufficiently. I don't offer myself as any kind of authority. Philosophy is not science. Philosophers do not discover new facts in the way that some scientists do, or even historians, and which most of us simply have to accept on their authority. One should never accept anything any philosopher says simply on his authority. Philosophy is not religion, it provides no new faith of its own, at

This paper was first presented to, and published by, the Center for the Study of Ethics in Society at Western Michigan University, Vol. 3, No. 2, December 1989. The talk is a summary of some of the views presented in full detail in Gert's book, Morality: A New Justification of the Moral Rules, *Oxford University Press, 1988. Used by permission of the author.*

least I do not. Other philosophers can speak for themselves, but I consider myself to be in the Socratic tradition. I am simply a midwife whose task is to help others deliver their own thoughts more clearly and precisely.

In order to do this I must show you that you do not really accept some of the views that you think you accept. But before I do this, I want to make a few things clear. I am not a moral skeptic or moral relativist. In fact I accept all of the standard moral views; I regard killing, cheating, etc., as bad, and relieving pain, helping people, etc., as good. My positive views about morality are so ordinary that I expect everyone to agree with everything I have to say, to wonder why I even bother to say it. I don't intend to say anything at all controversial, and if I seem to do so that will be because I haven't expressed myself clearly enough. I am completely superficial, everything is on the surface and if I seem to say anything profound, then I have been misunderstood. This goes for my positive views as well as my criticisms of others. I am saying this all right at the start so you won't expect anything controversial or profound in what follows.

The Golden Rule

First, to show you how noncontroversial my views are, I am going to discuss the Golden Rule, "Do unto others as you would have them do unto you." Most people claim that they think the Golden Rule is a good principle by which to live. But consider the following case: I am sleeping in my bedroom in Hanover, New Hampshire—a little town, and I don't lock my doors. Tonight that seems to be a mistake because I am awakened by a noise downstairs. I go out of the bedroom and look down over the balcony and there is a burglar frantically trying to find something of value and stuffing various items into a bag. I see him but he doesn't see or hear me. I go back in my room where I have a telephone and I am about to call the police. All of a sudden I think of the Golden Rule. Should I hang up the phone and go to bed? That's what the Golden Rule says to do, doesn't it? There is no question

at all that if I were a burglar I certainly wouldn't want anyone to call the police on me! Therefore if I act according to the Golden Rule I should not call the police on this burglar. That's what the Golden Rule tells us. You might object that the burglar himself is not following the Golden Rule. He would not want me to rob his house, so he is not following the Golden Rule. That is correct, but the Golden Rule does not say "Do unto others as you would

have them do unto you unless they have done unto you what they would not want done unto them." So the Golden Rule seems to tell you not to report the burglar. "Oh come on" you say, "there is something wrong with that interpretation." But I have simply given the Golden Rule a straightforward reading and on that reading it really is a silly rule. The only reason that people still think it is any good is that they haven't really thought about it at all.

Consider an example where someone has not done anything wrong. An encyclopedia salesman comes to the door and wants to sell you an encyclopedia. What do you have to do if you want to follow the Golden Rule? You have to buy it. Once the other salesmen in town know you follow the Golden Rule, you are going to have every one of them at your front door too. I can tell you from experience, because I used to sell encyclopedias, that there is no question of what encyclopedia salesmen want. Given that they want you to buy, if you accept that you should do unto others what you want others to do unto you, then you have to buy the encyclopedias. You can even imagine a sophisticated use of the Golden Rule in the ongoing dialogue between the sexes, where the boy says to the girl, "The Golden Rule says you should do unto me what...", and the girl says, "Well, you should do unto me...", and then the boy says, "Well, I said it first."

After consideration, everyone realizes that the Golden Rule is not really a very good guide to conduct. It seems to require conduct that everybody admits is not required and sometimes seems to require conduct that is clearly wrong. If followed literally, and how else are we to understand it, it requires all normal policemen not to arrest criminals, and all normal judges not to sentence them. Assuming that normal judges and policemen want neither to be caught nor sentenced, according to the Golden Rule, it follows that they ought not to arrest or sentence others. The Golden Rule also requires, and students might like this, that teachers not give flunking grades to students even if they deserve it. If you were a student you would not want to be flunked. But it also seems to require that a student get a better grade than those who do not deserve it, because if you were a student and deserved a better grade, you would want a better grade. So it now seems that the Golden Rule is really pretty useless if you are trying to find out what you ought to do.

The Golden Rule does have some useful functions for children, e.g., a six-year-old girl who starts beating up on her little four-year-old brother, taking his toy away at the same time. So you say to her, "Would you like someone to beat up on you and take away your toy?" She says, "No." Then you say, "Well, do not do it to others." Of course everyone knows it was wrong to beat up on a kid and take his toy. So the Golden Rule seems, even here, to be merely a rhetorical device and is not any help at all in finding out what you ought to do. The Golden Rule doesn't tell you anything that you don't already know except in cases where it tells you the wrong thing. It is really a useless and pointless rule to use as a guide to your conduct because it really doesn't tell you how you ought to act in any cases in which you have any doubt.

I am not denying that the Golden Rule, in some cases, tells us to do the moral thing. What I am saying is that in those cases, you already knew what was immoral before you applied the Golden Rule. If you are wondering whether to kill somebody, you don't need that Golden Rule to tell you, "I wouldn't want to be killed, therefore I shouldn't kill him." You knew it was wrong to kill him before you applied the Golden Rule. The Golden Rule is of no help at all because it gives you the wrong answers as often as it give you the right ones. Using procedures

that are not very reliable, that sometimes give you the right answer but just as often give you the wrong answer, is not very useful.

The Ten Commandments

Having shown the inadequacy of the Golden Rule, let us consider the Ten Commandments. You may remember that some people, even former President Reagan, regard the Ten Commandments as a list of completely universal moral rules that should be accepted by everyone as their guide to morality. He recommended that they be posted on the bulletin boards of all of the schools. But it is very doubtful that he knew all the Ten Commandments. Some know one or two, but very few know all ten. In fact, there are several different versions. For example, Luther has one version and Calvin has another even though they are very similar. Do the Ten Commandments really provide an adequate and universal moral guide? Some of the Ten Commandments may not be moral rules at all. For example, it is not clear whether the rule against worshipping idols has anything to do with morality. I am not in favor of worshipping idols. I do not, never have, never will, but not everything that we are against is necessarily immoral. I do not believe that worshipping idols has anything to do with morality. But because I don't want to make any claim that may be controversial, I shall ignore the question of whether worshipping idols is a moral matter.

Let us now consider the commandment against coveting thy neighbor's wife. It is a little sexist. It does not say anything about not coveting thy neighbor's husband, for it was addressed to men, not women, but that is not my concern here. It says, "Don't covet thy neighbor's wife" and then continues, "or his house, or his oxen, or his ass, or his manservant or his maidservant." Manservants and maidservants are polite translations of "male and female slaves." So in the official statement of one of the commandments it says don't covet thy neighbor's slaves, male or female, which seems to condone slavery. "Don't covet your neighbor's slaves" does not sound like a universal moral rule. Nor is it the kind of rule we want posted on every schoolroom bulletin board. Maybe this explains the Reagan administration's policy on South Africa. One might object, "No, no, no, it tells you *not to covet slaves,* so it's really against slavery." This objection is not very strong for it would lead one to say that because it tells you not to covet wives it has to be against marriage. Even if one grants this completely inadequate defense, it's of no avail because unfortunately there is another Commandment that clearly does not count as a completely universal moral rule. If any of the Ten Commandments allows immoral behavior then we cannot use the Ten Commandments as a guide to the moral life. A guide which we know is sometimes wrong is clearly of no use to us in settling doubtful cases.

Those who know the Ten Commandments know the immoral commandment: "But the seventh day is the sabbath of the Lord thy God. In it thou shall not do any work, thou, nor thy son, nor thy daughter, nor thy manservant, nor thy maidservant, nor thine oxen, nor thine ass, nor any of thy cattle, nor any stranger who is within thy gates. That thy manservant and maidservant shall rest as well as thou" (Deuteronomy V: 14). This commandment recommends the humane treatment of slaves. So it was a big advance over the practice of the times. Even the Greek philosophers Plato and Aristotle thought there were natural slaves. Aristotle said: "There are natural rulers and natural slaves." You can see that I am not just attacking ancient religion; ancient philosophers were no better. Nowadays we know better. We know that slavery is wrong. Even humane slavery, if that is possible. So even if the commandment about giving the slaves a day off is an improvement over the practice of the time, which it certainly was, nobody would accept it as expressing a timeless, universally acceptable moral rule. Imagine posting this is on your bulletin board: "Give your slaves a day off." Is that the kind of commandment we would want posted in the schoolroom as President Reagan recommends? I do not deny that

some of the Ten Commandments are perfectly good moral rules, e.g., "Do not kill." It actually doesn't say that but you can interpret it that way. All I am saying is that the fact that a rule is one of the Ten Commandments is not a good reason for accepting it as a universal moral rule. If the Ten Commandments has rules which are not good, the fact that a rule is one of the Ten Commandments doesn't tell you whether it is a good one or a bad one. So we can see that the Ten Commandments does not provide a universally adequate moral guide. You will note that I have shown the inadequacies of both the Golden Rule and the Ten Commandments without saying the slightest thing that is controversial. I have just told you what you already know.

The Categorical Imperative

Having eliminated the two most popular accounts of morality, I shall now mention one philosophical account, perhaps the most famous one of all, the Categorical Imperative, formulated by Immanuel Kant, regarded by some as the greatest philosopher of all time. The most popular formulation of the Categorical Imperative is, "Act only according to that maxim that you could thereby will to be a universal law." This can be paraphrased as "Don't do anything you could not will everyone to do." Kant shows how the Categorical Imperative rules out lying promises. They are immoral because you could not will that everyone make lying promises. If everyone knew that everyone was lying when they promised, nobody would expect the promise to be kept and then there would not really be any promises. So the Categorical Imperative shows you that lying promises are wrong. The Categorical Imperative proves it, but we have already seen that the Golden Rule correctly shows that you should not hit your little brother and take away his toy and that some of the Ten Commandments are genuine moral rules.

In order to provide an adequate moral guide the Categorical Imperative must classify as immoral all and only those acts which really are immoral. If it sometimes correctly tells you that an act is immoral, e.g., a lying promise, and sometimes incorrectly tells you that an act is immoral, then it is not better than these other popular guides. The Categorical Imperative does seem to classify as immoral acting on the maxim, "Never be the first to arrive at a party." If everybody acted on that rule there could not be any parties, and so it seems just like a maxim that allows lying promises. If one were interested, many maxims could be invented that would be impossible to make into universal laws, and using the Categorical Imperative, Kant would have to regard it as immoral to act on those maxims, but some of them might, in fact, even be maxims that it would be good manners to follow, e.g., "Never be the last to leave a party." It is impossible for everyone to act on that maxim, someone has to be last. It is clearly wrong to claim that acting on such a maxim is immoral. So we can see that the philosophical slogan is no better than the popular slogans in providing a universally adequate moral guide.

This attack on the Golden Rule, the Ten Commandments, and the Categorical Imperative is not an attack on morality. It's an attack on simplistic thinking about morality. It's an attack on the view that you can summarize morality in a one-sentence, or maybe a ten-sentence, slogan. It is amazing how many people, when shown the inadequacy of these slogans, conclude that morality has been shown to be inadequate, that ethical relativity and skepticism are the only possible positions. It is as if somebody, when you give them Newton's three laws of physics, concludes that since they are not completely adequate and do not account for everything, that shows that physics is inadequate.

To back up their sophistication about the subjectivity of values, people often quote Shakespeare's remark, "Nothing is good or bad, but thinking makes it so." Of course, Shakespeare was not a philosopher and besides, only a character says it, and so we don't know if Shakespeare believed it or not. But a lot of people quote this remark as if it proved that morality is subjective.

It is amazing how poorly people argue, how little they pay serious attention to whether or not they hold inconsistent views. What may make what I have said so far seem at all controversial is that I have pointed out the inconsistencies in views that people hold without ever realizing that they hold such inconsistent views.

Moral Theory

A moral theory is an attempt to go beyond slogans and to provide an adequate description of morality, one that does not result in inconsistencies. A good moral theory also shows how morality is related to our more general values and to impartiality and rationality. I have developed a moral theory which I think accurately describes morality, the moral system that we actually use when making moral judgments and deciding what to do in moral situations. What follows is based upon that theory, which is presented in far greater detail in my book, *Morality: A New Justification of the Moral Rules,* published by Oxford University Press in 1988 and now also available in paperback. (It may be relevant to point out here that there is not necessarily a conflict between morality and self-interest.)

Goods, Evils, and Rationality

Before I talk about morality at all I want to say something more about our general values, because "moral values" is not a redundant phrase. There are a lot of values besides moral values. I want to talk about those things we consider to be goods and evils, or benefits and harms, if you like that better. By an evil or a harm, I simply mean something that you would always avoid for yourself or your friends unless you had some reason for not avoiding it. I define a good or a benefit in a similar way, as something you would not avoid for yourself and your friends unless you had some reason to. I claim that, in the sense I have given to the terms, we all agree on what the goods and evils are, i.e., we all have the same basic values.

I have no argument at all for this claim. If you do not agree with me all I can do is try to clarify. If after I clarify and you understand and still disagree with me, there is nothing else for me to do. I have nothing further to say to you and you might as well stop reading this essay. In order to test whether or not there really is agreement, I am going to present the list of basic evils, a list of things that rational people, including you and your friends, avoid unless you have an adequate reason for not avoiding them. Here is the list:

Death
Pain
Disability
Loss of Freedom
Loss of Pleasure.

These evils differ from almost everything else in the world, because for anything else which does not involve these evils, we do not need any, let alone an adequate, reason for not avoiding them e.g., books.

If there is agreement on the evils, I do not think there will be any problem in getting agreement on the goods. Here is the list of goods (those things you would not avoid unless you had an adequate reason for doing so):

Abilities
Freedom
Pleasure.

The close relationship between the goods and evils should be apparent. It should also be apparent that we regard anyone who, without an adequate reason, does not avoid the evils or does avoid the goods as acting irrationally.

In order to explain what counts as an adequate reason we must first make clear what a reason is. A reason is a conscious belief that you or someone else will avoid suffering an evil, or will gain a good. So if you are acting rationally you wouldn't want to suffer any of the items on the list of evils unless you or someone else is going to avoid one of these evils or gain some good. Everyone admits that acting so as to avoid a good

or not to avoid an evil when no one, including yourself, is going to benefit in any way is irrational, e.g., killing yourself in order to make someone else suffer. It is also clear that causing yourself serious harm in order to gain some minor good, e.g., cutting off your arm to win a quarter bet, is also irrational. In order for your harming yourself to be rational, the reason you have must be adequate, i.e., the evil avoided or good gained must be equal to or greater than the harm caused. For example, it is not irrational to have your arm cut off in order to avoid the very high risk of death that would come from the spread of bone cancer in your unamputated arm.

This account of goods, evils, and rationality is really quite simple. We all agree that it may be rational to seek death in order to avoid intense permanent pain, e.g., some seriously ill people choose to die rather than continue to suffer such pain. Other people who are willing to undergo such pain in order to stay alive are also acting rationally. This shows that my claim that we all agree on what is good and evil is not a claim that we all agree on the ranking of the goods and evils. All disagreement about goods and evils is disagreement on the way we rank the evils and goods, it is never disagreement on whether something counts as a good or as an evil. When we do cost-benefit analysis there is not disagreement on whether something counts as a cost or as a benefit.

Although I do not claim that everybody agrees on the ranking of the goods and evils, by and large people tend to agree. A person who commits suicide to avoid going to the dentist is acting irrationally. But there are other times where one's illness and pain are serious enough that it is not irrational to prefer death. I cannot provide a procedure for ranking the goods and evils. Insofar as there are disagreements I shall not attempt to settle them because I do not want to say anything controversial. I admit that we sometimes disagree on what is better or worse, but claim that we always agree on what is good and bad. This account of what is a good and evil explains why we always choose goods over evils and it also explains what it means to say that we sometimes choose the lesser of two evils. We want to avoid both of them, but if we are forced to suffer one of them, we choose the lesser evil.

Morality

Once we see that there is complete agreement on what counts as the fundamental goods and evils, it may seem less implausible that there is also agreement on morality. Remember that I regard it as implausible that morality can be stated adequately in a single-sentence slogan. Indeed, you should not expect this essay to provide a complete account of morality, for morality can no more be adequately summarized in a short essay than can physics or biology. Besides if it did, you would have no reason to buy my book. But I am going to present the broad outline of the moral system we all use in making moral judgments.

Morality is like grammar; we all use it but we have difficulty in making it explicit. A philosopher is like a grammarian. What he does is make explicit the rules that we all use. What I am going to do is simply to make explicit the moral system that you all in fact use in making your moral judgments. I shall not say anything new at all. You can test whether what I say is correct by seeing if the outline that I give you is such that when you use it, it provides you with the moral judgments you always make, assuming that you are good moral people.

First, a moral system applies to all rational people, i.e., it applies to everybody whom we hold responsible for their actions. This means that it applies not only to philosophy majors and college graduates, but also to college freshmen and even high school students. But if morality applies to everyone, then a moral system has to be simple enough for everyone to understand it. We cannot judge people by a moral system if the system is so complicated that people can't understand it. So, since we judge high school students, and even younger children, by a moral system, this requires the moral system to be so simple that even they can understand it. If anybody

presents a moral theory that results in a moral system that requires one to take a philosophy class in order to understand it, this is enough to show that the theory is wrong. The theory could not be describing the moral system we actually use in judging people.

Since everybody is supposed to act as morality requires, i.e., to abide by the moral rules, we blame and punish them when they do not. But we never want anyone to act irrationally, so it cannot be irrational for people to act as morality requires. Otherwise we would sometimes blame or punish people for refusing to act irrationally. A system that is understood by everyone to whom it applies and which is not irrational for them to follow, is what I call a "public system." Games are such public systems, i.e., the rules apply to all the players in the game and all the players understand the rules and it is not irrational for any of them to follow them.

Morality differs from other public systems in at least one important way: it applies to all rational persons. Whereas the rules of a game apply only to the people playing, morality applies to everyone. Cheating is taken by many people to be the paradigm case of an immoral action because cheating seems to provide a model for all immoral action. But because one can cheat only those with whom one is participating in some shared activity, many philosophers have falsely concluded that morality applies only within a given society. Social contract theory and ethical relativity both rest on making the wrong analogy between cheating and morality. Morality is universal and does not depend upon any prior agreement, actual or hypothetical.

The Moral Rules

What are the rules of morality, i.e., the public system, that apply to all rational persons? What rules would a rational person who wants to avoid the evils want as part of a public system that applies to everyone? I claim that people would agree on the rules they would want to be part of a public system that applies to everyone. A list of these rules contains the following five rules:

Do not Kill
Do not Cause Pain
Do not Disable
Do not Deprive of Freedom
Do not Deprive of Pleasure.

Be sure to notice the close connection between these rules and the items on the list of evils. These first five rules just tell you "Don't cause anyone to suffer an evil." Since you don't want to suffer an evil, and you know that no other rational person does either, if you are putting forward a public system that applies to all rational persons, you obviously want these rules to be included in that system.

These five rules are not the only moral rules. There are, as luck and chance would have it, five more rules. These second five rules are also related to the evils, but less directly. I do not have the space here to provide the arguments showing how obedience to these rules is required for avoiding causing the suffering of evils, but I can recommend a book that has all these arguments in it. Even without consulting this book, I do not think anyone will be surprised by any of the second five rules. This is the list of the next five rules:

Don't Deceive
Keep Your Promise
Don't Cheat
Obey the Law
Do Your Duty—where Duty includes those actions you are required to do by your job, your position, your family, your circumstances, etc., e.g., a teacher has a duty to show up for class.

These are the ten moral rules that all rational persons would want to be part of the public system that applies to all rational persons. No one should be surprised by these ten rules. These are all obvious, simple rules that everyone is supposed to follow regardless of what their personal goal in life is. Careful attention to these rules shows that they primarily set limits on what one is morally allowed to do. They do not provide a positive goal for life. This is done by another part of the moral system, what I call *the moral ideals*. But before I say anything about moral ideals, I want to point out a few interesting features of the moral rules.

Notice that they are simple and general. They can be understood by everyone. They are all prohibitions, or can be stated as prohibitions, e.g., "Keep Your Promise" is exactly equivalent to "Don't Break Your Promise." Every one of those rules can be stated as a prohibition and with no change in meaning at all. What is not obvious from just looking at them is that they all have exceptions. The moral rules are not absolute, they have exceptions. They are, however, universal—they apply to everyone. Many people confuse universal and absolute. The moral rules are universal, they apply to everyone, but they are not absolute. They have exceptions, but these exceptions are also universal. What are the justified exceptions? Here, not surprisingly, people may disagree somewhat, just as they disagree on the ranking of the evils. In fact, it is this difference in the ranking of the evils that accounts for most moral disagreement when there is agreement on the facts. But almost all moral disagreements are in fact disagreements on the facts. Very seldom is there disagreement on the facts, including estimates on the probability of consequences, and disagreement on what morally ought to be done. In my seven years as a member of the Ethics Committee in a hospital, and as a consultant on ethical problems, I have not run across a single case, not one, where there was moral disagreement which was not based upon disagreement in the facts.

Philosophers tend to distinguish facts from values and claim that we all agree on the facts and disagree on the values. In my experience, the exact opposite is true. We all agree on our values and disagree about the facts. If you look carefully and precisely at what are presented as examples of moral disagreements, I think your own experience will confirm this claim. Take the example of Star Wars vs. Disarmament. Is there any disagreement in values? Does one side want to blow up the world and the other side save it? Of course not. Everyone wants to save the world.

One side thinks that Star Wars will save it, the other side thinks that disarmament will save it. They disagree about the probable consequences of different courses of action, or what the facts of the case are. They all have the same values—namely avoiding the death and destruction that will accompany any nuclear exchange. When people agree on the facts, they almost always agree on when it's justified to break a moral rule. This is because they agree that the justified exception has to be a part of the public system. If you are going to break a moral rule you have to be willing that everyone be publicly allowed to break the rule in the same circumstances. That this sounds a little like Kant's Categorical Imperative is not surprising, for the attraction of the Categorical Imperative is that it seems to capture the kind of impartiality that morality requires. This kind of impartiality does not require that we break a moral rule only when we would will that everyone actually break the rule in the same circumstances. Rather it requires that we break the rule only when we would be willing to publicly allow that everyone break it.

Let us consider applications of the procedure for justifying a violation of a moral rule that it can be broken justifiably when one would be willing to publicly allow everyone in the same circumstances to break that rule. First let us consider the question whether one can cause pain to someone, just for fun? Clearly not, for no rational person would be willing to publicly allow anyone to cause pain to another simply for the fun of it. But now consider whether one would be willing to allow someone to cause pain to another when it is necessary to do so to help them avoid death, and they consent to your causing that pain. Here it is clearly justifiable to break the moral rule because every rational person would be willing to publicly allow everyone to break the moral rule against causing pain to someone who gives consent when it is done to save their life. This is so obvious that it seems almost not worth saying. It is not obvious that it is justified to cause pain when it is necessary to save a person's life and they refuse consent. Not all rational persons would agree to publicly

allowing violating the rule against causing pain in these circumstances.

This explains why informed consent is so important in the practice of medicine. Doctors are breaking moral rules left and right, they are causing pain and disability and taking away freedom all the time. If what they do is not to count as immoral they must be justified in doing it. When you break a moral rule with regard to someone with their consent and for their benefit, everyone agrees that it is completely justified, because everyone would be willing to publicly allow such violations of the moral rules. Though we do not explicitly make use of the procedure that I have outlined, one can see that it explains not only all those cases that are clearly justified violations; it also explains those cases where people disagree on whether the violation is justified or not. These are the cases in which impartial rational persons can disagree on whether they would publicly allow such a violation. This summarizes what the moral theory says about the rules and when it is justified to violate them. I am aware that it may sound unfamiliar, but I think that you can see that it is all extremely simple and straightforward, that it simply makes explicit the procedure that you all use all the time.

The Moral Ideals

Now I am going to make explicit the moral ideals. Moral ideals are those precepts that tell you to help others, to prevent the suffering of pain and disability, etc. Following the moral ideals goes beyond what is required by the rules, but that does not mean that in a conflict between the rules and the ideals, one should always follow the rules. For example, everyone agrees that you can break a promise to meet someone at the movies, if it is necessary to save a life. The moral ideal of saving a life justifies your breaking this moral rule. The moral rules and moral ideals are both important, and sometimes one should take precedence over the other, sometimes the reverse. It depends on what rules and ideals are involved. It depends on the particular circumstances. But there is an important difference between the rules and the ideals. The rules tell you not to cause an evil, e.g., do not cause pain; the ideals tell you to prevent or relieve evil being suffered, e.g., relieve pain.

You will notice that the moral rules can be obeyed with regard to all people, all of the time, equally. You can obey the moral rules impartially with regard to all people all the time, twenty-four hours a day, seven days a week, fifty-two weeks a year. You can obey them when you are alone on a desert island, in fact, you cannot help but obey them when you are alone on a desert island. The situation is really different with regard to the moral ideals. You cannot be following the moral ideals twenty-four hours a day. You have to sleep sometime, and when you are sleeping you are not following the moral ideals. This is a significant difference between the moral ideals and the moral rules, e.g., all of you reading this essay are right now obeying all of the moral rules, but none of you right now are obeying any of the moral ideals. Reading this essay may lead you to follow moral ideals, but right at this minute, you are not following them, whereas you are obeying all of the moral rules.

This difference between the rules and the ideals leads to another difference: it is appropriate to punish people for not obeying the moral rules, but it is not appropriate to punish them for not following the moral ideals. When would you punish them? The moral rules differ from the moral ideals in that the moral rules should be enforced. When people say that morality cannot be enforced, another one of these wonderful slogans, they usually don't know what they're talking about. Everybody believes in the enforcement of the moral rules. It's only the moral ideals that should not be enforced. In fact, the moral rules are enforced by every criminal code in every civilized society in the world. There are rules against killing, causing pain, breaking promises, etc. To say that you should not enforce morality is a slogan as misleading as the slogans that I discussed at the beginning of this essay. I suspect that as much careful thought has been devoted to it as has been devoted to the Golden Rule by those who regard it as an adequate summary of morality or as a completely satisfactory moral guide.

Morality is too important to be summarized in terms of slogans. But that slogans are inadequate to summarize morality does not mean that only philosophers can properly understand what morality is. We all know what morality requires of us. It may be that we are not all that anxious to get completely clear about it.

Study Questions

1. State the Golden Rule in one of its standard forms. Give an example used by Gert to show that the Golden Rule is not a good moral principle. Do you think Gert's example is effective? Why?

2. What is the point of Gert's example maxim, "Never be the first to arrive at a party"? Do you think his argument succeeds? Why?

3. Does Gert provide support for his claim that we all agree on basic goods and evils? Why? Do you think he is right on this point? Why? Where do moral disagreements arise, according to Gert? Do you agree? Why?

4. What does Gert mean in saying that his ten moral rules are universal? Are these rules absolute, according to Gert? Is Gert using the term "absolute" in the same way as Stace?

5. Explain Gert's distinction between moral rules and moral ideals.

Canons of Police Ethics

INTERNATIONAL ASSOCIATION OF CHIEFS OF POLICE

Article 1. Primary Responsibility of Job

The primary responsibility of the police service, and of the individual officer, is the protection of the people of the United States through the upholding of their laws; chief among these is the Constitution of the United States and its amendments. The law enforcement officer always represents the whole of the community and its legally expressed will and is never the arm of any political party or clique.

Article 2. Limitations of Authority

The first duty of a law enforcement officer, as upholder of the law, is to know its bounds upon him in enforcing it. Because he represents the legal will of the community, be it local, state or federal, he must be aware of the limitations and proscriptions which the people, through law, have placed upon him. He must recognize the genius of the American system of government which gives to no man, groups of men, or institution, absolute power, and he must insure that he, as a prime defender of that system, does not pervert its character.

Article 3. Duty to be Familiar With the Law and with Responsibilities of Self and Other Public Officials

The law enforcement officer shall assiduously apply himself to the study of the principles of the laws which he is sworn to uphold. He will make certain of his responsibilities in the particulars of their enforcement, seeking aid from his superiors in matters of technicality or principle when these are not clear to him; he will make special effort to fully understand his relationship to other public officials, including other law enforcement agencies, particularly on matters of jurisdiction, both geographically and substantively.

Article 4. Utilization of Proper Means To Gain Proper Ends

The law enforcement officer shall be mindful of his responsibility to pay strict heed to the selection of means in discharging the duties of his office. Violations of law or disregard for public safety and property on the part of an officer are intrinsically wrong; they are self-defeating in that they instill in the public mind a like disposition. The employment of illegal means, no matter how worthy the end, is certain to encourage disrespect for the law and its officers. If the law is to be honored, it must first be honored by those who enforce it.

Article 5. Cooperation with Public Officials in the Discharge of Their Authorized Duties

The law enforcement officer shall cooperate fully with other public officials in the discharge of authorized duties, regardless of party affiliation or personal prejudice. He shall be meticulous, however, in assuring himself of the propriety, under the law, of such actions and shall guard against the use of his office or person, whether knowingly or unknowingly, in any improper or illegal action. In any situation open to question, he shall seek authority from his superior officer, giving him a full report of the proposed service or action.

Article 6. Private Conduct

The law enforcement officer shall be mindful of his special identification by the public as an upholder of the law. Laxity of conduct or manner in private life, expressing either disrespect for the law or seeking to gain special privilege, cannot but reflect upon the police officer and the police service. The community and the service require that the law enforcement officer lead the life of a decent and honorable man. Following the career of a policeman gives no man special perquisites. It does give the satisfaction and pride of following and furthering an unbroken tradition of safeguarding the American republic. The officer who reflects upon this tradition will not degrade it. Rather, he will so conduct his private life that the public will regard him as an example of stability, fidelity and morality.

Article 7. Conduct Toward the Public

The law enforcement officer, mindful of his responsibility to the whole community, shall deal with individuals of the community in a manner calculated to instill respect for its laws and its police service. The law enforcement officer shall conduct his official life in a manner such as will inspire confidence and trust. Thus, he will be neither overbearing nor subservient, as no individual citizen has an obligation to stand in awe of him nor a right to command him. The officer will give service where he can, and require compliance with the law. He will do neither from personal preference or prejudice but rather as a duly appointed officer of the law discharging his sworn obligation.

Article 8. Conduct in Arresting and Dealing with Law Violators

The law enforcement officer shall use his powers of arrest strictly in accordance with the law and with due regard to the rights of the citizen concerned. His office gives him no right to prosecute the violator nor to mete out punishment for the offense. He shall, at all times, have a clear appreciation of his responsibilities and limitations regarding detention of the violator; he shall conduct himself in such a manner as will minimize the possibility of having to use force. To this end he shall cultivate a dedication to the service of the people and the equitable upholding of their laws whether in the handling of law violators or in dealing with the law-abiding.

Article 9. Gifts and Favors

The law enforcement officer, representing government, bears the heavy responsibility of maintaining, in his own conduct, the honor and integrity of all government institutions. He shall, therefore, guard against placing himself in a position in which any person can expect special consideration or in which the public can reasonably assume that special consideration is being given. Thus, he should be firm in refusing gifts, favors, or gratuities, large or small, which can, in the public mind, be interpreted as capable of influencing his judgment in the discharge of his duties.

Article 10. Presentation of Evidence

The law enforcement officer shall be concerned equally in the prosecution of the wrong-doer and the defense of the innocent. He shall ascertain what constitutes evidence and shall present such evidence impartially and without malice. In so doing, he will ignore social, political, and all other distinctions among the persons involved, strengthening the tradition of the reliability and integrity of an officer's word.

The law enforcement officer shall take special pains to increase his perception and skill of observation, mindful that in many situations his is the sole impartial testimony to the facts of a case.

Article II. Attitude Toward Profession

The law enforcement officer shall regard the discharge of his duties as a public trust and recognize his responsibility as a public servant. By diligent study and sincere attention to self-improvement he shall strive to make the best possible application of science to the solution of crime and, in the field of human relationships, strive for effective leadership and public influence in matters affecting public safety. He shall appreciate the importance and responsibility of his office, and hold police work to be an honorable profession rendering valuable service to his community and his country.

Case 1.1

HOT WATER

You, as a fairly experienced corrections officer, think that you have discovered a way to use the "system" to make your job easier and your job performance more effective.

You are faced with the nightly problem of putting 94 mostly young, high-strung inmates to bed at 11:00 P.M. in an overcrowded dormitory. After the lights go out, you are immediately faced with enforcing several rules to maintain some level of quiet and safety in the darkened dorm. Your main goals are, you believe, to make certain that the men actually do go to their own beds and that the noise level abates enough to permit sleep. You make an effort to enforce the rules that lead to these goals.

One "lights-out" rule, however, strikes you as being somewhat less "important" than the others. This rule prohibits inmates from carrying water from the bathroom to their beds after 11:00 P.M. It was established years ago in response to a single incident involving one inmate who threw a cup of hot coffee into the face of a sleeping inmate in a darkened dorm. The victim was badly burned and the perpetrator was never discovered. Such an incident has not recurred in years, and the rule itself has not been strictly enforced, primarily because officers did not regard it as important and because it is difficult to enforce in a crowded dorm.

Knowing all of this, plus the fact that inmates really like to take coffee back to their beds, you adopt an unofficial policy of selective enforcement. When the dorm becomes quiet and people go to their own beds shortly after lights out, you tend to turn away and "not see" an occasional inmate carrying water to his bed. The inmates catch on quickly, and after a few days the dorm seems to quiet down and become more orderly within 5 to 10 minutes after lights out (as opposed to 15 or 20 in the past).

You feel pretty satisfied with the results, but questions remain. Most important, you are concerned about the possibility of another water-throwing incident. Have you done the right thing?

Questions for Discussion

1. Is your selective enforcement increasing the possibility of another water-throwing incident?

2. Considering the difficulty in enforcing this rule (when you try), how responsible would you be if another incident did occur?

3. Is the trade-off you have made—a more quiet dorm (which the inmates really do appreciate) versus the increased possibility, however slight, of an inmate being injured—valid?

4. How could this problem be solved without breaking the rules?

5. Could this "favor" to the inmates—providing a more hospitable atmosphere—create a form of trust between you and them? Defend your answer.

6. Could this "favor" to the inmates create a basis for blackmail in the future? Explain.

7. What would you do? Apply a utilitarian analysis to your decision. Apply the Categorical Imperative to your decision.

8. Reflect on the process of becoming a corrections officer and speculate on how this corrections officer came to this decision.

9. Apply Gert's Moral Rules to support or rebut the decision to allow the inmates to bring hot water to their beds.

10. Should we stop making rules by exception, recognizing that there are "nuts" in the world who shouldn't make it difficult for the rest of us? Give examples of other rules by exception.

11. Would you be willing to accept the consequences for breaking the rules?

Case 1.2

CREDIT WHERE CREDIT IS DUE

An informant has just left your office, and you now have the last piece of evidence you need for the biggest drug bust ever in your county. You can now approach the municipal court judge for arrest warrants, prepare and file felony complaints in municipal court, and mobilize every city police officer available to make arrests. Or you can take all your evidence to the county prosecutor so that she can present it to the grand jury and obtain secret indictments. This investigation has taken a long time, and a little more delay will not hurt anything.

But if these prosecutions begin with the secret indictments from the county common pleas court instead of felony complaints from the municipal court, the county sheriff's department will make the arrests and take all the credit. You know the sheriff will be present during the indictment arrests, and he will have photographs taken for the newspaper. The general public will never know that the city police did all the work, and your arrest statistics will not look as good as they should.

If you file the complaints, the municipal court clerk, the judge, the city prosecutor, the police officers, the public defender, and the defendants will spend a lot of time, effort and money on initial appearances, bond hearings, and preliminary hearings, and in the end the cases will go to the grand jury anyway. Since immediate arrests are not necessary, all that would be a waste, and it would give the county prosecutor much less time to organize and present the evidence to the grand jury than he would have otherwise. Both the city and county prosecutors have explained all this in a memo to your police department, and they have asked you to take cases straight to the grand jury whenever possible.

But you really need a good report from the chief on the next personnel review in order to get that promotion. The chief's brother is running against the incumbent for sheriff, and the chief will be very upset if you let the present sheriff take the credit for the arrests.

Questions for Discussion

1. There seems to be a lack of communication between the sheriff's department and the city police department. Is this protection of turf typical? If so, why?

2. Identify the officer's alternatives. What are the arguments, both pro and con, of each alternative?

3. Identify other incidents where several jurisdictions became involved in a criminal justice activity. What were the conflicts? How were they resolved?

4. Identify the personal, professional, and political considerations at play in this case. How might all (or most) of these considerations be resolved to everyone's satisfaction? Explain.

5. What would you do? Apply a utilitarian analysis to your decision. Apply the Categorical Imperative to your decision. Apply Gert's Moral Rules to support or rebut your decision.

Chapter 2

Due Process

"Let the jury consider their verdict," the King said, for about the twentieth time that day.

"No, no!" said the Queen. "Sentence first—verdict afterwards."

"Stuff and nonsense!" said Alice loudly. "The idea of having the sentence first!"

"Hold your tongue!" said the Queen, turning purple.

"I won't!" said Alice.

"Off with her head!" the Queen shouted at the top of her voice.

—*From* ALICE IN WONDERLAND

EVEN THOUGH THE KNAVE OF HEARTS, accused of stealing the Queen's tarts, merits a trial, Alice is summarily sentenced to death. The Queen of Hearts has no respect for due process, it seems. Or does she? Even Alice has a hearing, albeit short. And the Knave of Hearts has a trial. If the law of Wonderland is to have the sentence passed before the verdict is delivered, and that process is duly followed, isn't that all we mean by "due process"? The verdict against Alice will no doubt follow the removal of her head, all in due course!

An Overview of Due Process

The U.S. Constitution and the Bill of Rights not only introduced a new legal system, but in doing so, automatically circumscribed a new set of due process principles. These principles are subject to change as the Supreme Court and other courts interpret the law.[1] New York State Supreme Court Justice Sidney H. Asch traces the constitutional concept of due process to the English law concept of "the law of the land."[2]

Asch notes that while colonial documents contain the phrases "due process of law" and "the law of the land," neither phrase appears in the original Constitution of the United States. The Fifth Amendment to the Constitution adds the phrase, stating "... nor shall any person ... be deprived of life, liberty, or property, without due process of law ... " The definition of due process of law in *Black's Law Dictionary* refers to the right of a citizen to certain procedural actions prior to the deprivation of "... life, liberty, property or of any right granted him by statute ... "[3]

This definition is not purely formal. Note the all-important expression "prior to." This is a morally substantive limit on what can count as due process. By this definition, the Queen of Hearts violates due process in the cases of both the Knave of Hearts and Alice. The Queen attempts to give the Knave his due process *after* the deprivation, and she doesn't give Alice any due process at all.

Despite the provision for due process in the Bill of Rights (the Fifth Amendment), this applied only to the federal justice process. The states were not constitutionally required to observe due process until 1866, when the Fourteenth Amendment was adopted. Though many states had by that time enacted state legislation requiring due process, it was feared that the member states of the Confederacy would alter or ignore state-mandated due process in cases involving former slaves. Since slaves had been routinely denied any semblance of due process, the need for a Constitutional guarantee at the state level was clear.

Asch observes that it was only with the Fourteenth Amendment that the Federal government (the U.S. Supreme Court) became involved in setting standards of criminal procedure. The Court initially refused to apply the Fourteenth Amendment to cases involving claims of uneven administration of justice, but in 1927, the first state criminal case was reversed by the Supreme Court on grounds of lack of due process of law. A criminal conviction by a justice of the peace was reversed because the justice was paid only if he convicted the defendant. If he cleared the accused, he received nothing. The Court ruled that this system denied the accused person due process of law.[4] Several of the papers that you will read in this chapter discuss the due process decisions of the Supreme Court that have been issued since that time.

The Readings

The first selection in this chapter is "The Rule of Law" from John Rawls' influential book, *A Theory of Justice*. Rawls lays out the ethical foundation for due process only briefly, but in a very clear way. He first defines a legal system as "... a coercive order of public rules addressed to rational persons for the purpose of regulating their conduct and providing the framework for social cooperation." Because the boundaries of individual freedom depend on those rules being just, Rawls points out that liberty and the rule of law are very closely related. Rawls sees due process of law as fundamental to the maintenance of liberty because due process "insures that the legal order will be impartially and regularly maintained." The components of due process are seen by Rawls as "precepts of natural justice" that are "... reasonably designed to ascertain the truth, in ways consistent with the other ends of the legal system, as to whether a violation has taken place and under what circumstances." If due process fails, the legal order loses both its impartiality and its predictability. When this happens, liberty (what we may and may not do as a member of society) is threatened.

In the selection, *Rochin* v. *California* (1952), Justice Frankfurter discusses the Due Process Clause of the Fourteenth Amendment in detail regarding a case in which three deputy sheriffs entered the home of Rochin, a suspected narcotics seller, and forced their way into the suspect's bedroom where he was observed swallowing some capsules. The officers beat Rochin and then took him to a hospital where he was forcibly administered an emetic, causing him to vomit two capsules containing morphine. Rochin was convicted of possession of narcotics on the basis of the two capsules. The U.S. Supreme Court overturned the conviction as a violation of Rochin's right to due process under the Fourteenth Amendment.

Obtaining confessions is one of the major goals of law enforcement following arrest. A voluntary confession made by a knowing and mentally competent person is very effective in gaining a conviction. But confessions must be voluntary, not coerced, or they violate our Fifth Amendment right against self-incrimination, as well as the Fourteenth Amendment right to due process. Writing for the majority, Frankfurter says that

> due process of law is a summarized constitutional guarantee of respect for those personal immunities which, as Mr. Justice Cardozo twice wrote for the Court, are "so rooted in the traditions and conscience of our people as to be ranked as fundamental," *Snyder* v. *Massachusetts,* 291 U.S. 97, 105, or are "implicit in the concept of ordered liberty." *Palko* v. *Connecticut,* 302 U.S. 319, 325.

In this passage, Frankfurter clearly finds due process to be morally grounded in the concept of freedom, just as Rawls did many years later. We should note that freedom is not conditioned by some idea of social benefit. We presumably do not value freedom only if it maximizes the balance of good over bad in society. The reason is simple: good and bad are, at least in part, *defined in terms* of the presence of individual freedom. In this view, anyone who is willing to sacrifice due process on the altar of social benefit has put the cart before the horse.

One upshot of *Rochin* and other decisions upholding the right to due process is that until 1991, a coerced confession in a criminal trial was regarded as an absolute, uncorrectable error, thus demanding a new trial that does not use the coerced confession. For example, in *Blackburn* v. *Alabama* (1960), the Court writes that such an absolute view reflects the "strongly felt attitude of our society that important human values are sacrificed where an agency of the government, in the course of securing a conviction, wrings a confession out of an accused against his will."[5] In *Spano* v. *New York* (1959), the Court referred to "the deep-rooted feeling that the police must obey the law while enforcing the law; that in the end life and liberty can be as much endangered from illegal methods used to convict those thought to be criminals as from the actual criminals themselves."[6]

In *Arizona* v. *Fulminante* (1991),[7] many observers see a fundamental challenge to the absolute nature of the right to due process of law. In a highly segmented and close decision, the Court declared that admission of involuntary confessions is no longer an absolute error, but is subject to the "harmless error" review process established in

Chapman v. *California* (1967).[8] This means that even if an involuntary confession is admitted as evidence at trial, the trial process is not therefore necessarily invalidated, i.e., such admission may be a "harmless error." If a trial error is determined by a court to be harmless, the outcome of the trial may be left to stand.

In the Philip Jenkins selection, "Crime Control and Due Process," Jenkins explores the tension between what have been called the "crime control" and the "due process" models of criminal justice.[9] He examines these models as they have been implemented in the United States and in other countries, and concludes that the crime control model is less desirable than the due process model for a variety of reasons. Jenkins associates the crime control and the due process models with the conservative and liberal ends of the political spectrum. However, this may not be a useful division. The "crime control" attitude toward the Second Amendment right to keep and bear arms would certainly be one of weakening, and where possible ignoring, the Second Amendment. But such a perspective is not likely to be adopted by political conservatives. As a group, liberals are probably more likely to support the crime control/social benefit justification for limiting the extent of the Second Amendment.

Consequently, it may be more useful to look at the two models of criminal justice as that of the utilitarian versus the deontologist. The utilitarian stands ready to sacrifice any individual right (due process, freedom of speech, etc.) *if* doing so will benefit society as a whole. On the other hand, individual rights are regarded by the deontologist to have an internal justification. For example, the deontologist might hold that a person has a right to a fair trial *regardless* of the consequences. The utilitarian/deontologist distinction cuts across the political spectrum. Some utilitarians are conservatives, and some are liberals. The same holds true of deontologists.[10]

In the J. S. Fuerst and Roy Petty selection, "Due Process—How Much Is Enough?" the essential ingredient of *when* due process must occur is reviewed in terms of the Supreme Court's 1970 decision in *Goldberg* v. *Kelly*. In that case, a New York state welfare recipient, Mrs. Kelly, had her benefits terminated, but was provided with a right to a formal hearing if she wished to challenge the termination. The Court observed that her eligibility for support payments was a property right, which could not be abridged without due process of law. In short, the State of New York had acted much like the Queen of Hearts: the procedure must come *before* the deprivation, not afterwards. Nonetheless, as Fuerst and Petty argue, the form that due process takes is not necessarily built into the concept of due process of law itself. Fuerst and Petty believe that the adversarial model used in administrative hearings on social benefits is not only slow and cumbersome, but actually ineffective in producing fair results. Due process, Fuerst and Petty claim, can be more fairly and effectively achieved by adopting a European model of administrative hearing in which the presiding officer or judge plays the active role of evidence collection and conflict resolution. Fuerst and Petty believe that such an approach ". . . seems ideally suited for public housing authorities, child welfare agencies, state adoption agencies, [and] juvenile courts . . ."

To the criminal justice practitioner, the regular emergence of new due process requirements can be frustrating. Since due process is based on legal principle rather than the day-to-day realities of law enforcement and corrections, due process is sometimes a dirty word. If one is in the business of controlling crime, the crime control model of criminal justice is understandably a natural one. But, even though the good of society is a function of the rule of law, the law applies to everyone. And it is worth noting that federal laws passed over 100 years ago are enforced more and more frequently against criminal justice officers who go beyond the limits of due process.[11] These laws punish those who "willfully subject" others to "the deprivation of any rights, privileges or immunities secured or protected by the Constitution or law of the United States."[12]

The Benjamin J. Ferrell selection, "Duty to Intervene: An Officer's Dilemma," examines the recent case law surrounding 42 U.S.C. 1983. What legal responsibility does a police officer have to intervene in the wrongful actions of a fellow officer? Ferrell points out that section 1983 cases are now argued on the basis of *Byrd* v. *Brishke* (466 F.2nd 6), in which a U.S. Court of Appeals awarded damages to a citizen who was beaten, denied medical aid, falsely accused of violating the law, and held in a police facility for 48 hours. Police officers were held liable even though they did not personally take part in the beating. The reason: they neglected their duty to intervene in the wrongful acts of other officers. Ferrell then explains in careful detail the variations on this theme. For example, he takes note of the fact that if you, a junior officer, observe a fellow officer engaging in wrongful actions, you are not absolved of your duty to intervene just because your superior is also a witness to the acts and does not intervene. As Ferrell states, "the guiding principle is the nonfeasor officer must do whatever is REASONABLE [Ferrell's capitalization] under the circumstances to halt the wrongful conduct of the misfeasor *(Ware*, 709 F.2nd 345)." Ferrell thus raises the critical issue of individual discretion, our topic in Chapter 3.

Notes

1. The Bill of Rights (the first ten amendments) and the Fourteenth Amendment are included for reference at the end of this chapter.
2. Sidney H. Asch, *Police Authority and the Rights of the Individual.* (New York: Arco Publishing Company, 1971), p. 40.
3. *Black's Law Dictionary*, abridged 5th ed., s.v. "Due Process of Law."
4. Tumey v. Ohio, 273 U.S. 510 (1927).
5. 361 U.S. at 206, 207.
6. 360 U.S., at 320–321.
7. 111 S.Ct. 1246 (1991).
8. 386 U.S. 18.
9. See Herbert L. Packer, *The Limits of the Criminal Sanction.* (Stanford: Stanford University Press, 1968).
10. It is worth noting that in social and political philosophy, utilitarianism has had a strong following among Fascist and Marxist theorists, both groups being willing to subordinate the good of the individual citizen in order to achieve the good of society as a whole. Fascism and Marxism correspond to the extreme ends of the conservative/liberal spectrum, respectively.
11. *Ibid.*, p. 42.
12. 42 U.S.C. § 1981–1983, 1985 and 18 U.S.C. §§ 241, 242. These statutes, which originally date from the Civil War period, are included for reference at the end of this chapter.

The Rule of Law

JOHN RAWLS

I NOW WISH TO consider rights of the person as these are protected by the principle of the rule of law.[1] As before my intention is not only to relate these notions to the principles of justice but to elucidate the sense of the priority of liberty. I have already noted (§ 10) that the conception of formal justice, the regular and impartial administration of public rules, becomes the rule of law when applied to the legal system. One kind of unjust action is the failure of judges and others in authority to apply the appropriate rule or to interpret it correctly. It is more illuminating in this connection to think not of gross violations exemplified by bribery and corruption, or the abuse of the legal system to punish political enemies, but rather of the subtle distortions of prejudice and bias as these effectively discriminate against certain groups in the judicial process. The regular and impartial, and in this sense fair, administration of law we may call "justice as regularity." This is a more suggestive phrase than "formal justice."

Now the rule of law is obviously closely related to liberty. We can see this by considering the notion of a legal system and its intimate connection with the precepts definitive of justice as regularity. A legal system is a coercive order of public rules addressed to rational persons for the purpose of regulating their conduct and providing the framework for social cooperation. When these rules are just they establish a basis for legitimate expectations. They constitute grounds upon which persons can rely on one another and rightly object when their expectations are not fulfilled. If the bases of these claims are unsure, so are the boundaries of men's liberties. Of course, other rules share many of these features. Rules of games and of private associations are likewise addressed to rational persons in order to give shape to their activities. Given that these rules are fair or just, then once men have entered into these arrangements and accepted the benefits that result, the obligations which thereby arise constitute a basis for legitimate expectations. What distinguishes a legal system is its comprehensive scope and its regulative powers with respect to other associations. The constitutional agencies that it defines generally have the exclusive legal right to at least the more extreme forms of coercion. The kinds of duress that private associations can employ are strictly limited. Moreover, the legal order exercises a final authority over a certain well-defined territory. It is also marked by the wide range of the activities it regulates and the fundamental nature of the interests it is designed to secure. These features simply reflect the fact that the law defines the basic structure within which the pursuit of all other activities takes place.

Given that the legal order is a system of public rules addressed to rational persons, we can account for the precepts of justice associated with the rule of law. These precepts are those that would be followed by any system of rules which perfectly embodied the idea of a legal system. This is not, of course, to say that existing laws necessarily satisfy these precepts in all cases. Rather, these maxims follow from an ideal notion which laws are expected to approximate, at least for the most part. If deviations from justice as regularity are too pervasive, a serious question may arise whether a system of law exists as opposed to a collection of particular orders designed to advance the interests of a dictator or the ideal of a benevolent despot. Often there is no clear answer to this question. The point of thinking of a legal order as a system of public rules is that it enables us to derive the precepts associated with the principle of legality. Moreover, we can say that, other things equal, one legal order is more justly administered than another if it more perfectly fulfills the precepts of the rule of law. It will provide a more secure basis for liberty and a more effective means for organizing cooperative schemes. Yet because these precepts guarantee only the impartial and regular administration of rules, whatever these are, they are compatible with injustice. They impose rather weak constraints on the basic structure, but ones that are not by any means negligible.

Let us begin with the precept that ought implies can. This precept identifies several obvious features of legal systems. First of all, the actions which the rules of law require and forbid should be of a kind which men can reasonably be expected to do and to avoid. A system of rules addressed to rational persons to organize their conduct concerns itself with what they can and cannot do. It must not impose a duty to do what cannot be done. Secondly, the notion that ought implies can conveys the idea that those who enact laws and give orders do so in good faith. Legislators and judges, and other officials of the system, must believe that the laws can be obeyed; and they are to assume that any orders given can be carried out. Moreover, not only must the authorities act in good faith, but their good faith must be recognized by those subject to their enactments. Laws and commands are accepted as laws and commands only if it is generally believed that they can be obeyed and executed. If this is in question, the actions of authorities presumably have some other purpose than to organize conduct. Finally, this precept expresses the requirement that a legal system should recognize impossibility of performance as a defense, or at least as a mitigating circumstance. In enforcing rules a legal system cannot

regard the inability to perform as irrelevant. It would be an intolerable burden on liberty if the liability to penalties was not normally limited to actions within our power to do or not to do.

The rule of law also implies the precept that similar cases be treated similarly. Men could not regulate their actions by means of rules if this precept were not followed. To be sure, this notion does not take us very far. For we must suppose that the criteria of similarity are given by the legal rules themselves and the principles used to interpret them. Nevertheless, the precept that like decisions be given in like cases significantly limits the discretion of judges and others in authority. The precept forces them to justify the distinctions that they make between persons by reference to the relevant legal rules and principles. In any particular case, if the rules are at all complicated and call for interpretation, it may be easy to justify an arbitrary decision. But as the number of cases increases, plausible justifications for biased judgments become more difficult to construct. The requirement of consistency holds of course for the interpretation of all rules and for justifications at all levels. Eventually reasoned arguments for discriminatory judgments become harder to formulate and the attempt to do so less persuasive. This precept holds also in cases of equity, that is, when an exception is to be made when the established rule works an unexpected hardship. But with this proviso: since there is no clear line separating these exceptional cases, there comes a point, as in matters of interpretation, at which nearly any difference will make a difference. In these instances, the principle of authoritative decision applies, and the weight of precedent or of the announced verdict suffices.[2]

The precept that there is no offense without a law (*Nullum crimen sine lege*), and the requirements it implies, also follow from the idea of a legal system. This precept demands that laws be known and expressly promulgated, that their meaning be clearly defined, that statutes be general both in statement and intent and not be used as a way of harming particular individuals who may be expressly named (bills of attainder), that at least the more severe offenses be strictly construed, and that penal laws should not be retroactive to the disadvantage of those to whom they apply. These requirements are implicit in the notion of regulating behavior by public rules. For if, say, statutes are not clear in what they enjoin and forbid, the citizen does not know how he is to behave. Moreover, while there may be occasional bills of attainder and retroactive enactments, these cannot be pervasive or characteristic features of the system, else it must have another purpose. A tyrant might change laws without notice, and punish (if that is the right word) his subjects accordingly, because he takes pleasure in seeing how long it takes them to figure out what the new rules are from observing the penalties he inflicts. But these rules would not be a legal system, since they would not serve to organize social behavior by providing a basis for legitimate expectations.

Finally, there are those precepts defining the notion of natural justice. These are guidelines intended to preserve the integrity of the judicial process.[3] If laws are directives addressed to rational persons for their guidance, courts must be concerned to apply and to enforce these rules in an appropriate way. A conscientious effort must be made to determine whether an infraction has taken place and to impose the correct penalty. Thus a legal system must make provisions for conducting orderly trials and hearings; it must contain rules of evidence that guarantee rational procedures of inquiry. While there are variations in these procedures, the rule of law requires some form of due process: that is, a process reasonably designed to ascertain the truth, in ways consistent with the other ends of the legal system, as to whether a violation has taken place and under what circumstances. For example, judges must be independent and impartial, and no man may judge his own case. Trials must be fair and open, but not prejudiced by public clamor. The precepts of natural justice are to insure that the legal order will be impartially and regularly maintained.

Now the connection of the rule of law with liberty is clear enough. Liberty, as I have said, is a complex of rights and duties defined by institutions. The various liberties specify things that we may choose to do, if we wish, and in regard to which, when the nature of the liberty makes it appropriate, others have a duty not to interfere.[4] But if the precept of no crime without a law is violated, say by statutes being vague and imprecise, what we are at liberty to do is likewise vague and imprecise. The boundaries of our liberty are uncertain. And to the extent that this is so, liberty is restricted by a reasonable fear of its exercise. The same sort of consequences follow if similar cases are not treated similarly, if the judicial process lacks its essential integrity, if the law does not recognize impossibility of performance as a defense, and so on. The principle of legality has a firm foundation, then, in the agreement of rational persons to establish for themselves the greatest equal liberty. To be confident in the possession and exercise of these freedoms, the citizens of a well-ordered society will normally want the rule of law maintained.

We can arrive at the same conclusion in a slightly different way. It is reasonable to assume that even in a well-ordered society the coercive powers of government are to some degree necessary for the stability of social cooperation. For although men know that they share a common sense of justice and that each wants to adhere to the existing arrangements, they may nevertheless lack full confidence in one another. They may suspect that some are not doing their part, and so they may be tempted not to do theirs. The general awareness of these temptations may eventually cause the scheme to break down. The suspicion that others are not honoring their duties and obligations is increased by the fact that, in the absence of the authoritative interpretation and enforcement of the rules, it is particularly easy to find excuses for breaking them. Thus even under reasonably ideal conditions, it is hard to imagine, for example, a successful income tax scheme on a voluntary basis. Such an arrangement is unstable. The role of an authorized public interpretation of rules supported by collective sanctions is precisely to overcome this instability. By enforcing a public system of penalties government removes the grounds for thinking that others are not complying with the rules. For this reason alone, a coercive sovereign is presumably always necessary, even though in a well-ordered society sanctions are not severe and may never need to be imposed. Rather, the existence of effective penal machinery serves as men's security to one another. This proposition and the reasoning behind it we may think of as Hobbes's thesis.[5] (§ 42).

Now in setting up such a system of sanctions the parties in a constitutional convention must weigh its disadvantages. These are of at least two kinds: one kind is the cost of maintaining the agency covered say by taxation; the other is the danger to the liberty of the representative citizen measured by the likelihood that these sanctions will wrongly interfere with his freedom. The establishment of a coercive agency is rational only if these disadvantages are less than the loss of liberty from instability. Assuming this to be so, the best arrangement is one that minimizes these hazards. It is clear that, other things equal, the dangers to liberty are less when the law is impartially and regularly administered in accordance with the principle of legality. While a coercive mechanism is necessary, it is obviously essential to define precisely the tendency of its operations. Knowing what things it penalizes and knowing that these are within their power to do or not to do, citizens can draw up their plans accordingly. One who complies with the announced rules need never fear an infringement of his liberty.

It is clear from the preceding remarks that we need an account of penal sanctions however limited even for ideal theory. Given the normal conditions of human life, some such arrangements are necessary. I have maintained that the principles justifying these sanctions can be derived from the principle of liberty. The ideal conception shows in this case anyway how the nonideal scheme is to be set up; and this confirms the conjecture that it is ideal theory which is fundamental. We also see that the principle of responsibility is not founded on the idea that punishment is primarily retributive or denunciatory.

Instead it is acknowledged for the sake of liberty itself. Unless citizens are able to know what the law is and are given a fair opportunity to take its directives into account, penal sanctions should not apply to them. This principle is simply the consequence of regarding a legal system as an order of public rules addressed to rational persons in order to regulate their cooperation, and of giving the appropriate weight to liberty. I believe that this view of responsibility enables us to explain most of the excuses and defenses recognized by the criminal law under the heading of *mens rea* and that it can serve as a guide to legal reform. However, these points cannot be pursued here.[6] It suffices to note that ideal theory requires an account of penal sanctions as a stabilizing device and indicates the manner in which this part of partial compliance theory should be worked out. In particular, the principle of liberty leads to the principle of responsibility.

The moral dilemmas that arise in partial compliance theory are also to be viewed with the priority of liberty in mind. Thus we can imagine situations of an unhappy sort in which it may be permissible to insist less strongly on the precepts of the rule of law being followed. For example, in some extreme eventualities persons might be held liable for certain offenses contrary to the precept ought implies can. Suppose that, aroused by sharp religious antagonisms, members of rival sects are collecting weapons and forming armed bands in preparation for civil strife. Confronted with this situation the government may enact a statute forbidding the possession of firearms (assuming that possession is not already an offense). And the law may hold that sufficient evidence for conviction is that the weapons are found in the defendant's house or property, unless he can establish that they were put there by another. Except for this proviso, the absence of intent and knowledge of possession, and conformity to reasonable standards of care, are declared irrelevant. It is contended that these normal defenses would make the law ineffective and impossible to enforce.

Now although this statute trespasses upon

the precept ought implies can, it might be accepted by the representative citizen as a lesser loss of liberty, at least if the penalties imposed are not too severe. (Here I assume that imprisonment, say, is a drastic curtailment of liberty, and so the severity of the contemplated punishments must be taken into account.) Viewing the situation from the legislative stage, one may decide that the formation of paramilitary groups, which the passing of the statute may forestall, is a much greater danger to the freedom of the average citizen than being held strictly liable for the possession of weapons. Citizens may affirm the law as the lesser of two evils, resigning themselves to the fact that while they may be held guilty for things they have not done, the risks to their liberty on any other course would be worse. Since bitter dissensions exist, there is no way to prevent some injustices, as we ordinarily think of them, from occurring. All that can be done is to limit these injustices in the least unjust way.

The conclusion once again is that arguments for restricting liberty proceed from the principle of liberty itself. To some degree anyway, the priority of liberty carries over to partial compliance theory. Thus in the situation discussed the greater good of some has not been balanced against the lesser good of others. Nor has a lesser liberty been accepted for the sake of greater economic and social benefits. Rather the appeal has been to the common good in the form of the basic equal liberties of the representative citizen. Unfortunate circumstances and the unjust designs of some necessitate a much lesser liberty than that enjoyed in a well-ordered society. Any injustice in the social order is bound to take its toll; it is impossible that its consequences should be entirely canceled out. In applying the principle of legality we must keep in mind the totality of rights and duties that defines the liberties and adjust its claims accordingly. Sometimes we may be forced to allow certain breaches of its precepts if we are to mitigate the loss of freedom from social evils that cannot be removed, and to aim for the least injustice that conditions allow.

NOTES

1. For a general discussion, see Lon Fuller, *The Morality of Law* (New Haven, Yale University Press, 1964), ch. II. The concept of principled decisions in constitutional law is considered by Herbert Wechsler, *Principles, Politics, and Fundamental Law* (Cambridge, Harvard University Press, 1961). See Otto Kirchenheimer, *Political Justice* (Princeton, Princeton University Press, 1961), and J. N. Shklar, *Legalism* (Cambridge, Harvard University Press, 1964), pt. II, for the use and abuse of judicial forms in politics. J. R. Lucas, *The Principles of Politics* (Oxford, The Clarendon Press, 1966), pp. 106-143, contains a philosophical account.

2. See Lon Fuller, *Anatomy of the Law* (New York, The New American Library, 1969), p. 182.

3. This sense of natural justice is traditional. See H. L. A. Hart, *The Concept of Law* (Oxford, The Clarendon Press, 1961), pp. 156, 202.

4. It may be disputed whether this view holds for all rights, for example, the right to pick up an unclaimed article. See Hart in *Philosophical Review*, vol. 64, p. 179. But perhaps it is true enough for our purposes here. While some of the basic rights are similarly competition rights, as we may call them—for example, the right to participate in public affairs and to influence the political decisions taken—at the same time everyone has a duty to conduct himself in a certain way. This duty is one of fair political conduct, so to speak, and to violate it is a kind of interference. As we have seen, the constitution aims to establish a framework within which equal political rights fairly pursued and having their fair value are likely to lead to just and effective legislation. When appropriate we can interpret the statement in the text along these lines. On this point see Richard Wollheim, "Equality," *Proceedings of the Aristotelian Society*, vol. 56 (1955-1956), pp. 291ff. Put another way, the right can be redescribed as the right to try to do something under specified circumstances, these circumstances allowing for the fair rivalry of others. Unfairness becomes a characteristic form of interference.

5. See *Leviathan*, chs. 13-18. And also Howard Warrender, *The Political Philosophy of Hobbes* (Oxford, The Clarendon Press, 1957), ch. III; and D. P. Gauthier, *The Logic of Leviathan* (Oxford, The Clarendon Press, 1969), pp. 76-89.

6. For these matters, consult H. L. A. Hart, *Punishment and Responsibility* (Oxford, The Clarendon Press, 1968), pp. 173-183, whom I follow here.

Study Questions

1. What is formal justice? How is this concept related to the concept of "justice as regularity"? How does Rawls define a legal system?

2. List the precepts implied by the concept of a legal system. What precept places a limit on the use of discretion by those in the justice system?

3. How is the rule of law related to the concept of freedom? Why does Rawls think that prejudiced or unequal administration of the law is a threat to liberty? Use the Rodney King case to illustrate.

4. Rawls claims that a stable society requires "the coercive powers of government." How is the example of voluntary income tax used to support this claim? Do you agree with Rawls' claim? Why? Defend your position.

Rochin v. California

U. S. SUPREME COURT

MR. JUSTICE FRANKFURTER DELIVERED the opinion of the court.

Having "some information that [the petitioner here] was selling narcotics," three deputy sheriffs of the County of Los Angeles, on the morning of July 1, 1949, made for the two-story dwelling house in which Rochin lived with his mother, common-law wife, brothers and sisters. Finding the outside door open, they entered and then forced open the door to Rochin's room on the second floor. Inside they found petitioner sitting partly dressed on the side of the bed, upon which his wife was lying. On a "night stand" beside the bed the deputies spied two capsules. When asked "Whose stuff is this?" Rochin seized the capsules and put them in his mouth. A struggle ensued, in the course of which the three officers "jumped upon him" and attempted to extract the capsules. The force they applied proved unavailing against Rochin's resistance. He was handcuffed and taken to a hospital. At the direction of one of the officers a doctor forced an emetic solution through a tube into Rochin's stomach against his will. This "stomach pumping" produced vomiting. In the vomited matter were found two capsules which proved to contain morphine.

Rochin was brought to trial before a California Superior Court, sitting without a jury, on the charge of possessing "a preparation of morphine" in violation of the California Health and Safety Code, 1947, § 11,500. Rochin was convicted and sentenced to sixty days' imprisonment. The chief evidence against him was the two capsules. They were admitted over petitioner's objection, although the means of obtaining them was frankly set forth in the testimony by one of the deputies, substantially as here narrated.

On appeal, the District Court of Appeal affirmed the conviction, despite the finding that the officers "were guilty of unlawfully breaking into and entering defendant's room and were guilty of unlawfully assaulting and battering defendant while in the room," and "were guilty

342 U.S. 165 (1952). Some legal citations have been shortened or removed.

of unlawfully assaulting, battering, torturing and falsely imprisoning the defendant at the alleged hospital." 101 Cal. App. 2d 140, 143. One of the three judges, while finding that "the record in this case reveals a shocking series of violations of constitutional rights," concurred only because he felt bound by decisions of his Supreme Court. These, he asserted, "have been looked upon by law enforcement officers as an encouragement, if not an invitation, to the commission of such lawless acts." *Ibid.* The Supreme Court of California denied without opinion Rochin's petition for a hearing.[1] Two justices dissented from this denial, and in doing so expressed themselves thus: ". . . a conviction which rests upon evidence of incriminating objects obtained from the body of the accused by physical abuse is as invalid as a conviction which rests upon a verbal confession extracted from him by such abuse. . . . Had the evidence forced from the defendant's lips consisted of an oral confession that he illegally possessed a drug . . . he would have the protection of the rule of law which excludes coerced confessions from evidence. But because the evidence forced from his lips consisted of real objects the People of this state are permitted to base a conviction upon it. [We] find no valid ground of distinction between a verbal confession extracted by physical abuse and a confession wrested from defendant's body by physical abuse." 101 Cal. App. 2d 143, 149-150.

This Court granted certiorari, 341 U. S. 939, because a serious question is raised as to the limitations which the Due Process Clause of the Fourteenth Amendment imposes on the conduct of criminal proceedings by the States.

In our federal system the administration of criminal justice is predominantly committed to the care of the States. The power to define crimes belongs to Congress only as an appropriate means of carrying into execution its limited grant of legislative powers. U. S. Const., Art. I, § 8, cl. 18. Broadly speaking, crimes in the United States are what the laws of the individual States make them, subject to the limitations of Art. I, § 10, cl. 1, in the original Constitution, prohibiting

bills of attainder and *ex post facto* laws, and of the Thirteenth and Fourteenth Amendments.

These limitations, in the main, concern not restrictions upon the powers of the States to define crime, except in the restricted area where federal authority has preempted the field, but restrictions upon the manner in which the States may enforce their penal codes. Accordingly, in reviewing a State criminal conviction under a claim of right guaranteed by the Due Process Clause of the Fourteenth Amendment, from which is derived the most far-reaching and most frequent federal basis of challenging State criminal justice, "we must be deeply mindful of the responsibilities of the States for the enforcement of criminal laws, and exercise with due humility our merely negative function in subjecting convictions from state courts to the very narrow scrutiny which the Due Process Clause of the Fourteenth Amendment authorizes." *Malinski v. New York*, 324 U. S. 401, 412, 418. Due process of law, "itself a historical product," *Jackman v. Rosenbaum Co.*, 260 U. S. 22, 31, is not to be turned into a destructive dogma against the States in the administration of their systems of criminal justice.

However, this Court too has its responsibility. Regard for the requirements of the Due Process Clause "inescapably imposes upon this Court an exercise of judgment upon the whole course of the proceedings [resulting in a conviction] in order to ascertain whether they offend those canons of decency and fairness which express the notions of justice of English-speaking peoples even toward those charged with the most heinous offenses." *Malinski v. New York, supra*, at 416-417. These standards of justice are not authoritatively formulated anywhere as though they were specifics. Due process of law is a summarized constitutional guarantee of respect for those personal immunities which, as Mr. Justice Cardozo twice wrote for the Court, are "so rooted in the traditions and conscience of our people as to be ranked as fundamental," *Snyder v. Massachusetts*, 291 U. S. 97, 105, or are "implicit in the concept of ordered liberty." *Palko v. Connecticut*, 302 U. S. 319, 325.[2]

The Court's function in the observance of this settled conception of the Due Process Clause does not leave us without adequate guides in subjecting State criminal procedures to constitutional judgment. In dealing not with the machinery of government but with human rights, the absence of formal exactitude, or want of fixity of meaning, is not an unusual or even regrettable attribute of constitutional provisions. Words being symbols do not speak without a gloss. On the one hand the gloss may be the deposit of history, whereby a term gains technical content. Thus the requirements of the Sixth and Seventh Amendments for trial by jury in the federal courts have a rigid meaning. No changes or chances can alter the content of the verbal symbol of "jury"—a body of twelve men who must reach a unanimous conclusion if the verdict is to go against the defendant." On the other hand, the gloss of some of the verbal symbols of the Constitution does not give them a fixed technical content. It exacts a continuing process of application.

When the gloss has thus not been fixed but is a function of the process of judgment, the judgment is bound to fall differently at different times and differently at the same time through different judges. Even more specific provisions, such as the guaranty of freedom of speech and the detailed protection against unreasonable searches and seizures, have inevitably evoked as sharp divisions in this Court as the least specific and most comprehensive protection of liberties, the Due Process Clause.

The vague contours of the Due Process Clause do not leave judges at large.[4] We may not draw on our merely personal and private notions and disregard the limits that bind judges in their judicial function. Even though the concept of due process of law is not final and fixed, these limits are derived from considerations that are fused in the whole nature of our judicial process. See Cardozo, The Nature of the Judicial Process; The Growth of the Law; The Paradoxes of Legal Science. These are considerations deeply rooted in reason and in the compelling traditions of the legal profession. The Due Process Clause places upon this Court the duty of exercising a judgment, within the narrow confines of judicial power in reviewing State convictions, upon interests of society pushing in opposite directions.

Due process of law thus conceived is not to be derided as resort to a revival of "natural law."[5] To believe that this judicial exercise of judgment could be avoided by freezing "due process of law" at some fixed stage of time or thought is to suggest that the most important aspect of constitutional adjudication is a function for inanimate machines and not for judges, for whom the independence safeguarded by Article III of the Constitution was designed and who are presumably guided by established standards of judicial behavior. Even cybernetics has not yet made that haughty claim. To practice the requisite detachment and to achieve sufficient objectivity no doubt demands of judges the habit of self-discipline and self-criticism, incertitude that one's own views are incontestable and alert tolerance toward views not shared. But these are precisely the presuppositions of our judicial process. They are precisely the qualities society has a right to expect from those entrusted with ultimate judicial power.

Restraints on our jurisdiction are self-imposed only in the sense that there is from our decisions no immediate appeal short of impeachment or constitutional amendment. But that does not make due process of law a matter of judicial caprice. The faculties of the Due Process Clause may be indefinite and vague, but the mode of their ascertainment is not self-willed. In each case "due process of law" requires an evaluation based on a disinterested inquiry pursued in the spirit of science, on a balanced order of facts exactly and fairly stated, on the detached consideration of conflicting claims, see *Hudson County Water Co.* v. *McCarter*, 209 U. S. 349, 355, on a judgment not *ad hoc* and episodic but duly mindful of reconciling the needs both of continuity and of change in a progressive society.

Applying these general considerations to the circumstances of the present case, we are compelled to conclude that the proceedings by which this conviction was obtained do more than offend some fastidious squeamishness or private sentimentalism about combatting crime too energetically. This is conduct that shocks the conscience. Illegally breaking into the privacy of the petitioner, the struggle to open his mouth and remove what was there, the forcible extraction of his stomach's contents—this course of proceeding by agents of government to obtain evidence is bound to offend even hardened sensibilities. They are methods too close to the rack and the screw to permit of constitutional differentiation.

It has long since ceased to be true that due process of law is heedless of the means by which otherwise relevant and credible evidence is obtained. This was not true even before the series of recent cases enforced the constitutional principle that the States may not base convictions upon confessions, however much verified, obtained by coercion. These decisions are not arbitrary exceptions to the comprehensive right of States to fashion their own rules of evidence for criminal trials. They are not sports in our constitutional law but applications of a general principle. They are only instances of the general requirement that States in their prosecutions respect certain decencies of civilized conduct. Due process of law, as a historic and generative principle, precludes defining, and thereby confining, these standards of conduct more precisely than to say that convictions cannot be brought about by methods that offend "a sense of justice." See Mr. Chief Justice Hughes, speaking for a unanimous Court in *Brown* v. *Mississippi*, 297 U. S. 278, 285-286. It would be a stultification of the responsibility which the course of constitutional history has cast upon this Court to hold that in order to convict a man the police cannot extract by force what is in his mind but can extract what is in his stomach.[6]

To attempt in this case to distinguish what lawyers call "real evidence" from verbal evidence is to ignore the reasons for excluding coerced confessions. Use of involuntary verbal confessions in State criminal trials is constitutionally obnoxious not only because of their unreliability. They are inadmissible under the Due Process Clause even though statements contained in them may be independently established as true. Coerced confessions offend the community's sense of fair play and decency. So here, to sanction the brutal conduct which naturally enough was condemned by the court whose judgment is before us, would be to afford brutality the cloak of law. Nothing would be more calculated to discredit law and thereby to brutalize the temper of a society.

In deciding this case we do not heedlessly bring into question decisions in many States dealing with essentially different, even if related, problems. We therefore put to one side cases which have arisen in the State courts through use of modern methods and devices for discovering wrongdoers and bringing them to book. It does not fairly represent these decisions to suggest that they legalize force so brutal and so offensive to human dignity in securing evidence from a suspect as is revealed by this record. Indeed the California Supreme Court has not sanctioned this mode of securing a conviction. It merely exercised its discretion to decline a review of the conviction. All the California judges who have expressed themselves in this case have condemned the conduct in the strongest language.

We are not unmindful that hypothetical situations can be conjured up, shading imperceptibly from the circumstances of this case and by gradations producing practical differences despite seemingly logical extensions. But the Constitution is "intended to preserve practical and substantial rights, not to maintain theories." *Davis* v. *Mills*, 194 U. S. 451, 457.

On the facts of this case the conviction of the petitioner has been obtained by methods that offend the Due Process Clause. The judgment below must be

Reversed. . . .

MR. JUSTICE BLACK, concurring.

Adamson v. *California* 332 U. S. 46, 68-123, sets out reasons for my belief that state as well as federal courts and law enforcement officers must obey the Fifth Amendment's command that "No person ... shall be compelled in any criminal case to be a witness against himself." I think a person is compelled to be a witness against himself not only when he is compelled to testify, but also when as here, incriminating evidence is forcibly taken from him by a contrivance of modern science. Cf. *Boyd* v. *United States*, 116 U. S. 616; *Counselman* v. *Hitchcock*, 142 U. S. 547, 562; *Bram* v. *United States*, 168 U. S. 532; *Chambers* v. *Florida*, 309 U. S. 227. California convicted this petitioner by using against him evidence obtained in this manner, and I agree with MR. JUSTICE DOUGLAS that the case should be reversed on this ground.

In the view of a majority of the Court, however, the Fifth Amendment imposes no restraint of any kind on the states. They nevertheless hold that California's use of this evidence violated the Due Process Clause of the Fourteenth Amendment. Since they hold as I do in this case, I regret my inability to accept their interpretation without protest. But I believe that faithful adherence to the specific guarantees in the Bill of Rights insures a more permanent protection of individual liberty than that which can be afforded by the nebulous standards stated by the majority.

What the majority hold is that the Due Process Clause empowers this Court to nullify any state law if its application "shocks the conscience," offends "a sense of justice" or runs counter to the "decencies of civilized conduct." The majority emphasize that these statements do not refer to their own consciences or to their senses of justice and decency. For we are told that "we may not draw on our merely personal and private notions"; our judgment must be grounded on "considerations deeply rooted in reason and in the compelling traditions of the legal profession." We are further admonished to measure the validity of state practices, not by our reason, or by the traditions of the legal profession, but by "the community's sense of fair play and decency"; by the "traditions and conscience of our people"; or by "those canons of decency and fairness which express the notions of justice of English-speaking peoples." These

canons are made necessary, it is said, because of "interests of society pushing in opposite directions."

If the Due Process Clause does vest this Court with such unlimited power to invalidate laws, I am still in doubt as to why we should consider only the notions of English-speaking peoples to determine what are immutable and fundamental principles of justice. Moreover, one may well ask what avenues of investigation are open to discover "canons" of conduct so universally favored that this Court should write them into the Constitution? All we are told is that the discovery must be made by an "evaluation based on a disinterested inquiry pursued in the spirit of science, on a balanced order of facts."

Some constitutional provisions are stated in absolute and unqualified language such, for illustration, as the First Amendment stating that no law shall be passed prohibiting the free exercise of religion or abridging the freedom of speech or press. Other constitutional provisions do require courts to choose between competing policies, such as the Fourth Amendment which, by its terms, necessitates a judicial decision as to what is an "unreasonable" search or seizure. There is, however, no express constitutional language granting judicial power to invalidate *every* state law of *every* kind deemed "unreasonable" or contrary to the Court's notion of civilized decencies; yet the constitutional philosophy used by the majority has, in the past, been used to deny a state the right to fix the price of gasoline, *Williams* v. *Standard Oil Co.,* 278 U. S. 235; and even the right to prevent bakers from palming off smaller for larger loaves of bread, *Jay Burns Baking Co.* v. *Bryan*, 264 U. S. 504. These cases, and others,[7] show the extent to which the evanescent standards of the majority's philosophy have been used to nullify state legislative programs passed to suppress evil economic practices. What paralyzing role this same philosophy will play in the future economic affairs of this country is impossible to predict. Of even graver concern, however, is the use of the philosophy to nullify the Bill of Rights. I long ago concluded that the accordion-like qualities of this philosophy must inevitably imperil all the individual liberty safeguards specifically enumerated in the Bill of Rights.[8] Reflection and recent decisions[9] of this Court sanctioning abridgment of the freedom of speech and press have strengthened this conclusion.

MR. JUSTICE DOUGLAS, concurring.

The evidence obtained from this accused's stomach would be admissible in the majority of states where the question has been raised.[10] So far as the reported cases reveal, the only states which would probably exclude the evidence would be Arkansas, Iowa, Michigan, and Missouri.[11] Yet the Court now says that the rule which the majority of the states have fashioned violates the "decencies of civilized conduct." To that I cannot agree. It is a rule formulated by responsible courts with judges as sensitive as we are to the proper standards for law administration.

As an original matter it might be debatable whether the provision in the Fifth Amendment that no person "shall be compelled in any criminal case to be a witness against himself" serves the ends of justice. Not all civilized legal procedures recognize it.[12] But the choice was made by the Framers, a choice which sets a standard for legal trials in this country. The Framers made it a standard of due process for prosecutions by the Federal Government. If it is a requirement of due process for a trial in the federal courthouse, it is impossible for me to say it is not a requirement of due process for a trial in the state courthouse. That was the issue recently surveyed in *Adamson* v. *California*, 332 U. S. 46. The Court rejected the view that compelled testimony should be excluded and held in substance that the accused in a state trial can be forced to testify against himself. I disagree. Of course an accused can be compelled to be present at the trial, to stand, to sit, to turn this way or that, and to try on a cap or a coat. See *Holt* v. *United States*, 218 U. S. 245, 252-253. But I think that words taken from his lips, capsules taken from his stomach, blood taken from his veins are all inadmissible provided they are taken from him without his consent. They are inadmissible because of the command of the Fifth Amendment.

That is an unequivocal, definite and workable rule of evidence for state and federal courts. But we cannot in fairness free the state courts from that command and yet excoriate them for flouting the "decencies of civilized conduct" when they admit the evidence. That is to make the rule turn not on the Constitution but on the idiosyncrasies of the judges who sit here.

The damage of the view sponsored by the Court in this case may not be conspicuous here. But it is part of the same philosophy that produced *Betts* v. *Brady*, 316 U. S. 455, denying counsel to an accused in a state trial against the command of the Sixth Amendment and *Wolf* v. *Colorado*, 338 U. S. 25, allowing evidence obtained as a result of a search and seizure that is illegal under the Fourth Amendment to be introduced in a state trial. It is part of the process of erosion of civil rights of the citizen in recent years.

NOTES

1. The petition for a hearing is addressed to the discretion of the California Supreme Court and a denial has apparently the same significance as the denial of certiorari in this Court. Cal. Const., Art. VI, §§ 4, 4c; "Rules on Appeal," Rules 28, 29, 36 Cal. 2d 24-25 (1951). See 3 Stan. L. Rev. 243-269 (1951).

2. What is here summarized was deemed by a majority of the court, in *Malinski* v. *New York*, 324 U. S. 401, 412 and 438, to be "the controlling principles upon which this Court reviews on constitutional grounds a state court conviction for crime." They have been applied by this Court many times, long before and since the Malinski case.

3. This is the federal jury required constitutionally although England and at least half of the States have in some civil cases juries which are composed of less than 12 or whose verdict may be less than unanimous. See County Courts Act, 1934, 24 & 25 Geo. V, c. 53, § 93; Arizona State Legislative Bureau, Legislative Briefs No. 4, Grand and Petit Juries in the United States, v-vi (Feb. 15, 1940); The Council of State Governments, The Book of the States, 1950-1951, 515.

4. Burke's observations on the method of ascertaining law by judges are pertinent:

"Your committee do not find any positive law

which binds the judges of the courts in Westminster-hall publicly to give a reasoned opinion from the bench, in support of their judgment upon matters that are stated before them. But the course hath prevailed from the oldest times. It hath been so general and so uniform, that it must be considered as the law of the land." Report of the Committee of Managers on the Causes of the Duration of Mr. Hastings's Trial, 4 Speeches of Edmund Burke (1816) 200–201.

And Burke had an answer for those who argue that the liberty of the citizen cannot be adequately protected by the flexible conception of due process of law:

". . . the English jurisprudence has not any other sure foundation, nor consequently the lives and properties of the subject any sure hold, but in the maxims, rules, and principles, and juridical traditionary line of decisions. . . ." *Id.,* at 201.

5. Morris R. Cohen, "Jus Naturale Redivivum," 25 Philosophical Review 761 (1916), and "Natural Rights and Positive Law," Reason and Nature (1931), 401–426; F. Pollock, "The History of the Law of Nature," Essays in the Law (1922), 31–79.

6. As to the difference between the privilege against self-crimination protected, in federal prosecutions, under the Fifth Amendment, and the limitations which the Due Process Clause of the Fourteenth Amendment imposes upon the States against the use of coerced confessions, see *Brown v. Mississippi, supra,* at 285.

7. See n. 12 of dissenting opinion, *Adamson v. California, supra,* at p. 83.

8. *E.g., Adamson v. California, supra,* and cases cited in the dissent.

9. *American Communications Assn. v. Douds,* 339 U. S. 382; *Feiner v. New York,* 340 U. S. 315; *Dennis v. United States,* 341 U. S. 494.

10. See *People v. One 1941 Mercury Sedan,* 74 Cal. App. 2d 199 P. 2d 443 (pumping of accused's stomach to recover swallowed narcotic); *Rochin v. California,* 101 Cal. App. 2d 140 (pumping of accused's stomach to recover swallowed narcotic); *People v. Tucker,* 88 Cal. App. 2d 333 (blood test to determine intoxication); *State v. Ayres,* 70 Idaho 18 (blood test to determine intoxication); *Davis v. State,* 189 Md. 640 (blood typing to link accused with murder); *Skidmore v. State,* 59 New. 320 (examination of accused for venereal disease); *State v. Sturtevant,* 96 N. H. 99 (blood test to determine intoxication); *State v. Alexander,* 7 N. J. 585 (blood typing to establish guilt); *State v. Gatton,* 60 Ohio App. 192 (commenting on refusal to submit to blood test or urinalysis to determine intoxication); *State v. Nutt,* 78 Ohio App. 336 (commenting on refusal to submit to urinalysis to determine intoxication); but cf. *Booker v. Cincinnati,* 1 Ohio Supp. 152 (examination and urinalysis to determine intoxication); *State v. Cram,* 176 Ore. 577 (blood test to determine intoxication); *Commonwealth v. Statti,* 166 Pa. Super. 577 (blood typing linking accused to assault).

11. *Bethel v. State,* 178 Ark. 277 (examination for venereal disease); *State v. Height,* 117 Iowa 650 (examination for venereal disease); *State v. Weltha,* 228 Iowa 519 (blood test to determine intoxication, limiting rules on search and seizure); but cf. *State v. Benson,* 230 Iowa 1168 (comment on refusal to submit to blood test to determine intoxication); *People v. Corder,* 244 Mich. 274 (examination for venereal disease); but see *People v. Placido,* 310 Mich. 404, 408; *State v. Newcomb,* 220 Mo. 54 (examination for venereal disease); *State v. Matsinger,* 180 S. W. 856 (examination for venereal disease).

12. See Ploscowe, The Investigating Magistrate in European Criminal Procedure, 33 Mich. L. Rev. 1010 (1935).

Study Questions

1. What limitation on the Supreme Court does Justice Frankfurter think is important when reviewing a state criminal conviction involving a due process claim? What responsibility does Frankfurter believe the Court has regarding due process? On what does he base this belief? Do you agree with Frankfurter on this point? Why? Defend your position.

2. Is the concept of due process a precisely drawn and fixed concept like the concept of "jury," according to Frankfurter? Explain. Does Frankfurter believe that due process of law is determined simply by the beliefs and feelings of the judges who review the case? Why?

3. Frankfurter writes that the offensiveness of the police officers' treatment of Rochin goes beyond "squeamishness or private sentimentalism" and "is conduct that shocks the conscience." Do you agree? Why? Defend your position.

4. Is coercing incriminating words from a person's mouth the same as coercing incriminating capsules from a person's stomach? Why? Defend your position. What does Justice Douglas say about this in his concurring opinion?

5. Do you believe that a defendant in a criminal trial should be forced to testify against himself or herself, or compelled to present self-incriminating physical evidence? Why? Defend your position.

Crime Control and Due Process

PHILIP JENKINS

A DEFENDANT IN A modern criminal court has a wide variety of theoretical rights—at least in a Western country.... [These rights] had clear historical origins in the need to protect the innocent from a potentially repressive state. Many would argue that circumstances have now changed so that these rights are no longer needed. Even if they were still justified, the pressure from violent crime urgently demands reform. In this [paper] we will see why the due process rights under discussion still survive. As with the "right to be left alone," I will argue that these rights have a basis in practical necessity.

Herbert Packer has argued that there are two distinct models of the criminal justice process: crime control and due process.[1] They are both ideal descriptions—that is, neither exists in reality in this perfect form, but every system has some elements of both.

Crime Control

This is a conservative perspective, and a convenient summary of its assumptions was recently provided in a speech by President Reagan (see box 1). A crime control model would involve the people giving up some of their civil and legal rights in order to secure greater protection against crime. This model would emphasize speed and efficiency. It would make the process of justice resemble a conveyor belt, where an offender would enter the system at one end (arrest) and then reach conviction with speed and smoothness.

Box 1   Ronald Reagan and Crime Control

Conservative politicians have long made an issue of crime control, or "law and order." The slogan was rather discredited under the Nixon administration, when a number of law and order advocates suddenly found themselves at the receiving end of the system.

However, some very cogent remarks on crime control have been made recently by President Reagan, whose opinions on crime involve definite and wide-ranging theoretical implications. These remarks—such as a major speech he made in New Orleans in September 1981—are a good summary of the crime

Philip Jenkins, "Crime Control and Due Process," Crime and Justice: Issues and Ideas. (Pacific Grove: Brooks/Cole Publishing Co., 1984). Used by permission of Wadsworth, Inc. Chapter references have been removed and boxes have been renumbered.

control model and the conservative perspective on crime.[2]

The president argued that there are "rights of the accused," but also "rights of the innocent"—especially the victims of crime. In recent years the courts have allowed the rights of the accused to dominate the legal system so that victims have been forgotten. He wished to correct this imbalance by a number of measures:

• *Bail reform* would allow judges to keep defendants in jail before trial to prevent the commission of further crimes.

• *"The exclusionary rule* rests on the absurd proposition that a law enforcement error, no matter how technical, can be used to justify throwing an entire case out of court, no matter how guilty the defendant or how heinous the crime. The plain consequence of treating the wrongs equally is a grievous miscarriage of justice: the criminal goes free; the officer receives no effective reprimand; and the only ones who really suffer are the people of the community."

• *Organized crime* would be increasingly fought by the use of agencies like the IRS (which had been a very successful strategy under the Kennedys in the early 1960s: see box 2).

• *Drug trafficking* would be countered by increased use of the military to exclude drug importation, and by better domestic coordination of law enforcement agencies.

Apart from these specific criticisms, Reagan also launched a fundamental attack against liberal assumptions on the causation of crime. Crime is not directly caused by poverty. In fact, it often rises with prosperity. Criminals are simply evil, and they thrive on the inadequacies of the justice system:

• The truth is that criminals in America today get away with plenty, and sometimes—quite literally—they get away with murder.

• There has been a breakdown in the criminal justice system in America. It just plain isn't working.

• All too often, repeat offenders, habitual law breakers, career criminals—call them what you will—are robbing, raping and beating with impunity, and, as I said—quite literally—getting away with murder.

• The people are sickened and outraged. They demand that we put a stop to it.

He rejected contemporary social theories of crime:

• Many of the social thinkers of the 1950s and 60s who discussed crime only in the context of disadvantaged childhoods and poverty-stricken neighborhoods were the same people who thought that massive government spending could wipe away our social ills.

• The underlying premise in both cases was a belief that there was nothing permanent or absolute about any man's nature—that he was a product of his material environment, and that by changing that environment—with government as the chief vehicle of change through educational, health, housing and other programs—we could permanently change man and usher in a great new era.

• The solution to the crime problem will not be found in the social worker's files, the psychiatrist's note, or the bureaucrat's budget; it's a problem of the human heart, and it's there we must look for the answer.

His answer to these theories was in terms of "permanent truths" like:

• Right and wrong matters; individuals are responsible for their actions; retribution should be swift and sure for those who prey on the innocent.

• We must understand that basic moral principles lie at the heart of our criminal justice system; that our system of law acts as the collective moral voice of society....

Great attention would be paid in this system to making sure that the system is being used against the right people—that is, serious criminals against whom a good case could be developed. To avoid wasting the time of the court system, much more attention should be paid to ensuring that cases are properly prepared at the police stage. There is a great temptation for police agencies to prove their efficiency by impressive arrest statistics—even if most of the arrests are based on evidence too flimsy for a conviction. There have been experimental attempts to reduce the number of felony arrests, making sure that most of those would be adequately prepared and likely to lead to successful prosecution.

The crime control model would mean substantial changes at every stage of the current system. Above all, procedural irregularities would not lead to the failure of a prosecution or the exclusion of evidence. For example:

• An arresting officer might not be required to read a suspect his or her rights; and might be able to detain a suspect for a period without charges. Access to a lawyer might be restricted.

• Surveillance might be made much easier; evidence from illegal surveillance could be made available in court.

• The suspect's right to silence during interrogation could be removed.

• The law on searches and seizures could be altered to increase police powers.

• It is even possible to imagine an attack on the right to trial by jury. Of course, most criminal trials do not involve juries anyway, but juries could be restricted in cases involving (for instance) organized crime. Juries might convict by majority vote.

• Prosecutors might be allowed to appeal against a verdict of acquittal, on the model followed until recently in Canada.

• The accused might be "guilty until proven innocent," as in some European codes.

CONTROLLING ORGANIZED CRIME: A CASE STUDY

These sorts of change would be particularly appropriate for organized crime cases, which often drag on for months or years. Also, such cases involve an impressive array of legal talent using all their skill and experience to ensure that the most powerful criminals escape serious punishment. It is interesting that the only really successful campaigns against American organized

crime have both involved flagrant breaches of due process rules. In the late 1930s Thomas Dewey's campaign against "Murder Inc." made use of very dubious evidence. Again, in the early 1960s, Robert Kennedy's crusade against the Mafia broke almost every known rule of legal procedure; this was true despite the fact that Kennedy was a liberal. All that can be said in his defense is that it achieved wonderful results[2] (see box 2).

Box 2   The Kennedys and La Cosa Nostra

The 1950s were a great age for organized crime in America. "Syndicate" groups dominated the fast-growing casino industry in Nevada. Until 1958, they virtually ran Cuba, with Havana as a gambler's paradise. Meyer Lansky had developed a huge international drug ring and the financial structure to launder the profits; and finally, the large pension fund of the Teamsters' union was opened to Syndicate plunder. On the law enforcement side, J. Edgar Hoover's FBI denied the reality of organized crime, preferring to concentrate efforts on the (heavily infiltrated) American Communist party.

Matters began to change in 1960 with the election of President John F. Kennedy, who appointed his brother Robert attorney general. Together, the Kennedys began an unofficial war on organized crime, disproving the myth that it was beyond the reach of law enforcement.

The Kennedys distrusted the FBI, and so they took the effective step of employing the Internal Revenue Service against organized crime. This was a very dubious step, legally and constitutionally. IRS agents selected certain cities for "blitz" raids, where every major gambler and corrupt policeman in the town was arrested and prosecuted—a truly amazing and unprecedented step. By such actions (as in Pittsburgh) the government soon had plenty of material to show that the Mafia was only one group among a wide variety of organized crime gangs. Even where evidence was dubious, leading gangsters were served with substantial tax liens—Carlos Marcello in

New Orleans for $835,396; Santos Trafficante in Tampa for $300,000 (Blakey and Billings, 1981: 196–254).

Marcello is a splendid illustration of crime control in action. Until the Kennedys, his political power in Louisiana was thought to have put him beyond the power of the law. In 1956 he had attempted to solve an immigration visa problem by fraudulently obtaining a Guatemalan passport. In 1961 Robert Kennedy had him arrested and immediately deported without any due process. He was flown to Guatemala and "dumped there, without luggage and with little cash." The tax lien followed that, as insurance against his return (Ibid.: 241–244).

Surveillance was used on a massive scale against organized crime by the FBI, the IRS, and the Narcotics Bureau—often with dubious legality. At any one time the FBI had up to 100 bugs in operation in most metropolitan areas (Ibid.: 210)

This surveillance was used to intimidate as well as to gather information. Sam Giancana, who claimed to "own" Chicago, Miami, and Las Vegas, was subjected to twenty-four hour "lockstep" close surveillance. This destroyed his organized crime links, but also all his business activities and social activities (Ibid.: 254).

More simply, intensive prosecutorial activity resulted in the jailing of mobsters for extortion, conspiracy, or tax evasion. The number of indictments rose from 121 in 1961 to 615 in 1963 (Ibid.: 199).

Under the Kennedys' protection, highly illegal acts against mobsters included physical violence. One New York gangster from the Gambino family was detained by FBI men who "almost killed him . . . they crippled him" (Ibid.: 239).

By the middle of 1963 there were two possible responses from organized criminals. A handful wanted to resist, even to the point of killing the Kennedys. But the more common attitude was that of the Philadelphia *don* Angelo Bruno: "It is all over for us; I am going to Italy, and you should go too . . ." Only John Kennedy's assassination in November 1963 ended this short but extremely effective war. In 1978 a Senate

investigating committee suggested that there was good evidence for an organized crime role in his death (Summers 1980: 280).

Let us take a specific problem to illustrate the temptations of the crime control model. In the United States organized crime has a great deal more political influence than in any other Western industrialized nation. A major reason for this is mob influence in certain labor unions, notably the Teamsters. How could a justice system react to this situation?

The Teamsters' leadership has a long record of corruption. Four of its five presidents have been linked with organized crime. Specifically, its Central States Pension Fund (now worth about $3 billion) has served as an organized crime bank. In the early 1950s control of this fund went to Paul Dorfman, who had run Chicago labor racketeering as an ally of Al Capone. Paul ensured that the fund's insurance business passed through the hands of his son Allen Dorfman (1923–1983), who became the Teamsters' investment advisor. The Dorfmans brought this extremely rich resource into the hands of the criminal syndicates of Chicago and Cleveland, and recycled the proceeds of crime into legal investments—notably, in Las Vegas. When the fund was investigated in 1976, nearly $400 million was found to have been loaned to alleged associates of organized crime, such as Allen Glick and Alvin Malnik.

Allen Dorfman was one of the most powerful criminals in history—he was certainly among the wealthiest. He maintained his power for nearly thirty years, until his assassination in Chicago at the hands of mob rivals. There is a great temptation to suggest that the crime control idea is designed for such cases. Dorfman was obviously corrupt, but how could it be proved? Law enforcement officials no doubt wished they could treat mobsters in the same way that Castro had done when he came to power in 1959. He threw them into prison without trial and exiled them on release.

In 1982 Dorfman and some associates in the

Teamsters' leadership were in fact convicted of the serious charge of attempting to bribe a U.S. senator. Moreover, this conviction was achieved by legal methods, based on fourteen months of court-authorized wiretaps. In the final trial the prosecution used 2,000 reels of taped conversations, as well as the testimony of a number of organized crime "defectors." The case was based on incidents in 1979, but convictions were not handed down until the end of 1982; no doubt, there will be a lengthy appeals process.[3]

So major organized criminals are not beyond the reach of the U. S. justice system, even with all the due process protections it affords. But something like the Dorfman conviction can be achieved only with immense expenditure of money and time—on the part of the FBI, the Justice Department, and the courts. Even so, it can still take decades to convict someone whose wrongdoings were a matter of common public suspicion. Might there not be a case for reverting to the quick, cheap, and efficient methods used by Robert Kennedy (or even those of Castro)?

CONSIDERING THE VICTIM

In the crime control model it is results that matter. This is what voters hoped would happen, for example, when California attempted a major reform in its justice system in 1982. This "victim's bill of rights" would force the criminal to pay restitution.[4] Furthermore:

> It declares that students and teachers have an "inalienable right to attend campuses which are safe, secure and peaceful," and it would allow victims of crimes a right to be heard at the sentencing and parole hearings of criminals.
>
> But its principal result would be to give more authority to prosecutors in state courts. Beside limiting plea agreements and requiring all "relevant" evidence to be considered even if it was gathered in violation of standards set by the State Supreme Court, the proposal would do these things:
>
> Mandate a five-year sentence, in addition to the normal sentence, for those found guilty of repeat offenses of murder, rape,

> robbery, burglary, and certain other felonies.
>
> Require a judge to state why he is granting bail in serious felony cases.
>
> Allow prosecutors to disclose if a witness, including any defendants who testify, has a felony criminal record.
>
> Prohibit defendants from using a defense of "diminished capacity," because of intoxication, mental illness or disease, and narrow the use of insanity as a defense.
>
> Lower to 18 years from 21 the minimum age at which those convicted of serious felonies are sent to a state prison rather than a youth facility.

The values underlying this model are complex. Liberals would accuse its supporters of simply wanting to return to barbarism, but that is unfair. The crime control model is based, first, on a *consensus* view of society....

That is, all groups in society are in basic agreement about what constitutes crime and evil. Everybody—rich and poor—is equally in need of protection. To quote President Reagan:

> Theft is not a form of political or cultural expression; it is theft, and it is wrong. Murder is not forbidden as a matter of subjective opinion; it is objectively evil, and we must prohibit it. And no one but the thief and murderer benefits when we think and act otherwise.[5]

Failure to provide effective law and order can be seen as a form of discrimination against the poor. The rich and the middle class live in safer areas, whereas the poor and black live in high crime areas and constitute the largest body of victims.[6]

The desire to be protected from crime is a perfectly rational one: you may be prepared to give up a lot of rights to achieve that. Also, that is a respectable philosophical opinion. In 1651 the English philosopher Thomas Hobbes published his book *Leviathan*, which included a kind of contract theory. This assumed that in primitive times everyone was at war with everyone else. In this savagery "the life of man" was "nasty, brutish and short." Civilization came about when people got together to entrust power to a king or sovereign. In return for power, he had a duty to repress evil and preserve public security. Thus a "contract" exists between government and the governed. But suppose a government failed to provide this elementary security? This would mean that the contractual basis of society is null and void, and everyone has a right to private vengeance. The result would be renewed savagery, marked by vigilantes and private torture or execution of criminals. "Social wars" would thus break out again.

Finally, it may be that there is no alternative to crime control. Its theorists often argue that the experiences of the 1960s disproved a link between poverty and crime. Crime increased in times of prosperity, despite all the social spending in poor areas. If that failed, perhaps we should give "law and order" another chance.

Due Process

The crime control model clearly has its attractions. For instance, if we look at the Kennedy war on organized crime, it is very heartening to see men like Marcello or Giancana being hit hard for the first time in their lives. It is difficult to feel too sorry about the clear violations of their civil rights. In that particular case it is extremely difficult to see how else society could deal with organized crime except by a declaration of open war.

But in opposition to the crime control model, there stands a highly influential alternative, which Packer describes as the "due process" model. If crime control resembles a conveyor belt, this model is like an obstacle course. It emphasizes that the police have to observe the rules exactly at every stage of the process, or the evidence they acquire illegally will be excluded from court. It may even be that conviction will be impossible. In the United States this is associated particularly with the Warren Court of the 1950s and 1960s, and cases like *Mapp, Miranda*, and *Escobedo*. These clearly strengthened the exclusionary rule in situations of procedural irregularity.

However, we must understand that this was not a new invention of the Warren Court. Indeed, it is one of the oldest ideas of Anglo-American law. The fear was that if exact procedure was not followed, it would allow a government to make vague charges and become tyrannical. For instance, if someone charged that you robbed a certain bank on Second Avenue at 10:20 A.M. on the morning of Tuesday, April 30, you could respond to the charge. You could prove an alibi. But assume that someone said that you were responsible for various thefts in the state of Virginia between 1979 and 1981; how could you answer that? The burden of proof would be on you to show that you had never been in Virginia during those years. In case you think that is unlikely, there was an English trial in 1979–1980 in which a group of young anarchists were accused of conspiring with "persons unknown" at "places unknown" at unknown dates in the last few years to cause explosions. Go on—prepare your defense!

This sort of fear led courts to take fairly extreme positions on the exclusion of evidence. See, for instance, the case of *State* v. *Owen* in North Carolina (1810). Owen was charged that

> not having the fear of God before his eyes, but being moved and seduced by the instigations of the Devil ... with force and arms, at the city of Raleigh ... in and upon one Patrick Conway ... feloniously, willfully, and of his malice aforethought, did make an assault ... with a certain stick, of no value, which he the said John Owen in both his hands then and there had and held ... in and upon the head and face of him the said Patrick Conway ... did strike and beat ... giving to the said Patrick Conway, *then and there* with the pine stick aforesaid, in and upon the head and face of him the said Patrick Conway, several *mortal wounds,* of which said mortal wounds, the said Patrick Conway then and there instantly died.

Owen was found guilty, and appealed. His attorney argued that the indictment was defective, in that it did not "set forth the *length and depth* of the mortal wounds." A majority of the

Supreme Court of North Carolina regretfully agreed: "It appears from the books, that wounds capable of description must be described, that the Court may judge whether it be probable, that death might have been produced by them."[7] So the killer won a new trial on the smallest of technicalities. In comparison with this, the Warren Court was extremely moderate.

So the due process idea is deeply embedded in law. We can see the same principles of the supremacy of procedure in an English case of 1833. Briefly, the police broke up a demonstration that had gathered to demand political reform. In doing this, they failed to give proper warning (technically known as "reading the Riot Act"). In the ensuing fight a police officer was fatally stabbed. When this case went to the coroner's inquest, the jury found a verdict of justifiable homicide. They did not do this because they approved of violence against the police. Far from it: they described the killer as a "brutal fellow." However, if the police failed to follow procedure, they became just one body of armed thugs attacking a mob of demonstrators. This incident—the Calthorpe Street affair—did much to ensure that police in England and North America developed along legal and constitutional lines.[8] The criminal justice system inevitably uses force and coercion as part of its work. If it does not obey law in doing this, its personnel become no better than the criminals they face.

A supporter of the due process model would be well aware of the danger resulting if the idea is carried to ludicrous extremes. The "obstacle course" could become so difficult that no case could pass it, and anarchy would follow. However, the model could be defended on the following grounds.

First, the model has not been carried that far. Much evidence shows that the Miranda verdict, for instance, did not cut the conviction rate noticeably. The United States is far more concerned than most Western countries with the exclusionary principle and the need to observe rules, but even here the due process model does not exist in a pure form.[9]

Second, other countries have much more severe crime control models, and this is true not only of dictatorships. In (democratic) West Germany police need not obtain search warrants in most cases. Illegally obtained evidence is admissible in courts, except in very rare instances. Lawyers have no right to be present during the interrogation of a suspect. In England "Judges' Rules" specify how police should behave—for instance, how long suspects may be held without access to a lawyer. In practice these rules are simply ignored because there is no means to enforce them and no exclusionary rule.[10]

But the consequence of this is that conviction rates do not differ substantially in Britain, Germany, or the United States, so the due process model cannot be that disastrous for Americans (see boxes 3 and 4).

Box 3   The British Model

In many ways democratic Britain possesses a thorough crime control model. For example, in special political cases, the police can virtually revoke all due process rights under the "Prevention of Terrorism Act" of 1974. In the early 1980s calls for a "War on Crime" led to police pressure for a general reduction of defendants' rights. In essence these changes would just make legal what was already existing practice. To take some examples:

• The police would be able to search or arrest without warrants. They would also have much easier access to information about anybody's bank account.

• Anyone could be fingerprinted, without charge or arrest. The population of a whole town or area could be fingerprinted where the police claimed there was a need.

• The suspect could be held indefinitely without charge, and denied access to a lawyer.

In 1983 a proposed "Police and Criminal Evidence Bill" suggested great expansion of the right to search and seizure, even to the point of denying the right of confidentiality to lawyers, doctors, or clergy. If they had been dealing with a suspect as a client, their files could be confiscated or searched.

Apart from these proposed measures, existing police practices are controversial. For instance, there have been hundreds of (largely unexplained) deaths of suspects in police custody since 1970. Inquiries into police behavior are always carried out by other police officers, and very rarely lead to charges against officers. British police have become increasingly "trigger happy" (*New York Times*, May 22, 1983).

The prison system is equally unacquainted with U.S. due process rights. The prisons are dramatically overcrowded (some 25 percent over capacity). Prison discipline is severe; abuses are examined by "Boards of Visitors," usually sympathetic to the governor and the administration. Only recently has it been established that prisoners have a right of access to the courts to protest abuses.

The tight crime control model of Britain has led to predictable abuses. Police corruption has been a very serious problem, notably in London. In the early 1980s the inquiry known as "Operation Countryman" portrayed a situation at least as bad as that shown in New York by the Knapp Commission. Also, the lack of grievance mechanisms has caused public discontent. Police brutality did much to cause the major urban riots in Britain between 1976 and 1983 (notably in 1981); prison riots were severe in 1976 and 1978. But British police are campaigning for still greater powers (Evans, 1980; Scarman, 1982; Jenkins and Hutchings, 1982; Kettle and Hodges, 1982).

Box 4   Crime Control in France

France, like Britain, has long traditions of democracy. However, it has a crime control model of justice that would amaze law enforcement officials in the United States. For instance, only in 1981 did it abolish capital punishment—offenders were beheaded by means of the guillotine. As late as the 1950s criminals were still transported to the appalling penal colony of Devil's Island in South America. The French police are an extremely political body, with a long record of using torture and brutality against dissidents (notably in the 1960s). Civil disorders are dealt with by a tough riot squad, the CRS.

The loyalty of the police to the government is preserved by a kind of secret society to which leading police officials must belong (the S. A. C.). A national paramilitary force called the *Gendarmerie* is required to maintain detailed records on everyone in their locality. Patrol and surveillance are supposed to give highly aggressive and preventive policing.

But even with such a tightly controlled system, there was a feeling that the system was too soft on crime. From 1977, Justice Minister Alain Peyrefitte tried to pass a "Freedom and Security" law, which would cut discretion and make punishment tougher. Parole and suspended sentences would be abolished, and more emphasis would be put on the victim's rights. Efforts at rehabilitation would be more or less abandoned. Sentences were also made tougher, and the number of juveniles sent to prison rose dramatically. By 1981 some 7,000 people under the age of 18 were being imprisoned annually. The result of these conservative changes was a considerable rise in the prison population. By 1981 it was 42,000, in a system designed for 28,000.

In May 1981 France elected a new socialist government, the first nonconservative regime since 1958. The new minister of justice decided that the crime control system was on the verge of collapse and disorder. In only six months he freed about 20 percent of the prison population by pardon or parole; he also tried to reduce the use of capital punishment. The new government tried to make the police less of a military force. They were to be a civilian body on American or British lines, and there were experiments with putting officers on the beat, bringing them in touch with the community. Above all, they were expected to obey legality.

Conservatives still claimed that these reforms helped increase crime, terrorism, and disorder. However, others felt that the hard-line crime control policy had done nothing to cut crime and had made the penal system unworkable (based on articles in the *Guardian Weekly*, London, February 22, 1981; June 28, 1981; September 13, 1981; October 4, 1981; November 22, 1981; June 20, 1982; July 11, 1982; August 22, 1982; October 3, 1982).

Third, the United States definitely does not have a "soft" justice system. If we look at the number of prison inmates per 100,000 of general population, the tables would look something like this:

South Africa, USSR	600
United States	170
Britain	80
West Germany	67
France, Denmark, Belgium, Holland	30–40
Italy	22
Netherlands	13

Moreover, the figures look worse if we separate American blacks and whites. White Americans would fit somewhere between France and Germany; black Americans would be well up to the Soviet Union and South Africa. The American figures also continue to rise dramatically. Incidentally, the U.S. figure is identical to the imprisonment rate for Northern Ireland, an area in the middle of government repression and a bloody civil war.

Finally, it is widely feared that the crime control model in practice would be used against only certain crimes. The "frame 'em, frisk 'em, and fry 'em" theory emphasizes the consensus in society about the relative seriousness of crimes; but would that be used just for an all-out war on

street crimes, the crimes of the poor and of minorities? The Kennedys' use of crime control was so attractive because it attacked the powerful. It is very rare for law and order campaigns to focus on this sort of offense.

Total Control?

The reasons for having due process rights can be illustrated if we use the method of debate known as *reductio ad absurdum*. This means taking an argument to an outrageous extreme to show the flaws of a position. The people who hold that position will not believe it in so extreme a form, but they may be unable to see the flaws until they are made more glaring.

With the due process model, *reductio* is easy: we would so increase rights to the point where no one is convicted and no crime is punished. What about crime control? Let us assume that stopping crime must be the number-one priority of any civilized society, whatever rights must be given up. Let us devise a system in which the main goal is to cut crime massively, the only limitations being available technology and public expenditure. What would this system look like? (Incidentally, whenever I ask a group of people to devise such a system, I never cease to be amazed at the sadistic and dictatorial impulses that we all seem to have!)

A CRIME CONTROL MODEL WITHOUT LIMITS

One such model might be George Orwell's *1984* (published in 1948). This book was a satire on contemporary dictatorships, both Hitler's Germany and Stalin's Russia. A savage secret police operating from the "Ministry of Love" maintains thorough surveillance over all the people by a system of spies and informers. Children, who belong to party-run organizations, report any dubious behavior in their families—as do the superintendents of apartment blocks. Every room has a "telescreen" in it, which allows an observer to watch and supervise everything you do. Also thorough control of the media allows the shaping of attitudes through unscrupulous propaganda and remodelling of history.

This system is geared mainly for political dissidence, but the implications for crime control are obvious. Let us take up the theme of surveillance. First, there are nontechnological devices. In societies where a large number of people live closely together—for instance, in apartment blocks—certain individuals can be selected as "block wardens." In Cuba each block or street has its very observant "Committee for the Defense of the Revolution." Incidentally, you may have heard of the perfect society depicted in Thomas More's Utopia (1516). What is not generally realized is exactly how that "perfect" society fought crime and immorality. Essentially, it was by everyone spying on everyone else and having no privacy. Hardly a "utopian" solution!

But technology has revolutionized the possibilities for surveillance. Already the elements for a total system are there. In most countries (democratic or otherwise) every citizen has to have an identity card and number, and show it to the police when asked. It is a serious crime to be caught without it. In most European countries changes of address often have to be registered with the police. This use of identity cards and numbers might seem alien to inhabitants of North America or Britain, but is it really so unusual? Americans already make frequent use of their Social Security numbers, as well as credit cards. Offhand, I can think of over twenty numbers by which I am known in a variety of computer files, and I have never been charged with a criminal offense.[11]

What does this have to do with surveillance? Suppose there is a society in which there is only one type of number, and that is your Social Security, your identification, your bank account, your tax reference, your car registration, and your credit card. All these transactions are available to a central computer. Further, imagine that many more functions—such as buying gas—can be performed only with a credit card. You will then find that your monthly bill can readily be paid directly from your bank account, with a copy going directly to the IRS. You will also find that your account gives a precise picture of

your movements in a particular month. How can you deny that you were in Virginia on April 17 if you bought gas in Charlottesville on April 17 and had a meal in Richmond on April 18? What happens to alibis? If this seems unlikely, consider existing practice. Already in 1976, the British PNC (Police National Computer) at Hendon had centralized information on 25 million vehicles, 3 million fingerprints, and 5 million criminals (out of a total population of some 60 million).[12] And computers have come a long way since 1976 (see box 5).

Box 5   The Interstate Identification Index (III)

In 1983 the FBI began operating a communications system by which "inquiries about criminal suspects from anywhere in the USA will be funnelled through a FBI computer in Washington to the computers of 17 states" (Burnham, 1982: 120; Burnham, 1983). This system originated as far back as 1966, and in 1970 it was expanded to handle criminal history records. Ideally, it would provide law enforcement officers with instant access to criminal records. It is also "a nationwide electronic bulletin board where policemen can list the names of persons wanted for arrest and can post information about stolen property" (Burnham, 1982: 121).

The necessity of centralization is suggested by the huge scale of the data involved. The FBI's fingerprint records already cover some 21 million people, and state records contain 34 million criminal history records.

The problems with III are equally obvious. First, there are serious libertarian objections. As Senator Sam Ervin remarked, "For one man to have control of crime data might be more efficient. But this country wasn't based on the idea of efficiency so much: it was based on the idea of power diffused." Another critic suggested that the new system "could result in the absorption of state and local criminal data into a potentially abusive, centralized, Federally-controlled communications and computer information system" (quoted in Burnham, 1982: 127).

Such charges are aggravated by evidence

that the records kept are often out of date or inaccurate. For example, of the outstanding warrants reported by the FBI, 10.9 percent had already been cleared. In a survey of records supplied by the FBI's identification division, only a quarter of cases were found to be "complete, accurate and unambiguous" (Burnham, 1982: 126–128).

Compared to the centralization of data banks, the removal of all due process rights and protections would seem a minor step. If this were combined with a centralization of all American police forces and their records, a large step might have been taken toward *1984*. However, there are other steps you may care to take, such as compulsory mass fingerprinting, with records perhaps linked to individuals' numbers in the central computer. Greater use could be made of *agents provocateurs* (police agents who actively stir up illegal activity, and then expose it) or extensive telephone tapping. Warrants could be done away with, for instance, in access to bank accounts or tax records. Prisons would seem to offer huge scope for the application of new technology. . . . To quote a psychologist writing as long ago as 1970, "Criminals *can* be brainwashed—now," by use of aversion therapy, sensory deprivation, psychosurgery, and psychotropic drugs. Behavior can be modified, and the result can be used to control crime further. "Reconditioned" criminals could be sent out to contact their old associates and act as spies or provocateurs. Implanting electrodes in their brains could allow the police to track them (or indeed any offender) and to administer severe pain if they strayed into areas where they were not supposed to be.

In terms of technology there is one great problem with the system I have outlined here. It is too old-fashioned and not enough of a total control scheme. It is based on the ideas of a decade or more ago, and takes little account of recent developments. (Don't forget: the "Josephson Junction" microcomputer has already made the microchip obsolete.)

DRAWBACKS TO A CRIME CONTROL MODEL

Let us assume that this is a fairly perfect crime control scheme. What is wrong with it? Our aim was to create a society where fighting crime is the first social priority. Have we done that?

The first question must be "Who guards the guards?" In a totalitarian system there are no restraints on the power and discretion of the police authorities or the politicians who supervise them. White collar crime, corporate crime, and the "crimes of the powerful" continue unchecked. All the technology in the world is unlikely to change the aims of bureaucracy and the first goal is to concentrate on easier targets. Powerful criminals (such as the gangster Meyer Lansky) would remain friendly with leading politicians and bureaucrats. So the "perfect" system would not cure "crime in the suites." The restriction of democratic rights would also make it unlikely that such crimes would ever be exposed. With absolute power there would be enormous temptations on police and bureaucrats to engage in corruption and personal intimidation. No control system can restrain the powerful. Even in Hitler's Germany leaders of the police and army managed to arrange an almost-successful assassination plot against the Führer.

Would street crime be seriously reduced? In a system based on provocateurs and informers crime is not necessarily reduced: it is just monopolized by the friends and allies of the police. Totalitarian systems have often claimed to eliminate crime, but they can do that because they have an unchecked control over criminal statistics. There is enormous bureaucratic pressure simply to lie about the figures and show how efficient you have been. Also, some totalitarian systems have indeed cut violent crime. But they have often done this by legalizing it. Of course you can get thugs and psychopaths off the criminal statistics if you make them your secret police.

There would still have to be tremendous discretion. If your control system really did detect a great amount of crime, you could not prosecute everybody. How would you select? By bribery? Race? By the number of arrests you needed for this year's "quota"? Discretion is the gateway to corruption.

It might well be that the outcome of a crime control model would be essentially that demonstrated by a case study of Philadelphia in the 1930s (see box 6). Powerful criminals would become more powerful, poor offenders would suffer enormous injustices. Crime would not be reduced, just transferred up the social scale.

If this would not reduce crime, what would be its other consequences? First, the suppression of deviancy would tend to kill valuable social experiment and make society stagnant. Second, the justice system would lose much of the consent and legitimacy on which it is based, and that could make law enforcement actually more difficult. That point can be illustrated by a specific crime control proposal. In 1929 concern about gangsterism led the city of Chicago to call in an expert on policing to study the city force. This expert was Bruce Smith, who advocated disbanding the entire force and replacing it essentially with an army of occupation. A new force of college graduates would be recruited, preferably with no links to the community they served. They would live in barracks and act like a colonial constabulary.[13] Both race and class would divide them from the wider population.

This force would be honest, well intentioned and *less* effective than their corrupt predecessors. Why?

Box 6   Philadelphia 1935–1937

The Philadelphia police force has been subject to many charges of excessive brutality and racial discrimination, which has led to an extremely poor public image. In the 1930s the Philadelphia force provided an interesting example of the abuses of power that are possible in a crime control system. In these years the "due process" revolution was still a distant gleam, and abuses like the "third degree" interrogation were commonplace—not only in Philadelphia. The city was thoroughly controlled by the Republican machine in

alliance with the police force.

In 1935 a gambler named Nate Schaffner decided to "syndicate" the city—that is, to run organized crime as a monopoly. But why employ private enforcers when the city had such an excellent police force? Once Mayor J. Davis Wilson was elected, he immediately began to put the Schaffner scheme into effect. This had a number of stages (*Presentments*, 1937).

The police were purged. Honest officers found themselves dismissed or demoted. Some were used against vice and gambling, but very selectively. They were sent only against Schaffner's enemies to arrest or intimidate them. For instance, a special vice squad made many arrests until the gamblers caved in to Schaffner. Then the vice squad was transformed into a Christmas antipickpocketing detail. One honest officer, Captain Burns, was sent to devastate the gambling in certain areas of the city where the ward bosses were enemies of Wilson's.

The remaining police were wholly allied with Wilson and Schaffner. The detective force was used to wiretap and intimidate the mayor's political opponents. The uniformed patrolmen served as "bagmen" for the huge gambling operations that now got publicly under way. Gambling flourished openly, as did prostitution. The police ignored the casinos, even when they were held up by robbers a block from the police headquarters. When public pressure did lead to a raid, the police were sure to inform the club well in advance.

Some crimes were savagely punished and the crime control model was thoroughly used against the city's poor, blacks, and political dissidents. One attorney, the legendary "Chippy" Patterson, spent most of his time defending the framed and the intimidated from police persecution. (He gave his services free and, incidentally, was the only attorney in the city to address black defendants as "Mister.") Organized criminals also suffered, but only if they opposed Schaffner and Wilson. For instance, the gang of "Nig" Rosen was altogether expelled from the city for a number of years (Potter and Jenkins, unpublished).

Opponents of the new regime were savagely crushed. They were intimidated by the police or gangsters, and they were denounced by newspapers friendly to the "cabal." Only when Wilson's political machine split did a chance of reform appear. A grand jury was appointed, the state police were sent in, and Schaffner was broken.

Of course, the rigid control by a police-politicians-gambler alliance had not been broken. It just became less blatant, and control was transferred from one clique (Schaffner) to another (Rosen). And it stayed with Rosen for another twenty years (Potter and Jenkins, unpublished).

The public would see the police as an enemy force and would place no confidence in them. They would not give the police the respect and status their professional ideas led them to expect. The police might well turn in upon themselves and increasingly resort to corruption and brutality.

The community would tend to fear the police and not help them with the information that is essential to crime control. They might be reluctant to report crimes except in severe cases. Also, cooperation with the police (as in crime prevention programs) requires an element of trust.

If the police are seen as enemies, the public might resort to private justice. In Northern Ireland many Catholics see the police as an enemy army, so they are reluctant to turn offenders over to them. They turn to private forms of punishment, such as "kneecapping."

If the public does not trust and respect the justice system, they may well sympathize with criminals. There is therefore no element of condemnation for prisoners, who might be seen as victims. As in many peasant societies, criminals and bandits might be seen as heroes, whereas the law enforcement authorities are enemies. In Britain in the late 1970s, the antipolice feelings of young working-class people led them to chant the name of Harry Roberts at football matches. Harry Roberts was a London gangster who in 1966 murdered three police officers, in a country where the police are very rarely the victims of violence.

By contrast a force that achieves legitimacy and public consent may be more honest, because it has public respect, and more successful, because it will know its community very well. As examples of the types of policing, we may select Japan as a model of public support for authority. It is "heaven for a cop."[14] For the total failure of legitimacy, we might select the blacks of South Africa; or the Catholics of Northern Ireland (see box 7).

Box 7 The Failure of Legitimacy: Northern Ireland

Northern Ireland is a territory of about 1.5 million people, roughly 65 percent Protestant and 35 percent Catholic. The Protestants wish to be ruled by Britain (as at present); the Catholics want to join the Irish Republic in a United Ireland. In 1969 fighting between the two communities led to the intervention of the British Army. In the 1970s two main secret armies emerged: the Protestant UVF (Ulster Volunteer Force) and the Catholic IRA (Irish Republic Army). The IRA attacked the army and police, and both groups engaged in terrorist actions against civilians. Random killings of members of the other religion caused several hundred deaths. Also, bombs were used against civilian targets. In 1974 UVF bombs killed 32 people in Dublin; and the IRA killed 22 in a bar in Birmingham, England. By 1983 there had been almost 2,200 deaths.

How could the justice system respond to this challenge? The police and army claimed that they knew who the terrorists were, but it would be hard to get evidence against them. Even if they could build up a case, jurors would be intimidated. So a crime control model was used.

Surveillance. A massive computer system built up records on every home in the area, based on the collation of trivial facts. Suppose, for example, that the army arrested a man one night and asked for his identity. The army would then check the name he gave with the computer, and find, for example, that the man with this name lived in a house with a red carpet in the living room. The man would know this detail only if he was who he claimed to be (Ackroyd et al., 1977).

Internment. In 1971 hundreds of Republicans were arrested without charge and placed in prison camps. They had no due process rights, and some remained interned for several years, entirely on the unproven charges of the authorities.

Juries. Internment was unpopular, and so the authorities tried to replace it with something more normal. On the recommendation of Lord Diplock, internment would be ended. In future, people would be tried in courts, but there would be no juries allowed. He also recommended that statements or confessions made in police custody should be allowed, as long as the court was satisfied they had not been obtained by torture. There would be no exclusionary rule on evidence. By 1975 this had been put into practice, and all internees were released (Taylor, 1980).

Interrogation. The consequences of this reform were predictable. As early as 1971 the army had been torturing suspects by "sensory deprivation" techniques (like Soviet brainwashing). Now the police used torture to force confessions from suspects on a huge scale, and in very few cases did judges fail to accept this evidence. Suspects were beaten, burned, electrocuted, and they appeared in court with all kinds of wounds and bruises. But the judges almost invariably convicted them on the strength of their "confessions." These practices continue today (Ibid.).

What has been the consequence of all this? Almost certainly extreme crime control measures have made the situation worse:

• The Army and police are hated, whereas the private armies are respected—even when they engage in "organized crime" activities like extortion.

• Internment created a wave of support for the IRA and made the violence more severe.

• Even when a terrorist is jailed for a brutal offense, he receives tremendous sympathy as a victim. In 1981 many prisoners went on hunger strike and ten died, further increasing support for the revolutionaries. This support was partly financial, so groups like the IRA became better armed.

• Although many terrorists have been jailed, many more have been led to replace them because of their outrage at injustices. The crisis that began in 1969 shows no sign of fading away.

By carrying crime control ideas to an extreme, we can see some flaws in this otherwise attractive model:

1. It would tend to lose public support and consent.
2. The workings of bureaucracy would make it likely that only the crimes of the poor would be affected at all.
3. The conflict view suggests that the most serious crimes would actually grow worse in this model.
4. Above all, it is a very dubious proposition that the crime control model really would affect crime of any sort. The existence of due process rights—and the public confidence they give—might actually improve law enforcement.

So due process rights do not survive just because of sentimentality or force of habit. They are useful in fighting crime. They have one other major justification, which is perhaps the most basic of all. Briefly, if another person can be subject to procedural injustice, then so can you. If another person can be framed and wrongly convicted without hope of appeal, so can you. But if there are lots of safeguards for that other person, they are there for you if and when your time comes. Abandoning your civil rights is a rational decision if you believe that the police are never likely to make a mistake, or never find it in their interests to accuse an innocent person. Because the person they accuse might be you.

What Are Due Process Rights?

There are many specific rights that an individual possesses, but let us begin by stating in broad terms the guiding rules that should be observed.[15] Some commonly stated principles might include the following.

• Punishment should be applied only for conduct, not thought, status, or beliefs.

• Conduct can be defined as criminal only when it has previously been so defined by legislators. In Latin this is the legal maxim *nullum crimen, nulla poena, sine lege* ("No crime, no punishment, without law"). In other words, I may drink whiskey on December 10. Congress may on December 11 make a law forbidding the drinking of whiskey, but that cannot affect my actions on the previous day. If it did, it would be a retroactive (or *ex post facto*) law.

Those definitions must be stated precisely enough to leave little room for arbitrary conduct. You could, for example, make it a crime to join the Communist party. However, you should not make "communism" a crime if you then take it to include holding all sorts of different opinions. (Compare also Packer's opinions ...)

These would be general themes. For a list of appropriate specific rights, we might consider the two excellent statements of 1789 (the French "Declaration of the Rights of Man" and the American "Bill of Rights"). But are they all relevant today? For instance, the Fourth Amendment clause about the amount of detail required in search warrants arose out of a then newsworthy controversy in which a government had issued a vaguely worded warrant. Surely we do not still have to be bound by every minor detail of eighteenth-century documents? We can still have a system based on due process values, but differing in specific matters from a document like the Bill of Rights.

Maybe. On the other hand, it is striking how often attempts to change such specific details result in simply overturning the whole framework of due process ideas. What we often find is proof of the old saying that "hard cases make bad law." Laws produced as a sudden response to a horrible situation actually tend to make matters worse when applied to other cases. Let us take some examples, as they affect the areas of terrorism and organized crime.

First, I am taking it for granted that organized crime is gravely damaging to any society and that terrorism is a threat to any established society. However, let us look at responses that have emerged to these problems.

TERRORISM

In the discussion of Northern Ireland (see box 7), I showed that the crisis of the 1970s led to attempts to do away with the jury system and certain legal protections. Surely in this day and age an honest and professional judiciary and police force could be trusted not to abuse their powers? But this assumption was totally false. The result of abuses committed was to make a bloody situation far worse, far more violent. When special antiterrorist legislation is passed to suspend some civil rights (as in Britain or Germany), it is rarely used against terrorism, but very often against dissidents or other offenders.[16]

ORGANIZED CRIME

The problems of dealing with organized crime resemble those of terrorism: difficulty of proof, intimidation of jurors or witnesses. In the late 1960s the relative immunity of organized crime led to a campaign for action. In 1970 an "Organized Crime Control Bill" was passed by Congress. The law allowed the establishment of special Grand Juries, tightened up on immunity laws, allowed the detention of recalcitrant witnesses, and reduced defendant's rights in a number of other particulars. After all, were not special powers needed to fight this menace? However, in reality, the 1970 act was rarely used against organized crime. Far more often, it was used against political enemies of the Nixon administration. The new grand jury process was used for intelligence gathering by illegal means, and for punishing enemies by the contempt laws. Its targets were not Cosa Nostra families but Weatherman radicals and antiwar activists.[17]

So, even in such "hard cases" the Bill of Rights principles may retain a great deal of value.

NOTES

1. Packer (1968).
2. Smith (1982); Blakey and Billings (1981).
3. Moldea (1978); Brill (1978); Demaris (1981); *New York Times*, December 16, 1982; January 21, 1983.
4. *New York Times*, May 23, 1982. Copyright © 1982 by The New York Times Company.
5. Ibid., September 29, 1981. Copyright © 1981 by The New York Times Company.
6. Silberman (1978): 3–26, 159–224.
7. Friedman (1973): 133.
8. Thompson (1989): 206–208.
9. Wicker (1983).
10. Cole et al. (1981): 102; Holdaway (1979): 24–40.
11. Ackroyd et al. (1977).
12. Ibid.: 172.
13. Stead (1977): 197–199.
14. Bayley (1976).
15. See, for example, Katkin (1982); Packer (1968): 73.
16. Taylor (1980); Ackroyd et al. (1977).
17. Block and Chambliss (1981): 199–208.

REFERENCES

Ackroyd, C., Margolis, K., Rosenhead, J., and Shallice, T. 1977. *The Technology of Political Control*. London: Penguin.

Bayley, D. 1976. *Forces of Order*. Berkeley: University of California Press.

Blakey, G. R., and Billings, R. N. 1981. *The Plot to Kill the President*. New York: Times Books.

Block, A., and Chambliss, W. 1981. *Organizing Crime*. New York: Elsevier.

Brill, S. 1978. *The Teamsters*. New York: Simon and Schuster.

Cole, G. F., Frankowski, S. J., and Gertz, M. G. 1981. *Major Criminal Justice Systems*. Beverly Hills, Calif.: Sage.

Demaris, O. 1981. *The Last Mafiosi*. New York: Bantam.

Friedman, L. 1973. *History of American Law*. New York: Touchtone.

Holdaway, S., ed. 1979. *The British Police*. Beverly Hills, Calif.: Sage.

Katkin, D. 1982. *The Nature of Criminal Law*. Belmont, Calif.: Wadsworth.

Moldea, D. E. 1978. *The Hoffa Wars*. New York: Charter.

Packer, H. 1968. *The Limits of the Criminal Sanction*. Stanford, Calif.: Stanford University Press.

Silberman, C. E. 1978. *Criminal Violence, Criminal Times*. New York: Vintage.

Smith, R. N. 1982. *Thomas E. Dewey and His Times*. New York: Simon and Schuster.

Stead, P. J. 1977. *Pioneers in Policing*. Montclair, N.J.: Patterson Smith.

Taylor, P. 1980. *Beating the Terrorists*. London: Penguin Special.

Thompson, E. P. 1980. *Writing by Candlelight*. London: Merlin.

Wicker, T. 1983. "Exploding a Myth." *New York Times*, May 10.

Study Questions

1. Briefly describe the "crime control" and the "due process" models of criminal justice. Which model do you think would be more likely to be found in a repressive country such as Cuba or China? Why?

2. Which of the two models in Question 1 seems more firmly rooted in utilitarian ethical theory? Explain. Could both models be grounded in a utilitarian perspective? Explain.

3. What is the point of Jenkins' Ireland example? Do you agree with Jenkins? Why? Defend your position.

4. Should a person who is caught by the police committing a crime be given the same legal rights as a person charged on the basis of circumstantial evidence? Why? Defend your position. Does a prison inmate serving a life sentence for a vicious murder have a moral right to due process? Why? Defend your position.

5. Summarize Jenkins' chief arguments for and against the two models of criminal justice. Which model does Jenkins believe is better? Do you agree? Why? Defend your position.

Due Process—How Much Is Enough?

J. S. FUERST AND ROY PETTY

A PERVASIVE PROBLEM FOR those concerned with civil rights is how to extend those rights as widely as possible without interfering with the business of operating a government. Since 1960, we have witnessed growing concern about the conflict between the single-minded pursuit of civil rights and the effect of this pursuit on the government. The predominant attitude toward government services has become one of suspicion and hostility. As David Rothman has put it,

> From the perspective of professionals and administrators, civil libertarian lawyers have become so enamored of establishing rights that they completely forget the significance of anything else, whether it is patients' need for treatment, society's need for self-protection, or the community's need for housing.[1]

Why are these issues being raised now, at a time of increasing conservatism in the national government, in the federal courts, and indeed in the mood of the public at large? Why propose further limitations of any kind on personal rights and liberties when that process seems well under way?

One answer is that an unreasonable emphasis on rights rather than social needs serves the interests of the present administration, which identifies its opponents as civil libertarian purists with little administrative sense and no knowledge of administrative reality. Another is that experience indicates that it is not enough to try and find an equilibrium between the limiting of the discretion of social welfare administrators or the limitation of the expansion of

J. S. Fuerst and Roy Petty, "Due Process—How Much Is Enough?" The Public Interest, *vol. 79:1 (Spring 1985), pp. 96–110. © 1985 by National Affairs, Inc. Used by permission of the publisher.*

rights; what is needed is a supplementary strategy to accomplish the same ends.

In the past, liberals have tended to view any expansion of due process rights as a good thing, while putative conservatives have tended to think otherwise. But after a spate of recent cases—involving, for example, adoption, foster care, public housing, schools, and prisons—it is now clear that the issues are not that simple. Even staunch proponents of a strong civil-liberties position must begin to ask themselves two questions: First, how good is the expansion of due process rights in government-administered social programs when it begins to hamper or even cripple the benefits that the program in question is supposed to provide? Second, does the formalization of the process by which the state confers benefits and sanctions improve human welfare?

The Expansion of Due Process

The law in question is, of course, the simple command of the fourteenth amendment (taken from very similar wording in the fifth amendment): "...nor shall any state deprive any person of life, liberty, or property without due process of law." In earlier times, the principle meant in practice that before the government could hang you, jail you, or take your money or land, it had to go before a judge and convince him or a jury that it was fair and correct to do so. Concomitantly, legal definitions of what constituted "liberty" or "property" were quite narrow.

But in recent decades, the concept of "property" has become vastly more complicated as the government's role in providing or protecting property itself has increased. We now recognize as part of our wealth and property a bundle of rights and expectations that would never have been considered as such a few decades ago: the right to Social Security benefits if we are retired or disabled; the right to available welfare if we are destitute; the right to free public education if it is offered; the right to live in public housing if it is available and we qualify; the right to retain government jobs as long as our work is sat-

isfactory according to objective and fair standards. The extension of fifth and fourteenth amendment due process rights to protect these intangible properties came slowly.

One of the first to recognize that due process rights would have to be expanded to protect government benefits was Charles Reich. He observed, in his *Yale Law Journal* article "The New Property," that everyone in the nation had some substantial relationships with government in which government was holding all or most of the cards. He wrote:

> Government is a gigantic syphon. It draws in revenue and power, and pours forth wealth, money, benefits, services, contracts, franchises, and licenses. Government has always had this function but while in early times it was minor, today's distribution of largesse is on a vast, imperial scale.[2]

According to Reich, we had all come to expect and depend upon various kinds of benefits and services from government, and when we were unfairly deprived of these benefits or services by arbitrary action, it was just as damaging to us as if the government had seized our land or attacked our bank account. Reich proposed, quite simply, to expand the legal definition of "property" to include all expectations and aspects of unimpeded personal activity that related to action by government.

But what are "due process rights" to government benefits? Due process, after all, can have many components: the right of timely notice, the right of counsel, the right to call witnesses, the right to see the evidence against one, the right to confrontation or cross examination of witnesses, the right to a written record, the right to appeal, the right to an impartial judge, and the right to a fair and reasonable venue. The central question, of course—as U. S. Court of Appeals Judge Henry Friendly has observed—is not so much whether individuals are entitled to due process, but how many and which of these specific rights must be accorded and to whom, and under what circumstances.

The Role of the Courts

The due process revolution affecting government benefits is scarcely 15 years old. It can fairly be dated to the Supreme Court's decision in *Goldberg* v. *Kelly* (1970).

The state of New York had determined that Mrs. Kelly, who had been on welfare, was no longer eligible. She said they were wrong. The state stopped her benefits and told her that if she disagreed with this decision she had the right to a full, formal hearing on the facts of her case—later. But the Supreme Court said that her eligibility for welfare payments was a property right, and that no payments could be withheld until she had received due process of law. This meant that the state had to give her the opportunity to a full hearing *before* they cut off her benefits, not *after*.

In a sense, the *Goldberg* ruling was very narrow. The court said nothing about the adequacy of the procedure New York provided for those whose welfare payments were terminated; rather, it said only that the state could not stop Mrs. Kelly's payments until after she had had an opportunity to take advantage of that procedure. Narrow as it was, however, even this holding could substantially increase administrative burdens. Moreover, it could do so without providing guidance to states, which might find the burdens and costs of providing due process staggering. The late Justice Hugo Black recognized as much and noted in his dissent to *Goldberg* that "these ever-changing lists [of those who receive some forms of state or welfare assistance] put a constant administrative burden on government, and it certainly could not have reasonably anticipated that this burden would include the additional procedural expense imposed by the Court today."

Goldberg was followed by many similar decisions. Their effects on the operations of agencies and on the task of serving clients were soon reviewed.

One critic was Jerry Mashaw, who pointed out that an overzealous approach to due process might easily have deleterious effects on the treatment provided by state agencies.[3] As a result, he argued, due-process protections would favor not the neediest but only the most aggressive of recipients.

Mashaw observed that due process was best guaranteed to recipients of state benefits by the hiring of better-caliber professional employees, by reducing case loads, and by other general improvements in the structure of social welfare programs. To force such agencies to take a more and more defensive stance toward their clients was to reduce their abilities and incentives to be supportive, while further limiting their resources to do the job they were in business to do. Slapping more and more procedural requirements on administration had little or no effect on ultimate fairness. Mashaw argued that recipients were most likely to receive genuine "due process," that is, careful and unbiased review of the facts according to acceptable, humane standards, when agency officials were truly dedicated to serving their clients. In the absence of such dedication, no manner of formal due process mechanisms could do anything to improve conditions.

The Supreme Court and the inferior federal courts have not been impressed by this argument. As Justice Byron White said in *Stanley* v. *Illinois* (1977), which justified the placement of rather severe procedural restrictions on state-administered adoption proceedings:

> While difficulties might result from this opinion, the Constitution recognizes higher values than efficiency and speed. Indeed, the due process clause was designed to protect the fragile values of a vulnerable citizenry from the overbearing concern for efficiency that may characterize praiseworthy government officials no less and perhaps even more than mediocre ones.

The effect of this rhetoric on social services over the past decade or two has been like that of a wrecking ball. The *Stanley* decision, by requiring adoption agencies to attempt to locate and involve fathers of illegitimate children in adoption proceedings, has greatly drawn out the adoption process in some states, to the serious detriment of the children and families involved.

Similarly, in the area of juvenile court proceedings, Supreme Court and lower court decisions have changed what was once a flexible, protective, rehabilitation-oriented process into a sterile, rigid, and highly adversarial system that reproduces all the worst features of the adult criminal justice system—hardly an admirable model—in the name of due process for young offenders. The case of *In re Gault* (1967) declared that the Bill of Rights applied to minors as well as to adults and ordered that the full panoply of criminal court justice safeguards available to adults be imposed on the juvenile justice system. (In the words of Judge James Lincoln, presiding judge of the Detroit Juvenile Courts and head of the Juvenile Court Judges Association of the United States, "in the course of his opinion Justice Fortas took a ball bat and virtually clubbed the Juvenile Court out of existence.")

In the field of public housing, a series of court decisions in the 1970s robbed housing administrators of practically all discretion in the selection, management, and eviction of tenants by requiring strict guidelines for tenant selection, and elaborate, time-consuming adversary proceedings for evictions. The court's zeal in protecting the constitutional rights of potential new tenants and potential ex-tenants was admirable, but the burden of these decisions falls on other tenants and applicants—the great majority of public housing tenants and would-be tenants who followed the rules, did not commit crimes, and sought only a decent place to live. Formalizing the rules for evicting public housing tenants means that the process becomes much slower, more complicated, and expensive: As a result, even conscientious housing officials are more likely to avoid entering into eviction proceedings, and disruptive tenants can remain in place, forcing their law-abiding neighbors to move and causing idealistic and exemplary management employees to leave in frustration. Certainly the plight of families receiving public

assistance in many states is as bad as it was pre-*Goldberg*. Real assistance standards are lower (in terms of current price levels), and terminations of benefits have been more ruthless than ever with only a minuscule number of appeals along the lines of *Goldberg*. Sadly, a decade and a half of due process vigilance has not made life better for the recipients of government largesse. In fact, it can be argued that the insistence on "due process at any cost" has perhaps made things worse.

Goldberg's Other Progeny

Similarly, in public school administration, the imposition of due process requirements for suspensions and other disciplinary proceedings has made it more difficult for school administrators to defuse potentially destructive situations; the Supreme Court has ruled, for example, that even a 10-day suspension, imposed for the purpose of heading off imminent large-scale racial disturbances, was impermissible unless the students involved were given administrative hearings first (*Goss* v. *Lopez*, 1975).

Even state penitentiaries must provide a full array of due process rights to their prisoners in a great many circumstances, as a result of a long series of prisoners' rights cases in the Supreme Court. In *Vitek* v. *Jones* (1980), the court ruled that a prison administrator could not send an inmate to a state mental hospital for treatment without a formal adversarial hearing—even though the inmate had set fire to his mattress three times and was deemed by the consulting psychiatrist to be an imminent risk to the lives and safety of his fellow inmates. (This case illustrates particularly the conflict between psychiatrists and lawyers that Willard Gaylin describes ironically in *Doing Good*: "I fully understand the impulse of the adversarial movement to substitute for the hardnosed, belligerent, and tough minded psychiatrist, the attention of the gently, understanding, and empathetic lawyer.")

The court during the past few years has continued to favor the extension of civil rights over good social work practice. *Santosky* v. *Kramer*

(1982), for example, involved an upstate New York family which had a history of child neglect. The local social services agency had taken three of the children into custody (one only three days after he was born) out of fear that they might be harmed or endangered. The state eventually instituted "permanent neglect" proceedings against the parents, a necessary first step toward placing the young children for adoption. In New York, permanent neglect proceedings are extremely elaborate, much like a formal criminal trial; indeed, as the Supreme Court admitted, they are far more elaborate in most respects than the Constitution would seem to require. Yet the high court found after a detailed examination of the procedure required under the law that, despite the extensive social investigation conducted, the quantum of proof required by state law, which called for a preponderance of evidence rather than clear and convincing evidence, was too minimal to meet due process standards in taking children away from parents.

As a result of that decision, the determination of permanent neglect was overturned and the Santosky children remained unavailable for adoption. The Supreme Court's decision had nothing to do with the actual evidence presented against the Santoskys. The decision was concerned only with the weight of the evidence that might have been sufficient under state law, and whether that hypothetical level met constitutional standards. What actually took place at the Santoskys' hearing was considered irrelevant to the technical due process issue in controversy. The Constitution was thus vindicated. Under the banner of the "due process" clause the Santoskys, who have had, at last count, three of their five children removed to foster care, retain their formal designation as parents of Tina, John III, and Jed. The three children, who have been in foster care for nine years, will not be freed for adoption unless the state modifies its termination hearing policies and Ulster county reinstitutes permanent neglect proceedings against the parents. Jed is nine years old now and has lived with his natural parents for only the first three days of his life. As Justice Rehnquist in the Supreme Court said for the minority, "it is inconceivable to me that these procedures were unfair to petitioners. Only by its obsessive focus on the standard of proof and its almost complete disregard of the facts of the case could the majority find otherwise."

There have been inconsistent decisions in recent years, but the Santosky case is not unrepresentative of the federal courts' heightened sensitivity to real or imagined abuse of due process rights.

Preserving the Essence of Due Process

The command of the due process clause remains clear, expressing one of the oldest ideas of liberty. And it does not stretch logic to say that Mrs. Kelly had a "property" interest in her legitimate expectation of welfare benefits, or that those accused of being juvenile offenders or neglectful parents have similar interests that ought not to be unfairly taken from them by government. For expressing that idea and for attempting to make it available to millions of previously voiceless and powerless possessors of the "new property," the courts should be applauded. Yet substantial problems have arisen because of the implementation of that idea, and because the federal and state courts and public agencies (and even quasi-public agencies like universities or subsidized housing agencies, or hospitals receiving public monies) have interpreted the idea of due process in a manner that often hamstrings administration and does little or nothing to help the individuals involved.

No one argues that every single deprivation of property requires, for example, a full, formal, trial-type hearing. But if not, which elements can be detached without sacrificing the very idea of due process? The Supreme Court's answer to this question has varied greatly from case to case.

The only reliable and consistent principle found in most of the post-1970 due-process decisions was summarized by Justice White in one of many prisoners' rights cases, *Wolff* v. *McDonnell*

(1979). "Some kind of hearing is required at some time before a person is finally deprived of his property interests." That phrase was echoed in case after case, but the Court—unable to reconcile the leanings of individual Justices in certain cases or toward certain procedural devices —has been unable to adduce any other principles intrinsic to due process.

One who undertook to do exactly this was Judge Henry Friendly. Friendly took the phrase, "some kind of a hearing," and in 1975 made it the title of a practical and constructive piece of legal scholarship. In it, he simply enumerated all the elements of the traditional American adversarial model of legal fact-finding, and ranked them according to his own determination of importance. Like Justice White, he felt that "some kind of a hearing" was the most likely and reasonable starting point for assuring due process; and, accepting the adversarial model, he analyzed what ends the due process hearing was supposed to achieve and how successful or unsuccessful the different elements of that model were in furthering these ends. Finally, he began to set up a rough scale of state deprivation of property or liberty, and asked how many of the due process elements were required for each.

Friendly decided that three components were "fundamental" to any fair hearing: an unbiased judge; notice of the proposed action and reasons for it; and some chance for the individual to show why the action should not be taken. In more serious situations there might be added the right to call witnesses; to know the evidence against oneself; and to have the decision based on the evidence. While cross-examination—a hallmark of the American adversarial model—seems by its nature a separate sort of right, it is, as Judge Friendly acknowledged, the most time-consuming, tedious, and often least productive part of the model. Likewise (and as Justice White noted in *Wolff* v. *McDonnell*), there are times and places where cross-examination is just not possible. Additional factors may be necessary in the most serious situations, Friendly continued, including the right to counsel (about which the Supreme Court continues to be ambiguous);

the right to a record and statement of reasons for the decision; public attendance; and judicial review.

Friendly's purpose was a purely practical one. He was attempting to rescue the Supreme Court and give it a sane framework so that it could actually adapt quickly and easily. He used as his starting point the dictum in *Cafeteria Workers* v. *McElroy* (1961) that the degree of due process granted to any individual varies according to the relative gravity of individual versus state interests in that deprivation. Friendly contended that there was a sliding scale of rights that would apply differently in cases of varying seriousness. The difficulty, of course, occurs in the application, even as it does in *Cafeteria Workers* v. *McElroy*, which elicited dissenting opinions on the facts presented.

What Judge Friendly had recognized was that many of the elements of traditional American-style due process are in some respects counterproductive to the ultimate goal of reaching a decision that is as fair as possible with respect to both the individual and society. As the English judge Lord Loreburn said in 1911,

> I need not add that courts must act in good faith and listen to both sides, for that is a duty to anyone who decides anything. But I do not think they are bound to treat such a question as though it were sacred. They can obtain information, though it is best always to give a fair opportunity for relevant statements to those who are parties in the controversy. A hearing in essence demands that he who is entitled to it, shall have the right to support his allegations by arguments, however brief, and if need be, by proof however informal.

The problems involved in the confrontation of witnesses and cross-examination, as discussed in *Wolff* v. *McDonnell,* are rarely mentioned in the public housing cases or school cases where they are equally important. *Wolff* v. *McDonnell* raises the issue of whether or not the prisoner shall be able to question his accusers, guards, and other prisoners. The court makes the point that allowing for too much legalism and too much confrontation in the hearing can disrupt the institution as well as endanger other prisoners. Certainly this is also true about public housing, where the main problem in eviction cases involves tenants who do not want to talk about their neighbors for fear of reprisals.

Judge Marvin Frankel observed ten years ago that it is a fallacy to view all these procedural devices as intended solely to elicit truth. He pointed out that in fact lawyers use many of these procedural devices to keep information away from the fact-finder. Frankel noted that one of the major flaws of the adversarial process is that seeking the truth is not, in fact, the principal goal of parties in an American-style adversary hearing.

It is of no little interest that both Judge Friendly and Judge Frankel—considered among the best of both the appellate and trial benches—expressed admiration for the speedier, more informal, more flexible style of hearings common to European countries (unfortunately referred to in this country as the "inquisitorial" system), and somewhat wistfully expressed the hope that such methods might be tried here. Both Frankel and Friendly quote extensively from the work of Professor Bernard Schwartz and H. W. R. Wade, who advised that English lawyers should study American procedures in order to avoid the problems of cumbersome rigidity and potential for error in our system. To quote Lord Diplock's introduction to Schwartz and Wade: "The main value of such a study is to observe the horrible American examples of over-judicialization of administrative procedures and undue extension of judicial review and to learn not to do likewise."

Benefiting from the European Example

As Schwartz and Wade and others have observed, the English system (and most other European systems) of administrative law place little emphasis on adversarial methods. Rather, administrative hearings in social welfare settings are usually conducted by a lay judge, rather than a lawyer; and neither the government nor the individual is represented by counsel. Such a system is made possible by the ability of the English magistrate (as in many other countries) to be the most active participant in the hearing. It is he rather than the parties who conducts examination of witnesses and brings forth the evidence, eliminating the need for awkward rules of evidence or the cumbersome process of examination and cross-examination.

Perhaps the most notable difference between the American and English administrative processes is the dominant role played in the former by the legal profession. The use of laymen without legal representation as adjudicators, a practice that obtains in a number of British tribunals, is practically unknown in the United States. Even more important is the absence in America of a tradition of lay magistracy and lay tribunals such as that so firmly ingrained in British law.

By keeping their fact-finding system non-adversarial, European administrative hearings avoid the necessity of having lawyers play a dominant role in fact-finding and the resolution of disputes. An important reason for the growth in the complexity and rigidity of American due process hearings has been the activism of lawyers, particularly those in public interest organizations. Public interest lawyers have contributed much to protecting and defending the interests of those who would otherwise have no access to the legal system at all. But in the case of administrative due process they have, with the best of intentions, played a major role in creating an adjudicatory system so complicated and cumbersome that too often nobody benefits from its supposed protections.

Charles Reich once wrote, in an article subsequent to "The New Property," of the "desperate need for more lawyers" to help defend helpless citizens. Less than a decade later, an unsigned note in the Harvard Law Review would express a very different attitude toward public-interest lawyers:

The fact that these public interest lawyers often themselves select the interest to be represented provides another difficulty because the lawyer is not subject to any mechanism of accountability to insure his loyalty to scattered individuals whose interest he purportedly represents. Since there is no ready mechanism for establishing what is the preponderant interest of the day there is a danger that the lawyer will not advocate the interests of the greater class of the broad constituency supposedly represented, but rather his own perception of those of a few active members of that constituency. Public interest lawyers representing unorganized interests—and many of the cases are unorganized—have a marked personal preference for formal processes of decision including judicial review because a considerable portion of the psychological reward they receive for their work may depend upon a high visibility of their efforts and because dramatic court victories may assist fund-raising efforts.

The observation that public interest lawyers prefer formal procedures is accurate: That is the milieu in which they are educated and the environment in which they operate. As Harvard President Derek Bok recently observed, lawyers are trained "more for conflict than for the gentler arts of reconciliation and accommodation." Of course, such training is understandable, since these ideas of conflict and argument are central to the adversarial system—the faith that two enemies slugging it out before a passive observer is the best method of producing correct decisions. Perhaps in traditional civil or criminal litigation that faith is justified. In a typical case involving the provision or denial of benefits from an administrative social welfare agency, however, the pressure of counsel often seems to have the effect of converting an administrative hearing from a convocation of persons with the same general concerns into a formalized war of words and procedures, where neither judge nor prosecutor has any incentive, nor is even permitted, to help the defendant or be interested in his welfare. (Indeed, a lawyer's affection for formalized procedure appears to begin early. Last year, when hundreds of students at Harvard Law School turned out to protest a minor new rule about grades, they were heard chanting "*Goldberg* v.

Kelly"—meaning, of course, that the rule had been instated with insufficient regard for due process.)

When one compares the due process analysis of Judge Friendly with that of Schwartz and Wade, it becomes increasingly clear that the only necessary element of genuine due process in any individual case may be the presence of a tribunal which is unbiased and which has access to all the relevant information. The additional elements outlined by Judge Friendly, once the European model is examined, are revealed as little more than artificial devices to make up for the fact that the American judge or hearing officer is crippled by his passivity, by statute, or by tradition.

In Europe, by contrast, the hearing officer must produce his own evidence, ask his own questions, and call his own witnesses. The advocates present on either side are there merely to ensure that the hearing examiner does his own job fully and adequately, since he and he alone is responsible for finding all evidence and reaching a rational and justified result. The procedure is quite informal, resembling a discussion among parties all interested in obtaining truth and reaching accurate decisions. It is viewed as inappropriate to consider the parties in such administrative cases as adversaries at war with each other.

Such an approach seems ideally suited for public housing authorities, child welfare agencies, state adoption agencies, juvenile courts, and other agencies whose principal role is to be supportive of the people they are being paid to help, rather than being forced into the role of adversaries to the recipients of their benefits.

The key element in such a system would be a corps of truly independent examiners charged with reviewing each case of proposed termination of benefits. Such a group of examiners (they need not be lawyers—indeed it would be better if they were not) might well minimize the number of erroneous agency deprivations, and at substantially less cost, since the number of formal trial-type hearings would be reduced greatly.

American Adaptations

There are several promising experiments in flexible, speedy, delawyerized community justice now being carried out across the country. One of the oldest such programs is the Rochester (N.Y.) Center for Dispute Settlement, now in active operation for more than a decade. The center's emphasis is on settlement of problems through mediation and arbitration, in a non-adversarial setting, and it has been successful in doing so in many kinds of social service settings. For example, under a contract with the Rochester Housing Authority, the center has established a grievance procedure for public housing tenants. When disputes arise, tenants can take their complaints to an informal grievance program. If informal mediation fails to resolve the problem, the matter can be taken to a three-member arbitration panel. A measure of the program's success is that since 1981, 37 such hearings have been held with agreement reached. In eight of these, evictions have been agreed upon, and only two of those were appealed to the state courts; in both cases the agreements have been upheld.

A similar approach is taken by the Community Boards program in San Francisco. Started six years ago by attorney Raymond Shonholtz, the program follows European patterns by using citizen volunteers to hear, in an informal atmosphere, both criminal and civil complaints that have not already gone into the standard criminal or civil justice system. The program emphasizes small interpersonal disputes, but has handled landlord-tenant problems of all kinds. The community board program reports that about 85 percent of all the agreements arrived at are honored by the parties without further problems or resort to the court system—and in the past two years the 20 boards have heard more cases than the city's Municipal Court.

In the area of social service, the New York City Housing Authority has had remarkable success with its six-year-old Application Review Board, which provides an informal review for applicants who are turned down for public housing. The board, composed of three housing authority officials from the departments not connected with tenant selection, hears the complaints of those who think their applications were unfairly rejected. This is no small task. The New York City Housing Authority receives 29,000 applications for housing each year, of which 6,000 are rejected for a variety of reasons. All those who are rejected are given an opportunity to appeal the decision to the Application Review Board, and in 1983 a total of 911 rejected applications were reviewed by the board. Of those reviewed, 240 decisions were reversed, 240 were upheld, and the rest were remanded to the authority's tenant selection department for further study. Those who are ultimately rejected by the board may, of course, take their cases to the state courts—but officials report that only a very small percentage of board-rejected applicants ever do so.

The housing authority's board is far from being a rubber-stamp for the bureaucracy's decisions, and board chairman Arthur Wohl is universally admired as a hard-working, fair, and sympathetic adjudicator. The review board's efficiency is shown by the fact that the average turnover time for each appeal board case—from the time the review request is filed to the completion of the board's decision and disposition of the case—is only 60 days.

How to Rescue Due Process

That such local experiments can work successfully in varied and difficult settings is strong support for the idea that informal, flexible, delawyerized administrative adjudication could be adopted broadly in settling the disputes, large and small, that arise out of social service programs and other public agencies.

Such a corps of European-style "investigatory" judges might well be useful in almost every sort of administrative mass justice category—from school discipline to public housing to welfare payments—that is now handled under the complicated, confusing, and counter-productive guidelines for due process set up by the Supreme Court. Such a system could eliminate the need for constant multiyear litigation over such fine points as the theoretical burden of proof in a parental termination of rights hearing (*Santosky*) or the right of a school teacher to spank a student (*Ingraham* v. *Wright*, 1977).

In addition, a uniformly simple, quick, and informal system of examiners might well increase access to due process (while decreasing its burden on government agencies) in many ways: first, by materially increasing the chances that every individual case, no matter how small, can be accurately and fairly decided more proximately to the moment of deprivation; second, by preserving a simple record of evidence and judgment on which later appeal tribunals, if necessary, could confidently rely; third, by reducing the cost in time and money to government agencies for the conduct of due process hearings, thereby reducing disincentives to those agencies to provide hearings; and fourth, by providing a standard of uniformity and consistency—altogether lacking in the past decade—so that agencies and individuals alike will be more likely to know what their course of behavior ought to be, in advance of the need for a hearing.

While such a proposal may sound unrealistic, there are in fact precedents for it. At the turn of the last century many legal scholars despaired over the bewildering chaos of differing state laws and settled precedents in such areas as commercial contracts law or probate of wills; yet since that time the Uniform Commercial Code, the Uniform Probate Code, and many similar attempts at making specific categories of law unified and rational have had an immensely beneficial effect on the resolution of such legal disputes. It is not unrealistic at all to believe that an organization such as the American Law Institute, or perhaps an individual state, could be encouraged to develop a comprehensive new approach to due process that would achieve the goals of both efficiency and fair treatment.

We might begin by breaking down the supposed fences that exist between liberals and conservatives on the issue of due process. Instead of focusing on the Supreme Court's seemingly endless concern over whether too little or too much due process is being provided in individual cases, we should perhaps focus on the ways in which it may be provided without causing public agencies to drown under its weight. This should satisfy both the "liberal" concern with fairness and the "conservative" desire for efficiency.

"In Heaven there will be no law," observed the legal philosopher Grant Gilmore in 1974, "and the lion will lie down with the lamb.... In Hell there will be nothing but law, and due process will be meticulously observed." Professor Gilmore, himself a staunch advocate of the Bill of Rights, surely was not speaking of the idea of due process, but rather of the manner in which our legal system attempts to enforce it at immense pain and little gain to all parties involved. It is a manner which may debase the very idea that it seeks to uphold. That we must provide due process, the most simple and basic of our ancient liberties, to all who require it is beyond doubt; but how much better it would be if we could find a way to enforce it while striving, in Gilmore's terms, toward heaven rather than hell.

NOTES

1. David J. Rothman, "The State as Parent," *Doing Good: The Limits of Benevolence* (Pantheon Books: 1978), p. 172.
2. Charles Reich, "The New Property," *Yale Law Journal*, vol. 73, pp. 733–787.
3. Jerry Mashaw, "The Management Side of Due Process," *Cornell Law Review*, vol. 59 (1974), p. 772.

Study Questions

1. Fuerst and Petty align the two concerns of individual rights and social needs with conservatives and liberals. Which goes with which? Do you agree with Fuerst and Petty? Why? Defend your position.
2. Can you think of any counterexamples of the alignment of concern for social needs

with conservatives and the concern for individual rights with liberals? Discuss.

3. Do Fuerst and Petty agree or disagree with the expansion of due process in the juvenile justice system? Why? Do you agree with the authors' argument here? Why? Defend your position.

4. What components of a fair hearing are identified by Judge Henry Friendly? Do you think that cross-examination is an indispensable component of due process procedure? Would it be justifiable for a judge or arbitrator to make a determination in a trial or hearing on the basis of facts that were not presented as evidence in the hearing? Why? Defend your position.

5. Are Fuerst and Petty fundamentally opposed to the concept of due process? Explain. Do you agree with the authors? Why? Defend your position.

Duty to Intervene: An Officer's Dilemma

BENJAMIN B. FERRELL

OFFICERS HAVE THE RESPONSIBILITY to enforce the law and are accorded certain privileges in carrying out their duties. They may restrain liberty, invade privacy, and use physical force in appropriate situations. The exercise of these privileges is limited to those occasions in which they are required or authorized by law and must always be exercised by the officer in a reasonable manner. When an officer in carrying out his or her duties exceeds the limits of the privilege their actions are themselves wrongful and subject to restraint by other officers. Such wrongful acts by officers may not be a criminal violation, but they are often tortious and will give rise to a civil cause of action. This article examines the legal duty of an officer to intervene and stop the wrongful actions of other officers and the legal consequences that may result from such failure to so intervene.

A cause of action for failure to intervene may arise under common law tort principles and federal statutes. The federal statute most commonly involved in such actions is the Civil Rights Act, Title 42 United States Code section 1983.[1] This article will concentrate primarily on those events which have resulted in litigation filed pursuant to this statute. Certain threshold elements must be present in any situation to give rise to a cause of action under section 1983. These essential elements include actions taken by a person acting under the "color of state law" and the deprivation of a constitutional right. In addition the courts have held section 1983 "should be read against the background of tort liability," thus the usual case filed under section 1983 involves common law tort actions which have risen to constitutional proportions (Monroe, 365 U.S. 167)[2]

Therefore, if an officer is alleged to have failed to intervene to halt the wrongful actions of a fellow officer and those actions are of constitutional proportions, litigation may be

Benjamin B. Ferrell, "Duty to Intervene: An Officer's Dilemma," Journal of Contemporary Criminal Justice, *vol. 4:2 (May 1988), pp. 93–105. Used by permission of the publisher. Footnotes have been renumbered.*

brought under section 1983. Those actions which are wrongful, but not of constitutional proportions, may give rise to a cause of action under the tort laws of the state in which they occurred. Regardless of the law under which the suit is filed or the forum which decides the controversy, the officer who fails to intervene may be liable for such failure.

The liability of the nonfeasor officer for failing to intervene is not premised on the doctrine of respondent superior. The law considers an officer who neglects his duty in such a situation to be a direct participant in the tortious act (Davidson, 367 F.Supp. 482).[3]

General Principle of Law

The recognized rule in section 1983 cases in which claims are based upon the officers failing to intervene to protect the plaintiff from other officers who violate plaintiff's rights was pronounced in Byrd v. Brishke (466 F.2nd 6).[4] This case decided in 1972 by the United States Court of Appeals, Seventh Circuit, is regularly cited by the courts as the leading case on this point. The officers in this case denied the subject medical aid, beat and physically abused him, falsely accused him of violating the law, and held him in a police facility for forty-eight hours. Plaintiff based his damage claims upon the theory that even if the officers did not personally participate by beating him, they were liable in law for negligently or intentionally failing to protect the plaintiff from other officers who did violate his rights by beating him in their presence. Chief Judge Swygert in his opinion wrote:

> We believe it is clear that one who is given the badge of authority of a police officer may not ignore the duty imposed by his office and fail to stop other officers who summarily punish a third person in his presence or otherwise within his knowledge. That responsibility obviously obtains when the nonfeasor is a supervisory officer to whose direction the misfeasor officers are committed. So, too, the same responsibility must exist as to nonsupervisory officers who

are present at the scene of such summary punishment, for to hold otherwise would be to insulate nonsupervisory officers from liability for reasonably forseeable consequences of the neglect of their duty to enforce the laws and preserve the peace.

There are no opinions by the United States Supreme Court on this point, but the court has on numerous occasions denied certiorari in cases which have followed the Byrd principle.

Intervention

Certain conditions must exist to bring the principles of intervention to bear on an event. There must be a misfeasor officer,[5] who violates some protected right, a subject to whom the right belongs, and a nonfeasor officer who has the duty to stop the misfeasor from violating the rights of the subject. An officer has the duty of intervening to enforce the law whether the misfeasor is another officer or a citizen, however, this article treats only those situations involving misfeasor and nonfeasor officers.

The action of the misfeasor officers in Byrd was to "summarily punish a third person." The conduct calling for intervention is not so narrowly limited and other cases have applied the principle to various infringements of protected rights. Officer brutality is the most obvious misfeasance calling for intervention, but causes of action for failure to intervene may arise in illegal searches, arrests, and due process violations as well as investigations, pursuits, property deprivation, and a host of other situations where protected interests exist.

A subject charging that a nonfeasor officer violated his rights by failing to act affirmatively to prevent a misfeasor officer from acting assumes the misfeasor acted in a manner that violated the subject's rights. In Richardson v. City of Indianapolis (658 8 F.2nd 494)[7] the plaintiff claimed the non-shooting defendants violated the decedent's rights by failing to act affirmatively to prevent another officer from shooting the decedent. The court noting that the jury properly determined there was no violation of the decedent's civil rights by the officer who fired held there could be no liability on the part of the nonshooters for failure to prevent what the jury had determined was not a violation.

A general rule of tort law is that one is not liable for failing to act unless there is a legal duty to act. A nonfeasor officer, therefore, must have a duty to act in order to be liable for a failure to intervene. This duty to act exists as a matter of law if the nonfeasor is an officer (Byrd, 466 F.2nd 6). Occasions do arise in which the status of a nonfeasor is pertinent to the question of whether a duty to act exists. The dividing line appears to be when the individual assumes the "badge of authority" and accepts the duty to enforce the law. A trainee, not yet a sworn officer, on the scene for the purpose of familiarizing himself with police procedures and scheduled to become a member of the force the next day retained the status of a private citizen. "Thus, his conduct did not amount to state action. No basis existed for recovery under section 1983" (Russ, 538 F.2nd 799).[8] There was no basis for common law tort recovery as there was no evidence of any unlawful or negligent conduct on the trainee's part, as he had assumed no duty to protect the subject (Russ, 538 F.2nd 799).

The wrongful act of the misfeasor officer must be "in the presence" or "within the knowledge" of the nonfeasor officer (Byrd, 466 F.2nd 11). What constitutes "in the presence" is not limited to the immediate presence of the nonfeasor officer if he requested the assistance of the misfeasor officer and participated with him in some of the steps leading up to the tortious act. In Simms v. Reiner (419 F.Supp. 468)[9] Sheriff Knutell was refused admittance to a house to serve a civil warrant. He summoned assistance and Officer Reiner responded and was also refused admittance. Officer Reiner kicked open a door and entered the house. Officer Reiner encountered the plaintiff in the house and during an ensuing scuffle shot him.

There was no evidence (in Simms) that Sheriff Knutell physically abused the plaintiff, was armed, or was in the immediate presence of Officer Reiner or the plaintiff. The evidence did

establish, however, that the sheriff directly requested the assistance of Officer Reiner, was in his presence when Reiner entered the house without plaintiff's consent and followed him some distance into the house. The court held the officers had no right to make a forcible entry to serve a civil warrant even after being refused admittance. And in regard to Sheriff Knutell wrote, ". . . one who is given the badge of authority may not ignore the duty imposed by his office and assist or fail to stop other officers who engage in an unlawful entry or who summarily punish third persons in his presence or otherwise within his knowledge (Simms, 419 F.Supp. 468).

Officers, however, who did not help plan a raid or carry it out and who were not aware of the circumstances and whose involvement was limited to watching the side and rear of the house were not liable as they were not in any position to stop the misfeasor officers from making an unlawful entry (Hamrick, 439 F.Supp. 1170).[10] The burden is on the plaintiff to prove the presence or knowledge of the nonfeasor officer (Bracey, 494 F.2nd 571).[11]

While the tortious conduct must be in the presence or within the knowledge of the nonfeasor officer mere presence at the scene is not sufficient to impose liability. The nonfeasor officer must through his own conduct contribute to the violation of the subject's rights. Contributing conduct, however, may be an act of omission the same as an act of commission (Smith, 482 F.2nd 33).[12] Officers who were present when a subject was beaten, but were not personally involved in the administration of the beatings were nevertheless subject to liability for their "inaction" (Bruner, 684 F.2nd 422).[13] An officer, who did not strike the subject, but who was present and had knowledge of the beating by other officers is a participant if he "acquiesced" in it (Davidson, 386 F.Supp. 482).

An officer who functioned as a full partner in an investigation, accompanied the misfeasor officer to the subject's home, helped make an unlawful arrest and made no attempt to stop the physical abuse by the misfeasor officer is subject to liability for failing to intervene. The nonfeasor's "failure to intervene or object encouraged the illegal conduct of his partner" and "directly contributed to the violation of plaintiff's constitutional rights." (Schiller, 540 F.Supp. 605)[14]

The nonfeasor officer to be liable must have had time to perceive the nature and extent of the conduct and time to take some action to halt the wrongful deeds of the misfeasor officer. In Russ v. Ratliff (538 F.2nd 799) the appellate court upheld a jury verdict in favor of a highway patrolman for failing to intervene when a police officer shot and killed a prisoner. The evidence according to the appellate court revealed the entire incident lasted only a few seconds and the misfeasor's action in drawing and firing the weapon "stunned" the nonfeasor officer. The court opinions clearly draw a distinction between a situation where there was time for the other officers to intervene and those where the officers could not have intervened because the challenged events occurred within a few seconds (Richardson, 658 F.2nd 494).

The failure of a nonfeasor officer to intervene in the wrongful acts of a misfeasor may be the result of an intentional decision not to act or a negligent failure to take appropriate action. Whether the failure to act was intentional or the result of negligence the nonfeasor officer may be liable for failure to intervene. "While intentional torts ordinarily require some affirmative conduct, purposeful nonfeasance can also serve as the basis of liability for an intentional tort if the defendant owes the plaintiff a duty to act." (Bonner, 545 F.2nd 658;[15] Bruette, 554 F.Supp. 301)[16]

A failure to act which is not intentional raises the usual questions of fact and law involved in a negligence case. In a cause of action brought under Title 42 United States Code Section 1983 there must not only be a tort, but it must also be a tort of constitutional proportions. The degree of negligence required to establish a constitutional tort must be "gross negligence" (White, 592 F.2nd 381)[17] to the rights of the subject. The degree of negligence required was well stated in Anderson v. City of New York (657 F.Supp. 1571).[18]

Supervisory personnel have been found liable, based on a single violative incident, if they are present during the incident and fail to stop behavior violative of constitutional rights. Such failure to supervise, of so "grossly negligent" that it can be termed "deliberate indifference," can be of constitutional magnitude. Owen v. Haas, 601 F.2d 1242, 1247 (2d Cir.), cert. denied, 444 U.S. 980, 100 S.Ct 483, 62 L.Ed.2d 407(1979); Cattan, supra, 523 F.Supp. at 600-01. While this duty to supervise is most clearly attributable to supervisory personnel, it falls upon any officer witnessing unconstitutional behavior. (McQurter, 572 F.Supp. at 1415.)[19]

In determining a question of negligent failure to intervene the conduct of the nonfeasor officer is measured by the standard of reasonableness (Jennings, 476 F. 2nd 1275)[20]

A crucial consideration, in determining if an officer acted reasonably in failing to intervene, is what he knew or should have known about the situation and the actions of the misfeasor officer. An officer who participates in the planning of an operation or is fully informed as to the situation or whose actions help create the situation is in a more precarious legal predicament than one who must decide whether to assist or restrain his fellow officer from what he perceives after arrival on the scene (Hamrick, 539 F.Supp. 170; Schiller, 540 F.Supp. 605).

In Gagnon v. Ball (696 F.2nd 17)[21] Officers Ball and Laplaca were on a routine patrol together. Mrs. Gagnon ran toward their vehicle, waving a pellet gun, and shouting to the officers to "get" a man in a departing vehicle that had tried to assault her. Ball disarmed Mrs. Gagnon and without further inquiry arrested her and took her to headquarters. Mrs. Gagnon brought suit against both officers alleging that her constitutional rights had been denied by an unlawful arrest. The jury returned a verdict against both officers and the appellate court in upholding the verdict noted that Laplaca not only declined to intercede but also assisted Officer Ball in detaining her. In this case both officers observed the entire episode.

A different result was obtained in a case where an officer arrived on the scene in the middle of a noisy fracas unaware of what had occurred prior to his arrival and following the order of his superior made an arrest. The judge in deciding in favor of the arresting officer, primarily based his decision on the following of an order of a superior, but did note the officer was not present when the disturbance started (Vela, 703 F.2nd 147).[22] Whether an officer is fully aware of all the happenings is immaterial if he is able to make a determination from what can be observed after his arrival on the scene. If a suspect is subdued and under control when the officer arrives, but is still being subjected to excessive force and in need of medical assistance the failure to intervene may result in liability (McQurter, 572 F.Supp. 1401).

One clear cut situation in which liability will result is when a subject is undergoing custodial interrogation in the presence of several officers, poses no threat to their safety, and initiates no action. In this situation no officer could reasonably fail to intervene if another officer exerted physical force (Ware, 709 F.2nd 345).[23]

The affirmative duty of an officer to preserve law and order, and to protect the safety of persons in the community is applicable to all officers in all situations regardless of organizational rank, command position, or scene control directives. The duty to stop officers who punish or otherwise violate a person's rights clearly exists when the nonfeasor officer is a supervisory officer, but the same responsibility exists as to nonsupervisory officers who are present at the scene (Byrd, 466 F.2nd 11; Skevotilax, 586 F.Supp. 543).[24] This responsibility to intervene by nonsupervisory officers exists even if the misfeasor officer is a superior (Webb, 713 F.2nd 408).[25] It should also be noted that midlevel supervisors and lower echelon officers who are present when a misfeasor officer is violating a protected right are not relieved of responsibility to intervene because a superior officer on the scene fails to halt the wrongful conduct of the misfeasor (McQurter, 572 F.Supp. 1401). The courts have made no distinctions based upon hierarchical interests where federal, state, or local agencies or departments are all involved in the same incident (Coffy, 600 F.2nd 570;[26] Richardson, 658 F.2nd 494).

A confrontation in which the act of the misfeasor officer demands intervention to halt his wrongful conduct inevitably evokes other questions. How much and what type of intervention is required by the nonfeasor officer to meet the requirements of duty? Byrd and other cases make it plain there is a duty to intervene but they do not explicitly deal with the extent or type of intervention required (Putnam, 639 F.2nd 423).[27] The dilemma of the officer on the scene, especially if the misfeasor is a superior, is not eased by court decisions written from the perspective of declaring a positive duty to accomplish a negative result—an affirmative duty to prevent the commission of a wrongful deed. And the dilemma is further complicated in that the affirmative act may be one of omission as well as commission.

The guiding principle is the nonfeasor officer must do whatever is REASONABLE under the circumstances to halt the wrongful conduct of the misfeasor (Ware, 709 F.2nd 345). A rule of reasonableness is never specific, but it is a rule officers live with every day of their professional lives. Fortunately, officers do not usually have to be right to avoid liability, but they must always be reasonable. Just what is reasonable will depend on the facts and circumstances unless the situation is so gross as to constitute unreasonable conduct as a matter of law. It can be said, however, that no matter what the situation it is unreasonable for an officer to be non-observant or indifferent to the acts of his fellow officers. He must attempt to find out what has been going on and think out what his responsibilities are in the situation (McQurter, 572 F.Supp. 1401).

The sufficiency of an affirmative effort to intervene has not been an issue in most cases. The predominate situation in litigation is there was no effort at all to intervene. And courts have repeatedly noted the nonfeasor "failed to take any action" (King, 541 F.Supp. 1234);[28] "made no attempt" (Schiller, 540 F.Supp. 605); "made no objection" (Schiller 540 F.Supp. 605); "acquiesced" (Davidson, 386 F.Supp. 482); "declined to intercede" (Gagnon, 696 F.2nd 21); or "did not aid" (Skevotilax, 586 F.Supp. 542) while only a few cases have weighed the sufficiency of some action. In McQurter, one of the few cases, the court ruled that a mere question by the supervisory officer to a subordinate "if he wanted to get up off of him" was viewed as a failure by the superior to perform his duty (McQurter, 572 F.Supp. 1408). A reading of many cases leads one to conclude that some affirmative act, even though unsuccessful, might be considered reasonable under the circumstances. It is the complete failure by the nonfeasor officer to make any effort to stop the wrongful acts of the misfeasor that is sure to result in an adverse judicial decision.

An officer not present during a misfeasor's use of excessive force may arrive to find an injured subject in need of medical attention. "Prevailing standards of police work in this country today require that the officer on the scene render first aid to any injured subject and obtain the presence on the scene of any emergency professionals needed to assist in more aggravated cases." A failure to respond with the needed first aid treatment or to summon medical assistance is a neglect of duty likely to result in a liability judgment (McQurter, 572 F.Supp. 1408).

Circumstances often arise in which an officer to act in a reasonable manner must prioritize his actions. Performance of other tasks or duties, even though appropriate and needed, will not absolve an officer of the duty to intervene to halt a deprivation of rights. Crowd control, for example, at the scene of many arrests and accidents is a necessary and proper concern, but an officer may not shun his duty to intervene by merely engaging in the performance of another duty. The temper, conduct, and size of the crowd have, of course, a substantial influence on the sequence of the actions a reasonable officer should follow. An officer who encounters a small crowd that is not hostile or riotous but merely boisterous must make his paramount concern the constitutional rights of the subject (McQurter, 572 F. Supp. 1408).

The usual happenings giving rise to the duty to intervene involve a wrongful or illegal act by a misfeasor officer. There are occasions, however, when the result of the performance of a lawful duty in a lawful manner results in a third person being placed in jeopardy. When such jeopardy is created by the officers there is a duty to intervene and resolve the dangerous condition. A duty to intervene is clearly present when officers leave small children unattended in an automobile following the arrest of the driver. In such a situation the officers could not avoid knowing that, without their assistance, the small children would be exposed to weather and danger from traffic. This indifference in the face of known dangers constitutes gross negligence (White, 592 F.2nd 385).

Sometimes the best of intentions go awry and the officer carrying out a duty to intervene to halt the wrongful actions of a misfeasor negligently injures a bystander. An officer using force to intervene may be liable to a third person injured in the process. In such a situation the amount of force that would be reasonable in carrying out the duty to intervene is of critical importance. If the claim is asserted under Title 42 United States Code Section 1983, the tortious act injuring the bystander must rise to the level of a constitutional tort. The courts in making this determination will consider the amount of force exerted by the officer in carrying out his duty to intervene. Several factors must be considered in deciding if the intervening officer has negligently crossed the constitutional line. The factors which must be weighed include "the need for the application of force, the relationship between the need and the amount of force that was used, the extent of the injury inflicted, and whether force was applied in a good faith effort to maintain or restore discipline or maliciously and sadistically for the very purpose of causing harm" (Johnson, 481 F.2nd 1028).[29]

If the injury to the bystander is not of an aggravated nature and the force used to intervene is necessary, reasonable, limited and relatively controlled under the circumstances the tort will not be of constitutional dimensions and there will be no liability under the federal statute (Brudney, 414 F.Supp. 1190).[30]

Tortious wrongs give rise to a state law tort action regardless of the constitutional determination. State law tort liability is determined by the law of the state in which the tort occurred. While there exists some variations in the states the weight of authority holds an officer is liable for damages if he negligently injures a person by the exertion of force without the exercise of due care (Silver, p. 1–38).[31]

An officer is not relieved of the duty to intervene even though the failure to do so is caused by following the orders of a superior (King, 541 F.Supp. 1235). Although acting or failing to act pursuant to orders is not a defense in and of itself it may be relevant to a claim of good faith and the defense of qualified immunity (Putnam, 639 F.2nd 422). A defendant officer to establish a good faith qualified immunity in failing to intervene must have been reasonable in such failure and not have had any personal ill-will or malice toward the subject. An officer arriving on the scene in the midst of a fracas and ordered by a superior to arrest a suspect and observing no reasons to believe the arrest is not legal would not be liable for failing to intervene in the wrongful arrest or in making the arrest as ordered (Vela, 703 F.2nd 152).

Remedies

The remedies available in a failure to intervene cause of action may be equitable or legal and may be sought under state law or applicable federal statute (Schnell, 407 F.2nd 1086).[32] The equitable remedy most often sought is an injunction directing some action by a governmental entity, but individual officers may also be named as defendants. If the officer has a duty to prevent other officers from committing acts which deprive the subject of constitutional rights and fails to so halt the wrongful conduct the officer is a proper defendant in a case in which an equitable remedy is sought (Schnell, 407 F.2nd 1086).

Legal damages, which is the awarding of money to compensate the aggrieved party, may

be of three types: nominal, compensatory, and punitive. An officer who fails to intervene is considered a participant in the tort and thus a joint tortfeasor. The rule recognized in most state jurisdictions is that compensatory damages may not be apportioned among joint tortfeasors (20 ALR 3d 668).[33] Thus the successful plaintiff may look to one or all or any number of the defendants to satisfy his judgment. In a case filed under Title 42 United States Code Section 1983 federal law governs damage questions, but the same rule generally followed in the states is also followed in the United States courts (Davidson, 386 F.Supp. 482).

There is a wider divergence of opinion as to whether in an action against joint tortfeasors punitive damages may be apportioned against them. In those jurisdictions which apportion punitive damages the amount depends upon the differing degree of culpability or the existence or nonexistence of actual malice on the part of the defendants (20 ALR 3d 668). Thus where punitive damages are justified, but the degree of culpability is different, the amount of damages may differ among the joint tortfeasors and no punitive damages may be awarded against some of the defendants (20 ALR 3d 668).

Some jurisdictions have taken the view that punitive damages may not be apportioned among joint tortfeasors. In these jurisdictions punitive damages may not be awarded in varying amounts against some of the defendants and no damages against other defendants. Under this rule if punitive damages are justified against some defendants, but not others, the plaintiff may not recover against any of the jointly sued tortfeasors (20 ALR 3d 668).

The preferable rule in the United States courts is that each of the jointly sued tortfeasor's conduct will be independently assessed and punitive damages awarded against each one (Davidson, 386 F.Supp. 482).

When a municipal corporation is one of the defendants in a Title 42 United States Code Section 1983 action the general rule of joint and several liability applies so far as compensatory damages are concerned. A municipal defendant is not, however, liable for punitive damages in a suit brought under the federal statute (City of Newport, 453 U.S. 247).[34]

Conclusion

When an officer arrives on the scene and finds a fellow officer applying physical force against a subject the responding officer is in a dilemma. He must decide if his fellow officer needs assistance in subduing the subject or should he restrain his comrade from further violating the subject's constitutional rights. The duty imposed by the law is not changed if the first officer on the scene is superior to the responding officer, but one can easily see the growth of the dilemma if a junior officer responds and finds his supervisor applying what may be excessive force. The law, however, is clear that if an officer is using excessive force other officers on the scene have the duty to stop such action.

When and how officers should respond to this dilemma is a subject which needs much thought and consideration by the law enforcement community. The law thus far has been developed by intermediate appellate courts. The reported cases usually involve deliberate and gross violations of constitutional rights and no responses whatever by the observing officers. While the courts will not tolerate gross violations of constitutional rights they will weigh the actions of officers by the standard of reasonableness. Law enforcement agencies by developing regulations and training directives in how to handle this difficult dilemma could have a persuasive influence on what actions the courts find reasonable under the circumstances, especially in those encounters which fall in the grey area of questionable gross or deliberate indifference. It is only the officer whose life and safety is at risk during the encounter but his response will be evaluated by others in a judicial proceeding. A well thought out procedure by the law enforcement community of how an officer should reasonably respond to this dilemma would receive serious consideration by the courts.

NOTES

1. The Civil Rights Act, 42 United States Code section 1983.

> Every person who, under color of any statute, ordinance, regulation, custom, or usage of any State or Territory, subjects, or causes to be subjected, any citizen of the United States or any other person within the jurisdiction thereof to the deprivation of any rights, privileges, or immunities secured by the Constitution and laws, shall be liable to the party injured in an action at law, suit in equity, or other proper proceeding for redress. . . .

2. *Monroe* v. *Pape*, 365 U.S. 167 (1961).
3. *Davidson* v. *Dixon*, 386 F. Supp. 482 (1974).
4. *Byrd* v. *Brishke*, 466 F. 2d 6 (1972).
5. One who improperly does an otherwise proper or lawful act.
6. One who fails to perform a required duty.
7. *Richardson* v. *City of Indianapolis*, 658 F. 2d 494 (1981).
8. *Russ* v. *Ratliff*, 538 F. 2d 799 (1976).
9. *Simms* v. *Reiner*, 419 F. Supp. 468 (1976).
10. *Hamrick* v. *Lewis*, 539 F. Supp. 1170 (1982).
11. *Bracey* v. *Grenoble*, 494 F. 2d 571 (1974).
12. *Smith* v. *Ross*, 482 F. 2d 33 (1973).
13. *Bruner* v. *Dunaway*, 684 F. 2d 422 (1982).
14. *Schiller* v. *Strangis*, 540 F. Supp. 605 (1982).
15. *Bonner* v. *Coughlin*, 545 F. Supp. 568 (1976).
16. *Bruette* v. *Knope*, 554 F. Supp. 301 (1983).
17. *White* v. *Rochford*, 592 F. 2d 381 (1979).
18. *Anderson* v. *City of New York*, 657 F. Supp. 1571 (1987).
19. *McQurter* v. *City of Atlanta, Ga.* 572 F. Supp. 1401 (1983).
20. *Jennings* v. *Davis*, 476 F. 2d 1275 (1973).
21. *Gagnon* v. *Ball*, 696 F. 2d 21 (1982).
22. *Vela* v. *White*, 703 F. 2d 147 (1983).
23. *Ware* v. *Reed*, 709 F. 2d 345 (1983).
24. *Skevofilax* v. *Quigley*, 586 F. Supp. 543 (1984).
25. *Webb* v. *Hiyekel*, 713 F. 2d 408 (1983).
26. *Coffy* v. *Multi-county Narcotics Bureau*, 600 F. 2d 570 (1979).
27. *Putnam* v. *Gerloff*, 639 F. 2d 423 (1981).
28. *King* v. *Cuyler*, 541 F. Supp. 1234 (1982).
29. *Johnson* v. *Glick*, 481 F. 2d 1028 (1973).
30. *Brudney* v. *Ematrudo*, 414 F. Supp. 1190 (1976).
31. Silver, Isidore, 1987, *Police Civil Liability*, New York: Matthew Bender.
32. *Schnell* v. *City of Chicago*, 407 F. 2d 1086 (1969).
33. Punitive Damages—Apportionment, 20 ALR 666.
34. *City of Newport* v. *Fact Concerts, Inc.*, 453 U.S. 247 (1981).

Study Questions

1. To what does "section 1983" refer? What is the significance of *Byrd* v. *Brishke?* What is the "Byrd" principle?

2. Distinguish between the **misfeasor officer** and the **nonfeasor officer** in a situation involving the violation of a suspect's constitutional rights. Describe some of the conditions that must exist in order for a nonfeasor officer to be liable for failure to intervene.

3. According to Ferrell's discussion, could a junior officer have a supervisory responsibility over his or her superior officer if the superior officer engaged in tortious conduct toward a suspect? Discuss. If an officer fails to intervene because a superior officer gives a command to perform some other action, is the officer thereby relieved of the duty to intervene? Discuss.

4. Suppose that a police officer applies force, but does so without due care, negligently injuring the subject. The subject's claim under section 1983 is rejected because the force used was reasonable. Is the officer still liable for damages? Do you agree? Why? Defend your position.

5. Some persons might regard intervention as a violation of loyalty to one's fellow officers. Is intervening morally an act of loyalty or an act of disloyalty (or neither) in your opinion? Why? Defend your position.

The Bill of Rights

Amendment I

Congress shall make no law respecting an establishment of religion, or prohibiting the free exercise thereof; or abridging the freedom of speech, or of the press, or the right of the people peaceably to assemble, and to petition the Government for a redress of grievances.

Amendment II

A well regulated Militia, being necessary to the security of a free State, the right of the people to keep and bear Arms, shall not be infringed.

Amendment III

No Soldier shall, in time of peace be quartered in any house, without the consent of the Owner, nor in time of war, but in a manner to be prescribed by law.

Amendment IV

The right of the people to be secure in their persons, houses, papers, and effects, against unreasonable searches and seizures, shall not be violated, and no Warrants shall issue, but upon probable cause, supported by Oath or affirmation, and particularly describing the place to be searched, and the persons or things to be seized.

Amendment V

No person shall be held to answer for a capital, or otherwise infamous crime, unless on a presentment or indictment of a Grand Jury, except in cases arising in the land or naval forces, or in the Militia when in actual service in time of War or public danger; nor shall any person be subject for the same offense to be twice put in jeopardy of life or limb, nor shall be compelled in any criminal case to be a witness against himself, nor be deprived of life, liberty, or property, without due process of law; nor shall private property be taken for public use without just compensation.

Amendment VI

In all criminal prosecutions, the accused shall enjoy the right to a speedy and public trial, by an impartial jury of the State and district wherein the crime shall have been committed; which district shall have been previously ascertained by law, and to be informed of the nature and cause of the accusation; to be confronted with the witnesses against him; to have compulsory process for obtaining witnesses in his favor, and to have the assistance of counsel for his defense.

Amendment VII

In Suits at common law, where the value in controversy shall exceed twenty dollars, the right of trial by jury shall be preserved, and no fact tried by a jury shall be otherwise reexamined in any Court of the United States, than according to the rules of the common law.

Amendment VIII

Excessive bail shall not be required, nor excessive fines imposed, nor cruel and unusual punishments inflicted.

Amendment IX

The enumeration in the Constitution of certain rights shall not be construed to deny or disparage others retained by the people.

Amendment X

The powers not delegated to the United States by the Constitution, nor prohibited by it to the States, are reserved to the States respectively, or to the people.

Amendment XIV

Section 1. All persons born or naturalized in the United States and subject to the jurisdiction thereof, are citizens of the United States and of the State wherein they reside. No State shall make or enforce any law which shall abridge the privileges or immunities of citizens of the United States; nor shall any State deprive any person of life, liberty, or property, without due process of law; nor deny to any person within its jurisdiction the equal protection of the laws.

Section 2. Representatives shall be apportioned among the several States according to their respective numbers, counting the whole number of persons in each State, excluding Indians not taxed. But when the right to vote at any election for the choice of electors for President and Vice President of the United States, Representatives in Congress, the Executive and Judicial officers of a State, or the members of the Legislature thereof, is denied to any of the male inhabitants of such State, being twenty-one years of age, and citizens of the United States, or in any way abridged, except for participation in rebellion, or other crime, and basis of representation therein shall be reduced in the proportion which the number of such male citizens shall bear to the whole number of male citizens twenty-one years of age in such State.

Section 3. No person shall be a Senator or Representative in Congress, or elector of President and Vice President, or hold any office, civil or military, under the United States, or under any State, who, having previously taken an oath, as a member of Congress, or as an officer of the United States, or as a member of any State legislature, or as an executive or judicial officer of any State, to support the Constitution of the United States, shall have engaged in insurrection or rebellion against the same, or given aid or comfort to the enemies thereof. But Congress may by a vote of two-thirds of each House, remove such disability.

Section 4. The validity of the public debt of the United States, authorized by law, including debts incurred for payment of pensions and bounties for services in suppressing insurrection or rebellion, shall not be questioned. But neither the United States nor any State shall assume or pay any debt or obligation incurred in aid of insurrection or rebellion against the United States, or any claim for the loss or emancipation of any slave; but all such debts, obligations and claims shall be held illegal and void.

Section 5. The Congress shall have the power to enforce, by appropriate legislation, the provisions of this article.

42 U.S.C. §§ 1981–1983, 1985

§ 1981. EQUAL RIGHTS UNDER THE LAW

All persons within the jurisdiction of the United States shall have the same right in every State and Territory to make and enforce contracts, to sue, be parties, give evidence, and to the full and equal benefit of all laws and proceedings for the security of persons and property as is enjoyed by white citizens, and shall be subject to like punishment, pains, penalties, taxes, licenses, and exactions of every kind, and to no other.

§ 1982. PROPERTY RIGHTS OF CITIZENS

All citizens of the United States shall have the same right, in every State and Territory, as is enjoyed by white citizens thereof to inherit, purchase, lease, sell, hold, and convey real and personal property.

§ 1983. CIVIL ACTION FOR DEPRIVATION OF RIGHTS

Every person who, under color of any statute, ordinance, regulation, custom, or usage, of any State or Territory or the District of Columbia, subjects, or causes to be subjected, any citizen of the United States or other person within the jurisdiction thereof to the deprivation of any rights, privileges, or immunities secured by the Constitution and laws, shall be liable to the party injured in an action at law, suit in equity, or other proper proceeding for redress.

§ 1985. CONSPIRACY TO INTERFERE WITH CIVIL RIGHTS

Preventing officer from performing duties

(1) If two or more persons in any State or Territory conspire to prevent, by force, intimidation, or threat, any person from accepting or holding any office, trust, or place of confidence under the United States, or from discharging any duties thereof; or to induce by like means any officer of the United States to leave any State, district, or place, where his duties as an officer are required to be performed, or to injure him in his person or property on account of his lawful discharge of the duties of his office, or while engaged in the lawful discharge thereof, or to injure his property so as to molest, interrupt, hinder, or impede him in the discharge of his official duties;

Obstructing justice; Intimidating party, witness, or juror

(2) If two or more persons in any State or Territory conspire to deter, by force, intimidation, or threat, any party or witness in any court of the United States from attending such court, or from testifying to any matter pending therein, freely, fully, and truthfully, or to injure such party or witness in his person or property on account of his having so attended or testified, or to influence the verdict, presentment, or indictment of any grand or petit juror in any such court, or to injure such juror in his person or property on account of any verdict, presentment, or indictment lawfully assented to by him, or of his being or having been such juror; or if two or more persons conspire for the purpose of impeding, hindering, obstructing, or defeating, in any manner, the due course of justice in any State or Territory, with intent to deny to any citizen the equal protection of the laws, or to injure him or his property for lawfully enforcing, or attempting to enforce, the right of any person, or class of persons, to the equal protection of the laws;

Depriving persons of rights or privileges

(3) If two or more persons in any State or Territory conspire or go in disguise on the highway or on the premises of another, for the purpose of depriving, either directly or indirectly, any person or class of persons of the equal protection of the laws, or of equal privileges and immunities under the laws; or for the purpose of preventing or hindering the constituted authorities of any State or Territory from giving or securing to all persons within such State or Territory the equal protection of the laws; or if two or more persons conspire to prevent by force, intimidation, or threat, any citizen who is lawfully entitled to vote, from giving his support or advocacy in a legal manner, toward or in favor of the election of any lawfully qualified person as an elector for President or Vice President, or as a Member of Congress of the United States; or to injure any citizen in person or property on account of such support or advocacy; in any case of conspiracy set forth in this section, if one or more persons engaged therein do, or cause to be done, any act in furtherance of the object of such conspiracy, whereby another is injured in his person or property, or deprived of having and exercising any right or privilege of a citizen of the United States, the party so injured or deprived may have an action for the recovery of damages occasioned by such injury or deprivation, against any one or more of the conspirators.

18 U.S.C. §§ 241, 242

§ 241. CONSPIRACY AGAINST RIGHTS OF CITIZENS

If two or more persons conspire to injure, oppress, threaten, or intimidate any citizen in the free exercise or enjoyment of any right or privilege secured to him by the Constitution or laws of the United States, or because of his having so exercised the same; or

If two or more persons go in disguise on the highway, or on the premises of another, with intent to prevent or hinder his free exercise or enjoyment of any right or privilege so secured—

They shall be fined not more than $10,000 or imprisoned not more than ten years, or both; and if death results, they shall be subject to imprisonment for any term of years or for life.

§ 242. DEPRIVATION OF RIGHTS UNDER COLOR OF LAW

Whoever, under color of any law, statute, ordinance, regulation, or custom, willfully subjects any inhabitant of any State, Territory, or District to the deprivation of any rights, privileges, or immunities secured or protected by the Constitution or laws of the United States, or to different punishments, pains, or penalties, on account of such inhabitant being an alien, or by reason of his color, or race, than are prescribed for the punishment of citizens, shall be fined not more than $1,000 or imprisoned not more than one year, or both; and if death results shall be subject to imprisonment for any term of years or for life.

Case 2.1

FLIPPING A SUSPECT

"Unit 309."

"Unit 309. Go ahead."

"1307 S. Adams Avenue. See the man reference a burglary."

"Unit 309. En route."

"You think they'd give this to a one-man unit," John Miller said as he washed his doughnut down with a gulp of coffee.

"Yeah, right," Meredith Payton replied as she stood up from the stool of the doughnut shop. "Well, let's go fight crime."

It took them only a couple of minutes to get to the location, a rather run-down wood frame house on the "bad side" of town. The area had a reputation for heavy narcotics use as well as gambling. There was a numbers house somewhere in the neighborhood, but the vice officers had been unable to find it. It seemed a shame that low-level organized crime activity would prey on people who could hardly afford to feed their families as they tried to play just the right numbers and hit the big one. John and Meredith both knew that no one ever hit the big one and that the deck was stacked against the players.

"Let's get this over with," Meredith said. "It's your turn to write the report, I'll do the area canvass. Maybe one of the neighbors saw something."

Meredith got out of the cruiser to begin knocking on doors, while John met the complainant, who was standing in front of the house.

"What happened?" John asked the complainant.

"They broke into my house sometime today," replied Frank Jones, leading Miller to the back door of the house.

Miller began to think something was fishy. Very seldom are burglars able to break glass and have it shatter outside the door. "What did they get?" he asked.

"My refrigerator, stove, couch, two chairs, and a kitchen table," Jones replied. Miller noticed that the "small stuff"—stereo, television, and some jewelry—was untouched. He continued his investigation, getting Jones' statement, age, telephone number, and other information necessary to complete the report. He knew that it was just a matter of procedure since most of the burglaries went unsolved in this area and the complainant just needed a Case Number for his insurance company. He did get one little tidbit of information in the course of his interview: Jones had a history of arrests for narcotics possession.

Just as Miller was wrapping up his work, Payton came in and called him aside.

"You're not going to believe this, but there is an old lady living across the street who saw our victim loading furniture into a U-Haul truck this afternoon. She thought he was moving."

Miller and Payton walked over to Jones, who was nervously smoking a cigarette.

"Frank," Payton said sternly, "do you know that filing a false report is a first class misdemeanor?"

"Hey," Jones replied, "I swear to God, I was ripped off."

"Let me show you something," Miller said, leading Jones to the back door.

"How can someone break *in* your back door and have the glass break *out?*"

"Shit, I don't know, you're the cops, you figure it out," Jones replied.

"Cut the crap," interjected Payton. "The lady next door saw you loading the stuff in a U-Haul this afternoon."

"Damn." Jones knew he had been had.

"You're under arrest for filing a false crime report. Up against the wall."

While searching Jones, Miller found his works (hypodermic syringe, spoon cooker, and a couple of decks of suspect heroin) in Jones' sock. "Look here," he said, "felony time. You wanna tell me about it, Frank?"

"Aw, what the fuck," Frank replied, "I needed shit and I was out of cash. I figured I could pawn the stuff, make a report, and get the money from the insurance company my wife works for."

"You're gonna spend a long time in jail for a refrigerator," Payton said. "But, maybe we can work something out. You know that numbers house over there?"

"Yeah," said Jones, realizing he had just put his foot in his mouth.

"Well, I'll tell you what. I'm gonna hold onto this shit and you're gonna tell me all about that house, where it is, who runs it, who the bag man is, and anything else I wanna know. Then, if it all works out right, I'll lose your shit and no one will be the wiser. Deal?"

"Deal," replied Jones.

"Unit 309"

"Unit 309. Go ahead."

"Make it a 'no report,' the call was unfounded. Show us back in service."

"Unit 309. Clear."

Three weeks later, a major numbers racket was busted on the south side.

Questions for Discussion

1. In general, making a false crime report is a misdemeanor, but possession of heroin is a felony. Black's Law Dictionary defines "Misprision of Felony" as "The offense of concealing a felony committed by another, but without such previous concert with or subsequent assistance to the felon as would make the party concealing an accessory before or after the fact." Does your state have a similar statute making the actions of the officers a crime? Can the officers' decision be justified? Why? Defend your position.

2. Jones' possession of narcotics can be classified as a "victimless" crime. Do you think that the actions of the officers would have been different if there had been a victim (e.g., robbery, theft, assault, etc.)?

3. It seems that the officers are using Jones as a *means* to an *end*. Does this not violate the principles espoused by Kant?

4. Using the decision in *Rochin* v. *California*, do the actions of the officers violate Jones' due process rights? Why? Defend your position.

5. When is it an officer's prerogative to choose what offenses will be prosecuted? Construct a policy statement for these types of discretionary situations.

Case 2.2

THE MUSHFAKE MOSQUE

Mushfaking is a craft peculiar to, and extremely popular among, inmates in correctional institutions. This is probably due to the very time-consuming nature of the process. It involves building an object (a model boat, car, jewelry box, etc.) out of cardboard and inlaying the entire surface with wooden matchsticks and glue. This surface is then sanded and varnished, and further detail may be added with paint and more matchsticks (or even string and paper). The finished piece can be quite attractive and functional.

Most of the mushfake items in your lock (G-Dorm) are model ships and jewelry boxes. The level of craftsmanship of these items is very high. This, you suppose, reflects the fact that G-Dorm is a quiet dorm and that its residents, in prison terms, are generally sober, intelligent, and will apply themselves to whatever they do. They tend to be the elite inmates of the institution: college students, administrative clerks, etc. They also tend to stay out of trouble. In order to be assigned to G-Dorm, an inmate must have a very clean institutional record. Once assigned, if he receives a Class II ticket (a major infraction resulting in removal from the dorm), he will lose his bed and become ineligible for reinstatement for at least one year.

Needless to say, you have enjoyed your assignment in G-Dorm. You have come to know and genuinely like several of the men, and things have gone very smoothly until now. You are not sure why, but you have recently been assigned an inmate who, in your opinion, does not belong in a quiet dorm. His name is Walker, but he calls himself "Ahmad Jamal," and he is a self-described "Muslim militant."

You and the men in your dorm would be more likely to describe him as a royal pain in the neck. He has been a constant source of trouble and tension since his arrival. While dorm rules require a low tone of voice at all times, he is almost always loud and abrasive. While most of the residents are courteous and respectful of the rights of others, he is obnoxious and rude. As a practicing Christian, you and other like-minded residents find him especially odious when he launches into one of his harangues against the "evil nature of Christianity" and about the "arch-Satan," the United States. Inmate Walker has come very close to inciting more than a few fistfights in G-Dorm.

You and the other officers have written up Walker for some Class III (minor) offenses, especially for his loud tone of voice. He has thus far, however, been smart and lucky enough to avoid receiving a Class II ticket. His attitude and skill at avoiding major trouble are reflected, in your opinion quite appropriately, in his choice for a mushfake project. It is a mosque, complete with towers, onion domes, crescent moons, and drawers (it is also a jewelry box). You feel that it is purposefully and glaringly different from the other pieces in the dorm. It is deliberately built to be as large as, but no larger than, regulations permit (36" tall and 18" wide). As it sits on Walker's night table, you feel that it stands out like a sore thumb in G-Dorm, just like its owner. You wonder how long he, and his mosque, will remain in your lock.

You get a partial answer to this question when you come on duty on an early Sunday afternoon. You find two passes on your desk concerning Walker. One will permit him to go to the visiting room for a visit. The other will permit him to take his mosque to the visiting room (to be given to a visitor). A small step in the right direction, you think, as you enter your lock for the day and are greeted, as usual, by a contemptuous glance from Walker.

As the afternoon wears on, you spend most of your time sitting in front of the dorm, turned to your right, watching the Browns and Bears football game on an inmate's television. Most of the inmates are at the gym. Walker is showering for his visit. As you watch the game, you notice from the corner of your eye that inmate Hall, a man whom you both like and trust, is moving toward Walker's mosque, which is about 20 feet from you. He does nothing to draw your attention to him, but neither does he try to conceal his actions as he opens one of the drawers of the mosque and places a small rectangular white object into it. As he returns to his bed, you direct your attention back to the game. You sense that the other inmates in the dorm are watching you, waiting for your next move.

That you have just witnessed a plant of contraband is fairly obvious. When Walker takes the mosque to the visiting room it will, as is usual, be thoroughly searched by the visiting room officer. The contraband (a dollar bill? a small amount of marijuana?) will be discovered, and Walker will immediately receive a Class II ticket and be removed from G-Dorm. The plant itself was carried out in a manner that was obvious enough for you to see, yet subtle enough to preserve your deniability. The men in the dorm trusted you enough to let you in on this, and keep you safe from accountability at the same time. The scenario is easy to foresee, and it's risk free. Just watch the game and let it go, and you will be rid of Walker. Your lock will return to being a truly "quiet" dorm again.

The trouble is, you know that doing nothing in this situation is just plain wrong. You will be allowing Walker to be punished with a Class II ticket just because he has been a thorn in your and your dorm's side. You will also be allowing inmate Hall, the true possessor of the contraband, to avoid punishment and remain in G-Dorm. "Just what did Hall put into that drawer?" you wonder. How much more of whatever it was does he still possess? How much are you allowing your own undeniable prejudice against Walker's religion to affect your judgment? Amid these questions, you can't help but think how nice it would be to have Walker out of your dorm.

You stand up to do something about the situation, though you do not as yet have any idea what you will do. As you stand, Walker strides by on his way from the shower. He snorts loudly and flashes you a hateful look when he must make a slight detour around you to get to his aisle. You pause to consider the situation again. When Walker finishes dressing, he picks up his mosque, and walks in your direction toward the door. You, still a bit hesitant, are slow to open the door and Walker is perturbed. "Will you please open the door, off-fee-ser," he snarls, "You don't wanna make me late for my visit, do you?"

Questions for Discussion

1. What would you do? Defend your answer.
2. Does the fact that Walker's beliefs contradict your own have an impact on your decision? Are you allowing your own prejudices to influence your decision?
3. Is Walker's behavior a self-fulfilling prophecy?

4. Consider the following conclusion and support or reject the officer's decision.

"No," you reply, "not at all."

You open the door and let Walker march off to his fate. You sit back down to watch Cleveland rally to beat the Chicago Bears. You will later recall that watching this upset, and watching the officers coming to remove Walker's belongings, were the only two memorable events to occur in G-Dorm on that particular Sunday afternoon.

5. Using the decision in *Rochin* v. *California*, does your decision in question 1 above violate Walker's due process rights? Why? Defend your position.

6. Isn't what happened really better for all the inmates in the dorm?

7. Compare your answer in this case with your answer in "Flipping a Suspect." Did you support one and not the other? Is concealing evidence in "Flipping" appropriate? Justify your answers.

8. Would removing and destroying the contraband in Walker's presence and taking no action be an alternative? Why? Defend your position.

9. Would removing the contraband as soon as it was planted be appropriate? If so, what action should be taken against Hall?

10. What is *fair* and *equal* treatment?

Case 2.3

THE MEMO

DEPARTMENT OF CORRECTIONS

Classification: **CONFIDENTIAL**

To: Chief, Custodial Services
Chair, Board of Pardons and Parole

From: The Director

Subject: UNIONIZATION PROBLEMS

As you are aware, several inmates have been attempting to organize a labor union within three of our institutions. It is our position that an inmate union is inconsistent with the goals of the Department of Corrections.

Effective immediately, inmates who have been involved in union activities will be identified and transferred. Those who continue union activities and who come to the board for parole consideration will be denied parole. Those inmates who have not been involved in unionization activities will be afforded your usual consideration. It is our intention to have inmates involved in union activities "max out," thus deterring further union activities.

Thank you for your cooperation.

Questions for Discussion

1. Balance the rights of the inmates to organize for their common good versus the right of the Department of Corrections to control the institutions. Which right should take precedence?

2. Isn't this a "quick, cheap, and efficient" (Jenkins) way for dealing with criminals who attempt to organize?

3. Does this memo, in fact, deny due process rights to the inmates, or could an argument be made that inmates could gain early release by "playing the game?"

4. Using the decision in *Rochin* v. *California,* is the memo a violation of due process rights. Why? Defend your position.

5. In your opinion, should prisoners have the right to organize? Defend your answer.

6. Would "leaking" the memo be an appropriate action? Why? Defend your position.

Case 2.4

IT'S OUR POLICY

Section 03.01   Criminal Activity by Inmates Against Inmates

With the exception of an inmate death, all criminal activity in which an inmate is the victim and an inmate is the subject shall be investigated by the Custody Staff Supervisor. Disciplinary action will be taken against the offending inmate where appropriate and based on a preponderance of the evidence. In no event shall the victim inmate be permitted to file a report with a local law enforcement agency. Custody and Treatment staff shall make no reports or statements to outside agencies regarding the aforesaid activity.

Section 03.02   Criminal Activity by Inmates Against Staff

With the exception of great bodily harm or death, all criminal activity in which a staff member is the victim and an inmate is the subject shall be investigated by the Custody Staff Supervisor. Disciplinary action will be taken against the offending inmate where appropriate and based on a preponderance of the evidence. In no event shall the victim inmate be permitted to file a report with a local law enforcement agency. Custody and Treatment staff shall make no reports or statements to outside agencies regarding the aforesaid activity.

Questions for Discussion

1. Speculate on the purpose of this policy.

2. Refer to the Bill of Rights. Does the policy seem to conflict with any of these rights? If so, with which ones? Why?

3. Is this policy an attempt to avoid frivolous criminal investigations, or is it a denial of the due process rights of employees and inmates?

4. Using the decision in *Rochin* v. *California*, does the policy violate the due process rights of the employees or of the inmates? Why? Defend your position.

5. In this case, balance the rights of the individual (corrections officers and inmates) with the rights of the institution.

Case 2.5

PROTECTING THE INNOCENT

Steve and Janet are officers attached to the Youth Service Division of the municipal police department. They routinely deal with problems relating to the abuse and neglect of children and must work closely with Children's Protective Services. It is generally understood within the police department that the relationship with Children's Protective Services is important and one that both agencies need to work on from time to time.

During June of this past year, Steve and Janet had occasion to work with Children's Services in the removal of three children from the legal custody of their father and place them with their mother on a temporary basis, pending a hearing in family court. The father and mother had been divorced for about three years. She had initially given custody of the children to the father because he had a larger house and she was looking forward to independence without the pressures of motherhood.

The father was a veteran of the Vietnam conflict, was suffering from Post-Traumatic Stress Disorder, and had a history of drug and alcohol abuse. He has been unable to hold employment longer than a couple of months at a time since returning from Vietnam. He is considered to be disabled and is currently receiving S.S.I. In many respects, it is almost self-evident that he is incapable of being a good parent and, based on the testimony of the 11-year-old son who claims to have been physically abused by his father on many occasions, the removal of the children from their father's care was the correct thing to do. The other children are under 5 years of age and are unable to add a great deal of helpful testimony.

During the pick-up and removal of the children and the investigation that followed, Steve noted the absence of any physical evidence of abuse, but the father's highly emotional reaction to the charges and the removal of the children only seemed to confirm that he is too irrational and "hot headed" to be a parent. The municipal police department, Children's Services, and the court are all in agreement that the removal was the correct thing to do.

In the course of talking with the 11-year-old boy some time after he was placed in the custody of the mother, Steve and Janet learned that he had lied about being abused by his father because he wanted to live with his mother and had been very angry when his mother had abandoned him. He also indicated that while he did not like his father, his father had never actually been abusive or neglectful. Steve now feels that he must report what he has been told to the court for a reconsideration of custody, but Janet and the social worker with Children's Services feel that "well enough" should just be left alone and that it is in the "best interest of the children" to remain with their mother. Janet feels that, in the best interest of everyone concerned, Steve should forget what he has been told. Steve feels that the children's father has been deprived of his rights and accused of things he did not do and that, although he is not a model parent, he is not guilty of child abuse. Further, he is entitled to fair treatment under the law.

Questions for Discussion

1. Is the father's "highly emotional reaction" indicative of his emotional instability, or is it the natural response of a parent about to lose a child?

2. What is in the best interest of the 11-year-old boy? Weigh the utility of placement with an abandoning parent versus that of an emotionally unstable one.

3. Do the rights of the father outweigh the rights of the boy, or vice versa? If so, which should take precedence? If not, why not?

4. If you were Steve, what would you do?

5. Speculate on Janet's rationale for saying nothing.

Chapter 3

The Individual: Discretion and Decision-making

CRIMINAL JUSTICE PRACTITIONERS HAVE DEPARTMENTAL POLICIES, procedures, and rules, but a great deal of an officer's job also involves the exercise of discretionary authority. While no law specifically confers discretion on a corrections or police officer, it is difficult to imagine how an officer could function effectively without using discretion in everyday work. Prosecutors, prison directors, and supervisors expect discretion, as does the public.

If I am stopped by a police officer for going two miles over the speed limit, discretion may make sense, especially if everyone else on the highway was ten miles over the limit. Unfortunately, I may also expect discretion when I am twenty-five miles over the limit. What are the practitioner's limits to the exercise of discretion? Obvious misuses of discretionary authority include allowing personal bias to affect enforcement decisions, "not seeing" a prisoner commit a criminal act, or the use of discretion to conceal corruption.

Exercise of discretion generates problems and conflicts in the administrative areas of the criminal justice system. To the extent that individual discretion is encouraged, administrative control of individual practitioners is weakened. This is an important component in the professionalization of criminal justice practice because professionals are, by definition, substantially self-guided in their conduct. At the same time, many aspects of the relationship between the criminal justice system and its practitioners are rigidly hierarchical and authority-based. Most law enforcement agencies, for example, function more as military units than as engineering firms, medical clinics, or human services agencies. Thus, a criminal justice agency that develops policies that severely restrict discretion may nurture a "by-the-book" mentality among its practitioners. Such a perspective may discourage the critical reasoning that morally sensitive conduct demands. Even worse, highly detailed policies designed to curtail discretionary practice can serve as a shield for deliberately unethical conduct. This, of course, is directly related to the "Nuremburg defense" problem in assessing moral responsibility. The Nuremburg defense is named after the war crimes trials of Nazi officials held in Nuremburg after World War II. There, many of the accused argued that they were not morally responsible for the consequences of their actions since they "were just following orders."

Most of the issues that you will study in the readings and cases in this text are not clear-cut. The moral perspectives that you have developed as an adult will help you in your decision-making. You have no doubt internalized many ethical rules. But applying those rules (do the consequences count or not?), balancing them with your legal duties, and checking them against departmental policy (whose rules are trump?) can be a daunting prospect.

One approach that can be quite effective is the use of an **ethical checklist**. When you are examining the issues that arise in this book, and when you are working as a practitioner, run through the following list of questions:

• Does the action violate another person's Constitutional rights, including the right to due process of law? (Duties of justice)
• Does the action involve treating another person only as a means to an end? (Kant's Formula of the End-in-Itself)
• Is the action under consideration illegal? (Civic duties)
• Do you predict that your action will produce more bad than good for all persons affected? (Duties of nonmaleficence—do no wrong—and benevolence—do some good)
• Does the action violate department procedure or a professional ethical canon? (Duties of one's professional role)

If you answer "Yes" to any of these questions, the action you are considering is ethically *suspect*. This does not guarantee you an answer either way to the question, "Should I perform this action?" Philosophers are very adept at providing examples that might generate a "Yes" to all five questions, and yet seem morally acceptable, or even obligatory, to many people. Likewise, even if you answered all of the questions with "No" it wouldn't necessarily follow that the action is morally permissible. Despite these problems with the checklist above, the questions can help alert you to the possibility of ethical misconduct. If you answer "Yes" to two or more questions, the possibility rises dramatically. Even though we can generate hypothetical scenarios that seem to defy one's answers to the five questions, the frequency of problematic cases must be compared with that of cases that are handled successfully.

The Readings

The first selection, Peter Longo's "Criminal Investigation and the Classical Application of Ethics," recommends an **Aristotelian** approach to professional behavior. The Greek philosopher, Aristotle (384–322 B.C.), believed that moderation is the key guide to ethical behavior. As Longo points out, "overzealous behavior... has the potential to harm citizens." Longo focuses on Aristotle's insistence on individual responsibility, a perspective that is at the heart of this chapter. Although Aristotle placed great value on friendship, he believed that morality requires us to "honor truth above our friends." The rationalization that "everybody else does it" is simply not acceptable. Longo then illustrates the application of these points to a series of cases.

T. H. Cook's selection, "Toward a New Code of Police Ethics," is a detailed examination of the International Association of Chiefs of Police Law Enforcement Code of Ethics. (This code is included along with several other codes as reference material following the readings.) Though much of what Cook has to say applies to codes of ethics in probation and corrections, you should read the Law Enforcement Code first as background for Cook's paper. Cook argues that the Code goes far beyond moral duty, requiring virtual sainthood of the officer. Moreover, Cook believes that an "inflexible or unrealistically elevated level of moral expectation" contributes to stress and burnout among public servants. Cook also believes that the Code's "legalist" rejection of discretionary enforcement may provide a rationalization for the overly zealous officer. This is just the sort of officer who does not need additional encouragement in the form of "relentless prosecution" to take shortcuts where "zeal alone is not enough."

In Richard McCleary's paper, "How Structural Variables Constrain the Parole Officer's Use of Discretionary Powers," the role of discretion in the work of the parole officer is examined. The PO's decision-making process is determined in part by "organizational contexts and the costs of alternative decisions," according to McCleary. The major constraint on discretion is a result of differing views about the PO's role in the criminal justice system. McCleary quotes one PO as saying, "No DC [Department of Corrections] honcho in Springfield can tell me what's best for my clients." Parole officers tend to see themselves as counselors whose primary loyalties are to the parolee, not to the Department of Corrections. McCleary documents the results of this tension in terms of what the parole officer experiences as limits of use of discretion.

Unfortunately, as Lawrence Sherman points out in the selection, "Learning Police Ethics," codes and policy manuals that are laid down as department law are guaranteed to fail. It is Sherman's view that such approaches to police ethics may actually encourage unethical behavior among officers. Sherman's conclusion is substantiated by the real "code" that he believes officers acquire through socialization. For example, consider due process:

> Due process is only a means of protecting criminals at the expense of the law-abiding and should be ignored whenever it is safe to do so.

Sherman formulates several other parts of the "traditional code" governing police behavior, all equally pithy. His point is not that the task of making ethically sound decisions is impossible, but that it requires a specific effort and formal training to counteract the socialization of recruits to the "old" ways.

Criminal Investigation and the Classical Application of Ethics

PETER LONGO

ETHICS HAS BEEN DEBATED throughout the history of humankind and has recently been the focus of increased attention. Nationally, public officials who fail to follow exacting standards of ethics are being challenged by the media and the public. At the same time criminal justice forces are trying to handle increased crime and yet maintain ethics in enforcing the law. One would think that all of this debate and attention would have resulted in firm conclusions, but such is not the case. In fact, many questions remain. Is ethics a legal code? Is it proper upbringing? What is ethics? The student of criminal justice will spend a great amount of study time learning legal guidelines and mandates and countless hours mastering the art of criminal investigation. Yet it will not be enough to do what is legal and efficient. Criminal justice personnel will be called on in their discretionary decision making to do what is right.

It is this latter task, doing what is right, that serves as the focus of this reading. Some have called for a humanistic approach to the ethics debate (Gilbert, 1988), even though humanities tend to slow down our fast-paced world.[1] We are a society that enjoys fast food, fast cars, fast laughs; administrators are fixed on minute-manager theories and quick-fix solutions. Unfortunately, however, a quick-fix is usually short-lived. The lessons from the humanities, on the other hand, are deliberate and are aimed at endurance.

In response to this humanistic call, we will take several steps back into history, to revisit the well-known Greek and classical philosopher,

Aristotle. Aristotle's message of ethical behavior is priceless and of particular worth to criminal justice students. In all probability Aristotle did not know much about the particulars of criminal investigation, but he did understand a great deal about ethics and human nature. Additionally, his messages are clear and understandable and directly applicable to criminal justice matters, since criminal justice is, essentially, a study of human nature gone astray.

Potential Ethical Dilemmas

Let's imagine that you are a new police officer, called to investigate the disappearance and possible abduction of a twelve-year-old girl. Your investigative leads take you to a suspect within your jurisdiction, who fits the description on all points and has a previous record of kidnapping and child molestation. You apprehend the suspect, but your instincts tell you that the missing child is dead.

The suspect hears the Miranda warnings and chooses to remain silent. As you drive him to the location of the crime, the silence becomes uncomfortable. It is Christmas Eve, the snow is falling at a steady rate, and your thoughts wander from your own young daughter to the victim. Something must be done, but what?

This scenario was derived from a 1984 Supreme Court case, *Nix* v. *Williams*, better known in legal circles as the Christian burial case.[2] In the Nix case the officer gave an emotional speech about a proper Christian burial for

Peter Longo, "Criminal Investigation and the Classical Application of Ethics," in James N. Gilbert (ed.), Criminal Investigation: Essays and Cases. (New York: Macmillan, 1990), pp. 137–142. Reprinted with permission of Macmillan College Publishing Company. Copyright © 1990 by Macmillan College Publishing Company, Inc.

the victim, and the suspect responded by confessing to the homicide and telling the location of the body. The Supreme Court eventually ruled against the suspect's claim that the confession was unconstitutionally obtained from him. However, the exclusionary rule, which prevents the use of illegally obtained evidence in court proceedings, continues to present legal as well as ethical dilemmas. In the words of one New York judge, "The criminal is to go free because the constable has blundered."[3] The exclusionary rule has been modified through the years, but there are now many more legal gray areas that are often determined on a case by case basis.

Although the exclusionary rule is perhaps the most obvious ethical challenge to an investigator, it is by no means the only one. Investigators are called upon to obtain evidence in various forms and once again must not only know the legally required bounds and procedures, but must also act as ethical citizens. Police are highly unsupervised and experience great pressure to operate under an ends-justifies-the-means philosophy. In addition, there is always the temptation to do what peers are doing, even if it is wrong and/or illegal.

Aristotle's Ethical Framework for Criminal Investigation

Aristotle devotes less than two dozen lines to criminal law, yet those lines are quoted in thousands of volumes. In addition, Aristotle offers universal messages that have particular importance for criminal investigators.

As discussed previously, the exclusionary rule poses serious ethical dilemmas for criminal investigators. At times they may applaud the rule, at other times curse it. Aristotle clearly indicates that the law must be preserved and that it ultimately will lead us to a good life. That good life is based on ethical behavior, and Aristotle is harsh on lawbreakers.

The fact is that the greatest crimes are caused by excess and not by necessity. Men do not become tyrants in order that they may not

suffer cold; and hence great is the honour bestowed not on him who kills a thief, but on him who kills a tyrant.[4]

This passage has several important messages for criminal investigators. Generally, it urges moderate behavior. Moderation directly confronts overzealous behavior, which has the potential to harm citizens. According to Aristotle the greatest crimes stem from excess, not necessity. And excess, which is clearly a selfish act, breaks the spirit of the investigative community. Criminal investigators undoubtedly experience positive feelings when cases are broken, but the betrayal of one's ethics to solve a criminal investigation is inexcusable.

Aristotle's Understanding of Good

Good is probably easier to define in the technical field of criminal investigation than it is in the philosophical field of ethics. Good investigative methods include proper identification of a suspect, location and arrest of the suspect, protection of the chain of evidence, and so on. However, deriving a clear meaning of *good* in the abstract is a challenge. Aristotle gives *good* some universal meaning in his *Nicomachean Ethics,* which was originally intended for the statesman, or public servant. Criminal investigators can certainly be looked upon as public servants in the best sense of the phrase.

Aristotle states that "every art and every inquiry and similarly every action and choice is thought to aim at some good."[5] Thus, according to Aristotle's framework, criminal justice practitioners must aim each day to do what is good. Copleston, a scholar of Aristotle's work, adds to this notion, claiming that public servants should act "to make man, in a universal sense, happy."[6] Criminal investigators, then, are ethically bound to act on behalf of the citizens they serve even when that task is made unpleasant by an unfriendly judge, a difficult police chief, an obnoxious drunk, or some other less-than-desirable character. Aristotle urges equity, not necessarily equality. Thus, each situation and each individual must be evaluated, and then investigators must do what is good—a formidable charge.

Fortunately, the teachings of Aristotle do not demand immediate perfection. Aristotle believed that life is an ongoing adventure in which each activity offers a learning aspect. Centuries ago he realized the frailty of humankind, even though he did not excuse it. Instead he queries, "Shall we not, like archers who have a mark to aim at, be more likely to hit upon what we should?"[7] If criminal investigators continually aim at what is good, they will accomplish much.

Truth: An Individual Responsibility

American government has grown accustomed to hiding behind the group. According to David Truman, a political scientist, democracy is served by having lawmakers listen to groups, which are a mere reflection of individual behavior.[8] Even though this might be true, such a scheme keeps individuals from accepting responsibility and encourages the non-Aristotelian excuse "Everyone else was doing it." Political figures in Washington, D.C. have used this rationale, as have vast numbers of arrestees the world over.

The abdication of individual responsibility has had tragic consequences in both private and public sectors. The Valdez oil spill of 1989 showed how difficult it was to find an individual in the Exxon Corporation responsible. Individuals can hide in the bureaucratic maze of a corporate structure, blame the structure, and pay no ethical debt to society. The same loss of individual responsibility is at the heart of many police and/or correctional scandals. For example, the New York scandal that involved hundreds of police and was portrayed in the book and movie *Serpico* illustrates this point.[9] Large numbers of criminal investigators engaged in unlawful activities and then explained that so many others were doing it. The system, if it didn't tolerate, at least disguised such behavior. Aristotle's work swiftly condemns the group or pluralistic excuse:

We had perhaps better consider the universal good and discuss thoroughly what is meant by it, although such an inquiry is made an uphill one by the fact that the Forms have been introduced by friends of our own. Yet it would perhaps be thought to be better, indeed to be our duty, for the sake of maintaining the truth even to destroy what touches us closely, especially as we are philosophers; for, while both are dear, piety requires us to honour truth above our friends.[10]

This message is of critical importance: ethical duty lies with the individual, even if that duty damages friendship. Criminal investigators will encounter a police subculture, which may be fine unless it prevents ethical behavior. Perhaps a detective friend will plant drug evidence on a drug dealer to effect the arrest of an evil individual who has continually evaded legal arrest. Ultimately, each individual must decide whether "to honor truth."

Obtaining Excellence in Individual Ethics

The quest for ethical behavior is ongoing. Aristotle observes that ethical excellence involves both intellectual and moral aspects:

Intellectual excellence in the main owes both its birth and its growth to teaching (for which reason it requires experience and time), while moral excellence comes about as a result of habit, whence also its name is one that is formed by a slight variation from the word for habit. From this it is also plain that none of the moral excellences arises in us by nature; for nothing that exists by nature can form a habit contrary to its nature.[11]

In other words, experience and intellectual study can lead us to ethics, but it's not easy to be ethical. The ethical challenge is particularly difficult in the high-pressured world of criminal justice, where not only personal pressures, but also victims, the media, supervisors, and many others exert powerful influences. However, investigators can learn from their experiences and from study. Knowing all the legal mandates and achieving a sound moral base will result in ethical behavior.

Aristotle demands ethical behavior but knows that it is a never-ending challenge.

> Anyone can get angry ... that is easy ... or give or spend money; but to do this to the right person, to the right extent, at the right time, with the right aim, and in the right way, that is not for everyone, nor is it easy; that is why goodness is both rare, honorable, and noble.[12]

The criminal justice journey may be difficult, but it will also be honorable if investigators follow the path of ethical behavior, striving always for goodness.

Twentieth Century Examples

The relevance of Aristotle to criminal investigators is seen in examples of potential real-life situations. In each of the situations described here, imagine that you are a conscientious investigator—and look to Aristotle for guidance.

Imagine that you are asked to testify in a court of law about a known drug dealer. You know the harmful results of the suspect's actions, and you also know that you do not have sufficient evidence to support the particular charge. The bailiff calls you to take the stand. What do you do? Aristotle's advice is simple: tell the truth. The real challenge is to convict the drug dealer through truthful means; if you lie, the process of justice is a sham. Ah, but everyone lies. Aristotle says that this is no excuse. You are a public servant and must serve *all* the public.

Suppose that you have been called to an area known for its high crack-cocaine use. You visit an apartment where a single mother has overdosed on crack and has killed her two young children. Something must be done, you think as you hit the streets searching for crack dealers. Is it OK to be excessive in your search, just this once? Aristotle answers no; necessity does not justify excess. You have spent a great deal of time and energy learning how to investigate in a legal manner. Arrest the crack dealer, but do it right.

Imagine that you have been investigating a child pornography operation. You could save two weeks of intense work by lying to obtain a search warrant. That approach would make a great number of people happy, and your job as a public servant is to make people happy. What do you do? Aristotle suggests that you execute the search warrant legally, for a situation that tempts an investigator to lie for the good of a single case does not ultimately serve the entire community well. In an Aristotelian manner Justice Brandeis said in his dissent in *Olmstead* v. *United States*: "Our government is the potent, omnipresent teacher. For good or for ill, it teaches the whole people by its example. If the government becomes a lawbreaker, it breeds contempt for law; it invites every man to become a law unto himself; it invites anarchy."[13] Do not be deceived into making one person happy or one police chief happy at the expense of making the community happy.

You have been asked to investigate a complaint of domestic violence. You work your way through a neighborhood of crime ... crack dealers, drug pushing, prostitution. You are surrounded by human misery. You make your way to the door of the complainant. You knock, and a battered wife lets you in. The suspect has fled. You pursue the suspect and ultimately apprehend him. Is there anything wrong with letting the suspect feel a little of your anger and disgust? Once again, Aristotle cautions against excessive force. Responding in a manner consistent with a criminal lowers you to the level of the criminal. Instead, Aristotle says that public servants must treat humans as humans, even though not all humans act like humans. Criminal investigators will be frequently called upon to set the example. Aristotle's call is for ethical conduct.

Continuation of the Journey

Hopefully, the connection between classical ethics and criminal justice fieldwork has been made, but it must continue to be made. Ethical behavior requires ongoing practice and theory. Again, the words of Aristotle:

> But most people … take refuge in theory and think they are being philosophers and will become good in this way, behaving somewhat like patients who listen attentively to their doctors, but do none of the things they are ordered to do. And the latter will not be made well in body by such a course of treatment; the former will not be made well in soul by such a course in philosophy.[14]

It does an investigator no good to obtain a criminal justice education stressing legal investigative guidelines and then go out and violate the spirit of the law. The classical framework of Aristotle can serve both as a springboard for future discussions of investigative theories and as a practical guide to good actions, which will lead us ultimately to a good society.

NOTES

1. James Gilbert, "Investigative Ethics," in *Critical Issues in Criminal Investigation*, 2d ed., ed. M. Palmiotto (Cincinnati: Anderson, 1988).

2. *Nix v. Williams*, 467 U.S. 431 (1984).

3. *People v. Defore*, 150 N.E. 585 (1926), 587.

4. Aristotle, *Politics*, in *The Complete Works of Aristotle*, ed. Jonathan Barnes (Princeton: Princeton University Press, 1984), 1267(a): 13–16.

5. Aristotle, *Nicomachean Ethics* 1094(a): 1–2.

6. Frederick Copleston, *A History of Philosophy* (Garden City, NY: Image Books, 1962).

7. Aristotle, *Nicomachean Ethics* 1094(a): 24–25.

8. David Truman, *The Governmental Process* (New York: Knopf, 1951).

9. Peter Maas, *Serpico* (New York: Viking, 1973).

10. Aristotle, *Nicomachean Ethics* 1096(a): 12–16.

11. Ibid., 1103(a): 14–21.

12. Ibid., 1190(a): 20–30.

13. *Olmstead v. United States*, 277 U.S. 438 (1928), 485.

14. Aristotle, *Nicomachean Ethics* 11056(b): 12–18.

Study Questions

1. Longo states that criminal justice is basically a study of "human nature gone astray." Is there such a thing as *human nature*, in your view? How would you go about proving the existence of natural human characteristics, as opposed to learned behavior?

2. Explain what Aristotle means by the statement that "the greatest crimes are caused by excess and not by necessity." Do you agree with Aristotle? Why? Defend your position. Give examples in at least two areas of criminal justice practice in which the virtue of moderation is relevant.

3. Does Aristotle believe that some people are just naturally good, or can moral excellence be attained by anyone who tries? Do you agree with Aristotle? Why? Defend your position.

4. Is Longo's perspective on ethics in criminal justice a realistic one? Why? Defend your position.

Toward a New Code of Police Ethics

T. H. COOK

IT HAS NOW BEEN more than 30 years since the IACP [International Association of Chiefs of Police] adopted its well-known code of police ethics. Many changes have occurred during that time, both in American society and in police work. In view of these changes, it is now fitting that we should begin to reexamine the IACP code and determine whether it, too, is in need of change.

In reference to codes of police ethics, the late O. W. Wilson, who probably did more than anyone else to bring about the IACP code, stated that "...such a code is the first step toward true professionalization..." (O. W. Wilson, 1977, p. 9).[1] Many other authorities on professionalism, both inside and outside criminal justice, have echoed this sentiment.

The most widely acknowledged professions, such as law and medicine, have long had formal codes of professional ethics. Nursing, an emerging profession that relates to medicine in some of the same ways that law enforcement relates to criminal law, is well on its way toward developing not only an ethical code but an ethical consciousness. It is now recognized that not only doctors but also nurses must make life and death decisions, and entire courses on applied ethics are now commonplace in medical and nursing curricula. When higher education becomes mandatory for police employment, courses in ethics may become fashionable for pre-service law enforcement students as well, if only as a way for philosophers to shore up their enrollments.

But law enforcement is not yet a truly educated profession. So although many police agencies and most police academies pay lip service to the IACP code, and although short blocks of training on police ethics are now found in the curricula of most academies, remarkably little has been done in recent years to devise and disseminate a workable set of guidelines that might actually influence a contemporary officer's day-to-day behavior. Police conduct, like police discretion, is a topic that is often mentioned but little understood. The emphasis on rules to prevent misconduct and rules to prevent abuse of discretion and misuse of authority has obscured the need for guidelines to encourage rational decision-making, professional attitudes, or professional behavior.

It is the belief of this author that if a revised and updated code of police ethics were promulgated by an organization with the prestige of the IACP or the ACJS [Academy of Criminal Justice Sciences] (or by both organizations acting together), the broader implementation of the revised code might naturally follow. O. W. Wilson's professionalism was such that he would be pleased to know that another generation of colleagues is carrying his work forward (McLaren, 1973).[2] So let us now look at the code itself. The first paragraph of the IACP code reads as follows:

> As a law enforcement officer, my fundamental duty is to serve mankind; to safeguard lives and property; to protect the innocent against deception, the weak against oppression or intimidation, and the peaceful against violence or disorder; and to respect the Constitutional rights of all men to liberty, equality and justice.[3]

These opening statements, fortunately, are in need of little major revision whatsoever except for the sexism of the language. In 1957 they were not only profound but prophetic. The public service ideology was eventually espoused and internalized by most police agencies during the 1970s, and most of those individuals who disagreed with it have either been converted to it or weeded out of police work. The authority of the Bill of Rights was affirmed and expanded in the 1960s in a series of landmark cases that are likely to stand for some time as pillars of human rights. It is now virtually axiomatic that police officers are public servants and that they are legally and morally bound to protect the rights and freedoms as well as the lives and property of all human beings.

But are police officers *more than* public servants and legal guardians? Are they also saints in blue suits who stand as special moral exemplars: good Scouts, fearless and unflinching crime fighters, and soldiers of the Lord at the same time? The 1957 IACP code goes on to suggest that the police are all of these things and much more besides. If being a police officer is that exalted a duty and that sacred a trust, it is this author's opinion that only a saintly soldier or a soldierly saint could take the oath of office in good conscience. But do we want fanatics and zealots policing our streets? What we probably do want are reasonable, professional, competent, compassionate human beings who will use both their authority and their discretion wisely. With that possibility in mind, let us now examine the remaining paragraphs of the IACP code. The second paragraph reads as follows:

I will keep my private life unsullied as an example to all; maintain courageous calm in the face of danger, scorn, or ridicule; develop self-restraint; and be constantly mindful of the welfare of others. Honest in thought and deed in both my personal and official life, I will be exemplary in obeying the laws of the land and the regulations of my department. Whatever I see or hear of a confidential nature or that is confided to me in my official capacity will be kept ever secret unless revelation is necessary in the performance of my duty.

Obedience to the law and to department policy ought to go without saying as major professional obligations of all police officers. But what exactly is an "unsullied private life"? That may depend on personal taste and lifestyle as well as local social or cultural expectations. Even saints and soldiers have their idiosyncrasies, and some of them are best kept secret. What exactly are "honesty in thought and deed" and "constant mindfulness of the welfare of others"? How much of a personal life, how much privacy, and how much time for "R and R" is an officer permitted to have under such stringent rules? Not much if O. W. Wilson's own puritanism and workaholism are to be taken as our main example.

We now know, as Wilson and his generation did not, that an overly inflexible or unrealistically elevated level of moral expectation is one factor that often contributes to stress and burnout among police officers and other public servants. Suicides may even result from the extreme stress and guilt that ethical absolutism and personal perfectionism can place upon a person, as Wilson might have inferred from the death of his mentor August Vollmer (Stead, 1977).[4] Stress control and stress reduction are the current slogans of the police psychologist.

No less an authority than the Supreme Court in the recent *Garcia* decision has declared in effect that a public servant such as a police officer is "owned" by the public only during those 40 hours per week that the officer is actually scheduled to be working. The rest of the officer's time is the officer's own, and the public can purchase that time only by paying a much higher premium for services. Even deputy sheriffs, though not sheriffs themselves since by state constitutional mandate sheriffs are always on duty, come under the Garcia rule on overtime pay (cf. *Garcia,* 1985).[5]

Does this mean that rounding up stray criminals differs only in degree, but not in kind, from rounding up stray dogs, collecting garbage, or collecting subway tokens? Of course police work is different from these things. For most conscientious officers it can never be "just a job." It is at least a skilled and specialized career, and is striving to become a well-trained and educated profession.

But should off-duty police conduct, provided that it is legal, reasonably consistent with departmental policy, and reasonably consistent with local sociocultural expectations, come under closer scrutiny than that of most other public servants? Recent social and legal trends, as well as recent psychological research, tend to suggest that it largely should not, and this should be kept in mind in revising the IACP code.

The third paragraph reads as follows:

> I will never act officiously or permit personal feelings, prejudices, animosities, or friendships to influence my decisions. With no compromise for crime and with relentless prosecution of criminals, I will enforce the law courteously and appropriately without fear or favor, malice or ill will, never employing unnecessary force or violence and never accepting gratuities.

The second sentence of this paragraph is a virtual denial of police discretion. Some police departments have indeed chosen to officially permit minor gratuities such as free cups of coffee or "police discounts" on various items. But much more to the point is the passage about "no compromise for crime" and the "relentless prosecution of criminals." If this advice were seriously and exhaustively followed, our jails and prisons and courtrooms would be literally bursting at the seams and the Garcia ruling would have to be ignored to keep them that way. A more appropriate wording might be "with no compromise for serious crime while on duty, and with relentless prosecution of violent felons," because in some jurisdictions it is only the violent or recurrent felons that we have the resources or the desire to relentlessly prosecute. Are the police to be blamed for their inadequate resources, or for the lack of citizen cooperation, or for the innate flexibility of the criminal justice system? When the crime rate increases or a major crime goes unsolved, is it the fault of the police? Usually not, or at least not for the most part. Why enact an ethical code that makes police feel guilty about something they can't really control?

Admittedly there are some overzealous or overly officious officers who agree in their hearts with the literal words of this part of the IACP code, and wish that they could relentlessly prosecute or even persecute every criminal. These are J. Q. Wilson's "legalists," who fortunately are outnumbered by the other categories in his well-known taxonomy. The legalists are often the ones who end up as burnout cases, or who ironically end up taking the law into their own hands in order to catch elusive lawbreakers. Such officers hardly need any extra encouragement to rationalize either their own excessive zeal, or the shortcuts that they sometimes take when they realize that zeal alone is not enough. J. Q. Wilson's "watchmen" also have ample motives to exceed their authority, and along with the legalists might do well to content themselves with a combination of Wilson's "order maintenance" and "public service" orientations (Inciardi, 1987[6]; J. Q. Wilson, 1968[7]).

The fourth and final paragraph reads as follows:

> I recognize the badge of my office as a symbol of public faith, and I accept it as a public trust to be held so long as I am true to the ethics of police service. I will constantly strive to achieve these objectives and ideals, dedicating myself before God to my chosen profession . . . law enforcement.

"Constant striving" is hard enough in itself without promising to do it under the all-seeing eyes of the Divine Watchman. And does this last passage mean that an agnostic or, God forbid, an atheist or a Moslem or a Hindu, cannot be a good police officer? What about separation of church and state?

Ministers, indeed, have more in common with police officers than meets the eye. Both are public servants who exert a certain amount of social control. But that is all the more reason to keep religion and police work officially separate. Many officers who base their personal ideals and aspirations on religion or theology probably do have a stronger epistemic foundation for their ethical convictions than many who do not. But some of them are also more dogmatic, and consequently are less able to cope with the frustrations of revolving-door justice or with the discretionary decisions referred to above.

It takes many kinds of people to make up an effective police department, just as it takes many kinds of people to make democracy function in a pluralistic society. Most of all, what it takes is *people*, acting together in good faith toward a common goal, even though they disagree on some of their beliefs and values.

Let us resolve to keep it that way, and let us begin to revise our ethical guidelines to make it more evident that this is the case. The war on crime is mainly a war of attrition, and the casualties in this war are not only the crime victims and occasionally the criminals, but the minds and psyches of the police and of the general public as well. We all are casualties of that war when vigilantes and renegade cops become the leading heroes of the boob tube and the silver screen. Real police officers do have to set a better example than that. It is partly our duty as citizens and educators to instruct them how to do so.

NOTES

1. Wilson, O. W. (1977) *Police Administration*. Fourth edition. (New York: McGraw-Hill).

2. McLaren, R. C. (1973) "A Memorial to the Chief," *Police Chief* 18 (January 1973).

3. International Association of Chiefs of Police (1957) "Police Code of Ethics." (Gaithersburg, MD).

4. Stead, J. P., ed. (1977) *Pioneers in Policing*. (Montclair, NJ: Patterson Smith).

5. *Garcia vs. San Diego Metro*, 83 L.Ed. 8 (1985).

6. Inciardi, J. A. (1987) *Criminal Justice*. Second edition. (New York: Harcourt).

7. Wilson, J. Q. (1968) *Varieties of Police Behavior*. (Cambridge: Harvard Press).

Study Questions

1. Does professionalism require a code of ethics? Why? What should a code of ethics accomplish? Why?

2. Briefly describe in your own words the "public service" concept of policing stated in the *IACP Code of Ethics*. Does Cook agree with this perspective? Do you agree? Why? Defend your position.

3. Some people argue that ethical codes contain only ideals that one should *try* to live up to, rather than behaviors that one is *obligated* to accomplish. What does Cook have to say about such a view? Should a criminal justice practitioner simply *try* not to violate a subject's Constitutional rights, or does that practitioner have a moral obligation not to violate the Constitution? Why? Defend your position.

4. What do you think the IACP code intends by keeping one's "private life unsullied as an example to all"? Is off-the-job intoxication a violation? What about fornication (in jurisdictions where fornication is a misdemeanor) or sodomy (homosexual or heterosexual)? Is it a violation of the code if an officer grows and smokes marijuana in a jurisdiction where the amount involved is legal or is a misdemeanor? Defend your position.

5. What is Cook's main objection to paragraph three of the IACP code? Rewrite the paragraph so that it avoids the objection. Can it still function as a code of ethics?

How Structural Variables Constrain the Parole Officer's Use of Discretionary Powers

RICHARD McCLEARY

Introduction

Takagi and Robison (1968) have shown that the discretionary behavior of parole officers (POs) varies from individual to individual and from parole district to parole district. Most studies have attributed this variance to differences in PO types, and specifically, to psychological mechanisms such as personality and philosophy (See, e.g., Ohlin, Piven, & Pappenfort, 1956; Glaser, 1964; Havel, 1965). In contrast, the data presented here will show that what appears to be a free exercise of discretion on the part of the PO may actually be a structurally constrained, forced behavior. This finding is consistent with studies of related occupations (e.g., Sudnow, 1965; Scott, 1969), with studies of corrections bureaucracies at the policy-making level (e.g., Takagi, 1967; Kassebaum, Ward, & Wilner, 1971), and with widely accepted theories of behavioral specificity. Mischel's (1968) interpretation of these theories is typical:

> We should not expect a person to show similar behavior across situations if the consequences produced by the same behavior pattern in different situations are discrepant ... Consider for example the differences in the typical outcomes to an American girl for wearing slacks on a family picnic or wearing the same garment to her high school graduation (p. 178).

A PO's case decision, or his interaction with a parolee, is determined not only by the PO's personality, but also by organizational contexts and the costs of alternative decisions. In short, the PO often does what he *has* to do, not what he *wants* to do.

POs have always exercised two forms of discretionary power. First, POs could arbitrarily return their parolees to prison even if the parolees had broken no laws. Second, even if a law had been broken, the PO was not obliged to return his parolee to prison. While judicial reforms[1] have stripped Cook County POs of their power arbitrarily to return parolees to prison, their power to "save" certain parolees remains intact. When a parolee is arrested, for example, his PO may still attempt to negotiate the charges with the police and prosecutors. If the charges are reduced or dropped, the parolee will not be returned to prison. As this negotiation process is a discretionary decision on the part of the PO, however, it may happen that two parolees commit a crime together, yet depending on their POs, one may be returned to prison while the other remains free. The difference will ordinarily be the personal dispositions of the two POs, and perhaps more important, the structural constraints that differentially affect the two POs.

The structural constraints on discretion arise from a basic conflict between POs and their Department of Corrections (DC) superiors. The POs I met saw themselves as counselors or therapists[2] whose primary loyalty is to the client. One PO told me:

> I don't *owe* my clients anything but there is a matter of professional ethics that I have to consider. If one of my clients tells me something in confidence, I don't always pass it

along to the DC. I am a professional. I spent six years in school and another three years out there on the streets learning to do what I do. No DC honcho in Springfield can tell me what's best for my clients. When I make a case decision, I only think about what's best for my client. That's what being a professional means.

This comment was not atypical although many POs temper their statements to include those rare cases where the client is "obviously dangerous." DC officials tolerate and even encourage this attitude but insist at the same time that client-loyalty be subordinated to organizational loyalty.

The case of Richard illustrates the potential conflict between client and organizational loyalties. A former street gang member, Richard had been working at a "good" job for over eight months. According to Richard's PO, John, Richard was making an excellent adjustment to parole. One morning, John received a phone call from Richard's sister. She told John that Richard was carrying a pistol and that he might be planning an armed robbery. John and I visited Richard at his job that afternoon. Richard admitted carrying a pistol but denied that he was planning to use it in a robbery. He explained that his former gang was pressuring him to rejoin and that one gang member, "Seaweed," had threatened his life. Although carrying a pistol is a serious violation of parole, John did not ask Richard to surrender the pistol. In fact, no report of the phone call from Richard's sister or the meeting with Richard was ever made. John explained his decision this way:

> Seaweed's a bad dude. He's the gang enforcer. What I *should* do is put out a warrant for Richard. That would be best for me and best for the DC. It wouldn't be best for Richard though. I'm going to take a chance with him. I don't always do that. It depends on the dude and on the situation. If Richard gets caught with that piece, it's going to be front-page stuff and that'll be bad for the DC. It'll be bad for me because he might cop out and

say I gave him permission. What I'm counting on is that word'll get back to Seaweed. He'll stay clear if he knows Richard's got a piece. Another thing I'm counting on is that if Richard gets caught, he'll leave my name out of it. He's been cool with me before.

This case brings out three general points. First, organizational loyalty is usually related to publicity. As far as DC officials are concerned, a "good" PO is one who among other things does not embarrass the DC. Second, client-loyalty often forces the PO to do things that at least run the risk of generating adverse publicity. And third, the PO often jeopardizes his career through client-loyalty.

Few POs would have taken the risk that John took, yet most POs think of John as a "good" PO, a "real professional." DC officials, on the other hand, say that POs like John are neither "fair" nor "competent." These are euphemisms that DC officials use to describe organizational loyalty. While POs themselves do not admire *un*fairness or *in*competence in a literal sense, it turns out that they admire their peers who have been labeled unfair or incompetent. This is because by being fair and by being competent, the PO alters his relationship to his clients. He becomes an ideal DC employee rather than an ideal PO. The data presented here will show that in general, a PO's freedom of discretion varies as a function of his ability to manipulate these labels. Moreover, the data will show that the PO's exercise of discretionary power is determined not only by internal psychological mechanisms as earlier studies have shown, but also by three structural variables: the situation, the client, and the PO's reputation for fairness and competence.

Method

There are approximately 50 POs employed by the Illinois DC, Adult Field Services in Cook County. Six or seven POs will ordinarily work under one supervisor in a branch office. The half-dozen supervisors in turn work under three middle level managers. These managers and all other DC employees who are not supervisors or POs are called "DC officials." My field notes make direct reference to 42 POs, five branch office supervisors, and eleven DC officials.

Participant observer and interview data presented here have been collected regularly since September, 1974. My mode of entry into the field was direct. I presented myself at a branch office and asked permission of the supervisor to interview POs. Permission was given, and at a later date, was formalized through a written agreement with the Director of Adult Field Services, Cook County. The terms of this agreement (which I observed) were that I would not misrepresent myself to any PO or parolee and that I would not attempt to gain access to clinical data.

My role throughout the data collection phase was necessarily what Gold (1958) calls the "observer as participant." This role was not so restrictive as might be imagined, however. First, POs and graduate students have quite a bit in common at least as far as backgrounds are concerned. Furthermore, most POs have had the experience of "trying to collect data for a thesis." Consequently most of the POs I met were sympathetic and many went out of their way to help. In the beginning, for example, many POs introduced me to their friends. These natural friendship networks were instrumental for my introduction and acceptance into the branch offices.

The majority of my time in the field was spent accompanying POs on their "house call" rounds. I took notes of these experiences and usually expanded them the same day. I also spent time in the branch offices simply talking to POs and parolees. I usually reproduced these conversations from memory the same day. Most of the POs I met were not at all reluctant to answer my questions. Some appeared to enjoy the experience.

Many of the excerpts presented here as data are not actual interview or field note excerpts. The raw data have been "contaminated" in some cases to the extent that no general statement, behavior, or specific act can be attributed to a real person. At the same time, however, the "contamination" was not so complete as to change the underlying principle. The method of argument used here, analytic induction as outlined by Becker (1963), is supported by the original raw data.

Finally, there is no attempt made to disguise the parole agency studied here. My experiences with Federal and Wisconsin parole agencies convince me that the Illinois DC is no better or worse than the average. This article then is not meant to be an indictment of the Illinois DC or of any Illinois DC employee. The phenomena described here are general to all parole supervision agencies. Candid corrections officials will support this assertion.

The Data

FAIRNESS

POs are labeled fair or unfair strictly on the basis of their behavior in a given situation. A DC official described fairness this way:

> Don't forget that POs have two responsibilities, one to the ex-offender and one to the public. A fair PO stands behind his men 100% when they're innocent. When they're guilty, he turns his back on them. He balances his responsibility to the ex-offender with his responsibility to the public.

POs themselves interpret fairness more cynically. They have another name for it. One PO told me:

> Realistic is a better word for it. First off, I don't make distinctions between guilty and innocent men. I'll help a guilty man beat a rap if I can and if he deserves a break, and I'll watch an innocent man go down the tubes if I have to. It's not that I don't want to help, it's that I can't. I can make a certain amount of trouble for the State's Attorney but that's an unrealistic option. I'm only stalling off the inevitable. The State's Attorney's going to get my man anyway and I'm only making a powerful enemy by stalling. What I do in a case like that is co-operate.

Maybe I even give the State's Attorney some moral support. Then I come out of it with a reputation for being fair. But that's not being fair, that's just being realistic.

Being fair or being realistic means knowing when the situation is hopeless. Some examples of hopeless situations are:

Anything with a gun or where somebody gets hurt. Heroin's okay but selling heroin's the same as murder. The State's Attorney won't give my man a break in a case like that. He can't. The newspapers would crucify him.

A fair PO then is loyal to his clients only until the situation becomes hopeless. An unfair PO in the same situation continues to resist the inevitable and thereby risks adverse publicity. The net effect of unfair behavior is to focus public attention on the failures of prisons, parole boards, and parole supervision agencies. The entire DC suffers.

A few situations are absolutely hopeless (See Table 1) but most are only hopeless in degree. In marginal situations, the PO can continue to fight for his client, and in so doing, the PO is likely to win the respect of his peers. For example, a PO told me:

Look here. If you were on an operating table, would you want a realistic surgeon? No! An unrealistic surgeon keeps on working until your heart stops and he doesn't worry about getting blood on the walls. Of course, that's just talk. You can carry anything to extremes.

This was not an unusual comment. Many POs admire their peers who continue to fight for clients caught in hopeless situations. However, all POs realize that client-loyalty can be carried to an extreme.

The case of Lucas illustrates this principle well. One of Lucas' clients was arrested on a highly publicized weapons charge. This situation was absolutely hopeless but Lucas felt that extenuating circumstances[3] in the case demanded a reduced charge. When the prosecutor refused to negotiate the charge, Lucas deliberately stalled the disposition of the case. The client was eventually returned to prison but not before Lucas' futile efforts were noted by the press. At the beginning of this incident, a PO told me:

I wish Lucas would quit diddling around with the dude. If he was my client, he'd be back in Statesville already. Any dude gets caught in Cook County with a piece gets revoked. That's all there is to it. Lucas is just getting himself and a lot of other people in trouble. He's not going to save the dude.

Soon POs began to feel that Lucas' behavior was exposing them, not the DC, to public ridicule. A

Table 1 Only a Few Situations Are Absolutely Hopeless. Most Are Hopeless or Promising in Degree

Situation	Examples	Degree of Constraint on the PO
Absolutely hopeless	Murder Rape Weapons assault Narcotics sales	The PO has no freedom whatsoever. His behavior is totally constrained by the situation. If he "bucks the system," he will be denounced by his peers.
Marginally hopeless	Burglary Simple robbery	The PO has relatively little freedom.
Marginally promising	Narcotics possession Simple theft	The PO has a relatively great degree of freedom.
Absolutely promising	All misdemeanors "Victimless" felonies	Freedom is greatest. The parolee will not ordinarily be returned to prison in these situations unless his PO is forced to "sacrifice" him for some reason.

few days later when an exaggerated, sensationalized account of the case appeared in the newspapers, a PO said:

I've never been so pissed off in my life! Luke's done some crazy things before but never like this. Christ, the papers are making a federal case out of this. He's putting every one of us out there on front street. If he thinks he's going to get away with this, he's wrong. I'm not going to complain, but I know a half-dozen other POs who are.

As a result of lobbying by other POs, Lucas was relieved of his caseload and transferred to another parole district. Because POs think of such transfers as demotions, it can be said that Lucas' behavior was denounced by his peers and punished by his superiors.

In summary, a situation is realistic or unrealistic, hopeless or not, only in terms of its potential for generating adverse publicity. POs who refuse to abandon their clients in hopeless situations soon acquire reputations for being unfair, with consequences apparent later in the discussion. Finally, while POs generally admire peers who "buck the system," POs will denounce any peer who carries idealism to the extreme.

COMPETENCE

Fairness is a relatively clear and concrete term. Competence is not. A DC official told me, for example:

A competent PO knows when his clients are lying. He doesn't run around half-cocked, tilting at windmills. He's sure of his facts before he jumps on somebody. Frankly, one of the biggest problems we have is that some POs get too close to their clients. A PO like that isn't competent. You can't make good judgments when you're emotionally involved.

Other DC officials defined *in*competence similarly: A lapse in judgment resulting from an emotional involvement with a client. POs seem to be familiar with this notion but many dispute a key point one PO said:

You never know when a client's lying. Maybe you can test him out by asking him something you can check up on. If it turns out he lied, you know he's lying about other things too. But what if he passes your test? That doesn't mean he's not going to lie about other things. You never know when a client's lying but you never admit that. If somebody asks you about a client, you make something up and hope you get away with it. Anytime a PO says something definite about a client, the PO has to tell a lie.

POs routinely confess to "lying." Social psychologists might describe this behavior more sympathetically as a reinterpretation or reconstruction of reality: argumentation. For example, a PO might embellish a story before passing it along to the prosecutor:

Washington's not a criminal. He's sick. He needs treatment. The charge against him is substantially petty anyway. Would you call that a burglary? I'm going to try to get him probation on this. Then I'll get him into a drug rehabilitation program.

Brown didn't go along of his own accord. They forced him into it. I talked to Brown and I think I can get him to co-operate with you. If he testifies against the others, can you give him a break?

In effect then, when a PO tries to intercede with the prosecutor on behalf of a client, the PO is "lying." The point of this argument is that the PO's ability to "lie" depends on his reputation for competence. The better his reputation, the more credible are his "lies."

This point is best illustrated by the case of Tony, a PO who is no longer with the DC. Tony was contacted by a policeman who wanted information about one of Tony's clients. Tony told the policeman that he had seen the client that day and that the client was making excellent progress. It turned out later that the client had absconded and was in jail in another state. Tony could not have seen the client as he said he had. Tony's branch office supervisor explained the incident this way:

What happened was that Tony called up the parolee's brother and the brother lied to Tony. He said the parolee was at work but that everything was fine. That's what Tony should have put in his report—that he talked to the parolee's *brother*. Instead Tony was dumb enough to stake his career on the brother's word. Now what happened after that was that this detective tells everybody in the police department about Tony. Tony looks incompetent, I look incompetent, my boss looks incompetent, everybody in the DC up to and including the Director looks incompetent. We have to work with the police and that's hard when they think we're an incompetent outfit. Tony knows he's got a bad reputation. He should have known better. He never should have taken the word of the parolee's brother about something so important.

The POs who commented on this incident were familiar with the consequences of Tony's behavior but most emphasized another point. One PO said:

They don't really think Tony lied even though that's what really happened. He never called that guy's brother but they prefer to think he did. They want to think it's a case of a PO being chumped by one of his guys. They don't want to think Tony's dishonest. They want to think he's a chump. See, the police think that POs are a bunch of do-gooders. Tony's problem is that he's been tagged with that before, so they're always checking up on him. Hell, I vouch for some of my guys too but I don't have to worry about people laying for me like they lay for Tony. Tony's the type of PO who gets close to his guys. He goes out of his way to build up a rapport with his guys. People see him doing that and right away they think he's a do-gooder. Hell, I think Tony's one of the best POs I've ever known.

This was a typical view. Many POs actually suspected entrapment, that is, suspected that the policeman knew the parolee's whereabouts all along and called Tony only on the chance that Tony might "lie."

Another version of what "really happened" comes from Tony himself. He refused to discuss the case *per se* but offered this assessment of its long-range consequences:

I still sit in on plea bargaining sessions but they don't listen to me anymore. It's frustrating. The Public Defender's not looking out for my clients' interests and when I try to, the Public Defender and the State's Attorney tell me to butt out.

Tony resigned from the DC shortly after he made this comment. He felt that he could no longer represent his clients effectively. In fact, formal or informal plea bargaining sessions present the PO with his greatest opportunity to "lie" for his clients. When this forum is denied him, the PO is powerless.

Congruencies in these statements support some generalizations on the subject of competence. For example, it is apparent that competence is not a concrete entity. It is a mystique. Furthermore, while DC officials equate incompetence with gullibility, POs themselves have a more cynical, more complex interpretation. From their perspective, POs who have been labeled do-gooders are closely scrutinized. This scrutiny inevitably leads to the stigma of incompetence. Once a PO has been labeled incompetent, his ability to "lie" and thereby save his clients is destroyed.

In summary, POs cultivate reputations for competence. Once established, the reputation determines the PO's freedom of discretion. The reputation building process will be fully discussed below. First however, a final consequence of incompetence must be introduced.

PAPERWORK

There are two types of activity POs engage in: Activities that leave no permanent record and activities that require written justification. POs are free to do whatever they want to do so long as no one is looking, or equivalently, so long as no paperwork is generated. When behavior requires written justification, however, the PO's freedom is directly proportional to his ability to write self-serving reports. This point is dramatized by the statement of one PO:

> I had a nightmare once. The phone rang and when I picked it up, it was a newspaper reporter. One of my men ran amok down in the Loop. Then I woke up. I was glad it was only a dream. Whenever something like that happens, they have an inquiry. They subpoena your paperwork and you have to show that you were handling the case properly. They look for inconsistencies. If they find anything irregular, you're in for trouble.

A competent PO keeps excellent records as insurance against such events. He does not do this, however, without help.

The branch office supervisors are charged with collecting and verifying records and reports. The supervisor then plays a role similar to that of the bookkeeper in a branch office of a large corporation; he is in a position to tell his POs what irregularities catch the auditor's eye. POs realize this and take advantage of their supervisor's help whenever possible. Some examples:

> It's always best to hedge your language. Then later on nobody knows what the hell you meant. Terry keeps his eye on things like that. When I first started here, Terry handed my reports back with penciled corrections—like a teacher.
>
> Say like you're doing up an interview with a marginal man. You want to tell him certain things just for the record. Well, my supervisor knows what those things are, so I get him to help me write up my reports. Then when the marginal man screws up, my reports make it look like I busted my ass for him.
>
> If you read through the old reports, you see a lot that just say 'No Change Since Last Month.' Now that's an honest report but it makes you look second rate. POs who hand in reports like that are rookies or else they're not in tight with their supervisors.

POs call these practices "creative writing," "protection," or "C.Y.A."[4]

Fair, competent POs generally have close personal relationships with their supervisors. They speak openly about the "protection" system. The supervisors were also quite frank about this arrangement. One told me:

> When one of my POs comes in here with a problem, I show him how to handle the paperwork—how to protect himself. If the paperwork's not done, the PO isn't protected. When that happens, you get morale problems and attrition. Sooner or later, you get a new supervisor. The common denominator between me and the other supervisors is that we all came up through the ranks in a bureaucracy.

Another supervisor said:

> Suppose one of my POs has two options, x and y. If x is the safe, conservative way, I'd rather the PO do x. Unfortunately, some of my POs are very conscientious. They'll do y no matter what I say, and frankly, if they're going to do y anyway, I want them to do it the safest way possible. What I do is I sit down with the PO and help him write his report. On paper, I can make y look safer and more conservative than it really is.

On a few occasions, POs related anecdotes that suggested collusion of a greater magnitude and of a more determined nature. For example, one case that I was able to verify:

> Okay, now I don't do this myself but I know you can get away with backdating your reports. Your supervisor's got a date stamper you have to use. Like if a dude's on special board orders to report weekly but he misses a week. If the dude deserves a break, you can get away with handing in two reports the next week—but your supervisor's got to let you use his date stamper.

Such cases were atypical, however. Collusion is usually limited to the area of simple "protection." Supervisors and POs have a common interest there. In the event of official inquiry, both will want to have excellent, self-serving records.

Another reason why supervisors "protect" POs is that the "protected" PO appears to be more competent than he actually is. Of course, the competence of a PO reflects back on his supervisor. The data show nevertheless that supervisors do not "protect" incompetent POs. In the case of Tony, for example, one PO remarked:

> Tony should have made his report ambiguous. You never say you *saw* the parolee. Your reports are supposed to keep you out of trouble, not get you into trouble. If Tony had checked his reports through his supervisor first, he never would have got in trouble. My supervisor would never let me hand in a report like that.

What this PO said in effect is that Tony should have "protected" himself. Yet the data show that Tony's supervisor had previously refused to help Tony, and in fact, this is one of the reasons Tony resigned. In every case observed incompetent POs were refused "protection." One supervisor confirmed my suspicions, explaining:

> There are two different kinds of POs. I never ask one of my men if he's investigated a case thoroughly because some of them don't know what 'thoroughly' means. I know who does professional casework and who doesn't. I don't want the amateurs bothering me with their problems. There's no sense me going up the creek because of somebody else's incompetence.

Police and prosecutors ordinarily keep a sharp eye on POs suspected of being incompetent. Supervisors therefore take a greater risk "protecting" an incompetent PO. Furthermore, this outside attention often forces the supervisor himself to keep an eye on his incompetent POs. In Tony's case, for example, the supervisor was instructed by memo from a high DC official to scrutinize Tony's future behavior. In line with this point, one supervisor told me:

> My biggest problem is taking the flak for an incompetent PO. When I have an incompetent man working in this office, I have to watch him night and day. If he pulls some boneheaded stunt, I have to catch it before it gets out of the office. If somebody outside catches it, it looks like I'm not doing my job.

Another supervisor described a PO with a strong but undeserved reputation for incompetence this way:

> He's a shit magnet. Don't get me wrong. I like the kid but he's more trouble than he's worth. Actually, I guess he's a pretty good PO. He grates a lot of people in the police department the wrong way though and he's got a reputation for fouling up. When a PO gets a reputation like that, it makes more work for the supervisor.

Having an incompetent PO in the office means two things to the supervisor. First, the attention of police, prosecutors, and DC officials is focussed on the branch office. This will ordinarily disrupt or at least distress the normal office processes and especially the business of "protection." Second, having an incompetent PO in the office means that the supervisor himself faces potential embarrassment. To appear competent, the supervisor must catch "foul-ups" before they are brought to his attention by outsiders.

In summary, the PO's reputation for fairness and competence is an important structural constraint on his discretionary behavior. The PO's freedom is generally proportional to the strength of his reputation. This relationship between reputation and freedom follows from three principles. First, the incompetent PO ordinarily cannot "lie" successfully to outside agencies. Second, the incompetent PO cannot depend on his supervisor for "protection." And third, the incompetent PO may be subjected to close scrutiny from his own supervisor.

THE MYSTIQUE OF REP

Fairness and competence are reputations or labels, or as POs themselves say, "reps." Novice POs are usually considered fair until their behavior in a hopeless situation proves them otherwise. Thus POs do not actually have to *build* reps for fairness. On the other hand, novice POs are usually assumed to be *in*competent by DC officials, police, prosecutors, and branch office supervisors. The novice PO builds an increasingly stronger rep for competence as time passes and as he begins more and more to have successful interactions with outside agencies. Under optimal conditions, a novice PO will need a year or more to convince his peers, his supervisor, and important outsiders that he is competent.

The rep building process has three distinct components. To build a strong rep, the novice PO must be *informative, hyperfair,* and *selective.* These component terms will ordinarily describe the quality of the PO's relationships with outside agencies. When these terms are more closely analyzed, however, it is apparent that they also describe the quality of a PO's relationships with his clients. One point implicit to the rep building process then is that the PO's perception of a client will be a structural constraint on the PO's behavior.

To begin with, an *informative* PO is simply one who feeds information into the criminal justice system. Some of the information will be useful to the system but most of it will be use*less.* An example of useful information is the "tip." Many POs encourage their clients to become informants for this purpose.[5] One credentials conscious PO summed up this situation.

> The best degree to have so far as status is concerned is a Master's in Social Work. But I'd rather have three dependable snitches than three college degrees. When you come up with a hot tip, the boys downtown think you're on the ball.

A tip not only strengthens the PO's rep but also indebts the tip recipient to the PO. A PO who has amassed a number of favors with the police and prosecutor will ordinarily have enormous discretionary power.

The PO will more often feed useless information into the system, however. This information typically consists of trivial data the PO has collected from clients. For example, I overheard one PO tell a client:

> Look here, Ray. Why don't you give me your chick's address. I won't hassle her or anything but if they ever pick you up down there, I can say, 'Yeah, so what? I know where Ray is.

He's down there visiting his chick and her address is such-and-such.' Then I won't look like a chump. You know, it'll look like you asked my permission first.

While useless to the system, this information contributes to the overall air of competence the PO tries to exude. I have never met a PO who did not collect trivial data, and in fact, most POs keep notebooks or index card files near their telephones. The PO in this example was candid about the value of this information:

> Some POs will tell you they use this stuff to track down absconders but that's foolish. Absconders don't leave forwarding addresses. Collecting this stuff is like keeping two sets of books—one for me and one for the I.R.S. I use this stuff to bluff somebody once in a while but mostly I use it to make reports look intelligent.

Bluffing is always done with caution. If the PO's rep is strong enough, his bluffs are seldom called. An incompetent PO, on the other hand, cannot ordinarily bluff even his own supervisor.

The second rep building component is *hyperfairness.* A fair PO abandons his clients when the situation becomes hopeless but a hyperfair PO actually turns on his clients in hopeless situations. One PO told me:

> You know why Auslander likes me? Because every so often I help him burn one of my men. It's usually a case where I can't help the man anyway but Auslander doesn't know that. Then the next time I ask him to give one of my men a break, he thinks he owes me a favor. He's got the idea that when I think one of my men is guilty, I'm going to help him pull the switch. A rep like that doesn't hurt.

Like delivering a "hot tip," being hyperfair may indebt the police and the prosecutor to the PO.

A hyperfair PO co-operates with the prosecutor by lending moral support, by leaking clinical data that the prosecutor could not obtain legally, and in rare cases, by prejudicing the defense attorney. Many cases were observed in which the PO used his influence with his client to coerce a guilty plea. In one case reported by an informant but verified independently, a PO gave both the prosecutor and the defense attorney copies of a clinical report that diagnosed a client as a "violent psychopath." As a result, the defense attorney was prejudiced against the client and could not vigorously represent the client during plea bargaining.

A third and final component of the rep building process is *selectivity*. Like being hyperfair, being selective entails helping the prosecutor at the expense of the client. Unlike being hyperfair, however, being selective is not confined only to hopeless situations. Instead the selective PO underrepresents some clients and overrepresents others regardless of the leeway he possesses in the situation. In one case, for example, a PO testified as a character witness for a client. The PO later told me:

> I don't do that often. If I testify for a client, the judges know the client is all right. I've got a good rep with the judges because I'm selective. But if I testified for every one of my clients who got into a little scrape, the judges wouldn't trust me anymore. They'd think I'd turned into a Goddam social worker. You can't save everybody. If you try, you end up not being able to save anybody.[6]

The epithets "social worker" and "do-gooder" describe incompetent POs. To avoid these labels, and consequently, the stigma of incompetence, POs are forced to sacrifice some clients caught in marginal or absolutely realistic situations (See Table 1).

The major implication of selectivity is that the PO must decide which clients to save and which to sacrifice. The case of Brown and Jones is a good illustration of this phenomenon. Brown and Jones were involved in a highly publicized but nevertheless petty escape from County Jail. Whitney, a PO I was working with at that time, had both men in his caseload. I was particularly interested in what Whitney would do in this case because the charges against the men were trivial. The "escape" was a typical "walkaway," and under the circumstances, it

might have made more sense to prosecute the jailers. The morning after the jailbreak, I asked Whitney what he planned to do when Brown and Jones were recaptured. He said:

> That's a bitch. They were both in jail on lousy misdemeanors but now they got felony busts. Jailbreak's a one-to-six-year fall. I'm going to see what I can do for Brown but Jones can start packing his suitcase. He's going back to Statesville.

When I pressed Whitney for an explanation, he refused to discuss the case. However, Willy, another PO who was familiar with the case, said:

> That's simple. Jones is a smart ass. He was on his way back to the joint the day he got out. The other one, Brown, is a sincere client. He probably went along on the breakout because he was afraid of those other bums.

Willy told me that he had no trouble recognizing sincere clients:

> That's the easiest decision I have to make. A sincere client comes to me with his problems. He doesn't hold anything back. A sincere client's honest too. Some of these bums even lie to me about where they live. Most of them don't want my help anyway. I'm not going to chase a client around and kiss his ass. When a client's in trouble, I expect him to tell me about it—and not after it's too late to do anything.

Willy's statement appears to contradict an earlier assertion that the PO never knows when his client is lying. When I asked Willy explicitly whether "sincerity" was synonymous with "honesty," he said:

> No, it's more complicated than that but I can't explain it. It's just a feeling you get from working with a particular client. You know what I mean. He's *sincere*.

Not surprisingly, all POs agree that the difference between a "good" client and a "bad" client is sincerity. Yet no PO could define sincerity in concrete, objective terms. Later, a fairly straightforward definition began to emerge from the data. For example, I discovered that many POs had made statements like:

> When a man comes in here hooked on heroin and asks me to help, I get a really good feeling inside. That means he trusts me. That means I'm getting through to him. Whenever I get through to a man, I experience a real feeling of accomplishment.

In other words, sincerity is a *gratifier*. Helping a sincere client is more gratifying than helping an insincere client. Not only does the sincere client depend on his PO then, the sincere client is grateful to his PO.

In other cases, sincerity may refer to the client's *trustworthiness*. For example, in the case of Brown, Whitney had struck a bargain with the prosecutor: Brown would go free in return for his testimony against Jones and the other escapees. Had Brown reneged on his word at some point during the trial, the escapees would have been found not guilty; Whitney's reputation in the State's Attorney's office would have been damaged.

A case that illustrates this aspect of sincerity concerns a PO who perjured himself to provide a client with an alibi. After testifying, the PO told me:

> It wasn't something I did without thinking about it first. The dude is an apprentice—some sort of trade. He's two months away from finishing the program. I figured he needed a break. If I didn't testify, he would have gone back to the joint for five or six years. I'd have to start all over on him when he got out. He'd be too old for an apprenticeship by then. I'm glad I did it but it's not something I'd do for just anybody. You can only do that for a dude you really trust. If this dude had copped out after I testified, I'd be finished here. I knew this dude would stick to his story no matter what happened. We've got a really close relationship.

In other words, sincerity is a measure of trustworthiness. Although perjury is an extreme example, the general principle holds in all situations. For example, John trusted Richard not to get caught carrying a pistol, or if caught, not to mention John's prior knowledge; Whitney trusted Brown to deliver testimony; and in general, if a PO represents a client as being in need of some "treatment," the PO must trust the client to co-operate with the treatment program. More than one PO has told me that it is easiest to "save" a client with a record of drug or alcohol abuse. Such clients can be represented as "sick" rather than "criminal." But again, the client must be trusted to act "sick."[7]

Finally, recalling that POs idealize peers who become personally involved with clients, it is apparent that as far as POs themselves are concerned, a sincere client is an *ideal* client. He depends upon, is grateful to, and can be trusted by his PO. He accepts his PO as a friend and allows his PO to act out a professionally ideal role. Insincere clients, on the other hand, see their POs as distrusted adversaries.

HOW THE SYSTEM WORKS IN GENERAL

The preceding argument has dwelt on the PO's dealings with other criminal justice agencies. In fact, however, POs spend most of their time working with social welfare and non-criminal rehabilitation agencies. The PO's intercessionary role and the structural constraints that shape his case decisions are nevertheless unchanged.

The case of Reynaldo illustrates how the system works in general. When I first met Reynaldo, he was one of Bob's clients. Reynaldo wanted to earn a high school diploma, so he asked Bob to sponsor him for admission to a special education program. Bob refused without any explanation. A short time later, Reynaldo moved to another part of Chicago and was transferred to Whitney's case load. Whitney immediately sponsored Reynaldo for admission to the special program. When I discussed this change-about with Reynaldo, he expressed the opinion that Bob was prejudiced against Spanish-speaking parolees. Whitney disagreed with Reynaldo on this point, however:

> No, Bob's straight. You don't realize that a PO has to be careful about who he sponsors for some of these programs. If you send a real jag down, the program might take it out on

the rest of your caseload. I can't show you Reynaldo's records but he's got some things in his past that make him look like a bad risk for this program. I had to do some real talking to get him in. Now I've been around here a long time and I have some clout. I can afford to take a chance on Reynaldo. But Bob's a rookie. He has to be careful.

Narcotics offenders, check artists, and burglars are bad risks because of their relatively high recidivism rates. These parolees will often be denied access to the best programs for an obvious reason. I heard one PO tell a bad risk parolee:

Hey man, that program is expensive. You could be back in Statesville two weeks from now and all the money they spent on you would be wasted. You show me a year of good behavior on the streets and then I'll think about sponsoring you.

Parolees can also be denied opportunities because their "profiles" are not appropriate. For example:

Hooker needs a job bad. I'd send him down for this one but his profile's wrong. They're looking for young married dudes.

Profiles are most important when the agency has an unofficial "target" clientele. POs present their best faces to the agencies by scrupulously observing the "target" guidelines. If necessary, the agency can enforce its guidelines either indirectly, as Whitney explained, or directly, by complaining about a PO to the DC.[8] Such a complaint would affect the PO's rep, of course.

I observed the same phenomenon but in an exaggerated form when I examined the special "treatment" programs run by the DC *per se.* For example, the violent offender program calls for intensive supervision and counseling of parolees who are judged violent by absolute criteria. In practice, however, these criteria are so loosely interpreted that virtually every parolee in Cook County could be diagnosed "violent" by his PO and transferred to a special caseload. One PO who handles a violent offender caseload summarized this situation:

I don't have ten men in my caseload who are violent in any real sense. A lot of POs are using my caseload to build up their images. They have contests to see who can have the lowest return-to-prison rate. They get rid of their marginal cases by declaring them "violent." I don't care about my own return-to-prison rate but that kind of thing ruins the effectiveness of the violent offender program. My job is based on a twenty-man caseload. I'm supposed to have two eyeball contacts with every man every week. How can I do that with 55 men?[9]

So in the general case, the rep building process tends to corrupt the long-range goals of the organization. POs are encouraged to misuse the "treatment" milieu. A recent evaluation of Federal paraprofessional POs in Chicago (Gordon, 1976) found that paraprofessionals are more effective than professionals in some respects. This finding is consistent with the phenomenon described here. The effectiveness may come in part from the fact that paraprofessionals are not asked to demonstrate their competence in the usual way.[10]

In summary, a PO's freedom is proportional to his reputation for fairness and competence. As fairness is related to the situation, the situation will constrain behavior. As competence is related to the success of a PO's interactions with other agencies, and with his DC superiors, such factors as the PO's length of service and his past performance will constrain his behavior. And of course, in the process of building a rep, the PO is forced to label his clients. Thus the PO's own perception of a client constrains the PO's behavior. The description of the rep building dynamic has necessarily dwelt on the PO's interactions with other criminal justice agencies. However, the dynamic is general to all areas where the PO's role is intercessionary. Finally, the rep building dynamic has a corruptive effect on the long-range goals of the organization. Programs meant to "rehabilitate the client" or to "protect society" are used instead for rep building.

Conclusion

The findings presented here raise questions about the validity of most quantitative recidivism studies, and indeed, of recidivism statistics *per se*. Researchers typically look for differences or changes in recidivism rates across sections and across time. These differences or changes are then attributed to corresponding changes or differences in parolee characteristics, societal norms, or "rehabilitative treatments." Underlying such research is the assumption that the agent of failure lies in the parolee's social psychological history or biological constitution. These data show instead that the agent of failure may often lie in the structural dynamic of the parole supervision agency. Thus while a researcher may attribute an observed change in recidivism to an "effective treatment," it is just as likely that the change is due to some unknown shift in the structure of the parole agency.

The structural dynamic described here can be viewed as an extension and generalization of a phenomenon observed by Takagi (1967) in the Special Intensive Parole Unit experiment. During the late '50s and early '60s, the California DC randomly assigned parolees to 35 and 70-man caseloads. Although the DC expected the smaller caseloads to have lower recidivism rates, a preliminary evaluation showed no difference. According to Takagi, high DC officials decided at this point that a no-difference finding would be politically unacceptable. The POs assigned to the small caseloads were consequently told that they would be promoted strictly on the basis of their caseload recidivism rates: the lower the rate, the better the chance of promotion. A subsequent re-evaluation of the program found that the smaller caseloads were more effective than the larger caseloads in reducing recidivism (Havel & Sulka, 1962). What happened, of course, is that the researchers did observe a statistical difference but they incorrectly attributed this difference to the effectiveness of the treatment. In fact, the change was due entirely to a shift in the structural dynamic of the parole

agency, and particularly, to an abrupt change in the system of constraints that affect case decisions and PO parolee interactions.

Now to illustrate the relationship of this phenomenon to the Illinois DC, imagine that we have agreed upon some objective definition of recidivism; some parolees succeed, others fail. Clearly then, some parolees who by our definition are failures will be "saved" by their POs. Other parolees who are successes *ceteris paribus* will be abandoned or even sacrificed when the situation, the PO's perception, and the PO's reputation demand it. Still other parolees who, like Reynaldo, can become either successes or failures will be pushed in one direction or another by the PO's reputation. A measured recidivism rate is not only an aggregate of many objectively defined individual parole outcomes, it is also a unique indicator of the parole agency's structure. For all practical purposes, we may say that the parole agency "manufactures" successes and failures over and above the number provided by nature. Any change in the structural dynamic then is likely to affect the rate and quality of the manufacturing process.

The preceding argument should sensitize the reader to alternative explanations of recidivism statistics. The variance in this indicator from place to place and time to time may indeed mean that a treatment has been effective or that a societal norm has changed. However, there are also plausible organizational structure explanations. The prudent researcher will rule out these explanations before seriously considering others.

NOTES

1. Recent U.S. Supreme Court decisions have given parolees limited rights to due process consideration. Prior to 1973, for example, POs could detain a parolee in County Jail without filing an actual charge against the parolee; parolees could be returned to prison for "attitudinal" reasons. While POs still retain these powers in theory, they are exercised only in extreme emergencies. In practice, parolees are no longer returned to prison for technical violations (attitude, curfew, unauthorized

purchases) because the cost is prohibitive.

2. POs are officially designated as "Parole Counselors," parolees are semi-officially designated as "clients." One high DC official told me that he had never heard anyone say "parole officer" before.

3. Among other things, the parolee was believed completely innocent of the charge. This belief made the case unusual.

4. A PO told me that "C.Y.A." stands for California Youth Authority where the art of writing self-serving reports originated. The PO who told me this was quite serious. Other POs told me that "C.Y.A." stands for Cover Your Ass and this seems more plausible. Whatever, most POs use these initials in this context without questioning their literal meaning.

5. A major break in the infamous *Purolator Burglary* came about on a tip from a PO. This was unusual, however. Most tips concern narcotics traffic.

6. An anonymous academic tells me that professors behave similarly when writing recommendations: "If I think an applicant isn't going to be admitted anyway, I write a scathing—or worse—an adequate recommendation. This ensures that my glowing recommendations to the same department will have an optimum effect."

7. Furthermore, the parolee must be trusted to act "cured" after completing the program. One PO told me that he was able to place a client in a drug treatment program even though the client had never used drugs before; in other words, the client passed himself off as an addict to avoid being returned to prison. A social worker employed by the drug treatment program doubts that this could have happened. He admits nevertheless that POs often pass off minor users, or "chippers," as addicts. This places a strain on the program's already meager resources.

8. I have seen a number of written complaints from social welfare agencies about POs who send "bad risks" or "inappropriate profiles" to the program. POs seem to believe that the agencies want only those parolees who need help the least. Discrimination of this sort enhances the agencies' statistical performance, that is, inflates their success rates. POs call this type of discrimination "cherry picking."

9. Cf., footnote #7 above. This corruption is associated with every special program run by the DC. Incidentally, this emphasis on a low return-to-prison rate seems to originate with the POs themselves. The DC takes no note of the statistic when evaluating the PO's performance.

10. Personal communication, Margaret T. Gordon.

REFERENCES

Becker, Howard S.
1963 Outsiders: Studies in the Sociology of Deviance. New York: Free Press.

Glaser, Daniel T.
1964 The Effectiveness of a Prison and a Parole System. Indianapolis: Bobbs-Merrill.

Gold, Raymond L.
1958 "Roles in sociological field observations." Social Forces, 36:217-223.

Gordon, Margaret T.
1976 Involving Paraprofessionals in the Helping Process. Cambridge: Ballinger Publishers.

Havel, J.
1965 Special Intensive Parole Unit, Phase IV. Sacramento: Research Division, California Department of Corrections.

Havel, J. and E. Sulka
1962 Special Intensive Parole Unit, Phase III, Sacramento: Research Division, California Department of Corrections.

Kassebaum, G., D. Ward and D. Wilner
1971 Prison Treatment and Parole Survival. New York: John Wiley and Sons.

Mischel, W.
1968 Personality and Assessment. New York: John Wiley and Sons.

Ohlin, L. E., H. Piven and D. M. Pappenfort
1956 "Major dilemmas of the social worker in probation and parole." Journal of the National Probation and Parole Association, 2(3):211-225.

Scott, W. R.
1969 "Professional employees in a bureaucratic structure." In Amitai Etzioni (ed.), The Semi-Professions and Their Organization. New York: Free Press.

Sudnow, D.
1967 "Normal crimes: sociological features of the penal code in a public defender office." Social Problems, 12(3):255-276.

Takagi, P. T.
1967 Evaluation Systems and Deviations in a Parole Agency. Stanford University: Unpublished Ph.D. Dissertation.

Takagi, P. T. and J. Robison
1968 Case Decisions in a State Parole System. Sacramento: Research Division, California Department of Corrections.

Study Questions

1. Briefly describe the relationship between parole officer and parolee, as it is perceived by many parole officers, according to McCleary's research. What alternative relationships could properly exist, in your view? Which is the most desirable of all? Why? Defend your position.

2. Should there be any parole officer-parolee confidentiality? Why? Defend your position.

3. How far does McCleary believe client loyalty typically extends? Does a parole officer have a moral obligation of loyalty to the parolee? Why? Defend your position.

4. How do parole officers and Department of Corrections supervisors define a "fair" parole officer? A "competent" parole officer? How does this affect the amount of discretion available to the parole officer?

5. Should criminal justice practitioners be more restricted in the use of discretion? Why? Defend your position.

6. What does McCleary mean in saying that a parole agency "'manufactures successes and failures"? Does his research support this conclusion, in your view? Explain.

Learning Police Ethics

LAWRENCE SHERMAN

THERE ARE TWO WAYS to learn police ethics. One way is to learn on the job, to make your moral decisions in haste under the time pressures of police work. This is by far the most common method of learning police ethics, the way virtually all of the half million police officers in the United States decide what ethical principles they will follow in their work. These decisions are strongly influenced by peer group pressures, by personal self-interest, by passions and emotions in the heat of difficult situations.

There is another way. It may even be a better way. You can learn police ethics in a setting removed from the heat of battle, from the opinions of co-workers, and from the pressures of supervisors. You can think things through with a more objective perspective on the issues. You should be able to make up your mind about many difficult choices before you actually have to make them. And you can take the time to weigh all sides of an issue carefully, rather than making a snap judgment.

The purpose of this article is to provide a basis for this other, less common way of learning police ethics by making the alternative—the usual way of learning police ethics—as clear as possible. This portrait of the on-the-job method is not attractive, but it would be no more attractive if we were to paint the same picture for doctors, lawyers, judges, or college professors. The

Lawrence Sherman, "Learning Police Ethics," Criminal Justice Ethics, Vol. 1, No. 1 (Winter/Spring 1982), pp. 10–19. Used by permission of the author and The Institute for Criminal Justice Ethics, John Jay College of Criminal Justice, 899 Tenth Avenue, New York, NY 10102–0210.

generalizations we make are not true of all police officers, but they do reflect a common pattern, just as similar patterns are found in all occupations.

LEARNING NEW JOBS

Every occupation has a learning process (usually called "socialization") to which its new members are subjected. The socialization process functions to make most "rookies" in the occupation adopt the prevailing rules, values, and attitudes of their senior colleagues in the occupation. Very often, some of the existing informal rules and attitudes are at odds with the formal rules and attitudes society as a whole expects members of the occupation to follow. This puts rookies in a moral dilemma: should the rookies follow the formal rules of society or the informal rules of their senior colleagues?

These dilemmas vary in their seriousness from one occupation and one organization to the next. Young college professors may find that older professors expect them to devote most of their time to research and writing, while the general public (and their students) expects them to devote most of their time to teaching. With some luck, and a lot of work, they can do both.

Police officers usually face much tougher dilemmas. Like waiters, longshoremen, and retail clerks, they may be taught very early how to steal—at the scene of a burglary, from the body of a dead person, or in other opportunities police confront. They may be taught how to commit perjury in court to insure that their arrests lead to conviction, or how to lie in disciplinary investigations to protect their colleagues. They may be taught how to shake people down, or how to beat people up. Or they may be fortunate enough to go to work in an agency, or with a group of older officers, in which none of these violations of official rules is ever suggested to them.

Whether or not rookie police officers decide to act in ways the wider society might view as unethical, they are all subjected to a similar process of being taught certain standards of behavior. Their reactions to that learning as the years pass by can be described as their *moral careers:* the changes in the morality and ethics of their behavior. But the moral career is closely connected to the *occupational career:* the stages of growth and development in becoming a police officer.

This article examines the process of learning a new job as the context for learning police ethics. It then describes the content of the ethical and moral values in many police department "cultures" that are conveyed to new police officers, as well as the rising conflict within police agencies over what those values should be. Finally, it describes the moral career of police officers, including many of the major ethical choices officers make.

Becoming A Police Officer

There are four major stages in the career of anyone joining a new occupation:[1]

- the *choice* of occupation
- the *introduction* to the occupation
- the first *encounter* with doing the occupation's work
- the *metamorphosis* into a full-fledged member of the occupation

Police officers go through these stages, just as doctors and bankers do. But the transformation of the police officer's identity and self-image may be more radical than in many other fields. The process can be overwhelming, changing even the strongest of personalities.

CHOICE

There are three aspects of the choice to become a police officer. One is the *kind of person* who makes that choice. Another is the *reason* the choice is made, the motivations for doing police work. The third is the *methods* people must use as police officers. None of these aspects of choice appears to predispose police officers to be more or less likely to perform their work ethically.

Many people toy with the idea of doing police work, and in the past decade the applicants for policing have become increasingly diverse.

Once a predominately white male occupation, policing has accepted many more minority group members and attracted many more women. More college-educated people have sought out police work, but this may just reflect the higher rate of college graduates in the total population.

What has not changed, apparently, is the socioeconomic background of people who become police. The limited evidence suggests police work attracts the sons and daughters of successful tradespeople, foremen, and civil servants—especially police. For many of them, the good salary (relative to the educational requirements), job security, and prestige of police work represent a good step up in the world, an improvement on their parents' position in life.

The motivation to become a police officer flows naturally from the social position of the people who choose policing. People do not seem to choose policing out of an irrational lust for power or because they have an "authoritarian personality"; the best study on this question showed that New York City police recruits even had a *lower* level of authoritarian attitudes than the general public (although their attitudes become more authoritarian as they become adapted to police work, rising to the general public's level of authoritarian attitudes).[2] Police applicants tend to see police work as an adventure, as a chance to do work out of doors without being cooped up in an office, as a chance to do work that is important for the good of society, and not as a chance to be the "toughest guy on the block." Nothing in the motivation to apply for a police position seems to predispose police officers towards unethical behavior.

Nor do the methods of selecting police officers seem to affect their long-term moral careers. There was a time when getting on the force was a matter of bribery or political favors for local politicians, or at least a matter of knowing the right people involved in grading the entrance examinations and sitting on the selection committees. But in the 1980s the selection process appears to be highly bureaucratic, with impersonal multiple-choice tests scored by computers playing the most important role in the process.

To be sure, there are still subjective background investigations, personal interviews, and other methods that allow biases to intrude upon the selection process. But these biases, if anything, work in the direction of selecting people who have backgrounds of unquestioned integrity. Combined with the high failure rate among all applicants—sometimes less than one in twenty is hired, which makes some police departments more selective in quantitative terms than the Harvard Law School—the selection process probably makes successful applicants feel that they have been welcomed into an elite group of highly qualified people of very high integrity.

INTRODUCTION

But this sense of high ideals about police work may not last for long. The introduction to policing provided by most police academies begins to convey folklore that shows the impossibility of doing things "by the book" and the frequent necessity of "bending the rules."

Police recruit training has changed substantially over the past thirty years. Once highly militaristic, it has recently taken on more of the atmosphere of the college classroom. The endurance test-stress environment approach, in which trainees may be punished for yawning or looking out the window, may still be found in some cities, but it seems to be dying out. Dull lectures on the technical aspects of police work (such as how to fill out arrest reports) and the rules and regulations of the department are now often supplemented by guest lectures on theories of crime and the cultures of various ethnic groups.

But the central method of *moral* instruction does not appear to have changed. The "war story" still remains the most effective device for communicating the history and values of the department. When the instructor tells a "war story," or an anecdote about police work, the class discipline is relaxed somewhat, the interest and attention of the class increase, and an atmosphere of camaraderie between the class and the instructor is established. The content of the war story makes a deep impression on the trainees.

The war stories not only introduce police work as it is experienced by police officers—rather than as an abstract ideal—they also introduce the ethics of police work as something different from what the public, or at least the law and the press, might expect. Van Maanen recounts one excerpt from a police academy criminal law lecture that, while not a "story," indicates the way in which the hidden values of police work are conveyed:

I suppose you guys have heard of Lucky Baldwin? If not, you sure will when you hit the street. Baldwin happens to be the biggest burglar still operating in this town. Every guy in this department from patrolman to chief would love to get him and make it stick. We've busted him about ten times so far, but he's got an asshole lawyer and money so he always beats the rap.... If I ever get a chance to pinch the SOB, I'll do it my way with my thirty-eight and spare the city the cost of a trial.[3]

Whether the instructor would actually shoot the burglary suspect is open to question, although he could do so legally in most states if the suspect attempted to flee from being arrested [Mooted by Tennessee v. Garner. —eds.] . More important is the fact that the rookies spend many hours outside the classroom debating and analyzing the implications of the war stories. These discussions do help them decide how they would act in similar circumstances. But the decisions they reach in these informal bull sessions are probably more attributable to peer pressure and the desire to "fit in" to the culture of the department than to careful reflection on moral principle.

ENCOUNTER

After they leave the academy, the rookies are usually handed over to Field Training Officers (FTOs). In the classic version of the first day on patrol with the rookie, the FTO says, "Forget everything they taught you in the academy, kid; I'll show you how police work is really done." And show they do. The rookie becomes an observer of the FTO as he or she actually does police work. Suddenly the war stories come alive, and all the questions about how to handle tough situations get answered very quickly and clearly, as one police veteran recalls:

On this job, your first partner is everything. He tells you how to survive on the job ... how to walk, how to stand, and how to speak and how to think and what to say and see.[4]

The encounter with the FTO is only part of the rookie's "reality shock" about police work. Perhaps even more important are the rookie's encounters with the public. By putting on the uniform, the rookie becomes part of a visible minority group. The self-consciousness about the new appearance is heightened by the nasty taunts and comments the uniform attracts from teenagers and others.[5] The uniform and gun, as symbols of power, attract challenges to that power simply because they are there.[6] Other people seek out the uniform to manipulate the rookie to use the power on behalf of their personal interests. Caught frequently in the cross fire of equally unreasonable citizen demands, the rookie naturally reacts by blaming the public. The spontaneous reaction is reinforced by one of the central values of the police culture: the public as enemy.[7]

This is no different from the way many doctors view their patients, particularly patients with a penchant for malpractice suits. Nor is it different from the view many professors have of their students as unreasonable and thick-headed, particularly those who argue about grades. Like police officers, doctors and professors wield power that affects other people's lives, and that power is always subject to counterattack. Once again, Van Maanen captures the experience of the rookie:

[My FTO] was always telling me to be forceful, to not back down and to never try to explain the law or what we are doing to a civilian. I really didn't know what he was talking about until I tried to tell some kid why we have laws about speeding. Well, the more I tried to tell him about traffic safety, the angrier he got. I was lucky just to get his John Hancock on the citation. When I came back to the patrol car, [the FTO] explains to me just where I'd gone wrong. You really can't talk to those people out there, they just won't listen to reason.[8]

It is the public that transforms the rookie's self-conception, teaching him or her the pains of exercising power. The FTO then helps to interpret the encounters with the public in the light of the values of the police culture, perhaps leading the rookie even further away from the values of family or friends about how police should act.

The FTO often gives "tests" as he or she teaches. In many departments, the tests are as minor as seeing if the rookie will wait patiently outside while the FTO visits a friend. In other departments, the test may include getting the rookie involved in drinking or having sex on duty, a seriously brutal slugfest against an arrestee, or taking bribes for nonenforcement. The seriousness of the violations may vary, but the central purpose of the test does not: seeing if the rookie can keep his or her mouth shut and not report the violations to the supervisors. A rookie who is found to be untrustworthy can be, literally, hounded and harassed from the department.

Finally, in the encounter stage, the rookie gets the major reality shock in the entire process of becoming a police officer. The rookie discovers that police work is more social work than crime fighting, more arbitration of minor disputes than investigations of major crimes, more patching of holes in the social fabric than weaving of webs to catch the big-time crooks. The rookie's usual response is to define most of the assignments received as "garbage calls," not *real* police work. Not quite sure whom to blame for the fact that he or she was hired to do police work but was assigned everything else, the rookie blames the police executive, the mayor and city council, and even previous U.S. presidents (for raising public expectations). But most of all the rookie blames the public, especially the poor, for being so stupid as to have all these problems, or so smart as to take advantage of welfare and other social programs.

METAMORPHOSIS

The result of those encounters is usually a complete change, a total adaptation of the new role and self-conception as a "cop." And with that transformation comes a stark awareness of the interdependence cops share with all other cops. For all the independence police have in making decisions about how to deal with citizens, they are totally and utterly dependent on other police to save their lives, to respond to a call of an officer in trouble or need of assistance, and to lie on their behalf to supervisors to cover up minor infractions of the many rules the department has. This total change in perspective usually means that police accept several new assumptions about the nature of the world:

- loyalty to colleagues is essential for survival
- the public, or most of it, is the enemy
- police administrators are also the enemy
- any discrepancy between these views and the views of family and friends is due simply to the ignorance of those who have not actually done police work themselves

These are their new assumptions about the *facts* of life in police work, the realities which limit their options for many things, including the kinds of moral principles they can afford to have and still "survive," to keep the job, pay the mortgage, raise the kids, and vest the pension. This conception of the facts opens new police officers to learning and accepting what may be a new set of values and ethical principles. By the time the metamorphosis has been accomplished, in fact, most of these new values have been learned.

Content of Police Values Teaching

Through the war stories of the academy instructor, the actions and stories of the FTO, the bull sessions with other rookies and veterans, and the new officer's encounters with the public, a fairly consistent set of values emerges. Whether the officer accepts these values is another question. Most students of police work seem to agree that these are the values (or some of them) that are taught:

1. Discretion A: *Decisions about whether to enforce the law, in any but the most serious cases, should be guided by both what the law says and who the suspect is.* Attitude, demeanor, cooperativeness, and even race, age, and social class are all important considerations in deciding how to treat people generally, and whether or not to arrest suspects in particular.

2. Discretion B: *Disrespect for police authority is a serious offense that should always be punished with an arrest or the use of force.* The "offense" known as "contempt of cop" or P.O.P.O. (pissing off a police officer) cannot be ignored. Even when the party has committed no violation of the law, a police officer should find a safe way to impose punishment, including an arrest on fake charges.

3. Force: *Police officers should never hesitate to use physical or deadly force against people who "deserve it," or where it can be an effective way of solving a crime.* Only the potential punishments by superior officers, civil litigation, citizen complaints, and so forth should limit the use of force when the situation calls for it. When you can get away with it, use all the force that society should use on people like that—force and punishment which bleeding-heart judges are too soft to impose.

4. Due Process: *Due process is only a means of protecting criminals at the expense of the law-abiding and should be ignored whenever it is safe to do so.* Illegal searches and wiretaps, interrogation without advising suspects of their Miranda rights, and if need be (as in the much admired movie, *Dirty Harry*), even physical pain to coerce a confession are all acceptable methods for accomplishing the goal the public wants the police to accomplish: fighting crime. The rules against doing those things merely handcuff the police, making it more difficult for them to do their job.

5. Truth: *Lying and deception are an essential part of the police job, and even perjury should be used if it is necessary to protect yourself or get a conviction on a "bad guy."* Violations of due process cannot be admitted to prosecutors or in court, so perjury (in the serious five per cent of cases that ever go to trial) is necessary and therefore proper. Lying to drug pushers about wanting to buy drugs, to prostitutes about wanting to buy sex, or to congressmen about wanting to buy influence is the only way, and therefore a proper way, to investigate these crimes without victims. Deceiving muggers into thinking you are an easy mark and deceiving burglars into thinking you are a fence are proper because there are not many other ways of catching predatory criminals in the act.

6. Time: *You cannot go fast enough to chase a car thief or traffic violator, nor slow enough to get to a "garbage" call; and when there are no calls for service, your time is your own.* Hot pursuits are necessary because anyone who tries to escape from the police is challenging police authority, no matter how trivial the initial offense. But calls to nonserious or social-work problems like domestic disputes or kids making noise are unimportant, so you can stop to get coffee on the way or even stop at the cleaner's if you like. And when there are no calls, you can sleep, visit friends, study, or do anything else you can get away with, especially on the midnight shift, when you can get away with a lot.

7. Rewards: *Police do very dangerous work for low wages, so it is proper to take any extra rewards the public wants to give them, like free meals, Christmas gifts, or even regular monthly payments (in some cities) for special treatment.* The general rule is: take any reward that doesn't change what you would do anyway, such as eating a meal, but don't take money that would affect your job, like not giving traffic tickets. In many cities, however, especially in the recent past, the rule has been to take even those rewards that do affect your decisions, as long as they are related only to minor offenses—traffic, gambling, prostitution, but not murder.

8. Loyalty: *The paramount duty is to protect your fellow officers at all costs, as they would protect you, even though you may have to risk your own career or your own life to do it.* If your colleagues make a mistake, take a bribe, seriously hurt somebody illegally, or get into other kinds of trouble, you should do everything you can to protect them in the ensuing investigation. If your colleagues are routinely breaking the rules, you should never tell supervisors, reporters, or outside investigators about it. If you don't like it, quit—or get transferred to the police academy. But never, ever, blow the whistle.

The Rising Value Conflicts

None of these values is as strongly or widely held as in the past. Several factors may account for the breakdown in traditional police values that has paralleled the breakdown of traditional values in the wider society. One is the increasing diversity of the kinds of people who join police departments: more women, minorities, and college graduates. Another is the rising power of the police unions which defend individual officers who get into trouble—sometimes even those who challenge the traditional values. A third factor is the rise of investigative journalism and the romantic aura given to "bucking the system" by such movies as *Serpico*. Watergate and other recent exposés of corruption in high places—especially the attitude of being "above the law"—have probably made all public officials more conscious of the ethics of their behavior. Last but not least, police administrators have increasingly taken a very stern disciplinary posture towards some of these traditional police values and gone to extraordinary lengths to try to counteract them.

Consider the paramount value of loyalty. Police reformer August Vollmer described it in 1931 as the "blue curtain of secrecy" that descends whenever a police officer does something wrong, making it impossible to investigate misconduct. Yet in the past decade, police officers in Cincinnati, Indianapolis, New York, and elsewhere have given reporters and grand juries evidence about widespread police misconduct. In New York, police officers have even given evidence against their colleagues for homicide, leading to the first conviction there (that anyone can recall) of a police officer for murder in the line of duty. The code of silence may be far from breaking down, but it certainly has a few cracks in it.

The ethics of rewards have certainly changed in many departments over the past decade. In the wake of corruption scandals, some police executives have taken advantage of the breakdown in loyalty to assign spies, or "field associates," to corruption-prone units in order to detect bribe-taking. These officers are often recruited for this work at the police academy, where they are identified only to one or two contacts and are generally treated like any other police officer. These spies are universally hated by other officers, but they are very hard to identify. The result of this approach, along with other anti-corruption strategies, has been an apparent decline in organized corruption.[9]

The ethics of force are also changing. In the wake of well-publicized federal prosecutions of police beatings, community outrage over police shootings, and an explosion in civil litigation that has threatened to bankrupt some cities, the behavior and possibly the attitude of the police in their use of force have generally become more restrained. In Los Angeles, Kansas City, Atlanta, New York, Chicago, and elsewhere, the number of killings of citizens by police has declined sharply.[10] Some officers now claim that they risk their lives by hesitating to use force out of fear of being punished for using it. Even if excessive use of force has not been entirely eliminated, the days of unrestrained shooting or use of the "third degree" are clearly gone in many cities.

The increasing external pressures to conform to legal and societal values, rather than to traditional police values, have generated increasing conflict among police officers themselves. The divide-and-conquer effect may be seen in police officers' unwillingness to bear the risks of covering up for their colleagues, now that the risks are much greater than they have been. Racial conflicts among police officers often center on these values. At the national level, for example, the National Organization of Black Law Enforcement Executives (NOBLE) has been battling with the International Association of Chiefs of Police (IACP) since at least 1979 over the question of how restrictive police department firearms policies should be.

These conflicts should not be over-emphasized, however. The learning of police ethics still takes place in the context of very strong communication of traditional police values. The rising conflicts are still only a minor force. But they are at least one more contingency affecting the moral choices police officers face as they progress through their careers, deciding which values to adopt and which ethical standards to live by.

The Police Officer's Moral Career

There are four major aspects of moral careers in general that are directly relevant to police officers.[11] One is the *contingencies* the officer confronts. Another is the *moral experiences* undergone in confronting these contingencies. A third is the *apologia*, the explanation officers develop for changing the ethical principles they live by. The fourth and most visible aspect of the moral careers of police officers is the *stages* of moral change they go through.

CONTINGENCIES

The contingencies shaping police moral careers include all the social pressures officers face to behave one way rather than another. Police departments vary, for example, in the frequency and seriousness of the rule-breaking that goes on. They also vary in the openness of such rule-breaking, and in the degree of teaching of the *skills* of such rule breaking. It is no small art, for example, to coax a bribe offer out of a traffic violator without directly asking for it. Even in a department in which such bribes are regularly accepted, a new officer may be unlikely to adopt

the practice if an older officer does not teach him or her how. In a department in which older officers explicitly teach the techniques, the same officer might be more likely to adopt the practice. The difference in the officer's career is thus shaped by the difference in the contingencies he or she confronts.

The list of all possible contingencies is obviously endless, but these are some of the more commonly reported ones:

- the values the FTO teaches
- the values the first sergeant teaches
- the kind of citizens confronted in the first patrol assignment
- the level of danger on patrol
- whether officers work in a one-officer or two-officer car (after the training period)
- whether officers are assigned to undercover or vice work
- whether there are conflicts among police officers over ethical issues in the department
- the ethical "messages" sent out by the police executive
- the power of the police union to protect officers from being punished
- the general climate of civic integrity (or lack of it)
- the level of public pressure to control police behavior

Contingencies alone, of course, do not shape our behavior. If we were entirely the products of our environment, with no freedom of moral choice, there would be little point in writing (or reading) books on ethics. What contingencies like these do is push us in one direction or another, much like the waves in the ocean. Whether we choose to swim against the tide or flow with the waves is up to each of us.

MORAL EXPERIENCES

The moral experience is a major turning point in a moral career. It can be an agonizing decision about which principles to follow or it can be a shock of recognition as you finally understand the moral principles implicit in how other people are behaving. Like the person asleep on a raft drifting out to sea, the police officer who has a moral experience suddenly discovers where he or she is and what the choices are.

Some officers have had moral experiences when they found out the system they worked for was corrupt: when the judge dismissed the charges against the son of a powerful business executive, or when a sergeant ordered the officer not to make arrests at an illegal after-hours bar. One leading police executive apparently went through a moral experience when he was first assigned to the vice squad and saw all the money that his colleagues were taking from gamblers. Shocked and disgusted, he sought and obtained a transfer to a less corrupt unit within a few weeks.

Other officers have had moral experiences in reaction to particular incidents. One Houston police rookie was out of the academy for only several weeks when he witnessed a group of his senior colleagues beat up a Mexican-American, Joe Campos Torres, after he resisted arrest in a bar. Torres drowned after jumping or being pushed from a great height into a bayou, and no one knew how he had died when his body was found floating nearby. The officer discussed the incident with his father, also a Houston police officer, and the father marched the young officer right into the Internal Affairs Division to give a statement. His testimony became the basis of a federal prosecution of the other officers.

Other officers may have a moral experience when they see their ethics presented in public, outside of the police culture. New York City police captain Max Schmittberger, for example, who had been a bagman collecting graft for his superiors in New York's Tenderloin district, was greatly moved by the testimony of prostitutes he heard at the hearings of the Lexow Committee investigating police corruption in 1893. He told muckraking reporter Lincoln Steffens that the parade of witnesses opened his eyes to the reality of the corruption, so he decided to get on the witness stand himself to reveal even more details of the corruption.

No matter what contingencies occur to prompt a moral experience, the police officer faces relatively few choices about how to react. One option is to drift with the tide, letting things go on as they have been. Another option is to seek an escape route, such as a transfer, that removes the moral dilemma that may prompt the moral experience. A third option is to leave police work altogether, although the financial resources of police officers are not usually great enough to allow the luxury of resigning on principle. The fourth and most difficult option is to fight back somehow, either by blowing the whistle to the public or initiating a behind-the-scenes counterattack.

Not all moral experiences are prompted by criminal acts or even by violations of rules and regulations. Racist jokes or language, ethnic favoritism by commanders, or other issues can also prompt moral experiences. With some officers, though, nothing may ever prompt a moral experience; they may drift out to sea, or back to shore, sound asleep and unaware of what is happening to them.

APOLOGIA

For those officers with enough moral consciousness to suffer a moral experience, a failure to "do the right thing" could be quite painful to live with. "Even a bent policeman has a conscience," as a British police official who resigned on principle (inadequate police corruption investigations in London) once observed.[12] In order to resolve the conflict between what they think they should have done and what they actually did, officers often invent or adopt an acceptable explanation for their conduct. The explanation negates the principle they may have wished they actually had followed, or somehow makes their behavior consistent with that principle.

Perhaps the most famous apologia is the concept of "clean graft": bribes paid to avoid enforcement of laws against crimes that don't hurt people. Gambling and prostitution bribes were traditionally labeled as "clean graft," while bribes from narcotics pushers were labeled "dirty graft." (As narcotics traffic grew more lucrative, however, narcotics bribes were more often labeled "clean.")

The apologia for beating a handicapped prisoner in a moment of anger may draw on the police value system of maintaining respect for authority and meting out punishment because the courts will not. The apologia for stopping black suspects more often than white suspects may be the assumption that blacks are more likely to be guilty. No matter what a police officer does, he or she is apt to find *situationally justified* reasons for doing it. The reasons are things only the officer can understand because only the officer knows the full story, all the facts of the *situation*. The claim of situational expertise, of course, conveniently avoids any attempt to apply a general moral principle to conduct. The avoidance is just as effective in the officer's own mind as it would be if the apologia were discussed with the officer's spouse, clergyman, or parents.

Perhaps the most important effect of the apologia is that it allows the officer to live with a certain moral standard of behavior, to become comfortable with it. This creates the potential for further apologias about further changes in moral standards. The process can clearly become habit-forming, and it does. The progression from one apologia to the next makes up the stages of moral change.

STAGES

The stages of moral change are points on a moral continuum, the different levels of moral improvement or of the "slippery slope" of moral degeneration. Such descriptions sound trite and old-fashioned, but they are commonly used by officers who get into serious trouble—such as being convicted for burglary—to account for their behavior.

The officers caught in the Denver police burglary ring in 1961, for example, appear to have progressed through many stages in their moral careers before forming an organized burglary ring:

1. First they suffered moral experiences that showed them that the laws were not impartially enforced and that judges were corrupt.

2. Then they learned that other police officers were dishonest, including those who engaged in "shopping," i.e., stealing goods at the scene of a nighttime commercial burglary, with the goods stolen by the police thus indistinguishable from the goods stolen by others.

3. They joined in the shopping themselves and constructed an apologia for it ("the insurance pays for it all anyway").

4. The apologia provided a rationale for a planned burglary in which they were burglars ("the insurance still pays for it").

5. The final stage was to commit planned burglaries on a regular basis.

These stages are logically available to all police officers. Many, perhaps most, officers progress to Stage 3 and go no further, just as most professors steal paper clips and photocopying from their universities, but not books or furniture. Why some people move into the further stages and others do not is a problem for the sociology of deviance, not ethics. The fact is that some officers do move into the more serious stages of unethical conduct after most officers have established the custom in the less serious, but still unethical, stages.

Each aspect of police ethics, from force to time to due process, has different sets of stages. Taken together, the officer's movement across all the stages on all the ethical issues makes up his or her moral career in police work. The process is not just one way; officers can move back closer to legal principles as well as away from them. But the process is probably quite connected across different issues. Your moral stage on stealing may parallel your moral stage on force.

Learning Ethics Differently

This article has treated morality as if it were black and white, i.e., as if it consisted of clear-cut principles to be obeyed or disobeyed. Many issues in police ethics are in fact clear-cut, and hold little room for serious philosophical analysis. One would have a hard time making a rational defense of police officers stealing, for example.

But what may be wrong with the way police ethics is now taught and learned is just that assumption: that all police ethical issues are as clear-cut as stealing. They are not. The issues of force, time, discretion, loyalty, and others are all very complex, with many shades of gray. To deny this complexity, as the formal approaches of police academies and police rule books often do, may simply encourage unethical behavior. A list of "dos" and "don'ts" that officers must follow because they are ordered to is a virtual challenge to their ingenuity: catch me if you can. And in the face of a police culture that has already established values quite contrary to many of the official rules, the black-and-white approach to ethics may be naive.

As indicated above, an alternative approach may be preferred. This would consider both clear-cut and complex ethical issues in the same fashion: examining police problems in the light of basic moral principles and from the moral point of view. While there may be weaknesses in this alternative approach, it may well be the sounder road to ethical sensitivity in the context of individual responsibility.

NOTES

1. See John Van Maanen, "On Becoming a Policeman," in *Policing: A View from the Street,* eds. Peter Manning and John Van Maanen (Santa Monica, Calif.: Goodyear, 1978).

2. See John McNamara, "Uncertainties in Police Work: The Relevance of Recruits' Backgrounds and Training," in *The Police: Six Sociological Studies,* ed. David J. Bordua (New York: Wiley, 1967).

3. Van Maanen, "On Becoming a Policeman," p. 298.

4. Ibid, p. 301

5. See William Westley, *Violence and the Police* (Cambridge, Mass.: M.I.T. Press, 1979), pp. 159-60.

6. See William Ker Muir, Jr., *Police: Streetcorner Politicians* (Chicago: University of Chicago Press, 1977).

7. See Westley, *Violence,* pp. 48-108.

8. Van Maanen, "On Becoming a Policeman," p. 302.

9. See Lawrence Sherman, "Reducing Police Gun Use" (Paper presented at the International Conference on the Management and Control of Police Organizations, Breukelen, the Netherlands, 1980).

10. Ibid.

11. Cf. Erving Goffman, "The Moral Career of the Mental Patient," in *Asylum: Essays on the Social Situation of Mental Patients and Other Inmates* (Garden City, N.Y.: Anchor Books, 1961), pp. 127-69.

12. See Sherman, "Reducing Police Gun Use."

Study Questions

1. One of the eight traditional police values identified by Sherman is that "due process is only a means of protecting criminals at the expense of the law-abiding and should be ignored whenever it is safe to do so." Briefly describe a situation (real or hypothetical) that exemplifies this value. Do you generally agree with the value, or disagree? Why?

2. Why do people want to become police officers, according to Sherman? Why do you want to become a criminal justice practitioner? Do you think motivation varies for the different areas of criminal justice practice? Why?

3. Where should criminal justice ethics be learned, in your view?

4. Imagine that as a recruit, your field training officer embodies many, if not all, of the police values listed by Sherman. You believe that these values are wrong. How will you conduct yourself during the training period? Why?

Law Enforcement Code of Ethics

INTERNATIONAL ASSOCIATION OF CHIEFS OF POLICE

AS A LAW ENFORCEMENT OFFICER, my fundamental duty is to serve the community; to safeguard lives and property; to protect the innocent against deception, the weak against oppression or intimidation and the peaceful against violence or disorder; and to respect the constitutional rights of all to liberty, equality and justice.

I will keep my private life unsullied as an example to all and will behave in a manner that does not bring discredit to me or to my agency. I will maintain courageous calm in the face of danger, scorn or ridicule; develop self-restraint; and be constantly mindful of the welfare of others. Honest in thought and deed both in my personal and official life, I will be exemplary in obeying the law and the regulations of my department. Whatever I see or hear of a confidential nature or that is confided to me in my official capacity will be kept ever secret unless revelation is necessary in the performance of my duty.

I will never act officiously or permit personal feelings, prejudices, political beliefs, aspirations, animosities or friendships to influence my decisions. With no compromise for crime and with relentless prosecution of criminals, I will enforce the law courteously and appropriately without fear or favor, malice or ill will, never employing unnecessary force or violence and never accepting gratuities.

I recognize the badge of my office as a symbol of public faith, and I accept it as a public trust to be held so long as I am true to the ethics of police service. I will never engage in acts of corruption or bribery, nor will I condone such acts by other police officers. I will cooperate with all legally authorized agencies and their representatives in the pursuit of justice.

I know that I alone am responsible for my own standard of professional performance and will take every reasonable opportunity to enhance and improve my level of knowledge and competence.

I will constantly strive to achieve these objective and ideals, dedicating myself before God to my chosen profession ... law enforcement.

Code of Ethics

AMERICAN CORRECTIONAL ASSOCIATION

THE AMERICAN CORRECTIONAL ASSOCIA-TION expects of its members unfailing honesty, respect for the dignity and individuality of human beings; and a commitment to professional and compassionate service. To this end we subscribe to the following principles:

Relationships with clients/colleagues/ other professions/the public

• Members will respect and protect the civil and legal rights of all clients.

• Members will serve each case with appropriate concern for the client's welfare and with no purpose of personal gain.

• Relationships with colleagues will be of such character to promote mutual respect within the profession and improvement of its quality of service.

• Statements critical of colleagues or their agencies will be made only as these are verifiable and constructive in purpose.

• Members will respect the importance of all elements of the criminal justice system and cultivate a professional cooperation with each segment.

• Subject to the client's rights of privacy, members will respect the public's right to know, and will share information with the public with openness and candor.

• Members will respect and protect the right of the public to be safeguarded from criminal activity.

Professional conduct/practices

• No member will use his or her official position to secure special privileges or advantages.

• No member, while acting in an official capacity, will allow personal interest to impair objectivity in the performance of duty.

• No member will use his or her official position to promote any partisan political purposes.

• No member will accept any gift or favor of such nature to imply an obligation that is inconsistent with the free and objective exercise of professional responsibilities.

• In any public statement, members will clearly distinguish between those that are personal views and those that are statements and positions on behalf of an agency.

• Members will be diligent in their responsibility to record and make available for review any and all case information which could contribute to sound decisions affecting a client or the public safety.

• Each member will report, without reservation, any corrupt or unethical behavior which could affect either a client or the integrity of the organization.

• Members will not discriminate against any client, employee, or prospective employee on the basis of race, sex, creed, or national origin.

• Members will maintain the integrity of private information; they will neither seek personal data beyond that needed to perform their responsibilities, nor reveal case information to anyone not having proper professional use for such.

• Any member who is responsible for agency personnel actions will make all appointments, promotions, or dismissals only on the basis of merit and not in furtherance of partisan political interests.

Adopted August 1975 at the 105th Congress of Correction.

Code of Ethics

FEDERAL PROBATION OFFICERS' ASSOCIATION

AS A FEDERAL PROBATION OFFICER, I am dedicated to rendering professional service to the courts, the parole authorities, and the community at large in effecting the social adjustment of the offender.

I will conduct my personal life with decorum, will neither accept nor grant favors in connection with my office, and will put loyalty to moral principles above personal consideration.

I will uphold the law with dignity and with complete awareness of the prestige and stature of the judicial system of which I am a part. I will be ever cognizant of my responsibility to the community which I serve.

I will strive to be objective in the performance of my duties; respect the inalienable rights of all persons; appreciate the inherent worth of the individual, and hold inviolate those confidences which can be reposed in me.

I will cooperate with my fellow workers and related agencies and will continually attempt to improve my professional standards through the seeking of knowledge and understanding.

I recognize my office as a symbol of public faith and I accept it as a public trust to be held as long as I am true to the ethics of the Federal Probation Service. I will constantly strive to achieve these objectives and ideals, dedicating myself to my chosen profession.

September 12, 1960

Used by permission of the Federal Probation Officers' Association, Washington, D.C.

Case 3.1

THE FINAL PAT-DOWN

As a corrections officer, you are assigned to work in the main hall. Your job is to help maintain an orderly flow of inmates as they move back and forth between their locks and the dining hall. You are also to randomly select and stop certain inmates for a pat-down search. This is done to help stem the flow of contraband into the hall.

As you look down the hall, you see inmate Riddle leaving Six Dorm, your previous work assignment. You genuinely hate inmate Riddle. You suspect that he has been dealing in drugs and prostitution in Three Dorm. He has also been linked to an institution-wide protection scam that has resulted in some serious physical harm to inmates who have not cooperated with him. Although Riddle has thus far been clever enough to avoid being caught in any of these activities, he has received numerous minor conduct reports from you and other correctional officers who are aware of his activities. The pressure of these admittedly "bullshit" tickets and some serious family problems is beginning to show on Riddle's appearance and actions. The word is out that he is having an increasingly difficult time "keeping his cool."

This becomes noticeable to you as Riddle is stopped and patted down by the Six Dorm officer immediately outside the dorm. Even at this distance, you can see how angry Riddle is. He empties his pockets and raises his arms slowly, as if it were very difficult for him to comply with the order. The other officers notice this, too, and Riddle is stopped again at Four Dorm. This time, he is visibly shaking during the course of the search. He moves jerkily, as if contemplating striking out at someone. At One Dorm, he is stopped again. You can see that he can barely restrain himself during this search. He is ready, if stopped again, to explode and probably strike out, physically or verbally, at the officer.

He is now moving toward you. Although you are quite certain, after three searches, that he is not carrying any contraband, you are aware that you have the right to order him, or any other inmate, to stop and stand for a pat-down search. You also know that if you stop Riddle at this time, he might try to hit you. You are ready for this (you are on guard and other officers are standing nearby). As a matter of fact, you want Riddle to take a punch at you because it will finally give you a chance to write him up for a serious offense. He might even end up being reclassified to another institution, which would please you and most other officers very much.

But, as Riddle approaches, you hesitate for a moment. You wonder if this is the right way to dispose of Riddle.

Questions for Discussion

1. What would you do? Apply the ethical checklist to your decision.

2. Refer to the American Correctional Association's Code of Ethics. Assuming you decide to pat Riddle down, what portions of the Code do you appear to violate?

3. Discuss the benefits to the institution if Riddle is transferred. Do these outweigh the costs of having to prove that Riddle is, in fact, involved in corrupt activities?

4. Should morals/ethics be compromised just to create a favorable outcome?

5. Assume that you choose to pat Riddle down, he explodes, a fight ensues, and he is transferred. Later, you are asked why you patted him down (in light of the previous pat-downs). What will be your reply? Defend your answer.

Case 3.2

THE DISHWASHER*

David Morris, 27, and Sarah Morris, 23, are married, with three children ages 8 months, 2 years, and 3-1/2 years. He is working part-time as a dishwasher for a local restaurant. She works part-time as a nurse's aide in a local nursing home. Both are from out-of-state and have no family nearby for emotional or financial support.

David has had a series of convictions for relatively minor offenses including driving while intoxicated, driving under suspension, issuing bad checks, and domestic violence. The County Welfare Department has received allegations that the children are physically and possibly sexually abused by him. His latest conviction was on a combination of DUI and domestic violence charges. He was placed on probation for one year and ordered to attend marital and substance abuse treatment with his wife. He was fined $500, of which $450 was suspended on the condition that he comply with all terms of his probation, and sentenced to 30 days in jail with 27 days suspended.

Sarah recognizes the need for professional help if their marriage is to survive. At the same time, her patience is at an end and she has threatened divorce if David has any more problems with substance abuse or domestic violence.

As his probation officer, you have learned that David may be in violation of his probation. Both Sarah and the counseling agency have reported that he is not attending counseling sessions. Other probationers have mentioned that he is drinking heavily, a condition that figures into the allegations of physical and/or sexual abuse, according to County Welfare. Having dealt with David on probation before, you are not inclined to be lenient with him. Yet, you have some insight into the dynamics of substance abuse and know that his avoidance of treatment is a normal part of the denial process. You would like to see the family work on their problems and stay intact, but you strongly suspect that the allegations of abuse are well-founded. If the court finds him guilty of probation violation and revokes probation, he is liable to pay the full fine and serve all or part of the jail sentence ordered by the court.

Questions for Discussion

1. Should this probationer be brought before the court on a charge of probation violation? Why? Defend your position.

2. Apply the ethical checklist to your decision. Is your decision a correct one?

3. Refer to the Texas Adult Probation Officer's Code of Ethics. Does your decision violate any aspect of the Code? If yes, which one(s) and why?

4. Weigh the virtues of keeping the family together versus removing the father.

5. How much influence do you think that an individual's personal opinion has in situations like these?

6. If David is not brought before the court by you on a probation violation and he gets drunk and seriously injures his spouse or one of his children, are you at fault?

7. Is there actual "proof" of a violation in this case? Explain.

*The authors wish to thank R. Scott Distel for contributing this case.

Case 3.3

GOOD FRIENDS ARE HARD TO FIND

When I first joined the police department, I was told by a childhood friend, who was on the same department, "You will only have 'cop' friends, because nobody else understands us." My wife and I found this disquieting. As a result of that statement, we made an effort to cultivate friends outside of law enforcement, many of them being teachers, my wife's profession.

Making friends wasn't easy. It seemed that many people, upon discovering I was a police officer, took it upon themselves to blame me for all the troubles of the world and any violations that they had received from other officers. I can still recall attending a Halloween party shortly after I was sworn in. There was a woman there dressed as, of all things, a witch. She was a special education teacher and should have known better but, when she found out what I did, proceeded to tell my wife how all the police officers in the world were "assholes." Maybe my friend was right. Maybe we were predestined to have nothing but police officer friends. NO way. We found a way around it.

My wife and I made a policy of not telling new acquaintances what I did. We just said I worked in "public relations" for the city. After they would get to know us and realize that I was not a monster, we would tell them what I really did. It seemed to work and we began to cultivate a circle of close friends.

It was amazing to us how these friends bent their schedules to accommodate my shift work. Whenever a party was planned, we were the first ones contacted to make sure I was not working or could get the night off. Also, while I suspected that some of these friends were recreational drug users, they were always respectful of my sensitive position and practiced those activities when we were not around.

Two of these friends, Jim and Sandy, invited us to dinner one Friday night at their home. We arrived for drinks about 6:30 and Jim immediately presented me with my favorite, scotch on the rocks. He put on some music while my wife went to help Sandy in the kitchen. Jim and I sat in the living room. I needed something for my drink so that I would not leave rings on the coffee table. There was a wooden box on the table that I assumed contained coasters. When I opened the box, I didn't see coasters. What I did see were several joints.

When I put the lid back on the box, I looked up and saw the fear in Jim's eyes.

Questions for Discussion

1. What would you do if faced with this decision? Use the ethical checklist to assist you.
2. Discuss the ethics of deception with respect to keeping one's occupation a secret.
3. Reread the third paragraph of the Law Enforcement Officer's Code of Ethics. Should this apply in this situation? Why? Defend your position.
4. Speculate on why police officers tend to associate only with other police officers. Is it true? Is this true of other professions, such as engineers, professors, physicians, attorneys, etc.?

5. If you were aware that some of your friends were recreational drug users but did not use drugs in your presence, should you end your friendship with them? Why? Defend your position.

6. What are your ethical responsibilities with respect to your private life?

7. What would you have done if Jim had not been in the room?

Case 3.4

THE "TWO-HIT" FIGHT

Most fights in penal institutions involve only two inmates and are usually over very quickly. In fact, such encounters are referred to by inmates as "two-hit" fights, where inmate A hits inmate B and inmate B hits the floor. Such fights may be only random acts of violence, but more often they serve as a means of settling standing conflicts between the participants. Only on rare occasions are such fights witnessed by a corrections officer.

Inmate Jones was assigned to your dorm about a week ago. He is young, fairly muscular, and attractive enough to have already been hotly pursued by several of the older homosexuals in your dorm. Thus far, he has been able to rebuff the advances of all but one of his suitors, inmate Wilson. Wilson, who is not a particularly large or muscular man, is nevertheless being quite aggressive and persistent in this matter. You know that it will take more than a simple "No" from Jones to turn him away.

The inevitable confrontation finally occurs during morning clean-up in the dorm. You are doing paperwork in the day room when you hear Jones and Wilson begin to argue loudly. Wilson has cornered Jones, who was cleaning the sink area, and is demanding, you suppose, sexual favors. As you walk toward the bathroom to break up the argument you observe, through the window-lined hallway, that you are too late. Jones has delivered a totally effective haymaker to Wilson's jaw, knocking Wilson to the floor, his mouth bleeding slightly.

At this moment, you stop. You can still see Jones and Wilson, although they do not yet see you. You note that Wilson seems more surprised and frightened than physically harmed, and you think it unlikely that he will strike back at Jones. Jones, for his part, is calming down rapidly. He appears to have made his point, and you feel that he will not strike Wilson again unless he is challenged. At this point, Jones turns to leave the bathroom and it is time for you, as a corrections officer, to act.

You know what the proper procedure is: conduct reports should be immediately issued to both men, and both should be placed in segregation cells pending the outcome of a review hearing. But you wonder if such action in this situation is the right thing to do. As Jones walks toward the door (and you), you are faced with an immediate decision: intervene or ignore.

Questions for Discussion

1. What would you do in this situation? Use the ethical decision-making checklist to assist you.

2. Both men, especially Jones, would be penalized by official action. Is this appropriate?

3. Wasn't Jones justified in punching Wilson? Didn't Wilson deserve his fate?

4. Didn't the two inmates, in their own manner, resolve the underlying conflict, so that official action would only unnecessarily complicate the situation?

5. At what point should a correctional officer intervene in these situations?

6. Despite your personal beliefs, aren't rules and regulations written to be followed?

Case 3.5

IN THE BEST INTEREST OF THE CHILD

Tommy lives with his mother, Margaret, who is a single parent. Margaret has very limited abilities. Although she is not labeled developmentally delayed, she has low intellectual abilities. She has little education and has no employable skills. It is doubtful that she could obtain even high school skills in an adult education program or attain employment training. Her home is filthy, unhealthy, and unsafe. The bathroom plumbing has not worked in three weeks. Dog and cat excrement is everywhere. Clothing and bedding are piled in closets and in corners, unwashed. There is little in the refrigerator to eat. Dishes remain unclean and are gathering maggots and mold. Many papers and old rags are near the stove and the furnace.

Although Margaret is a nice woman and loves Tommy very much, she has few parenting skills; having limited awareness of her son's activities, she believes and accepts his excuses and misbehavior. When she needs to discipline him, she yells and screams, but does not follow through on consequences. Her mental health status is very poor, yet she fails to seek professional assistance.

It would appear that in the "best interest" of Tommy, you should report the unhealthy home conditions to the local housing authorities, report the unsafe home conditions to the Protective Services Department of Social Services, and file a petition in Juvenile Court to remove the minor from his unsafe home.

However, while Tommy's short-term interest may be served by this action, there is a strong possibility that such an action could have serious detrimental effects. This mother is emotionally fragile. If the city housing department condemns the home, the mother has no other place to live and other housing is very difficult to find. The Department of Social Services would put pressure on this mother to eliminate the filthy conditions. If her son is removed from her care, she would "fall apart."

You strongly sense that if Tommy's best interests are served, the mother is likely to attempt suicide.

Questions for Discussion

1. What would you do in this situation? Use the ethical decision-making checklist to assist you.

2. Contact your local Department of Social Services. What community alternatives are available in dealing with Tommy and his mother?

3. Would your decision be different if Tommy were 2 years old? 10 years old? 15 years old? Explain.

4. Which is more important, the best interests of the child or the fact that you are afraid of what the unstable parent might do to herself? Should that even be your concern? What about the unstable parent who might do harm to the child?

Chapter 4
Loyalty

DISCUSSIONS OF THE CONCEPT OF LOYALTY have a long history. You will recall Aristotle's claim in the previous chapter that truth should be honored above friendship. Loyalty is and has been one of the supreme virtues of the military and, for similar reasons, of criminal justice. The reasons for which loyalty is valued, however, are not limited to those circumstances involving life and death. Loyalty, for example, is highly prized in the corporate environment, even though the consequences of disloyalty are not likely to be fatal. (Indeed, violations of loyalty, e.g., in cases of whistle-blowing, may save lives.)

For the criminal justice practitioner, the issue of loyalty has a unique twist. Since an officer is sworn to execute the law, failure to disclose violations of the law committed by fellow officers on the grounds of loyalty is acting not only unethically, but potentially illegally (depending on those discretionary factors discussed in Chapter 3).

Loyalty is no doubt ranked highly as a virtue in criminal justice for reasons similar to those of the military, namely the life-and-death factor. Loyalty under such circumstances promotes actions that are not predicated on an evaluation of the consequences, but rather on a simple principle: act to protect, at virtually any cost, your fellows.

Loyalty so construed can become an exchange of protective favors. For example, one officer may drive by another officer's location to check on his or her welfare. In turn, that officer is expected to do the same, or perhaps return the favor in some other form. The form of that *quid pro quo* may be perfectly appropriate or it may require unethical or illegal action. At that point, we have the special case of an officer of the law becoming a violator of the law.

As Aristotle was aware, the real problem often emerges when the virtue of loyalty conflicts with the virtue of truth-telling. From a practical standpoint, this chapter and part of the next chapter (Truth) are concerned with the same issue: which virtue is the more important, loyalty or truth? This conflict can be seen in cases where blind loyalty leads to the harm of another person, or conceals a harm that has already occurred.

The Readings

In the selection, "Loyalty to Loyalty," the 19th century philosopher Josiah Royce defines loyalty as "the willing devotion of a self to a cause." He rejects the "common but false impression" that loyalty is necessarily associated with military virtues. Royce also objects to the general idea that duties of loyalty necessarily arise out of a group or organizational environment. "Loyalty," Royce says, "is perfectly consistent with originality." For Royce, loyalty is a supreme personal good. Consequently, the ordinary virtues of courage, honesty, humility, etc. are just "special forms of loyalty to loyalty." This is very evident in the following recommendation Royce makes to the reader:

> Let [your] cause so possess you that ... you can say ... "I am the servant of this cause, its reasonable, its willing, its devoted instrument, and, being such, I have neither eyes to see nor tongue to speak save as this cause shall command."

Royce separates good causes from evil causes by asking whether the cause is "essentially a *loyalty to loyalty*." That is, being loyal to one's cause must serve to promote like loyalty among others, not just those who are on my "team." If my actions are destructive of the loyalty of other persons, then my cause is evil. This is what Royce means by being loyal to the universal loyalty of mankind, namely, that such loyalty promotes rather than destroys the loyalty of others. Incidentally, you might have noticed that Royce's talk of "maximizing" loyalty could be regarded as a form of act utilitarianism in which loyalty is the supreme good, rather than happiness or economic preference.

Although Marcia Baron's paper, "The Moral Status of Loyalty," is concerned with loyal issues in the engineering profession, this selection is quite applicable to loyalty issues in other professions, including criminal justice practice. Baron poses two sets of questions concerning loyalty: (1) What is good about loyalty? Is acting loyally always good? and (2) How are conflicts among loyalties to be weighed?

With respect to the first set of questions, Baron examines competing definitions of loyalty. Some contemporary philosophers who have written about loyalty reject Royce's definition of loyalty as loyalty to *a cause*. The competing view is that being loyal is different from having an ideal or cause in the sense that being loyal to *my* spouse differs from viewing marital fidelity as an ideal. The ideal of marital fidelity doesn't distinguish among spouses, but my loyalty to my spouse does. Consequently, Baron argues, loyalties are always to specific people or groups of people.

Baron believes that loyalty raises serious moral difficulties. For example, it invites unfair discriminations among persons (the "old boy" system of hiring) and hence can easily lead to injustice. Worse, an appeal to loyalty as an explanation for action seems to be a dead-end, a "refusal to give a reason," in Baron's words. Loyalty seems to make us partial, rather than impartial, in our treatment of other persons, taking us backward in the process of ethical reasoning, rather than forward.

Baron then examines the desirable aspects of loyalty, concluding that conflicts among loyalties, or between loyalties and other duties, can be resolved. She proposes making a standard ethical distinction (first formulated by Kant[1]) between *duties of justice* and *duties of benevolence*. We owe duties of justice to everyone at the risk of infringing their rights, while duties of benevolence are general (owed to no one in particular) and hence can be omitted without violating a specific person's rights (though my regular failing of my duty to do good will certainly affect my standing as a morally good person). Baron argues persuasively that "duties of justice override considerations of loyalty . . . "because what I owe to everyone "supersedes what I may do to promote the welfare of my 'group' . . ."

In the selection, "Whistleblowing and Employee Loyalty," Ronald Duska argues that loyalty does not override the duty to blow the whistle on organizational wrongdoing, much less render whistleblowing impermissible, as some have argued.

Duska begins his analysis by considering the same question raised by Baron: What are the objects of loyalty? He rejects the "social atomist" view, in which one can be loyal only to specific persons, for a view more similar to Baron's, in which one can be loyal to individuals or to groups of persons. The key criterion is that loyalty "depends on ties that demand self-sacrifice with no expectation of reward." So, for example, the idea of being loyal to one's family (as a group) fits Duska's concept of loyalty, while the idea of loyalty to the corporation for which one works does not, since people do not work for a business with no expectation of reward.

From Duska's perspective it would seem that a person can be expected to demonstrate loyalty to a group or organization as long as one's participation is not based on a subsequent reward. Participation in charitable organizations would obviously meet this condition, but what about public service *jobs* by means of which one earns a living? Does it make sense to expect a corrections officer to be loyal to the Department of Corrections? Can loyalty even occur in such an organization, beyond loyalty to specific individuals? If it cannot, the entire dilemma regarding whistleblowing versus "departmental loyalty" dissolves. Whistleblowing dilemmas will still occur in cases involving loyalties to specific individuals, but even these dilemmas may be resolved if Baron's approach is accepted.

The final selection for this chapter is Mark S. Hamm's, "Whistleblowing in Corrections." Hamm approaches the subject of whistleblowing in terms of attempts at bureaucratic reform, such as when employees "challenge activities of their own agencies when they deem such activities to be improper." Hamm identifies three grounds on which whistleblowing may be based: (1) violations of bureaucratic norms such as discrimination on the basis of race or sex, abusive treatment of employees, misuse of authority, and incompetence; (2) inefficient or ineffective organizational policies (which presumably exceed some threshold of seriousness); and (3) violations of general moral principles such as misuse of authority to sexually intimidate, corruption, and other policies or organizational patterns of behavior that harm employees or the public.

Hamm focuses on the use of Kant's categorical imperative (the formula of the end-in-itself) as central to the third ground for whistleblowing being "the most important presupposition of all." He interprets the application of the formula of the end-in-itself to corrections policy in the following way:

> . . . corrections policy [should] be blind, in the sense that what is right or wrong does not depend on the particular interests of individual administrators, but on the insistence to treat staff and inmates as ends in themselves, never to use them for personal means.

Notes

1. Immanuel Kant, "Duties Towards Others," Louis Infield, trans., *Lectures on Ethics.* (Indianapolis: Hackett Publishing Company, 1981), pp. 191ff.

Loyalty to Loyalty

JOSIAH ROYCE

THE TWO FOREGOING LECTURES have been devoted to defending the thesis that loyalty is, for the loyal individual himself, a supreme good, whatever be, for the world in general, the worth of his cause. We are next to consider what are the causes which are worthy of loyalty.

I

But before I go on to this new stage of our discussion, I want, by way of summary of all that has preceded, to get before your minds as clear an image as I can of some representative instance of loyalty. The personal dignity and worth of a loyal character can best be appreciated by means of illustrations. And I confess that those illustrations of loyalty which my earlier lectures used must have aroused some associations which I do not want, as I go on to my further argument, to leave too prominent in your minds. I chose those instances because they were familiar. Perhaps they are too familiar. I have mentioned the patriot aflame with the war-spirit, the knight of romance, and the Japanese Samurai. But these examples may have too much emphasized the common but false impression that loyalty necessarily has to do with the martial virtues and with the martial vices. I have also used the instance of the loyal captain standing by his sinking ship. But this case suggests that the loyal have their duties assigned to them by some established and customary routine of the service to which they belong. And that, again, is an association that I do not want you to make too prominent. Loyalty is perfectly consistent with originality. The loyal man may often have to show his loyalty by some act which no mere routine predetermines. He may have to be as inventive of his duties as he is faithful to them.

Now, I myself have for years used in my own classes, as an illustration of the personal worth and beauty of loyalty, an incident of English history, which has often been cited as a precedent in discussions of the constitutional privileges of the House of Commons, but which, as I think, has not been sufficiently noticed by moralists. Let me set that incident now before your imagination. Thus, I say, do the loyal bear themselves: In January, 1642, just before the outbreak of hostilities between King Charles I and the Commons, the King resolved to arrest certain leaders of the opposition party in Parliament. He accordingly sent his herald to the House to demand the surrender of these members into his custody. The Speaker of the House in reply solemnly appealed to the ancient privileges of the House, which gave to that body jurisdiction over its own members, and which forbade their arrest without its consent. The conflict between the privileges of the House and the royal prerogative was herewith definitely initiated. The King resolved by a show of force to assert at once his authority; and, on the day following that upon which the demand sent through his herald had been refused, he went in person, accompanied by soldiers, to the House. Then, having placed his guards at the doors, he entered, went up to the Speaker, and, naming the members whom he desired to arrest, demanded, "Mr. Speaker, do you espy these persons in the House?"

You will observe that the moment was an unique one in English history. Custom, precedent, convention, obviously were inadequate to define the Speaker's duty in this most critical instance. How, then, could he most admirably express himself? How best preserve his genuine

Josiah Royce in The Philosophy of Josiah Royce, *John K. Roth, ed. (New York: Thomas Y. Crowell Company, 1971), pp. 289–301.*

personal dignity? What response would secure to the Speaker his own highest good? Think of the matter merely as one of the Speaker's individual worth and reputation. By what act could he do himself most honor?

In fact, as the well-known report, entered in the Journal of the House, states, the Speaker at once fell on his knee before the King and said: "Your Majesty, I am the Speaker of this House, and, being such, I have neither eyes to see nor tongue to speak save as this House shall command; and I humbly beg your Majesty's pardon if this is the only answer that I can give to your Majesty."

Now, I ask you not, at this point, to consider the Speaker's reply to the King as a deed having historical importance, or in fact as having value for anybody but himself. I want you to view the act merely as an instance of a supremely worthy personal attitude. The beautiful union of formal humility (when the Speaker fell on his knee before the King) with unconquerable self-assertion (when the reply rang with so clear a note of lawful defiance); the willing and complete identification of his whole self with his cause (when the Speaker declared that he had no eye or tongue except as his office gave them to him),— these are characteristics typical of a loyal attitude. The Speaker's words were at once ingenious and obvious. They were in line with the ancient custom of the realm. They were also creative of a new precedent. He had to be inventive to utter them; but once uttered, they seem almost commonplace in their plain truth. The King might be offended at the refusal; but he could not fail to note that, for the moment, he had met with a personal dignity greater than kingship,— the dignity that any loyal man, great or humble, possesses whenever he speaks and acts in the service of his cause.

Well—here is an image of loyalty. Thus, I say, whatever their cause, the loyal express themselves. When any one asks me what the worthiest personal bearing, the most dignified and internally complete expression of an individual is, I can therefore only reply: Such a bearing, such an expression of yourself as the Speaker adopted. Have, then, your cause, chosen by you just as the Speaker had chosen to accept his office from the House. Let this cause so possess you that, even in the most thrilling crisis of your practical service of that cause, you can say with the Speaker: "I am the servant of this cause, its reasonable, its willing, its devoted instrument, and, being such, I have neither eyes to see nor tongue to speak save as this cause shall command." Let this be your bearing, and this your deed. Then, indeed, you know what you live for. And you have won the attitude which constitutes genuine personal dignity. What an individual in his practical bearing can be, you now are. And herein, as I have said, lies for you a supreme personal good.

· · · · ·

III

... If loyalty is a supreme good, the mutually destructive conflict of loyalties is in general a supreme evil. If loyalty is a good for all sorts and conditions of men, the war of man against man has been especially mischievous, not so much because it has hurt, maimed, impoverished, or slain men, as because it has so often robbed the defeated of their causes, of their opportunities to be loyal, and sometimes of their very spirit of loyalty.

If, then, we look over the field of human life to see where good and evil have most clustered, we see that the best in human life is its loyalty; while the worst is whatever has tended to make loyalty impossible, or to destroy it when present, or to rob it of its own while it still survives. And of all things that thus have warred with loyalty, the bitterest woe of humanity has been that so often it is the loyal themselves who have thus blindly and eagerly gone about to wound and to slay the loyalty of their brethren. The spirit of loyalty has been misused to make men commit sin against this very spirit, holy as it is. For such a sin is precisely what any wanton conflict of loyalties means. Where such a conflict occurs, the best, namely, loyalty, is used as an instrument in order to compass the worst, namely, the destruction of loyalty.

It is true, then, that some causes are good, while some are evil. But the test of good and evil in the causes to which men are loyal is now definable in terms which we can greatly simplify in view of the foregoing considerations.

If, namely, I find a cause, and this cause fascinates me, and I give myself over to its service, I in so far attain what, for me, if my loyalty is complete, is a supreme good. But my cause, by our own definition, is a social cause, which binds many into the unity of one service. My cause, therefore, gives me, of necessity, fellow-servants, who with me share this loyalty, and to whom this loyalty, if complete, is also a supreme good. So far, then, being loyal myself, I not only get but give good; for I help to sustain, in each of my fellow-servants, his own loyalty, and so I help him to secure his own supreme good. In so far, then, my loyalty to my cause is also a loyalty to my fellows' loyalty. But now suppose that my cause, like the family in a feud, or like the pirate ship, or like the aggressively warlike nation, lives by the destruction of the loyalty of other families, or of its own community, or of other communities. Then, indeed, I get a good for myself and for my fellow-servants by our common loyalty; but I war against this very spirit of loyalty as it appears in our opponent's loyalty to his own cause.

And so, a cause is good, not only for me, but for mankind, in so far as it is essentially a *loyalty to loyalty*, that is, is an aid and a furtherance of loyalty in my fellows. It is an evil cause in so far as, despite the loyalty that it arouses in me, it is destructive of loyalty in the world of my fellows. My cause is, indeed, always such as to involve some loyalty to loyalty, because, if I am loyal to any cause at all, I have fellow-servants whose loyalty mine supports. But in so far as my cause is a predatory cause, which lives by overthrowing the loyalties of others, it is an evil cause, because it involves disloyalty to the very cause of loyalty itself.

IV

In view of these considerations, we are now able still further to simplify our problem by laying stress upon one more of those very features which seemed, but a moment since, to complicate the matter so hopelessly. Loyalty, as we have defined it, is the willing devotion of a self to a cause. In answering the ethical individualists, we have insisted that all of the higher types of loyalty involve autonomous choice. The cause that is to appeal to me at all must indeed have some elemental fascination for me. It must stir me, arouse me, please me, and in the end possess me. Moreover, it must, indeed, be set before me by my social order as a possible, a practically significant, a living cause, which binds many selves in the unity of one life. But, nevertheless, if I am really awake to the significance of my own moral choices, I must be in the position of accepting this cause, as the Speaker of the House, in the incident that I have narrated, had freely accepted his Speakership. My cause cannot be merely forced upon me. It is I who make it my own. It is I who willingly say: "I have no eyes to see nor tongue to speak save as this cause shall command." However much the cause may seem to be assigned to me by my social station, I must coöperate in the choice of the cause, before the act of loyalty is complete.

Since this is the case, since my loyalty never is my mere fate, but is always also my choice, I can of course determine my loyalty, at least to some extent, by the consideration of the actual good and ill which my proposed cause does to mankind. And since I now have the main criterion of the good and ill of causes before me, I can define a principle of choice which may so guide me that my loyalty shall become a good, not merely to myself, but to mankind.

This principle is now obvious. I may state it thus: In so far as it lies in your power, so choose your cause and so serve it, that, by reason of your choice and of your service, there shall be more loyalty in the world rather than less. And, in fact, so choose and so serve your individual cause as to secure thereby the greatest possible increase of loyalty amongst men. More briefly: *In choosing and in serving the cause to which you are to be loyal, be, in any case, loyal to loyalty.*

This precept, I say, will express how one

should guide his choice of a cause, in so far as he considers not merely his own supreme good, but that of mankind. That such autonomous choice is possible, tends, as we now see, not to complicate, but to simplify our moral situation. For if you regard men's loyalty as their fate, if you think that a man must be loyal simply to the cause which tradition sets before him, without any power to direct his own moral attention, then indeed the conflict of loyalties seems an insoluble problem; so that, if men find themselves loyally involved in feuds, there is no way out. But if, indeed, choice plays a part,—a genuine even if limited part, in directing the individual's choice of the cause to which he is to be loyal, then indeed this choice may be so directed that loyalty to the universal loyalty of all mankind shall be furthered by the actual choices which each enlightened loyal person makes when he selects his cause.

V

At the close of our first discussion we supposed the question to be asked, Where, in all our complex and distracted modern world, in which at present cause wars with cause, shall we find a cause that is certainly worthy of our loyalty? This question, at this very moment, has received in our discussion an answer which you may feel to be so far provisional,—perhaps unpractical,—but which you ought to regard as, at least in principle, somewhat simple and true to human nature. Loyalty is a good, a supreme good. If I myself could but find a worthy cause, and serve it as the Speaker served the House, having neither eyes to see nor tongue to speak save as that cause should command, then my highest human good, in so far as I am indeed an active being, would be mine. But this very good of loyalty is no peculiar privilege of mine; nor is it good only for me. It is an universally human good. For it is simply the finding of a harmony of the self and the world,—such a harmony as alone can content any human being.

In these lectures I do not found my argument upon some remote ideal. I found my case upon taking our poor passionate human nature just as

we find it. This "eager anxious being" of ours, as Gray calls it, is a being that we can find only in social ties, and that we, nevertheless, can never fulfill without a vigorous self-assertion. We are by nature proud, untamed, restless, insatiable in our private self-will. We are also imitative, plastic, and in bitter need of ties. We profoundly want both to rule and to be ruled. We must be each of us at the centre of his own active world, and yet each of us longs to be in harmony with the very outermost heavens that encompass, with the lofty orderliness of their movements, all our restless doings. The stars fascinate us, and yet we also want to keep our own feet upon our solid human earth. Our fellows, meanwhile, overwhelm us with the might of their customs, and we in turn are inflamed with the naturally unquenchable longing that they should somehow listen to the cries of our every individual desire.

Now this divided being of ours demands reconciliation with itself; it is one long struggle for unity. Its inner and outer realms are naturally at war. Yet it wills both realms. It wants them to become one. Such unity, however, only loyalty furnishes to us,—loyalty, which finds the inner self intensified and exalted even by the very act of outward looking and of upward looking, of service and obedience,—loyalty, which knows its eyes and its tongue to be never so much and so proudly its own as when it earnestly insists that it can neither see nor speak except as the cause demands,—loyalty, which is most full of life at the instant when it is most ready to become weary, or even to perish in the act of devotion to its own. Such loyalty unites private passion and outward conformity in one life. This is the very essence of loyalty. Now loyalty has these characters in any man who is loyal. Its emotions vary, indeed, endlessly with the temperaments of its adherents; but to them all it brings the active peace of that rest in a painful life,—that rest such as we found the mystic, Meister Eckhart, fully ready to prize.

Loyalty, then, is a good for all men. And it is in any man just as much a true good as my loyalty could be in me. And so, then, if indeed I seek a cause, a worthy cause, what cause could be more worthy than the cause of loyalty to loyalty; that is, the cause of making loyalty prosper amongst men? If I could serve that cause in a sustained and effective life, if some practical work for the furtherance of universal human loyalty could become to me what the House was to the Speaker, then indeed my own life-task would be found; and I could then be assured at every instant of the worth of my cause by virtue of the very good that I personally found in its service.

Here would be for me not only an unity of inner and outer, but an unity with the unity of all human life. What I sought for myself I should then be explicitly seeking for my whole world. All men would be my fellow-servants of my cause. In principle I should be opposed to no man's loyalty. I should be opposed only to men's blindness in their loyalty, I should contend only against that tragic disloyalty to loyalty which the feuds of humanity now exemplify. I should preach to all others, I should strive to practise myself, that active mutual furtherance of universal loyalty which is what humanity obviously most needs, if indeed loyalty, just as the willing devotion of a self to a cause, is a supreme good.

And since all who are human are as capable of loyalty as they are of reason, since the plainest and the humblest can be as true-hearted as the great, I should nowhere miss the human material for my task. I should know, meanwhile, that if indeed loyalty, unlike the "mercy" of Portia's speech, is not always mightiest in the mightiest, it certainly, like mercy, becomes the throned monarch better than his crown. So that I should be sure of this good of loyalty as something worthy to be carried, so far as I could carry it, to everybody, lofty or humble.

Thus surely it would be humane and reasonable for me to define my cause to myself,—if only I could be assured that there is indeed some practical way of making loyalty to loyalty the actual cause of my life. Our question therefore becomes this: Is there a practical way of serving the universal human cause of loyalty to loyalty? And if there is such a way, what is it? Can we see

how personally so to act that we bring loyalty on earth to a fuller fruition, to a wider range of efficacy, to a more effective sovereignty over the lives of men? If so, then indeed we can see how to work for the cause of the genuine kingdom of heaven.

VI

Yet I fear that as you have listened to this sketch of a possible reasonable cause, such as could be a proper object of our loyalty, you will all the while have objected: This may be a definition of a possible cause, but it is an unpractical definition. For what is there that one can do to further the loyalty of mankind in general? Humanitarian efforts are an old story. They constantly are limited in their effectiveness both by the narrowness of our powers, and by the complexity of the human nature which we try to improve. And if any lesson of philanthropy is well known, it is this, that whoever tries simply to help mankind as a whole, loses his labor, so long as he does not first undertake to help those nearest to him. Loyalty to the cause of universal loyalty—how, then, shall it constitute any practical working scheme of life?

I answer at once that the individual man, with his limited powers, can indeed serve the cause of universal loyalty only by limiting his undertakings to some decidedly definite personal range. He must have his own special and personal cause. But this cause of his can indeed be chosen and determined so as to constitute a deliberate effort to further universal loyalty. When I begin to show you how this may be, I shall at once pass from what may have seemed to you a very unpractical scheme of life, to a realm of familiar and commonplace virtuous activities. The only worth of my general scheme will then lie in the fact that, in the light of this scheme, we can, as it were, see the commonplace virtues transfigured and glorified by their relation to the one highest cause of all. My thesis is *that all the commonplace virtues, in so far as they are indeed defensible and effective, are special forms of loyalty to loyalty,* and are to be justified, centralized, inspired, by the one supreme effort to do good, namely, the effort to make loyalty triumphant in the lives of all men.

The first consideration which I shall here insist upon is this: Loyalty, as we have all along seen, depends upon a very characteristic and subtle union of natural interest, and of free choice. Nobody who merely follows his natural impulses as they come is loyal. Yet nobody can be loyal without depending upon and using his natural impulses. If I am to be loyal, my cause must from moment to moment fascinate me, awaken my muscular vigor, stir me with some eagerness for work, even if this be painful work. I cannot be loyal to barren abstractions. I can only be loyal to what my life can interpret in bodily deeds. Loyalty has its elemental appeal to my whole organism. My cause must become one with my human life. Yet all this must occur not without my willing choice. I must control my devotion. It will possess me, but not without my voluntary complicity; for I shall accept the possession. It is, then, with the cause to which you personally are loyal, as it was with divine grace in an older theology. The cause must control you, as divine grace took saving control of the sinner; but only your own will can accept this control, and a grace that merely compels can never save.

Now that such an union of choice with natural interest is possible, is a fact of human nature, which every act of your own, in your daily calling, may be used to exemplify. You cannot do steady work without natural interest; but whoever is the mere prey of this passing interest does no steady work. Loyalty is a perfect synthesis of certain natural desires, of some range of social conformity, and of your own deliberate choice.

In order to be loyal, then, to loyalty, I must indeed first choose forms of loyal conduct which appeal to my own nature. This means that, upon one side of my life, I shall have to behave much as the most unenlightened of the loyal do. I shall serve causes such as my natural temperament and my social opportunities suggest to me. I shall choose friends whom I like. My family, my community, my country, will be served partly because I find it interesting to be loyal to them.

Nevertheless, upon another side, all these my more natural and, so to speak, accidental loyalties, will be controlled and unified by a deliberate use of the principle that, whatever my cause, it ought to be such as to further, so far as in me lies, the cause of universal loyalty. Hence I shall not permit my choice of my special causes to remain a mere chance. My causes must form a system. They must constitute in their entirety a single cause, my life of loyalty. When apparent conflicts arise amongst the causes in which I am interested, I shall deliberately undertake, by devices which we shall hereafter study in these lectures, to reduce the conflict to the greatest possible harmony. Thus, for instance, I may say, to one of the causes in which I am naturally bound up:—

I could not love thee, dear, so much,
Loved I not honour more.

And in this familiar spirit my loyalty will aim to be, even within the limits of my own personal life, an united, harmonious devotion, not to various conflicting causes, but to one system of causes, and so to one cause.

Since this one cause is my choice, the cause of my life, my social station will indeed suggest it to me. My natural powers and preferences will make it fascinating to me, and yet I will never let mere social routine, or mere social tradition, or mere private caprice, impose it upon me. I will be individualistic in my loyalty, carefully insisting, however, that whatever else I am, I shall be in all my practical activity a loyal individual, and, so far as in me lies, one who chooses his personal causes for the sake of the spread of universal loyalty. Moreover, my loyalty will be a growing loyalty. Without giving up old loyalties I shall annex new ones. There will be evolution in my loyalty.

The choice of my cause will in consequence be such as to avoid unnecessary conflict with the causes of others. So far I shall indeed negatively show loyalty to loyalty. It shall not be my cause to destroy other men's loyalty. Yet since my cause, thus chosen and thus organized, still confines me to my narrow personal range, and since I can do so little directly for mankind, you may still ask whether, by such a control of my natural interests, I am indeed able to do much to serve the cause of universal loyalty.

Well, it is no part of the plan of this discourse to encourage illusions about the range of influence that any one poor mortal can exert. But that by the mere force of my practical and personal loyalty, if I am indeed loyal, I am doing something for the cause of universal loyalty, however narrow my range of deeds, this a very little experience of the lives of other people tends to teach me. For who, after all, most encourages and incites me to loyalty? I answer, any loyal human being, whatever his cause, so long as his cause does not arouse my hatred, and does not directly injure my chance to be loyal. My fellow's special and personal cause need not be directly mine. Indirectly he inspires me by the very contagion of his loyalty. He sets me the example. By his loyalty he shows me the worth of loyalty. Those humble and obscure folk of whom I have before spoken, how precious they are to us all as inspiring examples, because of their loyalty to their own.

From what men, then, have I gained the best aid in discovering how to be myself loyal? From the men whose personal cause is directly and consciously one with my own? That is indeed sometimes the case. But others, whose personal causes were apparently remote in very many ways from mine, have helped me to some of my truest glimpses of loyalty.

For instance: There was a friend of my own youth whom I have not seen for years, who once faced the choice between a scholarly career that he loved, on the one hand, and a call of honor, upon the other,—who could have lived out that career with worldly success if he had only been willing to conspire with his chief to deceive the public about a matter of fact, but who unhesitatingly was loyal to loyalty, who spoke the truth, who refused to conspire, and who, because his chief was a plausible and powerful man, thus deliberately wrecked his own worldly

chances once for all, and retired into a misunderstood obscurity in order that his fellow-men might henceforth be helped to respect the truth better. Now, the worldly career which that friend thus sacrificed for the sake of his loyalty is far from mine; the causes that he has since loyally served have not of late brought him near to me in worldly doings. I am not sure that he should ever have kept our interests in close touch with one another even if we had lived side by side. For he was and is a highly specialized type of man, austere, and a little disposed, like many scholars, to a life apart. For the rest, I have never myself been put in such a place as his was when he chose to make his sacrifice, and have never had his great choice set before me. Nor has the world rewarded him at all fairly for his fidelity. He is, then, as this world goes, not now near to me and not a widely influential man. Yet I owe him a great debt. He showed me, by the example of his free sacrifice, a good in loyalty which I might otherwise have been too blind to see. He is a man who does not love flattery. It would be useless for me now to offer to him either words of praise or words of comfort. He made his choice with a single heart and a clear head, and he has always declined to be praised. But it will take a long time, in some other world, should I meet him in such a realm, to tell him how much I owe to his example, how much he inspired me, or how many of his fellows he had indirectly helped to their own loyalty. For I believe that a good many others besides myself indirectly owe far more to him than he knows, or than they know. I believe that certain standards of loyalty and of scientific truthfulness in this country are to-day higher than they were because of the self-surrendering act of that one devoted scholar.

Loyalty, then, is contagious. It infects not only the fellow servant of your own special cause, but also all who know of this act. Loyalty is a good that spreads. Live it and you thereby cultivate it in other men. Be faithful, then, so one may say, to the loyal man; be faithful over your few things, for the spirit of loyalty, secretly passing from you to many to whom you are a stranger, may even thereby make you unconsciously ruler over many things. Loyalty to loyalty is then no unpractical cause. And you serve it not by becoming a mere citizen of the world, but by serving your own personal cause. We set before you, then, no unpractical rule when we repeat our moral formula in this form: Find your own cause, your interesting, fascinating, personally engrossing cause; serve it with all your might and soul and strength; but so choose your cause, and so serve it, that thereby you show forth your loyalty to loyalty, so that because of your choice and service of your cause, there is a maximum of increase of loyalty amongst your fellow-men.

Study Questions

1. Why does Royce think that the Speaker of the House of Commons demonstrated loyalty in his response to King Charles I? To whom or what was he being loyal?

2. What does Royce mean by being "loyal to loyalty"? Would the loyalty among Mafiosi to their "cause" meet Royce's definition?

3. What is the significance to Royce of the whistleblowing case he presents at the end of the selection?

4. How do you think Royce would analyze the conflict between loyalty to one's fellow officers and telling the truth?

Whistleblowing and Employee Loyalty

RONALD DUSKA

.... THERE ARE PROPONENTS ON both sides of the issue—those who praise whistleblowers as civic heroes and those who condemn them as "finks." Maxwell Glen and Cody Shearer, who wrote about the whistleblowers at Three Mile Island say, "Without the *courageous* breed of assorted company insiders known as whistleblowers—workers who often risk their livelihoods to disclose information about construction and design flaws—the Nuclear Regulatory Commission itself would be nearly as idle as Three Mile Island. . . . That whistleblowers deserve both gratitude and protection is beyond disagreement."[1]

Still, while Glen and Shearer praise whistleblowers, others vociferously condemn them. For example, in a now infamous quote, James Roche, the former president of General Motors said:

Some critics are now busy eroding another support of free enterprise—the loyalty of a management team, with its unifying values and cooperative work. Some of the enemies of business now encourage an employee to be *disloyal* to the enterprise. They want to create suspicion and disharmony, and pry into the proprietary interests of the business. However this is labelled—industrial espionage, whistleblowing, or professional responsibility—it is

Used by permission of the author.

another tactic for spreading disunity and creating conflict.[2]

From Roche's point of view, not only is whistleblowing not "courageous" and not deserving of "gratitude and protection" as Glen and Shearer would have it, it is corrosive and impermissible.

Discussions of whistleblowing generally revolve around three topics: (1) attempts to define whistleblowing more precisely, (2) debates about whether and when whistleblowing is permissible, and (3) debates about whether and when one has an obligation to blow the whistle.

In this paper I want to focus on the second problem, because I find it somewhat disconcerting that there is a problem at all. When I first looked into the ethics of whistleblowing it seemed to me that whistleblowing was a good thing, and yet I found in the literature claim after claim that it was in need of defense, that there was something wrong with it, namely that it was an act of disloyalty.

If whistleblowing is a disloyal act, it deserves disapproval, and ultimately any action of whistleblowing needs justification. This disturbs me. It is as if the act of a good Samaritan is being condemned as an act of interference, as if the prevention of a suicide needs to be justified.

In his book *Business Ethics,* Norman Bowie claims that "whistleblowing . . . violate(s) a *prima facie* duty of loyalty to one's employer." According to Bowie, there is a duty of loyalty that prohibits one from reporting his employer or company. Bowie, of course, recognizes that this is only a *prima facie* duty, that is, one that can be overridden by a higher duty to the public good. Nevertheless, the axiom that whistleblowing is disloyal is Bowie's starting point.[3]

Bowie is not alone. Sissela Bok sees "whistleblowing" as an instance of disloyalty:

The whistleblower hopes to stop the game; but since he is neither referee nor coach, and since he blows the whistle on his own team, his act is seen as a *violation of loyalty.* In holding his position, he has assumed certain

obligations to his colleagues and clients. He may even have subscribed to a loyalty oath or a promise of confidentiality. . . . Loyalty to colleagues and to clients comes to be pitted against loyalty to the public interest, to those who may be injured unless the revelation is made.[4]

Bowie and Bok end up defending whistleblowing in certain contexts, so I don't necessarily disagree with their conclusions. However, I fail to see how one has an obligation of loyalty to one's company, so I disagree with their perception of the problem and their starting point. I want to argue that one does not have an obligation of loyalty to a company, even a *prima facie* one, because companies are not the kind of things that are properly objects of loyalty. To make them objects of loyalty gives them a moral status they do not deserve and in raising their status, one lowers the status of the individuals who work for the companies. Thus, the difference in perception is important because those who think employees have an obligation of loyalty to a company fail to take into account a relevant moral difference between persons and corporations.

But why aren't companies the kind of things that can be objects of loyalty? To answer that we have to ask what are proper objects of loyalty. John Ladd states the problem this way. "Granted that loyalty is the wholehearted devotion to an object of some kind, what kind of thing is the object? Is it an abstract entity, such as an idea or a collective being? Or is it a person or group of persons?"[5] Philosophers fall into three camps on the question. On one side are the idealists who hold that loyalty is devotion to something more than persons, to some cause or abstract entity. On the other side are what Ladd calls "social atomists," and these include empiricists and utilitarians, who think that at most one can only be loyal to individuals and that loyalty can ultimately be explained away as some other obligation that holds between two people. Finally, there is a moderate position that holds that although idealists go too far in postulating some super-personal entity as an object of loyalty, loyalty is still an important and real relation that holds between people, one that cannot be dismissed by reducing it to some other relation.

There does seem to be a view of loyalty that is not extreme. According to Ladd, "'loyalty' is taken to refer to a relationship between persons—for instance, between a lord and his vassal, between a parent and his children, or between friends. Thus the object of loyalty is ordinarily taken to be a person or a group of persons."[6]

But this raises a problem that Ladd glosses over. There is a difference between a person or a group of persons and aside from instances of loyalty that relate two people such as lord/vassal, parent/child, or friend/friend, there are instances of loyalty relating a person to a group, such as a person to his family, a person to his team, and a person to his country. Families, countries, and teams are presumably groups of persons. They are certainly ordinarily construed as objects of loyalty.

But to what am I loyal in such a group? In being loyal to the group am I being loyal to the whole group or to its members? It is easy to see the object of loyalty in the case of an individual person. It is simply the individual. But to whom am I loyal in a group? To whom am I loyal in a family? Am I loyal to each and every individual or to something larger, and if to something larger, what is it? We are tempted to think of a group as an entity of its own, an individual in its own right, having an identity of its own.

To avoid the problem of individuals existing for the sake of the group, the atomists insist that a group is nothing more than the individuals who comprise it, nothing other than a mental fiction by which we refer to a group of individuals. It is certainly not a reality or entity over and above the sum of its parts and consequently is not a proper object of loyalty. Under such a position, of course, no loyalty would be owed to a company because a company is a mere mental fiction, since it is a group. One would have obligations to the individual members of the company, but one could never be justified in

overriding those obligations for the sake of the "group" taken collectively. A company has no moral status except in terms of the individual members who comprise it. It is not a proper object of loyalty. But the atomists go too far. Some groups, such as a family, do have a reality of their own, whereas groups of people walking down the street do not. From Ladd's point of view the social atomist is wrong because he fails to recognize the kinds of groups that are held together by "the ties that bind." The atomist tries to reduce these groups to simple sets of individuals bound together by some externally imposed criteria. This seems wrong.

There do seem to be groups in which the relationships and interactions create a new force or entity. A group takes on an identity and a reality of its own that is determined by its purpose, and this purpose defines the various relationships and roles set up within the group. There is a division of labor into roles necessary for the fulfillment of the purposes of the group. The membership, then, is not of individuals who are the same but of individuals who have specific relationships to one another determined by the aim of the group. Thus we get specific relationships like parent/child, coach/player, and so on, that don't occur in other groups. It seems then that an atomist account of loyalty that restricts loyalty merely to individuals and does not include loyalty to groups might be inadequate.

But once I have admitted that we can have loyalty to a group, do I not open myself up to criticism from the proponent of loyalty to the company? Might not the proponent of loyalty to business say: "Very well. I agree with you. The atomists are short-sighted. Groups have some sort of reality and they can be proper objects of loyalty. But companies are groups. Therefore companies are proper objects of loyalty."

The point seems well taken, except for the fact that the kinds of relationships that loyalty requires are just the kind that one does not find in business. As Ladd says, "The ties that bind the persons together provide the basis of loyalty." But all sorts of ties bind people together. I am a member of a group of fans if I go to a ball game. I am a member of a group if I merely walk down the street. What binds people together in a business is not sufficient to require loyalty.

A business or corporation does two things in the free enterprise system: It produces a good or service and it makes a profit. The making of a profit, however, is the primary function of a business as a business, for if the production of the good or service is not profitable, the business would be out of business. Thus nonprofitable goods or services are a means to an end. People bound together in a business are bound together not for mutual fulfillment and support, but to divide labor to make a profit. Thus, while we can jokingly refer to a family as a place where "they have to take you in no matter what," we cannot refer to a company in that way. If a worker does not produce in a company or if cheaper laborers are available, the company—in order to fulfill its purpose—should get rid of the worker. A company feels no obligation of loyalty. The saying "You can't buy loyalty" is true. Loyalty depends on ties that demand self-sacrifice with no expectation of reward. Business functions on the basis of enlightened self-interest. I am devoted to a company not because it is like a parent to me; it is not. Attempts of some companies to create "one big happy family" ought to be looked on with suspicion. I am not devoted to it at all, nor should I be. I work for it because it pays me. I am not in a family to get paid, I am in a company to get paid.

The cold hard truth is that the goal of profit is what gives birth to a company and forms that particular group. Money is what ties the group together. But in such a commercialized venture, with such a goal, there is no loyalty, or at least none need be expected. An employer will release an employee and an employee will walk away from an employer when it is profitable for either one to do so.

Not only is loyalty to a corporation not required, it more than likely is misguided. There is nothing as pathetic as the story of the loyal employee who, having given above and beyond

the call of duty, is let go in the restructuring of the company. He feels betrayed because he mistakenly viewed the company as an object of his loyalty. Getting rid of such foolish romanticism and coming to grips with this hard but accurate assessment should ultimately benefit everyone.

To think we owe a company or corporation loyalty requires us to think of that company as a person or as a group with a goal of human fulfillment. If we think of it in this way we can be loyal. But this is the wrong way to think. A company is not a person. A company is an instrument, and an instrument with a specific purpose, the making of profit. To treat an instrument as an end in itself, like a person, may not be as bad as treating an end as an instrument, but it does give the instrument a moral status it does not deserve; and by elevating the instrument we lower the end. All things, instruments and ends, become alike.

Remember that Roche refers to the "management team" and Bok sees the name "whistleblowing" coming from the instance of a referee blowing a whistle in the presence of a foul. What is perceived as bad about whistleblowing in business from this perspective is that one blows the whistle on one's own team, thereby violating team loyalty. If the company can get its employees to view it as a team they belong to, it is easier to demand loyalty. Then the rules governing teamwork and team loyalty will apply. One reason the appeal to a team and team loyalty works so well in business is that businesses are in competition with one another. Effective motivation turns business practices into a game and instills teamwork.

But businesses differ from teams in very important respects, which makes the analogy between business and a team dangerous. Loyalty to a team is loyalty within the context of sport or a competition. Teamwork and team loyalty require that in the circumscribed activity of the game I cooperate with my fellow players, so that pulling all together, we may win. The object of (most) sports is victory. But winning in sports is a social convention, divorced from the usual goings on of society. Such a winning is most times a harmless, morally neutral diversion.

But the fact that this victory in sports, within the rules enforced by a referee (whistleblower), is a socially developed convention taking place within a larger social context makes it quite different from competition in business, which, rather than being defined by a context, permeates the whole of society in its influence. Competition leads not only to victory but to losers. One can lose at sport with precious few consequences. The consequences of losing at business are much larger. Further, the losers in business can be those who are not in the game voluntarily (we are all forced to participate) but who are still affected by business decisions. People cannot choose to participate in business. It permeates everyone's lives.

The team model, then, fits very well with the model of the free market system, because there competition is said to be the name of the game. Rival companies compete and their object is to win. To call a foul on one's own teammate is to jeopardize one's chances of winning and is viewed as disloyalty.

But isn't it time to stop viewing corporate machinations as games? These games are not controlled and are not ended after a specific time. The activities of business affect the lives of everyone, not just the game players. The analogy of the corporation to a team and the consequent appeal to team loyalty, although understandable, is seriously misleading, at least in the moral sphere where competition is not the prevailing virtue.

If my analysis is correct, the issue of the permissibility of whistleblowing is not a real issue since there is no obligation of loyalty to a company. Whistleblowing is not only permissible but expected when a company is harming society. The issue is not one of disloyalty to the company, but of whether the whistleblower has an obligation to society if blowing the whistle will bring him retaliation.

NOTES

1. Maxwell Glen and Cody Shearer, "Going After the Whistle-blowers," *Philadelphia Inquirer*, Tuesday, August 2, 1983, Op-ed page, p. 11A

2. James M. Roche, "The Competitive System, to Work, to Preserve, and to Protect," *Vital Speeches of the Day* (May 1971): 445.

3. Norman Bowie, *Business Ethics* (Englewood Cliffs, N.J.: Prentice-Hall, 1982). pp. 140-143.

4. Sissela Bok, "Whistleblowing and Professional Responsibilities," *New York University Education Quarterly* 2 (1980): 3, and here p. 294.

5. John Ladd, "Loyalty," *The Encyclopedia of Philosophy* 5: 97.

6. *Ibid.*

Study Questions

1. What three topics are central to discussions of whistleblowing? On which of the three does Duska focus in his paper?

2. What is a *prima facie* duty? Does Duska believe that an employee has a *prima facie* duty to be loyal to the employer?

3. What are the three philosophical approaches regarding the objects of loyalty? Which approach does Duska take?

4. Loyalty is dependent on what characteristic, in Duska's view? How does this position affect the view that Duska has regarding *prima facie* duties to one's employer? Do you agree with Duska? Why?

The Moral Status of Loyalty

MARCIA BARON

Background

In a 1973 CBS report on Phillips Petroleum, Inc., one of its chief executives was asked to describe what sort of qualities his company looks for in prospective employees. He responded without hesitation that above all else, what Phillips wants and needs is loyalty on the part of its employees. A loyal employee, he elaborated. would buy only Phillips' products. (I take it that he did not mean this literally, but meant, rather, that the employee would not buy any products from a company other than Phillips if Phillips produced products of the same type.) Moreover, a loyal employee would vote in local, state, and national elections in whatever way was most conducive to the growth and flourishing of Phillips. And, of course, a loyal employee would never leave Phillips unless it was absolutely unavoidable. To reduce the likelihood of that happening, prospective employees were screened to make sure their respective wives did not have careers which might conflict with life-long loyalty to Phillips.[1]

Phillips does not appear to be anomalous in its expectations of loyalty, although times have changed somewhat since the early 1970s, thanks to the efforts of Ralph Nader and others. Nader and Mark Green (1979) report that the Gilman Paper Company of Saint Mary's, Georgia, demanded that their personnel manager find out who planned to vote against the candidate backed by the Gilman Company. The personnel manager refused to comply and finally quit, but another mill worker took on the task that the former had refused, and several people were subsequently fired for voting for the "wrong" candidate.[2]

Serious though the demand of loyalty is for all of those in business, the problem is particularly acute for engineers. Engineers are in a position of public trust. Compliance with the company's expectation of loyalty may, in some circumstances, have far-reaching consequences for those who trust the engineer to see to it that the product inspected by his or her department is safe.

Consider the following case reported by Kermit Vandivier (1972) in Robert Heilbroner's *In the Name of Profit.*[3] Rather than risk losing a sale by delaying delivery of the four-disk brake to the LTV Aerospace Corporation and explaining that, in the interest of safety, a new brake design would have to be drawn up, the B. F. Goodrich plant at Troy, Ohio opted to "fudge" the data from the qualifying tests. Vandivier, who was among the engineers told to co-operate "or else," entitles his essay in Heilbroner's book "Why Should My Conscience Bother Me?"[4] His task was to issue the formal qualification report on the brake. The brake had failed the tests abysmally, even after it was "helped along": fans were used to cool it during the test and a conveniently miscalibrated instrument was employed to measure the brake pressure. Vandivier buckled under the severe pressure of his superiors and reluctantly handed in the fraudulent report. Later, however, he submitted a letter of resignation, citing the "atmosphere of deceit and distrust in which it is impossible to work" (p. 28).

The resignation was to take effect a few weeks later, but the chief engineer informed Vandivier that in view of Vandivier's "'disloyalty,' " he had decided to accept the resignation "'right now' " (p. 29).

Vandivier and his cohorts were lucky. No one was (physically) injured when, predictably enough, the brakes failed. Such good fortune does not come to all those who succumb to the pressure and do what is said to be in the best interest of the company and to be required by loyalty. Many engineers who were loyal to Lee Iacocca and to Ford have more on their consciences than does Vandivier: between 1970 and 1977 Pinto crashes caused somewhere between 500 and 900 burn deaths. Yet the Pinto design was known to be faulty before any of the Pintos were sold (Dowie 1980; De George 1981).

THE ISSUES FOR ENGINEERS

While loyalty is a significant moral issue for everyone—why this is so will become evident shortly—it is of paramount importance that engineers come to grips with it since the impact of an engineer's decision to put loyalty to his or her company before (other) moral demands can have far-reaching and even life-and-death consequences. There are two clusters of abstract questions that a responsible engineer should ponder:

1. What, if anything, is good about loyalty? If it is good to be loyal, is it always good to be loyal? If there are circumstances in which it is wrong to act loyally, how can we identify or be on the alert for such circumstances?

2. What should one do if conflicting loyalties make demands on one? How, if at all, can one weigh the relative importance of one claim of loyalty against another?[5]

Let us first consider how the cluster of questions that 2 raises bears on engineering ethics. A look at the code of the National Society of Professional Engineers (NSPE), or virtually any other code of ethics for engineers, will make this plain. The NSPE Code begins: "The Engineer, to uphold and advance the honor and dignity of the engineering profession and in keeping with the high standards of ethical conduct ... will be honest and impartial, and will serve with devotion his employer, his clients, and the public...." Can an engineer, no matter how heroic, always serve *each* of these parties with devotion? Can he or she, in other words, always be loyal to all three? The answer is clearly "No." Loyalty to their clients required that the engineers at B. F. Goodrich live up to the trust that LTV placed in them: it required, among other things, that they adhere to the methods of qualification testing that the military specifies, rather than concoct their own "tests." Loyalty to the public required the Ford engineers to "blow the whistle," that is, to inform the public of the hidden danger in the Pinto, or perhaps collectively refuse to cooperate in completing the Pinto, given Iacocca's refusal to remodel the gas tank.

In order to answer the questions raised in 2 we must first address the more abstract ones which 1 raises. We cannot expect to make any headway in adjudicating between conflicting loyalties unless we first figure out how to evaluate the extent to which various claims of loyalty really do make a legitimate claim on us. To do this, we will analyze the concept of loyalty, isolate its positive features from its negative features and determine, within broad parameters, when it is right to act loyally and when, because of other moral considerations, it is wrong to do so. But first we must ask what loyalty is.

THE NATURE OF LOYALTY

In asking what loyalty is we have two aims: (1) to pin down what we shall mean, for the purposes of this discussion, when we use the words "loyal," "loyalty," and "loyally"; and (2) to try to capture the idea that most of us have when we speak of loyalty and the idea of loyalty that is relevant to the issues in engineering ethics, as indicated above. In other words, we want to avoid using the words in question loosely and vaguely: it is crucial that we be clear on what it is that we are talking about. In addition, though we do not need to take on the task of giving a full analysis of what loyalty is, we do not want to "change the subject" and end up discussing the moral status of something other than what is generally meant by "loyalty" when the term is used in connection with issues in engineering ethics.[6]

LOYALTY AND ITS OBJECTS

To accomplish our aims we must first decide what objects loyalty can take; that is, what sorts of things one can be loyal *to*. Immediately we encounter disagreement among those who have written on loyalty. Josiah Royce, a turn-of-the-century American philosopher and one of the few philosophers to write an entire book on loyalty, stipulates that the object of loyalty must be some *cause* or other. "Loyalty shall mean ... *The willing and practical and thoroughgoing devotion of a person to a cause* (16–17, Italics in text)," the cause being something "beyond your private self, greater than you are ... personal and ... superpersonal" (Royce 1908, pp. 55–56).

> Instances of loyalty are: The devotion of a patriot to his country, when this devotion leads him actually to live and perhaps to die for his country; the devotion of a martyr to his religion; the devotion of a ship's captain to the requirements of his office when, after a disaster, he works steadily for his ship, for the saving of his ship's company until the last possible service is accomplished, so that he is the last man to leave the ship, and is ready if need be to go down with his ship (Royce 1908, p. 17).

John Ladd, a contemporary philosopher, disagrees. So does another contemporary thinker, Andrew Oldenquist. In his *Encyclopedia of Philosophy* article on loyalty, Ladd differs from Royce as to the object of loyalty. Far from having as its objects impersonal and superpersonal causes, loyalty, Ladd thinks, is interpersonal. Both historically and in our ordinary moral language, "loyalty" is "taken to refer to a relationship between persons—for instance, between a lord and his vassal, between a parent and his children, or between friends. Thus the object of loyalty is ordinarily taken to be a person or group of persons" (Ladd 1967, p. 97). Loyalty, Ladd adds, is "also specific; a man is loyal to *his* lord, *his* father,

or *his* comrades. It is conceptually impossible to be loyal to people in general (to humanity) or to a general principle, such as justice or democracy" (p. 97).[7]

Oldenquist joins Ladd in rejecting the view that ideals can be the object of loyalty. His explanation makes it clear that the issue is a deep one, involving much more than the simple question of how we should use the term "loyalty." In his explanation, Oldenquist contrasts being loyal to something (or as he puts it, "having a loyalty") with having an ideal. The test by which one can distinguish loyalties from ideals is as follows:

> If I say that I ought to defend my country, I have a putative loyalty. But if I am willing to replace "my country" with, e.g.; "a democratic country" or "a Christian country," I have not a loyalty but an ideal; in this case what I am committed to is a kind of thing, not some particular thing. If I am unwilling to replace "my country" with a characterizing expression I have a genuine loyalty and not an ideal; my normative judgment is self-dependent (Oldenquist 1982, p. 175).

To put Oldenquist's point more generally, loyalties involve an ineliminable first person (possessive) pronoun: "my" (or "our"). This means that I can only be loyal to *my X*, but more importantly that to be loyal to my X, I must think of it under the description "my X" rather than merely as an X which has the qualities *a, b,* and *c*. The reason is that otherwise I am committed to a kind of X, not to this X. If I am committed to a kind of X but not to some particular X, then I do not yet have any reason for preferring my X to other X's of the same kind. And yet if I am loyal to my X (e.g., my country) I *do*, Oldenquist thinks, prefer it or value it more than other X's of the same kind (e.g., other democratic countries). So this must mean that if I have a loyalty to X, I value it as my X, not just as an X which is valuable independently of being mine. This is what Oldenquist means when he argues that the objects of loyalty contain "uneliminable [*sic*] egocentric particulars" (p. 175).

Ladd and Oldenquist thus seem roughly to agree on what sorts of objects loyalty can take.

Loyalties, on their view, are to people, not to ideals. Oldenquist might deny that one can only be loyal to people or groups of people, for he might deny that loyalty to one's country is really just loyalty to a group of people. But we can ignore such differences for now. We must focus instead on this question: What bearing does the disagreement between Royce, on the one hand, and Ladd and Oldenquist, on the other, have on the issues concerning loyalty in engineering ethics? Once we answer that question we can decide which characterizations of loyalty and its objects to accept for the purposes of this essay.

On Oldenquist's analysis, the demand that an engineer be loyal—if it really is a demand for loyalty—amounts to something like this: an engineer is to be loyal to his company because it is his company, and not solely because it is an important, socially useful company, or because he has been treated well by "the company" (i.e., the people who constitute it). His reasons for being loyal to it must include the fact that it is *his* company. Ladd would agree: the engineer must, to be loyal, be loyal to some particular group of people. In contrast, Royce's view is that this is elliptical and inaccurate. What the engineer is supposed to be loyal to, he thinks, is a cause—not a person, not a group of people, not an organization of people. Which characterization better captures (a) our ordinary conception of loyalty, and (b) the notion of loyalty which is relevant to engineering ethics? I believe that Ladd's and Oldenquist's characterization does. It outstrips Royce's characterizations with respect to both (a) and (b).

Consider (b) first. When Vandivier's superior at Goodrich told him that he was being disloyal, he surely did not mean that Vandivier was failing (either by having a cause to which he was disloyal or by having no cause) to fight for some cause—indeed, that is part of what Vandivier was doing in deciding to quit the company! What the superior meant is that he was being disloyal to his superiors and co-workers at Goodrich. The relevant notion of loyalty in that instance is loyalty to certain people or to a group

of people, not loyalty to an ideal or a cause.

The Ladd-Oldenquist characterization also accounts well for our ordinary use of "loyalty" and "loyal." A friend is loyal to another person, not to the cause of friendship, or to any other cause. The loyal dog is loyal to his master. When we speak of causes (or ideals) we are more apt to say that people are committed to them or devoted to them than that they are loyal to them.

THE CASE AGAINST LOYALTY

There are good philosophical reasons for worrying about the moral status of loyalty. Moral reasoning and moral conduct demand that one be impartial, that one not play favorites. Professors are not to give high grades to students just because they are family friends or members of the same political organization or Bible study group. Nor are jobs to be filled on the basis of whether the candidate is "my kind." Indeed, depending on the "kind" in question, it can be illegal to hire on that basis—and for good reason. If the members of group A have most of the power in a certain society and if out of loyalty to their co-members they try always to give the jobs to members of group A and to rent or sell residential property only to members of group A (or to reserve the only decent housing for members of group A), those who are not in group A will be, at the very best, second-class citizens.[8] Unfortunately, such scenarios are far from merely hypothetical.

What all this points to is the link between loyalty to X's and discrimination against non-X's. It is worth taking note of a special feature of the link between loyalty to X's and discrimination against non-X's: the link does not rely on any beliefs to the effect that non-X's are in some relevant (or irrelevant) respect inferior to X's. Whereas discrimination against non-X's commonly is nurtured by a belief that the people in question are less bright or lazier or somehow morally inferior, loyalty to X's provides its own potentially independent basis for discrimination. The "old buddy system" of hiring makes this clear: if, out of loyalty, I hire my nephews and sons-in-law whenever I can (and perhaps my nieces and daughters-in-law as well), I need not have anything against the better-qualified people whom I turn down. I need not believe that they are "a greater risk" or in some other respect less qualified. I simply am being loyal to my family. One problem with loyalty, then, is that it invites unfairness and threatens to contribute to social injustice.

There is a second and closely related reason for questioning the value of loyalty. Loyalty seems to eschew another central feature of morality: reliance on good reasons. If I am to justify some action that I took, I must be able to show that I had good reasons for taking it and that the reasons for taking it outweighed the reasons against taking it. Consider what happens if the action in question was performed out of loyalty. We have already seen that if I act from loyalty, I act partially; that is, I act on behalf of some particular person(s) or constellation of persons—my sister, my boss, my friend, my university, my company, my country. But putting partiality to one side, we note another feature of acting loyally: I act on behalf of one of these parties not because the party deserves it, because I promised it, because it will help the people in question while hurting no one else, but for a very different sort of reason (if indeed for a *reason* at all!): because the party is question is *my X*.

Recall Oldenquist's distinction between loyalties and ideals. If my reason for defending my country is that my country is democratic, then, he says, "I have not a loyalty but an ideal," for "what I am committed to is a kind of thing, not some particular thing." I have a genuine loyalty only if I am dedicated to X under the description "my X"; otherwise, I would have to say, any other X of the same kind (e.g., any democratic country) would have an equal claim on me. But what kind of reason is "Because it is mine"? If to act loyally is to act with a special regard for something because it is mine—only because it is mine—loyalty seems at best silly. Suppose someone asked me why I favor the type of government that I do favor or why I think so highly of

my thesis student. If to either question I responded, "Because it (s/he) is my____," the appropriate response would be an amused smile. And the only sensible way to comprehend my answer would be to regard it as a refusal to give a reason—perhaps an evasion. Hence it is hard to see how loyalty generates reasons. An appeal to loyalty seems to reject or evade the request for a reason. No wonder David Hume thought loyalty a virtue that holds "less of reason, than of bigotry, and superstition" (Hume 1888, p. 562). At its core this is just the sort of narrowness of vision that we are supposed to escape *through* moral reasoning!

This last point can be expanded on if we take a look at Hume's account of how moral reasoning enables us to be more impartial. Hume saw that while we are, as humans, very social creatures, our affections are partial. They pick and choose: we do not love everybody equally. It is natural to prefer certain people to others. He also noticed that we are more impressed by admirable men and women who live in our part of the world and our era, and more disturbed by horrible deeds done "close to home" than by those that happened hundreds of years ago. And yet, he noticed (speaking as a Briton), "we give the same approbation to the same moral qualities in China as in England" (p. 581). The fact that one wicked person lives in our town and another lives thousands of miles away does not prompt us to think of the first as more wicked, even though we *feel* more shaken up and more outraged by the spectacle of wicked deeds close to home. We don't say that cruelty of the same type and degree is worse if far away from us than if it is right in our neighborhood; yet our feelings towards the one instance of cruelty are quite different from our feelings towards the other instance. Hume noticed that what happens in such instances is that we take ourselves *beyond* those feelings by abstracting from them. We try to ignore the aspects of our feelings that are occasioned by the nearness or remoteness of the crime or character (or whatever) that is in question.

Our servant, if diligent and faithful, may excite stronger sentiments of love and kindness than Marcus Brutus, as represented in history; but we say not upon that account, that the former character is more laudable than the latter. We know, that were we to approach equally near to that renown'd patriot, he wou'd command a much higher degree of affection and admiration. Such corrections are common with regard to all the senses; and indeed 'twere impossible we cou'd ever make use of language, or communicate our sentiments to one another, did we not correct the momentary appearances of things, and overlook our present situation (Hume 1888, p. 582).

In moral reasoning we try to leave behind the irrelevant considerations. We try not to let such factors as the person's "looks" affect our judgment of guilt or innocence for a certain crime; in allocating academic honors or 4-H awards we try not to be affected in our decisions by considerations of how much we like the candidates, from which part of the country they hail, etc. Of course, I may *feel* like awarding the honor to the student who babysits my children, but I realize that the fact that she is our babysitter is not a good reason for favoring her over someone else who is a candidate for this honor. Hume would say that moral reasoning extends my natural sympathy—or if the "passions do not always follow our correction ... these corrections serve sufficiently to regulate our abstract notions, and are alone regarded, when we pronounce in general concerning the degrees of vice and virtue" (p. 585).

The trouble with loyalty is that it seems to force our sympathies back into their initial partiality. It seems to undo or oppose all the good that fair-minded moral reasoning strives to accomplish.

Yet a third and related problem with loyalty is that it seems to invite irresponsibility: acting out of loyalty to *X* without a concern for whether in doing so we act fairly, and without heeding the likely consequences of our action. In his ebullient praise of and call for loyalty, Josiah Royce (1908, p. 106) urges:

Let this so possess you that ... you can say ... "I am the servant of this cause, its reasonable, its willing, its devoted instrument; and being such, I have neither eyes to see nor tongue to speak save as this cause shall command." Let this be your bearing, and this your deed. Then, indeed, you ... have won the attitude which constitutes genuine personal dignity.

How can I act responsibly if I make myself a willing instrument of something else? If I say "No, I will not consider what dangers there are in nuclear power; I will promote the cause of my company without any regard to what happened at Browns Ferry," can I be acting responsibly? The answer is clearly "No." I cannot act responsibly if I avert my eyes from all warning signs. It is crucial that I remain open to new information and that I be willing to revise my plans—revise a design for a bridge or urge that the company alter its plans to keep the cost of the Pinto from exceeding two thousand dollars and the weight from exceeding two thousand pounds[9]—if I find that things are not quite as they seemed. To charge ahead despite indications that all will not go well is irresponsible. If loyalty demands such ostrich-like behavior, that only goes to show that loyalty needs to be tempered by other considerations.

It is worth noting that such instances of loyalty to one's company frequently end up hurting the company in the long run, as well as hurting consumers. This was the case, for instance, with the refusal to take seriously the very worrisome test results on the Corvair. The proposal to install a stabilizing bar in the rear of each car to correct the Corvair's tendency to flip over was long regarded as too costly—at fifteen dollars a car. When it finally was accepted and executed, it was too late for the Corvair to regain credibility. Losses in sales and legal expenses and out-of-court settlements for those maimed and killed were enormous (Wright 1980).

It is a sad fact about loyalty that it invites—according to Royce, *demands*—single mindedness. Single-minded pursuit of a goal is sometimes delightfully romantic, even a real inspiration. But it is hardly something to advocate to engineers, whose impact on the safety of the public is so very significant. Irresponsibility, whether caused by selfishness or by magnificently unselfish loyalty, can have most unfortunate consequences.

THE CASE FOR LOYALTY

The preceding pages expose loyalty's darker side. But there is also much to be said *for* loyalty, as the following examples will demonstrate.

Imagine a parent who, perhaps as a result of reading the previous section of this essay, felt that the mere fact that her son was *her son* was no reason for her to pay thousands of dollars a year for four years to send him to college, despite the fact that he is bright and eager to go to college. Imagine that she considers the idea of spending the money on him rather than using it to help bright orphans to get an education to be "irrational prejudice" in favor of her son. Clearly there would be something wrong here. It is terrific of her to devote large sums of money to the education of orphans; but what about her son? Surely she shouldn't regard him just as one of the promising young people in the world, as someone who has no greater claim to her pocketbook (and to her love and her attention) than anyone else.[10] To take a different example, imagine a parent who felt that there was no more reason to throw a birthday party for his six-year-old than for any other child. Here again, the fact that it is *his* child *should* make a difference to him.

From these considerations it emerges that "The Case Against Loyalty" stands in need of qualification. "Because it is my *X*" can, in some situations, for some instances of *X*, be a good reason for doing something for that person that one would not do for anyone else. "Because it is my child" is a good reason for me to spend much more time with him or her than with any other child (assuming that I have no other children) and, more generally, to make considerable sacrifices which I would not make for anyone else.

Consider, too, something that psychologists frequently point out: children need unconditional love, i.e., love that isn't conditional on the child's behavior. Yet someone who, disdaining the element of "blind affection" in loyalty, felt that the mere fact that it is his son was not sufficient reason to love him, would be incapable of unconditional love—unless his affections got the better of his judgment.

Parental responsibilities are not the only reason why loyalty is of great value. Relationships between equals—spouses, siblings, friends, lovers—could not flourish (or even count as *relationships* in the usual sense of the word) without the "favoritism" or "bias" which is central to loyalty. What kind of friend would I be if I were no more willing to help a friend in need than to help a stranger in the same way? And there are many other situations and instances of *X* for which "Because it is my *X*" is a good reason for the sort of favoritism which is at the heart of loyalty. "Because she is my friend" is a good reason for me to put in a good (but honest) word for her when she applies for a job in the company where I work, or to give her a lift to the airport—something that I would be less likely to do for a mere acquaintance (depending on the degree of need and the distance to the airport).

So far we have focussed on interpersonal, one-to-one relationships in presenting the case for loyalty. But loyalty is valuable in other arenas, as well. Memberships and fellowship in a community—be it a club, a church, an athletic team, a women's (or men's) support group, a town, (a division of) a company or university—is a significant part of human life. It would not be possible to feel that one is really a part of such a group if one did not have a special concern for that group because (at least *partly* because) it is one's group.

This is true even if one draws the important distinction between loyalty to the group and commitment to the ideal (if any) that it stands for. If I am in a local political action group and feel a real membership in and fellowship with that group, I would not be likely to quit that group for another which works for the same ideal. If I feel identification and affiliation with that group, if I am interested in its success or well-being as a group, I would feel a certain loyalty to it. This is a phenomenon that many of us experience in connection with the organizations for which we work—unless, of course, we are very unhappy with our work situations. And the organizations for which we work count on this feeling. They count on the fact that most of us will feel a certain amount of loyalty to the organization, and that this will help to deter us from quitting if some "nice opportunity" comes along. Despite its apparent lack of a rational basis, a bit of a "Rah! Rah!" attitude or a "I don't know why I'm attached to it; I just am" seems appropriate and desirable.

All of the above examples of loyalty emphasize the value of certain *attitudes and affections* which are central to loyalty. It can also be pointed out that many facets of human interaction would be impossible if we could not rely on each other to *act* loyally. Thus it is not just the *feeling* in loyalty that is important for human relationships, but also the *actions* which loyalty prompts. Friends would not confide in each other if they did not expect loyalty in the form of the keeping of these confidences.

The same is true on a large scale: a company needs to be able to count on its employees not to divulge trade secrets. Suppose that Engineer *A* and Engineer *B* are friends who are engaged in similar design projects at their respective businesses. Suppose, moreover, that the businesses are rivals. Under certain conditions it could be quite harmful to the company that employs Engineer *A* if she were to share with Engineer *B* the innovative plans that she and others at her company are working on. Her company depends on her special consideration for her company just because it is her company. In other words, it counts on her to be loyal. Imagine what would happen if Engineers *A* and *B* thought of the research that they were engaged in simply as research, and not as something that was being done for a certain company. It would be impossible for a company to compete successfully if too

much vital information were leaked. Of course in a much less capitalistic society, where businesses did not compete as ours do, trade secrets would not have the same importance. Only if there is competition, and only if that competition is important, does information have to be thought of as "owned." But that hardly justifies American Engineer *A* in sharing such information with American Engineer *B*, or vice versa.

Note that on a yet larger scale, where the "company" is a country, the vital information concerns defense matters, and the information is leaked to someone regarded by the government as an enemy, the person suspected of leaking the information is regarded as a traitor. It is important to recognize that the concept of a traitor only makes sense given a background expectation of loyalty. It is considered so very serious to be "disloyal" to one's country in this manner (leaking security information) that in the United States, at least, the punishment imposed is sometimes death.[11] If all countries were at perpetual peace with one another, if there were no animosity, then here again, the situation would not arise.

Expectations of loyalty from an employee last even after the employee quits one company to join another. The former company has to count on the former employee for a certain amount of loyalty. This becomes evident when one ponders the following hypothetical case, posed by Richard T. De George in his *Business Ethics* (1982, p. 204):

John Knosit was head of a research team of CDE Electric. His team was working on developing a cheaper and more effective filament for light bulbs. Six months ago, a rumor circulated in the industry that the team had made a breakthrough and all that was required was final testing. This would put CDE Electric far ahead of its competitors. Five months ago, X Electric hired John away from CDE, offering him $25,000 a year more than he had been getting. No mention was made of his work on the new filament. After being in his new position for three months, his superior approached him and said that X

Electric had hired him because of his work on the filament and that he would have to develop the filament quickly for X Electric or be fired. John knows how to develop the filament. Is he morally justified in developing it for X Electric?

Companies cannot control the departures of their employees: they can usually fire them at will, but they cannot force an employee to stay.[12] Nor can they keep someone from taking a job elsewhere (except, perhaps, by blackmailing, blackballing, or some other nefarious technique). Nor can they erase certain bits of information from the employee's memory. (Once again there are elaborate methods (hypnosis, electric shock "therapy"), but at least for the purposes of this paper, these are not worth regarding as options.) Companies simply must count on a certain modicum of loyalty on the part of those employees who, as employees, have important "trade secrets."

The dependence of companies on the loyalty of their employees is actually just an instance of a more general phenomenon. Our world is shaped by competition: there are goods which I—and my group—cannot have unless certain others do not get some of the same goods. Not everyone who applies for a fellowship gets it; not every team can win the championship. Those on the team count on each other to stick with the group, to aid it and not the opposing groups. A group member who refused to recognize the boundaries—i.e., who refused to think in terms of "us" and "them"—would, in some instances, be good cause for worry; a group leader who insisted on impartiality vis-à-vis other groups, on playing no favorites, would quickly be deposed. Imagine a department head in a university who refused additional travel money offered to the department by the Dean, on the grounds that a different department was more in need! Imagine a team captain who offered to have one of his best players take the place of someone on the opposing team who had been injured! Need we say more? These examples—as well as many others presented in this section—show that impartiality and a refusal to play (or have?) favorites can easily be overrated.

The Synthesis

At this stage we seem to be stuck in a dialectic, or a sort of tug-of-war. Loyalty seems so bad and yet so good. We must now tackle the really challenging question: Under what conditions is it wrong, on balance, to act as loyalty would demand—and under what conditions is it right to do so? What's a well-meaning, thoughtful engineer to do when faced with demands or expectations to be loyal, or when plagued by worries that a certain move (e.g., to quit a job she's recently begun for a more lucrative one) would be disloyal?

One answer will be based on a distinction commonly drawn in ethical theory: a distinction between *duties of justice* and *duties of benevolence*.

Among our duties of justice are duties to be fair, to be honest and to avoid inflicting or contributing to the needless suffering of others. These are strict duties; that is, they are duties which we owe to everyone. The violation of such a duty constitutes a violation of someone's right(s). If I deceive or rob someone, I violate his or her rights.[13]

Compare the duties just named with the duty to be kind and generous and to help those in need. I cannot help *everyone*; time, financial considerations, professional demands and the like preclude that. I can discharge the duty to help those in need without helping all who are in need. So it does not follow from the fact that I have a duty to be generous that I owe it to be generous to any particular person; more broadly, from the fact that I have duties of benevolence, it does not follow that I have a duty or duties of benevolence to any particular person. This being the case, no one to whom I have been unkind or ungenerous can correctly claim that (in itself) my lack of generosity or unkindness to him or her constituted a violation of his or her *rights*. It may be true that I've behaved badly, that I've been unkind and that this is an expression of a moral defect in my character; but if the duty that I failed to fulfill was a duty of benevolence and not a duty of justice, I have not violated anyone's rights. It may be true, of course, that I wasn't really behaving badly—I may simply have been unable to sacrifice my time or money to help this person in *these* circumstances, especially since I was helping a number of others. I am culpable only if I refuse the cases where people are most desperate and where the cost to me is quite low, *or* if I refuse far too often to help others and am just plain selfish. An example of the first type is the case of the thirty-eight witnesses who didn't bother even to call the police when Kitty Genovese slowly died in an alley from the wounds received in a stabbing. An example of the latter type would be someone who would perhaps phone the police in the sort of situation just described, but would never contribute to a charity or a political cause (unless, perhaps, the political cause was one which directly affected that person's interests), would never offer to give directions to someone who appeared to be lost, or help a blind person who, waiting to cross a busy street, is unaware that the light has turned green. The important thing for the reader to bear in mind, however, is simply that duties of justice are duties that one owes to everyone, and a failure to fulfill such duties to S constitutes an infringement of S's rights; whereas duties of benevolence are owed to no one in particular, and a failure to be benevolent to someone, no matter how culpable, does not in itself constitute a violation of that person's (or anyone else's) rights.

APPLYING THE DISTINCTION

Armed with the distinction between duties of justice and duties of benevolence, we can proceed to examine the duties of engineers vis-à-vis loyalty by asking: (1) Should an engineer act as loyalty directs if in doing so (s)he must violate a duty of justice, i.e., violate someone's rights? (2) Should one do what loyalty asks if in doing so one must violate a duty of benevolence?

It is vital to bear in mind that duties of justice and benevolence are matters of degree: some duties of justice (e.g., duties not to kill) are more important than others (e.g., a duty to keep one's promise to return a book to the library the next day), and likewise with duties of benevolence.

Moreover, it is sometimes hard to say whether a certain duty is a duty of justice, or instead, a duty of benevolence.[14] And sometimes it isn't clear whether an alleged duty is a duty at all. This should not worry us as long as we do not expect (or even hope) to find a mechanical solution to the problem of precisely when one should act as loyalty dictates. If we expect *parameters* for decision-making, the classifications of duties of justice and duties of benevolence should prove useful.

I will argue that duties of justice override considerations of loyalty[15] and that duties of benevolence (other than loyalty) sometimes do and sometimes do not. In part for the reasons why it is difficult to come up with any useful, general principles which rank duties of benevolence, it is not easy to say in advance when the claims of loyalty trump duties of benevolence. Some guidelines can be provided, however, for adjudicating among such conflicting claims. The guidelines will also be of assistance in situations where loyalties themselves conflict, or where demands of loyalty clash with the engineer's own wishes.

LOYALTY AND DUTIES OF JUSTICE

That duties of justice override considerations of loyalty becomes quickly apparent when we recall what we are counting as considerations of loyalty. A consideration of loyalty is a consideration that because X is mine—my company, team, club, neighborhood, etc.—I should promote it and should concern myself more with its needs than with the needs of other parties (except insofar as they are also, in some meaningful way, mine). How do such considerations compete with duties of justice? It is clear, I think, that my obligation to respect the rights of others has to come before considerations of what is best for my company, family, neighborhood, etc. What I owe to everyone must supersede what I may do to promote the welfare of my "group," or my spouse or friend or sibling.[16] None of this should be taken as denying that we should promote the welfare of our group, and more will be said shortly which will underscore the importance of such loyal actions. All that I have said so far is that duties of justice must come first.

If this is right, we now have an explanation (and justification) for our intuitions on such dilemmas in engineering ethics as the one in which Kermit Vandivier found himself, or that in which those who worked on the Pinto found themselves. If loyalty to the company—"My company, right or wrong"—mandated that the engineers at Ford who knew of the Pinto's built-in dangers keep quiet about them, it is nonetheless the case that the rights of the consumers to *know* about any unusual dangers in the car that they were driving (or thinking about buying) must come first.[17] The engineers at B. F. Goodrich had a duty of justice *not* to deceive those who had commissioned the qualification test (the test as specified by the military, not as "re-created" by employees of Goodrich). This duty of justice trumps considerations of loyalty to one's superiors or to the company.[18] Similarly, the thesis that duties of justice override considerations of loyalty explains our intuition that illegal dumping of hazardous wastes is wrong, especially if it threatens to contaminate the water supply, and that it is wrong not simply because it is illegal. It violates the right of those who drink the water to have drinking water which is safe—at least as safe as the government is willing to insist that it must be. But the thesis helps us out only in instances where the claims of loyalty clash with duties of justice. So, much more needs to be said....

NOTES

1. "The Corporation," CBS Reports, December 6, 1973.

2. Nader and Green do not indicate in what year this occurred. They said "recently" and their paper was first printed in 1973. For a plethora of stories of this sort, see Ewing(1977). One of the cases that Ewing reports is that of Louis V. McIntire, a chemical engineer who was fired by the Du Pont company when his supervisors came across the novel that he and his wife co-authored and published, *Scientists and Engineers: The Professionals Who Are Not*. The novel indirectly criticizes Du Pont by portraying in vivid detail a fictitious company, Logan

Chemical, which resembles Du Pont.

3. See also Vandivier (1980).

4. Vandivier (1972, p. 233). Vandivier was at the time actually a data analyst and instrumentation writer. He started at Goodrich as an instrumentation engineer.

5. Rather than address this question directly, I will leave it to the reader to ponder the matter after reading my essay.

6. Of course, it could be that the notion of loyalty that is relevant to engineering ethics is not what is usually meant by "loyalty." But I do not think that this will turn out to be the case.

7. Alasdair MacIntyre takes a similar view in his Lindlay Lecture "Is Patriotism a Virtue?" (Lawrence, Kans.: The University of Kansas, 1984). For discussions of MacIntyre's and Oldenquist's views, see Marcia Baron, "Patriotism and 'Liberal' Morality," in David Weissbord, ed., *Mind, Value, and Culture: Essays in Honor of E. M. Adams* (Atascadero, Calif.: Ridgeview Publishing Co., 1989) and Stephen Nathanson, "In Defense of 'Moderate' Patriotism," *Ethics*, vol. 99, no. 3 (April 1989), pp. 535–52.

8. It should be noted that like most motives the motive of loyalty rarely operates by itself, and so when I speak, here and elsewhere, of people acting from or out of loyalty, I should not be taken to mean that they are then motivated only by loyalty. Loyalty may mix with self-interest.

9. According to Dowie (1980, p. 170), all proposals to improve the Pinto's safety—one of which would have cost only one dollar per car and added only one pound to each car's weight—were rejected out of hand because Iacocca was determined not to exceed the "limits of 2,000" that he had set. See also the chronology of events in the development and production of the Pinto in the *Chicago Tribune* (1979).

10. I do not mean to imply that this evaluative judgment is valid independently of the social structure in which the woman and the son live. Within a different social framework where there was nothing resembling the nuclear family, adults (or perhaps only those who are parents) might regard themselves as having a duty of benevolence (explained below) to children in general, without any special duties to their children in particular.

11. Julius and Ethel Rosenberg were executed on June 19, 1953, amidst widespread protest and proclamation of their innocence. They were accused of having given the Soviet Union the secret of the atom bomb.

12. In some instances employers can ask new employees to sign "noncompetitive agreements" requiring that in the event that the engineer leaves

the company he or she may not work for any other company in the area for a certain length of time, both to be specified in the agreement. Feld (1980) sketches the conditions under which such a non-competition agreement is valid.

13. My use of "right" and "rights" here follows common philosophical usage. A right is, roughly, a title or a "trump." If you have a right to *X*, the fact that millions of people will be happier if your right isn't honored is irrelevant (assuming, of course, that you *really do* have a right to *X*). Your right trumps all considerations except competing rights. As Sharon Bishop Hill puts it (Hill 1975, p. 177), "The considerations [that a right] picks out as relevant mark off an area in which we do not allow considerations about either the general good or an individual's good to be decisive."

14. There are further problems with the distinction between duties of justice and duties of benevolence. First, the distinction is only as clear as the notion of rights, since duties of justice are duties to honor rights. And that notion is, at least in the opinion of many philosophers, itself riddled with problems. Secondly, it may not even be that clear, since if there are positive rights as well as negative rights—duties to do *X* for others as well as duties to refrain from doing *Y* to others—duties of justice may turn out to be duties to honor only a certain type of rights, viz., negative rights.

15. My position parallels and was to some extent inspired by Alan Goldman's position on the adversary system, as put forth in his discussion of legal ethics (1980).

16. Two clarifications are in order. First, things are different if the rights of (members of) my company, family, group are at stake. A subsistence right—a right to have the requisite food and shelter to stay alive—is at the *very least* in strong competition with a property right. Second, if two parties' rights compete and neither right appears to trump the other, it is presumably quite okay to favor one's loved ones. Hence, in a catastrophe in which, say, I can only save only one of two people, the other of whom will die without my aid, I do not act wrongly if I choose to save the person to whom I bear some special relation (friend, traveling companion, spouse, etc.). There is a growing literature in philosophy on these and related topics. See Anscombe (1967) and Bernard Williams (1976). In Baron (1984) I caution against some conclusions that Williams and others draw.

17. That at least some Ford engineers knew of the Pinto's dangers long before any accidents happened is documented by Mark Dowie (1980). See also De George (1981) and the *Chicago Tribune* (1979).

18. I have chosen my words carefully so as *not* to say that one must never act as loyalty directs if doing so violates someone's rights. I am inclined to this latter position, but I would not espouse it without thoroughly considering the complexities which arise because of the deplorable risk to whistleblowers—loss of job and, in some instances, profession. I will not discuss the question of whether an engineer should blow the whistle at great cost to herself or himself, since that is discussed in a different module in this series.

REFERENCES

Anscombe, G. E. M. 1967. "Who Is Wronged?" *Oxford Review* 5:16–17.

Baron, Marcia. 1984. "The Alleged Moral Repugnance of Acting from Duty." *The Journal of Philosophy* 81 (4): 197–220.

Baum, Robert, and Albert Flores, eds. 1980. *Ethical Problems in Engineering*, 2nd ed. Troy, N.Y.: The Center for the Study of the Human Dimensions of Science and Technology.

Chicago Tribune. 1979. "Ignored Pinto danger, secret memos." October 14, p. 1.

De George, Richard T. 1981. "Ethical Responsibilities to Engineers in Large Organizations: The Pinto Case." *Business and Professional Ethics Journal* 1(1):1–14.

———. 1982. *Business Ethics*. New York: MacMillan Publishing Company.

Dowie, Mark. 1980. "Pinto Madness." In *Ethical Problems in Engineering*, ed. Baum and Flores. vol. II, pp. 167–74.

Ewing, David. 1977. *Freedom Inside the Organization*. New York: E. P. Dutton.

Feld, Lipman G. 1980. "Responsibilities to Former Employers." In *Ethical Problems in Engineering*, ed. Baum and Flores, vol. I, pp. 166–67.

Goldman, Alan. 1980. *The Moral Foundations of Professional Ethics*. Totowa, N.J.: Rowman and Littlefield.

Heilbroner, Robert, ed. 1972. *In the Name of Profit*. Garden City, N.Y.: Doubleday and Company, Inc.

Hill, Sharon Bishop. 1975. "Self-Determination and Autonomy." In *Today's Moral Problems*, ed. Richard Wasserstrom, pp. 171–86. New York: MacMillan Publishing Company.

Hume, David. 1888. *Treatise of Human Nature*. (Many editions; citations here are to the Selby-Bigge edition.)

Ladd, John. 1967. "Loyalty." In *Encyclopedia of Philosophy*, ed. Paul Edwards, vol. V, pp. 97–98. New York: The MacMillan Company and The Free Press.

Nader, Ralph, and Mark Green. 1979. "Owing Your Soul to the Company Store." In *Ethical Issues in Business: A Philosophical Approach*, ed. Thomas Donaldson and Patricia H. Werhane, pp. 197-206. Englewood Cliffs, N.J.: Prentice Hall.

Oldenquist, Andrew. 1982. "Loyalties." *The Journal of Philosophy* 79(4):179-93.

Royce, Josiah. 1908. *The Philosophy of Loyalty*. New York: The MacMillan Company.

Vandivier, Kermit. 1972. "Why Should My Conscience Bother Me?" In *In the Name of Profit*, ed. Heilbroner, pp. 3-31.

_____. 1980. "Engineers, Ethics and Economics." In *Ethical Problems in Engineering*, ed. Baum and Flores, vol. II, pp. 136-38.

Williams, Bernard. 1976. "Persons, Character and Morality." In *The Identities of Persons*, ed. Amelie O. Rorty, pp. 197-215. Berkeley: University of California Press.

Wright, J. Patrick. 1980. "On a Clear Day You Can See General Motors." In *Ethical Problems in Engineering*, ed. Baum and Flores, vol. II, pp. 155-58.

Study Questions

1. What does Baron think are the objects of loyalty? How does this differ with Royce's view? Whose position is the more plausible in your view?

2. What serious problems does Baron see with treating loyalty as a moral virtue? What examples does Baron provide as reasons why loyalty is of great value?

3. Explain the difference between duties of justice and duties of benevolence. How does Baron apply this distinction to resolve moral dilemmas involving loyalty issues?

4. Do you think that Baron provides a realistic basis for resolving loyalty dilemmas? Why?

Whistleblowing in Corrections

MARK S. HAMM

WHILE THE ISSUE OF whistleblowing by employees within the corporate structure of American corrections has become more prominent in recent years, the practical use of whistleblowing as a reform measure remains ambiguous. Equally ambiguous is the motivation for employees to challenge corrections officials and their policies. Additionally, there has been little interest on the part of sociologists to understand the generic class of activities termed "bureaucratic opposition" and their implications for corrections. Obviously, the documentation necessary to understand whistleblowing in corrections is difficult to obtain except when such oppositions are revealed in newspapers, autobiographies, or court decisions. Furthermore, many correctional agencies have yet to establish routine procedures for the encapsulation and resolution of organizational conflict, making it all the more difficult to provide a sociological viewpoint on this issue.

Any attempt to effectuate change "from below," or to influence the circumstances within the correctional organization in which one is employed, necessitates considerable initiative,

Mark S. Hamm, "Whistleblowing in Corrections," Sociological Viewpoints, *Vol. 5:1 (1989), pp. 35-45. Used by permission of* Sociological Viewpoints.

energy, and risk taking. Why, then, do some corrections employees take such extraordinary measures within their organizations? What motivates these employees to overcome inertia and come to believe that they might and should struggle for reform? What kinds of initiative, risk-taking and strategy guide effective and constructive whistleblowing activities? This article will discuss possible answers to these questions To the extent that these answers are specified, it is expected that reformists will evaluate as necessary the process of whistleblowing in corrections.

Whistleblowing

The term "whistle-blower" was originated by Ralph Nader to categorize those public employees who challenge activities of their own agencies when they deem such activities to be improper (Rosenbloom, 1986). Perhaps the most famous case of whistleblowing in the criminal justice system is New York patrolman Frank Serpico's opposition to corruption in his own department. Serpico's whistleblowing touched off a wide-ranging investigation which culminated in numerous indictments as well as shakeups in the city's constabulary. Serpico's opposition is instructive in that it points to a basic feature of successful whistleblowing: it demonstrates a genuine concern for the public interest. Many other whistleblowing activities have not considered such a "whistleblowing ethic" and have failed. Not only have they failed, but they have somehow damaged their respective organizations in the process.

The process of whistleblowing begins with employees who wish to see a change in the policy or behavior of the organization which they consider abusive (Ewing, 1980; Gurr 1970; Near & Jensen, 1983; Peters & Branch, 1972; Weinstein, 1979). Additionally, they may seek to effect this change without themselves experiencing retaliation from the organization (Nader et al., 1972; Near & Jensen, 1983; Perrucci et al., 1980). Discontented employees thus attempt to alleviate organizational abuses by disputing bureaucratic injustices while at the same time trying to minimize their chances of becoming the victims of administrative retaliation.

Weinstein (1979) argues that any form of whistleblowing must be grounded in concrete situations that refer to ideal dimensions. Under such a formulation, these grounds provide the "good reasons" or bases for bureaucratic opposition. Without grounds, whistleblowings are merely clashes of self-interest. The use of grounds gives whistleblowings a sense of public meaning and purpose, and can be traced to three theoretical ideals. First, whistleblowings can be founded in resistance to purely bureaucratic norms, such as those drawn up by Max Weber (1958) in his theory of the ideal-typical organization. Such conditions as injustice, dishonor, and incompetence are infractions of organizational rules and provide a set of justifications for whistleblowing. Inefficient or ineffective policies violate the Weberian notion of "instrumental rationality" and provide a second set of grounds. Finally, whistleblowings may be grounded in wider moral norms such as fairness or in an ethical principle not to treat others as a means to serve the personal ends of an administrator (Weinstein, 1979).

Methodology

The method used in this study might best be described as "ethno-empirical." It draws upon several cases of whistleblowing which illustrate concretely the tension between ideal principle and administrative behavior. These cases were derived from interviews with correctional administrators and employees, prisoners, attorneys and members of a state's personnel commission. They all relate attempts to change a correctional bureaucracy by those who work or live within the organization but who do not have any authority. These attempts at "change from below" occur outside the normal administrative routine, and are used here to illustrate generalizations derived from theory about whistleblowing.

One major design limitation can be noted in this approach. All cases discussed in this article are examples where whistleblowing has had a positive effect on the correctional organization. Certainly, not all whistleblowings are good. Criminologists have long recognized that organizational conflict is endemic to corrections (Zald, 1962; Street et al., 1966; Powelson & Bendix, 1951; Weber, 1957; Sykes, 1971). Such conflict has often produced whistleblowings that have been motivated by nothing more than personal vengeance. As such, these attempts have no merit since they are simply clashes of self-interest and fail to demonstrate a desire to improve the performance and quality of public affairs. Additionally, the courts have noted that there are several deleterious effects of ill-conceived whistleblowing where whistleblowers attempt to serve their own self-interests rather than that of the public good. Instead, the investigation will only attempt to reveal a simple dialectic between bureaucratic ideal and administrative behavior.

Deviations from the Bureaucratic Ideal As Grounds for Whistleblowing

In Weber's (1958) discussion of the bureaucracy, workers are interpreted as mere functionaries who perform only their prescribed tasks and treat each organizational situation in accordance with the written rules. According to Weber, written rules are designed to refer specifically to the handling of cases, not people. As such, rules, rather than passions, are supposed to govern the bureaucrat's activities. Hence, rule compliance emerges as the primary goal of the organization.

The violation of organizational rules, either because of total disregard from them or because of subjective considerations, constitutes bureaucratic malfeasance or "organizational injustice." Such injustice violates not only bureaucratic norms, but the values of the constitutional republic. That is, it yields sexual, racial or religious discrimination; and, it involves using public resources for the advantages of specific groups. The following case example illustrates the conditions which present grounds for

malfeasance in a correctional organization.

Case Example: Corrections officer Gloria Z. began her whistleblowing when she asked the warden to show her a written policy of the institution that allowed him to set a double standard that permitted only male officers to transport prisoners. The warden failed to respond to both verbal and written requests to produce the written policy. After review, the State Personnel Board found that Officer Z was correct in contending that the enforcement of the prison's discriminatory transportation practice was based solely on convention, and recommended the development and implementation of a fair and non-discriminatory written transportation policy.

In this case, the grounds for bureaucratic malfeasance are further substantiated by the argument that the injustices of the correctional administration also violated the norms of efficiency. The rule infraction is considered as an abuse or misuse of authority that otherwise reduces or eliminates the efficiency of corrections operations. The common justification for hierarchical bureaucracy is that it promises greater efficiency than preceding or alternative forms of management (e.g., consensus, bargaining, voting, or contracting models). As applied to corrections, efficiency refers to the effective delivery of classification, custodial, and rehabilitative services. The defining characteristics of bureaucracy include the explicit division of labor, hierarchy of authority, conduct of office without regard for persons, and appointment and promotion of individuals to positions on the sole basis of their competency. These characteristics are designed to augment efficiency. Weber's model of bureaucracy stipulates that a specific set of rules will cover each of these characteristics and when such rules are violated, the organization is likely to become inefficient. Violation of the division of labor, as when the warden gave unauthorized support to the selection of a transportation officer, may therefore render the organization more inefficient. A vast literature attests to the application of the norm of competence (performance ability, skills, diligence, etc.) as essential for maximum efficiency. In the present case, efficiency begins with organizational activity conducted in accordance with a written transportation policy based upon the norm of competency, not on convention.

Another bureaucratic norm violation is incompetence. In a literal and formal sense, the superiors of an incompetent employee are the ones who violate the bureaucratic norm of competence. However, whistleblowings directed against incompetence usually focus on incompetent employees, not on those responsible for their appointment (Weinstein, 1979). The grounds for whistleblowing against incompetence are that the role incumbent is not discharging assigned duties. The opposition against organizational incompetence is strengthened with the employee's stated interests in career advancement, the desire to do meaningful and high quality work, and concern for the deleterious effect of inappropriate or self-defeating organizational behavior. The following case example represents conditions that constitute grounds for incompetence in the delivery of correctional services.

Case Example: Seven employees filed a class action grievance against the assistant warden of a medium security prison who began dumping all his office responsibilities on subordinates. The grievants alleged that the clerical subordinates were untrained to handle such responsibilities and, furthermore, that the assistant warden began to fill more and more of his day with unimportant activities such as playing basketball, engaging in frequent and lengthy conversations about non-corrections issues, and doing personal work while on duty. After review, the Personnel Board found that the assistant warden was delegating duties to clerical subordinates for which they were neither trained nor expected to perform according to their respective state position descriptions. Also the board recommended that the warden ensure that the assistant warden fulfill the responsibilities of his position and further suggested the possible disciplinary

actions that could result from using state time and property to benefit individual interests.

Another category of bureaucratic norm violation is the denial of respect or of honor to other persons, whether subordinate employees or members of the organization's clientele (Weinstein, 1979). The grounds for denial of respect are the subjection of persons to demands that are beyond their role requirements. These role requirements are defined by organizational rules. The following case example illustrates these grounds.

Case Example: Warden V. used institutional funds to purchase equipment for private use. This equipment was used to operate a section of the warden's cattle ranch. Warden V. insisted that corrections officers supervise inmate labor in the use of this equipment at his ranch. Also Warden V. frequently exhibited abusive temper tantrums directed towards both staff and inmates. Officers G. and M. filed an opposition claiming that the warden abused his authority and violated the rules. Further, his displays of temper were instances of both injustice and dishonor. After review, the Personnel Board found that the warden required officers G. and M. to act in ways that were undefined and irrelevant to their job descriptions, and that outbursts of temper added demands on the officers.

This case also elucidates the violation of rules specifying the rights of inmates. Requiring inmates to support the warden's corruption could have been opposed on the grounds of injustice, lack of respect, and dishonor. Of these criteria, dishonor is the strongest. When inmates are dishonored, either as a result of economic or psychological exploitation, some evidence suggests that oppositions can result in their favor especially when they are undertaken as action in behalf of prisoner unions (Browning, 1972; Huff et al., 1985; Irwin & Holder, 1973; Irwin, 1980; Ward, 1972).

The preceding discussion has attempted to examine the fundamental reason for whistleblowing in corrections: organizational abuse resulting from bureaucratic norm violations.

The following section will examine a second set of reasons for whistleblowing: abuses reflecting differences in values and in the interpretation of the policies designed to achieve the goals of corrections.

Disputes over Policy as Grounds for Whistleblowing

There are grounds other than bureaucratic norm violations on which whistleblowings are based. These grounds can be grouped together under the general rubric of disputes over organizational policy and focus on abusive rules rather than abusive persons. Policies may be judged to be objectionable because of four distinct reasons. First, they may contradict general bureaucratic norms. Second, they may be inconsistent with the particular goals that distinguish the organization from others. Third, policies may be opposed because they are held to violate general moral standards, such as those of a religious tradition, the general culture, or some transcendent position. Finally, policies may be disputed because they harm subordinate employees or clients in some way or because they harm the organization's relevant public (Weinstein, 1979). In a general sense, each of these reasons share a common ground for whistleblowing: the grievance is organization hypocrisy. The whistleblowers claim that the organization is not living up to its own standards or that policies and their implementation are not adequate to achieve its stated goal. For instance, Tom Murton's objections to the selling of prison materials and inmate labor at Tucker's Farm was, initially, nothing more than a whistleblowing grounded in a dispute over rehabilitation policies in the Arkansas Department of Corrections. Other problems notwithstanding, Murton's dissenting arguments were essentially based on a rehabilitative ideal, a notion to which the State Board of Corrections claimed to adhere. According to Murton, the practice of selling material and labor was contrary to the prison's major purpose, the rehabilitation of inmates (Murton, 1972).

Disputes over policy may also focus on internal issues of efficiency or external considerations of effectiveness (Weinstein, 1979). Behind some policy disputes concerning efficiency are oppositions to an incompetent administrator or other bureaucratic norm violations. Such disputes may also mask resistance to dishonor, as the following case example illustrates.

Case Example: In response to an increase in the frequency of runaways, the administration of a juvenile correctional institution implemented a security policy in which counselors and teachers were ordered to assist in head-counts, movements, and runaway investigations. Although employees in the counseling and teaching job classifications did not criticize the need for security checks, they did feel that this particular policy unduly harassed them, forced them to do an excessive amount of work, and left them less time for report-writing, lesson-planning, counseling, tutoring and informal interaction with the inmate population. After complaining to the superintendent without success, several employees initiated a whistleblowing against the institution. After review by the Personnel Board, the policy was changed to require that counselors and teachers should be responsible for headcounts only when inmates were assigned to their respective programs. All other security requirements were dropped for teachers and counselors.

In contrast to inefficient policies, ineffective policies are those which in some way are deemed inconsistent with organizational goals. The ground for a dispute over an ineffective policy is that the policy somehow subverts or is irrelevant to the goals of the organization. Public attention seems most keen to whistleblowings that are grounded in ineffective public policies (Nader et al., 1972; Peters & Branch, 1972), particularly where an employee attempts to redirect the organization towards its "proper" goal (Weinstein, 1979). The following case example represents the conditions necessary to establish the grounds for organizational ineffectiveness.

Case Example: After repeated verbal requests

to the administration, Dr. M., the prison psychiatrist, and Ms. S. and Ms. T., psychology therapists, filed a complaint with the warden of a maximum security prison charging that the administration was primarily interested in providing custodial services to inmates and keeping the cost of those services to a minimum. The three "oppositionists" represented the full staffing complement for psychological services at the prison, which served 984 inmates. The whistleblowers, who saw the most disturbed and obstreperous inmates on a day-to-day basis, sought policies that would provide them with assistance and thereby increase the quality of psychological care in the prison. Moreover, they argued that prevailing policies were judged to be ineffective regarding the delivery of full rehabilitative services. After review, the Personnel Board maintained that the warden of the institution should become more sensitive to the benefits of various "helping" professions and increase his line-item budget request for psychological services in the next fiscal year.

In the case, the prevailing policies of the prison were deemed abusive of inmates because they were ineffective as a means of achieving a goal of rehabilitation. Oppositions of this nature are sometimes indistinguishable from those which are judged to be unfair. As a reason for whistleblowing, fairness is considered to be a moral standard which applies to relations within the organization, yet it does not necessarily coincide with bureaucratic norms (Weinstein, 1979). Fairness does, however, coincide with those bureaucratic norms which prescribe equal treatment "without regard to persons" and hiring and promotion on the basis only of competence. Hence, whistleblowings against policies which explicitly discriminate against one group of employees, such as women or minority group members, are based on both moral and formal grounds. Historically, whistleblowings grounded in the struggle for fairness in public sector organizations have had relatively good chances for success for three reasons (Nader et al., 1972; Peters & Branch, 1972; Weinstein, 1979). First, the

perception of unfairness is often spurred by social changes external to the organization, such as the effects of the various liberation movements. Second, the moral purposes of the whistleblowers stimulate zeal and solidarity which are often absent in responses to purely bureaucratic norm violations. Finally, public administrators are typically less implacable and more apt to yield because discriminatory policies may contradict their own moral values and those of the society at large. Earlier in this article reference was made to correction officer Gloria Z. who disputed a discriminatory transportation policy. Her opposition was based upon the ground of bureaucratic malfeasance. The present discussion would indicate that such a violation could also be disputed on moral grounds of sexual discrimination.

Moral Imperative of Whistleblowing

The final grounds for whistleblowing to be discussed here are those charges of unfairness and of abuses grounded in policies which harm employees or clients and stem from a commitment to absolute moral principles, rather than from issues of efficiency and effectiveness. The most relevant moral principle which can serve as a ground for opposition is the prescription to treat people as ends-in-themselves, never as means only (Weinstein, 1979). Weinstein, whose work has been so liberally quoted in this article, has traced this ground to Immanuel Kant's principle of the "categorical imperative." This principle sets forth a bare minimum condition for moral action within an organization. It reads:

> Act so that you treat humanity, whether in your own person or in that of another, always as an end, never as a means only. (Weinstein, 1979:24).

Kant held that the idea that man is an "end," something whose worth is not dependent on what we can use him for, is the most important moral presupposition of all. Applied to corrections, the intent of the categorical imperative is to insist that corrections policy be blind, in the sense that what is right or wrong does not depend on the particular interests of individual administrators, but on the insistence to treat staff and inmates as ends in themselves, never to use them for personal means.

Whistleblowings grounded in an absolute moral principle can be very difficult to effect and can carry severe retaliatory implications for the oppositionist. Disclosures of "moral wrong doing" by Tom Murton at Tucker's Farm indicated that abuses were not isolated incidents of zealous correctional administrators at the Arkansas prison; rather, the abuses were part of an ongoing, immoral prison program that had continued over decades.[1] The Murton experience is instructive in that it provides an example of "blowing the whistle" from too close a distance to the abuses. The nature of the Arkansas Board of Corrections, including their legacy of failure to act certainly against the abuses at Tucker's Farm, made Murton's whistleblowing against "immoral" policies difficult to undertake. Essential to Murton's difficulty was his inability to merge his own struggle with public opposition against the Corrections Board (Murton, 1972). That Murton was forced to resign his position and risk his career indicates that the motivational ground for his opposition was something more than infractions of simple bureaucratic norms. Over and above Murton's personal conflicts with the Arkansas Board of Corrections, however, his story remains an invaluable lesson in exercising moral outrage against a corrupt and brutal system of imprisonment.

Conclusions

In his splendid review of whistleblowing in Federal government, Charles Peters (1972: ix) concluded that "Of all the wrong decisions I have seen made in government, wrong ideas and information have played no greater role than the failure of the men with the right ideas and information to press their cases courageously." Although it is only a preliminary consideration of the whistleblowing phenomenon in correc-

tions, the present analysis suggests that employees must first do their homework before they begin to "courageously press their cases" in the corrections profession. Most importantly, employees must be cognizant of the "whistleblowing ethic." That is, they must have a genuine concern for the public interest. In the absence of such an ethical standard, bureaucratic oppositions are nothing more than expressions of self-interest that can irrevocably damage both an individual's career and an organization's stability and effectiveness.

Once this ethical standard has been satisfied, organizational abuses can be fought based upon "grounds" associated with violations of bureaucratic norms, inefficient and ineffective policies, and immoral policies. As such, properly formulated whistleblowings—whether they are successful or not—are consistent with the rationality of bureaucracy. Accordingly, such activities are necessarily reformist because they attempt to induce a normative transformation of the social structure in which contemporary corrections is embedded.

NOTES

1. Murton's whistleblowing revealed abuses at Tucker's Farm such as extortion, torture and even murder. These abuses, and Murton's struggle to correct and eliminate them, are documented in the film "Brubaker."

REFERENCES

Browning, Frank. 1972. "Organizing Behind Bars" in Burton M. Atkins and Henry R. Glick (eds.), *Prisons, Protest, and Politics*. Englewood Cliffs, N.J.: Prentice Hall. 132–140.

Ewing, David W. 1980. "A Proposed Bill of Rights" in K. M. Rowland et al. (eds.), *Current Issues of Personnel Management*. Boston: Allyn and Bacon.

Gurr, Ted Robert. 1970. *Why Men Rebel*. Princeton: Princeton University Press.

Huff, Ronald C., Joseph E. Scott and Simon Dinitz. 1985. "Prisoners' Unions: A Cross National Investigation of Public Acceptance" in Robert M. Carter, Daniel Glaser and Leslie T. Wilkins (eds.), *Correctional Institutions*. New York: Harper and Row. 403–419.

Irwin, John and Willie Holder. 1973. "History of the Prisoners' Union", *The Outlaw: Journal of the Prisoners' Union*, 2, (January–February): 1.

Irwin, John. 1980. *Prisons in Turmoil*. Boston: Little, Brown and Co.

Murton, Tom. 1972. "Too Good for Arkansas" in Burton M. Atkins and Henry R. Glick (eds.), *Prisons, Protest, and Politics*. Englewood Cliffs, N.J.: Prentice Hall.

Nader, Ralph, P. J. Petkas and K. Blackwell (eds.). *Whistleblowing: The Report on the Conference of Professional Responsibility*. New York: Grossman.

Near, Janet P. and Tamila C. Jensen. 1983. "The Whistleblowing Process: Retaliation and Perceived Effectiveness". *Work and Occupations*. 10, No. 1, (February): 3–28.

Perrucci, Robert et al. 1980. "Whistleblowing: Professionals' Resistance to Organizational Authority". *Social Problems*, 28: 149–164.

Peters, Charles and Taylor Branch. 1972. *Blowing the Whistle: Dissent in the Public Interest*. New York: Praeger.

Powelson, Harvey and Reinhard Bendix. 1951. "Psychiatry in Prisons", *Psychiatry*, 14: 73–86.

Rosenbloom, David H. 1986. *Public Administration*. New York: Random House.

Sykes, Gresham M. *The Society of Captives: A Study of a Maximum Security Prison*. Princeton, N.J.: 1971. Princeton University Press.

Ward, David A. 1972. "Inmate Rights and Prison Reform in Sweden and Denmark". *Journal of Criminal Law, Criminology and Police Science*, 52, (June): 240–255.

Weber, George H. 1957. "Conflicts Between Professional and Non-Professional Persons in Institutional Delinquency Treatment," *Journal of Criminal Law, Criminology and Political Science*, 48: 26–43.

Weber, Max. "Bureaucracy" in H. H. Gerth and C. Wright Mills (eds.). 1958. *From Max Weber: Essays in Sociology*. New York: Oxford University Press.

Weinstein, Deena. 1979. *Bureaucratic Opposition: Challenging Abuses at the Workplace*. New York: Pergamon Press.

Zald, Mayer N., "The Correctional Institution for Juvenile Offenders: An Analysis of Organizational 'Character'". 1960. *Social Problems*, 8, No. 1, (Summer): 57–67.

Study Questions

1. What are the different types of "good reasons" for bureaucratic opposition that Hamm identifies?

2. In what sorts of cases does Hamm think whistleblowing is unjustified?

3. In your view, which is more important in justifying whistleblowing—the motivations of the whistleblower, or the circumstances from which the whistleblowing arises?

4. Suppose a policy maximizes organizational efficiency over the available alternatives, but only by treating prisoners and some employees in violation of Kant's formula of the end-in-itself. Should you blow the whistle on such a policy in Hamm's view? Do you agree with Hamm? Why?

5. Are acts of whistleblowing morally obligatory or supererogatory? Why?

Case 4.1

FOR THE LOVE OF THE BUREAU*

I became an FBI Agent at an early age. I was two years out of college and was in awe of the Director and his organizational supervisors. I was even more impressed with the media hype of the phenomenal success of both the Director himself and the Special Agents. During 16 weeks of training at Quantico, Virginia, and Washington, D.C., those perspectives were reinforced. We attended classes from 9 A.M. to 9 P.M. five days a week and shorter hours on Saturday and Sunday. Many practical courses as well as legally oriented subjects were taught, but underneath was the feeling of the infallibility of the Director and his organization. Yes, there was fear of incurring the wrath of the Director, but also the hope that good work would draw his commendations. Mr. Hoover personally signed the letters of censure or other administrative action, such as dismissal, as well as every commendation or financial award. More than 20 years of experience in the field did little to diminish my own vision of the Director and "The Bureau."

Late on Friday night in mid-summer, when I was a Senior Resident Agent, I received a telephone call from a supervisor in the Detroit Office who told me he was acting on behalf of an FBI Inspector. The crux of his conversation was that a man, then occupying a rented cottage 60 miles north of my office, had maliciously maligned the reputation and moral integrity of Mr. Hoover. While at a cocktail party in Washington, D.C., the man was alleged to have said that Mr. Hoover was a homosexual. The supervisor said the man must be confronted and told to "put up or shut up."[1] He refused to elaborate on those instructions. The Inspector entered the conversation and added only that I was to have the assistance of the "biggest" agents in my office. These two agents were to interview "the culprit" and I, as the third largest, was to drive the car. The interview was to be done very early the next morning, before 6:00 A.M. if possible.

All of our training emphasized that Agents never use physical force except to overcome situations where arrest was resisted or when life was threatened. There was some travel time involved, so along with two other agents we left in the early hours and arrived in the cottage by 5:30 A.M. On that trip, the ethics of such actions were questioned over and over, as were the vague instructions to say "put up or shut up." Was that an exact quote from the Director, or was it an interpretation of an overly zealous Inspector? Ultimately, it was agreed that the interview had to take place. It was also known to us that the interviewing agent was physically the largest, but was also the most diplomatic of the assigned Special Agents. The decision to carry out the request was based on (1) what we perceived as our duty, (2) our loyalty to the Director and those appointed to executive positions, and most of all, (3) what we perceived as the correct action in the eyes of all Special Agents. We also knew that a mishandling

*This case was written by a former FBI agent who wishes to remain anonymous.—eds.

would, at a minimum, jeopardize our ability to remain at our current location. At worst, it could result in a dismissal and/or prosecution for violation of civil rights. No thought was given to commendations. It was a true time of survival.

The interviewee was roused out of bed before 6:00 A.M. and the interview began. For me, waiting in the car, it was the moment of truth. I could order the other Agents away and face the consequences of failure to fulfill an order, or I could depend on diplomacy and/or physical dominance in the situation to prevail. I decided on the latter.

Fortunately for all of us, the man vehemently denied ever calling the Director a "homo" and in fact said that he was an admirer of the Director and a strong supporter of law enforcement, especially the FBI. He demanded to know the name of his accuser, which was not available, and finally concluded that he knew who accused him. The interview was concluded, and the Teletype prepared and sent. No further word was ever heard about the incident from the Inspector who had ordered the interview. He had left the Detroit office before any of the participating agents could find out more.

Ultimately, it was discovered that the man in the cottage was a Chicago resident on vacation. The purported allegation of homosexuality had been made many weeks before, and the Chicago office had received the original order to interview him but delayed until the man went on vacation. The Inspector who made the order in the Detroit area had his headquarters in the Chicago office. Chicanery was strongly suspected but impossible to prove.

Some would say ethics were compromised early, but those in the profession, at least those with practicality, would be unlikely to accuse the participants of unethical conduct. In short, survival will supersede ethics.

Notes

1. Apparently, this was a common practice under Hoover. [See Athan Theoharis, *From the Secret Files of J. Edgar Hoover.* (Chicago: I. R. Dee, 1991)—eds.].

Questions for Discussion

1. If you were the Agent, what would you do? Use the ethical decision-making checklist to assist you.

2. Discuss the ethics of using employees to do questionable investigations.

3. Is the author loyal to an individual, an organization, or both?

4. Using Hamm as a source, on what grounds should you blow the whistle on the supervisor?

5. Speculate on what might have happened to the author if he had refused to comply or had blown the whistle.

6. How did Hoover manage to maintain such absolute control over his subordinates?

7. The author makes the following statement: "In short, survival will supersede ethics." Do you agree? Why? Defend your position.

Case 4.2

BROTHERLY LOVE

William Adams had worked hard to get out of the ghetto. He had managed to beat all the odds. He avoided the dealers, pimps and other pitfalls that so often ruined intelligent young people. He worked hard in school and took part-time jobs to help support his mother and three brothers. He was graduated from high school with honors, attended the local junior college, and graduated *cum laude* in Criminal Justice from the State University. He felt at times that he owed his success to his role model, an African-American police officer who had "adopted" him when he was caught shoplifting at the age of six. All he wanted to do was to become a police officer like his mentor, get out of the inner city, and make a new life for himself and his family.

However, after finishing the police academy, he found himself back in his old neighborhood enforcing the law against the same people he had grown up with. He questioned his assignment, but was told by his superiors that the rookies got the worst assignments and that African-American police officers were needed in the inner city because of recent deteriorations in community relations due to white officer and African-American citizen conflicts.

What he never expected was to be alienated by two worlds: the "white man's" police culture, in which he was an often unaccepted minority, and his own culture, because he was now regarded by many as an "Uncle Tom," who enforced the rules of "the man."

Nevertheless, he managed to perform well, even under these difficult conditions. After he completed his three-month on-the-job training under the direction of a senior Field Training Officer, he finally got to work alone. He hoped to work hard, enforce the law firmly but fairly, and eventually become accepted by both cultures.

While patrolling his district one afternoon, he spotted James Thompson, a young man he had known in his youth. James had followed the exact opposite path that William had traveled. He had dropped out of school, been involved in a series of crimes as a juvenile, and been heavily involved in narcotics use. He had no job and lived wherever he could find a place to sleep—friends, family, or on the street. The odd thing was that James and William had stayed friends. James had never attempted to involve William in his criminal activities, and the time that they spent together in noncriminal activities was enjoyable. As William waited for the traffic light to change, he saw James go down an alley between two stores.

"I wonder what he is up to?" William thought as he drove down the alley looking for James. He wished he hadn't asked himself that question when he found William, crowbar in hand, trying to force open the back window of a clothing store.

Questions for Discussion

1. If you were the officer, what would you do? Use the ethical decision-making checklist to assist you.

2. When loyalties conflict, which loyalty—loyalty to family, culture, friends, organization, or society—should take precedence?

3. Discuss the advantages and disadvantages (both for the officer and the residents) of assigning Adams to his own neighborhood.

4. Is it appropriate to give rookies the worst assignments? Explain your answer.

5. Could/should Adams work with Thompson in the same fashion as Adams' mentor? Is there any comparison between Adams' work with Thompson and Adams' mentor? Remember: Adams was 6 years old when stopped by his police officer mentor, while Thompson is a young adult and is in the process of breaking and entering.

6. What is more important—the relationship and love that police officers have with their close friends, or their duty to the public and property they are sworn to protect?

7. What would be the effects of enforcement or nonenforcement on community relations?

8. Which is the "lesser of two evils" in this case?

9. Compare this case to "Good Friends are Hard to Find," that is, the case's element of cultural loyalty as a secondary issue to personal loyalty. Would this case present the same dilemma if the suspect were a complete stranger to William?

Case 4.3

THE DRUNKEN CAPTAIN

The city had just suffered through what was believed to be the worst winter storm of the century. Over three feet of snow had fallen in two days and the streets were lined with five- and six-foot-high walls of snow placed there by the plows. Jose Hernandez, a police officer for the past five years, felt that he and the two other patrol cars in his district were probably the only ones in the city out on this cold night.

He made his usual full stop at an intersection in a south side residential neighborhood, although he thought it wasn't necessary because the streets were deserted. Just as he began to pull into the intersection, he narrowly missed being struck by a late-model sedan traveling south at a high rate of speed and without its lights on. He immediately gave chase. He couldn't believe his eyes! The sedan was weaving down the road and bouncing off the snowbanks. He thought to himself, "This guy is either nuts or loaded."

He pulled his cruiser in behind the speeding sedan and activated his overhead lights. Fortunately, he gave himself plenty of room as the driver of the sedan made an "Elmer Fudd" stop—all brakes and no brains.

Officer Hernandez had hardly exited his cruiser when he detected "a strong odor of an alcoholic beverage." The driver of the sedan, a white male about 35, staggered from the car, supporting himself on the door frame. "I had to drive, offisher," he chuckled, "I was too drunk to walk."

This is going to be a good one, Officer Hernandez thought, as he observed the driver's bloodshot eyes, disheveled clothing, staggering walk, and disorientation.

"May I see your driver's license?" Hernandez asked.

When the driver opened his wallet, Hernandez' flashlight fell on the unmistakable badge of a captain on his department.

Questions for Discussion

1. If you were the officer, what would you do? Use the ethical decision-making checklist to assist you.

2. Police discretion can be described as the power to act in certain ways and to make certain decisions as part of the job since, in most cases, total enforcement of all violations would be impossible or impractical. At what point do offenses leave the arena of discretionary enforcement?

3. Have you ever been stopped and *not* been issued a traffic ticket for an offense that you did commit? Since you were guilty, did you insist that you be issued the ticket? Were you appreciative of the officer's discretion?

4. Duska states, "Loyalty depends on ties that demand self-sacrifice with no expectation of reward." Would your (non)enforcement action be subject to some kind of organizational reward or punishment?

5. Realistically, what do you think would happen if you arrested the captain? Should you not "cover for" your fellow officers?

6. Would your decision in this case be different if the captain had been drinking following a child abuse fatality? if he were an alcoholic? if he were a member of a different department?

7. Where does professional courtesy end and enforcement of the laws you are sworn to protect begin?

8. Suppose department policy requires a demotion (minimum) to termination (maximum) for any criminal conviction. Do you arrest the captain?

9. Would your decision in this case be different if the driver had been a police officer? a sergeant? a lieutenant? the chief?

10. Police "protect" each other in truly dangerous situations (confrontations with armed subjects, etc.). Should this protection extend to ignorance of misconduct by fellow officers? If so, to what extent? Explain.

11. Identify other professions that dictate off-duty conduct.

Case 4.4

OFFICER BOB

Officer Bob is nearing the end of a long and distinguished career as a corrections officer; he has received numerous commendations and was selected as Corrections Officer of the Year in 1972. As a relatively new corrections officer, you have learned of the great respect that both the officers and the supervisors have for this man. As one older officer put it, "Whenever I have doubts about this job, I think of Officer Bob; he makes me proud to be a corrections officer."

You, on the other hand, are beginning to have some doubts about Officer Bob. You have noted in recent conversations with him that his mind seems to wander a great deal and that his constant smile can often turn into a blank, uncomprehending stare. You have also noticed that he is a bit more friendly with the inmates than you would consider proper. The other officers with whom you have discussed this behavior have been quick to defend Bob. They point out his recent personal tragedy with the death of his wife, and the fact that he is only weeks away from retirement. "Bob has a lot on his mind," you are told. "He's still the best officer on the shift." You also feel a bit of resentment from the other officers toward a novice like yourself who would have the temerity to question Bob's ability. You think it best to drop the subject and overlook Bob's behavior.

It is now lock-up time in the cellblocks. At this time (10:00 P.M.) each evening, the inmates are locked in their cells for the night. This begins the last two hours of your shift. You are in "G" Block and Officer Bob is next door in "H" Block. As you stand in your utility closet, checking off the cleaning supplies your porters have just put away, you look through the closet windows. You can clearly see Officer Bob in his utility closet. He is standing next to Inmate Brown, a reputed homosexual and drug dealer. You notice them because they are standing so close to each other. Suddenly, you are startled to see Officer Bob reach into his coat pocket, pull out a small brown paper package, and give it to Inmate Brown. Brown smiles broadly and appreciatively at a likewise smiling Officer Bob. Brown then puts his arms around Bob's shoulders and kisses him full on the mouth. After this, Brown returns to his cell, and Bob leaves the closet.

At this point, you are reeling with shock and indecision. How should you handle this? If you confronted Bob, would he deny it? If you told a supervisor, would he believe it? You even question your own perception. Did you really see what you think you saw?

Minutes later, as you are about to leave your closet, you observe Officer Bob return to his utility closet. He is followed closely by a giggling Inmate Brown, who produces a small vial of white powder and a very small spoon. He uses the spoon to inhale some of the powder himself and then offers some to Officer Bob, who eagerly accepts it. Then, almost in the same instant, Brown puts down his powder and spoon and falls into the outstretched arms of Officer Bob. As both begin to sink to the floor, the lights in the closet go out.

You are in a state of shock and you look it. At least Lieutenant Davis thinks you do as he enters your lock and sees you stumbling out of your closet.

"What's the matter?" he asks. "Is something wrong?"

Quite a question, you think, considering what you have just seen. Your mind reels as your mouth struggles to form a response. You know that Lieutenant Davis is on his way to Control and will probably not check on Bob's cellblock again tonight. You also know that you can, if you wish, escort the lieutenant to Bob's closet, open the door (the lieutenant has a master key) and catch Bob "in the act." But, if you do, what would happen to Bob? How would it affect the other men on the shift? You know that Bob is very close to an otherwise well-deserved retirement and pension check. You also know how the other officers feel about Bob. Why should you let them down so hard? Why destroy Bob's career? How much more harm could he possibly do in the few weeks he has remaining as an employee?

Well, maybe a lot of harm, and not just the obvious damage to the security of the institution. Maybe the most damage that Bob could do with the remaining weeks of this employment would be to himself. At this point, perhaps, what Bob needs more than anything else is professional help. If you don't turn him in, you think, you might be denying him his last opportunity for such help before it is too late. And furthermore... No, there is no more time to consider your response. The lieutenant expects a simple "yes" or "no" answer to his question. What will your reply be?

Questions for Discussion

1. If you were the officer, what would you do? Use the ethical decision-making checklist to assist you.

2. Speculate on the reasons for Bob's change in behavior.

3. Answer the questions posed by the officer in the body of the case.

4. Weigh the effects of your action on the career and future of Officer Bob. What psychological impact would your decision have?

5. What do you think would happen to Officer Bob if you told the Lieutenant?

6. Where should the line be drawn between personal feelings toward a fellow officer and the professional integrity expected from one who is in a position of authority? Do you sacrifice the professional courtesy and amiable working relationship, including your co-worker's career and future, in order to "do the right thing" by turning him in to the supervisor?

7. What advice would you give a third person if he or she discovered Bob's action and told you about it in strict confidence?

8. Would your decision be different if Officer Bob were not a "few weeks from retirement"?

9. What if it were "Officer Barbara"?

Case 4.5

TO NARC OR NOT TO NARC

Mike had been with the county probation office for over 10 years. He was an eccentric kind of guy but everybody liked him. Very few people realized that most of his personality came from a bottle of gin. Who knew what he was really like?

Finally, Mike's behavior became noticeably strange. He quit talking to people and stayed in his office all day with the door shut. Everyone began to wonder what was the matter with him, including me. Finally, I asked someone who had worked closely with him for years and had watched the slow progression of alcoholism take its toll. Mike hid it so well that few others had any clue.

This was a man I had been out in the field with for hours at a time, with him behind the wheel, a gun on his hip, confronting dangerous and crazy felons. I could hardly believe that I had been so blind.

We have an office full of very young, very new probation officers. Should this be brought to somebody's attention? Suppose he takes one of these young officers out and something happens, or he wrecks the car and somebody gets hurt. Could I live with the guilt that I could have prevented it?

Nobody trusts anybody in this place. If I go through the chain of command, everybody might find out. Suppose *Mike* finds out; could he go over the edge? Would I be in danger? Could I live with being known as a *narc*?

Questions for Discussion

1. If you were the officer, what would you do? Use the ethical decision-making checklist to assist you.

2. Using Hamm as a guideline, on what grounds should you blow the whistle on the supervisor?

3. Duska states, "Loyalty depends on ties that demand self-sacrifice with no expectation of reward." Would your (non)enforcement action be subject to some kind of organizational reward or punishment?

4. Does your obligation to society outweigh your obligation to the organization?

5. Speculate on any alternatives you might have, short of blowing the whistle.

6. Did you ever see someone you knew cheating on a test, using drugs, or committing a criminal act? Did you "narc?" Why? Defend your position. Is your position consistent?

7. Is "narc" a dirty word? Why? Defend your position.

8. What if the drinking does not interfere with Mike's performance? Should action be taken?

Chapter 5

Truth

THE OLD SAW SAYS, "HONESTY IS the best policy." Is it conceivable that our system of law enforcement could operate on such a basis? For example, could an undercover investigation be conducted without dishonesty, lying, misrepresentation, and falsehood? A standard technique in the interrogation of a suspect involves extensive deception in order to elicit a confession. For example, if the suspect has a purported accomplice, the interrogator might leave the room for a minute or two and come back, telling the suspect that "your buddy is spilling his guts, and he names you as the shooter (holdup man, etc.). Why don't you come clean? Things will go easier for you." All of this is an outright lie, a "factual misrepresentation" in legal jargon. The alleged accomplice has not confessed anything, and in fact is in the process of being released. Things won't "go easier" for the suspect if he confesses; in fact, with complete silence and a good defense attorney, the suspect will be far better off in the end.

If truth-telling is a virtue, and lying is a fundamental moral wrong, then entire categories of criminal justice actions, such as interrogation, deceptive acts in undercover investigations, and so on, are morally wrong. Consider the "fine-tuning" of testimony by officers prior to trial—"getting their stories straight"—in order to ensure conviction. This may range from saying less than the whole truth to outright falsification of evidence and perjury. Must an officer tell the whole truth and sacrifice the conviction of a vicious criminal because of a minor investigative error? Or does such deception destroy the very function of law enforcement as a moral force in the society?

Aristotle argued that truth overrides friendship, but is truth itself sometimes subordinate to some other good? Kant is often regarded as answering with an unequivocal "No." In a celebrated example of applying (or misapplying!) his categorical imperative, Kant argues that if a would-be murderer comes to your door and asks you where the intended victim is, you must tell the truth, even if doing so results in the victim's death.[1] Thus, it is commonly held that Kant's categorical imperative generates a "zero tolerance" attitude regarding lying.[2]

The Readings

In the first selection for this chapter, "Truthfulness," Immanuel Kant takes a considerably different position regarding lying and truth-telling. Kant begins by discussing the psychological origins of lying in the human inclination to reserve and conceal one's faults from others. The essay is centered on the distinction between telling an *untruth* (a *falsiloquium*) and a lie (a *mendacium*). Kant believes that stating an untruth is not a lie if the hearer has no right to expect me to express my mind. Kant says, "If my enemy takes me by the throat and asks where I keep my money, I need not tell him the truth, because he will abuse it . . . "

Kant considers a coerced confession as no different in kind from the extortion of money. In both cases, it is morally permissible to tell an untruth. This is the only circumstance in which a white lie is justified. *If I am convinced that a truthful statement will be improperly used, I am under no moral obligation to speak the truth.* For example, if an undercover officer is asked a question where a truthful answer would endanger his or her own life or the lives of others, there is no moral obligation to tell the truth, in Kant's view. However, it is not clear how Kant would view the deception of the undercover operation itself. Cover stories told to innocent persons that are necessary to achieve the good ends of the deception would probably not be acceptable to Kant. He asks rhetorically, "If a lie does no harm to anyone and no one's interests are affected by it, is it a lie? Certainly." A lie is a lie, for Kant, regardless of whether one's intentions are good or bad, and is consequently morally wrong.

At any rate, Kant's above criterion for violating the duty to tell the truth should not be understood as implicitly utilitarian. It is not the consequences of the hearer's misuse of my truthful statement that bothers Kant. Rather, it is the fact that such misuse is itself a violation of the categorical imperative. The robber treats me only as a means, and he has no right to do that. It follows that he has no right to expect the truth from me, and I therefore have no duty to provide it. So, for Kant, lying by criminal justice officers would seem to be limited to cases where the person lied to is treating the officer only as a means. This leaves open the question of officers who are actively initiating the lying exchange.

In "Blue Lies and Police Placebos," Carl B. Klockars places police lying in the *persuasion* category of techniques of domination and control. Those four categories—authority, power, persuasion, and force—are used individually and jointly by police to overcome resistance to an officer and his or her goals. Klockars states that the moral justification offered for police lying is based on the principle of nonmaleficence (the avoidance of harm). Although criminal justice practitioners have a legal right to use force in their official duties, and since lying is morally preferable to the use of force, it follows that officers have the right to lie in the conduct of their official duties. Klockars describes the perspective of the courts toward lying as conceding that "while lying may be an offensive and morally dangerous means, it is certainly preferable to force."

The bulk of Klockars' paper is devoted to examining a series of examples of "placebos" and "blue" lies, both of which are viewed within police culture as being morally acceptable. In each case, the lie is used by the officer to persuade the hearer that the officer's perception of the circumstances is best. Placebos are lies that are intended to help the person lied to. Blue lies are used to control the hearer. In either type of lie, the "dupe" (a citizen, a judge, a fellow officer) is either benefited by the lie or is at least not harmed, and in all cases the public good is maximized.

Thus, all the examples can be regarded as relying on act utilitarian reasoning, in which the consequences of not lying are less desirable than those that result from lying. The subordination of truth-telling to other goods (the obligation to render aid, the obligation to protect the public, etc.) involves moral reasoning on the part of the officer. As Klockars notes, "[the officer] locates the justification of lying in genuine moral goods, not in mere self-interest, careerist ambitions, convenience, or the sale of more widgets." Nonetheless, Klockars concludes, police sensitivity to the harms that can result from lying is not great. This, of course, is an inherent danger in act utilitarian reasoning, namely, that some of the consequences will be ignored in the calculation, thus invalidating the results of the analysis.

Jerome H. Skolnick's selection, "Deception by Police," continues the examination of the utilitarian justification of police lying, especially in detection. Skolnick is especially sensitive to the paradoxical fact that "the end of truth justifies for the modern detective the means of lying," but clearly supports Sissela Bok's "backing away from the Kantian categorical imperative."

Skolnick states that lying occurs in all three stages of detection: investigation, interrogation, and testimony, but with decreasing acceptability in the respective stages. While lying to suspects is freely admitted by police and defended as morally acceptable, lying in court is neither admitted nor publicly defended. Moreover, Skolnick presents empirical evidence that testimonial lying by police is systematic, not a matter of individual aberration. For example, a study found that uniform police had been "fabricating grounds of arrest in narcotics cases in order to circumvent the requirements of *Mapp*.[3] Skolnick believes that such lies occur out of habit; lying is a "routine way of managing legal impediments." Skolnick appears to think that this process arises out of faulty utilitarian analysis. He says:

> ... the policeman characteristically measures the short-term disutility of the act of suppressing evidence, not the long-term utility of due process of law for protecting and enhancing the dignity of the citizen who is being investigated by the state.

Thus, when the officer sees that the law is working to suppress the truth in the interest of the criminal, "he usually attempts to construct the appearance of compliance, rather than allow the offender to escape apprehension."[4] Skolnick proposes adopting Sissela Bok's standard for justifying deception: would the officer be willing to argue, in public (without a mask and wig!) in favor of courtroom perjury, specifically to defend his or her own perjury?

Skolnick then examines deception in interrogation, the use of sophisticated psychological techniques and coercing confessions, and polygraph interrogation. He points out the well-known unreliability of high pressure psychological interrogation techniques and of polygraph testing, asking if psychological coercion isn't more morally offensive than deception in investigation. On the other hand, Skolnick asks why lying should be viewed as acceptable in an undercover drug operation, but not acceptable in the interrogation of a forcible rapist.

Skolnick seems to see this as an unresolvable inconsistency in the criminal justice system, and his conclusion can be read as one of pessimism. Crime control and due process are in irreconcilable conflict, but the supposed inconsistency need not be a crippling one. It may be more useful to view the conflict as an "in-house" quarrel between act utilitarians (law enforcement) and rule utilitarians (civil libertarians). In fact, Skolnick himself characterizes the opposing sides in these terms. As we already know, act utilitarianism has many weaknesses in practice that rule utilitarianism resolves. Consequently, Skolnick's pessimism may be premature.

The final selection is Thomas Barker and David L. Carter's paper, "Police Lies and Perjury: A Motivation-Based Taxonomy." Barker and Carter divide police lies into three categories: accepted lying, tolerated lying, and deviant lying. Accepted lies generally include what Klockars calls placebos and blue lies. Among their essential characteristics are the service of public interest (duty of benevolence) and avoidance of harm, including violations of Constitutional rights. Such lies are viewed as virtually unavoidable in police work.

Barker and Carter's second category, tolerated lies, includes deceiving the public about full enforcement, when in fact selective enforcement and discretion are the rule; lying to control domestic disturbances, when in fact there are no grounds for arrest; and lying during interrogation. Thus, this category can easily shade off at either end into blue lies or into truly deviant lying. Barker and Carter are very direct in their disagreement with act utilitarian reasoning, which encourages officers to tolerate lies "because it serves their ends—regardless of constitutional and ethical implications..."

The third category, deviant lies, includes lies that violate the law or department regulations. Barker and Carter state that deviant lies that violate the law (substantive or procedural) should not be permitted, but that such conduct is "well known" within the criminal justice system. They divide deviant lies further into two subcategories: those made in support of legitimate goals and those made in support of illegitimate goals. Barker and Carter feel that the central motivation for the first type of lies is officer frustration over the criminal justice process. The authors believe, nevertheless, that lying in court is a threat to civil liberties and "is as fundamentally improper as the criminal behavior of the accused." The second type of deviant lying involves lies told to avoid departmental disciplinary action, criminal prosecution, or civil suit. Protection of oneself or one's colleagues is the motivation for such lies. Consequently, the major moral rationalizations will be self-interest and loyalty to friends.

Barker and Carter appear to reject the utilitarian defense of police lying, stating at one point that the ends do not justify the means. However, the authors appear to believe that the point is moot, since deviant lying actually undermines the criminal justice process rather than providing operational work-arounds that ultimately benefit the public. They believe that police lying is directly linked to corruption, and that it works against organizational discipline rather than benefiting it. In short, on this account, there is not even an act utilitarian justification available for deviant lying (nor perhaps for tolerated lies either).

Notes

1. Immanuel Kant, "On a Supposed Right to Lie From Altruistic Motives," in Lewis White Beck (trans.), *The Critique of Practical Reason and Other Writings on Moral Philosophy*. (Chicago: University of Chicago Press, 1949).

2. For example, see Sissela Bok, *Lying: Moral Choice in Public and Private Life.* (New York: Vintage Books, 1979), and Jerome Skolnick, in this chapter. We will not deal with the issue of whether Kant misapplied the categorical imperative.
3. *Mapp v. Ohio,* 367 U.S. 643 (1961).
4. Jerome Skolnick, *Justice Without Trial.* Second edition. (New York: Wiley & Sons, 1975), p. 177, as quoted by Skolnick in the chapter selection.

Ethical Duties Towards Others: Truthfulness

IMMANUEL KANT

THE EXCHANGE OF OUR sentiments is the principal factor in social intercourse, and truth must be the guiding principle herein. Without truth social intercourse and conversation become valueless. We can only know what a man thinks if he tells us his thoughts, and when he undertakes to express them he must really do so, or else there can be no society of men. Fellowship is only the second condition of society, and a liar destroys fellowship. Lying makes it impossible to derive any benefit from conversation. Liars are, therefore, held in general contempt. Man is inclined to be reserved and to pretend. Reserve is *dissimulatio* and pretence *simulatio.* Man is reserved in order to conceal faults and shortcomings which he has; he pretends in order to make others attribute to him merits and virtues which he has not. Our proclivity to reserve and concealment is due to the will of Providence that the defects of which we are full should not be too obvious. Many of our propensities and peculiarities are objectionable to others, and if they became patent we should be foolish and hateful in their eyes. Moreover, the parading of these objectionable characteristics would so familiarize men with them that they would themselves acquire them. Therefore we arrange our conduct either to conceal our faults or to appear other than we are. We possess the art of simulation. In consequence, our inner weakness and error is revealed to the eyes of men only as an appearance of well-being, while we ourselves develop the habit of dispositions which are conducive to good conduct. No man in his true senses, therefore, is candid. Were man candid, were the request of Momus[I] to be complied with that Jupiter should place a mirror in each man's heart so that his disposition might be visible to all, man would have to be better constituted and to possess good principles. If all men were good there would be no need for any of us to be reserved; but since they are not, we have to keep the shutters closed. Every house keeps its dustbin in a place of its own. We do not press our friends to come into our water-closet, although they know that we have one just like themselves. Familiarity in such things is the ruin of good taste. In the same way we make no exhibition of our defects, but try to conceal them. We try to conceal our mistrust by affecting a courteous demeanour and so accustom ourselves to courtesy that at last it becomes a reality and we set a good example by it. If that were not so, if there were none who were better than we, we should become neglectful. Accordingly, the endeavour to appear good ultimately makes us really good. If all men were good, they could be candid, but as things are they cannot be. To be reserved is to be restrained in expressing one's mind. We can, of course, keep absolute silence. This is the readiest and most absolute method of reserve, but it is unsociable, and a silent man is not only unwanted in social circles but is also suspected; every one thinks him deep and disparaging, for if when asked for his opinion he remains silent people think that he must be taking the worst view or he would not be averse from expressing it. Silence, in fact, is always a treacherous ally, and therefore it is not even prudent to be completely reserved. Yet there is such a thing as prudent reserve, which requires not silence but careful deliberation; a man who is wisely reserved weighs his words carefully and speaks his mind about everything excepting only those things in regard to which he deems it wise to be reserved.

We must distinguish between reserve and secretiveness, which is something entirely different. There are matters about which one has no desire to speak and in regard to which reserve is easy. We are, for instance, not naturally tempted to speak about and to betray our own misdemeanours. Every one finds it easy to keep a reserve about some of his private affairs, but there are things about which it requires an effort to be silent. Secrets have a way of coming out, and strength is required to prevent ourselves betraying them. Secrets are always matters deposited with us by other people and they ought not to be placed at the disposal of third parties. But man has a great liking for conversation, and the telling of secrets adds much to the interest of conversation; a secret told is like a present given; how then are we to keep secrets? Men who are not very talkative as a rule keep secrets well, but good conversationalists, who are at the same time clever, keep them better. The former might be induced to betray some-

thing, but the latter's gift of repartee invariably enables them to invent on the spur of the moment something non-committal.

The person who is as silent as a mute goes to one extreme; the person who is loquacious goes to the opposite. Both tendencies are weaknesses. Men are liable to the first, women to the second. Someone has said that women are talkative because the training of infants is their special charge, and their talkativeness soon teaches a child to speak, because they can chatter to it all day long. If men had the care of the children, they would take much longer to learn to talk. However that may be, we dislike anyone who will not speak: he annoys us; his silence betrays his pride. On the other hand, loquaciousness in men is contemptible and contrary to the strength of the male. All this by the way; we shall now pass to more weighty matters.

If I announce my intention to tell what is in my mind, ought I knowingly to tell everything, or can I keep anything back? If I indicate that I mean to speak my mind, and instead of doing so make a false declaration, what I say is an untruth, a *falsiloquium*. But there can be *falsiloquium* even when people have no right to assume that we are expressing our thoughts. It is possible to deceive without making any statement whatever. I can make believe, make a demonstration from which others will draw the conclusion I want, though they have no right to expect that my action will express my real mind. In that case I have not lied to them, because I had not undertaken to express my mind. I may, for instance, wish people to think that I am off on a journey, and so I pack my luggage; people draw the conclusion I want them to draw; but others have no right to demand a declaration of my will from me. Thus the famous Law[2] went on building so that people might not guess his intention to abscond. Again, I may make a false statement (*falsiloquium*) when my purpose is to hide from another what is in my mind and when the latter can assume that such is my purpose, his own purpose being to make a wrong use of the truth. Thus, for instance, if my enemy takes me by the throat and asks where I keep my money, I need not tell him the truth, because he will abuse it; and my untruth is not a lie (*mendacium*) because the thief knows full well that I will not, if I can help it, tell him the truth and that he has no right to demand it of me. But let us assume that I really say to the fellow, who is fully aware that he has no right to demand it, because he is a swindler, that I will tell him the truth, and I do not, am I then a liar? He has deceived me and I deceive him in return; to him, as an individual, I have done no injustice and he cannot complain; but I am none the less a liar in that my conduct is an infringement of the rights of humanity. It follows that a *falsiloquium* can be a *mendacium*—a lie—especially when it contravenes the right of an individual. Although I do a man no injustice by lying to him when he has lied to me, yet I act against the right of mankind, since I set myself in opposition to the condition and means through which any human society is possible. If one country breaks the peace this does not justify the other in doing likewise in revenge, for if it did no peace would ever be secure. Even though a statement does not contravene any particular human right it is nevertheless a lie if it is contrary to the general right of mankind. If a man spreads false news, though he does no wrong to anyone in particular, he offends against mankind, because if such a practice were universal man's desire for knowledge would be frustrated. For, apart from speculation, there are only two ways in which I can increase my fund of knowledge, by experience or by what others tell me. My own experience must necessarily be limited, and if what others told me was false, I could not satisfy my craving for knowledge. A lie is thus a *falsiloquium in praejudicium humanitatis*, even though it does not violate any specific *jus quaesitum* of another. In law a *mendacium* is a *falsiloquium in praejudicium alterius*; and so it must be in law; but morally it is a *falsiloquium in praejudicium humanitatis*. Not every untruth is a lie; it is a lie only if I have expressly given the other to understand that I am willing to acquaint him

with my thought. Every lie is objectionable and contemptible in that we purposely let people think that we are telling them our thoughts and do not do so. We have broken our pact and violated the right of mankind. But if we were to be at all times punctiliously truthful we might often become victims of the wickedness of others who were ready to abuse our truthfulness. If all men were well-intentioned it would not only be a duty not to lie, but no one would do so because there would be no point in it. But as men are malicious, it cannot be denied that to be punctiliously truthful is often dangerous. This has given rise to the conception of a white lie, the lie enforced upon us by necessity—a difficult point for moral philosophers. For if necessity is urged as an excuse it might be urged to justify stealing, cheating and killing, and the whole basis of morality goes by the board. Then, again, what is a case of necessity? Everyone will interpret it in his own way, and, as there is then no definite standard to judge by, the application of moral rules becomes uncertain. Consider, for example, the following case. A man who knows that I have money asks me: 'Have you any money on you?' If I fail to reply, he will conclude that I have; if I reply in the affirmative he will take it from me; if I reply in the negative, I tell a lie. What am I to do? If force is used to extort a confession from me, if my confession is improperly used against me, and if I cannot save myself by maintaining silence, then my lie is a weapon of defence. The misuse of a declaration extorted by force justifies me in defending myself. For whether it is my money or a confession that is extorted makes no difference. The forcing of a statement from me under conditions which convince me that improper use would be made of it is the only case in which I can be justified in telling a white lie. But if a lie does no harm to anyone and no one's interests are affected by it, is it a lie? Certainly. I undertake to express my mind, and if I do not really do so, though my statement may not be to the prejudice of the particular individual to whom it is made, it is none the less *in praejudicium humanitatis.* Then, again, there are lies which cheat. To cheat is to make a lying promise, while a breach of faith is a true promise which is not kept. A lying promise is an insult to the person to whom it is made, and even if this is not always so, yet there is always something mean about it. If, for instance, I promise to send some one a bottle of wine, and afterwards make a joke of it, I really swindle him. It is true that he has no right to demand the present of me, but in Idea it is already a part of his own property.

Reservatio mentalis is a form of dissimulation and *aequivocatio* of simulation. If a man tries to extort the truth from us and we cannot tell it [to] him and at the same time do not wish to lie, we are justified in resorting to equivocation in order to reduce him to silence and to put a stop to his questionings. If he is wise, he will leave it at that. But if we let it be understood that we are expressing our sentiments and we proceed to equivocate we are in a different case; for our listeners might then draw wrong conclusions from our statements and we should have deceived them. Lies of this nature, if intended to lead to good, were called by the Jesuits *peccata philosophica* or *peccatilla.* Hence the modern terms 'peccadillo' and 'bagatelle'. But a lie is a lie, and is in itself intrinsically base whether it be told with good or bad intent. For formally a lie is always evil; though if it is evil materially as well, it is a much meaner thing. There are no lies which may not be the source of evil. A liar is a coward; he is a man who has recourse to lying because he is unable to help himself and gain his ends by any other means. But a stouthearted man will love truth and will not recognize a *casus necessitatis.* All expedients which take us off our guard are thoroughly mean. Such are lying, assassination, and poisoning. To attack a man on the highway is less vile than to attempt to poison him. In the former case he can at least defend himself, but, as he must eat, he is defenceless against the poisoner. A flatterer is not always a liar; he is merely lacking in self-esteem; he has no scruple in reducing his own worth and raising that of another in order to gain something by it. But

there exists a form of flattery which springs from kindness of heart. Some kind souls flatter people whom they hold in high esteem. There are thus two kinds of flattery, kindly and treacherous; the first is weak, while the second is mean. People who are not given to flattery are apt to be faultfinders.

If a man is often the subject of conversation, he becomes a subject of criticism. If he is our friend, we ought not invariably to speak well of him or else we arouse jealousy and grudge against him; for people, knowing that he is only human, will not believe that he has only good qualities. We must, therefore, concede a little to the adverse criticism of our listeners and point out some of our friend's faults; if we allow him faults which are common and unessential, while extolling his merits, our friend cannot take it in ill part. Toadies are people who praise others in company in the hope of gain. Men are meant to form opinions regarding their fellows and to judge them. Nature has made us judges of our neighbours so that things which are false but are outside the scope of the established legal authority should be arraigned before the court of social opinion. Thus, if a man dishonours some one, the authorities do not punish him, but his fellows judge and punish him, though only so far as it is within their right to punish him and without doing violence to him. People shun him, and that is punishment enough. If that were not so, conduct not punished by the authorities would go altogether unpunished. What then is meant by the enjoinder that we ought not to judge others? As we are ignorant of their dispositions we cannot tell whether they are punishable before God or not, and we cannot, therefore, pass an adequate moral judgment upon them. The moral dispositions of others are for God to judge, but we are competent judges of our own. We cannot judge the inner core of morality: no man can do that; but we are competent to judge its outer manifestations. In matters of morality we are not judges of our fellows, but nature has given us the right to form judgments about others and she also has ordained that we should judge ourselves in accordance with judgments that others form about us. The man who turns a deaf ear to other people's opinion of him is base and reprehensible. There is nothing that happens in this world about which we ought not to form an opinion, and we show considerable subtlety in judging conduct. Those who judge our conduct with exactness are our best friends. Only friends can be quite candid and open with each other. But in judging a man a further question arises. In what terms are we to judge him? Must we pronounce him either good or evil? We must proceed from the assumption that humanity is lovable, and, particularly in regard to wickedness, we ought never to pronounce a verdict either of condemnation or of acquittal. We pronounce such a verdict whenever we judge from his conduct that a man deserves to be condemned or acquitted. But though we are entitled to form opinions about our fellows, we have no right to spy upon them. Everyone has a right to prevent others from watching and scrutinizing his actions. The spy arrogates to himself the right to watch the doings of strangers; no one ought to presume to do such a thing. If I see two people whispering to each other so as not to be heard, my inclination ought to be to get farther away so that no sound may reach my ears. Or if I am left alone in a room and I see a letter lying open on the table, it would be contemptible to try to read it; a right-thinking man would not do so; in fact, in order to avoid suspicion and distrust he will endeavour not to be left alone in a room where money is left lying about, and he will be averse from learning other people's secrets in order to avoid the risk of the suspicion that he has betrayed them; other people's secrets trouble him, for even between the most intimate of friends suspicion might arise. A man who will let his inclination or appetite drive him to deprive his friend of anything, of his fiancee, for instance, is contemptible beyond a doubt. If he can cherish a passion for my sweetheart, he can equally well cherish a passion for my purse. It is very mean to lie in wait and spy upon a friend, or on anyone else, and to elicit information about him from menials by lowering ourselves to the level of our inferiors, who will thereafter not forget to regard themselves as our equals. Whatever militates against frankness lowers the dignity of man. Insidious, underhand conduct uses means which strike at the roots of society because they make frankness impossible; it is far viler than violence; for against violence we can defend ourselves, and a violent man who spurns meanness can be tamed to goodness, but the mean rogue, who has not the courage to come out into the open with his roguery, is devoid of every vestige of nobility of character. For that reason a wife who attempts to poison her husband in England is burnt at the stake, for if such conduct spread, no man would be safe from his wife.[3]

As I am not entitled to spy upon my neighbour, I am equally not entitled to point out his faults to him; and even if he should ask me to do so he would feel hurt if I complied. He knows his faults better than I, he knows that he has them, but he likes to believe that I have not noticed them, and if I tell him of them he realizes that I have. To say, therefore, that friends ought to point out each other's faults, is not sound advice. My friend may know better than I whether my gait or deportment is proper or not, but if I will only examine myself, who can know me better than I can know myself? To point out his faults to a friend is sheer impertinence; and once fault-finding begins between friends their friendship will not last long. We must turn a blind eye to the faults of others, lest they conclude that they have lost our respect and we lose theirs. Only if placed in positions of authority over others should we point out to them their defects. Thus a husband is entitled to teach and correct his wife, but his corrections must be well-intentioned and kindly and must be dominated by respect, for if they be prompted only by displeasure they result in mere blame and bitterness. If we must blame, we must temper the blame with a sweetening of love, goodwill, and respect. Nothing else will avail to bring about improvement.

NOTES

1. Momus, the god of mockery and censure, demanded that a little door be made in man's breast, that he might see his secret thoughts.

2. The reference is to John Law (1671-1729) and his Mississippi venture.

3. The last woman burnt in England suffered in 1789, the punishment being abolished in 1790. In point of fact, burning of women was considered more 'decent' than hanging and exposure on a gibbet.

Study Questions

1. Kant says that the "endeavor to appear good ultimately makes us really good." What is he getting at here? Do you agree? Why? Defend your position with an example in criminal justice practice.

2. Distinguish between a *falsiloquium* and a *mendacium*. Explain how Kant's thief example illustrates the distinction.

3. Distinguish among "false statement," "untruth," "lie," and "white lie," according to Kant, relating them to *"falsiloquium"* and *"mendacium,"* as appropriate. Do you find Kant's distinctions persuasive? Why? Defend your position.

4. Under what conditions does Kant believe that a white lie is morally justified? Is his position utilitarian? Do you agree with Kant on white lies? Why? Defend your position with an example from criminal justice practice and with a noncriminal justice example.

5. Does Kant think that it is possible to deceive someone without lying? Give an example. Is it morally permissible for a criminal justice practitioner to offer deceptive testimony under oath, as long as he or she never actually states a falsehood? Why? Defend your position with at least two examples. Would Kant agree with you? Explain.

Blue Lies and Police Placebos
The Moralities of Police Lying

CARL B. KLOCKARS

Most of them, in my judgment, were very honest fellows, at least within the bounds of reason.

—H. L. MENCKEN
Recollections of Notable Cops

WHETHER IT BE STOPPING a speeding car, restraining an angry or enthusiastic crowd, moving a group of street-corner loungers, quieting a family beef, turning off a cooling fire hydrant on a sultry, city summer day, or effecting capture of a felon or a runaway puppy, the work of police often requires that they overcome actual

Carl B. Klockars, "Blue Lies and Police Placebos," American Behavioral Scientist, Vol. 27:4 (March/April 1984), pp. 529-544. © 1984 Sage Publications, Inc. Reprinted by permission.

or potential resistance. In doing so they may be thought of as drawing upon one or more general types of domination and control: *authority, power, persuasion,* and *force.* This essay is about a single subspecies of one of those four types, lying, and the moral meanings police are inclined to attach to it. In large part, police derive those meanings from the relation lying enjoys to alternative means. Thus, we will begin by distinguishing those four means from one another and identifying the place of lying in a hierarchy of means of domination and control.

Authority. Authority is that form of domination and control marked by "unquestioning recognition by those who are asked to obey; neither coercion nor persuasion is needed" (Arendt, 1973: 116). Those who obey authoritative commands do so because they understand those commands as right and necessary: right because the person or institution issuing the command is entitled to do so; necessary because, sociologically speaking, genuine authority precludes serious consideration of alternatives. To wait patiently for a red light to turn green before proceeding, even when the way is obviously clear and there is no possibility of detection, is to evidence an authoritative relationship to the institutions of traffic control.

It is difficult if not impossible to know what proportion of police-citizen encounters are marked by relations of authority. This is so not only because relations of power may produce interactions that appear on the surface similar to relations of authority but also because many citizens are competent at acting as if an interaction is characterized by an authoritative relationship when in fact it is not. What is known, though, is that all three major movements in the history of American police, their militarization, their professionalization, and their legalization (that is, their coming to be understood as law enforcers or agents of the courts), are easily readable as direct attempts to encourage authoritative relations between police and citizens (Bittner, 1980; Fogelson, 1977; Haller, 1976; Miller, 1975). Despite the fact that all three movements have been suc-

cessful in some respects, all of them have met a peculiarly American mix of individualism, egalitarianism, and social heterogeneity fundamentally hostile to the enlargement of relations of authority.

Power. Power, according to Max Weber's (1958: 180) classic formulation, refers to "the chance of a man or a number of men to realize their own will in a communal action even against the resistance of others who are participating in the action." Power, understood in this way, shares at least one important characteristic with authority and is distinguished profoundly from authority by two others. The common feature is that both are *social* as opposed to individual forms of domination and control. They both depend upon persons acting in concert, sharing and coordinating meanings and actions. If a citizen complies with a police officer's order out of deference to police power, what is obeyed is not merely the police officer's command but the officer, the officers who will follow him or her, and the social, legal, economic, and political resources that will be brought to bear should the command be disobeyed.

Distinguishing power from authority are its relationship to (1) resistance and (2) probability. Power admits the contemplation and the calculation of the costs of resistance; authority, whose hallmark is unquestioning obedience, does not. This is not to say that obedience to power involves actual resistance. In fact, the second feature of power distinguishing it from authority is that power is a matter of the probability that *if* one resists one will be overcome. Power thus excludes those occasions when force or some other means of coercing compliance is actually employed.

Although it cannot be denied that police possess enormous amounts of legal, social, economic, political, and organizational resources that may be brought to bear in coercing individuals, the work of Muir (1977) has shown that in coercive relations police resources, rationality, respectability, and responsibility all undermine their power to coerce effectively. Muir (1977: 44-45) writes:

The reality, and the subtle irony, of being a policeman is that while he may appear to be the supreme practitioner of coercion, in fact he is first and foremost its most frequent victim.... Contrary to the more unflattering stereotypes of policemen, it is the citizen who virtually always initiates the coercive encounter. What is more, the citizen tends to enjoy certain inordinate advantages over the policeman in these transactions.... The citizen is, relative to the policeman, the more dispossessed, the more detached, the nastier, and the crazier.... The irony of the policeman's lot is that his authority, his status, his sense of civility, and his reasonableness impose terrible limits on his freedom to react to the extortionate practices of others.

Persuasion. Like power, persuasion as a means of domination and control acknowledges resistance. But, unlike power, it does not leave it potential, a matter of probabilities. Rather, persuasion actively engages resistance and seeks to overcome it by mobilizing signs, symbols, words, and arguments that induce in the mind of the person persuaded the belief that he or she ought to comply. The signs and symbols may evidence a police officer's claim to authority and power; the words and arguments may point to the rationality, desirability, or self-interest of compliant behavior. Whatever means of persuasion are used we do not speak of a person as being "persuaded" to do some thing until that person believes he or she ought to do it.

The lie, the statement intentionally uttered to deceive, is distinguishable from other means of persuasion such as the argument and tactics of rhetoric, polemic, and metaphor in two principal ways. First, it communicates a message the liar believes to be false. People often make false arguments by mistake, in which case such errors are not lies. False arguments may even be presented intentionally, as teachers of logic often do to show the errors of reason they contain, without qualifying as lies. What exempts them from classification as lies is that they fail to satisfy the second distinguishing feature of the lie: its intention to deceive. As a form of persuasion, what must also distinguish the lie is its attempt

to take from the mind of the person lied to its capacity to draw its own conclusions. This is not to say that the person lied to inevitably reaches a false conclusion or makes a wrong decision. Not only are lies often detected, but sometimes they can lead to a correct, right, or salutary conclusion even when they are not. Placebos sometimes cure.

Force. The fourth and final source a police officer can draw upon to gain compliance is force. It is a means of domination of a wholly different order than authority, power, or persuasion. For while authority, power, and persuasion all achieve mental domination and control, the domination and control force seeks is physical. When force is used to gain compliance, the will of the person coerced is irrelevant.

It is in their relation to the mind of the person coerced that force and the lie enjoy some special intimacies. Both assault its right to determine how the person lied to behaves: the lie by presenting it with a false reality, force by ignoring its will altogether. It is also their relation to the mind of the person coerced that renders the lie and force highly unreliable as long-term forms of domination. Lies are subject to detection and invite scrutiny, especially when they compel compliance that would not otherwise be given. Force risks failure as a means of control as soon as the individual applying it tires, weakens, or becomes inattentive. Finally, disrespectful as they are of the rights of mind, they are rarely approved of by persons on whom they are used and their use is rarely given legitimacy in societies that respect that right. In fact, in modern American society the only occupation given the legitimate right to use both force and lies is police.[1]

Police and the Legitimate Right to Lie

If "legitimacy" is understood to mean approval or acceptance by courts of law, the legitimacy of police lying is limited to lies told in the course of policing criminal or suspected criminal activities. This is so because, with few exceptions, the courts review police behavior only upon those occasions when charges are filed and the case is contested in court. Even then the courts grant legitimacy to police behavior in a highly limited way. In effect, what they say is that they will not refuse to punish persons who are found guilty merely because police behaved as they did. This implicit legal legitimacy is given to police lies as elaborate as the FBI's ABSCAM operation and as simple as the lies police interrogators tell (for example, your conspirator has confessed; your fingerprints were found at the scene; a witness has identified you in a line-up) when trying to obtain a confession (Klockars, 1983; Marx, 1980; Inbau and Reid, 1967). The only limitation on police lies of this type is that they not be of such a nature that they would induce an innocent person to commit a crime or falsely confess to having committed one.

The moral justification for allowing these kinds of lies is, in general, the principle of non-maleficence, the avoidance of harm. This principle, which is generally considered to override obligations to be truthful when the two are juxtaposed, justifies both the police use of lies and the police use of force in the pursuit of criminals. Moreover, it is also the source of limits on both force and lies, providing that no more of either be used than is necessary to prevent harm.

The fact is, however, that the courts have not attempted to restrict police lying in any substantial way beyond the requirement that it not create the harm of entrapment or induce a person to confess to a crime he or she did not commit. Police have no obligation to defend the necessity of their lies as, for example, courts require them to do when they seek authorization for permission to eavesdrop electronically or to wiretap (Report of the National Commission for the Review of Federal and State Laws Relating to Wiretapping and Electronic Surveillance, 1976).

There are various ways in which one might seek to explain the courts' reluctance to limit police lying. One might argue that there were actually some other moral principles involved, such as a claim that criminals by their acts had violated a social contract and thus had lost the right to be dealt with truthfully by the state and its agents (on this and other justifications for

lying, see Bok, 1978). This principle, in particular, would be difficult to reconcile with court requirements for Miranda warnings, which provide for a series of detailed, truthful cautions.

The more satisfactory approach involves appreciating the courts' attitude toward police lying in relationship to more profound concern with limiting police use of force. The courts' obligation to allow the use of force to prevent harm and at the same time to limit its use to only that amount necessary to prevent harm encourages the court to be very generous in its view of lying. While lying may be an offensive and morally dangerous means, it is certainly preferable to force.

Blue Lies and Police Placebos

Most police work does not involve pursuing criminals and most police spend only a small portion of their time at strict law enforcement tasks (Cumming et al., 1965; Webster, 1970). Thus, for most police officers, most of the time, courts' views on police lying, generous though they may be, are simply irrelevant. For legitimacy for the lies they tell in handling citizen complaints, writing reports, and maintaining and restoring order, the police look to their partners, peers, the occupational culture of policing, their experience, and the values they bring with them to the job. These sources, singly and in combination, are subject to variant readings, which produce individual differences in police perceptions of the legitimacy of particular lies. But despite those differences my field experience and published accounts of others suggest that certain types of lies receive general acceptance and approval. In examining a series of such generally acceptable police lies, I will attempt to articulate the morality that legitimates them.

POLICE PLACEBOS

The Smith brothers are two men in their middle 50s who have spent at least the past decade of their lives on skid row. They are familiar figures to the police, who refer to them as "10-81s," the police code for the mentally ill.

Among the Smith brothers' problems, as they see them, is that from time to time they are pursued by invisible agents from outer space. These agents have powers that are literally unbelievable. Among them is the ability to insert fine wires into a person's head, through which they can then control him.

The Smith brothers have managed to avoid this victimization largely through the efforts of a sympathetic police sergeant. The sergeant had the good sense to report the invasion to Washington, which immediately responded to his report by dispatching a squad of equally invisible investigators who were specially trained—and armed—to deal with just such intruders. Needless to say, this operation is highly confidential and outside of the Smith brothers, the sergeant, and a handful of persons in Washington with the highest of security clearances, no one knows about it.

The lie to the Smith brothers is a rather elaborate example of a police placebo. It is, however, worth reporting because it displays four features of placebos, as distinct from other types of police lies, in vivid detail. The first of these features is that the perception of the problem by the person who is lied to is wrong. In the Smith brothers' case, there is no question that the intruders they allege are pursuing them are illusions. Second, the lie sponsors the impression of effective or at least meaningful response to the problem as it is understood by the person who is lied to. Imaginary police respond to imaginary invaders. Third, the placebo must be given at least partly for the benefit of the person to whom it is given. While the lie the sergeant tells has the effect of quieting the Smith brothers and at least temporarily relieving the sergeant from the bother of their complaints, the Smith brothers are comforted by his response. Fourth, the use of the placebo assumes that the person to whom it is given will not be better served by some nondeceptive treatment. The sergeant has neither the time nor the ability to do more for the two terrified paranoids than to make their paranoia briefly less terrifying. Finally, although it is not an essential feature of the administration

of placebos, there tends to develop an attitude of humor or joking contempt toward the person who is duped by it. It is for this reason that the sergeant kept his creation of an invisible police secret from other police officers. What the sergeant knew is that had he told other police about it, they would have been unable to resist the fun of participating in the Smith brothers' deception. Of course, had they done so they would have eventually ruined his device.

Less elaborate but more common examples of police placebos include all sorts of promises to keep a close watch on an area or a dwelling after a person has been victimized or becomes fearful of being victimized by media reports of crime; assurances that burglaries with all the earmarks of a professional job were probably the work of "just kids"; advising a seriously injured child or widow of accident victim that the deceased is all right or receiving expert medical care; telling the family of a fatally injured accident victim that their loved one died instantly and painlessly when the officer knows the death was neither quick nor painless; and attribution of a decision not to effect an arrest to some generous or kindly motive rather than the futility of doing so in the face of inadequate evidence.

To police, such lies have a self-evident morality to them. They are in the best interest of the person duped by them and the police officer cannot help the situation otherwise. Police are also aware of the risks and dangers of placebos. They work only as long as the credibility of the liar and the lie are preserved. If placebos are generated unconvincingly or used indiscriminately, the context of credibility that makes them possible will be undermined.

BLUE LIES

The demonstrator was a middle-class white woman in her late forties. She had entered the abortion clinic anteroom and begun pleading with the women present not to go through with the acts of murder they were contemplating. The receptionist barred the door to the procedure room and called the cops.

When they arrived the woman had seated herself on the floor and refused to move. The press, including a photographer, was present. The woman stated that she had thought a lot about what she was doing and that she would not leave under her own power. If the police wanted her out of the clinic, they were going to have to carry her out.

The shorter of the two policemen in the anteroom, which by now had been cleared of both press and patients, kneeled down slowly next to her and explained. "Look, ma'am. I understand what you are trying to do here and even though it's against the law, I can respect it. But the problem is that this is my first day back to work after being off for a hernia operation. I've got 22 stitches and I'm afraid that if I have to carry you out of here they might just open up."

"You're not lying to me, are you?" asked the woman.

"No, I'm not," said the policeman. "I'll show you my stitches if you want," he offered, reaching for his belt.

"That's OK. I believe you. I don't want you to hurt yourself because of me. I'll go with you."

What I will call "blue lies," such as the one above, are different from police placebos in that they are told not to help or to comfort the person lied to but to control him or her. Police understand the legitimacy of such lies to derive in a general way from the legitimacy of their right to take control of the situation that prompts their intervention. In important respects the logic of this justification parallels that of the court with respect to police lies told in the pursuit of criminals: If resort to force is justified, not only are lies justified, but they are to be preferred to force.

The matter of justification of blue lies is, however, complicated in two principal ways. The first has to do with the fact that the police right to use force is extraordinarily broad. It would be difficult to imagine a more unsatisfactory or incompetent police officer than one who actually used force on every occasion he or she was entitled to do so. The same is true of police who see fit to lie when their authority, their power,

or their abilities at nondeceptive forms of persuasion will serve just as well. All considerations of the morality of force and lying aside, they are simply less reliable forms of domination than the others. Thus, in the police officer's view, to lie when one can achieve the same effect more efficiently and with less effort is not immoral but stupid. It follows from this same practical concern for the efficiency of the means used to control people that certain types of people, those the officer believes to be unresponsive to police authority, unimpressed by the potential of police power, and unmovable by other forms of persuasion, should be the most likely candidates for control through blue lies.

The second principal way in which the moral justification of blue lies differs from the courts' justification of lying in pursuit of criminals has to do with the fact that the problem of legitimacy for the police officer is much more complicated than it is for the court. He or she may find, for example, that the legal legitimacy required to do the work expected may be lacking:

> Before state legislatures enacted statutes giving limited authority to the police to stop and question persons suspected of criminal involvement, police nevertheless stopped and questioned people. It is inconceivable how any police agency could be expected to operate without doing so. But since the basis for their actions was unclear, the police—if they thought a challenge likely—would use the guise of arresting the individual on a minor charge (often without clear evidence) to provide a semblance of legality. Enactment of stopping and questioning statutes eliminated the need for this sham [Goldstein, 1977: 72].

Police officers may find the legitimacy of their moral conclusions in conflict with the legitimacy of the conclusions they, as police, are legally obliged to draw:

> Chacon's moral conclusion was that he was dealing with "a malevolent youth" and a "respectable old man." And he intended to take action according to the way he characterized the facts and to the moral principles

which were keyed to those characterizations.

The problem of his moral perceptions, however, was "complicated" by the fact that he was a policeman. As a policeman he had a second moral obligation: to square his moral perceptions with the legal implications of the situation. That is, his moral and legal judgments were not supposed to work at cross purposes. [Chacon's problem was that] there were no legal equivalents for "grandfather," "old man," "good worker," "asshole," and "disrespectful." In legal terms the perceptible facts were that the grandfather was in control of the "stick," the boy's head was bashed, and the grandfather was unscathed. These facts pointed to the legal conclusion that the grandfather ought to be arrested, not the youth. To resolve this contradiction of law and morals Chacon "put in" his report some untested inferences about provocation by the grandson.... The choices [Chacon] had made in formulating his moral perception of the matter had put him in the dilemma of being either a dishonest man or an immoral one [Muir, 1977: 197].

Or, they may find themselves obliged to perform acts the legitimacy of which neither compels nor persuades them:

The informal but consequential departmental policy was that all officers on the 12-8 shift should stop, question, and run a wanted check on an average of one person every two hours. Kenny's problem with the policy was that the sector he worked was largely rural and he either knew or knew the reason why anyone he saw out at that time of night was where he was. He regularly came up short of the quota, a fact his sergeant connected with every theft, vandalism, and burglary in the county.

To relieve this pressure Kenny took to spending a portion of each "graveyard" shift in graveyards, where the markers provided him with names and dates of birth which he could call in for wanted checks. Kenny's charade was short-lived. He decided that he had to terminate it when one of the recently deceased came back "wanted" and Kenny had to fabricate a minor scuffle and an excited chase to account for his escape.

The problem of finding oneself in situations in which different sources of legitimacy conflict is a common one. It recurs because policing is a moral occupation, because no wholly satisfactory way exists to resolve genuine conflict between equally legitimate moral aspirations, and because police, unlike the rest of us, cannot responsibly avoid situations that bring them into moral conflict. "Admittedly," to quote Bittner (1980: 8), "few are constantly mindful of the saying, 'He that is without sin among you, let him cast the first stone...', but only the police are explicitly required to forget it." These competing and conflicting moral legitimacies regularly place police officers in situations that require them to do "wrong" by one standard in order to do "right" by another.

BLUE LIES AND MORAL DILEMMAS

There are a number of ways police can attempt to escape the discomfort of such moral dilemmas, three of which are relatively common and more or less successful. The first is simply to fail or refuse to draw out the moral implications of one's acts. There are certainly police who "just do their job." For such police problems of morality are problems of manners, of learning how a "good" police officer should behave. For such people the occupational culture of policing is legitimate and authoritative.

There are, though, in every police agency a sufficient number of cynics, malcontents, rebels, and heretics to confuse and complicate the life of police officers who "just want to do their job." Hence, to maintain one's morality as a problem of manners requires a rather low profile and a selective circle of like-minded friends.

Exemption, a second strategy available to morally active police officers, involves finding a way of not having to play out the moral consequences of any particular decision by rendering it in some way exempt from moral implications. Let us examine a not uncommon type of police lie, a case of perjured testimony, to display how this strategy works.

Mike, an experienced and talented detective, was the chief investigating officer on a case that involved a series of rapes, kidnappings, and robberies that were all committed by the same person. In each of the cases the rapist knocked on the front door of the home, talked or forced his way in, and upon finding that the woman was alone or only small children were present, took her to a bedroom and raped her. In all, the rapist victimized five women in this way.

The third rape was, however, different from the others in that as he was raping his victim someone came to the front door and rang the bell. This frightened the rapist and he fled through a rear window, leaving behind him a shoe. Normally the shoe would have been placed with other physical evidence from the scene in a police evidence room, but Mike took possession of the shoe himself so that it might be used to give the rapist's scent to some specially trained tracking dogs who would follow it from the victim's home. The dogs followed the scent through city streets for some two miles before they lost it at the door of a popular after-hours club.

Instead of returning the shoe to the evidence room, Mike placed it in the back of one of the bottom drawers in his desk, a desk that is never locked. It sat in the desk drawer for weeks until Mike brought it out to compare it with a shoe that had been recovered in a search of the rapist's lodgings. It was a perfect mate to the shoe from Mike's desk. What Mike realized after he had made the match was that by keeping it in his unlocked desk drawer he had compromised if not destroyed the chain of continuity that would have to be established to introduce the shoe from the victim's home into evidence in court. What he did was forge an evidence receipt with the cooperation of the officer in charge of the evidence room to establish that the shoe had been there all the time.

Mike regards himself as an honest cop, takes pride in the quality and quantity of his work, is respected by other police officers as a man of integrity, and would be repulsed by the thought of planting evidence or arresting someone on a phony charge. "On the street" among people "in the life" he has a reputation as a detective who can be trusted to keep his word. He believes lying in court is wrong and would not do so, except under extraordinary circumstances. What is it about the above case that allows Mike to count it as a justifiable exception?

Three features of it figure into Mike's reasoning. A major factor is that Mike knows the truth. He knows that the shoe in his desk drawer is the same one he took from the crime scene. It is preposterous to suggest, as Mike assumes a defense attorney would, that he or someone else tampered with it so that it would match the shoe taken from the rapist's lodgings. Mike also knows from other evidence, including a complete confession, that the person he arrested for the crime is the one who committed it. Regardless of what the court should determine legally in this case, Mike knows that the man on trial is *factually* guilty of raping this woman and at least four others.[2]

Second, while Mike appreciates and endorses the courts' general concern for continuity of evidence and regards it as the obligation of a competent police officer to preserve that continuity, he finds the courts to be overzealous in their concerns and irrational in their reactions to minor errors. He doubts that they can be reasoned with or persuaded by rational means.[3] In short, Mike understands the courts' rules of evidence continuity as they apply to this case to be a mere technicality. What police mean by "technicality" is a procedural rule the violation of which does not affect a perpetrator's factual guilt and the innocent violation of which by police should be legally tolerated. When the court refuses to behave in this "rational" way, Mike and many other honest police officers like him find dealing falsely with the court to be morally justifiable.

Finally, it would be less than candid to fail to point out that there is an element of self-interest and self-protection to Mike's lie. He made a mistake and his lie covered it up. He could, however, have covered it up in a different way, by not introducing the shoe into evidence in court.

While the shoe proved to be a nice touch at the trial, the jury would undoubtedly have found the man guilty anyway. (They reached a guilty verdict on all counts in less than two hours, the last hour of which they spent eating lunch at the court's expense.) This inconsequential character of the shoe as evidence had the effect of making Mike's decision to lie easier. It was not necessary to introduce it, so he did not have to face the charge that the purpose of his lie was to cover his own error. He thus satisfied himself that he lied because the shoe was "legitimate" evidence that the jury had a right to see.

Had Mike been less sure of the rapist's factual guilt, had he had his own doubts about whether continuity had been broken for some corrupt purpose, had the evidence been of a sort that was crucial to conviction, and had he been responsible for the break in the chain of continuity that may have permitted tampering, Mike would have been presented with an altogether different moral occasion. Under such circumstances the choice would be between telling the truth and risking punishment for one's mistake and lying and risking sending an innocent man to jail. While there are police officers who would choose to lie under such circumstances, as there are police who steal from crime scenes, there is nothing that could be called a police morality that would justify their doing so.

Prioritization, a third way in which police escape the discomfort of situations that require them to do wrong by one standard in order to do right by another, is probably the most common. It is to escape the moral dilemma by finding that the values juxtaposed by it are not of equal weight. In justifying blue lies and police placebos, police come to understand that being truthful is a less pressing moral obligation than the obligation to do what can be done by lying:

Mike arrested a fairly wealthy local contractor for receiving stolen property. A search of the man's home and business produced more than a dozen items that could be identified as stolen and many others of highly questionable origins. The contractor was well connected. He had friends in the city's political hierarchy and knew a few police officers fairly well. Mike expected calls on the contractor's behalf.

The first one came from a police lieutenant who ran the department's shooting range. The contractor was a long-time hunting buddy of the lieutenant, who wanted to make sure that Mike understood that the contractor was his "personal friend."

"I hope not too personal," replied Mike. "I guess you know the guy's a faggot, huh?"

"Him? No. Really?" answered the lieutenant.

"Yup, no doubt about it. We found a whole bunch of faggot shit at his house. Hey, but look, don't worry. Nobody needs to know anything about that."

Mike's lie about the contractor's homosexuality effectively prevented the lieutenant from pressuring Mike further for special treatment of the contractor. Had he done so, he would have opened himself up to the suspicion that his relationship with the contractor was "too personal."

Mike's moral justification of his lie to the lieutenant is that his legal, moral, and professional obligations to press his case against the contractor outweigh his moral obligations to be truthful to a person who would have him corrupt them. There is also an amusing element to the way in which his creative lie skewers the lieutenant's corrupt intentions. Mike is, in fact, proud of his lie to the lieutenant and was praised for it when he shared it, selectively, with his police peers.

But while Mike's lie illustrates how police can become morally comfortable with lying and even enjoy it, it also illustrates how both the humor of the creative lie and its moral evaluation can be distorted. The contractor is slandered by Mike's lie. The lieutenant's behavior after being told the lie is evidence that the contractor's reputation among his friends is harmed more seriously by Mike's false allegation of his homosexuality than by the genuine evidence that he is a receiver of stolen goods. Neither Mike nor any of his police peers entered the harm done to the contractor into their moral evaluation of Mike's lie. Psychologically, such considerations should not be expected from persons who are attempting to send to jail the person harmed by their lie.

Mike's lie is also illustrative of a final point about lying as a means of social control. Lies can be and often are intrinsically appealing, exciting, and attractive. Each one generates a distorted reality that gives the liar a measure of control over the mind of the dupe. The work of the police requires them to learn to lie skillfully and in doing so exposes them to its seductions. It does so in a moral climate of such great complexity, and one so very different from that which nonpolice can enjoy, that those who manage to survive the moral hazards of a police career with a mature sense of their own dignity and integrity are as remarkable as they are rare.

Conclusion

Whether or not police lie more frequently than persons in any other occupation is an unanswerable empirical question. What is certain is that the coercive responsibility of their vocation obliges them to lie regularly and supplies them with a variety of moral justifications when they do. The most basic of these justifications derives from the police right to use force. It holds that in any situation in which police would be justified in using force to achieve legitimate ends, they would not only be justified in using lies, but lies would be a preferable alternative. In justification of other lies, those told to help people whose help is beyond the limits where police authority, power, persuasion, or force can be of assistance, police draw upon the ethics of placebo giving to justify their lies. It is an ethic that subordinates the placebo giver's moral obligation to be truthful to his or her obligation to help, comfort, and relieve pain in those who ask for assistance. In justifying still other types of lies, blue lies, police ethics either render them exempt from immoral implications by finding in their particulars extraordinary provocation or subordinating once again the moral obligation to be truthful to some moral obligation that takes priority to it.

It is important to stress that throughout this process of exempting and subordinating the obligation to be truthful the police officer's reasoning is moral. He or she locates the justification of lying in genuine moral goods, not in mere self-interest, careerist ambitions, convenience, or the sale of more widgets. However, as the police officer becomes comfortable with lies and their moral justification, he or she is apt to become casual with both. Lies often have an undeniably entertaining quality to them that can mask the harm they may inflict. Police sensitivity to these harms, particularly when the person victimized by them is disfavored by the norms of the occupational culture of policing, is likely to be minimal.

NOTES

1. Although I have in mind principally by "police" the folks who arrive when one calls the cops, I am prepared to include in the category special police occupations such as prison guards, keepers of mental institutions, and parents—all of whom are charged with policing small, specifically defined, and named populations within more or less restricted areas.

2. The factual guilt/legal distinction is noted in Skonick (1975: 182–183).

3. It is a matter of speculation, but Mike is probably quite right in assuming that the judge would have refused to admit the shoe into evidence no matter how reasonably Mike presented his case for continuity. Because the shoe was not essential, almost nothing would have persuaded a rational judge to permit its introduction and thereby open the case to an avenue of appeal. Had the shoe been a critical piece of evidence, a rational judge would be obliged to take arguments for its introduction seriously.

REFERENCES

Arendt, H. (1973) Crises of the Republic. Harmondsworth: Penguin.

Bittner, E. (1980) The Functions of Police in Modern Society. Cambridge, MA: Olegeschlager, Gunn & Hain.

Bok, S. (1978) Lying: Moral Choice in Public and Private Life. New York: Pantheon.

Cumming, E., I. Cumming, and L. Edell (1965) "Policeman as philosopher, guide, and friend." Social Problems 12: 276–286.

Fogelson, R. M. (1977) Big City Police. Cambridge, MA: Harvard Univ. Press.

Goldstein, H. (1977) Policing a Free Society. Cambridge, MA: Ballinger.

Haller, M. (1976) "Historical roots of police behavior. Chicago 1890–1925." Law and Society Rev. 12 (Winter): 303–323.

Inbau, F. and J. Reid (1967) Criminal Interrogations and Confessions. Baltimore: Williams & Wilkins.

Klockars, C. (1983) "The modern sting," in C. Klockars (ed.) Thinking About Police. New York: McGraw-Hill.

_____ (1980) "The Dirty Harry problem." Annals of the Amer. Academy of Pol. and Social Sci. 452 (November): 33–47.

Marx, G. (1980) "The new police undercover work." Urban Life 8 (January): 399–446.

Miller, W. (1975) "Police authority in London and New York City. 1830–1870." J. of Social History (Winter): 81–101.

Muir, W. K. (1977) Police, Streetcorner Politicians. Chicago: Univ. of Chicago Press.

Report of the National Commission for the Review of Federal and State Laws Relating to Wiretapping and Electronic Surveillance (1976) Washington, DC: Government Printing Office.

Skolnick, J. (1975) Justice Without Trial. New York: John Wiley.

Weber, M. (1958) "Class, status, and party." in H. Gerth and C. W. Mills (eds. and trans.) From Max Weber. New York: Oxford Univ. Press.

Webster, J. A. (1970) "Police task and time study." J. of Criminal Law, Criminology and Police Science 61: 94–100.

Study Questions

1. What is the principle of nonmaleficence? What role does this principle play in the moral justification of police lying? Is the principle powerful enough to justify lying, in your view? Why? Defend your position.

2. Explain the justification of lying that is grounded in the right to be dealt with truthfully by the state and its agents. What problem does Klockars see with this argument?

3. What does Klockars think is the most plausible explanation for judicial tolerance of police lying? What sort of ethical perspective must the judiciary be taking toward police lying, if Klockars' interpretation is correct?

4. What is a "police placebo"? What characteristics of a placebo are identified by Klockars? How do "blue lies" differ from placebos? How would Kant respond to these two categories of lies?

5. Of Klockars' rapist and contractor cases, which of the two involves the more objectionable lies, in your opinion? Why? What role does Mike's self-interest play in these cases? Is that relevant to the moral issues? Why? Defend your position.

Deception by Police

JEROME H. SKOLNICK

THE IDEAL OF LEGALITY implies that those convicted of crimes will not only be factually but legally guilty. A political commitment to legality is, after all, what distinguishes democratic governments from totalitarian ones. Yet, for every ideal there seems to be a practical challenge. The ideal of right to bail is challenged by the reality of the criminal's dangerousness, the presumption of innocence by the reality of factual guilt, the right to counsel by the triviality of certain offenses or the difficulties of providing counsel to those who have just been informed of their privilege against self-incrimination. Hard and fast rules limiting police conduct may challenge common sense, while the absence of such rules may invite arbitrary and abusive conduct. This paper discusses one of the most troubling and difficult questions pertaining to the ideal of legality: To what extent, if at all, is it proper for law enforcement officials to employ trickery and deceit as part of their law enforcement practices?[1]

Whatever the answer to that question—if indeed an answer can be formulated—it has to be measured against a hard reality of the criminal justice system. That reality is: Deception is considered by police—and courts as well—to be as natural to detecting as pouncing is to a cat. As we shall see, that is why it is so difficult both to control deceptive practices of detectives and to prescribe long-term measures to guarantee control.

A seminal, thought-provoking attempt has been made in Sissela Bok's important book on lying.[2] Bok does not deal explicitly with deception by detectives as she does with deception by

social scientists. But, she does refer to certain police practices in what must be regarded as the central chapter of her book—that on justification of deception, where she introduces standards for backing away from the Kantian categorical imperative.[3] Essentially, she argues for combining two standards for justifiable deception, insisting, first, on a public offering of justification for a lie and, second, on having the justification offered to an audience of reasonable persons. The chapter goes on to develop these notions in creative and original ways, but does not fully develop the implications of her guidelines for the detecting process. I would like to offer some observations which have been stimulated by her analysis about the detecting process itself.

The Normative Context of Detecting

Detecting occurs in the context of fluid moral constraints that are circumscribed by a tradition of due process of law, by ever-changing and not altogether clear interpretations of individual rights offered by the courts, and by the social organization of policing that develops its own moral norms and constraints. Finally, this amalgam of normative prescription is set within the context of an adversary system of justice.

If all that sounds complicated and confusing, it is. It suggests that, because of the multiple contexts of police action, there are unstable, even contradictory, norms. Is detecting to be considered akin to a poker game, where the players understand that deception is part of the game? It surely is not like the doctor-client, or even the

Jerome H. Skolnick, "Deception by Police," Criminal Justice Ethics, Vol. 1, No. 2 (Summer/Fall 1982), pp. 40–54. Used by permission of the author and The Institute for Criminal Justice Ethics, John Jay College of Criminal Justice, 899 Tenth Avenue, New York, NY 10019.

social scientist–subject relationship. The detective is not treating the subject, nor is the detective merely observing.

The detective deceives to establish grounds for convicting and punishing. The detecting process is informed and controlled by notions of fairness and dignity, but these notions, as embodied by law, are often unclear both in outcome and justification. The law often, but not always, supports police deception. The law permits the detective to pose as a consumer or purveyor of vice[4] but does not allow the policeman to employ certain ruses to gain entry without a search warrant[5] or to obtain a search warrant with a false affidavit.[6] The police subculture—the workaday normative order of police—permits, and sometimes demands, deception of courts, prosecutors, defense attorneys, and defendants but rarely, if ever, allows for deception of fellow policemen.[7] Police thus work within a severe but often agonizingly contradictory moral order which demands certain kinds of fidelities and insists upon other kinds of betrayals. The police milieu is normatively contradictory, almost to the point of being schizophrenogenic. Norms regarding deception, written and implied, abound in this moral order.

The Stages of Detecting

Deception occurs at three stages of the detecting process: investigation, interrogation, and testimony. If we place these three stages within the framework of a broad portrait of the moral cognition of the policeman, we observe that the acceptability of deception varies inversely with the level of the criminal process. Thus, deception is most acceptable to police—as it is to the courts—at the investigation stage, less acceptable during interrogation, and least acceptable in the courtroom.

If we inquire as to why that should be, the answer seems fairly obvious. Each stage is related to a set of increasingly stringent normative constraints. Courtroom testimony is given under oath and is supposed to be the truth, the whole truth, and nothing but the truth. Nobody is supposed to lie in a courtroom. When a policeman lies in court, he may be able to justify his deception on the basis of an alternative set of normative judgments (assuming that he is acting as a prosecution witness and is not himself the defendant), but he is still aware that courtroom lying violates the basic norms of the system he is sworn to uphold. Nevertheless, police do lie in the courtroom, particularly when they believe that judicial interpretations of constitutional limits on police practices are ill conceived or overly constraining in that they interfere with the policeman's ability to do his or her job as the police subculture defines it.

I shall argue in this paper that courtroom lying is justified within the police culture by the same sort of necessity rationale that courts have permitted police to employ at the investigative stage: The end justifies the means. Within an adversary system of criminal justice, governed by due process rules for obtaining evidence, the policeman will thus lie to get at the truth. The contradiction may be surprising, but it may be inevitable in an adversary system of justice where police perceive procedural due process norms and legal requirements as inconsistent obstacles to truth and the meting out of just desserts for the commission of crime.

Testimonial Deception

As I have indicated, it is difficult to prove a causal relationship between permissible investigative and interrogatory deception and testimonial deception. Police freely admit to deceiving suspects and defendants.[8] They do not admit to perjury, much less to the rationalization of perjury. There is evidence, however, of the acceptability of perjury as a means to the end of conviction. The evidence is limited and fragmentary and is certainly not dispositive. However, the evidence does suggest not only that a policeman will perjure himself—no surprise that—but that perjury, like corruption, does not lend itself to "rotten apple" explanations.[9] Perjury, I would suggest, like corruption, is systematic, and for much the same sort of reason

—police know that other police are on the take, and police know that other police are perjuring themselves. The following two items of evidence suggest that perjury represents a subcultural norm rather than an individual aberration.

Scholarly evidence of testimonial lying was revealed in a study conducted by Columbia law students in which they analyzed the effect of *Mapp* v. *Ohio*[10] on police practices in New York City. In *Mapp*, the Supreme Court held that the federal exclusionary rule in search and seizure cases was binding on the states. New York was the only large state that had not previously adopted the exclusionary rule as a matter of state law. (The exclusionary rule, of course, suppresses at trial evidence that was illegally obtained—usually in violation of the Fourth Amendment.) The students analyzed the evidentiary grounds for arrest and subsequent disposition of misdemeanor narcotics cases before and after the *Mapp* decision. Based on officers' accounts of the evidence for the arrest (see Table 1) the student authors concluded that

uniform police have been fabricating grounds of arrest in narcotics cases in order to circumvent the requirements of *Mapp*. Without knowledge of the results of this study, the two Criminal Courts judges and the two Assistant District Attorneys interviewed

doubted that a substantial reform of police practices had occurred since *Mapp*. Rather, they believe that police officers are fabricating evidence to avoid *Mapp*.[11]

Such lies came to be known as "dropsy" testimony since the police testified that those charged with drug possession were now dropping illicit drugs on the ground rather than keeping them where they were. Prior to *Mapp*, evidence obtained from unlawful searches of the person was admissible, even when illegally obtained. New York State was governed by the famous 1926 dictum of Judge Cardozo, who, while he was on the bench of the New York Court of Appeals, had dismissed the federal rule with the observation that under it "the criminal is to go free because the constable had blundered."[12] Obviously, the New York police had not been blundering prior to *Mapp*. Instead, they simply and routinely ignored the requirements of the Fourth Amendment.

In a more popular account, Robert Daley's fascinating *Prince of the City*, the former New York Deputy Police Commissioner writes of a surveillance showing that, on the one hand, defendants were guilty of hijacking television sets and that, on the other, cops were stealing some of the hijacked sets. The evidence was obtained through a legal wiretap. The detectives

Table 1 New York City Police Officers' Allegations Regarding Discovery of Evidence in Misdemeanor Narcotics Offenses, 1960–62

| | Percent of Arrests | | |
| How Evidence Found | Six-month period | | |
	Before Mapp	After Mapp	Difference
I. Narcotics Bureau			
(a) Hidden on person	35	3	−32
(b) Dropped or thrown to ground	17	43	+26
II. Uniform			
(a) Hidden on person	31	9	−22
(b) Dropped or thrown to ground	14	21	+ 7
III. Plainclothes			
(a) Hidden on person	24	4	−20
(b) Dropped or thrown to ground	11	17	+ 6

Original source: Comment, "Effect of *Mapp* v. *Ohio* on Police Search and Seizure Practices in Narcotics Cases," *Col. J. Law & Social Problems* 4 (1968): 94.

erased that part of the tape proving that the precinct cops had stolen some of the sets. Daley writes, "Tomorrow they would deny the erasure under oath.... It was the type of perjury that detectives...committed all the time in the interest of putting bad people in jail."[13]

The point here is not whether to deplore the police violations of the Fourth Amendment or the lying of police in the testimonial context; rather, it is to understand how police who engage in it themselves come to justify it, so that moral prescriptions might be given a better chance of being persuasive to police who do not find them compelling in practice.

The policeman lies because lying becomes a routine way of managing legal impediments—whether to protect fellow officers or to compensate for what he views as limitations the courts have placed on his capacity to deal with criminals. He lies because he is skeptical of a system that suppresses truth in the interest of the criminal. Moreover, the law permits the policeman to lie at the investigative stage, when he is not entirely convinced that the suspect is a criminal, but forbids lying about procedures at the testimonial stage, when the policeman is certain of the guilt of the accused. Thus, the policeman characteristically measures the short-term disutility of the act of suppressing evidence, not the long-term utility of due process of law for protecting and enhancing the dignity of the citizen who is being investigated by the state.

I quote at this point from a passage in *Justice without Trial* which recent discussions with police persuade me is still essentially valid:

> The policeman...operates as one whose aim is to legitimize the evidence pertaining to the case, rather than as a jurist whose goal is to analyze the sufficiency of the evidence based on case law.... The policeman respects the necessity for "complying" with the arrest laws. His "compliance," however, may take the form of post hoc manipulation of the facts rather than before-the-fact behavior. Again, this generalization does not apply in all cases. Where the policeman feels capable of literal compliance (as in the conditions

provided by the "big case"), he does comply. But when he sees the case law as a hindrance to his primary task of apprehending criminals, he usually attempts to construct the appearance of compliance, rather than allow the offender to escape apprehension.[14]

As I stated earlier, I am not aware of an ethical theory that would condone perjured testimony. Bok's standards for justifying deception would provide a useful guideline here, because the lying policeman would be required to justify courtroom perjury before a relevant public. This is precisely the sort of test I think Bok had in mind. Although police might justify perjury to each other over drinks after work or in the corridors of the locker room, I can scarcely imagine any policeman willing to justify such conduct in a public setting—unless he was perhaps on a television talk show, wearing a mask and wig. But any hesitation on the part of an officer to testify could be caused by fear of a perjury charge, not by moral scruples about lying in courtroom situations where criminals might go free.

Investigative Deception

Let us examine more closely the rationale for lying at the investigative stage. Here, police are permitted by the courts to engage in trickery and deception and are trained to do so by the police organization. One might properly conclude, from examining police practices that have been subjected to the highest appellate review, that the police are authoritatively encouraged to lie.[15]

Detectives, for example, are trained to use informers or to act themselves as informers or agents provocateurs when the criminal activity under investigation involves possession or sale of contraband. The contraband itself does not much matter. From an enforcement perspective, the problems involved in apprehending those who sell counterfeit money are almost identical to those involved in trapping dealers of illegal drugs. Years ago, when I studied a vice squad intensively, the squad was asked to help the United States Secret Service in apprehending a counterfeiting ring. They were asked because vice squads are especially experienced in law enforcement practices involving use of informants, deception, security of information, and, most generally, the apprehension of offenders whose criminality is proven by the possession for sale of illegal materials. A similar point can be made with respect to burglary enforcement. Victims (or police) rarely observe burglars in action. In fact, burglars are usually apprehended when detectives are able to employ a decoy or an informer who tells them that so-and-so is in possession of stolen goods.

The line between acceptable and unacceptable deception in such enforcement patterns is the line between so-called entrapment and acceptable police conduct. How does the law presently define entrapment? From my reading, the definition is hazy, murky, unclear. Two approaches are employed in legal writing about entrapment. One, the subjective approach, focuses upon the background, character, and intention of the defendant. Was he or she the sort of person who would have been predisposed to have committed the crime, even without the participation of the government official or agent? The objective test, by contrast, sets its sights on the nature of governmental participation. Justice Frankfurter, concurring in *Sherman v. United States,* presented the objective test as follows: "The crucial question, not easy to answer, to which the court must direct itself is whether the police conduct revealed in the particular case falls below standards to which common feelings respond, for the proper use of governmental power."[16] More recently, in *United States v. Russell,* Justice Rehnquist wrote the majority opinion affirming the prevailing rule—the subjective test—in a case where an undercover agent for the Federal Bureau of Narcotics and Dangerous Drugs told the suspect that he represented an organization that was interested in controlling the manufacture and distribution of methamphetamine.[17] The narcotics agent offered to supply Russell with a chemical that was an essential, hard-to-find ingredient in the manufacture of methamphetamine in return for half the drug produced. The agent told Russell that he had to be shown a sample of the drug in the laboratory where it was being produced before he would go through with the deal.

Russell showed him the laboratory and told the agent he and others had been making the drug for quite some time. The agent left and returned to the laboratory with the necessary chemical and watched while the suspects produced the drug. The narcotics agent did not actively participate in the manufacturing of the drug, but he was courteous and helpful to those who did. When a suspect dropped some aluminum foil on the floor, it was testified, the narcotics agent picked it up and put it into the cooker.

The majority of the court held that Russell was not "entrapped" because he had been an active participant in an illegal drug manufacturing enterprise that began before the government agent appeared on the scene and continued after the government agent left the scene. Russell was not an "unwary innocent," but an "unwary criminal." The subjective test, in short, permits police to engage in deceptive practices provided that the deception catches a wolf rather than a lamb.[18]

The objective test, focusing on the activities of the government, seems to suggest a more high-minded vision of the limits of police deception. By a high-minded vision, I mean to suggest one which conceives of significant limitations on police conduct in the interest of maintaining a civilized or moral constabulary. For example, a civilized police should not be permitted to torture a suspect in order to obtain a confession, even if it should turn out that the tortured party was an unwary criminal, that is, even if torture should produce the truth.[19] Nor, to cite a real case, would a civilized police be permitted to pump the stomach of a suspected narcotics dealer to show that pills that he had just swallowed contained morphine, even if that is exactly what the pills did contain.[20]

But the objective test may lose its objectivity when it relies on such concepts as "common feelings" or the "conscience of the community."[21] Although these concepts seem to imply enduring qualities or values, one could also argue that such concepts are variables. "Common feelings" might allow for far more latitude in police practices in a "high fear of crime" period than in a "low fear" period. Some might argue that values should be tested in the crucible of experience, and that flexibility is itself a virtue. The trouble is that one person's flexibility may be interpreted as another's lack of principle.

Moreover, "common feelings" may not be informative when we consider particular examples. I am reminded of a passage in Arthur Schlesinger's biography of Robert Kennedy, where Schlesinger tries to resolve the issue of whether Kennedy really knew about FBI wiretapping when he was Attorney General. Schlesinger relates a conversation between J. Edgar Hoover and Kennedy, where Hoover tells Kennedy that he had the situation "covered."[22] According to Schlesinger, Hoover felt that he had thus informed Kennedy of the wiretap, while Kennedy took the term "cover" to mean that a secret government informant had worked his way into the suspect's entourage.

Assuming for the purposes of argument that Kennedy did not know about the wiretapping, by what principle is a wiretap or bug to be considered less morally acceptable than a secret informant?[23] A wiretap or bug clearly invades expectations of privacy. But wiretaps and bugs enjoy two advantages over secret informants. First, the evidence they report as to what the defendant did or did not say is trustworthy. Second, and perhaps more important, a bug cannot encourage lawbreaking: It can neither advocate nor condone such conduct. It is not clear to me how an objective standard would distinguish between the two, and I find myself genuinely puzzled as to why informants are usually thought to be morally acceptable, while bugs are not. Indeed, an argument could be made that when the government attempts to modify dispositions (by employing secret informants who worm their way into the confidence of suspects, for example), that this is more violative of human dignity than the involuntary extraction of evidence from the body, even through stomach pumping. At least one whose stomach is being pumped can identify his adversary, while the secret informant "messes with the mind," as it were.

In any event, for the purpose of my more general argument it is enough to acknowledge that both legal tests of entrapment—objective and subjective—permit police to employ an enormous amount of routine deception, although the prevailing subjective test permits even more. Even in the dissenting opinion in *Russell*, Justice Stewart, supporting the objective test, writes that "the government's use of undercover activity, strategy, or deception is [not] necessarily unlawful. Indeed, many crimes, especially so-called victimless crimes, could not otherwise be detected."[24] In short, police are routinely permitted and advised to employ deceptive techniques and strategies in the investigative process. The police may occasionally trap a lamb, but the courts tacitly acknowledge that in the real world police deal mostly with wolves—and in the eyes of the courts a wolf might be wearing the clothing of either a congressman or a cocaine dealer.

Judicial permissiveness regarding investigative deception suggests how difficult it would be to defend a Kantian imperative against lying even in the abstract and how impossible it would be for any such defense to be accepted by courts, police, and the public. I shall conclude this discussion of investigative deception by suggesting a hypothesis: Judicial acceptance of deception in the investigation process enhances moral acceptance of deception by detectives in the interrogatory and testimonial stages of criminal investigation, and thus increases the probability of its occurrence.

This hypothesis does not suggest that every detective who deceives also perjures himself. It does suggest that deception in one context increases the probability of deception in the other. This hypothesis cannot be tested and therefore may not hold. It cannot be tested, because a true test would require an experimental design where we could manipulate the independent variable (authoritative permission to employ investigative trickery) and measure the dependent variable (courtroom perjury by police). Since we can neither manipulate the former nor measure the latter, the hypothesis, however plausible, must remain speculative.

Interrogatory Deception

In the remainder of this paper, I shall assume that the previously mentioned hypothesis is plausible and organize discussion around it. Thus, let us turn our attention to deception and interrogation—and here I shall confine my remarks to in-custody interrogation, although I recognize that the line between *custody* and *pre-custody* is unclear, and that the one between *conversation* and *interrogation* is also unclear. For the present, I simply want to make a historical reference to the in-custody interrogation problem which *Miranda v. Arizona*, decided in 1966, sought to resolve.[25] The holding of *Miranda* has now become so familiar as to be part of American folklore. The case held that the arrested person must be informed of his or her right to remain silent, must be warned that any statement he or she does make may be used as evidence, and must be told that he or she has the right to the presence of an attorney. The accused should also be informed that an attorney will be provided if he or she cannot afford one. The court also held that the government has a "heavy burden" to prove that a waiver of such rights was made voluntarily, knowingly, and intelligently.[26]

The *Miranda* decision was the evolutionary outcome of the Supreme Court's response to the admission, in state and federal courts, of confessions which, in the early part of the century, were based on overt torture, later on covert torture (the third degree), and later still on deception and psychological intimidation. Overt torture is exemplified by the facts in *Brown v. Mississippi*, where black defendants were beaten and whipped until they confessed. By 1936, the Supreme Court could no longer overlook the glaring fact that a confession so elicited was deemed admissible by the Supreme Court of the State of Mississippi.

But punitive in-custody interrogation was, of course, not confined to the South. The 1931 Wickersham Commission reported numerous instances of covert torture in many cities between 1920 and 1930.[27] The chief distinction between covert and overt torture is not in the severity of pain induced, but in its deniability. The Mississippi sheriffs did not deny whipping their black suspects. They were brutal but truthful. By contrast, the third degree classically involved deniable coercion: starving suspects, keeping them awake day and night, confining them in pitch-black, airless rooms, or administering beatings with instruments which left few, if any, marks. For example, a suspect might be hit over the head with a blackjack (though a telephone book would be placed between the blackjack and the head) or he might be hit with a rubber hose.[28]

Other types of in-custody interrogation might evoke forms of torture even more terrifying but also more deniable. Detectives in one police department reportedly hung suspects from their heels outside windows in tall buildings to induce confessions. Others simply required that defendants stand erect and be forbidden use of bathroom facilities. The dramatic impact of the sadism of the third degree[29] has tended to obscure the fact that, in using it, the police necessarily condoned systematic deception of the courts as well as torture of suspects. Thus, not only did the police subculture's norms of the period permit station house physical punishment of those whom the police might have felt deserved it, these norms also condoned wholesale perjury—disregard of the moral authority of the courts and of the oaths taken in them.[30]

Miranda overruled *Crooker v. California*,[31] and *Cicenia v. LaGay*,[32] both of which were cases where the accused asked to see a lawyer after he agreed to be interrogated. In Cicenia's case, not only did he ask to see a lawyer, but his lawyer, who had arrived at the police station, had asked to see his client. *Miranda* might well be interpreted as a case where the Supreme Court was concerned not only with whether a confession was coerced—that had long been a concern of the courts—but whether the right of the accused not to be coerced was being effectuated properly in the context of the adversary system. The dissenters in *Crooker*—Douglas, Warren, Black, and Brennan—took a strong position on the right to counsel at the pretrial stage, arguing:

> The right to have counsel at the pre-trial stage is often necessary to give meaning and protection to the right to be heard at the trial itself. It may also be necessary as a restraint on the coercive power of the police[33].... No matter how well educated, and how well trained in the law an accused may be, he is surely in need of legal advice once he is arrested for an offense that may exact his life[34].... The demands of our civilization expressed in the due process clause require that the accused who wants a counsel should have one at any time after the moment of arrest.[35]

The dissent also wrote that "the third degree flourishes only in secrecy."[36] It is quite clear, I think, that Justices Warren, Douglas, Black, and Brennan (and later Fortas, with whom they were to form a majority in *Miranda*) simply did not trust police to behave noncoercively when they had a suspect in custody; only counsel, they believed, would constrain police.

Ironically, compelling evidence for the view that police custody is inherently coercive was elicited from a 1962 book by professional police interrogators Fred E. Inbau and John E. Reid, entitled *Criminal Interrogation and Confessions*.[37] This book was a revision and enlargement of the second half of Inbau and Reid's earlier book, *Lie Detection and Criminal Investigation*.[38] The book is replete with suggestions for coercive and deceptive methods of interrogation, which the authors clearly considered necessary and proper for police conducting an investigation. Inbau and Reid were not advocates of the third degree. On the contrary, their book, seen in historical context, was a reformist document, representing a kind of dialectical synthesis between the polarities of third degree violence and civil liberties for protection of human dignity. Such a synthesis would have been progressive in the 1930s.

The benchmark test employed by Inbau and Reid was: "Although both 'fair' and 'unfair' interrogation practices are permissible, nothing shall be done or said to the subject that will be apt to make an innocent person confess."[39] A more philosophically based and sophisticated version of the Inbau and Reid position (and a more modern one) is Joseph Grano's "mental freedom" test of voluntariness. It is an objective test, asking "whether a person of ordinary firmness, innocent or guilty, having the defendant's age, physical condition, and relevant mental abnormalities (but not otherwise having the defendant's personality traits, temperament, intelligence, or social background), and strongly preferring not to confess, would find the interrogation pressures overbearing."[40] What might these pressures be?

It is worthwhile, I think, to quote substantially from the *Miranda* decision itself, partly to understand the impact Inbau and Reid's books had on the courts, and partly to understand what sorts of police trickery might or might not be regarded as coercive. Justice Warren wrote:

> The officers are told by the manuals that the principal psychological factor contributing to a successful interrogation is privacy—being alone with the person under interrogation." The efficacy of this tactic has been explained as follows:
>
> > If at all practicable, the interrogation should take place in the investigator's office or at least in a room of his own choice. The subject should be deprived of every psychological advantage. In his own home he may be confident, indignant, or recalcitrant. He is more keenly aware of his rights and more reluctant to tell of his indiscretions or criminal behavior within the walls of his home. Moreover his family and other friends are nearby, their presence lending moral support. In his office, the investigator possesses all the advantages. The atmosphere suggests the invincibility of the forces of the law.
>
> To highlight the isolation and unfamiliar surroundings, the manuals instruct the police to display an air of confidence in the

suspect's guilt and from outward appearance to maintain only an interest in confirming certain details. The guilt of the subject is to be posted as a fact. The interrogator should direct his comments toward the reasons why the subject committed the act, rather than court failure by asking the subject whether he did it. Like other men, perhaps the subject has had a bad family life, had an unhappy childhood, had too much to drink, had an unrequited desire for women. The officers are instructed to minimize the moral seriousness of the offense, to cast blame on the victim or on society. These tactics are designed to put the subject in a psychological state where his story is but an elaboration of what the police purport to know already—that he is guilty. Explanations to the contrary are dismissed and discouraged.

The texts thus stress that the major qualities an interrogator should possess are patience and perseverance.[41]

The manuals also suggest that suspects be offered legal excuses for their actions, says the *Miranda* Court. The interrogator is instructed to tell the suspect something like:

> Joe, you probably didn't go out looking for this fellow with the purpose of shooting him. My guess is, however, that you expected something from him and that's why you carried a gun—for your own protection. You knew him for what he was, no good. Then when you met him he probably started using foul, abusing language and he gave some indication that he was about to pull a gun on you, and that's when you had to act to save your own life. That's about it, isn't it, Joe?[42]

If the suspect does not respond to the understanding interrogator, notes the Court, another investigator is brought in—Mutt, the tough guy who plays against Jeff's nice guy role.

> In this technique, two agents are employed. Mutt, the relentless investigator, who knows the subject is guilty and is not going to waste any time. He's sent a dozen men away for this crime and he's going to send the subject away for the full term. Jeff, on the other hand, is

obviously a kindhearted man. He has a family himself. He has a brother who was involved in a little scrape like this. He disapproves of Mutt and his tactics and will arrange to get him off the case if the subject will cooperate. He can't hold Mutt off for very long. The subject would be wise to make a quick decision. The technique is applied by having both investigators present while Mutt acts out his role. Jeff may stand by quietly and demur at some of Mutt's tactics. When Jeff makes his plea for cooperation, Mutt is not present.[43]

Although *Miranda* is generally interpreted as focusing on the inherently coercive aspects of custodial interrogation, it should be noted that interrogatory tactics employ both deception and coercion. It is questionable whether custodial interrogation would be effective without deception. Indeed, deception appears to serve as custodial interrogation's functional alternative to physical coercion. Hence, deception and the inherent coercion of custody are inescapably related in modern interrogation.

Miranda generated enormous controversy. Studies were conducted by scholars and law reviews to try to demonstrate the impact of *Miranda*.[44] (It would be interesting to conduct a new round of studies to see if the findings of the older ones still hold.) Basically, the studies came to much the same conclusion: The *Miranda* warning did not appreciably reduce the amount of talking that a suspect would do, nor did *Miranda* significantly help suspects in making free and informed choices about whether to talk. A nice statement of how *Miranda* warnings could be rendered ineffectual, written by an author of the *Yale Law Journal*'s study of *Miranda*'s impact, appeared in the *Yale Alumni Magazine* in 1968.

> Even when detectives informed suspects of their rights without undercutting devices, the advice was often defused by implying that the suspect had better not exercise his rights, or by delivering the statement in a formalized, bureaucratic tone to indicate that the remarks were simply a routine, meaning-

less legalism. Instinctively, perhaps, detectives tended to create a sense of unreality about the *Miranda* warnings by bringing the flow of conversation to a halt with the statement, "...and now I am going to inform you of your rights." Afterwards, they would solemnly intone: "Now you have been warned of your rights," then immediately shift into a conversational tone to ask, "Now would you like to tell me what happened?" By and large the detectives regarded advising the suspect of his rights as an artificial imposition on the natural flow of the interrogation.[45]

Miranda also generated a substantial law review literature—some might say an industry—because the United States Supreme Court has been unwilling to set the only standard that would eliminate practically all the Miranda problems. That standard would be: Once the *Miranda* warnings are given, the accused is also given a lawyer who explains the implications of the warning.[46]

The privilege against self-incrimination existed before *Miranda*. The *Miranda* ruling essentially argues that, as part of due process, the government should not be permitted to make its case on the basis of the defendant's ignorance. Defendants must be informed of their rights. If we accept *Miranda* and take it seriously, we also must acknowledge that suspects do not—across the board—possess the legal acumen to waive their *Miranda* rights. In the late 1960s, at least, persons of "ordinary firmness" interpreted—or misinterpreted—their *Miranda* rights in such a way so as not to exercise them. From the perspective of those who would like to see *Miranda* overturned, that might not be a problem. But it also suggests that the average suspect, however "ordinarily firm," is not legally competent.

Those who are legally competent (lawyers) will routinely advise suspects to maintain silence. The continuing debate over *Miranda* reflects an ambivalence over enforcing the rule that the values expressed by the *Miranda* majority seem to call for: There can be no confession without a genuinely voluntary and knowledge-

able waiver, exercised after consultation with a lawyer. The *Crooker* minority was unquestionably correct in its assessment that people cannot fully understand the implications of legal warnings—offered, after all, in the rather coercive situation of arrest—without legal consultation. We apparently still prefer to offer the government an edge based on the defendant's ignorance. Knowledgeable defendants will remain silent. The ignorant will talk.

Grano's "ordinary firmness" test necessarily implies overruling *Miranda*. His test, which is oriented to crime control, would surely result in far more admissible evidence than a genuinely voluntary, lawyer-advised, waiver would. The present *Miranda* rule lies somewhere in between. Perhaps we tolerate *Miranda* because, on the whole, we have learned that it does not matter very much. Pressures of in-custody interrogation are such that, apparently, most suspects will talk despite the *Miranda* warning. In any event, most confessions are elicited in cases where there is a victim, where the confession is not the only evidence, and where the suspect is willing to plead guilty to a lesser offense.

Besides, once the suspect begins to talk, the very techniques the court sought to avoid are probably permissible. When a policeman says, in the kindliest of tones, "Look Joe, it will be better for you to confess," he is of course essentially deceiving the suspect into believing that he is the suspect's friend rather than his adversary.

In a recent article, Welsh S. White has argued that certain interrogation tactics are, nevertheless, likely to risk depriving the suspect of his constitutional rights.[47] Accordingly, White believes that the court should prohibit, via per se exclusions, "police conduct that is likely to render a resulting confession involuntary or to undermine the effect of required *Miranda* warnings or a suspect's independent right to an attorney."[48] What would some of these prohibitions be? One would be against deceiving a suspect about whether an interrogation was taking place, as in *Massiah v. United States*.[49] There, after indictment, one confederate, Colson, agreed to cooperate with the government, and deceptively interrogated his accomplice, Massiah. The resulting incriminatory statements were held inadmissible as a violation of the Sixth Amendment right to counsel. White argues that this right should be triggered at the point of arrest.

He also argues that statements elicited from "jail plants" should be prohibited, on grounds that someone who is experiencing the pressures of confinement is more likely to confide in a police agent.[50] Slightly different forms of trickery, which White also advocates prohibiting, are police misrepresentations of the seriousness of the offense or police use of threats or promises for confessing.

Finally, White argues for prohibition of "father figure" trickery, wherein a police officer falsely acts like a friend or counselor rather than an adversary. White offers as one example the famous Connecticut murder case, *State v. Reilly*, where the principal interrogating officer manipulated an eighteen-year-old into falsely confessing that he murdered his mother.[51] White treats the case primarily as an example of the officer pretending to be a father figure. White's discussion, however, omits entirely what two books about the case point to as the real culprit—the use of the polygraph during the interrogation of Reilly, who confessed after being told by the "father figure" that a machine, which could read his mind, had indicated that he actually was the murderer.[52]

The Polygraph as a Deceptive Device

Recall that Inbau and Reid were not only advocates of deceptive interrogation. They were also proponents and developers of polygraph examination techniques. The polygraph is an instrument which measures changes in blood pressure, pulse, respiration, and perspiration. Detection of lies via the examination of physical change is actually a throwback to early forms of trial by ordeal. There are reports of a deception test used by Hindus based on the observation that fear may inhibit the secretion of saliva.[53] To test

credibility, an accused was given rice to chew. If he could spit it out, he was considered innocent; but if it stuck to his gums, he was judged guilty. Until 1895, however, nobody had ever used a measuring device to detect deception. In that year, the Italian criminologist Cesare Lombroso used a combination of blood pressure and pulse readings to investigate crime. Before the First World War, others experimented with blood pressure and respiratory recordings. John A. Larson, perhaps the most scholarly of the Chicago-Berkeley group which sought to advance the "science" of lie detection, built an instrument in 1921 which he called a "polygraph." It combined all three measures—blood pressure, pulse, and respiration. His junior collaborator, Leonard Keeler, added galvanic skin response to the list. Contemporary lie detector machines basically employ all these measures, although there are some other technical improvements as well. For example, integrated circuits and other components reduce the margin of error in measurement.

According to a survey conducted by the *New York Times* in 1980, the lie detector is widely used by law enforcement groups:

> The Federal Bureau of Investigation conducted 1900 polygraph examinations in 1979, an increase of about 800 from 1978. The number of polygraph examinations administered by the Army, Navy, Marines and Air Force increased by 18 percent in two years, from 5710 to 6751. Polygraphs are finding a steadily growing market among state and local law enforcement agencies, litigants in civil cases and private retailers, who use the device to screen job applicants and combat pilferage.[54]

It is understandable but distressing that the use of the polygraph should be increasing. It is distressing because the validity of polygraph results is flawed by fundamental theoretical problems, not by technical ones. The increase in use is understandable, because even though the polygraph is not a dispositive truth-finding device, it is nevertheless an effective instrument of social control.

In the past, one problem of polygraph examination was imprecision of measurement. Thus, the machine recorded blood pressure, but there was a question as to whether it recorded blood pressure accurately. There is no doubt that imprecision of measurement was a problem in the past, but the problems with the lie detection process itself were far more fundamental and serious. These problems stem from the inadequacy of the theory behind lie detection. That theory involves the following premises: The act of lying leads to conscious conflict; conflict induces fear or anxiety; and these emotions are accompanied by measurable and interpretable physiological changes.[55]

But the assumptions of the theory are questionable. The act of lying does not always lead to conscious conflict. Some witnesses believe their own stories, even when they are false. Even when witnesses know they are lying, they may not experience much fear. Or, innocent witnesses may experience fear and anxiety just by being asked threatening questions. All this depends on witnesses' individual personalities, social backgrounds, what they are testifying to, and to whom they are testifying. Polygraph examiners acknowledge that subjects must "believe in" the lie detector.

Even if witnesses do experience fear and anxiety, these emotions may not consistently be expressed as changes in bodily response. If all bodily response rose and fell exactly with emotional states, the responses would have a precise relationship to each other. But that is not the case. Bodily responses do not vary regularly, either with each other or with emotional states. If they did, only a unigraph, not a polygraph, would be required. Four imprecise measures are not more accurate than one precise measure.

Since the relations among lying, conflict, emotion, and bodily responses are so fuzzy, the accuracy of the lie detector is not comparable to that of, say, blood tests or X rays. It is unlikely that a dozen lie detector examiners would consistently reach the same conclusions regarding truth or falsity if they depended only on the squiggles produced by a polygraph.

So why is the use of lie detectors sharply increasing? The fact that the polygraph is not reliable does not mean it is ineffective as a social control instrument. Crime suspects may confess when questioned by a skilled interrogator. When a suspect is strapped into what he or she would view as a technologically foolproof "lie detector," the coercive power of the interrogator is heightened. The interrogator is not an adversary, but an objective scientific observer. Even those suspicious of father figures may embrace the trappings of science.

Job applicants, in particular, are effectively "screened" with a lie detector. Consider the following lines of questioning. First, softballs: Is your name John Jones? Are you thirty-six years old? Were you born in New York City? Then, hardballs: Have you ever done anything you are ashamed of? Have you ever stolen anything? Have you ever known anyone who has stolen anything? Who? Have you ever engaged in homosexual acts? And so forth. This sort of questioning may well produce results.

There are thus two quite different empirical issues regarding the polygraph. Is it highly accurate, like X rays and blood tests? The answer is no. Is it effective in eliciting information from subjects who believe in it? The answer is yes. Whether the lie detector ought to be used by police—or by employers—is ultimately an ethical question. Should we allow deceptive, intrusive. yet nonviolent methods of interrogation in various institutions of a free society? Different people will have different answers to that question. But at least we should ask the right questions when considering the role of the so-called lie detector in American society.

The ethical problem is even more complicated because some who employ the lie detector actually believe that it detects lies, while others use it primarily as a technique of psychological intimidation. The police sergeant who told Peter Reilly that "this machine will read your mind" and then falsely persuaded Reilly that he had killed his own mother, thus eliciting from Reilly a critical but untrue confession, may himself have believed that the polygraph detects lies.

Did the sergeant also believe that the lie detector reads the mind?

The lie detector is symbolically scientific, and its technologically sophisticated trappings commend it to the most thoughtful and professional segments of the policing community. Thus, police use the polygraph because they believe in it. Yet the technique's results can convict innocent people, where old-fashioned techniques of deception would not. An instance of this, the case of F. B. Fay, is reported by psychophysiologist David T. Lykken.[56] Fay was asked by a police polygraphist in Toledo in 1978, "Did you kill Fred?" and "Before age twenty-four did you ever think about doing anyone bodily harm to get revenge?" It was assumed that, if Fay were innocent of Fred's murder, the second or "control" question would frighten Fay more, and that this would, in turn, "dampen" his autonomic reaction to the first or "relevant" question. Unfortunately for Fay, he responded more strongly to the "relevant" questions. The examiner, therefore, testified that Fay's denials were deceptive, and he was found guilty of murder and sentenced to prison for life. In October 1980, the actual killers were identified, and Fay was released after serving two and a half years.

In sum, then, we have to educate the law enforcement community as to the realistic limits of the polygraph. This will be difficult, partly because there is, as I have noted here, considerable controversy over use of the polygraph, and partly because, for the reasons I have already suggested, it is a uniquely valuable tool of interrogation. I myself have no hesitancy in stating where I stand on use of the instrument. I would argue against its use—first, because the false claims for its accuracy permit the highest degree of nonviolent coercion, and second, because cool nonreactors (sociopaths, skilled con men, the mildly self-drugged) can beat the test. Finally, if one of the important reasons for the *Miranda* rule is the inherent coerciveness of police interrogation, then how much more coercive is an interrogation by a questioner who is armed with a deceptively scientific instrument that can "read the mind"?

Conclusion

I have tried in this article to offer several observations about deception in the detecting process. First, I have suggested that detecting is a process moving from investigation, often through interrogation, to testimony. Police are offered considerable latitude by the courts during the investigation stage. This latitude to deceive, I have argued, carries over into the interrogation and testimonial stages as a subculturally supported norm. I have suggested that there is an underlying reason for this. When detectives deceive suspects in the course of criminal investigations or interrogations, they typically are not seeking to promote their own self-interest (as a detective would if he had lied about accepting bribes). On the contrary, the sort of deception employed to trap a narcotics dealer or dealer in stolen goods, or to elicit a confession from a murderer or rapist, is used for the public interest. The detective—and here I am speaking of the professional detective who explicitly condemns the use of physical violence but accepts employing psychological intimidation during interrogation—is also interested in eliciting truth. This results, I have suggested, in a paradox. The end of truth justifies for the modern detective the means of lying. Deception usually occurs in the interest of obtaining truth.

Both the detective and the civil libertarian, I have suggested, employ a utilitarian calculus. In so doing, each reveals the obvious limitations of such a calculus for resolving major issues of public policy. The detective measures the costs of the act of lying against the benefits to the crime victim and the general public. The civil libertarian is also concerned with the public interest but measures it in terms of rules protecting the long-range interests of all citizens in a system of governance, as opposed to the shorter range interests of punishing perpetrators.

The law reflects the tension between due process and crime control imperatives by establishing different—and inconsistent—standards for investigation and interrogation. At the investigative stage, the law's subjective test of entrapment comes perilously close to tests like Inbau and Reid's "innocent person" or Grano's more sophisticated "mental freedom" test: Both permit deceptive and coercive interrogation against wolves but not lambs.

Is there a moral justification for distinguishing between governmental deception at the investigative stage and at the interrogation stage? One could approach this issue by asking: What would be the rule of law regarding police deception in a moral society? It seems clear that in a moral society, authorities such as police would not be permitted to employ tactics that are generally regarded as immoral against those suspected, or accused, of a crime.

Indeed, we already have such rules: Police are not permitted to coerce a suspect physically. The police may, however, subject suspects to psychological coercion provided they consent to be interrogated. Unreliability is one reason we prohibit the admission of evidence obtained from physically coerced confessions. But we could have a rule distinguishing between a pure mea culpa confession and one which produces material evidence, such as a gun or a body. We do not have such rules partly because we deplore physically coercive tactics even when used against the guilty; we also do not have them because we fear that physical coercion would become a routine aspect of police interrogation. Physical coercion is clearly indistinguishable from deceit and trickery, and few of us would, really, I suspect, choose to be smashed in the face with a rifle butt, or hung from a high window, rather than be betrayed by a friend who is actually and secretly a police informant gathering incriminating evidence.

The more difficult question is whether deception—which we accept at the investigative stage—is as morally offensive as psychological coercion. Recall that earlier I discussed the distinction between gathering information by a secret informant and gathering it by electronic eavesdropping. I suggested there that I could not see any principle by which one was, on balance, worse than the other, even though we can perceive different sorts of objections to each. The wiretap or

bug clearly invades privacy, while the secret informant invades both privacy—in some ways more, in some ways less, than electronic eavesdropping—and personality. Not only is the secret informant privy to actions and conversations one would never consent to have had overheard; the secret informant also modifies personality by deliberately attempting to impair judgment. The wiretap is, in social science jargon, an "unobtrusive measurer." By contrast, the informant necessarily produces a reaction—speech, behavior—on the part of the observed, and may prove influential in determining that reaction.

If there is a distinction between investigative and interrogatory trickery and deceit, it has to be based on situational ethics, the morality of practical necessity. Practically speaking, it is impossible to enforce consensual crime statutes—bribery, drug dealing, prostitution—without employing deception. This need for deception may not be as clear at the interrogation stage. Often, evidence can be produced independently of confessions, and occasionally, false confessions are elicited.

But confessions may also be a practical necessity in many cases, particularly when dealing with the most serious sorts of criminals, such as murderers, rapists, and kidnappers. Miranda himself, it may be recalled, had confessed to the forcible kidnapping and rape of a nineteen-year-old woman. Why should situational ethics permit lying to a drug dealer but forbid in-custody conversational questioning of a forcible rapist? That question can be answered on historical and constitutional grounds, but it is hard to see how to make consistent common sense out of it.

I cannot here reconcile such inconsistencies, nor am I writing to lobby the Supreme Court. But I would like to conclude by suggesting that apparent inconsistency makes law look more like a game than a rational system for enforcing justice. Because of this appearance of inconsistency, police are not likely to take the stated rules of the game seriously and are encouraged to operate by their own codes, including those which affirm the necessity for lying wherever it seems justified by the ends.

NOTES

1. See generally, Welsh S. White, "Police Trickery in Inducing Confessions," *U. Pa L. Rev.* 127 (1979):581-629; Welsh S. White, "Interrogation without Questions: Rhode Island v. Innis and United States v. Henry," *Mich L. Rev.* 78 (1980):1209-51.

2. Sissela Bok, *Lying: Moral Choice in Public and Private Life* (New York: Pantheon, 1978).

3. See, for example, the discussion in Chapter VII, "Justification," of the group decision to deceive the public. Bok says it is based on the shared belief that the group's norms are good and that any means used to achieve group ends would also therefore be good (Bok, *Lying*, p. 97). See also the discussion of unmarked police cars as justifiable deception because the practice is publicized, while entrapment is not deemed justifiable unless the public agrees this is proper police behavior (Bok, *Lying*, pp. 98-99).

4. See, generally, Cory Marx, "Undercover Cops: Creative Policing or Constitutional Threat?" *Civ. Libs. Rev.* 4 (July/August 1977):34-44.

5. United States v. Ressler, 536 F. 2d 208 (1976), and list of cases cited in the body of that opinion.

6. Franks v. Delaware, 98 S. Ct. 2674 (1979).

7. As to "code of honor" regarding deception, see Lawrence W. Sherman, *Scandal and Reform: Controlling Police Corruption* (Berkeley and Los Angeles: University of California, 1978), pp. 46-67. As to existence of police subculture, see Ellwyn R. Stoddard, "A Group Approach to Blue-Coat Crime," in *Police Corruption: A Sociological Perspective*, ed. Lawrence W. Sherman (Garden City, N.J.: Doubleday, Anchor Books, 1974), pp. 277-304.

8. Jerome Skolnick, *Justice without Trial*, 2nd ed. (New York: Wiley & Sons, 1975), p. 177.

9. *The Knapp Commission Report*, City of New York Commission to Investigate Allegations of Police Corruption and the City's Anti-Corruption Procedures (New York, 1972), discussed in Sherman, *Scandal and Reform*, p. 160.

10. Mapp v. Ohio, 367 U.S. 643 (1961).

11. Quoted and discussed in Dallin Oaks, "Studying the Exclusionary Rule in Search and Seizure." *U. Chi. L. Rev.* 37 (1970):665-757.

12. People v. Defore, 242 N.Y. 13 (1926).

13. Robert Daley, *Prince of the City: The True Story of a Cop Who Knew Too Much* (Boston: Houghton Mifflin Co., 1978), p. 73.

14. Skolnick, *Justice*, pp. 214-215.

15. For a discussion of institutional support for trying to cover up misuse of force charges, see Paul Chevigny, *Police Power* (New York: Pantheon, 1969), p. 139. For case law and discussion of trickery and deception at the investigative stage, see Yale Kamisar, *Police Interrogation and Confessions* (Ann Arbor: University of Michigan Press, 1980).

16. Sherman v. United States, 356 U.S. 369 (1958).

17. United States v. Russell, 411 U.S. 423 (1973).

18. Welsh S. White, "Police Trickery."

19. Brown v. Mississippi, 297 U.S. 278 (1936).

20. Rochin v. California, 342 U.S. 165 (1952).

21. Ralph A. Rossum, "Entrapment Defense and the Teaching of Political Responsibility: The Supreme Court as Republican Schoolmaster," *Amer. J. Crim. L.* (1978):287-306.

22. Arthur M. Schlesinger, Jr., *Robert Kennedy and His Times* (Boston: Houghton Mifflin, 1978), p. 285.

23. Provisions for issuing a warrant to wiretap are stringent. The rule is that wiretaps may be conducted only after a warrant has been issued. Title III of 18 U.S.C. 2510-20 prescribes a careful procedure for obtaining a warrant to use electronic surveillance, and the federal law preempts state law on this subject. By contrast, an informant paid by the D.E.A., for example, may freely roam about southwestern Florida, working his way into any corner of the drug subculture, without specific judicial authorization. See Stuart Penn, "The Informer," *Wall Street Journal*, 10 May 1982.

24. United States v. Russell, 411 U.S. 423 (1973).

25. Miranda v. Arizona, 384 U.S. 486 (1966).

26. Lego v. Twomey, 404 U.S. 477 (1972) (Voluntariness must be proven by a preponderance of evidence).

27. *Report on Lawlessness in Law Enforcement*, National Commission on Law Observance and Enforcement (Washington, D.C.: United States Government Printing Office, 1931).

28. Ernest J. Hopkins, *Our Lawless Police: A Study of the Unlawful Enforcement of the Law* (1931; reprint ed., New York: Da Capo Press, 1972), pp. 236-63.

29. A list of such tactics is found in the Wickersham Report; see note 27.

30. Modern commentators claim that the most outrageous examples of the third degree tactics are no longer employed in American police departments. See Robert M. Fogelson, *Big City Police* (Cambridge, Mass.: Harvard University Press, 1977), p. 302.

31. Crooker v. California, 357 U.S. 433 (1958).

32. Cicenia v. LaGay, 357 U.S. 504 (1958).

33. Crooker v. California, 357 U.S. 433, 443 (1958).

34. Ibid., p. 446.

35. Ibid., p. 448.

36. Ibid., p. 443.

37. Fred E. Inbau and John E. Reid, *Criminal Interrogation and Confessions* (Baltimore: Williams and Wilkins Co., 1962).

38. Fred E. Inbau and John E. Reid, *Lie Detection*

and Criminal Interrogation. 3rd ed. (Baltimore: Williams and Wilkins Co., 1953).

39. Inbau and Reid, *Criminal Interrogations and Confessions,* p. 208.

40. Joseph Grano, "Voluntariness, Free Will, and the Law of Confessions," *Va. L. Rev.* 65 (1979):906.

41. Miranda v. Arizona, 384 U.S. 436, 449–50 (1966), citing Charles O'Hara *Fundamentals of Criminal Investigation* (Springfield, Ill.: Charles Thomas Publishing Co., 1956), p. 99.

42. Ibid., pp. 451–52, citing Inbau and Reid, *Criminal Interrogation and Confessions,* p. 40.

43. Ibid., p. 452, citing O'Hara, *Fundamentals,* p. 104, and Inbau and Reid, *Criminal Interrogation,* pp. 58–59.

44. Project, "Interrogations in New Haven: The Impact of Miranda," *Yale L.J.* 76 (1967):1519–1648; Richard H. Seeburger and R. Stanton Wettick, Jr., "Miranda in Pittsburgh—A Statistical Study," *U. Pitt. L. Rev.* 29 (1967):1–26; Cyril D. Robinson, "Police and Prosecutor Practices and Attitudes Relating to Interrogation," *Duke L.J.* 1968:425–524.

45. Richard E. Ayers, "Confessions and the Court," *Yale Alumni Magazine* (December, 1968): 18, 20. Cited in Yale Kamisar, Wayne R. LaFaye, and Jerold H. Israel, *Modern Criminal Procedure: Cases, Comments, Questions,* 5th ed. (St. Paul, Minn.: West Publishing Co., 1980), p. 632.

46. John Baldwin and Michael McConville, "Police Interrogation and the Right to See a Solicitor," *Crim. L. Rev.* 1979: 145–52; Welsh S. White, "Police Trickery."

47. Welsh S. White, "Police Trickery," p. 586.

48. Ibid., pp. 599–600.

49. Massiah v. United States, 377 U.S. 201 (1964).

50. United States v. Henry, 100 S.Ct. 2183 (1980).

51. State v. Reilly, No. 5285 (Conn. Super. Ct. Apr. 12, 1974), vacated 32 Conn. Supp. 349, 355 A.2d 324 (Super. Ct. 1976).

52. Donald S. Connery, *Guilty Until Proven Innocent* (New York: G.P. Putnam's Sons, 1977); Joan Barthel, *A Death in Canaan* (New York: E.P. Dutton, 1976).

53. David T. Lykken, *A Tremor in the Blood: Uses and Abuses of the Lie Detector* (New York: McGraw-Hill Book Co., 1981), p. 26.

54. Robert Pear, "As Use of the Polygraph Grows, Suspects and Lawyers Sweat," *New York Times,* 13 July 1980.

55. Jerome Skolnick, "Scientific Theory and Scientific Evidence: An Analysis of Lie Detection," *Yale L.J.* 70 (1961):699.

56. David T. Lykken, "Review: The Art and Science of the Polygraph Technique," *Contemporary Psychology* 26 (1981):480.

Study Questions

1. Skolnick claims that the police subculture sometimes demands "deception of courts, prosecutors, defense attorneys, and defendants." Briefly describe a hypothetical case of deception of each of these parties and comment on the moral justification, or lack of it, in each case.

2. Explain the distinction between legal guilt and factual guilt. What does this distinction have to do with a police officer lying in court? Should police officers lie in court when they see that the adversarial system will fail to get "the bad guys"? Why? Defend your position.

3. Explain Bok's standard of justifying deception before a relevant public using police perjury as an example. Does Skolnick think that police perjury is ever justified? How does Skolnick think police officers come to justify giving perjured testimony?

4. What is the moral status of investigative deception in Skolnick's view? Do you agree? Why? Defend your position. What connection does Skolnick see between judicial tolerance of investigative deception and other forms of police lying?

5. Is police interrogation inherently coercive, in your view? Should police be permitted to use "high tech" behavioral techniques of interrogation? Why? Defend your position.

6. What is your personal view of the Fifth Amendment right against self-incrimination and supporting case law such as *Miranda*? Does Skolnick agree with you?

Police Lies and Perjury: A Motivation-Based Taxonomy

THOMAS BARKER AND DAVID L. CARTER

LYING AND OTHER DECEPTIVE PRACTICES are an integral part of the police officer's working environment. At first blush, one's reaction to this statement might be rather forthright. Police officers should not lie. *If you can't trust your local police, who can you trust?* However, as with most issues, the matter is not that simple.

We are all aware that police officers create false identities for undercover operations. We know that they make false promises to hostage takers and kidnappers. We also know officers will strain the truth in order to spare the feelings of a crime victim and his/her loved ones. Police officers are trained to lie and be deceptive in these law enforcement practices. They are also trained to use techniques of interrogation which require deception and even outright lying.

Police officers learn much of this in the police academy, where they are also warned about the impropriety of perjury and the need to record all incidents fully and accurately in all official reports. The recruit learns that all rules and regulations must be obeyed. He/she learns of the danger of lying to internal affairs or a supervisor. The recruit is told to be truthful in his dealings with the non-criminal element of the public in that mutual trust is an important element in police community relations. Once the recruit leaves the academy—and some departments where officers work in the field before attending rookie school—the officer soon learns from his/her peers that police lying is the norm under certain circumstances.

Our purpose is to discuss the patterns of lying which might occur in a police organization, the circumstances under which they occur and the possible consequences of police lying.

Taxonomy of Police Lies

ACCEPTED LYING

Certain forms of police lying and/or deception are an accepted part of the police officer's working environment. The lies told in this category are accepted by the police organization because they fulfill a defined police purpose. Administrators and individual police officers believe that certain lies are necessary to control crime and to "arrest the guilty." In these instances, the organization will freely admit the intent to lie and define the acts as a legitimate policing strategy. On face value, most would agree with the police that lies in this category are acceptable and necessary. However, a troubling and difficult question is "to what extent, if at all, is it *proper* for law enforcement officials to employ trickery and deceit as part of their law enforcement practices?" (Skolnick, 1982, italics added). As we shall see, the answer to this question is not so easy. Acceptable lies may be very functional for the police but are they always proper, moral, ethical, and legal?

The most readily apparent patterns of "accepted" police lying are the deceptive practices that law enforcement officers believe are necessary to perform undercover operations or detect other forms of secret and consensual crimes. Police officers engaged in these activities must not only conceal their true identity but they must talk, act, and dress out of character, fabricating all kinds of stories in order to perform these duties. One could hardly imagine that FBI Special Agent Joseph Pistone could have operated for six years in the Mafia without the substantial number of lies that he had to tell (Pistone, 1987). However, the overwhelming majority of the undercover operations are neither as fascinating nor as dangerous as working six years with the Mafia or other organized crime groups. The most common police undercover operations occur in routine vice operations dealing with prostitution, bootlegging, gambling, narcotics, bribery of public officials (e.g., ABSCAM, MILAB, BRILAB) and sting operations.

These deceptive practices in undercover operations are not only acceptable to the law enforcement community but considered necessary for undercover operations to be effective. Nevertheless, such activities are not without problems. The "Dirty Harry" problem in police work raises the question as to what extent morally good police practices warrant or justify ethically, politically, or legally suspect means to achieve law enforcement objectives (Klockars, 1980). Marx also raises the issue that many of the tactics used by law enforcement officers in such recent undercover operations as ABSCAM, MILAB, BRILAB, police-run fencing or sting operations and anti-crime decoy squads may have lost sight of "the profound difference between carrying out an investigation to determine if a suspect is, in fact, breaking the law, and carrying it out to determine if an individual can be induced to break the law (Marx, 1985:106)." One congressman involved in the ABSCAM case refused the first offer of a cash bribe only later to accept the money after federal agents, concluding that he was an alcoholic, gave him liquor (Marx, 1985:104).

Encouraging the commission of a crime may be a legally accepted police practice when the officer acts as a willing victim or his/her actions facilitate the commission of a crime which was going to be committed in the first place. However, it is possible for "encouragement" to lead the suspect to raise the defense of entrapment.

According to *Black's Law Dictionary* entrapment is "the act of officers or agents of the government in inducing a person to commit a crime not contemplated by him, for the purpose of instituting a criminal prosecution against him (277)." For the defense of entrapment to prevail the defendant must show that the officer or his/her agent has gone beyond providing the encouragement and opportunity for the commission of a crime and through trickery, fraud, or other deception has induced the suspect to commit a crime. This defense is raised far more times than it is successful because the current legal criteria to determine entrapment is what is known as the "subjective test."

In the subjective test the predisposition of the offender, rather than the objective methods of the police, is the key factor in determining entrapment (Skolnick, 1982; Marx, 1985; Stitt and James, 1985). This makes it extremely difficult for a defendant with a criminal record to claim that he/she would not have committed the crime except for the actions of the officer. The "objective test" of entrapment raised by a minority of the Supreme Court has focused on the nature of the police conduct rather than the predisposition of the offender (Stitt and James, 1985). For example, the objective test probably would examine whether the production of crack by a police organization for use in undercover drug arrests is proper and legal. According to an Associated Press story, the Broward County Florida Sheriff's Department, not having enough crack to supply undercover officers, has started manufacturing their own crack. The sheriff's department chemist has made at least $20,000 worth of the illegal substance. Local defense attorneys have raised the issue of entrapment. In fact, one public defender stated:

> I think there's something sick about this whole system where the police make the product, sell the product and arrest people for buying the product (*Birmingham Post-Herald*, April 19, 1989:B2).

The issue of deception aside, this practice raises a number of ethical and legal issues concerning police practices. At what point do we draw the line to make a police undercover operation convincing?

In addition to the accepted practices of lying and deception required for undercover operations, members of the police community often believe that it is proper to lie to the media or the public when it is necessary to protect the innocent, protect the image of the department, or calm the public in crisis situations. The department's official policy may be one of openness and candor when dealing with the media. However, as a practical matter, members of the department may deny the existence of an investigation or "plant" erroneous information to protect an ongoing investigation (i.e., disinformation). The untimely revelation of facts may alert the suspects and drive them underground or cause them to cease their illegal activities. Nevertheless, one could argue that public exposure of certain criminal activities or the possibility of them might decrease the risk of injury to persons or property. This issue was raised in the recent terrorist bombing of PanAm Flight 103 over Lockerbie, Scotland. What was the best course of action? Tell the public of all threats against airliners—most of which were unfounded—and create fear? Or keep all threats confidential and hope that airline and government officials effectively deal with the threats?

In some crimes, such as kidnapping, the publication of accurate information, or any information at all, might lead to the murder of the victim. Therefore, under these circumstances, police administrators might view lies told to protect the victim as perfectly acceptable and necessary.

Police administrators are well aware of the possibility that the entire organization may be labeled deviant because of the deviant acts of its members. The "rotten apple" theory of police corruption has often been used as an impression management technique by police administrators who are aware of this possibility (Barker, 1977). It is easier to explain police deviance as a result of individual aberrations than to admit the possibility of systemic problems and invite public

scrutiny. However, candor and public scrutiny may be the best way to insure that corruption and other forms of police deviance do not occur or continue in an organization (see Cooper and Belair, 1978).

Thus, accepted lies are those which the organization views as having a viable role in police operations. The criteria for the lie to be accepted are:

• It must be in furtherance of a legitimate organizational purpose.

• There must be a clear relationship between the need to deceive and the accomplishment of an organizational purpose.

• The nature of the deception must be one wherein officers and the management structure acknowledge that deception will better serve the public interest than the truth.

• The ethical standing of the deception and the issues of law appear to be collateral concerns.

TOLERATED LYING

A second category of police lies are those which are recognized as "lies" by the police organization but are tolerated as "necessary evils." Police administrators will admit to deception or "not exactly telling the whole truth" when confronted with the facts. These types of situational or "white" lies are truly in the gray area of propriety and the police can provide logical rationales for their use. When viewed from an ethical standpoint they may be "wrong," but from the police perspective they are necessary (i.e., tolerated) to achieve organizational objectives or deal with what Goldstein has termed the basic problems of police work (Goldstein, 1977:9).

The basic problems of police work arise from the mythology surrounding police work; e.g., statutes usually require and the public expects the police to enforce all the laws all the time, the public holds the police responsible for preventing crime and apprehending all criminals, the public views the police as being capable of handling all emergencies, etc. (Goldstein, 1977). Most police administrators will not publicly admit that they do not have the resources, the training or the authority to do some of the duties that the public expects. In fact, many police administrators and police officers lacking the education and insight into police work would be hard pressed to explain police work, particularly discretionary decision-making, to outside groups. Therefore they resort to lies and deception to support police practices.

Police administrators often deny that their departments practice anything less than full enforcement of all laws rather than attempt to explain the basis for police discretionary decisions and selective enforcement. We continually attempt to deal with social problems through the use of criminal sanctions and law enforcement personnel. Mandatory sentencing for all offenders committing certain felony and misdemeanor offenses is often seen as a panacea for these offenses. For example, in recent years many politically active groups such as Mothers Against Drunk Drivers (MADD) had pressured legislators for stronger laws with mandatory enforcement in drunk driving cases. However, their sentiment in cases not involving accidents may not be shared by the general public (Formby and Smykla, 1984) or the police. One can only speculate as to the number of discretionary decisions still being made by police officers in DUI offenses in departments where full enforcement is the official policy. One of the authors learned of an individual who had two DUI offenses reduced and asked a police supervisor about it.

> *Barker:* The chief has said that all DUI suspects are charged and those over the legal blood alcohol level never have the charge reduced. In fact, he said this at a MADD meeting. Yet, I heard that [   ] had two DUI offenses reduced.

> *Supervisor:* That is true Tom. However, [   ] is helping us with some drug cases. MADD may not understand but they do not have to make drug busts.

The point of note is that the police, in response to political pressure, make a policy on DUI cases and vow that the policy will be followed. However, in this case, that vow was bro-

ken. The police made a discretionary judgment that the assistance of the DUI offender in drug investigations was of greater importance than a DUI prosecution. Thus, this policy deviation was tantamount to a lie to the MADD membership—a lie tolerated by the police department.

The public also expects the police to handle any disorderly or emergency situations. The American public believes that one of the methods for handling any problem is "calling the cops" (Bittner, 1972). However, in many of these order-maintenance situations the police do not have the authority, resources or training to deal with the problem. They often face a situation "where something must be done now" yet an arrest is not legally possible or would be more disruptive. The officer is forced to reach into a bag of tricks for a method of dealing with the crisis. Lying to the suspects or the complainants is often that method. For example, police officers may tell noisy teenagers to move along or be arrested when the officers have neither the intention nor legal basis for an arrest. They often tell complainants that they will follow up on their complaint or turn it over to the proper agency when they have no intention of doing it. The police see these lies as a way of handling "nuisance work" that keeps them from doing "real police work" or as a way of dealing with a problem beyond their means. In these cases, the lie is used as a tool of expediency—arguably an abuse of police discretion but one which is tolerated.

In domestic disturbances police officers face volatile situations where the necessary conditions for an arrest often are not present. Frequently there is a misdemeanor where the officer does not have a warrant, an offense has not been committed in his/her presence, and the incident occurred in a private residence. However, the officer may feel that something must be done. Consequently, the officer may lie and threaten to arrest one or both combatants, or take one of the parties out to the street or the patrol car to discuss the incident and arrest them for disorderly conduct or public intoxication when they reach public property. Another option is to make an arrest appear legal. Obviously, the latter strategy will not be a tolerated pattern of lying. It would fall into the pattern of deviant lying to be discussed later.

Officers soon learn that the interrogation stage of an arrest is an area where certain lies are tolerated and even taught to police officers. The now-famous *Miranda v. Arizona* case decided by the U.S. Supreme Court in 1966 quoted excerpts from Inbau and Reid's *Criminal Interrogation and Confession* text to show that the police used deception and psychologically coercive methods in their interrogation of suspects (George 1966:155-266). The latest edition of this same text gives examples of deceptive and lying practices for ... skilled interrogators to engage in (Inbau, Reid, Buckley, 1986).

As an illustration of these techniques, the reader is told that the interrogator should put forth a facade of sincerity so convincingly that "moisture may actually appear in his eyes" (p. 52). Another recommended effective practice of deception is that the interrogator have a *simulated* evidence case folder on hand during the course of the interrogation if an actual case file does not exist (p. 54). The interrogator may also make inferences such as a large number of investigators are working on the case and drew the same evidentiary conclusion about the suspect's guilt, even if, in reality, the interrogator is the only person working the case (p. 85). The inference is that the case against the suspect is strong because of the number of people involved in the investigation and the consequent weight of the evidence.

One particularly troublesome piece of advice for interviewing rape suspects is that:

> Where circumstances permit, the suggestion might be offered that the rape victim had acted like she might have been a prostitute and that the suspect had assumed she was a willing partner. In fact, the interrogator may even say that the police knew she had engaged in prostitution on other occasions ... (p.109).

As a final illustration, the book notes that an effective means to interrogate multiple suspects of a crime is "playing one offender against the other." In this regard it is suggested that the "interrogator may merely intimate to one offender that the other has confessed, or else the interrogator *may actually tell the offender so*" (emphasis added, p. 132).

It is difficult to say whether or not these tolerated forms of lying are "wrong"—many investigators would argue that they are not really "lies" but good interrogation techniques. One could also argue that the end justifies the means as long as the actions of the officers are not illegal. However, one can hypothesize that deception in one context increases the probability of deception in other contexts (c.f., Skolnick, 1982; Stitt and James, 1985). As a veteran police officer told one of the authors while they were discussing ways to convince a suspect to agree to a consent search ...

> *Barker:* That sure sounds like telling a lot of lies.
>
> *Officer:* It is not police lying; it is an art. After all, the criminal has constitutional protection. He can lie through his teeth. Why not us? What is fair is fair.

This attitude, which is borne in the frustrations of many officers, sets a dangerous precedent for attitudes related to civil liberties. When law enforcement officers begin to tolerate lies because it serves their ends—regardless of constitutional and ethical implications of those lies—then fundamental elements of civil rights are threatened.

DEVIANT POLICE LYING

The last example raises the possibility of the third category of policy lying—deviant lies. After all, "he (the suspect) can lie through his teeth. Why not us?" Deviant police lies are those which violate substantive or procedural law and/or police department rules and regulations. The deviant lies which violate substantive or procedural law are improper and should not be permitted. However, organization members (including supervisors), and other actors in the criminal justice system are often aware of their occurrence. Noted defense attorney Alan Dershowitz states that police lying is well known by actors in the criminal justice system. He clearly illustrates these as the "Rules of the Justice Game." In part, the rules include:

Rule IV: Almost all police lie about whether they violated the Constitution in order to convict guilty defendants.

Rule V: All prosecutors, judges, and defense attorneys are aware of Rule IV.

Rule VI: Many prosecutors implicitly encourage police to lie about whether they violated the Constitution in order to convict guilty defendants.

Rule VII: All judges are aware of Rule VI.

Rule VIII: Most trial judges pretend to believe police officers who they know are lying.

Rule IX   All appellate judges are aware of Rule VIII, yet many pretend to believe the trial judges who pretend to believe the lying police officers. (Dershowitz, 1983: xxi–xxii).

This may be an extreme position. However, other criminal defense attorneys believe that the police will lie in court. In fact, one study concluded that "the possibility of police perjury is a part of the working reality of criminal defense attorneys" (Kittel, 1986:20). Fifty-seven percent of the 277 attorneys surveyed in this study believed that police perjury takes place very often or often (Kittel, 1986:16). Police officers themselves have reported that they believe their fellow officers will lie in court (Barker, 1978). An English barrister believes that police officers have perjured themselves on an average of three out of ten trials (Wolchover, 1986).

As part of the research one of the authors asked an Internal Affairs (IA) investigator of a major U.S. police department about officer lying:

Carter: During the course of IA investigations, do you detect officers lying to you?

IA Investigator: Yes. all the time. They'll lie about anything, everything.

Carter: Why is that?

Investigator: To tell me what I want to hear. To help them get out of trouble. To make themselves feel better—rationalizing I guess. They're so used to lying on the job, I guess it becomes second nature.

An analysis of deviant lies reveals that the intent of the officer in telling deviant lies may be either in support of perceived legitimate goals, or illegitimate goals.

DEVIANT LIES IN SUPPORT OF PERCEIVED LEGITIMATE GOALS

The deviant lies told by the officer to achieve perceived legitimate goals usually occur to put criminals in jail, prevent crime, and perform various other policing responsibilities. The police officer believes that because of his/her unique experiences in dealing with criminals and the public he/she knows the guilt or innocence of those they arrest (Manning, 1978). Frequently, officers feel this way independently of any legal standards. However, the final determination of guilt or innocence is in the judicial process. The officer(s), convinced that the suspect is factually guilty of the offense, may believe that necessary elements of legal guilt are lacking, e.g., no probable cause for a "stop," no *Miranda* warning, not enough narcotics for a felony offense, etc. Therefore, the officer feels that he/she must supply the missing elements. One police officer told one of the authors that it is often necessary to "fluff up the evidence" to get a search warrant or insure conviction. The officer will attest to facts, statements, or evidence which never occurred or occurred in a different fashion. Obviously when he/she does this under oath, perjury has then been committed. Once a matter of record, the perjury must continue for the officer to avoid facing disciplinary action and even criminal prosecution.

Charges were dropped in a case against an accused cop killer and three Boston police officers were suspended with pay pending a perjury investigation. The perjury involved a Boston detective who "invented" an informant. The detective maintained that the informant gave critical information which was cited in the affidavit for a search warrant (*New York Times*, 1989:K9). The "no knock" search warrant's execution led to the death of a Boston detective. Similarly, the officer(s) who lies in these instances must employ creative writing skills in official reports to ensure that the written chronology of events are consistent with criminal procedures regardless of what actually occurred.

These lies are rationalized by the officer because they are necessary to ensure that criminals do not get off on technicalities. A central reason for these deviant lies is officer frustration. There is frustration with the criminal justice system because of the inability of courts and corrections to handle large caseloads. Frustration with routinized practices of plea negotiations and intricate criminal procedures which the officer may not fully understand. The officer sees the victims of crimes and has difficulty in reconciling the harm done to them with the wide array of due process protections afforded to defendants. Nevertheless, the officer has fallen into "the avenging angel syndrome" where the end justifies the means. The officer can easily rationalize lying and perjury to accomplish what is perceived to be the right thing. The officer's views are short-sighted and provincial. There is no recognition that such behavior is a threat to civil liberties and that perjury is as fundamentally improper as the criminal behavior of the accused.

DEVIANT LIES IN SUPPORT OF ILLEGITIMATE GOALS

Lies in this category are told to effect an act of corruption or to protect the officer from organizational discipline or civil and/or criminal liability. Deviant lies may be manifest in police perjury as the officer misrepresents material elements of an arrest or search in order to "fix" a criminal prosecution for a monetary reward. Lying and/or perjury in court is an absolute necessity in departments where corrupt acts occur on a regular basis. Sooner or later every

police officer who engages in corrupt acts or observes corrupt acts on the part of other officers will face the possibility of having to lie under oath to protect him/herself or fellow officers. Skolnick has suggested that perjury and corruption are both systematic forms of police deviance which occur for the same sort of reason: "Police know that other police are on the take and police know that other police are perjuring themselves" (Skolnick, 1982:42).

It is also possible that other forms of police deviance will lead to deviant lying. For example, the officer who commits an act of police brutality may have to lie on the report to his/her supervisor and during testimony to avoid the possibility of criminal sanction, a civil lawsuit, or department charges. The officer who has sex on duty, sleeps or drinks on duty may have to lie to a supervisor or internal affairs to avoid department discipline. The officer who causes an injury or death to a suspect which is not strictly according to law or police policy may have to lie to protect himself or his fellow officers from criminal and/or civil liability.

As an illustration, one of the authors assisted a police department which was under a federal court injunction related to an extensive number of civil rights violations for excessive force and harassment. During one series of inquiries, the following conversation occurred:

Carter: Did you ever talk to other accused officers before giving your deposition in these cases?

Officer: Of course. [NOTE: The tone of the response was almost incredulous.]

Carter: Would you discuss the facts of the allegation?

Officer: Sure. We had to be sure our stories were straight.

The implications from these statements and the continued conversations were clear: Officers were willing to lie during the sworn deposition to protect themselves and others. They would swear to the truth of facts which were plainly manufactured for their protection. Moreover, their remorse was not that they lied, but that they got caught in misconduct. Similarly, a police chief in West Virginia recently told a federal judge he lied to investigators in order to cover up for four officers accused of beating handcuffed prisoners (*Law Enforcement News*, March 15, 1989, p. 2). Again, the illegitimate goal of "protection" surfaces as a motive for lying.

The typical police bureaucracy is a complex organization with a myriad of rules and regulations. The informal organization, including many supervisors, overlooks these rules until someone decides to "nail someone." Given the plethora of rules and regulations in most large urban police departments it is virtually impossible to work a shift without violating one. It may be common practice to eat a free meal, leave one's beat for personal reasons, not wear one's hat when out of the car, to live outside the city limits, etc. All of these acts may be forbidden by a policy, rule, or regulation. When a supervisor decides to discipline an officer for violating one of these acts, the officer, and often fellow officers, may resort to lies to protect themselves and each other. After all, such "minor" lies are inherent in the "Blue Code." Manning observes that rule enforcement by police supervisors represents a mock bureaucracy where ritualistic and punitive enforcement is applied after the fact (Manning, 1978). The consequences of these seemingly understandable lies can be disastrous when discovered. The officer(s) may be suspended, reduced in rank, or dismissed. The same organization where members routinely engage in acceptable, tolerated, and deviant lying practices can take on a very moralistic attitude when it discovers that one of its own has told a lie to avoid internal discipline. Nevertheless, the lies told in these examples are told in support of the illegitimate goal of avoiding departmental discipline.

Conclusion

The effects of lying, even those which are acceptable or tolerated, are multifold. Lies can and do create distrust within the organization. When the public learns members of the police department lie or engage in deceptive practices,

this can undermine citizen confidence in the police. As we have seen, some police lies violate citizen's civil rights and others are told to cover up civil rights violations. Police lying contributes to police misconduct and corruption and undermines the organization's discipline system. Furthermore, deviant police lies undermine the effectiveness of the criminal justice system. What should the organization do to deal with the reality of police lies? An important first step is to establish a meaningful code of ethics and value statements for the organization. Importantly, this should go beyond the development of documents. The operational and managerial levels of the police department must know that the code of ethics and value statements are guides to police moral and ethical behavior. There should never become another set of rules and procedures to be used when necessary to "nail someone." Once ethics and values are embodied, it is essential to develop a support structure consisting of directives, training, and supervision. This will create a moral environment throughout the organization and establish parameters of acceptable behavior giving notice to employees about management.

REFERENCES

Barker, T. (1978). "An Empirical Study of Police Deviance Other Than Corruption," *Journal of Police Science and Administration* (6:3): 264-272.

_____ (1977). "Peer Group Support for Police Occupational Deviance," Criminology (15:3): 353-366.

Bittner, E. (1971). *The Functions of the Police in Modern Society*, Washington, DC: U.S. Government Printing Office.

Birmingham Post-Herald (1988). "Sheriff's Chemist Makes Crack," April 19: B2.

Black, H. C. (1983). *Black's Law Dictionary*, Abridged Fifth Edition. St. Paul, MN: West Publishing Co.

Cooper, G. R. and R. R. Belair (1978). *Privacy and Security of Criminal History Information: Privacy and the Media*. U.S. Department of Justice. Washington, DC: U.S. Government Printing Office.

Dershowitz, A. M. (1983). *The Best Defense*, New York: Vintage Books.

Formby, W. A. and J. O. Smykla (1984). "Attitudes

and Perception Toward Drinking and Driving: A Simulation of Citizen Awareness." *Journal of Police Science and Administration* (12:4): 379–384.

George, J. B. (1966). *Constitutional Limitations on Evidence in Criminal Cases*. Ann Arbor, Michigan: Institute of Continuing Legal Education.

Goldstein, H. (1977). *Policing A Free Society*. Cambridge, MA: Ballinger Publishing Company.

Inbau, F. E., J. E. Reid and J. P. Buckley (1986). *Criminal Interrogation and Confessions, 3rd Ed.*, Baltimore, MD: Williams and Wilkins.

Kittel, N. G. (1986). "Police Perjury: Criminal Defense Attorneys' Perspective," *American Journal of Criminal Justice* (Xl:1) (Fall): 11–22.

Klockars, C. B. (1980). "The Dirty Harry Problem," *The Annals*, 452 (November): 33–47.

Law Enforcement News (1989). March 15: 2.

Manning, P. K. (1978). "Lying, Secrecy and Social Control." In P. K. Manning and John Van Maanen (Eds.) *Policing: A View from The Street*, Santa Monica, CA: Goodyear Publishing Co. 238–255.

Marx, G. T. (1985). "Who Really Gets Stung? Some Issues Raised By The New Police Undercover Work." In Elliston, F. A. and M. Feldberg (Eds.) *Moral Issues in Police Work*. Totowa, NJ: Rowan and Allanheld.

New York Times (1989). "Dead Officer, Dropped Charges: A Scandal in Boston." March 20: K9.

Pistone, J. D. (1987). *Donnie Brasco: My Undercover Life in the Mafia*. New York, NY: Nail Books.

Skolnick, J. (1982). "Deception By Police," *Criminal Justice Ethics*, 1(2), (Summer/Fall): 40–54.

Stitt, B. G. and G. G. James (1985). "Entrapment An Ethical Analysis" in Elliston, F. A. and M. Feldberg (Eds.) *Moral Issues in Police Work*. Totowa, NJ: Rowman and Allanheld.

Wolchover, D. (1986). "Police Perjury in London." *New Law Journal* (Feb.): 180–184.

Study Questions

1. What is a taxonomy? Where in Barker and Carter's taxonomy of lying would they place deception used in an undercover operation? Do Barker and Carter believe that such deception is fundamentally morally wrong? Why?

2. Where in the taxonomy would you place Klockars' case involving the invention of a property room record for evidence mistakenly left in a desk drawer? Does self-interest play any role in this case?

3. What do Barker and Carter propose as a solution to the problem of police lying? Do you think their proposal has any merit? Why? Would you describe their approach as basically utilitarian, or deontological? Defend your answer.

Case 5.1

STREET ADJUSTMENT

Tom Allen has been a police officer for just over a year. He has managed to keep an excellent perspective in his job as a patrol officer, becoming neither badge heavy nor overly lax. For the past four months he has been paired with Ken Johnson, who has been on the department a little over three years. It is unusual to have permanent partners on this department, but the Sergeant has been impressed with Allen and Johnson's work product. They are one of the few two-man teams that have really seemed to click. They have had an outstanding record of quality enforcement and performance. They think alike and enjoy working together. Because of their high performance, they have been nicknamed "Reed and Malloy" after the characters on the television series "Adam-12."

Tom and Ken are partners in the true sense of the word. Not only do they work together, but they have become quite close socially, as have their wives. Since they have the same days off, it is not unusual for them to go hunting or fishing together, or out on a picnic with their wives and children. Although neither one of them has ever admitted it, they have a relationship that could best be described as brotherly love.

The night shift found them working together once again, and as dawn approached, it was a night that could be described as uneventful and quieter than most.

"Pull over behind that warehouse," Ken said. "I just spotted Bobby Dell. He's got to be up to no good."

Tom pulled up behind the warehouse and approached Dell on foot. While Dell did seem a little jumpy, he answered the officers' inquiries. Suddenly, and without warning, Dell sucker punched Officer Johnson, knocking him out cold. He then fled down an alley.

Officer Allen ran after him. Unfortunately for Dell, the alley ended in a parking lot surrounded by a high, barbed wire fence. Dell, knowing there was no escape, stopped, put his hands over his head, and said, "I give up." He offered no resistance as Allen placed the handcuffs on him, conducted a field search, and led him back to the patrol car.

As they approached the patrol car, Officer Johnson was in the process of getting up, dusting himself off, and wiping the blood from his nose. As Officer Allen opened the back door of the patrol car to place Dell inside, Johnson said, "Just a second." Johnson then took his nightstick and struck Dell in the face and again on the knees.

"That'll teach you to touch the 'brown gown,'" he said, as Dell fell to the ground. Johnson then turned to Allen and said, "That was one hell of a fall he took while you were chasing him. I don't think it was too bright of him to resist that violently when you finally caught him, either."

"But, he didn't resist," Allen replied.

"Yes he did, I saw the whole thing after I got up. That's how he got his injuries. We'll charge him with assault on a police officer, fleeing, and resisting arrest with violence. He'll plead, get time served, and never, ever touch another cop. Besides, it's 4:30 A.M. Who is gonna know? You write it up."

"Hey man, I can't falsify a report," Allen replied.

"Hey, look," said Johnson, "I fucked up. I just couldn't help myself, I was so pissed. If we don't write it up that way, it's my ass. I'll lose my job, house, and probably get sued. Look man, we work together, our wives are close, and there are no witnesses. No one will believe Dell and the whole thing will just blow over."

Questions for Discussion

1. If you were Officer Allen, what would you do? Use the ethical decision-making checklist to assist you.

2. Should a brief lapse in judgment be grounds for a lifetime punishment?

3. Consider the "late hit" in football or hockey. In what ways is this incident similar or different?

4. Using your decision in this case as a starting point, chart the many potential courses your decision could take.

5. According to Barker and Carter, which category(ies) of lying could apply in this case?

6. If Dell has done "it" once, will he do it again?

7. If Allen lets the incident go unreported, what should he do if a similar incident occurs in the future? Justify your answer.

8. Can one ever justify retaliation? Isn't the desire for vengeance a part of being human?

9. Who "sucker punched" whom? Do the handcuffs make a difference? Discuss.

Case 5.2

ASLEEP AT THE WHEEL

It is three in the morning and you are nearly halfway through your shift as an area patrol officer at your correctional institution. Your basic duties include checking the grounds, fences, and buildings for any unusual activity, which means, on this shift, *any* activity.

As you drive by the institution this time, however, something out of the ordinary catches your eye. You can't be sure, but you are almost certain that you see some kind of movement around the loading dock in the back of the kitchen. From your angle (ground level) it is quite difficult to make out what, if anything, the movement may have been. You decide to proceed to Tower Two, which has a good view of the loading dock, and find out if the tower officer has noticed anything.

After you stop and exit your vehicle, you recall that the tower officer this morning is R. V. Winkle. Out of habit, you pick up a handful of gravel and throw it at the windows of the tower. Officer Winkle, to be blunt, sleeps on duty. He is known for this but has thus far managed to avoid getting into serious trouble. This is due mostly to your and other officers like yourself covering up for him.

Once Officer Winkle is finally roused (it takes three handfuls of gravel), you direct his attention to the loading dock. He shines his spotlight at the dock and sees two inmates trying to hide behind some metal bread racks. Winkle then calls this information into Control, officers quickly appear on the dock, and the brief but unsuccessful escape attempt comes to an end.

A week later, as you are reporting for duty, you notice that Major Allison is making one of his very rare appearances at the third-shift officers' assembly. You wonder why. Your question is soon answered when Major Allison, referring to the escape attempt of a week before, presents a letter of commendation to Officer Winkle and thanks him, on behalf of the staff and the administration, for doing his job so well. Winkle, you note, gladly accepts the letter and the praise.

In a way, you're happy to see Winkle receive this letter. He is, after all, basically a nice guy. Such recognition will surely help improve the appearance of his rather spotty work record. It may even inspire him to be more conscientious in the future. On the other hand, you are unhappy that Winkle didn't mention you in his report of the incident. You were not even asked to fill out an incident report. You wonder if this time telling the truth is more important that officer loyalty. The fact of the matter is, you feel, Winkle just does not deserve this recognition and you do.

As your shift leaves the assembly area, you notice your shift Captain approaching you with an incredulous look on his face. He knows Winkle and he knows something is wrong in all of this. When he asks you if you were in the area of Tower Two on the morning of the escape attempt, you answer, "Yes."

"O.K.," your Captain says, "write me an incident report on the events of that morning, everything you did and observed, as best as you can remember."

"Yes, sir," you say, and you know that you must write a report. The question is, what will the report say?

Questions for Discussion

1. What would you do? Use the ethical decision-making checklist to assist you.
2. Does/should the supervisor have the right to expect you to express your mind?
3. Would your answer be different if this were Winkle's first sleeping episode?
4. According to Barker and Carter, which category(ies) of lying could apply in this case?
5. Don't we all have the obligation to tell it "as it is"? Why do we often feel guilty when we have to tell it "as it is"?

Case 5.3

TAIN'T NOBODY'S BIZNESS

It seemed as though he had been on probation forever. He wasn't exactly John Dillinger, or even Willie Sutton, but he was a thief. He stole some money from a convenience store where he worked. No prior record, just didn't know what came over him. (The bills were piling up, you know). But he was basically an O.K. guy so a couple of years on probation and several hundred dollars in restitution ought to repay his debt to society (and to the store).

He was a good probationer as probationers go. He always reported when it was time, he paid on his debt every month, and he stayed out of trouble. But he started looking pretty bad. He was sick all of the time, he was losing weight, he was always tired, and he acted depressed. He was sick so much that he couldn't hold a job, but he still made regular little payments and kept reporting through it all. Finally, he told me that he had AIDS. Not just HIV positive, but full-blown AIDS.

After that, things seemed to go downhill quickly. Chemotherapy, a lot of hospital stays, and the latest in experimental drugs. Nothing seemed to stop the progression of the disease. Finally, he went to live in an AIDS hospice. He knew he was terminal. I knew he was terminal. It seemed like the right time to terminate his probation.

Early termination of probation is normally a simple procedure. Usually, a judge will assume that I know what I'm doing. (After all, I am an experienced probation officer, I've had contact with the probationer for several years, and the judge hasn't seen the defendant since sentencing and doesn't know him from Adam.) Not this Judge. He has been a thorn in my (and the other probation officer's) side since he got on the bench. He is the personification of the term CYA (Cover Your Ass).

We generally have a standard format and "canned" entries for every occasion. This Judge doesn't like any of them. I don't think he has ever signed an entry without writing a lot of irrelevant comments on it first. He has to make sure that whatever the entry says, the responsibility falls on the probation officer, never on the Judge (who puts them on probation in the first place).

After I went to the Judge to beg and grovel to convince him that this defendant is *not* going back to work, he is *not* going to be able to pay all that restitution, and it *is* a problem for him to report, he decided that maybe an early term just might be in order (thanks, Judge). However, the "canned" early term entry states that the defendant has complied with the rules of probation. Unfortunately, this man owes money. So the Judge issues a new entry. It is 4:50 P.M. and I want to get the thing done so I can file it before 5:00. Judge does, I do, and then I am on my way home.

Then I read the entry. Not only did the Judge state that the defendant did not comply with probation, he also specified that the defendant has AIDS and further noted that he went to live in an AIDS hospice. He also noted the address of the home. All for the public record.

The next day, I went back to the clerk's office to retrieve the entry. After all, wasn't there a law about disclosing confidential medical information? Besides, this was *my* probationer. I was the one who had been with him in the hospital, listened to him when he was told he only had another six months to live, and gave him a shoulder to cry on. What right does the Judge have to plaster somebody's personal business all over the public record? The original entry never asked for anything so personal; it just said the defendant's probation was terminated.

I asked the clerk for the entry and told her the story. She dug out the entry. "Judge so-and-so?" she said, "I'm not tampering with anything he signed, he might come looking for it, you can't have it back, and I'll get in trouble." Then she put the file on the counter in front of me and walked away.

Questions for Discussion

1. If you were the officer, what would you do? Use the ethical decision-making checklist to assist you.

2. In this case, is "honesty the best policy"?

3. What harm does the removal of the AIDS reference cause, if any? What harm does leaving it cause, considering the probationer will probably die in six months anyway?

4. Why do you think that the judge entered the AIDS information?

5. According to Barker and Carter, which category(ies) of lying could apply in this case?

6. Does anyone, in good conscience, change official records? If so, how?

7. Are the judge's peculiarities and vindictiveness any reason for the probation officer's interpretation of the situation?

Case 5.4

CONFIDENTIALITY DILEMMA

You are employed as a juvenile probation officer and one of your clients is Paul, a 15-year-old, white male. Paul is not doing very well at home, is not attending school regularly, and has been caught by the police on the streets after curfew. You have recently been told, off the record and in violation of confidentiality, that Paul's mother has tested positive for the HIV virus. You are also concerned that Paul may have had an incestuous relationship with his mother.

You talk to the juvenile court judge and explain your problem. You need to find out if Paul is HIV positive, but do not wish to alarm him. The judge orders Paul to have a *complete* physical exam. Unfortunately, HIV testing requires counseling of the patient both prior to the test and after the test. The judge suggests that you go to the counseling and claim you are Paul. Thus, you would get the information without subjecting Paul to the trauma of the counseling.

Questions for Discussion

1. What would you do? Use the ethical decision-making checklist to assist you.
2. Weigh the costs of the deception versus the benefit of allowing a possible carrier of the AIDS virus to infect others. Apply Klockar's concept of "nonmaleficence" to this situation.
3. How could you get Paul tested without revealing your source?
4. Would you be remiss in your duties if you did not tell Paul of the possibility of HIV?
5. Paul might be rejected for placement if his condition is made known. Should you keep this information from a possible foster family or group home?
6. According to Barker and Carter, which category(ies) of lying could apply in this case?

Case 5.5

LAST SHIFT

This was a day of mixed emotions for those in the Planning and Research Unit of the Midland City Police Department, especially for Sergeant Pulley. Although the retirement of Lieutenant Ross meant a promotion for him, Pulley would probably miss Ross more than any other person in the close-knit unit. Ross had become Pulley's best friend on the job, and their families often spent time together. Pulley's wife, Claire, and Ross's wife, Paige, had became close. They even took a short trip together several months ago. On that trip, Pulley learned how much Paige was looking forward to her husband's retirement. They were looking forward to recapturing the time they had lost during the early years of their marriage, when Ross had worked long hours of overtime in the Homicide Unit. She often told of the day he was almost killed rescuing a small child from a burning house. It won him the medal of valor but cost him months of rehabilitation as the result of smoke inhalation. Pulley would probably miss the personal qualities of his Lieutenant even more: honesty, sincerity, loyalty, and a work ethic stronger than many rookies half his age.

On this Friday, the other three officers in the Planning Unit were off planning the evening's surprise retirement party for the Lieutenant. Only Ross, Pulley, and the Unit's longtime secretary, Cindy, were working. After completing his monthly patrol activity report, Pulley decided to pop into Ross's office to remind him that in three hours he would be an ex-cop and planning his cross country camping trip, the one Ross and Paige had planned for years.

As Pulley walked into Ross's outer office, he noticed that Cindy was away from her desk and that Ross's office door was closed. He listened for a moment and, not hearing any talking, knocked on the door. He knocked several times. There was no answer. After a few moments, he opened the door and saw Ross leaning back in his chair. Not knowing Ross to take naps at work, he took a closer look and suddenly realized that Ross was not breathing. As he moved to attempt cardiopulmonary resuscitation, he felt Ross's cold hand and knew he was much too late. After a few seconds, another realization struck Pulley. Ross had died at work, before his retirement took effect. With the strange pension system the city used, Paige would receive only half the amount she would normally get if Ross had lived past the end of the shift. Anger and frustration replaced the sick feeling Pulley had originally experienced. This was a gross injustice to such a fine officer, and as a result his devoted spouse would suffer yet again because of his job.

There must be something he could do to help his longtime friend. Suddenly it came to him. Only three hours left on the shift, no one else working, no meetings scheduled, no one likely to call or visit their out-of-the-way office. Maybe, with Cindy's help, they could help Ross "finish his last shift." She certainly would go along, as she knew both Ross and his wife very well. It was the least they could do for such fine people.

Questions for Discussion

1. If you were Pulley, what would you do? Use the ethical decision-making checklist to assist you.

2. Isn't the subordination of truth-telling to other goods appropriate in this case? If so, what other goods? If not, why?

3. Are the officer's actions in this case based on self-interest, career ambitions, or convenience? If not, could they be justified? Is the officer pursuing any "private-regarding benefits"?

4. Is allowing the death to "occur" after the shift justifiable to offset a poor retirement system?

5. Apply Bok's standard of public justification to your decision.

6. Would you consider Pulley's actions a "white lie"? Why? Defend your position.

7. Isn't Pulley's decision simply a lie intended to lead to good and thus a "peccadillo or bagatelle"?

Case 5.6

ICED OUT

I am a child guidance worker at a juvenile detention facility. When I first began my job there, I was idealistic. I believed good things would happen to the kids and staff if I maintained a positive outlook toward the residents and my coworkers. I quickly learned that this was not the case. There are many individuals in the "system" who are comfortable with tolerating injustices and abuses by both staff and administration in the juvenile facility. I suppose the reasons for this could be analyzed, but the fact remains that it doesn't matter what the reasons are; what concerns me and should concern many others is what is happening behind the closed doors of this detention facility.

Recently, I received a "letter of concern" from the administration for being late three times in one month. The times were one, two, and five minutes late, respectively. I do accept responsibility for my tardy behavior. What I cannot accept is the idea of focusing so much on this area when we have staff sleeping on the job on the overnight shift. Outside of hearing rumors about this, I recently caught one of my coworkers snoring on the job. He is a float, which means that he is responsible for covering three areas of the facility: two levels in detention and an open setting called Shelter Care. We have had two breakouts due to staff not monitoring the residents every 15 to 30 minutes on the overnight shift. The person I saw sleeping was the one who was working overnight when the breakouts occurred. The breakouts occurred approximately four and one-half hours before anyone knew about it. Now, if that person had done his job, the incident would not have happened. Consequently, he was fired, but he cried "Racism!" and grieved it with the union. He is now working at the facility again.

About two months ago, I went to the administration and voiced my concerns regarding people sleeping on the job, residents being slapped or handled roughly, use of profanity in front of the children, workers who sit on the job all day and let other workers carry the load, and other minor complaints. The administration listened patiently but that was the extent of their action regarding these occurrences. My coworkers immediately iced me out. There was a time when I had to physically restrain a male by myself, and when I called for back-up, I didn't receive help for almost three minutes. While that may not sound like a long time, when you have a child wailing on you and you are the only one on the floor monitoring 18 residents, it seems like an eternity. In that moment, I began to realize the cost of trying to change things and make them better. I later received a piece of paper with the letters cut out of a magazine to form racist and slanderous words toward me. It was left in my mailbox. When I presented the letter to the administration, rather than dealing with it, they asked me if I had sent it to myself. After that reaction, I knew nothing would change.

It is now two months later. All that has seemed to change are the faces of the residents. They still come and go.

Questions for Discussion

1. Assume that the author in this case was a white female, a white male, an African-American female, an African-American male, a Hispanic female, or a Hispanic male. Would your evaluation of the case be different? Why? Defend your position.

2. Is this a case of a concerned employee or one of "sour grapes"?

3. Why does the administration seem to want to placate both sides? What message does the administration seem to be sending?

4. After reading this case, are you more or less likely to blow the whistle?

Chapter 6

Corruption

GIFTS, TIPS, GRATUITIES, DOING FAVORS, smuggling drugs into a prison, accepting bribes, shakedowns and extortion, harassment and abuse of authority, selling seized property—are these actions on a continuum ranging from morally permissible to morally indefensible, or is the receipt of any benefit morally inappropriate for the criminal justice practitioner? There is a substantial ongoing debate in ethics literature and in the professional practice of business, law, medicine, and public service concerning these issues, at least in part because such practices are legal in some countries or jurisdictions but illegal in others. "Lubrication" payments, "palm greasing," the Christmas bottle of whiskey for the client or customer, "referral" fees, kickbacks, etc., may not be illegal in all circumstances. Nonetheless, many feel that such actions are morally tainted or suspicious.

At one end of the spectrum, of course, are out-and-out criminal activities of the criminal justice practitioner, including theft, robbery, narcotics trafficking in prisons, performing protection services for organized crime, and so on. Since these actions are not only illegal but are also serious moral wrongs, by definition they don't pose moral dilemmas. Corruption of this extreme kind is of course a serious administrative problem, and moral issues do arise in dealing with it. Invasion of privacy, employees' rights, and loyalty conflicts are just a few examples.

An example of the debate in criminal justice practice at the other end of the spectrum of corruption is the "free cup of coffee" issue. Accepting such a benefit is viewed by some criminal justice administrators as harmless in itself, but potentially the first step toward corruption. Other agencies feel that the free cup of coffee or half-price meal is corrupt in itself, while still others may view such activity as different in kind from bribery, and therefore appropriate.

We can make some progress here immediately by observing that the criminal justice practitioner serves the public as a whole, not any one individual. For example, if a grocer happens to benefit directly from the presence of a police officer on patrol, this protection is a result of the officer's duties to the citizens of the patrolled area, not a service provided by the officer to the grocer as an individual. Hence, the grocer owes the officer nothing and the officer cannot therefore accept any benefit, however small, from the grocer. For example, the officer should not accept a package of steaks from the grocer *as a police officer*. On the other hand, couldn't the grocer invite the officer (who is a friend) to dinner to enjoy those very same steaks? These questions are complicated by inconsistent public perceptions regarding gratuities. Gifts are common in the business world, and an honorarium for speaking at a trade show dinner is standard. Yet, an honorarium for a member of Congress making the same speech raises the hackles of many citizens, no doubt including the same persons who would happily write the honorarium check to the business person. As public servants, criminal justice practitioners face similar and conflicting public perceptions.

The Readings

The first selection in this chapter is taken from the International Association of Chiefs of Police, "Training Key #254: Police Corruption." This training material represents what might be regarded as the traditional view of corruption, namely, that all forms of corruption, from the free meal to the shakedown are deviant and are absolutely prohibited, and that officer training should explicitly teach these perspectives. Virtually all of the material in this reading applies to criminal justice practice in general and is not limited to law enforcement.

Bernard J. McCarthy's selection, "Patterns of Prison Corruption," begins with the observation that police corruption has received much more emphasis in the criminal justice literature than has corruption in correctional institutions and other areas of criminal justice practice. McCarthy argues that the virtual absence of literature on problems of corruption in the corrections area "impairs our ability to devise effective management control strategies." The purpose of his paper is to describe the range of corrupt activities observed in a single state department of corrections as a contribution to the systematic study of corruption in corrections.

McCarthy observes that corruption impacts both inmates and staff. Corrupt practices include "selective nullification" of rules and procedures, providing (usually by smuggling or theft) scarce goods and services to the inmate "economy," exploitation of inmates to enhance the perception of the staff member's job performance, and personal friendships between staff and inmates that encourage other corrupt actions.

Michael Johnston's paper, "Police Corruption," is a sociological analysis of corruption. Although his remarks refer to law enforcement, they are quite applicable to the entire range of criminal justice practice. Johnston divides corrupt acts into four categories: internal corruption, selective enforcement for personal gain, active criminality, and bribery and extortion. He limits his analysis to bribery and extortion, which he feels are the most significant forms of corruption and which are the most powerful influences on law enforcement.

Johnston's methodological approach applies three perspectives. The personalistic theory describes corruption of individual officers and delves into their social backgrounds, motivations, and personalities. The second theoretical perspective looks at corruption as an institutional phenomenon involving departmental bureaucratization, the conflict between police and other functions of the criminal justice system (the court system, in particular), and conflicts between the police and the public. The third perspective used by Johnston, and the one that he believes is the most useful, is the systemic view. This theoretical approach is concerned with conflicting values in society, especially vice and "personal" morality, and how those conflicts influence police behavior.

In examining the causes of corruption, Johnston quickly dismisses the "rotten apple" theory, in which a few deviant officers have a corrupting influence on an entire department. Johnston believes that such a view allows administrators to avoid department-wide corruption investigations, since all that need be done is to eliminate the rotten apples. In Johnston's words, rotten apples "are not corrupting the rest of the barrel; if anything, we ought to be looking at the barrel itself."

Most significantly, corruption is not so much a matter of deviance as it is a matter of conformity. And even if corruption were primarily caused by a few deviant persons, research has not been able to generate a profile that could be used to screen applicants. Thus, corruption is not a problem that can be solved by proper recruiting. As Johnston notes, even those studies that have identified common traits among police have isolated characteristics that are desirable in an officer, such as aggressiveness, impulsiveness, and risk-taking. However, it is not clear whether those traits are learned on the job or are brought in by the recruit. The upshot of all this, Johnston says, is that at least for pervasive, organized bribery and extortion, the "personalistic" model is of little use.

Johnston is more sanguine about the value of an institutional model of corruption, but he thinks that it is most useful in understanding "why some police officers are 'available' for corruption." It does not explain why officers form corrupt relationships with citizens outside the institution of law enforcement. Institutional sources of corruption include some familiar grounds—for example, the frustration and disillusionment with the criminal justice process. If an officer feels that his or her work is disregarded or disqualified on "technical" grounds, this may spawn an atmosphere where corruption can occur. Such conflicting demands also encourage or even require police to violate the law or departmental regulations. Although Johnston does not believe that such factors can explain a significant amount of corruption, he speculates that "it seems plausible that conflicting pressures, weak and ambiguous standards of conduct, strong temptations, and the necessity to break laws in the course of duty might encourage corruption."

The systemic model of corruption is based on the idea of fundamental value conflicts in society. Vice laws controlling alcohol, drugs, gambling, and prostitution, for instance, are not universally accepted by society, are inconsistent from state to state, and are viewed by many citizens, as well as by police, as victimless, unlike theft or crimes of violence. Johnston draws two conclusions from the vice example: first, society's ambivalence about vice "creates strong incentives" for law-breaking; and second, it encourages police not to enforce the law. In such an environment, bribes will be offered and accepted. Such corruption is a "win-win" situation in which everyone involved benefits and no one is harmed. As Johnston notes in this case, corruption seems "well suited to resolving the conflicts inherent in policing a complex society." Johnston goes on to examine the social costs and benefits of corruption in more detail, warning that while decriminalization may have positive benefits in some cases, we should not delude ourselves that the subsequent elimination of corruption would bear no costs.

Ellwyn R. Stoddard's selection, "The Informal 'Code' of Police Deviancy: A Group Approach to 'Blue-Coat Crime'," also rejects the individualistic account of police corruption. He examines the informal "code" of corruption in a police department and the means by which recruits were socialized into the department's practices. Stoddard concludes from his research that deviancy in an enforcement agency "is a reflection of values which are habitually practiced and accepted within [the] community." Officers who resisted the "code" were ostracized as "goofs."

Richard R. E. Kania's selection, "Should We Tell the Police to Say 'Yes' to Gratuities?" challenges the traditional view that it is always morally wrong for a police officer to accept gifts from citizens in the conduct of police work. Kania's conclusion is that the police, and sometimes other criminal justice personnel,

> ...should be encouraged to accept freely offered minor gratuities and that such gratuities should be perceived as the building blocks of positive social relationships between our police and the public, and not as incipient corrupters.

Kania first examines the standard arguments against the practice of police officers accepting gratuities. He finds two major arguments, one teleological and the other deontological. The teleological argument involves "slippery slope" reasoning, which asserts that even though taking a free meal, for example, may not be morally wrong, such actions have a corrupting effect on an officer, which will inevitably lead to serious wrong-doing. The metaphor of the slippery slope is that once you place your foot on the slippery slope, you will inevitably fall all the way down to the bottom. The slippery slope fallacy is an argument that incorrectly draws a conclusion from a premise that is held to lead inevitably, by either a chain of events or by facts, to that conclusion. For example, I might argue fallaciously that you shouldn't take aspirin. My argument is that aspirin is a pain-killer and before long, you'll need a stronger pain-killer, so you'll begin using Tylenol with codeine, and then you'll proceed to morphine, and before you know it, you'll be a heroin addict. So, taking aspirin is the foot on the slippery slope leading to heroin addiction. Slippery slope fallacies are very common in ordinary reasoning (think of the issues of gun control, capital punishment, drug abuse, abortion, free speech, government regulation of business, etc.).

In Kania's example, the basic idea is that if I accept the free meal, this obligates me to reciprocate at a later date. For instance, I might have to pay my "debt" by fixing a traffic ticket, and at the very least, I will be motivated to behave preferentially toward the gift-giver, instead of providing police services in an unbiased way. As Kania correctly observes, this line of reasoning is consequentialist (utilitarian) in nature.

The second argument against gifts and gratuities is what Kania calls the "unjustified enrichment" position. He identifies this rejection of gratuities as deontological in that accepting a gift or gratuity is held to be morally wrong in and of itself, regardless of the consequences. The wrongness of the action lies in the fact that the officer is unjustifiably enriched for performing a service he or she has already been paid by the public to do.

Drawing on anthropological data concerning gift-giving, Kania argues that refusing a free meal or a discount that has been genuinely offered in gratitude "would be to refuse the giver the opportunity to satisfy his sense of obligation." In other words, the perception of debt on the traditional account is backwards. The officer who accepts the gratuity does not incur a debt that must be paid later. The debt has already been incurred (a debt of gratitude for services, police visibility, etc.), and the holder is the gift-giver, not the officer.

Kania argues that the consequences of the officer rejecting a gratuity are undesirable, since by depriving the giver of the opportunity to pay a debt, police–community relations are adversely affected. Kania further discounts the argument that such minor gratuities are the first step toward major corruption, citing examples and studies that indicate that most officers do draw the necessary distinctions and do not slide into corruption.

Kania's argument centers on the claim that the morality of accepting a gift or gratuity depends on the perceptions of the giver and the police recipient. The result is that there will be a range of exchanges—from the morally wrong (a bribe being extorted, for example), to questionable cases involving mismatched perceptions of the exchange, to clearly ethical exchanges in which the gratuity is truly an expression of gratitude and nothing more. Kania concludes that expecting police to make such distinctions is not a great imposition because police officers are already in the habit of making critical moral choices. The difficulty lies in the unrealistic (and philosophically wrong-headed) training that recruits receive concerning gifts and gratuities. Kania says that "to generate unnecessary guilt in police faced with offers of trivial gifts and gratuities is folly.... New corruption is invited simply because corruption already is inferred..."

Training Key #254: Police Corruption

INTERNATIONAL ASSOCIATION OF CHIEFS OF POLICE

THE POLICE PROFESSION IS sometimes reluctant to openly discuss corruption. Extreme sensitivity about the subject has developed over the years because of the intense criticism law enforcement in general receives whenever specific instances of police corruption are uncovered. Yet corruption within law enforcement is no more prevalent than that in other professions or within the general public. This is true despite the fact that police officers are constantly exposed to situations where official power *could* be misused for personal gain.

Corruption in police departments is not limited to well-known cases in major cities. The potential for police corruption exists in all areas of the country, in both rural and urban settings. Police officers within all ranks of a department may be involved in corrupt activities. When corruption is widespread within an agency the likelihood is great that command personnel either condone or are involved in the misconduct.

What Is Corruption?

Substantial disagreement exists about what actually constitutes police corruption. Some authorities consider all instances of police misconduct as acts of corruption including such disparate cases as verbal abuse of citizens and organized "shakedowns" of criminals or businessmen. "Bribery" is often erroneously used in an all-inclusive manner to describe police corruption. One veteran officer defined corruption as the "three B's"—broads, booze, and bargains. The veteran's terse definition of corruption, while easily understood by all who have served as a police officer, does not adequately reflect or include the entire problem or the complexity of some forms of police corruption.

Generally, police corruption involves the misuse of official position either to commit or ignore an unauthorized act which may or may not violate the law. As payment for misusing his position, the officer expects at some point in time to receive something of value but not necessarily money. The payoff may take the form of services, status, influence, prestige, or future favoritism for the officer or someone else. Because such "debts" may be called in months or years after an officer has acted improperly, "invisible" corruption may exist in an agency. For example, the officer who agrees to tolerate illegal activity by a local politician may believe this action eventually will lead to a promotion.

Developing a working definition of police corruption requires that such misconduct be categorized. For purposes of this discussion, three general areas of corruption will be considered.

The first includes criminal acts in which officers not only tolerate statutory law but also misuse their position to carry out the crime. A second category to be considered is the violation of oath of office or misconduct in office. Finally, violations of departmental regulations in many cases involve corrupt behavior.

CRIMINAL ACTS

It is generally agreed that the depth of police corruption is the participation in crime by police officers who use their special skills, knowledge, or influence to avoid detection and apprehension. Whether an offense committed by an officer also entails corruption depends on the circumstances of the crime. The officer who uses his position to carry out a crime is part of the corruption problem, e.g., an officer who uses knowledge of his beat in committing a burglary. On the other hand, an officer who murders his wife during a family dispute commits a crime that is unconnected with the problem of corruption.

As with any other profession or the community at large, a certain percentage of police officers will engage in criminal activities. Every effort should be made to prevent these crimes by eliminating the conditions that contribute to their commission; however, a distinction must be made between crimes committed by officers which do not involve misuse of police authority and crimes which are linked with corrupt police practice.

MISCONDUCT IN OFFICE

The phrase "misconduct in office" refers to any willful malfeasance, misfeasance, or nonfeasance in office and may be considered within the context of police corruption when an officer acts with malice and aforethought to thwart justice.

Malfeasance is easily recognizable, consisting of any act by a police officer which without question violates the law. For example, an officer, who telephones a bookmaker to warn him of a pending raid has violated his oath of office and should face charges of "malfeasance," if not criminal conspiracy.

In contrast misfeasance by an officer is not always immediately obvious from his actions. Misfeasance is the improper performance of an official act. Misfeasance is usually observed in the performance of duty when an officer fails to use the degree of care, skill, or diligence which the circumstances reasonably demand. For example, operators of illegal gambling or prostitution businesses pay corrupt officers for protection from interruption of business, and, in general, arrest. However, such arrangements may allow for the officers to arrest members of the operation when necessary, e.g., to produce arrest statistics, alleviate pressures from outside of the police unit, or neutralize suspicions. Following such an arrest, the corrupt officer's testimony or evidence he obtained when making the arrest may be so weak that the court will dismiss the case or impose a small fine. Thus, the "accommodation arrest" is a sham arranged between the criminal and corrupt police officer.

Nonfeasance is the omission of an act which ought to be done. It is the neglect or refusal without sufficient excuse to perform an act which is an officer's legal duty to perform. Thus, if vice activity openly and flagrantly flourishes in a jurisdiction, the police can be accused of nonfeasance if they have not taken reasonable steps to curb the offenses.

More commonly, charges of nonfeasance are directed toward an individual officer rather than an entire agency. For example an officer who has not taken proper steps to stop the serving of liquor "after hours" at a bar on his beat is guilty of nonfeasance.

REGULATION VIOLATIONS

Violations of departmental regulations are unauthorized breaches of prescribed conduct. They may or may not be intentional and do not necessarily constitute corruption.

Well-written departmental regulations inform personnel of what is expected of them. Further, regulations must be enforced uniformly in all situations and be applied equally to all persons. Therefore regulations must reflect an element of universality that prohibits anyone from violating them. Through regulations a police officer knows how he is expected to act in fulfilling his responsibilities, how he should conduct himself, and what might result from failing to carry out the requirements of the department.

Very little disagreement exists among members of departments when specific regulations of conduct governing behavior are fair and reasonable. When rules are vague or unreasonable, the department's ability to control the activities of its officers decreases. In these cases, acceptable conduct becomes what the department will tolerate and what officers can "get away with." Impropriety and corrupt activity thrive in poorly run organizations where regulations have no real force in influencing behavior.

A common departmental regulation is one that prohibits the release of arrest records to private employers. In violation of this regulation, officers in certain jurisdictions check agency files for private employers to determine if job applicants have arrest records. Another regulation of many departments prohibits officers from working at certain part-time jobs—for example, as bartenders or private investigators. An officer working in either of these jobs might be tempted to use his police position to facilitate the part-time job. For example, as a bartender he may use his official position to enforce house rules. As a private investigator, he may utilize departmental information and resources during private investigations.

Officer Corruption

Corruption within a police department is caused by a multiplicity of constantly changing factors that vary among agencies. Personal gain appears to be a basic motivation for most police corruption. However, personal gain alone does not explain why corruption is a serious problem in some departments and virtually nonexistent in others.

Three interrelated elements that must be considered in the analysis of police corruption in any department are the individual, the agency or group, and the job.

THE INDIVIDUAL

To some observers, human behavior, particularly anti-social behavior, is understood almost exclusively in terms of "moral character" or the lack thereof. According to this view, an officer's misuse of authority reflects his personal anti-social tendencies as manifested in corrupt activity. Moreover, poor moral character is perceived as stemming from inadequate upbringing or genetic predisposition toward crime.

According to this view, the nature of police work attracts a substantial number of persons whose only interest in the profession is the opportunity for graft. This view stresses the careful selection of candidates for police work to eliminate undesirable personnel and poor risks.

THE GROUP

Other analyses of contributory factors related to police corruption consider the working environment of the police as much as the background or character of individual officers.

A police force functions as a closely-knit fraternity of officers who depend on one another for assistance and support both on and off the job. Mutual trust and dependence are a necessity for at any time during the course of a workday an officer's safety and perhaps his very life may depend on the actions of his fellow officers. These instances may be rare but when they do occur, each officer must be confident of the loyalty of the other. There can be no second thoughts in an emergency during which an officer's well-being is threatened.

The feeling of solidarity within a police agency is typically reinforced by the social isolation of police officers. The work schedule of police officers is not congruent with that of the 9 to 5 routine of most jobs. On holidays, weekends, and evenings, when most of the population is enjoying their leisure, police officers are at work. But the disparity between the working schedules of police officers and other citizens is an insignificant part of the police officer's social isolation. What makes him separate is the experience of his job and its tremendous influence over his perception, attitudes, and ability to form friendships outside of the police world.

An important part of the individual officer's attitude toward corruption is the so-called "code of silence," which has been described as an unwritten rule among police that constrains an officer from informing on or testifying against other officers. It is based on the intense feelings of loyalty to the group and mutual protectiveness against outsiders. It operates through peer pressure, and violations of the code are thought to result in being ostracized from the group. The "code of silence" is not absolute. There are limits to which most officers will avoid reporting acts of corruption. Whereas petty acts of corruption, such as free meals, may be protected by the code, extreme acts of corruption or criminality will be reported.

In practice, the code of silence leads to a perversion of ethics and makes corruption possible. It shields the corrupt police officer from exposure and condemns any colleague who would expose him. Chances are that peer pressure could stop or reduce corruption, and perhaps it does in many agencies. However, in certain departments, the pressure of the group protects rather than prevents corrupt activities.

Although most police officers do not engage in corrupt acts, their failure to report instances of misconduct supports the conditions that make widespread corruption possible. Honest in every other respect, the average police officer knowing about corrupt activities may either lie or equivocate about the misconduct of a fellow officer. Usually he will claim to have no knowledge about the allegation of improper conduct when confronted. When an honest officer is assigned a partner who is corrupt, the honest officer will simply request to work with a different officer or seek a transfer. He will avoid discussion of the real problem—corruption.

Police officers often delude themselves about the extent of corruption within their agencies.

They attempt to shield themselves from observing or thinking about the problem. Remaining "ignorant" of corruption relieves them from having to make the painful decision to recognize corruption and to report it.

THE JOB

The general conditions of police work cannot be overlooked when analyzing the causes of corruption. Police officers work alone or with a partner, and many of their contacts with suspects occur in isolation where the discretionary power of the officer can make the difference between freedom and arrest. Depending on the circumstances, the suspect, and the officer's attitude toward his job, his judgment can be influenced in either direction.

In the course of a police officer's intensive exposure to the worst side of humanity, he discovers that dishonesty and corruption are by no means restricted to those who are commonly considered as criminal. The officer encounters many individuals of good reputation engaging in practices equally dishonest and corrupt. An officer usually can cite specific instances of reputable citizens defrauding insurance agencies by false claims, hiding earnings to avoid taxes, or obtaining services or merchandise without payment.

Constant exposure to public immorality and the failures of the criminal justice system frequently create within police officers a cynical attitude toward their work and the general public. In the limitless encounters where the officer's discretion is the basis for action, this cynicism may lead an officer to manipulate the law in the name of expediency or for personal gain.

Another factor that affects an officer's attitude is the disparity between what is defined as illegal and which laws the public expects will be enforced. The entire area of so-called victimless crimes such as prostitution and gambling represents an intense source of frustration to police officers. In many jurisdictions, these illegal activities are condoned by the community and treated lightly by the courts. The attitude of the public can quickly become the attitude of the police in these instances, resulting in either corrupt practices or nonfeasance.

Roots of Corruption

Within the larger community of any police jurisdiction, the practice of exchanging gifts, swapping services, and extending professional "courtesies" is accepted by all citizens. It is a normal part of business relations for a salesman to offer a bargain to a steady customer or for a manufacturer to obtain favorable advertising space in a magazine or newspaper by paying "extra." Employees on public payrolls also receive gifts for professional services rendered.

The payment of money, goods, or services from businessmen to police officers is a widespread, traditional practice in many jurisdictions. The free meal is perhaps the most commonly received gratuity. The extra services businessmen expect in return for giving a gratuity may include such immediate acts as additional protection during business hours and after closing, police escorts to banks, and frequent patrol of the business vicinity.

This additional police protection of certain businesses detracts from the delivery of efficient and effective services to the general public. An even more serious outcome of accepting gratuities is that street-level decisions on allocations of police personnel are influenced by who is willing to pay extra for them rather than where they are most needed. "Favors" of this sort result in serious and improper displacement of police services and ultimately will represent a serious corruption hazard despite the fact that no criminal activity may be involved.

Businessmen offering gratuities may expect nothing more of the police than vague favor when needed. If accepting gratuities from businessmen is condoned, and granting of small favors is considered within a department to be of little or no overall consequence, real harm can result. Eventually, more serious forms of corruption will tend to be unrecognized or overlooked.

Study Questions

1. Distinguish among nonfeasance, misfeasance, malfeasance, and negligence.

2. According to the IACP, how important is peer pressure to conform a cause of police corruption? Do you think that this assessment is likely to be true in the other areas of criminal justice practice? Why? Defend your position.

3. What is your opinion of the justification of behavior that "Everyone else does it, so it must be morally acceptable"? Explain in detail why you think that this form of moral argument is valid or invalid. Use examples to defend your position.

4. What position does the IACP take regarding police acceptance of gratuities? What arguments are presented in defense of the position? Are the arguments ethical in nature, or are they more concerned with job effectiveness? Do you agree with the IACP here? Why? Defend your position.

Patterns of Prison Corruption

BERNARD J. McCARTHY

THE CORRUPTION OF PUBLIC EMPLOYEES represents a significant problem in the administration of criminal justice. Public officials engaging in corrupt practices undermine crime control efforts by enabling certain individuals to gain, by private purchase, immunity, or special consideration from the law. On another level, the exposure of corruption by public officials also leads to a loss of confidence and trust in the criminal justice system by the general public (NCCD, 1974).[1] While the significance of the problem is widely recognized, our understanding of the dimensions of the problem is limited, particularly in the field of criminal justice. The literature on corruption in criminal justice has focused almost exclusively on police practices. No such body of literature has developed with regard to the problem of corruption in other areas of criminal justice, particularly corrections.

This omission in the literature on corrections impairs our ability to devise effective management control strategies to reduce the incidence of employee misconduct. The need for a critical examination of this dark side of corrections is apparent when we consider the continuing public and political demand for accountability in the operation of government agencies, and the reports by the press on problems occurring in corrections, including accounts of employee misconduct, that have become almost routine. For example, in 1983 there were several different national news reports regarding correctional employees involved in various corrupt practices (accepting bribes, smuggling drugs, weapons, and other contraband; engaging in extortion, and sexually abusing inmates [New York Times Annual Index, 1983]).[2] Finally, corrections is a growing enterprise and, as its size expands, the likelihood of further employee corruption problems increases. A 1983 Department of Justice

Bernard J. McCarthy, "Patterns of Prison Corruption." Reprinted from the December 1984 issue of Corrections Today, with the permission of the American Correctional Association, Laurel, MD 02707.

study reported that there were over 4,300 adult correctional facilities, 2,000 probation agencies, and approximately 2,576 public and private juvenile custody facilities throughout the United States (*Report to the Nation on Crime and Justice,* 1983).[3] The American Correctional Association reports that 172,424 persons are employed in adult corrections, and 35,629 are working in the juvenile justice system (American Correctional Association, 1984).[4] Given the magnitude of corrections in the United States, the need for a critical examination of employee corruption problems is obvious. This paper takes a first step by attempting to describe the types of corrupt practices found in one agency.

The Case Study

The primary source of information for this study was provided by a content analysis of the case records compiled by the internal affairs unit of a state department of corrections. This basic source of information was supplemented by personal interviews with various staff members, cross-checks with official records compiled by other units within the agency (the division of personnel), and the administration of a self-report instrument to a sample of correctional officers.

Admittedly, this information source (the internal affairs records) cannot be expected to provide a total view of the problem, nor does it represent the full range of corruption within the agency. However, as researchers in the area of police corruption have suggested, the records of internal affairs units represent one of the best available sources of information for studying this form of hidden deviance (Meyer, 1976;[5] Sherman, 1979[6]).

For the purposes of this article, corruption is defined as the intentional violation of organizational norms (i.e., rules and regulations) by public employees for personal material gain. This definition is consistent with the general literature on corruption, particularly the literature on police corruption (Simpson, 1977).[7]

Several conditions must be present for an act

to be defined as corrupt. First, the action must involve employees involved in misconduct. Second, the offense must be in violation of the formal rules of the agency. Third, the offense must involve an employee receiving personal material gain through the misuse of his or her office. These conditions provide a basis for distinguishing corrupt practices from other forms of official misconduct.

During the 14-month review period the internal affairs unit handled 122 cases that allegedly involved employees in corrupt practices (out of a total of 180 cases pressed). A review of the allegations revealed four major offense categories plus a miscellaneous, or residual, category: Theft (n = 32), Embezzlement (n = 16), Trafficking (n = 16), Misuse of Authority (n = 54), Miscellaneous (n = 4).

Offense Categories

The offense categories were analyzed in terms of the characteristics of the offense, type of staff involvement, and organization.

THEFT

Allegations regarding employee theft comprised one-fourth of all cases; these offenses can generally be distinguished in terms of the victim involved. Petty forms of thievery were alleged by inmates who complained of losing both personal valuables and contraband (money or drugs). These items generally were claimed to have been stolen during cell searches or given to staff for safekeeping. Visitors also alleged that their possessions were stolen during routine visiting room searches. Staff were also victims of theft, losing such items as money, checks, etc. A final victim was the state: goods and materials that appeared to be stolen on a singular or opportunistic basis were reported as theft rather than embezzlement. This included the theft of a calculator, walkie talkie, food, tools, and other equipment.

It appears that charges of theft involving employees were usually directed at low-level staff. These individuals tend to act alone; the offense was rarely organized, non-hierarchical, and inmates were seldom involved as coconspirators. Among the items reported as stolen during the review period were: drugs, letters, checks, postal orders, inmate scrip (money), money (U.S.), tools, wallets, pocketbooks, calculators, radio equipment, cameras, color television sets, food, and construction materials. The type of victim involved usually determined the type of loss reported. It appeared that reports of losses of contraband by inmates and civilians (visitors) were raised when the victims were caught engaging in misconduct.

TRAFFICKING WITH INMATES

This offense involves the collaboration of staff with inmates and civilians to smuggle contraband into or out of correctional facilities for money, drugs, or services (usually of a sexual nature). Contraband is generally defined by the agency as any item not officially issued to the inmate that he cannot possess lawfully in prison.

Employees were suspected to be involved in smuggling the following items: drugs (pills, marijuana, heroin, cocaine, and benzedrex inhalers), alcohol, money, and weapons. Staff also appeared to be engaged in trafficking of other items (i.e., food, mail, reading materials), but were not subject to the formal sanctioning process, suggesting that less serious offenses were handled informally. This issue arose in interviews with staff.

The act of smuggling contraband items into a correctional facility varied considerably in degree of organization and scope of illicit activities. Generally, the more individuals involved, the more organized the operation and the more extensive the list of contraband items made available. The most sophisticated smuggling rings were organized hierarchically with inmates as ring leaders. In practice, operations ranged from a correctional officer bringing in alcohol for an inmate's personal use to large-scale, multistate conspiracies involving complex drug importation schemes. Staff involved in smuggling were usually line staff employees working

as correctional officers, although a few professionals (counselors and job placement officers) were implicated in a number of criminal conspiracies. The extent and role of staff involvement in smuggling also varied considerably; some employees merely served as "mules," picking up drugs at a prearranged location and transporting the contraband item to inmates for a carrying fee, while other employees coordinated the conspiracy, controlling the operation by directly selling items to inmates for a large profit or by using inmate intermediaries as salesmen or pushers.

In many cases the investigation of allegations of staff trafficking with inmates led to the discovery of other forms of misconduct. For example, the investigation of complaints that correctional officers were smuggling drugs into a correctional facility led to further charges that the officer misused his or her authority concerning the selective enforcement of rules and permissiveness towards his or her coconspirators. This suggests that if an employee is willing to smuggle drugs or weapons into a correctional facility, he or she is willing and able to commit other forms of misconduct (e.g., acceptance of gratuities) to maximize personal gain. Sums received by staff reportedly ranged from $35 for carrying one ounce of marijuana to $400 for obtaining a gun; pints of liquor were reportedly sold for $35 each.

EMBEZZLEMENT

In the present study, embezzlement is defined as "systematically converting state property or goods to one's own use," as opposed to simple forms of opportunistic and solitary acts of theft. In most cases, this offense involved low-level staff (usually correctional officers, shopkeepers, or clerks) and inmates embezzling money from administrative units where money or material transactions were made within the system. These offenses generally occurred in inmate canteens, commissaries, and prison warehouses. At another level, however, there were a few allegations of embezzlement involving higher-echelon staff.

Several administrators and other professionals responsible for special fund accounts were investigated during the report period.

Embezzlement involves both staff and inmates working alone or together to defraud the state. Complaints regarding embezzlement were received from prison canteens, commissaries, prison warehouses, inmate concession stands, inmate payrolls, and community donation fund accounts. The majority of complaints regarding embezzlement were discovered through staff audits. Only a few investigations were initiated through the receipt of specific complaints (usually anonymous).

Typically, embezzlement involved collusion among inmates and low-level staff who worked together in canteens, commissaries, etc. It appeared that some staff members became involved in a web of relationships (both social and criminal) with inmates.

MISUSE OF AUTHORITY

This offense refers to the intentional misuse of the discretion vested in one's position for personal material gain; it accounted for almost one-half of all complaints received by the unit. This finding is not surprising, since correctional employees (especially line staff) are afforded considerable discretion in using a system of rewards and punishments to manage inmates. These privileges are both formal (e.g., transfers, assignments to honor blocks, or influential jobs) and informal (e.g., overlooking minor infractions of institutional rules). Because of the conditions of confinement (that involve relative levels of deprivation) and the frequency of low visibility decisions by staff, the potential for misuse of this authority is great.

Based on a review of the cases and staff interviews, misuse of authority appears to involve five basic offenses directed against inmates. One form of misuse of authority anticipated, but not found, in this study involves charges of staff vs. staff, e.g., gratuities provided to superiors for days off, promotions, or transfer to preferred shifts or jobs.

1. *Acceptance of gratuities for special consideration for legitimate privileges:* Under this category, employees would solicit or receive gratuities, usually money or drugs, from inmates for favorable consideration for transfer requests, cell and job assignments, and admission into special programs. For example, a correctional officer in charge of a work release program allegedly solicited a $20 fee from an inmate for finding him a job.

2. *Acceptance of gratuities for special consideration for protection of illicit activities:* This category involves employees involved in protecting, permitting, or engaging in illicit activities of inmates. These include "selling" the rights of franchises to illicit businesses (gambling, drugs, prostitution) in a section of a facility (e.g., a particular dormitory), protecting illicit activities from discovery or competition from other inmates (loan sharks, drug sales, prostitution), and actual involvement in criminal conspiracies with and without inmate collusion (e.g., selling of escapes, extortion of inmates and their families, forgery of money orders).

3. *Mistreatment/harassment or extortion of inmates:* This offense involves an employee using his or her authority in a punitive way toward an inmate in order to secure personal gain, rather than the provision of special privileges to inmates. This misuse of authority has been described as a form of extortion where the threat or abuse of power is used in order to secure payment (Key, 1936).[8] This offense includes setting up certain inmates for shakedowns and personally punishing inmates when they refuse to provide special services or obey specific directions. Allegations also involve inmates' complaints that correctional officers were using their authority to stamp out some of the competition in drug smuggling rings among inmates, or for purposes of personal revenge.

4. *Mismanagement:* This offense is a catch-all

category that covers charges against staff (usually administrators) that they mismanaged a unit or division for personal gain or aggrandizement. Allegations regarding prison industries and the operation of individual correctional facilities were received. Complaints were generally initiated by inmates regarding mismanagement by prison officers that resulted in personal gain, such as the use of prison industries for private profit. In only one instance did a staff member raise charges against supervisors. Another major investigation appeared to have been prompted by inmates writing to the local newspaper about their charges.

5. *Miscellaneous:* This final group includes a number of unrelated offenses that involved allegations of serious employee misconduct. These included several suspicious deaths of employees, charges of sexual coercion of a female employee by her supervisor, the sale of drugs in the community by employees, and several cases where prospective employees had attempted to conceal their prior criminal backgrounds.

Impact of Corruption

With respect to *inmates,* the two most direct functions of corruption are: first, the selective nullification of rules, regulations, and procedures designed to control and restrict the offender; and second, the provision of scarce commodities to the ongoing inmate underground economy of the correctional system. In terms of their immediate living situation, certain inmates are provided the opportunity to gain some control over their conditions of confinement and thereby minimize the rigors of incarceration. Generally, it can be anticipated that, as long as inmates are kept under conditions of severe material deprivation, the demand for illicit goods and services will remain high. A third consequence of corruption is exploitation.

Corruption serves several functions for *staff.*

These functions can be specified in terms of activities designed to augment personal income or assist personnel with the performance of their job responsibilities, and as a method to develop or maintain friendships with inmates. Employees who misuse their discretionary authority for private gain can do so in a number of ways. They can aggressively seek out opportunities (e.g., sale of drugs) or simply decide to accept unsolicited requests from inmates. The amount of material gain is dependent on the willingness of the staff member to participate in different types of corrupt practices.

Staff members may also participate in corrupt arrangements with inmates as a result of work-related pressures. As Cloward (1960)[9] has noted, line staff frequently work out informal accommodations with inmates as a form of social control within the prison. Corruption may also serve to develop or strengthen personal ties between certain employees and inmates. Friendships may develop and the staff member may engage in corrupt practices as a favor to a particular inmate.

Some of the dysfunctions of corruption include threatening the security of an institution (and the safety of staff) by smuggling weapons and escape implements. The introduction of contraband and the sale of special privileges may undermine institutional discipline. Also, staff involvement in corrupt practices may diminish inmate and staff confidence and respect in the administration of the prison and call into question the legitimacy of the correctional process.

This paper was based on an exploratory case study of corruption in corrections. The purpose of the study was threefold: first, to examine the forms of corruption occurring in an institutional environment; second, to provide the basis for informed action designed to control the problem by identifying patterns of corruption; and third, to contribute to the systematic study of corruption and its impact on the criminal justice system by providing an initial overview of the problem in prisons.

NOTES

1. National Council on Crime and Delinquency (NCCD). "Policy Statement on Corruption," *Crime and Delinquency.* October, 1974.

2. New York Times. *Annual Index.* 1983.

3. United States Department of Justice. *Report to the Nation on Crime and Justice: The Duty.* Washington, DC: Bureau of Justice Statistics, 1983.

4. American Correctional Association. *Directory 1984.* College Park, MD, 1984.

5. Meyer, J. C., "Definitional and Etiological Issues in Police Corruption: An Assessment and Synthesis of Competing Perspectives," *Journal of Police Science and Police Administration,* Volume 4, 1976.

6. Sherman, W. "Obtaining Access to Police International Affairs Files," *Criminal Law Bulletin.* September–October, 1979.

7. Simpson, A. *The Literature of Police Corruption.* New York, NY: John Jay Press, 1977.

8. Key, V. O. *Techniques of Political Graft in the United States.* Chicago, IL: University of Chicago Press, 1936.

9. Cloward, R. *Theoretical Studies in the Social Organization of the Prison.* New York, NY: Social Science Research Council, 1960.

Study Questions

1. Why do you think that the criminal justice literature on corruption has focused almost exclusively on police corruption? Are police officers more susceptible occupationally to corruption than correctional officers, or is there some other explanation? Defend your position.

2. What did McCarthy find to be the most common form of corruption in the institution he studied? What do you think that prison administrators should do to reduce this type of corruption?

3. Incarceration of offenders is often justified on the basis of its alleged deterrent effect on citizens who would otherwise break the law. If the severe and unpleasant limitations on freedom that are experienced by inmates are truly a deterrent, why is there any corruption in correctional facilities, let alone extensive corruption? Defend your position.

4. Is the sexual harassment of one correctional officer by another officer a form of corruption, in your opinion? Why? Defend your position. Does your concept of corruption agree with McCarthy's? Explain.

Police Corruption

MICHAEL JOHNSTON

A POLICE OFFICER AND his partner stop for lunch at a small diner. Both in uniform, they sit at the counter and eat a full meal. When they are done, they wave at the owner and leave, paying nothing. Neither the owner nor the police officers give the matter much thought, for the owner routinely gives free lunch to the officers working the district.

A rookie patrol officer and his veteran partner investigate a break-in at a liquor store. When they arrive at the scene they find

Michael Johnston, Political Corruption and Public Policy in America. *(Monterey: Brooks/Cole Publishing Company, 1982), Ch. 4 (pp. 72–107). © 1982 by Wadsworth, Inc. Used by permission of the publisher.*

several other patrol cars, a broken window, and a ransacked store. The rookie notices that his veteran colleagues are taking a great deal of interest in the remaining liquor. Some of them are taking bottles back to their cars. One veteran hands a couple of bottles to the rookie: "Here kid, have yourself a party. It's all covered by insurance anyway." The young cop pauses a moment, then takes the liquor out to his car.

Several years of hard work in an inner-city precinct have finally paid off for a patrolman: he has been designated captain's bagman. On the first and 15th of every month, he makes the rounds of the book joints, speakeasies, and numbers writers in the district, collecting protection money. Back at the precinct, the money is divided into shares. The captain, lieutenant, and sergeant get the most, but even for some patrol officers the illegal take exceeds $1000 per month.

City police are charged with responsibility for enforcing the law. Yet at least some police officers, in almost every city of any size, break the law. All of the cases mentioned previously are examples of actual police misconduct. They vary in seriousness and the frequency with which they occur, but in each case department regulations and public laws are being broken.

... I will examine typical patterns of police corruption, their causes and effects, and some possible strategies for policing the police. The analysis will be guided by three theoretical approaches. First, the personalistic perspective suggests that police corruption is either a "rotten apple" problem or a systematic one. In the "rotten apple" theory, a few dishonest officers spoil the image of a basically honest department. If the corruption is systematic, the personalistic perspective suggests that corruption is caused by the social background of police recruits, their motivations, and their personalities. Second, institutional factors affecting the development and persistence of corruption include bureaucratization of large police departments, the role of the police in the broader criminal justice system, and the difficulties of maintaining "police pro-

fessionalism." Finally, the systemic view directs our attention to value and culture conflicts in society, particularly over vice and personal morality. The systemic view points to crime and vice as big business and to peer-group socialization processes through which veteran officers teach recruits how to resolve the dilemmas of police work. As with the analysis of machine politics, I will argue that the systemic approach is the most useful of the three. I will also suggest, however, that institutional factors are important as well, especially when viewed in the wider systemic setting.

Police in the City

Urban police officers live and work at that crucial pressure point where law and society meet. Their lot is one of tension, ambiguity, and conflicting demands from many segments of the community. They are isolated from the rest of the community by their work schedules, their uniforms, and the power and danger that go with the job. Police work quickly becomes an all-encompassing way of life for the officers and their families. Yet we depend heavily upon them. As August Vollmer put it in 1936, we expect our police:

> ... to have the wisdom of Solomon, the courage of David, the patience of Job and the leadership of Moses, the kindness of the Good Samaritan, the strategy of Alexander, the faith of Daniel, the diplomacy of Lincoln, the tolerance of the Carpenter of Nazareth, and, finally, an intimate knowledge of every branch of the natural, biological, and social sciences. If he had all these, he *might* be a good policeman.[1]

When police are wrong, then, it is serious business. If we can no longer depend upon the police to protect us and our property, what happens then? If police powers of arrest, coercion, and violence are used in arbitrary and capricious ways, what happens to our rights and civil liberties? When police scandals are revealed, many citizens who have always trusted the police—frequently to the point of taking them for granted—respond with fear and bitterness. Life in the city becomes more dangerous and unpredictable when it turns out that the police officer is really *not* our friend.

BACKGROUND

Police corruption emerged, it seems, almost as soon as there were police. Sherman notes that charges of corruption forced Henry II of England to relieve several sheriffs of their duties as early as 1170, and that the Paris police engaged in bribery, extortion, and active thievery from the end of the Dark Ages until the French Revolution.[2] The Sûreté of Paris, founded in 1817, recruited thieves as police, on the assumption that they could best catch other thieves. As Sherman explains, however, "The arrest of several Sûreté men for burglary showed that thieves as detectives were still thieves."[3] New York City authorities reorganized their police in 1845 but made the mistake of leaving the appointment of officers to elected ward representatives. Not only did police ignore election irregularities; often, they worked out lucrative crime-and-kickback schemes with ward officials and criminals. In 1857 the New York state legislature created a new police force accountable to the governor. The result was an actual battle at City Hall between the old and new police, with the army intervening to stop the mayhem. The new, state-controlled police force, once firmly in power, quickly developed corrupt practices of its own.[4]

Administrative reforms reduced police corruption somewhat in London and Paris beginning in the late 1800s, though both cities have had periodic outbreaks of scandal.[5] In New York, police corruption continues today. The Lexow Commission investigation in 1892 unearthed organized extortion, bribery, sale of office, and corruption in the enforcement of gambling, liquor, and prostitution laws. Seventy years later the Knapp Commission reported that many of these activities continued to flourish and that they had been joined by extensive corruption in drug-law enforcement.[6] Many observers, in fact, have noted that police corruption in New York seems to go through 20-year cycles of public apathy, scandal, investigation, "reform," and apathy again.

Other American cities have had police scandals. In the early 1960s, for example, corrupt activities—including active police burglary rings—were discovered in Chicago, Denver, and Des Moines. As of late 1979, charges of police misconduct were being investigated in such places as Atlanta, Miami, Nye County (Nevada), Chicago, Dade County (Florida), Miami Beach, Los Angeles, and New Britain, Connecticut. Allegations in these cases range from one officer's actively soliciting clients for an attorney (Miami) to a systematic graft operation involving the Chicago police motor pool.[7] Police corruption still flourishes and poses serious dilemmas for urban law enforcement agencies.

Police Corruption: Types and Techniques

Police encounter the full range of human activity in the course of their work, and as a result, police corruption assumes many forms. The seriousness of wrongdoing varies as well. The "free lunch" described previously is a common violation of departmental regulations and the law, but it is not as serious as the systematic bribery and extortion involving the captain's bagman. Corruption also varies in the number of officers involved and the degree to which it is organized. In this section I will set out some general categories of police corruption and then focus on bribery/extortion practices, which will be my primary concern.

WHAT IS POLICE CORRUPTION?

I define police corruption as actions *on the part of an officer that exploit the powers of law enforcement in return for considerations of private-regarding benefit and that violate formal standards governing his or her conduct.* "Actions" can include decisions *not* to act. "Private-regarding benefit" covers a wide range of rewards, tangible and otherwise, that accrue to the officer, colleagues, family, and friends. "Formal standards" can be public laws, departmental regulations, or both.

Obviously, our definition of corruption is a

broad one. It puts free lunch into the same category as police burglary rings, at least for the moment. It does, however, distinguish corruption from other forms of misconduct, such as police brutality, and from such violations of department regulations as sleeping or drinking while on duty. The latter actions break laws or department regulations and could be said to yield certain private-regarding benefits, but they do not in themselves necessarily constitute exploitation of the role of police officer. They are the sorts of misconduct in which many people could engage.

Generally speaking, there are four major categories of police corruption:

1. internal corruption;
2. selective enforcement or non-enforcement of the law;
3. active criminality; and
4. bribery and extortion.

These categories blur considerably in practice. A motorcycle cop who takes a $20 bill in exchange for not writing a speeding ticket is engaging in bribery or extortion, depending upon who initiated the illicit transaction. The cop is also practicing selective non-enforcement. Moreover, the boundaries between many sorts of corruption and legitimate conduct are indistinct. There exist some situations in which selective enforcement is wholly legitimate. Still, these four categories of corruption enable us to catalog the types and practices of police corruption.

Internal corruption. Some kinds of police corruption do not directly involve the public but instead take place among officers or subunits of a department. In some departments radio operators routinely expect, and get, "Christmas money" from patrol officers.[8] Part of the motivation is simple good will, but radio dispatchers can also cover up for officers who go out of service for a time without authorization or who do not wish to take calls in certain neighborhoods. These special arrangements are against regulations and may produce slow or inadequate police service, but as corruption they are usually of minor concern. Another sort of internal corruption is the practice, found in some cities, of paying sergeants, lieutenants, and captains to secure choice assignments or to avoid disciplinary action. Officers may also give or sell portions of drugs confiscated in arrests to each other for use as evidence in other cases, for planting on suspects, for paying off informers, or even for personal use. The Chicago motor pool case—in which police cars were sold at cut rates to officers while still in good condition, forcing the department to buy new cars[9]—is yet another example of internal corruption. Just as the governmental bottleneck is the focus of corrupt techniques of influence because important decisions are at stake, a police department is a complex organization with internal bottlenecks of its own.

Selective enforcement or non-enforcement of the law. Discretion is the essence of good police work. Incidents rarely fall neatly into categories specified by the law. Officers must routinely make quick judgments as to what has happened and what, if anything, should be done. If police did not enjoy wide discretion, they would be highly ineffective and would quickly alienate the communities they are supposed to serve. Legitimate discretion can, however, be abused or exploited. Traffic cops stopping speeders do not have to write tickets. They can issue verbal or written warnings. Many motorists know this, and some will offer a $20 bill to "aid" the officer in exercising discretion. Some officers, on the other hand, will use their powers of discretion to extort the money, thereby teaching the unsophisticated citizen that the law is often a matter of judgment and negotiation. Similarly, an officer who confronts small-time numbers runners or drug users can arrest them or let them go free. If they are freed, it makes a great deal of difference whether they were let go in exchange for valuable information or for money. Whether or not discretion is used corruptly depends, for analytical purposes, on whether or not the officer is pursuing private-regarding benefits. In practice, though, even this may be difficult to judge. An officer who aggressively uses her discretionary powers to get information from numbers runners may eventually arrest higher-ups in the operation and thus be doing a good job. But if she does this solely to win promotion to a plain-clothes detective squad where she hears bribe money comes easy, she is beginning to abuse her discretion for private gain.

Police discretion constitutes a particularly sensitive kind of bottleneck. Officers who detain citizens have them at their mercy, if only for a short time, for they can decide to use (or not use) significant powers of search and seizure, arrest, and violence. Abuses in these situations are difficult to detect because they happen quickly and are often concealed by both officer and citizen. Discretion is an essential part of police work, but it is also a root of the corrupt practice of selective law enforcement.

Active criminality. When allegations of an organized police burglary ring in Des Moines surfaced during the early 1960s, a story made the rounds that one of the physical-fitness tests for prospective recruits was how fast they could run the 100-yard dash with a television set under each arm. In point of fact, only a small percentage of any modern police force gets involved in the active planning and committing of crimes. But active criminality does take place, typically involving burglary and the sale of stolen goods. It is for many people a particularly disturbing type of police corruption.

Many of the powers and procedures that enable police to combat crime also enable them to commit crime. Police have access to all sorts of places, public and private, at all times of the day or night. Most of us do not question their right to be there. An officer trying the back door of a liquor store late at night is probably just making sure the lock is secure. But maybe something less honorable is going on. American police are armed, and they have two-way radios to keep track of the location and movement of other police. Both tools could be quite useful in pulling off burglaries. A uniform and a badge are symbols of trust, but they can also be used to deceive us or to allay our suspicions and caution. Most police use these powers in service of the law. Even those who are involved in other forms

of corruption often regard active criminality as breaking the norms of "acceptable" misconduct.[10] Not all officers feel that way, though, and when active police criminality does come to light the result frequently is great public outcry. As the Des Moines anecdote suggests, people develop a widespread cynicism about all police—honest or otherwise.

Bribery and extortion. Bribery and extortion refer to practices in which law enforcement roles are exploited specifically to raise money. For analytical purposes, bribery is initiated by the citizen, extortion by the officer. In practice, the distinction is rarely clear,[11] for frequently these transactions are products of unspoken mutual expectations. In such an atmosphere, it makes little difference who initiates the deal. In fact, the systemic approach will suggest that often there are strong environmental pressures on both police and public to resolve potential conflicts through corruption.

Practices of bribery and extortion vary widely, ranging from a few officers who take whatever might come their way to systematic protection rings. Sherman divides these and other corrupt practices into three categories, based on whether or not they are pervasive and organized. He also outlines the typical "sources" of corruption present in each case, as shown in Table 1.

Type I corruption—non-pervasive and unorganized—includes departments in which most officers are honest, but where a few will take a bribe if the opportunity arises. There is no systematic bribery or extortion. If a contractor gives an officer a few dollars to ignore a truck parked on a sidewalk, the money is pocketed and the matter ends there. Lone offenders seeking to beat the rap on minor offenses are a major source of Type I corruption, as Sherman's table suggests. In practice, a Type I department is about as "clean" a police force as we could expect to find in a major city.

Type II corruption is no more organized than Type I, but it involves a majority of the department. Here too, officers take whatever a day's work may bring their way and keep it for

Table 1 Sherman's three types of police corruption[12]

Type	Extent	Organization	Sources Lone criminals	Public	Rackets
I	Small	Little	X		
II	Large	Little	X	X	
III	Large	Much	X	X	X

themselves and partners. When a majority of a department "takes," however, opportunities to make money can become more frequent. Motorists may be more likely to try to buy their way out of tickets, for example, if they have reason to think that 70% of the police will go for the offer than if they think their chances are only 20%. The general public becomes a source of Type II bribery, particularly in nations where the police issue various licenses, permits, and certificates.[13]

Corruption in a Type III case is pervasive and organized. Money is taken on a systematic basis from persons engaged in gambling, prostitution, drugs, and illegal liquors in return for police "protection."[14] Other, perhaps less well organized shakedown operations may be directed at motorists, construction contractors, trucking firms who send overweight trucks through the city, bars, and restaurants. Money is collected monthly or every two weeks by a "bagman" and divided among all officers in the deal. Shares are awarded to patrol officers; a share and a half or a double share may go to commanding officers. A single share, called a "steady note" in some cities, can be quite sizable. The Knapp Commission heard of shares ranging from $400 per month per officer in quieter Manhattan districts to more than $1500 per month for some Harlem detectives. Because this money is tax free, it represents a sizable income supplement, exceeding in some cases an officer's legitimate take-home pay. New officers who want in on the deal may be put on a two- or three-month probation to test their trustworthiness. Later, if they leave the district, they may get that probation-time

money as "severance pay." Ring members who find new protection clients frequently are given the first take from the new source as a "finder's fee." Discussions may be held on where to find new clients or whether or not to raise a client's regular assessment. A majority of a precinct's officers may be involved in the corruption. Those who are not involved know what is going on. Lone offenders and the general public are occasional sources of money for Type III bribery and extortion, but here two new and much more significant elements enter into the process—organized crime and vice. Many "protection" clients have direct or indirect organized crime connections. Vice is big business; substantial investments and big profits are at stake. Its scale, organization, and racket connections put Type III police corruption in a class by itself.

SCOPE OF THE ANALYSIS

Internal corruption, selective enforcement, active criminality, and bribery and extortion all pose serious policy problems and analytical challenges. My primary focus, however, will be the bribery/extortion problem, and, in particular, the pervasive organized practices of Type III cases. I will focus on bribery and extortion in part simply to cut the general subject of police corruption down to size. But I also focus on bribery and extortion because they are the most significant forms of police corruption. They are widespread and assume similar forms in many cities. More than other kinds of corruption, bribery and extortion are forms of influence, shaping the law enforcement service that society gets.

HOW MUCH CORRUPTION?

No one knows the full extent of police wrongdoing. Normally, the parties to a corrupt transaction have an interest in keeping it secret. Even when police scandal is unearthed, we discover only part of the corruption. Albert J. Reiss' study of police behavior in four large northern cities, however, gives us some idea of the scope of the problem. Reiss' researchers rode with police officers—who knew they were being observed—for several weeks during the summer of 1966. The observers counted, among other things, all instances in which officers committed felonies and misdemeanors other than assault. They found that roughly 20% of the officers took part in criminal violations of the law.[15] These officers may not typify big-city police, and the precincts involved did tend to be high-crime areas. But if 20% of a group of officers *who knew they were being observed* indulged in some form of lawbreaking, how much police wrongdoing must there be overall?

Reiss' observers also found that small favors of the "free lunch" variety were commonplace. Thirty-one percent of the businesspeople surveyed in high-crime areas acknowledged giving free merchandise or special discounts to the police. Many businesspeople extend these favors believing that they will receive extra police protection, an assumption Reiss finds generally unsupported by fact. Reiss' conclusions, based on his own and other data, give us an overall idea of the scope of police misconduct: "(D)uring any year a substantial minority of all police officers violate the criminal law, a majority misbehave toward citizens in an encounter, and most engage in serious violations of the rules and regulations of the department."[17]

What causes police corruption? The next section takes up this question, beginning with the personalistic approach.

Personalistic Views on Police Corruption

There are three major personalistic explanations for police corruption. They all emphasize individual officers as the ultimate causes of police crime, but they differ in their degrees of rigor, in the variables they emphasize, and in the ends to which they are used by analysts and administrators. They are, first, the "rotten apple" metaphor; second, a recruitment perspective; and third, a "police personality" explanation.

"ROTTEN APPLES"?

Whenever evidence of police misconduct surfaces in a major city, someone is sure to bring forth the notion that corruption is merely the doing of a few "rotten apples" in an otherwise honest department. Typically, these assertions come from the police chief, followed by police commissioners, police union leaders, and the mayor or city manager. The "rotten apple" argument has a natural attraction for these people. It is in their interest that the public, prosecutors, and the press not regard the police as totally and systematically corrupt. Many citizens believe in "rotten apples" too, for the notion that all or most of our guardians cannot be trusted is a frightening one indeed.

"Rotten apple" metaphors, however, simply cannot account for significant cases of police corruption. In Type III cases they are wrong by definition, because a majority of the force is involved in systematic corruption. Even in cases involving only a few officers, "rotten apple" ideas are of little value. They assume that a few deviants indulge in corruption because of some defect in themselves. Yet the deviants typically turn out to be much like other cops—unexceptional in background, personality, and (with the exception of the wrongdoing itself, fairly typical in their career paths. Their motives for joining the force are much like other officers'. When they recount how they came to indulge in corruption, they often describe a gradual process of learning on the job.[18] "Rotten apples" are not corrupting the rest of the barrel; if anything, we ought to be looking at the barrel itself.

The "rotten apple" view rests on fallacies that are of more than theoretical significance. They are a distinct hindrance to understanding and—where necessary—combatting police corruption. "Rotten apple" arguments are often employed as an excuse for not vigorously uncovering corruption in a department; if only a few deviants are involved, why not just handle the problem on a case-by-case basis? Similarly, the excuse can be used to limit investigations already in progress, protecting important figures while passing off the dismissal of a handful of patrol officers as a systematic cleanup. This view diverts our attention from fundamental problems in department organization and in police work itself. Indeed, much police corruption may be not so much deviance as conformity. The "rotten apples" view shifts responsibility away from top administrators and covers up the uneasy relationship between the police and the rest of the criminal justice system. It implies that all we have to do to fight police corruption is to carefully recruit people who do not have certain "defects"— despite the fact that vastly improved recruitment standards have not prevented corruption.

RECRUITMENT

Even if we discount the notion that isolated deviants are the cause of police corruption, it is still possible that personal traits shared widely within a department are at the root of corruption. If we found that police officers are recruited from social strata particularly susceptible to corruption, then we might have a more supportable personalistic explanation of police corruption than the "rotten apples" perspective.

Urban police officers are indeed recruited from distinct segments of the population. In the last 10 or 15 years, minority and women's organizations have made unrepresentative police recruitment a significant issue in many cities by citing problems of police brutality, police–community relations, and discrimination in hiring, firing, and promotion.

During the mid-1960s Arthur Neiderhoffer studied the New York City police to learn about the causes and consequences of what he termed "police cynicism." One of his concerns was recruitment: who became police officers, and what were their backgrounds? Not surprisingly, Neiderhoffer found the NYPD at the time almost exclusively to be a male preserve. There were, however, other distinctive patterns as well. Officers tended to come from White European (and frequently Roman Catholic) "ethnic" families. Neiderhoffer obtained data on membership in ethnic fraternal police organizations and found that of the more than 20,000 officers who belonged to one of these fraternal groups in 1965, 42% belonged to the Irish group, 25% to the Italian, and 5.4% to the Polish organization. These memberships are hardly a perfect indicator of police ethnicity, but the predominance of Irish and Italian officers is striking.[19]

Police recruits came from families of decidedly modest occupational and financial status, as Neiderhoffer observed: "For the past fifteen years (leading up to 1967), during a cycle of prosperity, the bulk of police candidates has been upper lower class with a sprinkling of lower middle class; about ninety-five percent has had no college training.[20] Data on the occupations of recruits' fathers revealed that 86.9% of the recruits came from the working class, broadly defined. Seven percent were sons of police officers. Police recruits tended in addition to be of average or better size and weight, above-average physical stamina and agility, and slightly above-average intelligence (mean IQ of 105). The percentage of applicants accepted in typical years ranged from 4% (Los Angeles) to 15% (New York).[21]

Some change in this picture has taken place over the last decade. Women, Blacks, and Puerto Ricans have joined city police departments in increasing numbers. Recruitment policies, height and weight requirements, and training procedures have been revised. It is not unusual today to see many sorts of people patrolling the streets. Still, changes occur only gradually; most police officers are still White males from working-class and lower middle-class families.

What does this have to do with police corruption? Maybe officers from lower-status families are more likely to take a bribe. Strong desires to climb the status ladder might make these sorts of officers more receptive to making money whenever they can. Lack of advanced schooling and a rough-and-tumble adolescence might leave

a young officer unaware—or even contemptuous—of standards of law and morality. Working-
class origins are also sometimes presumed to
produce certain attitudes, such as bigotry,
authoritarianism, selfishness, and shortsighted-
ness, any of which might lead to wrongdoing.
Police recruiting procedures may be filling difficult and complex jobs with people who are all
too ordinary, as Neiderhoffer suggests:

> The end result of the process of elimination
> (of potential police recruits) is to accentuate
> the medium and mediocre at the expense of
> the independent and exceptional. Working-
> class background, high-school education or
> less, average intelligence, cautious personal-
> ity—these are typical features of the modern
> police recruit. Only in his superior physical
> endowment does he stand above the
> world.[22]

When police scandal erupts, critics and concerned citizens often point to the social composition of the police force as a possible cause.
Typical recommendations include stricter
recruiting and training procedures and higher
educational standards, such as two years of college or more. Are these prescriptions based on a
sound explanation of police corruption?

I think not. It is true that many or most corrupt officers are White working-class "ethnic"
males without extensive education. But so are
most of the *honest* cops. Until recently there simply has not been enough variety in police officers' backgrounds for us to compare the
corruptibility of differing types of recruits. It
will be interesting to see whether the women
and minorities now entering police work will
turn up in the ranks of the corrupt. I am fairly
certain that a significant number of them will.
Even if they do not become as corrupt as established officers, it will not necessarily be because
they are "less corruptible." Especially in Type III
cases, suspicious old-style officers may simply be
reluctant to let them in on the action.

I think it fallacy, too, that those from the classic police background are somehow more corruptible than the rest of us. Strong desires for
status and financial and job security are hardly

exclusive properties of the working class. If
Watergate, white-collar crime, and illegal political contributions by business-people have taught
us anything, it is that high-status people, too,
will also bend or break the law to serve their private purposes. As for attitudes, Neiderhoffer's
research on "police cynicism"—arguably an
important part of an officer's decision to break
the law—found that college educated officers
were considerably more cynical than others.[23] It
may even be that working-class recruits are *better*
adapted to police work than, say, middle-class
college graduates. Neiderhoffer suggests that
they have been less insulated from street life and
more thoroughly tested than their college
trained counterparts.[24]

Whether or not Neiderhoffer's observations
are correct is a question that must await future
study. It seems unlikely, though, that an ethnic
working-class background in itself makes a person more corruptible than others, or that stiffer
entrance requirements will necessarily produce
an honest department. And as a practical matter,
if society decides it wants a college educated
police force, it had better be prepared to pay for
it. The recruitment and retention of college educated police will cost a lot more in salaries than
we offer now.

POLICE PERSONALITY

The "police personality" issue is partly a question of personal background, since the selection
of applicants and recruitment standards influences the department's psychological makeup.
But "police personality" can develop within the
department, too, if training and on-the-job
socialization perpetuate certain attitudes. There
is such a thing as a police subculture in many
departments.[25] There is evidence that applicants
are judged in part on how well they are likely to
fit in with the subculture,[26] and that they are
further socialized into it as they learn the job.[27]
Is there a "police personality," whatever its
source? If there is, could it lead to corruption?

Controversy over police behavior during the
last decade or so has spawned a great deal of
research into personalities and attitudes of police

officers. Joel Lefkowitz, in his very useful review of this research, notes that between the extreme views of police as heroes and police as ordinary people reside a number of images of police attitudes:

> Somewhere in the middle ground of informed opinion are those who feel that there exists a constellation of traits and attitudes or a general perspective on the world which particularly characterizes the policeman. This constellation is presumably comprised of such interrelated traits as authoritarianism, suspiciousness, physical courage, cynicism, conservatism, loyalty, secretiveness, and self-assertiveness. In addition these authors uniformly are of the opinion that these traits are fostered by occupational demands and do not especially characterize those who become police candidates before their exposure to the life of a policeman [citations omitted].[28]

Lefkowitz concludes that there *is* a "police personality."[29] Police officers tend to be somewhat more suspicious and defensive and feel more isolated than most people. They are not, however, especially cynical, dogmatic, or authoritarian in outlook, compared to many other occupational groups, and may be even less so than most lower middle- or working-class men. Police officers tend to be somewhat more impulsive, aggressive, and willing to take risks than people in other occupational groups. To some extent they prefer working under close supervision and are "more easily influenced by a status figure" than most other people.[30] As for the sources of these traits, Lefkowitz rightly observes that studies of police personality do not show conclusively whether the attitudes are brought to the force by recruits or learned on the job. Lefkowitz concludes that there is support for the notion that attitudes are learned in the process of police work, but he reminds us that police applicants are largely a self-selected group and come disproportionately from a social class that itself exhibits many of the psychological traits found in the police personality.

Does the police personality explain police corruption? I would argue that it does not. Many of the traits noted previously—aggressiveness, risk taking, willingness to take orders, even suspiciousness and impulsiveness—would seem to be *desirable* qualities in police officers. None of them seems inherently linked to corruption. If police attitudes are merely a reflection or distillation of the personality traits of a particular class, and if those traits are linked to corruption, then we might expect to find widespread corruption within that class. I am not convinced that in reality we would find such corruption. If on the other hand police personality grows out of police work itself, then—whether or not the attitudes seem tied to corruption—our attention is directed to the nature of the work and to its role in shaping behavior and attitudes.

This is where personalistic explanations for police corruption ultimately break down. Corruption takes place in actual police work situations. Pressures, opportunities, and frustrations are all part of the job, as are contacts with other people. Even if we could show that some personal or psychological characteristic somehow predisposes an officer to "turn corrupt"—a notion the evidence seems to deny—much would still depend upon pressures and opportunities growing out of dealings with other police, with the institutional workings of the police department, and with members of the public. This is especially true in the case of pervasive, organized bribery and extortion, my main concern here. The personalistic approach makes no provision for these pressures and opportunities and thus is an inadequate (or, in the "rotten apple" case, a downright pernicious) attempt at explanation. In the next two sections I will examine these pressures and opportunities in the dimensions of police work.

The Institutional Approach

Urban police departments are awkward organizational hybrids. Chains of command are organized on a quasi-military basis, yet most of the force works beyond the reach of effective supervision. Administrators seek "professionalization," yet the majority of the situations encountered on the street require on-the-spot decisions for which established guidelines are little help. Police officers work at the intake point of the criminal justice system, where the standards of "justice" differ sharply from the vision pursued by the rest of that system. Perhaps it is the way we organize police work—rather than the specific people we recruit—that leads to blue-coat crime.

In this section I discuss a set of related propositions about police departments as institutions. They raise four major problems: (1) the organizational difficulties of policing urban areas; (2) the police role in the criminal justice system; (3) the tension between professional and bureaucratic standards of conduct; and (4) the role of commanders and administrators in spreading or preventing corruption. These institutional problems create the "bottleneck" in which the police work. They do not so much explain how corruption begins as point to *sustaining* factors.

PROBLEMS OF POLICING THE CITY

Sherman has discussed five problems in urban policing that can be regarded as institutional preconditions of corruption.[31] Some of them are inherent in the nature of the work, others developed in practice. They are wide officer discretion, low managerial visibility of police activities, low public visibility, peer group secrecy, and managerial secrecy. Each of these problems makes it easier for corruption to occur.

Wide discretion. Police officers do not simply "enforce the law." Every police encounter is a complex and possibly dangerous situation involving human beings, and often their property, health, and safety. Officers in many instances must act immediately and make critical decisions based on only the sketchiest information. This is true not just in service and emergency situations—rushing an expectant mother to the hospital, tending to the injured in a brawl—but in law enforcement encounters as well. Laws can be vague. What really constitutes "loitering," "creating a nuisance," or (one of my favorite legal locutions) "tippling and reveling"? There is a wide range of legitimate police

responses. Officers must decide whether to arrest people or let them go, whether to write a ticket or give a verbal or written warning, whether or not to use force, how much to use. The rookie officer quickly encounters still more ambiguities. She may be certain that a man was an eyewitness to an event, but if he doesn't want to talk she will have to decide how much threatening or cajoling is in order to get the information. If the witness does talk, the officer must judge if what he says has any value.

Wide officer discretion is unavoidable, given the difficulties of dealing with people and the way we draft our laws. For the most part, it is desirable, too. But leaving that much room for individual judgment can also contribute to corruption. Officers can put police discretion to legitimate or illegitimate uses. The boundary between the two areas is anything but distinct. Many citizens are aware of this and will offer cash, gifts, and other favors to officers to help them exercise their "judgment." A traffic cop who accepts a speeder's promise to obey the limits and issues only a verbal warning may be acting legitimately; one who makes the same decision in exchange for a $20 bill is not. Or what of a patrol officer who has been buying auto parts from a store at a "police discount" and who does not ticket cars parked there illegally? The public is not hurt much, and nothing in officers' orders compels them to ticket every illegally parked car they see. Every officer ignores minor offenses at times to tend to more important business. These are probably cases of corruption, although minor ones, and wide officer discretion is a part of it. Discretion does not make corruption inevitable, but it enables an officer to conceal many illegitimate decisions. It can also foster belief among citizens and police that when the law becomes a matter of judgment, it goes up for sale. When this belief is widespread, corruption becomes safer and easier for all involved.

Low managerial visibility. Most patrol officers work on their own or with a single partner. They operate beyond the supervision of sergeants, lieutenants, and captains because they are dispersed throughout a district and are constantly on the move. Police officers are not soldiers. Despite the quasi-military chain of command and such innovations as two-way radio, the fact is that most police supervisors most of the time cannot know what their officers are doing. Sherman observes: "Since supervisors rarely observe line officers as they make decisions, controls on their use of discretion are relatively weak, and always after the fact."[32]

Low public visibility. If police supervisors have little knowledge of police activities, most of the public has even less. As frequently as we see police officers cruising down the street or writing parking tickets, we seldom see them investigating a crime or arresting anyone for anything more consequential than speeding. Much significant police activity takes place beyond the view of all but a few members of the public—those directly involved and perhaps a handful of bystanders. If we *do* see police in action we may have no way of knowing what is really going on. As noted earlier, if we saw an officer fiddling with the lock on a store late at night, we could not say for sure whether his or her motives were legitimate. Low public visibility, like low managerial visibility, offers many opportunities to conceal illicit decisions and behavior.

Peer group secrecy. Afficionados of police novels and movies have heard much about the ways police stick together and develop a distinctive belief system and vocabulary. Popular treatments of this "brotherhood" at times romanticize and exaggerate it for dramatic effect, but the police subculture is a fact, and along with it comes peer group secrecy.

There is nothing wrong or unusual about the growth of subcultures. Doctors and lawyers have them. So do college professors. But the police subculture stands apart from others in its comprehensiveness and strength. By "comprehensiveness," I mean that it seems to contain and teach a much more inclusive set of attitudes about politics, society, and self than do other subcultures. "Strength" refers partly to the effective socialization of newcomers. CBS's "60 Minutes," for example, televised a story in 1977 about a Florida

sociologist and criminology scholar who took on part-time police work. In short order he became more police officer than sociologist in his activities, work schedule, and circle of acquaintances. Many of his beliefs and attitudes changed markedly, gravitating toward those of his fellow officers. "Strength" also refers to the sanctions and disapproval directed against those who threaten to break the rules of the subculture. These sanctions range from social ostracism to violence and can effectively bring "oddballs" back into line.

This is where peer group secrecy comes into play. The person most likely to see corrupt cops at work is another cop. Yet in many or most cases he or she will do nothing about it and will tell no one. Fear of retaliation plays a part in this, but so do bonds of friendship, an "us against the world" attitude toward the public and press, and the fact that an officer must ultimately be able to trust and be trusted by his or her colleagues. Outsiders and administrators will thus find information on corruption difficult to get. They will find it virtually impossible to get officers to testify against their colleagues. Honest officers may spend an entire career working with colleagues whom they know are "taking" and do nothing about it. Those who try to fight corruption, such as detectives Frank Serpico and Robert Leuci[34] in New York, will find themselves in grave danger.

It might seem that peer group secrecy and the police subculture are simply the aggregate result of personalistic factors. Peer group secrecy is, however, very much an institutional factor. It derives much of its special strength and comprehensiveness from the way police departments operate. The uniform, the gun and night stick, and the use of force separate police from civilians. Public resentment of police work (no one likes to be arrested or given a ticket), guidelines for police conduct laid down by the courts, and public controversy over police conduct and personnel policies have contributed to a cohesiveness that can approach garrison mentality. Police personnel work odd hours and rotating shifts (perhaps one six-day week on a "daylight" shift, one week of "nightwork," one week on the "graveyard" shift, and one week off), which means that most of their friends are apt to be other officers. Finally, the work itself involves long hours of tedium and paperwork, punctuated by short episodes of action and possibly great danger. These factors bind police together, make them feel isolated from and misunderstood by the rest of society, and encourage peer group secrecy.

Managerial secrecy. Sherman's fifth precondition for police corruption involves the values and actions of commanding and administrative officers. Most "top cops" are former patrol officers who have risen through the ranks. Though some change has occurred in recent years, few administrators enter a department at the top. All who have climbed the ladder are intimately acquainted with the patrol officer's lot and with the values of the subculture. Administrators and commanders are often reluctant to investigate and discipline officers on charges of corruption unless revelations of scandal and external pressure compel it. Even when they do take action, it is often less than vigorous.[35] Proactive strategies against corruption—active investigation and continuing efforts to stop wrongdoing before it starts—are rare in most departments.

Managerial secrecy also includes resentment of "interference" by the public, press, or politicians. Allegations by the press frequently are ignored. If a response is necessitated by the emergence of sensational evidence, the "rotten apple" explanation is revived and thrown out for public consumption. Formal inquiries, such as the Knapp investigation, are bitterly resented at all levels of the department. Similar resentment is found in many institutions—college professors, for example, do not like to have state legislators tell them what to teach—but in police departments managerial secrecy is strengthened by the values of the police subculture, by the anxieties that allegations of corruption provoke, and by the vigor with which the press often pursues the corruption issue once it has surfaced.

Sherman's five institutional problems are not in themselves a theory of police corruption.[36]

They do, however, highlight institutional aspects of city policing that are preconditions to corruption. Each opens up opportunities for corruption and its concealment, and each is a more or less direct product of the way our police forces are organized. More will be said later about how these opportunities are converted into actual misconduct.

POLICE IN THE CRIMINAL JUSTICE SYSTEM

Most of the cases entering our criminal justice system begin with some sort of police encounter. As noted at the outset, police work where law and society meet. They are "intake officers" for a complex social and institutional system made up of courts, penal institutions, parole and probation officials, lawyers, judges, victims of crime, and (at least indirectly) the public. How an officer acts in a given encounter—indeed, whether he or she acts at all—is of immense concern to all parts of the system. For a suspect, it may be a matter of freedom or imprisonment; for the public, safety or continued victimization; for the courts, a manageable load of well prepared cases or chaos; and for the officer, commendation or condemnation, safety or injury. All of these concerns weigh against each other in an environment of ambiguity and wide discretion.

The police officer's role in the criminal justice system creates two serious dilemmas. One concerns the means of providing justice, the other the ends. The dilemma of means involves conflicting professional and bureaucratic standards of police conduct. The dilemma of ends is one of differing conceptions of justice itself. The police officer resolves these dilemmas by making informal and unsatisfying compromises on behalf of a system to which he or she may have little commitment. This situation, I feel, is a cause of corruption.

MEANS OF POLICING: PROFESSIONALISM VERSUS BUREAUCRATIZATION

Reiss has discussed the influence of professional and bureaucratic norms on police conduct. He suggests that in many situations these norms are irreconcilable—that an officer simply cannot satisfy both sets of demands. What are these conflicting standards, and where do they originate?

Reiss writes that a profession

> is commonly regarded as a special kind of occupation where technical knowledge is gained through long, prescribed training. The knowledge itself is regarded as a systematic body of theory and practice. The professional person adheres to a set of professional norms that stipulate the practitioner should do technically competent work in the "client's" interest. As Wilensky notes, at the core of professionalism is devotion to an ideal that "... the client's interest more than personal or commercial profit should guide decisions when the two are in conflict.[37]

The "professionalized" police officer, then, is a well trained, judicious decision-maker, able to handle authoritatively the many situations encountered on the street within a wide range of discretion. "Authoritatively" is an important word here, for professionals who have reached a decision based on their best judgment naturally wish to see that decision stick. "Professionalized" police departments emphasize education for officers, sophisticated crime-detection techniques, computerized data processing, and advanced communications systems. Professionalism as a managerial approach also allows and encourages commanders to insulate themselves from outside "interference." For the officer on the beat, professionalism is a source of status as well as of freedom to make judgments; the professional officer is not just the city's uniformed errand boy.

Bureaucratization poses a direct threat to professionalism and places the patrol officer in an acute dilemma. Reiss again:

> A *bureaucracy* requires the standardization of rules by a central authority in the expectation that universalism will prevail in the applications of those rules. This contradicts the concept that in a profession, the professional must be able to exercise discretion in the application of standards, particularly to meet the requirements of a particular case. A *command organization* threatens professional status because it expects men to follow orders regardless of their judgment. The professional ideal holds that orders are antithetical to the exercise of discretion.[38]

Bureaucratization is a necessary aspect of urban policing, but the city police officer is still caught between the conflicting pressures of professionalism and bureaucracy. In most police encounters, the two cannot be reconciled. Consider the case of a narcotics detective who carefully cultivates a set of informants. Relationships here are delicate and based on a number of understandings. The officer may "have something" on the informant and use the threat of arrest to get information. Or she may trade drugs or money for tips and leads. Here is the dilemma: if the officer follows her department's regulations on dealing with informants—which may require her officially to record the informant's name and may prohibit exchanging drugs or money for information—she will quickly find she has no informants. The department also requires her to ring up a certain quota of drug arrests each month, and to get arrests she needs information. What does she do? In most cases she will disregard the regulations—and often break laws—to get information and make arrests. The tension between professionalism and bureaucratization often forces a "good cop" to break the law in order to produce arrests.

Ends of policing: What is justice? Police conceptions of justice often differ markedly from those employed in the rest of the criminal justice system, worsening the tensions of professionalism and discretion. The most visible of these value conflicts are matters of procedure. The U.S. Supreme Court's *Miranda* and *Escobedo* decisions, which laid down safeguards for the rights of the accused, were highly unpopular with most police. In the popular arena this was a "law and order" issue, but it also reflects more basic differences between the police and the courts. As noted previously, professionals seek to make *authoritative* decisions and do not welcome others' efforts to change decisions or to lay down rules of decision-making. Police often feel that legislators and courts create vague, unworkable, and hastily constructed laws and procedures while holding police conduct up to minute and arbitrary scrutiny. Officials in the court system may regard police as bumbling, overzealous in the use of force, insensitive to the subtleties of the law, and cavalier when it comes to the requirements of due process. The result, as Reiss points out, is sharply contrasting notions of procedural justice: "Matters that the police want defined by rules, the courts want to leave open to discretion. And what the courts want defined by rules, the police want to leave open to discretion."[39]

Contrasts exist, too, in conceptions of the substance of justice. Some officers might feel that legislators and the courts ask the police to apply unenforceable laws to activities such as gambling and prostitution, while violent crimes such as rape and muggings are ignored, their perpetrators freed by the courts on technicalities. Or, some might feel that the courts come down hard on the "ordinary guy" while letting the hardened offender and the affluent white-collar criminal off with a slap on the hand. Most frustrating might be the numerous cases in which an officer simply *knows* that a person has been committing crimes but that the evidence will not stand up in court. These conflicting substantive notions of justice are certainly debatable; when it comes to conflict between police and courts I find myself agreeing with the courts more often than not. But it is undeniable that many police officers feel their values of right and wrong, their hard work in putting together a case, and their first-hand knowledge of the community are constantly being disregarded and even repudiated by the criminal justice system they are asked to serve. The result is tension and resentment.

Two major consequences of these tensions can pave the way for police corruption. One is disillusionment with the criminal justice process and an accompanying lack of commitment to the standards defining police roles and conduct within that system. The second, more concrete consequence is that conflicting demands upon the police lead to actual police misconduct. "Misconduct" here refers not to corruption but rather to violations of law and departmental regulations that are more or less compelled by the conflicting pressures of police work. Police officers in many situations must literally break some laws if they are to enforce others.

One good example involves the enforcement of vice laws. One way police departments insulate themselves from the contradictory demands of other parts of the criminal justice system is by adopting a narrow definition of police responsibilities. For example, police departments regard a crime as "cleared" when an arrest is made, whether or not the accused is eventually convicted. Once the case has been "cleared" it is in the hands of the courts. Thus, when public outcry forces a crackdown on gambling, prostitution, or drug traffic, it is arrests and not convictions that department brass normally seeks. In New York City in 1970, Rubinstein reports, more than 9000 gambling arrests produced only 70 jail terms. During one period in the late 1960s, 73 numbers raids in Brooklyn resulted in 356 arrests. Of these cases, 198 were dropped, and 63 produced acquittals. Only 77 persons were fined. (The average fine was $113, mere pocket change for people involved in gambling.) Five went to jail and served an average of 17 days, 12 sentences were suspended, and one person went to prison for a year.[40]

The message to officers on the street is clear. To advance within the department, one must make vice arrests, and one must not worry too much about *how* one makes the arrest or whether it will stand up in court. As we have seen, making arrests requires information, and on the street, information is not just given away. Officers may buy vice information with money, drugs, or protection from arrest. They can extort it through violence or the threat of violence, or they can "steal" it through arrangements such as illegal wiretaps and entrapment. For years many members of New York's elite Special Investigating Unit carried bags of heroin wherever they went, for at any time they might have been able to use them to deal with an informant.[41] Looked at in one way, these practices are necessary parts of good police work. They may, however, also break the law.

Some officers may indulge in this sort of wrongdoing for years without ever "taking." For at least a few others, though, it seems plausible that conflicting pressures, weak and ambiguous standards of conduct, strong temptations, and the necessity to break laws in the course of duty might encourage corruption. These institutional factors can open the door to corruption for officers who, for whatever reasons, are already inclined to partake of it.

"COMMAND CORRUPTION"

So far the discussion has focused on corruption among low-ranking police officers who work the streets. But a concern with institutional sources of police corruption naturally directs our attention to the command structure and to the fact that commanding officers themselves can be corrupted. Before we conclude our review of the institutional perspective on police corruption, let us briefly discuss corruption among commanders.

Everyone in a police department works for someone else. Even the chief or commissioner, despite his or her desires for political and professional independence, works for the mayor. A patrol officer, of course, is at the bottom of the heap. Knowing this, anyone engaged in an illegal enterprise who is being bothered by an honest cop can try to "get to" the honest cop's boss. Perhaps a sergeant, lieutenant, captain, or someone even higher up has already been corrupted, having risen through the ranks with old habits intact. Perhaps the superior is taking a "steady note" or is simply receptive to a good offer. Whatever the situation, a friendly commanding officer can do many things to get an honest patrol officer off your back. William F. Whyte, in his study of Boston's "Cornerville," reported a case in which a commander transferred an inconveniently honest officer to a cemetery beat. Similar actions might include assigning an officer to extra work without pay, posting him or her in a precinct far from home, assigning kinds of work he or she does not like, and even conferring or withholding promotions. "The

threat of transfer," Whyte observed, "is particularly effective with those officers who become attached to the district in which they are assigned...."[42]

Police commanders, then, can be of great help to someone who commands a gambling or other crime related organization. In fact, there are some significant similarities between police and crime organizations. Both have a stake in monitoring and controlling gambling and related vice activities, although their reasons for control are at least nominally at odds. Both have hierarchical command structures operated in a quasi-military manner. Each is a "brotherhood" of sorts, set off from outsiders. Both divide overall responsibilities into territorial jurisdictions; both have an interest in occupying that "turf," but neither wants to fight over it constantly. Both employ violence and coercion as needed, and—perhaps most important—both exist in the "no man's land" between society's public morality and its private vices.

Given these similarities, it is not surprising that Whyte found extensive cooperation between gambling "managers" and police commanders. In exchange for money, favors, and occasional political support, police commanders restrained anti-gambling activities. When, for public relations reasons, a raid had to be conducted, commanders would tip off their counterparts in the gambling organizations. That way, important individuals and large sums of money could be protected. Gambling bosses could even put these sporadic raids to disciplinary use by making sure troublesome subordinates would be on the scene to be arrested. This cooperation meant larger profits for gambling operators, extra income for police commanders, and a general reduction in conflict and violence between both.

Thus, we should remember that police corruption can occur higher up in the department. Not only does "command corruption" enable some officers to get in on the take and persuade other officers to wink at misconduct, it can also hinder reform if corruption is ever revealed. New York's Frank Serpico tried at first to fight police corruption by talking to his superiors, but he got little response. At least some commanders were involved in corruption themselves. Many more were reluctant to rock the boat. Actions of commanders, then, can be an important determinant of how much corruption exists; and as we shall see later on, they can be critical in determining the success or failure of efforts at reform.

The ways we have chosen to organize urban policing have, I think, a significant bearing upon corruption among the police. Aspects of police work such as wide officer discretion, low public visibility, and managerial secrecy open up opportunities for wrongdoing. Conflicting pressures of professionalism and bureaucratization create ambiguous standards of behavior. The department's uneasy relationship with the rest of the criminal justice system forces many good officers to break the law just to do their jobs. Commanding officers' behavior is significant throughout—a commander who is on the take can make life miserable for an honest officer, and a merely indifferent commander can make police corruption very difficult to detect and eradicate.

Institutional factors, however, do not provide a full explanation of police corruption. They do give us a description of the critical bottleneck that the police officer or commander controls through his or her power to make important decisions. The institutional perspective identifies conflicting sets of values and expectations that bear upon officers' decisions and that magnify the importance of officers as decision-makers. It also points out forces that sustain corruption once it has begun. What is still missing, however, is an account of how corrupt transactions are initiated—of how opportunities are turned into actual corruption. The institutional perspective explains why some police officers are "available" for corruption, but the sort of bribery and extortion that is my primary concern takes at least two parties. It involves the motives and actions of private parties—citizens who enter into corrupt transactions. Relationships between police and private parties are the

subject of the systemic view, and it is to that which I now turn.

Systemic Perspectives on Police Corruption

... I suggested that one reason why the police are so interesting and why police corruption is so important is that police work where law and society meet. In the preceding section of this chapter I outlined some of the institutional pressures bearing upon that critical point. In this section I will look at pressures upon the police that come from the societal side. Institutional forces create the bottleneck that the police officer controls; the systemic view points to people and interests trying to get at things they want. If they want things that are illegal they must somehow neutralize the police officer's power to stop them. Corruption is a form of influence well suited to that task.

VICE AND MORALS: AMBIVALENCE OR HYPOCRISY?

Systemic pressures that make for police corruption begin in our ambivalence about ourselves. Americans are particularly fond of turning questions of private conduct into matters of public policy. We regulate such matters as who may drink alcoholic beverages, what sorts of literature may be sold, and who may indulge in what sorts of sexual behavior with whom. Taking drugs of many sorts and most forms of gambling are illegal in most of the nation. Our public concern with others' morality and personal behavior has deep cultural and historic roots and has often reflected class, ethnic, and religious frictions. Prohibition, for example, was a native-versus-immigrant issue in many cities and was also proposed as a law that would force the improvident workingman to sober up and go home to the wife and kids. Behavior that one person enjoys often proves objectionable to someone else. In such cases we typically pass regulatory laws and send the police out to enforce them.

These laws create problems for both police and public. Vice laws are often arbitrary and vary widely from place to place. "Playing a number" at the drugstore is against the law; buying a state lottery ticket in the same store is not. A person of legal age can walk into any bar in Pennsylvania and buy a six-pack to go; a Connecticut bartender who sells beer to go can land in jail. In some states, liquor and other vice laws are matters of local or county option, further confusing the matter. For many people and police officers, vice laws are a nuisance.

A more serious problem is that many people simply do not obey vice laws. This is frequently true in cases of deep value conflicts, where one segment of a community has legally imposed its own morality upon others. Another difficulty is the fact that some citizens (and some police) regard many vice activities as essentially "victimless," unlike crimes of theft or violence. If someone wants to discreetly buy an after-hours drink, play a number, or buy a "dirty" book, the argument runs, who is being hurt? As long as people are people, there will be a strong demand for life's forbidden pleasures, and as long as people like money someone will be willing to supply such pleasures for the right price.[43] The result is the growth of illicit vice industries selling liquor, sex, drugs, and opportunities to gamble to the millions who wish to indulge. Many people underestimate the scale of these industries, assuming that vice is supplied by fly-by-night operators who can easily be driven out of business by the passage of an ordinance. This is not so; vice in America is a highly profitable multibillion dollar enterprise. It is supported and patronized by all kinds of citizens, not just a degenerate few. As Gail Sheehy demonstrated in her study of prostitution in New York, investments in vice come from, and a share of the profits flows back to, prestigious "mainstream" individuals and businesses.[44] Making prostitution, pornography, gambling, and other vice activities illegal does not make them go away; if anything, it makes them more profitable. Making these activities illegal also forces the police to stand between supply and demand and try to keep the two apart.

Society's ambivalence about vice creates strong incentives for people to break the law. It also encourages the police not to enforce the law because it is often so difficult. Vice laws govern activities in which people are generally involved of their own volition,[45] and—unlike crimes of theft or violence—in which none of the parties has a direct interest in seeing the law enforced. Completing this picture is the fact that participants in vice—sometimes the consumer, more often the entrepreneur or other police—will offer police bribes and other incentives to look the other way. Consumers caught gambling may put up cash to avoid arrest, fines, and embarrassment. Vice entrepreneurs have investments and high profits at stake; they make more than enough money to bribe the cops and may simply regard "protection money" as part of their overhead costs. They may spend several thousand dollars a month to keep the police at bay in the same way a grocer pays for heat and electricity. Especially in Type III cases, invitations to "take" will come from other officers, who will test young recruits to see if they are interested and "reliable."

These direct offers of bribe money and other incentives help convert passive opportunities for wrongdoing into actual corruption. Such pressures are systemic in that they emanate from interactions with the public, from society's ambivalence about vice, and from the workings of the underground economy that the ambivalence has fostered. In almost every police encounter with the public—and especially in contacts involving vice and the money it entails—there is a potential conflict over what the officer should do. One mechanism that neatly resolves this conflict is corruption.

Corruption benefits all of the direct parties to vice transactions, at least in the short run. The consumer procures his or her gratification, the entrepreneur buys protection, and the police officer makes some money. Corruption also does away with the need for violence or coercion. It is an attractive way of avoiding tasks that could never be accomplished anyway, such as the complete eradication of prostitution or of numbers games. There will always be vice, an officer may conclude, so what difference does it make if you "take" or not? The public need never know. Police can arrest a few minor lawbreakers to meet their quotas, vice entrepreneurs can keep their activities sufficiently discreet, and nobody has to talk about the money. Corruption is well suited to resolving the conflicts inherent in policing a complex society.

The systemic view yields a picture of the forces and actions that convert opportunities into corrupt behavior. It suggests that police corruption is rooted not in the kinds of people who become officers but rather in their interaction with society. Coupled with the pressures and contradictions of the institutional setting, this analysis creates a picture of the bottleneck situation out of which police corruption develops. Institutional factors define the bottleneck, systemic forces set up the pressures within it, and both drive the police officer toward corruption.

HOW TO ACCOUNT FOR THE HONEST COP?

The systemic and institutional perspectives are so all-encompassing that we are forced to consider why there exist any honest police officers at all. Many small and medium-sized cities probably have only moderate levels of police corruption, and frequently it is not well organized. Even the most corrupt big city departments have many officers who have never taken a dime. If systemic and institutional pressures have so much to do with police corruption, how do we account for those who remain honest?

This question, I think, has both many answers and no answer. Why any one officer does or does not get involved in corrupt practices may be impossible to say; certainly some officers will be more resistant to corrupting pressures than others. Not all officers, however, are exposed equally to these pressures. Vice activity is an integral component in the corruption problem, yet not all police are involved in vice work. Some may do traffic or communications duty, and others may serve the bureaucracy. A substantial share of the officers on the street work in quiet residential districts and may have little to do

with the dilemmas of enforcing the vice laws. Some of those who do encounter systemic pressures as patrol or plain-clothes officers may decide to transfer to other sorts of work, and many more may not indulge in corruption themselves but choose to tolerate the corrupt actions of partners and colleagues.

One important factor influencing the way an officer will react to the pressures of the job is peer group socialization. We have already seen the kind of peer group secrecy that exists in police work, and it is also true that many of the most important norms of conduct are learned not in the Police Academy but on the job. These informal norms become crucial in high-pressure situations where formal standards of conduct are unworkable, ambiguous, or non-existent. It is in those situations that pressures making for police corruption tend to converge.

On-the-job socialization—the values and behavior a police officer learns from his or her colleagues—is a critical influence on corruption. New recruits and veterans alike need the guidance and support of others who understand:

> The policeman needs the support of his colleagues. It is not only that he needs them to come to his aid when his safety and well-being are threatened; he needs their understanding. They are the only ones who have "been there"; they are the only ones who know the ambiguities of the trade and require no lengthy explanations and excuses in the recounting of his experiences. In exchange for the understanding, every man who chooses to remain a policeman will put up with a great deal.[46]

Much of this peer group socialization—especially that encountered by the new recruits—is of necessity negative in character. Many of the rules the recruit has learned in the Police Academy—dress and equipment regulations, paper work procedures, the niceties of evidence, search and seizure, and interrogation processes—are widely disregarded out in the precincts. Some of these rules, as discussed previously, must be disregarded if an officer is to meet his or her arrest quotas. From more experienced colleagues young officers quickly learn what they can "get away with" and what minimal standards of activity must be met. Other attitudes are learned as well. Cynicism, authoritarianism, and a feeling that most people dislike the police have been suggested as attitudes learned from colleagues, though the evidence on this is far from conclusive.

Peer group socialization can lead to corruption in at least two ways. First, new recruits can learn an informal code of conduct that teaches that certain types of wrongdoing are widely practiced and thus acceptable. Wrongdoing within these boundaries will generally be kept secret by others, even if they do not take part in corrupt activities. The substance of the "code"— that is, which activities are or are not sanctioned—may vary from department to department and account for some variations in degree of corruption. The code is not a carte blanche to steal; it usually declares certain types of behavior off limits. Stoddard writes of an officer who first indulged in the sorts of shakedowns and bribery and extortion allowed by the "code" and then moved on to active criminality—planning and carrying out burglaries. He made this transition thinking that he was still within the code, and that he hence enjoyed the support of his colleagues. He assumed many of them were doing the same sorts of things. When he was finally arrested, he was surprised to learn that he had very little company: few fellow officers were engaged in active criminality, and most sharply disapproved of his conduct. Planning and carrying out burglaries was a violation of the code, and as a result few police officers got involved in it.[47]

The second way that peer group socialization can lead to corruption is through a process of "testing." Veteran officers may test a young recruit by offering him or her part of a take or by setting up situations in which the new officer must decide whether or not to join in questionable behavior (such as the hypothetical liquor store example ...). Testing may be initiated by veterans actively involved in corruption who want to know if the recruit wants to join or will at least remain quiet. The testing may also be

done by officers not deeply involved in corruption who simply want to serve notice that one's primary allegiance must be to one's colleagues on the street, come what may. New recruits are dependent upon veterans for knowledge, help in time of danger, and emotional support. Understandably, they very much want acceptance. In testing situations, then, we would expect many of them to go along with the deal, at least for the moment. It seems plausible to suggest that—for at least a few—this is where corruption begins.

Peer group socialization helps us understand how institutional pressures and systemic temptations lead to corrupt behavior in specific instances. Indeed, socialization may be the main mechanism through which new officers learn the full extent of institutional and systemic dilemmas—and the commonly accepted ways to resolve them. Some of these ways involve corruption, others do not. Perhaps certain kinds of socialization could even inhibit corruption; the Knapp Commission's recommendations for New York rested at least partly on this assumption.[48] This and other possible remedies for police corruption will be discussed later....

So far I have laid out and discussed three general approaches to the explanation of police corruption. I have suggested that although the individualistic approach has serious flaws, institutional and systemic factors combined can give us a fairly clear and useful account of the development and persistence of police corruption. It is time now to examine the consequences of police corruption—to spell out its costs and possible benefits, to identify those who win or lose, and to speculate on its implications for law enforcement in modern society.

Consequences of Police Corruption

Police corruption, like machine politics, is a regressive form of influence in its direct effects, benefiting "haves" at the expense of "have nots." As for the kind and quality of law enforcement a corrupt police force delivers, the answers are more complex. At the very least, police corruption poses questions about the kinds of laws we enact and about how we enforce them. Some analysts have suggested that police corruption even has some broadly beneficial latent functions.

WHO WINS, WHO LOSES?

Corruption of the police is a form of influence. All of us break laws at one time or another, and some of us get caught. Those who are caught—whether for running a red light or for dealing in heroin—presumably have an interest in avoiding a ticket, fine, or trip to jail. In some unknown percentage of these cases either the civilian or police officer initiates a corrupt transaction. Here is where the regressive consequences of police corruption begin. The currency of corruption is money, or things money can buy, such as meals or consumer goods. Some people can afford the cost of corrupt influence; most of us cannot. Police corruption, then, is in its most serious forms a kind of influence accessible to only a few.

These few are not necessarily the conventionally affluent, although a surgeon can probably more easily afford to fix a ticket than a waitress can. In pervasive, organized corruption, the "haves" tend to be those engaged in lucrative but illegal vice activities. Higher-ups in these fields frequently do become affluent. Less prominent figures, such as a petty numbers runner who may spend $200 a week or more on police protection, may simply depend on a large cash flow to buy off the cops. Both types are "haves" in the sense that they can devote much more money to illegal influence than can the rest of us. People who cannot or will not employ money and material incentives must rely on the call of duty and the law to influence police behavior. When they encounter officers who are "taking," they presumably have far less influence than those who make pay-offs. When corrupt officers comprise a significant portion of an area's police, people in the "have-not" majority lose in two ways. First, they are deprived of at least some of the police protection they are entitled to receive. Second, when caught in illegal acts they will likely suffer heavier sanctions than will those who pay, even though the latter are often engaged in far more serious offenses.

These inequalities and the central role of money in police corruption become more apparent if we make a rough accounting of the winners and losers in police corruption, much as we did for machine politics. This accounting appears in Table 2.

Table 2 Beneficiaries and losers in police corruption (gains and losses in parentheses)

Major Beneficiaries	Minor Beneficiaries	Minor Losers	Major Losers
• Organized crime *(protection, money)* • Vice entrepreneurs *(protection, money)* • Groups of police officers (Type III cases) *(money)*	• Lone offenders who pay *(nonenforcement of laws)* • Individual police officers (Types I, II) *(money, gifts, "police discounts")* • Vice "investors" (e.g., owners of buildings renting to vice operators) *(money)* • Businesspeople paying small incentives (e.g., free meals, "police discounts") *(added police presence, nonenforcement of parking ordinances)* • Vice consumers *(opportunities to partake of vice)*	• Area residents, "taxpayers" *(loss of services, possibly more crime)* • Businesspeople who cannot/ do not pay *(reduced police presence, possible harassment)* • Lone offenders who cannot/do not pay *(relatively harsher law enforcement)*	• Inner-city neighborhoods, other vice locations *(stronger organized crime, increased vice and its detrimental neighborhood effects)* • General citizenry *(loss of trust in an accountable police force)* • Victims of increased crime *(crime losses, injury)*

The accounting is rough and tentative but reflects a consistent pattern. Major and minor benefits go to people who can pay the price; costs fall most heavily upon those who cannot or will not. Police corruption is a regressive and undemocratic form of influence. Table 2 also reflects the central role of money in the economy of police corruption. Corrupt officers sell protection for cash, and protection makes vice and other illegal activities more profitable. Some of the costs to the losers are monetary as well, though usually indirect and long term. A businessperson who cannot pay, for example, may suffer higher crime losses, or loss of business due to vigorous enforcement of parking restrictions.

CORRUPTION, THE POLICE, AND SOCIETY

What are the effects of corruption upon the quality of law enforcement and upon the more general role of police in modern society? Here the answers are not clear. One effect of corruption is that certain illegal activities are tolerated and made more profitable; in this sense the quality of law enforcement is diminished. I have also suggested (Table 2) that areas where vice operations flourish—particularly inner-city neighborhoods—suffer the adverse consequences of these sorts of activities. Society as a whole loses trust in its police, a critical factor when we consider their powers of search and seizure, arrest, and coercion. It is also possible that police corruption leads to increased crime, even in parts of the city away from the corruption and in types of activity not directly related to the bribery and extortion. For example, corruption may allow the drug trade to flourish, resulting in more burglaries by addicts. Or the presence of a corrupt and alienated police force that the public holds in contempt may encourage potential lawbreakers to act on their temptations. Solid understanding of these "ripple effects" must await further research.

As with machine politics, however, we should not dismiss police corruption out of hand as totally harmful. Some effects may be insignificant. The motorist who buys her way out of a speeding ticket with $20 has evaded formal "justice," to be sure; but she has also paid a fine of sorts and has suffered the unnerving experience of getting caught. The experience will probably make some people slow down, at least for a while. Others, of course, will go right back to speeding. Either way, speeders stopped by the police—whether they pay a bribe or take a ticket—make up only a small percentage of all those who break the speed limit. A possible positive by-product of corruption in the vice area could be a reduction in tension and violence if police and vice operators have worked out a *modus vivendi*.

Some consequences of police corruption may be neutral, or even beneficial. Dorothy H. Bracey suggests not only that police corruption has several important latent functions that help us understand why corruption is so persistent but that it "functions to fulfill societal and cultural goals, i.e., contributes to the maintenance of the social system."[49] How can this be? Bracey proposes several functional consequences of police corruption. Corruption can promote "solidarity, mutual trust, and *esprit de corps*"[50] in the ranks by creating a shared and secret pattern of behavior open only to police officers. This kind of solidarity presumably would develop only in cases of pervasive, organized corruption, Bracey notes. A small number of corrupt officers, or even many officers "accepting bribes unbeknownst to each other," she suggests, will not increase department morale and solidarity. Indeed, they may weaken it.

Bracey points out other latent functions of police corruption.[51] Corruption is a sort of "training device" or "rite of passage" by which veterans initiate and socialize young recruits into the "brotherhood." Corruption "reaffirms the status of superior officers at the same time that it increases their solidarity with their subordinates," and it is a "stabilizing factor" ironing out potential cultural conflicts over vice, morals, and regulatory laws. Corruption is a "facilitator of business," allowing licit and illicit enterprises to flourish despite a maze of arbitrary and often conflicting laws. The cost of bribing an officer, together with the information a good detective can extract by offering to ignore a criminal suspect's wrongdoing, make corruption a form of "para-legal law enforcement" and "crime control." Corruption in the form of small bribes enables people to obtain services otherwise unavailable, as in the case of a restaurateur who gets an escort to the bank with his day's receipts in exchange for free meals. It offers compensation for the low income and status of police work. Corrupt practices persist in part because they ease lasting problems of law enforcement. Any attempt to combat police wrongdoing must recognize this fact, Bracey tells us; anticorruption programs must include alternative ways of addressing these problems. Bracey's analysis quite rightly suggests that police corruption must be viewed within its wider institutional and systemic setting and cannot simply be condemned without analysis.

Police corruption poses difficult questions about the quality of law enforcement the public demands and the kind of service it can legitimately expect to get. We have, I think, placed demands upon our police that are contradictory and can never be satisfied. We expect the police to regulate matters of personal morality while respecting the privacy and civil liberties of suspects. We expect them to crack down on clandestine activities while scrupulously obeying regulations on how they may obtain information and gather evidence. We hold them responsible for enforcing myriad regulations dealing with economic enterprise while somehow remaining immune to the pressures and temptations these laws inevitably create. We cannot have things both ways, and one result of these tensions and contradictions is corruption.

As long as we choose to police our cities and regulate individual behavior as we currently do, we will probably have to live with a certain amount of police corruption. Our options do not include having a crime-free urban society and a totally honest police force. We cannot have either one, let alone both. Our choices are instead more like cost-benefit calculations: what

sorts of social behavior *must* we police, and what can we live with? How much police corruption is tolerable, and how much is too much? Might we not actually benefit from certain kinds of police corruption, and might there not be situations in which the corrupt cop is also the best cop? Failure to examine these questions in a realistic way may leave us in the sort of dilemma Robert Daley describes in New York, where extensive prosecutions had turned the narcotics detective force inside out:

> There came a day when Assistant U.S. Attorney Rudolph Giuliani, trying to put together a major narcotics investigation with new narcotics detectives newly assigned to him, realized that they were all inept. They couldn't conduct a surveillance without calling in that they were lost. They never played hunches.
>
> A great detective, Giuliani thought, should be a man of imagination and fearlessness. A man with a sense of adventure, a man not limited by procedure. In his new detectives, all these qualities were absent, so that he asked himself almost in despair: Where have all the great detectives gone? The answer that came back to him was this one: I put them all in jail.[52]

Police Corruption: What To Do About It?

I will discuss anti-corruption policies in fairly brief fashion, for a number of reasons. My purpose here is analysis, not prescription; and, as the preceding section suggested, I see a total eradication of police corruption as neither possible nor entirely desirable. Instead, our policy choices in the police corruption area must be tested against a wide set of goals and considerations involving competing conceptions of morality, due process, and the uses and limits of public power. Such a test is beyond the scope of this work. Anti-corruption programs have also been elsewhere proposed and analyzed in much greater detail than would be possible here.[53]

Many of the popularly discussed remedies for police corruption—revised training and recruitment, more intensive screening at the appointment and promotion stages, psychologi-cal testing, and the like—rest on an implicit per-sonalistic theory of police misconduct. As I have suggested, however, institutional and sys-temic forces have more to do with the develop-ment and persistence of police corruption than do individuals' characteristics. Let us briefly look at the sorts of anti-corruption policies these theories might suggest.

INSTITUTIONAL STRATEGIES

Institutional factors define the bottleneck that police officers control. There is a limited amount we can do to change that fact; police officers, after all, are appointed to enforce the law, and that often means changing people's behavior and making unpopular decisions. It may, however, be possible to modify some of the institutional pressures bearing upon police behavior.

One institutional change might be the appointment of departmental inspectors with continuing responsibility for police corruption, but who are responsible to the mayor or city manager rather than to the chief of police. Inspectors' staffs could be a mixture of civilians and law enforcement officers, weakening some of the subcultural bonds between investigators and investigated, especially if the law enforce-ment veterans are hired from outside the depart-ment rather than from the ranks. A continuing investigative effort could also avoid the cycles of scandal, reform, and apathy that have occurred in many cities. This sort of investiga-tive office, of course, would be extremely unpopular throughout the force and would evoke resistance similar to that in many cities against proposals for civilian review.

Another administrative adaptation might be to widen the range of salaries and work situa-tions available to patrol officers: the higher salaries and better beats would be used as incen-tives and rewards for exemplary police work. In most departments today, patrol officers move up a fairly short ladder of salaries and work situa-tions more or less on the basis of seniority rather than performance. As a result, there are few distinct incentives to excel and few penalties for substandard work, short of outright failure. Creation of a new rank of Master Patrol Officer, as has been proposed in New York and else-where, could confer added benefits on exem-plary officers and serve as a clear message that good police work is rewarded. This step might be an expensive one, however, both in terms of direct salary payments and the bureaucratic bur-den of added evaluation of police performance. People who equate low municipal expenditures with efficiency might be unwilling to bear the added expense. Further, strict evaluation would run headlong into the problems of officer dis-cretion and low managerial visibility, while wrongdoing might still be protected by peer group secrecy. It might also be very difficult in practice to decide who should be rewarded.

A third institutional strategy focuses on com-manding officers. Sherman argues persuasively that commanders' commitment to fighting cor-ruption is crucial to the success of anti-corrup-tion policies.[54] This viewpoint is supported by most of the officers with whom I have discussed corruption. Clearly, if captains and higher administrators are involved in corruption them-selves, if they discourage the efforts of would-be reformers, or if they simply decide to do noth-ing, the cause of corruption is aided. Conversely, a leadership committed to fighting systematic corruption can do a number of things. Comman-ders can support continuing investigations and create incentives for and offer protection to hon-est officers who will act against corruption. Commanders can cooperate with elected offi-cials and the public in soliciting information and suggestions about police conduct in the city's neighborhoods. Such anti-corruption procedures must be backed up with strong leadership by example; notice must be served that certain kinds of behavior will not be tolerated. These leader-ship strategies will never eliminate all corrup-tion, but they could have an influence on how new recruits resolve the dilemmas of police work. It is also true, however, that an intensifi-cation of command controls over police behav-ior may exacerbate the tensions between bureaucratization and professionalism, and between the police and the rest of the criminal justice system.

Related to the issue of commanders' behavior is that of command recruitment. As earlier observations on peer group and managerial secrecy suggest, commanders recruited through the ranks might be less likely to take a hard line on corruption than those hired from outside the department. Lateral entry has increased somewhat in recent years; a comparison of commanders' handling of corruption cases and their career paths might prove quite interesting.

Two other institutional strategies involve the department's relationship with the rest of the criminal justice system. First, perhaps we could reduce the gap in values, expectations, and procedures between the police and the courts. The police department could adopt a more general view of the vice business, for example. It could emphasize *quality* of vice arrests over quantity; the officer who nets a "big fish" or who prepares cases so well that convictions generally result, could be rewarded, instead of simply being asked to bring in a certain quota of arrests each month. Quota systems encourage bad arrests, falsification of evidence, and repeated roundups of "small fry" who are of little consequence in the vice trade. Police officers understandably can become cynical after years of this and may conclude that so long as they meet their quotas not much else matters. The courts, to reduce the value gap, could examine the difficulty of enforcing vice and other sorts of laws and revise their expectations and guidelines accordingly. This is not a proposal to "unleash the police," with all the dangers to civil liberties that might entail, but rather a suggestion that the officer's judgment and street experience be accorded greater credence.[55] Increased cooperation between the police and the courts, however, is much more easily described than accomplished. The obstacles to such coordination range from contrasting training to a wide gulf of social class differences.

The second suggestion concerning the criminal justice system grows out of the first. If officers must break some laws to gather the information necessary to enforce others, and if this sort of lawbreaking can lead to corruption, perhaps we should change the rules governing the obtaining of information. I am not advocating a wholesale repeal of restrictions on interrogation or a curtailing of civil liberties. I am suggesting, for example, that police departments be allowed to aid officers in paying and protecting informants, so that narcotics detectives would not get into the business of holding and distributing drugs to keep informants happy. Or, closer police relationships with prosecutors and the courts could reduce the necessity for detectives to wiretap illegally. We must move with great caution in this area of gathering evidence, for some restrictions are essential to our rights of privacy and the presumption of innocence. But squarely confronting the difficulties of enforcing some of our laws might enable us to reduce an officer's need to break others.

SYSTEMIC STRATEGIES

The systemic perspective suggests anti-corruption policies fewer in number but broader in scope. Foremost among them is to decriminalize many so-called "victimless crimes." If people partake of gambling, prostitution, pornography, and certain kinds of drugs of their own volition, and if enforcing the laws against them leads to corruption, then what good is the law? If police inspection of bars and restaurants fosters corrupt relationships, why not get the police out of the inspection business? Most of these "crimes" hurt no one, the argument runs, and the laws enacted against them do not so much protect society as impose one group's morality upon others. In any event, vice is big business. To try to stop these activities with laws no one believes in will never work, according to the argument. So why not decriminalize, license, and even tax these activities and take the police out of the bottleneck?

At first glance, this argument makes sense. Many vice activities *are* victimless in an immediate sense; doing away with laws against them might well reduce police bribery and extortion. Viewed in a broader perspective, however, vice is not really victimless at all. Gambling drains off income from many families and communities that can ill afford it. Hard drug abuse ruins lives and may cause crimes. Prostitution is accompanied by robberies and other crimes; many prostitutes are runaway teenagers recruited under pressure of financial need, drug habits, or violence, not by free choice. Feminist groups have recently contended that pornography engenders violence against women, though hard evidence has yet to be gathered. As for "nuisance regulations," many involve legitimate public interests, such as the maintenance of clean restaurants.

The costs and benefits of decriminalization are difficult to compare, if only because the costs are public and the benefits very much private. We might still decide to decriminalize some kinds of vice despite their ripple effects, whether out of libertarian conviction or the belief that the difficulties and futility of enforcing vice laws outweigh their presumed benefits. My point is that if we pursue decriminalization as an anti-corruption strategy, we should not delude ourselves that such a policy would have no costs. It might well reduce police corruption, but there would come a point beyond which its indirect costs would decisively outweigh the presumed benefits.

A related systemic proposal is to keep certain kinds of laws but assign their enforcement to someone other than the police. Why not let the health department license taverns and let the state police or FBI fight the drug trade? The problem here is fairly clear: police corruption might be reduced, but someone else would be put into the same kind of bottleneck. The locus of corruption would shift—tavernkeepers would now pay off the health inspectors—but the amount of corruption would not change. Indeed, the quality of law enforcement would deteriorate, at least for a time, as new authorities would be moving into new territory with almost no information to go on.

The final recommendation suggested by the systemic perspective is perhaps the most difficult of all, but it may hold some promise. The recommendation is that the public and its elected offi-

cials have a continuing and comprehensive concern and understanding for the complexities and contradictions of the police officer's lot. This involves careful thought about the laws we enact, the social and economic roots of crime, and the inherent conflicts involved in enforcing any law upon a highly skeptical and individualistic public. It even involves asking whether we could live up to the standards we impose on others. A former Denver police officer who resigned in disgrace during a police scandal made this sort of point when he was asked what should be done about police corruption: "Take an interest in the policeman, his family, his tensions, his fears, his standing in the community, and his future and you'll be buying yourself the best possible insurance policy."[56]

This approach would not necessarily make big-city police forces honest overnight, or indeed ever. It might, however, reduce the alienation and estrangement between ourselves and the people we have chosen as our guardians. Intangible as this strategy is, it might ease some of the systemic pressures that cause much of our police corruption.

Summary

No one knows how much police corruption takes place, but we do know that it is a widespread problem. Departments vary in the pervasiveness and degree of organization of police misconduct. In some cities, only a few officers are involved, and they "take" only when an offer comes their way. In other cities, organized rings rake in thousands of dollars each month in effective and systematic schemes of extortion. Personalistic, institutional, and systemic explanations can be offered to account for police corruption; I suggest that the latter two in combination best account for blue-coat crime. Police corruption, like machine politics, is regressive in its distribution of costs and benefits, aiding haves at the expense of have-nots, but it also raises some fundamental questions about the kinds of laws we enact and the obstacles we place in the way of their enforcement.

Total eradication of police corruption is probably neither possible nor desirable, but the institutional and systemic analyses offer at least a few suggestions for policy-makers concerned about corruption.

NOTES

1. August Vollmer, *The Police and Modern Society* (Berkeley, Calif.: University of California Press, 1936), p. 222.

2. Lawrence W. Sherman, *Police Corruption: A Sociological Perspective* (New York: Doubleday, 1974), pp. 40-41. A number of works on the general issue of police corruption are listed in the Selected Bibliography at the end of this book.

3. *Ibid.*, p. 41.

4. *Ibid.*, pp. 43-44.

5. *Ibid.*, pp. 41-43. V. O. Key, "Police Graft," *American Journal of Sociology*, 40:5 (March 1935), pp. 624-636.

6. New York City, Knapp Commission, *The Knapp Commission Report on Police Corruption* (New York: George Braziller, 1973). A useful summary of the commission's findings and principal recommendations appears on pp. 1-34.

7. *New York Times* Information Bank, July 1-October 1, 1979. The *NYT* Information Bank for the entire year 1978 contains more than 350 reports of police misconduct, not including reports from New York City itself.

8. Jonathan Rubinstein, *City Police* (New York: Farrar, Strauss and Giroux, 1973), p. 103.

9. *Chicago Tribune*, August 28, 1979, p. 1; August 29, 1979, p. 1.

10. Ellwyn R. Stoddard, "The Informal 'Code' of Police Deviancy: A Group Approach to 'Blue-Coat Crime,'" *Journal of Criminal Law, Criminology, and Police Science*, 59:2 (1968), pp. 201-213.

11. A discussion of the way the courts have come to handle the bribery/extortion distinction appears in Herbert J. Stern, "Prosecutions of Local Political Corruption Under the Hobbs Act: The Unnecessary Distinction Between Bribery and Extortion," *Seton Hall Law Review*, 3:1 (Fall 1971), pp. 1-17.

12. From *Police Corruption: A Sociological Perspective*, by L. W. Sherman, p. 11. (Copyright © 1974 by L. W. Sherman (New York: Doubleday, 1974). Reprinted by permission.)

13. *Ibid.*, pp. 9-10; see also David H. Bayley, *The Police and Political Development in India* (Princeton, N.J.: Princeton University Press, 1969).

14. This discussion is based upon Sherman, *Police Corruption*, pp. 10-12; Knapp Commission, pp. 61-69,

71-87; Rubinstein, pp. 390-423; and Key, *passim*.

15. Albert J. Reiss, *The Police and the Public* (New Haven, Conn.: Yale University Press, 1971)., pp. 156, 160.

16. *Ibid.*, pp. 161-162.

17. *Ibid.*, p. 169. (From *The Police and the Public*, by A. J. Reiss. Copyright © 1971 by Yale University Press. This and all other quotations from this source are reprinted by permission.)

18. See, for example, the recollections of "Officer Smith," who was dismissed from a midwestern police department because of his involvement in active criminality, as reported in Stoddard, op. cit.; and the similar account of an ex-cop in Denver, reported in Mort Stern, "What Makes a Policeman Go Wrong?" *Journal of Criminal Law, Criminology, and Police Science*, 53:1 (March 1962), pp. 97-101.

19. Arthur Neiderhoffer, *Behind the Shield: The Police in Urban Society* (Garden City, N.Y.: Doubleday, 1967), pp. 134-136. The large number of Irish officers bears out the age-old stereotype of the red-headed cop with a brogue. Irish-Americans have gone into police work in great numbers for several generations. Neiderhoffer quotes the "half-serious" observation of a former New York Police Commissioner that "if it weren't for the Irish, there would be no police. And if it weren't for the Irish, there would be no need for them." Neiderhoffer estimated, overall, that in the mid-1960s about 11,000 members (40%) of the New York police were Irish-American; this, in a city whose total population was at most about 10% Irish. *Ibid.*, pp. 135-136.

20. *Ibid.*, p. 37.

21. *Ibid.*, pp. 33-38. Working-class job categories as designated by Neiderhoffer included Clerical; Sales; Protective Service; Skilled, Semi-Skilled, and Unskilled Workers; Services; and Farm Workers.

22. *Ibid.*, p. 38.

23. *Ibid.*, pp. 103-151, and 231-242, for Neiderhoffer's complete attitudinal findings.

24. *Ibid.*, pp. 37-38. Neiderhoffer wrote his analysis before many women began to become police officers, but his generalizations seem likely to apply to working and middle-class women, at least somewhat, as well as to men.

25. See, for example, H. Carlson, R. E. Thayer, and A. C. Germann, "Social Attitudes and Personality Differences among Members of Two Kinds of Police Departments," *Journal of Criminal Law, Criminology and Police Science*, 62 (1971), pp. 564-567; J. P. Clark, "Isolation of the Police: A Comparison of the British and American Situations," *Journal of Criminal Law, Criminology, and Police Science*, 56 (1965), pp. 307-319; D. J. Dodd, "Police Mentality and Behavior," *Issues in Criminology*, 3:1 (1967), pp. 47-67; Joel Lefkowitz, "Attitudes of Police Toward Their

Job," in J. R. Snibbe, and H. M. Snibbe, Eds., *The Urban Policeman in Transition* (Springfield, Ill.: Charles C. Thomas, 1973), pp. 202-232; and R. C. Trojanowicz, "The Policeman's Occupational Personality," *Journal of Criminal Law, Criminology, and Police Science*, 62 (1971), pp. 551-559.

26. Thomas C. Gray, "Selecting for a Police Subculture," pp. 46-54 in Jerome H. Skolnick and Thomas C. Gray, Eds., *Police in America* (Boston: Little, Brown, 1975).

27. See, for example, Charles Bahn, "The Psychology of Police Corruption: Socialization of the Corrupt," *Police Journal*, 48 (January 1975), pp. 30-36; J. A. McNamara, *Role Learning for Police Recruits: Some Problems in the Process* (Ann Arbor, Mich.: University Microfilms, 1967); James Q. Wilson, "Generational and Ethnic Differences among Career Police Officers," *American Journal of Sociology*, 69:5 (1964), pp. 522-528.

28. Joel Lefkowitz, "Psychological Attributes of Policemen: A Review of Research and Opinion," Journal of Social Issues, 31:1 (Winter 1975), p. 6; see also Richard R. Bennett and Theodore Greenstein, "The Police Personality: Test of the Predispositional Model," *Journal of Police Science and Administration*, 3 (1975); R. W. Balch, "The Police Personality: Fact or Fiction?", *Journal of Criminal Law, Criminology, and Police Science*, 63 (1972), pp. 106-119; M. Rokeach, M. G. Miller, and J. A. Snyder, "The Value Gap Between Police and Policed," *Journal of Social Issues*, 27:2 (1971), pp. 155-171.

29. Lefkowitz, "Psychological Attributes of Policemen," pp. 7-20.

30. *Ibid.*, p. 12.

31. Sherman, Police Corruption, pp. 12-14.

32. *Ibid.*, p. 12.

33. Peter Maas, *Serpico: The Cop Who Defied the System* (New York: Viking Press, 1973).

34. Robert Daley, *Prince of the City: The True Story of a Cop Who Knew Too Much* (Boston: Houghton Mifflin, 1978).

35. Maas, Chapters 10-13 and 15; Knapp Commission, Chapters 17-20.

36. Sherman lists a sixth dilemma or precondition—a pervasive status problem—which I would agree is closely linked to corruption. I have not described it here because its roots seem to be more systemic and personalistic than institutional, although departmental recruitment policies do indeed have their status implications. The status problem is not wholly absent from this analysis, however, for a pervasive feeling that police work is underpaid, misunderstood, and looked down upon by the general public is one aspect of the peer group socialization process to be taken up in the section on systemic perspective. For data on how

police compare to other occupational groups in terms of public perceptions, see J. B. Rotter and D. K. Stein, "Public Attitudes toward the Trustworthiness, Competence and Altruism of Twenty Selected Occupations," *Journal of Applied Social Psychology*, 1 (1971), pp. 334-343.

37. Reiss, pp. 121-122; see, in general, Chapter III. Quotation included from Harold L. Wilensky, "The Professionalization of Everyone?" *American Journal of Sociology*, 70:2 (September 1964), pp. 138-140.

38. Reiss, pp. 123-124.

39. *Ibid.*, p. 132.

40. Rubinstein, pp. 378-379.

41. *Ibid.*, pp. 379-380; Daley, pp. 201-204 and *passim*.

42. William F. Whyte, *Street Corner Society: The Social Structure of an Italian Slum* (Chicago: University of Chicago Press, 2nd ed. 1955), pp. 124-126.

43. See, on this point, Gay Talese, *Honor Thy Father* (New York: World Publishing Co., 1971), p. 72. Here, Talese describes young Bill Bonanno's feeling that his father, racketeer Joseph Bonanno, was not really a criminal but rather was merely catering to the tastes and demands of a hypocritical society. See also Jacob Chwast, "Value Conflicts in Law Enforcement," *Crime and Delinquency*, 11:2 (April 1965), pp. 151-161.

44. Gail Sheehy, *Hustling: Prostitution in Our Wide-Open Society* (New York: The Delacorte Press, 1973), esp. Chapter 5, "The Landlords of Hell's Bedroom," pp. 116-154.

45. The major exceptions to this generalization are many prostitutes, and drug addicts who are unable to quit their habits.

46. Rubinstein, p. 454.

47. Stoddard, op. cit.

48. Knapp Commission, pp. 65-66.

49. Dorothy Heid Bracey, "A Functional Approach to Police Corruption," Criminal Justice Center Monograph No. 1 (The John Jay Press, 1976), p. 5.

50. *Ibid.*, p. 8.

51. *Ibid.*, pp. 9, 11, 13, 17, 19, 20, 21, 23.

52. Daley, p. 292 (material in parentheses added).

53. Knapp Commission, Chapters 17-23; W. P. Brown, *A Police Administration Approach to the Corruption Problem* (New York: State University of New York, 1971); Lawrence Sherman, *Scandal and Reform: Controlling Police Corruption* (Berkeley: University of California Press, 1978).

54. Sherman, *Scandal and Reform* and "Police Corruption Control: Environmental Context Versus Organizational Policy," pp. 107-126 in David H. Bayley, Ed., *Police and Society* (Beverly Hills, Calif.: Sage Publications, 1977).

55. Even with an "unleashed" police force roaming

the streets, not much of a fundamental nature would change. Crime would still be profitable, people would still want to spend money on illicit pleasures, and cities would still be difficult places to police. Corruption would if anything *increase*

under these circumstances, as more coercive and arbitrary police behavior would increase both the suspect's incentives to offer a bribe and the officer's powers of extortion.

56. M. Stern, p. 101.

Study Questions

1. What are the four types of corruption identified by Johnston? Give two examples of each type.

2. What is the "rotten apple" explanation of police corruption? Does Johnston believe that it is useful in understanding corruption? What is his argument here?

3. Johnston cites Lawrence Sherman's five institutional preconditions of corruption. What are they? Which do you believe is the most significant? Why? Which poses the greatest moral danger to the police or corrections recruit, in your view? Why?

4. What is "testing" in Johnston's use of the term? How should a recruit respond to testing? Defend your position, identifying it as utilitarian or deontological in perspective.

5. How would you fight corruption? Defend your position.

The Informal "Code" of Police Deviancy: A Group Approach to "Blue-Coat Crime"

ELLWYN R. STODDARD

IT HAS BEEN ASSERTED by various writers of criminology, deviant behavior, and police science that unlawful activity by a policeman is a manifestation of personal moral weakness, a symptom of personality defects, or the recruitment of individuals unqualified for police work. In contrast to the traditional orientation, this paper is a sociological examination of "blue-coat crime"[1] as a functioning informal social system whose norms and practices are at variance with legal statutes. Within the police group itself, this pattern of illicit behavior is

referred to as the "code."

Following an examination of these contrasting viewpoints, this case study will provide data to ascertain the existence of the "code," its limitations and range of deviancy, and the processes through which it is maintained and sanctioned within the group. The guiding hypothesis of this study is that illegal practices of police personnel are socially prescribed and patterned through the informal "code" rather than being a function of individual aberration or personal inadequacies of the policeman himself.

Ellwyn R. Stoddard, "The Informal 'Code' of Police Deviancy: A Group Approach to 'Blue-Coat Crime'," Journal of Criminal Law, Criminology, and Police Science, *Vol. 59, #2 (1968), pp. 201-213.* Copyright © *by Northwestern University School of Law. Used by permission of the author.*

The Individualistic Approach

Three decades ago August Vollmer emphasized that the individual being suited to police work was the factor responsible for subsequent deviancy among officers. This approach implicitly assumes inherent personality characteristics to be the determinant which makes a police recruit into a good officer or a bad one.[2] A current text of police personnel management by German reaffirms the individualistic orientation of Vollmer, and suggests that the quality of police service is ultimately dependent upon the individual police officer. There is no evidence of an awareness of group pressures within his analysis.[3]

A modified version of this individualistic approach is the view that perhaps the individual chosen had already become "contaminated" prior to being hired as a member of the force, and when presented with chances for bribery or favoritism, the "hard core guy, the one who is a thief already, steps in."[4]

A third factor, stressed by Tappan,[5] is the poor screening method at the recruitment stage. Such an officer might have had inadequate training, insufficient supervision, and poor pay and is ripe for any opportunity to participate in lucrative illicit enterprises. This author then goes into great detail to show the low intelligence and educational level of police officers. Another author adds that improved selection and personality evaluation have improved the quality of the police considerably over the past 20 years,[6] thereby attacking this problem directly. One recent author wrote that low salaries make more difficult the attraction of applicants with the moral strength to withstand temptations of "handouts" and eventual corruption.[7] Sutherland and Cressey, although aware that graft is a characteristic of the entire police system[8] rather than of isolated patrolmen, stress the unqualified appointments of police officials by corrupt politicians as the source of police deviancy. They state:

Another consequence of the fact that police departments often are organized for the welfare of corrupt politicians, rather than of society, is inefficient and unqualified personnel. This is unquestionably linked with police dishonesty, since only police officers who are "right" can be employed by those in political control. Persons of low intelligence and with criminal records sometimes are employed.[9]

The Group Approach

In contrast to the individualistic approach of these foregoing authors, the emphasis on the social context in which police deviancy flourishes has preoccupied the sociological criminologists. The present case study would clearly reflect this latter orientation.

Barnes and Teeters mention police deviancy in conjunction with organized syndicated crime.[10] Korn and McCorkle,[11] Cloward,[12] and Merton[13] see political and police corruption as a natural consequence of societal demands for illegal services. When these desired services are not provided through legal structures, they are attained through illegal means. However, documentation in support of these theoretical explanations is sketchy and limited in scope. Bell suggests that "crime is an American way of life." In the American temper there exists a feeling that "somewhere, somebody is pulling all the complicated strings to which this jumbled world dances." Stereotypes of big crime syndicates project the feeling that laws are just for "the little guys." Consequently, while "Americans have made such things as gambling illegal, they don't really in their hearts think of it as wicked."[14] Likewise, the routine discovery of an average citizen in overt unlawful activity rarely inflames the public conscience to the degree that it does when this same deviant behavior is exhibited by a police officer. Thus, the societal double standard demands that those in positions of trust must exhibit an artificially high standard of morality which is not required of the average citizen.

A measure of role ambivalence is an inevitable part of the policeman occupation in a democratic society. While he is responsible to protect the members of his society from those who would do them harm, the corresponding powers for carrying out this mandate are not delegated.[15] To perform his designated duties, the conscientious policeman often must violate the very laws he is trying to enforce. This poses a serious dilemma for the police officer since his attempt to effectively discourage violation of the law among the general public is often hinged to extra-legal short-cut techniques[16] which are in common practice by his law enforcement cohorts. For example, the use of "illegal" violence by policemen is justified by them as a necessary means to locate and harass the most vicious criminals and the Organized Syndicates.[17] These procedures are reinforced through coordinated group action.

> The officer needs the support of his fellow officers in dangerous situations and when he resorts to practices of questionable legality. Therefore, the rookie must pass the test of loyalty to the code of secrecy. Sometimes this loyalty of colleagues has the effect of protecting the law-violating, unethical officer.[18]

Such illegal practices which are traditionally used to carry out a policeman's assigned tasks might well be readily converted to the aims of personal gain.

In these tight informal cliques within the larger police force, certain "exploratory gestures"[19] involving the acceptance of small bribes and favors can occur. This is a hazy boundary between grateful citizens paying their respects to a proud profession, and "good" citizens involved in corruption wishing to buy future favors. Once begun, however, these practices can become "norms" or informal standards of cliques of policemen. A new recruit can be socialized into accepting these illegal practices by mild, informal negative sanctions such as the withholding of group acceptance. If these unlawful practices are embraced, the recruit's membership group—the police force—and his reference group—the clique involved in illegal behavior—are no longer one and the same. In

such circumstances the norms of the reference group (the illegal-oriented clique) would clearly take precedence over either the formal requisites of the membership group (police department regulations) or the formalized norms (legal statutes) of the larger society.[20] When such conflicts are apparent a person can

> 1) conform to one, take the consequences of non-conformity to the other. 2) He can seek a compromise position by which he attempts to conform in part, though not wholly, to one or more sets of role expectations, in the hope that sanctions applied will be minimal.[21]

If these reference group norms involving illegal activity become routinized with us they become an identifiable informal "code" such as that found in the present study. Such codes are not unique to the police profession. A fully documented case study of training at a military academy[22] in which an informal pattern of behavior was assimilated along with the formal standards clearly outlined the function of the informal norms, their dominance when in conflict with formal regulations, and the secretive nature of their existence to facilitate their effectiveness and subsequent preservation. The revelation of their existence to those outside the cadet group would destroy their integrative force and neutralize their utility.

This same secrecy would be demanded of a police "code" to insure its preservation. Although within the clique the code must be well defined, the ignorance of the lay public to even its existence would be a requisite to its continuous and effective use.[23] Through participation in activity regimented by the "code" an increased group identity and cohesion among "code" practitioners would emerge.

> Group identity requires winning of acceptance as a member of the inner group and, thereby, gaining access to the secrets of the occupation which are acquired through informal contacts with colleagues.[24]

Lack of this acceptance not only bars the neophyte from the inner secrets of the profession, but may isolate him socially and professionally from his colleagues and even his superiors. There is the added fear that, in some circumstance in which he would need their support, they would avoid becoming involved, forcing him to face personal danger or public ridicule alone.

The social structure in which law enforcement is maintained has a definite bearing on what is considered normal and what is deviant behavior. The pattern of "Blue-Coat Crime" (i.e., the "code") seems far more deviant when compared to the dominant middle-class norms of our society as when compared to lower class values. Whyte maintains that in the Italian Slum of Cornerville, the primary function of the police department is not the enforcement of the law, but the regulation of illegal activities ...

> ... an outbreak of violence arouses the "good people" to make demands for law enforcement ... even when they disturb police racketeer relations. Therefore, it is in the interest of the departments to help maintain a peaceful racket organization ... By regulating the racket and keeping peace, the officer can satisfy the demands for law enforcement with a number of token arrests and be free to make his adjustment to the local situation.[25]

Since an adjustment to the local situation might well involve adopting some of the "code" practices, the successful police rookie is he who can delicately temper three sets of uncomplementary standards: 1) the "code" practices adopted for group acceptance, 2) the societal standard regulating the duties and responsibilities of the police profession and 3) his own system of morality gained from prior socialization in family, religious, educational and peer-group interaction.

METHODOLOGICAL CONSIDERATIONS

The difficulties connected with any intensive investigation into the "code" are self evident. The binding secrecy which provides the source of its power would be disrupted if the "code" were revealed to an "outsider." Thus, standard sociological research methods were ineffective in this type of investigation. The traditional ethnographic technique of using an informant familiar with the "code" and its related practices made available the empirical data within this study. Obviously, data from a single informant do not begin to meet the stringent scientific criteria of reliability for the purpose of applying the conclusions from this case to police agencies in general. It is assumed that subsequent research will establish whether this is a unique episode or more of a universal phenomenon. However, the decision to enrich the literature with this present study in spite of its methodological deficiencies was felt to be justified inasmuch as an intensive search through the professional literature revealed no empirical accounts dealing directly with deviant policemen.[26]

Because of the explosive nature of such materials on the social, political and economic life of the persons involved, the use of pseudonyms to maintain complete anonymity is a precaution not without precedent, and was a guarantee given by the director of this study in return for complete cooperation of the informant.[27] The informant was a police officer for 3-1/2 years before he was implicated in charges of Robbery and Grand Larceny. He was subsequently tried and convicted, serving the better part of a year in prison. At the time of these interviews, he had been released from prison about three years.

The initial design of this study attempted to correlate these empirical data with two journalistic accounts[28] but the subjective handling of those stories neutralized any advantage gained from an increased number of informants. The present design is based exclusively on the single informant.

THE CODE AND ITS PRACTICES

Some of these terms used to describe police deviance are widely used, but because of possible variations in meaning they are defined below.[29] These practices are ordered so that those listed first would generally elicit the least fear of legal prosecution and those listed last would invoke major legal sanctions for their perpetration.

Mooching—An act of receiving free coffee, cigarettes, meals, liquor, groceries, or other items either as a consequence of being in an underpaid, undercompensated profession *or* for the possible future acts of favoritism which might be received by the donor.

Chiseling—An activity involving police demands for free admission to entertainment whether connected to police duty or not, price discounts, etc.

Favoritism—The practice of using license tabs, window stickers or courtesy cards to gain immunity from traffic arrest or citation (sometimes extended to wives, families and friends of recipient).

Prejudice—Situations in which minority groups receive less than impartial, neutral, objective attention, especially those who are less likely to have "influence" in City Hall to cause the arresting officer trouble.

Shopping—The practice of picking up small items such as candy bars, gum, or cigarettes at a store where the door has been accidentally unlocked after business hours.

Extortion—The demands made for advertisements in police magazines or purchase of tickets to police functions, or the "street courts" where minor traffic tickets can be avoided by the payment of cash bail to the arresting officer with no receipt required.

Bribery—The payments of cash or "gifts" for past or future assistance to avoid prosecution; such reciprocity might be made in terms of being unable to make a positive identification of a criminal, or being in the wrong place at a given time when a crime is to occur, both of which might be excused as carelessness but no proof as to deliberate miscarriage of justice. Differs from mooching in the higher value of a gift and in the mutual *understanding* regarding services to be performed upon the acceptance of the gift.

Shakedown—The practice of appropriating expensive items for personal use and attributing it to criminal activity when investigating a break in, burglary, or an unlocked door. Differs from shopping in the cost of the items and the ease by which former ownership of items can be determined if the officer is "caught" in the act of procurement.

Perjury—The sanction of the "code" which demands that fellow officers lie to provide an alibi for fellow officers apprehended in unlawful activity covered by the "code."

Premeditated Theft—Planned burglary, involving the use of tools, keys, etc., to gain forced entry or a pre-arranged plan of unlawful acquisition of property which cannot be explained as a "spur of the moment" theft. Differs from shakedown only in the previous arrangements surrounding the theft, not in the value of the items taken.

Mooching, chiseling, favoritism and *prejudice* do not have rigid interpretations in the "code." Their presence appears to be accepted by the general public as a real fact of life. Since the employment of one of these practices can be done while in the normal routine of one's duties, such practices are often ignored as being "deviant" in any way. Ex-Officer Smith sees it in this light:

> ...the policeman having a free cup of coffee? I have never thought of this as being corrupt or illegal because this thing is just a courtesy thing. A cup of coffee or the old one—the cop on the beat grabbing the apple off the cart—these things I don't think shock too many people because they know that they're pretty well accepted.

But when asked about the practice of *mooching* by name, it assumed a different character of increased importance to Smith!

> I think mooching is accepted by the police and the public is aware of it. My opinion now, as an ex-policeman, is that mooching is one of the underlying factors in the larger problems that come ... it is one of the most basic things. It's the easiest thing to accept and to take in stride because it's so petty. I think that it is the turning point a lot of times.

The "Sunday Comics" stereotype of policemen initiating mooching, bribery and favoritism is incorrect according to Smith's experience:

> Generally, the policeman doesn't have to ask for things, he just finds out about them. Take for example the theaters. I know the Roxy theatres would let the policeman in on his badge, just about anytime. It's good business because it puts the owner in a closer relationship with the policeman, and the policeman is obligated to him. If they had a break-in, a fire, or a little favor such as double parking out front to unload something, they'd expect special consideration from the policeman.
>
> When I walked the east side beat the normal thing was for bartenders to greet me and offer me a pack of cigarettes or a drink. When I walked the beat I was pretty straight laced, there were a few bartenders that I felt were just trying to get along with me, and I loosened up a little with those people. One bartender gave me cigars when he found out that I didn't smoke cigarettes. I always accepted them; he always pointed out there wasn't any obligation. Some of the beat men accepted cigarettes, some cigars, some took cash, and these men know when they're dealing with bootleggers, and why they're being paid. Different businessmen in the loop area give policemen Christmas presents every year.

Shopping and *shakedown*, *extortion* and *bribery* are all clearly unlawful, but in these practices the manner in which they are carried out contains a measure of safety to the policeman should his presence or behavior be questioned. A policeman's investigative powers allows him entry into an open building in which a "suspected robbery" has occurred, and various types of articles such as cigarettes and the like cannot be traced to any given retail outlet. Hence, his presence on such occasions is not *suspected;* rather, it is *expected!* Also, should a clumsy job of *shopping* or *shakedown* result in witnesses reporting these unlawful practices, the "code" requires that participating officers must commit *perjury* to furnish an alibi for those colleagues observed in illegal activities. This is both for the protection of the deviant officer and to preclude public disclosure of the widespread involvement of fellow officers in "code" practices. How extensive is *shopping* and *shakedown* as practiced by a department?

> As far as the Mid-City department is concerned I would say that 10 percent of the department would go along with anything, including deliberate forced entries or felonies. But about 50 percent of them would openly go along with just about anything. If they found a place open or if there had been a break-in or if they found anything they could use and it was laying there, they'd help themselves to it.
>
> Whenever there's an open door or window, they call for all the cars and they shake the whole building down—loot it!

Would those policemen involved in shopping and shakedown participate in something more serious? According to ex-officer Smith, they would.

> Most of the policemen who shop or go along with shopping would go along with major theft, if it just happened. I think where you've got to draw the line is when you get into premeditated, deliberate thefts. I think this is where the big division comes.
>
> In shopping, the theft just happens. Premeditated theft is a cold, deliberate, planned thing.

Here Smith points out the limits of the "code" which, though condoning any level of theft that "just happens," cannot fully support *premeditated theft.*

> I think in premeditated theft that the general police attitude is against it, if for no other reason just for the matter of self-preservation, and survival. When you get to a premeditated, deliberate thing, then I think your police backing becomes pretty thin.

At the time when Smith was engaged in the practice of *premeditated theft* in Mid-City, it looked somewhat differently to him than it did later. When he took an objective look , he was aware of just how little this extreme deviancy *actually was practiced.*

When I was involved in it, it seemed like all the people around me were involved in it, and participating in it. It looked more to me like the generally accepted thing then, than it does now, because actually the clique that I was in that did this sort of thing was a small one. I'm not discounting the fact that there may have been a lot of other small cliques just like this.

Looking at his behavior as an outsider, after his expulsion, Smith saw it in this light:

After taking a long, hard look at my case and being real honest about it, I'd have to say that the [premeditated theft like mine] is the exception. The longer I'm away from this thing the more it looks like this.

In Mid-City, *extortion* was not generally practiced and the "code" prescribed "street courts" (i.e., bribery for minor traffic offenses) as outside the acceptable pattern.

[Extortion is] something that I would classify as completely outside the law [here in Mid-City], something that in certain areas has been accepted well on the side of both the public and the police. There's a long standing practice that in Chicago if you are stopped for a traffic violation if you had a five dollar bill slipped in your plastic holder, or your billfold, the patrolman then asks for your license, and if that's in there you'll very rarely be issued a summons. Now this thing was something that was well known by truck-drivers and people who travel through that area.

Smith maintains that the "code" is widespread, although from the above analysis of extortion it can be clearly seen that specific practices have been traditionally practiced and accepted in certain areas, yet not found acceptable in another community. Would this mean that the bulk of these "code" practices occur in police departments other than the one in which Smith served his "apprenticeship" in "Blue-Coat Crime"? Our informant says "yes" and offers the following to substantiate his answer:

I think generally the Mid-City police department is like every police department in the world. I think the exceptions are probably in small towns or in a few cities that have never been touched by corrupt politics, if there are any. But I think that generally they are the same everywhere,[30] because I have talked to policemen from other cities. I know policemen in other cities that I've had contact with that were in those things. I've discussed open things, or out and out felonies, with policemen from Kansas City on. And I know that at least in that city that it happens, and it's a matter of record that it happens in Denver and Chicago. And I think that this happens in all cities.

From a scientific point of view, other than the incidence of police scandals from time to time, there is no evidence to confirm or deny this one ex-officer's opinion regarding the universal existence of the "code."

THE RECRUIT'S INITIATION INTO THE "CODE" CLIQUE

Bucher describes a profession as a relatively homogeneous community whose members share identity, values, definitions of role, and interest. Socialization of recruits consists of inducting them into the "common core."[31] This occurs on two levels: the formal, or membership group, and the informal, or the reference group.

In the Mid-City police department the failure to socialize most of the new recruits into the "code" would constitute a threat to those who presently practice it. Thus, all "code" practitioners have the responsibility of screening new recruits at various times to determine whether they are "alright guys," and to teach by example and mutual involvement the limitations of "code" practices. If the recruit accepts such training, he is welcomed into the group and given the rights and privileges commensurate with his new status. If he does not, he is classified as a "goof" and avoided by the rest.

In a journalistic account of police deviancy, it was argued that if corruption exists in the political structures controlling police department appointments, this "socialization" into deviancy begins at the point of paying for the privilege of making an application or of buying an appointment.[32] Although Smith did not "buy" his appointment, he cited the existence of factions having influence in recruit appointments, even within the structure of a Civil Service Commission.

> There are four different requirements to the whole thing. One is your written test, one is your agility, one is your physical examination, and the fourth is the oral examination which is given by the civil service commission. I really crammed before I took the test. When I took the test it was a natural for me, it was a snap. I scored a 94 on my test for the police department. With my soldiers preference, which gives you 5 points, I scored a 99.[33] I passed my agility test and my physical. I could have had a 100 score, I could have been a gymnast, gone through the agility test and made everyone else look silly and still I could have failed in the oral exam. And this is the kicker where politics comes in.
>
> There are three old men that are aligned with different factions, different people on and off the department, different businessmen that have power, different groups, different lodges and organizations and all these things influence these men, these three people that make up the civil service board.

The existence of the "code" had hurt the level of morale generally in the Mid-City department. In fact, the breakdown of each new recruit's morale is an important step in gaining his acceptance of the "code."[34]

> The thing that hurt the morale was the fact that a large percentage of the people on the department were involved in illegal practices to some degree. And actually you take a man that has just joined the department, has good intentions[35] and is basically honest, and in this, to a man that's never been dishonest and hasn't stepped over the line, there aren't degrees. It's all either black or white. And the illegal activity I know shocks a lot of these young men.... because it was the thing to do. It's a way to be accepted by the other people. It's a terrible thing the way one policeman

will talk about another. Say an old timer will have a new man working with him and he'll tell you, "You've got to watch him, because *he's honest!*"

For a recruit to be accepted in the Mid-City police department he must accept the informal practices occurring in the department. Illegal activity is pursued within the police force as the dominant "norm" or standard.

To illustrate the group pressure on each policeman who dares to enforce the law as prescribed in the legal statutes, the following account is typical.

> We'll take a classic example—Mr. Sam Paisano. Now when I was on the force I knew that whenever I worked in the downtown area, I could go into Sam's restaurant and order my meal and never have to pay a dime. I think that just about every patrolman on the force knew that. If I had run across Sam doing anything short of murder, I think I would have treaded very lightly. Even if I hadn't accepted his free meals. Say I had turned it down; still if I stopped this man for a minor traffic violation, say I caught him dead to rights, I'd be very reluctant to write this man a ticket because I'd suffer the wrath of the other men on the force. I'd be goofing up their meal ticket. Now he in turn knows this. The rest of the officers wouldn't waste any words about it, they'd tell you right off—"You sure fouled up our meal ticket". The old timers would give you a cold shoulder. If it came to the attention of the gold braid, your immediate superiors, they'd make sure you had a little extra duty or something. In most cases if you did this just to be honest, just to be right, it would go badly for you.
>
> This special treatment of Mr. Paisano wasn't something that you concealed, or that you were ashamed of because it was the normal accepted thing to do. I'd have been more ashamed, and I'd have kept it quiet if I'd stopped such a man as this, because I'd have felt like some kind of an oddball. I would have been bucking the tide, I'd have been out of step.

Yet, such general practices must be converted to

individual participation at some point, and to be effective this involvement must be on a primary group relationship basis. Smith's account of his introduction to the "code" follows the first steps of the assimilating process.

> The first thing that I can recall seeing done [which was illegal] was on the night shift when I first went on patrol. The old timers were shaking buildings down and helping themselves to whatever was in the building. The first time I saw it happen I remember filing through the check-out counter at a supermarket, seeing all the officers grabbing their cigarettes or candy bars, or whatever they wanted and I passed through without anything.
>
> I got in the car and this old timer had, of all the petty things, two of these 25 or 30 cent candy bars and he sat them down in the seat and told me to have some. I told him I really didn't want any. And he asked me if "that shook me up" or something. And I told him, "Well, it sort of surprised me." He said that everybody did it and that I should get used to that.
>
> As it went on it progressed more. Well, in fact, he justified it at the time by telling me he had seen the same market one time, when there had been a legitimate break-in and one particular detective had been so busy loading the back seat of his car full of hams and big pieces of beef that he was tumbling and falling down back and forth from the cooler to the alley, and he didn't even know who was around him he was so busy carrying things out. And he named this officer and I don't doubt it because I've seen the same officer do things in that same nature.
>
> And this was the first direct contact I had with anything like this.

The old timers would test the new recruits with activities which could be laughed off if they were reported, such as the 30 cent candy bar taken from the supermarket in the above account.

The old timers would nose around 'til they found out whether a young guy was going to work with them and "be right" as far as they were concerned, or whether he was going to resist it and be straight as far as the rest of the world was concerned.

If the recruit cooperated, the practices were extended and the rookie became involved. Once he was involved there was no "squealing" on fellow policemen breaking the law. Then he could have some personal choice as to how far he personally wished to go. However, those who were straight-laced and wanted to stay honest had their problems too. Social isolation appears to be a powerful sanction as can be seen from Smith's information.

> There are a few policemen that are straight-laced all the way. I can remember one policeman who might have made an issue of another policeman taking something. He had that attitude for the first six months that he was on the force but by that time, he had been brow beaten so bad, he saw the writing on the wall. He knew better than to tell anything. In addition to brow beating, this man in very short order was put in a position where they had him on the information desk, or kicked around from one department to another, 'cause nobody wanted to work with him. This kind of a man they called "wormy," because anything that would happen he'd run to the braid.
>
> This fellow, I knew, wanted to be one of the boys, but he wanted to be honest, too. As it turned out, this guy was finally dismissed from the force for having an affair with a woman in his squad car. Just a couple of years before that he would have had a fit if he thought that somebody was going to take a drink on duty, or fool around with a woman, or steal anything. For this reason this man spent a lot of time on the information desk, working inside, and by himself in the squad car.

Negative sanctions were applied against "goofs" who advocated following the legitimate police ethic. Group acceptance by senior officers was the reward to a recruit accepting the "code," and the "code" was presented to the recruit as the police way of life having precedence over legal responsibilities.

This small fraction that ... are honest and would report illegal activity, are ostracized. Nobody will work with them. They look at them like they're a freak, talk about them like they're a freak, and they are a freak.

The goofs that would talk about doing things the way they should be done, they had to be ignored or put down. There were older policemen that as they found out I would go along with certain things, pressed to see how much further I would go. And showed me that they went farther, whether I cared to or not. So naturally I went along quite a ways with some of them. And I don't really remember how we first became aware of how far the other person would go. I think this is just a gradual thing.

The existence of a social system of an informal nature working quietly under the facade of the formal police department regulations has been clearly demonstrated in Mid-City. One further note in explaining the motivations of policemen toward illegal activities involves the condition of low salaries. Smith's department pay scale and working conditions would suggest that economic pressures were a factor in condoning or rationalizing "code" practices.

The pay wasn't good. I went on the department and earned $292 a month. The morale of the force was as low as that of any group that I've ever been around. There was constant complaining from all of them about everything.

The training programs were set up so that you would have to come in on your own time and weren't compensated for it. . . . They dictated to you how you lived your whole life, not only what you did during the eight hours you were a policeman but how you'd live your whole life. This as much as anything hurt the morale.

But when Smith was asked directly, "With the policeman's low salary, do illegal activities become necessary to keep up financially?" he discounted it as a major factor.[36]

I don't think this is the case. I don't think there are very many policemen that I knew, and I knew all of them, that were social climbers or that tried to keep up with the Jones, by illegal activities anyway.

Actually most of the police officers think that they are even above those people that have money, because they have power. Those people with money are pretty well forced to cater to a policeman. And you'll find that very few people ever tell a policeman what they think of him, whether they like him or not. They know that a policeman will do him harm. The businessmen, especially the bigger businessmen, pamper the policeman. They will treat them with respect when they face them.

SANCTIONS FOR PRESERVATION OF THE "CODE"

Normally, practitioners of the "code" would consist of a united group working to protect all fellow patrolmen from prosecution. However, Smith had exceeded the "code" limits[37] by committing *premeditated theft*, and in order to protect the "code" from being exposed during the scandal involving Smith and two accomplices, the "clique" socially and spatially isolated themselves from the three accused policemen.

Everybody ran for cover, when the thing hit the front page of the newspapers. I've never seen panic like there was at that time. These people were all ready to sell out their mother to save their own butts. They knew there was no holding back, that it was a tidal wave. They were grabbing just anything to hang on. The other policemen were ordered to stay away from us, myself and the other men involved. They were ordered to stay away from the trials. They were told to keep their noses out of this thing, that it would be handled.

There were a few policemen who came around during this time. Strangely the ones who came around were the ones who didn't go in for any of the illegal activity. They didn't have anything to worry about. Everybody else ran and hid.

During a time like this, group consensus is required to preserve the "code." A certain amount of rationalization is necessary to mollify past illicit activity in light of present public exposure. Smith continues:

> I think if they had really gone by the book during the police scandal, that 25 percent of the policemen would have lost their jobs. I've talked to some of them since, and the worst violators all now have themselves convinced that they weren't guilty of a thing.
>
> I've never referred to myself as this before, but I was their goat, their scapegoat. The others stuck together and had support. I got what I deserved, but if I compare myself with the others, I got a real raw deal.

Preservation of the "code" occurs when policemen work with another person who has similar intentions and begin to "trust" one another in illegal activities without fear of the authorities being informed. A suggestion of rotating young officers from shift to shift to weaken the "code" had been given public discussion. To this, Smith reacted thusly:

> I think that the practice of rotating young officers will serve a purpose. It will eliminate a lot of things because you just can't take a chance with somebody that you don't know. If you don't know but what the next person they throw you with might be a CID ... short for Criminal Investigation Department. They're spies! Say there are just 10 percent of the men on the department that wouldn't go along with anything, and they are switching around with the new system, you don't know when you're going to catch one of them and if you do you're a cooked goose. The old system you were 90 percent sure of the people you were with.

This same process used to preserve the illegal "code" as a group phenomenon is also the same process used to develop and promote the acceptable professional ethics of the police. A situation in which it is "normal" for a policeman to "squeal on his fellow patrolmen," would undermine professional ethics. Personal insecurity would mount with the constant fear of just being accused with or without supporting evidence.

Such an anarchical system lends itself to intrigue, suspicion and an increased possibility of each officer being "framed." Thus, these same procedures which would effectively reduce the continuation of the "code" would also prove dysfunctional to the maintenance of the ethics which are the core of the police profession itself. These concurrent processes reflect the dual standards extant in society at large.

DIFFICULTIES INVOLVED IN BREAKING THE "CODE"

If a "code" does exist in a law enforcement agency, one of the major factors which protects it from attack is secrecy. This factor is compounded by public acceptance of the traditional view of illegal behavior as only an individualistic, moral problem.

Another shield of the "code" from attack is the apathy resulting from the myriad of complex demands and responsibilities placed upon the average citizen. So many things touch him with which he must become involved that he does not pursue problems which do not directly concern him. Inextricably connected with this is the realistic fear of retaliation, either through direct harassment by the police or indirectly through informal censures.[38]

Smith says that only a real big issue will provoke an apathetic public to action.

> Everybody's looking out for number one. And the policeman can do you harm. It's such a complex thing, there are so many ways, so many different people are affected by the police—most people will back off. Most people are afraid to do anything, if it looks like it's going to affect them adversely.

If the police have carefully practiced *prejudice* in their day-to-day operations, the chances are slim that the persons against whom these illegal practices were committed possess either the social or political power to break the "code" before the system could retaliate. Knowing this fact keeps most of the persons with any knowledge of the "code's" operation silent indeed.

The rigid procedures of obtaining legal

evidence and the dangers of committing a *false arrest* are gigantic deterrents to bringing accusations against any suspicious person, especially a policeman. Ex-Officer Smith discusses the realistic problems involved in attempting to enforce legal statutes against *shopping* or other aspects of the "code":

I think that any law against *shopping* would be hard to enforce against a police officer. You'd really have to have the evidence against him and really make it public, 'cause it would be soft pedaled all the way otherwise. Let's say you see a police officer in a restaurant taking a pack of cigarettes or let's say it's something other than a pack of cigarettes, something that you can prove came from the restaurant. And along comes a radio news unit and you stop the unit and say you just saw a policeman steal a pack of cigarettes or something bigger. When other police arrive on the scene the newsman would probably pull the other policemen off to the side and tell them that their buddy just took a pack of cigarettes and that goofball [the informer] wants to make trouble about it. You insist that they shake down the policeman and they find the item. Here you're in pretty good shape. In this case you'd have a policeman in a little bit of trouble. I don't think he'd lose his job or do any time over it, but I'd say there would be some scandal about it. Unless you were real hard headed they'd soft pedal it.

Let's back up a little and say the policeman threw the item back into the restaurant, and then you made your accusation. Then you're in trouble, 'cause when they shake him down and he doesn't have a thing. Now you're a marked man, because every policeman in town will know that you tried to foul up one of their boys. Even the honest policemen aren't going to like what you did. In other words, they are tightly knit, and they police this city by fear to a certain extent.

In Mid-City only those who are involved in practicing the "code" are equipped with the necessary information to expose its operations. Whether one *can* inform on his fellow officers is directly connected with the degree of his illegal involvement prior to the situation involving the unlawful event.

It all depends upon how deeply you are involved. If you've been a guy who has gone along with a free cup of coffee, the gratuities, the real petty things and you'd happen to drive up on a major theft, drive up on another policeman with his shoulder against the door, then you might take action. However, if you had gone a little farther, say you'd done some shopping, then you're forced to look the other way. It's like a spider spinning a web, you're drawn in toward the center.

It appears obvious that those who are involved in the "code" will be the least useful instruments for alleviating the problem. Only the professionally naive would expect a "code" practitioner to disclose the "code's" existence, much less reveal its method of operation, since his own position is so vulnerable.

Summary of Findings

From data furnished by a participant informant, an informal "code" of illegal activities within one police department was documented. The group processes which encouraged and maintained the "code" were identified. It was found that the new recruits were socialized into "code" participation by "old timers" and group acceptance was withheld from those who attempted to remain completely honest and not be implicated. When formal police regulations were in conflict with "code" demands among its practitioners, the latter took precedence. Since the "code" operates under conditions of secrecy, only those who participate in it have access to evidence enough to reveal its method of operation. By their very participation they are implicated and this binds them to secrecy as well. In this study the public indignation of a police scandal temporarily suspended the "code" but it flourished again when public apathy returned.

Although some individual factors must be considered in explaining police deviancy, in the present study the sanction of group acceptance was paramount. This study clearly demonstrates the social genesis of the "code," the breeding ground for individual unlawful behavior. From evidence contained herein, an individualistic orientation to police deviancy may discover the "spoiled fruit" but only when the "code" is rooted out can the "seedbed" of deviancy be destroyed.

From related research in group deviancy, it can be stated that the social organization of a given community (including its respectable citizens) is the milieu in which a "code" flourishes. Thus, a police department is an integral element of that complex community structure, and deviancy found in an enforcement agency is a reflection of values which are habitually practiced and accepted within that community. This was found to be true in the present study.

The findings of this case study should not be interpreted as applicable to all police departments nor should it be a rationalization for the existence of an illicit "code" anywhere. Rather, it is a very limited effort to probe the very sensitive area of "Blue-Coat Crime" and describe its operation and method of perpetuation in one enforcement agency.

NOTES

1. This concept is a restricted modification of Sutherland's term "White Collar Crime." Edwin H. Sutherland, "White Collar Criminality," *5 Amer. Soc. Rev.* 1–12 (1940). However, the stress of Sutherland's thesis is the lowering of social morale *of the larger society* by the violation of trust by those holding these social positions. The present emphasis is upon the group participating in those violations and *their* reactions, morale and behavior, rather than the consequences accruing the larger society as a result of these illegal actions. The same violation of trust might produce a degree of disorganization and lowering of morale among nonparticipants, while producing a heightened morale and cohesion among all of those in the norm-violating clique.

2. August Vollmer, *The Police and Modern Society* 3–4 (1936).

3. A. C. German, *Police Personnel Management* 3–4 (1958).

4. Mort Stern, "What Makes a Policeman Go Wrong? An Ex-Member of the Force Traces the Steps on Way from Law Enforcement to Violating," by a former Denver police officer, as told to Mort Stern, *Denver Post*, October 1, 1961. Reprinted in 53 *J. Crim. L., C. & P. S.* 97–101 (1962).

A similar reaction is given by James F. Johnson, a former state trooper, Secret Service agent, security officer and private investigator in World Telegram and Sun, March 10, 1953, quoted in Tappan, *Crime, Justice and Correction* 290 (1960).

5. Tappan, *Ibid.* 309ff.

6. Wilson, "Progress in Police Administration," 42 *J. Crim. L., C. & P. S.* 141 (1951).

7. Johnson, *Crime, Correction and Society* 452 (1964).

8. The Lexow Committee in New York (1894–1895), and the Seabury Committee a generation later found the same situation of *departmental* corruption quoted in Sutherland & Cressey, *Principles of Criminology* 338 (6th ed. 1960).

9. Sutherland & Cressey, *Ibid.*

10. Barnes & Teeters, *New Horizons in Criminology* 245–247 (2d ed. 1958).

11. Korn & McCorkle, *Criminology and Penology* 85–86, 125–136 (1959).

12. Richard A. Cloward, "Illegitimate Means, Anomie, and Deviant Behavior," 24 *Amer. Soc. Rev.* 167 (1959).

13. Merton, *Social Theory and Social Structure,* Chaps. 1, 4, and 5 (Revised and enlarged ed. 1958).

14. Bell, "Crime as an American Way of Life," 13 *Antioch Rev.* 140–144 (1953).

15. Sutherland & Cressey, *op. cit.* 331.

16. This dilemma is presently being compounded by recent Supreme Court decisions involving police powers and personal civil rights. The fear of an emergent police state (which may or may not be valid) leads the present Justices to feel that freedom of the individual will result when police powers no longer encroach upon individual rights. The paradox is that the police are required to fulfill their traditional protection duties in spite of these new formal procedures designed to limit their investigative activities. To fulfill the social expectations of "catching criminals, dope peddlers, etc.," the policeman must adopt certain extra-legal procedures strictly on an informal basis, while appearing on the surface to be adhering to the formal limitations imposed upon him. See Arthur Neiderhoffer's recent monograph *Behind the Shield: The Police in Urban Society* (1967).

17. Westley, "Violence and the Police," 59 *Amer. J. Soc.* 34–41 (1953).

18. Westley, "Secrecy and the Police," 34 *Social Forces* 254–257 (1956).

19. This concept was taken from Cohen, *Delinquent Boys: The Culture of the Gang* 60 (1955).

20. Sherif & Sherif, *An Outline of Social Psychology* 630–631, 638. For a sophisticated treatment of reference group theory see Chapters 4, 16, and 18. (Revised ed. 1956).

21. Stouffer, "An Analysis of Conflicting Social Norms," 14 *Amer. Soc. Rev.* 707 (1949).

22. Dornbush, "The Military Academy as an Assimilating Institution," 33 *Social Forces* 316–321 (1955).

23. Moore & Tumin, "Some Social Functions of Ignorance," 14 *Amer. Soc. Rev.* 791 (1949).

24. Johnson, *op. cit.* 445–446.

25. Whyte, *Street Corner Society* 138–139 (Enlarged ed. 1955).

Another author conceptualized this problem by delineating it as two separate police functions. "Law enforcement" has specific formal legal procedures whereas "keeping the peace" is vague and without a clear-cut mandate. This study updates by three decades the classic work of Whyte. See Egon Bittner, "The Police on Skid-Row: A Study of Peace Keeping," 32 *Amer. Soc. Rev.* 699–715 (1967).

26. Many authors have written of police deviancy as tangential to their central theme. However, persistent search failed to reveal recent empirical studies focusing directly on the deviant policeman himself. Most applicable were Westley's *Violence and the Police, op. cit.,* and *Secrecy and the Police, op. cit.,* although even here the data were gained from policemen still "in favor," who might well have reservations about revealing the full extent to which the "Code" was practiced.

27. A graduate assistant from the Department of Sociology, Mr. Ivy L. Gilbert approached ex-officer "Smith" as a friend, and under guidance of the present author was able to gain "Smith's" cooperation for a scientific study. Taped interviews over a period of several months were recorded and transcribed by Gilbert. Many of these materials were used in Gilbert's Master's Thesis, *A Case Study of Police Scandal: An Investigation into Illegitimate Norms of a Legitimate Enforcement Agency* (June, 1965).

28. One article is a composite of personal experience as a police reporter, David G. Wittels, "Why Cops Turn Crooked," *Saturday Evening Post,* April 23, 1949, p. 26ff; the other is an account of a former Denver policeman as retold by a news editor, Mort Stern, *op. cit. supra* note 4.

29. The majority of these terms and definitions are modified from those listed by Gilbert, *op. cit.* 3–4, and discussed by German, *op. cit. supra* note 3 at p. 173.

30. Smith's evaluations are heavily influenced by his experience. He was a patrolman in a police department totaling about 250 personnel, serving a metropolitan area of a quarter of a million persons.

However, other sources have suggested that when a community gets larger than 80,000 people, political corruption and graft are inevitable. Wittels, *op. cit.,* 26.

31. Rue Bucher and Anselm Strauss, "Professions in Progress," 64 *Amer. J. Soc.* 325–326 (1961).

32. One Policeman reported having paid $300.00 to take the police examination. He also was required to pledge his family's vote to the "right" party. After some wait, he took a "special exam," then more waiting lists, and a final $300.00 to the party fund was required before he was hired. Then he had to purchase his own uniform on contract at the "right" store. Before this man became a member of the department, by his participation in the recruitment process, he was an involved member practicing the "code." Wittels, *op. cit.* 105–107, 111.

33. In spite of Smith's remarkable test level, he was left off a list of highest 10 eligible applicants, and some three months later was put on the list through the influence of his father, a respected member of the police department with many years of unblemished service. Otherwise, he may never have been placed on the appointment list.

34. This is not unlike the planned removal of old civilian standards and values when a new soldier recruit is given basic training. The formal regulations are presented to him, but in company with "old Salts" he learns how the system can be worked and what a person must do to participate in it.

35. One writer corroborates this by stating that young recruits who show traits of being ambitious, as well as those with family responsibilities, are the most susceptible to graft. The pressures toward success and achievement are clearly indicated by either or both of these factors. Wittels, *op. cit.* 27.

36. To evaluate Smith's statement on economic pressures, an additional personal datum is relevant. Smith used most of his money from *premeditated theft* for his "habit"—a racing car. He later declared he probably wouldn't have participated in this crime *so much* had it not been for the "habit." His responses did not seem to indicate that he *began* theft for racing money, but that he *continued* it to counter the economic drain created by owning and driving the racing machine.

37. One officer reports that he wondered why he was not promoted—perhaps they thought he was lazy. He was tagging cars of all violators, and even reported a broken sidewalk belonging to an "organization" man. He couldn't get ahead. He made a couple of outstanding arrests and was made a

detective. Later, he ran a "vice" raid against a "protected" place, and was back as a rookie on a beat in
"Siberia." He finally took some payoffs and cooperated and eventually became a Police Captain, but
exceeding the "Code" limits, was caught and prosecuted. Either not accepting the "code," or exceeding its limits, had negative effects. Wittels, *op. cit.*
III–122.

38. The campaigning attack on the "untouchable"
image of J. Edgar Hoover and the FBI has made
political news. The very act of exposing methods
used by Hoover's organization, which though
admittedly effective were clearly unlawful, caused
the political downfall of an otherwise popular
politician in the November 1966 Nevada election.

Study Questions

1. Explain Stoddard's distinction between individualistic and sociological theories of
police deviance. Which perspective does Stoddard take? What does Stoddard mean by a
police "code"? Do you think that criminal justice practitioners operate according to such a
code? Discuss.

2. What is police "shopping"? How does Stoddard's informant distinguish morally
between shopping and premeditated theft? Do you think that this distinction is successful?
Analyze the argument that accepting gratuities leads to more serious forms of corruption.
Defend your analysis.

3. What is a "goof," as the term is used by Stoddard's informant? In your view, what are
the two most significant sanctions that might be imposed against a goof by practitioners
of the police code? If (or when) you are confronted by a police or corrections "code," will
you be a goof? Why? Defend your position.

4. What problems does Stoddard identify in eliminating a "code" in a criminal justice
agency? Do community values play any role in the values practiced by the agency, according to Stoddard? Do you agree? Why?

Should We Tell the Police to Say "Yes" to Gratuities?

RICHARD R. E. KANIA

MOST CRIMINAL JUSTICE EDUCATORS are
strongly opposed to public officials accepting
minor gratuities. Arthur Aubry, Jr., for example,
includes "[e]nforcement of the law courteously
and appropriately at all times without fear or
favor, never employing unnecessary force, and
never accepting gratuities of any sort"[1] among his
seventeen ethical principles for police officers.

McMullan states that "a public official is *corrupt*
if he accepts money or money's worth for doing
something that he is under a duty to do anyway,
that he is under a duty not to do, or to exercise a
legitimate discretion for improper reasons."[2]
And the International Association of Chiefs of
Police has promulgated a widely reprinted "Law
Enforcement Code of Ethics"[3] advocating the

*Richard Kania, "Should We Tell the Police to Say 'Yes' to Gratuities?", Criminal Justice Ethics, Vol. 7,
No. 2 (Summer/Fall 1988), pp. 37–49. Used by permission of the author and The Institute for Criminal
Justice Ethics, John Jay College of Criminal Justice, 899 Tenth Avenue, New York, NY 10019.*

absolute prohibition of the acceptance of gratuities. Many leading government and criminal justice reformers advance similar views, arguing that even the most trivial gratuity is a temptation that can only lead our public officials into further unethical conduct.[4]

Voices occasionally argue that minor gratuities do not necessarily result in adverse consequences.[5] Others have claimed that such gratuities may have some positive effects for the social system.[6] The criticism directed at U.S. Attorney General Edwin Meese III during his Senate confirmation hearings—for having accepted gifts from Korean officials—recently revived this debate in the media: supporters of the Reagan Administration scoffed at the idea that minor gifts corrupt their recipients while critics of the Administration and of Mr. Meese argued otherwise.

For the criminal justice community, especially those interested in police practices, this ethical question has been a perennial topic of discussion. But however much the issue has been discussed, it seems never to have been subjected to an in-depth analysis. The ethical impropriety of accepting minor gratuities has been treated as though it were established fact, with only the degree of impropriety being in question.[7] What debate there has been has focused on the relative seriousness of the ethical violation, the response the criminal justice system should make in dealing with this pattern of misconduct, and the consequences that acceptance of such gratuities will have for the more serious corruption of police officers or other justice officials.[8]

It is my view that this discussion has gone on too long without a reconsideration of the initial assumptions that accepting minor gratuities is inherently wrong, or improperly obligates the police recipients to the givers, or inevitably leads recipients into genuine corruption. In contrast to the prevailing view, I take the position that *the police* especially, and, under certain circumstances, other justice officials *should be encouraged to accept freely offered minor gratuities and that such gratuities should be perceived as the building blocks of positive social relationships between our police and the public,* and not as incipient corrupters. Such a change in our perception of gratuities can be justified by a fuller understanding of the motives of their givers. Some, if not most, minor gratuities are offered to repay or reward the police *for services already rendered.* It is true that these services are the legal due of the givers, having been paid for by their taxes. But the givers need not see it this way, and may indeed feel they still owe a debt to the police. Thus the police need not assume that the gifts they receive are intended to generate subsequent indebtedness to the givers. This "heretical" viewpoint should be evaluated as objectively as the other issues related to the corruption problem, and if the evaluation indicates that there is merit in the alternative view, then criminal justice educators and police trainers should approach the topic of acceptance of gratuities more open-mindedly than in the past. Perhaps trainers and educators should even promote the acceptance of minor gratuities within certain carefully qualified contexts, under carefully crafted guidelines and standards.

Slippery Slopes, Camels' Noses, and Unjustified Enrichment

Certainly many will disagree with this heretical position. Their objections dominate the literature on gratuities. Several arguments have been marshalled against the practice of accepting gratuities, generally falling into two basic lines of ethical reasoning: the "slippery slope" and the unjustified enrichment strategies.

The slippery slope analogies are far more common. Generally stated, the argument claims that although taking minor gratuities may not be a serious ethical problem, it begins a process of gradual subversion of the recipient's integrity. Eventually the acceptance of petty gratuities leads to more serious unethical conduct. This line of reasoning is essentially teleological. The acceptance of gratuities is not seen as wrong in itself, but the associated consequences of bias, favoritism, and bribery are evil. The relatively innocent gratuity, the free cup of coffee, is, to introduce another popular metaphor, the nose of the camel of corruption, trying to find a way inside the tent of law enforcement.[9]

Consequentialist theorists argue that the police officer who accepts minor gratuities becomes obligated to provide preferential treatment to the gift givers, and is thus no longer capable of providing equal and unbiased police services. This favoritism is a serious unethical consequence of gratuity giving, whether accepting minor gratuities is also ethically wrong in and of itself.[10]

A second school of thought takes the even more uncompromising position that any gratuity is in and of itself wrong because it is an unjustified enrichment for doing services already fully compensated and, in fact, paid for by the public. Advocates of this position assert that public employees are entitled to nothing beyond their basic compensation for doing their duty. This is a deontological ethical position, which stands apart from any particular consequences of the act. Accepting gratuities is wrong even if no subsequent bribery, bias, or favoritism ever results.

On Becoming a Heretic

My "heretical" position on this matter arises from the ethical deliberations I had within myself while serving as a police officer. I was faced with having to accept or decline unsolicited minor gratuities from merchants on my foot patrol beat. Like most police officers who have completed a modern, progressive police academy program, I knew that the conventional ethical standard obliged me to forego taking any gratuities and that it was even more unethical to solicit such gifts. At the academy the "why" was explained in terms of the probability of progressing to more serious, more unacceptable graft, as if the taking of a single gratuity were infectious.

When I arrived on the street, paired with a veteran officer, I was quickly shown that the supposedly unethical behavior was the social norm for the police and the merchants alike.

Were all these police corrupt? By the literal application of the ethical standard which I had learned in the police course, they indeed were. But were they really? Their behavior generally suggested otherwise. Although the officers whom I observed took minor gratuities without much hesitation, they provided no inappropriate or illegal favors in return.

The memory of police academy training was there to explain: the merchants were potential favor seekers who eventually would call in their chits. It recalled George C. Homan's observation: "Persons that give much to others try to get much from them, and persons that get much from others are under pressure to give much to them."[11] The police were seen as selling their souls bit by bit, against a future act of overt favoritism or corruption which the merchant or restaurateur would demand of them.

But this did not seem to be a frequent outcome, for these chits were not being called in. The merchants and restaurateurs occasionally did ask the police to perform special services for them, but none of the requests were out of line with what might normally be expected from any police officer, corrupted or pure. This failure of verification did not mean that I was witnessing a failure of the police academy faith, but it did make me suspect that there was more to the issue than had been explained at the academy. Perhaps the temptations of the merchants had been carried out in some other spirit. Perhaps there was no intention of calling in those chits for illegal favoritism or overtly corrupt police action. If these possibilities were to be accorded validity, then alternative explanations of the merchants' behavior were required. What other motivation might they have if not the future corruption of police officers?

I found a possible answer in the writings of a social anthropologist and in the offhand remarks of a short-order cook on the midnight shift in a restaurant on my beat. The social anthropologist was Edmund Leach, who wrote, "If I give you a present you will feel morally bound to give something back. In economic terms you are in debt to me, but in communicative terms the sense of reciprocal obligation is an expression of a mutual feeling that we both belong to the same social system."[12] Of course, I could have supposed that it was the police officer who was accruing the debt. That is how the short-order cook provided the missing analytical link. I tried to argue the cook out of giving me a free meal on a night-watch. The cook would have none of it and refused payment. I even reminded the cook that the owner gave only a percentage discount. In response, the cook replied that the owner did not work the midnight crowd, and had a lot less to be grateful to the police for. The short-order cook was grateful to the police; he felt that he was in a state of indebtedness to the police. The gratuities were not gifts given in expectation of future rewards, but, as Leach had explained, in repayment of the debt already owed by the late night cook.

Who Owes Whom? The Cohesive Value of Gift Exchange

My rationale for suggesting that police accept minor gratuities rests on the assumption that merchants and restaurateurs feel a genuine sense of debt toward the police who visit them. Offering these police minor gratuities helps settle the imbalance which merchants perceive. It is the giver who is indebted, not the police recipient.

What are the police doing that generates this debt? In the foregoing example they were visiting the establishment frequently on their rounds, providing the security that the short-order cook sought. Was this not a service that every police officer routinely was obliged to provide? Yes, most certainly it was. Did that fact in any way reduce the perception of the cook that he owed this officer and others in the police department a personal debt? No, it did not. I, true to my training, felt no debt was owed me, and so felt uncomfortable in accepting the free meals.[13]

An analogy can be drawn between gratuities given to police and "tips" given to salaried workers who provide personal services to which a consumer has a basic right as a consequence of

doing business with the workers' employer. Tip-giving consumers feel socially obligated to tip when excellent service is rendered. Tip recipients accept the gifts in the recognition that they have performed to the satisfaction of the tipper. Neither need feel that the other has any subsequent claim on him/her after the transaction is concluded. Opponents of this analogy argue that it does not hold because the police are paid their wages to provide everyone with equally good public service. However, direct police service is not distributed evenly in society. There are heavy consumers of police service, just as there are citizens who rarely, if ever, require direct police assistance. Equality in the actual provision of police service never occurs and is an unrealistic expectation, even if, in the abstract, police protection is extended equally. The real imbalance in the consumption of direct police service underlies the sense of debt felt by some heavy consumers of police service, and provides an ethical rationale for the giving and accepting of gratuities.

To refuse a gift genuinely offered in gratitude would be to refuse the giver the opportunity to satisfy his sense of obligation. As the French social anthropologist Marcel Mauss explained, "A gift not yet repaid debases the man who accepted it, particularly if he did so without thought of return."[14] It would be a rejection of that "expression of a mutual feeling that we both belong to the same social system" of which Leach writes.

Police officers may indeed have both an ethical and pragmatic obligation to accept such gifts. They are morally obligated to maintain good relations with law-abiding members of the community. To decline the gifts is to insult the givers, alienating them from the police. Alienation must be avoided for practical, pragmatic reasons. If citizens feel alienated, the police are less able to perform their duties. Of course, other means could be provided to enable citizens feeling a sense of indebtedness to repay police assistance. Gifts to police-sponsored benefits, rather than to police officers individually, and non-material recognition in the form of letters of appreciation have been suggested in lieu of personal gratuities.[15] But the former fails to fulfill the giver's need precisely because it is impersonal, while the debt is quite personal. The letter of appreciation is entirely appropriate, but it is an option that is not open to everyone. Effective letter-writing is not a uniformly distributed talent. The free cup of coffee, meal discount, or small gift is personal, immediate, and easily provided from resources at hand. Thus they are the most efficient means of achieving and maintaining social cohesion and avoiding alienation.

The point I am making about social cohesion is far from original. Many others beside Mauss and Leach have made the point that gift exchange has a cohesive value. Yet this social cohesion has been identified in corrupt transactions as well as legal ones. Dorothy Bracey shows an awareness of it in her examination of police corruption. Following the rules of value-neutrality in functional analysis, she does not dwell on the propriety or impropriety of these small scale "corrupters." Instead she identifies both harmful and useful aspects of the practice and finds increased social cohesion as one of several possible positive attributes of these exchanges.[16] Charles Kaut, studying institutionalized official "gift" exchange practices in the Philippines, comes to similar conclusions. Gratuities do increase social cohesion independently of their alleged corrupting influences.[17]

Many who have studied the problem with an open mind have been able to play devil's advocate, citing the positive features of gratuity acceptance, without necessarily encouraging police to accept them.[18] If positive features in the giving and receiving of gratuities do exist, then a broader teleological approach in ethical reasoning might be more appropriate, one more utilitarian in nature, that looks to the balance between advantages and disadvantages in accepting gratuities.[19]

This broader utilitarian reasoning which I am now encouraging has generally been discounted or ignored amid the claims about the probabilities of slippery slopes and camels' noses. This is especially disconcerting because there is evidence

to show that the slippery slope argument is a fallacy.[20] The New York City Police investigated by the Knapp Commission felt that the slope was not irresistible: they made a sharp distinction between the unacceptably corrupt "meat eaters" and the acceptably corrupt "grass eaters".[21] Subsequent research on police attitudes and opinions confirms that police make and adhere to distinctions between acceptable and unacceptable practices, even though these distinctions do not conform to the statutory distinctions between legal and corrupt practices. Michael Banton found that some police clearly reject the notion that a gratuity obligates them to the donors.[23] The knowledge that police officers can draw and stay within the lines between grass-eating and meat-eating corrupt practices may mean nothing to those who argue that both meat- and grass-eating are intolerably corrupt. But if we are evaluating the consequentialist arguments, ought we not to examine *all* the consequences of the rule? Its violation may carry some police down slippery slopes to favoritism and bribery. But its violation can also produce worthwhile social cohesion and provide indebted citizens an opportunity to express their genuine appreciation. True, its nonviolation may protect some police from temptation and corruption. And the loss of social cohesion could be remedied in other ways. But is this justification enough? Does its faithful observance produce only favorable consequences?

Empirical studies of the consequences of faithfully following the rules against taking gratuities are very rare; there may be none.[24] There do not appear to be many police who never violate the rule against taking gratuities. One study of sworn officers in three small police departments found no one who would "report a fellow officer for" free coffee, free movie access, a discounted or free meal.[25] So common were "free meals, discounts, small favors such as cigarettes or free drinks or similar" in the multi-cities, participation observation studies of Donald Black[26] and Albert Reiss[27] on actual police practices, that the final reports made no effort to record them in the results of police misconduct. Yet several probable negative consequences of following the rule can be suggested.

Consequences of Following the Published Formal Norms

What might occur if a police officer declined to accept a minor gratuity offered by a merchant or restaurateur? Ideally, the police ought to be protected from more serious vice. Realistically and empirically, however, this is not likely to be the only result, even if it were to be one result of such rule-abiding behavior. At best, experience demonstrates that an awkward situation might develop. The merchant might become politely insistent, and if the officer persisted in resisting the offer, ill will might result. The police officer might bargain away the gift, by disclaiming an interest in it, or by throwing up departmental policy as a barrier to its acceptance, perhaps to find the gift-giver offering clever ways to avoid the restrictions. The officer might stall by deferring acceptance or otherwise declining to take possession of the gift, while not actually refusing it. If the officer remained adamant about refusing the gift, however, harm might be inflicted on the social relationship between officer and merchant.

I have had personal experience of some of these techniques and have witnessed others. In one case, I was offered a Christmas gift from the manager of a small, privately owned department store, a $10.00 gift certificate made out in my name. I declined to accept it, citing departmental policy, only to discover the same certificate in my mail at home a few days later, modified to have "Mrs." inserted before my name. That same Christmas I was offered a bottle of Scotch at a tavern-restaurant, declined by saying that I did not drink Scotch, and then was confronted with questions about my drinking preferences. My only escape was a lie about not drinking alcohol, which made the tavern manager uneasy in my presence thereafter. Perhaps my most effective escape was to defer acceptance of the gift until I was out of uniform or off duty, and then fail to

collect it. This technique usually was successful, but it did not represent an actual refusal of the gift or denial of its acceptability. I had accepted these gifts in principle, as it were, and delayed only in taking delivery.

What if an officer does not employ such games to avoid the unauthorized gifts? What if he completely refuses, flatly spurning the offer? I had a junior officer assigned to me for training, an officer of unquestionably strong moral character who accepted the academy creed at face value. He steadfastly refused even the most minor discounts from restaurateurs, and twice became embroiled in arguments over the matter in my presence. On the second occasion, the argument actually became heated, and the inflexible officer accused the restaurant owner of trying to corrupt the police force. At that point, the officer was verbally evicted from the establishment and told not to return. The argumentative officer was called an "ass-hole" to his face and, in my opinion, had earned the label for his rigid refusal to accept an inconsequential discount. In the few months left of that inflexible but ethical officer's appropriately short, difficult, but uncorrupted police career, he found it necessary to bring a bag lunch and eat in the car while his "corrupted" partners ate at discount in neighborhood eateries. This deviation from the "unethical" behavior of his peers served to provide the businesses of his patrol sector less on-site protection than was provided by the "corrupt" police who continued to accept meal discounts in the spirit in which they were offered. Although an isolated case does not an empirical proof make, it does illustrate one of the possible consequences of rejecting a minor gratuity, originally offered in a spirit of genuine gratitude.

Are All Proffered Gratuities Expressions of Gratitude?

The position I am proposing here does not assume that all gratuities are offered in a spirit of genuine gratitude. Certainly it seems unlikely that they would be. Some givers give with ulterior motives, just as the police academy warnings have suggested. An equally serious concern is that the gifts are offered out of a sense of obligation, habit, or worse still, necessity.

In some cities the practice of gathering in gifts is undertaken with the zeal of tax collecting on a 100 percent commission basis. The merchants likewise view the visiting police officers as free-lance tax collectors.[28] In such cases, the practice of gift giving and acceptance has become so institutionalized that both parties see it as a compulsory social requirement rather than a gift freely given.[29] The police can—and occasionally do—carry self-solicitous activities too far, and merchants sometimes make official complaints.[30] Obviously such abuse of merchants is totally indefensible, and does not fall within the scope of what could properly be called a gift or gratuity.

If the motives of the giver are improper and the police officer accepts the benefit with knowledge and acceptance of those motives, then the exchange is unethical, as the police academy instructs. If the police officer solicits "freebies" and is a "moocher" then his conduct is, as Banton observed, a form of extortion.[31] That too is totally unethical, as all will recognize. But these two unethical scenarios do not exhaust all the possibilities of motives and interpretations in an exchange situation.

The ethical quality of an exchange is a relative matter, requiring some understanding of the intention and perceptions of both the giver and the recipient. A giver can perceive his/her offer as expressing a gift in a genuine sense of appreciation, as expressing a gift from a sense of social obligation, as making an investment to secure future good will from the recipient, as placing a deposit on future services or favors, as paying off the recipient to gain an illegal advantage, or as surrendering something of value under pressure from an official who might otherwise cause the giver harm. The recipient, too, may view the object or service offered in one of several ways. He/she may accept the gift as an expression of gratitude, as a ritual offering to achieve or maintain positive social ties, as a

credit against future services to be provided, or as an inducement to overlook law violations. Or, the gift can be extorted from the giver as protection from harassment or arrest, be it justified or falsely arranged. Moreover, there can be situations when the perceptions of one of the parties do not match the perceptions of the other. Some of the potential combinations may be completely innocent and fully ethical, merely innocuous, or completely improper and therefore unethical. To decide which of these combinations should be criticized and which should be condoned or even encouraged, we need to understand the motivations of both actors in the exchange and, furthermore, to decide whose perception should determine the moral character of the exchange.

THE PERCEPTION OF THE GIVER

1. *Reward Given:* The giver is acknowledging that a significant legal and ethical service has been rendered to him/her by the police recipient. The reward is a token which serves to honor and repay that positive service.

2. *Gift Given:* The giver is acknowledging that an ongoing social, legal, and ethical relationship exists between him/herself and the police recipient. The gift is a token that expresses appreciation for this continuing pattern of valued, reliable service rendered by the police recipient. From the point of view of the giver, it helps settle a social debt owed to the police officer.

3. *Gratuity Given:* The giver is acknowledging that an ongoing legal and ethical relationship exists between him/herself and the law enforcement agency of which the recipient is a member. The gratuity is a token that serves to foster and maintain that positive relationship with the recipient and other police officers. Thus the token is given to continue a pattern of reliable service rendered by the department over an extended period of time.

4. *Investment Made:* The giver is offering a token to indicate that he/she is interested in establishing a special relationship between him/herself and the law enforcement agency of

which the recipient is a member and that the investment is a token which serves to initiate that preferred relationship with the recipient and other police officers. The giver hopes to place the police recipient into social debt. The benefits the giver envisions receiving in return need not be illegal or unethical but exceed normal standards of or entitlements to police services.

5. *Bribe Offered:* The giver is making a payment to acquire a specific illegal or unethical police service or to preclude the lawful exercise of a proper police function. No positive, integrative social relationship derives from the exchange. The bribe is the purchase price of the service actively sought. It is understood to conclude the immediate interaction without any further obligation by either party, although additional transactions may follow. The transaction clearly is unethical.

6. *Arrangement Initiated:* The giver is making a payment to acquire or continue ongoing illegal or unethical police services or to preclude the future lawful exercises of police functions. The payment is an installment on the purchase price of the services actively and repetitively sought. It is understood to be one in a series of illegal transactions. An integrative (although illicit) social relationship will derive from the exchange. The transactions clearly are unethical.

7. *Shakedown Paid:* The giver is coerced into offering a payment to the law enforcement official to avoid the threat of the lawful exercise of a proper police function or an unlawful abuse of police authority. No positive, integrative social relationship derives from the exchange. Future payoffs may be solicited from the giver, but the transaction is intended to conclude the immediate interaction. The transaction clearly is unethical.

THE PERCEPTION OF THE POLICE RECIPIENT

A. *Reward Received:* The recipient is aware that a legal and ethical service has been rendered to the giver and that the reward is a token that serves to honor and repay that positive service.

The token is accepted in a shared recognition of the significance to the giver of the service, even if that service is only part of the legal and professional expectations associated with the recipient's office.

B. *Gift Received:* The recipient is aware that an ongoing social, legal, and ethical relationship exists between him/herself and the giver and that the gift is a token that serves to repay the debt that the giver feels exists and to maintain that positive social relationship. The token is accepted in a shared recognition of a pattern of reliable service over an extended period of time, even if that service is only part of the legal and professional expectations associated with the recipient's office.

C. *Gratuity Received:* The recipient is aware that an ongoing legal and ethical relationship exists between the police department and the giver and that the gratuity is a token which serves to maintain that positive social relationship. The token is accepted in a shared recognition of a pattern of reliable service over an extended period of time, even if that service is only part of the legal and professional expectations associated with the department's mission.

D. *Understanding Reached:* The police recipient accepts the token as an investment made by the giver to establish a special relationship between the giver and the law enforcement agency of which the recipient is a member. The police recipient acknowledges that he/she has been placed in social debt. The relationship he/she envisions may or may not be fully legal or ethical, but the act of acceptance is unethical because the relationship agreed to places the giver in a special, preferred status vis-à-vis access to valued police services.

E. *Bribe Accepted:* The recipient is accepting a payment to provide a specific illegal or unethical police service or to preclude the lawful exercise of a proper police function. No positive, integrative social relationship derives from the exchange. The bribe is accepted as the purchase price of the service provided. It concludes the immediate interaction without any further obligation by the recipient, although additional transactions may follow. The transaction clearly is unethical and illegal.

F. *Installment Collected:* The recipient is collecting a payment "on the pad" for ongoing illegal or unethical police services or to preclude the future lawful exercises of police functions. The payment is an installment on the purchase price of the services being provided. It is understood to initiate or continue an ongoing series of illegal transactions. An integrative (although illicit) social relationship will derive from the exchange. The transaction clearly is unethical and also is illegal.

G. *Bribe Extorted:* The recipient is seeking out a payment to provide a specific illegal or unethical police service or to preclude the lawful exercise of a proper police function under the officer's control. The officer is compelling the recipient to enter into the bargain. No positive, integrative social relationship derives from the exchange. The payment is demanded as the purchase price of the service offered. It is understood to conclude the immediate interaction without an ongoing commitment to provide the same service again, although additional transactions may follow and a coercive paid arrangement may be compelled. The transaction clearly is unethical and also is illegal.

Whose View Determines Ethical Quality?

These perceptions give rise to a dual scale of exchange-based relationships, some of which, in my view, are clearly ethical, some questionable, and some indisputably unethical. They may be appropriately reciprocal, that is, the giver and the recipient may have the same interpretation of the exchange, or they may be mismatched, which introduces an ambiguity into the exchange. Some of the more likely combinations are presented in Table 1.

If both police officers and gift-givers see the gift the same way, as an ethical repayment of a debt owed the police, no problems arise and no ethical violation exists. However, as Table 1

demonstrates, mismatches in perceptions will occur. I believe that the perception of the recipient toward the exchange is more critical than that of the giver in the categorization of an exchange as ethical or unethical.[32] However, the perception of the giver also is quite relevant, for it can be the source of ambiguity and future friction between the giver and recipient. That is a significant concern with which both giver and recipient must be prepared to deal if the exchange is not to generate conflict at a later time.

Although it is my opinion that the intent and perceptions of the giver are not as important to the characterization of the exchange as those of the recipient, the officer must act in a manner that emphasizes his, not the giver's, perspective. Otherwise, it is the giver's perception that will govern the exchange. The acceptance is ethical for the police officer so long as he/she takes the gift either as a ritual offering to seal a social relationship or as a true reciprocal gift for police services properly provided. If the gift is accepted as a payment for future legal or quasi-legal services, then the officer is committing him/herself to an unspecified obligation that he/she owes to no other citizen. This is a violation of the special trust that exists between the police officer and the general public. If the officer enters into the exchange with the perception that he/she does owe a special obligation to a single citizen, then that sense of exclusive obligation is what makes the acceptance unethical.

When the perceptions of the giver and the recipient do not coincide, ambiguity exists and problems arise, as actual experiences reveal. When I was still a police officer, frequently I was offered small tokens from merchants on my foot beat. Initially I interpreted these as gratuities but occasionally found it necessary to reject some offers that seemed to be investments. One lounge in particular routinely offered me free liquor, which I always declined. After I had put aside the blue uniform for other employment, I returned there only to have the offer repeated. Even after making it clear that I no longer

Table 1   Relationships of Giver's Perceptions to Police's Perceptions

Nominal Category	The Giver's Perception	The Police Perception
The True Reward 1-A (fully ethical)	A Reward Given: Offered in gratitude for a major contribution or heroic act by the police.	A Reward Received: Accepted in acknowledgment of the significance of the act to the giver.
The True Gift 2-B (fully ethical)	A Gift Given: Offered to express genuine gratitude for a pattern of valued, legitimate police services previously rendered to the giver.	A Gift Received: Accepted without further obligation, a debt thus having been repaid to the recipient police officer by the giver.
The Ambiguous Gift 2-C (fully ethical)	A Gift Given: Offered to express genuine gratitude for a pattern of valued, legitimate police services previously rendered to the giver.	A Gratuity Received: Accepted in a spirit of continuing reciprocal social obligation meant to maintain legal ties.
The True Gratuity 3-C (fully ethical)	A Gratuity Given: Offered to express a wish that legitimate police services provided to the giver be continued.	A Gratuity Received: Accepted in a spirit of continuing reciprocal social obligation meant to maintain legal ties.
The Uncalled Debt 3-D (unethical only for the police)	A Gratuity Given: Offered to express a wish that legitimate police services provided to the giver be continued.	An Understanding Reached: Accepted in credit for unspecified future legal, quasi-legal, or illegal favors or advantages.
The Bad Investment 4-C (ethical only for police)	An Investment Made: Offered to promote future legal advantages, secure favors, or otherwise gain the giver special status.	A Gratuity Received: Accepted in a spirit of continuing reciprocal social obligation meant to maintain legal ties.
The Understanding 4-D (unethical)	An Investment Made: Offered to promote future legal advantages, secure favors, or otherwise gain the giver special status.	An Understanding Reached: Accepted in credit for unspecified future legal, quasi-legal, or illegal favors and advantages.
The Bribe 5-E (unethical and illegal)	A Bribe Offered: Offered to exempt present illegal actions or omissions from police investigation, arrest, or interference.	A Bribe Accepted: Accepted to overlook or ignore present illegal activities or omissions of the gift-giver.
An Arrangement 6-F (unethical and illegal)	An Arrangement Made: Offered to exempt present ongoing illegal actions or omissions from police investigation, arrest, or interference.	An Installment Collected: Accepted to overlook or ignore ongoing illegal activities or omissions of the gift-giver.
The Shakedown 7-G (unethical and illegal)	A Shakedown Paid: Paid unwillingly to secure protection from police enforcement activities or threats of harassment.	A Bribe Extorted: Demanded to overlook or ignore present or future illegal activities or to avoid overt harassment.

served as a police officer, the "gift" offer stood. This suggested that the previous offers had not been intended as "investments" after all. I had been inappropriately suspicious of the owner's motives. In the case of another officer, the reverse was true. Having become accustomed to free meals at one restaurant, an officer returned there some time after being assigned to another beat. The bill for the full price was presented, and the officer did not have sufficient cash to pay. He had to summon another officer there to help him out with the payment. What he had been taking as a "gratuity" or "gift" had been an "investment" that the manager no longer had to keep up.

Another example from my own experience is especially enlightening. At one cafeteria where officers were treated to substantial discounts and occasional free meals, two officers were approached by the evening manager who was holding a city parking ticket. The evening manager asked the officers if either had written the ticket. One had. The officer concerned commented that he had not recognized the manager's car. He added that he would have given him the opportunity to take corrective action if he had recognized it, allowing him to feed the elapsed meter. This was a common police courtesy of that department, although one easily criticized for its potential for biased application and abuse. When the manager asked if the officer "could do something about the ticket," the officer sought to reject the suggestion of after-the-fact ticket fixing. He responded by saying that, if the man would put the fine into the ticket envelope and seal it, the officer would take it to the police station when he ended his duty tour, thus saving the man postage or a special trip. The evening manager appeared annoyed, but did precisely what the officer suggested. The officer and his companion officer both left the cafeteria suspecting that their free and discounted meals there were a thing of the past. To the officers' surprise, that was not the case. After eating elsewhere for a few days, trying to avoid an anticipated unpleasant scene, one of the officers returned to the establishment

while making routine rounds. The evening manager made a point of apologizing to the officer, and commented that he was concerned that his behavior had upset the police so that they were avoiding eating at his place of business. (This was an accurate perception).[33]

Initially the evening manager had viewed the exchange as an "investment." The officers' behavior had challenged that perception, making it clear that they had accepted the meals only as a "gratuity." This episode worked to the advantage of the police not only by correcting the manager's misconception but also by establishing the ethical viewpoint of the officers.

Of course, another set of circumstances might have arisen had the officers not been resolute in their perception of the intent of the earlier exchanges. Had the officers yielded to the expectations of the manager, the exchange would have been converted from a problematically ethical to an unethical one. For this reason I contend that the police officer should be responsible for determining and asserting the character and the ethical quality of any such exchange.

The police officer who allows the giver to set the ethical terms of the exchange relationship has abrogated his responsibilities. Yet as we currently educate our police officers in police academies and college classrooms, we teach them to do precisely that. The academics and trainers who assert that the expectations of the givers determine the relationship deny the individual police officer control over the character of that relationship. Worse yet, the closed-minded position that any and every gratuity is corrupting creates a psychological stigma that virtually all police officers must bear. If one free cup of coffee makes a public official corrupt, then nearly all police are corrupt. Because I refused to accept the logic of this label, I now challenge this inference. But what of the many police who accept the label and continue to violate the rule? Might we not anticipate a "self-fulfilling prophecy," an application of labeling theory to law enforcers? To return this decision to the police officers who wish to be viewed and wish to view themselves as uncorrupted, teachers and trainers need to take into account the police officers' points of view, not to eliminate them from consideration.

How is the recipient to manage the difficult situations that he or she will daily face? I contend that the police recipient first must be shown that the simple acceptance of gifts and gratuities does not ipso facto make him or her corrupt. To continue advancing that old, uncritical line of reasoning is to compel the officer to make the wrong choice in such cases. We know that most will accept the gifts and gratuities, making them, in this uncompromisingly rigid view, "corrupt." The situation parallels that described by labeling theorists. If the taker of minor gifts is defined as corrupt, the recipient who takes a gift in good faith is thereby categorized as fallen. A further decline from grace would be a small step to take, as the slippery slope analogy implies.

Conclusion

Can we rely upon our police to make distinctions between legitimate gratuities and unethical offers on their own or without close ethical monitoring? An argument could be made on either side of the question. Police officers are compelled to make critical ethical distinctions daily—decisions about the use of intentional violence or deadly force, discretionary decisions about arrests, searches, and seizures, decisions about intervention in domestic and personal conflicts at the fringes of the criminal law, and a hundred other matters.

To trust them with another ethical decision should not overburden their abilities to make such decisions. However, just as we do not send our police onto the streets of our communities unschooled in the prevailing public attitudes about these other ethical questions, we should not ignore the matter of minor gratuities. Those whose duty is to train, teach, and educate our criminal justice practitioners have an obligation to do so wisely, with a full understanding of the consequences of their instructions for those who

are required to carry them out. It seems reasonable that the expectations we have of them and the guidance we give them be as real and realistic as the situations into which we thrust them when they are called upon to make these ethical distinctions.

The basic assumption of critics of gratuities is that the gratuity is offered to create a sense of obligation in the police officer. But it can be argued with equal plausibility that the donor gives in order to satisfy his/her own sense of obligation to the police officer. The recipient of the "tip" knows that this small bonus is a reward for services previously provided, not a payment for future services as yet unspecified. The merchants or restaurateurs offering police officers gratuities may be seen, and usually will see themselves, as expressing appreciation, not engaging in subtle corruption. Why should ethical theorists seek to portray the practice otherwise?

The current ethical instructions concerning gifts and gratuities are neither realistic nor advantageous to sincere police officers seeking to make hard ethical choices. However, if one were to educate the officer to another point of view, such as that proposed in this paper, that taking gifts with an ethical intent does not automatically corrupt, then the officer who wishes to remain untainted by corruption would be fortified in his or her own self-esteem. To generate unnecessary guilt in police faced with offers of trivial gifts and gratuities is folly. No advantage for the criminal justice system can be demonstrated in such procedural restrictions. New corruption is invited simply because corruption already is inferred from situations where no corrupting influence was intended.

NOTES

An earlier version of this paper was presented to the Academy of Criminal Justice Sciences in Orlando, Florida, in 1986. The author wishes to acknowledge and thank Drs. Charles Kaut, Dorothy Bracey, Thomas Barker, and Reed Adams for their helpful ideas but accepts personal responsibility for the heresy offered herein.

1. Aubry, Jr., "The Value of Ethics in the Police Service," 12 *Police* 41 (1967).

2. McMullan, "A Theory of Corruption," 9 *Soc. Rev.* 183–184.

3. Reprinted in S. Walker, *The Police in America: An Introduction* 245 (1983).

4. Aubry, Jr., *supra* note 1, at 42.

5. Feldberg, "Gratuities, Corruption, and the Democratic Ethos of Policing: The Case of the Free Cup of Coffee," in *Moral Issues in Police Work* 267–76 (F. Elliston & M. Feldberg eds. 1985).

6. See, e.g., Bracey, "A Functional Approach to Police Corruption," *John Jay College Criminal Justice Center Monographs No. 1* (1976); "Police Corruption in Britain and America: A Functional Approach, 1 *Police Stud.* 16–23 (1978); "Corruption as a Response to Legal Innovation," paper presented at the annual meeting of the American Anthropological Association, Washington, D.C. (Dec. 5, 1980). See also Kaut, "Utang Na Loob: A System of Contractual Obligation Among Tagalos," 17 *Sw. J. of Anthropology* 256 (1961), and E. Leach, *Culture and Communication: The Logic by Which Symbols are Connected* (1976).

7. See, e.g., Stoddard, "The 'Informal Code' of Police Deviancy: A Group Approach to 'Blue-Coat Crime," 59 *J. of Crim. L., Criminology, & Police Sci.* 203, 205 (1968), and T. Barker and J. Roebuck, *An Empirical Typology of Police Corruption* 21–24 (1973).

8. Cohen, "Exploiting Police Authority," 5 *Crim. Justice Ethics,* Summer/Fall 1986, at 23.

9. J. Kleinig, "The Slippery Slope Problem," Lecture 23, at 1–3 (1987) (unpublished lecture notes, John Jay College of Criminal Justice, The City University of New York).

10. *Id.* at 1.

11. Homan, "Social Behavior As Exchange," 63 *Am. J. Soc.* 606 (1958).

12. E. Leach, *supra* note 6, at 6.

13. A legitimate and compelling argument can still be raised against the practice if the police ignore non-givers and frequent only those commercial establishments that offer gratuities. Proper discipline and supervision can overcome the tendency to gravitate toward donors. For example, some police departments have policies that require police officers to select different eating places each day, that prohibit loitering at any single place of business, or that require officers to visit each open business during his/her rounds.

14. M. Mauss, *The Gift: Forms and Functions of Exchange in Archaic Societies* 63 (I. Cunnison trans. 1967).

15. Both John Kleinig in a personal letter (Oct. 5, 1987) and an anonymous reviewer of an earlier version of this paper have made these suggestions.

16. Bracey, *supra* note 6, "A Functional Approach to Police Corruption."

17. Kaut, *supra* note 6.

18. J. Kleinig, *supra* note 9.

19. Proponents of the more restrictive deontological ethical posture occasionally associated with the criticism of gratuity acceptance are unlikely to be mollified. Even if the acceptance of gratuities had only socially positive consequences, the fact that they constituted unauthorized enrichment would nonetheless make their acceptance wrong.

20. Feldberg, *supra* note 5, at 268–70.

21. The Knapp Commission, *The Knapp Commission Report on Police Corruption,* 65–66 (1972).

22. See e.g., Fishman, "Measuring Police Corruption," *John Jay College Criminal Justice Center Monographs No. 10* (1978), and R. Kania, *Discipline in Small Police Forces: An Ethnographic Examination of Bureaucratic Social Control* (1982) (Ph.D. diss. U. Va).

23. M. Banton, *The Policeman in the Community,* 58, 223 (1964).

24. I am unable to find any.

25. R. Kania, *supra* note 22, at 63.

26. D. Black, *Police Encounters and Social Organization: An Observation Study* (1968) (Ph.D. diss., U. Mich.).

27. A. Reiss, Jr., *The Police and the Public,* 159ff. (1971).

28. The motion picture *Freebie and the Bean* (1974) (edited and produced by Richard Rush, screenplay by Robert Kaufman) illustrates most vividly a heavy-handed, mooching police officer's abuse of merchants.

29. Cohen, *supra* note 8, at 30.

30. Meyer, Jr., "A Descriptive Study of Police Corruption," 40 *Police Chief,* Aug. 1973, at 38–41.

31. M. Banton, *supra* note 23, at 221.

32. An anonymous reviewer of an earlier version of this paper remarked in opposing my arguments, "A policy of no gratuities is the only workable policy because it requires a reform only of the police and not of society." Turning this line of reasoning to my advantage, police policy makers have some control over the indoctrination of the police and virtually none over the indoctrination of the public at large. This being so, it makes more sense to view the gift as the honest giver offers it, and to train our police accordingly.

33. Michael Banton reports a similar scenario in which "a man ... because he had given the police free meals, thought he could ignore the parking regulations; he was promptly disabused by this idea, and officers stopped visiting his premises." See *supra* note 23, at 58.

Study Questions

1. What is a slippery slope argument? How is such an argument connected with the issue of corruption? Why are slippery slope arguments often of questionable value?

2. What good consequences does Kania believe can result from accepting a minor gift or gratuity? What examples does Kania cite to prove that undesirable consequences may result from refusing a gift or gratuity? Do you think that Kania's argument is successful? Why?

3. What is the deontological objection to accepting minor gifts and gratuities? How does Kania respond to this objection? Do you think Kania successfully refutes this objection? Why?

Case 6.1

THE SURE THING

It's too darned hot, you conclude, to make a decision like that tonight. Maybe, in the time remaining on the shift, you could try to review, as rationally as possible, the events of the past several months. What the hell happened, you wonder, and why?

The moment that changed your life, more significantly than you could imagine even at the time, was when you were told that your five-year-old daughter had a brain tumor. She responded well to the surgery and appeared to be recovering until you and your wife noticed that her eyesight seemed to be rapidly deteriorating. The doctor confirmed this and concluded that your daughter's only chance to avoid going completely blind would require her to undergo a long and perhaps risky drug treatment. Furthermore, the doctor informed the two of you, the drugs were quite expensive and also experimental in nature and thus not covered by your insurance. You and your wife agreed to the treatment.

Nothing, however, prepared you for the shock of the drug bills that followed. Only by working an exhausting number of overtime hours were you able to come close to paying for the prescription. It was during this period also that you put your name in as a candidate for the new sergeant's position (with a significant raise in pay). You had been a corrections officer at Madison Correctional Institution for over nine years and had an excellent work record. You felt that you deserved the promotion and had a good chance at it.

Five weeks ago, however, after a particularly long and tiring number of overtime days, you just plain fell dead asleep on the job. You were found that way by the Shift Captain and written up. You expected the hearing officer to show some compassion in determining your discipline, considering the amount of overtime you had worked before the incident and, more important, the reason for the overtime. The hearing officer, with no real explanation, chose to ignore your work record and your financial problems, and elected to impose the maximum penalty available. You received a

10-day suspension, without pay (a severe blow to your tight financial situation), and a two-year written letter of reprimand in your personnel file. This ended your chances for the current promotion.

Stories of such events spread quickly in prison. It was less than one week after you returned to work that you had your first conversation with Inmate Root. Inmate Root is a local boy, educated, intelligent, and generally a slick operator. He was well aware of your problems and came to the point quickly. Your cellblock, he implied, might be a good place from which to conduct his "business" (undoubtedly drug dealing). He was concerned, however, about your reputation as an excellent shakedown officer. He wanted you to maintain this reputation, but not at the risk of having his "inventory" discovered. His solution was simple. Every day, at the beginning of the shift, you would find a small piece of paper in your top desk drawer. On the paper would be two cell numbers—one circled, one not. The uncircled cell, if searched, would probably yield a small but respectable amount of contraband (a marijuana cigarette, cafeteria food, etc.). The cell with the circled number should, at all costs, not be searched. The circled number would change weekly since, as Root explained, it was not safe for him to keep his "inventory" in one cell too long. The noncircled number would change nightly. As compensation for your services, each Sunday you would find an unaddressed, unstamped envelope containing a cash "stipend" in your mailbox (Root had several local contacts).

You were still bitter from your suspension and the loss of your promotion, but you found it difficult to agree to such a proposition. Root sensed this and pressed further. He handed you a small slip of paper with two numbers written on it, a circled 22 and a plain 8.

"This is for tomorrow night," he said. "Use it or throw it away. It's up to you. But remember, if things go 'smoothly' this week, you should definitely check out your mailbox Sunday morning."

The next night you shook down Cell 8 and found a jar of peanut butter from the cafeteria. You did not shake down Cell 22. At the beginning of your shift the following night, you found another numbered piece of paper in your top desk drawer. You followed the same procedure with similar results. As it happened, the rest of the week went "smoothly" and early on Sunday morning you discovered a plain white envelope in your mailbox containing $500 in cash. This was obviously no small operation.

When you returned to work tonight, Inmate Root was there to meet you. He was obviously pleased with the way things went the week before. He explained that last week was just a trial run, a test, and that his "inventory" was not yet in your cellblock. The move would be difficult and risky. Before he was willing to make such a commitment, he needed a commitment from you.

"You know your part in the operation, you know what your compensation will be," Root says, "and I need a decision this week. If you're in, we start real operations next week. If you're not, you won't hear another word about it, period."

So here you are now, sitting in this hot and foul-smelling cellblock, trying to make the decision of your life. Your daughter's doctor has recently told you that the drug regimen, which seems to be helping, may have to continue for another year to be permanently effective. By then, even with overtime, you know you might be in a financial bind from which you could never recover. You also consider how much an extra

$500 each week would help (the irony of using drug money to pay drug bills does not escape you, either). You know that you are already too far in to turn Root over to the administration (screw them anyway, they took away two weeks of your pay at a desperate time). You also know that it is not too late to back out. But, so much money and so little involvement on your part. No carrying in, no carrying out. It's not even dealing, really. It could be safe, you think, as safe as it gets—a sure thing.

Questions for Discussion

1. Using Kania's taxonomy of gifts and gratuities, is this conduct ethical?
2. Discuss the severity of the discipline for sleeping on duty.
3. Why did the officer fall into that pattern of misconduct?
4. Support or reject the officer's rationale for involvement in the corrupt activities. Defend your answer by using the "checklist" approach.

Case 6.2

TRAFFIC ASSIST

It was a night a police officer would like to forget: starting the shift with 15 calls holding. They were all routine reports: burglaries, minor thefts, hot rods, abandoned vehicles. All routine and all time-consuming. For officer K. C. Cooper, the shift couldn't be over quickly enough. All she could think of was to get the paperwork done, check out, take a quick shower, get into civilian clothes, meet her date, and head off to the party.

As Cooper cruised down the expressway, she noticed an elderly gentleman struggling to change a tire. She might have ignored it, being so close to shift change, but the old guy's rear end was sticking out in the traffic lane and she knew the car could easily get clipped in the heavy traffic.

She made a U-turn through the median and then another back up the road, activated her red lights, and pulled in behind the motorist, making sure she used the cruiser to give her a lane of protection.

The whole tire change took about 10 minutes. The old man was very thankful. He had been unable to get the lug nuts off and expressed doubt that he was strong enough to put the spare tire on, even if he had gotten the flat one off.

As soon as K. C. was finished, the old man reached into his pocket and pulled out a $20 bill.

"Take this, it is the least I can do," he said.

"I can't," K. C. replied, "it's just part of the job."

"Look," the old man said, looking somewhat offended, "It would have cost me $50 to have road service come out here and change this tire even if I had survived the traffic and been able to call them. Now, thanks to your help, I won't be late for my meeting. I know you guys are underpaid. Just take the $20 and buy yourself a bottle. I insist."

Questions for Discussion

1. Using Kania's taxonomy, is this conduct ethical?
2. What would you do in this situation? Assume there was no department policy to guide you.
3. What does the Code of Ethics direct you to do?
4. What if Cooper accepted the money and then donated it to charity?

Case 6.3

THE GOLDEN RETRIEVERS

Bill and Mary owned a liquor store. It was in the inner city. They gave me free booze.

It didn't start out that way. I was dispatched one night to a burglary at their store. It was the usual smash and grab. Someone broke the window and took as much liquor as they could carry before the alarm company called the police. Bill and Mary came to the store at our request. We needed them to board up the window and to tell us what was taken. What started as a "routine" burglary report turned into a different type of relationship.

I stopped at their store a couple of days after the burglary to get some follow-up information. While standing at the counter of the store, I was suddenly confronted with what was, without a doubt, the largest Golden Retriever I had ever seen. King looked like a giant, furry clerk. He stood on his hind legs, paws on the counter, and barked at me. In later visits, while in the back storeroom, I would be entertained by King's lurking behind the counter and jumping up and barking at the unsuspecting, and terrified, customers. Since I also had a Golden Retriever, the Whitcombs and I seemed to "click."

Bill and Mary Whitcomb had owned the 23rd Avenue liquor store for years. They stayed behind when all the other business owners had long ago abandoned the deteriorating area for greener pastures. They treated their customers (mostly alcoholics who would buy the liquor and get a cup of ice free) with respect. They were kind people and didn't look down on their clientele.

They were also an interesting couple. For some reason, they never sold the business. They always were upbeat. As time passed and I got to know them better, I would often stop in the store from time to time while on patrol. On paydays, I would stop by on my way home, with my Golden Retriever, to visit them. While the dogs kept guard behind the counter, I would sip coffee and chat, ever mindful of our location and keeping an eye out through the numerous peepholes surreptitiously cut in the walls behind the liquor bottles.

The holes were there for a purpose. Behind most were handguns. Behind a couple were shotguns. They took this situation rather matter-of-factly. But there was an undercurrent of concern. Several years ago, both their sons were murdered in an armed robbery at the store. Yet, they carried on.

I am not really sure how it happened. There was never any suggestion of impropriety. I never asked for favors and they never asked for special treatment. But as the months progressed and my visits (both on duty and off) increased, they always gave me a little something. At first, it was a cigar. Later, it was a little off the price of a bottle. Finally, it was an extra bottle along with my purchase. I don't know why I took the gifts. They weren't paying me for extra police protection. I just thought that they were nice people. I made an extra effort to keep an eye on their place for no particular reason. I could have bought my liquor cheaper nearer to home, but Bill and Mary were more like friends than people in my patrol area.

Questions for Discussion

1. Using Kania's taxonomy, is this conduct ethical?
2. Using the Code of Ethics, is this conduct ethical?
3. Is this corruption, or friendship?
4. Is there an implicit perception on the part of at least one of the parties that this is liquor for "officer presence"? What other "underlying" problems are evident here?
5. How would the public perceive this relationship?
6. Assuming that these were (1) "true gifts," (2) "ambiguous gifts," (3) "true gratuities," or (4) "bad investments," at what point, according to Kania, would they become unethical for the officer?

Case 6.4

THAT EARL

As the newly appointed Assistant to the Deputy Warden of Programs at Mid-State Correctional Institution, you are still amazed at the amount of time that must be devoted to staff meetings. You find most of these meetings unproductive, and some of them are boring enough to remind you of the long nights you spent in the locks where you began your career as a third-shift correctional officer.

Today's meeting, you are informed, will be a routine labor–management discussion of issues affecting employees. You have yet to attend such a meeting but anticipate, based upon what you have heard through the rumor mill, that the proceedings will consist of a good deal more arguing and wrangling than discussion.

As you enter the meeting room, you are not surprised to see the employee representative, Officer Earl D. Fox. Officer Fox, a 22-year corrections veteran, is well respected and is regarded as a tough-minded union steward. He is also vice-president of the officers' union local. You fully expect today's discussion to be a lively one.

As per instructions from your supervisor, you close and lock the door behind you as you enter and take your seat. Your supervisor breaks the initial, and somewhat uncomfortable, silence by speaking directly to you.

"We feel that you've been in management long enough to be included in one of our special meetings with Earl. It will be much easier for you and the rest of us if, for this first time out, you just sit and observe the meeting and save your questions until the end."

Although you are somewhat surprised by these conditions, you agree to them. As the meeting proceeds you sense that this will be a day full of surprises—and it is! Officer Fox is the first to speak and, while the others take notes, he details the confidential proceedings of the past two closed union executive board meetings. There follows a discussion of general and specific policies and plans of the union with suggestions on how the administration might counter them. Officer Fox is then given suggestions as to proposals he might make at the next executive board meeting in order to steer the union in the "right" direction. He agrees to try, and states that he will report the results to management as soon as possible.

After hearing Officer Fox betray the union local, the rest of the meeting does not seem so surprising to you. Once the topic of the union agenda has been exhausted, Officer Fox informs the group about matters that individual employees, many of whom confide in him regularly, have told him and that management might find useful. The meeting concludes with a discussion of which disciplinary cases Officer Fox, as a union steward, would be allowed to win in order to maintain his reputation among the men as the toughest steward on the block.

At the conclusion of the meeting your supervisor asks you to stay over for a few minutes. As the others file out, you begin to understand how the administration has been able to outmaneuver the union so successfully over the past few years. You also recall the respect you had for Officer Fox when you were a correctional officer and the times when you shared your opinions about the institution and the administration with him.

"Of course," your supervisor says, "none of what you have heard here today leaves this room. As far as anyone else is concerned, this has been a normal, loud, labor-management relations meeting." You nod in agreement and, as you get up to leave, your supervisor says, not quite apologetically, "Don't worry about it, guy. We need spies like Earl to let us know what our employees are up to. He helps us; we take care of him, too. What can I say? Welcome to the real world."

As you leave work that day, you are stopped by one of your friends from your days as a correctional officer.

"Old Foxy said you were in the labor-management thing today," he laughs. "Said he really gave you guys hell."

"Sure did," you manage to choke out.

"That Earl," your friend continues, "he's just one helluva guy."

"Sure is," you reply.

Questions for Discussion

 1. In your view, what are Earl's motives?
 2. Are you in a no-win situation? What are your possible choices? What are the potential results of each choice?
 3. What would you do? Defend your response using the "checklist" approach.

Case 6.5

RECORDS CHECK

Officer Jennifer Smyth had worked hard for the five years she had been on the Stevensville Police Department. She was one of the first women on the force and was a single mother of two. This combination had caused her some tough times during the first few years she was on the job. It was just recently that she gained enough seniority to bid on an open day-shift slot. The only drawback of the opening was the requirement that she spend at least two shifts a week working the desk, handling bookings and walk-in reports. She felt that it was worth the inconvenience, even though it meant being off the streets. Now at least she would have time to spend with her children. It would also give her some more time to work her second job, as an insurance investigator handling mostly accident investigations.

After her first week on the job, Joe Stacy, an insurance agent she normally dealt with, called. He told her that now, since she spent a few days a week working the desk, he could help her earn a little extra money. He explained that several times a week, he met with clients whose driving record might make them poor insurance risks. The problem was that he either had to take their word with regard to their driving record or make them wait three days for the Motor Vehicle Record (MVR) to be returned. Either way the company often lost out: they either issued policies to poor drivers, or told people to wait and lost their business to another agency. Joe suggested that Officer Smyth could alleviate the problem by running the MVRs through the police computer and calling him with the results. He would give her $30 for each one she ran. Officer Smyth told Joe she would call him back with an answer.

After hanging up she began to think. The extra money would come in real handy with the children getting ready to start school in the fall. But she believed that it was either against department rules or possibly even a crime to use the police computer system for nonpolice matters. She had noticed, however, that no one at the station paid much attention to who used the computer or why, and she had never heard of anyone getting in the jackpot for misuse of the computer system.

She picked up the phone to call Joe back and tell him . . . ?

Questions for Discussion

1. Using Kania's taxonomy, is this conduct ethical? Defend your position.
2. Using the Code of Ethics, is this conduct ethical? Defend your position.
3. Is there a conflict of interest in this case?
4. Identify the ethical, departmental, and criminal violations that might arise from this situation.

Chapter 7

Force

ACCORDING TO THOMAS HOBBES, HUMAN LIFE outside of society, in a state of nature, would be "solitary, poor, nasty, brutish, and short." Hobbes believed that every person's natural right to use force to protect his own interests would perpetuate a continual state of civil war if there were no organized limitations on that right. In Hobbes' view, society is constructed to relocate each person's right to use force. This right is removed from the individual and vested in the society at large. The power is in turn delegated to specific groups in the society, primarily the military and the criminal justice system. The loss of the individual right to use force against another person occurred thousands of years ago, when societies began to control the practice of blood-feuding. For example, prior to the 7th century B.C., the Greeks considered murder to be a private affair between the murderer and the family of the victim. The codification of Athenian law by Draco in 621 B.C. removed the right to blood vengeance from the individual and replaced it with a corresponding state right to punish. Even then, the family of the victim was still allowed to carry out the prosecutorial process.[1]

Today, in addition to the police and the military, other social entities retain a more limited right to exercise force. These include parents and legal guardians, public school officials, and physicians. The individual's right to use force against others is not nonexistent, of course, but is severely limited by law—for example, in the right of self-defense, the right of a spouse (typically the husband) to kill an adulterous third party, and the act of citizen's arrest (though this should not be regarded as strictly an individual action).

The individual and the societal use of force are similar: the goal is to stimulate, modify, or deter some act or set of actions by another person or group of persons. However, the right of individual citizens and others, such as physicians and public school officials, to use force is limited to those acts specified by case law and statutory law. Citizens may exercise force against others only in very limited situations. The school principal's capacity to use corporal punishment derives from the parents' right to punish, together with the concept of *in loco parentis*. The surgeon's capacity to commit a technical battery is constrained by the concept of informed consent. Except in unusual cases of emergency, that consent must be explicit and fully informed.

In sharp contrast, the criminal justice practitioner's right to use force is typically broad and nonspecific. It overlaps other persons' right to force and extends far beyond those very limited and specific circumstances to include any actions that are controlled by criminal law and civil law. For example, the right of a police officer to take into custody a person who presents a danger to himself will very likely involve the use of force. Similarly, a corrections officer may use force if it is necessary to maintain order and carry out the policies of the prison.

When and where force is necessary is not always clear. Consider the act of **arrest**. A police officer may arrest a person if he or she has probable cause to believe that the person has committed a crime. What constitutes an arrest, and under exactly what conditions an arrest has occurred, is not a simple question. Sidney H. Asch points out that

> ... a mere statement by a police officer, asserting an arrest, followed by acquiescence by the person to whom the words are spoken, [may] be considered an arrest in the eyes of law ... even though force has not been used and the person arrested has not even been touched.[2]

This shows that the use of force is not intrinsic to the act of arrest, even if force is commonly used. Similarly, the use of force may be sufficient to maintain prison order, but it does not follow that it is necessary. Just because certain criminal justice practices typically involve the use of force does not mean that such force is necessary and hence justified.

The morally acceptable level of force used by the criminal justice practitioner, as well as in other public sector jobs permitting force, seems to be determined by the nature of the forceful act itself rather than by its consequences. The reasoning here is straightforward: If force is used to obtain evil ends, then there is no moral dilemma; it is where force is used to obtain what everyone acknowledges to be *good* ends that the moral issues arise. If only the consequences were relevant in justifying force, few puzzles would arise.

The Readings

Carl B. Klockars examines these dilemmas in the first selection, "The Dirty Harry Problem." The title refers to the well-known Clint Eastwood character, Inspector Harry "Dirty Harry" Callahan, as well as to the "Dirty Hands" problem in philosophical literature. All Dirty Harry cases involve using dirty means to accomplish good ends, and as such, pose a classical challenge to act utilitarian reasoning. Klockars' discussion is not limited to the "dirty" use of force, but includes any dirty means used by a police officer to accomplish a good end. Klockars defines "dirty" to mean actions that are widely perceived to be intrinsically offensive and that involve breaking prevailing rules of social order.

It is important to understand that not all dirty conduct involves the Dirty Harry problem. For example, if a police officer focuses on the factual guilt of a suspect, he or she is likely to see dirty acts not as means, "but as ends in themselves—as punishment of guilty people whom the police believe deserve to be punished." Klockars argues that the Dirty Harry dilemma arises only if there is a reasonable probability that the dirty means is sufficient to accomplish the ends and that *only* those dirty means will accomplish the end (the means are necessary). But those dirty means are merely the conditions necessary for the dilemma to arise. Klockars says

> the troublesome issue in the Dirty Harry problem is not whether under some utilitarian calculus a right choice can be made, but that the choice must always be between at least two wrongs. And in choosing to do either wrong, the policeman inevitably taints or tarnishes himself.

Klockars examines three models of policing in the context of resolving the Dirty Harry dilemma: the professional or bureaucratic model, the peacekeeper model, and the craftsman model. Klockars believes that all of these models fail to resolve the dilemma. The dilemma cannot be resolved because the choice confronting the officer is a moral choice, not a technical or occupational choice. Having said this, Klockars appears to nonetheless believe that using dirty means is the morally wrong choice, and that officers should be punished for resorting to dirty means.

The second selection is the U.S. Supreme Court's decision in *Tennessee* v. *Garner* (1985). *Garner* reveals a dramatic change in the way in which force may be used to arrest a person. Prior to *Garner*, any necessary force, excluding deadly force, could be used to arrest a misdemeanant in most states, and *any* necessary force could be used to arrest a felony suspect. It has generally been held that if resistance to arrest endangers the officer or another person, deadly force may be used regardless of the offense causing the arrest. Despite this tradition in common law, the Court observes that most police departments in the United States forbid the use of deadly force against nonviolent suspects, even if they are suspected of a felony.

Garner involves a relatively straightforward case in which a 15-year-old boy, Edward Garner (unarmed and slight of build), was shot in the head and killed by a police officer. Garner was about to escape capture for a suspected nighttime burglary, and ignored the officer's command to halt by attempting to climb over a fence. Garner's father brought action in a Federal District Court, seeking damages for violation of the decedent's Constitutional rights under 42 U.S.C. § 1983. The District Court ruled that the officer's actions were justified under a Tennessee statute. The Court of Appeals reversed on grounds that the statute violated the Fourth and Fourteenth Amendments.

In upholding the Court of Appeals decision, the U.S. Supreme Court (both majority and dissenters) agreed that the shooting of Garner was a *seizure* under the Fourth Amendment, and all members of the Court agreed that the issue was whether that seizure passes the test of "reasonableness" required by the Fourth Amendment. This requirement calls for the balancing of public interest against individual liberty. That is, the Fourth Amendment doesn't guarantee that citizens will be secure against the government searching their homes or their bodies, or seizing evidence to be used against them. As citizens, we are simply protected against "unreasonable searches and seizures." What the Court found in *Garner* is that using deadly force against a fleeing felon is not *always* reasonable; it depends on the circumstances.

The determination of reasonableness by balancing individual rights against governmental interests has a long history in case law. In *Garner*, the Court cites not only the suspect's "fundamental interest in his own life," but also the interest that the individual and society have in the judicial determination of guilt and punishment. Deadly force frustrates these interests. On the other hand, the Court points to the government's interest in effective law enforcement and the importance of a credible threat to promote peaceful submission of suspects to the arresting officer. The Court concludes that in the balance,

> it is not better that all felony suspects die than that they escape. Where the suspect poses no immediate threat to the officer and no threat to others, the harm resulting from failing to apprehend him does not justify the use of deadly force to do so.

Lee H. Bowker's selection, "The Victimization of Prisoners by Staff Members," is concerned with documenting the broad category of staff–prisoner victimization in prisons. This category consists of acts committed by individuals or groups of correctional officers that go beyond official institutional policies and state and federal laws. Bowker concedes that determining whether an administrative policy is itself victimizing, or potentially so, requires knowledge of the rationale behind the policy. Since such knowledge is rarely available, administrative responsibility for victimization is difficult to assign.

Bowker's discussion covers physical brutality, sexual assault and sexual coercion, brutality in children's institutions, psychological victimization, economic victimization, and social victimization. Bowker discusses two theories about why prisoners are victimized by corrections personnel: the "total institutions" theory and the role theory. The first tends to look at all confinement institutions as miniature totalitarian societies in which social control by the authorities is the supreme good. Bowker rejects this account, favoring the "role" theory evidenced in the famous Haney, Banks, and Zimbardo Stanford Prison Experiment.[3] Bowker reports that his own research has revealed that civilian volunteers introduced into the correctional setting "can engage in types of behavior that are psychologically victimizing," behavior that Bowker calls "power-tripping."

Agnes L. Baro's paper, "Tolerating Illegal Use of Force Against Inmates," examines the circumstances surrounding the systematic use of inmate beating in Hawaii's Oahu Community Correctional Center in the early 1980s. Baro reports on the external investigations into the pattern of beatings and the evident reluctance of the criminal justice system in Hawaii to charge correctional officers or administrators or to discipline those involved. As a result, Baro states, the use of illegal force against inmates continued throughout the 1980s, resulting in Hawaii becoming the first state to be sued by the Department of Justice under the 1981 Civil Rights of Institutionalized Persons Act.

Baro expresses concern about the endorsement of prison brutality precisely because the systematic beating of prisoners appears to have produced very "orderly" prisons, i.e., prisons in which intimidation of staff by prisoners and other disturbances are rare, and in which prison employees are "treated with respect." The end result has been that attempts at reform have been defeated, and wardens who tolerated brutality have been promoted.

The final reading in this chapter, the U.S. Supreme Court's decision, *Hudson* v. *McMillian* (1992), involves the constitutionality of beating prison inmates as long as the injuries caused are not serious. The Court ruled that the Eighth Amendment does not hinge on the seriousness of the injury caused to the prisoner. As a very recent decision, it is difficult to determine the ramifications of *Hudson*, but it is clear from the language of the decision that the concept of the Eighth Amendment protection against cruel and unusual punishment has been sharpened.

This case concerns Keith Hudson, serving time for armed robbery, who was beaten by two corrections officers under the observation of a third officer. The beating followed a verbal exchange between Hudson and McMillian. Hudson was removed from his cell, placed in shackles and handcuffs, taken to an unused corridor, and beaten about the face, chest, and stomach. Hudson's injuries were later described by the district court as "minor."

Hudson filed a civil suit under 42 U.S.C. § 1983, charging violation of his Eighth Amendment right not to be subjected to cruel and unusual punishment. The specific question the Court addresses in *Hudson* is whether excessive physical force is cruel and unusual punishment when the prisoner does not suffer "significant" injury. The Court of Appeals had agreed that the beating of Hudson was objectively unreasonable, clearly excessive, and involved "the unnecessary and wanton infliction of pain" as required by the Supreme Court's 1986 decision in *Whitley* v. *Albers*, 475 U.S. 312. Yet, the Court of Appeals reversed the Magistrate's original finding, which was in favor of Hudson, on the grounds that Hudson's beating did not cause significant injury.

In *Hudson*, the Supreme Court relies heavily on the *Whitley* criterion of "unnecessary and wanton infliction of pain," observing that the absence of serious injury *is* relevant to an Eighth Amendment inquiry in determining such preliminary conditions as whether force was needed, how much was needed, and the perception of the threat observed by officials. The Court's point, however, is that while the seriousness of the injury is relevant, it is not determinative. This conclusion is based on the argument that "contemporary standards of decency" must be considered in Eighth Amendment claims.[4]

Some persons in our society are opposed to prison reform and claim that "prison is supposed to be a horrible place," and the like, but the Court clearly rejects this view in *Hudson*. "Routine discomfort" is permissible, though, and the Court does agree that "[not] every malevolent touch by a prison guard gives rise to a federal cause of action." Nonetheless, the Court's qualification of this perspective is crucial: *de minimus* use of force is acceptable, *"provided that* the use of force is not of a sort 'repugnant to the conscience of mankind' (emphasis added)." Moreover, the Court specifically rejects the claim that excessive force cases are no different from cases involving conditions of confinement, stating that there *is* a difference "between punching a prisoner in the face and serving him unappetizing food . . . "

The Court also briefly considers the argument that Hudson's Eighth Amendment right was not violated because the beating was not punishment at all in the legal sense of the word. This approach is rejected not only on precedent but because the Court of Appeals accepted the Magistrate's original determination that the beating was part of a pattern of institutional behavior qualifying as punishment.

In a separate concurring opinion, J. Blackmun rejects the "inherently self-interested" argument offered jointly by several state attorneys general that the "significant injury" test is necessary to prevent an excessive number of court filings by prison inmates. Blackmun is almost incredulous that the interpretation of "an explicit constitutional protection is to be guided by pure policy preferences for the paring down of prisoner petitions." Blackmun argues that the right to file a court action is a prisoner's most fundamental political right.

Two additional selections have been included in this chapter as reference materials regarding the use of force, the Ohio Department of Corrections "Policy on Use of Force" and the Los Angeles Police Department "Policy on Use of Force." These policies can be regarded as representative of similar policies in other states and jurisdictions. Although use-of-force policies for police officers may show minor variations from one jurisdiction to another, all must conform to the requirements of *Garner*, for example. Of course, this does not apply to the use of force in a correctional institution. There, for instance, deadly force may be used to "prevent or halt" a felony.

Notes

1. Compare this with the view held by some persons today that the prosecution of violent crime is essentially a service that the state provides to the victim or the victim's family. In such a view, the state *per se* has no interest in prosecuting crime. Rather, the state merely represents a fundamentally private interest of the victim or victim's family to exact revenge. For example, the media coverage of the 1991 rape trial of William Kennedy Smith cast the prosecutor as having failed to adequately represent her "client," the alleged victim. Recent legislation in some states, allowing testimony regarding the impact of the crime on the victim's family, seems to be based, at least in part, on the perception that personal retribution is relevant to criminal justice. As another example, a prosecutor might consult the family of a victim of drunk driving regarding the level of charges to be brought against the driver. Such practices may reveal social ambivalence about the individual's right to use force, i.e., that the right is still owned by the citizen but is administered by an agent, the state.

2. Sidney H. Asch, *Police Authority and the Rights of the Individual.* (New York: Arco Publishing Company, 1971), p. 49.

3. Craig Haney, Curtis Banks, and Philip Zimbardo, "Interpersonal Dynamics in a Simulated Prison," *International Journal of Criminology and Penology*, Vol. 1:1 (1973), pp. 69–97.

4. See *Estelle v. Gamble*, 429 U.S. 97 (1976), in which the Supreme Court ruled that denial of medical treatment to a prisoner was cruel and unusual if (and only if) the medical need was serious.

The Dirty Harry Problem

CARL B. KLOCKARS

WHEN AND TO WHAT extent does the morally good end warrant or justify an ethically, politically, or legally dangerous means for its achievement? This is a very old question for philosophers. Although it has received extensive consideration in policelike occupations and is at the dramatic core of police fiction and detective novels, I know of not a single contribution to the criminological or sociological literature on policing which raises it explicitly and examines its implications.[1] This is the case in spite of the fact that there is considerable evidence to suggest that it is not only an ineluctable part of police work, but a moral problem with which police themselves are quite familiar. There are, I believe, a number of good reasons why social scientists have avoided or neglected what I like to call the Dirty Harry problem in policing, not the least of which is that it is insoluble. However, a great deal can be learned about police work by examining some failed solutions, three of which I consider in the following pages. First, though, it is necessary to explain what a Dirty Harry problem is and what it is about it that makes it so problematic.

The Dirty Harry Problem

The Dirty Harry problem draws its name from the 1971 Warner Brothers film *Dirty Harry* and its chief protagonist, antihero Inspector Harry "Dirty Harry" Callahan. The film features a number of events which dramatize the Dirty Harry problem in different ways, but the one which does so most explicitly and most completely places Harry in the following situation. A 14-year-old girl has been kidnapped and is being held captive by a psychopathic killer. The killer, "Scorpio," who has already struck twice, demands $200,000 ransom to release the girl, who is buried with just enough oxygen to keep her alive for a few hours. Harry gets the job of delivering the ransom and, after enormous exertion, finally meets Scorpio. At their meeting Scorpio decides to renege on his bargain, let the girl die, and kill Harry. Harry manages to stab Scorpio in the leg before he does so, but not before Scorpio seriously wounds Harry's partner, an inexperienced, idealistic, slightly ethnic, former sociology major.

Scorpio escapes, but Harry manages to track him down through the clinic where he was treated for his wounded leg. After learning that Scorpio lives on the grounds of a nearby football stadium, Harry breaks into his apartment, finds guns and other evidence of his guilt, and finally confronts Scorpio on the 50-yard line, where Harry shoots him in the leg as he is trying to escape. Standing over Scorpio, Harry demands to know where the girl is buried. Scorpio refuses to disclose her location, demanding his rights to a lawyer. As the camera draws back from the scene Harry stands on Scorpio's bullet-mangled leg to torture a confession of the girl's location from him.

As it turns out, the girl is already dead and Scorpio must be set free. Neither the gun found in the illegal search, nor the confession Harry extorted, nor any of its fruits—including the girl's body—would be admissible in court.

The preceding scene, the heart of *Dirty Harry*, raises a number of issues of far-reaching significance for the sociology of the police, the first of which will now be discussed.

Carl B. Klockars, "The Dirty Harry Problem," The Annals of The American Academy of Political and Social Science, *Vol. 451 (November 1980), pp. 33–47. Used by permission of The American Academy of Political and Social Science and the author.*

The Dirty Harry Problem I:
The End of Innocence

As we have phrased it previously, the Dirty Harry problem asks when and to what extent does the morally good end warrant or justify an ethically, politically, or legally dangerous means to its achievement? In itself, this question assumes the possibility of a genuine moral dilemma and posits its existence in a means–ends arrangement which may be expressed schematically as follows:

MEANS

		Morally Good (+)	Morally Dirty (–)
E	Morally good (+)	A + +	B – + The Dirty Harry Problem
N			
D			
S	Morally dirty (–)	C + –	D – –

It is important to specify clearly the terms of the Dirty Harry problem not only to show that it must involve the juxtaposition of good ends and dirty means, but also to show what must be proven to demonstrate that a Dirty Harry problem exists. If one could show, for example, that box B is always empirically empty or that in any given case the terms of the situation are better read in some other means–ends arrangement, Dirty Harry problems vanish. At this first level, however, I suspect that no one could exclude the core scene of Dirty Harry from the class of Dirty Harry problems. There is no question that saving the life of an innocent victim of kidnapping is a "good" thing nor that grinding the bullet-mangled leg of Scorpio to extort a confession from his is "dirty."[2]

There is, in addition, a second level of criteria of an empirical and epistemological nature that must be met before a Dirty Harry problem actually comes into being. They involve the connection between the dirty act and the good end. Principally, what must be known and, importantly, known before the dirty act is committed, is that it will result in the achievement of the good end. In any absolute sense this is, of course, impossible to know, in that no acts are ever completely certain in their consequences. Thus the question is always a matter of probabilities. But it is helpful to break those probabilities into classes which attach to various subcategories of the overall question. In the given case, this level of problem would seem to require that three questions be satisfied, though not all with the same level of certainty.

In *Dirty Harry*, the first question is, Is Scorpio able to provide the information Dirty Harry seeks? It is an epistemological question about which, in *Dirty Harry*, we are absolutely certain. Harry met Scorpio at the time of the ransom exchange. Not only did he admit the kidnapping at that time, but when he made the ransom demand, Scorpio sent one of the girl's teeth and a description of her clothing and underwear to leave no doubt about the existence of his victim.

Second, we must know there are means, dirty means and nothing other than dirty means, which are likely to achieve the good end. One can, of course, never be sure that one is aware of or has considered all possible alternatives, but in *Dirty Harry* there would appear to be no reason for Scorpio in his rational self-interest to confess to the girl's location without being coerced to do so.

The third question which must be satisfied at this empirical and epistemological level concedes that dirty means are the only method which will be effective, but asks whether or not, in the end, they will be in vain. We know in *Dirty Harry* that they were, and Harry himself, at the time of the ransom demand, admits he believes that the girl is already dead. Does not this possibility or likelihood that the girl is dead destroy the justification for Harry's dirty act? Although it surely would if Harry knew for certain that the girl was dead, I do not think it does insofar as even a small probability of her being saved exists. The reason is that the good to be achieved is so unquestionably good and so passionately felt that even a small possibility of its achievement demands that it be tried. For example, were we to ask, If it were your daughter would you want Harry to do what he did? it would be this passionate sense of unquestionable good that we are trying to dramatize. It is for this reason that in philosophical circles the Dirty Hands problem has been largely restricted to questions of national security, revolutionary terrorism, and international war. It is also why the Dirty Harry problem in detective fiction almost always involves murder.

Once we have satisfied ourselves that a Dirty Harry problem is conceptually possible and that, in fact, we can specify one set of concrete circumstances in which it exists, one might think that the most difficult question of all is, What ought to be done? I do not think it is. I suspect that there are very few people who would not want Harry to do something dirty in the situation specified. I know I would want him to do what he did, and what is more, I would want anyone who policed for me to be prepared to do so as well. Put differently, I want to have as police officers men and women of moral courage and sensitivity.

But to those who would want exactly that, the Dirty Harry problem poses its most irksome conclusion. Namely, that one cannot, at least in the specific case at hand, have a policeman who is both just and innocent. The troublesome issue in the Dirty Harry problem is not whether under some utilitarian calculus a right choice can be made, but that the choice must always be between at least two wrongs. And in choosing to do either wrong, the policeman inevitably taints or tarnishes himself.

It was this conclusion on the part of Dashiell Hammett, Raymond Chandler, Raoul Whitfield, Horace McCoy, James M. Cain, Lester Dent, and dozens of other tough-guy writers of hard-boiled detective stories that distinguished these writers from what has come to be called the "classical school" of detective fiction. What

these men could not stomach about Sherlock Holmes (Conan Doyle), Inspector French (Freeman Wills Crofts), and Father Brown (Chesterton), to name a few of the best, was not that they were virtuous, but that their virtue was unsullied. Their objection was that the classical detective's occupation, how he worked, and the jobs he was called upon to do left him morally immaculate. Even the most brilliant defender of the classical detective story, W. H. Auden, was forced to confess that that conclusion gave the stories "magical function," but rendered them impossible as art.[3]

If popular conceptions of police work have relevance for its actual practice—as Egon Bittner and a host of others have argued that they do[4]—the Dirty Harry problem, found in one version or another in countless detective novels and reflected in paler imitations on countless television screens, for example, "Parental Discretion is Advised," is not an unimportant contributor to police work's "tainted" quality. But we must remember also that the revolution of the tough-guy writers, so these writers said, was not predicated on some mere artificial, aesthetic objection. With few exceptions, their claim was that their works were art. That is, at all meaningful levels, the stories were true. It is this claim I should next like to examine in the real-life context of the Dirty Harry problem.

The Dirty Harry Problem II: Dirty Men and Dirty Work

Dirty Harry problems arise quite often. For policemen, real, everyday policemen, Dirty Harry problems are part of their job and thus considerably more than rare or artificial dramatic exceptions. To make this point, I will translate some rather familiar police practices, street stops and searches and victim and witness interrogation, into Dirty Harry problems.

GOOD ENDS AND DIRTY MEANS

The first question our analysis of street stops and searches and victim and witness interrogation must satisfy is, For policemen, do these activities present the cognitive opportunity for the juxtaposition of good ends and dirty means to their achievement? Although the "goodness" question will be considered in some detail later, suffice it to say here that police find the prevention of crime and the punishment of wrongful or criminal behavior a good thing to achieve. Likewise they, perhaps more than any other group in society, are intimately aware of the varieties of dirty means available for the achievement of those good ends. In the case of street stops and searches, these dirty alternatives range from falsifying probable cause for a stop, to manufacturing a false arrest to legitimate an illegal search, to simply searching without the fraudulent covering devices of either. In the case of victim or witness interrogations, dirty means range from dramaturgically "chilling" a *Miranda* warning by an edited or unemphatic reading to Harry's grinding a man's bullet-shattered leg to extort a confession from him.

While all these practices may be "dirty" enough to satisfy certain people of especially refined sensitivities, does not a special case have to be made, not for the public's perception of the "dirtiness" of certain illegal, deceptive, or subrosa acts, but for the police's perception of their dirtiness? Are not the police hard-boiled, less sensitive to such things than are most of us? I think there is no question that they are, and our contention about the prevalence of Dirty Harry problems in policing suggests that they are likely to be. How does this "tough-minded" attitude toward dirty means affect our argument? At least at this stage it seems to strengthen it. That is, the failure of police to regard dirty means with the same hesitation that most citizens do seems to suggest that they juxtapose them to the achievement of good ends more quickly and more readily than most of us.

THE DIRTY MEANS MUST WORK

In phrasing the second standard for the Dirty Harry problem as "The dirty means must work," we gloss over a whole range of qualifying conditions, some of which we have already considered. The most critical implied in *Dirty Harry* is

that the person on whom dirty means are to be used must be guilty. It should be pointed out, however, that this standard is far higher than any student of the Dirty Hands problem in politics has ever been willing to admit. In fact, the moral dilemma of Dirty Hands is often dramatized by the fact that dirty means must be visited on quite innocent victims. It is the blood of such innocents, for example, whom the Communist leader Hoerderer in Sartre's *Dirty Hands* refers to when he says, "I have dirty hands. Right up to the elbows. I've plunged them in filth and blood. But what do you hope? Do you think you can govern innocently?"[5]

But even if cases in which innocent victims suffer dirty means commonly qualify as Dirty Harry problems, and by extension innocent victims would be allowable in Dirty Harry problems, there are a number of factors in the nature and context of policing which suggest that police themselves are inclined toward the higher "guilty victim" standard. Although there may be others, the following are probably the most salient.

1. The Operative Assumption of Guilt. In street stops and searches as well as interrogations, it is in the nature of the police task that guilt is assumed as a working premise. That is, in order for a policeman to do his job, he must, unless he clearly knows otherwise, assume that the person he sees is guilty and the behavior he is witnessing is evidence of some concealed or hidden offense. If a driver looks at him "too long" or not at all or if a witness or suspect talks too little or too much, it is only his operative assumption of guilt that makes those actions meaningful. Moreover, the policeman is often not in a position to suspend his working assumption until he has taken action, sometimes dirty action, to disconfirm it.

2. The Worst of all Possible Guilt. The matter of the operative assumption of guilt is complicated further because the policeman is obliged to make a still higher-order assumption of guilt, namely, that the person is not only guilty, but dangerously so. In the case of street stops and searches, for instance, although the probability

of coming upon a dangerous felon is extremely low, policemen quite reasonably take the possibility of doing so as a working assumption on the understandable premise that once is enough. Likewise the premise that the one who has the most to hide will try hardest to hide it is a reasonable assumption for interrogation.

3. The Great Guilty Place Assumption. The frequency with which policemen confront the worst of people, places, and occasions creates an epistemological problem of serious psychological proportions. As a consequence of his job, the policeman is constantly exposed to highly selective samples of his environment. That he comes to read a clump of bushes as a place to hide, a roadside rest as a homosexual "tearoom," a sweet old lady as a robbery looking for a place to happen, or a poor young black as someone willing to oblige her is not a question of a perverse, pessimistic, or racist personality, but of a person whose job requires that he strive to see race, age, sex, and even nature in an ecology of guilt, which can include him if he fails to see it so.[6]

4. The Not Guilty (This Time) Assumption. With considerable sociological research and conventional wisdom to support him, the policeman knows that most people in the great guilty place in which he works have committed numerous crimes for which they have never been caught. Thus when a stop proves unwarranted, a search comes up "dry," or an interrogation fails, despite the dirty means, the policeman is not at all obliged to conclude that the person victimized by them is innocent, only that, and even this need not always be conceded, he is innocent this time.

DIRTY MEANS AS ENDS IN THEMSELVES

How do these features of police work, all of which seem to incline police to accept a standard of a guilty victim for their dirty means, bear upon the Dirty Harry problem from which they derive? The most dangerous reading suggests that if police are inclined, and often quite rightly inclined, to believe they are dealing with factually, if not legally, guilty subjects, they become likely to see their dirty acts, not as means to the achievement of good ends but as ends in themselves—as punishment of guilty people whom the police believe deserve to be punished.

If this line of argument is true, it has the effect, in terms of police perceptions, of moving Dirty Harry problems completely outside of the fourfold table of means-ends combinations created in order to define it. Importantly as well, in terms of our perceptions, Dirty Harry problems of this type can no longer be read as cases of dirty means employed to the achievement of good ends. For unless we are willing to admit that in a democratic society a police arrogates to itself the task of punishing those who they think are guilty, we are forced to conclude that Dirty Harry problems represent cases of employing dirty means to dirty ends, in which case nobody, not the police and certainly not us, is left with any kind of moral dilemma.

The possibility is quite real and quite fearsome, but it is mediated by certain features of police work, some of which inhere in the nature of the work itself and others, imposed from outside, which have a quite explicit impact on it. The most important of the "naturalistic" features of policing which belie the preceding argument is that the assumption of guilt and all the configurations in the policeman's world which serve to support it often turn out wrong. It is precisely because the operative assumption of guilt can be forced on everything and everyone that the policeman who must use it constantly comes to find it leads him astray as often as it confirms his suspicions.

Similarly, a great many of the things policemen do, some of which we have already conceded appear to police as less dirty than they appear to us—faked probable cause for a street stop, manipulated *Miranda* warnings, and so forth—are simply impossible to read as punishments. This is so particularly if we grant a hard-boiled character to our cops.

Of course, neither of these naturalistic restrictions on the obliteration of the means-ends schema is or should be terribly comforting. To the extent that the first is helpful at all assumes a certain skill and capacity of mind that we may not wish to award to all policemen. The willingness to engage in the constant refutation of one's working worldview presumes a certain intellectual integrity which can certainly go awry. Likewise, the second merely admits that on occasion policemen do some things which reveal they appreciate that the state's capacity to punish is sometimes greater than theirs.

To both these "natural" restrictions on the obliteration of the means-ends character of Dirty Harry problems, we can add the exclusionary rule. Although the exclusionary rule is the manifest target of *Dirty Harry*, it, more than anything else, makes Dirty Harry problems a reality in everyday policing. It is the great virtue of exclusionary rules —applying in various forms to stops, searches, seizures, and interrogations— that they hit directly upon the intolerable, though often, I think, moral desire of police to punish. These rules make the very simple point to police that the more they wish to see a felon punished, the more they are advised to be scrupulous in their treatment of him. Put differently, the best thing Harry could have done for Scorpio was to step on his leg, extort his confession, and break into his apartment.

If certain natural features of policing and particularly exclusionary rules combine to maintain the possibility of Dirty Harry problems in a context in which a real danger appears to be their disappearance, it does not follow that police cannot or do not collapse the dirty means-good ends division on some occasions and become punishers. I only hold that on many other occasions, collapse does not occur and Dirty Harry problems, as defined, are still widely possible. What must be remembered next, on the way to making their possibility real, is that policemen know, or think they know, before they employ a dirty means that a dirty means and only a dirty means will work.

ONLY A DIRTY MEANS WILL WORK

The moral standard that a policeman know in advance of resorting to a dirty means that a dirty means and only a dirty means will work,

rests heavily on two technical dimensions: (1) the professional competence of the policeman and (2) the range of legitimate working options available to him. Both are intimately connected, though the distinction to be preserved between them is that the first is a matter of the policeman's individual competence and the second of the competence of the institutions for which (his department) and with which (the law) the policeman works.

In any concrete case, the relations between these moral and technical dimensions of the Dirty Harry problem are extremely complicated. But a priori it follows that the more competent a policeman is at the use of legal means, the less he will be obliged to resort to dirty alternatives. Likewise, the department that trains its policemen well and supplies them with the resources— knowledge and material—to do their work will find that the policemen who work for them will not resort to dirty means "unnecessarily," meaning only those occasions when an acceptable means will work as well as a dirty one.

While these two premises flow a priori from raising the Dirty Harry problem, questions involving the moral and technical roles of laws governing police means invite a very dangerous type of a priori reasoning:

> Combating distrust [of the police] requires getting across the rather complicated message that granting the police specific forms of new authority may be the most effective means for reducing abuse of authority which is now theirs; that it is the absence of properly proscribed forms of authority that often impels the police to engage in questionable or outright illegal conduct. Before state legislatures enacted statutes giving limited authority to the police to stop and question persons suspected of criminal involvement, police nevertheless stopped and questioned people. It is inconceivable how any police agency could be expected to operate without doing so. But since the basis for their actions was unclear, the police—if they thought a challenge likely—would use the guise of arresting the individual on a minor charge (often without clear evidence) to provide a semblance of

legality. Enactment of stopping and questioning statutes eliminated the need for this sham.[7]

Herman Goldstein's preceding argument and observations are undoubtedly true, but the danger in them is that they can be extended to apply to any dirty means, not only illegal arrests to legitimate necessary street stops, but dirty means to accomplish subsequent searches and seizures all the way to beating confessions out of suspects when no other means will work. But, of course, Goldstein does not intend his argument to be extended in these ways.

Nevertheless, his a priori argument, dangerous though it may be, points to the fact that Dirty Harry problems can arise wherever restrictions are placed on police methods and are particularly likely to do so when police themselves perceive that those restrictions are undesirable, unreasonable, or unfair. His argument succeeds in doing what police who face Dirty Harry problems constantly do: rendering the law problematic. But while Goldstein, one of the most distinguished legal scholars in America, can follow his finding with books, articles, and lectures which urge change, it is left to the policeman to take upon himself the moral responsibility of subverting it with dirty and hidden means.

COMPELLING AND UNQUESTIONABLE ENDS

If Dirty Harry problems can be shown to exist in their technical dimensions—as genuine means-ends problems where only dirty means will work—the question of the magnitude and urgency of the ends that the dirty means may be employed to achieve must still be confronted. Specifically, it must be shown that the ends of dirty means are so desirable that the failure to achieve them would cast the person who is in a position to do so in moral disrepute.

The two most widely acknowledged ends of policing are peace keeping and law enforcement. It would follow, of course, that if both these ends were held to be unworthy, Dirty Harry problems would disappear. There are arguments challenging both ends. For instance, certain radical critiques of policing attempt to reduce the peace-keeping and law-enforcing functions of the police in the United States to nothing more than acts of capitalist oppression. From such a position flows not only the denial of the legitimacy of any talk of Dirty Harry problems, but also the denial of the legitimacy of the entire police function.[8]

Regardless of the merits of such critiques, it will suffice for the purpose of this analysis to maintain that there is a large "clientele," to use Albert Reiss's term, for both types of police function.[9] And it should come as no surprise to anyone that the police themselves accept the legitimacy of their own peace-keeping and law-enforcing ends. Some comment is needed though, on how large that clientele for those functions is and how compelling and unquestionable the ends of peace keeping and law enforcement are for them.

There is no more popular, compelling, urgent, nor more broadly appealing idea than peace. In international relations, it is potent enough to legitimate the stockpiling of enough nuclear weapons to exterminate every living thing on earth a dozen times over. In domestic affairs, it gives legitimacy to the idea of the state, and the aspirations to it have succeeded in granting to the state an absolute monopoly on the right to legitimate the use of force and a near monopoly on its actual legitimate use: the police. That peace has managed to legitimate these highly dangerous means to its achievement in virtually every advanced nation in the world is adequate testimony to the fact that it qualifies, if any end does, as a good end so unquestionable and so compelling that it can legitimate risking the most dangerous and dirtiest of means.

The fact is, though, that most American policemen prefer to define their work as law enforcement rather than peace keeping, even though they may, in fact, do more of the latter. It is a distinction that should not be allowed to slip away in assuming, for instance, that the policeman's purpose in enforcing the law is to keep the peace. Likewise, though it is a possibility, it will not do to assume that police simply enforce the law as an end in itself without meaning and without purpose or end. The widely discretionary behavior of working policemen and the enormous underenforcement of the law which characterizes most police agencies simply belie that possibility.

An interpretation of law enforcement which is compatible with empirical studies of police behavior—as peace keeping is—and police talk in America—which peace keeping generally is not—is an understanding of the ends of law enforcement as punishment. There are, of course, many theories of punishment, but the police seem inclined toward the simplest: the belief that certain people who have committed certain acts deserve to be punished for them. What can one say of the compelling and unquestionable character of this retributive ambition as an end of policing and policemen?

Both historically and sociologically there is ample evidence that punishment is almost as unquestionable and compelling an end as peace. Historically, we have a long and painful history of punishment, a history longer in fact than the history of the end of peace. Sociologically, the application of what may well be the only culturally universal norm, the norm of reciprocity, implies the direct and natural relations between wrongful acts and their punishments.[10] Possibly the best evidence for the strength and urgency of the desire to punish in modern society is the extraordinary complex of rules and procedures democratic states have assembled which prevents legitimate punishment from being administered wrongfully or frivolously.

If we can conclude that peace and punishment are ends unquestionable and compelling enough to satisfy the demands of Dirty Harry problems, we are led to one final question on which we may draw from some sociological theories of the police for assistance. If the Dirty Harry problem is at the core of the police role, or at least near to it, how is it that police can or do come to reconcile their use of—or their failure to use—dirty means to achieve unquestionably good and compelling ends?

Public Policy and Police Morality: Three Defective Resolutions of the Dirty Harry Problem

The contemporary literature on policing appears to contain three quite different types of solution or resolution. But because the Dirty Harry problem is a genuine moral dilemma, that is, a situation which will admit no real solution or resolution, each is necessarily defective. Also, understandably, each solution or resolution presents itself as an answer to a somewhat different problem. In matters of public policy, such concealments are often necessary and probably wise, although they have a way of coming around to haunt their architects sooner or later. In discovering that each is flawed and in disclosing the concealments which allow the appearance of resolution, we do not urge that it be held against sociologists that they are not philosophers nor do we argue that they should succeed where philosophers before them have failed. Rather, we only wish to make clear what is risked by each concealment and to face candidly the inevitably unfortunate ramifications which must proceed from it.

SNAPPY BUREAUCRATS

In the works of August Vollmer, Bruce Smith, O. W. Wilson, and those progressive police administrators who still follow their lead, a vision of the perfect police agency and the perfect policeman has gained considerable ground. Labeled "the professional model" in police circles—though entirely different from any classical sense of profession or professional—it envisions a highly trained, technologically sophisticated police department operating free from political interference with a corps of well-educated police responding obediently to the policies, orders, and directives of a central administrative command. It is a vision of police officers, to use Bittner's phrasing, as "snappy bureaucrats,"[11] cogs in a quasi-military machine who do what they are told out of a mix of fear, loyalty, routine, and detailed specification of duties.

The professional model, unlike other solutions to be considered, is based on the assumption that the policeman's motives for working can be made to locate within his department. He will, if told, work vice or traffic, juvenile or homicide, patrol passively or aggressively, and produce one, two, four, or six arrests, pedestrian stops, or reports per hour, day, or week as his department sees fit. In this way the assumption and vision of the professional model in policing is little different from that of any bureaucracy which seeks by specifying tasks and setting expectations for levels of production—work quotas—to coordinate a regular, predictable, and efficient service for its clientele.

The problem with this vision of *sine ira et studio* service by obedient operatives is that when the product to be delivered is some form of human service—education, welfare, health, and police bureaucracies are similar in this way—the vision seems always to fall short of expectations. On the one hand the would-be bureaucratic operatives—teachers, social workers, nurses, and policemen—resent being treated as mere bureaucrats and resist the translation of their work into quotas, directives, rules, regulations, or other abstract specifications. On the other hand, to the extent that the vision of an efficient and obedient human service bureaucracy is realized, the clientele of such institutions typically come away with the impression that no one in the institution truly cares about their problems. And, of course, in that the aim of bureaucratization is to locate employees' motives for work within the bureaucracy, they are absolutely correct in their feelings.

To the extent that the professional model succeeds in making the ends of policing locate within the agency as opposed to moral demands of the tasks which policemen are asked by their clients to do, it appears to solve the Dirty Harry problem. When it succeeds, it does so by replacing the morally compelling ends of punishment and peace with the less human, though by no means uncompelling, ends of bureaucratic performance. However, this resolution certainly does not imply that dirty means will disappear, only that the motives for their use will be career advancement and promotion. Likewise, on those occasions when a morally sensitive policeman would be compelled by the demands of the situational exigencies before him to use a dirty means, the bureaucratic operative envisioned by the professional model will merely do his job. Ambitious bureaucrats and obedient timeservers fail at being the type of morally sensitive souls we want to be policemen. The professional model's bureaucratic resolution of the Dirty Harry problem fails in policing for the same reason it fails in every other human service agency: it is quite simply an impossibility to create a bureaucrat who cares for anything but his bureaucracy.

The idealized image of the professional model, which has been responded to with an ideal critique, is probably unrealizable. Reality intervenes as the ideal type is approached. The bureaucracy seems to take on weight as it approaches the pole, is slowed, and may even collapse in approaching.

BITTNER'S PEACE

A second effort in the literature of contemporary policing also attempts to address the Dirty Harry problem by substituting an alternative to the presently prevailing police ends of punishment. Where the professional model sought to substitute bureaucratic rewards and sanctions for the moral end of punishment, the elegant polemics by Egon Bittner in *The Functions of Police in Modern Society* and "Florence Nightingale in Pursuit of Willie Sutton: A Theory of the Police" seek to substitute the end of peace. In beautifully chosen words, examples, and phrasing, Bittner leads his readers to conclude that peace is historically, empirically, intellectually, and morally the most compelling, unquestionable, and humane end of policing. Bittner is, I fear, absolutely right.

It is the end of peace which legitimates the extension of police responsibilities into a wide variety of civil matters—neighborhood disputes, loud parties, corner lounging, lovers' quarrels, political rallies, disobedient children, bicycle registration, pet control, and a hundred other types of tasks which a modern "service" style police department regularly is called upon to perform. With these responsibilities, which most "good" police agencies now accept willingly and officially, also comes the need for an extension of police powers. Arrest is, after all, too crude a tool to be used in all the various situations in which our peace-keeping policemen are routinely asked to be of help. "Why should," asks Herman Goldstein in a manner in which Bittner would approve, "a police officer arrest and charge a disorderly tavern patron if ordering him to leave the tavern will suffice? Must he arrest and charge one of the parties in a lovers' quarrel if assistance in forcing a separation is all that is desired?"[12] There is no question that both those situations could be handled more peacefully if police were granted new powers which would allow them to handle those situations in the way Goldstein rhetorically asks if they should. That such extensions of police powers will be asked for by our most enlightened police departments in the interests of keeping the peace is absolutely certain. If the success of the decriminalization of police arrests for public intoxication, vagrancy, mental illness, and the virtually unrestricted two-hour right of detention made possible by the Uniform Law of Arrest are any indication of the likelihood of extensions being received favorably, the end of peace and its superiority over punishment in legitimating the extension of police powers seem exceedingly likely to prevail further.

The problem with peace is that it is not the only end of policing so compelling, unquestionable, and in the end, humane. Amid the good work toward the end of peace that we increasingly want our police to do, it is certain that individuals or groups will arise who the police, in all their peace-keeping benevolence, will conclude, on moral if not political or institutional grounds, have "got it coming." And all the once dirty means which were bleached in the brilliant light of peace will return to their true colors.

SKOLNICK'S CRAFTSMAN

The third and final attempt to resolve the Dirty Harry problem is offered by Jerome Skolnick, who in *Justice Without Trial* comes extremely close to stating the Dirty Harry problem openly when he writes:

> ... He (the policeman) sees himself as a craftsman, at his best, a master of his trade ... [he] draws a moral distinction between criminal law and criminal procedure. The distinction is drawn somewhat as follows: The substantive law of crimes is intended to control the behavior of people who wilfully injure persons or property, or who engage in behaviors having such a consequence, such as the use of narcotics. Criminal procedure, by contrast, is intended to control authorities, not criminals. As such, it does not fall into the same moral class of constraint as substantive criminal law. If a policeman were himself to use narcotics, or to steal, or to assault, *outside the line of duty*, much the same standards would be applied to him by other policemen as to the ordinary citizen. When, however, the issue concerns the policeman's freedom to carry out his *duties*, another moral realm is entered.[13]

What is more, Skolnick's craftsman finds support from his peers, department, his community, and the law for the moral rightness of his calling. He cares about his work and finds it just.

What troubles Skolnick about his craftsman is his craft. The craftsman refuses to see, as Skolnick thinks he ought to, that the dirty means he sometimes uses to achieve his good ends stand in the same moral class of wrongs as those he is employed to fight. Skolnick's craftsman reaches this conclusion by understanding that his unquestionably good and compelling ends, on certain occasions, justify his employment of dirty means to their achievement. Skolnick's craftsman, as Skolnick understands him, resolves the Dirty Harry problem by denying the dirtiness of his means.

Skolnick's craftsman's resolution is, speaking precisely, Machiavellian. It should come as no surprise to find the representative of one of the classic attempts to resolve the problem of Dirty Hands to be a front runner in response to Dirty Harry. What is worrisome about such a resolution? What does it conceal that makes our genuine dilemma disappear? The problem is not that the craftsman will sometimes choose to use dirty means. If he is morally sensitive to its demands, every policeman's work will sometimes require as much. What is worrisome about Skolnick's craftsman is that he does not regard his means as dirty and, as Skolnick tells us, does not suffer from their use. The craftsman, if Skolnick's portrait of him is correct, will resort to dirty means too readily and too easily. He lacks the restraint that can come only from struggling to justify them and from taking seriously the hazards involved.

In 1966, when *Justice Without Trial* first appeared, Skolnick regarded the prospects of creating a more morally sensitive craftsman exceedingly dim. He could not imagine that the craftsman's community, employer, peers, or the courts could come to reward him more for his legal compliance than for the achievement of the ends of his craft. However, in phrasing the prospects in terms of a Dirty Harry problem, one can not only agree with Skolnick that denying the goodness of unquestionably good ends is a practical and political impossibility, but can also uncover another alternative, one which Skolnick does not pursue.

The alternative the Dirty Harry problem leads us to is ensuring that the craftsman regards his dirty means as dirty by applying the same retributive principles of punishment to his wrongful acts that he is quite willing to apply to others! It is, in fact, only when his wrongful acts are punished that he will come to see them as wrongful and will appreciate the genuine moral—rather than technical or occupational—choice he makes in resorting to them. The prospects for punishment of such acts are by no means dim, and considerable strides in this area have been made. It requires far fewer resources to punish than to reward. Secondly, the likelihood that juries in civil suits will find dirty means

dirtier than police do is confirmed by police claims that outsiders can not appreciate the same moral and technical distinctions that they do. Finally, severe financial losses to police agencies as well as to their officers eventually communicate to both that vigorously policing themselves is cheaper and more pleasing than having to pay so heavily if they do not. If under such conditions our craftsman police officer is still willing to risk the employment of dirty means to achieve what he understands to be unquestionably good ends, he will not only know that he has behaved justly, but that in doing so he must run the risk of becoming genuinely guilty as well.

A Final Note

In urging the punishment of policemen who resort to dirty means to achieve some unquestionably good and morally compelling end, we recognize that we create a Dirty Harry problem for ourselves and for those we urge to effect such punishments. It is a fitting end, one which teaches once again that the danger in Dirty Harry problems is never in their resolution, but in thinking that one has found a resolution with which one can truly live in peace.

NOTES

1. In the contemporary philosophical literature, particularly when raised for the vocation of politics, the question is commonly referred to as the Dirty Hands problem after J. P. Sartre's treatment of it in *Dirty Hands* (Les Maines Sales, 1948) and in *No Exit and Three Other Plays* (New York: Modern Library, 1950). Despite its modern name, the problem is very old and has been taken up by Machiavelli in *The Prince* (1513) and *The Discourses* (1519) (New York: Modern Library, 1950); by Max Weber, "Politics as a Vocation," (1919) in *Max Weber: Essays in Sociology*, eds. and trans. H. Gerth and C. W. Wills (New York: Oxford University Press, 1946); and by Albert Camus, "The Just Assassins," (1949) in *Caligula and Three Other Plays* (New York: Alfred A. Knopf, 1958). *See* Michael Walzer's brilliant critique of these contributions, "Political Action: The Problem of Dirty Hands" *Philosophy and Public Affairs*,

2(2) (winter 1972). Likewise the Dirty Hands/Dirty Harry problem is implicitly or explicitly raised in virtually every work of Raymond Chandler, Dashiell Hammett, James Cain, and other *Tough Guy Writers of The Thirties,* ed. David Madden (Carbondale, IL: Southern Illinois University Press, 1968), as they are in all of the recent work of Joseph Wambaugh, particularly *The Blue Knight, The New Centurions,* and *The Choirboys.*

2. "Dirty" here means both "repugnant" in that it offends widely shared standards of human decency and dignity and "dangerous" in that it breaks commonly shared and supported norms, rules, or laws for conduct. To "dirty" acts there must be both a deontologically based face validity of immorality and a consequentialist threat to the prevailing rules for social order.

3. W. H. Auden, "The Guilty Vicarage," in *The Dyer's Hand and Other Essays* (New York: Alfred A. Knopf, 1956) pp. 146–58.

4. Egon Bittner, *The Functions of Police in Modern Society* (New York: Jason Aronson, 1975) and "Florence Nightingale in Pursuit of Willie Sutton," in *The Potential For Reform Of the Criminal Justice System,* vol. 3, ed. H. Jacob (Beverly Hills, CA: Sage Publications, 1974) pp. 11–44.

5. Sartre, *Dirty Hands,* p. 224.

6. One of Wambaugh's characters in *The Choirboys* makes this final point most dramatically when he fails to notice that a young boy's buttocks are flatter than they should be and reads the child's large stomach as a sign of adequate nutrition. When the child dies through his mother's neglect and abuse, the officer rightly includes himself in his ecology of guilt.

7. Herman Goldstein, *Policing a Free Society* (Cambridge, MA: Ballinger Publishing, 1977), p. 72.

8. *See,* for example, John F. Galliher, "Explanations of Police Behavior: A Critical Review and Analysis," *The Sociological Quarterly,* 12:308–18 (summer 1971); Richard Quinney, *Class, State, and Crime* (New York: David McKay, 1977).

9. Albert J. Reiss, Jr., *The Police and the Public* (New Haven, CT: Yale University Press, 1971), p. 122.

10. These two assertions are drawn from Graeme Newman's *The Punishment Response* (Philadelphia: J. B. Lippincott Co., 1978).

11. Bittner, p. 53.

12. Ibid., p. 72.

13. Jerome Skolnick, *Justice Without Trial,* 2nd ed. (New York: John Wiley & Sons, 1975), p. 182.

Study Questions

1. What is the "Dirty Harry" problem? What does it have to do with utilitarianism?

2. What are the conditions under which the Dirty Harry problem can arise? Why does Klockars believe it is a moral dilemma? Do you agree with Klockars that there is a genuine dilemma? Why?

3. If force is used by an officer to administer punishment, is this a Dirty Harry problem, in Klockars' view? Why?

4. What are the three models of policing described by Klockars? Why does he think each one fails to solve the Dirty Harry problem? Do you agree with Klockars? Why?

5. In your view, does Klockars contradict himself in saying both (1) that the Dirty Harry problem poses an unsolvable moral dilemma and (2) that officers who use dirty means to achieve good ends should be punished? Defend your answer. Do you think that Klockars is primarily a utilitarian or a deontologist? Why?

Tennessee v. Garner

U.S. SUPREME COURT *(with dissenting opinion)*

JUSTICE WHITE delivered the opinion of the Court.

This case requires us to determine the constitutionality of the use of deadly force to prevent the escape of an apparently unarmed suspected felon. We conclude that such force may not be used unless it is necessary to prevent the escape and the officer has probable cause to believe that the suspect poses a significant threat of death or serious physical injury to the officer or others.

I

At about 10:45 p.m. on October 3, 1974, Memphis Police Officers Elton Hymon and Leslie Wright were dispatched to answer a "prowler inside call." Upon arriving at the scene they saw a woman standing on her porch and gesturing toward the adjacent house.[1] She told them she had heard glass breaking and that "they" or "someone" was breaking in next door. While Wright radioed the dispatcher to say that they were on the scene, Hymon went behind the house. He heard a door slam and saw someone run across the back yard. The fleeing suspect, who was appellee-respondent's decedent, Edward Garner, stopped at a 6-feet-high chain link fence at the edge of the yard. With the aid of a flashlight, Hymon was able to see Garner's face and hands. He saw no sign of a weapon, and, though not certain, was "reasonably sure" and "figured" that Garner was unarmed. App. 41, 56; Record 219. He thought Garner was 17 or 18 years old and about 5'5" or 5'7" tall.[2] While Garner was crouched at the base of the fence, Hymon called out "police, halt" and took a few steps toward him. Garner then began to climb over the fence. Convinced that if Garner made it

over the fence he would elude capture,[3] Hymon shot him. The bullet hit Garner in the back of the head. Garner was taken by ambulance to a hospital, where he died on the operating table. Ten dollars and a purse taken from the house were found on his body.[4]

In using deadly force to prevent the escape, Hymon was acting under the authority of a Tennessee statute and pursuant to Police Department policy. The statute provides that "[i]f, after notice of the intention to arrest the defendant, he either flee or forcibly resist, the officer may use all the necessary means to effect the arrest." Tenn. Code Ann. § 40-7-108 (1982).[5] The Department policy was slightly more restrictive than the statute, but still allowed the use of deadly force in cases of burglary. App. 140-144. The incident was reviewed by the Memphis Police Firearm's Review Board and presented to a grand jury. Neither took any action. *Id.*, at 57.

Garner's father then brought this action in the Federal District Court for the Western District of Tennessee, seeking damages under 42 U.S.C. § 1983 for asserted violations of Garner's constitutional rights. The complaint alleged that the shooting violated the Fourth, Fifth, Sixth, Eighth, and Fourteenth Amendments of the United States Constitution. It named as defendants Officer Hymon, the Police Department, its Director, and the Mayor and city of Memphis. After a 3-day bench trial, the District Court entered judgment for all defendants. It dismissed the claims against the Mayor and the Director for lack of evidence. It then concluded that Hymon's actions were authorized by the Tennessee statute, which in turn was constitutional. Hymon had employed the only reasonable and practicable means of preventing Garner's escape.

471 U.S. 1 (1985). Some legal citations have been shortened or removed.

Garner had "recklessly and heedlessly attempted to vault over the fence to escape, thereby assuming the risk of being fired upon." App. to Pet. for Cert. A10.

The Court of Appeals for the Sixth Circuit affirmed with regard to Hymon, finding that he had acted in good-faith reliance on the Tennessee statute and was therefore within the scope of his qualified immunity. 600 F. 2d 52 (1979). It remanded for reconsideration of the possible liability of the city, however, in light of *Monell* v. *New York City Dept. of Social Services*, 436 U.S. 658 (1978), which had come down after the District Court's decision. The District Court was directed to consider whether a city enjoyed a qualified immunity, whether the use of deadly force and hollow point bullets in these circumstances was constitutional, and whether any unconstitutional municipal conduct flowed from a "policy or custom" as required for liability under *Monell.* 600 F. 2d, at 54–55.

The District Court concluded that *Monell* did not affect its decision. While acknowledging some doubt as to the possible immunity of the city, it found that the statute, and Hymon's actions, were constitutional. Given this conclusion, it declined to consider the "policy or custom" question. App. to Pet. for Cert. A37–A39.

The Court of Appeals reversed and remanded. 710 F. 2d 240 (1983). It reasoned that the killing of a fleeing suspect is a "seizure" under the Fourth Amendment,[6] and is therefore constitutional only if "reasonable." The Tennessee statute failed as applied to this case because it did not adequately limit the use of deadly force by distinguishing between felonies of different magnitudes—"the facts, as found, did not justify the use of deadly force under the Fourth Amendment." *Id.,* at 246. Officers cannot resort to deadly force unless they "have probable cause ... to believe that the suspect [has committed a felony and] poses a threat to the safety of the officers or a danger to the community if left at large." *Ibid.*[7]

The State of Tennessee, which had intervened to defend the statute, see 28 U.S.C. § 2403(b), appealed to this Court. The city filed a petition for certiorari. We noted probable jurisdiction in the appeal and granted the petition. 465 U.S. 1098 (1984).

II

Whenever an officer restrains the freedom of a person to walk away, he has seized that person. *United States* v. *Brignoni-Ponce,* 422 U.S. 873, 878 (1975). While it is not always clear just when minimal police interference becomes a seizure, see *United States* v. *Mendenhall,* 446 U.S. 544 (1980), there can be no question that apprehension by the use of deadly force is a seizure subject to the reasonableness requirement of the Fourth Amendment.

A

A police officer may arrest a person if he has probable cause to believe that person committed a crime. *E. g., United States* v. *Watson,* 423 U.S. 411 (1976). Petitioners and appellant argue that if this requirement is satisfied the Fourth Amendment has nothing to say about *how* that seizure is made. This submission ignores the many cases in which this Court, by balancing the extent of the intrusion against the need for it, has examined the reasonableness of the manner in which a search or seizure is conducted. To determine the constitutionality of a seizure "[w]e must balance the nature and quality of the intrusion on the individual's Fourth Amendment interests against the importance of the governmental interests alleged to justify the intrusion." *United States* v. *Place,* 462 U.S. 696, 703 (1983); see *Delaware* v. *Prouse,* 440 U.S. 648, 654 (1979); *United States* v. *Martinez-Fuerte,* 428 U. S. 543, 555 (1976). We have described "the balancing of competing interests" as "the key principle of the Fourth Amendment." *Michigan* v. *Summers,* 452 U.S. 692, 700, n. 12 (1981). See also *Camara* v. *Municipal Court,* 387 U. S. 523, 536–537 (1967). Because one of the factors is the extent of the intrusion, it is plain that reasonableness depends on not only when a seizure is made, but also how it is carried out. *United States* v. *Ortiz,* 422 U.S. 891, 895 (1975); *Terry* v. *Ohio,* 392 U.S. 1, 28–29 (1968).

Applying these principles to particular facts, the Court has held that governmental interests did not support a lengthy detention of luggage, *United States* v. *Place, supra,* an airport seizure not "carefully tailored to its underlying justification," *Florida* v. *Royer,* 460 U.S. 491, 500 (1983) (plurality opinion), surgery under general anesthesia to obtain evidence, *Winston* v. *Lee,* 470 U.S. 753 (1985), or detention for fingerprinting without probable cause, *Davis* v. *Mississippi,* 394 U.S. 721 (1969); *Hayes* v. *Florida,* 470 U.S. 811 (1985). On the other hand, under the same approach it has upheld the taking of fingernail scrapings from a suspect, *Cupp* v. *Murphy,* 412 U.S. 291 (1973), an unannounced entry into a home to prevent the destruction of evidence, *Ker* v. *California,* 374 U.S. 23 (1963), administrative housing inspections without probable cause to believe that a code violation will be found, *Camara.* v. *Municipal Court, supra,* and a blood test of a drunken-driving suspect, *Schmerber* v. *California,* 384 U.S. 757 (1966). In each of these cases, the question was whether the totality of the circumstances justified a particular sort of search or seizure.

B

The same balancing process applied in the cases cited above demonstrates that, notwithstanding probable cause to seize a suspect, an officer may not always do so by killing him. The intrusiveness of a seizure by means of deadly force is unmatched. The suspect's fundamental interest in his own life need not be elaborated upon. The use of deadly force also frustrates the interest of the individual, and of society, in judicial determination of guilt and punishment. Against these interests are ranged governmental interests in effective law enforcement.[8] It is argued that overall violence will be reduced by encouraging the peaceful submission of suspects who know that they may be shot if they flee. Effectiveness in making arrests requires the resort to deadly force, or at least the meaningful threat thereof. "Being able to arrest such individuals is a condition precedent to the state's entire system of law enforcement." Brief for Petitioners 14.

Without in any way disparaging the importance of these goals, we are not convinced that the use of deadly force is a sufficiently productive means of accomplishing them to justify the killing of nonviolent suspects. Cf. *Delaware* v. *Prouse, supra,* at 659. The use of deadly force is a self-defeating way of apprehending a suspect and so setting the criminal justice mechanism in motion. If successful, it guarantees that that mechanism will not be set in motion. And while the meaningful threat of deadly force might be thought to lead to the arrest of more live suspects by discouraging escape attempts,[9] the presently available evidence does not support this thesis.[10] The fact is that a majority of police departments in this country have forbidden the use of deadly force against nonviolent suspects. See *infra,* at 18-19. If those charged with the enforcement of the criminal law have abjured the use of deadly force in arresting nondangerous felons, there is a substantial basis for doubting that the use of such force is an essential attribute of the arrest power in all felony cases. See *Schumann* v. *McGinn,* 307 Minn. 446, 472, 240 N. W. 2d 525, 540 (1976) (Rogosheske, J., dissenting in part). Petitioners and appellant have not persuaded us that shooting nondangerous fleeing suspects is so vital as to outweigh the suspect's interest in his own life.

The use of deadly force to prevent the escape of all felony suspects, whatever the circumstances, is constitutionally unreasonable. It is not better that all felony suspects die than that they escape. Where the suspect poses no immediate threat to the officer and no threat to others, the harm resulting from failing to apprehend him does not justify the use of deadly force to do so. It is no doubt unfortunate when a suspect who is in sight escapes, but the fact that the police arrive a little late or are a little slower afoot does not always justify killing the suspect. A police officer may not seize an unarmed, nondangerous suspect by shooting him dead. The Tennessee statute is unconstitutional insofar as it authorizes the use of deadly force against such fleeing suspects.

It is not, however, unconstitutional on its

face. Where the officer has probable cause to believe that the suspect poses a threat of serious physical harm, either to the officer or to others, it is not constitutionally unreasonable to prevent escape by using deadly force. Thus, if the suspect threatens the officer with a weapon or there is probable cause to believe that he has committed a crime involving the infliction or threatened infliction of serious physical harm, deadly force may be used if necessary to prevent escape, and if, where feasible, some warning has been given. As applied in such circumstances, the Tennessee statute would pass constitutional muster.

III

A

It is insisted that the Fourth Amendment must be construed in light of the common-law rule, which allowed the use of whatever force was necessary to effect the arrest of a fleeing felon, though not a misdemeanant. As stated in Hale's posthumously published Pleas of the Crown:

> "[I]f persons that are pursued by these officers for felony or the just suspicion thereof ... shall not yield themselves to these officers, but shall either resist or fly before they are apprehended or being apprehended shall rescue themselves and resist or fly, so that they cannot be otherwise apprehended, and are upon necessity slain therein, because they cannot be otherwise taken, it is no felony." 2 M. Hale, Historia Placitorum Coronae 85 (1736).

See also 4 W. Blackstone, Commentaries *289. Most American jurisdictions also imposed a flat prohibition against the use of deadly force to stop a fleeing misdemeanant, coupled with a general privilege to use such force to stop a fleeing felon. *E. g., Holloway* v. *Moser,* 193 N. C. 185, 136 S. E. 375 (1927); *State* v. *Smith,* 127 Iowa 534, 535, 103 N. W. 944, 945 (1905); *Reneau* v. *State,* 70 Tenn. 720 (1879); *Brooks* v. *Commonwealth,* 61 Pa. 352 (1869); *Roberts* v. *State,* 14 Mo. 138 (1851); see generally R. Perkins & R. Boyce, Criminal Law 1098–1102 (3d ed. 1982); Day, Shooting the Fleeing Felon: State of the Law, 14 Crim. L. Bull. 285, 286–287 (1978); Wilgus, Arrest Without a Warrant,

22 Mich. L. Rev. 798, 807–816 (1924). But see *Storey* v. *State,* 71 Ala. 329 (1882); *State* v. *Bryant,* 65 N. C. 327, 328 (1871); *Caldwell* v. *State,* 41 Tex. 86 (1874).

The State and city argue that because this was the prevailing rule at the time of the adoption of the Fourth Amendment and for some time thereafter, and is still in force in some States, use of deadly force against a fleeing felon must be "reasonable." It is true that this Court has often looked to the common law in evaluating the reasonableness, for Fourth Amendment purposes, of police activity. See, *e. g., United States* v. *Watson,* 423 U. S. 411, 418–419 (1976); *Gerstein* v. *Pugh,* 420 U. S. 103, 111, 114 (1975); *Carroll* v. *United States,* 267 U. S. 132, 149–153 (1925). On the other hand, it "has not simply frozen into constitutional law those law enforcement practices that existed at the time of the Fourth Amendment's passage." *Payton* v. *New York,* 445 U. S. 573, 591, n. 33 (1980). Because of sweeping change in the legal and technological context, reliance on the common-law rule in this case would be a mistaken literalism that ignores the purposes of a historical inquiry.

B

It has been pointed out many times that the common-law rule is best understood in light of the fact that it arose at a time when virtually all felonies were punishable by death.[11] "Though effected without the protections and formalities of an orderly trial and conviction, the killing of a resisting or fleeing felon resulted in no greater consequences than those authorized for punishment of the felony of which the individual was charged or suspected." American Law Institute, Model Penal Code § 3.07, Comment 3, p. 56 (Tentative Draft No. 8, 1958) (hereinafter Model Penal Code Comment). Courts have also justified the common-law rule by emphasizing the relative dangerousness of felons. See, *e. g., Schumann* v. *McGinn,* 307 Minn., at 458, 240 N. W. 2d, at 533; *Holloway* v. *Moser, supra,* at 187, 136 S. E., at 376 (1927).

Neither of these justifications makes sense today. Almost all crimes formerly punishable by death no longer are or can be. See, *e. g., Enmund*

v. *Florida*, 458 U.S. 782 (1982); *Coker* v. *Georgia*, 433 U.S. 584 (1977). And while in earlier times "the gulf between the felonies and the minor offences was broad and deep," 2 Pollock & Maitland 467, n. 3; *Carroll* v. *United States, supra*, at 158, today the distinction is minor and often arbitrary. Many crimes classified as misdemeanors, or nonexistent, at common law are now felonies. Wilgus, 22 Mich. L. Rev., at 572–573. These changes have undermined the concept, which was questionable to begin with, that use of deadly force against a fleeing felon is merely a speedier execution of someone who has already forfeited his life. They have also made the assumption that a "felon" is more dangerous than a misdemeanant untenable. Indeed, numerous misdemeanors involve conduct more dangerous than many felonies.[12]

There is an additional reason why the common-law rule cannot be directly translated to the present day. The common-law rule developed at a time when weapons were rudimentary. Deadly force could be inflicted almost solely in a hand-to-hand struggle during which, necessarily, the safety of the arresting officer was at risk. Handguns were not carried by police officers until the latter half of the last century. L. Kennett & J. Anderson, The Gun in America 150–151 (1975). Only then did it become possible to use deadly force from a distance as a means of apprehension. As a practical matter, the use of deadly force under the standard articulation of the common-law rule has an altogether different meaning—and harsher consequences—now than in past centuries. See Wechsler & Michael, A Rationale for the Law of Homicide: I, 37 Colum. L. Rev. 701, 741 (1937).[13]

One other aspect of the common-law rule bears emphasis. It forbids the use of deadly force to apprehend a misdemeanant, condemning such action as disproportionately severe. See *Holloway* v. *Moser*, 193 N. C., at 187, 136 S. E., at 376; *State* v. *Smith*, 127 Iowa, at 535, 103 N. W., at 945. See generally Annot., 83 A. L. R. 3d 238 (1978).

In short, though the common-law pedigree of Tennessee's rule is pure on its face, changes in the legal and technological context mean the rule is distorted almost beyond recognition when literally applied.

C

In evaluating the reasonableness of police procedures under the Fourth Amendment, we have also looked to prevailing rules in individual jurisdictions. See, *e. g., United States* v. *Watson*, 423 U.S., at 421–422. The rules in the States are varied. See generally Comment, 18 Ga. L. Rev. 137, 140–144 (1983). Some 19 States have codified the common-law rule,[14] though in two of these the courts have significantly limited the statute.[15] Four States, though without a relevant statute, apparently retain the common-law rule.[16] Two States have adopted the Model Penal Code's provision verbatim.[17] Eighteen others allow, in slightly varying language, the use of deadly force only if the suspect has committed a felony involving the use or threat of physical or deadly force, or is escaping with a deadly weapon, or is likely to endanger life or inflict serious physical injury if not arrested.[18] Louisiana and Vermont, though without statutes or case law on point, do forbid the use of deadly force to prevent any but violent felonies.[19] The remaining States either have no relevant statute or case law, or have positions that are unclear.[20]

It cannot be said that there is a constant or overwhelming trend away from the common-law rule. In recent years, some States have reviewed their laws and expressly rejected abandonment of the common-law rule.[21] Nonetheless, the long-term movement has been away from the rule that deadly force may be used against any fleeing felon, and that remains the rule in less than half the States.

This trend is more evident and impressive when viewed in light of the policies adopted by the police departments themselves. Overwhelmingly, these are more restrictive than the common-law rule. C. Milton, J. Halleck, J. Lardner, & G. Abrecht, Police Use of Deadly Force 45–46 (1977). The Federal Bureau of Investigation and the New York City Police Department, for example, both forbid the use of firearms except when necessary to prevent death or grievous bodily harm. *Id.*, at 40–41; App. 83. For accreditation by the Commission on Accreditation for Law Enforcement Agencies, a department must restrict the use of deadly force to situations where "the officer reasonably believes that the action is in defense of human life . . . or in defense of any person in immediate danger of serious physical injury." Commission on Accreditation for Law Enforcement Agencies, Inc., Standards for Law Enforcement Agencies 1–2 (1983) (italics deleted). A 1974 study reported that the police department regulations in a majority of the large cities of the United States allowed the firing of a weapon only when a felon presented a threat of death or serious bodily harm. Boston Police Department, Planning & Research Division, The Use of Deadly Force by Boston Police Personnel (1974), cited in *Mattis* v. *Schnarr*, 547 F. 2d 1007, 1016, n. 19 (CA8 1976), vacated as moot *sub nom. Ashcroft* v. *Mattis*, 431 U.S. 171 (1977). Overall, only 7.5% of departmental and municipal policies explicitly permit the use of deadly force against any felon; 86.8% explicitly do not. K. Matulia, A Balance of Forces: A Report of the International Association of Chiefs of Police 161 (1982) (table). See also Record 1108–1368 (written policies of 44 departments). See generally W. Geller & K. Karales, Split-Second Decisions 33–42 (1981); Brief for Police Foundation et al. as *Amici Curiae*. In light of the rules adopted by those who must actually administer them, the older and fading common-law view is a dubious indicium of the constitutionality of the Tennessee statute now before us.

D

Actual departmental policies are important for an additional reason. We would hesitate to declare a police practice of long standing "unreasonable" if doing so would severely hamper effective law enforcement. But the indications are to the contrary. There has been no suggestion that crime has worsened in any way in jurisdictions that have adopted, by legislation or departmental policy, rules similar to that announced today. *Amici* note that "[a]fter extensive research and consideration, [they] have concluded that

laws permitting police officers to use deadly force to apprehend unarmed, non-violent fleeing felony suspects actually do not protect citizens or law enforcement officers, do not deter crime or alleviate problems caused by crime, and do not improve the crime-fighting ability of law enforcement agencies." *Id.*, at 11. The submission is that the obvious state interests in apprehension are not sufficiently served to warrant the use of lethal weapons against all fleeing felons. See *supra*, at 10–11, and n. 10.

Nor do we agree with petitioners and appellant that the rule we have adopted requires the police to make impossible, split-second evaluations of unknowable facts. See Brief for Petitioners 25; Brief for Appellant 11. We do not deny the practical difficulties of attempting to assess the suspect's dangerousness. However, similarly difficult judgments must be made by the police in equally uncertain circumstances. See, *e. g., Terry* v. *Ohio*, 392 U.S., at 20, 27. Nor is there any indication that in States that allow the use of deadly force only against dangerous suspects, see nn. 15, 17–19, *supra*, the standard has been difficult to apply or has led to a rash of litigation involving inappropriate second-guessing of police officers' split-second decisions. Moreover, the highly technical felony/misdemeanor distinction is equally, if not more, difficult to apply in the field. An officer is in no position to know, for example, the precise value of property stolen, or whether the crime was a first or second offense. Finally, as noted above, this claim must be viewed with suspicion in light of the similar self-imposed limitations of so many police departments.

IV

The District Court concluded that Hymon was justified in shooting Garner because state law allows, and the Federal Constitution does not forbid, the use of deadly force to prevent the escape of a fleeing felony suspect if no alternative means of apprehension is available. See App. to Pet. for Cert. A9–A11, A38. This conclusion made a determination of Garner's apparent dangerousness unnecessary. The court did find, however, that Garner appeared to be unarmed, though Hymon could not be certain that was the case. *Id.*, at A4, A23. See also App. 41, 56; Record 219. Restated in Fourth Amendment terms, this means Hymon had no articulable basis to think Garner was armed.

In reversing, the Court of Appeals accepted the District Court's factual conclusions and held that "the facts, as found, did not justify the use of deadly force." 710 F. 2d, at 246. We agree. Officer Hymon could not reasonably have believed that Garner—young, slight, and unarmed—posed any threat. Indeed, Hymon never attempted to justify his actions on any basis other than the need to prevent an escape. The District Court stated in passing that "[t]he facts of this case did not indicate to Officer Hymon that Garner was 'non dangerous.'" App. to Pet. for Cert. A34. This conclusion is not explained, and seems to be based solely on the fact that Garner had broken into a house at night. However, the fact that Garner was a suspected burglar could not, without regard to the other circumstances, automatically justify the use of deadly force. Hymon did not have probable cause to believe that Garner, whom he correctly believed to be unarmed, posed any physical danger to himself or others.

The dissent argues that the shooting was justified by the fact that Officer Hymon had probable cause to believe that Garner had committed a nighttime burglary. *Post,* at 29, 32. While we agree that burglary is a serious crime, we cannot agree that it is so dangerous as automatically to justify the use of deadly force. The FBI classifies burglary as a "property" rather than a "violent" crime. See Federal Bureau of Investigation, Uniform Crime Reports, Crime in the United States 1 (1984).[22] Although the armed burglar would present a different situation, the fact that an unarmed suspect has broken into a dwelling at night does not automatically mean he is physically dangerous. This case demonstrates as much. See also *Solem* v. *Helm,* 463 U.S. 277, 296–297, and nn. 22–23 (1983). In fact, the available statistics demonstrate that burglaries only rarely involve physical violence. During the 10-year period

from 1973–1982, only 3.8% of all burglaries involved violent crime. Bureau of Justice Statistics, Household Burglary 4 (1985).[23] See also T. Reppetto, Residential Crime 17, 105 (1974); Conklin & Bittner, Burglary in a Suburb, 11 Criminology 208, 214 (1973).

V

We wish to make clear what our holding means in the context of this case. The complaint has been dismissed as to all the individual defendants. The State is a party only by virtue of 28 U.S.C. § 2403(b) and is not subject to liability. The possible liability of the remaining defendants—the Police Department and the city of Memphis—hinges on *Monell* v. *New York City Dept. of Social Services,* 436 U.S. 658 (1978), and is left for remand. We hold that the statute is invalid insofar as it purported to give Hymon the authority to act as he did. As for the policy of the Police Department, the absence of any discussion of this issue by the courts below, and the uncertain state of the record, preclude any consideration of its validity.

The judgment of the Court of Appeals is affirmed, and the case is remanded for further proceedings consistent with this opinion.

So ordered.

JUSTICE O'CONNOR, with whom THE CHIEF JUSTICE and JUSTICE REHNQUIST join, dissenting.

The Court today holds that the Fourth Amendment prohibits a police officer from using deadly force as a last resort to apprehend a criminal suspect who refuses to halt when fleeing the scene of a nighttime burglary. This conclusion rests on the majority's balancing of the interests of the suspect and the public interest in effective law enforcement. *Ante,* at 8. Notwithstanding the venerable common-law rule authorizing the use of deadly force if necessary to apprehend a fleeing felon, and continued acceptance of this rule by nearly half the States, *ante,* at 14, 16–17, the majority concludes that Tennessee's statute is unconstitutional inasmuch as it allows the use of such force to apprehend a burglary suspect who is not obviously armed or otherwise dangerous. Although the circumstances of this case are unquestionably tragic and unfortunate, our constitutional holdings must be sensitive both to the history of the Fourth Amendment and to the general implications of the Court's reasoning. By disregarding the serious and dangerous nature of residential burglaries and the long-standing practice of many States, the Court effectively creates a Fourth Amendment right allowing a burglary suspect to flee unimpeded from a police officer who has probable cause to arrest, who has ordered the suspect to halt, and who has no means short of firing his weapon to prevent escape. I do not believe that the Fourth Amendment supports such a right, and I accordingly dissent.

II

For purposes of Fourth Amendment analysis, I agree with the Court that Officer Hymon "seized" Garner by shooting him. Whether that seizure was reasonable and therefore permitted by the Fourth Amendment requires a careful balancing of the important public interest in crime prevention and detection and the nature and quality of the intrusion upon legitimate interests of the individual. *United States* v. *Place,* 462 U.S. 696, 703 (1983). In striking this balance here, it is crucial to acknowledge that police use of deadly force to apprehend a fleeing criminal suspect falls within the "rubric of police conduct ... necessarily [involving] swift action predicated upon the on-the-spot observations of the officer on the beat." *Terry* v. *Ohio,* 392 U.S. 1, 20 (1968). The clarity of hindsight cannot provide the standard for judging the reasonableness of police decisions made in uncertain and often dangerous circumstances. Moreover, I am far more reluctant than is the Court to conclude that the Fourth Amendment proscribes a police practice that was accepted at the time of the adoption of the Bill of Rights and has continued to receive the support of many state legisla-

tures. Although the Court has recognized that the requirements of the Fourth Amendment must respond to the reality of social and technological change, fidelity to the notion of *constitutional*—as opposed to purely judicial—limits on governmental action requires us to impose a heavy burden on those who claim that practices accepted when the Fourth Amendment was adopted are now constitutionally impermissible. See, *e. g., United States* v. *Watson,* 423 U.S. 411, 416–421 (1976); *Carroll* v. *United States,* 267 U.S. 132, 149–153 (1925). Cf. *United States* v. *Villamonte-Marquez,* 462 U.S. 579, 585 (1983) (noting "impressive historical pedigree" of statute challenged under Fourth Amendment).

The public interest involved in the use of deadly force as a last resort to apprehend a fleeing burglary suspect relates primarily to the serious nature of the crime. Household burglaries not only represent the illegal entry into a person's home, but also "pos[e] real risk of serious harm to others." *Solem* v. *Helm,* 463 U.S. 277, 315–316 (1983) (BURGER, C. J., dissenting). According to recent Department of Justice statistics, "[t]hree-fifths of all rapes in the home, three-fifths of all home robberies, and about a third of home aggravated and simple assaults are committed by burglars." Bureau of Justice Statistics Bulletin, Household Burglary 1 (January 1985). During the period 1973–1982, 2.8 million such violent crimes were committed in the course of burglaries. *Ibid.* Victims of a forcible intrusion into their home by a nighttime prowler will find little consolation in the majority's confident assertion that "burglaries only rarely involve physical violence." *Ante,* at 21. Moreover, even if a particular burglary, when viewed in retrospect, does not involve physical harm to others, the "harsh potentialities for violence" inherent in the forced entry into a home preclude characterization of the crime as "innocuous, inconsequential, minor, or 'nonviolent.'" *Solem* v. *Helm, supra,* at 316 (BURGER, C. J., dissenting). See also Restatement of Torts § 131, Comment *g* (1934) (burglary is among felonies that normally cause or threaten death or serious bodily harm); R. Perkins & R. Boyce, Criminal Law 1110 (3d ed.

1982) (burglary is dangerous felony that creates unreasonable risk of great personal harm).

Because burglary is a serious and dangerous felony, the public interest in the prevention and detection of the crime is of compelling importance. Where a police officer has probable cause to arrest a suspected burglar, the use of deadly force as a last resort might well be the only means of apprehending the suspect. With respect to a particular burglary, subsequent investigation simply cannot represent a substitute for immediate apprehension of the criminal suspect at the scene. See President's Commission on Law Enforcement and Administration of Justice, Task Force Report: The Challenge of Crime in a Free Society 97 (1967). Indeed, the Captain of the Memphis Police Department testified that in his city, if apprehension is not immediate, it is likely that the suspect will not be caught. App. in No. 81-5605 (CA6), p. 334. Although some law enforcement agencies may choose to assume the risk that a criminal will remain at large, the Tennessee statute reflects a legislative determination that the use of deadly force in prescribed circumstances will serve generally to protect the public. Such statutes assist the police in apprehending suspected perpetrators of serious crimes and provide notice that a lawful police order to stop and submit to arrest may not be ignored with impunity. See, e. g., Wiley v. Memphis Police Department, 548 F. 2d 1247, 1252-1253 (CA6), cert. denied, 434 U.S. 822 (1977); Jones v. Marshall, 528 F. 2d 132, 142 (CA2 1975).

The Court unconvincingly dismisses the general deterrence effects by stating that "the presently available evidence does not support [the] thesis" that the threat of force discourages escape and that "there is a substantial basis for doubting that the use of such force is an essential attribute to the arrest power in all felony cases." Ante, at 10, 11. There is no question that the effectiveness of police use of deadly force is arguable and that many States or individual police departments have decided not to authorize it in circumstances similar to those presented here. But it should go without saying that the effectiveness or popularity of a particular police practice does not determine its constitutionality. Cf. Spaziano v. Florida, 468 U.S. 447, 464 (1984) ("The Eighth Amendment is not violated every time a State reaches a conclusion different from a majority of its sisters over how best to administer its criminal laws"). Moreover, the fact that police conduct pursuant to a state statute is challenged on constitutional grounds does not impose a burden on the State to produce social science statistics or to dispel any possible doubts about the necessity of the conduct. This observation, I believe, has particular force where the challenged practice both predates enactment of the Bill of Rights and continues to be accepted by a substantial number of the States.

Against the strong public interests justifying the conduct at issue here must be weighed the individual interests implicated in the use of deadly force by police officers. The majority declares that "[t]he suspect's fundamental interest in his own life need not be elaborated upon." Ante, at 9. This blithe assertion hardly provides an adequate substitute for the majority's failure to acknowledge the distinctive manner in which the suspect's interest in his life is even exposed to risk. For purposes of this case, we must recall that the police officer, in the course of investigating a nighttime burglary, had reasonable cause to arrest the suspect and ordered him to halt. The officer's use of force resulted because the suspected burglar refused to heed this command and the officer reasonably believed that there was no means short of firing his weapon to apprehend the suspect. Without questioning the importance of a person's interest in his life, I do not think this interest encompasses a right to flee unimpeded from the scene of a burglary. Cf. Payton v. New York, 445 U.S. 573, 617, n. 14 (1980) (WHITE, J., dissenting) ("[T]he policeman's hands should not be tied merely because of the possibility that the suspect will fail to cooperate with legitimate actions by law enforcement personnel"). The legitimate interests of the suspect in these circumstances are adequately accommodated by the Tennessee statute: to avoid the use of deadly force and the consequent risk to his life, the suspect need merely obey the valid order to halt.

A proper balancing of the interests involved suggests that use of deadly force as a last resort to apprehend a criminal suspect fleeing from the scene of a nighttime burglary is not unreasonable within the meaning of the Fourth Amendment. Admittedly, the events giving rise to this case are in retrospect deeply regrettable. No one can view the death of an unarmed and apparently nonviolent 15-year-old without sorrow, much less disapproval. Nonetheless, the reasonableness of Officer Hymon's conduct for purposes of the Fourth Amendment cannot be evaluated by what later appears to have been a preferable course of police action. The officer pursued a suspect in the darkened backyard of a house that from all indications had just been burglarized. The police officer was not certain whether the suspect was alone or unarmed; nor did he know what had transpired inside the house. He ordered the suspect to halt, and when the suspect refused to obey and attempted to flee into the night, the officer fired his weapon to prevent escape. The reasonableness of this action for purposes of the Fourth Amendment is not determined by the unfortunate nature of this particular case; instead, the question is whether it is constitutionally impermissible for police officers, as a last resort, to shoot a burglary suspect fleeing the scene of the crime.

Because I reject the Fourth Amendment reasoning of the majority and the Court of Appeals, I briefly note that no other constitutional provision supports the decision below. In addition to his Fourth Amendment claim, appellee-respondent also alleged violations of due process, the Sixth Amendment right to trial by jury, and the Eighth Amendment proscription of cruel and unusual punishment. These arguments were rejected by the District Court and, except for the due process claim, not addressed by the Court of Appeals. With respect to due process, the Court of Appeals reasoned that statutes affecting the fundamental interest in life must be "narrowly drawn to express only the legitimate state interests at stake." 710 F. 2d, at 245. The Court of Appeals concluded that a statute allowing police use of deadly force is narrowly drawn and therefore constitutional only if the use of such force is limited to situations in which the suspect poses an immediate threat to others. *Id.,* at 246-247. Whatever the validity of Tennessee's statute in other contexts, I cannot agree that its application in this case resulted in a deprivation "without due process of law." Cf. *Baker* v. *McCollan,* 443 U.S. 137, 144-145 (1979). Nor do I believe that a criminal suspect who is shot while trying to avoid apprehension has a cognizable claim of a deprivation of his Sixth Amendment right to trial by jury. See *Cunningham* v. *Ellington,* 323 F. Supp. 1072, 1075-1076 (WD Tenn. 1971) (threejudge court). Finally, because there is no indication that the use of deadly force was intended to punish rather than to capture the suspect, there is no valid claim under the Eighth Amendment. See *Bell* v. *Wolfish,* 441 U.S. 520, 538-539 (1979). Accordingly, I conclude that the District Court properly entered judgment against appellee-respondent, and I would reverse the decision of the Court of Appeals.

III

Even if I agreed that the Fourth Amendment was violated under the circumstances of this case, I would be unable to join the Court's opinion. The Court holds that deadly force may be used only if the suspect "threatens the officer with a weapon or there is probable cause to believe that he has committed a crime involving the infliction or threatened infliction of serious physical harm." *Ante,* at 11. The Court ignores the more general implications of its reasoning. Relying on the Fourth Amendment, the majority asserts that it is constitutionally unreasonable to "use deadly force against fleeing criminal suspects who do not appear to pose a threat of serious physical harm to others. *Ibid.* By declining to limit its holding to the use of firearms, the Court unnecessarily implies that the Fourth Amendment constrains the use of any police practice that is potentially lethal, no matter how remote the risk. Cf. *Los Angeles* v. *Lyons*, 461 U.S. 95 (1983).

Although it is unclear from the language of the opinion, I assume that the majority intends the word "use" to include only those circumstances in which the suspect is actually apprehended. Absent apprehension of the suspect, there is no "seizure" for Fourth Amendment purposes. I doubt that the Court intends to allow criminal suspects who successfully escape to return later with § 1983 claims against officers who used, albeit unsuccessfully, deadly force in their futile attempt to capture the fleeing suspect. The Court's opinion, despite its broad language, actually decides only that the shooting of a fleeing burglary suspect who was in fact neither armed nor dangerous can support a § 1983 action.

The Court's silence on critical factors in the decision to use deadly force simply invites second-guessing of difficult police decisions that must be made quickly in the most trying of circumstances. Cf. *Payton* v. *New York*, 445 U.S., at 619 (WHITE, J., dissenting). Police are given no guidance for determining which objects, among an array of potentially lethal weapons ranging from guns to knives to baseball bats to rope, will justify the use of deadly force. The Court also declines to outline the additional factors necessary to provide "probable cause" for believing that a suspect "poses a significant threat of death or serious physical injury," *ante*, at 3, when the officer has probable cause to arrest and the suspect refuses to obey an order to halt. But even if it were appropriate in this case to limit the use of deadly force to that ambiguous class of suspects, I believe the class should include nighttime residential burglars who resist arrest by attempting to flee the scene of the crime. We can expect an escalating volume of litigation as the lower courts struggle to determine if a police officer's split-second decision to shoot was justified by the danger posed by a particular object

and other facts related to the crime. Thus, the majority opinion portends a burgeoning area of Fourth Amendment doctrine concerning the circumstances in which police officers can reasonably employ deadly force.

IV

The Court's opinion sweeps broadly to adopt an entirely new standard for the constitutionality of the use of deadly force to apprehend fleeing felons. Thus, the Court "lightly brushe[s] aside," *Payton* v. *New York, supra,* at 600, a longstanding police practice that predates the Fourth Amendment and continues to receive the approval of nearly half of the state legislatures. I cannot accept the majority's creation of a constitutional right to flight for burglary suspects seeking to avoid capture at the scene of the crime. Whatever the constitutional limits on police use of deadly force in order to apprehend a fleeing felon, I do not believe they are exceeded in a case in which a police officer has probable cause to arrest a suspect at the scene of a residential burglary, orders the suspect to halt, and then fires his weapon as a last resort to prevent the suspect's escape into the night. I respectfully dissent.

NOTES

1. The owner of the house testified that no lights were on in the house, but that a back door light was on. Record 160. Officer Hymon, though uncertain, stated in his deposition that there were lights on in the house. *Id.,* at 209.

2. In fact, Garner, an eighth-grader, was 15. He was 5′4″ tall and weighed somewhere around 100 or 110 pounds. App. to Pet. for Cert. A5.

3. When asked at trial why he fired, Hymon stated:

"Well, first of all it was apparent to me from the little bit that I knew about the area at the time that he was going to get away because, number 1, I couldn't get to him. My partner then couldn't find where he was because, you know, he was late coming around. He didn't know where I was talking about. I couldn't get to him because of the fence here, I couldn't have jumped this fence and come up, consequently jumped this fence and caught him before he got away because he was already up on the fence, just one leap and he was already over the fence, and so there is no way that I could have caught him." App. 52.

He also stated that the area beyond the fence was dark, that he could not have gotten over the fence easily because he was carrying a lot of equipment and wearing heavy boots, and that Garner, being younger and more energetic, could have outrun him. *Id.*, at 53-54.

4. Garner had rummaged through one room in the house, in which, in the words of the owner, "[a]ll the stuff was out on the floors, all the drawers was pulled out, and stuff was scattered all over." *Id.*, at 34. The owner testified that his valuables were untouched but that, in addition to the purse and the 10 dollars, one of his wife's rings was missing. The ring was not recovered. *Id.*, at 34-35.

5. Although the statute does not say so explicitly, Tennessee law forbids the use of deadly force in the arrest of a misdemeanant. See *Johnson* v. *State*, 173 Tenn. 134, 114 S. W. 2d 819 (1938).

6. "The right of the people to be secure in their persons ... against unreasonable searches and seizures, shall not be violated...." U.S. Const., Amdt. 4.

7. The Court of Appeals concluded that the rule set out in the Model Penal Code "accurately states Fourth Amendment limitations on the use of deadly force against fleeing felons." 710 F. 2d, at 247. The relevant portion of the Model Penal Code provides:

"The use of deadly force is not justifiable ... unless (i) the arrest is for a felony; and (ii) the person effecting the arrest is authorized to act as a peace officer or is assisting a person whom he believes to be authorized to act as a peace officer; and (iii) the actor believes that the force employed creates no substantial risk of injury to innocent persons; and (iv) the actor believes that (1) the crime for which the arrest is made involved conduct including the use or threatened use of deadly force; or (2) there is a substantial risk that the person to be arrested will cause death or serious bodily harm if his apprehension is delayed." American Law Institute, Model Penal Code § 3.07(2)(b) (Proposed Official Draft 1962).

The court also found that "[a]n analysis of the facts of this case under the Due Process Clause" required the same result, because the statute was not narrowly drawn to further a compelling state interest. 710 F. 2d, at 246-247. The court considered the generalized interest in effective law enforcement sufficiently compelling only when the suspect is dangerous. Finally, the court held, relying on

Owen v. *City of Independence* 445 U.S. 622 (1980), that the city was not immune.

8. The dissent emphasizes that subsequent investigation cannot replace immediate apprehension. We recognize that this is so, see n. 13, *infra;* indeed, that is the reason why there is any dispute. If subsequent arrest were assured, no one would argue that use of deadly force was justified. Thus, we proceed on the assumption that subsequent arrest is not likely. Nonetheless, it should be remembered that failure to apprehend at the scene does not necessarily mean that the suspect will never be caught.

In lamenting the inadequacy of later investigation, the dissent relies on the report of the President's Commission on Law Enforcement and Administration of Justice. It is worth noting that, notwithstanding its awareness of this problem, the Commission itself proposed a policy for use of deadly force arguably even more stringent than the formulation we adopt today. See President's Commission on Law Enforcement and Administration of Justice, Task Force Report: The Police 189 (1967). The Commission proposed that deadly force be used only to apprehend "perpetrators who, in the course of their crime threatened the use of deadly force, or if the officer believes there is a substantial risk that the person whose arrest is sought will cause death or serious bodily harm if his apprehension is delayed." In addition, the officer would have "to know, as a virtual certainty, that the suspect committed an offense for which the use of deadly force is permissible." *Ibid.*

9. We note that the usual manner of deterring illegal conduct—through punishment—has been largely ignored in connection with flight from arrest. Arkansas, for example, specifically excepts flight from arrest from the offense of "obstruction of governmental operations." The commentary notes that this "reflects the basic policy judgment that, absent the use of force or violence, a mere attempt to avoid apprehension by a law enforcement officer does not give rise to an independent offense." Ark. Stat. Ann. § 41-2802(3)(a) (1977) and commentary. In the few States that do outlaw flight from an arresting officer, the crime is only a misdemeanor. See, *e. g.*, Ind. Code § 35-44-3-3 (1982). Even forceful resistance, though generally a separate offense, is classified as a misdemeanor. *E. g.*, Ill. Rev. Stat., ch. 38, ¶ 31-1 (1984); Mont. Code Ann. § 45-7-301 (1984); N. H. Rev. Stat. Ann. § 642:2 (Supp. 1983); Ore. Rev. Stat. § 162.315 (1983).

This lenient approach does avoid the anomaly of automatically transforming every fleeing misdemeanant into a fleeing felon—subject, under the common-law rule, to apprehension by deadly force—solely by virtue of his flight. However, it is in real tension with the harsh consequences of flight in cases where deadly force is employed. For example, Tennessee does not outlaw fleeing from arrest. The Memphis City Code does, § 22-34.1 (Supp. 17, 1971), subjecting the offender to a maximum fine of $50, § 1-8 (1967). Thus, Garner's attempted escape subjected him to (a) a $50 fine, and (b) being shot.

10. See Sherman, Reducing Police Gun Use, in Control in the Police Organization 98, 120-123 (M. Punch ed. 1983); Fyfe, Observations on Police Deadly Force, 27 Crime & Delinquency 376, 378-381 (1981); W. Geller & K. Karales, Split-Second Decisions 67 (1981); App. 84 (affidavit of William Bracey, Chief of Patrol, New York City Police Department). See generally Brief for Police Foundation et al. as *Amici Curiae.*

11. The roots of the concept of a "felony" lie not in capital punishment but in forfeiture. 2 F. Pollock & F. Maitland, The History of English Law 465 (2d ed. 1909) (hereinafter Pollock & Maitland). Not all felonies were always punishable by death. See *id.,* at 466-467, n. 3. Nonetheless, the link was profound. Blackstone was able to write: "The idea of felony is indeed so generally connected with that of capital punishment, that we find it hard to separate them; and to this usage the interpretations of the law do now conform. And therefore if a statute makes any new offence felony, the law implies that it shall be punished with death, *viz.* by hanging, as well as with forfeiture...." 4 W. Blackstone, Commentaries *98. See also R. Perkins & R. Boyce, Criminal Law 14-15 (3d ed. 1982); 2 Pollock & Maitland 511.

12. White-collar crime, for example, poses a less significant physical threat than, say, drunken driving. See *Welsh* v. *Wisconsin,* 466 U.S. 740 (1984); *id.,* at 755 (BLACKMUN, J., concurring). See Model Penal Code Comment, at 57.

13. It has been argued that sophisticated techniques of apprehension and increased communication between the police in different jurisdictions have made it more likely that an escapee will be caught than was once the case, and that this change has also reduced the "reasonableness" of the use of deadly force to prevent escape. E. g., Sherman, Execution Without Trial: Police Homicide and the Constitution, 33 Vand. L. Rev. 71, 76 (1980). We are unaware of any data that would permit sensible evaluation of this claim. Current arrest rates are sufficiently low, however, that we have some doubt whether in past centuries the failure to arrest at the scene meant that the police had missed their only chance in a way that is not presently the case. In 1983, 21% of the offenses in the Federal Bureau of

Investigation crime index were cleared by arrest. Federal Bureau of Investigation, Uniform Crime Reports, Crime in the United States 159 (1984). The clearance rate for burglary was 15%. *Ibid.*

14. Ala. Code § 13A-3-27 (1982); Ark. Stat. Ann. § 41-510 (1977); Cal. Penal Code Ann. § 196 (West 1970); Conn. Gen. Stat. § 53a-22 (1972); Fla. Stat. § 776.05 (1983); Idaho Code § 19-610 (1979); Ind. Code § 35-41-3-3 (1982); Kan. Stat. Ann. § 21-3215 (1981); Miss. Code Ann. § 97-3-15(d) (Supp. 1984); Mo. Rev. Stat. § 563.046 (1979); Nev. Rev. Stat. § 200.140 (1983); N. M. Stat. Ann. § 30-2-6 (1984); Okla. Stat., Tit. 21, § 732 (1981); R. I. Gen. Laws § 12-7-9 (1981); S. D. Codified Laws §§ 22-16-32, 22-16-33 (1979); Tenn. Code Ann. § 40-7-108 (1982); Wash. Rev. Code § 9A.16.040(3) (1977). Oregon limits use of deadly force to violent felons, but also allows its use against any felon if "necessary." Ore. Rev. Stat. § 161.239 (1983). Wisconsin's statute is ambiguous, but should probably be added to this list. Wis. Stat. § 939.45(4) (1981-1982) (officer may use force necessary for "a reasonable accomplishment of a lawful arrest"). But see *Clark* v. *Ziedonis,* 368 F. Supp. 544 (ED Wis. 1973), aff'd on other grounds, 513 F. 2d 79 (CA7 1975).

15. In California, the police may use deadly force to arrest only if the crime for which the arrest is sought was "a forcible and atrocious one which threatens death or serious bodily harm," or there is a substantial risk that the person whose arrest is sought will cause death or serious bodily harm if apprehension is delayed. *Kortum* v. *Alkire,* 69 Cal. App. 3d 325, 333, 138 Cal. Rptr. 26, 30-31 (1977). See also *People* v. *Ceballos,* 12 Cal. 3d 470, 476-484, 526 P. 2d 241, 245-250 (1974); *Long Beach Police Officers Assn.* v. *Long Beach,* 61 Cal. App. 3d 364, 373-374, 132 Cal. Rptr. 348, 353-354 (1976). In Indiana, deadly force may be used only to prevent injury, the imminent danger of injury or force, or the threat of force. It is not permitted simply to prevent escape. *Rose* v. *State,* 431 N. E. 2d 521 (Ind. App. 1982).

16. These are Michigan, Ohio, Virginia, and West Virginia. *Werner* v. *Hartfelder,* 113 Mich. App. 747, 318 N. W. 2d 825 (1982); *State* v. *Foster,* 60 Ohio Misc. 46, 59-66, 396 N. E. 2d 246, 255-258 (Com. Pl. 1979) (citing cases); *Berry* v. *Hamman,* 203 Va. 596, 125 S. E. 2d 851 (1962); *Thompson* v. *Norfolk & W. R. Co.,* 116 W. Va. 705, 711-712, 182 S. E. 880, 883-884 (1935).

17. Haw. Rev. Stat. § 703-307 (1976); Neb. Rev. Stat. § 28-1412 (1979). Massachusetts probably belongs in this category. Though it once rejected distinctions between felonies, *Uraneck* v. *Lima,* 359 Mass. 749, 750, 269 N. E. 2d 670, 671 (1971), it has since adopted the Model Penal Code limitations with regard to private citizens, *Commonwealth* v. *Klein,* 372 Mass.

823, 363 N. E. 2d 1313 (1977), and seems to have extended that decision to police officers, *Julian* v. *Randazzo*, 380 Mass. 391, 403 N. E. 2d 931 (1980).

18. Alaska Stat. Ann. § 11.81.370(a) (1983); Ariz. Rev. Stat. Ann. § 13-410 (1978); Colo. Rev. Stat. § 18-1-707 (1978); Del. Code Ann., Tit. 11, § 467 (1979) (felony involving physical force *and* a substantial risk that the suspect will cause death or serious bodily injury *or* will never be recaptured); Ga. Code § 16-3-21(a) (1984); Ill. Rev. Stat., ch. 38, ¶ 7-5 (1984); Iowa Code § 804.8 (1983) (suspect has used or threatened deadly force in commission of a felony, or would use deadly force if not caught); Ky. Rev. Stat. § 503.090 (1984) (suspect committed felony involving use or threat of physical force likely to cause death or serious injury, *and* is likely to endanger life unless apprehended without delay); Me. Rev. Stat. Ann., Tit. 17-A, § 107 (1983) (commentary notes that deadly force may be used only "where the person to be arrested poses a threat to human life"); Minn. Stat. § 609.066 (1984); N. H. Rev. Stat. Ann. § 627.5(II) (Supp. 1983); N. J. Stat. Ann. § 2C-3-7 (West 1982); N. Y. Penal Law § 35.30 (McKinney Supp. 1984-1985); N. C. Gen. Stat. § 15A-401 (1983); N. D. Cent. Code § 12.1-05-07.2.d (1976); 18 Pa. Cons. Stat. § 508 (1982); Tex. Penal Code Ann. § 9.51(c) (1974); Utah Code Ann. § 76-2-404 (1978).

19. See La. Rev. Stat. Ann. § 14:20(2) (West 1974); Vt. Stat. Ann., Tit. 13, § 2305 (1974 and Supp. 1984). A Federal District Court has interpreted the Louisiana statute to limit the use of deadly force against fleeing suspects to situations where "life itself is endangered or great bodily harm is threatened." *Sauls* v. *Hutto*, 304 F. Supp. 124, 132 (ED La. 1969).

20. These are Maryland, Montana, South Carolina, and Wyoming. A Maryland appellate court has indicated, however, that deadly force may not be used against a felon who "was in the process of fleeing and, at the time, presented no immediate danger to

...anyone...." *Giant Food, Inc.* v. *Scherry,* 51 Md. App. 586, 589, 596, 444 A. 2d 483, 486, 489 (1982).

21. In adopting its current statute in 1979, for example, Alabama expressly chose the common-law rule over more restrictive provisions. Ala. Code § 13A-3-27, Commentary, pp. 67-68 (1982). Missouri likewise considered but rejected a proposal akin to the Model Penal Code rule. See *Mattis* v. *Schnarr,* 547 F. 2d 1007, 1022 (CA8 1976) (Gibson, C. J., dissenting), vacated as moot *sub nom. Ashcroft* v. *Mattis,* 431 U.S. 171 (1977). Idaho, whose current statute codifies the common-law rule, adopted the Model Penal Code in 1971, but abandoned it in 1972.

22. In a recent report, the Department of Corrections of the District of Columbia also noted that "there is nothing inherently dangerous or violent about the offense," which is a crime against property. D. C. Department of Corrections, Prisoner Screening Project 2 (1985).

23. The dissent points out that three-fifths of all rapes in the home, three-fifths of all home robberies, and about a third of home assaults are committed by burglars. *Post,* at 26-27. These figures mean only that if one knows that a suspect committed a rape in the home, there is a good chance that the suspect is also a burglar. That has nothing to do with the question here, which is whether the fact that someone has committed a burglary indicates that he has committed, or might commit, a violent crime.

The dissent also points out that this 3.8% adds up to 2.8 million violent crimes over a 10-year period, as if to imply that today's holding will let loose 2.8 million violent burglars. The relevant universe is, of course, far smaller. At issue is only that tiny fraction of cases where violence has taken place and an officer who has no other means of apprehending the suspect is unaware of its occurrence.

Study Questions

1. According to the Court, what constitutes an officer seizing a person? What does this have to do with the use of deadly force?

2. What are the "competing interests" to be balanced in applying the Fourth Amendment? Does the Court minority agree with the majority that there are competing interests in *Garner*?

3. Precisely what is the Court's conclusion regarding the use of force against felony suspects? On what premises is this conclusion based? Do you think the Court has drawn a valid conclusion on the basis of the premises? Why?

4. Why does the Court minority believe that Garner's Fourth Amendment rights were not violated? Is this primarily a factual dispute or a philosophical one, in your judgment? How would the majority respond to this counterargument?

The Victimization of Prisoners by Staff Members

LEE H. BOWKER

THE DOCUMENTATION ON STAFF-PRISONER victimization in America's prisons is extensive but shallow. Most of this material describes victimization in prisons for men, with a smaller amount of documentation for institutions containing delinquent boys and very little information on staff-prisoner victimization in institutions for females. The treatment of the subject is superficial in that incidents tend to be mentioned only in passing (or as part of a polemical piece of writing), and they are not presented or analyzed in any great detail. Like other prison victimization reports, they tend to be recorded factually and not related to any general theoretical framework. Another general problem with documentation on staff-prisoner victimization is that the quality of the reporting of incidents is often difficult to determine. Reports are almost always limited to the views of one of the participants or observers, with no corroboration from others. Even when reports are written by social scientists, they usually consist of second and third-person accounts derived from interviews rather than direct observation by the scientists.

Material on the victimization of prisoners by staff members is also beset by definitional problems. How does one separate the victimization of prisoners by individual staff members from the "fair" application of institutional policies by correctional officers?

This problem is particularly severe when dealing with historical material for which institutional standards of appropriate treatment are not available. Victimization is generally thought of as consisting of acts committed by individuals and groups that go beyond the conditions imposed upon prisoners by official institutional policies and state laws. In the modern prison, this definitional problem is not such a serious one because the official policies of the state and federal correctional systems are generally quite humane. Excessively victimizing behavior by staff members is usually clearly against the regulations of the institution. This is not the same as saying that offenders against these institutional regulations will be punished. In many correctional systems, it is probable that a careful staff member can engage in extensive victimizing behavior toward prisoners before he or she will be officially reprimanded for it. Even then, it is extremely unlikely that a staff member will ever be terminated for such behavior.

Definitional problems still exist in those jurisdictions that continue to use physically harsh means of punishing prisoners, and also in any correctional institutions where "goon squads" are used. The goon squads are groups of physically powerful correctional officers who "enjoy a good fight" and who are called upon to rush to any area of the prison where it is felt that muscle power will restore the status quo. If a prisoner is ripping up things in his cell and refuses to be quiet, the goon squad may be called and three or four of these correctional officers will forcibly quiet him, administering a number of damaging blows to the head and body. If there is a fight between two prisoners, the goon squad may break it up. Should a prisoner refuse to report to the hospital when he is ordered to do so, he may be dragged from his cell and deposited in the hospital waiting room. Mentally ill prisoners who are acting out are almost always initially dealt with by goon squads

Lee H. Bowker, Prison Victimization. *(New York: Elsevier Science Publishing Co., Inc., 1980), Ch. 7, pp. 101–127. Reprinted by permission of the author.*

rather than by qualified therapeutic personnel or even by orderlies under the direction of such personnel. It is difficult to draw the line between the necessary application of force where human life or the social order are extensively threatened, and the misuse of violence by goon squad members.

Aside from goon squads and the few states that officially permit physically harsh means of punishment, we can define the behavior of a correctional officer as victimizing or nonvictimizing by comparing questionable incidents with the body of official regulations and policies that is usually summarized in a handbook distributed to all correctional officers. If the behavior goes beyond the regulations and policies, then it is victimizing. If it does not, then it is difficult to accuse the officer of being an aggressor in all but the most extreme cases.

However clear we may be able to make the definition of victimization by line staff members, there is no way to create a similarly precise definition for wardens and other top-level correctional administrators. When they implement a policy or regulation that is victimizing or potentially victimizing, they must take responsibility for having created a definition of the situation within which correctional officers may carry out what amounts to victimizing behavior as they perform their duties in conformance with institutional regulations. Few of these regulations are proclaimed by correctional administrators simply out of sadism. Instead, these administrators balance one evil against another, and decide to implement a potentially victimizing regulation because they feel that this regultion will solve more problems than it creates. This means that, except for cases at the periphery of reasonable judgment, we cannot easily judge an administrative action to be victimizing unless we know the rationale behind that action and have some objective set of data about conditions in the institution that informed the administrative decision. Since this kind of information is almost never available, we are left with a murky situation in which administrative responsibility for prisoner victimization

can usually be assigned in only the most tentative fashion. With these qualifications in mind, we will proceed to examine the documentation on staff-prisoner victimization in correctional institutions.

Physical Victimization

However unpleasant prisons may be today, historical materials make it clear that they were infinitely worse in the past. Clemmer tells us that it was once common for correctional officers to assault prisoners with clubs and their fists, but by the late 1930s, perhaps in response to a new state law, the frequency of these attacks had declined to the point at which they occurred "only rarely."[1] Conley shows how the emphasis on custody and industrial productivity encouraged brutality and corruption in the Oklahoma prison system from the early 1900s through the 1960s. In addition to the usual beatings, officers used deliberate tortures such as forcing the men to eat in the hot sun during the summer when shade was nearby and handcuffing prisoners to the bars in their cells (with knotted rags in their mouths) so that when their legs collapsed, their body was suspended only by the handcuffs. When wardens ordered that physical victimization of prisoners by correctional officers be suspended, these officers adapted by moving to techniques of psychological victimization.[2]

The decrease in brutality by correctional officers that Clemmer describes as having occurred in Illinois in the 1930s did not reach some southern prisons until the 1970s. The mistreatment of prisoners in the Arkansas prison system has been documented in books such as *Killing Time, Life in the Arkansas Penitentiary*[3] and *Inside Prison U.S.A.*[4] The latter includes a description of the infamous "Tucker telephone," as well as blow-by-blow accounts of beatings. In the Tucker telephone, a naked prisoner was strapped to a table and electrodes were attached to his big toe and his penis. Electrical charges were then sent through his body which, in "long distance calls," were timed to cease just before the prisoner became unconscious. Murton and Hyams state that in some cases, "the sustained current not only caused the inmate to lose consciousness but resulted in irreparable damage to his testicles. Some men were literally driven out of their minds."[5] In testimony under oath, a 15-year-old prisoner accused the superintendent of an Arkansas institution of kicking and hitting him in the back and stomach while another staff member held him on the ground. The superintendent did not confirm this allegation, but he admitted driving a truck at 40 miles per hour with three prisoners draped over the hood and then jamming on the brakes to catapult them to the ground as a unique method of punishment.[6]

Reports from Louisiana,[7] Mississippi,[8] Virginia[9] and Florida[10] confirm that the habitual mistreatment of prisoners is not limited to the Arkansas prison system. The brutalization of prisoners by correctional officers outside of the south seems to be less extensive and also less statistically innovative. Some of the incidents reported from northern prisons make little sense, such as the prisoner who was killed by the use of chemical gassing weapons when he was locked in a solitary security cell[11] or the three prisoners who were handcuffed to overhead pipes as punishment for being too "noisy" during sleeping hours.[12] Most of the incidents reported from these facilities seem to be associated with unusual occurrences such as prison riots, protests and punitive transfers. These incidents all involve some sort of prisoner challenge to the authority of prison staff members, and the challenge is sometimes met with violence as a way of reestablishing administrative authority. For example, prisoners being transferred from one Ohio penitentiary to another after a period of considerable unrest alleged severe guard brutality. One prisoner asserted that he was handcuffed and chained, taken into a bus, and then beaten on the head by a correctional officer with a blackjack and left unconscious. Another prisoner alleged that while handcuffed, he was dragged into the bus where he suffered kicks and other blows about the back, legs, hips and groin. The worst incident described by the prisoners

told the story of a prisoner who first had Mace sprayed in his face while he was still in his cell, and then was beaten with chains, blackjacks and fists by five correctional officers who then spit on him, slammed his head against the cell door, and took him to the bus, where he was subjected to further assault.[13]

When 500 prisoners at the Pendleton Reformatory in Indiana refused to return to their cells on a winter day in 1972, the correctional officers used tear gas and shotguns to force them back. None of the prisoners was shot because the shotguns were discharged into the air rather than at the prisoners. This change in policy was probably due to an earlier incident at the Reformatory in which "46 men [prisoners] were wounded, many critically, from shots in the head, in the back, through the chest, in the legs, feet, thigh, through the groin, in the side—in fact some who tried to throw up their hands in the traditional gesture of surrender had their hands shattered and are minus fingers."[14] In a related incident, a group of black prisoners refused to return to their cells, and one black prisoner raised his hand in the black power salute. A guard was heard to say, "That one is mine!" and the young man was fatally riddled with five bullets. Testimony before the United States Senate later revealed that approximately 50% of the correctional officers involved in the incident belonged to the Ku Klux Klan.[15]

Excessive violence used during a prisoner altercation may not be legitimate, but it is understandable. There are few parents who have not gone too far in punishing their children when they were angry. A more serious problem occurs when prisoners are brutalized for an extended period of time after a riot as punishment for having participated. A classic example of this occurred after the disaster at Attica in New York. Correctional administrators, in violation of a court order, refused to admit a group of doctors and lawyers to the prison as observers on the pretext that they needed to have an opportunity to assess the prison's condition. During the time that the observers were deliberately excluded, extreme violence occurred, involving the vanquished prisoners. The Second Circuit Federal Court of Appeals finally issued an injunction against further reprisals and physical abuse and found that in the four days beginning with the recapture of Attica, the state troopers and correctional personnel struck, prodded and assaulted injured prisoners, some of whom were on stretchers. Other prisoners were stripped naked and then forced to run between lines of correctional officers who beat them with clubs, spat upon them, burned them with matches, and poked them in the genitals—among other things.[16]

The Attica reprisals are well documented, but Toch is generally skeptical of other prisoner reports of organized brutality by correctional officers. He takes a different approach, looking at official records of officer-prisoner violence in New York State for the year 1973. A total of 386 incidents were recorded in the official file, and these involved 547 prisoners and 1,288 employees. The relative number of officers and prisoners in these incidents is meaningful in itself in that it indicates the more than two-to-one odds that prisoners face in these altercations. One might argue that with odds such as these, there is little excuse for causing excessive injury to the prisoners. In fact, there were no injuries at all in one-third of the reports. The most common action cited was a "hold," which included such maneuvers as half-nelsons, pulls and choking. Toch believes that correctional officer violence is routinely justified by formulas similar to those used to justify police brutality, and that it is really based on correctional officer subcultural norms favoring violence against prisoners. These norms develop because of the pervasive fear of prisoners that is part of the correctional officer subculture. This same subcultural phenomenon makes it almost impossible to convince a correctional officer to testify against one of his fellow employees, so corroborating testimony is rarely obtained in investigations of officer brutality, except from other prisoners. Toch also links officer violence to official regulations that forbid the forming of meaningful interpersonal relationships between officers and prisoners. Such

regulations leave officers with only naked force as a way of enforcing order and also create what Toch characterizes as a "trench warfare climate" in prisons.[17] Whether one concentrates on the day-to-day routinized violence or the extreme brutality that is sometimes associated with prison disturbances and transfers, the conclusion is the same. It is that although most correctional officers in most prisons do not engage in any form of brutality and are only concerned with defending themselves against attack, there are enough officers who have values and beliefs that favor brutality and enough incidents that seem to require some sort of a show of force by officers so that there is a steady stream of minor unnecessary or excessive acts of violence in America's prisons, punctuated by occasional acts in which officers go far beyond any reasonable standard of the application of necessary force.

If an officer who favors the brutalization of prisoners is careful, he or she can limit the application of excessive force to incidents that fit the prison's definition of the appropriate use of force to maintain prison discipline or prevent escapes. Complaints lodged against such a correctional officer will invariably be dismissed by the warden who will rule that the violence was appropriately applied within institutional regulations. In fact, it may be claimed that had officers not used violence in the incident, they would have been delinquent in the performance of stated duties and subject to dismissal. This kind of rationale also makes it difficult for a prisoner to receive a fair hearing in court, where the warden's testimony carries considerable weight with judges and juries. As an example of this, I was close to a case in which a mentally ill prisoner was climbing a fence separating two prison yards and was fatally shot in the head by a prison officer who had commanded him to stop. The officer, who was stationed in a tower, probably was unaware of the mental condition of the prisoner and might not have taken that into account in any case. More importantly, he did not need to shoot the prisoner, as going from one prison yard to another does not constitute a risk of escape. Since the prisoner was unarmed, a shot in the leg rather than the head would have been more than sufficient even had he been climbing a fence on the boundary of the prison compound. The warden chose to ignore these arguments and immediately supported the action of the officer, saying that it was appropriate and required by institutional regulations. The local officials outside of the prison also accepted the judgment of the warden and declined prosecution in the case. There is nothing more serious than murder, and if this can be so easily justified by correctional officials one can appreciate the wide variety of possibly victimizing acts that are similarly justified annually in the United States.

THE INVOLVEMENT OF CORRECTIONAL OFFICERS IN SEXUAL AGGRESSION

There are three ways that correctional officers can be involved in sexual aggression against prisoners. The first is to carry out the aggression themselves. This is occasionally hinted at, but has been well documented only for isolated cases that involved female and adolescent male victims. The second type of involvement is for correctional officers to permit a sexual attack in their presence and then to enjoy the spectacle. Although occasionally mentioned in passing, the best example of this sort of behavior in the literature comes from an institution for the retarded rather than from a prison.[18] The final form of correctional officer involvement in sexual attacks on prisoners is passive participation by deliberately failing to carry out one's custodial responsibilities. In this behavior, the officer does not adequately control an area or deliberately stays away from a site in which it is known that sexual assaults regularly occur. Although seemingly less severe than the first two forms of staff participation in sexual assaults, this third type is the most important because its occurrence is much more common than the first two types. As Sagarin and MacNamara conclude, prison rapes hardly seem possible "without the connivance, or at least deliberate inattention, of prison authorities.[19]

Cole[20] and Wooden[21] cite numerous examples of sexual assaults on juveniles by correctional officers. Boys and girls may be forced to submit to sexual advances by threats of violence or they may be manipulated to cooperate by promises of favors. Bartollas et al. quote a youthful prisoner:

> He had intercourse with me about every two weeks. I did not want to do it, but he talked about getting me out of [here] faster and I wanted to get out because I had been here a long time. I think the reason I did it was I just came back from AWOL and I thought I had a long time to go so I thought I would get out of here.[22]

These authors also show how a staff member can subtly approach the topic of participation in sexual relations with a prisoner so that they can not be quoted as having made a direct overture or threat. Another prisoner that they interviewed told them how a staff member began to talk to him about people they knew in common and then switched to the prisoner's homosexuality in what appeared at first to be an attempt to help him. Then the staff member began to talk about the sexual acts that he enjoyed himself and linked that to sexual acts that the prisoner enjoyed. At this point it was clear to the prisoner that he was being manipulated into committing homosexual acts although the staff member had not made a specific quotable overture.[23]

The occasional reports of sexual assaults carried out against girls and women by jailers, sheriffs, deputies and other correctional officials[24] were taken more seriously after the national publicity given to the case of Joanne Little.[25] Like many other county jails and understaffed correctional facilities, the Beaufort County Jail in North Carolina employed no female staff members to care for its occasional female prisoners. The autopsy report of the Beaufort County Medical Examiner made clear that the 62-year-old jailer had been killed by Ms. Little while he was forcing her to engage in sexual relations with him. Little stabbed him seven times with an icepick and then escaped, only to turn herself in to the police at a later date.[26] It is unlikely that Little was the first prisoner to be sexually approached by this jailer. Unfortunately, professional standards in rural local jails are so variable and documentation so completely lacking that it is impossible to make even "a ball park estimate" of the national incidence of this form of sexual victimization.

The only documented case of a correctional staff member forcing prisoners to engage in sexual behavior with one another is contained in Cole's book, *Our Children's Keepers*. He quotes a 15-year-old boy as saying that two counselors forced a friend of his to go into another room and have sexual intercourse with a known homosexual prisoner. When the friend refused to do so, he was taken into another room and beaten. The counselors then came out and brought in the homosexual prisoner, following which the two prisoners had sexual relations for the amusement of the counselors. In the words of the observer, "They get a kick out of somebody going through it—then they make fun of him in front of everybody else."[27] We cannot give too much credence to this report in view of the way in which it was obtained. It is included here merely as an example of how such events may occur in correctional institutions.

The contribution to sexual assaults between prisoners that is made by correctional officers who fail to carry out adequately their duties is legendary. There are relatively few prisons that are so poorly constructed and so greatly understaffed that it is absolutely impossible for staff members to keep prisoners under sufficient surveillance to prohibit sexual aggression. When Davis asked 26 correctional employees to take polygraph tests, 25 refused, presumably because they felt they were guilty of failing to carry out their assigned duties in situations that led directly to the sexual assault of prisoners in documented cases. Davis describes sexual assaults that were made possible because the officers in charge did not adequately patrol their areas. It is easy for skeptics to dismiss many of the reports of correctional officer complicity in prisoner sexual assaults, but the kind of documentation provided by Davis convinces us of this complicity beyond the shadow of a doubt. In one incident,

a prisoner was reported as having screamed for over an hour while he was being gang-raped in his cell within hearing distance of a correctional officer who not only ignored the screams but who laughed at the victim afterward. Prisoners who reported this incident passed polygraph examinations while the accused officer refused to take the test.[28]

Extreme examples of officer involvement in inmate sexual behavior include a southern institution in which a prisoner could buy a homosexual partner from a correctional officer or even from the deputy warden[29] and the use of homosexual prisoners as "gifts" from staff members to prisoner leaders who helped them keep the institution quiet.[30] One ex-prisoner claims to have been presented to "an entire wing of the prison, as a bonus to the convicts for their good behavior. In this wing, any prisoner who wanted his services, at any time and for any purposes, was given it; the guards opened doors, passed him from one cell to another, provided lubricants, permitted an orgy of simultaneous oral and anal entry, and even arranged privacy."[31]

It is easy to see why some authors place heavy blame on correctional officers for their contribution to prison sexual assaults.[32] The only objective observer who defends them is Lockwood, who feels that the combination of sexually aggressive prisoners, overcrowded conditions, management and program needs that require prisoners to intermingle, and legal limitations imposed by the courts creates a situation in which the ability of correctional officers to prevent sexual victimization is sharply attenuated.[33]

BRUTALITY IN CHILDREN'S INSTITUTIONS

Professional standards in institutions for delinquent youth appear to be much more variable than professional standards in state correctional systems for adults. Although there are many exemplary institutions in which not even the slightest hint of staff brutality would ever be tolerated, these exist close by other institutions in which a wide range of staff aggression toward prisoners is not only tolerated but encouraged. It is impossible to estimate accurately a national rate of staff-prisoner victimization in juvenile institutions, but the impression one gets from reading the literature is that this form of victimization is probably more prevalent in juvenile institutions than in adult institutions. Cole tells about a staff member in a Louisiana institution who assaulted prisoners with a hosepipe and big sticks. The staff member combined the beatings with economic victimization when he extracted a portion of all the gifts received by prisoners through the mail.[34] Quoting descriptions of beatings derived from accounts collected by James,[35] Chase concludes that there are more American children being mistreated in institutions than in their homes.[36] The severity of this indictment is accentuated by the most recent report on American child abuse, which presents 507,494 incidents of child abuse reported to official agencies in 1977, a reporting rate of 2.3 cases per 1,000 population.[37]

The John Howard Association's report on the Illinois Youth Centers at St. Charles and Geneva provides rare detail on the physical abuse of youngsters by staff members. Of 46 youths between the ages of 14 and 19 whom they interviewed at St. Charles, 23 stated that they had been slapped, kicked, punched, had their arms twisted or were struck with an object by a staff member. About half of the youths stated that they had witnessed staff members committing such acts against other youngsters. Many of the staff members also admitted the use of extensive corporal punishment, and there were several staff members who were consistently named as physical abusers of children. One staff member admitted striking youngsters on different occasions with a stick, a fishing pole and his hands. These situations did not involve the use of necessary restraint to subdue a youth who was attacking a staff member or another youth. Instead, it was a matter of general brutality when staff members were in bad moods.[38] This kind of gratuitous punishment differs in degree, but not in kind, from the vicious brutality suffered by youngsters in reformatories more than a century ago.[39]

Reports of beating of institutionalized children are from all parts of the nation, from the deep south[40] to the relatively well-funded institutions that are found in Massachusetts. A Harvard student posing as a delinquent at a Massachusetts institution observed an incident in which a youngster's hair was used to mop up urine from the floor.[41] Feld showed that staff brutality was higher in custody-oriented institutions than in treatment-oriented institutions. The former institutions were characterized by acts such as choking and physical beatings, whereas the more benign treatment-oriented staff members limited themselves to beatings with a plastic baseball bat and other minor physical punishments.[42]

The most detailed analysis of staff-prisoner victimization in juvenile institutions was carried out by Bartollas et al. in their study of an Ohio reformatory. A number of forms of staff-prisoner victimization at this institution were actually supported by the informal staff normative code, a code analogous to the convict code among the prisoners. The "acceptable" forms of staff exploitation were psychological and social in nature, although physical victimization was not supported by the staff normative code. For example, direct physical brutality was defined as unacceptable when a leader was intoxicated, upset because of a personal problem, using weapons against the youth or deliberately trying to seriously injure a youngster. It was also unacceptable to encourage directly (as opposed to passively) the victimization of one prisoner by another, to aid escapes (which led to increased punishment for the escapee when he was caught), and to sexually exploit the boys for one's own pleasure. The tie-in of homosexual gratification to rewards such as cigarettes, protection from peers, or promise of early release was defined as particularly offensive behavior under the staff normative code and was dealt with informally by staff members whenever a rumor about sexual exploitation was substantiated. Informal sanctions usually led to the resignation of the offending staff member.[43]

Psychological Victimization

We have already mentioned Conley's observation that correctional officers in the Oklahoma State Penitentiary who were temporarily forbidden to physically brutalize prisoners switched to psychological forms of victimization. For example, officers conducting shakedowns would deliberately break open little boxes that contained a prisoner's personal trinkets instead of asking him for the key. They would also harass the prisoners by "making noise in the cell house so they couldn't sleep, refusing personal requests, failing to respond to an inmate's call for help if he was ill or a victim of an assault, and otherwise constantly hounding the individuals."[44] These forms of psychological victimization can be perpetrated on individual prisoners who have been marked for special mistreatment or on all prisoners as a matter of personal policy.

The author once observed the classic example of psychological victimization in which the sergeant placed letters to a prisoner where the prisoner could see them but not reach them, and then claimed that there were no letters for that prisoner. The prisoner became quite agitated as a result and eventually developed considerable paranoia about his mail. In each incident, the officer tormented him throughout the day and then gave him the letters in the evening saying that he had just discovered them. Eventually, the prisoner lost control completely and was cited for a disciplinary infraction, which may well have been the officer's goal in the manipulation. A more elegant form of the game is described by Heise as "The Therapeutic 'No.'" In this game, staff members deliberately say "no" to a prisoner who has come with a legitimate request in an attempt to force an explosive or angry response.[45]

A very sophisticated form of the psychological victimization of prisoners by staff members occurs when correctional officers use their special knowledge of the outside world to heighten prisoner anxieties about their loved ones, their release date or other subjects of paramount importance. An example of this, reported from a women's institution, involved a prisoner whose son was in foster care while she was incarcerated. The officer she worked for would wait until she was within hearing distance and then begin a conversation with a second correctional officer about how commonly foster children were mistreated. These discussions went on endlessly, concentrating on subjects such as starvation, corporal punishment and sexual victimization. The prisoner was not allowed to speak, nor could she report the incidents to the administration. How could she prove that the officers were deliberately practicing psychological victimization against her? These incidents, along with the mishandling of a medical condition by the prison physician, almost agitated her enough to attempt an escape.[46]

Staff members are also privy to another source of potentially victimizing information about prisoners—the data in their central files. Information in these files contains not only the complete criminal records of prisoners but also material from social investigations, institutional reports and other items revealing the most intimate details of their lives—details that are often irrelevant to any criminal prosecution. It is common in some institutions for correctional officers to uncover this material to embarrass prisoners. Homosexual behavior, low-status crimes such as sexual offenses against minors, self-destructive acts and bouts with mental illness are examples of the kinds of subjects that officers sometimes extract from central files to use against prisoners. This method of psychological victimization is not confined to correctional institutions, for Goffman also observed it in a mental hospital.[47] A variation on the game occurs when officers pass on derogatory labels that have been affixed to unlucky prisoners by their colleagues in crime, such as "rat," "snitch," and "punk."[48]

The number of forms that psychological victimization of prisoners by staff members can take is almost limitless. New examples are constantly being reported in the literature or revealed in testimony given in the nation's courts. In Nevada, a warden put a pistol to the neck of a prisoner and said, "Move or I'll kill you," when it was not necessary for him to do so because the deputy warden was already walking the prisoner down the corridor to solitary confinement.[49] An officer in a California penitentiary who had been asked for help by a prisoner who was coughing blood gave him a note that said, "Yell for help when the blood is an inch thick, all over the floor, and don't call before that."[50] It is likely that if the officer had judged the prisoner's condition to be serious, he would have summoned medical help. The psychological victimization in this incident occurs because the officer deliberately pretends that he will never summon help while the prisoner is alive. An injunction was granted in New York State against the assignment of male guards at a women's prison, which occurred as a result of testimony that these officers deliberately came into shower rooms to watch the women as they were naked and also deliberately watched them when they were on the toilet.[51] In one of the most gruesome incidents revealed in a Senate subcommittee hearing, an Ohio correctional officer collected pet cats from the prisoners and then "dashed their brains out in sight of the whole prison population."[52] Being deprived of their children, prisoners often invest fatherly and motherly emotion in their pets so that this act of brutality symbolized multiple infanticide to many of the prisoners who could not avoid seeing it.

In the history of prisons in America, groups of prisoners sometimes mutilated themselves in protest against mistreatment by staff members. The mass cuttings of heel tendons described by Keve[53] are no longer common on the American prison scene. Likewise, the self-mutilations accomplished by Peruvian prisoners as a result of severe beatings administered by criminal justice personnel are not replicated in this country.[54] Today, self-destructive behavior by prisoners is much more likely to be an individual act than an act of group protest. Mattick is probably correct that self-destructive behavior is declining as a percentage of all prison violence.[55] The highest rate of self-mutilations known in contemporary American prisons occurred at Angola Prison in Louisiana in a ten-month period in 1974. A total of 107 self-mutilation cases were heard by the disciplinary board during this period, an average of about ten per month.[56] The despair felt by prisoners who damaged themselves has been well documented in the literature.[57] This has been linked to physical victimization by correctional officers,[58] but there has been little recognition in the literature of the ways in which psychological victimization by prison officers can also contribute to suicidal and other self-damaging acts. One occasionally hears comments to the effect that psychologically disturbed and inadequate prisoners are more likely to be "picked on" by staff members than well-adjusted, highly prisonized inmates. In institutions where this is true, the deliberate mistreatment by staff members of prisoners who are already highly disturbed may be sufficient to precipitate self-destructive incidents.

Occasions in which prisoners harm themselves primarily because of psychological victimization by correctional officers are probably relatively rare in the United States. A more common contribution to prisoner self-destruction that is made by correctional officers is the lack of sensitivity to the needs of prisoners who are approaching potentially self-destructive personal crises. Because correctional officers are usually poorly trained in interpersonal relations, most of them neither recognize nor are sufficiently motivated to assist prisoners undergoing psychological breakdowns. For every officer who sadistically torments such prisoners, there are hundreds who fail to give adequate support or to call in qualified medical personnel in a situation that is gradually deteriorating. This is not a matter of victimization at the individual level but is instead a reflection of policies and funding priorities in state legislatures and other funding bodies.

Economic Victimization

Prison officers and other staff members in correctional institutions may be involved in economic victimization of a very direct sort, such as eating a prisoner's food or wearing his or her clothing. Most institutions guard against this sort of direct economic victimization. It is probably more common for prison officers to victimize economically their charges indirectly by being involved in contraband operations and loansharking. For example, the director of the Omaha Urban League alleged in 1974 that prison officers were regularly bringing in drugs and reaping profits from the drug traffic in a midwestern penitentiary.[59] The warden of the federal penitentiary in Atlanta said that nothing could be done to halt the alleged staff corruption in that institution unless the culprits were actually caught in the act. At the same hearing, one of his prisoners testified that 95% of all marijuana in the prison was provided by staff members.[60] A Tampa newspaper, investigating the homosexual attack and murder of a 19-year-old prisoner, mentioned that the prisoners who assaulted the victim were middlemen for a loan racket run by the officer who was supervising the area in which the prisoner was raped and killed. Testimony revealed that the victim had been subjected to sexual assault before his death as punishment because the correctional officer believed that he was "snitching" on him for selling ham from the kitchen for private profit. In addition to the assault by prisoners, it was alleged that the victim had been beaten by several correctional officers four days before he died and had begged to be placed in the isolation unit but that his request was denied.[61]

When a staff member is involved in a sub rosa economic system of the prison, it is possible to "burn" prisoners with impunity because they cannot possibly report the crime to the administration without revealing their own involvement in the illegal activity. If the prisoner is a member of a powerful gang or clique, pressures can be brought to bear on correctional officers to keep them from this sort of economic victimization. On the other hand, sophisticated officers are careful never to burn any prisoner who has this kind of backing. Instead, they victimize only the isolated prisoners who enlist their help in sub rosa economic transactions. Such a prisoner, who

gives an officer some money to smuggle out of the prison for his wife, may find out that the officer has pocketed it instead of delivering it, or perhaps that a portion of it was subtracted as an additional payment for delivery beyond the amount already agreed upon.

The definition of victimization becomes contorted out of all recognition in the case of the officer who regularly participates in sub rosa smuggling activities with prisoners but who keeps his record clean by occasionally reporting unsophisticated prisoners to the administration for attempting to bribe him. Victimization in this instance consists of enforcing the regulations that the officer should have been enforcing in a setting in which the regulations were habitually ignored. One officer who allegedly charged up to $300 a trip to "pack" contraband in and out of the prison made enough money over his career to establish an independent business in the free community. This "horse" (a slang term for prison officers who smuggle contraband into the institution) was probably able "to stay in business" for such a long time because he only "packed" for powerful, trustworthy prisoners and systematically wrote infraction tickets on every other prisoner who approached him.

We cannot leave the subject of the economic victimization of prisoners by staff members without mentioning drug testing, industrial victimization and the suppression of prisoner unions. These topics do not fit our definition of victimization because they refer to institutional policy and, in some cases, enacted law. Many prison industries are operated under less than safe conditions in order to maximize productivity. Once a major problem in America's prisons,[62] this lingers on today in industrial programs that continue to use equipment that is antiquated and unsafe.

The testing of dangerous drugs by prisoners, which has been rapidly declining in recent years, is another form of institutional victimization that is outside our technical definition. Beginning with a 1904 study of bubonic plague by Colonel R. P. Strong,[63] prisoners were paid a pittance (if anything) but offered minor administrative favors in return for participating in highly dangerous experiments. Even these small rewards were more than sufficient motivation to recruit prisoners for medical and drug-testing experiments because the prisoners were artificially economically disadvantaged by policies and laws that forbade them to be paid more than a few cents an hour. Was it really necessary to apply radiation to the testicles of prisoners so that later they would become sterile? Prisoners, whom I know personally, were involved in such an experiment, claiming they were not adequately informed of the consequences at the time that they agreed to participate. Some of them would now like to lead normal married lives and have children, but their criminal records largely rule out adoption and their participation in the radiation experiment leaves them unable to conceive their own children. In an excellent treatment of the subject, Meyer shows how the pharmaceutical companies and the general public have benefited over the years from low-cost prisoner experiments. The victimizing nature of these experiments has been given credence by their abolition under contemporary federal standards for drug-testing experiments.[64]

The substandard wages that are generally paid to men and women working in prison industries are also economically victimizing, although such wages do not constitute victimization under our definition of the subject. However, technical victimization creeps into this situation when prisoners attempt to organize unions, following the model that is accepted in free society, and they are prevented from doing so when administrative actions such as punitive transfers, punitive segregation and unjust parole board "flops" (parole board decisions to increase sentence length) are used to suppress the formation of prisoner unions.[65] Although prisoner unions are permitted in some European nations (such as KRUM, organized in Sweden in 1966), the only way for prisoner unions to survive in the United States is if they have a power base outside of the institution. The San Francisco-based Prisoners' Union, which was co-founded by John Irwin, is an example of this kind of an organization. Whether it will have any significant national impact remains to be seen.

Social Victimization

The most blatant form of social victimization carried out against prisoners by correctional officers is racial discrimination. Two other forms of victimization that are essentially social in nature are the nonperformance of stated duties and the deliberate handing over of supervisory responsibilities to prisoners who then use their staff-sanctioned power to abuse others. Reports of correctional officer discrimination against black prisoners abound in the literature.[66] These reports include evidence of discrimination in job assignments[67] and disciplinary hearings.[68] Racial discrimination becomes mixed with religious discrimination when groups such as the Black Muslims are denied their religious rights.[69] Carroll describes an incident in which kissing between a prisoner and a visitor, which was officially prohibited but always permitted for uniracial couples, resulted in the abrupt termination of a visit when a black prisoner kissed his white visitor.[70] Carroll also observed correctional officers admitting white visitors to inmate organizations without searches, but systematically searching visitors to black organizations and conducting bodily postvisit searches of black prisoners three times as often as similar searches of white prisoners.[71] All of these reports pale in comparison with the allegations of virulent racism by correctional officers at Soledad prison in California.[72]

When a staff member turns over supervisory activities to a prisoner, all of the other prisoners in that jurisdiction are subject to a potential victimization. We have already seen some examples of sexual victimization that occurred because of this form of staff behavior. I cite only two additional examples here. Testimony in a federal court alleged that a prisoner in a Texas institution had been set up as a "prison enforcer" for which he was rewarded with special privileges such as a homosexual in his cell to service his sexual needs and the authority to assault other prisoners at any time in the service of maintaining institutional order.[73] The other example comes from the juvenile institution studied by Bartollas et al. Staff members in this institution often catered to the needs of "heavy" (physically powerful) prisoners in return for their cooperation in running the reformatory. These favored prisoners were permitted to unlock the doors of their fellow prisoners with the staff's keys. This gave the "heavies" license to victimize other prisoners in return for their allegiance to staff members.[74]

The social victimization of prisoners as a class of individuals occurs when correctional officers and other staff members neglect to carry out their stated duties. Bartollas and his associates described staff members who stayed in their offices, perhaps taking naps, thus leaving the weaker prisoners open to all sorts of victimization by their peers.

Other staff members discriminated directly against scapegoats by giving them all the menial work details in the cottage, seldom talking with them, or permitted other youths to victimize them openly in the presence of staff.[75]

Prisoners are beginning to realize that they can file legal actions against correctional staff members who refrain from carrying out their duties in ways that lead to prisoner victimization. A recent issue of Corrections Compendium reports several such cases filed under 42 U.S.C. 1983. One of the complainants had suffered sexual abuse and alleged a history of incidents over a period of two years because of inadequate supervision by institutional staff members. The other alleged that one prisoner had been killed and another injured by a fire that broke out in an Arkansas jail while the sheriff had gone to a basketball game, leaving the jail unattended.[76] There is increasing recognition that such actions by correctional staff members constitute a serious form of victimization.

Two theoretical explanations for the victimization of prisoners by correctional officers have been advanced in the literature. These are the total institutions theory and the role theory. Actually there is very little difference between these two approaches. Total institutions theory looks at institutions as a whole and emphasizes the similarities between prisons, mental hospitals and other total institutions. In contrast, role theory emphasizes the role played by correctional officers and argues that citizens can be rapidly socialized to play the role of correctional officer.

The creation of total institutions theory is generally credited to Goffman in his book, *Asylums*, in which he discusses social and psychological assaults upon inmates by staff members. In Goffman's conception, the psychological victimization of inmates by staff members is part of the overall process of mortification, in which the inmates' attachment to civilian life is stripped away. The exasperating thing about much of the unnecessary psychological victimization that goes on is that the staff justifies the victimization in terms of institutional needs.[77] Following this same line of analysis, Hartmann has identified the existence of the staff role of the "key jingler" for persons who deliberately use power in a manner that is debilitating to the inmates. These individuals are concerned with "throwing their weight around" rather than promoting the welfare of the inmates under their control.[78]

The maximum security prison is conceptualized as a miniature totalitarian state by Burns. The six basic features of a totalitarian regime—totalitarian ideology, a single party typically led by one person, a terroristic police, a communications monopoly, a weapons monopoly and a centrally directed economy—are systematically applied to maximum security prisons in Burns' analysis. In this model, staff members who are in a position of great authority will be sorely tempted to practice brutality, blackmail, bribery and favoritism. Terroristic police practices are part of the social control mechanism for keeping inmates in line.[79] If Burns' conception of the maximum security prison as a totalitarian regime is correct, then we would expect that those correctional officers who are better integrated with the culture of the prison and more socially involved in it would be more brutal and totalitarian than those officers who exist at the periphery of the staff subculture. An exploratory investigation by Shoemaker and Hillery suggests that this may be true in some institutions. However, the correlations they found were significant in only one of three institutions (and that was a boarding school rather than a maximum security prison),[80] so their evidence does not lend more than minimal support to the theory advanced by Burns.

Role theory as applied to the victimization of prisoners by officers received support from the Stanford Prison Experiment conducted by Haney et al.[81] In this experiment, college students who had been authenticated as psychologically normal were paid to role-play guards and inmates in a pseudoprison in the basement of a Stanford building. Everyone involved was aware of the fact that the experiment was artificial, although it was very well staged. Commenting on this experiment, Zimbardo says:

At the end of six days we had to close down our mock prison because what we saw was frightening. It was no longer apparent to most of the subjects (or to us) where reality ended and the roles began. The majority had indeed become prisoners or guards, no longer able to clearly differentiate between role-playing and self. There were dramatic changes in virtually every aspect of their behavior, thinking, and feeling. In less than a week the experience of imprisonment undid (temporarily) a lifetime of learning: human values were suspended, self-concepts were challenged and the ugliest, most base, pathological side of human nature surfaced. We were horrified because we saw some boys (guards) treat others as if they were despicable animals, taking pleasure in cruelty, while other boys (prisoners) became servile, dehumanized robots who thought only of escape, of their own individual survival and of their mounting hatred for the guards.[82]

In the Stanford experiment, approximately one-third of the staff members became tyrannical in their arbitrary use of power over the inmates. They developed creative ways of breaking the spirit of the prisoners who were in their charge. Although the other two-thirds of the staff members were not tyrannical, there was never a case in which one of them interfered with a command given by any of the tyrannical guards. They never even tried to pressure the other staff members into behaving more reasonably. The experiment was called off because of the possibility that some of the subjects were being severely damaged by their experiences. Three of them had to be released in the first four days because they had severe situational traumatic reactions, such as confusion in thinking, severe depression and hysterical crying.

This experiment devastates the constitutional sadism theory of staff brutality, which is, in any case, not represented in the serious literature on staff-inmate victimization. The realization that any normal human being can take on the negative characteristics commonly associated with the worst of prison officers leads us to look more carefully at how roles are structured in the prison situation. A study of mine shows that even civilian volunteers who become quasistaff members of a correctional institution can engage in types of behavior that are psychologically victimizing. In a volunteer program administered by me in which all but two of the staff members were volunteers from the external community, there were many cases of power-tripping and sexual enticement by the staff members, with power-tripping being primarily engaged in by males, and sexual enticement by females, although the reverse was true in some cases. The power-tripper enjoys a feeling of control over the lives of prisoners and manipulates them in therapy groups and in administrative situations so as to make them more dependent and more anxious than they would otherwise be. Power-trippers are sure that inmates should do what they are told, and they imply that they have a great deal more power over the inmates' release date than is actually the case.

Sexual enticement occurs when the volunteer staff member dresses, talks and acts in a sexually suggestive way while within the prison. Pseudoromances are encouraged in which the prisoners are led to believe that the staff members have a real interest in them, while the staff members in actuality are merely gratifying themselves by being admired and sought after. When the relationship goes too far, the prisoners are often subjected to disciplinary actions because the victimizing staff member claims that it was "all the prisoner's fault." In addition, some prisoners become so emotionally involved that when the relationship falls apart, they become suicidal. Others come looking for their "lovers" when they are released from prison, only to find out that these staff members have no intention of following up on the promises they made while the prisoners were safe behind bars.[83]

Is the role of the prison guard so compulsive that a certain percentage of the people who play it will be invariably motivated to abuse prisoners in one way or another? The comments by Zimbardo and my experiences say yes, and this idea is also consistent with a report by Jacobs and Kraft, that suggests the possibility that racial differences among guards are suppressed by the "master status" of the prison officer.[84] However, an obscure publication on correctional institutions in Wisconsin offers contrary evidence. This report by Ross describes what happened during a 16-day period when members of the Wisconsin State Employees Union went on strike and National Guard Units took over the administration of the prisons. The National Guardsmen were in the prisons for more than twice the period of time of Zimbardo's experiment, yet they were not institutionalized by the experience. Instead of becoming brutal and mistreating the inmates, they treated them like decent human beings. They relaxed the disciplinary regime and at the same time reduced the number of incidents of violence among inmates.[85]

It is probable that the reason the National Guardsmen's behavior did not deteriorate during their time as correctional officers was that they never conceived of themselves as playing the role of prison officers. They had a different role to play—the role of National Guardsmen acting in an emergency. In addition, they had a network of relations with each other that existed before they had entered the prison and that strengthened their resistance to the negative process of institutionalization. With these kinds of social supports, it is possible that the National Guardsmen could have had tours of duty of one or two years in length without ever adopting the more negative aspects of the role of the prison officer. International studies of prison camps in which the prisoners are able to live rather normal lives under the supervision of military units also offer some evidence in support of the idea that the military role can take precedence over the prison officer role and minimize the appeal of engaging in behavior that is at least psychologically victimizing if not physically brutal.

NOTES

1. Donald Clemmer, *The Prison Community* (New York: Holt, Rinehart and Winston, 1940), p. 204.

2. John A. Conley, "A History of the Oklahoma Prison System, 1907–1967," Ph.D. dissertation, Michigan State University, 1977.

3. Bruce Jackson, *Killing Time, Life in the Arkansas Penitentiary* (Ithaca, NY: Cornell University Press, 1977).

4. Tom Murton and Joe Hyams, *Inside Prison, U.S.A.* (New York: Grove Press, 1969).

5. Ibid., p. 7.

6. Prison brutality revealed during the federal hearing, *The Freeworld Times* 1 (January 1972):2.

7. Fear, Angola's punishment camp terrorizes prisoners, *Southern Coalition Report on Jails and Prisons* 5 (Spring 1978):3.

8. Stephen Gettinger, Mississippi: Has come a long way but it had a long way to come, *Corrections Magazine* 5 (June 1979):8; *Corrections Digest* 4 (December 12, 1973):3.

9. Philip J. Hirschkop and Michael A. Millemann, The prison life of Leroy Jones, in Burton M. Atkins and Henry R. Glick (Eds., *Prisons, Protest, and Politics* (Englewood Cliffs, NJ: Prentice-Hall, 1972), pp. 55–59.

10. Jessica Mitford, *Kind and Usual Punishment* (New York: Random House, 1971), pp. 41–42.

11. Oklahoma prison guards indicted for inmate

gassing incident, *Corrections Digest* 6 (February 5, 1975):2.

12. Federal jury convicts prison guards of brutality, *Corrections Digest* 5 (March 6, 1974):2–3.

13. 'Dedicated' with violence, *The Freeworld Times* 1 (August 1972):8–9.

14. Rioters killed, *The Freeworld Times* 1 (February 1972):6, 9.

15. Ibid., p. 6.

16. Mitford (1971), p. 290.

17. Hans Toch, *Police, Prisons, and the Problem of Violence* (Washington, DC: U.S. Government Printing Office, 1977), pp. 65–67.

18. Robert Bogdan and Steven J. Taylor, *Introduction to Qualitative Research Methods* (New York: Wiley, 1975).

19. Edward Sagarin and Donal E. J. MacNamara, The homosexual as a crime victim, *International Journal of Criminology and Penology* 3 (1975):21.

20. Larry Cole, *Our Children's Keepers: Inside America's Kid Prisons* (New York: Grossman, 1972).

21. Kenneth Wooden, *Weeping in the Playtime of Others: America's Incarcerated Children* (New York: McGraw-Hill, 1976).

22. Clemens Bartollas, Stuart J. Miller and Simon Dinitz, *Juvenile Victimization: The Institutional Paradox* (New York: Wiley, 1976), p. 214.

23. Ibid., p. 214.

24. Gene Kassebaum, Sex in prison, violence, homosexuality, and intimidation are everyday occurrences, *Sexual Behavior* 2 (January 1972):39–45.

25. The case of Joanne Little, *Crime and Social Justice* 3 (Summer 1975):42–45. For a more recent case, see Women press for change at Tutwiler, *Southern Coalition Report on Jails and Prisons* 5 (Fall 1978):3.

26. Woman's killing of jailer raises inmate abuse questions, *Corrections Digest* 5 (December 11, 1974):11–12.

27. Cole (1972), p. 8.

28. Alan J. Davis, Sexual assaults in the Philadelphia prison system and sheriff's vans, *Trans-Action* 6 (December 1968):11.

29. Jack Griswold, Mike Misenheimer and Art Powers, *An Eye for an Eye* (New York: Holt, Rinehart and Winston, 1970), pp. 42–43, cited in Anthony M. Scacco Jr., *Rape in Prison* (Springfield IL: C. C. Thomas, 1975), p. 32.

30. Sagarin and MacNamara (1975).

31. Ibid., pp. 21–22.

32. See, for example, Davis (1968) and Scacco (1975).

33. Daniel Lockwood, *Prison Sexual Violence* (New York: Elsevier, 1980), p. 140.

34. Cole (1972), p. 64.

35. Howard James, Children in trouble, *Christian Science Monitor* (April 5, 12, 19, 26, and May 10, 24, 1969), cited in Naomi F. Chase, *A Child Is Being Beaten* (New York: McGraw-Hill, 1976), pp. 154, 160.

36. Chase (1976), p. 151.

37. *National Analysis of Official Child Abuse and Neglect Reporting* (Washington, DC: Government Printing Office, 1969).

38. John Howard Association, *Illinois Youth Centers at St. Charles and Geneva* (Chicago: John Howard Association, 1974).

39. See, for example, Cliff Judge and Roma Emmerson, Some children at risk in Victoria in the 19th century, *Medical Journal of Australia* 1 (1974): 490–495.

40. John Vodicka, Louisiana warden indicted for beatings of juveniles, *Southern Coalition Report on Jails and Prisons* 5 (Summer 1978):1.

41. Wooden (1976), p. 108.

42. Barry C. Feld, *Neutralizing Inmate Violence* (Cambridge, MA: Ballinger, 1977).

43. Bartollas et al. (1976).

44. Conley (1977), p. 237.

45. Robert E. Heise, *Prison Games* (Fort Worth: privately published, 1976).

46. Kenneth Dimick, *Ladies in Waiting Behind Prison Walls* (Muncie, IN: Accelerated Development, 1977), pp. 46–47.

47. Erving Goffman, *Asylums* (Garden City, NY: Doubleday, 1961).

48. Heise (1976).

49. *Corrections Digest* 3 (November 1, 1972), pp. 11–12.

50. Mitford (1971), p. 148.

51. Injunction granted against assignment of male guards at Bedford Hills, *Corrections Compendium* 2 (October 1977), p. 3.

52. Mitford (1971), pp. 268–269.

53. Paul W. Keve, *Prison Life and Human Worth* (Minneapolis: University of Minnesota Press, 1974).

54. H. H. A. Cooper, Self-mutilation by Peruvian prisoners, *International Journal of Offender Therapy* 15 (1971):180–188.

55. Hans Mattick, The prosaic sources of prison violence, in Jackwell Susman, *Crime and Justice, 1971–1972* (New York: A.M.S. Press, 1974):179–187.

56. A. Astrachan, Profile/Louisiana, *Corrections Magazine* 2 (September–October 1975):9–14.

57. See, for example, R. S. Esparza, Attempted and committed suicide in county jails, in Bruce Danto (Ed.), *Jailhouse Blues* (Orchard Lake, MI: Epic Publications, 1973), pp. 27–46; James L. Claghorn and Dan R. Beto, Self-mutilation in a prison hospital, *Corrective Psychiatry and Journal of Social Therapy* 13 (1967):133–141; Robert Johnson, *Culture and Crisis in Confinement* (Lexington, MA: D. C. Heath, 1976); Hans Toch, *Men in Crisis* (Chicago: Aldine, 1975); *Living in Prison: The Ecology of Survival* (New York: Free Press, 1977).

58. R. J. Wicks, Suicide prevention—A brief for

corrections officers, *Federal Probation* 36 (September 1972):29–31.

59. Nebraska prisoners speak-out, *The Freeworld Times* 3 (January–February 1974):7.

60. Danger, death, corruption at Atlanta federal prison detailed in Senate testimony, *Corrections Digest* 9 (October 6, 1978):3–4.

61. Inmate death linked to guard rackets, *The Freeworld Times* 2 (May 1973):15.

62. See Conley (1977) for historical examples of excessive industrial accidents caused by deliberate administrative inattention to matters of safety.

63. Gilbert F. McMahon, The normal prisoner in medical research, *Journal of Clinical Pharmacology* 71 (February–March 1972):72.

64. Peter B. Meyer, *Drug Experiments on Prisoners, Ethical, Economic, or Exploitative?* (Lexington, MA: D. C. Heath, 1976).

65. C. Ronald Huff, Unionization behind the walls, *Criminology* 12 (1974):175–193; Prisoners' union: A challenge for state corrections, *State Government* 48 (1975):145–149.

66. Haywood Burns, The black prisoner as victim, in Michele G. Hermann and Marilyn G. Haft (Eds.), *Prisoners' Rights Sourcebook* (New York: Clark Boardman, 1973), pp. 25–31.

67. Ronald Goldfarb, *Jails: The Ultimate Ghetto of the Criminal Justice System* (Garden City, NY: Doubleday, 1976), p. 405.

68. Erik O. Wright, *The Politics of Punishment: A Critical Analysis of Prisons in America* (New York: Harper and Row, 1973), p. 127.

69. James B. Jacobs, *Stateville: The Penitentiary in Mass Society* (Chicago: University of Chicago Press, 1977), p. 59.

70. Leo Carroll, *Hacks, Blacks, and Cons* (Lexington, MA: D. C. Heath, 1974), pp. 123–124.

71. Ibid., pp. 127–128.

72. George Jackson, *Soledad Brother: The Prison Letters of George Jackson* (New York: Bantam, 1970).

73. This week: Texas prison faces federal court test, *Corrections Digest* 9 (October 6, 1978):2–3.

74. Bartollas et al. (1976), pp. 208–209.

75. Ibid., pp. 207–209.

76. Sheriff may be liable for acts of his subordinates, and Leaving prisoners unattended can lead to civil rights violation, *Corrections Compendium* 2 (June 1978):5.

77. Goffman (1961).

78. Carl Hartman, The key jingler, *Community Mental Health Journal* 5 (1969): 199–205.

79. Henry Burns, Jr., A miniature totalitarian state: Maximum security prison, *Canadian Journal of Criminology and Corrections* 11 (July 1969):153–164.

80. Donald J. Shoemaker and George A. Hillery, Jr., "Violence and Commitment in Custodial Settings," paper presented at the annual meeting of the American Sociological Association, 1978.

81. Craig Haney, Curtis Banks and Philip Zimbardo, Interpersonal dynamics in a simulated prison, in Robert G. Leger and John R. Stratton (Eds.), *The Sociology of Corrections* (New York: Wiley, 1977), pp. 65–92.

82. Philip Zimbardo, Pathology of imprisonment, *Society* 9 (6) (1972):4.

83. Lee H. Bowker, Volunteers in correctional settings: Benefits, problems, and solutions, in *Proceedings of the American Correctional Association* (Washington, DC: American Correctional Association, 1973), pp. 298–303.

84. James B. Jacobs and Lawrence J. Kraft, Integrating the keepers: A comparison of black and white prison guards in Illinois, *Social Problems* 25 (1978):304–318.

85. Beth Ross, *Changing of the Guard: Citizen Soldiers in Wisconsin Correctional Institutions* (Madison: League of Women Voters of Wisconsin, 1979).

Study Questions

1. How does Bowker define staff-prisoner victimization? What are the definitional problems he encounters? Do you think these definitional problems indicate a basically utilitarian perspective or a deontological perspective on Bowker's part?

2. In Bowker's view, would a prison in which homosexual rape regularly occurs very likely indicate staff complicity? What are some of the possible motives reported in the studies Bowker cites?

3. What kinds of psychological victimization does Bowker report? How would you compare the morality of psychological abuse as opposed to physical abuse of inmates? Defend your position.

4. Should correctional officers receive extensive training in interpersonal relations, or should staff-prisoner interpersonal relations be de-emphasized and/or prohibited, in your view? Why?

Tolerating Illegal Use of Force Against Inmates

AGNES L. BARO

ON MONDAY, DECEMBER 14, 1981, the Hawaii National Guard, the Honolulu Police Department, and employees from the Halawa High Security Facility (HHSF) assisted Oahu Community Correctional Center (OCCC) staff in a major search and seizure. This event is known locally as "the '81 shakedown." It lasted five days, cost the state well over a quarter of a million dollars, and led to a series of investigations spanning a three-year period.

Most important, the '81 shakedown taught Hawaii's correctional officers that prisoners could be controlled and order could be maintained through the systematic use of corporal punishment. This is not to say that all officers agreed or participated in what would become institutionalized terrorism, but there is enough historical evidence to support the allegation that inmate beatings were tolerated by officials at all levels of the Hawaii state government.

The history of the '81 shakedown began in 1960 with the first prison riot in over 40 years. After the riot, the new state government replaced the territorial-era prison director and hired a "mainland expert" as its Corrections Division administrator. However, the new administrator was not given any formal authority to hire or fire wardens. Instead, an elaborate patronage system evolved whereby obviously incompetent wardens were protected no matter how dirty or dangerous their prisons became.

Throughout most of the 1960-to-1980 period, Oahu Prison (the state's largest facility) was so poorly managed that escapes, staff intimidation, drugs and weapons, and inmate assaults on each other and on staff were endemic. Attempts to reform this prison included a 1975 takeover by

the lieutenant governor. Over 40 employees were transferred to other state jobs (dismissals are rare in Hawaii government), but the warden kept his job and did not retire until 1981.

During June of 1980, two inmates were murdered and one seriously wounded in armed battles staged within Oahu Prison's Old Cellblock. The battles were followed by three days of disturbances. In August 1980, inmates at the HHSF also rioted. Thus, staff who participated in the '81 shakedown had relatively recent experiences of facing heavily armed, out-of-control inmates. Perhaps more significantly, they worked in a prison system that had been largely controlled by inmates for 20 years. Staff intimidation and assault were common experiences.

Evidence of mounting tension during 1981 includes a June disturbance when inmates forced correctional officers out of the Old Cellblock and held it under siege for 10 hours. In September 1981, a mentally ill inmate was beaten to death by other inmates. Two days later, officers abandoned the cellblock when attempts to seize drugs and a pistol failed; one lieutenant was injured by an inmate wielding a two-foot-long machete.

The warden of Oahu Prison retired in July 1981, but his successor resigned after only 90 days. Once a new warden had been appointed, planning for a major shakedown began.

During the first day, approximately 350 inmates were moved out of the Old Cellblock into a large recreation field where they would spend the night. Some inmates drew attention to themselves by verbally harassing HHSF officers stationed on the perimeter. They also set fire to the tent set up by the Hawaii National Guard.

The authors would like to express their gratitude to Professor Baro for preparing this paper expressly for inclusion in this book.

This behavior prompted the HHSF warden to ask the OCCC warden for control of the strip searches and for permission to "discipline" inmates (Senate Judiciary Committee, 1983, p. 387).[1] Permission was granted.

On the second day of the shakedown, OCCC relinquished control of the strip searches and provided staff to identify inmates who had harassed the HHSF officers. Those present in the strip-search area included the HHSF warden and his top staff. Closed-circuit television cameras and an intercom that linked the area with Central Control were turned off.

While the strip searches were going on, staff in the medical unit became concerned about the number and types of injuries they were treating. One inmate was beaten so badly that he was sent to a private hospital.

Despite objections from the OCCC medical staff, some injured inmates were removed prior to being treated and were transferred directly to the HHSF. The OCCC physician reported going to the strip-search area and pleading with the OCCC warden to stop the beatings, but the beatings continued. At this time, the medical unit administrator went to Central Control and asked why the television cameras were turned off. She also expressed concern about the inmate injuries. However, she was told that a deputy attorney general was in the strip-search area and that she should not be concerned about illegal uses of force.

The events that took place on the third day of the shakedown can only be characterized as a correctional officer riot. On this day, the OCCC security staff had command of the strip-search area. Once again, television and intercom communication with Central Control was cut off. According to one officer-witness, "There was ... chaos inside there, guys went berserk" (Ombudsman, 1983, p. 25).[2]

The chaos consisted of inmates being driven through lines of snarling and biting police dogs, correctional officers beating inmates, and fights between officers who had disagreements about which inmates (if any) should be beaten. One officer reported rescuing a smaller inmate by throwing him over his shoulder and running down a corridor. Here is his description of what happened to "the kid":

> First they went tune him up. I seen guys walk up to him when he came down for the search and they went whack him, two or three whacks, big guys. But he no say nothing, the kid, he took the licking. I figure pau [finished] already, whack him four or five times, pau. Then after that, the other guys start jumping in, start hitting him this and that, just like one prisoner of war. The mob go crazy (Ombudsman, 1983, pp. 87–88).

An OCCC unit manager was in the kitchen during the period of chaos. The kitchen is not far from the strip-search area but it is not in direct line of sight. Since employees had opened the doors for better ventilation, the manager could hear what he described (to the author) as "a fear-and-pain type of screaming." At one point, he left the kitchen and walked toward the strip-search area. He reported to the author that he saw "two guards holding an inmate while a third beat him with a baton." The manager also reported seeing officials from the State Attorney General's Office and two OCCC administrators witnessing the beating.

On the weekend following the shakedown, rumors began to circulate among newspaper and television reporters that there were injured inmates who were being denied medical treatment.

The assistant Corrections Division administrator was assigned to investigate. After visiting inmates transferred to the high-security facility, she called for an outside investigation (Senate Judiciary Committee, 1983, p. 7). However, the governor told the press that "initial assessments from the attorney general and the Department of Social Services and Housing indicate that there is no substantial evidence of any brutality at the prison" (Senate Judiciary Committee, 1983, p. 9). He also refused to launch an external investigation. However, under considerable pressure, he did appoint a "blue ribbon panel," and the state ombudsman and Senate Judiciary Committee conducted extensive investigations.

Meanwhile, the assistant corrections administrator was ordered to continue her internal investigation. She did not complete her task until March of 1982. At that time, she sent her report to the attorney general's office. One of the deputy attorney generals who was at the prison during the shakedown immediately released a summary of her report to the press. The assistant administrator reported (to the author) that this deputy attorney general "altered my report" by putting the word "minor" in front of words such as "lacerations and bruises." During the ensuing Senate Judiciary Committee hearings, the deputy also refused to submit her original report even after he had been subpoenaed to do so.

The results of both the Senate Judiciary Committee and the ombudsman's investigations indicated that at least 44 inmates had been beaten. Evidence against both wardens and supervisory staff as well as 22 officers was provided to correctional officials. Seven months later (April of 1984), an in-house panel recommended that disciplinary action should be taken against 32 employees, including the wardens. However, after conferring with the attorney general, the prison system director decided to drop all charges against the employees.

The reaction from the ombudsman was unprecedented. For the first time in 15 years, he issued a special report. In what became a front-page battle, the ombudsman confronted the director and warned that the decision not to discipline prison employees would "adversely affect the Department and the public in years to come" (Ombudsman, 1984, p. 15).[3] He also quoted Winston Churchill to remind the director that "we cannot say the past is past without surrendering the future."

The ombudsman's remarks were prophetic. The use of illegal force against inmates resulting in serious injury continued throughout the 1980s. According to one prison manager, "Six months after the shakedown we had control of our inmates but not of our officers; just to stop an inmate beating was an accomplishment because there were no administrative remedies" (reported to author).

By 1983, the U.S. Attorney General was concerned enough to write the governor of Hawaii to complain that state officials were "failing to protect inmates against excessive and inappropriate" uses of force, which resulted in what he called "a pattern and practice of brutality." The response from the governor and the state attorney general was to deny the U.S. Department of Justice investigatory access to Hawaii's prisons.

Hawaii became the first state to be sued by the Department of Justice under the 1981 Civil Rights of Institutionalized Persons Act. However, because the Department of Justice could not get access to substantiate allegations, the suit was dismissed. In a peace-making gesture, the governor then granted access. After a year of investigation, the department announced that inmates at the OCCC were controlled by "fear and violence" and that there was "a pattern of unjustified staff violence at all levels throughout the facility." U.S. Attorney General William Bradford Reynolds also noted that OCCC was probably the only prison in the country where inmates were in protective custody because they needed protection from staff (Altonn, 1985).[4]

Regardless of the interest taken by the Department of Justice and regardless of a successful American Civil Liberties Union (ACLU) lawsuit, inmate beatings in Hawaii prisons continued well into 1989. The physical abuse of inmates at the Halawa Correctional Facility received front-page attention in 1989 when the ACLU threatened to sue over 20 separate incidents that had occurred during the past year. In an act of courage unique to this particular bureaucracy, the prison medical director told the press that medical workers had treated 20 inmates who had "clearly been beaten" (Tswei, 1989).[5]

Since I worked for the Hawaii prison system for six of the post-1981-shakedown years, I have often questioned my own degree of complicity in the reign of terror. Not having had any direct line authority, I can let myself off the hook somewhat by claiming a lack of power. Nevertheless, the fact remains that I occupied several very important positions (i.e., chief planner, educational services officer, and training administrator). Thus, I was not without influence or access to top administrators.

Perhaps conveniently, I never witnessed an inmate beating, but I did see injured inmates. They always made me feel better when they claimed they had fallen or had other "accidents." Perhaps they were telling the truth. I really don't know.

What I do know is that during the 1980s, Hawaii's prisons were among the most orderly in the country. By "orderly," I mean that staff were rarely intimidated, there were few disturbances, and employees were treated with a great deal of respect. In fact, I'm always amazed when I visit prisons in other states and witness inmates being disrespectful to staff.

I will admit that I enjoyed working in such an "orderly" prison system, but I did not enjoy my constant fear for inmate safety or the feeling that my professional values were little more than rhetoric. Some people shared my fear, anger, and shame. A few even used their administrative power to try to get rid of the worst wardens and staff. In the end, the wardens were promoted and the reformers were defeated by a political system and culture that tolerated the abuse of prisoners. I make this allegation after having studied the prison system, political system, and political culture for over five years. In fact,

I earned a Ph.D. by doing so.

The point I most want to make is that people in democratic societies get whatever prison system they are willing to tolerate. I think this point has been made by almost every historian who has studied prisons. In this way, the people of Hawaii are not very different from the people of Arkansas or Texas. It is simply a matter of degrees of tolerance. Similarly, I doubt that I am any different from prison employees in states with similar histories. But should we refuse to work in these states?

REFERENCES

1. Senate Judiciary Committee (1983). *Special Investigation*. Honolulu: Senate of the State of Hawaii.

2. Ombudsman (1983). *Investigation of allegations of the use of unreasonable force against inmates during the shakedown of the Oahu Community Correctional Center from December 14 through December 18, 1981*. Honolulu: Office of the Ombudsman.

3. Ombudsman (1984). *Opinion of the Ombudsman regarding the decision of the Director of the Department of Social Services and Housing to dismiss all cases from the 1981 Oahu Community Correctional Center shakedown* (Special Report Number One). Honolulu: Office of the Ombudsman.

4. Altonn, Helen (1985, January 3). U.S. claims staff violence at Oahu prison. *Honolulu Star-Bulletin*, p. A-1.

5. Tswei, Suzanne (1989, July 9). Beatings, abuses by guards alleged at two state prisons. *Honolulu Star-Bulletin & Advertiser*, p. A-1.

Study Questions

1. What were the Oahu prison conditions like between 1960 and 1980? What was the "shakedown" response to those conditions? What consequences did it have for the prison during the 1980s?

2. What events does Baro cite to justify the allegation that inmate beatings were tolerated by officials at every level in Hawaii? What moral perspective could be offered to justify such tolerance? Do you think the justification would be acceptable, given the circumstances described by Baro? Why?

3. Is the practice of inmate beating in the Oahu case a Dirty Harry problem, as described by Klockars? Why?

Hudson v. McMillian

U.S. SUPREME COURT *(with dissenting opinion)*

JUSTICE O'CONNOR delivered the opinion of the Court.

This case requires us to decide whether the use of excessive physical force against a prisoner may constitute cruel and unusual punishment when the inmate does not suffer serious injury. We answer that question in the affirmative.

I

At the time of the incident that is the subject of this suit, petitioner Keith Hudson was an inmate at the state penitentiary in Angola, Louisiana. Respondents Jack McMillian, Marvin Woods, and Arthur Mezo served as corrections security officers at the Angola facility. During the early morning hours of October 30, 1983, Hudson and McMillian argued. Assisted by Woods, McMillian then placed Hudson in handcuffs and shackles, took the prisoner out of his cell, and walked him toward the penitentiary's "administrative lockdown" area. Hudson testified that, on the way there, McMillian punched Hudson in the mouth, eyes, chest, and stomach while Woods held the inmate in place and kicked and punched him from behind. He further testified that Mezo, the supervisor on duty, watched the beating but merely told the officers "not to have too much fun." App. 23. As a result of this episode, Hudson suffered minor bruises and swelling of his face, mouth, and lip. The blows also loosened Hudson's teeth and cracked his partial dental plate, rendering it unusable for several months.

Hudson sued the three corrections officers in Federal District Court under 42 U.S.C. § 1983, alleging a violation of the Eighth Amendment's prohibition on cruel and unusual punishments and seeking compensatory damages. The parties consented to disposition of the case before a Magistrate, who found that McMillian and Woods used force when there was no need to do so and that Mezo expressly condoned their actions. App. 26. The Magistrate awarded Hudson damages of $800. *Id.,* at 29.

The Court of Appeals for the Fifth Circuit reversed. 929 F. 2d 1014 (1990). It held that inmates alleging use of excessive force in violation of the Eighth Amendment must prove: (1) significant injury; (2) resulting "directly and only from the use of force that was clearly excessive to the need"; (3) the excessiveness of which was objectively unreasonable; and (4) that the action constituted an unnecessary and wanton infliction of pain. 929 F. 2d, at 1015. The court determined that respondents' use of force was objectively unreasonable because no force was required. Furthermore, "[t]he conduct of McMillian and Woods qualified as clearly excessive and occasioned unnecessary and wanton infliction of pain." *Ibid.* However, Hudson could not prevail on his Eighth Amendment claim because his injuries were "minor" and required no medical attention. *Ibid.*

We granted certiorari, 499 U.S. __ (1991), to determine whether the "significant injury" requirement applied by the Court of Appeals accords with the Constitution's dictate that cruel and unusual punishment shall not be inflicted.

II

In *Whitley* v. *Albers,* 475 U.S. 312 (1986), the principal question before us was what legal standard

---

The text of this decision was taken from the slip opinion and may contain minor differences from the forthcoming United States Reports version. Cf. 112 S.Ct. 995 (1992).

should govern the Eighth Amendment claim of an inmate shot by a guard during a prison riot. We based our answer on the settled rule that "'the unnecessary and wanton infliction of pain ... constitutes cruel and unusual punishment forbidden by the Eighth Amendment.'" *Id.,* at 319 (quoting *Ingraham* v. *Wright,* 430 U.S. 651, 670 (1977)) (internal quotation omitted).

What is necessary to establish an "unnecessary and wanton infliction of pain," we said, varies according to the nature of the alleged constitutional violation. 475 U.S., at 320. For example, the appropriate inquiry when an inmate alleges that prison officials failed to attend to serious medical needs is whether the officials exhibited "deliberate indifference." See *Estelle* v. *Gamble,* 429 U.S. 97, 104 (1976). This standard is appropriate because the State's responsibility to provide inmates with medical care ordinarily does not conflict with competing administrative concerns. *Whitley, supra,* at 320.

By contrast, officials confronted with a prison disturbance must balance the threat unrest poses to inmates, prison workers, administrators, and visitors against the harm inmates may suffer if guards use force. Despite the weight of these competing concerns, corrections officials must make their decisions "in haste, under pressure, and frequently without the luxury of a second chance." 475 U.S., at 320. We accordingly concluded in *Whitley* that application of the deliberate indifference standard is inappropriate when authorities use force to put down a prison disturbance. Instead, "the question whether the measure taken inflicted unnecessary and wanton pain and suffering ultimately turns on 'whether force was applied in a good faith effort to maintain or restore discipline or maliciously and sadistically for the very purpose of causing harm.'" *Id.,* at 320–321 (quoting *Johnson* v. *Glick,* 481 F. 2d 1028, 1033 (CA2), cert. denied *sub nom. John* v. *Johnson,* 414 U.S. 1033 (1973)).

Many of the concerns underlying our holding in *Whitley* arise whenever guards use force to keep order. Whether the prison disturbance is a riot or a lesser disruption, corrections officers must balance the need "to maintain or restore discipline" through force against the risk of injury to inmates. Both situations may require prison officials to act quickly and decisively. Likewise, both implicate the principle that "'[p]rison administrators ... should be accorded wide-ranging deference in the adoption and execution of policies and practices that in their judgment are needed to preserve internal order and discipline and to maintain institutional security.'" 475 U.S., at 321–322 (quoting *Bell* v. *Wolfish,* 441 U.S. 520, 547 (1979)). In recognition of these similarities, we hold that whenever prison officials stand accused of using excessive physical force in violation of the Cruel and Unusual Punishments Clause, the core judicial inquiry is that set out in *Whitley:* whether force was applied in a good-faith effort to maintain or restore discipline, or maliciously and sadistically to cause harm.

Extending *Whitley's* application of the "unnecessary and wanton infliction of pain" standard to all allegations of excessive force works no innovation. This Court derived the *Whitley* test from one articulated by Judge Friendly in *Johnson* v. *Glick, supra,* a case arising out of a prisoner's claim to have been beaten and harassed by a guard. Moreover, many Courts of Appeals already apply the *Whitley* standard to allegations of excessive force outside of the riot situation. See *Corselli* v. *Coughlin,* 842 F. 2d 23, 26 (CA2 1988); *Miller* v. *Leathers,* 913 F. 2d 1085, 1087 (CA4 1990) (en banc), cert. denied, 498 U.S. __ (1991); *Haynes* v. *Marshall,* 887 F. 2d 700, 703 (CA6 1989); *Stenzel* v. *Ellis,* 916 F. 2d 423, 427 (CA8 1990); *Brown* v. *Smith,* 813 F. 2d 1187, 1188 (CA11 1987). But see *Unwin* v. *Campbell,* 863 F. 2d 124, 130 (CA1 1988) (rejecting application of *Whitley* standard absent "an actual disturbance").

A

Under the *Whitley* approach, the extent of injury suffered by an inmate is one factor that may suggest "whether the use of force could plausibly have been thought necessary" in a particular situation, "or instead evinced such wantonness with respect to the unjustified infliction of harm as is tantamount to a knowing willingness that it occur." *Whitley,* 475 U.S., at 321. In determining whether the use of force was wanton and unnecessary, it may also be proper to evaluate the need for application of force, the relationship between that need and the amount of force used, the threat "reasonably perceived by the responsible officials," and "any efforts made to temper the severity of a forceful response." *Ibid.* The absence of serious injury is therefore relevant to the Eighth Amendment inquiry, but does not end it.

Respondents nonetheless assert that a significant injury requirement of the sort imposed by the Fifth Circuit is mandated by what we have termed the "objective component" of Eighth Amendment analysis. See *Wilson* v. *Seiter,* 501 U.S., ___, ___ (1991). *Wilson* extended the deliberate indifference standard applied to Eighth Amendment claims involving medical care to claims about conditions of confinement. In taking this step, we suggested that the subjective aspect of an Eighth Amendment claim (with which the Court was concerned) can be distinguished from the objective facet of the same claim. Thus, courts considering a prisoner's claim must ask both if "the officials act[ed] with a sufficiently culpable state of mind" and if the alleged wrongdoing was objectively "harmful enough" to establish a constitutional violation. *Id.,* at ___, ___.

With respect to the objective component of an Eighth Amendment violation, *Wilson* announced no new rule. Instead, that decision suggested a relationship between the requirements applicable to different types of Eighth Amendment claims. What is necessary to show sufficient harm for purposes of the Cruel and Unusual Punishments Clause depends upon the claim at issue, for two reasons. First, "[t]he general requirement that an Eighth Amendment claimant allege and prove the unnecessary and wanton infliction of pain should ... be applied with due regard for differences in the kind of conduct against which an Eighth Amendment objection is lodged." *Whitley, supra,* at 320. Second, the Eighth Amendment's prohibition of cruel and unusual punishments "'draw[s] its

meaning from the evolving standards of decency that mark the progress of a maturing society,'" and so admits of few absolute limitations. *Rhodes* v. *Chapman,* 452 U.S. 337, 346 (1981) (quoting *Trop* v. *Dulles,* 356 U.S. 86, 101 (1958) (plurality opinion)).

The objective component of an Eighth Amendment claim is therefore contextual and responsive to "contemporary standards of decency." *Estelle,* 429 U.S., at 103. For instance, extreme deprivations are required to make out a conditions-of-confinement claim. Because routine discomfort is "part of the penalty that criminal offenders pay for their offenses against society," *Rhodes, supra,* at 347, "only those deprivations denying 'the minimal civilized measure of life's necessities' are sufficiently grave to form the basis of an Eighth Amendment violation." *Wilson, supra,* at ___ (quoting *Rhodes, supra,* at 347) (internal citation omitted). A similar analysis applies to medical needs. Because society does not expect that prisoners will have unqualified access to health care, deliberate indifference to medical needs amounts to an Eighth Amendment violation only if those needs are "serious." See *Estelle* v. *Gamble, supra,* at 103-104.

In the excessive force context, society's expectations are different. When prison officials maliciously and sadistically use force to cause harm, contemporary standards of decency always are violated. See *Whitley, supra,* at 327. This is true whether or not significant injury is evident. Otherwise, the Eighth Amendment would permit any physical punishment, no matter how diabolic or inhuman, inflicting less than some arbitrary quantity of injury. Such a result would have been as unacceptable to the drafters of the Eighth Amendment as it is today. See *Estelle, supra,* at 102 (proscribing torture and barbarous punishment was "the primary concern of the drafters" of the Eighth Amendment); *Wilkerson* v. *Utah,* 99 U.S. 130, 136 (1879) ("[I]t is safe to affirm that punishments of torture ... and all others in the same line of unnecessary cruelty, are forbidden by [the Eighth Amendment]").

That is not to say that every malevolent touch by a prison guard gives rise to a federal cause of action. See *Johnson* v. *Glick,* 481 F. 2d, at 1033 ("Not every push or shove, even if it may later seem unnecessary in the peace of a judge's chambers, violates a prisoner's constitutional rights"). The Eighth Amendment's prohibition of "cruel and unusual" punishment necessarily excludes from constitutional recognition *de minimis* uses of physical force, provided that the use of force is not of a sort "'repugnant to the conscience of mankind.'" *Whitley, supra,* at 327 (quoting *Estelle, supra,* at 106) (internal quotation marks omitted).

In this case, the Fifth Circuit found Hudson's claim untenable because his injuries were "minor." 929 F. 2d, at 1015. Yet the blows directed at Hudson, which caused bruises, swelling, loosened teeth, and a cracked dental plate, are not *de minimis* for Eighth Amendment purposes. The extent of Hudson's injuries thus provides no basis for dismissal of his § 1983 claim.

B

The dissent's theory that *Wilson* requires an inmate who alleges excessive use of force to show serious injury *in addition* to the unnecessary and wanton infliction of pain misapplies *Wilson* and ignores the body of our Eighth Amendment jurisprudence. As we have already suggested, the question before the Court in *Wilson* was "[w]hether a prisoner claiming that conditions of confinement constitute cruel and unusual punishment must show a culpable state of mind on the part of prison officials and, if so, what state of mind is required." *Wilson, supra,* at ___. *Wilson* presented neither an allegation of excessive force nor any issue relating to what was dubbed the "objective component" of an Eighth Amendment claim.

Wilson did touch on these matters in the course of summarizing our prior holdings, beginning with *Estelle v. Gamble, supra. Estelle,* we noted, first applied the Cruel and Unusual Punishments Clause to deprivations that were not specifically part of the prisoner's sentence. *Wilson,* 501 U.S., at ___. As might be expected from this primacy, *Estelle* stated the principle underlying the cases discussed in *Wilson:* punishments "incompatible with the evolving standards of decency that mark the progress of a maturing society" or "involv[ing] the unnecessary and wanton infliction of pain" are "repugnant to the Eighth Amendment." *Estelle, supra,* at 102-103 (internal quotations omitted). This is the same rule the dissent would reject. With respect to the objective component of an Eighth Amendment claim, however, *Wilson* suggested no departure from *Estelle* and its progeny.

The dissent's argument that claims based on excessive force and claims based on conditions of confinement are no different in kind, *post,* at 8-9, and n. 4, is likewise unfounded. Far from rejecting *Whitley*'s insight that the unnecessary and wanton infliction of pain standard must be applied with regard for the nature of the alleged Eighth Amendment violation, the *Wilson* Court adopted it. See *Wilson, supra,* at ___. How could it be otherwise when the constitutional touchstone is whether punishment is cruel and unusual? To deny, as the dissent does, the difference between punching a prisoner in the face and serving him unappetizing food is to ignore the "'concepts of dignity, civilized standards, humanity, and decency'" that animate the Eighth Amendment. *Estelle, supra,* at 102 (quoting *Jackson v. Bishop,* 404 F. 2d 571, 579 (CA8 1968)).

C

Respondents argue that, aside from the significant injury test applied by the Fifth Circuit, their conduct cannot constitute an Eighth Amendment violation because it was "isolated and unauthorized." Brief for Respondents 28. The beating of Hudson, they contend, arose from "a personal dispute between correctional security officers and a prisoner," and was against prison policy. *Ibid.* Respondents invoke the reasoning of courts that have held the use of force by prison officers under such circumstances beyond the scope of "punishment" prohibited by the Eighth Amendment. See *Johnson v. Glick, supra,* at 1032 ("[A]lthough a spontaneous attack by a guard is 'cruel' and, we hope, 'unusual,' it does not fit any ordinary concept of 'punishment'"); *George v. Evans,* 633 F. 2d 413, 416 (CA5 1980) ("[A] single, unauthorized assault by a guard does not constitute cruel and unusual punishment ..."). But see *Duckworth* v. *Franzen*, 780 F. 2d 645, 652 (CA7 1985) ("If a guard decided to supplement a prisoner's official punishment by beating him, this would be punishment ..."), cert. denied, 479 U.S. 816 (1986).

We take no position on respondents' legal argument because we find it inapposite on this record. The Court of Appeals left intact the Magistrate's determination that the violence at issue in this case was "not an isolated assault." App. 27, n. 1. Indeed, there was testimony that McMillian and Woods beat another prisoner shortly after they finished with Hudson. *Ibid.* To the extent that respondents rely on the unauthorized nature of their acts, they make a claim not addressed by the Fifth Circuit, not presented by the question on which we granted certiorari, and, accordingly, not before this Court. Moreover, respondents ignore the Magistrate's finding that Lieutenant Mezo, acting as a supervisor, "expressly condoned the use of force in this instance." App. 26.

The judgment of the Court of Appeals is

Reversed.

JUSTICE STEVENS, concurring in part and concurring in the judgment.

In *Whitley* v. *Albers*, 475 U.S. 312 (1986), the Court held that injuries to prisoners do not constitute cruel and unusual punishment when they are inflicted during a prison disturbance "that indisputably poses significant risks to the safety of inmates and prison staff" unless force was applied "'maliciously and sadistically for the very purpose of causing harm.'" *Id.*, at 320–321 (citation omitted). The Court's opinion explained that the justification for that particularly high standard of proof was required by the exigencies present during a serious prison disturbance. "When the 'ever-present potential for violent confrontation and conflagration' ripens into actual unrest and conflict," *id.*, at 321 (citation omitted), then prison officials must be permitted to "take into account the very real threats the unrest presents to inmates and prison officials alike." *Id.*, at 320.

Absent such special circumstances, however, the less demanding standard of "'unnecessary and wanton infliction of pain'" should be applied. *Estelle* v. *Gamble*, 429 U.S. 97, 104 (1976) (quoting *Gregg* v. *Georgia*, 428 U.S. 153, 173 (1976) (opinion of Stewart, Powell, STEVENS, JJ.)); see *Unwin* v. *Campbell*, 863 F. 2d 124, 135 (CA1 1988) (opinion of Campbell, C. J.) ("where institutional security is not at stake, the officials' license to use force is more limited; to succeed, a plaintiff need not prove malicious and sadistic intent"); see also *Wyatt* v. *Delaney*, 818 F. 2d 21, 23 (CA8 1987). This approach is consistent with the Court's admonition in *Whitley* that the standard to be used is one that gives "due regard for differences in the kind of conduct against which an Eighth Amendment objection is lodged." 475 U.S., at 320. In this case, because there was no prison disturbance and "no need to use any force since the plaintiff was already in restraints," App. 27, the prison guards' attack upon petitioner resulted in the infliction of unnecessary and wanton pain. *Id.*, at 28.

Although I think that the Court's reliance on the malicious and sadistic standard is misplaced, I agree with the Court that even this more demanding standard was met here. Accordingly, I concur in Parts I, II(A), II(B), and II(C) of the Court's opinion and in its judgment.

JUSTICE BLACKMUN, concurring in the judgment.

The Court today appropriately puts to rest a seriously misguided view that pain inflicted by an excessive use of force is actionable under the Eighth Amendment only when coupled with "significant injury," *e.g.*, injury that requires medical attention or leaves permanent marks. Indeed, were we to hold to the contrary, we might place various kinds of state-sponsored torture and abuse—of the kind ingeniously designed to cause pain but without a telltale "significant injury" entirely beyond the pale of the Constitution. In other words, the constitutional prohibition of "cruel and unusual punishments" then might not constrain prison officials from lashing prisoners with leather straps, whipping them with rubber hoses, beating them with naked fists, shocking them with electric currents, asphyxiating them short of death, intentionally exposing them to undue heat or cold, or forcibly injecting them with psychosis-inducing drugs. These techniques, commonly thought to be practiced only outside this Nation's borders, are hardly unknown within this Nation's prisons. See, *e.g.*, *Campbell* v. *Grammer*, 889 F. 2d 797, 802 (CA8 1989) (use of high-powered fire hoses); *Jackson* v. *Bishop*, 404 F. 2d 571, 574–575 (CA8 1968) (use of the "Tucker Telephone," a hand-cranked device that generated electric shocks to sensitive body parts, and flogging with leather strap). See also *Hutto* v. *Finney*, 437 U.S. 678, 682, n. 5 (1978).

Because I was in the dissent in *Whitley* v. *Albers*, 475 U.S. 312, 328 (1986), I do not join the Court's extension of *Whitley*'s malicious-and-sadistic standard to all allegations of excessive force, even outside the context of a prison riot. Nevertheless, I otherwise join the Court's solid opinion and judgment that the Eighth Amendment does not require a showing of "significant injury" in the excessive-force context. I write separately to highlight two concerns not addressed by the Court in its opinion.

I

Citing rising caseloads, respondents, represented by the Attorney General of Louisiana, and joined by the States of Texas, Hawaii, Nevada, Wyoming, and Florida as *amici curiae*, suggest that a "significant injury" requirement is necessary to curb the number of court filings by prison inmates. We are informed that the "significant injury requirement has been very effective in the Fifth Circuit in helping to control its system-wide docket management problems." Brief for Texas, Hawaii, Nevada, Wyoming, and Florida as *Amici Curiae* 15.

This audacious approach to the Eighth Amendment assumes that the interpretation of an explicit constitutional protection is to be guided by pure policy preferences for the paring down of prisoner petitions. Perhaps judicial

overload is an appropriate concern in determining whether statutory standing to sue should be conferred upon certain plaintiffs. See, *e.g.*, *Associated General Contractors of Ca.lifornia, Inc.* v. *Carpenters*, 459 U.S. 519, 529–546 (1983) (identifying "judge-made rules" circumscribing persons entitled to sue under § 4 of the Clayton Act); *Blue Chip Stamps* v. *Manor Drug Stores*, 421 U.S. 723, 737–749 (1975) (identifying judicial "policy" considerations limiting standing under § 10(b) of the Securities Exchange Act of 1934). But this inherently self-interested concern has no appropriate role in interpreting the contours of a substantive constitutional right.

Since the burden on the courts is presumably worth bearing when a prisoner's suit has merit, the States' "concern" is more aptly termed a "conclusion" that such suits are simply without merit. One's experience on the federal bench teaches the contrary. Moreover, were particular classes of cases to be nominated for exclusion from the federal courthouse, we might look first to cases in which federal law is not sensitively at issue rather than to those in which fundamental constitutional rights are at stake. The right to file for legal redress in the courts is as valuable to a prisoner as to any other citizen. Indeed, for the prisoner it is more valuable. Inasmuch as one convicted of a serious crime and imprisoned usually is divested of the franchise, the right to file a court action stands, in the words of *Yick Wo* v. *Hopkins*, 118 U.S. 356, 370 (1886), as his most "fundamental political right, because preservative of all rights."

Today's ruling, in any event, does not open the floodgates for filings by prison inmates. By statute, prisoners—alone among all other § 1983 claimants—are required to exhaust administrative remedies. See 94 Stat. 352, 42 U.S.C. § 1997e(a); *Patsy* v. *Board of Regents of Florida*, 457 U.S. 496, 507–512 (1982). Moreover, prison officials are entitled to a determination before trial whether they acted in an objectively reasonable manner, thereby entitling them to a qualified immunity defense. *Procunier* v. *Navarette*, 434 U.S. 555, 561–562 (1978); see also *Harlow* v. *Fitzgerald*, 457 U.S. 800, 817–818 (1982) (unsubstantiated

CHAPTER 7: FORCE

allegations of malice are insufficient to overcome pretrial qualified immunity). Additionally, a federal district court is authorized to dismiss a prisoner's complaint *in forma pauperis* "if satisfied that the action is frivolous or malicious." 28 U.S.C. § 1915(d). These measures should be adequate to control any docket-management problems that might result from meritless prisoner claims.

II

I do not read anything in the Court's opinion to limit injury cognizable under the Eighth Amendment to physical injury. It is not hard to imagine inflictions of psychological harm—without corresponding physical harm—that might prove to be cruel and unusual punishment. See, *e.g.*, *Wisniewski* v. *Kennard*, 901 F. 2d 1276, 1277 (CA5) (guard placing a revolver in inmate's mouth and threatening to blow prisoner's head off), cert. denied, __ U.S. __ (1990). The issue was not presented here, because Hudson did not allege that he feared that the beating incident would be repeated or that it had caused him anxiety and depression. See App. 29.

As the Court makes clear, the Eighth Amendment prohibits the unnecessary and wanton infliction of "pain," rather than "injury." *Ante*, at 2–3. "Pain" in its ordinary meaning surely includes a notion of psychological harm. I am unaware of any precedent of this Court to the effect that psychological pain is not cognizable for constitutional purposes. If anything, our precedent is to the contrary. See *Sierra Club* v. *Morton*, 405 U.S. 727, 734 (1972) (recognizing Article III standing for "aesthetic" injury); *Brown* v. *Board of Education*, 347 U.S. 483, 494 (1954) (identifying school children's feelings of psychological inferiority from segregation in the public schools).

To be sure, as the Court's opinion intimates, *ante*, at 7, *de minimis* or nonmeasurable pain is not actionable under the Eighth Amendment. But psychological pain can be more than *de minimis*. Psychological pain often may be clinically diagnosed and quantified through well

established methods, as in the ordinary tort context where damages for pain and suffering are regularly awarded. I have no doubt that to read a "physical pain" or "physical injury" requirement into the Eighth Amendment would be no less pernicious and without foundation than the "significant injury" requirement we reject today.

JUSTICE THOMAS, with whom JUSTICE SCALIA joins, dissenting.

We granted certiorari in this case "limited to the following question," which we formulated for the parties:

> "'Did the Fifth Circuit apply the correct legal test when determining that petitioner's claim that his Eighth Amendment rights under the Cruel and Unusual Punishment Clause were not violated as a result of a single incident of force by respondents which did not cause a significant injury?'" 500 U.S. __, __ (1991).

Guided by what it considers "the evolving standards of decency that mark the progress of a maturing society," *ante*, at 6 (internal quotations omitted), the Court today answers that question in the negative. I would answer it in the affirmative, and would therefore affirm the judgment of the Fifth Circuit. I respectfully dissent.

I

The magistrate who found the facts in this case emphasized that petitioner's injuries were "minor." App. 26, 28. The three judges of the Fifth Circuit who heard the case on appeal did not disturb that assessment, and it has not been challenged here. The sole issue in this case, as it comes to us, is a legal one: must a prisoner who claims to have been subjected to "cruel and unusual punishment" establish at a minimum that he has suffered a significant injury? The Court today not only responds in the negative, but broadly asserts that *any* "unnecessary and wanton" use of physical force against a prisoner *automatically* amounts to "cruel and unusual punishment," whenever more than *de minimis* force is involved. Even a *de minimis* use of force, the Court goes on to declare, inflicts cruel and unusual punishment where it is "repugnant to the conscience of mankind." *Ante*, at 7 (internal quotations omitted).[1] The extent to which a prisoner is *injured* by the force—indeed, whether he is injured at all—is in the Court's view irrelevant.

In my view, a use of force that causes only insignificant harm to a prisoner may be immoral, it may be tortious, it may be criminal, and it may even be remediable under other provisions of the Federal Constitution, but it is not "cruel and unusual punishment." In concluding to the contrary, the Court today goes far beyond our precedents.

A

Until recent years, the Cruel and Unusual Punishment Clause was not deemed to apply at all to deprivations that were not inflicted as part of the sentence for a crime. For generations, judges and commentators regarded the Eighth Amendment as applying only to torturous punishments meted out by statutes or sentencing judges, and not generally to any hardship that might befall a prisoner during incarceration. In *Weems* v. *United States*, 217 U.S. 349 (1910), the Court extensively chronicled the background of the amendment, discussing its English antecedents, its adoption by Congress, its construction by this Court, and the interpretation of analogous provisions by state courts. Nowhere does *Weems* even hint that the Clause might regulate not just criminal sentences but the treatment of prisoners. Scholarly commentary also viewed the Clause as governing punishments that were part of the sentence. See T. Cooley, Constitutional Limitations *329 ("It is certainly difficult to determine precisely what is meant by cruel and unusual punishments. Probably any punishment *declared by statute* for an offence which was punishable in the same way at the common law, could not be regarded as cruel or unusual in the constitutional sense. And probably any new statutory offence may be punished to the extent and in the mode permitted by the *common law* for offences of similar nature. But those degrading punishments which in any State had become obsolete before its existing

constitution was adopted, we think may well be held forbidden by it as cruel and unusual") (emphasis added). See also 3 J. Story, Commentaries on the Constitution of the United States 750–751 (1833).

Surely prison was not a more congenial place in the early years of the Republic than it is today; nor were our judges and commentators so naive as to be unaware of the often harsh conditions of prison life. Rather, they simply did not conceive of the Eighth Amendment as protecting inmates from harsh treatment. Thus, historically, the lower courts routinely rejected prisoner grievances by explaining that the courts had no role in regulating prison life. "[I]t is well settled that it is not the function of the courts to superintend the treatment and discipline of prisoners in penitentiaries, but only to deliver from imprisonment those who are illegally confined." *Stroud* v. *Swope*, 187 F. 2d 850, 851-852 (CA9), cert. denied, 342 U.S. 829 (1951). See also *Sutton* v. *Settle*, 302 F. 2d 286, 288 (CA8 1962) (*per curiam*), cert. denied, 372 U.S. 930 (1963); *United States ex rel. Atterbury* v. *Ragen*, 237 F. 2d 953, 954-956 (CA7 1956), cert. denied, 353 U.S. 964 (1957); *Banning* v. *Looney*, 213 F. 2d 771 (CA10 1954) (*per curiam*); *Sarshik* v. *Sanford*, 142 F. 2d 676 (CA5 1944). It was not until 1976—185 years after the Eighth Amendment was adopted—that this Court first applied it to a prisoner's complaint about a deprivation suffered in prison. *Estelle* v. *Gamble*, 429 U.S. 97 (1976).

B

We made clear in *Estelle* that the Eighth Amendment plays a very limited role in regulating prison administration. The case involved a claim that prison doctors had inadequately attended an inmate's medical needs. We rejected the claim because the inmate failed to allege "acts or omissions sufficiently harmful to evidence *deliberate indifference* to *serious* medical needs." *Id.*, at 106 (emphasis added). From the outset, thus, we specified that the Eighth Amendment does not apply to every deprivation, or even every unnecessary deprivation, suffered by a prisoner, but *only* that narrow class of deprivations involving "serious" injury inflicted by prison officials acting with a culpable state of mind. We have since described these twin elements as the "objective" and "subjective" components of an Eighth Amendment prison claim. See *Wilson v. Seiter*, 501 U.S. __, __ (1991) (slip op., at 3-4).

We have never found a violation of the Eighth Amendment in the prison context when an inmate has failed to establish either of these elements. In *Rhodes v. Chapman*, 452 U.S. 337 (1981), for instance, we upheld a practice of placing two inmates in a single cell on the ground that the injury alleged was insufficiently serious. Only where prison conditions deny an inmate "the minimal civilized measure of life's necessities," *id.*, at 347, we said, could they be considered "cruel and unusual punishment." Similarly, in *Whitley v. Albers*, 475 U.S. 312 (1986), we held that a guard did not violate the Eighth Amendment when he shot an inmate during a prison riot because he had not acted with a sufficiently culpable state of mind. When an official uses force to quell a riot, we said, he does not violate the Eighth Amendment unless he acts "'maliciously and sadistically for the very purpose of causing harm.'" *Id.*, at 320-321 (quoting *Johnson v. Glick*, 481 F. 2d 1028, 1033 (CA2) (Friendly, J.), cert. denied *sub nom. John v. Johnson*, 414 U.S. 1033 (1973)).

We synthesized our Eighth Amendment prison jurisprudence last Term in *Wilson, supra*. There the inmate alleged that the poor conditions of his confinement *per se* amounted to cruel and unusual punishment, and argued that he should not be required in addition to establish that officials acted culpably. We rejected that argument, emphasizing that an inmate seeking to establish that a prison deprivation amounts to cruel and unusual punishment always must satisfy *both* the "objective component ... (was the deprivation sufficiently serious?)" *and* the "subjective component (did the officials act with a sufficiently culpable state of mind?)" of the Eighth Amendment. *Id.*, at __ (slip op., at 3-4). Both are necessary components; neither suffices by itself.

These subjective and objective components, of course, are implicit in the traditional Eighth Amendment jurisprudence, which focuses on penalties meted out by statutes or sentencing judges. Thus, if a State were to pass a statute ordering that convicted felons be broken at the wheel, we would not separately inquire whether the legislature had acted with "deliberate indifference," since a statute, as an intentional act, necessarily satisfies an even higher state-of-mind threshold. Likewise, the inquiry whether the deprivation is objectively serious would be encompassed within our determination whether it was "cruel and unusual."

When we cut the Eighth Amendment loose from its historical moorings and applied it to a broad range of prison deprivations, we found it appropriate to make explicit the limitations described in *Estelle, Rhodes, Whitley*, and *Wilson*. "If the pain inflicted is not formally meted out *as punishment* by the statute or the sentencing judge, some mental element must be attributed to the inflicting officer before it can qualify," *Wilson*, 501 U.S., at __ (slip op., at 5) (emphasis in original)—thus, the subjective component. Similarly, because deprivations of all sorts are the very essence of imprisonment, we made explicit the serious deprivation requirement to ensure that the Eighth Amendment did not transfer wholesale the regulation of prison life from executive officials to judges. That is why, in *Wilson*, we described the inquiry mandated by the objective component as: "[W]as the deprivation *sufficiently serious?*" *Id.*, at __ (slip op., at 3) (emphasis added). That formulation plainly reveals our prior assumption that a serious deprivation is *always* required. Under that analysis, a court's task in any given case was to determine whether the challenged deprivation was "sufficiently" serious. It was not, as the Court's interpretation today would have it, to determine whether a "serious" deprivation *is required at all.*[2]

C

Given *Estelle, Rhodes, Whitley*, and *Wilson*, one might have assumed that the Court would have little difficulty answering the question presented in this case by upholding the Fifth Circuit's "significant injury" requirement.[3] Instead, the Court announces that "[t]he objective component of an Eighth Amendment claim is ... contextual and responsive to contemporary standards of decency." *Ante*, at 6 (internal quotation omitted). In the context of claims alleging the excessive use of physical force, the Court then asserts, the serious deprivation requirement is satisfied by no serious deprivation at all. "When prison officials maliciously and sadistically use force to cause harm, contemporary standards of decency always are violated." *Ibid*. Ascertaining prison officials' state of mind, in other words, is the *only* relevant inquiry in deciding whether such cases involve "cruel and unusual punishment." In my view, this approach is an unwarranted and unfortunate break with our Eighth Amendment prison jurisprudence.

The Court purports to derive the answer to this case from *Whitley*. The sum and substance of an Eighth Amendment violation, the Court asserts, is ""'"the unnecessary and wanton infliction of pain."'" *Ante*, at 2–3 (quoting *Whitley*, 475 U.S., at 319). This formulation has the advantage, from the Court's perspective, of eliminating the objective component. As noted above, however, the only dispute in *Whitley* concerned the subjective component; the prisoner, who had been shot, had self-evidently been subjected to an objectively serious injury. *Whitley* did not say, as the Court does today, that the *objective* component is contextual, and that an Eighth Amendment claim may succeed where a prisoner is not seriously injured. Rather, *Whitley* stands for the proposition that, assuming the existence of an objectively serious deprivation, the culpability of an official's state of mind depends on the context in which he acts. "*Whitley* teaches that, *assuming the conduct is harmful enough to satisfy the objectiue component of an Eighth Amendment claim*, see *Rhodes* v. *Chapman*, 452 U.S. 337 (1981), whether it can be characterized as 'wanton' depends upon the constraints facing the official." *Wilson, supra*, at __ (slip op., at 8) (emphasis modified). Whether officials subject a prisoner to the "unnecessary and wanton infliction of pain" is simply one way to describe the *state of mind inquiry* that was at issue in *Whitley* itself.

As *Wilson* made clear, that inquiry is *necessary* but not *sufficient* when a prisoner seeks to show that he has been subjected to cruel and unusual punishment.

Perhaps to compensate for its elimination of the *objective* component in excessive force cases, the Court simultaneously makes it harder for prisoners to establish the *subjective* component. As we explained in *Wilson*, "deliberate indifference" is the baseline mental state required to establish an Eighth Amendment violation. 501 U.S., at __ (slip op., at 8–9). Departure from this baseline is justified where, as in *Whitley*, prison officials act in response to an emergency; in such situations their conduct cannot be characterized as "wanton" unless it is taken "maliciously and sadistically for the very purpose of causing harm." 475 U.S., at 320–321 (internal quotation omitted). The Court today extends the heightened mental state applied in *Whitley* to *all* excessive force cases, even where no competing institutional concerns are present. The Court simply asserts that "[m]any of the concerns underlying our holding in *Whitley* arise whenever guards use force to keep order." *Ante*, at 3 (emphasis added). I do not agree. Many excessive force cases do not arise from guards' attempts to "keep order." (In this very case, the basis for petitioner's Eighth Amendment claim is that the guards hit him when there was no need for them to use any force at all.) The use of excessive physical force is by no means invariably (in fact, perhaps not even predominantly) accompanied by a "malicious and sadistic" state of mind. I see no justification for applying the extraordinary *Whitley* standard to *all* excessive force cases, without regard to the constraints facing prison officials. The Court's unwarranted extension of *Whitley*, I can only suppose, is driven by the implausibility of saying that minor injuries imposed upon prisoners with anything less than a "malicious and sadistic" state of mind can amount to "cruel and unusual punishment."

D

The Court's attempts to distinguish the cases expressly resting upon the objective component are equally unconvincing. As noted above, we have required an extreme deprivation in cases challenging conditions of confinement, *Rhodes* v. *Chapman*, 452 U.S. 337 (1981). Why should such an objectively serious deprivation be required there and not here? The Court's explanation is that "routine discomfort is 'part of the penalty that criminal offenders pay for their offenses against society.'" *Ante*, at 6 (quoting *Rhodes*, *supra*, at 347). But there is quite a gap between "routine discomfort" and the denial of "the minimal civilized measure of life's necessities" required to establish an Eighth Amendment violation. In the Court's view, then, our society's standards of decency are not violated by anything short of uncivilized conditions of confinement (no matter how malicious the mental state of the officials involved), but are automatically violated by any malicious use of force, regardless of whether it even causes an injury. This is puzzling. I see no reason why our society's standards of decency should be more readily offended when officials, with a culpable state of mind, subject a prisoner to a deprivation on one discrete occasion than when they subject him to continuous deprivations over time. If anything, I would think that a deprivation inflicted continuously over a long period would be of greater concern to society than a deprivation inflicted on one particular occasion.[4]

The Court's attempted distinction of *Estelle* is also unpersuasive: "Because society does not expect that prisoners will have unqualified access to health care, deliberate indifference to medical needs amounts to an Eighth Amendment violation only if those needs are 'serious.'" *Ante*, at 6. In my view, our society similarly has no expectation that prisoners will have "unqualified" freedom from force, since forcibly keeping prisoners in detention is what prisons are all about. Why should the seriousness of injury matter when doctors maliciously decide not to treat an inmate, but not when guards maliciously decide to strike him?

At bottom, of course, there is no conclusive way to refute the Court's assertions about our society's "contemporary notions of decency."

That is precisely why this Court has long insisted that determinations of whether punishment is cruel and unusual "should be informed by objective factors to the maximum possible extent," *Rhodes*, *supra*, at 346 (internal quotations omitted).

The Court attempts to justify its departure from precedent by saying that if a showing of serious injury were required, "the Eighth Amendment would permit any physical punishment, no matter how diabolic or inhuman, inflicting less than some arbitrary quantity of injury." *Ante*, at 6. That statement, in my view, reveals a central flaw in the Court's reasoning. "[D]iabolic or inhuman" punishments *by definition* inflict serious injury. That is not to say that the injury must be, or always will be, *physical*. "Many things—beating with a rubber truncheon, water torture, electric shock, incessant noise, reruns of 'Space 1999'—may cause agony as they occur yet leave no enduring injury. The state is not free to inflict such pains without cause just so long as it is careful to leave no marks." *Williams* v. *Boles*, 841 F. 2d 181, 183 (CA7 1988). Surely a prisoner who alleges that prison officials tortured him with a device like the notorious "Tucker Telephone" described by JUSTICE BLACKMUN, *ante*, at 1, has alleged a serious injury. But petitioner has not alleged a deprivation of this type; the injuries he has alleged are entirely physical and were found below to be "minor."

Furthermore, to characterize the serious injury requirement as "arbitrary" is not to explain why it should be eliminated in this particular context while it remains applicable to all other prison deprivations. To be sure, it will not always be obvious which injuries are "serious." But similarly, it will not always be obvious which medical needs are "serious," or which conditions of confinement deny "the minimal civilized measure of life's necessities." These determinations are, however, required by the Eighth Amendment, which prohibits *only* those punishments that are "cruel and unusual." As explained above, I think our precedents clearly establish that a prisoner seeking to prove that he has been subjected to "cruel and unusual" punishment must always show that he has suffered a serious deprivation.

If the Court is to be taken at its word that "the unnecessary and wanton infliction of pain" upon a prisoner *per se* amounts to "cruel and unusual punishment," the implications of today's opinion are sweeping. For this formulation replaces the objective component described in our prior cases with a "necessity" component. Many prison deprivations, however, are not "necessary," at least under any meaningful definition of that word. Thus, under today's analysis, *Rhodes* was wrongly decided. Surely the "double celling" of inmates was not "necessary" to fulfill the State's penal mission; in fact, the prison in that case had been designed for individual cells, but was simply overcrowded. 452 U.S., at 343. We rejected the prisoners' claim in *Rhodes* not because we determined that double-celling was "necessary," but because the deprivations alleged were not sufficiently serious to state a claim of cruel and unusual punishment. After today, the "necessity" of a deprivation is apparently the only relevant inquiry beyond the wantonness of official conduct. This approach, in my view, extends the Eighth Amendment beyond all reasonable limits.

II

Today's expansion of the Cruel and Unusual Punishment Clause beyond all bounds of history and precedent is, I suspect, yet another manifestation of the pervasive view that the Federal Constitution must address all ills in our society. Abusive behavior by prison guards is deplorable conduct that properly evokes outrage and contempt. But that does not mean that it is invariably unconstitutional. The Eighth Amendment is not, and should not be turned into, a National Code of Prison Regulation. To reject the notion that the infliction of concededly "minor" injuries can be considered either "cruel" or "unusual" "punishment" (much less cruel *and* unusual punishment) is not to say that it amounts to acceptable conduct. Rather, it is to recognize that primary responsibility for preventing and punishing such conduct rests not

with the Federal Constitution but with the laws and regulations of the various States.

Petitioner apparently could have, but did not, seek redress for his injuries under state law.[5] Respondents concede that if available state remedies were not constitutionally adequate, petitioner would have a claim under the Due Process Clause of the Fourteenth Amendment. Cf. *Davidson* v. *Cannon,* 474 U.S. 344, 348 (1986); *Hudson* v. *Palmer,* 468 U.S. 517, 532–534 (1984); *Parratt* v. *Taylor,* 451 U.S. 527, 541 (1981). I agree with respondents that this is the appropriate, and appropriately limited, federal constitutional inquiry in this case.

Because I conclude that, under our precedents, a prisoner seeking to establish that he has been subjected to "cruel and unusual punishment" must always show that he has suffered a serious injury, I would affirm the judgment of the Fifth Circuit.

NOTES

1. This point is pure dictum, because the force here was surely not *de minimus.*

2. While granting petitioner relief on his Eighth Amendment claim, the Court leaves open the issue whether isolated and unauthorized acts are "punishment" at all. This will, of course, be the critical question in future cases of this type. If we ultimately decide that isolated and unauthorized acts are not "punishment," then today's decision is a dead letter. That anomaly simply highlights the artificiality of applying the Eighth Amendment to prisoner grievances, whether caused by the random misdeeds of prison officials or by official policy.

3. I do not believe that there is any substantive difference between the "serious deprivation" requirement found in our precedents and the Fifth Circuit's "significant injury" requirement.

4. Moreover, by distinguishing this case from "conditions" cases, the Court resurrects a distinction that we have repudiated as "not only unsupportable in principle but unworkable in practice." *Wilson* v. *Seiter,* 501 U.S. — - —, and n. 1 (1991) (slip op., at 4–5, and n. 1). When officials use force against a prisoner, whether once or every day, that is a "condition" of his confinement. It is unwise, in my view, to make the very existence of the serious deprivation requirement depend on whether a particular claim is characterized as one challenging a "condition" or one challenging a "specific act." Cf.

McCarthy v. *Bronson,* 500 U.S. __, __ (1991) (slip op., at 6) ("conditions of confinement" under 28 U.S.C. § 636(b)(1)(B) includes not only challenges to ongoing prison conditions but also challenges to "isolated incidents" of excessive force, in part because "the distinction between cases challenging ongoing conditions and those challenging specific acts of alleged misconduct will often be difficult to identify").

5. According to respondents:

"Louisiana state courts are open to prisoners for the purpose of suing prison personnel who have caused them unjustified wrongs. For example, see *Parker* v. *State,* 282 So. 2d 483, 486–87 (La. 1973), *cert. denied,* 414 U.S. 1093 (1973); *Anderson* v. *Phelps,* 451 So. 2d 1284, 1285 (La. Ct. App. 1st Cir. 1984); *McGee* v. *State,* 417 So. 2d 416, 418 (La. Ct. App. 1st Cir.), *writ denied,* 420 So. 2d 871 (La. 1982); *Neathery* v. *State,* 395 So. 2d 407, 410 (La. Ct. App. 3d Cir. 1981); *Shields* v. *State Through Dep't of Corrections,* 380 So. 2d 123 (La. Ct. App. 1st Cir. 1979), *writ denied,* 382 So. 2d 164; *Craft* v. *State,* 308 So. 2d 290, 295 (La. Ct. App. 1st Cir.), *writ denied,* 319 So. 2d 441 (La. 1975), *cert. denied,* 423 U.S. 1075, 96 S. Ct. 859, 47 L. Ed. 2d 84 (1975); *Lewis* v. *Listi,* 377 So. 2d 551, 553 (La. Ct. App. 3d Cir. 1979); *Bastida* v. *State,* 269 So. 2d 544, 545 (La. Ct. App. 1st Cir. 1972); *Adams* v. *State,* 247 So. 2d 149, 151 (La. Ct. App. 1st Cir. 1971); *St. Julian* v. *State,* 98 So. 2d 284 (La. Ct. App. 1st Cir. 1957); *Nedd* v. *State,* 281 So. 2d 131, 132 (La. 1973), *cert. denied,* 415 U.S. 957, 94 S. Ct. 1484, 39 L. Ed. 2d 572 (1974); *Mack* v. *State,* 529 So. 2d 446, 448 (La. Ct. App. 1st Cir. 1988), *writ denied,* 533 So. 2d 359 (La. 1988); *Walden* v. *State,* 430 So. 2d 1224 (La. Ct. App. 1st Cir. 1983), *writ denied,* 435 So. 2d 430 (La. 1983); *White* v. *Phelps,* 387 So. 2d 1188 (La. Ct. App. 1st Cir. 1980); *Hampton* v. *State,* 361 So. 2d 257, 258 (La. Ct. App. 1st Cir. 1978); *Davis* v. *State,* 356 So. 2d 452, 454 (La. Ct. App. 1st Cir. 1977); *Betsch* v. *State,* 353 So. 2d [358], 359 (La. Ct. App. 1st Cir. 1977), *writ refused,* 354 So. 2d 1389 (La. 1978); *Williams* v. *State,* 351 So. 2d 1273 (La. Ct. App. 1st Cir. 1977); *Jones* v. *State,* 346 So. 2d 807, 808 (La. Ct. App. 1st Cir.), *writ refused,* 350 So. 2d 671 (La. 1977); *Walker* v. *State,* 346 So. 2d 794, 796 (La. Ct. App. 1st Cir.), *writ denied,* 349 So. 2d 879 (La. 1977); *Raney* v. *State,* 322 So. 2d 890 (La. Ct. App. 1st Cir. 1975); and *Bay* v. *Maggio,* 417 So. 2d 1386 (La. Ct. App. 1st Cir. 1982)." Brief for Respondents 42–43, n.38.

Petitioner has not disputed the existence or adequacy of state-law remedies for his injuries.

Study Questions

1. Did the Court of Appeals for the Fifth Circuit find the beating of Hudson to involve "unnecessary and wanton infliction of pain"? Does the Supreme Court agree? Do you agree? Why?

2. What is the "core judicial inquiry" in cases of excessive use of force by prison officials, according to the Supreme Court?

3. Do you think that prison inmates should ever be beaten? Why? If so, under what circumstances? Can the beating of an inmate under restraint ever be justified? Why?

Policy on Use of Force

OHIO DEPARTMENT OF REHABILITATION AND CORRECTION

5120-9-01 USE OF FORCE

(A) As the legal custodians of a large number of inmates, some of whom are dangerous, prison officials and employees are confronted with situations in which it is necessary to use force to control inmates.

This rule identifies the circumstances when force may be used lawfully.

(B) As used in this rule and rule 5120-9-02 of the Administrative Code:

(1) "Excessive force" means an application of

Ohio Administrative Code, Chapter 5120-9-01.

force which, either by the type of force employed, or the extent to which such force is employed, exceeds that force which is reasonably necessary under all the circumstances surrounding the incident.

(2) "Force" means any violence, compulsion, or constraint physically exerted by any means upon or against a person or thing.

(3) "Deadly force" means any force which carries a substantial risk that it will proximately result in the death of any person. Examples of deadly force include, but are not limited to, the following:

    (a) Discharging a firearm in the immediate vicinity of and directed toward another person;

    (b) Striking another person on the head with an instrument;

    (c) Applying force or weight to the throat or neck of another.

(4) "Physical harm to persons" means any injury, illness, or other physiological impairment regardless of its gravity or duration.

(5) "Serious physical harm to persons" means any of the following:

    (a) Any mental illness or condition of such gravity as would normally require hospitalization or prolonged psychiatric treatment;

    (b) Any physical harm which carries a substantial risk of death;

    (c) Any physical harm which involves some permanent incapacity, whether partial or total, or which involves some temporary, substantial incapacity;

    (d) Any physical harm which involves some permanent disfigurement or which involves some temporary, serious disfigurement;

    (e) Any physical harm which involves acute pain of such duration as to result in substantial suffering, or which involves any degree of prolonged or intractable pain.

(6) "Risk" means a significant possibility, as contrasted with a remote possibility, that a certain result may occur or that certain circumstances may exist.

(7) "Substantial risk" means a strong possibility, as contrasted with a remote or significant possibility, that a certain result may occur or that certain circumstances may exist.

(8) "Immobilizing restraint" means any appliance which secures the arms and/or legs of an inmate to a bed in such a way that the inmate is prevented from rising from his or her bed, using toilet facilities or eating. "Immobilizing restraint" shall include, but is not limited to, what is known as "four-way restraints."

(C) There are six general situations in which a staff member may legally use force against an inmate:

    (1) Self-defense from an assault by an inmate;

    (2) Defense of third persons, such as other employees, inmates, or visitors, from an assault by an inmate;

    (3) Controlling or subduing an inmate who refuses to obey prison rules and regulations;

    (4) Prevention of crime, such as malicious destruction of state property or prison riot;

    (5) Prevention of escape; and

    (6) Controlling an inmate to prevent self-inflicted harm.

Use of immobilizing restraints as defined in paragraph (B)(7) above shall be governed exclusively by the provisions of paragraphs (I), (J), (K), and (L) of this rule.

(D) Force or physical harm to persons shall not be used as prison punishment. This paragraph shall not be construed to affect or limit the disciplinary measures authorized in rules 5120-9-06 and 5120-9-07 of the Administrative Code.

(E) The superintendent, administrator, or staff member of a correctional institution is authorized to use force, other than deadly force, when and to the extent he reasonably believes that such force is necessary to enforce the lawful rules and regulations of the institution and to control violent behavior.

(F) The superintendent, administrator, or staff member is authorized to use force, including deadly force, when and to the extent he reasonably believes that such force is the least force necessary to do any of the following:

    (1) Protect self from death or serious physical harm from the unlawful use of force by an inmate or another person;

    (2) Protect another against death or serious physical harm from the unlawful use of force by an inmate or another person when there is a reasonable belief that the protected person would be justified in using such force if able;

    (3) Disperse or apprehend rioters whose conduct is creating a substantial risk of serious physical harm to other persons;

    (4) Prevent or halt a felony about to be or being committed; and

    (5) Prevent or halt an escape about to be or being committed, or to apprehend an inmate who has escaped.

(G) Whenever possible, an appropriate warning shall be given prior to the use of deadly force. In no event shall a warning shot with a firearm be appropriate within a building.

(H) Whenever, in the judgment of the shift supervisor, any application of force may have exceeded "slight force" as set forth in rule 5120-9-02 of the Administrative Code, a medical examination of the inmate shall be conducted as soon as practicable following the incident.

(I) Immobilizing restraints may be ordered by the shift supervisors as a last resort to control and protect an inmate who threatens suicide, who experiences a violent episode of mental instability, or who needs to be completely subdued for a very short period of time after behaving violently toward another person. Immobilizing restraints shall not be used as punishment.

(J) The duration of the restraint of an inmate in immobilizing restraints shall be categorized as "initial," "extended" or "authorized."

(1) "Initial" restraint of no more than three hours may be ordered by a shift supervisor;

(2) "Extended" restraint shall be approved by a physician. This extension of the initial period of restraint shall not be longer in duration than eight hours. The physician's approval must be obtained either personally or by telephone within the initial three-hour period;

(3) "Authorized" restraint exceeding the extended period must receive the prior approval of a physician, who must first examine the inmate. The authorized period shall not exceed eight hours. Such authorization shall be based on a personal examination with reference made to the inmate's medical chart. The inmate may not be restrained beyond any authorized period without further personal examination and authorization by a physician.

(K) An inmate placed in immobilizing restraints shall be released or placed in lesser restraints unless the responsible physician finds that his behavior mandates otherwise. Release from immobilizing restraints may also be ordered at any time by the shift supervisor or the superintendent or his designee.

(L) The superintendent shall designate areas in the institution where inmates may be restrained in immobilizing restraints.

Policy on Use of Force

LOS ANGELES POLICE DEPARTMENT

240.10 Use of Force

In a complex urban society, officers are daily confronted with situations where control must be exercised to effect arrests and to protect the public safety. Control may be achieved through advice, warnings, and persuasion, or by the use of physical force. While the use of reasonable physical force may be necessary in situations which cannot be otherwise controlled, force may not be resorted to unless other reasonable alternatives have been exhausted or would clearly be ineffective under the particular circumstances. Officers are permitted to use whatever force that is reasonable and necessary to protect others or themselves from bodily harm....

245 Employee-Involved Use of Force Incidents
245.05 Reportable Use of Force Incident—Defined

A reportable use of force incident is defined as an incident in which any on-duty Department employee, or off-duty employee whose occupation as a Department employee is a factor, uses a nonlethal control device or any physical force to:

- Compel a person to comply with the employee's directions; or,
- Overcome resistance by a suspect during an arrest or a detention; or,
- Defend any person from an aggressive action by a suspect.

Los Angeles Police Department, Manual of the Los Angeles Police Department, *1991, vol. 1, pp. 98, 108, 109; vol. 4, p. 332.*

Exceptions: The following incidents are *not* reportable under the provisions of this Section:

- The use of a firm grip control only, which does not result in an injury; or,
- That force necessary to overcome passive resistance due to physical disability or intoxication which does not result in an injury; e.g., the use of a wrist lock to assist an intoxicated person to a standing position; or,
- An incident investigated by the Officer-Involved Shooting Section, Robbery-Homicide Division.

245.10 Reporting Use of Force Incidents

An employee who becomes involved in a reportable use of force incident or discharges a TASER or a chemical irritant control device for any reason other than an approved training exercise shall:

- Complete a Use of Force Report, Form 1.67.2;
- Report the full details of the use of force incident in the related Department arrest or crime report;
- Use an Employee's Report, Form 15.7, to report the full details of the use of force incident when a crime or arrest report is *not* required;
- Ensure that each page of all copies of the related report has the words USE OF FORCE in the left margin.

Off-duty employees who become involved in a reportable use of force incident shall notify their supervisor or watch commander without unnecessary delay. Notification shall be made to the Watch Commander, Detective Headquarters Division, when the employee's location of assignment is closed.

Note: Off-duty employees completing use of force related reports shall submit a copy to their supervisor no later than their next regularly scheduled tour of duty....

556 Use of Firearms
556.10 Preamble to the Policy on the Use of Firearms

The use of a firearm is in all probability the most serious act in which a law enforcement officer will engage. It has the most far-reaching consequences for all of the parties involved. It is, therefore, imperative not only that the officer act within the boundaries of legal guidelines, ethics, good judgment, and accepted practices, but also that the officer be prepared by training, leadership, and direction to act wisely whenever using a firearm in the course of duty.

A reverence for the value of human life shall guide officers in considering the use of deadly force. While officers have an affirmative duty to use that degree of force necessary to protect human life, the use of deadly force is not justified merely to protect property interests.

It is in the public interest that a police officer of this Department be guided by a policy which the people believe to be fair and appropriate and which creates public confidence in the Department and its individual officers.

This policy is not intended to create doubt in the mind of an officer at a moment when action is critical and there is little time for meditation or reflection. It provides basic guidelines governing the use of firearms so that officers can be confident in exercising judgment as to the use of deadly force. Such a policy must be viewed as an administrative guide for decision-making before the fact and as a standard for administrative judgment of the propriety of the action taken. It is not to be considered a standard for external judgment (civil or criminal litigation) of the propriety of an action taken. This is a matter of established law and also a process for courts and juries reviewing specific facts of a given incident.

556.20 Necessity That Officers Be Armed

As long as members of the public are victims of violent crimes and officers in the performance of their duties are confronted with deadly force, it will remain necessary for police officers to be properly armed for the protection of society and themselves.

556.25 Reason for the Use of Deadly Force

An officer is equipped with a firearm to protect himself or others against the immediate threat of death or serious bodily injury or to apprehend a fleeing felon who has committed a violent crime and whose escape presents a substantial risk of death or serious bodily injury to others.

556.30 Protection of General Public

Regardless of the nature of the crime or the justification for firing at a suspect, officers must remember that their basic responsibility is to protect the public. Officers shall not fire under conditions that would subject bystanders or hostages to death or possible injury, except to preserve life or prevent serious bodily injury. Firing under such conditions is not justified unless the failure to do so at the time would create a substantial immediate threat of death or serious bodily injury.

556.35 Minimizing the Risk of Death

An officer does not shoot with the intent to kill; he shoots when it is necessary to prevent the individual from completing what he is attempting. In the extreme stress of a shooting situation, an officer may not have the opportunity or ability to direct his shot to a nonfatal area. To require him to do so, in every instance, could increase the risk of harm to himself or others. However, in keeping with the philosophy that the minimum force that is necessary should be used, officers should be aware that, even in the rare cases where the use of firearms reasonably appears necessary, the risk of death to any person should be minimized.

556.40   The Use of Deadly Force

An officer is authorized the use of deadly force when it reasonably appears necessary:

- To protect himself or others from an immediate threat of death or serious bodily injury, or
- To prevent a crime where the suspect's actions place persons in jeopardy of death or serious bodily injury, or
- To apprehend a fleeing felon for a crime involving serious bodily injury or the use of deadly force where there is a substantial risk that the person whose arrest is sought will cause death or serious bodily injury to others if apprehension is delayed.

Officers shall not use deadly force to protect themselves from assaults which are not likely to have serious results.

Firing at or from moving vehicles is generally prohibited. Experience shows such action is rarely effective and is extremely hazardous to innocent persons.

Deadly force shall only be exercised when all reasonable alternatives have been exhausted or appear impracticable.

556.50   Justification Limited to Facts Known to Officer

Justification for the use of deadly force must be limited to what reasonably appear to be the facts known or perceived by an officer at the time he decides to shoot. Facts unknown to an officer, no matter how compelling, cannot be considered at a later date to justify a shooting.

556.55   Suspected Felony Offenders

An officer shall not fire at a person who is called upon to halt on mere suspicion and who simply runs away to avoid arrest. Nor should an officer fire at a "fleeing felon" if the officer has any doubt whether the person fired at is in fact the person against whom the use of deadly force is permitted under this policy.

556.60   Youthful Felony Suspects

This Department has always utilized extreme caution with respect to the use of deadly force against youthful offenders. Nothing in this policy is intended to reduce the degree of care required in such cases.

556.70   Shooting at Fleeing Misdemeanants

Officers shall not use deadly force to effect the arrest or prevent the escape of a person whose only offense is classified solely as a misdemeanor under the Penal Code.

556.75   Firing Warning Shots

Generally, warning shots should not be fired. . . .

572   Use of Chemical Agents

To minimize injury to suspects, officers, and others or to avoid property damage, the use of a chemical agent, such as tear gas, may be necessary in circumstances where a serious danger to life and property exists and other methods of control or apprehension would be ineffective or more dangerous.

The field commander at a police situation has the responsibility for determining the need for the use of a chemical agent and the authority to direct its deployment. In no event, however, can authorization for the use of a chemical agent be given by an officer below the rank of Sergeant or Detective. The use of a chemical agent for crowd or riot control must be authorized by an officer of the rank of Commander or higher.

573   Use of Nonlethal Control Devices

To reduce the number of altercations-related injuries to officers and suspects, the Department authorizes the use of selected nonlethal control devices.

Approved nonlethal control devices may be used to control a violent or potentially violent suspect when lethal force does not appear to be justifiable and/or necessary; and attempts to subdue the suspect by other conventional tactics have been or will likely be ineffective in the situation at hand; or there is a reasonable expectation that it will be unsafe for officers to approach to within contact range of the suspect.

Chemical irritant spray *shall* be possessed and maintained by all uniformed field personnel who have completed designated training in its use. Non-uniformed personnel *may* possess chemical irritant spray subject to the same training requirements.

The TASER shall be used *only* by personnel who have completed the Department's TASER training program.

Officers who use nonlethal control devices shall ensure that medical treatment is obtained, if needed, for the person(s) upon whom the nonlethal control device is used. TASER cassette darts which penetrate the skin shall be removed by trained medical personnel only.

Case 7.1

MARIJUANA FOR DINNER

Officer Mark Barrett worked the midnight shift of a large metropolitan police department in the southeast. Because "cutback management" had taken its toll on his squad, it was not unusual to start a shift with 15 or 20 calls holding and only four one-officer cars and one two-officer car to handle the load. Thus, any time an officer made an arrest, it was necessary to check out of service for at least two hours in order to transport the prisoner to jail, complete the booking process, and wrap up the paperwork. It also left the patrol zone short. It seemed that for the last few weeks the "dirt-bags" had learned that, because of the manpower shortage, they were able to win in cases of police–citizen confrontation.

While completing a routine check of a park late one night, Officer Barrett observed a white male subject duck behind a tree when he saw the patrol car. Officer Barrett approached the subject to determine why he was in the park after hours. The man had what Officer Barrett can best describe as an "attitude," that is, he was somewhat belligerent and uncooperative. During the course of the inquiry, Officer Barrett noticed that the man had a joint over his ear. Officer Barrett thought, "What a jerk." When he confronted the man, he stated, "So, what's the big deal?"

Officer Barrett quickly reviewed his options. First, he could arrest the man for possession of a marijuana cigarette. The problem was he would have to leave his zone one officer short, the case was a misdemeanor, and, since the average marijuana seizure on his department is over two pounds, he would look kind of silly arresting for only one joint. The second was to release the man and ignore the offense. The problem with that was that the guy had an attitude and he didn't want him to think he could run roughshod over any officer that stopped him. He was faced with a real dilemma. What could he do short of arrest but more than an outright release?

He handed the joint back to the subject and said, "We've got a problem. You have this joint and I've got to arrest you."

"How's about I just throw it down the sewer?" replied the suspect.

"Can't, that's littering."

"What can I do, then?"

"Bon appetit."

"Huh?" replied the suspect.

"Eat hearty."

"Aw, come on," replied the suspect.

"It's that, or jail."

As officer Barrett drove away, the subject was left standing in the park with a green tongue and sticks, seeds, leaves, and wrapping paper working their way through his digestive system. His attitude, however, was much improved.

Questions for Discussion

1. What would you do? Apply the ethical decision-making checklist to help you.

2. Balance the utility of making an arrest versus the danger to fellow officers by leaving the district for several hours. Does the severity of the offense matter? Why? Defend your position.

3. Should "attitude" influence an officer's decision in this case? Explain.

4. What if the suspect was driving under the influence? Would that make a difference? Explain.

Case 7.2

TALK OR DIE

"Attention all units. Burglary in progress, possible assault. 207 Ohio Avenue. Complainant advises she heard glass breaking and her elderly neighbor screaming. Unit 602, respond on a '3'."

This was not Officer Gary Williams' call, but since he was in the area, he began to cruise the streets near the location waiting for some description of the subject(s) as the other units arrived on the scene.

"Unit 602. BOLO." [BOLO is an acronym for "Be on the look-out."]

"Unit 602. Go ahead."

"Be advised, victim is DOA. Subjects will be wanted reference homicide, sexual assault and burglary. Victim is an 80-year old female. Advise homicide and the lab. Complainant observed two subject(s) leaving the scene. Subject #1 is a white male, approximately six feet tall. Subject fled the scene just prior to this unit's arrival. He was wearing only a green jacket, underpants, and army boots. Subject #2 is a white male. No other description."

"Unit 602. Clear."

Williams continued to cruise the area, hoping to get lucky. Usually the subjects are long gone by the time units respond, but maybe this call would be different. He heard 602 request a dog to search the area. Since the units had responded and set up a perimeter quicker than usual, maybe with luck, the subject might still be inside.

About 10 minutes later, he heard the K-9 units advise they were beginning to check the area. Within 10 seconds Williams saw "Mr. Underwear" bounding across the street about 30 feet in front of his headlights. "The son of a bitch is mine," he thought as he jumped out of his cruiser and began to run after him. Luck was with him. You just can't be fleet-footed in big, loose army boots. Williams grabbed the guy, cuffed him, led him back to the cruiser, and put him in the back seat.

"Where's your partner, asshole?"

"I don't know what you're talking about."

"The guy that was with you when you dicked that old lady."

"Shit, man, I don't know what you're talking about."

"Look, motherfucker," Williams said, unsnapping his holster, "you've got two choices. Tell me the name of your partner and go to jail, or die."

"What you talking about man, you just can't shoot me."

"Wanna bet? You've got 10 seconds to decide. Talk, or the handcuffs come off and you become a fleeing forcible felon. I'll have no choice but to 'off' you."

"You wouldn't."

"Eight seconds."

"That's murder, man!"

"Five seconds."

"Nobody was with me!"

"Three seconds."

"All right, all right, man, just put the gun away, I'll talk."

Questions for Discussion

1. Apply Klockars' features of a Dirty Harry problem to this case to determine whether or not a Dirty Harry problem exists. Defend your assessment.

2. Assume the officer was bluffing. Can the actions of the officer be justified? Explain.

3. Do you think that the use of force in this case was justified?

4. Review the readings in Chapter 5: Truth. Would the officer be justified in testimonial deception as to the legality of the confession?

Case 7.3

TO INSURE PROMPT SERVICE

You are employed as a waitress for a nationally known restaurant chain, one that is famous for the many people who "eat and run," leaving you to pay the bill. It is the policy of the restaurant to serve police officers free coffee. This is done for the purpose of occasioning police presence and also in gratitude for the difficult, sometimes thankless, job that the officers do. Late one evening, one of your customers leaves the restaurant without paying his bill. You manage to get the license plate number of the customer's car and call the police with the number, as well as a description of the customer.

Within minutes, Officer Jackson (one of your regular customers) returns with "Joe Stiff." Since it is the policy of the restaurant not to press criminal charges, Joe pays his bill and turns to leave. He is stopped by Officer Jackson.

"You're going to give your waitress a tip for all her trouble, aren't you?" Officer Jackson says.

The authors would like to thank Ruth Osborne for contributing this case.

Stiff opens his wallet and takes out a dollar bill. At the sight of this, Officer Jackson grabs Joe's wrist and repeats, "You *will* give your waitress a *tip* for all the TROUBLE you've caused her."

Stiff puts the dollar back and gives you a five-dollar bill.

As Officer Jackson leaves to go back on patrol, he turns to Stiff and says, "Have a nice day."

Questions for Discussion

1. Discuss the relationship between the restaurant and the police. Apply the concepts in Kania's article to the situation.

2. What type of force is employed against the customer? Is this a discretionary action by the officer, or inappropriate use of force?

Case 7.4

THE LATE HIT

You are a young, inexperienced, probationary corrections officer assigned to the Disciplinary and Administrative Segregation Cell Block at your state's maximum security prison. The D-AS Block houses two types of prisoners who cannot be placed in the general population. The first type is the prisoner who needs protection from the general population. Usually, this prisoner has been repeatedly victimized and is either unwilling or unable to protect himself. The second type is the prisoner who poses a danger to the general population: the violent, impulsive, and/or sadistic inmate who cannot or will not be controlled by the correctional staff.

One such inmate in the second category is Ho Chang. Ho is an expert in the martial arts and is doing three consecutive life terms for murder. In addition, it is strongly suspected that Ho was responsible for the deaths of at least two inmates, although there was never enough evidence to bring him up on charges. Ho has assaulted numerous inmates and staff but, since he is a lifer with no chance for parole and your state does not have the death penalty, additional sentences are of little value. Ho's method of operation is to lull his victim into a false sense of security and then brutally assault him when his guard is down.

Whenever it is necessary to remove Ho from his cell the standard operating procedure is to have him put his hands and feet through the bars for cuffing prior to opening the cell door. When the cell door is opened, Ho backs out of the cell and is shackled. A minimum of four officers are necessary whenever Ho is removed. In addition, a yellow line has been painted on the floor outside of Ho's cell to indicate the extent of his reach.

Today, you and three "veteran" officers are assigned to escort Ho while he takes his weekly shower. You are very nervous, and you unconsciously telegraph this to Ho. Without warning, Ho drops to the floor and, in spite of the shackles, kicks you with both his feet. You are knocked to the floor.

Instantly, the other three officers are on top of Ho. He is pinned to the floor in a matter of seconds. Once Ho is controlled, Sgt. Ethan Finch kicks Ho twice in the groin and once in the rib cage. Ho is then literally thrown back into his cell.

You are unhurt. You are also taken aback by the violence meted out to Ho after he was under control. Later, you discreetly approach Sgt. Finch.

"Sergeant, what you did to Ho wasn't right."

"Look kid, he kicked you. We kicked him. The man in the striped shirt comes out, calls offsetting penalties, and we call it a day. Just a late hit, that's all."

Questions for Discussion

1. Did Ho precipitate his own punishment?
2. Can Finch's actions be justified? Take the perspective of Ho and then of the officer kicked.
3. Can Finch's actions be classified as "brutality"? Why? Defend your position.

Chapter 8

Punishment

THE PHILOSOPHICAL LITERATURE ON PUNISHMENT IS enormous and covers many subtopics. Although the definition of punishment is of some interest, most work centers on two large questions: Can punishment be morally justified at all; and if so, what is the justification? We will assume an uncontroversial definition of punishment, following Stanley I. Benn, namely, that punishment is the deliberate infliction of suffering or deprivation on a person "by an agent authorized by the system of rules against which an offense has been committed."[1]

This definition rules out cases of suffering that are not punishment. For example, the social disgrace and embarrassment suffered by a corporate executive who has been convicted of a "white collar" crime might be claimed by some people to be "punishment enough." And even though such suffering may have great rehabilitative and deterrent effect, it is not punishment. The suffering of shame and the deprivation of privacy are consequences of the executive's wrongful behavior, but they were not deliberately imposed on the criminal by an agent of the state. The consequences were *caused* by the behavior itself, and by its exposure to the public.

Another example of suffering that would not in itself qualify as punishment would be treatment for burns suffered in a prison fire. The painfulness of the treatment could not be considered punishment *per se*, since as Benn notes, the unpleasantness of it is coincidental to some other purpose (healing the burn). The suffering or deprivation involved in punishment must be intrinsic to the act of punishment. For example, torturous treatment that was exactly the same in nature and suffering as the burn treatment would be punishment in the proper sense; indeed, it would be cruel and unusual in the Eighth Amendment meaning of the term. In this case, the pain and suffering is the purpose of the treatment, rather than a mere by-product.

Many readers are probably familiar with the two types of theories of punishment: the retributive justification and the utilitarian justification. This categorization is essentially the familiar deontological/teleological distinction found in moral theories. The retributivist believes that the punishment of wrong-doing is right in itself. The justification does not come from some source external to the act of punishment. This does not mean that the retributivist necessarily denies the need for justification itself, but rather that the justification of punishment does not lie in some other good. In Michael Davis' words, "retributive theories are primarily theories of justice, not social control.[2]

As you might expect, Kant defended the retributive theory of punishment. His statement of the thesis is very clear:

> Juridical Punishment can never be administered merely as a means for promoting another Good either with regard to the Criminal himself or to Civil Society, but must in all cases be imposed only because the individual on whom it is inflicted *has committed* a Crime.[3]

This statement is not vacuous, as some have thought, because Kant has a specific account of the nature of the goodness of punishment—what Kant calls the "principle of equality." Applied to punishment, the principle means that "the undeserved evil which any one commits on another, is to be regarded as perpetrated on himself."[4] Kant goes on to identify this application of the principle of equality as "the right of retaliation" (*lex talionis*). Echoes of Kant's definition of retribution can be heard in A. C. Ewing's statement of the retributive theory:

> ... the primary justification of punishment is always to be found in the fact that an offense has been committed which deserves punishment, not in any future advantage to be gained by its infliction.[5]

Even though retribution, retaliation, revenge, and vengeance all have similar meanings in English, some philosophers argue that there are important distinctions among these terms. For example, Joel Feinberg says that the retributive theory should not be confused with what he calls *vengeance theories*. Feinberg defines such vengeance theories as holding that the justification of punishment lies in "vindictive satisfaction in the mind of the beholder [of the punishment]."[6] Feinberg identifies three versions of the vengeance theory: the escape-valve version, in which punishment provides vicarious release of aggressive feelings toward the criminal; the hedonistic version, which locates the justification of punishment in the pleasure people experience in seeing the criminal suffer; and the romantic version, in which justification is felt to reside in the emotions of hate and anger felt toward the criminal. The last two versions Feinberg regards as scarcely defensible, while the first version of the vengeance theory is nothing more than a species of the utilitarian theory of punishment. This shows, incidentally, why at least some vengeance theories should not be confused with the deontologically-grounded retributive theory.

The utilitarian justification of punishment generally appears in either of two forms. The first type appeals to the reforming effects of punishment on the criminal. The state is justified in imposing suffering on a person because doing so will decrease the likelihood of that person acting wrongly in the future. If a particular punishment cannot be shown to have a corrective or rehabilitative effect on the convict, it is unjustified and hence morally wrong. If the punishment is predictably corrective, the familiar utilitarian analysis must begin. Since punishment is by definition an evil visited upon a person, those bad consequences must be weighed against the good consequences—for instance, the criminal actions that will never happen because of the corrective action of the punishment.

These calculations, either on an act or rule utilitarian account, are extremely difficult in that the good effects are the future *absence* of criminality. For example, how do we know what would have happened if an 18-year-old auto thief were not punished? Can we correctly say that the two years in prison failed to rehabilitate if the person is again arrested for auto theft? How do we know that the criminal would not have "graduated" to armed robbery, had it not been for the prison term?

The idea that one may justifiably be punished to reduce the likelihood of future misconduct presents several other problems for the utilitarian. First, it seems to allow punishment if any future misconduct will be reduced. If harsh punishment for car theft deters future armed robbery, then perhaps harsh punishment for shoplifting will do the same. The goal of the punishment seems to be completely disconnected from the action bringing it about. Surely a punishment should be commensurate with the seriousness of the offense. Even worse, utilitarians must face the problem of apparent justification of punishing someone who has committed no offense at all, but who predictably will commit one soon. If we have a statistically reliable profile for armed robbers, why wait until a robbery is actually committed? If the punishment is an effective deterrent, then there seems to be little reason for waiting until the crime occurs when it could have been completely prevented.

This is known as the problem of punishment of the innocent. In its most extreme form, this criticism of the utilitarian justification of punishment has been posed as follows: If we can deter other people from committing crimes by harshly punishing this one innocent person as an example, don't the good consequences to society far outweigh the suffering and deprivation experienced by the innocent person? Of course, we must make sure that the public *believes* that the convict is truly guilty, but whether the convict is actually guilty or not will not have any bearing on the deterrent effect of the punishment. Would such a punishment be morally justified?

A more modest form of the same problem occurs in what many people believe to be a justifiable goal of punishment: the deterrence of other persons from committing the same crime. In this view, we are justified in punishing Jones for armed robbery even if the punishment will predictably have no corrective effect on Jones. As long as *other* would-be armed robbers are deterred from that crime by the example of Jones' punishment, the punishment is justified. You can see that this approach is only a step away from the problem of punishment of the innocent. Both cases justify punishment, not because of any effect it has on the behavior of the convict, but because of the effect it has on the behavior of others. In both cases, it is not clear that the convict is being treated as anything other than a means. If a utilitarian defense of punishment is going to succeed at all, it seems that some good must accrue to the subject of the punishment. This is a significant conclusion. A punishment that is a wonderful deterrent to others, but *only* a deterrent to others violates Kant's formula of the End-in-Itself.

Furthermore, if rehabilitation is an essential component of a utilitarian justification of punishment, then suffering and deprivation no longer seem to be necessary components of punishment. But if we can rehabilitate a criminal with little or no suffering—for example, with brain surgery—is the criminal getting "what he or she deserves"? If the utilitarian rejects the idea that only those who deserve to be punished should be punished, then we seem to be back to punishing the innocent for the greater good, and punishing people who are likely to commit a crime but actually haven't.

The general issue of desert (what one deserves) is related directly to the issue of moral responsibility. The issue of moral responsibility in turn rests on the issue of free will and determinism. These larger philosophical problems cannot be adequately addressed in this chapter, but in practical terms you can see how they underlie the legal questions of the insanity defense, diminished capacity, and mitigating circumstances that relate directly to moral responsibility.

The Readings

General Punishment

The first selection, J. D. Mabbott's "Punishment," directly challenges the utilitarian theory of punishment. Mabbott states that he will defend a pure retributive theory, but the thesis is not the usual. He says

> No punishment is morally retributive or reformative or deterrent. Any criminal punished for any one of these reasons is certainly unjustly punished. The only justification for punishing any man is that he has broken a law.

Mabbott argues that by connecting punishment with law-breaking rather than with moral wrong-doing, traditional objections to the retributive theory are avoided. Since in this view punishment is not intended to balance or negate moral wrong, the questions of *how* to punish in a way that balances moral wrong never arises.

Mabbott then attacks utilitarian justifications of punishment, e.g., reform of the criminal and deterrence of others. In fact, Mabbott seems to think it is implausible to suppose that the punishment of a particular person could have a deterrent effect, so deterrence could hardly justify *that particular punishment.*

Although Mabbott's position is quite distinct from Kant's, both versions of retributivism force us to look at the justification of punishment on an individual basis. We can't say, "Most punishments are justified," as a pure utilitarian might. If we are to treat each person as an end, we must look at each punishment and ask, "Is *this* punishment justifiable?" Even on utilitarian grounds, this formal condition may eliminate virtually all appeals to deterrence as a justification for a specific punishment. Only in those cases where the punishment of a specific person is highly publicized is any deterrent effect *from that punishment* likely to occur. It is logically absurd to suppose that a punishment did have a deterrent effect on a potential wrong-doer when none of the potential wrong-doers were aware that the punishment occurred.[7]

The second selection, John Rawls' "Justifying Punishment," is taken from Rawls' seminal paper on utilitarianism, "Two Concepts of Rules." Rawls argues that the utilitarian justification of punishment can be rescued from the criticisms of the retributivists, and in fact, that the utilitarian and retributivist justifications are compatible.

Rawls' position is based on utilizing a long-standing distinction between justifying a practice and justifying a particular action falling under a practice. Utilitarian justifications are relevant to *practices*, while retributive justifications are applicable to particular punishments. Rawls uses the following example: The question, "Why was *J* put in jail yesterday?" is different from the question, "Why do people put other people in jail?" The answer to the first question might be, "Because he robbed a bank, was tried and found guilty," while the answer to the second question would probably be something like, "Because it protects society from dangerous people." While the judicial process is therefore basically retributivist, Rawls says, the ideal legislative process is utilitarian.

Rawls argues that this distinction solves the utilitarian's problem of punishment of the innocent because it recognizes the retributivist's valid claim that no one can be justly punished unless he has broken the law. At the same time, Rawls' solution accommodates the utilitarian's insistence that people not be punished just for the sake of punishment, but rather that a penal system must be shown to benefit society. Rawls then considers two objections to his revision of utilitarianism: that it justifies too little, and that it justifies too much.

Capital Punishment

The question of abolishing capital punishment in the United States was a live issue for many decades prior to the U. S. Supreme Court's decision in *Gregg* v. *Georgia* (1976). In that decision, the Court ruled that "the punishment of death does not invariably violate the Constitution" (428 U. S. 169). Up to that time, it appeared that the United States might follow the vast majority of industrialized nations that have abolished the death penalty. Aside from some Third World countries and fundamentalist theocracies like Iran, only the former Soviet Union and South Africa still maintain capital punishment. After a long hiatus, executions have resumed in the United States, in compliance with the requirements of review for arbitrariness and caprice, and the balancing of aggravating and mitigating circumstances stated both in *Gregg* and in the earlier decision in *Furman* v. *Georgia* (1972). Consequently, the vast literature concerning the constitutionality of the death penalty is now moot.

On the other hand, the morality of capital punishment remains unchanged as an important issue throughout the country. In *Gregg,* the Court appears to sidestep the moral issue by deferring to the state legislatures to select any lesser penalties: "We may not require the legislature to select the least severe penalty possible so long as the penalty selected is not cruelly inhumane or disproportionate to the crime involved" (428 U.S. 175). We can therefore expect the death penalty debate to continue, at least in those states that continue to execute. *Furman* contains several powerful arguments against capital punishment in general, even though the Court's decision in that case was limited to the constitutionality of Georgia's imposition of the death penalty. Many of the arguments that persuaded the majority in *Furman* are echoed by Blackmun's dissenting opinion in *Gregg* v. *Georgia.*[8]

Sidney Hook's selection, "The Death Sentence," is a limited defense of the death penalty in two types of cases. Although Hook believes the usual justifications for capital punishment such as deterrence or community outrage are unsuccessful, he argues that there are cases in which capital punishment is justified. The first instance is where a defendant sentenced to life imprisonment for murder asks to be executed. In such cases, Hook believes that the convict's wishes should be respected. One difficulty that arises with this view is that such an action seems to be a judicially assisted suicide rather than a punishment.[9] The second case for capital punishment is where, in

Hook's view, execution is the only solution to dealing with repeat murderers—persons who have been punished for murder and who kill again.

The second selection on capital punishment is Hugo Adam Bedau's paper, "How to Argue About the Death Penalty." Bedau approaches the issue by first arguing that four widely debated factual questions do have likely answers. Those questions are as follows: (1) Is the death penalty a better deterrent to murder than imprisonment? (2) Is the death penalty administered arbitrarily or in a racially discriminatory way? (3) Could an innocent person be executed for a crime he or she did not commit, under our current system? (4) Do persons who are imprisoned for a capital crime, but not executed, commit another capital crime? Bedau thinks the answers to these questions are No, Yes, Yes, and Yes, respectively. However, even if everyone agreed with these answers, Bedau says that the death penalty debate would remain unresolved.

Bedau proposes instead that we consider capital punishment from the perspective of the social goals that punishment should achieve, limited by "acknowledged moral principles." Bedau thus rejects a pure retributivist view in which punishment is good for its own sake. If punishment is properly a means to achieve some end, what are those ends? Bedau proposes two. First, punishment should contribute to the reduction of crime, and second, punishment should be economical in the sense that it should not waste valuable resources if equally effective cheaper means are available. Bedau also considers other goals, including rectification of harm, venting of public anger, and the moral improvement of the convict, but thinks these are problematic.

The utilitarian goals proposed by Bedau are circumscribed by deontological constraints. Bedau identifies six constraints, including death as the less preferable punishment if there is a feasible alternative, the severity of fair punishment being commensurate with the gravity of the crime, etc. He concludes that while the death penalty is a means to certain social goals, it is not the only, or the best, means. The moral status of capital punishment is in conflict with the general preference that governmental power over individuals should not be expanded, and that where governmental power is wielded, it should enhance "the autonomy and liberty of those directly affected." Finally, Bedau says, the death penalty is not a symbol of justice, but rather of "brutality and stupidity." Bedau draws this conclusion from the conflict between the claim that all murderers deserve death and the fact that so very few actually get it.

The final selection in this chapter is James W. Marquart and Julian B. Roebuck's "Prison Guards and Snitches: Social Control in a Maximum Security Institution." This paper examines a particular administrative prison policy of inmate control through the use of an informer-privilege system. Marquart and Roebuck point out that the "stool pigeon" is a negative image embedded in prison folklore. While some research has been done on the personal characteristics of "rats," the authors' purpose is to study "how officials use inmate intelligence as a management strategy."

Because each guard was responsible for 400 inmates in the Texas prison researched, corrections officers delegated guard "authority" to a system of inmate snitches, who in turn developed their own networks of informers. In fact, the inmate "guard" hierarchy involved four levels of inmate reporting responsibilities! The authors describe the system as "totalitarian" and one that "virtually destroyed any chances among the ordinary inmates (as individuals or groups) to unite or engage in collective dissent, protests, or violence." Despite its overall effectiveness, the snitch system of prisoner control treated the ordinary inmates as nonpersons "who lived in continuous fear, loneliness, isolation, and tension." Not only could head snitches effect punishment indiscriminately against inmates, they were powerful enough to bring about the discharge of low-ranking prison guards.

Although this form of prisoner control was declared to be corrupt and deviant in *Ruiz* v. *Estelle* (1980), and is no longer in use, *de facto* systems of inmate-run "enforcement" systems continue to exist in many correctional institutions.

Notes

1. Stanley I. Benn, "Punishment," in Paul edwards (ed.), *The Encyclopedia of Philosophy* (New York: Macmillan Publishing Co., and The Free Press), vol. 7, p. 29.
2. Michael Davis, "Recent Work in Punishment Theory," *Public Affairs Quarterly*, vol. 4:3 (July 1990), p. 219. This paper contains a very useful overview of the philosophy of punishment by one of the leaders in the field, as well as a bibliography.
3. Immanuel Kant, *The Philosophy of Law*, W. Hastie, trans. (Edinburgh: T. & T. Clark, 1887), p. 194.
4. *Ibid.*, p. 195.
5. A. C. Ewing, *The Morality of Punishment* (London: Kegan Paul, 1929), p. 13.
6. Joel Feinberg (ed.), *Reason and Responsibility*. Third Edition (Encino, CA: Dickenson Publishing Co., 1975), p. 421.
7. This simply shows that knowledge of another's punishment is a necessary condition for being deterred from that crime *by that punishment*. Knowledge of punishment is obviously not a sufficient condition for deterrence, though. Hugo Bedau recounts the plausible, if apocryphal, story of the public hanging of pickpockets in England. The events were supposed to be a favorite among pickpockets, who worked the crowds with great success.
8. In *Furman* and *Gregg*, it is important to remember that in the former, four of nine justices argued that capital punishment does not violate the Eighth Amendment prohibition of cruel and unusual punishment, while in *Gregg*, those four were joined by Justices Stewart and White, who had agreed in *Furman* that capital punishment in Georgia was then unconstitutional. The seventh vote in *Gregg* was Justice Stevens, who had replaced Justice Douglas in the interim.

   Although space limitations prevented reproducing these decisions here, they are widely available in applied ethics readers. For a very accessible treatment of capital punishment, including an excerpt from *Gregg*, see Jeffrey Olen and Vincent Barry, *Applying Ethics*, Third Edition (Belmont: Wadsworth Publishing Company, 1989), Ch. 7. Also see the exchange between Michael Davis ("The Death Penalty, Civilization, and Inhumaneness") and Jeffrey Reiman ("The Death Penalty, Deterrence, and Horribleness: Reply to Michael Davis") in *Social Theory and Practice*, vol. 16:2 (Summer 1990), pp. 245–259 and pp. 261–272, respectively.
9. See Hugo Adam Bedau, "Death as a Punishment," in Hugo Adam Bedau (ed.), *The Death Penalty in America*, Revised Edition (Garden City: Anchor Books, 1967), p. 219.

Punishment

J. D. MABBOTT

I PROPOSE IN THIS paper to defend a retributive theory of punishment and to reject absolutely all utilitarian considerations from its justification. I feel sure that this enterprise must arouse deep suspicion and hostility both among philosophers (who must have felt that the retributive view is the only moral theory except perhaps psychological hedonism which has been definitely destroyed by criticism) and among practical men (who have welcomed its steady decline in our penal practice).

The question I am asking is this. Under what circumstances is the punishment of some particular person justified and why? The theories of reform and deterrence which are usually considered to be the only alternatives to retribution involve well-known difficulties. These are considered fully and fairly in Dr. Ewing's book *The Morality of Punishment,* and I need not spend long over them. The central difficulty is that both would on occasion justify the punishment of an innocent man, the deterrent theory if he were believed to have been guilty by those likely to commit the crime in future, and the reformatory theory if he were a bad man though not a criminal. To this may be added the point against the deterrent theory that it is the threat of punishment and not punishment itself which deters, and that when deterrence seems to depend on actual punishment, to implement the threat, it really depends on publication and may be achieved if men believe that punishment has occurred even if in fact it has not. As Bentham saw, for a Utilitarian apparent justice is everything, real justice is irrelevant.

Dr. Ewing and other moralists would be inclined to compromise with retribution in the face of the above difficulties. They would admit that one fact and one fact only can justify the punishment of this man, and that is a *past* fact, that he has committed a crime. To this extent reform and deterrence theories, which look only to the consequences, are wrong. But they would add that retribution can determine only *that* a man should be punished. It cannot determine how or how much, and here reform and deterrence may come in. Even Bradley, the fiercest retributionist of modern times, says "Having once the right to punish we may modify the punishment according to the useful and the pleasant, but these are external to the matter; they cannot give us a right to punish and nothing can do that but criminal desert." Dr. Ewing would maintain that the whole estimate of the amount and nature of a punishment may be effected by considerations of reform and deterrence. It seems to me that this is a surrender which the upholders of retribution dare not make. As I said above, it is publicity and not punishment which deters, and the publicity though often spoken of as "part of a man's punishment" is no more part of it than his arrest or his detention prior to trial, though both these may be also unpleasant and bring him into disrepute. A judge sentences a man to three years' imprisonment, not to three years *plus* three columns in the press. Similarly with reform. The visit of the prison chaplain is not part of a man's punishment nor is the visit of Miss Fields or Mickey Mouse.

The truth is that while punishing a man and punishing him justly, it is possible to deter others, and also to attempt to reform him, and if

J. D. Mabbott, "Punishment," Mind, *vol. 48 (1939), pp. 152–167. Reprinted by permission of Oxford University Press.*

these additional goods are achieved the total state of affairs is better than it would be with the just punishment alone. But reform and deterrence are not modifications of the punishment, still less reasons for it. A parallel may be found in the case of tact and truth. If you have to tell a friend an unpleasant truth you may do all you can to put him at his ease and spare his feelings as much as possible while still making sure that he understands your meaning. In such a case no one would say that your offer of a cigarette beforehand or your apology afterwards are modifications of the truth still less reasons for telling it. You do not tell the truth in order to spare his feelings, but having to tell the truth you also spare his feelings. So Bradley was right when he said that reform and deterrence were "external to the matter," but therefore wrong when he said that they may "modify the punishment." Reporters are admitted to our trials so that punishments may become public and help to deter others. But the punishment would be no less just were reporters excluded and deterrence not achieved. Prison authorities may make it possible that a convict may become physically or morally better. They cannot ensure either result; and the punishment would still be just if the criminal took no advantage of their arrangements and their efforts failed. Some moralists see this and exclude these "extra" arrangements for deterrence and reform. They say that it must be the punishment *itself* which reforms and deters. But it is just my point that the punishment *itself* seldom reforms the criminal and never deters others. It is only "extra" arrangements which have any chance of achieving either result. As this is the central point of my paper, at the cost of laboured repetition I would ask the upholders of reform and deterrence two questions. Suppose it could be shown that a particular criminal had not been improved by a punishment and also that no other would-be criminal had been deterred by it, would that prove that the punishment was unjust? Suppose it were discovered that a particular criminal had lived a much better life after his release and that many would-be criminals believing him to have been guilty were

influenced by his fate, but yet that the "criminal" was punished for something he had never done, would these excellent results prove the punishment just?

It will be observed that I have throughout treated punishment as a purely legal matter. A "criminal" means a man who has broken a law, not a bad man; an "innocent" man is a man who has not broken the law in connection with which he is being punished, though he may be a bad man and have broken other laws. Here I dissent from most upholders of the retributive theory— from Hegel, from Bradley, and from Dr. Ross. They maintain that the essential connection is one between punishment and moral or social wrong-doing.

My fundamental difficulty with their theory is the question of *status*. It takes two to make a punishment, and for a moral or social wrong I can find no punisher. We may be tempted to say when we hear of some brutal action "that ought to be punished"; but I cannot see how there can be duties which are nobody's duties. If I see a man ill-treating a horse in a country where cruelty to animals is not a legal offence, and I say to him "I shall now punish you," he will reply, rightly, "What has it to do with you? Who made you a judge and ruler over me?" I may have a duty to try to stop him and one way of stopping him may be to hit him, but another way may be to buy the horse. Neither the blow nor the price is a punishment. For a moral offence, God alone has the *status* necessary to punish the offender; and the theologians are becoming more and more doubtful whether even God has a duty to punish wrong-doing.

Dr. Ross would hold that not all wrong-doing is punishable, but only invasion of the rights of others; and in such a case it might be thought that the injured party had a right to punish. His right, however, is rather a right to preparation, and should not be confused with punishment proper.

This connection, on which I insist, between punishment and crime, not between punishment and moral or social wrong, alone accounts for some of our beliefs about punishment, and also meets many objections to the retributive theory as stated in its ordinary form. The first point on which it helps us is with regard to retrospective legislation. Our objection to this practice is unaccountable on reform and deterrence theories. For a man who commits a wrong before the date on which a law against it is passed, is as much in need of reform as a man who commits it afterwards; nor is deterrence likely to suffer because of additional punishments for the same offence. But the orthodox retributive theory is equally at a loss here, for if punishment is given for moral wrong-doing or for invasion of the rights of others, that immorality of invasion existed as certainly before the passing of the law as after it.

My theory also explains, where it seems to me all others do not, the case of punishment imposed by an authority who believes the law in question is a bad law. I was myself for some time disciplinary officer of a college whose rules included a rule compelling attendance at chapel. Many of those who broke this rule broke it on principle. I punished them. I certainly did not want to reform them; I respected their characters and their views. I certainly did not want to drive others into chapel through fear of penalties. Nor did I think there had been a wrong done which merited retribution. I wished I could have believed that I would have done the same thing myself. My position was clear. They had broken a rule; they knew it and I knew it. Nothing more was necessary to make punishment proper.

I know that the usual answer to this is that the judge enforces a bad law because otherwise law in general would suffer and good laws would be broken. The effect of punishing good men for breaking bad laws is that fewer bad men break good laws.

[*Excursus on Indirect Utilitarianism*. The above argument is a particular instance of a general utilitarian solution of all similar problems. When I am in funds and consider whether I should pay my debts or give the same amount to charity, I must choose the former because repayment not only benefits my creditor (for the benefit to him might be less than the good done

through charity) but also upholds the general credit system. I tell the truth when a lie might do more good to the parties directly concerned, because I thus increase general trust and confidence. I keep a promise when it might do more immediate good to break it, because indirectly I bring it about that promises will be more readily made in future and this will outweigh [the] immediate loss involved. Dr. Ross has pointed out that the effect on the credit system of my refusal to pay a debt is greatly exaggerated. But I have a more serious objection of principle. It is that in all these cases the indirect effects do not result from my wrong action—my lie or defalcation or bad faith—but from the publication of these actions. If in any instance the breaking of the rule were to remain unknown then I could consider only the direct or immediate consequences. Thus in my "compulsory chapel" case I could have considered which of my culprits were law-abiding men generally and unlikely to break any other college rule. Then I could have sent for each of these separately and said "I shall let you off if you will tell no one I have done so." By these means the general keeping of rules would not have suffered. Would this course have been correct? It must be remembered that the proceedings need not deceive everybody. So long as they deceive would-be law-breakers the good is achieved.

As this point is of crucial importance and as it has an interest beyond the immediate issue, and gives a clue to what I regard as the true general nature of law and punishment, I may be excused for expanding and illustrating it by an example or two from other fields. Dr. Ross says that two men dying on a desert island would have duties to keep promises to each other even though their breaking them would not affect the future general confidence in promises at all. Here is certainly the same point. But as I find that desert island morality always rouses suspicion among ordinary men I should like to quote two instances from my own experience which also illustrate the problem.

(i) A man alone with his father at his death promises him a private and quiet funeral. He finds later that both directly and indirectly the keeping of this promise will cause pain and misunderstanding. He can see no particular positive good that the quiet funeral will achieve. No one yet knows that he has made the promise nor need anyone ever know. Should he therefore act as though it had never been made?

(ii) A college has a fund given to it for the encouragement of a subject which is now expiring. Other expanding subjects are in great need of endowment. Should the authorities divert the money? Those who oppose the diversion have previously stood on the past, the promise. But one day one of them discovers the "real reason" for this slavery to a dead donor. He says "We must consider not only the value of this money for these purposes, since on all direct consequences it should be diverted at once. We must remember the effect of this diversion on the general system of benefactions. We know that benefactors like to endow special objects, and this act of ours would discourage such benefactors in future and leave learning worse off." Here again is the indirect utilitarian reason for choosing the alternative which direct utilitarianism would reject. But the immediate answer to this from the most ingenious member of the opposition was crushing and final. He said, "Divert the money but keep it dark." This is obviously correct. It is not the act of diversion which would diminish the stream of benefactions but the news of it reaching the ears of benefactors. Provided that no possible benefactor got to hear of it no indirect loss would result. But the justification of our action would depend entirely on the success of the measures for "keeping it dark." I remember how I felt and how others felt that whatever answer was right this result was certainly wrong. But it follows that indirect utilitarianism is wrong in all such cases. For its argument can always be met by "Keep it dark."

The view, then, that a judge upholds a bad law in order that law in general should not suffer is indefensible. He upholds it simply because he has no right to dispense from punishment.

The connection of punishment with law-breaking and not with wrong-doing also escapes moral objections to the retributive theory as held by Kant and Hegel or by Bradley and Ross. It is asked how we can measure moral wrong or balance it with pain, and how pain can wipe out moral wrong. Retributivists have been pushed into holding that pain *ipso facto* represses the worse self and frees the better, when this is contrary to the vast majority of observed cases. But if punishment is not intended to measure or balance or negate moral wrong then all this is beside the mark. There is the further difficulty of reconciling punishment with repentance and with forgiveness. Repentance is the reaction morally appropriate to moral wrong and punishment added to remorse is an unnecessary evil. But if punishment is associated with law-breaking and not with the moral evil the punisher is not entitled to consider whether the criminal is penitent any more than he may consider whether the law is good. So, too, with forgiveness. Forgiveness is not appropriate to law-breaking. (It is noteworthy that when, in divorce cases, the law has to recognize forgiveness it calls it "condonation," which is symptomatic of the difference of attitude.) Nor is forgiveness appropriate to moral evil. It is appropriate to personal injury. No one has any right to forgive me except the person I have injured. No judge or jury can do so. But the person I have injured has no right to punish me. Therefore there is no clash between punishment and forgiveness since these two duties do not fall on the same person nor in connection with the same characteristic of my act. (It is the weakness of vendetta that it tends to confuse this clear line, though even there it is only by personifying the family that the injured party and the avenger are identified. Similarly we must guard against the plausible fallacy of personifying society and regarding the criminal as "injuring society," for then once more the old dilemma about forgiveness would be insoluble.) A clergyman friend of mine catching a burglar red-handed was puzzled about his duty. In the end he ensured the man's punishment by information and evidence, and at the same time showed his own forgiveness by visiting the man in prison and employing him when he came out. I believe any "good Christian" would accept this as representing his duty. But obviously if the punishment is thought of as imposed *by* the victim or *for* the injury or immorality then the contradiction with forgiveness is hopeless.

So far as the question of the actual punishment of any individual is concerned this paper could stop here. No punishment is morally retributive or reformative or deterrent. Any criminal punished for any one of these reasons is certainly unjustly punished. The only justification for punishing any man is that he has broken a law.

In a book which has already left its mark on prison administration I have found a criminal himself confirming these views. *Walls Have Mouths* by W. F. R. Macartney, is prefaced, and provided with appendices to each chapter, by Compton Mackenzie. It is interesting to notice how the novelist maintains that the proper object of penal servitude should be reformation,[1] whereas the prisoner himself accepts the view I have set out above. Macartney says "To punish a man is to treat him as an equal. To be punished *for an offence against rules* is a sane man's right."[2] It is striking also that he never uses "injustice" to describe the brutality or provocation which he experienced. He makes it clear that there were only two types of prisoner who were *unjustly* imprisoned, those who were insane and not responsible for the acts for which they were punished[3] and those who were innocent and had broken no law.[4] It is irrelevant, as he rightly observes, that some of these innocent men were, like Steinie Morrison, dangerous and violent characters, who on utilitarian grounds might well have been restrained. That made their punishment no whit less unjust.[5] To these general types may be added two specific instances of injustice. First, the sentences on the Dartmoor mutineers. "The Penal Servitude Act ... lays down specific punishments for mutiny and incitement to mutiny, which include flogging.... Yet on the occasion of the only big mutiny in an English prison, men are not dealt with by the Act specially passed to meet mutiny in prison, but are taken out of gaol and tried under an Act expressly passed to curb and curtail the Chartists—a revolutionary movement."[6] Here again the injustice does not lie in the actual effect the sentences are likely to have on the prisoners (though Macartney has some searching suggestions about that also) but in condemning men for breaking a law they did not break and not for breaking the law they did break. The second specific instance is that of Coulton, who served his twenty years and then was brought back to prison to do another eight years and to die. This is due to the "unjust order that no lifer shall be released unless he has either relations or a job to whom he can go: and it is actually suggested that this is really for the lifer's own good. Just fancy, you admit that the man in doing years upon years in prison had expiated his crime: but, instead of releasing him, you keep him a further time—perhaps another three years—because you say he has nowhere to go. Better a ditch and hedge than prison! True, there are abnormal cases who want to stay in prison, but Lawrence wanted to be a private soldier, and men go into monasteries. Because occasionally a man wants to stay in prison, must every lifer who has lost his family during his sentence (I was doing only ten years and I lost all my family) be kept indefinitely in gaol after he has paid his debt?"[7] Why is it unjust? Because he has paid his debt. When that is over it is for the man himself to decide what is for his own good. Once again the reform and utilitarian arguments are summarily swept aside. Injustice lies not in bad treatment or treatment which is not in the man's own interest, but in restriction which, according to the law, he has not merited.

It is true that Macartney writes, in one place, a paragraph of general reflection on punishment in which he confuses, as does Compton Mackenzie, retribution with revenge and in which he seems to hold that the retributive theory has some peculiar connection with private property. "Indeed it is difficult to see how, in society as it is to-day constituted, a humane prison system could function. All property is sacred, although the proceeds of property may well be reprehensible, therefore any offence against property is sacrilege and must be punished. Till a system eventuates which is based not on exploitation of man by man and class by class, prisons must be dreadful places, but at least there might be an effort to ameliorate the more savage side of the retaliation, and this could be done very easily."[8] The alternative system of which no doubt he is thinking is the Russian system described in his quotations from *A Physician's Tour in Soviet Russia*, by Sir James Purves-Stewart, the system of "correctional colonies" providing curative "treatment" for the different types of criminal.[9] There are two confusions here, to one of which we shall return later. First, Macartney confuses the retributive system with the punishment of one particular type of crime, offences against property, when he must have known that the majority of offenders against property do not find themselves in Dartmoor or even in Wandsworth. After all his own offence was not one against property—it was traffic with a foreign Power—and it was one for which in the classless society of Russia the punishment is death. It is surely clear that a retributive system may be adopted for any class of crime. Secondly, Macartney confuses injustice within a penal system with the wrongfulness of a penal system. When he pleads for "humane prisons" as if the essence of the prison should be humanity, or when Compton Mackenzie says the object of penal servitude should be reform, both of them are giving up punishment altogether, not altering it. A Russian "correctional colony," if its real object is curative treatment, is no more a "prison" than is an isolation hospital or a lunatic asylum. To this distinction between abolishing injustice in punishment and abolishing punishment altogether we must now turn.

It will be objected that my original question "Why ought X to be punished?" is an illegitimate isolation of the issue. I have treated the whole set of circumstances as determined. X is a citizen of a state. About his citizenship, whether willing or unwilling, I have asked no questions. About the government, whether it is good or bad, I do not enquire. X has broken a law. Concerning the law, whether it is well-devised or not, I have not asked. Yet all these questions are surely relevant before it can be decided whether a particular punishment is just. It is the essence of my position that none of these questions is relevant. Punishment is a corollary of law-breaking by a member of the society whose law is broken. This is a static and an abstract view but I see no escape from it. Considerations of utility come in on two quite different issues. Should there be laws, and what laws should there be? As a legislator I may ask what general types of action would benefit the community, and, among these, which can be "standardized" without loss, or should be standardized to achieve their full value. This, however, is not the primary question since particular laws may be altered or repealed. The choice which is the essential *prius* of punishment is the choice that there should be laws. The choice is not Hobson's. Other methods may be considered. A government might attempt to standardize certain modes of action by means of advice. It might proclaim its view and say "Citizens are requested" to follow this or that procedure. Or again it might decide to deal with each case as it arose in the manner most effective for the common welfare. Anarchists have wavered between these two alternatives and a third—that of doing nothing to enforce a standard of behaviour but merely giving arbitrational decisions between conflicting parties, decisions binding only by consent.

I think it can be seen without detailed examination of particular laws that the method of law-making has its own advantages. Its orders are explicit and general. It makes behaviour reliable and predictable. Its threat of punishment may be so effective as to make punishment unnecessary. It promises to the good citizen a certain security in his life. When I have talked to businessmen about some inequity in the law of liability they have usually said "Better a bad law than no law, for then we know where we are."

Someone may say I am drawing an impossible line. I deny that punishment is utilitarian; yet now I say that punishment is a corollary of law and we decide whether to have laws and which laws to have on utilitarian grounds. And surely it is only this corollary which distinguishes law from good advice or exhortation. This is a misunderstanding. Punishment is a corollary not of law but of law-breaking. Legislators do not choose to punish. They hope no punishment will be needed. Their laws would succeed even if no punishment occurred. The criminal makes the essential choice: he "brings it on himself." Other men obey the law because they see its order is reasonable, because of inertia, because of fear. In this whole area, and it may be the major part of the state, law achieves its ends without punishment. Clearly, then, punishment is not a corollary of law.

We may return for a moment to the question of amount and nature of punishment. It may be thought that this also is automatic. The law will include its own penalties and the judge will have no option. This, however, is again an initial choice of principle. If the laws do include their own penalties then the judge has no option. But the legislature might adopt a system which left complete or partial freedom to the judge, as we do except in the case of murder. Once again, what are the merits (regardless of particular laws, still more of particular cases) of fixed penalties and variable penalties? At first sight it would seem that all the advantages are with the variable penalties; for men who have broken the same law differ widely in degree of wickedness and responsibility. When, however, we remember that punishment is not an attempt to balance moral guilt this advantage is diminished. But there are still degrees of responsibility; I do not mean degrees of freedom of will but, for instance, degrees of complicity in a crime. The danger of allowing complete freedom to the judicature in fixing penalties is not merely that it lays too heavy a tax on human nature but that it would lead to the judge expressing in his penalty the degree of his own moral aversion to the crime. Or he might tend on deterrent grounds to punish more heavily a crime which was spreading and for which temptation and

opportunity were frequent. Or again on deterrent grounds he might "make examples" by punishing ten times as heavily those criminals who are detected in cases in which nine out of ten evade detection. Yet we should revolt from all such punishments if they involved punishing theft more heavily than blackmail or negligence more heavily than premeditated assault. The death penalty for sheep-stealing might have been defended on such deterrent grounds. But we should dislike equating sheep-stealing with murder. Fixed penalties enable us to draw these distinctions between crimes. It is not that we can say how much imprisonment is right for a sheep stealer. But we can grade crimes in a rough scale and penalties in a rough scale, and keep our heaviest penalties for what are socially the most serious wrongs regardless of whether these penalties will reform the criminal or whether they are exactly what deterrence would require. The compromise of laying down maximum penalties and allowing judges freedom below these limits allows for the arguments on both sides.

To return to the main issue, the position I am defending is that it is essential to a legal system that the infliction of a particular punishment should *not* be determined by the good *that particular punishment* will do either to the criminal or to "society." In exactly the same way it is essential to a credit system that the repayment of a particular debt should not be determined by the good that particular payment will do. One may consider the merits of a legal system or of a credit system, but the acceptance of either involves the surrender of utilitarian considerations in particular cases as they arise. This is in effect admitted by Ewing in one place where he says "It is the penal system as a whole which deters and not the punishment of any individual offender."[10]

To show that the choice between a legal system and its alternatives is one we do and must make, I may quote an early work of Lenin in which he was defending the Marxist tenet that the state is bound to "wither away" with the establishment of a classless society. He considers the possible objection that some wrongs by man against man are not economic and therefore that the abolition of classes would not *ipso facto* eliminate crime. But he sticks to the thesis that these surviving crimes should not be dealt with by law and judicature. "We are not Utopians and do not in the least deny the possibility and inevitability of excesses by *individual persons,* and equally the need to suppress such excesses. But for this no special machine, no special instrument of repression is needed. This will be done by the armed nation itself as simply and as readily as any crowd of civilized people even in modern society parts a pair of combatants or does not allow a woman to be outraged."[11] This alternative to law and punishment has obvious demerits. Any injury not committed in the presence of the crowd, any wrong which required skill to detect or pertinacity to bring home would go untouched. The lynching mob, which is Lenin's instrument of justice, is liable to error and easily deflected from its purpose or driven to extremes. It must be a mob, for there is to be no "machine." I do not say that no alternative machine to ours could be devised but it does seem certain that the absence of all "machines" would be intolerable. An alternative machine might be based on the view that "society" is responsible for all criminality, and this curative and protective system developed. This is the system of Butler's "Erewhon" and something like it seems to be growing up in Russia except for cases of "sedition."

We choose, then, or we acquiesce in and adopt the choice of others of, a legal system as one of our instruments for the establishment of the conditions of a good life. This choice is logically prior to and independent of the actual punishment of any particular persons or the passing of any particular laws. The legislators choose particular laws within the framework of this predetermined system. Once again a small society may illustrate the reality of these choices and the distinction between them. A Headmaster launching a new school must explicitly make both decisions. First, shall we have any rules at all? Second, what rules shall we have? The first decision is a

genuine one and one of great importance. Would it not be better to have an "honour" system, by which public opinion in each house or form dealt with any offence? (This is the Lenin method.) Or would complete freedom be better? Or should he issue appeals and advice? Or should he personally deal with each malefactor individually, as the case arises, in the way most likely to improve his conduct? I can well imagine an idealistic Headmaster attempting to run a school with one of these methods or with a combination of several of them and therefore without punishment. I can even imagine that with a small school of, say, twenty pupils all open to direct personal psychological pressure from authority and from each other, these methods involving no "rules" would work. The pupils would of course grow up without two very useful habits, the habit of having some regular habits and the habit of obeying rules. But I suspect that most Headmasters, especially those of large schools, would either decide at once, or quickly be driven, to realize that some rules were necessary. This decision would be "utilitarian" in the sense that it would be determined by consideration of consequences. The question "what rules?" would then arise and again the issue is utilitarian. What action must be regularized for the school to work efficiently? The hours of arrival and departure, for instance, in a day school. But the one choice which is now no longer open to the Headmaster is whether he shall punish those who break the rules. For if he were to try to avoid this he would in fact simply be returning to the discarded method of appeals and good advice. Yet the Headmaster does not decide to punish. The pupils make the decision there. He decides actually to have rules and to threaten, but only hypothetically, to punish. The one essential condition which makes actual punishment just is a condition he *cannot* fulfill—namely that a rule should be broken.

I shall add a final word of consolation to the practical reformer. Nothing that I have said is meant to counter any movement for "penal reform" but only to insist that none of these reforms have anything to do with punishment.

The only type of reformer who can claim to be reforming the system of punishment is a follower of Lenin or of Samuel Butler who is genuinely attacking the *system* and who believes there should be no laws and no punishments. But our great British reformers have been concerned not with punishment but with its accessories. When a man is sentenced to imprisonment he is not sentenced also to partial starvation, to physical brutality, to pneumonia from damp cells and so on. And any movement which makes his food sufficient to sustain health, which counters the permanent tendency to brutality on the part of his warders, which gives him a dry or even a light and well-aired cell, is pure gain and does not touch the theory of punishment. Reformatory influences and prisoners' aid arrangements are also entirely unaffected by what I have said. I believe myself that it would be best if all such arrangements were made optional for the prisoner, so as to leave him in these cases a freedom of choice which would make it clear that they are not part of his punishment. If it is said that every such reform lessens a man's punishment, I think that is simply muddled thinking which, if it were clear, would be mere brutality. For instance, a prisoners' aid society is said to lighten his punishment, because otherwise he would suffer not merely imprisonment but also unemployment on release. But he was sentenced to imprisonment, not imprisonment *plus* unemployment. If I promise to help a friend and through special circumstances I find that keeping my promise will involve upsetting my day's work, I do not say that I really promised to help him and to ruin my day's work. And if another friend carries on my work for me I do not regard him as carrying out part of my promise, nor as stopping me from carrying it out myself. He merely removes an indirect and regrettable consequence of my keeping my promise. So with punishment. The Prisoners' Aid Society does not alter a man's punishment nor diminish it, but merely removes an indirect and regrettable consequence of it. And anyone who thinks that a criminal cannot make this distinction and will regard all the inconvenience to him that comes to him as punishment, need only talk to a prisoner or two to find out how sharply they resent these wanton additions to a punishment which by itself they will accept as just. Macartney's chapter on "Food" in the book quoted above is a good illustration of this point, as are also his comments on Clayton's administration. "To keep a man in prison for many years at considerable expense and then to free him charged to the eyes with uncontrollable venom and hatred generated by the treatment he has received in gaol, does not appear to be sensible." Clayton "endeavoured to send a man out of prison in a reasonable state of mind. 'Well, I've done my time. They were not too bad to me. Prison is prison and not a bed of roses. Still they didn't rub it in....'"[12] This "reasonable state of mind" is one in which a prisoner on release feels he has been punished but not *additionally* insulted or ill-treated. I feel convinced that penal reformers would meet with even more support if they were clear that they were not attempting to alter the system of punishment but to give its victims "fair play." We have no more right to starve a convict than to starve an animal. We have no more right to keep a convict in a Dartmoor cell "down which the water trickles night and day"[13] than we have to keep a child in such a place. If our reformers really want to alter the system of punishment, let them come out clearly with their alternative and preach, for instance, that no human being is responsible for any wrong-doing, that all the blame is on society, that curative or protective measures should be adopted, forcibly if necessary, as they are with infection or insanity. Short of this let them admit that the essence of prison is deprivation of liberty for the breaking of law, and that deprivation of food or of health or of books is unjust. And if our sentimentalists cry "coddling of prisoners," let us ask them also to come out clearly into the open and incorporate whatever starvation and disease and brutality they think necessary *into the sentences they propose.*[14] If it is said that some prisoners will prefer such reformed prisons, with adequate food and aired cells, to the outer world, we may retort that their numbers are probably not greater than those of the masochists who like to be flogged. Yet we do not hear the same "coddling" critics suggest abolition of the lash on the grounds that some criminals may like it. Even if the abolition from our prisons of all maltreatment other than that imposed by law results in a few down-and-outs breaking a window (as O. Henry's hero did) to get a night's lodging, the country will lose less than she does by her present method of sending out her discharged convicts "charged with venom and hatred" because of the additional and uncovenanted "rubbing it in" which they have received.

I hope I have established both the theoretical importance and the practical value of distinguishing between penal reform as we know and approve it—that reform which alters the accompaniments of punishment without touching its essence—and those attacks on punishment itself which are made not only by reformers who regard criminals as irresponsible and in need of treatment, but also by every judge who announces that he is punishing a man to deter others or to protect society, and by every juryman who is moved to his decision by the moral baseness of the accused rather than by his legal guilt.

NOTES

1. p. 97.
2. p. 165. My italics.
3. pp. 165–166.
4. p. 298.
5. p. 301.
6. p. 255.
7. p. 400.
8. pp. 166, 167.
9. p. 229.
10. A. C. Ewing, *The Morality of Punishment* (London: Routledge and Kegan Paul, Ltd., 1929), p. 66.
11. *The State and Revolution* (Eng. trans.), p. 93. Original italics.
12. p. 152.
13. *Op. cit.*, p. 258.
14. "One of the minor curiosities of jail life was that they quickly provided you with a hundred worries which left you no time or energy for worrying about your sentence, long or short.... Rather as if you were thrown into a fire with spikes in it, and the spikes hurt you so badly that you forget about the fire. But then your punishment would *be* the spikes not the fire. Why did they pretend it was only the fire, when they knew very well about the spikes?" (From *Lifer* by Jim Phelan, p. 40.)

Study Questions

1. What does Mabbot mean when he says that reform and deterrence "are not modifications of the punishment"? Explain how his "unpleasant truth" case illustrates his point. Do you agree? Why? Defend your position.

2. According to Mabbot, does punishment *itself* ever reform a convict? Explain. In your view, could the punishment of Jones itself ever deter someone from committing the crime committed by Jones? Explain. What conditions would have to exist in order for the deterrent effect of *Jones'* punishment to actually occur? Would this deterrent effect morally justify punishing Jones? Why? Defend your position.

3. Mabbot states that a correctional institution, if its real object is curative treatment, is *not* a prison (a place of punishment). Do you agree? Why? Defend your position, commenting on the so-called "medical model" of corrections.

4. Why does Mabbot believe that the view that prison reform lessens the punishment is "simply muddled thinking"? Do you agree with Mabbot? Why? Defend your position.

Two Concepts of Rules

JOHN RAWLS

IN THIS PAPER I WANT to show the importance of the distinction between justifying a practice[1] and justifying a particular action falling under it, and I want to explain the logical basis of this distinction and how it is possible to miss its significance. While the distinction has frequently been made,[2] and is now becoming commonplace, there remains the task of explaining the tendency either to overlook it altogether, or to fail to appreciate its importance.

To show the importance of the distinction I am going to defend utilitarianism against those objections which have traditionally been made against it in connection with punishment and the obligation to keep promises. I hope to show that if one uses the distinction in question then one can state utilitarianism in a way which makes it a much better explication of our considered moral judgments than these traditional objections would seem to admit.[3] Thus the importance of the distinction is shown by the way it strengthens the utilitarian view regardless of whether that view is completely defensible or not.

To explain how the significance of the distinction may be overlooked, I am going to discuss two conceptions of rules. One of these conceptions conceals the importance of distinguishing between the justification of a rule or practice and the justification of a particular action falling under it. The other conception makes it clear why this distinction must be made and what is its logical basis.

I

The subject of punishment, in the sense of attaching legal penalties to the violation of legal rules, has always been a troubling moral question.[4] The trouble about it has not been that people disagree as to whether or not punishment is justifiable. Most people have held that, freed from certain abuses, it is an acceptable institution. Only a few have rejected punishment entirely, which is rather surprising when one considers all that can be said against it. The difficulty is with the justification of punishment: various arguments for it have been given by moral philosophers, but so far none of them has won any sort of general acceptance; no justification is without those who detest it. I hope to show that the use of the aforementioned distinction enables one to state the utilitarian view in a way which allows for the sound points of its critics.

For our purposes we may say that there are two justifications of punishment. What we may call the retributive view is that punishment is justified on the grounds that wrongdoing merits punishment. It is morally fitting that a person who does wrong should suffer in proportion to his wrongdoing. That a criminal should be punished follows from his guilt, and the severity of the appropriate punishment depends on the depravity of his act. The state of affairs where a wrongdoer suffers punishment is morally better than the state of affairs where he does not; and it is better irrespective of any of the consequences of punishing him.

What we may call the utilitarian view holds that on the principle that bygones are bygones and that only future consequences are material to present decisions, punishment is justifiable only by reference to the probable consequences of maintaining it as one of the devices of the social order. Wrongs committed in the past are,

John Rawls, "Two Concepts of Rules," The Philosophical Review, *vol. 54 (1955), 3–32. This is a revision of a paper given at the Harvard Philosophy Club on April 30, 1954.*

as such, not relevant considerations for deciding what to do. If punishment can be shown to promote effectively the interest of society it is justifiable, otherwise it is not.

I have stated these two competing views very roughly to make one feel the conflict between them: one feels the force of *both* arguments and one wonders how they can be reconciled. From my introductory remarks it is obvious that the resolution which I am going to propose is that in this case one must distinguish between justifying a practice as a system of rules to be applied and enforced, and justifying a particular action which falls under these rules: utilitarian arguments are appropriate with regard to questions about practices, while retributive arguments fit the application of particular rules to particular cases.

We might try to get clear about this distinction by imagining how a father might answer the question of his son. Suppose the son asks, "Why was *J* put in jail yesterday?" The father answers, "Because he robbed the bank at *B*. He was duly tried and found guilty. That's why he was put in jail yesterday." But suppose the son had asked a different question, namely, "Why do people put other people in jail?" Then the father might answer, "To protect good people from bad people" or "To stop people from doing things that would make it uneasy for all of us; for otherwise we wouldn't be able to go to bed at night and sleep in peace." There are two very different questions here. One question emphasizes the proper name: it asks why *J* was punished rather than someone else, or it asks what he was punished for. The other question asks why we have the institution of punishment: why do people punish one another rather than, say, always forgiving one another?

Thus the father says in effect that a particular man is punished, rather than some other man, because he is guilty, and he is guilty because he broke the law (past tense). In his case the law looks back, the judge looks back, the jury looks back, and a penalty is visited upon him for something he did. That a man is to be punished, and what his punishment is to be, is settled by its being shown that he broke the law and that the

law assigns that penalty for the violation of it.

On the other hand we have the institution of punishment itself, and recommend and accept various changes in it, because it is thought by the (ideal) legislator and by those to whom the law applies that, as a part of a system of law impartially applied from case to case arising under it, it will have the consequence, in the long run, of furthering the interests of society.

One can say, then, that the judge and the legislator stand in different positions and look in different directions: one to the past, the other to the future. The justification of what the judge does, *qua* judge, sounds like the retributive view; the justification of what the (ideal) legislator does, *qua* legislator, sounds like the utilitarian view. Thus both views have a point (this is as it should be since intelligent and sensitive persons have been on both sides of the argument); and one's initial confusion disappears once one sees that these views apply to persons holding different offices with different duties, and situated differently with respect to the system of rules that make up the criminal law.[5]

One might say, however, that the utilitarian view is more fundamental since it applies to a more fundamental office, for the judge carries out the legislator's will so far as he can determine it. Once the legislator decides to have laws and to assign penalties for their violation (as things are there must be both the law and the penalty) an institution is set up which involves a retributive conception of particular cases. It is part of the concept of the criminal law as a system of rules that the application and enforcement of these rules in particular cases should be justifiable by arguments of a retributive character. The decision whether or not to use law rather than some other mechanism of social control, and the decision as to what laws to have and what penalties to assign, may be settled by utilitarian arguments; but if one decides to have laws then one has decided on something whose working in particular cases is retributive in form.[6]

The answer, then, to the confusion engendered by the two views of punishment is quite simple: one distinguishes two offices, that of the judge and that of the legislator, and one distinguishes their different stations with respect to the system of rules which make up the law; and then one notes that the different sorts of considerations which would usually be offered as reasons for what is done under the cover of these offices can be paired off with the competing justifications of punishment. One reconciles the two views by the time-honored device of making them apply to different situations.

But can it really be this simple? Well, this answer allows for the apparent intent of each side. Does a person who advocates the retributive view necessarily advocate, as an *institution*, legal machinery whose essential purpose is to set up and preserve a correspondence between moral turpitude and suffering? Surely not.[7] What retributionists have rightly insisted upon is that no man can be punished unless he is guilty, that is, unless he has broken the law. Their fundamental criticism of the utilitarian account is that, as they interpret it, it sanctions an innocent person's being punished (if one may call it that) for the benefit of society.

On the other hand, utilitarians agree that punishment is to be inflicted only for the violation of law. They regard this much as understood from the concept of punishment itself.[8] The point of the utilitarian account concerns the institution as a system of rules: utilitarianism seeks to limit its use by declaring it justifiable only if it can be shown to foster effectively the good of society. Historically it is a protest against the indiscriminate and ineffective use of the criminal law.[9] It seeks to dissuade us from assigning to penal institutions the improper, if not sacrilegious, task of matching suffering with moral turpitude. Like others, utilitarians want penal institutions designed so that, as far as humanly possible, only those who break the law run afoul of it. They hold that no official should have discretionary power to inflict penalties whenever he thinks it for the benefit of society; for on utilitarian grounds an institution granting such power could not be justified.[10]

The suggested way of reconciling the retributive and the utilitarian justifications of punishment seems to account for what both sides have wanted to say. There are, however, two further questions which arise, and I shall devote the remainder of this section to them.

First, will not a difference of opinion as to the proper criterion of just law make the proposed reconciliation unacceptable to retributionists? Will they not question whether, if the utilitarian principle is used as the criterion, it follows that those who have broken the law are guilty in a way which satisfies their demand that those punished deserve to be punished? To answer this difficulty, suppose that the rules of the criminal law are justified on utilitarian grounds (it is only for laws that meet his criterion that the utilitarian can be held responsible). Then it follows that the actions which the criminal law specifies as offenses are such that, if they were tolerated, terror and alarm would spread in society. Consequently, retributionists can only deny that those who are punished deserve to be punished if they deny that such actions are wrong. This they will not want to do.

The second question is whether utilitarianism doesn't justify too much. One pictures it as an engine of justification which, if consistently adopted, could be used to justify cruel and arbitrary institutions. Retributionists may be supposed to concede that utilitarians *intend* to reform the law and to make it more humane; that utilitarians do not *wish* to justify any such thing as punishment of the innocent; and that utilitarians may appeal to the fact that punishment presupposes guilt in the sense that by punishment one understands an institution attaching penalties to the infraction of legal rules, and therefore that it is logically absurd to suppose that utilitarians in justifying *punishment* might also have justified punishment (if we may call it that) of the innocent. The real question, however, is whether the utilitarian, in justifying punishment, hasn't used arguments which commit him to accepting the infliction of suffering on innocent persons if it is for the good of society (whether or not one calls this punishment). More generally, isn't the utilitarian committed in principle to accepting many practices which he, as a morally sensitive person, wouldn't want to accept? Retributionists are inclined to hold that there is no way to stop the utilitarian principle from justifying too much except by adding to it a principle which distributes certain rights to individuals. Then the amended criterion is not the greatest benefit of society *simpliciter,* but the greatest benefit of society subject to the constraint that no one's rights may be violated. Now while I think that the classical utilitarians proposed a criterion of this more complicated sort, I do not want to argue that point here.[11] What I want to show is that there is *another* way of preventing the utilitarian principle from justifying too much, or at least of making it much less likely to do so: namely, by stating utilitarianism in a way which accounts for the distinction between the justification of an institution and the justification of a particular action falling under it.

I begin by defining the institution of punishment as follows: a person is said to suffer punishment whenever he is legally deprived of some of the normal rights of a citizen on the ground that he has violated a rule of law, the violation having been established by trial according to the due process of law, provided that the deprivation is carried out by the recognized legal authorities of the state, that the rule of law clearly specifies both the offense and the attached penalty, that the courts construe statutes strictly, and that the statute was on the books prior to the time of the offense.[12] This definition specifies what I shall understand by punishment. The question is whether utilitarian arguments may be found to justify institutions widely different from this and such as one would find cruel and arbitrary.

This question is best answered, I think, by taking up a particular accusation. Consider the following from Carritt:

> ...the utilitarian must hold that we are justified in inflicting pain always and only to prevent worse pain or bring about greater happiness. This, then, is all we need to con-

sider in so-called punishment, which must be purely preventive. But if some kind of very cruel crime becomes common, and none of the criminals can be caught, it might be highly expedient, as an example, to hang an innocent man, if a charge against him could be so framed that he were universally thought guilty; indeed this would only fail to be an ideal instance of utilitarian 'punishment' because the victim himself would not have been so likely as a real felon to commit such a crime in the future; in all other respects it would be perfectly deterrent and therefore felicific.[13]

Carritt is trying to show that there are occasions when a utilitarian argument would justify taking an action which would be generally condemned; and thus that utilitarianism justifies too much. But the failure of Carritt's argument lies in the fact that he makes no distinction between the justification of the general system of rules which constitutes penal institutions and the justification of particular applications of these rules to particular cases by the various officials whose job it is to administer them. This becomes perfectly clear when one asks who the "we" are of whom Carritt speaks. Who is this who has a sort of absolute authority on particular occasions to decide that an innocent man shall be "punished" if everyone can be convinced that he is guilty? Is this person the legislator, or the judge, or the body of private citizens, or what? It is utterly crucial to know who is to decide such matters, and by what authority, for all of this must be written into the rules of the institution. Until one knows these things one doesn't know what the institution is whose justification is being challenged; and as the utilitarian principle applies to the institution one doesn't know whether it is justifiable on utilitarian grounds or not.

Once this is understood it is clear what the counter-move to Carritt's argument is. One must describe more carefully what the institution is which his example suggests, and then ask oneself whether or not it is likely that having this institution would be for the benefit of society in the long run. One must not content oneself with the vague thought that, when it's a question of *this* case, it would be a good thing if *somebody* did something even if an innocent person were to suffer.

Try to imagine, then, an institution (which we may call "telishment") which is such that the officials set up by it have authority to arrange a trial for the condemnation of an innocent man whenever they are of the opinion that doing so would be in the best interests of society. The discretion of officials is limited, however, by the rule that they may not condemn an innocent man to undergo such an ordeal unless there is, at the time, a wave of offenses similar to that with which they charge him and telish him for. We may imagine that the officials having the discretionary authority are the judges of the higher courts in consultation with the chief of police, the minister of justice, and a committee of the legislature.

Once one realizes that one is involved in setting up an *institution,* one sees that the hazards are very great. For example, what check is there on the officials? How is one to tell whether or not their actions are authorized? How is one to limit the risks involved in allowing such systematic deception? How is one to avoid giving anything short of complete discretion to the authorities to telish anyone they like? In addition to these considerations, it is obvious that people will come to have a very different attitude towards their penal system when telishment is adjoined to it. They will be uncertain as to whether a convicted man has been punished or telished. They will wonder whether or not they should feel sorry for him. They will wonder whether the same fate won't at any time fall on them. If one pictures how such an institution would actually work, and the enormous risks involved in it, it seems clear that it would serve no useful purpose. A utilitarian justification for this institution is most unlikely.

It happens in general that as one drops off the defining features of punishment one ends up with an institution whose utilitarian justification is highly doubtful. One reason for this is that punishment works like a kind of price

system: by altering the prices one has to pay for the performance of actions it supplies a motive for avoiding some actions and doing others. The defining features are essential if punishment is to work in this way; so that an institution which lacks these features, e.g., an institution which is set up to "punish" the innocent, is likely to have about as much point as a price system (if one may call it that) where the prices of things change at random from day to day and one learns the price of something after one has agreed to buy it.[14]

If one is careful to apply the utilitarian principle to the institution which is to authorize particular actions, then there is *less* danger of its justifying too much. Carritt's example gains plausibility by its indefiniteness and by its concentration on the particular case. His argument will only hold if it can be shown that there are utilitarian arguments which justify an institution whose publicly ascertainable office and powers are such as to permit officials to exercise that kind of discretion in particular cases. But the requirement of having to build the arbitrary features of the particular decision into the institutional practice makes the justification much less likely to go through. . . .

III

So far I have tried to show the importance of the distinction between the justification of a practice and the justification of a particular action falling under it by indicating how this distinction might be used to defend utilitarianism against two long-standing objections. One might be tempted to close the discussion at this point by saying that utilitarian considerations should be understood as applying to practices in the first instance and not to particular actions falling under them except insofar as the practices admit of it. One might say that in this modified form it is a better account of our considered moral opinions and let it go at that. But to stop here would be to neglect the interesting question as to how one can fail to appreciate the significance of this rather obvious distinction and can take it for granted that utilitarianism has the consequence that particular cases may always be decided on general utilitarian grounds.[21] I want to argue that this mistake may be connected with misconceiving the logical status of the rules of practices; and to show this I am going to examine two conceptions of rules, two ways of placing them within the utilitarian theory.

The conception which conceals from us the significance of the distinction I am going to call the summary view. It regards rules in the following way: one supposes that each person decides what he shall do in particular cases by applying the utilitarian principle; one supposes further that different people will decide the same particular case in the same way and that there will be recurrences of cases similar to those previously decided. Thus it will happen that in cases of certain kinds the same decision will be made either by the same person at different times or by different persons at the same time. If a case occurs frequently enough one supposes that a rule is formulated to cover that sort of case. I have called this conception the summary view because rules are pictured as summaries of past decisions arrived at by the *direct* application of the utilitarian principle to particular cases. Rules are regarded as reports that cases of a certain sort have been found on *other* grounds to be properly decided in a certain way (although, of course, they do not *say* this).

There are several things to notice about this way of placing rules within the utilitarian theory.[22]

1. The point of having rules derives from the fact that similar cases tend to recur and that one can decide cases more quickly if one records past decisions in the form of rules. If similar cases didn't recur, one would be required to apply the utilitarian principle directly, case by case, and rules reporting past decisions would be of no use.

2. The decisions made on particular cases are logically prior to rules. Since rules gain their point from the need to apply the utilitarian principle to many similar cases, it follows that a particular case (or several cases similar to it) may exist whether or not there is a rule covering that

case. We are pictured as recognizing particular cases prior to there being a rule which covers them, for it is only if we meet with a number of cases of a certain sort that we formulate a rule. Thus we are able to describe a particular case as a particular case of the requisite sort whether there is a rule regarding *that* sort of case or not. Put another way: what the *A*'s and the *B*'s refer to in rules of the form 'Whenever *A* do *B*' may be described as *A*'s and *B*'s whether or not there is the rule 'Whenever *A* do *B*', or whether or not there is any body of rules which make up a practice of which that rule is a part.

To illustrate this consider a rule, or maxim, which could arise in this way: suppose that a person is trying to decide whether to tell someone who is fatally ill what his illness is when he has been asked to do so. Suppose the person to reflect and then decide, on utilitarian grounds, that he should not answer truthfully; and suppose that on the basis of this and other like occasions he formulates a rule to the effect that when asked by someone fatally ill what his illness is, one should not tell him. The point to notice is that someone's being fatally ill and asking what his illness is, and someone's telling him, are things that can be described as such whether or not there is this rule. The performance of the action to which the rule refers doesn't require the stage setting of a practice of which this rule is a part. This is what is meant by saying that on the summary view particular cases are logically prior to rules.

3. Each person is in principle always entitled to reconsider the correctness of a rule and to question whether or not it is proper to follow it in a particular case. As rules are guides and aids, one may ask whether in past decisions there might not have been a mistake in applying the utilitarian principle to get the rule in question, and wonder whether or not it is best in this case. The reason for rules is that people are not able to apply the utilitarian principle effortlessly and flawlessly; there is need to save time and to post a guide. On this view a society of rational utilitarians would be a society without rules in which each person applied the utilitarian

principle directly and smoothly, and without error, case by case. On the other hand, ours is a society in which rules are formulated to serve as aids in reaching these ideally rational decisions on particular cases, guides which have been built up and tested by the experience of generations. If one applies this view to rules, one is interpreting them as maxims, as "rules of thumb"; and it is doubtful that anything to which the summary conception did apply would be called a *rule*. Arguing as if one regarded rules in this way is a mistake one makes while doing philosophy.

4. The concept of a *general* rule takes the following form. One is pictured as estimating on what percentage of the cases likely to arise a given rule may be relied upon to express the correct decision, that is, the decision that would be arrived at if one were to correctly apply the utilitarian principle case by case. If one estimates that by and large the rule will give the correct decision, or if one estimates that the likelihood of making a mistake by applying the utilitarian principle directly on one's own is greater than the likelihood of making a mistake by following the rule, and if these considerations held of persons generally, then one would be justified in urging its adoption as a general rule. In this way *general* rules might be accounted for on the summary view. It will still make sense, however, to speak of applying the utilitarian principle case by case, for it was by trying to foresee the results of doing this that one got the initial estimates upon which acceptance of the rule depends. That one is taking a rule in accordance with the summary conception will show itself in the naturalness with which one speaks of the rule as a guide, or as a maxim, or as a generalization from experience, and as something to be laid aside in extraordinary cases where there is no assurance that the generalization will hold and the case must therefore be treated on its merits. Thus there goes with this conception the notion of a particular exception which renders a rule suspect on a particular occasion.

The other conception of rules I will call the practice conception. On this view rules are pic-tured as defining a practice. Practices are set up for various reasons, but one of them is that in many areas of conduct each person's deciding what to do on utilitarian grounds case by case leads to confusion, and that the attempt to coordinate behavior by trying to foresee how others will act is bound to fail. As an alternative one realizes that what is required is the establishment of a practice, the specification of a new form of activity; and from this one sees that a practice necessarily involves the abdication of full liberty to act on utilitarian and prudential grounds. It is the mark of a practice that being taught how to engage in it involves being instructed in the rules which define it, and that appeal is made to those rules to correct the behavior of those engaged in it. Those engaged in a practice recognize the rules as defining it. The rules cannot be taken as simply describing how those engaged in the practice in fact behave: it is not simply that they act as if they were obeying the rules. Thus it is essential to the notion of a practice that the rules are publicly known and understood as definitive; and it is essential also that the rules of a practice can be taught and can be acted upon to yield a coherent practice. On this conception, then, rules are not generalizations from the decisions of individuals applying the utilitarian principle directly and independently to recurrent particular cases. On the contrary, rules define a practice and are themselves the subject of the utilitarian principle.

To show the important differences between this way of fitting rules into the utilitarian theory and the previous way, I shall consider the differences between the two conceptions on the points previously discussed.

1. In contrast with the summary view, the rules of practices are logically prior to particular cases. This is so because there cannot be a particular case of an action falling under a rule of a practice unless there is the practice. This can be made clearer as follows: in a practice there are rules setting up offices, specifying certain forms of action appropriate to various offices, establishing penalties for the breach of rules, and so on. We may think of the rules of a practice as defining

offices, moves, and offenses. Now what is meant by saying that the practice is logically prior to particular cases is this: given any rule which specifies a form of action (a move), a particular action which would be taken as falling under this rule given that there is the practice would not be *described* as that sort of action unless there was the practice. In the case of actions specified by practices it is logically impossible to perform them outside the stage-setting provided by those practices, for unless there is the practice, and unless the requisite proprieties are fulfilled, whatever one does, whatever movements one makes, will fail to count as a form of action which the practice specifies. What one does will be described in some *other* way.

One may illustrate this point from the game of baseball. Many of the actions one performs in a game of baseball one can do by oneself or with others whether there is the game or not. For example, one can throw a ball, run, or swing a peculiarly shaped piece of wood. But one cannot steal base, or strike out, or draw a walk, or make an error, or balk; although one can do certain things which appear to resemble these actions such as sliding into a bag, missing a grounder and so on. Striking out, stealing a base, balking, etc., are all actions which can only happen in a game. No matter what a person did, what he did would not be described as stealing a base or striking out or drawing a walk unless he could also be described as playing baseball, and for him to be doing this presupposes the rule-like practice which constitutes the game. The practice is logically prior to particular cases: unless there is the practice the terms referring to actions specified by it lack a sense.[23]

2. The practice view leads to an entirely different conception of the authority which each person has to decide on the propriety of following a rule in particular cases. To engage in a practice, to perform those actions specified by a practice, means to follow the appropriate rules. If one wants to do an action which a certain practice specifies then there is no way to do it except to follow the rules which define it. Therefore, it doesn't make sense for a person to raise the question whether or not a rule of a practice correctly applies to *his* case where the action he contemplates is a form of action defined by a practice. If someone were to raise such a question, he would simply show that he didn't understand the situation in which he was acting. If one wants to perform an action specified by a practice, the only legitimate question concerns the nature of the practice itself ("How do I go about making a will?").

This point is illustrated by the behavior expected of a player in games. If one wants to play a game, one doesn't treat the rules of the game as guides as to what is best in particular cases. In a game of baseball if a batter were to ask "Can I have four strikes?" it would be assumed that he was asking what the rule was; and if, when told what the rule was, he were to say that he meant that on this occasion he thought it would be best on the whole for him to have four strikes rather than three, this would be most kindly taken as a joke. One might contend that baseball would be a better game if four strikes were allowed instead of three; but one cannot picture the rules as guides to what is best on the whole in particular cases, and question their applicability to particular cases as particular cases.

3 and 4. To complete the four points of comparison with the summary conception, it is clear from what has been said that rules of practices are not guides to help one decide particular cases correctly as judged by some higher ethical principle. And neither the quasi-statistical notion of generality, nor the notion of a particular exception, can apply to the rules of practices. A more or less general rule of a practice must be a rule which according to the structure of the practice applies to more or fewer of the kinds of cases arising under it; or it must be a rule which is more or less basic to the understanding of the practice. Again, a particular case cannot be an exception to a rule of a practice. An exception is rather a qualification or a further specification of the rule.

It follows from what we have said about the practice conception of rules that if a person is engaged in a practice, and if he is asked why *he* does what *he* does, or if he is asked to defend what he does, then his explanation, or defense, lies in referring the questioner to the practice. He cannot say of *his* action, if it is an action specified by a practice, that he does it rather than some other because he thinks it is best on the whole.[24] When a man engaged in a practice is queried about his action he must assume that the questioner either doesn't know that he is engaged in it ("Why are you in a hurry to pay him?" "I promised to pay him today") or doesn't know what the practice is. One doesn't so much justify one's particular action as explain, or show, that it is in accordance with the practice. The reason for this is that it is only against the stage-setting of the practice that one's particular action is described as it is. Only by reference to the practice can one *say* what one is doing. To explain or to defend one's own action, as a particular action, one fits it into the practice which defines it. If this is not accepted it's a sign that a different question is being raised as to whether one is justified in accepting the practice, or in tolerating it. When the challenge is to the practice, citing the rules (saying what the practice is) is naturally to no avail. But when the challenge is to the particular action defined by the practice, there is nothing one can do but refer to the rules. Concerning particular actions there is only a question for one who isn't clear as to what the practice is, or who doesn't know that it is being engaged in. This is to be contrasted with the case of a maxim which may be taken as pointing to the correct decision on the case as decided on *other* grounds, and so giving a challenge on the case a sense by having it question whether these other grounds really support the decision on this case.

If one compares the two conceptions of rules I have discussed, one can see how the summary conception misses the significance of the distinction between justifying a practice and justifying actions falling under it. On this view rules are regarded as guides whose purpose it is to indicate the ideally rational decision on the given particular case which the flawless application of the utilitarian principle would yield.

One has, in principle, full option to use the guides or to discard them as the situation warrants without one's moral office being altered in any way: whether one discards the rules or not, one always holds the office of a rational person seeking case by case to realize the best on the whole. But on the practice conception, if one holds an office defined by a practice then questions regarding one's actions in this office are settled by reference to the rules which define the practice. If one seeks to question these rules, then one's office undergoes a fundamental change: one then assumes the office of one empowered to change and criticize the rules, or the office of a reformer, and so on. The summary conception does away with the distinction of offices and the various forms of argument appropriate to each. On that conception there is one office and so no offices at all. It therefore obscures the fact that the utilitarian principle must, in the case of actions and offices defined by a practice, apply to the practice, so that general utilitarian arguments are not available to those who act in offices so defined.[25]

Some qualifications are necessary in what I have said. First, I may have talked of the summary and the practice conceptions of rules as if only one of them could be true of rules, and if true of any rules, then necessarily true of *all* rules. I do not, of course, mean this. (It is the critics of utilitarianism who make this mistake insofar as their arguments against utilitarianism presuppose a summary conception of the rules of practices.) Some rules will fit one conception, some rules the other; and so there are rules of practices (rules in the strict sense), and maxims and "rules of thumb."

Secondly, there are further distinctions that can be made in classifying rules, distinctions which should be made if one were considering other questions. The distinctions which I have drawn are those most relevant for the rather special matter I have discussed, and are not intended to be exhaustive.

Finally, there will be many border-line cases about which it will be difficult, if not impossible, to decide which conception of rules is applicable. One expects border-line cases with any concept, and they are especially likely in connection with such involved concepts as those of a practice, institution, game, rule, and so on. Wittgenstein has shown how fluid these notions are.[26] What I have done is to emphasize and sharpen two conceptions for the limited purpose of this paper.

IV

What I have tried to show by distinguishing between two conceptions of rules is that there is a way of regarding rules which allows the option to consider particular cases on general utilitarian grounds; whereas there is another conception which does not admit of such discretion except insofar as the rules themselves authorize it. I want to suggest that the tendency while doing philosophy to picture rules in accordance with the summary conception is what may have blinded moral philosophers to the significance of the distinction between justifying a practice and justifying a particular action falling under it; and it does so by misrepresenting the logical force of the reference to the rules in the case of a challenge to a particular action falling under a practice, and by obscuring the fact that where there is a practice, it is the practice itself that must be the subject of the utilitarian principle.

It is surely no accident that two of the traditional test cases of utilitarianism, punishment and promises, are clear cases of practices. Under the influence of the summary conception it is natural to suppose that the officials of a penal system, and one who has made a promise, may decide what to do in particular cases on utilitarian grounds. One fails to see that a general discretion to decide particular cases on utilitarian grounds is incompatible with the concept of a practice; and that what discretion one does have is itself defined by the practice (e.g., a judge may have discretion to determine the penalty within certain limits). The traditional objections to utilitarianism which I have discussed presuppose the attribution to judges, and to those who have made promises, of a plenitude of moral authority to decide particular cases on utilitarian grounds. But once one fits utilitarianism together with the notion of a practice, and notes that punishment and promising are practices, then one sees that this attribution is logically precluded.

That punishment and promising are practices is beyond question. In the case of promising this is shown by the fact that the form of words "I promise" is a performative utterance which presupposes the stage setting of the practice and the proprieties defined by it. Saying the words "I promise" will only be promising given the existence of the practice. It would be absurd to interpret the rules about promising in accordance with the summary conception. It is absurd to say, for example, that the rule that promises should be kept could have arisen from its being found in past cases to be best on the whole to keep one's promise; for unless there were already the understanding that one keeps one's promises as part of the practice itself there couldn't have been any cases of promising.

It must, of course, be granted that the rules defining promising are not codified, and that one's conception of what they are necessarily depends on one's moral training. Therefore it is likely that there is considerable variation in the way people understand the practice, and room for argument as to how it is best set up. For example, differences as to how strictly various defenses are to be taken, or just what defenses are available, are likely to arise amongst persons with different backgrounds. But irrespective of these variations it belongs to the concept of the practice of promising that the general utilitarian defense is not available to the promisor. That this is so accounts for the force of the traditional objection which I have discussed. And the point I wish to make is that when one fits the utilitarian view together with the practice conception of rules, as one must in the appropriate cases, then there is nothing in that view which entails that there must be such a defense, either in the practice of promising, or in any other practice.

Punishment is also a clear case. There are many actions in the sequence of events which constitute someone's being punished which pre-suppose a practice. One can see this by consider-ing the definition of punishment which I gave when discussing Carritt's criticism of utilitarian-ism. The definition there stated refers to such things as the normal rights of a citizen, rules of law, due process of law, trials and courts of law, statutes, etc., none of which can exist outside the elaborate stage-setting of a legal system. It is also the case that many of the actions for which people are punished presuppose practices. For example, one is punished for stealing, for tres-passing, and the like, which presuppose the insti-tution of property. It is impossible to say what punishment is, or to describe a particular instance of it, without referring to offices, actions, and offenses specified by practices. Pun-ishment is a move in an elaborate legal game and presupposes the complex of practices which make up the legal order. The same thing is true of the less formal sorts of punishment: a parent or guardian or someone in proper authority may punish a child, but no one else can.

There is one mistaken interpretation of what I have been saying which it is worthwhile to warn against. One might think that the use I am making of the distinction between justifying a practice and justifying the particular actions falling under it involves one in a definite social and political attitude in that it leads to a kind of conservatism. It might seem that I am saying that for each person the social practices of his society provide the standard of justification for his actions; therefore let each person abide by them and his conduct will be justified.

This interpretation is entirely wrong. The point I have been making is rather a logical point. To be sure, it has consequences in matters of ethical theory; but in itself it leads to no par-ticular social or political attitude. It is simply that where a form of action is specified by a practice there is no justification possible of the particular action of a particular person save by reference to the practice. In such cases the action is what it is in virtue of the practice and to explain it is to refer to the practice. There is no inference whatsoever to be drawn with respect

to whether or not one should accept the prac-tices of one's society. One can be as radical as one likes but in the case of actions specified by prac-tices the objects of one's radicalism must be the social practices and people's acceptance of them.

I have tried to show that when we fit the utilitarian view together with the practice con-ception of rules, where this conception is appro-priate,[27] we can formulate it in a way which saves it from several traditional objections. I have further tried to show how the logical force of the distinction between justifying a practice and justifying an action falling under it is connected with the practice conception of rules and cannot be understood as long as one regards the rules of practices in accordance with the summary view. Why, when doing philosophy, one may be inclined to so regard them, I have not discussed. The reasons for this are evidently very deep and would require another paper.

NOTES

1. I use the word "practice" throughout as a sort of technical term meaning any form of activity specified by a system of rules which defines offices, roles, moves, penalties, defenses, and so on, and which gives the activity its structure. As examples one may think of games and rituals, trials and par-liaments.

2. The distinction is central to Hume's discussion of justice in *A Treatise of Human Nature*, bk. III, pt. II, esp. secs. 2-4. It is clearly stated by John Austin in the second lecture of *Lectures on Jurisprudence* (4th ed.; London, 1873), I, 116ff. (1st ed., 1832). Also it may be argued that J. S. Mill took it for granted in *Utilitarianism*; on this point cf. J. O. Urmson, "The Interpretation of the Moral Philosophy of J. S. Mill," *Philosophical Quarterly*, Vol. III (1953). In addition to the arguments given by Urmson there are several clear statements of the distinction in *A System of Logic* (8th ed.; London, 1872), bk. VI, ch. xii pars. 2, 3, 7. The distinction is fundamental to J. D. Mabbott's important paper, "Punishment," *Mind*, n.s., vol. XLVIII (April, 1939). More recently the distinction has been stated with particular emphasis by S. E. Toulmin in *The Place of Reason in Ethics* (Cambridge, 1950), see esp. ch. xi, where it plays a major part in his account of moral reasoning. Toulmin doesn't explain the basis of the distinction, nor how one might overlook its impor-tance, as I try to in this paper, and in my review of

his book (*Philosophical Review,* Vol. LX [October, 1951]), as some of my criticisms show, I failed to understand the force of it. See also H. D. Aiken, "The Levels of Moral Discourse," *Ethics,* vol. LXII (1952), A. M. Quinton, "Punishment," *Analysis,* vol. XIV (June, 1954), and P. H. Nowell-Smith, *Ethics* (London, 1954), pp. 236-239, 271-273.

3. On the concept of explication see the author's paper *Philosophical Review,* Vol. LX (April, 1951).

4. While this paper was being revised, Quinton's appeared; footnote 2 supra. There are several respects in which my remarks are similar to his. Yet as I consider some further questions and rely on somewhat different arguments, I have retained the discussion of punishment and promises together as two test cases for utilitarianism.

5. Note the fact that different sorts of arguments are suited to different offices. One way of taking the differences between ethical theories is to regard them as accounts of the reasons expected in different offices.

6. In this connection see Mabbott, *op. cit.,* pp. 163-164.

7. On this point see Sir David Ross, *The Right and the Good* (Oxford, 1930), pp. 57-60.

8. See Hobbes's definition of punishment in Leviathan, ch. xxviii; and Bentham's definition in *The Principle of Morals and Legislation,* ch. xii, par. 36, ch. xv, par. 28, and in *The Rationale of Punishment,* (London, 1830), bk. I, ch. i. They could agree with Bradley that: "Punishment is punishment only when it is deserved. We pay the penalty, because we owe it, and for no other reason; and if punishment is inflicted for any other reason whatever than because it is merited by wrong, it is a gross immorality, a crying injustice, an abominable crime, and not what it pretends to be." *Ethical Studies* (2nd ed.; Oxford, 1927), pp. 26-27. Certainly by definition it isn't what it pretends to be. The innocent can only be punished by mistake; deliberate "punishment" of the innocent necessarily involves fraud.

9. Cf. Leon Radzinowicz, *A History of English Criminal Law: The Movement for Reform 1750-1833* (London, 1948), esp. ch. xi on Bentham.

10. Bentham discusses how corresponding to a punitory provision of a criminal law there is another provision which stands to it as an antagonist and which needs a name as much as the punitory. He calls it, as one might expect, the *anaetiosostic,* and of it he says: "The punishment of guilt is the object of the former one: the preservation of innocence that of the latter." In the same connection he asserts that it is never thought fit to give the judge the option of deciding whether a thief (that is, a person whom he believes to be a thief, for the judge's belief is what the question must always turn upon) should hang or not, and so the law writes the provision: "The judge shall not cause a thief to be hanged unless he have been duly convicted and sentenced in course of law" (*The Limits of Jurisprudence Defined,* ed. C. W. Everett [New York, 1945], pp. 238-239).

11. By the classical utilitarians I understand Hobbes, Hume, Bentham, J. S. Mill, and Sidgwick.

12. All these features of punishment are mentioned by Hobbes; cf. *Leviathan,* ch. xxviii.

13. *Ethical and Political Thinking* (Oxford, 1947), p. 65.

14. The analogy with the price system suggests an answer to the question how utilitarian considerations insure that punishment is proportional to the offense. It is interesting to note that Sir David Ross, after making the distinction between justifying a penal law and justifying a particular application of it, and after stating that utilitarian considerations have a large place in determining the former, still holds back from accepting the utilitarian justification of punishment on the grounds that justice requires that punishment be proportional to the offense, and that utilitarianism is unable to account for this. Cf. *The Right and the Good,* pp. 61-62. I do not claim that utilitarianism can account for this requirement as Sir David might wish, but it happens, nevertheless, that if utilitarian considerations are followed penalties will be proportional to offenses in this sense: the order of offenses according to seriousness can be paired off with the order of penalties according to severity. Also the absolute level of penalties will be as low as possible. This follows from the assumption that people are rational (i.e., that they are able to take into account the "prices" the state puts on actions), the utilitarian rule that a penal system should provide a motive for preferring the less serious offense, and the principle that punishment as such is an evil. All this was carefully worked out by Bentham in *The Principles of Morals and Legislation,* chs. xiii-xv.

21. So far as I can see it is not until Moore that the doctrine is expressly stated in this way. See, for example, *Principia Ethica,* p. 147, where it is said that the statement "I am morally bound to perform this action" is identical with the statement "*This action will produce the procedure the greatest possible amount of good in the Universe*" (my italics). It is important to remember that those whom I have called the classical utilitarians were largely interested in social institutions. They were among the leading economists and political theorists of their day, and they were not infrequently reformers interested in practical affairs. Utilitarianism historically

goes together with a coherent view of society, and is not simply an ethical theory, much less an attempt at philosophical analysis in the modern sense. The utilitarian principle was quite naturally thought of, and used, as a criterion for judging social institutions (practices) and as a basis for urging reforms. It is not clear, therefore, how far it is necessary to amend utilitarianism in its classical form. For a discussion of utilitarianism as an integral part of a theory of society, see L. Robbins, *The Theory of Economic Policy in English Classical Political Economy* (London, 1952).

22. This footnote should be read after sec. 3 and presupposes what I have said there. It provides a few references to statements by leading utilitarians of the summary conception. In general it appears that when they discussed the logical features of rules the summary conception prevailed and that it was typical of the way they talked about moral rules. I cite a rather lengthy group of passages from Austin as a full illustration.

John Austin in his *Lectures on Jurisprudence* meets the objection that deciding in accordance with the utilitarian principle case by case is impractical by saying that this is a misinterpretation of utilitarianism. According to the utilitarian view "... our conduct would conform to *rules* inferred from the tendencies of actions, but would not be determined by a direct resort to the principle of general utility. Utility would be the test of our conduct, ultimately, but not immediately: the immediate test of the rules to which our conduct would conform, but not the immediate test of specific or individual actions. Our rules would be fashioned on utility; our conduct, on our rules" (vol. I, p. 116). As to how one decides on the tendency of an action he says: "If we would try the tendency of a specific or individual act, we must not contemplate the act as if it were single and insulated, but must look at the class of acts to which it belongs. We must suppose that acts of the class were generally done or omitted, and consider the probable effect upon the general happiness or good. We must guess the consequences which would follow, if the class of acts were general; and also the consequences which would follow, if they were generally omitted. We must then compare the consequences on the positive and negative sides, and determine on which of the two the *balance* of advantage lies.... If we truly try the tendency of a specific or individual act, we try the tendency of the class to which that act belongs. The *particular* conclusion which we draw, with regard to the single act, implies a *general* conclusion embracing all similar acts ... To the rules thus inferred, and lodged in the memory, our conduct would conform *immediately*

if it were truly adjusted to utility" (*ibid.*, p. 117). One might think that Austin meets the objection by stating the practice conception of rules; and perhaps he did intend to. But it is not clear that he has stated this conception. Is the generality he refers to of the statistical sort? This is suggested by the notion of tendency. Or does he refer to the utility of setting up a practice? I don't know; but what suggests the summary view is his subsequent remarks. He says: "To consider the specific consequences of single or individual acts, would *seldom* [my italics] consist with that ultimate principle" (*ibid.*, p. 117). But would one ever do this? He continues: "... this being admitted, the necessity of pausing and calculating, which the objection in question supposes, is an imagined necessity. To preface each act or forbearance by a conjecture and comparison of consequences, were clearly *superfluous* [my italics] and mischievous. It were clearly superfluous, inasmuch as the *result of that process* [my italics] would be embodied in a known *rule*. It were clearly mischievous, inasmuch as the *true* result would be expressed by that rule, whilst the process would probably be faulty, if it were done on the spur of the occasion" (*ibid.*, pp. 117-118). He goes on: "If our experience and observation of particulars were not *generalized*, our experience and observation of particulars would seldom avail us in *practice*.... The inferences suggested to our minds by repeated experience and observation are, therefore, drawn in *principles*, or compressed into *maxims*. These we carry about us ready for use, and apply to individual cases promptly ... without reverting to the process by which they were obtained; or without recalling, and arraying before our minds, the numerous and intricate considerations of which they are *handy abridgments* [my italics].... True theory is a *compendium* of particular truths.... Speaking then, generally, human conduct is inevitably *guided* [my italics] by *rules*, or by *principles* or *maxims*" (*ibid.*, pp. 117-118). I need not trouble to show how all these remarks incline to the summary view. Further, when Austin comes to deal with cases "of comparatively rare occurrence" he holds that specific considerations may outweigh the general. "Looking at the reasons from which we had inferred the rule, it were absurd to think it inflexible. We should therefore dismiss the *rule*; resort directly to the *principle* upon which our rules were fashioned; and calculate *specific* consequences to the best of our knowledge and ability" (*ibid.*, pp. 120-121). Austin's view is interesting because it shows how one may come close to the practice conception and then slide away from it.

In *A System of Logic*, bk. VI, ch. xii, par. 2, Mill distinguishes clearly between the position of judge and legislator and in doing so suggests the distinction between the two concepts of rules. However, he distinguishes the two positions to illustrate the difference between cases where one is to apply a rule already established and cases where one must formulate a rule to govern subsequent conduct. It's the latter case that interests him and he takes the "maxim of policy" of a legislator as typical of rules. In par. 3 the summary conception is very clearly stated. For example, he says of rules of conduct that they should be taken provisionally, as they are made for the most numerous cases. He says that they "point out" the manner in which it is least perilous to act; they serve as an "admonition" that a certain mode of conduct has been found suited to the most common occurrences. In *Utilitarianism*, ch. ii, par. 24, the summary conception appears in Mill's answer to the same objection Austin considered. Here he speaks of rules as "corollaries" from the principle of utility; these "secondary" rules are compared to "landmarks" and "direction-posts." They are based on long experience and so make it unnecessary to apply the utilitarian principle to each case. In par. 25 Mill refers to the task of the utilitarian principle in adjudicating between competing moral rules. He talks here as if one then applies the utilitarian principle directly to the particular case. On the practice view one would rather use the principle to decide which of the ways that make the practice consistent is the best. It should be noted that while in par. 10 Mill's definition of utilitarianism makes the utilitarian principle apply to morality, i.e., to the rules and precepts of human conduct, the definition in par. 2 uses the phrase "actions are right in *proportion* as they *tend* to promote happiness" [my italics] and this inclines towards the summary view. In the last paragraph of the essay "On the Definition of Political Economy," *Westminster Review* (October, 1836), Mill says that it is only in art, as distinguished from science, that one can properly speak of exceptions. In a question of practice, if something is fit to be done "in the majority of cases" then it is made the rule. "We may ... in talking of art *unobjectionably* speak of the *rule* and the *exception,* meaning by the rule the cases in which there exists a preponderance ... of inducements for acting in a particular way; and by the exception, the cases in which the preponderance is on the contrary side." These remarks, too, suggest the summary view.

In Moore's *Principia Ethica*, ch. v, there is a complicated and difficult discussion of moral rules. I will not examine it here except to express my suspicion that the summary conception prevails. To be sure, Moore speaks frequently of the utility of rules as generally followed, and of actions as generally practiced, but it is possible that these passages fit the statistical notion of generality which the summary conception allows. This conception is suggested by Moore's taking the utilitarian principle as applying directly to particular actions (pp. 147-148) and by his notion of a rule as something indicating which of the few alternatives likely to occur to anyone will generally produce a greater total good in the immediate future (p. 154). He talks of an "ethical law" as a prediction, and as a generalization (pp. 146, 155). The summary conception is also suggested by his discussion of exceptions (pp. 162-163) and of the force of examples of breaching a rule (pp. 163-164).

23. One might feel that it is a mistake to say that a practice is logically prior to the forms of action it specifies on the grounds that if there were never any instances of actions falling under a practice then we should be strongly inclined to say that there wasn't the practice either. Blue-prints for a practice do not make a practice. That there is a practice entails that there are instances of people having been engaged and now being engaged in it (with suitable qualifications). This is correct, but it doesn't hurt the claim that any given particular instance of a form of action specified by a practice presupposes the practice. This isn't so on the summary picture, as each instance must be "there" prior to the rules, so to speak, as something from which one gets the rule by applying the utilitarian principle to it directly.

24. A philosophical joke (in the mouth of Jeremy Bentham): "When I run to the other wicket after my partner has struck a good ball I do so because it is best on the whole."

25. How do these remarks apply to the case of the promise known only to father and son? Well, at first sight the son certainly holds the office of promisor, and so he isn't allowed by the practice to weigh the particular case on general utilitarian grounds. Suppose instead that he wishes to consider himself in the office of one empowered to criticize and change the practice, leaving aside the question as to his right to move from his previously assumed office to another. Then he may consider utilitarian arguments as applied to the practice; but once he does this he will see that there are such arguments for not allowing a general utilitarian defense in the practice for this sort of case. For to do so would make it impossible to ask for and to give a kind of promise which one often wants to be able to ask for and to give. Therefore he will not want to change the practice, and so as a promisor he has no option but to keep his promise.

26. *Philosophical Investigations* (Oxford, 1953), I, pars. 65-71, for example.

27. As I have already stated, it is not always easy to say where the conception is appropriate. Nor do I care to discuss at this point the general sorts of cases to which it does apply except to say that one should not take it for granted that it applies to many so-called "moral rules." It is my feeling that relatively few actions of the moral life are defined by practices and that the practice conception is more relevant to understanding legal and legal-like arguments than it is to the more complex sort of moral arguments. Utilitarianism must be fitted to different conceptions of rules depending on the case, and no doubt the failure to do this has been one source of difficulty in interpreting it correctly.

Study Questions

1. What does Rawls mean by distinguishing the moral justification of a practice or rule from the justification of a particular action that falls under a practice? Use lying as an example to explain the distinction.

2. Briefly describe Rawls' characterizations of the retributivist and the utilitarian justifications of punishment. How do these two forms of justification match up with the distinction mentioned in question 1 above? How does Rawls believe the retributivist and utilitarian justifications match with the roles of the judge and the legislator? Do you agree? Why? Defend your position.

3. Why is a careful definition of "institution" necessary to Rawls' defense of utilitarianism against the "punishment-of-the-innocent" argument? How does the hypothetical institution of *telishment* fit into Rawls' defense? Is Rawls' defense successful? Why? Defend your position.

4. Explain Rawls' distinction between the *summary* and the *practice* conception of rules. How does the practice conception of a rule save utilitarianism from the punishment-of-the-innocent criticism?

The Death Sentence

SIDNEY HOOK

IS THERE ANYTHING NEW that can be said for or against capital punishment? Anyone familiar with the subject knows that unless extraneous issues are introduced a large measure of agreement about it can be, and has been, won. For example, during the last 150 years the death penalty for criminal offenses has been abolished, or remains unenforced, in many countries; just as important, the number of crimes punishable by death has been sharply reduced in all countries. But while the progress has been encouraging, it still seems to me that greater clarity on the issues involved is desirable: Much of the continuing polemic still suffers from one or the other of the twin evils of vindictiveness and sentimentality. Sentimentality, together with a

Sidney Hook, "The Death Sentence," in Hugo Adam Bedau (ed.), The Death Penalty in America, *Revised Edition (Garden City, NY: Doubleday, 1967), pp. 146-154. The version in Bedau is from* The New Leader, *vol. 44 (April 3, 1961), pp. 18-20, with three paragraphs added. Cf. the original version, which appeared in* The New York Law Forum *(August 1961), pp. 278-283, as an address before the New York State District Attorney's Association. Reprinted with permission of* The New Leader *and Ernest B. Hook.*

great deal of confusion about determinism, is found in Clarence Darrow's speeches and writings on the subject. Darrow was an attractive and likeable human being but a very confused thinker. He argued against capital punishment on the ground that the murderer was always a victim of heredity and environment—and therefore it was unjust to execute him. ("Back of every murder and back of every human act are sufficient causes that move the human machine beyond their control.") The crucifiers and the crucified, the lynch mob and its prey are equally moved by causes beyond their control and the relevant differences between them are therewith ignored. Although Darrow passionately asserted that no one knows what justice is and that no one can measure it, he nonetheless was passionately convinced that capital punishment was unjust.

It should be clear that if Darrow's argument were valid, it would be an argument not only against capital punishment but against all punishment. Very few of us would be prepared to accept this. But the argument is absurd. Even if we are all victims of our heredity and environment, it is still possible to alter the environment by meting out capital punishment to deter crimes of murder. If no one can help doing what he does, if no one is responsible for his actions, then surely this holds just as much for those who advocate and administer capital punishment as for the criminal. The denunciation of capital punishment as unjust, therefore, would be senseless. The question of universal determinism is irrelevant. If capital punishment actually were a deterrent to murder, and there existed no other more effective deterrent, and none as effective but more humane, a case could be made for it.

Nor am I impressed with the argument against capital punishment on the ground of its inhumanity. Of course it is inhumane. So is murder. If it could be shown that the inhumanity of murder can be decreased in no other way than by the inhumanity of capital punishment acting as a deterrent, this would be a valid argument for such punishment.

I have stressed the hypothetical character of these arguments because it makes apparent how crucially the wisdom of our policy depends upon the alleged facts. Does capital punishment serve as the most effective deterrent we have against murder? Most people who favor its retention believe that it does. But any sober examination of the facts will show that this has never been established. It seems plausible, but not everything which is plausible or intuitively credible is true.

The experience of countries and states which have abolished capital punishment shows that there has been no perceptible increase of murders after abolition—although it would be illegitimate to infer from this that the fear of capital punishment never deterred anybody. The fact that "the state with the very lowest murder rate is Maine, which abolished capital punishment in 1870," may be explained by the hypothesis that fishermen, like fish, tend to be cold blooded, or by some less fanciful hypothesis. The relevant question is: what objective evidence exists which would justify the conclusion that if Maine had not abolished capital punishment, its death rate would have been higher? The answer is: no evidence exists.

The opinion of many jurists and law enforcement officers from Cesare Beccaria (the eighteenth century Italian criminologist) to the present is that swift and certain punishment of some degree of severity is a more effective deterrent of murder than the punishment of maximum severity when it is slow and uncertain. Although this opinion requires substantiation, too, it carries the weight which we normally extend to pronouncements by individuals who report on their life experience. And in the absence of convincing evidence that capital punishment is a more effective and/or humane form of punishment for murder than any other punishment, there remains no other reasonable ground for retaining it.

This is contested by those who speak of the necessity for capital punishment as an expression of the "community need of justice," or as the fulfillment of "an instinctive urge to punish injustice." Such views lie at the basis of some forms of the retributive theory. It has been alleged that the retributive theory is nothing more than a desire for revenge, but it is a great and arrogant error to assume that all who hold it are vindictive. The theory has been defended by secular saints like G. E. Moore and Immanuel Kant, whose dispassionate interest in justice cannot reasonably be challenged. Even if one accepted the retributive theory or believed in the desirability of meeting the community need of justice, it doesn't in the least follow that this justifies capital punishment. Other forms of punishment may be retributive, too.

I suppose that what one means by community need or feeling and the necessity of regarding it, is that not only must justice be done, it must be seen to be done. A requirement of good law is that it must be consonant with the feeling of the community, something which is sometimes called "the living law." Otherwise it is unenforceable and brings the whole system of law into disrepute. Meeting community feeling is a necessary condition for good law, but not a sufficient condition for good law. This is what Justice Holmes meant when he wrote in *The Common Law* that "The first requirement of a sound body of law is that it should correspond with the actual feelings and demands of the community, whether right or wrong." But I think he would admit that sound law is sounder still if in addition to being enforceable it is also just. Our moral obligation as citizens is to build a community feeling and demand which is right rather than wrong.

Those who wish to retain capital punishment on the ground that it fulfills a community need or feeling must believe either that community feeling *per se* is always justified, or that to disregard it in any particular situation is inexpedient because of the consequences, *viz.*, increase in murder. In either case they beg the question—in the first case, the question of justice, and in the second, the question of deterrence.

One thing is incontestable. From the standpoint of those who base the argument for retention of capital punishment on the necessity of satisfying community needs there could be no justification whatsoever for any *mandatory* death sentence. For a mandatory death sentence attempts to determine in advance what the community need and feeling will be, and closes the door to fresh inquiry about the justice as well as the deterrent consequences of any proposed punishment.

Community need and feeling are notoriously fickle. When a verdict of guilty necessarily entails a death sentence, the jury may not feel the sentence warranted and may bring in a verdict of not guilty even when some punishment seems to be legally and morally justified. Even when the death sentence is not mandatory, there is an argument, not decisive but still significant, against any death sentence. This is its incorrigibility. Our judgment of a convicted man's guilt may change. If he has been executed in the meantime, we can only do him "posthumous justice." But can justice ever really be posthumous to the victim? Rarely has evidence, even when it is beyond reasonable doubt, the same finality about its probative force as the awful finality of death. The weight of this argument against capital punishment is all the stronger if community need and feeling are taken as the prime criteria of what is just or fitting.

What about heinous political offenses? Usually when arguments fail to sustain the demand for capital punishment in ordinary murder cases, the names of Adolf Hitler, Adolf Eichmann, Joseph Stalin and Ilse Koch are introduced and flaunted before the audience to inflame their feelings. Certain distinctions are in order here. Justice, of course, requires severe punishment. But why is it assumed that capital punishment is, in these cases, the severest and most just of sentences? How can any equation be drawn between the punishment of one man and the sufferings of his numerous victims? After all, we cannot kill Eichmann six million times or Stalin twelve million times (a conservative estimate of the number of people who died by their order).

If we wish to keep alive the memory of political infamy, if we wish to use it as a political lesson to prevent its recurrence, it may be educationally far more effective to keep men like Eichmann in existence. Few people think of the dead. By the same token, it may be necessary to execute a politically monstrous figure to prevent him from becoming the object of allegiance of a restoration movement. Eichmann does not have to be executed. He is more useful alive if we wish to keep before mankind the enormity of his offense. But if Hitler had been taken alive, his death would have been required as a matter of political necessity, to prevent him from becoming a living symbol or rallying cry of Nazi die-hards and irreconcilables.

There is an enormous amount of historical evidence which shows that certain political tyrants, after they lose power, become the focus of restoration movements that are a chronic source of bloodshed and civil strife. No matter how infamous a tyrant's actions, there is usually some group which has profited by it, resents being deprived of its privileges, and schemes for a return to power. In difficult situations, the dethroned tyrant also becomes a symbol of legitimacy around which discontented elements rally who might otherwise have waited for the normal processes of government to relieve their lot. A *mystique* develops around the tyrant, appeals are made to the "good old days," when his bread and circuses were used to distract attention from the myriads of his tortured victims, plots seethe around him until they boil over into violence and bloodshed again. I did not approve of the way Mussolini was killed. Even he deserved due process. But I have no doubt whatsoever that had he been sentenced merely to life imprisonment, the Fascist movement in Italy today would be a much more formidable movement, and that sooner or later, many lives would have been lost in consequence of the actions of Fascist legitimists.

Where matters of ordinary crime are concerned these political considerations are irrelevant. I conclude, therefore, that no valid case has so far been made for the retention of capital punishment, that the argument from deterrence is inconclusive and inconsistent (in the sense that we do not do other things to reinforce its deterrent effect if we believe it has such an effect), and that the argument from community feeling is invalid.

However, since I am not a fanatic or absolutist, I do not wish to go on record as being categorically opposed to the death sentence in all circumstances. I should like to recognize two exceptions. A defendant convicted of murder and sentenced to life should be permitted to choose the death sentence instead. Not so long ago a defendant sentenced to life imprisonment made this request and was rebuked by the judge for his impertinence. I can see no valid grounds for denying such a request out of hand. It may sometimes be denied, particularly if a way can be found to make the defendant labor for the benefit of the dependents of his victim as is done in some European countries. Unless such considerations are present, I do not see on what reasonable ground the request can be denied, particularly by those who believe in capital punishment. Once they argue that life imprisonment is either a more effective deterrent or more justly punitive, they have abandoned their position.

In passing, I should state that I am in favor of permitting *any* criminal defendant, sentenced to life imprisonment, the right to choose death. I can understand why certain jurists, who believe that the defendant wants thereby to cheat the state out of its mode of punishment, should be indignant at the idea. They are usually the ones who believe that even the attempt at suicide should be deemed a crime—in effect saying to the unfortunate person that if he doesn't succeed in his act of suicide, the state will punish him for it. But I am baffled to understand why the absolute abolitionist, dripping with treacly humanitarianism, should oppose this proposal. I have heard some people actually oppose capital punishment in certain cases on the ground that: "Death is too good for the vile wretch! Let him live and suffer to the end of his days." But the absolute abolitionist should be the last person in the world to oppose the wish of the lifer, who regards this form of punishment as torture worse than death, to leave our world.

My second class of exceptions consists of those who having been sentenced once to prison for premeditated murder, murder again. In these particular cases we have evidence that imprisonment is not a sufficient deterrent for the individual in question. If the evidence shows that the prisoner is so psychologically constituted that, without being insane, the fact that he can kill again with impunity may lead to further murderous behavior, the court should have the discretionary power to pass the death sentence if the criminal is found guilty of a second murder.

In saying that the death sentence should be *discretionary* in cases where a man has killed more than once, I am *not* saying that a murderer who murders again is more deserving of death than the murderer who murders once. Bluebeard was not twelve times more deserving of death when he was finally caught. I am saying simply this: that in a sub-class of murderers, i.e., those who murder several times, there may be a special group of sane murderers who, knowing that they will not be executed, will not hesitate to kill again and again. For *them* the argument from deterrence is obviously valid. Those who say that there must be no exceptions to the abolition of capital punishment cannot rule out the existence of such cases on *a priori* grounds. If they admit that there is a reasonable probability that such murderers will murder again or attempt to murder again, a probability which usually grows with the number of repeated murders, and still insist they would *never*

approve of capital punishment, I would conclude that they are indifferent to the lives of the human beings doomed, on their position, to be victims. What fancies itself as a humanitarian attitude is sometimes an expression of sentimentalism. The reverse coin of sentimentalism is often cruelty.

Our charity for all human beings must not deprive us of our common sense. Nor should our charity be less for the future or potential victims of the murderer than for the murderer himself. There are crimes in this world which are, like acts of nature, beyond the power of men to anticipate or control. But not all or most crimes are of this character. So long as human beings are responsible and educable, they will respond to praise and blame and punishment. It is hard to imagine it but even Hitler and Stalin were once infants. Once you *can* imagine them as infants, however, it is hard to believe that they were already monsters in their cradles. Every confirmed criminal was once an amateur. The existence of confirmed criminals testifies to the defects of our education—where they can be reformed—and of our penology—where they cannot. That is why we are under the moral obligation to be intelligent about crime and punishment. Intelligence should teach us that the best educational and penological system is the one which prevents crimes rather than punishes them; the next best is one which punishes crime in such a way as to prevent it from happening again.

Study Questions

1. What is Hook's view regarding the inhumanity of punishment? Would you regard this view as utilitarian or as deontological? Explain.

2. What is the "satisfaction of community feelings" defense of capital punishment? Why is this defense inconsistent with the concept of mandatory death sentencing, according to Hook? Do you agree with Hook? Why? Defend your position.

3. Under what circumstances does Hook believe capital punishment to be justified? Explain. Do you agree with Hook? Why? Defend your position.

4. Hook states that next to prevention, the best penological system "is one which punishes crime in such a way as to prevent it from happening again." Do you see any problems with this claim? Defend your position.

How to Argue About the Death Penalty

HUGO ADAM BEDAU

I

ARGUMENT OVER THE DEATH penalty—especially in the United States during the past generation—has been concentrated in large part on trying to answer various disputed *questions of fact*. Among them two have been salient: Is the death penalty a better deterrent to crime (especially murder) than the alternative of imprisonment? Is the death penalty administered in a discriminatory way, and, in particular, are black or other nonwhite offenders (or offenders whose victims are white) more likely to be tried, convicted, sentenced to death, and executed than whites (or offenders whose victims are nonwhite)? Other questions of fact have also been explored, including these two: What is the risk that an innocent person could actually be executed for a crime he did not commit? What is the risk that a person convicted of a capital felony but not executed will commit another capital felony?

Varying degrees of effort have been expended in trying to answer these questions. Although I think the current answers are capable of further refinement, I also think anyone who studies the evidence today must conclude that the best current answers to these four questions are as follows. (1) There is little or no evidence that the death penalty is a better deterrent to murder than is imprisonment; on the contrary, most evidence shows that these two punishments are about equally (in)effective as deterrents to murder. Furthermore, as long as the death penalty continues to be used relatively rarely, there is no prospect of gaining more decisive evidence on the question. (2) There is evidence that the death

penalty has been and continues to be administered, whether intentionally or not, in a manner that produces arbitrary and racially discriminatory results in death sentencing. At the very least, this is true in those jurisdictions where the question has been investigated in recent years. (3) It is impossible to calculate the risk that an innocent person will be executed, but the risk is not zero, as the record of convicted, sentenced, and executed innocents shows. (4) Recidivism data show that some murderers have killed after a conviction and prison sentence for murder; so there is a risk that others will do so as well.

Let us assume that my summary of the results of research on these four questions is correct, and that further research will not significantly change these answers. The first thing to notice is that even if everyone agreed on these answers, this would not by itself settle the dispute over whether to keep, expand, reduce, or abolish the death penalty. Knowing these empirical truths about the administration and effects of the death penalty in our society does not entail knowing whether one should support its retention or abolition. This would still be true even if we knew with finality the answers to *all* the factual questions that can be asked about it.

There are two reasons for this. The facts as they currently stand and as seen from the abolitionist perspective do not point strongly and overwhelmingly to the futility of the death penalty or to the harm it does, at least as long as it continues to be used only in the limited and restricted form of the past decade: confined to the crime of murder, with trial courts empowered to exercise "guided discretion" in sentencing, with defense counsel able to introduce

Hugo Adam Bedau, "How to Argue About the Death Penalty," Israel Law Review, *Vol. 25, 1991,* pp. 466–480. *Used by permission of the author and* Israel Law Review.

anything as mitigating evidence, and with automatic review of both conviction and sentence by some appellate court. Nor do the facts show that the alternative of life imprisonment is on balance a noticeably superior punishment. For example, the evidence of racial discrimination in the administration of the death penalty, while incontestable, may be no worse than the racial discrimination that occurs where lesser crimes and punishments are concerned. No one who has studied the data thinks that the administration of justice for murder approaches the level of racial discrimination reached a generation ago in the South by the administration of justice for rape. Besides, it is always possible to argue that such discrimination is diminishing, or will diminish over time, and that, in any case, since the fault does not lie in the capital statutes themselves—they are color-blind on their face—the remedy does not lie in repealing them.

But the marginal impact of the empirical evidence is not the major factor in explaining why settling disputes over matters of fact does not and cannot settle the larger controversy over the death penalty itself. As a matter of sheer logic, it is not possible to deduce a policy conclusion (such as the desirability of abolishing the death penalty) from any set of factual premises, however general and well supported. Any argument intended to recommend continuing or reforming current policy on the death penalty must include among its premises one or more normative propositions. Unless disputants over the death penalty can agree about these normative propositions, their agreement on the general facts will never suffice to resolve their dispute.

II

Accordingly, the course of wisdom for those interested in arguing about the death penalty is to focus attention on the normative propositions crucial to the dispute, in the hope that some headway may be made in narrowing disagreement over their number, content, and weight. If this is to be done effectively, the context of these norms in general political ideology needs to be fixed. Suffice it to say here that I proceed from within the context of liberal pluralistic constitutional democracy and the conception of punishment appropriate therein.

Logically prior to the idea of punishment is the idea of a crime. What counts as a criminal harm depends in part on our conception of persons as bearers of rights deserving respect and protection. In this setting, liability to punishment and its actual infliction serve the complex function of reinforcing compliance with a set of laws deemed necessary to protect the fundamental equal rights of all members of society. The normative propositions relevant to the death penalty controversy are interwoven with the basic purposes and principles of liberal society, including the recognition and protection of individual rights to life and liberty, and to security of person and property.

These norms can be divided into two groups: those that express relevant and desirable *social goals* or *purposes*, and those that express relevant and respectable *moral principles*. Punishment is thus a practice or institution defined through various policies—such as the death penalty for murder—and intended to be the means or instrument whereby certain social goals are achieved within the constraints imposed by acknowledged moral principles.

Reduction of crime, or at least prevention of an increase in crime, is an example of such a goal. This goal influences the choice of punishments because of their impact (hypothesized or verified) on the crime rate. No one, except for purists of a retributive stripe, would dissent from the view that this goal is relevant to the death penalty controversy. Because of its relevance, there is continuing interest in the outcome of research on the differential deterrent efficacy of death versus imprisonment. The only questions normally in dispute are what that research shows (I have summarized it above) and how important this goal is (some regard it as decisive).

Similarly, that no one should be convicted and sentenced to death without a fair trial (i.e., in violation of "due process of law") is a principle of law and morality generally respected. Its general acceptance explains the considerable reformation in the laws governing the death penalty in the United States that have been introduced since 1972 by the Supreme Court. The Court argued that capital trials and death sentencing were in practice unfair (in constitutional jargon, they were in violation of the Eighth and Fourteenth Amendments, which bar "cruel and unusual punishments" and require "equal protection of the laws," respectively). State legislatures and thoughtful observers agreed. Here again the only questions concern how important it is to comply with this principle (some regard it as decisive) and the extent to which the death penalty currently violates it (I have remarked on this point above, too).

The chief use of a moral principle in the present setting is to constrain the methods used in pursuit of policy (as when respect for "due process" rules out curbstone justice as a tactic in crime fighting). However, identifying the relevant goals, acknowledging the force of the relevant principles, and agreeing on the relevant general facts will still not suffice to resolve the dispute. The relative importance of achieving a given goal and the relative weight of a given principle remain to be settled, and disagreement over these matters is likely to show up in disagreement over the justification of the death penalty itself.

If this is a correct sketch of the structural character of debate and disagreement over the death penalty, then (as I noted earlier) the best hope for progress may lie in looking more carefully at the nonfactual normative ingredients so far isolated in the dispute. Ideally, we would identify and evaluate the policy goals relevant to punishment generally, as well as the moral principles that constrain the structure and content of the penalty schedule. We would also settle the proper relative weights to attach to these goals and constraints, if not in general, then at least for their application in the present context. Then, with whatever relevant general facts are at our disposal, we would be in a position to draw the appropriate inferences and resolve the entire

dispute, confident that we have examined and duly weighed everything that reason and morality can bring to bear on the problem.

As an abstract matter, therefore, the question is whether the set of relevant policies and principles, taken in conjunction with the relevant facts, favors reduction (even complete abolition) of the death penalty, or whether it favors retention (or even extension) of the death penalty. Lurking in the background, of course, is the troubling possibility that the relevant norms and facts underdetermine the resolution of the dispute. But let us not worry about sharks on dry land, not yet.

III

Where choice of punishments is concerned, the relevant social goals, I suggest, are few. Two in particular generally commend themselves:

(G1) Punishment should contribute to the reduction of crime; accordingly, the punishment for a crime should not be so idle a threat or so slight a deprivation that it has no deterrent or incapacitative effects; and it certainly should not contribute to an increase in crime.

(G2) Punishments should be "economical"—they should not waste valuable social resources in futile or unnecessarily costly endeavors.

The instrumental character of these purposes and goals is evident. They reflect the fact that society does not institute and maintain the practice of punishment for its own sake, as though it were a good in itself. Rather, punishment is and is seen to be a means to an end or ends. The justification of a society's punitive policies and practices must therefore involve two steps: first, it must be shown that these ends are desirable; second, it must be shown that the practice of punishment is the best means to these ends. What is true of the justification of punishment generally is true a fortiori of justifying the death penalty.

Endorsement of these two policy goals tends to encourage support for the death penalty. Opponents of capital punishment need not reject these goals, however, and its defenders cannot argue that accepting these goals vindicates their preferred policy. Traditionally, it is true, the death penalty has often been supported on the ground that it provides the best social defense and is extremely cheap to administer. But since the time of Beccaria and Bentham, these empirical claims have been challenged, and rightly so. If support for the death penalty today in a country such as the United States rests on the high priority placed on these goals, then there is much (some would say compelling) evidence to undermine this support. The most that can be said solely by reference to these goals is that recognition of their importance can always be counted on to kindle interest in capital punishment, and to that extent put its opponents on the defensive.

Whether punishment is intended to serve only the two goals so far identified is disputable. An argument can be made that there are two or three further goals:

(G3) Punishment should rectify the harm and injustice caused by crime.

(G4) Punishment should serve as a recognized channel for the release of public indignation and anger at the offender.

(G5) Punishment should make convicted offenders into better persons rather than leave them as they are or make them worse.

Obviously, anyone who accepts the fifth goal must reject the death penalty. I shall not try here to argue the merits of this goal, either in itself or relative to the other goals of punishment. Whatever its merits, this goal is less widely sought than the others, and for that reason alone is less useful in trying to develop rational agreement over the death penalty. Its persuasive power for those not already persuaded against the death penalty on other grounds is likely to be slight to zero. Although I am unwilling to strike it from the list of goals that punishment in general is and should be practiced to achieve, it would be unreasonable to stress its pre-eminence in the present context.

The proposed third goal is open to the objection that rectification of injustice is not really a goal of punishment, even if it is a desirable goal in other settings. (Indeed, it is widely believed that rectification is not a goal of punishment but of noncriminal tort judgments.) But even if it is a goal of punishment generally, it seems irrelevant to the death penalty controversy, because neither death nor imprisonment (as practiced in the United States) rectifies anything. Nonetheless, this goal may be indirectly important for the death penalty controversy. To the extent that one believes punishments ought to serve this goal, and that there is no possible way to rectify the crime of murder, one may come to believe that the fourth goal is of even greater importance than would otherwise be the case. Indeed, striving to achieve this fourth goal and embracing the death penalty as a consequence is quite parallel to striving to achieve the fifth goal and consequently embracing its abolition.

Does this fourth goal have a greater claim on our support than I have allowed is true of the fifth goal, so obviously incompatible with it? Many would say that it does. Some would even argue that it is this goal, not any of the others, that is the paramount purpose of punishment under law. Whatever else punishment does, its threat and infliction are to be seen as the expression of social indignation at deliberate harm to the innocent. Preserving a socially acceptable vehicle for the expression of anger at offenders is absolutely crucial to the health of a just society.

There are in principle three ways to respond to this claim insofar as it is part of an argument for capital punishment. One is to reject it out of hand as a false proposition from start to finish. A second is to concede that the goal of providing a visible and acceptable channel for the emotion of anger is legitimate, but to argue that this goal could at best justify the death penalty only in a very small number of cases (the occasional Adolf Eichmann, for example), since otherwise its importance would be vastly exaggerated. A third response is to concede both the legitimacy and the relative importance of this goal, but to point out that its pursuit, like that of all other goals, is nonetheless constrained by moral principles (yet to be examined), and that once these principles are properly employed, the death penalty ceases to be a permissible method of achieving this goal. I think both the second and third objections are sound, and a few further words here about each are appropriate.

First of all, anger is not the same as resentment or indignation, since the latter feeling or emotion can be aroused only through the perceived violation of some moral principle, whereas the former does not have this constraint. But whether the feeling aroused by a horrible murder is really only anger rather than indignation is just the question whether the principles of morality have been violated or not. Knowing that the accused offender has no legal excuse or justification for his criminal conduct is not enough to warrant the inference that he and his conduct are appropriate objects of our unqualified moral hostility. More about the context of the offense and its causation must be supplied; it may well be that in ordinary criminal cases one rarely or never knows enough to reach such a condemnatory judgment with confidence. Even were this not so, one has no reason to suppose that justified anger at offenders is of overriding importance, and that all countervailing considerations must yield to its pre-eminence. For one thing, the righteous anger needed for that role is simply not available in a pluralistic secular society. Even if it were, we have been assured from biblical times that it passes all too easily into self-righteous and hypocritical repression by some sinners or others.

Quite apart from such objections, there is a certain anomaly, even irony, in the defense of the death penalty by appeal to this goal. On the one hand, we are told of the importance of a publicly recognized ritual for extermination of convicted murderers as a necessary vent for otherwise unchanneled disruptive public emotions. On the other hand, our society scrupulously rejects time-honored methods of execution that truly do express hatred and anger at offenders: beheading, crucifixion, dismemberment and even hanging and the electric chair are disappearing. Execution by lethal injection, increasingly the popular option, hardly seems

appropriate as the outlet of choice for such allegedly volatile energies! And is it not ironic that this technique, invented to facilitate life-saving surgery, now turns out to be the preferred channel for the expression of moral indignation?

IV

If the purposes or goals of punishment lend a utilitarian quality to the practice of punishment, the moral principles relevant to the death penalty operate as deontological constraints on their pursuit. Stating all and only the principles relevant to the death penalty controversy is not easy, and the list that follows is no more than the latest approximation to the task.... With some overlap here and there, these principles are six:

(P1) No one should deliberately and intentionally take another's life where there is a feasible alternative.

(P2) The more severe a penalty is, the more important it is that it be imposed only on those who truly deserve it.

(P3) The more severe a penalty is, the weightier the justification required to warrant its imposition on anyone.

(P4) Whatever the criminal offense, the accused and convicted offender does not forfeit all his rights and dignity as a person. Accordingly, there is an upper limit to the severity—cruelty, destructiveness, finality—of permissible punishments, regardless of the offense.

(P5) Fairness requires that punishments should be graded in their severity according to the gravity of the offense.

(P6) If human lives are to be risked, the risk should fall more heavily on wrong-doers (the guilty) than on others (the innocent).

I cannot argue here for all these principles, but they really need no argument from me. Each is recognized implicitly or explicitly in our practice; each can be seen to constrain our conduct as individuals and as officers in democratic institutions. Outright repudiation or cynical disregard of any of these principles would disqualify one from engaging in serious discourse and debate over punishment in a liberal society. All can be seen as corollaries or theorems of the general proposition that life, limb, and security of person—of *all* persons—are of paramount value. Thus, only minimal interference (in the jargon of the law, "the least restrictive means") is warranted with anyone's life, limb, and security in order to protect the rights of others.

How do these principles direct or advise us in regard to the permissibility or desirability of the death penalty? The first thing to note is that evidently none directly rules it out. I know of no moral principle that is both sufficiently rigid and sufficiently well established for us to point to it and say: "The practice of capital punishment is flatly contradictory to the requirements of this moral principle." (Of course, we could invent a principle that would have this consequence, but that is hardly to the point.) This should not be surprising; few if any of the critics or the defenders of the death penalty have supposed otherwise. Second, several of these principles do reflect the heavy burden that properly falls on anyone who advocates that certain human beings be deliberately killed by others, when those to be killed are not at the time a danger to anyone. For example, whereas the first principle may permit lethal force in self-defense, it directly counsels against the death penalty in *all* cases without exception. The second and third principles emphasize the importance of "due process" and "equal protection" as the finality and incompensability of punishments increase. The fourth principle draws attention to the nature and value of persons, even those convicted of terrible crimes. It reminds us that even if crimes know no upper limit in their wantonness, cruelty, destructiveness, and horror, punishments under law in a civilized society cannot imitate crimes in this regard. Punishment does operate under limits, and these limits are not arbitrary.

The final two principles, however, seem to be exceptions to the generalization that the principles as a group tend to favor punishments other than death. The fifth principle seems to entail that if murder is the gravest crime, then it

should receive the severest punishment. This does not, of course, *require* a society to invoke the death penalty for murder—unless one accepts *lex talionis* ("a life for a life, an eye for an eye") in a singularly literal-minded manner. Since *lex talionis* is not a sound principle on which to construct the penalty schedule generally, appealing to this interpretation of the fifth principle here simply begs the question. Nevertheless, the principle that punishments should be graded to fit the crime does encourage consideration of the death penalty, especially if it seems that there is no other way to punish murder with the utmost permissible severity.

Of rather more interest is the sixth principle. Some make it the cornerstone of their defense of the death penalty. They argue that it is better to execute all convicted murderers, lest on a future occasion any of them murder again, than it is to execute none of them, thereby averting the risk of executing any who may be innocent. A policy of complete abolition—at least in the United States today—would result in thousands of convicted killers (only a few of whom are innocent) being held behind bars for life. This cohort would constitute a permanent risk to the safety of many millions of innocent citizens. The sole gain to counterbalance this risk is the guarantee that no lives (innocent or guilty) will be lost through legal executions. The practice of executions thus protects far more innocent citizens than the same practice puts in jeopardy.

This argument is far less conclusive than it may at first seem. Even if we grant it full weight, it is simply unreasonable to use it (or any other argument) as a way of dismissing the relevance of principles that counsel a different result, or as a tactic to imply the subordinate importance of those other principles. If used in this manner, the sixth principle would be thoroughly transformed. It has become a disguised version of the first policy goal (viz., Reduce crime!) and in effect would elevate that goal to pre-eminence over every competing and constraining consideration. The argument also fosters the illusion that we can in fact reasonably estimate, if not actually calculate, the number of lives risked by a policy of abolition as opposed to a policy of capital punishment. This is false; we do not and cannot reasonably hope to know what the risk is of convicting the innocent, even if we could estimate the risk of recidivist murder. We therefore cannot really compare the two risks with any precision. Finally, the argument gains whatever strength it appears to have by tacitly ignoring the following dilemma. If the policy of killing the convicted in order to reduce risk to the innocent is to achieve maximum effect, then death must be the *mandatory* penalty for everyone convicted of murder (never mind other crimes). But such a policy cannot really be carried out. It flies in the face of two centuries of political reality, which demonstrates the impossibility of enforcing truly mandatory death penalties for murder and other crimes against the person. The only realistic policy alternative is some version of a *discretionary* death penalty. However, every version of this policy actually tried has proved vulnerable to criticism on grounds of inequity in its administration as critic after critic has shown. Meanwhile, history tells us that our society is unable to avoid all risk of recidivist murder.

The upshot is that we today run both the risk of executing the innocent and the risk of recidivist murder, even though it is necessary to run only one of these risks.

V

What has our examination of the relevant goals and principles shown about the possibility of resolving the death penalty controversy on rational grounds? First, the death penalty is primarily a means to one or more ends or goals, but it is not the only (and arguably not the best) means to them. Second, several principles of relevance to sound punitive policy in general favor (although they do not demand) abolition of the death penalty. Third, there is no goal or principle that constitutes a conclusive reason favoring either side in the dispute. Unless, of course, some one goal or principle is interpreted or weighted in such a manner (cf. the fifth goal, or

the fifth principle). But in that case, one side or the other will refuse to accept it. Finally, the several goals and principles of punishment that have been identified have no obvious rank order or relative weighting. As they stand, these goals and principles do indeed underdetermine the policy dispute over capital punishment. Perhaps such a ranking could be provided by some comprehensive socioethical theory. But the failure of every known such theory to secure general acceptance so far does not bode well for prompt and rational resolution of the controversy along these lines.

Despite the absence of any conclusive reasons or decisive ranking of principles, we may take refuge in the thought … that a preponderance of reasons does favor one side rather than the other. Such a preponderance emerges, however, only when the relevant goals and principles of punishment are seen in a certain light, or from a particular angle of vision. Perhaps this amounts to one rather than another weighting of goals and principles but without conscious reliance upon any manifest theory. In any case, I shall mention three such considerations that are important in my assessment of the moral objections to the death penalty.

The first and by far the most important concerns the role and function of power in the hands of government. It is in general preferable, *ceteris paribus,* that such power over individuals should shrink rather than expand. Where such power must be used, then let it be devoted to constructive rather than destructive purposes, thus enhancing the autonomy and liberty of those directly affected. But the death penalty contradicts this concern; it is government power used in a dramatically destructive manner upon individuals in the absence of any compelling social necessity. No wonder it is the ultimate symbol of such power.

Another consideration that shapes my interpretation of the goals and principles of evaluation is an orientation to the *future* rather than to the past. We cannot do anything for the dead victims of crime. (How many of those who oppose the death penalty would continue to do so if *mirabile dictu*, executing the murderer brought the victim back to life?) But we can—or at least we can try to—do something for the living: we can protect the innocent, prevent illegitimate violence, and help those in despair over their own victimization. None of these constructive tasks involves punishing anyone for expressive, vindictive, or retributive reasons. The more we stress these factors in our choice of punishments, the more we orient our punitive policies toward the past—toward trying to use government power over the lives of a few as a socially approved instrument of moral bookkeeping.

Finally, the death penalty projects a false and misleading picture of man and society. Its professed message for those who support it is this: justice requires killing the convicted murderer. So we focus on the death that all murderers supposedly deserve and overlook our inability to give a rational account of why so few actually get it. Hence, the lesson taught by the practice of capital punishment is really quite different. Far from being a symbol of justice, it is a symbol of brutality and stupidity. Perhaps if we lived in a world of autonomous Kantian moral agents, where all the criminals freely expressed their rational will in the intention to kill others without their consent or desert, then death for the

convicted murderer might be just (as even Karl Marx was inclined to think). But a closer look at the convicts who actually are on our death rows shows that these killers are a far cry from the rational agents of Kant's metaphysical imagination. We fool ourselves if we think a system of ideal retributive justice designed for such persons is the appropriate model for the penal system in our society.

Have I implicitly conceded that argument over the death penalty is irrational? If I am right that the death penalty controversy does not really turn on controversial social goals or controversial moral principles, any more than it does on disputed general facts, but instead turns on how all three are to be balanced or weighed, does it follow that reason alone cannot resolve the controversy, because reason alone cannot determine which weighting or balancing is the correct one? Or can reason resolve this problem, perhaps by appeal to further theory, theory that would deepen our appreciation of what truly underlies a commitment to liberal institutions and a belief in the possibilities for autonomy of all persons? I think it can—but this is the right place to end the present investigation because we have reached the launching platform for another one.

Study Questions

1. What four factual questions regarding the death penalty are identified by Bedau? What answers are available from research, according to Bedau? Are these answers reasonably close to the facts as you understand them? Explain.

2. Bedau states that "as a matter of sheer logic, it is not possible to deduce a policy conclusion (such as the desirability of abolishing the death penalty) from any set of factual premises." What does Bedau mean? What are the implications here for the death penalty debate?

3. What are the five general social goals of punishment identified by Bedau? Discuss his assessment of those goals, and agree or disagree with Bedau at each point. Defend your position.

4. Which, if any, of the six moral principles of punishment does Bedau think are incompatible with the death penalty? Explain. How does Bedau defend his opposition to the death penalty? Do you agree with Bedau? Why? Defend your position.

5. In the United States, only a very few persons convicted of premeditated murder are executed. If all of those convicted of premeditated murder deserve death, is it just to execute only a few and allow the rest to live? Why? Defend your position.

Prison Guards and Snitches
Social Control in a Maximum Security Institution

JAMES W. MARQUART AND JULIAN B. ROEBUCK

IN PRISON VERNACULAR "RATS," "snitches," "stool pigeons," "stoolies," or finks refer to inmates who "cooperate" with or discretely furnish information to staff members. By and large, the popular imagery and folk-beliefs surrounding these inmates are particularly negative. Typically, prison movies present "rats" as the weakest, most despicable and pitiful creatures in the prisoner society. "Rats" are usually depicted as outcasts or isolates that undermine the solidarity of the cons by breaking the inmate "code" of silence (see Sykes, 1958). Whenever a "rat" appears in a movie scene, groups of inmates stop talking, disband, or mumble obscenities.[1] Some prison researchers, like McCleery (1960), contend that uncovering snitches is an obsession for the majority of inmates. This may be true in many correctional institutions because "rats" are often the victims of "accidents" or savage reprisals from other prisoners, as evidenced by the New Mexico prison riot in 1980. The inmates in many other prisons have developed an inmate society, enabling them to define, label, and punish "rats" as deviants.

The sociology of confinement, especially prison role research, has for decades noted the negative perception of "rats" by the other inmates (see Bowker, 1977). Yet, despite the fascination with and knowledge of "rats," prison researchers (unlike police researchers) have offered little systematic research on snitches.[2] Johnson (1961) and Wilmer (1965) are the only prison investigators who have examined inform-

ing, but their work focuses on the types and personal attributes of "rats" rather than informing as a mechanism of social control. Perhaps the best descriptions of the exchange relationships between staff members and stool pigeons come from former inmates (see Bettelheim, 1943; Solzhenitsyn, 1975; and Charriere, 1970). Nevertheless, little is known about how officials use inmate-intelligence as a management strategy.

This paper examines a southwestern state penitentiary control system wherein a network of "paid" inmate informants functioned as surrogate guards. Although known "rats" may be typically loathed and disparaged by the staff and captives in most institutions, the "rats" in the prison under study were hated, but also envied, feared, and respected. No stigma was attached to their deviant role. We focus on the snitch recruitment process, the types of intelligence gathered, the informers' payoff and the use of this intelligence to maintain social order—in short the dynamics of this guard-surrogate guard society.

Setting and Method of Study

The data were collected at the Johnson Unit,[3] a maximum security recidivist prison within the Texas Department of Corrections (TDC), that housed nearly 3200 inmates over the age of twenty-five (47% black, 36% white, and 17% hispanic). Many of these hard-core offenders had been convicted of violent crimes. Johnson had a

James W. Marquart and Julian B. Roebuck, "Prison Guards and Snitches: Social Control in a Maximum Security Institution," in Kenneth C. Haas and Geoffrey P. Alpert (eds), The Dilemmas of Corrections: Contemporary Readings, *Second Edition (Prospect Heights, IL: Waveland Press, 1986). pp. 158–176. Copyright © 1991 by Waveland Press, Inc., Prospect Heights, Illinois. Reprinted with permission from the publisher.*

system-wide reputation for tight disciplinary control, and inmate trouble-makers from other TDC prisons were sent there for punishment. Structurally, the prison had eighteen inside cell blocks (or tanks) and twelve dormitories branching out from a single central hall—a telephone pole design. The Hall, the main thoroughfare of the prison, was a corridor almost one quarter of a mile long, measuring sixteen feet wide by twelve feet high.

The data for this paper are derived from field research conducted from June 1981 through January 1983. The first author entered Johnson as a guard, a role which enabled him to observe and analyze first-hand the social control system. A number of established field techniques were used: participant observation, key informants, formal and informal interviews, and the examination of prison and inmate documents and records. The investigator directly observed and participated in the daily routine of prison events (work, school, meals, sick call, cell and body searches, counts, etc.) as well as various unexpected events (fights, stabbings, suicide attempts, drug trafficking). He also observed and examined officer/officer and officer/inmate (snitch) interaction patterns, inmate/officer transactions, leadership behavior, rule violations, disciplinary hearings, and the administration of punishment. With time, he established rapport with guards and inmates, gaining the reputation of a "good officer." (He was even promoted to sergeant in November 1982).

During the fieldwork, the observer developed, as did most ranking guards, a cadre of "rats" and channeled their information to supervisors (sergeants, lieutenants, captains, majors). These inmates routinely brought him information about prisoners (e.g., weapons, gambling, stealing) and even other officers (e.g., sleeping on the job, drug smuggling, having sex with inmates). The vast majority of snitches were shared, but the "rats" dealt primarily with officers who had the reputation of using good judgment (not overreacting, keeping cool) when handling sensitive information. Enmeshed in the intelligence network, the researcher fre-

quently discussed these matters with the officers and "rats."

The Snitch System

Johnson employed 240 officers and housed nearly 3,200 inmates. One guard was generally assigned to supervise four cellblocks totalling 400 prisoners. Obviously this situation obviated individual inmate supervision. Therefore, to facilitate control and order, staff members enlisted the "official" aid of the inmate elites as informers and surrogate guards. These snitches, called building tenders (BTs) and turnkeys, in turn cultivated their own inmate snitches. Johnson was managed via a complex information network facilitating a proactive as well as a reactive form of prisoner management. These surrogate guards acted with considerable authority.

STRUCTURE AND WORK ROLE

The BT system involved four levels of inmates. The top of the hierarchy consisted of the "head" building tenders. In 1981, each of the eighteen cell blocks had one building tender designated by the staff as the "head" BT. These BTs were responsible for all inmate behavior that occurred in "their" particular block. Block "ownership" was recognized by inmates and staff members alike who referred informally but meaningfully, for example, to "Watson's tank" or "Robinson's tank." Head BTs were the block's representatives to the staff and were held accountable for any problems that occurred therein. Besides procuring information (described in the next section), head BTs mediated problems (e.g., lover's quarrels, petty stealing, gambling, fighting, dirty or loud cell partners) within the living areas. They listened to and weighed each inmate's version of an argument or altercation. In most cases, the head BT warned the quarrelers to "get along with each other" or "quit all the grab-assing around." In some cases, they even let two antagonists settle their differences in a "supervised" fistfight. However, those inmates who could not or would not get along with the others were usually beaten and then moved to another cell block. BTs unofficially and routinely settled the mundane problems of prison life in the blocks without the staff's knowledge but with their tacit approval (see Marquart and Crouch, 1983).[4]

The second level of the system consisted of the rank and file building tenders. In every block (or dormitory), there were generally between three and five inmates assigned as BTs, totalling nearly 150 in the prison. BTs "worked the tank" and maintained control in the living areas by tabulating the daily counts, delivering messages to other inmates for the staff, getting the other inmates up for work, procuring information, and protecting the officers from attacks by the ordinary inmates. BTs also socialized new inmates into the system; that is, they educated them to "keep the noise down, go to work when you are called, mind your own business, stop 'grab-assing around,' and tell us [BTs] when you have a problem." BTs broke up fights, issued orders to the other inmates, protected weak inmates from exploitation, protected the officers, and passed on information to the head BT and staff members.

Finally, the BTs unofficially disciplined erring inmates. For example, if an inmate was found stealing another's property, he was apt to receive a slap across the face, a punch in the stomach, or both. If the erring inmate continued to steal, he was summarily beaten and, with the staff's approval, moved to another cell block. The BTs were "on call" twenty-four hours a day and the head BT assigned the others to shifts (morning, evening, and night). It was an unwritten rule that cell block guards were not to order the BTs to sweep the floors, wash windows, or perform other menial tasks. Those officers who violated this "rule" were informed on and frequently disciplined (e.g., reassigned to gun towers, never assigned to that particular block again). This further underscores the building tenders' proprietorship of the tanks as well as their ability and power to curtail the lower ranking guards' authority and behavior.

The third level consisted of inmate runners or strikers. Runners were selected and assigned to work in the blocks by BTs on the basis of their loyalty, work ability, and willingness to act as informants. They also worked at regular jobs throughout the prison (e.g., laundry, shops, kitchen). Runners performed the janitorial work of the block such as sweeping, cleaning windows, and dispensing supplies to the cells. More importantly, runners, who were also called hitmen, served as the physical back-up for the BTs by assisting in breaking up fights and quelling minor disturbances. As a reward for their services, runners enjoyed more mobility and privileges within the block than the other inmates (but less than the BTs). Many runners were also friends or acquaintances of the BTs in the free world, and some were their consensual homosexual partners. Some blocks had three or four runners, while others had seven, eight, or even nine. Altogether, there were approximately 175 to 200 runners.

The fourth level of the BT system consisted of turnkeys, numbering 17 in 1981. The Hall contained seven large metal barred doors, riot barricades that were manned by turnkeys in six-hour shifts. Turnkeys shut and locked these doors during fights or disturbances to localize and prevent disturbances from escalating or moving throughout the Hall. These inmates actually carried the keys (on long leather straps) which locked and unlocked the barricades. Every morning, turnkeys came to the central picket (a room containing all the keys for the prison and riot gear) and picked up keys for "their" barricades. Turnkeys routinely broke up fights, provided assistance to the BTs, and physically protected the officers from the ordinary inmates. These doorkeepers passed along information to the BTs about anything they heard while "working a gate." When off duty they lived in the blocks where they assisted the BTs in the everyday management of inmates. Turnkeys occupied a status level equal to that of the BTs.

SELECTION OF BTS AND TURNKEYS

As "managers" of the living areas and Hall, these inmate-agents obviously performed a dangerous task for the staff. Vastly outnumbered, BTs and turnkeys ruled with little opposition from the ordinary inmates. In fact, most of the ordinary inmates feared their "overseers" because of their status and physical dominance. They were formally selected by the staff to perform an official job within the living areas. Unwritten but "official" departmental policy existed on the appointment of inmates to BT and turnkey positions. The staff at Johnson (and other Texas prisons) recommended certain inmates as BTs/turnkeys to the Classification Committee (a panel of four TDC officials all with prison security backgrounds).[5] This committee then reviewed the inmate records and made the final selections. Recommendations to the Classification Committee from the staff were not always honored and less than half of those recommended were selected for BT/turnkey jobs. One supervisor, an active participant in the recruitment process at Johnson, expressed a typical preference:

> I've got a personal bias. I happen to like murderers and armed robbers. They have a great deal of esteem in the inmate social system, so it's not likely that they'll have as much problem as some other inmate because of their esteem, and they tend to be more aggressive and a more dynamic kind of individual. A lot of inmates steer clear of them and avoid problems just because of the reputation they have and their aggressiveness. They tend to be aggressive, you know, not passive.

The BTs and turnkeys were physically and mentally superior inmates, "natural leaders" among their peers. All were articulate and had physical presence, poise, and self-confidence. Generally, they were more violent, prisonized, and criminally sophisticated than the ordinary inmates. Of the eighteen head BTs, eight were in prison for armed robbery, five for murder (one was an enforcer and contract style killer), one for attempted murder, one for rape, one for drug trafficking, and two for burglary. Their average age was thirty-nine and they were serving an average prison sentence of thirty-two years. Of the seventeen turnkeys, three were murderers, three were armed robbers, six were burglars, two were drug traffickers, one was a rapist and one was doing time for aggravated assault. Their

average age was thirty-one and they were serving an average sentence of twenty-two years. All were physically strong, rugged, prison-wise, and physically imposing. BTs and turnkeys were older than most prisoners and often they were violent recidivists similar to the inmate leaders noted by Clemmer (1940) and Schrag (1954). In contrast, the average TDC inmate in 1981 had been given a twenty-one year sentence and was between twenty-two and twenty-seven years old. Almost half (48%) were property offenders or petty thieves.

Information Acquisition

The most important means of controlling inmates' behavior in the cell blocks was the presence of BTs. These inmate-agents, while carrying out their other duties, spent most of their time sitting around the entrance to the block talking with other inmates, especially the runners. Conversations with and observations of other prisoners enabled the BTs to gather a variety of intelligence about inmates' moods, problems, daily behaviors, friends, enemies, homosexual encounters, misbehaviors, plans, plots and overall demeanor.

The runners, who worked throughout the prison, had more contact with the ordinary inmates than did the BTs. This contact facilitated eavesdropping and the extracting of information. For example, while mopping the runs (walkways on each tier), runners talked to and observed the inmates already in their cells. At work, these inmates listened to, watched, talked to, and interacted with the others. Runners secured and relayed to the BTs information on work strikes, loan sharking, stealing of state property, distilling liquor, tattooing, homosexual acts, and escape and revenge plans.

INFORMATION SOURCES IN THE CELL BLOCKS

Though informing was expected from runners, they were not formally instructed to inform. A head BT explains this situation:

> You don't pick these people and tell them

now you've got to go in there and tell me what's going on inside the dayroom [a TV and recreation area in each living area]. By becoming a runner it is expected that you will tell what's going on; it's an unspoken rule that you will inform on the rest of the people in here. If you hear something you are going to come to me with it.

With the runners' information, the BTs penetrated the tank social system. Ordinary prisoners knew they were under constant surveillance and thus were amenable to the prisoner social control system—a system based on inmate intelligence reports, regimentation, strict rules, and certain punishments. For example, when the BTs found out that two or more inmates were "cliquing up" for any purpose, they immediately told the staff, who disbanded the group through cell changes.

Atomized and lacking solidarity, the ordinary inmates "ratted" on each other, especially when they felt the need for protection. Ordinary inmates rarely, if ever, sought out the staff to solve a block problem because this brought punishment from the BTs. Instead they sought the counsel and help of the BTs, the power block they were forced to deal with. From the ordinary inmates, the BTs learned about a variety of things such as gambling pools, illicit sex, petty thievery, tattooing paraphernalia, liquor making, weapons, and numerous other forms of contraband, misbehavior, and planned misbehavior (e.g., plots of revenge, possible attacks on an overbearing guard). This knowledge enabled the guards to take a proactive stance, thereby preventing rule violations. Not all block residents were informers. Those who snitched did so for several reasons.

Like anyone else, prisoners react negatively to certain repugnant behaviors and situations. Most were followers and refrained from taking action themselves. Citizens often call the police, for example, about a neighbor's barking dog or loud stereo rather than complain directly to the neighbor. Inmates took similar action. They told the BTs about various illegalities (especially those that threatened them in any way) because

they knew the problem would be resolved in the block without involving themselves or attracting official intervention. The BTs usually took swift action when resolving problems. For example, one inmate told the BTs in his block that his cellmate was making sexual advances to him. After investigating the claims, the BTs solved this problem by beating the sexually aggressive inmate and, with staff approval, moving him to another block. In another cell block, an inmate told the head BT that his cell partner was scaring him by turning off the cell's light bulb. The BT struck the pranking inmate on the head with a pipe and threatened to have him moved to another block. The prankster "got his message."

Inmates were not always straightforward and sometimes informed for revenge. For example, some inmates informed on those they desired to see the BTs punish and/or move to another cell block. Some inmates "planted" contraband in their enemies' cell and then "tipped off" the BTs. Some inmates gave the BTs false information about other inmates, a variety of snitching called "dropping salt" or "crossing out." However, revenge-informing was restricted because the BTs were especially aware of this maneuver—and severely punished the disclosed instigator. Those who gave spurious information of any kind (or who deceived the BTs in any way) played a dangerous game. If discovered, they were beaten. The BTs (like the guards) weighed and checked the informer's information, considered his motive, and noted the relationship between him and the one informed upon before taking action.

Some ordinary inmates reported illegalities to the BTs in return for favors and to get on their good sides. For example, when an inmate told the BTs about someone who was fashioning a weapon, he expected something in return. Favors assumed many forms such as selection as a runner or maybe even a job recommendation. BTs often recommended "helpful" inmates to the staff for jobs in the garment factory, shops, laundry, or showrooms—and these allies served as additional snitches.

A number of ordinary inmates "ratted" on

other inmates as a sort of game playing device. They planned a scenario, informed, and then sat back and enjoyed the action and reaction. Several inmates told me that this kind of game playing relieved their boredom at others' expense. The BTs received most of their information from regular legitimate snitches. However, in some cases when the regular channels did not suffice, they resorted to threats and the terrorization of ordinary inmates to gather information.

BTs, like guards, could not be everywhere at once and therefore relied on stool pigeons. For example, BTs could not observe homosexuality in the cells, but their snitches could. Bob, a head BT, sums up the situation: "The tanks are run through an information system. Whether this information comes from runners or even other inmates, this is how trouble is kept down." The BTs' snitching system was officially recognized as part of the prisoner control system whereas their snitches' behavior was informal, though expected.

INFORMATION GATHERED OUTSIDE THE BLOCK

Runners and ordinary inmates worked throughout the prison and routinely informed the BTs about activities in the work areas, school, hospital, laundry, dining rooms, and shower rooms. Gary, a head BT, described this activity:

We [BTs] all have our people, but we don't fuck with each other's people. If you walk down the Hall and hear somebody say "he's one of mine" that means that that particular inmate owes some type of allegiance to a particular BT. The reason he owes that allegiance or loyalty is perhaps he [a BT] got him a job someplace, got him out of the field and into the Garment Factory. These people are loyal to me. I put them there not for me but for the Man [the warden] and they tell me what's going on in that particular place. If you don't help me then I'll bust you. I got Bruce the job in the Issue Room [clothing and supply room]. I own Bruce because I got him that job. He tells me if clothing is being stolen or if inmates are trying to get more than they deserve.

Misbehavior, plots, and plans were not confined solely to the living areas and the BTs had extended "ears" in all areas where inmates interacted. Consequently, they kept abreast of developments everywhere and relatively little happened without their knowledge.

Turnkeys were not isolated from this spy network because they too had snitches. The turnkeys worked in the prison corridor and therefore gathered much information about illegal behavior outside the cell blocks. They acquired information about weapons, drugs, or other contraband being passed in the Hall, a vital area in the prison because large numbers of inmates were in constant movement there from one point to another. The turnkeys had to keep a constant vigil in the Hall to keep out unauthorized inmates and to maintain order in a very fluid and potentially explosive situation. The Hall was divided into the north and south ends and inmates who lived on the north end were forbidden to walk to the south end and vice versa. No inmates were permitted in the Hall who were not enroute to an official designation. Turnkeys generally knew in which end of the building inmates lived and vigorously watched for "trespassers." Holding down the illegal inmate Hall traffic suppressed contraband peddling as well as general disorder.

EFFICIENCY OF THE SYSTEM

At first glance, this snitching system appears cumbersome and inadequate because (apparently) BTs' and turnkeys' snitches could end up snitching on one another and the guards, creating an amorphous situation without accuracy, consistency, or legitimacy. However, the system worked effectively because the BTs and turnkeys, for the most part, knew "whose snitch was whose." Loyalty to key individuals and reciprocity were the key conditions underpinning the snitch system. BTs and turnkeys interacted amongst themselves and generally knew whose "people" were working where, and their grapevine facilitated the necessary communication. Some snitches were "shared" or owed allegiance to several BTs (or turnkeys). The snitches did not owe their allegiance to the guards or to the BTs as a group, but rather to a particular BT or the BTs who ran their cell block or who were in close supervisory contact with them. When a BT's snitch was "busted," he was expected to intervene with the staff to help his snitch get off or obtain light punishment. The snitches were not completely immune from the rules, but they had an edge over other inmates in circumventing certain rules and in receiving lighter punishments when caught in rule breaking.

Types of Information

The major organizational role of the BTs and turnkeys was to gather information on ordinary inmates' behavior, but they did not report every rule violation and violator. They screened all information and passed to the staff only intelligence about actual or potentially serious rule infractions. As Jerry, a head BT, says:

> Look, we don't tell the Man [Warden] about everything that goes on in the tanks. That makes it look bad if I'm running down to the Major's office[6] and telling somebody, old so and so, he's playing his radio too loud, or so and so, he's got an antenna that goes from his cell up to the window. That shows the Man up there that I don't have control of that tank and I can't let that happen. That makes me look bad.

The BTs handled "misdemeanors" or petty rule violations themselves in the blocks. The BTs and turnkeys regularly informed the staff about five types of serious rule violations, commonly called "Major's Office Business."

"MAJOR'S OFFICE BUSINESS"

First and foremost, the BTs and turnkeys were constantly on guard to detect escape plans because TDC considered escape the most serious of all violations. For example, one night when the first author was on duty, a cell block officer found several saw marks on the bars of a cell's air vent which provided access to the cell house plumbing area and ceiling fans. Should an inmate stop the fan, he could conceivably climb

to the roof and perhaps escape. When a shift supervisor arrived to examine the marks, the block's BTs were assembled and asked about the situation. They knew of no hacksaw blades in the block and doubted that the two suspected inmates were the types to be preparing for an escape. They suggested that the cell's previous occupants were the most likely culprits. In any event, the BTs assisted several officers (including the researcher) in searching the inmates' belongings for escape tools. Nothing was found and everyone was allowed to go back to bed.

Second, BTs informed the staff about ordinary inmates' homosexual behavior. The staff considered this behavior serious because it frequently led to envy, fights, lover's quarrels, retaliation, stabbings, as well as to the buying and selling of "punks." Homosexuality also went against the legal and moral rules of the prison system. The guards, a moralistic conservative group, despised homosexuality and punished it severely, officially or otherwise. BTs were very adept at discovering this form of illicit behavior. For example, one night while I was on the third shift (9:45 to 5:45 A.M.), the head BT on 13-block informed a captain that one well-known homosexual (or "bitch") had entered the wrong cell on the second tier. I accompanied the shift supervisor and head BT as they slowly crept along the walkway and caught the inmates "in the act." Both were charged and punished. The BTs made sure the inmates entered their own cells and not someone else's, thus also keeping stealing to a minimum.

Third, the inmate-agents told the staff about inmates who strong-armed weaker inmates into paying protection, engaging in homosexual acts, or surrendering their property. Extortion or strong-arming was considered serious because of the potential for violence and the prison's legal obligation to protect inmates from exploitation and physical harm. In most cases, these problems were handled informally within the blocks (i.e., a warning). If the behavior persisted, the offending inmate was generally beaten up ("tuned up") and reported to the staff. Staff members usually gave the erring inmate a few slaps across the face or kicks in the buttocks and transferred him to another cell block.

Fourth, BTs and turnkeys informed the staff about drug trafficking. The introduction of drugs into the population was extremely difficult but occasionally small quantities were smuggled inside. Again, the inmate-agents kept this activity to a minimum and assisted the staff in making "drug busts." For example, one head BT and a turnkey briefed the staff about an inmate who worked outside the prison compound (farm operation) and who was supplying marijuana cigarettes to a certain block. Plans were devised to catch the inmate with his supplies. As he came in from work the next day, another guard and the investigator detained and searched him. Although no marijuana was found, it was later reported to us that the "dealer" quit trafficking because he knew he was being watched.

The BTs and turnkeys also told ranking staff members about guards who brought in drugs. In fact, one head BT was notorious for convincing (or entrapping) officers, especially new recruits, to smuggle narcotics into the institution. If the officer agreed, and some did, the staff was informed, and plans were made to catch the unsuspecting officer. Officers caught bringing in drugs (or any other contraband such as pornography) to the inmates were immediately dismissed. The BTs in one block even assisted the staff in apprehending an officer who was homosexually involved with an inmate. This officer was promptly terminated.

Last, the BTs and turnkeys informed staff members about inmates who manufactured, possessed, or sold weapons, especially knives. Inmates with weapons obviously placed the officers and their inmate agents in physical jeopardy. One day, John, the head BT on 18-block, came to the Major's Office and told the captain about a knife in the eighth cell on the first row of "his" block. Two officers, two BTs, and the researcher searched the cell and found a knife wedged in between the first bunk and the cell wall. The owner of the weapon received a disciplinary hearing, spent fifteen days in solitary

confinement, and was then moved to another cell block. It was common for the BTs to help the guards search suspected inmates' cells because they knew the tricks and places that inmates used to conceal weapons. Many officers learned how to search cells from the BTs. On another occasion a turnkey told the first author that an inmate, who had just exited a dining hall, was carrying a knife in his ankle cast. The cast was searched and a small homemade knife was found. The turnkey later revealed to the investigator that one of his snitches spotted the inmate putting the "shank" in his cast just prior to leaving the block for the dining hall.

ROUTING OF INFORMATION

The actual passage of information did not always follow a formal chain of command. Though runners and ordinary inmates "reported" directly to the BTs and turnkeys, these latter inmates relayed information only to those ranking officers (sergeants, lieutenants, captains, majors, wardens) with whom they had developed a personal relationship. Some guards were trusted by few if any inmate-snitches and were essentially left out of the informer process. Others who had displayed sufficient consistency and common sense in handling sensitive information were trusted, respected, and admired by the inmate elites. Inmate-agents actively sought alliances with these officers. Indeed, only a "man" could be trusted with confidential information. Such officers were briefed each day about events on and off their work shifts. Some of these inmate-agents were so loyal to a particular staff member that they refused to "deal" with other officers in that particular staff member's absence.

Staff members who had a cadre of inmate-agents "working" for them were in a better position to anticipate and control problems in the prison. Somewhat ironically, therefore, inmates were in a position to confer status on officers and even to affect indirectly their promotions. Some officers often gave their favorite BT or turnkey special jobs generally performed only by staff members. These jobs included stakeouts, shadowing, or entrapping a suspected inmate or officer to gather evidence about rule violations or plans of wrongdoing. These special assignments brought the staff member and inmate together in an even tighter, symbiotic relationship, leading sometimes to mutual trust and friendship. Some of these snitches were so fanatical in their loyalty that they openly stated they would kill another inmate if so ordered by "their" officer.

AN OPEN SYSTEM OF INFORMING

Unlike "rats" in prison movies, BTs and turnkeys did not hide the fact that they were snitches. It was not uncommon to see some of these inmate-agents point out the misdeeds of another inmate to a guard in the presence of other inmates. It was quite common to see BTs and turnkeys "escort" their officer "friends" as companions and bodyguards while these guards were making their rounds. While accompanying "his" officer, the inmate-agent openly informed the staff member about what was "going on" in a particular cell block or work area. The "betrayer-betrayed" relationship was not hidden and when the guards searched an inmate's cell or body, the suspected inmate knew full well in most cases who had "tipped off" the staff. One could argue that the BTs and turnkeys were not "rats" because they officially, voluntarily, and openly worked for the staff. Following this reasoning, the only "real" snitches were the BTs' and turnkeys' informers who were ordinary inmates. These inmates were mildly stigmatized by other inmates, but rarely punished because all inmates feared the BTs' presence and wrath.

Although informing occurred throughout the prison, the Major's Office was the official focal point of such activity. This office, located directly off the main corridor, was the place BTs-turnkeys conducted their "business;" that is, turned in intelligence reports and discussed plans of action. This site was divided into two rooms; the front part (off the Hall) housed the inmate bookkeepers and the back room contained two desks for the major and captains. Disciplinary court was convened in the back room where such punishments as slapping, punching, kicking, stomping, and blackjacking were administered.

The staff and their "inmate-guards" socialized here as well as conducted the daily "convict business." Throughout the day, BTs and turnkeys came in to visit their bookkeeper friends and mingle with the ranking guards. Together, in this office area, the guards and their inmate-agents drank coffee, smoked, discussed the point spreads for sporting events, joked, chatted, engineered practical jokes, roughhoused, and ate food from the prison canteen. Whenever a captain, major, or warden entered, these inmates (sometimes there were eight or nine) would, if sitting, stand and say "hello sir." However, all was not fun and games. These inmates also kept the staff abreast of what was "going on," especially in terms of Major's Office business. All day, a steady stream of these inmate-agents filed in and out. BTs and turnkeys entered this office at will. However, the Major's Office was off-limits to the ordinary inmates except for official reasons. It was a status symbol for the "rats" to hang around this office and interact with the guards.

The Informer's Payoff

Skolnick (1966: 124), in his account of police informants, maintains that "the informer-informed relationship is a matter of exchange in which each party seeks to gain something from the other in return for certain desired commodities." Similarly, BTs and turnkeys expected to receive rewards for the information they proferred beyond a sense of accomplishment for a job well done.

In addition to status and influence, BTs and turnkeys also enjoyed a number of privileges which flowed from and defined their position. Some of these privileges appear relatively minor, yet they loomed large in a prison setting. The privileges included such scarce resources as specially pressed clothes and green quilted jackets. Ordinary inmates, meanwhile, wore white, ill-fitting coats. Some BTs possessed aquariums and such pets as cats, owls, rabbits, and turtles. BT cell block doors were rarely closed, permitting BTs to move freely about the block and to receive "visits" in their cells from friends and homosexuals. The latter were not threatened or forced to engage in sexual behavior; they voluntarily moved in to share the benefits. Head BTs roamed the halls and spent considerable time in and around the Major's Office.

Furthermore, BTs were able to eat whenever they desired and often ate two or three times in one meal period. Part of this special freedom stemmed from the fact that BTs and turnkeys were on call 24 hours a day. Nonetheless it was viewed by them and others as a special privilege. These inmate-agents were permitted to carry weapons with which to protect themselves and the guard force. These weapons, usually kept concealed, included wooden clubs, knives, pipes, blackjacks, "fistloads," and hammers. A special privilege was relative immunity from discipline. For example, if a fight occurred between a BT (or turnkey) and another inmate, the non-BT might receive several nights in solitary or ten days in cell restriction; the BT might receive a reprimand or, more likely, no punishment at all. This differential treatment reflected the understanding that the BT was probably "taking care of business." The BTs also used their influence to persuade the staff to "go lightly" on their runners who faced disciplinary cases for "helping the Man." In short, the BTs and turnkeys did "soft" time. Because of their position and privileges, the BTs-turnkeys were hated, but also feared, envied and respected by the other prisoners.

On an interpersonal level, many of the BT-turnkey-officer relationships transcended a simple *quid pro quo* of exchange of favors for instrumental purposes. That is, upper level staff members called their favorite BTs and turnkeys by their first names. Sometimes, they even took the word of a head BT over that of a cell block officer. In this way, the status differential between the staff members and their inmate

agents was decreased. As one supervisor put it:

> Look, these guys [BTs-turnkeys] are going to be here a while and they get to know the cons better than us. I can't depend on some of these officers, you know how they are, they're late, they're lazy, they want extra days off, or just don't show up. Hell, you've got to rely on them [BTs and turnkeys].

This preferential treatment of a subset of inmates caused frustration and low morale among many low ranking officers, contributing to a high turnover rate among the guard staff, especially weak guards.[7]

Inmates, Information, and Social Control

The prison staff's primary duty is to maintain social order and prevent escapes. Although Johnson's barb-wire fences, lights, alarm system, perimeter patrol car, and rural isolation reduced the possibility of escapes and mass disorder, routine control and order were achieved proactively by penetrating and dividing the inmate population. Walls, fences, and alarms were the last line of defense as well as symbolic forms of social control. Moreover, the staff's guns, tear gas, and riot gear were also an end of the line means of control and were infrequently utilized. The prison guards, like police officers, rarely employed weapons to achieve order.

The day-to-day maintenance of order at Johnson depended on the cooperation of inmate elites, a snitching system, and the terrorization of the ordinary inmates. The constant surveillance and terrorization of ordinary inmates prevented them from acquiring the solidarity necessary for self-protection and the cohesion needed for organized resistance. Although the ordinary inmates were atomized, they lived in a regimented and predictable environment. The staff's power, authority, and presence permeated the institution.

The role and identity of the inmate-agents was not hidden and they did not suffer from role strain or spoiled identities. Even though the ordinary inmates surreptitiously called the BTs-turnkeys "dogs" among themselves, they avoided physical confrontations with the "dogs" at all costs. They lacked the influence, prestige, power and organization necessary to stigmatize the BTs'-turnkeys' status or define their roles as deviant (see Lofland, 1969). To compound deviancy, one must be caught committing an inappropriate act, and snitching by the BTs and turnkeys was not considered inappropriate (see Matza, 1969: 148-9). At Johnson, informing was a means to enhance one's status and well-being. The inmate-agents were pro-staff and openly sided with and protected the guards. As one building tender stated: "I'm proud to work for the Man [Warden] because I know who butters my bread." They rationalized away their snitching behavior by denigrating and dehumanizing the ordinary inmates, referring to them as "scum" and "born losers." Ordinary inmate-snitches were looked down upon but rarely punished.

The guard staff used this snitch system to penetrate the inmate population and thereby act proactively to reduce the likelihood of such breaches of prison security as escapes, murders, rapes, narcotic rings, mob violence, loansharking, protection rackets, excessive stealing, and racial disruption. The officers, protected by the elites, were rarely derogated or attacked and never taken hostage or murdered. The staff was rarely caught off guard. This totalitarian system virtually destroyed any chances among the ordinary inmates (as individuals or groups) to unite or engage in collective dissent, protests, or violence. Those ordinary inmates who were docile and went along with the system were generally protected and left alone. This proactive system was so successful that only two inmate murders and one riot occurred from 1972 through 1982.

The aggressive use of co-opted snitches was not, however, without problems. Ordinary inmates under this system were non-persons who lived in continuous fear, loneliness, isolation, and tension. They never knew when they

might be searched or, for that matter, disciplined on the basis of another inmate's accusation. BTs and turnkeys were not above occasionally falsely accusing "insubordinate" inmates of wrongdoing. The staff routinely backed up their allies. Some "unruly" inmates were "set up" by the BTs (e.g., having a knife thrown in their cell while they were at work) and then reported to the staff. Every ordinary inmate was suspect and even lower ranking guards were sometimes terminated solely on the word of a head BT. Furthermore, a federal judge, as part of the class action civil suit *Ruiz* v. *Estelle* (1980), stated that this form of prisoner control at TDS was corrupt and deviant in terms of progressive penology. The snitch system at Johnson is now defunct and the staff no longer uses BTs and turnkeys (see Marquart, 1984).

Conclusion

This paper examined the structure and workings of an informer-privilege system within a penitentiary for older recidivists. At Johnson, the official informers, called BTs and turnkeys, worked for and openly cooperated with the staff. These snitches, the most aggressive, older, and criminally sophisticated prisoners, were not deviants or outcasts. In turn, they cultivated additional snitches and, with the staff's help, placed these allies in jobs or positions throughout the institution. Ordinary inmate behavior as well as that of lower ranking guards was under constant scrutiny. Therefore, the staff knew almost everything that occurred within the institution, permitting proactive control and thereby preventing in many instances, violent acts, group disturbances, and escapes.

The ordinary inmates considered the inmate-guards "rats." However, they lacked the influence, prestige, and power to define and label them as such—to impute deviancy to the BT-turnkey role. Selection as a BT or turnkey was not assignment to a deviant category, but rather to an elite corp of pro-staff inmates. Within this system, the only deviants were the unruly ordinary inmates and weak lower ranking guards. Both of these groups were stigmatized and labeled deviant by the staff and their inmate-agents within the prison. From the standpoint of progressive penologists and reform-minded citizens, this entire system would be considered deviant, inhumane, and morally corrupt. Although the system described in this paper may be unusual, it remains to be seen if and how other prison staffs co-opt elite inmates to help maintain social order. Past prison research has demonstrated some informal alliances between prison staffs and inmate elites. However, the form of this alliance may vary widely from prison to prison.

NOTES

1. Perhaps the epitome of the hatred of "rats" was in the movie "Stalag 17" (1952) wherein William Holden was falsely accused of being a "plant" in a German POW camp during World War II.
2. The use of informants in police work, especially in vice and narcotic operations, has been well-documented (see Greene, 1960; Skolnick, 1966; Westley, 1970).
3. Johnson is a pseudonym.
4. For a more thorough analysis of the BT/turnkey system see Marquart (1983).
5. The exact format or guidelines used by the Classification Committee is not known. However, this committee was composed primarily of security personnel and these members probably exerted the greatest voice in the selection process.
6. The Major's Office is simply an office area where the ranking guards (sergeants, lieutenants, captains, majors and wardens) conducted disciplinary hearings and other forms of prison "business."
7. Weak guards were easily bullied by the inmates, could not or would not enforce order, failed to break up fights, failed to fight inmates, and were basically ignored and laughed at by the other guards and inmates.

REFERENCES

Bettelheim, B.
   1943 "Individual and mass behavior in extreme situations." Journal of Abnormal and Social Psychology.

Charriere, H.
   1970 Papillon. New York: Basic Books.
Clemmer, D.C.
   1940 The Prison Community. New York: Holt, Rinehart and Winston.
Greene, E.
   1960 War on the Underworld. London: John Long.
Johnson, E.H.
   1961 "Sociology of Confinement: Assimilation and the prison 'rat.'" The Journal of Criminal Law, Criminology, and Police Science. 51: 528–533.
Lofland, J.
   1969 Deviance and Identity. Englewood Cliffs, NJ: Prentice Hall.
Marquart, J. W.
   1984 The Impact of Court-Ordered Reform in a Texas Penitentiary: The Unanticipated Consequences of Legal Intervention. Paper presented at the Southern Sociological Society Annual meetings in Knoxville (April).
Marquart, J. W. and B. M. Crouch
   1983 Coopting the Kept: Using Inmates for Social Control in a Southern Prison. Paper presented before the American Society of Criminologists Annual meetings in Toronto.
Matza, D.
   1969 Becoming Deviant. Englewood Cliffs, NJ: Prentice Hall.
McCleery, R.
   1960 "Communication patterns as bases of systems of authority," in Theoretical Studies in Social Organizations of the Prison. New York: Social Science Research Council.
Ruiz v. *Estelle*, 503 F. Supp. 1265 (S.D. Texas) 1980.
Schrag, C.
   1954 "Leadership among prison inmates," American Sociological Review. 19: 37–42.
Skolnick, J. H.
   1966 Justice Without Trial: Law Enforcement in Democratic Society.
Solzhenitsyn, A. I.
   1975 The Gulag Archipelago II. New York: Harper and Row.
Sykes, G.
   1958 The Society of Captives. Princeton, N.J.: Princeton University Press.
Westley, W.
   1970 Violence and the Police. Cambridge, MA: MIT Press.
Wilmer, H. A.
   1965 "The role of a 'rat' in prison." Federal Probation 29 (March): 44–49.

Study Questions

1. What are "BTs" and "turnkeys"? How were the BTs organized at Johnson Unit?

2. From an administrative perspective, what moral value seems to dominate the snitch system? Explain. What moral values are sacrificed? Explain.

3. From an inmate perspective, what moral values are most protected under the snitch system? What values are least significant? Explain.

4. Given your understanding of mainstream contemporary correctional theory, what was wrong with the Johnson system? Does the success of the system reveal a theoretical inadequacy, in your view? Why? Defend your position.

5. Describe your ethical reaction to the snitch system. Assess the system from a utilitarian perspective and then from a deontological perspective. Do you agree with the Court's decision to terminate the system? Why? Defend your position.

Case 8.1

THE STROP

Jay Barros was a delinquent. He would even admit it freely. He'd done just about everything and had been on probation and in and out of institutions for years. The psychologists had long ago classified him as a typical sociopath: no conscience, never learning from the past, impulsive, and manipulative.[1]

Harold "Red" Chapman was a probation officer. He was also an ex-cop. He didn't counsel his charges; he supervised them with an iron hand. He had one rule: any misconduct and you get violated. No questions, no excuses. It was odd, though, he didn't violate that many kids. Most of his probationers led pretty straight lives when they were on Red's caseload.

Jay knew he had messed up. He had been cutting classes, been caught drinking, and didn't come home for three straight days. Jay's mother had called Red to report on Jay's behavior, and Red had called Jay into his office for a conference. Jay figured that it was back to the state Boy's School, again, as he walked into Red's office and shut the door behind him.

"Sit down and shut up," Red said in a stern voice. "We're gonna talk. As I see it, you've got two choices. Your first choice is a quick trip to the detention center and an even quicker trip out to the Boy's School. But that's a lot of paperwork on my end."

"Yeah, and what's my second choice?" Jay asked, beginning to think that if he played his cards right he might just get out of this. Red reached into his lower drawer and brought out a piece of leather two and one-half inches wide and three feet long.

"This is a strop. Barbers use them to sharpen razors. I use this one to adjust attitudes. That's your second choice. Ten with the strop and you walk out of here. It's your choice." Jay stood up and grabbed his ankles.

Note

1. For additional information on the sociopathic personality, see Hervey Cleckley, *The Mask of Sanity: An Attempt to Clarify Some Issues About the So-called Psychopathic Personality* (Saint Louis: C. V. Mosby Co., 1964).

Questions for Discussion

1. Did Barros choose his punishment?

2. *Jackson v. Bishop* (404 F. 2nd 571) held that whipping was in violation of the Eighth Amendment. Do you agree or disagree that the strop, in this case, was a less severe punishment than incarceration?

3. What other alternatives are there to the incarcerate-or-whip dichotomy?

4. Some states (e.g., Michigan) outlaw any type of corporal punishment against students. Other states (e.g., Ohio) allow paddling of students under very strict procedural guidelines. Which state is correct, in your view? Why? Defend your position.

Case 8.2

SIGN, SIGN, EVERYWHERE A SIGN

THE COURT: Mr. Jones, you have been found guilty of criminal sexual conduct in the second degree. For this, you can be placed in the State Penitentiary for up to 15 years.

Before I announce my sentence, I want to review both the circumstances of the offense and your personal background. Your offense is heinous. It involves one of the most unforgivable actions by a member of our community, because you molested a young child who had been placed in your care and was your responsibility. This was a vulnerable young child of only six years. Being responsible for her care while her parents were away, and having in your hands received the trust of her very fragile personality, you took advantage of your position of responsibility and touched her repeatedly about her breasts, buttocks, and vagina.

There was no weapon involved in this case. You didn't need that in order to assert your authority. You did, nevertheless, leave bruises on her genital area—bruises caused by your thoughtless and dangerous actions, and driven by this misdirected lust. As a result of your actions, the victim's family and the victim have been psychologically traumatized and will require counseling. You have changed all of their lives in a way that is unalterable. Finally, it has come to light during the course of the counseling of this child that you have done this on other occasions as well.

This isn't the first time you have been in contact with the legal system. In spite of your relatively young age—19 years—you have been in trouble with the law since the age of 13. As a juvenile, you were adjudicated a delinquent the first time for being truant from school. That was followed by an adjudication for a break-in and one for making annoying phone calls. The record indicates that those phone calls were made to a young girl of the age of 10 in your neighborhood.

Since becoming an adult, you have been convicted of indecent exposure and possession of a weapon. You also have a misdemeanor conviction for assault and battery.

Mr. Jones, you have demonstrated to this Court that you are a dangerous person. There is no question in my mind that the twin goals of punishment for you and protection for society must be uppermost in my mind when I fashion a sentence for you. If the sentence is significant enough, I should hope that it would deter you, and others who may be like-minded as you, from committing offenses such as this that prey on innocent victims. I intend to get my message across to you in no uncertain terms that your behavior simply won't be tolerated by a civilized society. You don't have much time to straighten your life out, Mr. Jones, before you spend the rest of your life institutionalized behind bars.

You have been on probation before and you have successfully completed that probation. For that reason, and also because of your young age and because you have expressed extreme remorse for this offense, I am not going to incarcerate you immediately. I am going to place you on probation and impose certain restrictions on your activity. I will impose a jail sentence to be served at the end of your probation. However, the jail sentence will be subject to review by the court. If you have followed the rules of probation, it will not be necessary to serve that jail sentence.

Therefore, the Court's sentence is as follows: You are placed on probation for a period of five years. During this period of time you must undergo psychological counseling for your sexual deviancy. You must pay for all the costs of counseling for the victim and her family. Since you have a job and her family is unemployed, this is the only opportunity that is available to try to reconstruct this young lady's personality. They can't afford it. If you are incarcerated, this very important goal could not be achieved. Moreover, you must engage in 150 hours of community service. Your community service will be spent on the maintenance staff of a senior citizens home, and you will receive no wages for the work that you perform. Finally, you must place a sign on the front of your home, no smaller than three feet by five feet, that states: "I am a convicted child molester. I am seeking treatment for my offense. All children are warned to stay away from this home." You may not be in the company of any child under the age of 18 during the period of your probation.

Finally, you are sentenced to spend one year in the Metro County Jail. This period of incarceration is to be served during your last year of probation and it is subject to review by the court. If you have performed each and every term of your probation order satisfactorily and completely, this period of incarceration will be suspended.

That concludes this sentence. Next case.

Questions for Discussion

1. Isn't this a form of "mental whipping" and the same punishment as in "The Strop"?
2. Is this punishment "fair" from the point of view of the defendant? the victim? the community?
3. There are several elements to this sentence. Analyze each from an ethical perspective.
4. Did the punishment fit the crime?
5. Comment on the judge's use of Mr. Jones' juvenile record in the sentencing decision. Does your state's juvenile/criminal code allow for this?

Case 8.3

DEATH WATCH

You are an experienced correctional officer and are well respected by your peers, supervisors, and administration. You have held virtually every position in the maximum security prison where you work, including death row. You have been a sergeant for the past three years and have recently been promoted to lieutenant. Things are going well for you and you see no reason why you should not be promoted to captain and then to the Head of Custody Services.

The Warden of your institution has instituted a management rotation system for all mid-managers. In this system, each mid-manager spends a minimum of six months in each department within the prison structure. The Warden feels that each mid-manager should be intimately familiar with all facets of prison management and you feel that this is an excellent (and quite progressive) management style.

Your most recent assignment has been to supervise and coordinate the "Death Watch" team.[1] This team has the responsibility for the supervision of the condemned prisoner for the 48 hours prior to execution and for the execution itself. This elite team is well-trained and professional in its duties. You are assigned to take an active part in the team's preparation for and administration of the death sentence.

However, you are opposed (both morally and religiously) to the death penalty. You feel that the death penalty is wrong. You also know that if you fail to complete this assignment, you will no doubt remain a lieutenant for the remainder of your career. If you participate in the forthcoming execution, this portion of your management training will be completed and you will no doubt progress professionally as planned.

Note

1. For a description of life on death row and the activities of the modern-day execution team, see Robert Johnson, *Death Work: A Study of the Modern Execution Process* (Pacific Grove, Calif.: Brooks/Cole Publishing Company, 1990).

Questions for Discussion

1. May a moral duty ever override a legal duty? If so, under what conditions?

2. What would you do? Defend your position.

3. Balance the benefit of standing by one's convictions versus the potential effect on one's career.

4. Compare and contrast the actions of this corrections officer and those of a police officer using deadly force.

Case 8.4

MONDAY MORNING MEMOS

You are involved with electronic surveillance/monitoring of probationers. You have just installed new equipment that allows for voiceprint identification of your clients and also measures their blood alcohol content almost simultaneously. Thus, you can monitor the whereabouts of your clients and also determine whether those who are to abstain from the use of alcohol are complying. Your probation officers also make random checks on clients at their places of residence and business and are allowed to ask them to submit to tests for drugs and/or alcohol.

It is Monday morning and you are presented with two "Technical Violation of Probation" reports. It is your decision as to whether these offenders are to be referred to the court for violation hearings or warned and given another chance.

Case #1. Dale Richardson is a 33-year-old white male. He is employed as an office administrator. He has had one prior conviction for fleeing the police, a misdemeanor. He was placed on probation after forging checks drawn on his company in the amount of $400. Richardson stated that he was drinking heavily at the time and was unable to meet some gambling debts. Since he had agreed with his wife that he would not gamble, he forged the name of his company's comptroller on four $100 checks. He is on probation for three years and must make restitution to his employer. In addition, as a condition of probation, he must abstain from alcohol and attend AA meetings. When investigators contacted him at home Saturday evening, his blood alcohol reading was 0.13 (legally intoxicated). This is the second time in six months that he has failed the Breathalyzer.

Case #2. Sally Vincent is a 25-year-old white female. She is employed as an attendant in a coin-operated laundry. She has been arrested once in the past for soliciting prostitution. She was placed on probation for stealing $375 in cash from a man with whom she is alleged to have had sex. Vincent admitted to using the money to obtain drugs. She is on two years probation and must refrain from use of alcohol or drugs. Two probation officers visited her at her residence ten days ago and obtained a urine sample. It tested positive for marijuana. She failed one previous drug test eight months ago.

Questions for Discussion

1. Would you refer either of the probationers to the court for a formal violation hearing? Explain.

2. Would you give either of the probationers a warning only? Explain.

3. Compare your responses in cases 1 and 2 above. Were they the same or different? If they were the same, why? If they were different, why? Explain.

Chapter 9

Race, Gender, and Discrimination

MORE THAN ANY OTHER SOCIAL ISSUES of violence in recent years, those of sex and race stand out. The Skinhead beating death of Mulugeta Seraw, a dark-skinned visitor to Portland, Oregon; the beating death of homosexual Navy man Allen Schindler by another enlisted man; the 1983 pooltable gang rape in New Bedford, Massachusetts; and the fatal racial assault on Michael Griffith in Howard Beach, New York—all are part of the social landscape of the past 15 years.

It would be a mistake to suppose, though, that race and gender problems are limited to isolated acts of violence committed by a tiny fraction of the population. In his influential study of race in the United States, Andrew Hacker begins with the observation that race has been "an American obsession" since the beginning of European colonization. The separation of black Americans and white Americans "... is pervasive and penetrating. As a social and human division, it surpasses all others—even gender—in intensity and subordination."[1]

Historian Nell Irvin Painter described the tremendous influence of such black stereotypes as "oversexed-black-Jezebel" and "black-beast-rapist" in the Senate confirmation hearings on Clarence Thomas' nomination to the U.S. Supreme Court.[2] The clash of testimony between Thomas and his former co-worker, law professor Anita Hill, combined in one media mess some of the most complex issues of race and gender.

Several questions come to mind immediately. What is race? Exactly what is racial discrimination or harassment? What is sexual harassment? Can sexual or racial harassment truly occur unintentionally? How should a victim respond to what he or she perceives to be harassment? (Recall that Clarence Thomas characterized the public examination of sexual harassment charges against him as an "electronic lynching.") What of the alleged denial of Islamic dietary needs of Muslim inmates at the Ohio State Penitentiary at Lucasville prior to the 1993 riots?

In another area of continuing controversy, race and sex still confer tremendous economic advantages on white males regardless of educational level; yet programs designed to reduce this inequity are widely regarded (by white males) as "reverse discrimination." Exactly what is reverse discrimination, and does it constitute the same injustice as the discrimination that it seeks to eliminate?

Ethical problems like these are intertwined with factual issues. For example, are police officers in City X really more likely to stop black drivers in the "white" part of town, thus reinforcing the local patterns of *de facto* segregation? Is there a department policy prohibiting such enforcement patterns? Is the policy monitored? What is the level of compliance?

It is not only criminal justice practitioners who face such phenomena as openly racist organizations with a potential for violence (both civilian and inside prisons) and unorganized, violent "hate" crimes. As citizens in a society in which deeply-rooted racial and sexual prejudices remain, you must face also such prejudices as they may exist in you, in your fellow workers, and in agency policies. The readings and cases in this chapter are designed to stimulate your thinking about racial and sexual discrimination, and other forms of discrimination as well.

The Readings

Racial and Gender Discrimination

The first two readings offer a perspective of secondary social status and discrimination from the "receiving end." In "Being Black in America," Andrew Hacker first explores the question of the value of being white and the comparable disvalue of being black through a parable called "The Visit." Hacker asks the reader to imagine being visited by an official who explains that you were to have been born black rather than white. Once discovered, this mistake must be rectified, so at midnight you will become black, retaining all of your personality and knowledge, but physically unrecognizable to those who know you. The official tells you that you will live another 50 years—as a black American. He is willing to compensate you handsomely for the consequences of the mistake and asks you to name the sum. How much money would you ask for as just compensation for the error? Hacker then draws a vivid portrait of what you might learn if you were to spend part of your life in a black body in America. Consider the matter of finding a place to live under conditions that Hacker describes as "residential apartheid." He says,

> ...black Americans have no illusions about the hurdles they will face. If you look outside your designated areas, you can expect chilly receptions, evasive responses, and outright lies: a humiliating experience, rendered all the more enraging because it is so repeated and prolonged.

Only a small minority of black householders prefer living in a black neighborhood; some 85 percent prefer an equal mixture. Yet, Hacker observes, research clearly shows that white householders begin moving out when a neighborhood becomes more than 8 percent black. Once "white flight" begins, the area is on its way to becoming all black. This phenomenon occurs even when the incoming black householders are of the same economic and social standing as the white householders. "No matter what your talents or attainments," Hacker says, "you are seen as infecting a neighborhood simply because of your race. This is the ultimate insult of segregation."

In "Barriers to Equality: The Power of Subtle Discrimination to Maintain Unequal Opportunity," Mary P. Rowe explores what she calls "discriminatory microinequities" that contribute to occupational segregation and prevent women and minorities from ever moving into the top leadership positions traditionally held by white males. Microinequities are "tiny, damaging characteristics of an environment" that are too small to take to court, even though their impact on the victim is far from trivial. According to Rowe, microinequities are unjust actions that, in the workplace, are "the framework for discrimination against everyone who is obviously 'different' from the person making decisions..." Microinequities would include such actions as the racist or sexist joke, a remark about the foolishness of Martin Luther King Day, the girlie calendar, the lack of an introduction to an important visitor, remarks about physical appearance, etc. Rowe argues that microinequities are damaging because they are a kind of unpredictable punishment. They are fundamentally irrational because "... they occur in the context of merit, and of striving for excellence, but do not have anything to *do* with excellence or merit."

Although all persons, regardless of race or sex, are subject to microinequities, Rowe shows that women and minorities are statistically more vulnerable to such actions because of the power relationships in American society. Since those with less power in an organization are more likely to be women or minority members, those persons are disproportionately more likely to have trouble coping with inequities (Rowe's example: "What do you mean, did I speak up when he insulted me? Are you kidding? He's my boss!").

Affirmation Action and Reverse Discrimination

Perhaps no social justice issue in the workplace has been as divisive as antidiscrimination legislation and case law. Although racial and sexual discrimination probably remain the most bitterly disputed, other physical characteristics, such as age, physical handicap, height, weight, and physical attractiveness, have also been the basis of unfair discrimination.

First, we should be clear that there is fair or just discrimination, as well as unfair discrimination. A person who is wheelchair-bound cannot serve on a firefighting crew, and we justly discriminate against such persons when hiring firefighters. But a wheelchair-bound person can be an extremely capable member of a SCUBA team. (In fact, the diving instructor of one of the authors is wheelchair-bound and is a certified expert in a wide range of diving specialties.) Imagine a wheelchair-bound person who applies for an opening on the police dive team. To dismiss such a person's application out of hand would be, all other things being equal, to unfairly discriminate against that officer.

The ability to perform the job for which one applies is a necessary condition for being considered for that job, and those who fail to meet that necessary condition are obviously not unjustly discriminated against when they are rejected. No one denies this much. The real disputes arise regarding a different criterion—"best qualified." In fact, it is safe to say that the concept of **merit** embedded in these two words is at the center of the most bitter disputes surrounding antidiscrimination policy and affirmative action programs.

Two major problems surround the meritocratic criterion "best qualified" as applied to hiring and promotion. The first problem is that despite the frequent lip service paid to this criterion, as a society we do not appear to value merit as much as we say we do. How many family farms hire the "best qualified" helpers rather than brother Joe, sister Sue, or neighbor Ned? Does the local shoe store conduct a nationwide search to find the "best qualified" salesperson? Was twice-elected Ronald Reagan *really* the best qualified person in the United States to be President from 1981 to 1989? Was Roger Smith, CEO of General Motors during its decline in the 1980s, really the "best qualified"? And did he really merit his multimillion-dollar draw on the firm's coffers? Was Daryl Gates the "best qualified" person available to be Los Angeles' Chief of Police?

In fact, as a society we rarely, if ever, choose the best qualified person for a specific job. Instead, we choose people because we're related to them, because we know them or their family, because they're the only one to respond to the job advertisement, because we believe they need the job more than someone else, because they've got six months more on their union card than another candidate, because they espouse the same values that we do, because they're socially attractive (not too fat, not too short) or have a good camera presence, because they're the same sex or race as we are, and so on. We are content with our choices as long as there is reasonable evidence that the person can do the job at some minimally satisfactory level.

Consider the common criterion of seniority, which has been used extensively throughout the business world and the public service sector.[3] For example, two job candidates may be equally qualified to be a dispatcher. Yet, if one of the applicants has been on the force for 12 years and the other has been on the force for 11 years, the applicant with the seniority will get the job, at least under many union contracts. Even in jobs where seniority is not contractually recognized, it may function as a *de facto* criterion in promotion decisions. Such a decision clearly involves nonmerit criteria, since we assumed that both were equally qualified to perform the job. In fact, under many seniority systems, seniority can "trump" other qualifications, so that a less qualified, but more senior, employee will be selected. Does this mean that seniority systems are inherently unfair just because they involve nonmerit considerations? What about the good consequences that result from a seniority system, such as lower employee turnover, professional pride in long service, devotion to the employing firm or agency, etc.? This does not mean that such criteria are inappropriate, but it does suggest that there is a fair amount of hypocrisy in the sudden devotion to the "best qualified" criterion that has emerged in recent years. Guiding such discussions on the basis of self-interest is not likely to produce morally significant conclusions.

The second problem with the criterion of "best qualified" is more serious. What do we mean when we say that Jones is the best qualified person for the job? Do we mean that Jones will predictably outperform all other competing candidates *on the job*, or do we mean that Jones simply ranks above the other candidates in the hiring or promotion process? If all the candidates will perform the job in roughly equal ways, what advantage should Jones be given over other candidates? In such a case, *all* of the candidates are qualified, so perhaps random selection would be the only fair way to choose.[4] If we hire Smith over Jones in this case, does it really make sense to say that we hired someone who was less qualified than another candidate? Is there any sense in which I *deserve* a job more than you simply because I scored higher on the promotion exam, even though either of us would perform satisfactorily on the job?

Where do affirmative action programs fit into this discussion? These programs are society's attempt to change the racial and sexual bias that exists. They are designed to reduce and eventually eliminate unfair discrimination in the workplace. For example, suppose that in a county prison, female prison guards are paid less than their male counterparts because the county commissioners believe that "most of the women are not the primary family breadwinners." Since their spouses already have jobs, the women "don't need" the money as much as the male guards, most of whose spouses do not work. This has been, and still is, a very common form of sexual discrimination in the public and private sectors. Equal pay for equal work still does not exist in the United States. Women and racial minorities with college degrees can be expected to earn only a fraction of what white males with the same educational background will earn.

Ironically, discriminating against a woman because she is the second income in the family signals another defection from the "hire-only-on-merit" camp. In such a case, the ground for preferring the male applicant is not qualifications at all, but *need*. This shows at a stroke that an affirmative action program designed to provide equality of opportunity to female applicants may be perfectly consistent with merit-based hiring. Thus, the view held by some people in our society—that affirmative action programs are fundamentally inconsistent with merit-based hiring and promotion—is clearly false.

Jobs that have been traditionally white and/or male are another target of affirmative action programs. Here again the goal of the programs is to eliminate discrimination. To determine whether hiring and promotion practices are discriminatory, we need only to look at the facts. Discrimination is not simply a matter of deliberate bigotry practiced by hate-spewing white males. In fact, few cases of discrimination could be so described. Instead, discrimination is usually a pattern or history of unthinking choices or choices made on irrelevant grounds. This is one of the reasons why antidiscrimination legislation typically refuses to rely on intention.

For example, if the chief (a male, naturally!) always seems to hire young white female dispatchers, is this discriminatory against males, black women, and older women? There is certainly the suspicion of discrimination regardless of the chief's protests. In fact, he may be a very nice person in every sense. But if qualified males, black women, and older women are available in the labor pool but just never seem to get the job, year after year, opportunity after opportunity, that's discrimination. And, that's what affirmative action programs are designed to remedy.

If our society were blind to race, sex, age, and other characteristics irrelevant (except in very limited cases) to job performance, we could expect to see a relatively random distribution of these characteristics throughout the job market. Individual job preferences will no doubt prevent completely random distribution as long as children are taught that nationality, race, sex, religion, etc. are important social categories. Cultural differences among those categories will very likely be reflected in job preferences (or, perhaps job preferences define in part cultural categories). For example, we do not teach our children that having an even number of letters in one's last name is an important characteristic and so we could expect to find this characteristic randomly distributed across all occupations and positions. Still, most proponents of affirmative action agree that proportional representation is not a goal of affirmative action programs. Representation is simply a criterion for identifying those firms and agencies whose job practices are unfairly discriminatory.

A major complaint made against affirmative action programs is that they are in themselves discriminatory. The act of reducing the effects of discrimination against one group of people in some cases is held to require unfair discrimination against the historically favored group. This is termed "reverse discrimination."

For example, if a corrections agency has never appointed a woman as warden, despite the regular application of qualified female candidates, an affirmative action program might set a target that 10 percent of all wardens will be women within a period of six years.[5] The women will have to be qualified for the position, but it may mean that a male candidate who is perceived as being "better qualified" will not receive the appointment in competition with a well-qualified woman. Consequently, the charge goes, the male candidate is the victim of "reverse discrimination." He has been passed over *because,* and only because, he is a man. With his qualifications, in a sex-blind society, he presumably would have received the appointment. To discriminate against someone on the basis of sex is morally wrong, the argument continues, so therefore, reverse discrimination being just as wrong as the discrimination under attack, affirmative action (of this sort) is morally wrong.

Lisa Newton, in the selection, "Reverse Discrimination as Unjustified," puts the point as follows:

> ... when the employers and the schools *favor* women and blacks, the *same* [emphasis added] injustice is done. Just as the previous discrimination did, this reverse discrimination violates the public equality which defines citizenship ...

Newton argues therefore that the injustice of reverse discrimination in affirmative action programs is just as bad as the racial or sexual discrimination that the programs are designed to eliminate: "It destroys justice, law, equality, and citizenship itself."

Richard Wasserstrom rejects this perspective in his paper, "A Defense of Programs of Preferential Treatment." He attacks two major arguments that purport to show that affirmative action programs are unfair or unjust. He argues first that it is mistaken to think that the reverse discrimination effects of an affirmative action program are just as bad as racist and sexist treatment. What made slavery and segregation wrong, Wasserstrom says, was *not* the fact that people were treated on the basis of an irrelevant characteristic (race), but rather that the *practices themselves* were morally wrong. Affirmative action programs do not rely on the idea that white males are not fully human, that they lack important moral characteristics, or that they are fundamentally weaker or inferior to blacks and females. Nor do affirmative action programs supply an additional advantage to groups of persons who already have the upper hand. Wasserstrom concludes that "whatever may be wrong with today's affirmative action programs ..., it should be clear that the evil, if any, is just not the same."

Wasserstrom then considers the second major argument against affirmative action, namely, the claim that qualifications are the only relevant consideration in distributing social goods. Wasserstrom argues that basing claims of desert on rules is suspect "unless and until the rule which creates the claim is itself shown to be a justified one." What this means is that it doesn't follow that Jones *deserves* the promotion more than Smith just because we have a rule that says, "Always promote the person who has the highest score on the examination." What must be done first is to show that the rule itself is justified, for example, on the basis of the superior consequences of following it rather than some other rule. Wasserstrom uses the example of law school admissions based solely on academic criteria. Would admitting only the most qualified students be socially effective? We know very little about the relation between being a good law student and being a good lawyer, Wasserstrom says, so how can we be confident that qualifications alone would lead to a better legal system?

The final selection is Edwin C. Hettinger's paper, "What Is Wrong with Reverse Discrimination?" Hettinger argues that most accounts of what is morally wrong with reverse discrimination don't succeed. At the very best, reverse discrimination "is unjust in a relatively weak sense." Since racism and sexism are far greater injustices in our society, it follows that programs that reduce racism and sexism at the cost of some mild injustices are morally acceptable. Hettinger bases this argument on the premise that "... social policies which involve minor injustice are permissible ... when they are required in order to overcome much greater injustice ... "

Hettinger argues against Lisa Newton's attack on affirmative action in much the same way as Wasserstrom. He points out that the motives of racial and sexual discrimination are morally wrong, while those of affirmative action programs are not. Not only the motives, but also the consequences, of discrimination differ from the consequences of affirmative action. Therefore, Hettinger concludes, if discrimination and affirmation action programs are different in motive and different in consequence, how could they be morally equivalent?

Notes

1. Andrew Hacker, *Two Nations: Black and White, Separate, Hostile, Unequal* (New York: Charles Scribner's Sons, Ballantine Books, 1992), p. 3.
2. Nell Irvin Painter, "Hill, Thomas, and the Use of Racial Stereotype," in Toni Morrison (ed., with Introduction), *Race-ing Justice, En-gender-ing Power: Essays on Anita Hill, Clarence Thomas, and the Construction of Social Reality* (New York: Pantheon Books, 1992), pp. 204 ff.
3. Seniority is the basis for the so-called "Peter Principle," which states that an employee will rise through the hierarchy of ranks or positions, eventually attaining a position in which the employee is incompetent. While experience obviously cannot be discounted, merit or competence is not linearly related to years on the job.
4. In allocating scarce medical resources, all competing candidates who qualify for a benefit—a kidney, for instance—will be selected by a process that is inherently random. First come–first served, for example, randomly selects a recipient for the one available organ, since the time of the medical need for the organ is randomly distributed. If your need happens to develop a week before mine, you get the organ. The economic need for a job may not be significantly different in ethical terms from the need for medical care when both are scarce goods.
5. Contrary to popular belief, this is not a quota system. It is a system of numerical goals in which both sexes compete for the same position, but in which one's sex is deemed a legitimate consideration in the hiring or promotion process. Quota systems, which are illegal, bar candidates from competing for a job unless they are of the desired race or sex. In *University of California v. Bakke* (1978), the Supreme Court agreed that the Medical School's setting aside of seats in the freshman class for minority applicants was unfairly discriminatory—it was a quota system. But the Court went on to say that the *consideration* of race in the admissions process was not unfairly discriminatory, as long as all seats were available to all applicants on a competitive basis.

Being Black in America

ANDREW HACKER

MOST WHITE AMERICANS WILL say that, all things considered, things aren't so bad for black people in the United States. Of course, they will grant that many problems remain. Still, whites feel there has been steady improvement, bringing blacks closer to parity, especially when compared with conditions in the past. Some have even been heard to muse that it's better to be black, since affirmative action policies make it a disadvantage to be white.

What white people seldom stop to ask is how they may benefit from belonging to their race. Nor is this surprising. People who can see do not regard their vision as a gift for which they should offer thanks. It may also be replied that having a white skin does not immunize a person from misfortune or failure. Yet even for those who fall to the bottom, being white has a worth. What could that value be?

Let us try to find out by means of a parable: suspend disbelief for a moment, and assume that what follows might actually happen.

THE VISIT

You will be visited tonight by an official you have never met. He begins by telling you that he is extremely embarrassed. The organization he represents has made a mistake, something that hardly ever happens.

According to their records, he goes on, you were to have been born black: to another set of parents, far from where you were raised.

However, the rules being what they are, this error must be rectified, and as soon as possible. So at midnight tonight, you will become black. And this will mean not simply a darker skin, but the bodily and facial features associated with African ancestry. However, inside you will be the person you always were. Your knowledge and ideas will remain intact. But outwardly you will not be recognizable to anyone you now know.

Your visitor emphasizes that being born to the wrong parents was in no way your fault. Consequently, his organization is prepared to offer you some reasonable recompense. Would you, he asks, care to name a sum of money you might consider appropriate? He adds that his group is by no means poor. It can be quite generous when the circumstances warrant, as they seem to in your case. He finishes by saying that their records show you are scheduled to live another fifty years—as a black man or woman in America.

How much financial recompense would you request?

When this parable has been put to white students, most seemed to feel that it would not be out of place to ask for $50 million, or $1 million for each coming black year. And this calculation conveys, as well as anything, the value that white people place on their own skins. Indeed, to be white is to possess a gift whose value can be appreciated only after it has been taken away. And why ask so large a sum? Surely this needs no detailing. The money would be used, as best it could, to buy protection from the discriminations and dangers white people know they would face once they were perceived to be black.

Of course, no one who is white can understand what it is like to be black in America. Still, were they to spend time in a black body, here are some of the things they would learn.

In the eyes of white Americans, being black encapsulates your identity. No other racial or national origin is seen as having so pervasive a personality or character. Even if you write a book on Euclidean algorithms or Renaissance sculpture, you will still be described as a "black author." Although you are a native American, with a longer lineage than most, you will never be accorded full membership in the nation or society. More than that, you early learn that this nation feels no need or desire for your physical presence. (Indeed, your people are no longer in demand as cheap labor.) You sense that most white citizens would heave a sigh of relief were you simply to disappear. While few openly propose that you return to Africa, they would be greatly pleased were you to make that decision for yourself.

Your people originated in Africa, and you want to feel pride in your homeland. After all, it was where humanity began. Hence your desire to know more of its peoples and their history, their culture and achievements, and how they endure within yourself. W. E. B. Du Bois said it best: "two thoughts, two unrecognizable stirrings, two warring ideals in one black body."[1]

Yet there is also your awareness that not only America, but also much of the rest of the world, regards Africa as the primal continent: the most backward, the least developed, by almost every modern measure. Equally unsettling, Africa is regarded as barely worth the world's attention, a region no longer expected to improve in condition or status. During its periodic misfortunes—usually famine or slaughter—Africa may evoke compassion and pity. Yet the message persists that it must receive outside help, since there is little likelihood that it will set things right by itself.

Then there are the personal choices you must make about your identity. Unless you want to stress a Caribbean connection, you are an American and it is the only citizenship you have. At the same time, you realize that this is a white country, which expects its inhabitants to think and act in white ways. How far do you wish to adapt, adjust, assimilate, to a civilization so at variance with your people's past? For example, there is the not-so-simple matter of deciding on your diction. You know how white people talk and what they like to hear. Should you conform to those expectations, even if it demands denying or concealing much of your self? After all, white America gives out most of the rewards and prizes associated with success. Your decisions are rendered all the more painful by the hypocrisy of it all, since you are aware that even if you make every effort to conform, whites will still not accept you as one of their own.

So to a far greater degree than for immigrants from other lands, it rests on you to create your own identity. But it is still not easy to follow the counsel of Zora Neale Hurston: "Be as black as you want to be." For one thing, that choice is not always left to you. By citizenship and birth, you may count as an American, yet you find yourself agreeing with August Wilson when he says "We're a different people." Why else can you refer to your people as "folks" and "family," to one another as "sisters" and "brothers," in ways whites never can?[2]

There are moments when you understand Toni Morrison's riposte, "At no moment in my life have I ever felt as though I were an American."[3] This in turn gives rise to feelings of sympathy with figures like Cassius Clay, H. Rap Brown, Lew Alcindor, and Stokely Carmichael, who decided to repatriate themselves as Muhammad Ali, Jamil Abdullah al-Amin, Kareem Abdul-Jabbar, and Kwame Touré.

Those choices are not just for yourself. There will be the perplexing—and equally painful—task of having to explain to your children why they will not be treated as other Americans: that they will never be altogether accepted, that they will always be regarded warily, if not with suspicion or hostility. When they ask whether this happens because of anything they have done, you must find ways of conveying that, no, it is not because of any fault of their own. Further, for reasons you can barely explain yourself, you must tell them that much of the world has decided that you are not and cannot be their equals; that this world wishes to keep you apart, a caste it will neither absorb nor assimilate.

You will tell your children this world is wrong. But, because that world is there, they will have to struggle to survive, with scales weighted against them. They will have to work harder and do better, yet the result may be less recognition and reward. We all know life can be unfair. For black people, this knowledge is not an academic theory but a fact of daily life.

You find yourself granting that there are more black faces in places where they were never seen before. Within living memory, your people were barred from major league teams; now they command the highest salaries in most professional sports. In the movies, your people had to settle for roles as servants or buffoons. Now at least some of them are cast as physicians, business executives, and police officials. But are things truly different? When everything is added up, white America still prefers its black people to be performers who divert them as athletes and musicians and comedians.

Yet where you yourself are concerned, you sense that in mainstream occupations, your prospects are quite limited. In most areas of employment, even after playing by the rules, you find yourself hitting a not-so-invisible ceiling. You wonder if you are simply corporate wallpaper, a protective coloration they find it prudent to display. You begin to suspect that a "qualification" you will always lack is white pigmentation.

In theory, all Americans with financial means and a respectable demeanor can choose where they want to live. For over a generation, courts across the country have decreed that a person's race cannot be a reason for refusing to rent or sell a residence. However, the law seems to have had little impact on practice, since almost all residential areas are entirely black or white. Most whites prefer it that way. Some will say they would like a black family nearby, if only to be able to report that their area is integrated. But not many do. Most white Americans do not move in circles where racial integration wins social or moral credit.

This does not mean it is absolutely impossible for a black family to find a home in a white area. Some have, and others undoubtedly will. Even so, black Americans have no illusions about the hurdles they will face. If you look outside your designated areas, you can expect chilly receptions, evasive responses, and outright lies: a humiliating experience, rendered all the more enraging because it is so repeated and prolonged. After a while, it becomes too draining to continue the search. Still, if you have the income, you will find an area to your liking; but it will probably be all black. In various suburbs and at the outer edges of cities, one can see well-kept homes, outwardly like other such settings. But a closer view shows all the householders to be black.

This is the place to consider residential apartheid—and that is what it is—in its full perspective. Black segregation differs markedly from that imposed on any other group. Even newly arrived immigrants are more readily accepted in white neighborhoods.

Nor should it be assumed that most black householders prefer the racial ratios in areas where they currently reside. Successive surveys have shown that, on average, only about one in eight say they prefer a neighborhood that is all or mostly black, which is the condition most presently confront. The vast majority—some 85 percent—state they would like an equal mixture of black and white neighbors.[4] Unfortunately, this degree of racial balance has virtually no chance of being realized. The reason, very simply, is that hardly any whites will live in a neighborhood or community where half the residents are black. So directly or indirectly, white Americans have the power to decide the racial composition of communities and neighborhoods. Most egregious have been instances where acts of arson or vandalism force black families to leave. But such methods are exceptional. There are other, less blatant, ways to prevent residential integration from passing a certain "tipping" point.

Here we have no shortage of studies. By and large, this research agrees that white residents will stay—and some new ones may move in—if black arrivals do not exceed 8 percent. But once the black proportion passes that point, whites begin to leave the neighborhood and no new ones will move in. The vacated houses or apartments will be bought or rented by blacks, and the area will be on its way to becoming all black.

What makes integration difficult if not impossible is that so few whites will accept even a racial composition reflecting the overall national proportion of 12 or 13 percent. In this regard, one or two attempts have been made to impose ceilings on the number of black residents in housing projects and developments, so as not to frighten away whites. Starrett City in New York has used this strategy, as has Atrium Village in Chicago.[5] According to some legal readings these procedures are unconstitutional, since they treat racial groups differently. Those administering such "benign quotas" have found they must maintain two sets of waiting lists. This has been necessary to ensure that the next families chosen for vacant apartments will preserve the prevailing racial ratio. Given the preference of most blacks for integrated housing, quite a few tend to apply, and they invariably outnumber the whites on the list. The result is that black applicants have to wait longer, and are less likely to get their first choice of accommodation.

Whites and blacks who want to achieve and maintain interracial housing—itself a rarity—find they are forced to defend "benign quotas" that are biased against some blacks, since there are fewer "black" places. Racial quotas also tend to put blacks on the spot. On the one hand, few are willing to publicly support a ceiling for people of their race. Even so, most of the black householders already in residence would prefer that the racial ratio remain stabilized. After all, they themselves underwent a wait because they wanted to live in a racially integrated setting. Yet preserving the equation pits them against other blacks impatient to get in.

If many whites say they support racial inte-

gration in principle, even if this only means a token black neighbor, at least as many do not want any blacks living near them at all. One question, certainly, is how far this resistance is based solely on race, or whether the reasons have more to do with culture or class. White people themselves vary in income and other symbols of status, and every section of the nation has hierarchies among white neighborhoods. Even in an area where everyone earns essentially the same income, many residents would not want a homosexual couple on their block, or a neighbor who parked a business van ("PARAGON PEST CONTROL") in his driveway every night. Simply being a fellow white is not enough to make a person a desired neighbor.

This granted, we can try to isolate the element of race by positing some "ideal" black neighbors: persons with professional credentials or those who hold administrative positions in respected organizations. Give them sophisticated tastes; make them congenial in demeanor; and have them willing to care about their property and the area as a whole. And allow, further, that a fair number of whites might not object to having one or two such households nearby. Why, then, would such open-minded neighbors start worrying if the number of black families—granting that all of them are impeccably middle class—seems to be approaching a racial "tipping" point?

The first reason is that there is no assurance that the black proportion will stay below the "tipping" figure. Word gets around among black families when a "white" neighborhood appears willing to accept a measure of integration. Rental and real estate agents are also quick to note this fact and begin recommending the area to black customers. As a result, whenever homes and apartments become vacant, a visible number of those coming to look at them appear to be black. Nor should this be surprising. Some black Americans want more interracial exposure for themselves and their children. Others may not share this wish, but they know that better schools and safer streets are more apt to be where whites are.

As has been noted, the white exodus gets underway even before the black proportion reaches ten percent.[6] And the turnover can be all but total within a single year. Moreover, this happens even when the blacks who move in have the same economic and social standing as the white residents. What is it, then, that makes white Americans unwilling to risk having black neighbors? Some of the reasons are familiar and openly stated. Others involve fears less easily articulated or admitted.

To the minds of most Americans, the mere presence of black people is associated with a high incidence of crime, residential deterioration, and lower educational attainment. Of course, most whites are willing to acknowledge that these strictures do not apply to all blacks. At the same time, they do not want to have to worry about trying to distinguish blacks who would make good neighbors from those who would not. To which is added the suspicion that if more black families arrive, it would take only one or two undesirables to undermine any interracial amity.

Even if all one's black neighbors were vouchsafed to be middle class or better, there may still be misgivings about their teenaged children. To start, there is the well-known wariness of white parents that their children—especially their daughters—could begin to make black friends. Plus the fear that even less intimate contacts will influence the vocabulary and diction, even the academic commitments, of their own offspring. And if white parents are already uneasy over the kinds of music their children enjoy, imagine their anxieties at hearing an even greater black resonance. Along with the worry that some of the black youths on the block might display a hostile demeanor, clouding the congenial ambience most Americans seek.

Americans have extraordinarily sensitive antennae for the colorations of neighborhoods. In virtually every metropolitan area, white householders can rank each enclave by the racial makeup of the residents. Given this knowledge, where a family lives becomes an index of its social standing. While this is largely an economic matter, proximity to blacks compounds this assessment. For a white family to be seen as living in a mixed or changing neighborhood can be construed as a symptom of surrender, indeed as evidence that they are on a downward spiral.

If you are black, these white reactions brand you as a carrier of contaminations. No matter what your talents or attainments, you are seen as infecting a neighborhood simply because of your race. This is the ultimate insult of segregation. It opens wounds that never really heal and leaves scars to remind you how far you stand from full citizenship.

Except when you are in your own neighborhood, you feel always on display. On many occasions, you find you are the only person of your race present. You may be the only black student in a college classroom, the only black on a jury, the sole black at a corporate meeting, the only one at a social gathering. With luck, there may be one or two others. You feel every eye is on you, and you are not clear what posture to present. You realize that your presence makes whites uncomfortable; most of them probably wish you were not there at all. But since you are, they want to see you smile, so they can believe that you are being treated well. Not only is an upbeat air expected, but you must never show exasperation or anger, let alone anything that could look like a chip on your shoulder. Not everyone can keep such tight control. You don't find it surprising that so many black athletes and entertainers seek relief from those tensions.

Even when not in white company, you know that you are forever in their conversations. Ralph Ellison once said that to whites, you are an "invisible man."[7] You know what he meant. Yet for all that, you and your people have been studied and scrutinized and dissected, caricatured, and pitied or deplored, as no other group ever has. You see yourself reduced to data in research, statistics in reports. Each year, the nation asks how many of your teenagers have become pregnant, how many of your young men are in prison. Not only are you continually on view; you are always on trial.

What we have come to call the media looms large in the lives of almost all Americans. Television and films, newspapers and magazines, books and advertising, all serve as windows on a wider world, providing real and fantasized images of the human experience. The media also help us to fill out our own identities, telling us about ourselves, or the selves we might like to be.

If you are black, most of what is available for you to read and watch and hear depicts the activities of white people, with only rare and incidental allusions to persons like yourself. Black topics and authors and performers appear even less than your share of the population, not least because the rest of America doesn't care to know about you. Whites will be quick to point out that there have been successful "black" programs on radio and television, as well as popular black entertainers and best-selling authors. Yet in these and other instances, it is whites who decide which people and productions will be underwritten, which almost always means that "black" projects will have to appeal to whites as well. You some times sense that much that is "black" is missing in artists like Jessye Norman and Toni Morrison, Paul Robeson, and Bill Cosby, who you sense must tailor their talents to white audiences. You often find yourself wishing they could just be themselves, among their own people.

At the same time, you feel frustration and disgust when white America appropriates your music, your styles, indeed your speech and sexuality. At times, white audiences will laud the originality of black artists and performers and athletes. But in the end, they feel more comfortable when white musicians and designers and writers—and athletic coaches—adapt black talents to white sensibilities.

Add to this your bemusement when movies and television series cast more blacks as physicians and attorneys and executives than one will ever find in actual hospitals or law firms or corporations. True, these depictions can serve as role models for your children, encouraging their aspirations. At the same time, you do not want white audiences to conclude that since so many of your people seem to be doing well, little more needs to be done.

Then there are those advertisements showing groups of people. Yes, one of them may be black, although not too black, and always looking happy to be in white company. Still, these blacks are seldom in the front row, or close to the center. Even worse, you think you have detected a recent trend: in advertisements that include a person of color, you see Asians being used instead of blacks.

To be sure, textbooks and lesson plans now include allusions to "contributions" made by Americans of many ancestries. Children are taught how the Chinese built the railroads, and that Hispanics have a vibrant and varied culture. Even acknowledging these nods, the curriculums of the nation's schools and colleges focus mainly on the achievements of white people. The emphasis is on English origins, and that those settlers brought their institutions and ideas from the British Isles. Most Americans with European ancestors can identify with this "Anglo-Saxon" past. Descendants of slaves do not find it as easy. Whether black children are alienated by the content of the curriculum is a matter of controversy, which will be considered later on. At this point, it can be said that few teachers attempt to explain how the human beings consigned to slavery shaped the structure and sensibilities of the new nation. Apart from brief allusions to a Sojourner Truth or a Benjamin Banneker, your people appear as passive victims and faceless individuals.

In much the same vein, white children can be led to see how the travails of Shakespeare's heroes shed light on the human condition. Or that Jane Austen's heroines have messages for Americans of today. Nor is this impossible for black Americans. Ralph Ellison, raised in rural Alabama, recalled that reading Ezra Pound and Sigmund Freud gave him a broader sense of life. Jamaica Kincaid has cited Charlotte Brontë as her first literary influence. Yet no matter how diligently you think about these authors and their ideas, you find that much of your life is not reflected in European learning. You often feel that there is a part of yourself, your soul, that Europe cannot reach.[8]

Well, what about assimilation? Here you receive the same message given immigrants: if you wish to succeed, or simply survive, adapt to the diction and demeanor of the Anglo-American model. But even if you opt for that path, you will never receive the acceptance accorded to other groups, including newcomers arriving from as far away as Asia and the Middle East. In the view of those who set the rules, if you are of African origin, you will never fully fit the image of a true American. Notice how even blacks who espouse conservative opinions are regarded more as curiosities than serious citizens.

Whether you would like to know more white people is not an easy question to answer. So many of the contacts you have with them are stiff and uneasy, hardly worth the effort. If you are a woman, you may have developed some cordial acquaintances among white women at your place of work, since women tend to be more relaxed when among themselves. Still, very few black men and women can say that they have white "friends," if by that is meant people they confide in or entertain in their homes.

Of course, friendships often grow out of shared experiences. People with similar backgrounds can take certain things for granted when with one another. In this respect, you and white people may not have very much in common. At the same time, by no means all your outlooks and interests relate to your race. There probably are at least a few white people you would like to know better. It just might be that some of them would like to know you. But as matters now stand, the chances that these barriers will be broken do not appear to be very great.

Societies create vocabularies, devising new terms when they are needed, and retaining old ones when they serve a purpose. Dictionaries list words as obsolete or archaic, denoting that they are no longer used or heard. But one epithet survives, because people want it to. Your vulnerability to humiliation can be summed up in a single word. That word, of course, is "nigger."

When a white person voices it, it becomes a knife with a whetted edge. No black person can hear it with equanimity or ignore it as "simply a word." This word has the force to pierce, to wound, to penetrate, as no other has. There have, of course, been terms like "kike" and "spic" and "chink." But these are less frequently heard today, and they lack the same emotional impact. Some nonethnic terms come closer, such as "slut" and "fag" and "cripple." Yet, "nigger" stands alone with its power to tear at one's insides. It is revealing that whites have never created so wrenching an epithet for even the most benighted members of their own race.

Black people may use "nigger" among themselves, but with a tone and intention that is known and understood. Even so, if you are black, you know white society devised this word and keeps it available for use. (Not officially, of course, or even in print; but you know it continues to be uttered behind closed doors.) Its persistence reminds you that you are still perceived as a degraded species of humanity, a level to which whites can never descend.

You and your people have problems, far more than your share. And it is not as if you are ignorant of them, or wish to sweep them under a rug. But how to frame your opinions is not an easy matter. For example, what should you say about black crime or addiction or out-of-wedlock pregnancies? Of course, you have much to say on these and other topics, and you certainly express your ideas when you are among your own people. And you can be critical—very critical—of a lot of behavior you agree has become common among blacks.

However, the white world also asks that black people conduct these discussions in public. In particular, they want to hear you condemn black figures they regard as outrageous or irresponsible. This cannot help but annoy you. For one thing, you have never asked for white advice. Yet whites seem to feel that you stand in need of their tutelage, as if you lack the insight to understand your own interests. Moreover, it makes sense for members of a minority to stand together, especially since so many whites delight in magnifying differences among blacks. Your people have had a long history of being divided and conquered. At the same time, you have no desire to be held responsible for what every person of your color thinks or does. You cannot count how many times you have been asked to atone for some utterances of Louis Farrakhan, or simply to assert that he does not speak for you. You want to retort that you will choose your own causes and laments. Like other Americans, you have no obligation to follow agendas set by others.

As it happens, black Americans can and do disagree on racial matters, not to mention a host of other issues. Thus a survey conducted in 1990 found that 78 percent of those polled said they preferred to think of themselves as "black," and another 20 percent chose "African-American," while the remaining 2 percent stayed with "Negro."[9] Another study by a team of black social scientists found that less than a quarter of the blacks they polled felt that black parents should give their children African names.[10] Indeed, on a wide range of matters, there is no fixed, let alone official, black position. Yet it is amazing how often white people ask you to tell them how "black people" think about some individual or issue.

Then there are the accusations of inconsistency. As when you seem to favor taking race into consideration in some areas, but not in others. Or that you support a double standard, which allows separate criteria to be used for blacks in employment or education. Well, as it happens, you do believe:

• That discrimination against blacks remains real and calls for radical remedies; yet you cannot take seriously the argument that these compensatory actions will cause whites to suffer from "reverse" discrimination.

• That blacks have every right to attend predominantly white schools; yet once they are there, they should not be taken to task for spending much of their time with classmates of their own race.

• That it is important to preserve historically black colleges; yet you would feel entitled to object if some other schools were to designate themselves as "historically white."

• That racism is often the key reason why white voters rally behind white candidates; yet when blacks support a candidate of their own race, you do not see this as expressing racism.

• That while you reject censorship, you would prefer that a book like *Huckleberry Finn* not be assigned in high school classes, since its ubiquitous use of "nigger" sustains a view of blacks that can only hurt your people. Nor are you persuaded that the typical teacher can make clear Mark Twain's intentions, or put them in perspective, for white teenagers.

It will often seem to you as if black people's opinions are constantly under scrutiny by the white world. Every time you express an opinion, whites seem to slap it on their dissecting table, showing that blacks want the best of both ways. In fact, you have answers on these issues, but whites take so much delight in citing alleged "inconsistencies" that they hardly hear what you have to say.

You may, by a combination of brains and luck and perseverance, make it into the middle class. And like all middle-class Americans, you will want to enjoy the comforts and pleasures that come with that status. One downside is that you will find many white people asking why you aren't doing more to help members of your race whom you have supposedly left behind. There is even the suggestion that, by moving to a safer or more spacious area, you have callously deserted your own people.

Yet hardly ever do middle-class whites reflect on the fact that they, too, have moved to better neighborhoods, usually far from poorer and less equable persons of their own race or ethnic origins. There is little evidence that middle-class whites are prepared to give much of themselves in aid of fellow whites who have fallen on misfortune. Indeed, the majority of white Americans have chosen to live in sequestered suburbs, where they are insulated from the nation's losers and failures.

Compounding these expectations, you find yourself continually subjected to comparisons with other minorities or even members of your own race. For example, you are informed that blacks who have emigrated from the Caribbean earn higher incomes than those born in the United States.[11] Here the message seems to be that color by itself is not an insurmountable barrier. Most stinging of all are contrasts with recent immigrants. You hear people just off the boat (or, nowadays, a plane) extolled for building businesses and becoming productive citizens. Which is another way of asking why you haven't matched their achievements, considering how long your people have been here.

Moreover, immigrants are praised for being willing to start at the bottom. The fact that so many of them manage to find jobs is taken as evidence that the economy still has ample opportunities for employment. You want to reply that you are not an immigrant, but as much a citizen as any white person born here. Perhaps you can't match the mathematical skills of a teenager from Korea, but then neither can most white kids at suburban high schools. You feel much like a child being chided because she has not done as well as a precocious sister. However, you are an adult, and do not find such scolding helpful or welcome.

No law of humanity or nature posits a precise format for the family. Throughout history and even in our day, households have had many shapes and structures. The same strictures apply to marriage and parental relationships. All this requires some emphasis, given concerns expressed about "the black family" and its presumed disintegration. In fact, the last several decades have seen a weakening of domestic ties in all classes and races.

Black Americans are fully aware of what is happening in this sphere. They know that most black children are being born out of wedlock and that these youngsters will spend most of their growing years with a single parent. They understand that a majority of their marriages will dissolve in separation or divorce, and that many black men and women will never marry at all. Black Americans also realize that tensions between men and women sometimes bear a violence and bitterness that can take an awful toll.

If you are black, you soon learn it is safest to make peace with reality: to acknowledge that the conditions of your time can undercut dreams of enduring romance and "happily ever after." This is especially true if you are a black woman, since you may find yourself spending many of your years without a man in your life. Of course, you will survive and adapt, as your people always have. Central in this effort will be joining and sustaining a community of women—another form of a family—on whom you can rely for love and strength and support.

If you are a black woman, you can expect to live five fewer years than your white counterpart. Among men, the gap is seven years. Indeed, a man living in New York's Harlem is less likely to reach sixty-five than is a resident of Bangladesh. Black men have a three times greater chance of dying of AIDS, and outnumber whites as murder victims by a factor of seven. According to studies, you get less sleep, are more likely to be overweight, and to develop hypertension. This is not simply due to poverty. Your shorter and more painful life results, in considerable measure, from the anxieties that come with being black in America.[12]

If you are a black young man, life can be an interlude with an early demise. Black youths do what they must to survive in a hostile world, with the prospect of violence and death on its battlefields. Attitudes can turn fatalistic, even suicidal: gladiators without even the cheers of an audience.

When white people hear the cry, "the police are coming!" for them it almost always means, "help is on the way." Black citizens cannot make the same assumption. If you have been the victim of a crime, you cannot presume that the police will actually show up; or, if they do, that they will take much note of your losses or suffering. You sense police officials feel that blacks should accept being robbed or raped as one of life's everyday risks. It seems to you obvious that more detectives are assigned to a case when a white person is murdered.

If you are black and young and a man, the arrival of the police does not usually signify help, but something very different. If you are a teenager simply socializing with some friends, the police may order you to disperse and get off the streets. They may turn on a search light, order you against a wall. Then comes the command to spread your legs and empty out your pockets, and stand splayed there while they call in your identity over their radio. You may be a college student and sing in a church choir, but that will not overcome the police presumption that you have probably done something they can arrest you for.

If you find yourself caught up in the system, it will seem like alien terrain. Usually your judge and prosecutor will be white, as will most members of the jury, as well as your attorney. In short, your fate will be decided by a white world.

This may help to explain why you have so many harsh words for the police, even though you want and need their protection more than white people do. After all, there tends to be more crime in areas where you live, not to mention drug dealing and all that comes in its wake. Black citizens are at least twice as likely as whites to become victims of violent crimes. Moreover, in almost all of these cases, the person who attacks you will be black.[13] Since this is so, whites want to know, why don't black people speak out against the members of their race who are causing so much grief? The reason is partly that you do not want to attack other blacks while whites are listening. At least equally important is that while you obviously have no taste for violence, you are also wary of measures that might come with a campaign to stamp out "black crime." ... At this point you might simply

say that you are not sure you want a more vigorous police presence, if those enforcers are unable to distinguish between law-abiding citizens and local predators. Of course, you want to be protected. But not if it means that you and your friends and relatives end up included among those the police harass or arrest.

The national anthem sings of America as "the land of the free." The Pledge of Allegiance promises "liberty and justice for all." The Declaration of Independence proclaims that all human creatures are "created equal."

If you are black, you cannot easily join in the anthem's refrain, reciting the pledge, or affirming that your country is committed to equality. While you grant that the United States is "your" country, you may define your citizenship as partial and qualified. It is not that you are "disloyal," if that means having your first allegiance elsewhere. Rather, you feel no compelling commitment to a republic that has always rebuffed you and your people.

We know from surveys that during the Cold War era, black Americans felt less antipathy toward nations then designated as our enemies, since they saw themselves less threatened by the Soviet Union or Cuba or China than did most white Americans. Nor were they so sure why they or their children were asked to risk their lives fighting people of color in places like Vietnam and Panama and the Middle East. And if the United States finds itself increasingly at odds with Islamic countries or other movements in the Third World, even more black Americans may find themselves wondering where their own allegiances lie.

As you look back on the way this nation has treated your people, you wonder how so many have managed to persevere amid so much adversity. About slavery, of course, too much cannot be said. Yet even within living memory, there were beaches and parks—in the North as well as in the South—where black Americans simply could not set foot. Segregation meant separation without even a pretense of equal facilities. In Southern communities that had only a single public library or swimming pool, black residents and taxpayers could never borrow a book or go for a swim. Indeed, black youths were even forbidden to stroll past the pool, lest they catch a glimpse of white girls in their bathing costumes.

How did they endure the endless insults and humiliations? Grown people being called by their first names, having to avert their eyes when addressed by white people, even being expected to step off a sidewalk when whites walked by. Overarching it all was the terror, with white police and prosecutors and judges possessing all but total power over black lives. Not to mention the lynchings by white mobs, with victims even chosen at random, to remind all blacks of what could happen to them if they did not remain compliant and submissive.

You wonder how much of that has changed. Suppose, for example, you find yourself having to drive across the country, stopping at gasoline stations and restaurants and motels. As you travel across the heart of white America, you can never be sure of how you will be received. While the odds are that you will reach your destination alive, you cannot be so sure that you will not be stopped by the police or spend a night in a cell. So you would be well advised to keep to the speed limit, and not exceed it by a single mile. Of course, white people are pulled over by state troopers; but how often are their cars searched? Or if a motel clerk cannot "find" your reservation, is it because she has now seen you in person? And are all the toilet facilities at this service station really out of order?

The day-to-day aggravations and humiliations add up bit by bitter bit. To take a depressingly familiar example, you stroll into a shop to look at the merchandise, and it soon becomes clear that the clerks are keeping a watchful eye on you. Too quickly, one of them comes over to inquire what it is you might want, and then remains conspicuously close as you continue your search. It also seems that they take an unusually long time verifying your credit card. And then you and a black friend enter a restaurant, and find yourselves greeted warily, with

what is obviously a more anxious reception than that given to white guests. Yes, you will be served, and your table will not necessarily be next to the kitchen. Still, you sense that they would rather you had chosen some other eating place. Or has this sort of thing happened so often that you are growing paranoid?

So there is the sheer strain of living in a white world, the rage that you must suppress almost every day. No wonder black Americans, especially black men, suffer so much from hypertension. (If ever an illness had social causes, this is certainly one.) To be black in America means reining in your opinions and emotions as no whites ever have to do. Not to mention the forced and false smiles you are expected to contrive, to assure white Americans that you harbor no grievances against them.

Along with the tension and the strain and the rage, there come those moments of despair. At times, the conclusion seems all but self-evident that white America has no desire for your presence or any need for your people. Can this nation have an unstated strategy for annihilating your people? How else, you ask yourself, can one explain the incidence of death and debilitation from drugs and disease; the incarceration of a whole generation of your men; the consignment of millions of women and children to half-lives of poverty and dependency?[14] Each of these debilities has its causes; indeed, analyzing them has become a minor industry. Yet with so much about these conditions that is so closely related to race, they say something about the larger society that has allowed them to happen.

This is not to say that white officials sit in secret rooms, plotting the genocide of black America. You understand as well as anyone that politics and history seldom operate that way. Nor do you think of yourself as unduly suspicious. Still, you cannot rid yourself of some lingering mistrust. Just as your people were once made to serve silently as slaves, could it be that if white America begins to conclude that you are becoming too much trouble, it will find itself contemplating more lasting solutions?

REFERENCES

1. W. E. B. Du Bois, *The Souls of Black Folk* (1903) in *W. E. B. Du Bois: Writings,* edited by Nathan Huggins (The Library of America, 1986).

2. August Wilson, quoted in *New York Times* (April 15, 1990).

3. Toni Morrison, quoted in *New York Times* (January 15, 1986).

4. *New York Times* (April 1, 1987).

5. *New York Times* (July 24, 1987).

6. Gerald Jaynes and Robin Williams, eds., *A Common Destiny: Blacks and American Society* (National Academy Press, 1989).

7. Ralph Ellison, *Invisible Man* (Random House, 1952).

8. W. E. B. Du Bois: *Writings,* edited by Nathan Huggins (The Library of America, 1986).

9. *Political Trendletter* (Joint Center for Political and Economic Studies, March 1991).

10. Communication from Professor Richard Allen, University of Michigan, September 2, 1989. Also see his article in the *American Political Science Review* (June 1989).

11. Thomas Sowell, "The Fallacy of Racial Politics," *Harpers* (June 1984).

12. Colin McCord and Harold Freeman, "Excess Mortality in Harlem," *New England Journal of Medicine* (January 18, 1990).

13. Catherine Whitaker, *Black Victims* (Bureau of Justice Statistics, 1990).

14. In 1990, when a sample of black Americans were asked if they thought that the government was deliberately encouraging drug use among black people, 64 percent felt that this might be true. When asked if they suspected that AIDS had been purposely created by scientists to infect black people, 32 percent believed there might be some truth in this view. New York Times (October 29, 1990).

Study Questions

1. What is the point of Hacker's parable, "The Visit"? Make a list of what you perceive to be the major consequences of becoming black for the last 50 years of your life. How much compensation would you request? Why? Defend your position. (Note: You should analyze Hacker's parable regardless of your race.)

2. What does "apartheid" mean? Explain what Hacker means by "residential apartheid." Does this phenomenon exist in your area? If you are white (black), would you live in an area where half the residents are black (white)? Why? Defend your position on the basis of a specific moral theory.

3. Hacker states that "white reactions" brand black persons as carriers of contamination. What does Hacker mean here? Give two examples of reactions that would fall under this category.

4. In 1992, Cincinnati Reds owner Marge Schott was barred from participating in professional baseball for one year for using racial slurs, including referring to a Reds player as a "nigger." Why does Hacker think that this racial epithet is so hurtful? How should you react to a white person who uses the word "nigger" casually in conversation with other white persons? Why? Justify your response.

5. Describe contact with the criminal justice system from the perspective of a white person, and then from the perspective of a black person. Assess any differences that you find.

Barriers to Equality
The Power of Subtle Discrimination to Maintain Unequal Opportunity

MARY P. ROWE

"She cannot represent us in Washington; she isn't even pretty!"

"Don't try to build a career in that company, Aaron; they are very traditional. Because of who you are, you will never make it to the top...."

"Check his work for a few weeks, will you, Henry? His grades are good, but you can't tell with someone from a black college."

Introduction

In recent years there has been much discussion of the glass ceiling, the invisible barrier that keeps women and African Americans, Latinos and other minorities, from going to the top of traditionally "Anglo," male institutions. There is also an emergent discussion about whether Caucasians (as well as blacks and women) can make it to the top in companies run by Asians. Glass *walls* are equally impenetrable; glass walls keep women and minorities barred from certain occupations within society and within institutions; it is easy for each of us to observe occupational segregation in our own places of work.

There are of course several reasons for the glass barriers. For example, an important difficulty for women is the need for family supports, like adequate leaves and child care. It is the hypothesis of this article that subtle discrimination also contributes much to the glass barriers; it is the practical (not necessarily conscious) manifestation of the fact that senior managers want to choose people like themselves to succeed them. I believe that subtle discrimination is now, in most workplaces, the principal scaffolding for segregation in the United States, the framework for discrimination against everyone who is obviously "different" from the person making decisions about whatever is the matter at hand.

Most major U.S. institutions have long since begun to address major manifestations of prejudice. In many companies, a major act of discrimination that could immediately be proven would immediately be rectified, if brought to the attention of senior management. However, subtle barriers maintain their strength, by for example, not inviting African Americans to strategy meetings, leaving women home from field trips, blaming problems on the person who is obviously different, expecting failure from the person of difference. As we enter the 1990s, a decade in which it is expected that only about one in ten of all net new entrants into the U.S. labor force will be an Anglo white male, diversity will be the most important aspect of the U.S. labor force, and the glass barriers will become even more critical. Subtle discrimination is a timely topic for all training programs on workplace civility, on valuing differences, and on harassment.

There has been much discussion of whether discrimination works by keeping minority people out, or by affecting the minority person so that he or she behaves in an unacceptable or unproductive fashion. Blame the aggressor? Or blame the victim? This paper suggests that discrimination maintains itself in a wide variety of

Mary P. Rowe, "Barriers to Equality: The Power of Subtle Discrimination to Maintain Unequal Opportunity," Employee Responsibilities and Rights Journal, *vol. 3:2, pp. 153–163. Copyright © 1990 Plenum Publishing Corporation. Used by permission of the publisher.*

ways, working within the dominant culture and within the person discriminated against. The mechanism functions through a wide variety of "micro" events, or in the terms of this paper, microinequities.

The analysis is drawn from seventeen years as ombudsman to MIT and as a consultant to companies in North America. All the quotations that follow are real. Nearly all are from 1989. Although some will find the examples banal and trivial, for the persons who were the objects of each example these sentences were full of pain. Indeed, this is the point of the article.

What Are Microinequities? Why Look at Them?

It will become obvious, from the discussion that follows, that each person is his or her own expert on what constitutes a microinequity in any given instance. Discriminatory microinequities are tiny, damaging characteristics of an environment, as these characteristics affect a person not indigenous to that environment. They are distinguished by the fact that for all practical purposes one cannot do anything about them; one cannot take them to court or file a grievance. They are actions which are unjust toward individuals, when reasonable people would agree the particular treatment of the individual occurs only because of a group characteristic unrelated to creativity and work performance (for example, sex, race, religion, age, or country of origin). *("You cannot send her to represent us in that negotiation; most of their top people are European. She will be treated politely but she won't be taken seriously."* ... *"Would the Senator's staff be convinced by a black lobbyist?")*

These are the situations where a minority person is not introduced; when mail is addressed to a male rather than a female technical manager, because it is presumed that he is technically more competent. These are the comments about physical appearance *("You make me think about tepees and tomahawks.")* in talking with a Native American colleague. These are the presumptions, uncountered by Anglo male superiors, that a

Latina cannot negotiate the contract in Japan; or that it is professionally acceptable to show sex films at a professional conference *("It's OK. We warned the ladies about the porn flicks, so if they want to, they can stay away from the evening meetings.")*. This is the hand on the knee from a senior vice-president at the banquet table; these are the disrespectful comments to an African-American member of the board *("Martin Luther King Day is just a foolish and costly gesture to yet another special interest group.")*. These are the two-sided stereotypes about technical ability *("Hey, Paul Wu, you made a mistake in math! How come? I thought you guys never made a mistake!"* ... *"We hired an Hispanic engineer and he was incompetent; never again.")*. This is the supercompetent, white American who will never make it to the top of a Japanese company, though he was brought up in Japan, is bilingual, and can "pass" on the telephone.

There is a useful literature about where these phenomena come from, why people overlook or fear or put down those whom they perceive to be "not like us." In studies of racism Dr. Chester Pierce calls many of these microevents, "microaggressions" (Barbour, 1970).[1] Jean-Paul Sartre has written about these phenomena as the expectations of anti-Semites about what it means to be a Jew (Sartre, 1965).[2] One may think of subtle discrimination as a projection of our negative feelings about ourselves, or as a scapegoating process, supported by myths and by selective perception which supports the myths. This article is about the *effects* of subtle discrimination and how it works.

Microinequities are fiendishly efficient in perpetuating unequal opportunity, because they are in the air we breathe, in the books we read, in the television we all watch, and because we cannot change the personal characteristic that leads to the inequity. Microinequities are woven into all the threads of our work life and of U.S. education. They are "micro," not at all in the sense of trivial, but in the sense of miniature. I write about these events, in this paper, with a focus on racism and sexism. However, the same points may be made with respect to nationality, religion, age, handicap, sexual orientation, and many other dimensions of diversity, especially as the U.S. internationalizes and becomes more heterogeneous.

How Do the Minutiae of Discrimination Maintain the Glass Barriers?

I know of no systematic, scientific study of "microinequities," but one can suggest many hypotheses as to why such behavior may do damage. I personally do believe these inequities cause serious damage; I believe they are the major explanation for glass barriers. I will therefore set forth my hypotheses. *I believe that microinequities exert their influence both by walling out the "different" person, and by making the person of difference less effective:*

• Microinequities sometimes cause damage because they predispose a manager to even worse behavior. Thus "seeing through" an "invisible" African-American, or paying no attention to support staff women, may make them feel like part of the furniture. This habit may also lead to underpaying minorities and women, because the senior person has little idea what the "invisible people" actually contribute. It may also lead to overlooking someone who might be the best-qualified person for promotion. Every experienced manager has seen examples where a senior person will start recruiting from outside, while not "seeing" the woman in front of him who has been a significant contributor, and who could be promoted (*"What really hurt was that then I was expected to train him to do the job."*).

• In addition to the above, some microinequities cause extended damage, because at the time they occur they are preventing better behavior from occurring. If an executive assistant is unreasonably overloaded with routine or personal work for a supervisor, she may be prevented from doing the kind of creative work that would have prepared her for promotion (*"I would like to be taking on the accounting, but he just sees me as the person who bought his wife's Christmas presents so skillfully."*).

• Microinequities may also have a negative

Pygmalion quality. That is, the expectation of poor performance, or the lack of expectation of good performance, may do damage because managers and students and employees have a strong tendency to do what is expected of them. The Asian-American who is expected to be docile may later be thought not to be sufficiently assertive (*"He just called me in whenever he needed error-free, technical work on no notice and with no back talk. I would stay up all night. At the end of the year my evaluation said I didn't speak up enough."*).

• Microinequities cause damage in part because they are a kind of "punishment" which cannot be predicted, in any functional sense; microinequities are *irrational*. That is, by and large, they occur in the context of merit, and of striving for excellence, but do not have anything to *do* with excellence or merit. This is, of course, by definition what makes them "inequities"; that the punishment occurs in the context of work but *without relevance to performance* (*"It was the damnedest thing; he got off the phone from talking with his daughter, and he blew up at me (the only woman in the group) about a budget proposal that I did not have anything at all to do with!"*). It is therefore important to look at such phenomena in the context of what we know from behavior modification theory. As an intermittent, unpredictable, "negative reinforcement," microinequities have peculiar power as a negative learning tool (unpredictable, intermittent reinforcement being a powerful type of reinforcement). Moreover, because one cannot change the provocation for negative reinforcement (for example, one's race or gender), one inevitably feels some helplessness.

• Microinequities are often difficult to detect or be sure about (*"I can't put my finger exactly on it. But white institutions are just cold."*). This means for one thing that it is hard for the subject to take effective action (*"Tell me, how can I fight a wisp of fog?"*). It also means that frequent targets of inequities, like Latinos, Native Americans, Asian-Americans, African-Americans, and women, may constantly range through emotions, from legitimate anger (which may or may not have a constructive outlet), to paranoia. The constant experience of being uncertain, about whether one was "left out" or put down, inevitably leads to some displaced and misplaced anger *("I spend my day going through changes.")*. Any misplaced anger itself is a problem, because it may in turn offend innocent (or not innocent) bystanders. Uncertainty may also lead to ignoring *real* insults in such a way that they persist.

• Microinequities are also often not intentional in any conscious or even unconscious way, even when objective observers would agree that they exist—that an injury really took place. This is another reason they are hard for a victim to respond to *("I know that no one meant for me to feel out of place. But I could not stand the belly dancers at the dinner. I hated the annual sales meeting after that.")*. We are all socialized to believe that *intent* to injure is an important part of injury, and it is certainly critical to our actually dealing with injuries at the hands of others. Faced with a microaggression, the victim may not be certain of the motives of the aggressor, and may be unwilling to engage in hostility where no injury was intended. Under conditions of uncertainty about motives, most victims are sometimes in the position of either not getting angry when they should (which reinforces the aggression and may weaken the victim's professional image and self-image) or of protesting some times when no injury was *consciously* intended even though it actually occurred. The latter situation is occasionally salutary for all concerned, especially if the aggressor reacts by acknowledging that an injury took place. But sometimes the aggressor is totally unaware of aggressing, even though observers would agree that injury took place. The aggressor may then respond to protest with bewilderment, frustration, humiliation, anger, or feelings of betrayal. Or, what is worse, the aggressor may then undermine the minority person who challenged him *("He said that my joke was racist. Do you think he is really on the team?")*.

• Microaggressions and inequities grow in infinite variety. It is hard to stay ahead of the proliferation of types, let alone the number of petty injuries. For this reason minorities and women may find themselves being too alert for some new kind of insult, because of past frustration. And every experienced manager is familiar with apparently inappropriate anger from someone who was probably responding to "the last war" and not the present one *("I blew it. It was one too many. He just asked who could possibly have done this brilliant work. I did not realize it was a compliment. I felt totally insulted and blew up; I cannot believe I did that.")*.

• Microinequities also cause damage in part because they take up time and energy. Sorting out what is happening, and then dealing with one's pain and anger, take work *("The worst thing, after she was so mean, was not being able to concentrate; I could not seem to think straight that whole week.")*. Moreover, studies show that extra time is also required of many minorities and women to help deal with the pain caused by microinequities suffered by *other* minorities and women, because people of difference turn to each other for advice and solace *("I get calls from people almost every night, about what happened to them that day.")*.

• Communications between genders and among different ethnic groups are sometimes more difficult than between persons who are alike. It is also harder to make sound judgments about persons of difference. Microinequities worsen difficult communications, and difficult communications also increase subtle discrimination. It is obvious that none of us knows what it was like to be brought up as a member of the other sex or of a different race. And the forms of racism and sexism are so specific that each group is isolated from the other's experience, and therefore may not intuitively understand the pain of others. Thus, small inequities can add to the fact that cross-group communications are already slower and more difficult; and that cross-group judgments are harder to make well. For example, a white supervisor may find it hard to evaluate the leadership abilities of a person of color—and then, through prejudice, also fail to give constructive criticism and adequate feedback *("Nobody ever criticized my work or made any suggestions. They just never promoted me.*"). This sometimes happens quite consciously when a white male supervisor is afraid to mention a performance problem (*"She seems so touchy!"*). The lack of communication and subtle discrimination then feed off each other and may lead to a downward spiral (*"If she weren't black, she would have been fired long ago, but nobody has ever said a thing to her."*). It is becoming increasingly common not only to find this difficulty between minorities and nonminorities, but also *between* minority groups. For example, Asian-Americans and African-Americans may have difficulty making and then expressing appropriate judgments about each other's work, because of strong differences in cultural background exacerbated by subtle discrimination.

• Microaggressions seem petty, in a world where available redress may often seem heavy-handed or too clumsy a tool. This is a problem even for those who appear to have some power. Formal grievances, going to court, and appeal to the CEO are heavy weapons; using them is often thought to carry high cost. The perceived lack of *appropriate* modes of redress therefore helps to perpetuate microaggressions. This is especially true where the aggrieved person does not want to lose privacy or professional image. What can an African-American vice-president do, if someone he is negotiating with sneers in private? What can a female plant manager do, if the boss stares directly at her bosom whenever they are alone? Until the person of difference learns how to handle these events effectively (which takes work), the apparent lack of redress is, at best, frustrating (*"I am a first-rate engineer. I do not want to be known as a 'harassment case'; I do not see that there is anything I can do about his touching me."*).

Do Microaggressions Do More Harm to Minorities and Women than to White Men?

Don't microproblems just "happen to everyone" (*"Haven't you just been describing the general inhumanities of large organizations?"*)? Is this really discrimination (*"I harass everybody, Mary. I don't discriminate."*)? This question sometimes arises when an employer has done an employee attitude survey on racism or sexism without a white male control group; white males may protest (*"We also get treated terribly. We just don't complain about it; we get on with the job."*). Let me raise here hypotheses as to why microproblems may be worse for minorities and women than for the "average" white male. (I do not mean to say that male Caucasians are impervious to mean behavior.) Some of the hypotheses as to why micro-inequities may do more damage to minorities and women are, of course, analogous to the hypotheses as to why they do damage at all.

• "General" harassment often takes a specifically sexist form when applied to women, a racist form when applied to African-Americans, and so on. Instead of saying to some average white male, *"Your work on this project has been inexcusably sloppy, you blinking idiot; you'll never make it that way!,"* the remark may come out, *"My God, you think no better than my wife; why don't you go home and have babies!",* or, *"We will never be able to make up for the generations of Southern schools that produced you!"* The harassment of African-Americans piles up in allusions to race, the harassment of women as allusions to sex roles and sex, instead of being randomly applied, or appropriately focused on work. Like the dripping of water, random drops may do little damage; endless drops in one place can have profound effects (*"I got A's in college, and here I am losing all self-esteem; I feel as if I can't do anything right."*). This is especially important where the "micro" problem is sexualized behavior, and where the object of the aggression was sexually abused in childhood (or saw someone like themselves sexually abused). Thus the estimated 20%–35% of women and 5%–15% of men who were sexually abused in childhood may be especially vulnerable to even quite minor sexualizations in the workplace (*"I know this sounds crazy, but I feel as if I had been raped."*).

• Many minorities and women were socialized to respond disproportionately swiftly to disapproval. Parents often teach their daughters to cooperate rather than to compete with men. Some African-American parents teach their children to be sensitive and cautious about anger and criticism from white males. And I find it is sometimes difficult to persuade Asians and Asian-Americans to resist harassment that whites and other U.S. minorities will no longer put up with. Conversely one can find many white males who were explicitly socialized to expect hard knocks, to compete ferociously and openly, even (or especially) when injured, and to have a very high pain threshold. It would be hard to prove that either kind of socialization is "right" or "wrong" in absolute terms, but it is easy to see how these cultural paths run afoul of each other. If a white male supervisor shouts angrily for five minutes at a young woman, she may not wholly "recover" from the attack for weeks or months ("*I never asked him a question again. I avoided him whenever I could until I got out of there.*"). Later, in a discussion with the supervisor, one may hear that he's completely forgotten his "random grouchiness," or thought it was trivial. Thus, behavior that might be trivial or survivable for the average white male may be quite destructive to others, in a manner that has nothing directly to do with the work at hand.

• Microinequities are more often reported where more powerful people have offended less powerful people. (I think no one knows whether they originate more in this direction than in the reverse. Perhaps power is corrupting; perhaps aggressive underdogs are always eliminated over time or, more likely, more powerful people ignore or are not so easily injured by microinsults from below. Perhaps the generally higher pay and status of the more powerful gives adequate recompense.) It is generally the less powerful who have most difficulties in coping with inequities, since less powerful people by definition have less influence. It is especially difficult to stop an aggressor who is a supervisor ("*What do you mean, did I speak up when he insulted me? Are you kidding? He's my boss!*"). Disproportionate numbers of less powerful people are minority and female; these groups are therefore statistically more vulnerable to microinequities.

• In a traditionally white male atmosphere it is much harder to get certain kinds of microinequities to stop, because the slights are culturally so "normal" that they simply are not noticed. Many whites are acutely uncomfortable around persons of color; they ignore them or fail to look at and address them—but do not notice that they are doing so. Sexy calendars on walls; "humorous" surveys and cartoons about sex; "humorous" mimicry of the handicapped and of other races; ethnic and sexist jokes; and the use of sex in ads, announcements, and in computer hacking, are so ubiquitous that many whites and many men literally do not notice them ("*I complained about some extremely offensive girlie calendars in the machine shop. He said, 'What calendars?' He did not even see them!*").

• Traditionally white male environments may even reinforce certain kinds of discriminatory behavior that are perceived as actively enjoyable, like the aggressive and humiliating recounting of sex and ethnic jokes, or AIDS or handicap jokes ("*You should see Chris. Chris does a spaz routine, dragging his leg on the street. It'll really crack you up.*"). This reinforcement may directly interfere with the pursuit of excellence. ("*The recruiting team got a reference that said: 'She is not very creative. Of course you can hire her if you want, but if I were looking for someone new in the lab, I'd rather have her body than her mind.' Can you believe it? They did not return the reference; they said, 'Let's hire her!'*")

• There is a more acute role-modeling problem for persons of difference, because of their constantly witnessing microinequities against others like themselves. That is, disproportionately more Latinos, African-Americans and women see people "like them" put down or ignored or ill-served by their superiors and elders ("*After what happened to Carlos, I just gave up.*"). This point may be clearer when one remembers that in most work environments, the principal (if unintended) same-sex and same-race role models, for persons of color and women, are clerical workers and hourly workers, and these are the groups most frequently reporting microinequities. This inadvertent, damaging role-modeling is even stronger because nearly all minorities and women are continuously being taken to be holding the lower level jobs traditionally held by minorities and women, even if they are managers ("*I am constantly being taken to be a file clerk,*" says an African-American woman engineer. "*I constantly feel a struggle to develop my own self-image, but it is not affirmed by most of the world around me, as it is for my majority male colleagues.*").

• It is often harder for minorities and women to find mentors to help them deal with microinequities. There are so few senior minorities and women in most organizations that junior members of the community cannot, on the average, find the same amount of high-status, same-race, same-sex mentorship that white males can find. Frequently the higher-status women and minorities try to compensate by spending extra time as same-sex, same-race mentors. It is, however, almost inevitable that the burden of dealing with microinequities falls on senior people who are already somewhat disproportionately drained of energy by caring for others. This is of course an especially powerful support to glass barriers ("*I went to see a brother in upper management, and told him what had happened to me. He just stood looking out of the window, clenching his fists.*").

• There is another reason why it is sometimes hard to find an appropriate mentor when a woman and/or minority person is offended by a microproblem. If one goes to a white male, he may or may not understand. If one goes to a friend of the same race and sex, he or she may be just wonderful in helping one to deal with it, or may not be helpful at all. ("*I told her he put his hands under my blouse. She asked me if I were wearing a slinky black blouse that day.*"). That is, listeners of the same sex and race may be so discouraged and bitter, or so full of denial, that they are worse than useless.

In sum, I believe that it is often more difficult for minorities and women to find adequate help in dealing with racism and sexism, than for majority men to deal with "general inhumanities." I believe many minority and women managers, students, and employees have a

disproportionate need for supportive white male mentorship, and are disproportionately injured when an advisor or teacher or supervisor assigned to them is just generally unfriendly. Let us take a hypothetical example, Awilda Hernandez, who is a management trainee in a Midwest bank. She has a need for support, if only because she will inevitably live through many microinequities. She needs someone to advise her about advancement in an Anglo male environment, because it is foreign to her. The support that she gets from back home is not likely to be professional support. She is, in other words, less well supported by the general society and may be less well supported by her family than if she were a white male. If her supervisor turns out to be generally inattentive, grouchy, or cold ("*What do you mean, am I a mentor? Cream rises to the top; mentorship is a bloody waste of my time.*"), she has been deprived of a mentor in circumstances where she, more than others, needed a mentor. The situation will be compounded if she is afraid to ask for a new advisor or does not know how to find substitute help.

This paper has suggested many reasons why the problems of microinequities for minorities and women go beyond the general inhumanities of large organizations. The point may be clearer if you will imagine (this is a real example) being a solo, young, white, male, child-care worker in a large, conservative, inner-city daycare system. The "general harassment" might include sincere questions and snide comments on your sexuality. Other white males might find you odd. Women might distrust your skills ("*Wait, Jim, let me show you how to do that.*") or your interest in children ("*Are you married?*"). You might be in fact inept, in some ways, your first year. You might be very sensitive to just run-of-the-mill anger from your cross-sex, perhaps cross-race, supervisor. You might find the constant assumption that women-are-better to be very oppressive—the ads, the jokes, the pictures of women and children on the walls, the many fathers deprived of custody. You might have no one like yourself to turn to. You might get to hate always being asked to fix things ("*I was constantly being asked why I wanted to be there, as if I might molest the children, or drop a baby.").*

I believe that discriminatory behavior itself causes pain, and also may constitute for minorities and women a situation they cannot control, evade, or ameliorate (or, as we have said, they may see it that way). Continued experience of destructive situations that cannot be improved can start unhappy cycles of behavior ranging from declining self-esteem (which makes one feel still less efficacious in changing the environment) to withdrawal, resignation, poor work, fantasies of violence, and so on (*"I struggled for days to deal with my anger at what he said; I will never forget that bastard as long as I live. If I ever find myself in a position to do him in, you can bet I will do my best."*). At the very least it either takes a lot of energy to deal with an environment perceived as hostile, or it takes lots of energy to maintain one's level of denial of difficulties.

In my own environment, as in all others in the U.S., I believe microinequities cause stress. Over the years there have been occasional, unpublished studies at the Massachusetts Institute of Technology about the performance of men and women, for example the in-house surveys of "sex-blind" admissions. These studies typically show that women and men do randomly as well as each other. However, women also regularly report high stress levels and lower self-esteem, for example, in a study of the academic environment for male and female graduate students (Committee on Women Student Interests, 1987, unpublished). Small departmental studies report pain from microinequities (e.g., Barriers to Equality, 1984, unpublished). Persons of color also report pain from microinequities (Racial Climate Report, 1988, unpublished).

Are Microinequities Ever Useful?

Occasionally one will find someone who believes that hardship is good for people; creativity requires incessant pain; harassment inspires excellence (*"My parents were immigrants; I made it through—so can everyone else."*).

It is hard to respond to these ideas because individual situations vary so much. The speaker who remembers having survived terrible hurdles may also have had exceptional health and energy, or a wonderfully supportive parent or uncle or religion, or extended family—or may be the only person of his or her type ever to have survived that background—or may have come through "successful," but terribly scarred.

I think most of us believe that challenge is good (in the right doses), that creativity requires intense concentration and effort, and that excellence itself, and high expectations, inspire excellence. But most people believe that intermittent positive reinforcement—the carrot—is more powerful than the stick. I personally do not believe our world to be so devoid of sticks that we need more of them. And there seem to me to be enough good reasons to believe that microinequities cause *damage* that we should try to ameliorate them. The Law of Parsimony would suggest that it is simplest to assume that human ability is randomly distributed (*"We could double the numbers of excellent managers and scientists in the U.S., if we knew how to provide real equal opportunity for minorities and women."*). Is this not a sufficient incentive for us to try to undo damage that occurs? Is it not more reasonable to assume that people survive in spite of damage rather than because of it?

What Can Be Done?

I do not believe that subtle discrimination can or should be legislated, made the subject of formal policy, or dragged into formal grievance procedures. Obviously anyone who feels unjustly treated should have safe, accessible, and credible complaint-handlers to talk with. All workplaces should provide confidential advisers such as ombudsmen, to provide support and to help in devising effective plans to address individual concerns. Many employees and managers need support to analyze their concerns, in part to be able to *differentiate* subtleties from actionable problems. There are of course rare circumstances where the behavior described here could be taken to court. But, by definition, subtle discrimination is not appropriate for formal grievances.

What an employer can do is recognize the importance of microinequities. Subtle discrimination is an appropriate topic for employee attitude surveys, for company newsletters, for staff meetings. An employer can encourage responsible networks of minorities and women to support each other in discussing such problems, to present noon-time workshops, to join mentoring programs, to learn how to deal effectively with discrimination, and how to report it when necessary. Supervisors can look for microinequities and discuss them in a low-key way as they happen. Subtle discrimination is a timely subject for explicit discussion in management training programs which focus on topics like performance evaluation and harassment. It is a wonderful topic for consciousness-raising cartoons (*"That's a splendid idea, Miss Dickinson. I wonder if one of the men would like to suggest it?"*). A good place to talk about these topics is in programs on valuing differences, and on diversity in the workplace. Probably the best place is anywhere that people are willing to raise the subject with someone unlike themselves.

NOTES

1. Pierce, C. (1970). Offensive mechanisms. In Barbour, F. (Ed.), *The Black 70's.* Boston: Sargent.
2. Sartre, J. P. (1965). *Anti-Semite and Jew.* New York: Schocken Books.

Study Questions

1. What is the "glass ceiling"? Explain the "glass" metaphor. How does it relate to inequality of opportunity? How do we know that "glass" barriers exist? Explain.
2. Briefly define "microinequity" and give your own example. Have you ever committed such an action? Explain. Have you ever suffered such an action? Explain.
3. According to Rowe, how do "small" discriminatory acts maintain glass barriers?
4. What is the role of intent to injure in understanding microinequities? In your opinion, does any harm occur if no harm was intended? Why? Defend your position with examples.

Reverse Discrimination as Unjustified

LISA H. NEWTON

I HAVE HEARD IT argued that "simple justice" requires that we favor women and blacks in employment and educational opportunities, since women and blacks were "unjustly" excluded from such opportunities for so many years in the not so distant past. It is a strange argument, an example of a possible implication of a true proposition advanced to dispute the proposition itself, like an octopus absent-mindedly slicing off his head with a stray tentacle. A fatal confusion underlies this argument, a confusion fundamentally relevant to our understanding of the notion of the rule of law.

Two senses of justice and equality are

Lisa H. Newton, "Reverse Discrimination as Unjustified," Ethics, *vol. 83:4 (July 1973), pp. 308–312.*
© *University of Chicago Press. Used by permission of the author and the publisher.*

involved in this confusion. The root notion of justice, progenitor of the other, is the one that Aristotle (*Nichomachean Ethics* 5.6; *Politics* 1.2; 3.1) assumes to be the foundation and proper virtue of the political association. It is the condition which free men establish among themselves when they "share a common life in order that their association bring them self-sufficiency"— the regulation of their relationship by law, and the establishment, by law, of equality before the law. Rule of law is the name and pattern of this justice; its equality stands against the inequalities—of wealth, talent, etc.— otherwise obtaining among its participants, who by virtue of that equality are called "citizens." It is an achievement—complete, or, more frequently, partial—of certain people in certain concrete situations. It is fragile and easily disrupted by powerful individuals who discover that the blind equality of rule of law is inconvenient for their interests. Despite its obvious instability, Aristotle assumed that the establishment of justice in this sense, the creation of citizenship, was a permanent possibility for men and that the resultant association of citizens was the natural home of the species. At levels below the political association, this rule-governed equality is easily found; it is exemplified by any group of children agreeing together to play a game. At the level of the political association, the attainment of this justice is more difficult, simply because the stakes are so much higher for each participant. The equality of citizenship is not something that happens of its own accord, and without the expenditure of a fair amount of effort it will collapse into the rule of a powerful few over an apathetic many. But at least it has been achieved, at some times in some places; it is always worth trying to achieve, and eminently worth trying to maintain, wherever and to whatever degree it has been brought into being.

Aristotle's parochialism is notorious; he really did not imagine that persons other than Greeks could associate freely in justice, and the only form of association he had in mind was the Greek *polis*. With the decline of the *polis* and the shift in the center of political thought, his notion of justice underwent a sea change. To be exact, it ceased to represent a political type and became a moral ideal: the ideal of equality as we know it. This ideal demands that all men be included in citizenship— that one Law govern all equally, that all men regard all other men as fellow citizens, with the same guarantees, rights, and protections. Briefly, it demands that the circle of citizenship achieved by any group be extended to include the entire human race. Properly understood, its effect on our associations can be excellent: it congratulates us on our achievement of rule of law as a process of government but refuses to let us remain complacent until we have expanded the associations to include others within the ambit of the rules, as often and as far as possible. While one man is a slave, none of us may feel truly free. We are constantly prodded by this ideal to look for possible unjustifiable discrimination, for inequalities not absolutely required for the functioning of the society and advantageous to all. And after twenty centuries of pressure, not at all constant, from this ideal, it might be said that some progress has been made. To take the cases in point for this problem, we are now prepared to assert, as Aristotle would never have been, the equality of sexes and of persons of different colors. The ambit of American citizenship, once restricted to white males of property, has been extended to include all adult free men, then all adult males including ex-slaves, then all women. The process of acquisition of full citizenship was for these groups a sporadic trail of half-measures, even now not complete; the steps on the road to full equality are marked by legislation and judicial decisions which are only recently concluded and still often not enforced. But the fact that we can now discuss the possibility of favoring such groups in hiring shows that over the area that concerns us, at least, full equality is presupposed as a basis for discussion. To that extent, they are full citizens, fully protected by the law of the land.

It is important for my argument that the moral ideal of equality be recognized as logically distinct from the condition (or virtue) of justice in the political sense. Justice in this sense exists *among* a citizenry, irrespective of the number of the populace included in that citizenry. Further, the moral ideal is parasitic upon the political virtue, for "equality" is unspecified—it means nothing until we are told in what respect that equality is to be realized. In a political context, "equality" is specified as "equal rights"—equal access to the public realm, public goods and offices, equal treatment under the law—in brief, the equality of citizenship. If citizenship is not a possibility, political equality is unintelligible. The ideal emerges as a generalization of the real condition and refers back to that condition for its content.

Now, if justice (Aristotle's justice in the political sense) is equal treatment under law for all citizens, what is injustice? Clearly, injustice is the violation of that equality, discriminating for or against a group of citizens, favoring them with special immunities and privileges or depriving them of those guaranteed to the others. When the southern employer refuses to hire blacks in white-collar jobs, when Wall Street will only hire women as secretaries with new titles, when Mississippi high schools routinely flunk all black boys above ninth grade, we have examples of injustice, and we work to restore the equality of the public realm by ensuring that equal opportunity will be provided in such cases in the future. But of course, when the employers and the schools *favor* women and blacks, the same injustice is done. Just as the previous discrimination did, this reverse discrimination violates the public equality which defines citizenship and destroys the rule of law for the areas in which these favors are granted. To the extent that we adopt a program of discrimination, reverse or otherwise, justice in the political sense is destroyed, and none of us, specifically affected or not, is a citizen, a bearer of rights—we are all petitioners for favors. And to the same extent, the ideal of equality is undermined, for it has content only where justice obtains, and by destroying justice we render the ideal meaningless. It is, then, an ironic paradox, if not a contradiction in terms, to assert that the ideal of

equality justifies the violation of justice; it is as if one should argue, with William Buckley, that an ideal of humanity can justify the destruction of the human race.

Logically, the conclusion is simple enough: all discrimination is wrong prima facie because it violates justice, and that goes for reverse discrimination too. No violation of justice among the citizens may be justified (may overcome the prima facie objection) by appeal to the ideal of equality, for that ideal is logically dependent upon the notion of justice. Reverse discrimination, then, which attempts no other justification than an appeal to equality, is wrong. But let us try to make the conclusion more plausible by suggesting some of the implications of the suggested practice of reverse discrimination in employment and education. My argument will be that the problems raised there are insoluble, not only in practice but in principle.

We may argue, if we like, about what "discrimination" consists of. Do I discriminate against blacks if I admit none to my school when none of the black applicants are qualified by the tests I always give? How far must I go to root out cultural bias from my application forms and tests before I can say that I have not discriminated against those of different cultures? Can I assume that women are not strong enough to be roughnecks on my oil rigs, or must I test them individually? But this controversy, the most popular and well-argued aspect of the issue, is not as fatal as two others which cannot be avoided: if we are regarding the blacks as a "minority" victimized by discrimination, what is a "minority"? And for any group—blacks, women, whatever—that has been discriminated against, what amount of reverse discrimination wipes out the initial discrimination? Let us grant as true that women and blacks were discriminated against, even where laws forbade such discrimination, and grant for the sake of argument that a history of discrimination must be wiped out by reverse discrimination. What follows?

First, are there other groups which have been discriminated against? For they should have the same right of restitution. What about American

Indians, Chicanos, Appalachian Mountain whites, Puerto Ricans, Jews, Cajuns, and Orientals? And if these are to be included, the principle according to which we specify a "minority" is simply the criterion of "ethnic (sub) group," and we're stuck with every hyphenated American in the lower-middle class clamoring for special privileges for *his* group—and with equal justification. For be it noted, when we run down the Harvard roster, we find not only a scarcity of blacks (in comparison with the proportion in the population) but an even more striking scarcity of those second-, third-, and fourth-generation ethnics who make up the loudest voice of Middle America. Shouldn't they demand *their* share? And eventually, the WASPs will have to form their own lobby, for they too are a minority. The point is simply this: there is no "majority" in America who will not mind giving up just a bit of their rights to make room for a favored minority. There are only other minorities, each of which is discriminated against by the favoring. The initial injustice is then repeated dozens of times, and if each minority is granted the same right of restitution as the others, an entire area of rule governance is dissolved into a pushing and shoving match between self-interested groups. Each works to catch the public eye and political popularity by whatever means of advertising and power politics lend themselves to the effort, to capitalize as much as possible on contemporary popularity until the restless mob picks another group to feel sorry for. Hardly an edifying spectacle, and in the long run no one can benefit: the pie is no larger—it's just that instead of setting up and enforcing rules for getting a piece, we've turned the contest into a free-for-all, requiring much more effort for no larger a reward. It would be in the interests of all the participants to reestablish an objective rule to govern the process, carefully enforced and the same for all.

Second, supposing that we do manage to agree in general that women and blacks (and all the others) have some rights of restitution, some right to a privileged place in the structure of opportunities for a while, how will we know

when that while is up? How much privilege is enough? When will the guilt be gone, the price paid, the balance restored? What recompense is right for centuries of exclusion? What criterion tells us when we are done? Our experience with the Civil Rights movement shows us that agreement on these terms cannot be presupposed: a process that appears to some to be going at a mad gallop into a black takeover appears to the rest of us to be at a standstill. Should a practice of reverse discrimination be adopted, we may safely predict that just as some of us begin to see "a satisfactory start toward righting the balance," others of us will see that we "have already gone too far in the other direction" and will suggest that the discrimination ought to be reversed again. And such disagreement is inevitable, for the point is that we could not *possibly* have any criteria for evaluating the kind of recompense we have in mind. The context presumed by any discussion of restitution is the context of rule of law: law sets the rights of men and simultaneously sets the method for remedying the violation of those rights. You may exact suffering from others and/or damage payments for yourself if and only if the others have violated your rights: the suffering you have endured is not sufficient reason for them to suffer. And remedial rights exists only where there is law: primary human rights are useful guides to legislation but cannot stand as reasons for awarding remedies for injuries sustained. But then, the context presupposed by any discussion of restitution is the context of preexistent full citizenship. No remedial rights could exist for the excluded: neither in law nor in logic does there exist a right to *sue* for a standing to sue.

From these two considerations, then, the difficulties with reverse discrimination become evident. Restitution for a disadvantaged group whose rights under the law have been violated is possible by legal means, but restitution for a disadvantaged group whose grievance is that there was no law to protect them simply is not. First, outside of the area of justice defined by the law, no sense can be made of "the group's rights," for no law recognizes that group or the individuals in it, qua members, as bearers of rights (hence *any* group can constitute itself as a disadvantaged minority in some sense and demand similar restitution). Second, outside of the area of protection of law, no sense can be made of the violation of rights (hence the amount of the recompense cannot be decided by any objective criterion). For both reasons, the practice of reverse discrimination undermines the foundation of the very ideal in whose name it is advocated; it destroys justice, law, equality, and citizenship itself, and replaces them with power struggles and popularity contests.

Study Questions

1. How does Newton define justice in the political sense? Why can't the ideal of equality ever justify a violation of justice, according to Newton? What conclusion does Newton draw from this regarding reverse discrimination? Do you agree? Why? Defend your position.

2. Describe as best you can what Newton means by the expression "reverse discrimination." How do you use the expression? Do you agree with Newton that "the same injustice is done" when a woman is favored by an employer as when a woman is harmfully discriminated against by an employer? Why? Defend your position.

3. Newton poses the question, "What amount of reverse discrimination wipes out the initial discrimination?" Does Newton think that there is an answer to this question? In your view, is the purpose of affirmative action to "wipe out" the debt of wrongful discrimination in the past? Why? Defend your position.

4. Newton claims that "restitution for a disadvantaged group whose grievance is that there was no law to protect them simply is not [possible]." How does Newton defend this statement? Is her argument successful? Defend your position.

A Defense of Programs of Preferential Treatment

RICHARD WASSERSTROM

MANY JUSTIFICATIONS OF PROGRAMS of preferential treatment depend upon the claim that in one respect or another such programs have good consequences or that they are effective means by which to bring about some desirable end, e.g., an integrated, equalitarian society. I mean by "programs of preferential treatment" to refer to programs such as those at issue in the *Bakke* case—programs which set aside a certain number of places (for example, in a law school) as to which members of minority groups (for example, persons who are non-white or female) who possess certain minimum qualifications (in terms of grades and test scores) may be preferred

Richard Wasserstrom, "A Defense of Programs of Preferential Treatment," National Forum: The Phi Kappa Phi Journal, LVIII (Winter 1978), 15–18. Copyright © Richard A. Wasserstrom. Used by permission of the publisher.

for admission to those places over some members of the majority group who possess higher qualifications (in terms of grades and test scores).

Many criticisms of programs of preferential treatment claim that such programs, even if effective, are unjustifiable because they are in some important sense unfair or unjust. In this paper I present a limited defense of such programs by showing that two of the chief arguments offered for the unfairness or injustice of these programs do not work in the way or to the degree supposed by critics of these programs.

The first argument is this. Opponents of preferential treatment programs sometimes assert that proponents of these programs are guilty of intellectual inconsistency, if not racism or sexism. For, as is now readily acknowledged, at times past employers, universities, and many other social institutions did have racial or sexual quotas (when they did not practice overt racial or sexual exclusion), and many of those who were most concerned to bring about the eradication of those racial quotas are now untroubled by the new programs which reinstitute them. And this, it is claimed, is inconsistent. If it was wrong to take race or sex into account when blacks and women were the objects of racial and sexual policies and practices of exclusion, then it is wrong to take race or sex into account when the objects of the policies have their race or sex reversed. Simple considerations of intellectual consistency—of what it means to give racism or sexism as a reason for condemning these social policies and practices—require that what was a good reason then is still a good reason now.

The problem with this argument is that despite appearances, there is no inconsistency involved in holding both views. Even if contemporary preferential treatment programs which contain quotas are wrong, they are not wrong for the reasons that made quotas against blacks and women pernicious. The reason why is that the social realities do make an enormous difference. The fundamental evil of programs that discriminated against blacks or women was that these programs were a part of a larger social universe which systematically maintained a network of institutions which unjustifiably concentrated power, authority, and goods in the hands of white male individuals, and which systematically consigned blacks and women to subordinate positions in the society.

Whatever may be wrong with today's affirmative action programs and quota systems, it should be clear that the evil, if any, is just not the same. Racial and sexual minorities do not constitute the dominant social group. Nor is the conception of who is a fully developed member of the moral and social community one of an individual who is either female or black. Quotas which prefer women or blacks do not add to an already relatively overabundant supply of resources and opportunities at the disposal of members of these groups in the way in which the quotas of the past did maintain and augment the overabundant supply of resources and opportunities already available to white males.

The same point can be made in a somewhat different way. Sometimes people say that what was wrong, for example, with the system of racial discrimination in the South was that it took an irrelevant characteristic, namely race, and used it systematically to allocate social benefits and burdens of various sorts. The defect was the irrelevance of the characteristic used—race—for that meant that individuals ended up being treated in a manner that was arbitrary and capricious.

I do not think that was the central flaw at all. Take, for instance, the most hideous of the practices, human slavery. The primary thing that was wrong with the institution was not that the particular individuals who were assigned the place of slaves were assigned there arbitrarily because the assignment was made in virtue of an irrelevant characteristic, their race. Rather, it seems to me that the primary thing that was and is wrong with slavery is the practice itself—the fact of some individuals being able to own other individuals and all that goes with that practice. It would not matter by what criterion individuals were assigned; human slavery would still be wrong. And the same can be said for most if not all of the other discrete practices and institutions which comprised the system of racial discrimination even after human slavery was abolished. The practices were unjustifiable—they were oppressive—and they would have been so no matter how the assignment of victims had been made. What made it worse, still, was that the institutions and the supporting ideology all interlocked to create a system of human oppression whose effects on those living under it were as devastating as they were unjustifiable.

Again, if there is anything wrong with the programs of preferential treatment that have begun to flourish within the past ten years, it should be evident that the social realities in respect to the distribution of resources and opportunities make the difference. Apart from everything else, there is simply no way in which all of these programs taken together could plausibly be viewed as capable of relegating white males to the kind of genuinely oppressive status characteristically bestowed upon women and blacks by the dominant social institutions and ideology.

The second objection is that preferential treatment programs are wrong because they take race or sex into account rather than the only thing that does matter—that is, an individual's qualifications. What all such programs have in common and what makes them all objectionable, so this argument goes, is that they ignore the persons who are more qualified by bestowing a preference on those who are less qualified in virtue of their being either black or female.

There are, I think, a number of things wrong with this objection based on qualifications, and not the least of them is that we do not live in a society in which there is even the serious pretense of a qualification requirement for many jobs of substantial power and authority. Should anyone claim, for example, that the persons who comprise the judiciary are there because they are the most qualified lawyers or the most qualified persons to be judges? Would anyone claim that Henry Ford II is the head of the Ford Motor Company because he is the most qualified person for the job? Part of what is wrong with even talking about qualifications and merit is that the

argument derives some of its force from the erroneous notion that we would have a meritocracy were it not for programs of preferential treatment. In fact, the higher one goes in terms of prestige, power and the like, the less qualifications seem ever to be decisive. It is only for certain jobs and certain places that qualifications are used to do more than establish the possession of certain minimum competencies.

But difficulties such as these to one side, there are theoretical difficulties as well, which cut much more deeply into the argument about qualifications. To begin with, it is important to see that there is a serious inconsistency present if the person who favors "pure qualifications" does so on the ground that the most qualified ought to be selected because this promotes maximum efficiency. Let us suppose that the argument is that if we have the most qualified performing the relevant tasks we will get those tasks done in the most economical and efficient manner. There is nothing wrong in principle with arguments based upon the good consequences that will flow from maintaining a social practice in a certain way. But it is inconsistent for the opponent of preferential treatment to attach much weight to qualifications on this ground, because it was an analogous appeal to the good consequences that the opponent of preferential treatment thought was wrong in the first place. That is to say, if the chief thing to be said in favor of strict qualifications and preferring the most qualified is that it is the most efficient way of getting things done, then we are right back to an assessment of the different consequences that will flow from different programs, and we are far removed from the considerations of justice or fairness that were thought to weigh so heavily against these programs.

It is important to note, too, that qualifications—at least in the educational context—are often not connected at all closely with any plausible conception of social effectiveness. To admit the most qualified students to law school, for example given the way qualifications are now determined—is primarily to admit those who have the greatest chance of scoring the highest grades at law school. This says little about efficiency except perhaps that these students are the easiest for the faculty to teach. However, since we know so little about what constitutes being a good, or even successful lawyer, and even less about the correlation between being a very good law student and being a very good lawyer, we can hardly claim very confidently that the legal system will operate most effectively if we admit only the most qualified students to law school.

To be at all decisive, the argument for qualifications must be that those who are the most qualified deserve to receive the benefits (the job, the place in law school, etc.) because they are the most qualified. The introduction of the concept of desert now makes it an objection as to justice or fairness of the sort promised by the original criticism of the programs. But now the problem is that there is no reason to think that there is any strong sense of "desert" in which it is correct that the most qualified deserve anything.

Let us consider more closely one case, that of preferential treatment in respect to admission to college or graduate school. There is a logical gap in the inference from the claim that a person is most qualified to perform a task, e.g., to be a good student, to the conclusion that he or she deserves to be admitted as a student. Of course, those who deserve to be admitted should be admitted. But why do the most qualified deserve anything? There is simply no necessary connection between academic merit (in the sense of being the most qualified) and deserving to be a member of a student body. Suppose, for instance, that there is only one tennis court in the community. Is it clear that the two best tennis players ought to be the ones permitted to use it? Why not those who were there first? Or those who will enjoy playing the most? Or those who are the worst and, therefore, need the greatest opportunity to practice? Or those who have the chance to play least frequently?

We might, of course, have a rule that says that the best tennis players get to use the court before the others. Under such a rule the best players would deserve the court more than the poorer ones. But that is just to push the inquiry back one stage. Is there any reason to think that we ought to have a rule giving good tennis players such a preference? Indeed, the arguments that might be given for or against such a rule are many and varied. And few if any of the arguments that might support the rule would depend upon a connection between ability and desert.

Someone might reply, however, that the most able students deserve to be admitted to the university because all of their earlier schooling was a kind of competition, with university admission being the prize awarded to the winners. They deserve to be admitted because that is what the rule of the competition provides. In addition, it might be argued, it would be unfair now to exclude them in favor of others, given the reasonable expectations they developed about the way in which their industry and performance would be rewarded. Minority-admission programs, which inevitably prefer some who are less qualified over some who are more qualified, all possess this flaw.

There are several problems with this argument. The most substantial of them is that it is an empirically implausible picture of our social world. Most of what are regarded as the decisive characteristics for higher education have a great deal to do with things over which the individual has neither control nor responsibility, such things as home environment, socioeconomic class of parents, and, of course, the quality of the primary and secondary schools attended. Since individuals do not deserve having had any of these things vis-à-vis other individuals, they do not, for the most part, deserve their qualifications. And since they do not deserve their abilities they do not in any strong sense deserve to be admitted because of their abilities.

To be sure, if there has been a rule which connects, say, performance at high school with admission to college, then there is a weak sense in which those who do well at high school deserve, for that reason alone, to be admitted to college. In addition, if persons have built up or relied upon their reasonable expectations concerning performance and admission, they have a claim to be admitted on this ground as well. But it is certainly not obvious that these claims of desert are any stronger or more compelling than the competing claims based upon the needs of or advantages to women or blacks from programs of preferential treatment. And as I have indicated, all rule-based claims of desert are very weak unless and until the rule which creates the claim is itself shown to be a justified one. Unless one has a strong preference for the status quo, and unless one can defend that preference, the practice within a system of allocating places in a certain way does not go very far at all in showing that that is the right or the just way to allocate those places in the future.

A proponent of programs of preferential treatment is not at all committed to the view that qualifications ought to be totally irrelevant. He or she can agree that, given the existing structure of an institution, there is probably some minimal set of qualifications without which one cannot participate meaningfully within the institution. In addition, it can be granted that the qualifications of those involved will affect the way the institution works and the way if affects others in the society. And the consequences will vary depending upon the particular institution. But all of this only establishes that qualifications, in this sense, are relevant, not that they are decisive. This is wholly consistent with the claim that race or sex should today also be relevant when it comes to matters such as admission to college or law school. And that is all that any preferential treatment program—even one with the kind of quota used in the *Bakke* case—has ever tried to do.

I have not attempted to establish that programs of preferential treatment are right and desirable. There are empirical issues concerning the consequences of these programs that I have not discussed, and certainly not settled. Nor, for that matter, have I considered the argument that justice may permit, if not require, these programs as a way to provide compensation or reparation for injuries suffered in the recent as well as distant past, or as a way to remove benefits that are undeservedly enjoyed by those of the dominant group. What I have tried to do is show that it is wrong to think that programs of preferential treatment are objectionable in the centrally important sense in which many past and present discriminatory features of our society have been and are racist and sexist. The social realities as to power and opportunity do make a fundamental difference. It is also wrong to think that programs of preferential treatment are in any strong sense either unjust or unprincipled. The case for programs of preferential treatment could, therefore, plausibly rest both on the view that such programs are not unfair to white males (except in the weak, rule-dependent sense described above) and on the view that it is unfair to continue the present set of unjust—often racist and sexist—institutions that comprise the social reality. And the case for these programs could rest as well on the proposition that, given the distribution of power and influence in the United States today, such programs may reasonably be viewed as potentially valuable, effective means by which to achieve admirable and significant social ideals of equality and integration.

Study Questions

1. Wasserstrom attacks two arguments that attempt to prove that preferential treatment programs are unfair. Briefly describe the first argument. How does Wasserstrom attack it? Do you think his criticism succeeds? Why? Defend your position.

2. How would Wasserstrom respond to Newton's claim that "the *same* injustice is done" [italics added] by affirmative action programs as by the discriminatory practices those programs are designed to eliminate? Assume that affirmative action programs are inherently evil. Are they just as evil as slavery, apartheid or Jim Crow laws, sexual harassment, or race/sex-based blackballing? Why? Defend your position.

3. Wasserstrom points out that slavery would still be wrong regardless of how slaves were selected (e.g., if slaves were selected randomly without racial or sexual preference). What does this show about the connection between the justness of a practice and racial/sexual preference? Explain.

4. Briefly describe the second argument which attempts to show that preferential treatment programs are unjust. How does Wasserstrom attack this argument? Is the attack successful? Why? Defend your position.

5. Should race, sex, state or country of origin, high school sports performance, or musical skills be considered by the admissions committee of a selective (non-open admissions) college, or do only the most academically qualified applicants deserve admission? Why? Does anyone *deserve* to go to college? Why? Does anyone *deserve* a job or promotion? Why? Defend your position.

What Is Wrong with Reverse Discrimination?

EDWIN C. HETTINGER

MANY PEOPLE THINK IT obvious that reverse discrimination is unjust. Calling affirmative action reverse discrimination itself suggests this. This discussion evaluates numerous reasons given for this alleged injustice. Most of these accounts of what is wrong with reverse discrimination are found to be deficient. The explanations for why reverse discrimination is morally troubling show only that it is unjust in a relatively weak sense. This result has an important consequence for the wider issue of the moral justifiability of affirmative action. If social policies which involve minor injustice are permissible (and perhaps required) when they are required in order to overcome much greater injustice, then the mild injustice of reverse discrimination is easily overridden by its contribution to the important social goal of dismantling our sexual and racial caste system.[1]

By 'reverse discrimination' or 'affirmative action' I shall mean hiring or admitting a slightly less well qualified woman or black, rather than a slightly more qualified white male,[2] for the purpose of helping to eradicate sexual and/or racial inequality, or for the purpose of compensating women and blacks for the burdens and injustices they have suffered due to past and ongoing sexism and racism.[3] There are weaker forms of affirmative action, such as giving preference to minority candidates only when qualifications are equal, or providing special educational opportunities for youths in disadvantaged groups. This paper seeks to defend the more controversial sort of reverse discrimination defined above. I begin by considering several spurious objections to reverse discrimination.

Edwin C. Hettinger, "What Is Wrong with Reverse Discrimination?" Business & Professional Ethics Journal, *vol. 6:3 (Fall 1987), pp. 39–55. Used by permission of the author.*

In the second part, I identify the ways in which this policy is morally troubling and then assess the significance of these negative features.

Spurious Objections

I. REVERSE DISCRIMINATION AS EQUIVALENT TO RACISM AND SEXISM

In a discussion on national television, George Will, the conservative news analyst and political philosopher, articulated the most common objection to reverse discrimination. It is unjust, he said, because it is discrimination on the basis of race or sex. Reverse discrimination against white males is the same evil as traditional discrimination against women and blacks. The only difference is that in this case it is the white male who is being discriminated against. Thus if traditional racism and sexism are wrong and unjust, so is reverse discrimination, and for the very same reasons.

But reverse discrimination is not at all like traditional sexism and racism. The motives and intentions behind it are completely different, as are its consequences. Consider some of the motives underlying traditional racial discrimination.[4] Blacks were not hired or allowed into schools because it was felt that contact with them was degrading, and sullied whites. These policies were based on contempt and loathing for blacks, on a feeling that blacks were suitable only for subservient positions and that they should never have positions of authority over whites. Slightly better qualified white males are not being turned down under affirmative action for any of these reasons. No defenders or practitioners of affirmative action (and no significant segment of the general public) thinks that contact with white males is degrading or sullying, that white males are contemptible and loathsome, or that white males—by their nature—should be subservient to blacks or women.

The consequences of these two policies differ radically as well. Affirmative action does not stigmatize white males; it does not perpetuate unfortunate stereotypes about white males; it is not part of a pattern of discrimination that makes being a white male incredibly burdensome.[5] Nor does it add to a particular group's "already overabundant supply" of power, authority, wealth, and opportunity, as does traditional racial and sexual discrimination.[6] On the contrary, it results in a more egalitarian distribution of these social and economic benefits. If the motives and consequences of reverse discrimination and of traditional racism and sexism are completely different, in what sense could they be morally equivalent acts? If acts are to be individuated (for moral purposes) by including the motives, intentions, and consequences in their description, then clearly these two acts are not identical.

It might be argued that although the motives and consequences are different, the act itself is the same: reverse discrimination is discrimination on the basis of race and sex, and this is wrong in itself independently of its motives or consequences. But discriminating (i.e., making distinctions in how one treats people) on the basis of race or sex is not always wrong, nor is it necessarily unjust. It is not wrong, for example, to discriminate against one's own sex when choosing a spouse. Nor is racial or sexual discrimination in hiring necessarily wrong. This is shown by Peter Singer's example in which a director of a play about ghetto conditions in New York City refuses to consider any white applicants for the actors because she wants the play to be authentic.[7] If I am looking for a representative of the black community, or doing a study about blacks and disease, it is perfectly legitimate to discriminate against all whites. Their whiteness makes them unsuitable for my (legitimate) purposes. Similarly, if I am hiring a wet-nurse, or a person to patrol the women's change rooms in my department store, discriminating against males is perfectly legitimate.

These examples show that racial and sexual discrimination are not wrong in themselves. This is not to say that they are never wrong; most often they clearly are. Whether or not they are wrong, however, depends on the purposes, consequences, and context of such discrimination.

2. RACE AND SEX AS MORALLY ARBITRARY AND IRRELEVANT CHARACTERISTICS

A typical reason given for the alleged injustice of all racial and sexual discrimination (including affirmative action) is that it is morally arbitrary to consider race or sex when hiring, since these characteristics are not relevant to the decision. But the above examples show that not all uses of race or sex as a criterion in hiring decisions are morally arbitrary or irrelevant. Similarly, when an affirmative action officer takes into account race and sex, use of these characteristics is not morally irrelevant or arbitrary. Since affirmative action aims to help end racial and sexual inequality by providing black and female role models for minorities (and non-minorities), the race and sex of the job candidates are clearly relevant to the decision. There is nothing arbitrary about the affirmative action officer focusing on race and sex. Hence, if reverse discrimination is wrong, it is not wrong for the reason that it uses morally irrelevant and arbitrary characteristics to distinguish between applicants.

3. REVERSE DISCRIMINATION AS UNJUSTIFIED STEREOTYPING

It might be argued that reverse discrimination involves judging people by alleged average characteristics of a class to which they belong, instead of judging them on the basis of their individual characteristics, and that such judging on the basis of stereotypes is unjust. But the defense of affirmative action suggested in this paper does not rely on stereotyping. When an employer hires a slightly less well qualified woman or black over a slightly more qualified white male for the purpose of helping to overcome sexual and racial inequality, she judges the applicants on the basis of their individual characteristics. She uses this person's sex or skin color as a mechanism to help achieve the goals of affirmative action. Individual characteristics of the white male (his skin color and sex) prevent him from serving one of the legitimate goals of employment policies, and he is turned down on

this basis.

Notice that the objection does have some force against those who defend reverse discrimination on the grounds of compensatory justice. An affirmative action policy whose purpose is to compensate women and blacks for past and current injustices judges that women and blacks on the average are owed greater compensation than are white males. Although this is true, opponents of affirmative action argue that some white males have been more severely and unfairly disadvantaged than some women and blacks.[8] A poor white male from Appalachia may have suffered greater undeserved disadvantages than the upper-middle class woman or black with whom he competes. Although there is a high correlation between being female (or being black) and being especially owed compensation for unfair disadvantages suffered, the correlation is not universal.

Thus defending affirmative action on the grounds of compensatory justice may lead to unjust treatment of white males in individual cases. Despite the fact that certain white males are owed greater compensation than are some women or blacks, it is the latter that receive compensation. This is the result of judging candidates for jobs on the basis of the average characteristics of their class, rather than on the basis of their individual characteristics. Thus compensatory justice defenses of reverse discrimination may involve potentially problematic stereotyping.[9] But this is not the defense of affirmative action considered here.

4. FAILING TO HIRE THE MOST QUALIFIED PERSON IS UNJUST

One of the major reasons people think reverse discrimination is unjust is because they think that the most qualified person should get the job. But why should the most qualified person be hired?

a. Efficiency. One obvious answer to this question is that one should hire the most qualified person because doing so promotes efficiency. If job qualifications are positively correlated with job performance, then the more qualified person will tend to do a better job. Although it is not always true that there is such a correlation, in general there is, and hence this point is well taken. There are short term efficiency costs of reverse discrimination as defined here.[10]

Note that a weaker version of affirmative action has no such efficiency costs. If one hires a black or woman over a white male only in cases where qualifications are roughly equal, job performance will not be affected. Furthermore, efficiency costs will be a function of the qualifications gap between the black or woman hired, and the white male rejected: the larger the gap, the greater the efficiency costs.[11] The existence of efficiency costs is also a function of the type of work performed. Many of the jobs in our society are ones which any normal person can do (e.g., assembly line worker, janitor, truck driver, etc.). Affirmative action hiring for these positions is unlikely to have significant efficiency costs (assuming whoever is hired is willing to work hard). In general, professional positions are the ones in which people's performance levels will vary significantly, and hence these are the jobs in which reverse discrimination could have significant efficiency costs.

While concern for efficiency gives us a reason for hiring the most qualified person, it in no way explains the alleged injustice suffered by the white male who is passed over due to reverse discrimination. If the affirmative action employer is treating the white male unjustly, it is not because the hiring policy is inefficient. Failing to maximize efficiency does not generally involve acting unjustly. For instance, a person who carries one bag of groceries at a time, rather than two, is acting inefficiently, though not unjustly.

It is arguable that the manager of a business who fails to hire the most qualified person (and thereby sacrifices some efficiency) treats the owners of the company unjustly, for their profits may suffer, and this violates one conception of the manager's fiduciary responsibility to the shareholders. Perhaps the administrator of a hospital who hires a slightly less well qualified black doctor (for the purposes of affirmative action) treats the future patients at that hospital unjustly, for doing so may reduce the level of health care they receive (and it is arguable that they have a legitimate expectation to receive the best health care possible for the money they spend). But neither of these examples of inefficiency leading to injustice concern the white male "victim" of affirmative action, and it is precisely this person who the opponents of reverse discrimination claim is being unfairly treated.

To many people, that a policy is inefficient is a sufficient reason for condemning it. This is especially true in the competitive and profit oriented world of business. However, profit maximization is not the only legitimate goal of business hiring policies (or other business decisions). Businesses have responsibilities to help heal society's ills, especially those (like racism and sexism) which they in large part helped to create and perpetuate. Unless one takes the implausible position that business' only legitimate goal is profit maximization, the efficiency costs of affirmative action are not an automatic reason for rejecting it. And as we have noted, affirmative action's efficiency costs are of no help in substantiating and explaining its alleged injustice to white males.

b. The Most Qualified Person Has a Right to the Job. One could argue that the most qualified person for the job has a right to be hired in virtue of superior qualifications. On this view, reverse discrimination violates the better qualified white male's right to be hired for the job. But the most qualified applicant holds no such right. If you are the best painter in town, and a person hires her brother to paint her house, instead of you, your rights have not been violated. People do not have rights to be hired for particular jobs (though I think a plausible case can be made for the claim that there is a fundamental human right to employment). If anyone has a right in this matter, it is the employer. This is not to say, of course, that the employer cannot do wrong in her hiring decision; she obviously can. If she hires a white because she loathes blacks, she does wrong. The point is that her wrong does not consist in violating the right some candidate has to her job (though this would violate other rights of the candidate).

c. The Most Qualified Person Deserves the Job. It could be argued that the most qualified person should get the job because she deserves it in virtue of her superior qualifications. But the assumption that the person most qualified for a job is the one who most deserves it is problematic. Very often people do not deserve their qualifications, and hence they do not deserve anything on the basis of those qualifications.[12] A person's qualifications are a function of at least the following factors: (a) innate abilities, (b) home environment, (c) socio-economic class of parents, (d) quality of the schools attended, (e) luck, and (f) effort or perseverance. A person is only responsible for the last factor on this list, and hence one only deserves one's qualifications to the extent that they are a function of effort.[13]

It is undoubtedly often the case that a person who is less well qualified for a job is more deserving of the job (because she worked harder to achieve those lower qualifications) than is someone with superior qualifications. This is frequently true of women and blacks in the job market: they worked harder to overcome disadvantages most (or all) white males never faced. Hence, affirmative action policies which permit the hiring of slightly less well qualified candidates may often be more in line with considerations of desert than are the standard meritocratic procedures.

The point is not that affirmative action is defensible because it helps insure that more deserving candidates get jobs. Nor is it that desert should be the only or even the most important consideration in hiring decisions. The claim is simply that hiring the most qualified person for a job need not (and quite often does not) involve hiring the most deserving candidate. Hence the intuition that morality requires one to hire the most qualified people cannot be justified on the grounds that these people deserve to be hired.[14]

d. The Most Qualified Person Is Entitled to the Job. One might think that although the most qualified person neither deserves the job nor has a right to the job, still this person is entitled to the job. By 'entitlement' in this context, I mean a natural and legitimate expectation based on a type of social promise. Society has implicitly encouraged the belief that the more qualified candidate will get the job. Society has set up a competition and the prize is a job which is awarded to those applying with the best qualifications. Society thus reneges on an implicit promise it has made to its members when it allows reverse discrimination to occur. It is dashing legitimate expectations it has encouraged. It is violating the very rules of a game it created.

Furthermore, the argument goes, by allowing reverse discrimination, society is breaking an explicit promise (contained in the Civil Rights Act of 1964) that it will not allow race or sex to be used against one of its citizens. Title VII of that Act prohibits discrimination in employment on the basis of race or sex (as well as color, religion, or national origin).

In response to this argument, it should first be noted that the above interpretation of the Civil Rights Act is misleading. In fact, the Supreme Court has interpreted the Act as allowing race and sex to be considered in hiring or admission decisions.[15] More importantly, since affirmative action has been an explicit national policy for the last twenty years (and has been supported in numerous court cases), it is implausible to argue that society has promised its members that it will not allow race or sex to outweigh superior qualifications in hiring decisions. In addition, the objection takes a naive and utopian view of actual hiring decisions. It presents a picture of our society as a pure meritocracy in which hiring decisions are based solely on qualifications. The only exception it sees to these meritocratic procedures is the unfortunate policy of affirmative action. But this picture is dramatically distorted. Elected government officials, political appointees, business managers, and many others clearly do not have their positions solely or even mostly because of their qualifications.[16] Given the widespread acceptance in our society of procedures which are far from meritocratic, claiming that the most qualified person has a socially endorsed entitlement to the job is not believable.

5. UNDERMINING EQUAL OPPORTUNITY FOR WHITE MALES

It has been claimed that the right of white males to an equal chance of employment is violated by affirmative action.[17] Reverse discrimination, it is said, undermines equality of opportunity for white males.

If equality of opportunity requires a social environment in which everyone at birth has roughly the same chance of succeeding through the use of his or her natural talents, then it could well be argued that given the social, cultural, and educational disadvantages placed on women and blacks, preferential treatment of these groups brings us closer to equality of opportunity. White males are full members of the community in a way in which women and blacks are not, and this advantage is diminished by affirmative action. Affirmative action takes away the greater than equal opportunity white males generally have, and thus it brings us closer to a situation in which all members of society have an equal chance of succeeding through the use of their talents.

It should be noted that the goal of affirmative action is to bring about a society in which there is equality of opportunity for women and blacks without preferential treatment of these groups. It is not the purpose of the sort of affirmative action defended here to disadvantage white males in order to take away the advantage a sexist and racist society gives to them. But noticing that this occurs is sufficient to dispel the illusion that affirmative action undermines the equality of opportunity for white males.[18]

Legitimate Objections

The following two considerations explain what is morally troubling about reverse discrimination.

I. JUDGING ON THE BASIS OF INVOLUNTARY CHARACTERISTICS

In cases of reverse discrimination, white males are passed over on the basis of membership in a group they were born into. When an affirmative action employer hires a slightly less well qualified black (or woman), rather than a more highly qualified white male, skin color (or sex) is being used as one criterion for determining who gets a very important benefit. Making distinctions in how one treats people on the basis of characteristics they cannot help having (such as skin color or sex) is morally problematic because it reduces individual autonomy. Discriminating between people on the basis of features they can do something about is preferable, since it gives them some control over how others act towards them. They can develop the characteristics others use to give them favorable treatment and avoid those characteristics others use as grounds for unfavorable treatment.[19]

For example, if employers refuse to hire you because you are a member of the American Nazi Party, and if you do not like the fact that you are having a hard time finding a job, you can choose to leave the party. However, if a white male is having trouble finding employment because slightly less well qualified women and blacks are being given jobs to meet affirmative action requirements, there is nothing he can do about this disadvantage, and his autonomy is curtailed.[20]

Discriminating between people on the basis of their involuntary characteristics is morally undesirable, and thus reverse discrimination is also morally undesirable. Of course, that something is morally undesirable does not show that it is unjust, nor that it is morally unjustifiable.

How morally troubling is it to judge people on the basis of involuntary characteristics? Notice that our society frequently uses these sorts of features to distinguish between people. Height and good looks are characteristics one cannot do much about, and yet basketball players and models are ordinarily chosen and rejected on the basis of precisely these features.

To a large extent our intelligence is also a feature beyond our control, and yet intelligence is clearly one of the major characteristics our society uses to determine what happens to people.

Of course there are good reasons why we distinguish between people on the basis of these sorts of involuntary characteristics. Given the goals of basketball teams, model agencies, and employers in general, hiring the taller, better looking, or more intelligent person (respectively) makes good sense. It promotes efficiency, since all these people are likely to do a better job. Hiring policies based on these involuntary characteristics serve the legitimate purposes of these businesses (e.g. profit and serving the public), and hence they may be morally justified despite their tendency to reduce the control people have over their own lives.

This argument applies to reverse discrimination as well. The purpose of affirmative action is to help eradicate racial and sexual injustice. If affirmative action policies help bring about this goal, then they can be morally justified despite their tendency to reduce the control white males have over their lives.

In one respect this sort of consequentialist argument is more forceful in the case of affirmative action. Rather than merely promoting the goal of efficiency (which is the justification for businesses hiring naturally brighter, taller, or more attractive individuals), affirmative action promotes the nonutilitarian goal of an egalitarian society. In general, promoting a consideration of justice (such as equality) is more important than is promoting efficiency or utility.[21] Thus in terms of the importance of the objective, this consequentialist argument is stronger in the case of affirmative action. If one can justify reducing individual autonomy on the grounds that it promotes efficiency, one can certainly do so on the grounds that it reduces the injustice of racial and sexual inequality.

2. BURDENING WHITE MALES WITHOUT COMPENSATION

Perhaps the strongest moral intuition concerning the wrongness of reverse discrimination is

that it is unfair to job seeking white males. It is unfair because they have been given an undeserved disadvantage in the competition for employment; they have been handicapped because of something that is not their fault. Why should white males be made to pay for the sins of others?

It would be a mistake to argue for reverse discrimination on the grounds that white males deserve to be burdened and that therefore we should hire women and blacks even when white males are better qualified.[22] Young white males who are now entering the job market are not more responsible for the evils of racial and sexual inequality than are other members of society. Thus, reverse discrimination is not properly viewed as punishment administered to white males.

The justification for affirmative action supported here claims that bringing about sexual and racial equality necessitates sacrifice on the part of white males who seek employment. An important step in bringing about the desired egalitarian society involves speeding up the process by which women and blacks get into positions of power and authority. This requires that white males find it harder to achieve these same positions. But this is not punishment for deeds done.

Thomas Nagel's[23] helpful analogy is state condemnation of property under the right of eminent domain for the purpose of building a highway. Forcing some in the community to move in order that the community as a whole may benefit is unfair. Why should these individuals suffer rather than others? The answer is: Because they happen to live in a place where it is important to build a road. A similar response should be given to the white male who objects to reverse discrimination with the same "Why me?" question. The answer is: Because job seeking white males happen to be in the way of an important road leading to the desired egalitarian society. Job-seeking white males are being made to bear the brunt of the burden of affirmative action because of accidental considerations, just as are homeowners whose property is used in order to build a highway.

This analogy is extremely illuminating and helpful in explaining the nature of reverse discrimination. There is, however, an important dissimilarity that Nagel does not mention. In cases of property condemnation, compensation is paid to the owner. Affirmative action policies, however, do not compensate white males for shouldering this burden of moving toward the desired egalitarian society. So affirmative action is unfair to job seeking white males because they are forced to bear an unduly large share of the burden of achieving racial and sexual equality without being compensated for this sacrifice. Since we have singled out job seeking white males from the larger pool of white males who should also help achieve this goal, it seems that some compensation from the latter to the former is appropriate.[24]

This is a serious objection to affirmative action policies only if the uncompensated burden is substantial. Usually it is not. Most white male victims of affirmative action easily find employment. It is highly unlikely that the same white male will repeatedly fail to get hired because of affirmative action.[25] The burdens of affirmative action should be spread as evenly as possible among all the job seeking white males. Furthermore, the burden job seeking white males face—of finding it somewhat more difficult to get employment—is inconsequential when compared to the burdens ongoing discrimination places on women and blacks.[26] Forcing job seeking white males to bear an extra burden is acceptable because this is a necessary step toward achieving a much greater reduction in the unfair burdens our society places on women and blacks. If affirmative action is a necessary mechanism for a timely dismantlement of our racial and sexual caste system, the extra burdens it places on job seeking white males are justified.

Still the question remains: Why isn't compensation paid? When members of society who do not deserve extra burdens are singled out to sacrifice for an important community goal, society owes them compensation. This objection loses

some of its force when one realizes that society continually places undeserved burdens on its members without compensating them. For instance, the burden of seeking efficiency is placed on the shoulders of the least naturally talented and intelligent. That one is born less intelligent (or otherwise less talented) does not mean that one deserves to have reduced employment opportunities, and yet our society's meritocratic hiring procedures make it much harder for less naturally talented members to find meaningful employment. These people are not compensated for their sacrifices either.

Of course, pointing out that there are other examples of an allegedly problematic social policy does not justify that policy. Nonetheless, if this analogy is sound, failing to compensate job-seeking white males for the sacrifices placed on them by reverse discrimination is not without precedent. Furthermore, it is no more morally troublesome than is failing to compensate less talented members of society for their undeserved sacrifice of employment opportunities for the sake of efficiency.

Conclusion

This article has shown the difficulties in pinpointing what is morally troubling about reverse discrimination. The most commonly heard objections to reverse discrimination fail to make their case. Reverse discrimination is not morally equivalent to traditional racism and sexism since its goals and consequences are entirely different, and the act of treating people differently on the basis of race or sex is not necessarily morally wrong. The race and sex of the candidates are not morally irrelevant in all hiring decisions, and affirmative action hiring is an example where discriminating on the basis of race or sex is not morally arbitrary. Furthermore, affirmative action can be defended on grounds that do not involve stereotyping. Though affirmative action hiring of less well qualified applicants can lead to short run inefficiency, failing to hire the most qualified applicant does not violate this person's rights, entitlements, or deserts. Additionally, affirmative action hiring does not generally undermine equal opportunity for white males. Reverse discrimination is morally troublesome in that it judges people on the basis of involuntary characteristics and thus reduces the control they have over their lives. It also places a larger than fair share of the burden of achieving an egalitarian society on the shoulders of job seeking white males without compensating them for this sacrifice. But these problems are relatively minor when compared to the grave injustice of racial and sexual inequality, and they are easily outweighed if affirmative action helps alleviate this far greater injustice.[27]

NOTES

I thank Cheshire Calhoun, Beverly Diamond, John Dickerson, Jasper Hunt, Glenn Lesses, Richard Nunan, and Martin Perlmutter for helpful comments.

1. Thomas Nagel uses the phrase "racial caste system" in his illuminating testimony before the Subcommittee on the Constitution of the Senate Judiciary Committee, on June 18, 1981. This testimony is reprinted as "A Defense of Affirmative Action" in Ethical Theory and Business, 2nd edition, ed. Tom Beauchamp and Norman Bowie (Englewood Cliffs, NJ: Prentice-Hall 1983), pp. 483-487.

2. What should count as qualifications is controversial. By 'qualifications' I refer to such things as grades, test scores, prior experience, and letters of recommendation. I will not include black skin or female sexism in my use of 'qualification,' though there are strong arguments for counting these as legitimate qualifications (in the sense of characteristics which would help the candidate achieve the legitimate goals of the hiring or admitting institution). For these arguments see Ronald Dworkin, "Why Bakke Has No Case," The New York Review of Books, November 10th, 1977.

3. This paper assumes the controversial premise that we live in a racist and sexist society. Statistics provide immediate and powerful support for this claim. The fact that blacks comprise 12% of the U.S. population, while comprising a minuscule percentage of those in positions of power and authority, is sufficient evidence that our society continues to be significantly racist in results, if not in intent. Unless one assumes that blacks are innately less able to attain, or less desirous of attaining these positions

to a degree that would account for this huge underrepresentation, one must conclude that our social organizations significantly disadvantage blacks. This is (in part) the injustice that I call racism. The argument for the charge of sexism is analogous (and perhaps even more persuasive given that women comprise over 50% of the population). For more supporting evidence, see Tom Beauchamp's article "The Justification of Reverse Discrimination in Hiring" in Ethical Theory and Business, pp. 495-506.

4. Although the examples in this paper focus more on racism than on sexism, it is not clear that the former is a worse problem than is the latter. In many ways, sexism is a more subtle and pervasive form of discrimination. It is also less likely to be acknowledged.

5. This is Paul Woodruff's helpful definition of unjust discrimination. See Paul Woodruff, "What's Wrong With Discrimination," Analysis, vol. 36, no. 3, 1976, pp. 158-160.

6. This point is made by Richard Wasserstrom in his excellent article "A Defense of Programs of Preferential Treatment," National Forum (The Phi Kappa Phi Journal), vol. viii, no. 1 (Winter 1978), pp. 15-18. The article is reprinted in Social Ethics, 2nd edition, ed. Thomas Mappes and Jane Zembaty (New York: McGraw-Hill, 1982), pp. 187-191. The quoted phrase is Wasserstrom's.

7. Peter Singer, "Is Racial Discrimination Arbitrary?" Philosophia, vol. 8 (November 1978), pp. 185-203.

8. See, for example, Robert Simon, "Preferential Hiring: A Reply to Judith Jarvis Thomson," Philosophy and Public Affairs, vol. 3, no. 3 (Spring 1974).

9. If it is true (and it is certainly plausible) that every black or woman, no matter how fortunate, has suffered from racism and sexism in a way in which no white male has suffered from racism and sexism, then compensation for this injustice would be owed to all and only blacks and women. Given this, arguing for affirmative action on the grounds of compensatory justice would not involve judging individuals by average features of classes of which they are members. Still it might be argued that for certain blacks and women such injustices are not nearly as severe as the different type of injustice suffered by some white males. Thus one would have to provide a reason for why we should compensate (with affirmative action) any black or woman before any white male. Perhaps administrative convenience is such a reason. Being black or female (rather than white and male) correlates nicely with the property of being more greatly and unfairly disadvantaged, and thus race and sex are useful rough guidelines for determining who most

needs compensation. This does, however, involve stereotyping.

10. In the long run, however, reverse discrimination may actually promote overall societal efficiency by breaking down the barriers to a vast reservoir of untapped potential in women and blacks.

11. See Thomas Nagel, "A Defense of Affirmative Action," p. 484.

12. This is Wasserstrom's point. See "A Defense of Programs of Preferential Treatment," in *Social Ethics,* p. 190.

13. By 'effort' I intend to include (1) how hard a person tries to achieve certain goals, (2) the amount of risk voluntarily incurred in seeking these goals, and (3) the degree to which moral considerations play a role in choosing these goals. The harder one tries, the more one is willing to sacrifice, and the worthier the goal, the greater are one's deserts. For support of the claim that voluntary past action is the only valid basis for desert, see James Rachels, "What People Deserve," in *Justice and Economic Distribution,* ed. John Arthur and William Shaw (Englewood Cliffs, NJ: Prentice-Hall, 1978), pp. 150–163.

14. It would be useful to know if there is a correlation between the candidate who is most deserving (because she worked the hardest) and the one with the best qualifications. In other words, are better qualified candidates in general those who worked harder to achieve their qualifications? Perhaps people who have the greatest natural abilities and the most fortunate social circumstances will be the ones who worked the hardest to develop their talents. This raises the possibility, suggested by John Rawls, that the ability to put forward effort is itself a function of factors outside a person's control. See his *A Theory of Justice* (Cambridge, MA: Harvard University Press, 1971), pp. 103–104. But if anything is under a person's control and hence is something a person is responsible for, it is how hard she tries. Thus if there is an appropriate criterion for desert, it will include how much effort a person exerts.

15. See Justice William Brennan's majority opinion in *United Steel Workers and Kaiser Aluminum* v. *Weber,* United States Supreme Court, 443 U.S. 193 (1979). See also Justice Lewis Powell's majority opinion in *University of California* v. *Bakke,* United States Supreme Court, 438 U.S. 265 (1978).

16. This is Wasserstrom's point. See "A Defense of Programs of Preferential Treatment," p. 189.

17. This is Judith Thomson's way of characterizing the alleged injustice. See "Preferential Hiring," *Philosophy and Public Affairs,* vol 2, no. 4 (Summer 1973).

18. If it is true that some white males are more severely disadvantaged in our society than are some women and blacks, affirmative action would increase the inequality of opportunity for these white males. But since these individuals are a small minority of white males, the overall result of affirmative action would be to move us closer toward equality of opportunity.

19. James Rachels makes this point in "What People Deserve," p. 159. Joel Feinberg has also discussed related points. See his *Social Philosophy* (Englewood Cliffs, NJ: Prentice-Hall, 1973), p. 108.

20. He could work harder to get better qualifications and hope that the qualifications gap between him and the best woman or black would become so great that the efficiency cost of pursuing affirmative action would be prohibitive. Still he can do nothing to get rid of the disadvantage (in affirmative action contexts) of being a white male.

21. For a discussion of how considerations of justice typically outweigh considerations of utility, see Manuel Velasquez, *Business Ethics* (Englewood Cliffs, NJ: Prentice-Hall, 1982), Chapter Two.

22. On the average, however, white males have unfairly benefited from the holding back of blacks and women, and hence it is not altogether inappropriate that this unfair benefit be removed.

23. Nagel, "A Defense of Affirmative Action," p. 484.

24. It would be inappropriate to extract compensation from women or blacks since they are the ones who suffer the injustice affirmative action attempts to alleviate.

25. This is a potential worry, however, and so it is important to insure that the same white male does not repeatedly sacrifice for the goals of affirmative action.

26. Cheshire Calhoun reminded me of this point.

27. Of course one must argue that reverse discrimination is effective in bringing about an egalitarian society. There are complicated consequentialist arguments both for and against this claim, and I have not discussed them here. Some of the questions to be addressed are: (1) How damaging is reverse discrimination to the self-esteem of blacks and women? (2) Does reverse discrimination promote racial and sexual strife more than it helps to alleviate them? (3) Does it perpetuate unfortunate stereotypes about blacks and women? (4) How long are we justified in waiting to pull blacks and women into the mainstream of our social life? (5) What sorts of alternative mechanisms are possible and politically practical for achieving affirmative action goals (for instance, massive early educational funding for children from impoverished backgrounds)?

Study Questions

1. How does Hettinger define reverse discrimination/affirmative action? Give an example. What does Hettinger mean by "weaker forms" of affirmative action (that he is not interested in discussing)? Give an example.

2. In what ways does reverse discrimination differ from racism and sexism, according to Hettinger? Do you think that Hettinger succeeds in showing that reverse discrimination is *not* "just as bad" as racism and sexism? Why? Defend your position.

3. What is the compensatory justice defense of affirmative action? Does Hettinger think that this defense is successful? Explain.

4. Briefly state the five traditional reasons listed by Hettinger for why it is unfair not to hire the most qualified person for a job. Does Hettinger think any of these reasons prove that affirmative action programs are unfair? Explain. Do you agree with Hettinger? Why? Defend your position.

5. What does Hettinger believe *is* morally problematic with affirmative action? How serious is the wrong, in Hettinger's view? Do you agree? Why? Defend your position.

6. Explain Thomas Nagel's eminent domain example. Is his reasoning utilitarian or deontological? Explain.

Case 9.1

THE HEADHUNTER AND THE SHOO-FLY[1]

You find it hard to believe. It is the beginning of your 21st week of police training. It's all downhill from here. You graduate a week from Friday. Nothing to do now but listen to the various supervisors from your department tell you about the policy and procedure manual. No more tests, no more pressure. In less than two weeks, you'll be sworn in and, although you will be a rookie, you will no longer be a trainee. You are really looking forward to graduation. While you don't know for sure, you think you might be graduating #1 and just might have been voted the top police trainee by the members of your class. Quite an honor. You managed to get along with everyone: classmates, training advisors, and instructors. No hint of being a "brown-nose" or company person.

When you arrive home at the end of the day, the following message is on your answering machine:

"This is Captain Kabat of Internal Affairs. I'll expect you in my office at 8:00 A.M. tomorrow morning."

You wonder what you did. A trip to Internal Affairs could only mean one thing. The Headhunters were out to get you. You know that, until you are off probation, you serve at the will of the Chief of Police. Any conduct they don't like, anything from being arrested to looking at your sergeant the wrong way, can get you fired. No reason, no explanation, no excuses. You do not sleep much that night.

You arrive at Internal Affairs at 7:30 the next morning. The 30 minutes spent outside the Captain's office seem like 30 years. Finally, the door opens and Kabat motions you into his office.

"First off, you are not in any kind of trouble."

You feel the tension drain from your body and start to relax for the first time since last night.

"In fact, we need your help."

"Yes, sir." You wonder what they could possibly need you for.

"Once in a while, we spot what we feel to be an outstanding police trainee in an academy class. This trainee, we feel, deserves our special attention. He is one who will go far in this department and, at the same time, can be a help to us."

"Yes, sir."

"You're being assigned to II Platoon B Squad after your graduation. The squad is supervised by Sgt. Betty Wyn. While she has never violated any department policy, some of the *men* on the squad have some serious reservations about her ability to supervise them, *if you know what I mean*."

"Yes, sir." You are beginning to think you are a broken record.

"All you are to do is watch her. Make notes. We will talk on the phone every so often. I want to know everything she does."

"Yes, sir."

Within six months, you have accumulated enough minor and/or technical violations of department policy to get her demoted back to patrol officer. She resigns shortly thereafter.

Three weeks later, you are again called into Captain Kabat's office.

"You're being transferred to III Platoon A Squad. The squad is supervised by Sgt. Sam Skelton. While he has never violated any department policy, some of the *white men* on the squad have some serious reservations about his ability to supervise them, *if you know what I mean*."

"Yes, sir."

Note

1. "Headhunter" is a term that describes a police officer who works in internal affairs and investigates police misconduct.

Questions for Discussion

1. What forces acted on this recruit officer that led him to his decision?
2. What types of discrimination are readily identifiable in this case?
3. Speculate on Kabat's motivation.
4. Should the rookie officer go over the Captain's head? If so, how? If not, why not?

Case 9.2

PRACTICAL JOKING, INITIATION, DISCRIMINATION, OR HAZING?

Chief Samantha Clinton was a good cop. She started as a patrol*man* when the prevailing attitude of the department was that women police officers were only good as secretaries, matrons, or juvenile officers. Unlike her fellow officers of the class of '64, she had to prove herself. A female officer was presumed to be incapable of doing the job of patrol*man*. That is why they called the position patrol*man*. The male officers were assumed to be capable of doing the job and had to prove that they couldn't.

It started the very first day on the job. Her field training officer (FTO) gave her the keys to the squad car and told her to inventory the trunk—check for flares, first aid kit, etc. As the light came on in the trunk, the first thing she saw was a very large snake. She was not sure who was more startled. Fortunately, she recognized the critter as a rat snake—ugly, but harmless. She gently picked it up and walked back into the station, handed it to her somewhat startled FTO, and returned to her inventory duties—all to the amusement of the other officers.

That wasn't the last time she was a "victim" of squad antics. But she noticed that she was not the only one. All the rookies were victims. In a sense, it was a rite of passage. A snake in the trunk, being sent to maintenance for a sawdust pump, told to go to the gun shop for a "group tightener" to put on the end of the service weapon to improve shooting, shaving cream in the hat just prior to inspection, etc. She noticed another thing. The officers who took the jokes in stride were readily accepted; those who complained were not. While she was not sure if this was right, she put up with it, the jokes subsided, and she was accepted as a member of the squad. As the years passed, she even became an active participant in setting up the rookies. Even as a sergeant and later a lieutenant, she would look the other way at these breaks in the tension. Funny thing, she noticed, these practical jokes never interfered with the work of the squad. They did a good job and were productive. The jokes always came during a slow time or as a release after a particularly stressful event.

When Clinton was promoted to chief of police, she had to deal with many of the same old prejudices among her peers. She was the first female chief of a large metropolitan area and was again breaking new ground. In addition to the usual duties of a chief of police, the city manager was concerned that the department was substantially under-represented with respect to minorities. In fact, minority officers represented only about 3% of the department, and of 300 officers, only one sergeant was African-American, one Hispanic. She was the only female above the rank of patrol officer.

She spent the next four years recruiting qualified minority candidates and at the start of the fifth year minorities were well represented in the department. But there was a problem.

For the past several months, there has been an undercurrent of dissent among the members of the African-American Law Enforcement Officers Association (AALEOA) and the Hispanic-American Law Enforcement Officers Association

(HALEOA). They have alleged, and at least one independent study has confirmed, that there is an undercurrent of racism among the command officers and supervisors in the department. In response to this concern, Chief Clinton initiated a series of in-service training seminars focused on cultural diversity and sensitivity. Each officer of the department has completed at least 16 hours of training.

However, members of AALEOA and HALEOA continue to voice their concern that they are discriminated against and not accepted by supervisors and command officers. Further, some allege that they have been the victims of various "pranks" by senior officers and supervisors.

Some of her supervisors and command officers have hinted to her that the pranks and other assignments are not racially based, that this is the rite of passage suffered by all new police officers. The members of AALEOA and HALEOA (all junior officers hired in the last four years) are equally convinced that the problems are racially motivated.

Questions for Discussion

1. In your view, is the activity practical joking, initiation, discrimination, or hazing? Explain.
2. Is there a possibility that morale would be lower/higher/stay the same if this activity was stopped?
3. Speculate on the value and use of humor as a means of stress relief where the humor involves humiliation of a fellow officer.

Case 9.3

TWO PREGNANT TEENAGERS

You are a probation officer in a Midwestern juvenile court.

JULIA

Julia is a 15-year-old female offender on your caseload. Julia has become pregnant. Both Julia and her mother agree that an abortion is the most suitable alternative.

According to the social work code of ethics, a social worker should show respect for the rights and prerogatives of clients and make every effort to foster maximum self-determination on the part of the client. You, however, do not favor abortion.

DONNA

Donna is a 16-year-old, female juvenile offender on your caseload. She has recently become pregnant.

Donna's mother will not give Donna specific permission for an abortion, but will not stand in the way of her obtaining one. The mother sees nothing wrong with her daughter having a child. Donna's mother had her first child at the age of 16 and another child would increase the welfare payment to the home.

Donna wants an abortion. She has made significant progress in accepting how she got involved in delinquency and is making changes in her life. Within the past year, she has greatly improved her school attendance and grades. She is now working part-time after school and hopes to attend a junior college after her high school graduation next year. Donna can see from her own childhood that teenage girls are not capable and mature enough to raise a child. Donna has been exposed to sexual behavior from an early age—seeing her mother prostitute herself, and being sexually molested at the ages of 5 and 11 by her father and her mother's boyfriend, respectively.

You feel that if the pregnancy is carried to term, Donna will be pressured to keep the child. This, you feel, would destroy this young girl's life and would destroy all that you have tried so hard to achieve.

You know that Donna could obtain a legal abortion without the consent of her mother by petitioning the juvenile court judge in her county of residence.

There are two juvenile court judges in the district. One listens to all the evidence before deciding whether to grant an adolescent an abortion: the circumstances, competency, and the maturity of the youth. The other does not believe in abortion under any circumstances, not only refusing to grant any abortion, but refusing to invoke a self-disqualification in any choice hearings as provided by state law.

You feel an abortion is in Donna's best interest.

Questions for Discussion

Julia

1. Must you respect and approve of the client's wishes?

2. Must you provide specific information on how to obtain an abortion when the client does not have this information?

3. Must the social worker arrange for the abortion when the client is unable to do so for herself (the client has no telephone, no transportation to a clinic 60 miles away, and no knowledge of resources)?

Donna

1. Should you divulge the legal avenues for an abortion to Donna?

2. Could this be perceived to be "in the best interests of the child" even if it violates the wishes of the mother and the judge?

3. Should you attempt to intervene in the scheduling of the court hearing in order to be assigned the judge who will listen and evaluate the case fairly?

4. Are you allowing the court to "fairly" do its job?

Both

1. Should the probation officer be required to do everything in his/her power to fulfill the client's wishes?

2. What is more important (or what should be more important), respecting the rights and prerogatives of your clients, or your own?

Case 9.4

SHOOT 'TIL YOU WIN

The weapons qualification rules at your state's corrections training academy have been the same for years. Students are given two days of instruction and practice in the firing of a 12-gauge shotgun and a .38 special revolver. Then the students are given three opportunities to qualify on the range. Those who are not able to score the minimum number of points after three attempts will be dismissed from the academy and barred from reapplying for one year.

Students at the academy, up until about six months ago, have been about 95% male, with the few female students going on to work in the state's only institution for female inmates. However, a recent Federal Circuit Court ruling mandated that female corrections officers be permitted to work in male institutions. As a result, the number of female students at the academy has increased a great deal, as have your problems as the chief range instructor.

Before this most recent ruling, it was quite rare for any students, male or female, to fail the weapons qualification course. Since the court order (unfortunately), there have been over a dozen dismissals from the academy for lack of a qualifying score, all female trainees. You know that you will hear more about this trend. The Monday morning following the latest dismissal, you do.

Ed Johnson, the assistant director of the academy, summons you to his office. He comes right to the point.

"The special master (the representative of the federal court responsible for monitoring the state's compliance with court orders) is not very happy about these latest dismissals. He implied that we are sandbagging, that we are using the weapons qualification thing to slow down the hiring of female corrections officers. Worse yet, he said that if the number of these dismissals does not decrease dramatically, and soon, he will come to the academy and personally review our weapons qualification program."

You explain to Johnson that you are not at all afraid of having an outside review of your program. You genuinely feel that your program is tightly and accurately run and that it is extremely fair to the participating students.

"That's not the point," Johnson replies. "The fact of the matter is I don't want this special master guy down here. I don't want it to appear that we are in any way trying to buck the court order."

After a moment of silence, you ask Johnson, "What should I do?"

"Look," he continues, "you and I both know that the state has made an all-out effort to recruit female corrections officers since the court order. Maybe it is a cultural thing, I don't know, but a lot of these people are just not as 'familiarized' with the weapons as men."

You respond that, in your opinion, the two-day training period is more than enough for this "familiarization."

"I tend to agree," Johnson replies. "Besides, our director would probably not allow us to spend more money on additional training time."

After another moment of silence, you again ask Johnson what he expects of you.

Johnson is hesitant. "Think about ... 'modifying' the minimum passing score for female students."

"Lowering it?" you ask.

"Modifying it," he replies. "Consider also allowing the female students a 'sufficient' number of qualification attempts."

"More than three?" you ask.

"Whatever is sufficient," he replies.

Then, almost as if on cue, Johnson's intercom buzzes and he is summoned to an "urgent" meeting with the institution's communications director.

"Be back in my office at three," he says. "We will talk then."

You know what Johnson will want to hear at your next meeting. You also truly believe that implementing his suggestions would constitute a genuine disservice to the men and women who have worked hard to qualify and to the profession itself. You have about four hours to think about it.

Questions for Discussion

1. What would you do? Justify your decision.
2. Firearms ability is a physical ability. Some states have dual physical ability standards, one for males and one for females. In your view, is this fair? Why? Defend your position.
3. Is there ever any justification for a double standard? Explain.

Case 9.5

ZIG-ZAGGED

Your dilemma originated in another institution and the initial scandal was dying down before your current problems began. It all started with the revelation that several white officers in your state's maximum security institution were actively involved in the "White Lightning Brotherhood," an extremely racist (anti-black, anti-Semitic) organization. The affair was extensively covered by the news media, and the identifying mark of the group, a lightning bolt tattoo on the back of the hand, became a familiar sight in print and on television. Most of the officers involved in the group lost their jobs, and the Department of Corrections has since taken great pains to strongly reassert its position against racism.

Your workplace, Monroe Correctional Institution (M.C.I.), remained largely unaffected by the scandal until two weeks ago last Monday, the day Officer Duncan reported to work with his new tattoo. Officer Duncan had been to a "ZZ Top" concert that weekend and was a great a fan of the group. He was such a fan that, after the concert and a few beers, he went to the local tattoo parlor and had the official logo of the group, a stylized "ZZ," tattooed on his lower arm. He was proud of his tattoo, a visible sign of his admiration of his favorite musical group.

Officer Duncan's tattoo was plainly visible, and when he came to work that first day, he enjoyed showing it to his fellow officers. He was assigned to Three Dorm that day and, as was usual in that job, worked in close proximity to several African-American inmates. None of them commented on his tattoo, if they noticed it at all.

His tattoo was observed later that day, however, by Major Fuddle, the chief of security at M.C.I. Major Fuddle, a temperamental and rather abrasive man, was nearing retirement. He had an honorable career in corrections. The only flaw in his record were charges that he had, in the past, held racist views and had tolerated racist behavior among his staff. He had even been disciplined for this (several years ago), and he was now very anxious to "stay clean" on this subject until he could "slide" into retirement. When the major saw Duncan's tattoo, he saw only lightning bolts. He also saw an ungrateful bastard of an employee who was trying to ruin his career and thwart his retirement plans. He loudly gave Officer Duncan a direct order to have the tattoo removed "yesterday" and then angrily stalked off to his office. Officer Duncan, stunned as he was by this outburst, was able to collect his thoughts enough to contact his union steward, who then spoke to the major and other members of the administration.

The next day, Major Fuddle and Institutional Inspector Burns, along with Officer Grey, Duncan's steward, came to your office. Burns began.

"Warden, the best we can do in this situation is to give Duncan two weeks to remove the tattoo. During that time, he would be assigned to outside posts with no inmate contact. If the tattoo is not removed in those two weeks, we believe Duncan should be terminated."

Officer Grey then spoke. "I'm sure you are aware, sir, that Officer Duncan's tattoo is a representation of two Zs, not a lightning bolt."

"It looks like two damn lightning bolts!" huffed the major.

"And," continued Officer Grey, "it is located on his lower forearm and not on the back of his hand."

"I agree," replied Burns, "that Duncan's tattoo does not look exactly like the ones in the newspapers. But in my opinion, it is similar enough to be possibly interpreted as a racist symbol and could lead to problems in this institution."

"And make us look like hell," added Major Fuddle.

Officer Grey spoke again. "You know sir, that Officer Duncan doesn't have a racist bone in his body. He is a good officer, loves rock 'n roll and his family, and is probably uninterested enough in current events to have never even heard of the White Lightning Brotherhood."

You nod in agreement, knowing Officer Duncan, and knowing this to be true.

"Look sir," Officer Grey concludes, "Duncan really wants to keep that tattoo, but he also wants, and needs, to keep his job. He will do what he is told, but please try to be fair to him and not react hastily to a hypothetical threat to the institution's security. Let him keep his tattoo."

"Our position remains firm," Burns replies.

"Damn right," adds the major as the meeting concludes.

So now you, as the warden, must make a decision in the matter. You want to do the right thing *and* be fair.

Questions for Discussion

1. Why should Fuddle be concerned in light of the fact that the tattoo was not apparently offensive to the inmates who saw it?

2. Do you think that the major was overreacting?

3. If you were the warden, what would your decision be? Explain.

Chapter 10

The Institution: Criminal Justice Administration

MANAGEMENT THEORISTS AND SPECIALISTS IN ORGANIZATIONAL behavior regularly point out that their field of inquiry is general, rather than limited to businesses, as is often thought. The management of a business, a corrections agency, a county court system, a not-for-profit foundation, and a university all share a similar range of features and problems. They all face short-term tactical problem-solving issues just as they require long-range strategic planning. All organizations have information systems. They all face problems of income-generation and budgeting, as well as the attendant problems of marketing and public relations. A law enforcement agency must meet payroll and deal with labor issues just as surely as any business. Several problems specific to the employment area were examined in Chapter 9.

Ethical issues that arise in the context of the management of an organization are thus already familiar. In looking at specific cases, however, the assumption has already been made that organizations, as well as individuals in organizations, can be said to have moral responsibilities. While this assumption may appear to be obviously true, many philosophers have challenged the idea that the actions of any organization, *per se,* are subject to moral appraisal. John Ladd, for example, argues that bureaucratic organizations are constructed by people to help them accomplish certain goals.[1] According to this view, decisions may be attributed to the organization itself, rather than to a collection of individuals, and hence may be assessed solely in terms of the policies and principles that constitute the organization. Ladd says, "If we think of an organization as a machine, it is easy to see why we cannot reasonably expect it to have any moral obligations to people or for them to have any to it."[2] On the other hand, if an organization can be held to be morally responsible, apart from the actions of the persons who make up the organization, it must also have moral rights of some sort. Such a view could be based on the premise that moral duties and moral rights are inseparable: it is impossible to assign one without assigning the other. Others might object to this line of reasoning by pointing to alleged cases of owners of moral rights who have no moral duties, e.g., babies and young children, or even animals.

While the philosophical literature at this time has been concerned primarily with the question of the moral responsibilities of businesses, there appears to be no reason why such discussions do not bear directly on other organizations, including those that make up the criminal justice system. Ladd's paper, for instance, deals with the general category of bureaucratic organizations, both private and public. There does not appear to be a moral difference between a corporation that engages in racially discriminatory hiring and a corrections agency that engages in the same discriminatory actions. Is there an important difference between corporate officers who knowingly design, manufacture, and market a product that exposes the buyer to a deadly hazard and a prison in which physical and mental brutality are deliberately employed by prison administrators, as Elizabeth Baro reported in Chapter 7? If Ford Motor Company were a state-owned cooperative allegedly working to the benefit of the public, would the marketing of the Pinto be any less wrong?

The moral assessment of the actions of agencies of the state seems just as defensible as the moral assessment of corporate actions. If we assume for the sake of argument that organizations can be moral agents of some sort, what features should we expect to find? Thomas Donaldson, speaking of corporations, says that

> In order to qualify as a moral agent, a corporation would need to embody *a process of moral decision-making.* . . . this process seems to require, at a minimum:
>
>   1. The capacity to use moral reasons in decision-making.
>   2. The capacity of the decision-making process to control not only overt corporate acts, but also the structure of policies and rules.[3]

The presence of a decision-making process is crucial here. Ladd's conception of the formal organization as a machine means that decision-making *per se* is strictly limited by the policies and rules that define the goals of the organization. Thus, a purely mechanical decision-making process, which allows only certain types of considerations to enter into the analysis, is not what Donaldson has in mind. Decision-making in the sense of moral agency must allow *all* considerations into the mix, including moral considerations, and it must allow for the possibility of redefining policies and goals. This is the point of the second requirement quoted above.

An organization that behaves as "a well-oiled machine" is thus not a good model for morally responsible conduct. This does not mean that organizations that can be correctly viewed as moral agents will be poorly managed or chaotic and unpredictable. It does mean that the central issue of discretion, which was introduced in Chapter 3 at the level of individual action, is also characteristic of administrative decision-making.

For any organization, the moral problems that are often closest to home are those involving employees. If charity begins at home, so also does ethically sound organization behavior begin internally. Organizations that treat their employees merely as means to achieve organizational goals are not likely to abandon that principle in their relations with others. To the extent that criminal justice agencies resemble military organizations, those agencies may be particularly susceptible to "mission"-oriented thinking, in which individuals are not treated as morally autonomous beings.

The Readings

The first selection, David Ewing's "A Proposed Bill of Rights," attempts to lay out a set of substantive rights of employees, many of which are already in place in leading organizations. It contains speech protection, including whistleblowing speech or speech contrary to management views, protection of privacy, protection against black-listing, etc. Most important, Ewing proposes the procedural right to due process, which functions internally before an impartial arbitrator. As Ewing points out, without a due process right, the other rights would have to be enforced externally through the courts, which Ewing thinks would be inefficient. A few of the rights discussed by Ewing have since then appeared via case law. These include restrictions on drug testing, the banning of polygraph testing in hiring, and the continued application of antidiscrimination laws to the workplace.

Burton Atkins and Mark Pogrebin's selection "Discretionary Decision-Making in the Administration of Justice," focuses directly on discretion in the criminal justice system as a whole, including the police, prosecution, judiciary, prison administration, and parole. Atkins and Pogrebin point out that there is a ripple effect throughout the system that originates with a police officer's discretionary judgment. Thus, cases that do go to court and end in conviction involve scrutiny of discretion. However, since the majority of criminal cases are plea-bargained and are never tried in court, most discretionary judgments made by law enforcement are never reviewed by other criminal justice system decision-makers. The authors state that police administrators have generally failed to issue formal discretionary policy guidelines "in order to avoid ambiguity in the line officer's use of discretion."

Prosecutorial discretion in the charging decision generally lacks a system of "internal rationalization and accountability," according to Atkins and Pogrebin. While there are typically statutory requirements to prosecute all offenders, it is widely acknowledged that total enforcement is both impractical and undesirable. The subsequent widespread practice of plea bargaining has an unclear legal status. While a few courts appear to condone plea bargaining, there are few legal limitations and "little policy" regarding either prosecutorial discretion to charge or plea negotiations. Since the courts are hesitant to supervise prosecutorial discretion, this entire area of decision-making has undergone little review.

Atkins and Pogrebin also find little control on the use of discretion in the judicial actions of setting bail, trial conduct, and sentencing. They cite many indications of enormous disparity among judges, with only a few states attempting to remedy the consequences through legislatively fixed sentencing and appellate review of trial judge sentencing. A major problem with judicial discretion appears to be the lack of training and preparation for being a judge, and hence for exercising judicial discretion. The authors say that "few attorneys who become judges have had much, if any, criminal law practice."

Discretion in prison administration has the lowest public visibility of all the stages of the criminal justice process. Legislative restraint is negligible, and essentially tosses the ball into the prison administrator's court, allowing correctional agencies to make and enforce any rules necessary for disciplining inmates, for instance. Atkins and Pogrebin interpret this legislative abrogation of duty as one of the causes of increasing judicial intervention in corrections. The most thoroughgoing intervention might be the judicial condemnation of the entire Arkansas penal system in *Holt* v. *Sarver.*[4]

The authors speculate that discretionary abuse in prisons is a principal cause of failure to reform prisoner attitudes toward wrongful behavior. They learn from the very system intended to rehabilitate their social values that the legal system does not in fact practice what it preaches.

The final selection, Mark S. Hamm's "A Vignette on Loyalty: The Rehabilitative Ideal and Corruption in Prison Administration," is a personal view of a former high-level corrections administrator. Hamm recounts his success in helping to reform the Arizona juvenile corrections system, and later, the adult system. Nonetheless, within a few years, Hamm was fired for reasons that are unclear, and virtually all of the reforms instituted under Hamm's leadership were terminated. Prison violence has resumed, and prisoner control is the dominant perspective in the Arizona system. Hamm remains committed to the rehabilitative or "medical" model of corrections, which seeks to identify the causes of criminal behavior and to provide a truly correctional environment within prisons. Hamm's account points up the power held by senior administrators to effect change, even where there is no correctional ideal at work. Consequently, the change may be for better or for worse.

Notes

1. John Ladd, "Morality and the Ideal of Rationality in Formal Organizations," *The Monist,* October 1970, pp. 488–516, cf. 491–492.
2. Ibid., p. 507.
3. Thomas Donaldson, *Corporations and Morality* (Englewood Cliffs: Prentice-Hall, 1982), p. 30.
4. 300 F. Supp. 825 (1969).

A Proposed Bill of Rights

DAVID W. EWING

WHAT SHOULD A BILL of rights for employees look like?

First, it should be presented in the form of clear and practical injunctions, not in the language of desired behavior or ideals.

In 1789, when James Madison and other members of the first U.S. Congress settled down to write the Bill of Rights (the first ten amendments to the Constitution), Madison insisted on using the imperative "shall" instead of the flaccid "ought," which had been used in the declarations of rights by the states, from which the

David W. Ewing, Freedom Inside the Organization: Bringing Civil Liberties to the Workplace *(New York: E.P. Dutton, 1977), Ch. 9 (pp. 144–151). Copyright © 1977 by David W. Ewing. Used by permission of Dutton Signet, a division of Penguin Books USA Inc.*

ideas for the federal Bill of Rights were taken. For instance, where Virginia's historic Declaration of Rights of 1776 stated that "excessive bail ought not to be required," and where the amendments proposed in 1788 by Virginia legislators were identically worded, the amendment proposed by Madison (and later accepted) read: "Excessive bail shall not be required...."

The imperative has precisely the same advantage in a bill of rights for members of a corporation, government bureau, university administration or other organization. An analogy is a traffic light. It does not contain various shades of red but just one shade which means clearly and unequivocally, "Stop." Nor does a stop sign say "Stop If Possible" or "Stop If You Can." It says simply, "Stop."

Second, as a general rule, it is wise to phrase a bill of rights in terms of negative injunctions rather than positive ones. A bill of rights does not aim to tell officials what they can do so much as it aims to tell them what they cannot do. It is not like the delegation of powers found in constitutions. Here again it is instructive to recall the writing of the federal Bill of Rights in 1789. Madison insisted that the positive grants of government powers had been well provided for in the main body of the Constitution and did not need to be reiterated in the first ten amendments.

In addition, a "Thou shalt not" type of commandment generally can be more precise than a "Thou shalt" type of commandment; the latter must be worded and interpreted to cover many possibilities of affirmative action. Since it is more precise, a "Thou shalt not" injunction is more predictable—not quite as predictable as a traffic light, but more so than most positive injunctions can be.

Also, since it is more limited, a negative injunction is less of a threat to the future use of executive (and legislative) powers. For instance, the injunction "Congress shall make no law respecting an establishment of religion" (first item in the U.S. Bill of Rights) inhibits Congress less, simply because it is so precise, than a positive command such as "Congress shall respect various establishments of religion" (rejected by the Founding Fathers when proposed in the 1789 discussions), which is more protean and expansible.

Third, an organization's bill of rights should be succinct. It should read more like a recipe in a cookbook than the regulations of the Internal Revenue Service. It is better to start with a limited number of rights that apply to familiar situations and that may have to be extended and amended in a few years than try to write a definitive listing for all time. Rights take time to ingest.

Fourth, a bill of rights should be written for understanding by employees and lay people rather than by lawyers and personnel specialists. It should not read like a letter from a credit company or a Massachusetts auto insurance policy. If an organization desires to make everything clear for experts, it could add a supplement or longer explanation that elaborates in technical terms on the provisions and clarifies questions and angles that might occur to lawyers.

Fifth, a bill of rights should be enforceable. Existence as a creed or statement of ideals is not enough. While creeds indeed may influence behavior in the long run, in the short run they leave too much dependent on good will and hope.

The bill of rights that follows is one person's proposal, a "working paper" for discussion, not a platform worked out in committee ... The slight variations in style are purposeful—partly to reduce monotony and partly to suggest different ways of defining employee rights and management prerogatives.

1. *No organization or manager shall discharge, demote, or in other ways discriminate against any employee who criticizes, in speech or press, the ethics, legality, or social responsibility of management actions.*

Comment: This right is intended to extend the U.S. Supreme Court's approach in the *Pickering* case[1] to all employees in business, government, education, and public service organizations.

What this right does not say is as important as what it does say. Protection does not extend to employees who make nuisances of themselves or who balk, argue, or contest managerial decisions on normal operating and planning matters, such as the choice of inventory accounting method, whether to diversify the product line or concentrate it, whether to rotate workers on a certain job or specialize them, and so forth. "Committing the truth," as Ernest Fitzgerald called it, is protected only for speaking out on issues where we consider an average citizen's judgment to be as valid as an expert's—truth in advertising, public safety standards, questions of fair disclosure, ethical practices, and so forth.

Nor does the protection extend to employees who malign the organization. We don't protect individuals who go around ruining other people's reputations, and neither should we protect those who vindictively impugn their employers.

Note, too, that this proposed right does not authorize an employee to disclose to outsiders information that is confidential.

This right puts publications of nonunionized employees on the same basis as union newspapers and journals, which are free to criticize an organization. Can a free press be justified for one group but not for the other? More to the point still, in a country that practices democratic rites, can the necessity of an "underground press" be justified in any socially important organization?

2. No employee shall be penalized for engaging in outside activities of his or her choice after working hours, whether political, economic, civic, or cultural, nor for buying products and services of his or her choice for personal use, nor for expressing or encouraging views contrary to top management's on political, economic, and social issues.

Comment: Many companies encourage employees to participate in outside activities, and some states have committed this right to legislation. Freedom of choice of products and services for personal use is also authorized in various state statutes as well as in arbitrators' decisions. The third part of the statement extends the protection of the First Amendment to the employee whose ideas about government, economic policy, religion, and society do not conform with the boss's. It would also protect the schoolteacher who allows the student newspaper to espouse a view on sex education that is rejected by the principal, ... the staff psychologist who endorses a book on a subject considered taboo in the board room, and other independent spirits.

Note that this provision does not authorize an employee to come to work "beat" in the morning because he or she has been moonlighting. Participation in outside activities should enrich employees' lives, not debilitate them; if on-the-job performance suffers, the usual penalties may have to be paid.

3. No organization or manager shall penalize an employee for refusing to carry out a directive that violates common norms of morality.

Comment: The purpose of this right is to ... afford job security (not just unemployment compensation) to subordinates who cannot perform an action because they consider it unethical or illegal. It is important that the conscientious objector in such a case hold to a view that has some public acceptance. Fad moralities—messages from flying saucers, mores of occult religious sects, and so on—do not justify refusal to carry out an order. Nor in any case is the employee entitled to interfere with the boss's finding another person to do the job requested.

4. No organization shall allow audio or visual recordings of an employee's conversations or actions to be made without his or her prior knowledge and consent. Nor may an organization require an employee or applicant to take personality tests, polygraph examinations, or other tests that constitute, in his opinion, an invasion of privacy.

Comment: This right is based on policies that some leading organizations have already put into practice. If an employee doesn't want his working life monitored, that is his privilege so long as he demonstrates (or, if an applicant is willing to demonstrate) competence to do a job well.

5. No employee's desk, files, or locker may be examined in his or her absence by anyone but a senior manager who has sound reason to believe that the files contain information needed for a management decision that must be made in the employee's absence.

Comment: The intent of this right is to grant people a privacy right as employees similar to that which they enjoy as political and social citizens under the "searches and seizures" guarantee of the Bill of Rights (Fourth Amendment to the Constitution). Many leading organizations in business and government have respected the principle of this rule for some time.

6. *No employer organization may collect and keep on file information about an employee that is not relevant and necessary for efficient management. Every employee shall have the right to inspect his or her personnel file and challenge the accuracy, relevance, or necessity of data in it, except for personal evaluations and comments by other employees which could not reasonably be obtained if confidentiality were not promised. Access to an employee's file by outside individuals and organizations should be limited to inquiries about the essential facts of employment.*

Comment: This right is important if employees are to be masters of their employment track records instead of possible victims of them. It will help to eliminate surprises, secrets, and skeletons in the clerical closet.

7. *No manager may communicate to prospective employers of an employee who is about to be or has been discharged gratuitous opinions that might hamper the individual in obtaining a new position.*

Comment: The intent of this right is to stop blacklisting. The courts have already given some support for it.

8. *An employee who is discharged, demoted, or transferred to a less desirable job is entitled to a written statement from management of its reasons for the penalty.*

Comment: The aim of this provision is to encourage a manager to give the same reasons in a hearing, arbitration, or court trial that he or she gives the employee when the cutdown happens. The written statement need not be given unless requested; often it is so clear to all parties why an action is being taken that no document is necessary.

9. *Every employee who feels that he or she has been penalized for asserting any right described in this bill shall be entitled to a fair hearing before an impartial official, board, or arbitrator. The findings and conclusions of the hearing shall be delivered in writing to the employee and management.*

Comment: This very important right is the organizational equivalent of due process of law as we know it in political and community life. Without due process in a company or agency, the rights in this bill would all have to be enforced by outside courts and tribunals, which is expensive for society as well as time-consuming for the employees who are required to appear as complainants and witnesses. The nature of a "fair hearing" is purposely left undefined here so that different approaches can be tried, expanded, and adapted to changing needs and conditions.

Note that the findings of the investigating official or group are not binding on top management. This would put an unfair burden on an ombudsperson or "expedited arbitrator," if one of them is the investigator. Yet the employee is protected. If management rejects a finding of unfair treatment and then the employee goes to court, the investigator's statement will weigh against management in the trial. As a practical matter, therefore, employers will not want to buck the investigator-referee unless they fervently disagree with the findings.

In Sweden, perhaps the world's leading practitioner of due process in organizations, a law went into effect in January 1977 that goes a little farther than the right proposed here. The new Swedish law states that except in unusual circumstances a worker who disputes a dismissal notice can keep his or her job until the dispute has been decided by a court.

Every sizable organization, whether in business, government, health, or another field, should have a bill of rights for employees. Only small organizations need not have such a statement—personal contact and oral communications meet the need for them. However, companies and agencies need not have identical bills of rights. Industry custom, culture, past history with employee unions and associations, and other considerations can be taken into account in the wording and emphasis given to different provisions.

For instance, Booz, Allen and Hamilton, the well-known consulting company, revised a bill of rights for its employees in 1976 (the list included several of the rights suggested here).

One statement obligated the company to "Respect the right of employees to conduct their private lives as they choose, while expecting its employees' public conduct to reflect favorably upon the reputation of the Firm." The latter part of this provision reflects the justifiable concern of a leading consulting firm with outward appearances. However, other organizations—a mining company, let us say, or a testing laboratory—might feel no need to qualify the right of privacy because few of their employees see customers....

NOTE

1. *Pickering* v. *Board of Education*, 391 U.S. 563 (1968).

Study Questions

1. Why does Ewing believe that a bill of rights should be composed of negative injunctions rather than positive injunctions?

2. Describe Ewing's position on organizational "free speech" rights. Is it acceptable, too limited, or too broad, in your view? Defend your position.

3. What is Ewing's view of privacy rights in the workplace? Do you agree with Ewing? Why? Do public sector employees have less of a right to privacy than private sector employees, in your view? Why? Defend your position.

4. Why is a due process right in the workplace so important, in Ewing's view? Is Ewing's recommended due process right workable? Why? Do you think that due process requires an adversarial court-based mechanism? Why? Defend your position.

Discretionary Decision-Making in the Administration of Justice

BURTON ATKINS AND MARK POGREBIN

ONE OF THE MOST demanding intellectual tasks that observers of any institution or process must undertake—be it public or private, political or nonpolitical—is that of analytically and empirically distinguishing symbol and myth from reality. As Max Lerner so aptly expressed it several decades ago, we react, in many ways, like children to our surroundings—imbued with myths that provide us comfort as we contend with the realities of our environment.[1]

Our legal system is shaped by innumerable myths and symbols. Perhaps the most significant

Burton Atkins and Mark Pogrebin, "Discretionary Decision-Making in the Administration of Justice," in Burton Atkins and Mark Pogrebin (eds.), The Invisible Justice System: Discretion and the Law, Second Edition (Cincinnati: Anderson Publishing Company, 1982), pp. 3-15. Copyright © 1978, 1982 by Anderson Publishing Co. Used by permission of the publisher.

one within our constitutional framework is that of due process. As it has evolved in a constitutional context, due process generally refers to rules of fundamental fairness that dictate the broad assumptions and values guiding our criminal justice system. Due process also denotes a belief in governmental limitation, of barriers to whimsical authority by political officials. It suggests an adherence to the old adage that ours "is a government of laws, not of men"; that our system of justice is premised upon rules and upon structure, not upon the personal idiosyncrasies of public officials. We take great comfort in the symbol of due process, we virtually pay it homage and we seem to feel more secure in the knowledge that our criminal justice system is operating by norms of regularity and restraint.

Against this symbolic frame of reference, the issue of discretionary decision-making in the criminal justice system poses substantial tensions. Discretion refers to a situation in which an official has latitude to make authoritative choices not necessarily specified within the source of authority which governs his decision-making. Kenneth Culp Davis, a recognized commentator on discretion, argues that a public officer exercises discretion "... whenever the effective limits of his power leave him free to make a choice among possible courses of action or inaction."[2] Discretionary justice thus suggests latitude of decision-making rather than formality or certainty. It suggests that, unlike the symbolic idea of due process, idiosyncrasy rather than rules may guide decision-making within the administration of criminal justice.

Discretion is exercised in the police officer's decision to apprehend a suspect, the prosecutor's decision to file, dismiss or reduce formal charges, the judge's decision to admit a defendant to bail, release on recognizance, grant or deny trial motions, suspend sentence, release on probation, impose severe or minimal sentence in prison, and the parole board's decision whether or not to release a prisoner from incarceration. It is a critical element at almost every point in our criminal justice system. Yet, our legal system's reliance on discretionary decisions is not unique. As Davis has observed, all legal systems in history have utilized such power.[3] But it is not simply its existence which draws our attention to discretionary decision-making. Rather, discretion is important because it maintains a flexible, individualized system of justice. Nevertheless, it is a system vulnerable to abuse. Roscoe Pound wrote: "A balance between rules of law and discretion which will give effect both to the general security and general life with the least impairment of either is perhaps the most difficult problem in the science of law."[4] The question, then, is not how to avoid all discretion, since discretion and justice are not incompatible concepts, but, in the words of Justice Charles Brietel of the New York Court of Appeals, "... how to control it so as to avoid the unequal, the arbitrary, the discriminatory, and the oppressive."[5]

If discretionary decisions are inevitable, then the issue is not whether or not they *should* occur but rather determining the degree of impact the exercise of discretion has upon the administration of justice. The invisible system of justice that lies beyond the formal scriptures of the law derives its energy from the failure of statutory law or any administrative code of regulation to specify all contingencies of decision-making. The essential problem becomes that of discovering the elusive balance between structuring decisions and providing for individualized justice.

Davis has suggested three concepts that can be applied to the task of limiting or regulating discretion. The first is confining discretion. This refers to keeping "... discretionary power within designated boundaries."[6] This may be accomplished through statutory or administrative rule-making. Confining, in other words, refers to setting the limits beyond which decisions may not reach. Discretion may also be structured by controlling boundaries established by the confining process.[7] Finally, discretion may be checked by imposing the supervisory controls of one decision-maker upon another.[8] These concepts are useful because they provide a starting point for conceptualizing the issue of discretion.

Yet their intrinsic limitation is that they presume the problem of discretion to be similar, if not identical, in a variety of institutions. The use of discretionary judgments by all those involved in the various components of our legal system is not a clear case of right or wrong, lawful or unlawful.

Each part of the criminal justice system utilizes discretion in different ways for a variety of reasons. Because each part of the legal structure is primarily concerned with its own particular needs and functions, it becomes difficult to resolve conflicts that involve the actual utilization of discretionary judgments or the authority to exercise it. The variety of contexts in which discretion may be employed, and the details concerning its actual exercise, are endemic to our justice system because each component of the system is organized more for its own purposes and concerns than formulated for the common good of the criminal justice system....

Police

Contrary to myth, most police work does not necessarily involve cornering bank robbers and muggers on the streets. A considerable amount of police activity is directed towards service functions, areas of activity which entail a particularly high degree of discretionary judgment. Police officers have considerable discretion to invoke or refrain from invoking arrest when they confront low visibility offenses or crimes which have little impact on anyone but those directly involved. Much discretionary behavior stems from the ambiguity of criminal statutes. It remains, in most instances, a matter of judgment for patrolmen to determine whether or not particular activities fall within the legal sanction, and if so, whether or not the particular circumstances require arrest. As one observer has noted:

The law contains certain guidelines about the boundaries of legality. Within these boundaries, however, there is located a vast array of activities that are not important since determined by considerations of legality....

The effective reasons for the action are not located in the formulas of statutes but in considerations that are related to established practices of dealing informally with problems.[9]

Discretionary decisions by actors at one point in the system can have important effects on decisions made elsewhere. When law enforcement agents, for example, choose not to invoke their arrest powers for routine, low visibility and particular victimless crimes, their decisions define the outer limits of sanctions to be imposed by the political system regardless of what the statutory law may provide. In this context, the police become law interpreters since their discretionary judgments on the streets give concrete meaning to vagrancy, prostitution, gambling, and intoxication laws. As Joseph Goldstein has argued in a now classic article, a patrolman's discretionary judgments on the streets ultimately affect others in the system who make decisions—prosecutors, grand jury, judges, probation officers, correction authority and parole and pardon boards.[10]

Discretionary policy judgments not to arrest a suspect who has committed a low visibility offense, moreover, are rarely subject to review by other decision-makers in the system. There are some situations, however, in which police discretion is scrutinized by other participants in the criminal justice process. One circumstance is judicial assessment of the evidence, circumstances of arrest, and confessions. A court decision to accept or reject a police officer's discretionary judgments helps to establish the limit of the officer's legal behavior. Yet, the vast majority of criminal cases are plea bargained and never come before a judge and jury in an open trial. In reality, then, the discretionary judgments that law enforcement officers make in deciding whether or not to arrest are rarely scrutinized by other decision-makers in the legal process. This is particularly troublesome when illegal discretionary decisions are made. Rosset and Cressey have observed that:

When there is no announced norm to govern decisions, it is hard to know what evidence is relevant and what procedure is appropriate. Where there is no defined process for making decisions, it is difficult to discern what standards are being used. Rules and norms become little more than suggestions to the decision-maker. When a policeman decides not to make an arrest, or a prosecutor declines to file a charge against a person accused of a crime, the official is on his own, because there is not likely to be a formal hearing or other procedure. In these situations there are few determinative legal criteria to effectively bind the official because his decision is not subject to review.[11]

The President's Task Force on Police proposed that police departments develop clearly stated policies that would enable police to have specific guidance for those situations which often require the exercise of discretion. The report stated that:

> Policy should cover such matters, among others, as the issuance of orders to citizens regarding their movements or activities, the handling of minor disputes, the safeguarding of the rights of free speech and free assembly, the selection and use of investigative methods, and the decision whether or not to arrest in specific situations involving specific crimes.[12]

More than a decade after this recommendation was made, there are still very few police departments that issue formal guidelines on the use of discretionary policy to the rank and file patrolman. The same problems still exist because of the unwillingness of police administrators to state departmental discretionary policies as clearly as possible in order to avoid ambiguity in the line officer's use of discretion. The absence of clear guidelines which would aid the patrolman in his everyday encounters with suspects and complainants perpetuates the ambiguity of his responsibilities. Instead of attempting to make decisions based on familiar departmental policy, he continues to depend on his personal judgments which often have little or no legal basis. It is to the policeman's disadvantage that

he is forced to make factual judgments rather than legal judgments due to the lack of stated normative administrative guidelines in the exercise of discretionary judgments.

On what basis are discretionary judgments made? What cognitive processes, in other words, affect the latitude of decision-making by the police officer? Surprisingly little research has been conducted on this issue. Many studies are now available which describe the policeman's working environment and how discretion is exercised, but few scholars have directed their attention to the variables that affect discretionary judgments. One exception is a study of police discretion by James O. Finckenhauer. In his study, Finckenhauer examined the effect of education upon the discretionary judgments of police recruits. His procedure was to offer the subjects ten hypothetical scenarios representing a variety of problems a police officer might confront. The hypothetical situations involved legal violations relating to prostitution, gambling, obscenity, and pornography. That is, each situation posed a technical legal violation which allowed the police officer to arrest the violator, take some official action other than arrest, or do nothing. Finckenhauer found some differences in college and non-college educated recruits' reactions to these hypothetical situations, particularly that "... college educated police officers are less likely to advocate involving the criminal process in such situations."[13]

Finckenhauer's research is important because it suggests that education does have an effect upon how discretion operates in the administration of justice. These findings also are in conformity with, and lend support to, goals set by the Task Force on the Police, part of the President's Commission on Law Enforcement and Administration of Justice, which has suggested that the quality of police departments was ultimately tied to the educational level of recruits brought into the system.[14] Besides the obvious implication linking education to police professionalism, Finckenhauer's research clearly suggests that discretionary decision-making involves a behavioral component. In other words, how discretionary judgments are made and in what circumstances they are not likely to be maximized and minimized, relates to each decision-maker's cognitive processes. While the psychological dimension of decision-making is related to discretion within the legal system, little research has been done directly applying behavioral concepts to police and prosecutorial decision-making.[15]

Prosecution

A prosecutor's discretion is extensive. It encompasses the power to selectively prosecute suspected offenders, to give strength to, or emasculate, law enforcement policies by not prosecuting violations of certain laws, to drop charges once having initiated a prosecution, and, of course, to plea bargain with a defendant.

Probably the least publicly visible aspect of prosecutorial discretion is the charging decision. While most jurisdictions have statutes which require prosecution of all offenders, and frequently dictate that prosecutors shall "diligently enforce"[16] all law within their jurisdiction, the fact remains that total enforcement may be both impractical and undesirable as a matter of public policy. Undoubtedly, some discretion has to be exercised if only because limited resources of money, personnel, and time prevent a prosecutor from initiating a complaint against all offenders. Apart from resource limitations, prosecutors may be motivated by political ambition or even corruption. Thus, the decision to charge or not to charge may be tied to their own personal motivations.

The disparity between what statutes provide and what political realities dictate similarly affects the removal of prosecutors who have abused their discretionary powers. State statutes provide for removal of prosecutors by courts, voters, governors, and legislatures. For the most part, however, these processes are ineffective checks to prosecutorial discretion.[17] In some instances, courts may suggest that prosecutorial

action is mandatory in certain circumstances. Nevertheless, most jurisdictions have taken the position that a prosecutor's charging decision is beyond judicial scrutiny.[18] Some courts, in fact, have gone further, interpreting statutes conferring authority on prosecutors quite broadly so as to actually legitimize discretion not to prosecute.[19]

The decision to charge a defendant is frequently made with the ultimate aim of plea bargaining. The informal negotiation towards a plea stems from a promise by the prosecutor to reduce the original charge, often comprised of multiple charges, to a lesser criminal offense if the defendant agrees to enter a guilty plea. Excessive plea bargaining discretion has been the focus of reform policy that seeks to place restraints on the prosecutor's flexibility in dealing with criminal defendants. Some jurisdictions, for example, have experimented with a policy precluding plea bargaining for drug violations.[20] Need for controls, however, extends to other aspects of prosecutorial decision-making. Remington and Rosenblum, for example, argue that although the prosecutor's discretion is widely acknowledged, little attention has been devoted to developing a system of internal rationalization and accountability. Remington and Rosenblum advocate the formulation of institutionalized procedures making it possible for discretion to be utilized, but in a manner which is visible and subject to review in order to insure that it is not abused.[21]

Courts have, for the most part, remained curiously silent on plea bargaining. However, some courts have begun to confront the plea bargaining issue directly, but unfortunately, emerging judicial policy has provided little beyond a tacit recognition that plea bargaining is a catalyst for an efficient, or perhaps more accurately, expeditious administration of justice. A few courts have been candid in their approval of plea bargaining. For example, in *U.S.* v. *Wiley,* a federal district court noted that:

If, in one year, 248 judges are to deal with 35,517 defendants, the district courts must encourage pleas of guilty. One way to encourage pleas of guilty is to establish or announce a policy that, in the ordinary case, leniency will not be granted to a defendant who stands on trial.[22]

The Supreme Court has similarly condoned plea bargaining. In *Brady* v. *U.S.*, the Court ruled that a guilty plea conditional upon a prosecutor's leniency does not violate the Fifth Amendment protection against self-incrimination.[23] In *Santobello* v. *New York,* the United States Supreme Court implicitly recognized that plea negotiations were an essential component of the administration of justice.[24] The current position of the federal courts on the issue of plea bargaining was set forth in *North Carolina* v. *Alford* which held "the standard was and remains whether the plea represents a voluntary and intelligent choice among the alternative courses of actions open to the defendant."[25] Still, there is little policy primarily concerned with the procedural exercise of prosecutorial discretion to charge or not to charge a defendant, or policies designed to guide discretionary judgments affecting the process of plea negotiation. The Supreme Court had, however, taken some initial steps toward a policy in the *Santobello* decision when it ruled that prosecutors must adhere to promises made to defendants in plea bargaining. Yet as even Chief Justice Burger had recognized (while a member of the federal court of appeals), courts may only be capable of performing a limited role in curtailing prosecutorial discretion:

> Few subjects are less adapted to judicial review than the exercise by the Executive of his discretion in deciding when and whether to institute criminal proceedings or what precise charge should be made, or whether to dismiss a proceeding once brought.[26]

Whereas courts have some power to check abuses of police discretion, the interplay between judicial and prosecutorial discretion is more ambiguous. It is a given fact that prosecutors have considerable authority in negotiating pleas. This discretion is bolstered by the hesitancy of courts to interfere with bargains struck between prosecutor and defendant. In some circumstances, however, the courts will intervene. The circumstances surrounding *United States* v. *Ammidown* represent one such instance.[27] In this case, the defendant, Ammidown, had pleaded guilty to second degree murder after having been initially charged in the first degree for planning his wife's rape and murder by a friend. Federal District Judge John Sirica, however, refused to accept the negotiated plea on the grounds that the crime was so heinous that the public interest would not accept a mere "tap on the wrist."[28] At Sirica's insistence, the defendant pleaded guilty to the charge in the original indictment and was found guilty of first degree murder. Ammidown then appealed his conviction to the court of appeals for the District of Columbia. In vacating the judgment and sentence, the court of appeals sought to formulate policy that would guide judicial discretion as it affects prosecutorial plea bargaining. The essentials of this policy are that a bargain may be rejected only if (1) it is inherently unfair to the defendant; (2) it represents an abuse of prosecutorial discretion, or (3) it interferes with a judge's sentencing prerogative without any overriding prosecutorial interest.

Ammidown is actually only one of a series of decisions in which federal courts have opted for a presumption in favor of prosecutorial discretion in plea bargaining. The emerging doctrine appears to be that prosecutors will be given a generally free rein in plea bargaining but the judiciary will nevertheless reserve the right to intervene when the prosecutor abuses his discretion. Courts have occasionally taken a more extreme view that the judiciary has no power whatsoever to oversee prosecutorial discretion because of the separation of powers doctrine. This argument, adopted by Chief Justice Burger in *Newman* v. *U.S.*[29] when he sat on the court of appeals, was based on the idea that prosecutors are executive officials subject only to executive controls over their internal decision-making process. Yet, *Ammidown* seems to reflect the drift of opinion at least within the federal courts. It would be reasonable to conclude that the political and organizational necessities of prosecutorial decision-making combined with a hesitancy by the courts to impose judicial supervision provide the conditions in which prosecutorial discretion can flourish.

The Judiciary

Judicial discretion, like police and prosecutorial discretion, is inevitable. The issue here is probably more complex since certain strains of jurisprudence are tied to interpretations of judicial behavior that view a judge as a legal automaton applying statutory and common law rules to particular cases in a rather mechanical fashion. Ultimately, this formalistic view of decision-making would have to reject the notion of judicial discretion since the concept implies ambiguity and flexibility, whereas mechanical jurisprudence emphasizes certainty and even rigidity in judges' opinions.[30] The mechanical theory is also founded upon the assumption that judicial decision-making is qualitatively different from other kinds of political decision-making. However, discretion may best be interpreted as the inevitable result of a human decision-making process that applies with equal force to judicial and nonjudicial institutions.

A trial judge has considerable discretion in setting bail, conducting a trial, and imposing sentence. The function of bail is to secure a defendant to the court's authority. At least in theory, the amount of security required to bind a defendant should be dependent upon his financial status, opportunity for employment, and roots in the community. Unfortunately, the bail process rarely works as intended. The root of the problem is that judges and court-support personnel usually do not, and perhaps cannot, process the kinds of information relevant to fitting the amount of bail to the particular circumstances of each defendant. This is not meant to suggest that the imposing of bail, or for that matter, the determination of whether or not a defendant should be released on his own recognizance, is entirely haphazard. In some instances, it may be. But more often, judges develop their own *modus operandi* in relationship to how much the amount of bail should be and how it should be set, but also in relation to the function that pretrial release or detention should serve. Not surprisingly, then, judicial discretion has a considerable impact upon the bail decision since each judge has his own perception of the seriousness of a crime and of the defendant's moral character. It is not at all uncommon for judges to set their own bail rate schedules. In some instances, these schedules are idiosyncratic in that they reflect the judges' perception of the seriousness of offenses and not society's view of the severity of crime. One study conducted in New York, for example, found that judges generally imposed higher bail in robbery and burglary offenses than in sex-related offenses even though the latter are crimes against persons as opposed to crimes against property. In fact, the view of the New York judges that robbery and burglary offenses should be treated more severely than sex-related crimes, even though burglaries do not necessarily involve any contact with the victim, suggests a priority of legal values that might very well be questioned.[31]

It would be erroneous, however, to suggest that the judge proceeds entirely by whim. As Suffet has suggested in his study of bail setting interaction, the actual determination of bail is the result of an exchange relationship between judge, prosecutor, and defense attorney.[32] In the end, like the policeman and prosecutor, a judge's discretion is frequently controlled by his role relationship with other actors in the system. Nevertheless, how this bail decision is reached and the impact of discretionary powers within the process can have an enormous impact upon the defendant. In one respect, the bail system as it operates in most areas discriminates against defendants because of economic statutes, particularly when judges impose bail based upon the type of offense with little or no consideration for the characteristics of the defendant, the amount of money necessary to bind him to the court's jurisdiction, or even whether or not the defendant should be released on personal recognizance. For defendants who must experience pretrial detention because of an inability to raise bond, the repercussion can be serious indeed. There is some evidence to suggest that these defendants receive more severe sentences because of their handicap in preparing defenses within the confines of a jail. Equally as damaging is the fact that those who are ultimately released or found innocent by the court nevertheless have no recourse from the social stigma of jail or the economic inconvenience of having lost their jobs through the ordeal.

As much, if not more, discretion exists in the sentencing process. Numerous studies have documented the scope of this problem. For example, one study of sentencing discretion and disparity in federal district court found that judges in North Carolina imposed an average sentence of 77.6 months upon narcotics violators, whereas those in South Carolina, working within the same statutory parameters and generally within the same geographic area within the United States, sentenced narcotics violators to an average of 56.3 months in jail. A similar tendency was found for forgery convictions. One federal district court in Texas sentenced forgers to an average of 43 months. Yet, another in the same state sentenced forgers to only 27.2 months.[34] This amount of sentencing discretion is not limited to felony offenses in federal courts. One study of the New York City Magistrate Court found considerable variation in intoxication, sanitary law, and speed ordinance violations over a 15-year period. For example, New York judges varied from 1.3% to 73.4% in the percent of intoxication cases discharged; from 18.8% to 87.6% in the rate for imposing fines for sanitary law violations; and from 1.0% to 79.0% for the frequency with which speed ordinance violators received suspended sentences.[35]

The causes of sentencing disparity and discretion lie in the combined effect of legislative policies that impose maximum and minimal thresholds for sentence, indeterminate sentences, and the judge's perceptions of the utility of certain legal policies. Few legislative policies exist that are designed to limit judicial discretion. Some states, however, have recently experimented with "flat-time" sentencing in which a judge must impose a legislatively fixed sentence for certain kinds of offenses. Appellate review of trial judge sentencing, considered by many commentators to be a more viable solution than flat-time laws, is virtually non-existent in our country. Appellate courts in Arizona, Connecticut, Hawaii, Iowa, Massachusetts, Nebraska, New York and Oregon do have power to review and modify sentences alleged to be too severe, but these are more the exception than the rule. In six other states, courts are empowered to "reverse, affirm, or modify" criminal court judgments, but the "suitability" of a particular sentence is normally unreviewable. Federal appellate courts generally face similar constraints.[36]

While appellate review might appear as an attractive solution to abuses in sentencing discretion, several limitations of the process must be recognized. One is that while many jurisdictions might favor the appellate review process, they commit themselves to an exponential increase in criminal appeals at a time when many courts are seeking ways of reducing the seemingly endless number of appeals. Organizational demands, in other words, may place some restraints on this approach. Another problem is that appellate review does not necessarily reduce discretion in sentencing. Instead, it creates another layer of discretionary decision-making intended to check decisions of trial judges. There is also evidence that few sentences would actually be changed. For example, the New York experience with appellate review of sentencing has shown that about 90% of appeals raised on grounds of legality, propriety, or excessiveness were affirmed. By contrast, slightly more than 5% were modified and slightly less than 5% were actually reversed.[37] Obviously, appellate judges are not prone to disturb a trial judge's sentence except in the most extreme situations.

If a certain amount of discretion is inevitable in judicial sentencing powers, there is still the problem of contending with the idiosyncratic role behavior of judges. Since judges are human, they will obviously be susceptible to human frailties such as bias and bigotry. In theory, a judge's sentencing decision is supposed to be premised upon legally relevant criteria such as the severity of the crime and whether or not the defendant has a prior criminal record. Supposedly irrelevant are such factors as the defendant's demeanor in court, his deference or lack thereof towards judicial authority, and even his attire in court. Nevertheless, it has been proven that sentencing decisions are related to legally irrelevant criteria. One study of Detroit Traffic Court, for example, found an inverse relationship between the defendants' mode of dress and whether or not they received a jail sentence as opposed to receiving a fine or suspended sentence. Those defendants whose attire was more dignified were less likely to be jailed. This relationship held even where the severity of offense was taken into account. Although the relationship was not statistically significant, the Detroit data also suggests that defendants' demeanor was also related to the magnitude of fines imposed; that to the extent defendants failed to use honorific titles, expressed disrespect for the court and the like, they were more likely to receive larger fines.[38]

While justice is supposedly blind to legally irrelevant criteria, it is clear that maintaining the tenuous balance between discretionary justice and discretionary abuse involves more than simply drafting model penal codes or model sentencing acts. It may entail some type of cue-taking and consensus-building among judges. On-the-job socialization to agreed upon sentencing norms may reduce some disparity. But more fundamental problems remain. Most proposals have not dealt with the process by which lawyers become judges and how ill-equipped many lawyers are to undertake the burdens of judicial decision-making. Few law school graduates are trained in legal aspects of sentencing, no less the psychological dimensions of the process. Few attorneys who become judges have had much, if any, criminal law practice. As federal judge Marvin Frankel has observed, too much attention has been paid in the sentencing debate to what the judge should do, and too little attention to the problem of who the judges are:

The most notable thing about this group... is that its members have mostly remained unencumbered by any exposure to, or learning about, the problems of sentencing. Characterized by their dominant attributes, our judges are men (mostly) of no longer tender years who have not associated much with criminal defendants, who have not seemed shrilly unorthodox, who have not lived recently in poverty, who have been modestly or more successful in their profession. They are likely to have had more than an average lawyer's amount of experience in the courtroom, though it is a little remarkable how large a percentage of those who go on the bench lack this credential. They are unlikely to have defended more than a couple of criminal cases, if that many. They are more likely to have done a stint as prosecutors, usually as a brief chapter in the years shortly after law school. However much or little they have been exposed to the criminal trial process, most people ascending (as we say) to the bench have paid only the most fleeting and superficial attention to matters affecting the sentences of convicted defendants. In this respect, the pattern set in the law school is carried forward and reenforced.[39]

Prison Administration

Considerable discretion exists in prison administration. It is at the last stages of the criminal justice process that we find the lowest public visibility in discretionary decision-making. Prisons, far removed from the public eye, have until recently been generally free to utilize their administrative authority in any manner they thought consistent with their control policies and goals. Perhaps the most flagrant examples of abuse in discretionary decision-making have occurred in the procedures adopted for disciplining inmates. For years now, prisoner behavior has been guarded by petty rules which are, for the most part, unwritten and vague. Quite often these rules are arbitrarily and discriminately enforced. Even with the numerous federal court cases that have recently begun to restrain some of the discretionary abuses of prisoner rights, corrections still has a major problem of finding ways to combine the need for flexibility and discretion in decision-making with the need to make fair and sensible decisions.

A major cause for extensive discretionary decision-making among correctional officials stems from the lack of restraint placed upon administrators by statutory law. Legislatures grant broad authority with hardly any restrictions on the exercise of administrative authority. The grant of authority given to prison officials by legislation is usually broad. The statutes normally stipulate that correction departments can make and enforce all rules regarding regulating and disciplining inmates. In other words, the content of the rules, as well as their interpretation, is left to the discretion of the prison administrators. Many states grant broad power to allow officials to freely alter such rules as it may become expedient. For the most part, the statutory language allows the officials to use their own judgment in deciding when such alterations should be imposed.[40] For example, under the old indeterminate sentencing law in California before the recent change to a more determinate sentencing system, the California Adult Authority was charged with overseeing the administration of the indeterminate sentencing procedure and parole system. It was given extensive authority to grant and revoke paroles, to fix length of sentences, to establish the conditions of parole, and to restore a prisoner's political and civil rights to the extent that the Authority saw fit. Through its statutes, the California legislature had imposed no restraints upon, and had created no standards for, the Adult Authority's decision-making.[41]

This statutory ambiguity providing prison officials with vast discretionary power has, at the same time, contributed to the erosion of the "hands-off" doctrine. This doctrine had been used extensively by courts to justify their reluctance to intervene in the administration of correctional institutions. Now courts have become more aware of prisoner demands, in part because legislatures had virtually abrogated their responsibility in providing external controls over prison administrators.

Courts have also begun to accept the proposition that correctional abuses often deny prisoners their constitutional rights. This modified position is indicative of the recognition by courts that the imposition of arbitrary punishment in the form of disciplinary hearings often deprives prisoners of certain rights such as earned good time and other institutionally earned privileges. Proceeding from this assumption, courts have ruled, for example, that prison officials cannot unreasonably censor prisoners' mail in violation of the First Amendment;[42] that prisons must adopt minimum housing standards for inmates;[43] that restraints may be placed upon disciplinary procedures employed by prison officials;[44] and that the religious freedom of incarcerated offenders must be protected under certain conditions.[45] In fact, *Holt v. Sarver* went so far as to declare the entire Arkansas penitentiary system to be in violation of the Eighth Amendment protection against cruel and unusual punishment.[46]

Perhaps the most auspicious Supreme Court decision has been *Wolff v. McDonnell.*[47] In *Wolff,* the court ruled that certain constitutional rights should be afforded to prisoners prior to punishment by prison officials. While the inmates do not have the right to confront their accusers and are not entitled to counsel, a hearing is nevertheless required. While this is a limited protection at best, it does indicate that the Supreme Court is not going to allow the "hands-off" doctrine to hamper all attempts at curtailing discretionary abuses in prisons. To the extent that *Wolff* and other precedents effectively limit disciplinary practices, an area usually considered to be entirely within the domain of the prison administrators, they establish the constitutional basis necessary for extending judicial supervision to other spheres of internal decision-making. This trend towards more judicial intervention should not be interpreted as suggesting that abuses will necessarily be curtailed at a pace commensurate with judicial supervision. Judicial policy evolves slowly and one cannot always predict just how vigorously future courts will defend the interest of prisoners. The exercise of discretionary power remains a real problem. At the very least, however, prisoners now may have access to grievance mechanisms when abusive discretionary decisions are alleged to occur.

Positive judicial intervention could have some unforeseen benefits beyond the curtailment of discretionary abuse. It may well be that the imposition of external control mechanisms will limit disciplinary situations that lead to inmate frustration and violence. The Attica prison revolt of 1971 is the most vivid example of problems that were smoldering long before the riot occurred—problems that still exist unabated in other prisons around the country.

Regardless of the preconceptions that the public may have concerning the effect of a prison sentence on modifying criminal behavior or the threat of jail as a deterrent to crime, two facts emerge from even a casual observation of the American penal system. First, a large proportion of prison inmates are recidivists, a fact that suggests that prison environments do little to alter an individual's penchant for violating societal norms. In this context, it would seem reasonable to hypothesize that discretionary abuse on the part of prison administrators undermines any attempt by authorities to instill within inmates' minds a sense of equity or justice regarding the legal system. In the final analysis, the purpose of rehabilitation must be to reshape prisoners' values towards society. Yet it would seem that abused discretionary power would very likely reinforce prisoners' attitudes that the system is corrupt, and that survival either in or outside the penitentiary depends as much upon illegal means as it does upon legal ones.

Parole

The parole decision represents another critical point in the system in which enormous discretionary power occurs. Considerable variations in parole board decision-making existing across the United States are fueled, in part, by the belief among many officials that the granting of parole is a purely administrative task to be performed without judicial or legislative interference. The granting of parole has been alluded to in one study as decision-making by "an act of grace."[48] To the extent that such a perception permeates decision-making in parole boards, it certainly impedes any attempt to balance discretionary abuse with decision-making structure and rules. One of the few existing nationwide surveys of parole board decision-making found that less than half of the parole boards studied adhered to standards suggested by the Presidential Task Force Report on Corrections as minimally necessary for limiting discretionary abuse. The study showed, for example, that as of 1972, 60% did not permit counsel at the parole hearing; 69% did not permit inmates to present witnesses at the hearing; 78% did not record the reasons for the parole decision; only 40% made verbatim transcripts of the proceedings; and only 43% informed the inmate directly of the decision.[49] With such practices in effect, it is clearly difficult to impose restraints upon parole boards, particularly when the absence of complete records of the proceedings makes it virtually impossible for courts, or any institution for that matter, to review the boards' decisions. The fluidity of decision-making in parole boards is not limited to the state board. The United States Parole Board had been accused of exactly the same type of amorphous decision-making that allows discretionary abuse to flourish. As Kenneth Culp Davis has written:

> In granting or denying parole, the board makes no attempt to structure its discretionary power through rules, policy statements, or guidelines; it does not structure through statements of findings and reasons; it has no system of precedents; the degree of openness of proceedings and records is about the least possible; and procedural safeguards are almost totally absent. Moreover, checking of discretion is minimal; board members do not check each other by deliberating together

about decisions; administrative check of board decisions is almost non-existent; and judicial review is customarily unavailable[50]

Although courts have imposed some restraints on prison discipline and administration, they have been more hesitant to extend judicial control over the process by which correction officials grant or deny a prisoner release on parole. Typical of their response is the one made in *Scarpa* v. *United States Board of Parole,* where the court of appeals ruled that due process rights do not attach at parole hearings and that "... in the absence of flagrant, unwarranted, or unauthorized action by the Board, it is not the function of the courts to review such proceedings."[51] Another court of appeals similarly augmented the Board of Parole's discretionary powers when it wrote that "the question of parole is ... a matter entirely for the judgment and discretion of the Board of Parole."[52] As far back as 1935, the Supreme Court has held that parole is not a right but an "act of grace" and that due process standards do not apply.[53]

While courts cling to this "hands-off" doctrine, it may appear that the seeds for change already exist. One important inference of *Wolff* v. *McDonnell,* for example, is that the arbitrary disciplining of an inmate may delay the timing of his ultimate release from prison. If the denial of a request for parole is the consequence of the inmate's failure to conform to prison regulations and if, in fact, disciplinary actions taken against a prisoner occurred in the absence of due process safeguards, or even if the decision to deny parole is interpreted as simply another form of disciplinary action, the necessary linkages are established to extend the due process cloak to the parole hearing. In this context, *Wolff* clearly emerges as a critical decision.

Another source for change is that the Supreme Court has been willing in recent years to extend constitutional guarantees to individuals seeking what has traditionally been referred to as privileges rather than rights. For instance, *Goldberg* v. *Kelley*[54] suggests that this legal dichotomy may no longer be a barrier. In that case, the court ruled that a welfare recipient had the right to a hearing, conforming to due process standards, before welfare benefits could be terminated. The decision is premised on the fact that due process standards need not be negated simply because a privilege was involved. When tied to the Court's decision in *Morrissey* v. *Brewer*[55] that parole revocation must be guided by due process, it would seem but a short step to extending the doctrine backwards to the initial parole decision.[56]

If and when parole is granted, the offender is placed under the supervision of a parole officer. At this stage of the system, the parolee has the obligation to abide by the rules agreed to as a condition of release from the correctional institution. Here too, the authorities have a wide latitude of discretionary authority in their supervision of the offender. A report on the New York parole system found that the parole officer can exercise a great deal of discretion in seeing that the parole agreement is satisfied.[57] In general, the parole officer prizes his right to use his discretion because it helps to maintain the current parole system. Because the parole agreement entered into by the offender contains so many technical rules, nearly all parolees violate parole at one time or another. If an officer were forced to recommend revocation for all violations of parole rules and regulations, he would be revoking a large majority of his caseload back to prison for only minor infractions. It must be understood that parole revocation cuts across both the discretionary release decision on the part of the parole board and the community supervision aspects of parole.

The Supreme Court decision of *Morrissey* v. *Brewer*[58] provides the revocated parolee with many rights. The due process requirements imposed upon a revocation hearing included (1) written notice to the parolee of alleged violations; (2) providing the parolee an opportunity to appear in person at the hearing and to bring witnesses and evidence; (3) the right of confronting and cross-examining hostile witnesses;

(4) a neutral and detached hearing body; and (5) a written statement by the revocation board concerning reasons for its decision and providing the evidence to support the conclusions. The Court nevertheless left many issues unresolved in *Morrissey*. Whether or not evidence obtained by a parole agent in an unauthorized search is admissible at a revocation hearing was not considered by the Court. Nor did the Supreme Court decide the issue of whether an indigent parolee is entitled to appointed counsel. However, *Morrissey* represents an initial attempt, and thus a very important step, towards imposing some restraints upon parole decision-making....

A proper understanding of how our legal system operates cannot be conveyed by a single tack, be it legal, political, sociological, or criminological. The legal scholar, for example, may see the problem of discretionary abuse as stemming from ambiguity in existing statutes. Solutions, accordingly, flow from a desire to correct existing legislative deficiencies or by proposing new legislation. The further development and refinement of judicial policies might appear of equal importance. The sociologist, on the other hand, may interpret the issue of discretionary decision-making from the perspective of interaction among actors within the criminal justice system. Social scientists, be they sociologists or political scientists, might view the issue from an empirical paradigm and thereby utilize empirical evidence tested with sophisticated statistical techniques to explore the complexities of discretion.

The fact that the quality of our system of justice depends, in large part, on the discretionary decisions of others is an uncomfortable reality. Our system of justice is not staid; the decisions that define its character are often the result of complicated, subtle, and sometimes irrational processes. They reflect a critical interplay between formal and informal legal norms, political events, organizational necessities, and psychological motives. In short, within the formal structure of criminal justice, they constitute the invisible system of *human* justice.

NOTES

1. Max Lerner, "Constitution and Court as Symbols," *Yale L. Rev.*, 46 (June, 1937), pp. 1290–1294.
2. Kenneth Culp Davis, *Discretionary Justice: A Preliminary Inquiry* (Baton Rouge: LSU Press, 1969), p. 4.
3. Kenneth Culp Davis, "Discretionary Justice," *J. Legal Ed.*, 23 (1970), pp. 58–59.
4. Roscoe Pound, "Discretion, Dispensation and Mitigation: The Problem of the Individual Special Case," *N.Y.U. L. Rev.*, 35 (1960), p. 925.
5. Justice Charles Breitel, "Controls in Criminal Law Enforcement," *U. Chi. L. Rev.*, 27 (Spring 1960), p. 427.
6. K. Davis, p. 97.
7. *Ibid.*
8. *Ibid.*, p. 142.
9. E. Bittner, "Police Discretion in Emergency Apprehension of Mentally Ill Persons," *Soc. Prob.*, 14 (Spring, 1967), p. 278.
10. J. Goldstein, "Police Discretion not to Invoke the Criminal Process: Low Visibility Decisions in the Administration of Justice," *Yale L. Rev.*, 69 (1960).
11. A. Rosett and D. Cressey, *Justice by Consent* (Philadelphia: Lippincott, 1976), p. 190.
12. President's Commission on Law Enforcement and Administration of Justice, *Task Force Report: The Police* (Washington, D.C., Government Printing Office, 1967) pp. 19–20.
13. James Finckenauer, "Higher Education and Police Discretion," *J.P.S. and Ad.* 3 (1975), pp. 450–457.
14. *Task Force Report: The Police*, 1967, p. 126.
15. Certainly an exception to this is considerable work done on the psychological and group dimensions of judicial choice. Useful summaries of this research can be found in Glendon Schubert, (ed.), *Judicial Behavior: A Reader in Theory and Research* (Chicago: Rand McNally, 1964).
16. Private Prosecution: A Remedy for District Attorney's Unwarranted Inaction," *Yale L. Rev.*, 65 (1955), p. 209.
17. *Ibid.*, p. 211.
18. *Ibid.*, p. 213.
19. *See* comment, "Prosecutorial Discretion in the Initiation of Criminal Complaints," *S. Calif. L. Rev.*, 42 (1969), p. 523.
20. Thomas Church, "Plea Bargaining and the Courts: Analysis of a Quasi-Experiment," *Law and Society Rev.*, (Spring, 1976), pp. 377–401.
21. F. Remington and Rosenblum, "The Criminal Law and the Legislative Process," *U. Ill. L. Forum*, 481 (1960), p. 497.
22. 184 F. Supp. 679, N.D. Ill., (1960).

23. 397 U.S. 742, 1970.

24. 404 U.S. 257, 260, 1971.

25. 400 U.S. 25, 1970.

26. Newman v. U.S., 382 F. 2d 479, 1967 D.C. cir.

27. 497 F. 2d 615, D.C. cir 1973.

28. Cited at p. 618 of *Ammidown*.

29. Newman v. U.S., *loc. cit.*

30. For a discussion of the "No Discretion" thesis, see Ronald Dworkin, "Judicial Discretion," *Journal of Philosophy*, 60 (1963), p. 624; *see also* Rolf Sartorius, *Individual Conduct and Social Norms* (1975) and Sartorius "Social Policy and Judicial Legislation," *Am. Phil. Q.*, 8 (1971), p. 151. For a review of their work, and a contrary position, *see* Kent Greenwalt, "Discretion and Judicial Decision: The Elusive Quest for the Fetters that Bind Judges," *Columbia L. Rev.*, 75 (1975), pp. 359-399.

31. Charles E. Ares, Anne Rankin, and Herbert Sturz, "The Administration of Bail in New York," *N.Y.U. L. Rev.*, 38 (1963).

32. Frederick Suffet, "Bailsetting: A Study in Courtroom Interaction," *Crime and Delinquency*, (October, 1966), pp. 318-331.

33. Compelling Appearance in Court: Administration of Bail in Philadelphia," *U. P. L. Rev.*, 102 (1954) pp. 1031-1043; 1051-1054.

34. Julian C. D'Esposoto, Jr., "Sentencing Disparity: Causes and Cures," *J. C. L. C. and P. S.*, 60 (1969), p. 183.

35. *See* Albert Somit, Joseph Tanenhaus and Walter Wilke, "Aspects of Judicial Sentencing Behavior," *U. Pittsburgh L. Rev.*, 21 (1960), pp. 613-621.

36. Charles B. Burr, II, "Appellate Review as a Means of Controlling Criminal Sentencing Discretion—A Workable Alternative?" *U. Pittsburgh L. Rev.*, 33 (Fall 1971), pp. 5-6.

37. James D. Hopkins, "Reviewing Sentencing Discretion: A Method of Swift Appellate Action," *UCLA L. Rev.*, 23 (1976) p. 498.

38. *See* Dean Jaros and Robert I. Mendelsohn, "The Judicial Role and Sentencing Behavior," *MW. J. Political Science*, 11 (November, 1967), pp. 471-488.

39. Marvin E. Frankel, *Criminal Sentences* (New York: Hill and Wang), 1973, pp. 13-14.

40. For further discussion, *see* W. Anthony Fitch and Julian Tepper, "Structuring Correction and Decision-Making: A Traditional Proposal," *Catholic U. L. Rev.*, 22 (1973), p. 776.

41. *See* Douglas J. Hitchcock, "The California Adult Authority—Indeterminate Sentencing and the Parole Decision as a Problem in Administrative Discretion," *U. Calif. at Davis L. Rev.*, 5 (1972), p. 373.

42. Procunier v. Martinez, 416 U.S. 396, 1974.

43. Holt v. Sarver, 300 F. Supp. 825, 1969.

44. Clutchett v. Procunier, 328 F. Supp. 767, 1971.

45. Banks v. Havener, 324 F. Supp. 27, 1964.

46. *See* Holt v. Sarver, *loc. cit.*

47. 418 U.S. 539, 1974.

48. V. O'Leary, M. Gottfredson and A. Gelman, "Contemporary Sentencing Proposals," *Crim. L. Bul.*, 11 (Sept.-Oct., 1975), pp. 555-586.

49. V. O'Leary and J. Nuffield, "Parole Decision Making Characteristics," *Crim. L. Bul.*, 8 (Oct., 1972), pp. 651-680.

50. Kenneth Culp Davis, *Discretionary Justice: A Preliminary Inquiry* (Baton Rouge: LSU Press, 1969), p. 126.

51. 477 F. 2d 278 5th cir 1973, p. 283.

52. Cagle v. Harris, 349 F. 2d 404 8th cir 1965.

53. Escoe v. Zerbst, 295 U.S. 490, 1935. Other recent federal court decisions rejecting the extension of constitutional rights at parole hearings are Menchino v. Oswald, 430 F. 2d 403 2nd cir. 1970; Barnes v. United States, 445 F. 2d 260 8th cir. 1971; and Buchanan v. Clark, 446 F. 2d 1379, 5th cir 1971.

54. 397 U.S. 254, 1970.

55. 408 U.S. 471, 1972.

56. For a fuller treatment of problems in this area, *see* Plotkin, 1975.

57. "Report on the New York Parole: A Summary by Citizens' Inquiry on Parole and Criminal Justice," *Crim. L. Bul.*, 11 (May-June, 1975), pp. 273-303.

58. 408 U.S. 471, 1972.

Study Questions

1. How do Atkins and Pogrebin define "discretion"? How does discretion contrast with due process, according to the authors?

2. Do Atkins and Pogrebin think that discretion in the criminal justice system should be eliminated, or merely controlled? Explain. Do you agree with their assessment here? Why? Defend your position.

3. Where in the criminal justice system is discretion most visible to the public? Where is it least visible? What are some of the major causes of the extent of discretionary decision-making in those areas?

4. Do Atkins and Pogrebin appear to support or reject a "hands-off" policy toward use of discretion? Discuss. Do you agree with their assessment? Why? Defend your position.

A Vignette on Loyalty:
The Rehabilitative Ideal and Corruption in Prison Administration

MARK S. HAMM

THE WORD LOYALTY WAS translated from Early Latin into the Old French *loial*, meaning "steadfast in allegiance to one's government," or "faithful to a person, ideal, or custom." Likewise, *vignette* is based on an Old French term, *vigne*, meaning "a literary sketch having the intimate charm and subtlety attributed to a portrait."

A vignette on loyalty, then, is an intimate and "charming" account of a writer's faithful allegiance to a government ideal. A vignette on loyalty must be unabashedly personal—like a self-portrait—and desperately clear about the persons and customs that constitute the subtle shadings of the images presented by the author. My vignette is on maintaining faith in an ideal while working for a public organization that has become corrupt.

I. Faith in Rehabilitation

I began my study of crime and justice at Indiana University during the late 1960s at the tail end of what is commonly referred to as the "golden era" of American criminology. There, I was strongly influenced—as were hundreds of other students at IU during that era—by Professor Alfred R. Lindesmith, a world-renowned expert on heroin addiction. At the time, Lindesmith's book, *The Addict and the Law* (Indiana University Press, 1965), was considered the most respected sociological analysis on the subject ever published in the United States.

Lindesmith's thesis was nothing short of revolutionary: Addiction to narcotics is a medical problem that can be most effectively controlled by physicians, not by agents of the criminal justice system. Lindesmith was a courageous champion of this thesis. Earlier in his career, he had published a series of articles in *The Nation*, detailing what he called "the moral bankruptcy of our narcotics laws." In response, former Bureau of Narcotics chief Harry J. Anslinger visited IU President Herman B. Wells, and attempted to persuade Wells that Lindesmith should be dismissed from his faculty post for expressing views that were anti-American.

Lindesmith was also an extraordinary teacher with great humanity. Long before the emergence of radical criminology and its hybrids—the *criminology of peacemaking, feminist criminology,* and *left realist criminology*—Lindesmith demonstrated an unwavering compassion for society's underdogs. For example, I recall being a student in Lindesmith's seminar on deviance during the fall of 1969 when the media and then-President Richard M. Nixon had all but condemned Charles Manson to death for the notorious Tate-LaBianca murders. Lindesmith was skeptical of such precipitous decision-making, and delivered an impassioned series of lectures highly critical of the circus-like atmosphere surrounding the Manson trial.

Yet from Lindesmith I learned a lesson that was far more practical than simply railing against social injustices. That is, no matter how wicked or deviant a criminal, punishment—in the absence of treatment—serves little purpose in terms of effective crime control. Instead, crime control comes through the painstaking process of matching specific causes of crime with specific cures (i.e., the well-known "medical model" of criminal justice). Under this formulation,

This essay was written expressly for inclusion in this book.

junkies can be treated with methadone, thieves can be treated by rearranging the array of people they associate with, and so forth. In other words, there is a *scientific* method of crime control that is based on a humane system of treatment.

At the time, there were few textbooks on corrections. Yet students of the era were not without models of effective rehabilitation. In fact, rehabilitation dominated the literature of penology published during the mid- to late 1960s. My first lessons in prison rehabilitation came through my interest in the Cuban Revolution and Fidel Castro.

During the late 1960s I became a member of the Venceremos Brigade, an international youth group dedicated to supporting the Cuban Revolution in both theory and practice. Most of the books used in university courses during this period were romanticized accounts of life in Cuba during the first 10 years of Castro's Revolutionary Government. Included within this literature were descriptions of a system of penology that was impeccably sensitive to the human rights of prisoners. In particular, I became fascinated with Cuba's agricultural programs. Under this system, prisoners spent their days working on farms, riding horses, caring for livestock, and tending crops.

During this period of Cuban history, Fidel Castro (himself a former prisoner) was a frequent visitor to Cuban prisons, where he passionately implored offenders to participate in their rehabilitation plan, thereby contributing to Cuba's revolutionary struggle for social justice throughout the Third World. Those prisoners who went along with this system of penology were given a remarkably high level of medical attention, academic education, recreation, and conjugal visits. Prisoners were paid the same wages as Cubans who held comparable jobs in the community, and they were even afforded the opportunity to play an occasional game of baseball with Fidel himself (the Maximum Leader is a pitcher known for his wicked fast ball!).

And so, it was the confluence of these idealized values—*compassion* and *service*—learned primarily from Lindesmith and Castro, that congealed into my full-throttled belief in prison rehabilitation. In time, I took these values to Arizona, where I started my education in government.

II. From Death Row to the State Capital

I began my career in corrections at the Arizona State Prison in Florence, a maximum security institution, during the fall of 1974. My assignment was to teach G.E.D. classes to prisoners confined to what was formerly called Death Row. (Two years earlier, in *Furman* v. *Georgia*, the U.S. Supreme Court had declared a moratorium on capital punishment in America, thereby commuting all death sentences to life imprisonment.) Yet I quickly learned that these prisoners—condemned for life—cared little about the G.E.D. diploma. They were wrestling with more important matters.

For comfort and emotional stability, these prisoners turned to the moral philosophies espoused in such texts as *The Bible*, Martin Buber's *I and Thou*, and *A Kierkegaard Anthology*. Black prisoners often turned to George Jackson's *Soledad Brother* and Eldridge Cleaver's *Soul on Ice*. From these condemned men, I learned that *hope* came through mental survival. And such survival was possible only if they indulged themselves in theology and philosophy.

Unlike Cuban prisoners, the condemned men of the Arizona State Prison had no access to horses, pigs, cows, chickens, or pineapple groves. There were no conjugal visits, no meaningful educational program, and certainly no baseball games with the nation's President, Gerald Ford. There were only ideas and the struggle for hope.

By 1976, the newly elected Carter administration had implemented a series of criminal justice reforms that opened up rehabilitation programs throughout the nation's prisons. One of these reforms was the U.S. Title I Program, which aimed to improve literacy among prisoners. After leaving the Arizona State Prison in 1975, I became a "Title I teacher" at the Arizona Youth Center, located in the spectacular Santa Catalina Mountains north of Tucson.

For the next five years, I became a combined social studies teacher, drug counselor, and agricultural supervisor for the institution. I also coached the basketball team, taught guitar and harmonica lessons, and developed a mountain survival course. Essentially, I was allowed free rein to engage in all manner of rehabilitation, and was rewarded for such efforts because rehabilitation was the guiding principle of the institution's philosophy.

In 1979, I moved to Phoenix and became the Principal of Adobe Mountain School. At the time, Adobe Mountain was one of the largest juvenile correctional institutions in the West. When I arrived, Adobe was filled to capacity with gang members and other violent (and not so violent) youth from Phoenix, Tucson, Los Angeles, San Diego and various points in between. But there were no rehabilitation programs. In fact, there was no real system of correctional management.

During my first day on the yard, I saw more than 300 inmates who did nothing but go to meal call, watch television, or play ping-pong or pool. Dozens of inmates were allowed to sleep all day long. The grass around the compound had not been cut in weeks, and was nearly two feet tall. Treatment staff did not follow a schedule, and their rehabilitative efforts were limited to sporadic individual counseling and tutoring sessions. Violence was rampant within the population, and to make matters worse, the former Superintendent of the school was under a Grand Jury indictment on charges of corruption, including a charge of sexual abuse against a female inmate (Adobe was a 400-plus-bed co-ed facility).

Such problems were not unusual within the Arizona Department of Corrections in those days. In 1977, the Florence prison experienced its most bloody riot in history. And in the summer of 1978, inmates Gary Tison and Randy Greenwalt escaped from Florence and went on a killing rampage that was unprecedented in Arizona history. To complicate matters, the Tison/Greenwalt escape had been linked to an organized crime network in Phoenix.

It was during these days that my staff and I transformed Adobe Mountain School into what the U.S. Department of Justice would one day call a "vibrant educational enterprise ... and a model of correctional treatment." By 1980, every student at the school was enrolled in a minimum of six classes per day. These included classes in reading, math, social studies, and life skills; agriculture, physical education, business machines, woodworking, and air-conditioning repair; cosmetology, computers, electronics assembly, music and art therapy; bookkeeping, beekeeping, solar energy, sex education, moral philosophy and outdoor survival.

We created an "Institutional Improvement Group" composed of inmates, staff, and administrators. Together we remodeled the antiquated Adobe facility with floor tile, carpet, and Native American art work. Solar energy panels were installed on each of the dormitories; a large garden provided an ample supply of vegetables for evening meals; and pecan seedlings were germinated in a newly acquired greenhouse and sold to agricultural enterprises in the greater Phoenix valley. The profits, in turn, were used to implement a tattoo removal program for gang members.

I began to gain media support for the Adobe Mountain reforms. During the summer of 1980, I was interviewed by Phoenix, Los Angeles, and Tucson radio and television reporters; and the reforms were detailed in a front-page feature of the *Phoenix Republic*. In essence, I was able to show concrete evidence of improvement at the school: The lawn was mowed, everyone was busy, the institution was clean and productive. But most importantly, violence and administrative corruption had ceased.

Because of this, a member of the Arizona Legislature introduced a provision into State law mandating that Arizona's Wildlife Preserve be established at Adobe Mountain School. This meant that the wild javelina, deer, rattlesnakes, antelope, eagles, and gila monsters captured by the State's Wildlife Department would come under my supervision, and therefore, under the care of street kids who had never been exposed to any of these magnificent creatures—their conception of nature, moreover, was limited to what they had seen in public parks. By 1981, the Adobe reforms had captured the attention of Arizona politicians.

III. *Administrative Politics and the Rehabilitative Ideal*

In the wake of the Florence riot, the Tison/Greenwalt rampage, and the allegations of DOC contacts with organized crime, Arizona Governor Bruce Babbitt came to realize that cleaning up the embattled prison system was necessary for his 1980 reelection and, therefore, for his future political aspirations. (In 1988, Babbitt would make a run as a Democratic candidate for President of the United States.) Given these times, and the complexity of these issues, Babbitt could not have made a wiser decision than to select Ellis C. MacDougall to become the newly appointed director of corrections for the State of Arizona.

During the 1970s, Ellis MacDougall was one of the most respected penologists in the nation. MacDougall had served as commissioner of corrections in four states—Maine, Mississippi, Georgia, and Alabama—and was the president of the American Correctional Association. Ellis was Jimmy Carter's campaign manager in the 1972 Georgia governor's race, a tenured professor in criminal justice at the University of South Carolina, and one of the nation's most outspoken advocates of offender rehabilitation.

The MacDougall style of prison administration was, to say the least, *dynamic*. Within months of his appointment, MacDougall had dismantled the "old boy" network in the Arizona DOC by calling for the resignations of four wardens, and by rearranging the entire administrative structure of the department. For the first time in the history of American corrections, MacDougall appointed a woman (Camile Graham) to run the adult division of his prison system.

The MacDougall reforms were wide sweeping and his impact on the media was astonishing.

During these days, Ellis wore his full head of white hair down to his shoulders. The media described him as "a modern-day General Custer" and he became a frequent visitor to Arizona prisons. MacDougall's favorite tactic was to show up unannounced in the middle of the night by way of a Department of Public Safety helicopter directed to land in the middle of the prison compound. There, long hair blowing in the desert wind, Ellis would take on all comers. It was often said that Ellis' ego was bigger than the Grand Canyon. Yet this scale could be matched by Ellis' vengeance against corruption, lazy management, and prisoners who fight the system and each another.

The most important MacDougall reforms, however, were made in the infrastructure of the agency. During his tenure, Ellis commissioned a group of university researchers to design one of the first computer-based management information systems in the field of corrections. He also approved and actively encouraged other university-based research projects and implemented a series of prison industry programs that interfaced with the private sector.

Having set reforms in place to control wardens and prisoners with managed intimidation and management information systems, Ellis set out to cement his relationship with the Arizona Legislature and Governor Babbitt. He did so by showcasing Adobe Mountain School as his ideal form of correctional management. As a result, I was put into regular contact with Ellis, Governor Babbitt, and members of the Arizona Legislature. My job was to explain how rehabilitation works in a correctional institution.

This effort was perceived as effective, and on June 5, 1981, I was appointed assistant director of the Arizona Department of Corrections. Now, my job was to administer all educational programs in the state's prison system. This included the administration of $7 million in community college contracts for prisoner education and $4 million in federal aid.

Thus, it became my responsibility to travel the state, monitoring, aiding and abetting the delivery of rehabilitation services. By mid-1982, our staff had developed a comprehensive special education program for prisoners, implemented a computerized management information system to track prisoner involvement in treatment programs, and secured a contract with a New York City publishing house for the free distribution of more than 100,000 books to prison libraries. Then an event took place that would change my life forever.

IV. The Million-Dollar Heist

In late August 1982, Ellis summoned me to his office, where I was introduced to the Arizona Director of Public Safety, a legislator from South Phoenix, and the Arizona Inspector General. I had just returned from a two-day inspection of the educational programs at the Fort Grant prison. "We've got a problem at Fort Grant," said Ellis. "Somebody stole more than $1 million in community college money. The receipts and computer printouts [evidence of the theft] are buried beneath the patio of the warden's house. Evidently, somebody took a jackhammer, buried the evidence, and cemented over it."

I told Ellis that I had heard this story the previous day from a freelance journalist who had traveled to Fort Grant to interview me, but I put little stock in the allegation. However, I said that I would look into it further, and Ellis apologized for having to distract me from what he called "more important matters."

I returned to Fort Grant the next day where the warden and I proceeded to dynamite his patio in search of lost receipts and printouts. We found nothing. I immediately informed Ellis of this and he thanked me for the information. This would be the last official conversation I ever had with Ellis MacDougall.

Over the next month, I worked with the Department's deputy director of internal affairs and deputy director of administration in an effort to discover information about the missing money. Although we found no evidence of any theft, the media intensified their coverage of the allegations surrounding the Fort Grant incident.

And during the first week of October, I was visited in my office by the director of internal affairs. Acting on orders from Director MacDougall, he summarily fired me from the Arizona Department of Corrections because of the controversy surrounding the alleged theft. My career in corrections was suddenly over.

V. Reflections on Loyalty and Corruption

No formal charges were ever brought against me for the $1 million heist. Indeed, just as quickly as I was fired, the media, the Department of Corrections, and the Department of Public Safety curiously lost interest in the entire affair. To this day, I do not know if there was ever, in fact, a theft of community college money; and if there was, I do not know who benefited from the heist. Over the course of the next year and a half (1982–1983), I appealed my dismissal to the Arizona Personnel Division, and in 1984 I was reinstated as an educational director within the Juvenile Division. Yet my reputation was sufficiently tarnished, and I would never walk the corridors of power again. In 1985, I resigned my position and quietly left Arizona and its prison system behind me.

Today, I am a tenured professor of criminology at Indiana State University. I live peacefully in a log cabin on the outskirts of Bloomington where, among other things, I write about prisons and their potential for rehabilitating inmates. I find myself, once again, inspired and sustained by the *criminology of humanity* I learned so long ago from Alfred Lindesmith and Fidel Castro. My loyalty to the rehabilitative ideal has never been stronger.

I am kindred in spirit with scholars such as Francis Cullen, Paul Gendreau, Jerome Miller, and Patricia VanVoorhis, who have created an eloquent body of literature on the effectiveness of prison rehabilitation; with William Chambliss, Marjorie Zatz, H. Michael Erisman, and Gaston Fernandez, who, despite popular opinion on the subject, continue to document the extraordinary struggles and achievements of the Cuban Revolution; and with William Bowers, Marla

Sandys, and Hal Pepinsky, who continue to provide meaningful evidence to support the fact that capital punishment is a ludicrous public policy.

As for the Arizona Department of Corrections, I harbor no ill will. I hold the agency responsible only for changing the organizational ethos that led to my fall from grace. I came to the organization steeped in the rehabilitative ideal. I practiced it well and had no personal agenda. I have never stolen from public resources; I do not possess the criminal know-how or ideology to do so. Yet the agency overlooked these facts in favor of *someone's* self-interest(s).

To be sure, it is entirely possible that a theft was committed. With more than $7 million in community college money at hand, it is also possible that this theft was quite large. If so, such a crime would have to be (1) covered up and (2) resolved as swiftly as possible without going to court.

No, I was not fired because of my performance; by all manner of evaluation I was an effective and efficient administrator who got along with fellow employees and did not cause problems. I was fired for another reason. Perhaps it was because I knew too much about the theft. (Importantly, shortly after my dismissal, Bob Zorn, the Fort Grant warden who helped me dynamite his patio, was also fired.) If so, I became a convenient scapegoat for this crime—my career, and the rehabilitative ideal, sacrificed on the altar of administrative corruption.

In the long run, however, I have suffered little from this public sacrifice. I don't know if the same can be said for the Arizona Department of Corrections. Recently, I toured the Arizona prison system. The reform-minded MacDougall has been gone for years. He was replaced by the director of public safety, Arizona's top law enforcement agent. The national trend toward punishment and "boot camp" training is clearly evident in these institutions. At Florence, nearly 100 men are now confined to Cellblock 6—Death Row—where they await execution. The Arizona Youth Center and Adobe Mountain School have been renamed. They are no longer schools; now they are called juvenile institutions. Inmates spend most of their days doing institutional maintenance and participating in paramilitary maneuvers. On my visit to Adobe Mountain, I watched a work crew of more than 50 inmates—dressed in paramilitary uniforms—spend the entire afternoon mindlessly raking rocks from one side of the compound to the other. I saw another crew of 50 who spent the afternoon picking up litter along Interstate 10.

There are no longer moral philosophy classes at Adobe; the greenhouse and solar energy panels have been dismantled and destroyed; there are no gardens, no music classes, and no tattoo removal programs; and there is no wildlife, no art, and no instruction in computers, electronics assembly, or sex education. Once again, violence is a problem and administrators are dedicated not to an ideal, but to simply maintaining institutional control so as to curry favor with the central office bureaucracy. For all intents and purposes, the rehabilitative ideal is dead.

VI. Conclusions

There are, I suppose, at least two morals to this story. The first is that individual values are important. When passionately embraced, values will sustain us when government acts to usurp good administration. Being loyal to values does not necessarily lead to success in public administration. In the ceaseless flux of modern correctional practice, government elites may oppose, support, or exploit our good intentions. The marvelous thing about values is that they operate on a personal level—they are fundamental beliefs about humankind that transcend the bureau-pathologies of modern government. It is our personal loyalty to values that sustains us when government has abandoned them in favor of self-interests.

The second moral operates on an organizational level. Values are necessary for good public administration. Unlike the boot camp model of contemporary corrections, the *rehabilitative ideal* is a value that has deep roots in academic sociology and political science. It is a value system that offers an effective crime control strategy. It is the absence of this value system, I believe, that is the moral cause of what has gone wrong in our prisons today.

SELECTED BIBLIOGRAPHY

Clarke, James W. (1989) *Last Rampage: The Escape of Gary Tison*. Boston: Little, Brown & Co.

Cullen, Francis T. and Karen E. Gilbert (1982) *Reaffirming Rehabilitation*. Cincinnati: Anderson.

Gendreau, Paul and Robert R. Ross (1987) "Revivification of Rehabilitation: Evidence from the 1980s." *Justice Quarterly* 3: 349–407.

Hamm, Mark S. (1989) "Political Rehabilitation in Cuban Prisons: The Plan Progressivo." *Journal of Correctional Education* 40: 72–79.

——— (1991) "The Abandoned Ones: A History of the Oakdale/Atlanta Prison Riots." In *Crimes by the Capitalist State: An Introduction to State Criminality*, edited by Gregg Barak. Albany, NY: State University of New York Press.

Lindesmith, Alfred R. (1956) "Traffic in Dope." *The Nation*, April 21.

——— (1957) "Dope: Congress Encourages the Traffic." *The Nation*, March 16.

——— (1958) "Our Immoral Drug Laws." *The Nation*, June 21.

Lockwood, Lee (1969) *Castro's Cuba, Cuba's Fidel*. New York: Vintage Books.

MacDougall, Ellis C. (1976) "Corrections Has Not Been Tried." *Criminal Justice Review* 1: 63–76.

Szulc, Tad (1986) *Fidel: A Critical Portrait*. New York: Avon.

Study Questions

1. What relationship does Hamm find between punishment and crime control? How does the "medical" model of corrections fit into this discussion? Do you agree with Hamm? Why? Defend your position.

2. Describe the reforms instituted by Hamm at the Adobe Mountain School in 1979. Were they appropriate to the goals of juvenile corrections, in your view? Discuss.

3. Do a brief literature search on Ellis MacDougall. What correctional ideas stand out? Does prison reform require the efforts of individuals such as Hamm or MacDougall, or can it be achieved entirely through policy? Discuss.

4. Describe the changes made at Adobe Mountain School after Hamm left the Arizona system. Do you agree with the changes? Why? Defend your position.

5. Discuss the clash between prison reform and the "punishment/boot camp" model of the 1980s with your instructor. Should state-level corrections administration be assigned to a law enforcement official, as it was in Arizona? Why? What ethical issues regarding rehabilitation could arise?

Case 10.1

PROTECTING YOUR TURF*

The position of senior resident agent in a small Midwestern city entailed substantial liaison responsibilities. It was well known among law enforcement personnel that the FBI was severely handicapped because of the lack of agents and because support staff were located only in the headquarters city. Without a doubt, help and cooperation from the local police kept the image of the FBI alive. The FBI, often underfunded by Congress, could not be efficient, but was under severe pressure to produce statistics showing convictions of criminals who committed federal offenses and also to report recoveries. Everyone knew that when the director went before congressional budget hearings, those statistics would be the main factors in obtaining funds.

One of the investigative fields handled by the FBI, and more specifically by the resident agents, was bank robberies. In all honesty, many were solved by local and state authorities; however, the FBI agents followed up after the apprehensions to gather evidence and interview witnesses because the detective facilities of the local law enforcement agencies were less adequate and many times heavily loaded, sometimes even more so than the federal agencies. Many times, the perpetrator was caught and ready to confess in any court, but the FBI tried by every means possible to have the criminal brought into federal court, even though the penalty was often less severe than conviction in state court. Recoveries in those cases were claimed by both the local agency and the FBI. Those recoveries, fines, restitutions, and so forth, served both agencies in their budget preparations.

In several instances the local prosecutor wanted to prosecute in a state court, often using the argument of more severe penalties, i.e., exclusive of the federal law and capital offense provision when the victim was killed, injured, or kidnapped. A senior resident agent was expected to overcome that kind of argument, knowing that the prosecutor often wanted the conviction to promote his image and get the publicity, not only for reelection purposes, but also because many prosecutors aspire to be judges. Good conviction records can result in future judicial positions.

Any person in that position might be tempted to accomplish his end by insisting on local prosecution. It is difficult to assess motivation, but it is fair to say that many times the prosecutor felt that the crime was solved by local agencies dealing directly with his office and that federal agents did little more than report the results to the U.S. Attorney.

Thus, the pressure on the senior resident agent in dealing with the many prosecutors in his area becomes an ethical question. He is aware of his agency's demands and of the desires of the U.S. Attorney for a high conviction rate. The resident agent weighs that knowledge and the solution of the case. If the FBI did the investigation and ultimately solved the case, the prosecution should clearly be in federal court.

*This case was written by a former FBI agent who wishes to remain anonymous.

However, if the locals apprehended the violators and made a strong case, a real problem will arise.

In such circumstances, ordinary ethical behavior says that the case should be prosecuted locally, but the resident agent feels that to remain in his position and to meet the demands from his superiors he must use arguments that perhaps are less than ethical. One plausible argument is to point out that most state prisons, as well as the court dockets, are already overcrowded, and that federal prosecution would be less expensive to local taxpayers. The next most effective argument is that the federal law, specifically the Federal Reserve Act, covers embezzlements, fraud, etc., committed in banks—not all banks, but most of them. This means that in most cases, investigation for successful prosecution requires the use of a qualified accountant. It is rare that a local prosecutor has such expertise in his office or even in any agency where he could request such assistance. Hiring a CPA, or another qualified expert, could well drain the budget of most prosecutors. So the dilemma for the senior resident agent is whether he can ethically point out that if the local prosecutor insists on prosecuting bank robberies, he can also take responsibility for enforcement of laws governing embezzlements and related crimes within the banks. The FBI, in contrast, does have the accountant agents available to prosecute such criminal violations. The fact is that the FBI is not going to stop investigations under the Federal Reserve Act because convictions and recoveries, fines, etc., usually far exceed the bank robbery statistics. The local prosecutors would not be told that.

So it comes down to ethics. Federal prosecution seems to be a practical solution because it does have advantages to all concerned, except to local prosecutors' personal goals. Ethical practitioners in any profession should exercise extreme caution in stretching or omitting the truth. In the above scenario, the real truth was more than stretched. Clear-cut ethical conduct is, then, like beauty—it is in the eyes of the beholder. Pragmatic behavior often supersedes ethical standards. Subsequent evaluation and judgment form an easy basis for condemnations. Intent and motivation should be considered, but maliciousness or other harm should be weighed as a mitigating circumstance in some cases and as an aggravating circumstance in others.

Even today, looking back as the senior resident agent who used just such a questionable approach in settling turf quarrels, I certainly could be admonished, congratulated, or anything in between. For instance, a number of cases were tried in local courts when murder or felony murder was involved because there was a clear-cut mandatory life or death sentence. These were judgment calls, which fortunately were never questioned by anyone but me as I examined my own ethical behavior.

Questions for Discussion

1. Identify the personal, professional, and political considerations at play in this case. How might all (or most) of these considerations be resolved to everyone's satisfaction? Explain.

2. What would you do? Apply a utilitarian analysis to your decision. Apply the Categorical Imperative to your decision. Apply Gert's Moral Rules to support/counter your decision.

Case 10.2

NEIGHBORHOOD CRIMINAL EVICTION

The drug problem was getting totally out of hand. As Chief Andres Gonzales was driving down Plumb Street with his family three weeks ago, he saw at least two drug deals go down. To make matters worse, the dealers weren't even doing the selling. They would stand 50 or 60 feet away and watch as the "Munchkins," children no more than 10 or 11 years old, did the deals for them. Something more had to be done.

The Plumb Street neighborhood used to be a good place to live. Most of the residents were middle class people who worked for the city's largest employer, National Chemical. Three years earlier, "The National" was purchased by a large West Coast conglomerate, and operations at the local plant were greatly curtailed. As a result, unemployment in the Plumb Street neighborhood increased dramatically and with it an increase in criminal activity. Still, it was a close-knit area. The residents worked closely with the police department in attempts to keep the neighborhood a nice place to live. They formed the Plumb Street Neighborhood Association, a Community Watch Program, and a Neighborhood Citizens Patrol in an effort to keep down the criminal activity. A Community Police Officer was assigned to the area to coordinate activities. Still, there seemed to be no significant impact on the criminal and drug activity in the area. Two weeks ago, Chief Gonzales called a meeting of the Plumb Street Neighborhood Association. After four hours of debate and discussion, he emerged from the meeting with the following list of drug and crime control propositions to be implemented after two weeks of public hearings and notices:

1. Each resident of the Plumb Street neighborhood over the age of 8 shall be issued a photo identification card to be carried with them at all times.

2. Any person in the Plumb Street neighborhood shall display the identification card to a police officer upon request.

3. Persons in the Plumb Street neighborhood without identification and not an invited guest of a resident shall leave the neighborhood.

4. Any resident may request the police department to check on suspicious persons. The police shall respond and identify the person.

5. Police may establish checkpoints from time to time to limit ingress of nonresidents or nonguests.

6. "Cruising" past the same location more than once in a three-hour period shall be prohibited.

Yesterday, after two weeks of public hearings (in which no persons objected), the Neighborhood Criminal Eviction Program was implemented.

Questions for Discussion

1. Should citizens be allowed to set restrictions upon themselves to limit their victimization?

2. Should the rights of nonresidents be curtailed in the pursuit of safety?

3. Apply a Kantian perspective to the crime control propositions set forth in this case.

Case 10.3

TRUTH OR SCARE

It has been several weeks since your transfer to Mudville Correctional Institution and the assumption of your new job as deputy warden of programs. You feel satisfied with what you have observed thus far and feel that no major changes will be required in either your department's procedures or personnel. One area, nominally under the control of your department, that you have yet to evaluate is the institution's Scared Straight program.

Mudville's Scared Straight program is considered to be one of the most successful in the state. There is a long waiting list of youth groups who wish to attend. The effectiveness of the program in lowering the recidivism rates of the participating juveniles, which has always been good, has increased significantly during the past few years. You are looking forward to seeing your first presentation this Friday. You are also pleased that you have been able to convince Major Slug, the institutional head of security, to attend the program for the first time. Major Slug, you have gathered from the short time you have known him, has little love for the inmates or their "do-gooder" service programs. You hope Friday's presentation will modify some of his views.

The program begins with a mock orientation and processing of the juveniles into the system. The juveniles are issued orange coverall uniforms, made to stand at attention, and in general treated in a rough boot camp fashion. During this phase, there is also much open sexual taunting of the juveniles by the inmates. Then the juveniles are each assigned an identification number, ordered to remember it, and told to "forget they ever had a name." It is not uncommon for at least one juvenile offender to faint dead away from sheer terror during this part of the program.

After the juveniles are "processed in," they are given a tour of the inmates' living quarters. A strict, military-style discipline is also maintained during this phase of the program.

The tour then proceeds to the auditorium for its final and longest phase. Here, several volunteer inmate "counselors" speak to the assembled group. The first few inmates talk about their past lives of crime, how they thought they were "bad muthahs" on the street, how they now wish they had respected their parents, etc. Your problems begin when the inmates turn to the topic of their lives inside the prison. Security in the institution, one speaker states, is a "joke." "If you come in here," he says, "you can expect to be robbed and punked out[1] in the first week, count on it." Another speaker rails against the quality of the institution's food, hinting that this is due to corruption. The next speaker addresses the topic of vocational training in the institution. "Don't expect to learn a skill in this joint, they don't teach you nothin' in these classes here." Other speakers, who work in the penal industries, attack the administration for the low pay ($22 a month) that they receive for their labors. "Our state is in the prison business," one inmate says. "It uses slave labor at slave wages to make money on the products it sells."

The same basic anti-administration themes are repeated by a few more speakers and then the program concludes. You are surprised and angry about what you have heard. You feel that most of the inmate counselors presented a genuinely unfair and untrue characterization of prison life. Major Slug, you noted, left the program in a rage before it was finished. You wonder how he will deal with this open and public verbal attack on the security of his institution each week. For your part, you resolve to investigate the situation further before you act.

The next day, you call the director of social services, a Ms. Wallace, into your office. You begin by asking her questions about the structure of the Scared Straight program. You are told that the only actual inmate-employee of the program is inmate Garcia (the rest are volunteers). It is Garcia who coordinates the program, secures the inmate volunteers and, you believe, sets the overall tone of the presentation. He and Ms. Wallace encourage the inmates to express their anger and frustration with the penal system. You state that, in your opinion, this practice has led to some very unfair attacks on the security and programs of the institution. Ms. Wallace concedes that some of the inmates' anti-administration statements are "exaggerated." On the other hand, she firmly believes that they are justified by the program's great effect on juvenile recidivism rates.

Later that day you speak to inmate Garcia. Your belief that Garcia is the force behind the anti-administration tone of the program is quickly confirmed. Garcia is an intelligent and motivated convict-activist. He tells you, and your further research confirms this, that both he and the program are greatly respected by many prominent professionals in the criminal justice field who have viewed the program and who, he suggests, share his basic view of the penal system. "I believe that our program presents a true picture of prison life," Garcia says. "If you want me to change anything, you will have to give me a direct order to do so." Of course, both he and you know that he will refuse to obey that type of direct order, immediately lose his job, and face disciplinary action. The constitutional and public relations problems that would follow would be, you suspect, considerable.

Two days later, there is a large-scale and intensive shakedown of Three Block. The search is supposedly the result of an inmate-informant's tip regarding drug-related activity in that lock. A pound of marijuana is found in the bathroom area. Some smaller amounts of various drugs are found in a few cells also, including two marijuana cigarettes in the cell of inmate Garcia. You hear the details of this only after you happen to see Major Slug personally escorting Garcia to the segregation unit. When the major passes by you, he smiles and winks, but says nothing. Since then, he has seemed hesitant to discuss the Three Block search with you.

Inmate Garcia, of course, denies that the marijuana cigarettes are his and asserts that they were planted in his cell by the officers conducting the search. You know that it will be almost impossible for Garcia to prove this allegation. You also know that Major Slug can be quite impulsive and aggressive, although you won't let yourself believe he could do something so foolish. Still, you wonder.

As you sit at your desk, you consider your options. The penalty for holding such a small amount of drugs will not be severe. Under normal circumstances, an inmate would receive five days in the hole and then return to his former lock and job assignment. But Garcia's job involves a special position of trust. You know that you have every right to dismiss Garcia from his job based upon his drug-related rule infraction (and probably incur a minimum amount of flack from his outside supporters). On the other hand, with Garcia fired, you are certain the program would collapse. You don't know how long it would take to rebuild such an effective and popular program. You know that the program has helped many troubled juveniles. You sincerely believe, however, that the program's false and distorted view of life in prison is more of a problem than just bad publicity. You believe that it perpetuates the worst of the negative stereotypes of prison and in the long run could do great harm to not only the prison but the entire criminal justice system. You consider all of these factors (and try not to think about Major Slug's search).

What should you do?

Note

1. A sexual assault on an immature, young, and naive inmate by an older, aggressive inmate.

Questions for Discussion

1. Would the inmates be doing a disservice to the juveniles by downplaying the conditions of the prison?

2. Is it all right to exaggerate (or lie) for the purpose of deterring future criminal activity on the part of these children? Refer to the chapter on Truth for assistance.

3. Is the purpose of the program to criticize the institution, or to salvage a potentially criminal person?

4. Is the program an appropriate outlet for the inmates' anger and frustration?

Case 10.4

WHAT ABOUT BETSY?

"And do you, Betsy, take Luke to be your lawful wedded husband?"

Sheriff Cruse sat in the front pew of the church. It was hard to believe that Betsy was actually getting married. She was like a daughter to him, he thought. In fact, since her parents were killed two years ago, he had become her surrogate father.

He was honored when she asked him to "give her away."

He reflected on the day he first met Betsy. He was just turning the corner down the main hallway of the sheriff's office. Rushing in the opposite direction, her arms full of case files and her mind miles away, came Betsy. The resultant collision must have been a sight to behold—files flying, his coffee drenching his uniform and the timid little clerk.

The accident was to become a benefit. Sheriff Cruse kept an eye on Betsy for the next couple of years. He watched her develop into one of the most competent and trusted employees in the records section. She was promoted to supervisor. She completed her college degree in public administration. She had a natural ability for organization and was single-handedly responsible for increasing the efficiency of her department by almost 100 percent. All this with no complaints on the part of her employees. She was, without a doubt, an ideal employee and supervisor.

When the position of administrative assistant to the sheriff became available, Cruse immediately thought of Betsy. His current assistant, Mrs. Phillips, was an institution at the office, and was retiring after almost thirty years. She would be a tough act to follow. Sheriffs may come and go, Cruse thought, but it always seemed that Mrs. Phillips would go on forever. She *was* the sheriff's office. When he offered the position to Betsy, she didn't hesitate and accepted at once.

Betsy made Mrs. Phillips look almost incompetent. Her transition had none of the usual problems. It was as if she had been in the position for years. In short, she made the sheriff look good. She was efficient, handled his appointments in a businesslike yet friendly manner, and had wonderful human relations skills. Just like the records section when she was the supervisor, Cruse's office was running smoothly. And, Betsy got along well with everyone. The sheriff, in all the years he had been there, had never heard anyone say anything critical about Betsy.

As the wedding ceremony progressed, he thought how lucky the groom was. He was getting a wonderful wife. Betsy wasn't doing badly, either. The sheriff did not usually approve of in-house relationships. For some reason, when those couples fought or broke up, the department usually suffered as it went through the period when her side didn't speak to his side, and vice versa. Yet, Betsy and Luke seemed to avoid those pitfalls. There was never anything short of pure professionalism while they were working. They both possessed the highest moral and ethical standards of anyone the sheriff had ever met.

"And do you Luke, take Betsy, to be your lawful wedded wife?"

Of 347 deputies, Luke was the best, bar none. He was the only deputy in the history of the department to turn down a promotion. He studied and passed the promotional exam. He was head and shoulders above the next highest candidate. He had proven supervisory skills. When his sergeant was shot last year, he took over the squad. Like Betsy's records section, Luke's squad's efficiency increased, and he was also well liked and respected by his peers and other supervisors. He didn't turn down the promotion because he distrusted management or didn't want to become "one of them." He just liked working the road. And he was good at it. His stats were high and complaints were few and usually unfounded. (A citizen did complain about him one time and, while the complaint was minor, it was sustained. Rather than deny and fight it, Luke simply admitted his mistake.) The sheriff often wondered what it would be like to have an entire department of deputies like Luke. The perfect department, he thought. It was funny, Cruse thought, even when Luke wore his "hat" as union steward and chief negotiator at contract time, he was still a consummate professional. They had been through some knock-down, drag-out, marathon negotiating sessions and, like the prosecutor and defense attorney, always walked out of the session as they had come in—no animosity, no irritation.

"By the power vested in me by this church and this state, I now pronounce you man and wife."

Now it was official. Tough union negotiations were approaching. Your administrative assistant has access to a great deal of confidential information about the union and other administrative matters. She is now married to the chief union negotiator.

What about Betsy?

Questions for Discussion

1. Is there a conflict of interest here? Why? Defend your position.
2. Is it appropriate to assume that there will be indiscretions with respect to the office of the sheriff?
3. Should Betsy be transferred, or should the sheriff wait until a complaint is made?

Case 10.5

A MORAL RIGHT

One of the nice things about being a supervisor, Sandra Otte thought as she walked into her condo on this Friday evening, is that there weren't that many after-hours calls from clients in crisis or police officers who have arrested one of her probationers. Now, although she had a great deal more responsibility, the after-hours calls were limited to her probation officers who had major problems. She was proud of the fact that she supervised 10 professionals who carried out their duties with a minimum of supervision. As she sat in her easy chair, Steen, her pet cat, settled contentedly into her lap.

Her game plan was a simple one. Catch the evening news and spend the remainder of the weekend reading. As the evening news came into focus, she knew that her game plan was about to be dramatically altered.

Erieville had been the focus of a recent effort by a large group of Right-to-Life activists to halt abortions at the New Women's Clinic. On the other hand, the local, state, and national chapters of the National Organization for Women were equally opposed to Right to Life's goal. The confrontations and emotions had escalated in recent days, and many felt violence was imminent. Tonight's news coverage focused on the attempts of the Right-to-Life members to block the entrance to the clinic by forming a "human chain." At the center of the chain was Johann Farnsworth, one of Sandra's senior probation officers. Within seconds, a spokesperson for the New Women's Clinic announced to the demonstrators that they were closing their doors for the day. The demonstrators then disbanded without incident.

Other than Johann's opposition to abortion under any circumstance, he has been an excellent employee. The only real problem in his performance came within a few days of his joining the staff. Johann had a bumper sticker on his car that said "Pro-Abortion? Too Bad Your Mother Wasn't." After Sandra consulted with her supervisor and the judge, it was agreed that this type of judgmental bumper sticker was not consistent with the nonjudgmental setting that much of the agency's client counseling provided. Johann agreed to cover up the bumper sticker. Sandra made it clear that she was not dictating Johann's personal values. She was just preventing a negative impact that those values might have on his clients. In fact, Sandra sympathized with Johann.

When Sandra learned that Right to Life was going to target Erieville and that Johann was the president of the local chapter, it was necessary for her to remind him that county policy dictates that employees not participate in public political activities. Additionally, increasing tension between the demonstrating groups resulted in a restraining order against any demonstrations within 100 feet of the entrance to a clinic.

As Sandra watched the demonstrators disperse, it appeared that no arrests would be made or police action taken. However, she had just observed one of her employees violating policy and a court order. She now had to spend the rest of the weekend pondering what action to take on Monday.

Questions for Discussion

1. Should an employer be allowed to set limits on an employee's off-duty activities? Under what circumstances and to what extent?

2. Johann was in violation of a court order prohibiting demonstrating within 100 feet of the clinic. No arrests or police actions were taken at the time of the demonstration. Should Sandra take action?

3. Assume that Sandra failed to report her observations. Would that be a cover-up?

Chapter 11

Ethics and the Realities of Life: Surviving the Vortex

"I'M A MORAL PERSON. I KNOW right from wrong. Why should I study ethics?" From the sterility of the classroom or the safety of the armchair, this may appear to be a logical argument. One can liken this position to that of a sports fan attending a football game. From the safety of the 50-yard line, many observations can be made about the ineptness of the receiver or the inadequacy of the quarterback who failed to see an obvious opening. Yet, if we were to afford our "armchair quarterback" the luxury of joining the players on the field, calling the play, taking the snap, and then facing several large persons from the opposition intent on permanently embedding our critic into the turf, an entirely new perspective would emerge.

The same holds true in the ethical decision-making arena. In the classroom, away from external influences and those with vested interests in the decision, taking the correct moral course is relatively easy. However, like our sports critic, when on the field and facing the realities of life, unintended outcomes often result.

What forces could lead an otherwise ethical person to an unethical (and possibly illegal) decision? In this final chapter, William Tafoya gives us some insight. He analyzes how a police officer fell prey to what Tafoya calls a vortex: a whirlpool that consumes everything (or everyone) caught in its motion.

The reader may tend to dismiss this case as an anomaly. However, one would do well to keep in mind that the officer who was caught in this vortex was equally convinced that he would never, under any circumstances, participate in the behavior described below.

The Vortex

WILLIAM TAFOYA

Introduction

Several years ago, a group of police officers from a major metropolitan police department were terminated for their involvement in the attempted cover-up of the beating and subsequent death of a black motorist. Recently, in a different large city a similar incident occurred with even more widespread consequences. In the wake of the beating of Rodney King by members of the Los Angeles Police Department in 1991, much has been publicized. How much has been learned? What has changed? This case study should be instructive. It should demonstrate that regardless of how far policing has progressed, much more remains to be accomplished.

One of the former officers involved in the earlier incident sought me out. It is not the first time he has confided his past in someone, but it may be the first time the events he describes have been systematically verified. Following our initial discussion in 1991 and then in greater depth following the interview itself, open source information was used to validate the interpretation presented by this former police officer. He and the others terminated were dismissed for lying under oath during the administrative inquiry of the incident.

The irony, however, is not that they lied and were caught. What is incongruous is that even though this officer realized that what he was doing was wrong, he felt *compelled* to lie. Even though he sensed the cover-up would fail, he nevertheless believed he must go along with the attempt to do so. What a paradox. Why would an intelligent person do that?

We generally believe that those who lie or commit criminal acts are of low moral character or are otherwise lacking in something the rest of us possess. The tragedy is that such ethical dilemmas may occur and be resolved in the same manner with greater frequency than anyone would like to believe. *That* is the real issue. That is the message of this case study. This issue has been ignored for far too long.

The interview that follows was conducted in two sessions in 1992. One of the most striking aspects of this person's experience is that the typical "excuses" or explanations for such behavior—inferior early childhood environment, poor adult role models, educational deprivation, etc.—are absent. This individual enjoyed an exceptional "middle-America" upbringing. One expects from such a person a heightened sense of morality. Today this person not only espouses principles but evidences integrity in his behavior. While he is not employed by a law enforcement agency, he is in a very responsible position that enables him to counsel and consult with young people interested in criminal justice and policing.

The lesson intended to be conveyed in this exposition is that it is not merely the inadequately prepared who are susceptible to legal or ethical impropriety. We all are.

A full review of the facts of the case is beyond the scope of this inquiry. Rather, the case will focus on the various forces that led this officer to his decision. To protect the privacy of innocent parties and to avoid the recrimination of others, the names of persons and places have been disguised.

For the reader's convenience, the following convention is used:

Q = question of the interviewer, the author;

A = answer of person interviewed, the former police officer.

This essay was written expressly for inclusion in this book.

Interview One

Question (Q): Something has been bothering you for a long time. Tell me about it.

Answer (A): It concerns the beating and subsequent death of a motorist and my involvement in the attempted cover-up.

Q: Many years have passed since then. Why have you not been able to put the matter behind you?

A: Because I did some things that go against my basic character, upbringing, and sense of justice. I was talked into doing something that I would not have thought possible. It is something I have had to live with; it has not been easy.

Q: Have recent nationally publicized events brought back to consciousness your experience?

A: The beating of Rodney King has not created any more anxiety for me, but I can't help reflecting on the parallels. For example, a lot of people who analyzed the Rodney King incident have concluded it was racially motivated. I don't think it was. In that regard the Rodney King incident was similar to the one in which I was involved.[1]

Q: Was the situation in which you were involved racially motivated?

A: No. In my case a group of officers surrounded a man and beat him because he ran, not because he was black, although that was alleged.

Q: Do you see other similarities between the two incidents?

A: Yes, I think so. In both incidents there was a group of officers—including me—standing around in the background while a smaller group of officers did the actual beating. In that regard the two incidents were identical.

Q: Do you think that some time in the future the officers involved in the Rodney King beating are going to feel the way you do now?

A: That's an interesting question. I watched the television coverage of the LAPD officers coming out of the courtroom in Simi Valley at the start of their state trial. Three of the four had very arrogant looks on their faces as if thinking, "This isn't going to be anything; we're going to get through it." But the fourth officer—he appeared to be the youngest—looked terrified, scared to death. You could see the look on his face. He looked to me like somebody who said, "I screwed up." He realized the gravity of the situation. I remember thinking, "This guy realizes that he is in big trouble."

Q: Did you identify with him?

A: Yes, I really did. I thought, "You poor kid."

Q: Can you recall what happened immediately prior to the incident?

A: *(Laughs.)* If I had stayed at the doughnut shop, I'd never have been involved. I was working alone that night and went over to the doughnut shop in City B to have a cup of coffee when I heard a call go out over the [police] radio to an officer I knew and liked. I responded because I was close by; I was first on the scene. Shortly thereafter the officer assigned the call arrived. He and I spoke briefly, when the sergeant rolled up. Moments later a motorist pulled up to the intersection. I don't know why, but when he did—fully aware of our presence—he loudly revved the engine of his vehicle; he really drew attention to himself unnecessarily. Had he just pulled away from the intersection we wouldn't have gone after him; we were preoccupied with the assigned call.

Q: Had any of several decisions of a number of people—the motorist, the sergeant, you—been made differently, the outcome might have been different. Sheer coincidence?

A: I'd never been there!

Q: Tell me what you recall from the week preceding the incident. What was going on in your life personally?

A: That's an interesting question. I don't recall anything.

Q: Nothing extraordinary? Nothing bothersome that had occurred very recently?

A: No.[2]

Q: I am trying to get at your state of mind at

the time of the incident involving the motorist.

A: Maybe I wasn't the police type, but I always tried to keep a good attitude. I tried never to be negative toward the people I came into contact with. I always tried to approach people in a positive manner. I loved my job. I loved going to work. I loved the excitement. I loved the fact that ... *(Suddenly recalls.)* I don't think it was the week before, maybe a little earlier. I got a commendation for it. I saved a lady's life. I found her on a toilet in a restroom at 2:00 A.M.; she wasn't breathing. It wasn't even my district. When I heard the call I was near; I just crossed into the other district. I gave her mouth-to-mouth and revived her. Saved her. You know, it was a good feeling. I liked doing that kind of police work. I enjoyed it. I didn't go out with the attitude that I was going to put everybody in jail. I probably let more people go than I arrested. I tried to treat everybody with respect.

Q: Would you agree or disagree with the following characterization: "This couldn't possibly happen to me. I'm not like that; I'm not that kind of person."

A: That is an accurate statement. I grew up in a little Christian Reformed community. I'm a religious person. I know what the truth is. I know you are supposed to be honest. That is probably what has bothered me more than anything else. I know what I did was wrong. I knew it was wrong when I did it. I was sick with myself; still am.

Q: You realized—at the time—that what you were doing was wrong?

A: I knew what was going down at the time. That's why I got the hell off the scene as quickly as I could. Okay, I should have written the report because I caught the guy.

Q: You left the scene quickly?

A: Alright. After the beating I knew what was gonna go on. I knew what they [the officers who did the beating] were gonna want from me.

Q: You knew they were going to expect you to be part of the cover-up?

A: After they beat the guy, I knew there was no way they could just sweep it under the rug.

Q: How much time passed between the time of the incident and your going to Internal Affairs?

A: Six or seven hours.

Q: So it wasn't immediately. You had time to think about it and yet you participated in the cover-up attempt.

A: Yes. Immediately after I realized what was going on. I didn't want to be part of it. I left the scene and tried to hide. I listened to the radio traffic for the rest of the night. Officers who had been involved talking back and forth: meet me there, change the call to this, change the call to that. And I knew what was going to happen when I rolled up behind the station at the end of the shift. I just *knew*.

Q: Think back to the moment you walked out of Internal Affairs. What went through your mind?

A: I remember distinctly. I couldn't believe what I had just done. I was scared. I had been intimidated. I stood by and watched my fellow officers beat a man senseless, officers I knew had a propensity for the use of excessive force.

Q: Did you fear retaliation?

A: Yes. This goes back a long way, before I joined the police department. I was socialized early and often in the police culture by friends who were police officers. From them I heard repeatedly that the most important lesson to be learned was sticking together. One friend, [Fred], suggested that if I ever saw anything I thought was improper—and was a rookie—I should keep quiet, go back to the car, and make like I was writing a report; stuff like that.

In the police academy, I remember this very distinctly. We were taking a traffic test and I noticed that some of the questions were repetitive or the answers were obvious in other parts of the test. The test was intentionally too easy. Some of us [discussed this after the exam and decided to] mention it to the instructor. The training sergeant responded: "What a bunch of Hand-ups." I had never heard that phrase before.

A woman in our training academy class had previously done an internship with the department's Detective Bureau. She seemed to know everything there was to know about law enforcement. We asked her about what it meant. She said rather sarcastically that "Hand-up" is the worst insult one police officer can give another. A "Stand-up" cop is one who covers for a fellow officer. Everybody likes such officers, trusts them. Such officers go to bat for one another. But a "Hand-up" cop is likely to tell the truth and not cover for a fellow officer. It was then that I first began to understand that in the police culture, telling the truth was not always a virtue.

When a Stand-up cop is in trouble, every cop in the world materializes out of thin air to help at the scene. When an officer gets a reputation as a Hand-up cop, he is shunned. If such an officer gets in trouble and calls for backup, other officers respond to cover only if dispatched to do so and even then they take wrong turns, their car seems to stall, or they are delayed in some other way, okay? Get it?

I remember a situation after I had been on the road just four or five weeks. I saw something I didn't think was right so I turned around and went back to my patrol car. I made like I was writing a report. And from that time forward, they all worried a little bit about me. If anybody was likely to tell the truth, they speculated I was the most likely to do so.

Do you see the dilemma for a cop? It isn't enough to walk away. Keeping one's mouth shut is not sufficient. Doing that signals that "I can't be trusted." You must participate to be completely accepted. And police

officers are tested—regularly—to ensure they are Stand-ups.

That is why they got on me especially hard that morning at the end of shift. They were afraid that I would be scared and tell the truth. I had no one to turn to. I was relatively new on the squad; I wasn't really tight with anybody. Everyone around me had a vested interest in this thing.

Q: If you could go back and change just one thing, to whom would you reach out?

A: That's interesting. I never thought about that before, but it would have to be the commander who recommended that I be fired. I know that sounds strange, but I had a really interesting relationship with him. I first met him one morning when I got a call on a lady with a gun outside a bar. I was the only one available at the time. Everybody else was tied up on other calls; no one could clear to cover me. The only backup available was the senior officer, the commander. I can still remember that as I was dealing with one subject the commander rolled up and said "Whatta ya got?" I said, "That lady's got a gun; search her." ... So here I am, a year on the road, a rookie, ordering the midnight operations commander to search this gal. He came up with a gun, too. After that we had a pretty good relationship.

In retrospect I'm certain he knew what was going down. He knew what was happening and really went out of his way to try to save me; I believe he did all he could. But ultimately he was the one who recommended that I be fired. Even after telling me for six weeks that he was only going to give me 45 days and a transfer. When I learned that he recommended that I be fired I really felt let down. I was very, very hurt by what he had done. I felt I had really been jerked around.

I realize now that he had to do what he did. He had to pull the plug. I'd like to go back to talk to him.

Q: He was available; he was at the time. Why

did you choose not to call him?

A: I didn't think about it—then.[3]

Q: Is there someone else to whom you could have reached out? Spouse? Sibling? Parents? Best friend?

A: I wasn't thinking clearly enough at that moment. At the basic academy, if somebody—an instructor, counselor, somebody, *anyone,* had said "If you are ever in a difficult situation, call me; here's my number," I probably would have called that person. But no one did that. I didn't have anyone I felt would understand or with whom I could share my fears and concerns—not even, or perhaps especially, my wife.

Q: The Code of Silence?

A: Yeah. I wanted to be a Stand-up cop, not a Hand-up cop. And I was scared to death as well. Word got back to me sometime during the course of the week—even before the motorist died. After the guy died, somebody told me that they heard that someone said that if I told the truth I'd be found face down in a ditch.[4]

But, when I made the decision to go in [to Internal Affairs] and do it [lie], the guy wasn't dead yet. I think I was hoping that he wasn't gonna die; it would all just blow over. I still think about what I would have done if the guy had been killed outright. If he had been dead on the scene, I probably would have told the truth.

To this day I struggle with this. I'd like to believe that had the man been killed outright I would not have lied in the first place, that I would have done the right thing. But a part of me—given my state of mind at the time—says that I would not have had the courage to tell the truth. I wish I could go back in time to find out. I guess I was damned if I did and damned if I didn't.

Q: Did you rationalize that since he was going to live that somehow made it [the beating] okay?

A: No. It didn't make it okay. No! No! I did rationalize that the thing might blow over, okay? But that didn't justify the beating.

What happened was wrong and there was no question about that. There was no way I could excuse that.

Q: Did you feel the motorist deserved the beating, that he brought it on himself?

A: What they were doing was teaching him a lesson. But it got out of hand. It's like a late hit in football. It wasn't right, but it was something that was done. Once in a while you got caught and you got penalized for it. But it was part of the game.

I think this was a police riot; the police lost control. In that regard there are some parallels to the Rodney King beating. There was the group that was taking out all of their frustrations and anxieties on the guy. And there was another group—the group I was in—standing around thinking, "What are these guys doing?" And doing nothing about it, like being in suspended animation.

I think there are lots of similarities with small group violence that gets out of hand, and the psychology of a mob that loses control. In a riot there is the anonymity of the group. There is a contagion and escalation. I think that's what happened to those guys. You come out of a high speed chase and you're hyped, wired. No one said stop.

Q: When the officers started beating the motorist, what means did they use?

A: It's really a blur. I can't really identify who did what. It sounds kinda weird, I know. I should be able to say so and so did this and so and so did that, but I can't. I can't identify who or what specifically was going on.

Q: You've tried to sort this out before, haven't you? Do you think it stays a blur because it's easier to cope with now if you let the specifics remain unclear?

A: Pardon me?

Q: Is it convenient? Is it easier to live with not being able to sort it all out?

A: I think it's because things happened so fast I can't sort them all out. I don't think I'm repressing it. I remember thinking, "I can't believe this is happening." I mean, I had never seen a group of officers descend on somebody like that before.

Q: Is it fair to say that the beating went beyond the bounds of what was necessary under the circumstances?

A: Yeah, no question there.

Q: Is that what prompted you to try to stop it?

A: The initial thing was trying to get the cuffs on him. Then a bunch of the officers were on the guy. What I recall trying to stop was Officer A hitting the motorist with his nightstick. The guy was down and Officer A was standing over him, swinging at him. That was just unbelievable. I hollered, "Cool it; take it easy," or something like that, trying to get him to stop hitting the guy. In retrospect, it was probably pretty feeble, because Officer A seemed not to hear me and kept at it. I didn't say or do anything else. No one else tried to stop it either. I just stood there gawking. If anything stands out in my mind now it is Officer A standing over that guy, swinging the nightstick down, repeatedly hitting him.

Q: Do you recall what the victim was doing? Do you object to my referring to him as a victim?

A: No, at that point he was a victim. I don't recall him resisting at all. Officer B said the guy hit him; I don't know. It was like, like tunnel vision. Then everybody was in there. I didn't see the guy resisting.[5]

Q: Would you describe the victim's behavior as passive?

A: He was down. He had lots of officers around him. It was not something that occurred over a long period of time. It happened very quickly. It is very difficult for me to sort out. If someone had been there with a video camera, maybe. But, I also wanted to distance myself from what happened as soon as I could. I didn't want anything to do with it.

Q: How long did the beating take?[6]

A: It was all over in less than a minute. Jumping out of the cars, cuffing him, and stomping him. Then there were some late hits as well.

Q: Tell me about when you walked away from the scene.

A: After the beating was over, the victim was propped up against a patrol car. I looked at him and at that moment realized the guy is black. As my vision focused more intently, I saw that his head was extremely bloody. I remember hearing myself say, "Oh, my God." I meant it was really bad; they nailed him.

Q: Did you hear any racial epithets directed at the victim?

A: No, none. No one stood over him and said, "Take that, nigger," or, "I'm beating you only because you're black."

Q: Was there any dialogue directed to the victim?

A: Not that I recall. Nothing stands out in my mind that was said to or about the victim by any of the officers.

Q: Was the victim placed in a patrol car when the beatings were concluded?

A: No, he was propped up against a patrol car, but an ambulance transported him to the hospital.

Q: What transpired after the victim was taken away in the ambulance? What happened at the scene?

A: A radio call went out; a car was needed to clear to handle it. I don't remember what the call was, but I said I'd take it. I caught the motorist. I was first on the scene. *That* report should have been mine. But I didn't want anything to do with it. So when the dispatcher asked if any unit could clear for the new call, I said I would handle it and I went back in service. I just wanted to get out of there.

Q: It was very convenient for you to use another call to avoid dealing with the situation.

A: Oh yeah! I think that was the only lucky thing that happened to me that night. The pressure was off a bit because as they were sizing things up, they probably were thinking that I had a pretty good attitude about everything. But Officer F was new. They didn't know him so attention shifted away from me as I was clearing and focused on him. That's why I cleared. I cleared because I did not want to be involved further.

Q: How long was it from that point until the end of the shift?

A: I'm shivering; I feel as though I'm reliving it right this moment. Seven hours.

Q: You listened to the [police] radio traffic for the remainder of the shift?

A: Yeah, I hear the thing [incident] being changed from this to that and one thing to another. I hear one unit call for a meet with another unit. "Meet me at such and such and so forth." I knew what was going on. They were trying to figure out what they were going to do.

Q: Since you kept listening to the radio traffic, you still didn't feel detached from the incident. End of shift; you went to go home. Tell me about what happened next. Was there an attempt to contact you before the end of your shift?

A: No, but when I pulled into the station at the end of shift, they were there, waiting for me.

Q: Who made the first statement to you?

A: I think it was Officer A.

Q: You said that Officer A beat the motorist. Was he the principal in this event?

A: He was *a* principal, but the sergeant was the leader. But they were all kind of standing around, making a comment here and there. Then they said, "Here is what we are gonna do; here is what we are gonna say." They were going to say the guy resisted arrest and then went crazy, that he was up and down.

Q: Who said that to you?

A: Geez, I don't remember. It was like they were all there and each one was supporting whatever was being said to me.

Q: Who was there?

A: Well, it is amazing, but it's like all the individuals have become an entity; they ceased to be individuals in my mind.

Q: It is easier for you to deal with what happened when you think about it as "an entity"; it disperses the responsibility of individuals.

A: Yes.

Q: Having never done this [an in-depth interview], perhaps specifics will start to come back to you, provoke you to sort things out with a bit more specificity. After the interview and over the next few days, as things occur to you, as they pop into your mind, make a note or two about that issue. Then listen to this audio tape recording and fill in the blanks for yourself. This is just a suggestion. But there are still some gaps I believe you need to fill. This isn't going to go away today; it isn't going to end for you tomorrow. There are too many questions left unanswered. Over the course of this interview, you've used the phrase "that's interesting," several times. That choice of words suggests to me that you had not previously thought about those particular issues before. You haven't sorted them out.

A: Well, I never talked to anyone about this in a nonadversarial setting before. That's why I wanted to do this interview.

Q: Not even your wife?

A: First off, my wife, God love her, I mean, I don't think another woman would have stayed with me. (*Poise begins to falter.*) I should have trusted her. I think that if I had gone home that morning, I would have told her. But I was so [expletive] scared. I had made the [expletive] lie. I went in and lied to Internal Affairs. Then I was had. Now I'm a perjurer. Under duress, or whatever, it happened. I made a false statement. Now I'm done; now I'm committed. Now I can't get out of it.

I remember the next night, sitting at home and opening the City A Newspaper 1. There was an article, dealing with the incident. And I started reading—maybe, my God, maybe I was calling for help (*composure continues to waver*)—but I pointed at that article and said, "That wasn't the way it really happened."

Q: What was her reaction?

A: We had—*have*—a good marriage; still do. And we had an understanding. If I didn't volunteer information about work, she didn't ask. My brother has that kind of relationship with his wife, too. He didn't want to talk about what he did on the job and his wife didn't want to know. I liked to talk and my wife likes to listen, but if I didn't volunteer, she didn't push. That's the way it was that night.

Sometimes after a rough day I just wanted to sit and relax for a while. We might talk, but not necessarily about work. I don't recall what she said when I made that comment, but she knew not to ask unless I went further and I didn't.

I told her the day after I made my statement to Homicide. I lived through that whole week...

Q: Alone?

A: Alone. The morning I went to give a statement to Homicide, I got a call at home from Officer A before I went in. But my wife answered the phone and told him I was still asleep. I wish she would have woke me up; she didn't. She just left a note saying that he called. I always wondered what he was going to tell me before I went to Homicide.

At Homicide everything was laid out the way they (the conspirators) said it would. They said they (the Homicide investigators) would play Good Guy, Bad Guy, with me. They said they were gonna take me to the district attorney. They said I should just stick to my story no matter what. We all had to stick together. And that's the way it happened; that's what I did.

Q: Sticking together; that was a constant intonation?

A: Through those few days, all right. Stick to your story. And they talked to me a lot because, you know, they all were saying, just stick to your story. I think it was one night in City B, Officer A kept saying, "Don't change your story. Nobody's gonna know."

That very morning in City A Newspaper 2 on the front page was an article which indicated to me that the cover-up was falling apart. Officer A and I were both covering

City B. He told me to stick to my story. He said that what he did on the scene was correct. I think that by then he had convinced himself that the lie was the truth.

They (the conspirators) kept saying just stick to your story. If they take you over to the district attorney's office and they threaten to indict you, just stick to your story. If you do that, things will be fine. So there was a lot of that.

Q: Did you feel ashamed?

A: Oh, God! *(Becomes very emotional.)* What I did. I'm still ashamed of what I did. A comment a good friend made haunts me. He said, "Integrity is like virginity. Once you lose it, it's gone." *(Begins to cry.)*

Q: That's not true. I disagree with that statement.

A: Maybe I'm being too hard on myself, but I also remember clearly when I first testified against Officer A. That was the day they fired me. I remember being called in, sitting on the witness stand. And this is something I remember very clearly; I'll never forget it. The defense attorney says to me, "Officer, it still is Officer, isn't it?" I was fired after my testimony, so I was still employed at that time. I said yes and he said, "Have you ever lied? Have you ever told a lie?" I said yes. He said, "Oh, you did?" in a raised and exaggerated manner, feigning being offended. Maybe he was.

It really became demeaning for me. He pressed on, "Did you lie under oath?" I said yes. "An oath to God?" he said. I was humiliated. I never felt worse in my life, not before and not since. Again, that's why I try so hard now. That's why I'm letting you do this to me. I suppose I'm trying to to make amends. This is a catharsis for me. I've gotta stop somebody else, some other police officer, from doing this. I don't want somebody else to go through what I did.

I've been incredibly fortunate to have recovered fairly well; I got a second chance. Sometimes I think I shouldn't have. After I was fired and moved away from City A, a retired FBI agent took me under his wing, so to speak. I've got to do for other police officers what so many people have done for me. I've got to make sure, somehow, that nobody goes through what I went through. I would not wish on my worst enemy what I've felt all these years. I'm still living with a hell of a lot of guilt.

Q: What could your department have done? What should they have done to help you avoid succumbing to the Code of Silence?

A: Training. Reinforce the training. And have someone to whom you could turn—an ombudsman. Someone in the department who you could talk to before you sign anything or are sworn to give testimony. Not an attorney, not legal advice, but someone with a behavioral science background. Someone who understands what a person goes through emotionally.

Looking back at the [basic academy] training I got, we had good guy/bad guy training advisors. Two sergeants. One played the role of the bad guy, the other played the role of the good guy. Those roles imprinted on my thinking very quickly. I'm sure those roles were intentional. I remember in the first few days, if I had anything routine, I'd go to the bad-guy sergeant. But if I had a real problem, I'd go to the good-guy sergeant because he was nice, less threatening, less intimidating. Ironically, it was the good-guy sergeant who made the comment about Hand-up cops. Because he was the good guy, that made an impression. Had the bad-guy sergeant made that statement, I might not have taken it to heart. But it was the good-guy sergeant, the training advisor with whom I identified and respected.

And there was my friend [Fred], someone I respected, who before I became a police officer, told me to go back to the patrol car and pretend to write a report.

Q: Those are very powerful implications about what was expected of you.

A: Yeah; I'm not sure the system can be beat. In my case at least, the psychological coaching to be a Stand-up cop was coming from people I really respected. Reinforcement of that ideology is continuous and widespread. I went into the police academy a moral person; I had taken ethics classes before I became a police officer. I came out of the police academy confused about what was acceptable and what was unacceptable behavior as a police officer.

Q: Is such behavior generally tolerated?

A: If things get out of hand but the officers involved are basically good cops and they just lose their temper; yeah, thumping someone would be excused.[7]

Q: Besides training, reinforcement of appropriate behavior, and ombudsman services, what else should a police department do to help its officers avoid such dilemmas?

A: Well, I think if they would admit that these things happen out there, that would help. I think it's important to talk about the socialization process and about cynicism.

Q: You are not a cynic but this experience could have done that.

A: I think that's an important point. I'll bet that lots of police officers who go through something like this, if they weren't cynics before, sure became cynics after. For a long time I had a real hatred for some of the people involved. I felt as though I was hung out to twist in the wind. Members of my old squad shunned me. I felt that the department left me high and dry. I was being pulled every which way by the prosecution. The department fired me. That hurt—a lot!

There was a lieutenant I didn't particularly like. One day about two weeks after I was suspended he said, "You know they are going to fire you, don't you?" I said no, they are going to give me a suspension and a transfer. That is what the commander told me. He [the commander] said, "Don't do anything, don't talk to anybody; I'll take care of you." The lieutenant responded, "They *are* going to fire you; hell, they've *got* to fire you."

And I thought, what a jerk, I never liked him; I don't think he likes me. That's why he's saying that. He might have been an egotist, but he was the only one who told me the truth the entire time. I didn't get any support from the department. I guess they had to distance themselves. They had to cut their losses. In retrospect, you know, they had to do what they did. I'd have probably done the same thing. You can't keep people on who have done something like that, no matter what their record. Even if they were great cops that everyone liked.

Q: What else could a police department do? You have clearly exemplified the police socialization process, promotion of the Stand-up-cop mind set. How can the reverse message be conveyed? How can a negative connotation be attached to Stand-up cop behavior? How can the characterization of the Hand-up cop become morally just and correct?

A: The word "correct" is so subjective. The *correct* thing to do is taking care of your fellow officers. Going one-on-one with someone, having the stuffing beat out of you, rolling around on the street, hollering for emergency back-up; that teaches you the *correct* behavior. They [one's fellow officers] are all there. Woosh! Just like magic. They appear seemingly out of thin air—*if* you are one of them—a Stand-up cop. That is what they respect. If they don't respect you they won't be there when you need them. You learn to appreciate that.

Consider an example: In the course of an arrest, the guy resists arrest, hits your partner, then runs off. You catch the guy and bring him back handcuffed. Your partner takes out his nightstick and pops the guy. What am I going to do? Virtually everyone to whom I pose this situation says they would write the report omitting the nightstick part. They would say the guy took a hell of a fall resisting arrest. Most people

think this would be no big deal because the guy was an asshole. That's their attitude.

I think that in most police departments there's this fear of Internal Affairs investigations. That they are going to get you. There is a paranoia about being called up there; right or wrong, no one wants to go before Internal Affairs.

We need to get police departments to the point where if an officer, an otherwise good officer, screws up—like the example I just used—that officer automatically goes to the sergeant. The department says, okay, we've got to do damage control. You were wrong. You are going to get a penalty for it. You are going to get disciplined for what you've done.

Then the department goes to the guy who got thumped and says, okay, our officer made a mistake. What do you want as compensation? Attorneys won't like this at all. But, a department should support an otherwise good officer.

But what happens is that maybe for fear of a lawsuit or just embarrassment, they deny everything and hang the officer out to dry. So the word gets around that the only way to protect yourself is to be a Stand-up cop. Cover at all costs. One lie leads to another, and it becomes increasingly more complicated. All of a sudden you are in too far and there is no way out. What did you call it, a vortex? Yeah, it's like being sucked into a giant whirlpool.

I tell people that the truth is always the best personal policy. If you lie, you've got to remember every detail; otherwise you get tripped up. If you tell the truth all the way, you don't have that problem, because it will always come out the same. If you lie you'll get fired for that. Plus, you haven't gotten out of what caused you to lie in the first place. Lying is really a losing proposition all around. That's what's gotta be conveyed to young cops. Never lie.

Don't listen when someone says, "Forget

everything you learned in the police academy." You've got to follow the academy guidelines and the department has got to support its officers, not just punish them when it all comes out in the [news]papers or on television.

Q: Let's change gears here. Let's talk about your wife's reaction when you went home and said you didn't have a job.

A: Well, I think my wife suspected something was going wrong, but as I said, she is a very supportive woman.

Q: There were never any recriminations from her?

A: No. Not once. Never have been. She supported me 100 percent the entire time. I think I might have eaten my gun if it hadn't been for her. I've never told anybody this, but there was more than one time during the investigation that I thought about suicide. I seriously considered that option.

Q: You felt so badly about what had happened that you didn't think you could live with it?

A: Yeah.

Q: Tell me about your relationship with your wife then and now.

A: Great then. Great now. Sometimes I think there is more strength that comes out of adversity. My wife is a wonderful woman. She was very supportive through the whole ordeal. While I was testifying in the case, she had to have a biopsy; the doctors were checking for cancer. At the height of this thing, she's having surgery. The judge let me go home so I could be with her for the surgery and so I could be with her when she got home. She's really been wonderful, Bill. I probably don't tell her often enough how much I love her. She's a wonderful woman; our life together is wonderful.

Q: Has she ever asked you why you did not confide in her?

A: I think most women would have. I think most would have left and would have been justified in doing so. No, she never has. When this happened, we had only been married about three years. As a matter of fact it

happened two days before our anniversary. By the time I had a chance to talk to her I had already lied; I had made a false statement. I was committed.

Q: Why didn't you recant?

A: They got me in there [Internal Affairs] the first thing in the morning. I didn't have much time for reflection, to think it through. Things just happened too fast.

Q: When did you finally tell your wife what actually happened?

A: When the guy died and after I made a statement to Homicide. It was a Monday. The guy died four days later. Things were falling apart. The whole cover-up was just crumbling. There were articles in the [news] papers. It was all deteriorating. A former sergeant of mine called me at home and told me they wanted me at Homicide at 1:00 P.M. that day. I said, "What's it about?" He said it was about the motorist thing. I asked him if he could tell me what is going on. He said he couldn't, but that it was heavy. So I went down to Homicide at 1:00 [P.M.]. The homicide commander and my commander were there. They started playing good guy/bad guy with me. My commander says to me, "Come on tell me the truth, let me help you out." The homicide commander—he's playing the bad guy. So it's unfolding exactly like the guys [the conspirators] have been telling me it was going to happen. I'm sitting there sticking to my story. Then they haul me over to the district attorney's office. Before we left, I called the FOP [Fraternal Order of Police] and told them I thought I needed a lawyer. They told me not to say anything.

At the district attorney's office I didn't say anything and they cut me loose. Somebody from the FOP came over there and picked me up. They took me over to an attorney's office. The first words out of my mouth at the attorney's office were, "I need a drink." He gave me one. Then I said, "I witnessed a murder." He was the first person that I told the truth to. He stares at me as if from a defense posture. He says, "Well, they can't use your Internal Affairs statement against you in criminal court so you are okay there. He reassured me and then told me to go home and he'd figure out what's going on.

I went to bed; I was worn out. About 7:00 [P.M.] my wife came in and woke me up; my commander was on the phone. He said, "I want you down at Homicide right now." He said it was in my best interest. He wasn't nasty about it. He was almost begging me. So I said let me talk to my attorney. I called him and he said let's go see what's going on. No sooner had I hung up with my attorney than the commander is calling me back seeing if I was going down to Homicide.

At Homicide they said, "We have someone in the other room who is going to make a statement, to tell the truth." I'm thinking, yeah, sure. Let me see who it is. They said okay. I walk to the doorway and I see Officer C sitting there. So I think this is one of those situations where they're bringing me by the door to show me someone who is refusing to make any statements but they're trying to break me. I mean, I'm paranoid at the time; I really am. So I ask them to let me talk to him. I walked up to Officer C and ask him, "Are you telling the truth?" He said "Yeah." I said "Fine." That's all I needed. I needed to have somebody else tell the truth. I sat down and made my statement.

I think my commander saved me, I really do. I think he was looking out for me. I don't know what time I got out of there; 10:30 or 11:00 P.M. My commander and I went over to a bar in City C. We had a couple of drinks. He was supportive. I don't remember the gist of the conversation, but I remember the booth we were sitting in. He told me to go home, get some sleep, and not to say anything to anyone. He seemed supportive. I don't know if he was concerned about me or protecting the investigation. At that point I wasn't sure who he was looking out for, me or the department.

Q: When you left the commander, what did you do then?

A: I went home. No, actually I made one other stop on the way home. I stopped at the home of some friends who lived in City C. Very good friends; people with whom my wife and I spent Sundays, at their pool. I really had a good relationship with [Jim]. I knocked on their door. They were asleep and didn't answer the door. It's kinda funny; I was gonna tell him. I figured he was the kind of person I could talk to. Then I went home, sat down with my wife, and told her what happened and what I had done.

Q: What was her reaction?

A: She gave me a big hug. She was very supportive.

Q: Did she question you, or did she sit passively listening to what you were saying?

A: I think she just listened.

Q: Were you making eye contact with her as you told her?

A: That's an interesting question. I don't think so. I was sitting on the couch, holding her hand, kind of looking down. I don't think I made eye contact with her at all.

Q: Was that a conscious decision?

A: I don't think I deliberately avoided looking at her. I was not Machiavellian about any of it. I didn't feel as though I had control of anything at this point; I was in a daze.

Q: Are you in control now?

A: It's been a lot of years; that's an awful long time. I don't feel as though I've got closure yet. I don't think I am going to wake up and find out it was all just a bad dream. It happened and I'm still having problems with it.

Q: Let's go back to something you said earlier. I think your self-image is very important to you and you still don't feel worthy. I believe you internalized the phrase about integrity being like virginity; once you've lost it, you can't get it back.

Let me expand on what I said earlier. In my opinion you have a great deal of character. If you were unprincipled you would have let go a long time ago. The fact that it still bothers you after all this time *and* that you have taken steps to try to have others benefit from your experience is a clear indication to me that you are a very decent person. Closure may not be right around the corner, but the fact that you are sharing such personal thoughts so openly now suggests that the healing process is well on its way. You have been very forthright and have not skirted any of my questions. *And,* whether or not you realize it, you have been making direct eye contact with me. All this ...

A: *(Interrupts angrily, weeping.)* Yeah? When I was 23, why the [expletive] did I do what I did? That's what's haunting me. You know, you're telling me what everybody else tells me, Bill. How can all of you do this? Do you know what I'm saying? The other FBI agent, he said the same thing. Not the same words, but essentially recognized me as being a good person. People gave me jobs, they gave me chances. The people who elected me an officer of my professional association, etc., etc. All of you say I am a moral person. I don't see the person you see! You don't see the person I see!

Q: You believe the other shoe *should* fall, don't you? "The system" condemned you, but you have convinced yourself that was not enough. You say you want closure, but what you expect, what you *think* you deserve is recrimination from people you respect. That hasn't happened so you are trying to get that now. You *want* someone—me—to say, "I'm not buying any of your explanation. You were wrong, plain and simple. You know you were wrong and I'm not going to forgive you for what you did."

You feel you should be getting what your sense of morality tells you that you deserve but did not get. You know you were wrong, but in your own mind, your punishment was not severe enough. Those in whom you have confided recognize your sincerity. That is why they support you. If you tried to

excuse or justify your behavior, that would be obvious and *would* get you what you *think* you deserve.

A: The other thing that still bothers me is that the others were all acquitted. Officer A stuck to his story!

Q: The most innocent person involved received the most severe penalty?

A: Interesting. That word again. Yeah, Officer A said he was sticking to his story and nobody was gonna know.

Did you see the thing on TV a couple of weeks ago about the City D beating? The police beat this guy to death. If you look at the video tape of Officer A's testimony in my case and compare that with the video tape of the officer's testimony in the City D beating of this white guy, they are identical. They are even down on the ground in the same position. They're talking about the guy going for his gun. Both officers are talking about how the guy is hitting them. I'm looking at this and say to myself, "You [expletive]; you're lying. They are using the same defense Officer A did and they got acquitted too!

The only good thing about my case was that recently Officer A was arrested and charged with a life felony. He is facing a life felony. Everyone who stuck to their story got away with it. It worked. The rest of us are admitted liars. This is stupid; it's incredible!

Q: What I would like to do now is take a break. I'd like for you to reflect on what you have told me and what I have asked. You may have some questions for me when we get together again.

A: Okay.

Second Session of the Interview Continues

Q: Didn't you get *any* support back then?

A: [Jim] got me the job at [XYZ Trucking] in City A. I had never done anything with trucks, but I worked hard and was rather quickly made a supervisor there. Shortly after I was promoted, [Jim] got a memo from the main office saying that he should not have hired anyone involved with the City A incident. Both he and another man in the home office were friends that I met while I was a police officer. So, it was the Monday after the acquittal [of the conspirators] when the employees circulated a petition asking that I be fired and then gave it to management. The new manager told me about the petition and demand. He said he would not fire me, but asked me to take a couple of days off until things quieted down. When I came back to work two days later I was informed that I was being terminated for failing to report to work for two days without proper notice. Interestingly, they gave me two weeks severance pay even though I had only been employed there for three months.

Q: Have you kept tabs on what's happened in City A over the years?

A: Once in a while friends will send me newspaper clippings. Like when Officer A was arrested. But other than that I haven't had much contact. I used to subscribe to the local paper, but I stopped doing that a long time ago. I couldn't tell you who the chief of police is now.

Q: Tell me about the threats you and your wife received.

A: My wife got a couple phone calls. One I remember very distinctly. It was the night before my wife's surgery. I had just returned to City A from the trial in City B. I had only been home 15 minutes and was taking things out of my suitcase when the phone rang. She answered it and the caller said "Tell the cop we know where he is; we're gonna kill him," and then hung up. That really scared her.

The first threat I received after I was fired as a police officer. It might have been by one of my fellow employees at [XYZ Trucking]. I have no proof of that, but a coworker who worked in the office came up

to me and said "I got a call to tell the cop we know where he lives and we're gonna kill him." It may not have been those precise words; I can't remember exactly. And he might have received that call as he said, but I don't think so. I think he was delivering his own message or a message from a clique with whom he associated at [XYZ Trucking].

Q: Tell me about what contact you had with the FBI during this incident.

A: None, really. Surprisingly, even on the lawsuits and the federal investigation, I went right to the Grand Jury. The federal prosecutor, a Civil Rights Division guy, came in from Washington, DC. I was never interviewed by the FBI. My only contact with anyone from the Bureau was the agent who walked with me to and from court a couple of times as well as to and from the offices of the U.S. Attorney. But I think he was assigned to be a kind of mother hen, to make sure I wasn't accosted during those times.

Q: Since our first session, did you take any notes?

A: You know that's interesting. You asked me to do that. After we parted company, I did just that for a couple of hours. Since we started again I've been free-associating. Here's a note I made earlier: "I've probably done more to benefit law enforcement since leaving the City A police department because I am not nearly so myopic as I was then and I'm devoting myself to helping others avoid making the same mistake I made."

Q: Excellent. Now you are looking at yourself objectively, not merely castigating yourself.

A: Funny that you should mention that.

Q: If there is some force in the universe keeping a ledger on us, in your log there has got to be more pluses than minuses. That one event is a negative, but it was not something you instigated. You were not the officer swinging the club. In fact, you tried to stop it, but couldn't find a way to do so, and then you got caught up in trying to protect your fellow officers. That said, what you have done with your life, it seems to me, far outweighs the necessity for the kind of recrimination that you feel is your due.

A: Something else that I made a note about. I have never had career closure. I miss being a police officer. If there was a way I could go back, even now, that I could go back to work if only for six months, to prove that I am not the kind of person they made me out to be, I would go back—in a minute.

If I could go back on the road and into that district tomorrow I could do the job; all these years would be like a day because I could do my work. If I could somehow do that, it would give me closure. Most ex-police officers walk away because they wanted to. I didn't have that luxury. The circumstances under which I left are painful.

You asked me about Sergeant B. I thought about him. I expressed my concerns to him that morning behind the station. I said to him, "You know what happened out there was not right?" This is the first time I've thought about that. I've never thought about that the entire time. Maybe it's a seed you planted when you asked me to take notes and reflect.

Q: Sergeant B was not your supervisor, is that correct?

A: Correct, he was not. Sergeant A was, but he had gone home before the end of the shift.

Q: Anything else?

A: Well you planted a couple of seeds that took sprout. (*Smiles and begins chuckling.*) Do the people there think they made a mistake when they fired me?

Q: You think so, don't you?

A: If they do, why haven't they bothered to tell me? (*Begins to cry.*)

Q: The fear of civil litigation is a very strong incentive for letting sleeping dogs lie.

A: I'm not that kind of person!

Q: They did not know that at the time, had no

way of knowing, and don't know now. *Perceiving* oneself to have been wronged in the past is a powerful inducement for some to want to reopen the case, seek reinstatement, file a multimillion-dollar lawsuit, etc. That often happens even when the person is wrong but can't accept it, even over a period of time as long as yours.

I'm confident your vulnerability was evident to the people who interviewed you at the time. They sensed that you felt you were guilty. If so, it is likely they also wagered you would accept their judgment and not contest that decision.

Consider an administrator's point of view. Here's a very bad situation with everyone denying responsibility, a victim who dies, and at best, a difficult case to make. Think of the public pressure. The administrator knows the public wants something done quickly. Somebody has to take the blame. And here's an officer who lies but subsequently admits guilt in trying to cover up. You've heard the phrase, better a bird in the hand than two in the bush.

A: They did fire everyone even remotely involved. They fired almost everybody who was on duty that night. I think there were only one or two officers who were on duty that night who didn't get fired. Everyone on that shift was paranoid and felt guilty by association.

Q: Frankly, you *are* guilty of that for which you were fired, aren't you?

A: Yes.[8]

Q: What bothers you is not that you were fired, but that the *more* guilty received the *same* penalty and should have received more severe punishment. In your eyes, therefore, they got off too easily. Isn't that the case?

A: Yes.

Q: Consider where they are now and what they are doing today. Consider where you are, what you are doing, and who you are today. You have vindicated *yourself.* You have risen above what happened. Have they?

A: I think I feel a little better about it all.

Q: One other thing. You should give more consideration to and reflect on your relationship with your association. You said that you feel very good about the fact that when you were nominated for office, you felt compelled to tell them what happened and asked if they were sure you could be trusted. You were elected, weren't you? You are very highly regarded by your colleagues. What higher compliment can a person receive than the confidence of one's peers? There is little that you could do that would give you a higher stamp of approval. Their confidence was not bestowed casually. And, more importantly, you have demonstrated their trust in you was well founded.

A: You know, all of a sudden, I don't feel alone anymore.

Q: It's time you stopped carrying this burden. You are contributing to society in a meaningful way. You have turned your life around. You have not become a cynic. You have done something very positive with your life personally and professionally, and you have influenced others because of your victimization.

A: Am I a victim too? That is another point I was thinking about. (*Tears run down his cheeks.*) Up until this interview I have always looked at myself more as a "subject" than as a "victim."

Q: In spite of what happened, what you have contributed to society has been very positive. You have not tried to minimize, excuse, or rationalize your behavior. Now—in this interview—you are saying: Here is what happened. I cannot legitimize it given my background and upbringing. Who knows how many people who read about your experience may avoid the vortex.

A: Something else I now recall is the officer I assisted on that first call that night. A couple of days later he came up to me and said he had heard that I tried to stop the beating. He said he really respected me for that. I'd forgotten about that until now. That really makes me feel better now than it did at the time.

Q: Anything else?

A: Someone one once told me that on the culpability ladder, I was on the bottom rung. Yet, I was sued for several million dollars. I was not defended by City A; I spent $8,000—proceeds from the sale of my house—to defend myself in that suit. I left City A very depressed. But I was fortunate.

After the verdicts, I remember watching on television, the civil unrest begin and the burning. People died then. I felt very badly; I remember wondering if I had contributed to that as well.

Q: Have you heard me talk about the potential for the repeat of massive, nationwide civil unrest?

A: Yes and it scares the hell out of me. I'm not looking forward to the end of [this] decade, with all those crack babies coming of [crime prone] age. And all the homeless, hungry children who could become sociopaths. That's really frightening.

In retrospect, maybe I *don't* want to be a cop right now. (*Smiles.*) It seems like things are getting nastier; people are getting to be a lot meaner and more willing to use violence than they used to when I first entered policing. Maybe what I am doing now is a more important contribution.

Q: Hold your hands out in front of you, please, parallel with the floor.

(*During the first session, the former officer fidgeted unconsciously, and as he reached for a glass of water his hands trembled. For the past several minutes, he has been calm and seems more relaxed. His hands are steady as he holds them out.*)

A: My hands are not cold anymore.

Q: Do you feel better now?

A: I'll never get over it; there will always be hurt. But all of a sudden I really do—honestly—feel better.

Q: This interview, when it is published, will

serve as a very tangible exposition of your experience. It details how such a thing can happen and will suggest how to deal with it.

A: That's the bottom line. Accountability demands that a police department support its people and not permit the Stand-up cop to be the hero. The Stand-up cop is not the good guy. The person of courage is the one who recognizes things are getting out of hand and prevents matters from getting worse. The person of courage is the one who realizes what his partner is telling him is true. That officer knows he's in trouble. He knows he's going to be in more trouble. But he is not going to compound it by lying. He's going to tell the truth and take what's coming to him and then get on with his life and career.

That's the message that has got to come out of my experience. For me, the moral of this story is: It *can* happen to you. But you can avoid great shame, embarrassment and indignity by not making matters worse. Stand up on behalf of justice!

Conclusions

What lessons can be learned from the experience of this former police officer? How can future law enforcement officers avoid inappropriate, unprofessional, and illegal behavior? Structured discourse concerning the potential for misbehavior is, of course, essential. But while training and education have been readily available for more than three decades, sufficiently candid or persuasive dialogue may not have been.

Since the mid-1960s a block of instruction on ethics has been included in most law enforcement basic academy and advanced officer training courses. Starting in the late 1970s a lecture on the topic was presented to all FBI National Academy students. In 1982 that one lecture was replaced by an elective course, "Ethics, Discipline and the Police," taught by now-retired FBI Agent Hillary Robinette. Ethics courses have

also long been available in the philosophy departments of many universities and colleges. More recently the topic has been recommended to be included in graduate criminal justice degree curricula (Felkenes, 1987).

With such wide coverage of this important subject, why does corruption and brutality continue to plague law enforcement? Are law enforcement agencies simply failing to screen out the "bad apples," candidates predisposed to inappropriate, unprofessional, and illegal behavior? Most of the men and women who swear to uphold the Constitution and enforce their state's statutes, take that oath with unswerving intention to do precisely that. Nor can background be cited as being at fault.

In most cases those who succumb to peer pressure—as in the case discussed here—are actually products of exemplary upbringing. So why? One reason is that few acknowledge they might succumb to unethical behavior. It is seen as the problem of the other guy. And more than one institution that has traveled this rocky road knows how defensive people can be at the suggestion they might go astray. Having been burned, the path of least resistance is to talk around—and not directly nor too specifically—about the problem of the potential for the excessive use of force.

The mode educational level of most police middle managers and numerous police chiefs today is a bachelor's degree. Academic writing is not beyond them. The thoughts of scholars who have studied and published on this issue need closer examination and reflection by police policymakers. The insights of Muir, 1977; Felkenes, 1982, 1984; Schmalleger and Gustafson, 1981; Sherman, 1982; Heffernan and Stroup, 1985; Delattre, 1989; Braswell, et al., 1991; Cohen and Feldberg, 1991; and Souryal, 1992, for example, are noteworthy.

The important message conveyed in traditional pedagogic exchanges needs to be made more explicit, direct, *and* realistic if a more positive outcome is expected "on the street," given the diverse and changing nature of society

(Bozza, 1992, 1993). This can be achieved through the use of state-of-the-art technology, such as videotaped role playing exercises and simulations, interactive video and teleconferencing, computer-based training (CBT), or cutting-edge technology, such as artificial intelligence and virtual reality. Case studies and Socratic sessions should also prove to be useful adjuncts to traditional teaching methods.

Forecasts of increased violence through the remainder of this decade and into the 21st century do not bode well for the future of policing (Tafoya, in press). If these forecasts are even remotely accurate, the number of situations in which police officers will encounter ethical and moral quandaries—of the kind described here—will almost certainly increase in proportion to the amount of violence with which they will be confronted and must contend throughout the remainder of the 1990s.

How effectively the next generation of police officers deals with the dilemma of the "Stand-up cop" will be a direct reflection on the courage—or lack thereof—demonstrated by present-day law enforcement administrators, recruiters, trainers, and educators. There is much that police managers and supervisors can blame on insufficient funding, a handy excuse for inadequate response or inappropriate behavior. But with regard to misconduct, the buck cannot legitimately be passed to politicians nor the budget blamed: no one bears greater responsibility than police administration.

Several years ago the author discussed with an executive the punitive action to be taken against a law enforcement officer for violation of an organizational regulation. The executive said, "I don't want to do this, but the matter was brought to my attention. I am *forced* to take action." An appropriate response is important. But the conventional wisdom of the deterrent effect notwithstanding, mere administrative and/or prosecutive actions do little to alter inappropriate behavior in the work environment. And it is there that the "Stand-up cop" thrives; being caught is the price of "doing business."

The executive who fails to take action equitably *and* who fails to consistently speak out against the "Stand-up-cop" mentality sends a clear, tacit message that such conduct is condoned, or worse, encouraged by management. That kind of notice to the troops reinforces the efficacy of inappropriate behavior of the few, and compromises or drives out of the organization those who disdain such conduct. It is not enough to take action when conduct goes public or becomes organizationally embarrassing.

One promising response to inappropriate police behavior was initiated statewide in California by means of a telecourse, aired in July 1993, that focused on the role of the bystander officer. Produced under the auspices of California's Commission on Peace Officer Standards and Training (POST), this particular undertaking is but the first in a series of telecourses and other training initiatives planned by POST that will concentrate on ways in which to overcome police misconduct and excessive use of force. This "Tactical Intervention" telecourse was based on the research of University of Massachusetts at Amherst psychologist Ervin Staub. He encourages officers to intervene when fellow officers use excessive force. Dr. Staub argues that "You have to [provide training] in a way that does not undermine [police officers'] loyalty to each other, but changes what loyalty means—stopping excess violence rather than hiding it behind a code of silence" (Goleman, 1993).

It is also important to understand that the norms of acceptable behavior in the police culture dictate that rookies should be seen and not heard. Thus, veteran officers frequently take the position that there is nothing they can learn from rookies; rookies must learn from senior officers. Rookies quickly get the message; they adapt and adjust. That is, they keep their mouths shut. While it is acceptable behavior for a seasoned officer to say to a rookie, "Don't do that!" the reverse is not. If Dr. Staub's message gets through, senior officers will come to realize—and maybe start advising rookies—that, in a bystander mode, they should not hesitate to say "enough is enough." This very literally is in the best interest of an officer caught up in the heat of the moment. In a physical confrontation adrenalin is pumping; the officer is on automatic pilot. That is precisely when objectivity by *someone else*—a bystander officer—is needed. *That* is covering a fellow officer. This simple act of courage of a bystander officer may mitigate the need to take the next step that inexorably leads to the vortex. Officers, regardless of seniority, need to turn 180 degrees the "Stand-up cop" mentality. Officers who really care about each other cover one another in an appropriate manner—not by covering up, but by preventing a situation from escalating.

If decision-makers avoid confronting this issue in a forthright manner today, police officers will find themselves in consternation—as the person interviewed was for many years—in the future. The tragedy is that those who despair will be not *just* the officers involved but also their families, friends, and neighbors. And if they suffer, so will the calling to which so many have honorably given their lives. That will be the legacy of police policymakers who resist change and cling to the status quo. This is not hyperbole or an overstatement. No matter how uncomfortable this issue may be to deal with, failing to do so literally invites disaster. For the individual such an experience can be tragic, both personally and professionally. Vicarious-liability lawsuits can make the experience financially devastating for the agency and the community as well (Kappeler, 1993).

But the fear of a lawsuit should not be the primary criterion upon which an agency initiates steps to confront the complex issue of the excessive use of force. In 1814, to a correspondent with whom he was discussing morality and ethics, Thomas Jefferson quoted French philosopher Claude Adrien Helvetius:

> The humane man is he to whom the sight of misfortune is insupportable, and who to rescue himself from this spectacle, is *forced* [emphasis mine] to succor the unfortunate object.

Jefferson goes on to express the belief that we are all imbued not only with compassion for others but also with a sense of responsibility to those in obvious need of assistance. What he called "a moral instinct" prompts and even compels us to come to the aid of those who are victimized in our presence (Padover, 1956:232–233). Taking this bull by the horns should not be done because it is politically correct or for fear of the ticking time bomb of litigation. It should be done because it is the right thing to do.

Alvin Toffler (1970), renowned futurist and social critic, in his classic *Future Shock*, noted that if we do something we affect the future in one way. If we do nothing we affect the future in another way. By our actions or *inactions* we affect the future.

NOTES

1. This interview took place one month before the riots in Los Angeles that followed the announcement of the not guilty verdict in the state trial of the four Los Angeles police officers charged in the 1991 beating of Rodney King. Two of the four were convicted in a federal trial in 1993 of violating Rodney King's civil rights.

2. He subsequently recalled an incident from the prior week. He stopped a black juvenile. He does not recall why he stopped the young man, but as he was letting him go the young man asked, "You're not a member of the Hit Squad, are you?" He said that bothered him a great deal; it was the first time he became aware of the squad's reputation in that neighborhood.

3. At the Basic Academy and thereafter, officers in this department are drilled in the sanctity of Chain of Command. Violating that principle—bypassing a sergeant and a lieutenant to seek the counsel of a commander—would have been unthinkable.

4. Subsequently determined to have been Officer D, one of the major conspirators.

5. The tunnel vision effect is exemplified by an incident recalled after the interview: In a prior one-on-one altercation, the officer called for an emergency back-up. Later, as he began writing his report of the incident, he could recall only one officer being there—the first one to arrive. It was subsequently established that there were 20 officers on the scene.

6. It has been established that the incident took place in less than 60 seconds.

7. The psychological literature is full of cases that explain aberrant behavior as the actions of sociopaths, the antisocial personality, or what I call an intellectual shrug of the shoulders. [The *Diagnostic and Statistical Manual of Mental Disorders* (DSM-III-R) describes the antisocial personality disorder as: "A lack of socialization along with behavior patterns that bring a person repeatedly into conflict with society; incapacity for significant loyalty to others or to social values; callousness; irresponsibility; impulsiveness; and inability to feel guilt or learn from experience or punishment. Frustration tolerance is low and such people tend to blame others or give plausible rationalizations for their behavior" (Stone, 1993:121).] But that cannot be used to explain this person's conduct. His life-long experience *should* have adequately prepared him and enabled him to resist the intimidation and do what was appropriate. But it didn't. Based on what he has told me and what I have read about this incident, it is as if he were caught in an emotional *vortex* that sucked him in. He was drowning and knew it, but was unable to escape.

The timeliness of the investigation suggests that there was an effective organizational mechanism in place to deal with such matters and that action was taken promptly. It appears this department did the right thing. They seem to have followed the *letter* of their established administrative procedures. Yet, that this person received such powerful verbal cues strongly suggests that there was a difference between what the department *said* was expected of its officers and what was *actually* expected. This evidences a chink in the knight's armor that may be more widespread than generally realized or acknowledged.

8. It has been determined that at the time, there was an independent hearing of this and the other firings. The examiner found all the terminations to have been justified.

RECOMMENDED READINGS

Albee, Richard L. (1989) "How Will Ethical Issues Impact 21st Century Law Enforcement?" Unpublished [Command College] paper, Sacramento, CA: Commission on Peace Officer Standards and Training (POST), #8-0132. Information about this and other POST papers cited below may be obtained from CA POST, Sacramento, CA, at (916) 227-2823.

Boyd, Thomas D. (1993) "A Model for Development of Police Officer Understanding of and Adherence to Ethical Standards," Unpublished [Command College] paper, Sacramento, CA: Commission on Peace Officer Standards and Training (POST), #16-0313.

Boyle, Daniel B. (1993) "Police Violence: Addressing the Issue," *FBI Law Enforcement Bulletin*, 62:6 (June):17-21.

Bozza, Charles M. (1992) "The Future of Diversity in America: The Law Enforcement Paradigm Shift," *Journal of Contemporary Criminal Justice*, 8:3 (August):208-216.

Bozza, Charles M. (1993) "Inside the Ring of Fire," *Police Futurist*, 1: (April): 7-11.

Braswell, Michael C., Belinda R. McCarthy and Bernard J. McCarthy, eds. (1991) *Justice, Crime and Ethics.* Cincinnati: Anderson Publishing Company.

Bryan, John S. (1988) "Police Integrity in the Year 2000: What Are the Influences for Change and How Will They Be Managed?" Unpublished [Command College] paper, Sacramento, CA: Commission on Peace Officer Standards and Training (POST), #7-0110.

Cockerham, Bruce E. (1990) "Value Diversity in Entry-Level Officers: The Impact on California Law Enforcement by the Year 2000," Unpublished [Command College] paper, Sacramento, CA: Commission on Peace Officer Standards and Training (POST), #10-0181.

Cohen, Howard S. and Michael Feldberg (1991) *Power and Restraint: The Moral Dimension of Police Work.* New York: Praeger.

Collins, Harry R. (1991) "Police Corruption in California by the Year 2000: Influencing Positive Change Through Programmed Prevention," Unpublished [Command College] paper, Sacramento, CA: Commission on Peace Officer Standards and Training (POST), #12-0240.

Delattre, Edwin J. (1989) *Character and Cops: Ethics in Policing.* Washington, DC: American Enterprise Institute.

Felkenes, George (1984) "Attitudes of Police Officers Towards Their Professional Ethics," *Journal of Criminal Justice*, 12:211-220.

Felkenes, George (1987) "Ethics in the Graduate Criminal Justice Curriculum," *Teaching Philosophy*, 10:1 (March):23-36.

Freeman, Carole A. (1990) "The Ethical Decision Making Process by 2000: Forces for Change in the Organizational Conscience," Unpublished [Command College] paper, Sacramento, CA: Commission on Peace Officer Standards and Training (POST), #9-0163.

Goleman, Daniel (1993) "Studying the Pivotal Role of Bystanders," *New York Times* (Tuesday, June 22):B5.

Heffernan, William and Timothy Stroup (1985) *Police Ethics: Hard Choices in Law Enforcement.* New York: John Jay Press.

Homer (750 B.C.) *The Iliad,* in contemporary verse by Robert Fitzgerald. Philadelphia: Franklin Library, 1979.

Homer (750 B.C.) *The Odyssey,* in contemporary verse by Robert Fitzgerald. Philadelphia: Franklin Library, 1979.

Kappeler, Victor E. (1993) *Critical Issues in Police Civil Liability.* Prospect Heights, IL: Waveland Press.

Muir, William (1977) *Police: Streetcorner Politicians.* Chicago: University of Chicago Press.

Nielsen, Eric (1988) "Anger Management: A Training Program for Reducing Incidents of Police Misconduct," Paper presented at the World Conference on Police Psychology, December, 1985, at the FBI Academy, Quantico, VA; appears in *Police Psychology: Operational Assistance,* edited by James T. Reese and James M. Horn. Quantico, VA: FBI Academy: 319-325.

Padover, Saul K. (1956) *A Jefferson Profile: As Revealed in His Letters.* New York: John Day.

Pate, Anthony and Sampson Annan (1993) "Complaints of Police Use of Excessive Force: A National Study," Paper presented at the Annual Meeting of the Academy of Criminal Justice Sciences, March 16-20, Kansas City, Missouri.

Plato (340 B.C.) *Selected Dialogues,* translated by Benjamin Jowett. Philadelphia: Franklin Library, 1983; see esp. "Protagoras" and "The Republic."

Pollock-Byrne, Joycelyn M. (1988) "Book Review Essay: Ethics and Criminal Justice," *Justice Quarterly,* 5:3 (September):475-485.

Reese, James T. (1986) "Policing the Violent Society: The American Experience," *Stress Medicine,* 2:233-240.

Reese, James T. (1988) "Psychological Aspects of Policing Violence," Paper presented at the World Conference on Police Psychology, December, 1985, at the FBI Academy, Quantico, VA; appears in *Police Psychology: Operational Assistance,* edited by James T. Reese and James M. Horn. Quantico, VA: FBI Academy: 347-361.

Reese, James T. and Harvey A. Goldstein, eds. (1986) *Psychological Services for Law Enforcement.* Washington, DC: U.S. Government Printing Office.

Robinette, Hillary M. (1987) *Burnout in Blue: Managing the Police Marginal Performer.* New York: Praeger.

Robinette, Hillary M. (1985) "The Police Problem Employee," in *Police Management Today: Issues and Case Studies,* edited by James Fyfe. Washington, DC: International City Management Association: 181-193.

Robinette, Hillary M. (1993) "Police Supervision Tomorrow," Paper presented at the Annual Symposium of the Society of Police Futurists International, May 3-5, Baltimore, Maryland.

Schaefer, Robert (1985) "Maintaining Control: A Step Towards Personal Growth," *FBI Law Enforcement Bulletin,* 54:3 (March): 10-14.

Schmalleger, Frank (1991) *Criminal Justice Ethics: An Annotated Bibliography and Research Guide.* Westport, CT: Greenwood.

Schmalleger, Frank (1990) *Ethics in Criminal Justice: A Justice Professional Reader.* Bristol, IN: Wyndham Hall.

Schmalleger, Frank and Robert Gustafson, eds. (1981) *The Social Basis of Criminal Justice: Ethical Issues for the 80's.* University Press of America.

Sherman, Lawrence (1982) "Learning Police Ethics," *Criminal Justice Ethics,* 1:1:10-19.

Souryal, Sam S. (1992) *Ethics in Criminal Justice: In Search of Truth.* Cincinnati: Anderson.

Souryal, Sam S. and Dennis W. Potts (1993) "'What Am I Supposed to Fall Back On?': Cultural Literacy in Criminal Justice Ethics," *Journal of Criminal Justice Education,* 4:1 (Spring): 15-41.

Staub, Ervin (1989) *The Roots of Evil.* Cambridge, England: Cambridge University Press.

Stone, Evelyn M., ed. (1988) *American Psychiatric Glossary,* 6th ed. Washington, DC: American Psychiatric Press.

Tafoya, William L. (in press) *Crime in the 21st Century.* Chicago: Office of International Criminal Justice, University of Illinois at Chicago; see also: "A Delphi Forecast of the Future of Law Enforcement," Ph.D. Dissertation, University of Maryland, 1986 [University Microfilms International #DA87-12267; National Criminal Justice Reference Service (NCJRS) #109101].

Toffler, Alvin (1970) Future Shock. New York: Random House.

Index